DEBATING THE WOMAN QUESTION IN THE FRENCH THIRD REPUBLIC, 1870–1920

Karen Offen offers a magisterial reconstruction and analysis of the debates around relations between women and men, how they are constructed, and how they should be organized that raged in France and its French-speaking neighbors from 1870 to 1920. The "woman question" encompassed subjects from maternity and childbirth, and the upbringing and education of girls to marriage practices and property law, the organization of households, the distribution of work inside and outside the household, intimate sexual relations, religious beliefs and moral concerns, government-sanctioned prostitution, economic and political citizenship, and the politics of population growth. The book shows how the expansion of economic opportunities for women and the drop in the birth rate further exacerbated the debates over their status, roles, and possibilities. With the onset of the First World War, these debates were temporarily placed on hold but they would revive by 1916 and gain momentum during France's postwar recovery.

KAREN OFFEN (Ph.D., Stanford University) is a historian and independent scholar affiliated as a Senior Scholar with the Michelle R. Clayman Institute for Gender Research at Stanford University in California.

NEW STUDIES IN EUROPEAN HISTORY

Edited by

PETER BALDWIN, *University of California, Los Angeles*
CHRISTOPHER CLARK, *University of Cambridge*
JAMES B. COLLINS, *Georgetown University*
MIA RODRÍGUEZ-SALGADO, *London School of Economics and Political Science*
LYNDAL ROPER, *University of Oxford*
TIMOTHY SNYDER, *Yale University*

The aim of this series in early modern and modern European history is to publish outstanding works of research, addressed to important themes across a wide geographical range, from southern and central Europe, to Scandinavia and Russia, from the time of the Renaissance to the present. As it develops the series will comprise focused works of wide contextual range and intellectual ambition.

A full list of titles published in the series can be found at: www.cambridge.org/newstudiesineuropeanhistory

DEBATING THE WOMAN QUESTION IN THE FRENCH THIRD REPUBLIC, 1870–1920

KAREN OFFEN

Dear Brigid,
    A "companion-in-arms" for
many years at Stanford +
in the Bay Area — you rock!

        Hugs!
        Karen Offen
        8 May 2018

CAMBRIDGE
UNIVERSITY PRESS

CAMBRIDGE
UNIVERSITY PRESS

University Printing House, Cambridge CB2 8BS, United Kingdom

One Liberty Plaza, 20th Floor, New York, NY 10006, USA

477 Williamstown Road, Port Melbourne, VIC 3207, Australia

314–321, 3rd Floor, Plot 3, Splendor Forum, Jasola District Centre,
New Delhi – 110025, India

79 Anson Road, #06–04/06, Singapore 079906

Cambridge University Press is part of the University of Cambridge.

It furthers the University's mission by disseminating knowledge in the pursuit of
education, learning, and research at the highest international levels of excellence.

www.cambridge.org
Information on this title: www.cambridge.org/9781107188044
DOI: 10.1017/9781316946336

© Karen Offen 2018

First published 2018

Printed in the United Kingdom by Clays, St Ives plc

A catalogue record for this publication is available from the British Library.

Library of Congress Cataloging-in-Publication Data
NAMES: Offen, Karen., author.
TITLE: Debating the woman question in the French Third Republic, 1870-1920 / Karen Offen.
DESCRIPTION: Cambridge ; New York, NY : Cambridge University Press, [2017] |
Series: New studies in European history | Includes bibliographical references and index.
IDENTIFIERS: LCCN 2017004387 | ISBN 9781107188044 (Hardback : alk. paper) |
ISBN 9781316638408 (pbk. : alk. paper)
SUBJECTS: LCSH: Women–France–Social conditions–19th century. | Women–France–Social
conditions–20th century. | Women's rights–France–History–19th century. |
Women's rights–France–History–20th century. | Feminism–France–History–19th century. |
Feminism–France–History–20th century. | France–History–Third Republic, 1870-1940.
CLASSIFICATION: LCC HQ1613 .O339 2017 | DDC 305.40944/09034–dc23
LC record available at https://lccn.loc.gov/2017004387

ISBN 978-1-107-18804-4 Hardback
ISBN 978-1-316-63840-8 Paperback

To Marilyn Jacoby Boxer,
with my heartfelt gratitude for forty-five years of friendship,
collegiality, and sisterhood

Contents

vii

Preface

France, is, in the opinion of the entire world, the paradise of woman.

Inaugural issue of *Femina* (1 February 1901)

The generative function – with all its physiological and moral consequences – is certainly the most serious thing, the primordial and dominant thing about feminine existence. Adversaries and partisans of feminist theories agree on this fact. And it is somewhat curious to attest that this generative function furnishes both sides with their supreme argument, their climactic point, in support of their reasoning. But, insofar as the first insist on seeing in this [function] only a cause of woman's essential and irremediable inferiority and a rationale for her subordination (a primitive notion, worthy of barbarous times when the "right of the strongest" was the only rule), the second, inspired by the modern ideal of justice, would like it to become, for she who accomplishes it, a source of material and moral advantages, independence, influence, and well-being; and in its name they formulate their principal demands.

Nelly Roussel
"Pour les Mères," *L'Almanach Féministe, 1907*

In contrast to my earlier volume *The Woman Question in France, 1400–1870,* which spans multiple centuries by focusing on emerging themes during the centuries of French monarchies, this volume will reconstruct and interrogate, by honing in on chronological slices, the explosion of debates on the woman question during the first fifty years of the Third Republic. It will demonstrate just how important the debates on the woman question became during this period, when progressive Frenchmen attempted to construct a new democratic form of government and when women (and their male allies) frontally challenged masculine domination in French society by campaigning for women's equality in law and education, parity and partnership in the institution of marriage, equal opportunities in the labor force, and control over their own bodies and fertility as well as over their own earnings. The introductory quotations, for instance, epitomize the vast differences in opinion on the situation of women in early twentieth-century France.

This is not a book about "images of women" or masculine stereotypes of women, or about women as "muse" for male creativity; in my study real women talk – and often they talk back to and contest views of the female sex that seem demeaning, destructive, or even downright dangerous. Nor is it, strictly speaking, a history of French feminism, or of the organized feminist campaigns – or of the antifeminist opposition. Others have contributed to this literature. My book is rather about the debate, about conflict, about struggle, a "war" whose weapons were words, and arguments that collided and sent sparks flying in many directions; it is about those men and women who spoke up, who engaged in polemics for and against the emancipation of women in French society.

Although, technically speaking, the proclamation of the Republic took place in September 1870 (following the defeat of Napoléon III by the German armies at Sedan), the Constitution was only enacted in 1875. The republicans only won control of the two-chamber parliament in 1878 and the presidency in 1879, but the new regime would not become firmly implanted in France until the end of the 1880s and into the 1890s. Thus, this book actually begins in approximately 1872, following the extraordinary eruption and vicious suppression of the Paris Commune (discussed in my companion volume), which had serious implications and detrimental consequences for the subsequent revival of the woman question debates. I track those debates through the Great War to 1920, which marked the fiftieth anniversary of the Third Republic's founding. In my epilogue (Chapter 15), I briefly bring the story up to 1949, with the publication of Simone de Beauvoir's *The Second Sex*, to which my own book effectively serves as a "prequel."

I characterized the preceding volume as one about *Reconnaissance*. Here I have deliberately labeled the four parts of this volume, covering five decades but sliced into four sequential chronological periods (1872–1889, 1890–1900, 1901–1914, and 1914–1920) as *Familiarization, Encounter, Climax*, and *Anti-Climax*, which might be imagined as representing four stages in a human sexual "relationship."

The chapters in these four parts will demonstrate that virtually all the significant issues concerning male–female relations were placed on the table for debate, if not by 1914, then certainly by 1920. The break points correspond to important turning points in the political, economic, and social history of the French Third Republic that had a direct effect on the debates, such as the centennial of the French Revolution in 1889 and the Paris Exposition of 1900, both of which witnessed the advent and application of the new label of "feminism," the eruption of major women's rights congresses (some government-sponsored), the organization and lobbying efforts of local, regional, and national women's rights groups, the outbreak of war in 1914, the making of peace in 1919, and finally, in 1920, the Republic's fiftieth anniversary celebration. The debates on the woman question are in fact tightly aligned with and deeply entwined with each of these developments. I treat these debates in a comprehensive and fully contextualized manner, to the extent that my sources, all published in their time, will allow. Doubtless, more sources remain to be recovered, especially in the daily press of Paris and the provinces as well as that of francophone Belgium and Switzerland. These debates transcended the borders of France proper and found participants throughout French-speaking areas of Europe.

A problem with earlier historical treatments of "feminism" – and, more broadly, women's history – is that historians have lumped these decades together (e.g., 1870-1914, or even 1870-1940); this practice has foreclosed the possibility/opportunity for the rich, deep contextualized reconstruction and analysis that the investigation of shorter periods can allow. My objective here is partly to demonstrate the interconnectedness (these days, some say "entanglement") of the various themes and topics, and to engage readers to more closely follow through time the development and distinctive inflections of the arguments and issues, and to experience vicariously the personalities of the debaters, to feel the heat and intensity of the debates, just as though they had been participant observers in that specific period of time.

In this volume, in particular, the "devil" is in the details, as found in the great amount of newly recovered published evidence. Attention to these details allows readers to track change and/or continuity in the debates over time and among the participants. It also allows, with the careful attention to chronology, to demonstrate the fits and starts, and the crosscutting of the multiple themes and topics.

Several colleagues have suggested that I end the book in 1914, with the outbreak of World War I. This would certainly conform to standard practice among historians – but as in the case of bridging the French Revolution, a bridge is needed here as well, to the immediate postwar period and to the fiftieth anniversary of the regime. In fact, the woman question debates took a critical turn during the Great War, given the conundrum of the plummeting French birth rate coupled with the need for young women and mothers to seek employment in order to keep the

French economy going in wartime, especially by working in the munitions factories. Meanwhile, their menfolk were being slaughtered by the thousands (at least 1.3 million Frenchmen died in this war, and hundreds of thousands more were wounded or disabled for life). Questions about women's patriotism and their inclination to pacifism provoked much discussion in the French press. Feminists anticipated that, once the war was over, French women would have sufficiently proved their patriotism through their war work and would be rewarded with full citizenship. Very important debates center on these issues.

Instead, in the immediate postwar years (1919–1922), even as the French public was slowly coming around to embrace women's equal citizenship, the loosening of legal restrictions on wives, the inevitability of women's workforce participation, etc., the resistant right-wingers in the French Senate (many of whom were younger professed republicans) would slam the door to full citizenship in their faces. It is my conviction that the immediate aftermath of the war – and the fifty-year anniversary of the founding of the Republic in 1920 – provides a far more suitable place to end the book. As I explain in the epilogue *all* the issues are on the table; after that the arguments, both in favor of women's emancipation and against, become extremely repetitive. Had I extended the book to the end of the Third Republic and included all these subsidiary debates – which others (Christine Bard, Françoise Thébaud, Paul Smith, Mary Louise Roberts, Siân Reynolds, Geoff Read, and Elisa Camiscioli, among others) have already addressed eloquently and in considerable detail – completion of the manuscript would be still be "pending," and nothing much would have been gained.

Both of my anonymous readers expressed concern about "how the relationship between these middle- and upper-class metropolitan women and those subjugated in the colonies works in the French feminist story." The fact is that the colonial issue, as concerns the plight and condition of indigenous women, does not appear much in the *debates* on the woman question in early Third Republic France, except in the form of denunciations of their confinement, their lack of education and opportunities, and invocations of France's "civilizing mission" to come to their rescue. It does emerge to a degree in the 1900s during the debates over legalizing paternity suits by unwed mothers. At that time the question is a political question: whether in the colonies paternity suits might also be filed by indigenous unwed mothers against French men with whom they are cohabiting (due, not least, to the absence of, or at least severe shortage of, French wives or potential wives). I do address this particular issue in the appropriate chapter.

In contrast to the British case, however, where scholars have documented the engagement of numbers of English and Irish women resident in the British colonies – particularly in India – in campaigns to end the subordination of indigenous women by abolishing *sati* and other customs that severely discriminate against women, this was not the case for France. That is not to say that a few feminists, such as Hubertine Auclert, were not distressed over the condition of women in Algeria (which was actually a French *département* in the 1890s), or that others (such as Madame Luce in Algiers) would not attempt to provide indigenous girls with educational opportunities. But this did not fuel important public debates on the woman question in France's imperial territories for many decades. The evidence I have encountered supports the conclusion that the thrust of French debate on the woman question before 1900 was overwhelmingly directed toward resolving the complex of issues that made Francophone women's lives miserable *in metropolitan* France, as well as in the French-speaking part of Belgium and in the Suisse Romande. More concern about the plight of indigenous women in the French colonies – and what might be done to alleviate it – manifests itself after World War I, as pressure mounts during the 1920s and 1930s for the dissolution of colonial empire. France's mainstream feminists do weigh in heavily by the time of the colonial exposition of 1931, but those debates lie beyond the scope of this volume. That would be another book, one that others have already begun to write.

As in the earlier volume, I have drawn from key arguments made in my own publications (particularly those that concern the defining and locating feminism in France, and exploring feminism's close connections to depopulation and nationalism) for material to repurpose here, but no chapter here reprints an earlier article as such. Wherever appropriate, I have acknowledged my borrowings in the bibliographical footnotes. This book has no formal bibliography; however, the footnotes are both bibliographical and historiographical, and both primary and secondary sources are cited in order of publication rather than alphabetically. I have tried to make the references as explicit and transparent as possible, so that others can easily consult the evidence if they so desire and verify (or dispute) the conclusions I have reached. Copies of the primary materials on which the book is based will be deposited in the Special Collections archive of the Stanford University Libraries. All translations from the French are mine unless otherwise attributed in the notes.

This book, like my earlier publications *European Feminisms* and the volume that accompanies this one – *The Woman Question in France,*

1400–1870 – is a synthetic work of interpretative history grounded in primary sources. Such work is possible only by building on the earlier contributions and insights of my colleagues in French and European history, literature, art, and culture. Rather than thanking them here individually for their contributions and insights, or relegating such recognition to the endnotes (as one reviewer suggested), I have chosen to acknowledge their work (and that of other "authorities") in the body of the text. This strategy indicates not only that I have read their books and articles but also that I have taken their findings and observations into account. No one should doubt that this book is grounded in decades of collaborative, collegial feminist scholarship, both by women and by men. By thus acknowledging the scholars whose research and insights has contributed greatly to the underpinnings of my book, I also demonstrate what a major contribution their practice of women's and gender history has made to reorienting the discipline of history more generally – and, in particular, to reconceptualizing French history from a gendered perspective.

I have not neglected "quarrels" or disagreements with other historians in the text. I prefer to think of such disagreements as legitimate debates about interpretation. It is, of course, also possible to relegate these to the endnotes, but I think that engaging arguments about interpretation, with evidence in hand, remains a critical component of the best practice of historical writing, and that highlighting the occasions where historians differ should not be avoided. This practice also serves to draw the reader into the ongoing conversations about interpretations of evidence.

Acknowledgments

I would first like to acknowledge those French history colleagues in the United States, in Great Britain, and especially in France, who have been members of the cheerleading squad since the 1970s and 1980s – you know who you are and I hope some of you will be asked to review one or both of my volumes on the woman question debates. I won't name you here because, first, the list is quite long and, second, I know how book review editors automatically exclude acknowledged – and extremely knowledgeable – close associates when they are choosing reviewers. This ploy will make them work harder.

Thanks also go to the directors and staff (over the years) and former scholars at the Clayman Institute for Gender Research at Stanford, especially my sister Senior Scholars, the late Susan Groag Bell, Edith B. Gelles, and Marilyn Yalom, for their encouragement and support over many decades. Thanks also to the participants in Stanford's French Culture Workshop who have vetted several of these chapters.

No one can do this kind of historical research without the help of unsung heroines and heroes in the libraries and archives. Here I would like to acknowledge the best friends a historian could ever have in the Stanford University Libraries: super sleuth Sarah B. Sussman, Curator for French and Italian at Green Library, who (like Mary Jane Parrine before her) takes seriously my requests for book acquisitions, and the resourceful Joe Leggette, Media and Reserves Specialist, who knows where all the old French newspaper and book microfilms are hidden. Joe has also kept the antique microfilm readers and printers in working condition so that I could rely on them. In France, I owe deep gratitude to Annie Metz, director of the *Bibliothèque Marguerite Durand* (BMD), who has repeatedly come to my rescue in long-distance consultations as well as being helpful during my visits to Paris (thank heaven for the new microfilm reader-printer-scanner at the BMD and for the staff's decision to make *La Fronde* available online). I thank Annie too for realizing (after my power-point presentation at Sciences Po on Mme Ghénia Avril de Sainte-Croix, (a French feminist who figures prominently in this volume) that the lovely oil portrait in the basement archive at the BMD is actually a long-sought early portrait of her when she was still Mlle de Sainte-Croix.

It takes financial resources as well as time to research and write histories of underresearched topics. To those who provided (over several decades) the fellowships and grants that supported various phases of my research – the National Endowment for the Humanities, the Rockefeller Foundation, and the John Simon Guggenheim Memorial Foundation, as well as the Marilyn Yalom Fund at Stanford's Clayman Institute – I once again acknowledge my heartfelt gratitude. Special thanks as well to the Raymundo Fund for providing major financial support of my work and to my family for understanding (or at least, tolerating) my obsession with restoring to memory the European woman question debates, especially those in France and the Francophone world.

I would especially like to thank the staff at Cambridge University Press, beginning with Lewis Bateman, who initially took on my book(s) before his retirement in May 2016 and who chose the two anonymous readers for the press. These heroic colleagues went over my chapters in exacting detail. The care they devoted to my manuscript is a great gift and their suggestions for improving the final version are deeply appreciated. I also thank Michael Watson at Cambridge University Press's UK office for shepherding both books through the publication process. Thanks go to the production crew, beginning with Robert Judkins at Cambridge University Press, to Divya Arjunan of SPI Global, and to Julia Ter Maat in Singapore for her careful copyediting. I also appreciate the great care with which Robert Swanson at Arc Indexing, Inc., prepared the index for this volume.

Finally, I am deeply grateful to my longtime friend and colleague Marilyn Jacoby Boxer, whom I have known and worked with closely for over forty years, following our initial meeting in 1972 in the BMD, when she and I were just beginning to research aspects of French women's history. Marilyn, whose career in academia took a very different path than mine, has read through this entire manuscript more than once (not to mention reading and critiquing the rest of my work over the years, a gift that I have attempted to reciprocate whenever possible); she has saved me from some serious gaffes even as she has suggested hundreds of improvements. In many respects this book is also her book, and I dedicate it to her.

General Introduction
What Do Women Want?

"What do women want?" The pioneering Austrian physician and psycho-analyst Sigmund Freud (who translated Harriet Taylor Mill's 1851 essay on the enfranchisement of women into German and lived in Paris in the 1880s) was not the first to pose this celebrated question, nor was he the first to offer answers. Had he been in Paris from 1869 to 1878, he would have easily encountered the debates on the woman question. Certainly when he did reside there, in 1885–1886, these debates were in full swing. Indeed, Maria Deraismes (1828–1894) had already posed – and responded to – this very question in the first issue (10 April 1869) of *Le Droit des Femmes*.[1] She provided some explicit answers: equal rights, liberty, a choice of social roles and responsibilities, educational opportunities to develop women's intellect and skills, the right to work and equal pay for equal work – and, in particular, a single standard of morality for both sexes.

Had Freud followed the discussions in *Le Droit des Femmes*, or in its successor *L'Avenir des Femmes*, or read Léon Richer's subsequent publications on the disabilities of married women in the law during the 1870s and from late 1879 on in the restored *Le Droit des Femmes*, or had he attended (or even read about) the international women's rights congresses held in Paris in 1878 and 1889, he – like most other publicly aware individuals – would have known exactly what French women wanted, along with the broader goals women's rights advocates pursued. These more general goals included: (1) the freedom for women to assume and carry out their responsibilities as fully accredited *citoyennes*; (2) to channel the significant influence and power they knew they already possessed as embodied women into positive accomplishments; and (3) joint governance, in the family and in society, with men. The achievement of any and all of these goals required

---

[1] Maria Deraismes, "Ce que veulent les femmes," *Le Droit des Femmes*, n° 1 (10 April 1869), 1–2. This article is reprinted in Maria Deraismes, *Ce que veulent les femmes: Articles et discours de 1869 à 1894*, ed. O[dile] Krakovitch (Paris: Syros, 1980).

government intervention – a change in the rules – that would grant adult women, especially wives, decision-making authority.

Would a major change in regimes in France bring with it progress toward these goals? Could a secular Republic, which since the French Revolution signified a regime that should – and must – act on its professed principles of liberty, equality, and fraternity, apply its concept of justice and the "rights of man" to women – "*la moitié de l'humanité*" [half of humanity] in Deraismes's terminology (as in that of the French Revolution) – by enacting major changes in married women's legal status and providing educational and economic opportunities for all girls and women? Could the French, living under a Republic, ensure a happy ending to the debates on the woman question by dismantling what Deraismes had, like her revolutionary predecessors, called "masculine aristocracy"? Could they agree to extend equal citizenship to the other half of humankind?

Such questions had already confronted the male proponents of a Third Republic as they attempted to construct a new, more liberal regime in response to what they saw as the authoritarianism of the Second Empire. In 1869 in her tract *La Femme et les moeurs: Liberté ou Monarchie* [Women and Morals: Liberty or Monarchy] André Léo invoked the principles of the French Revolution, framed women's rights as human rights, and called for women's complete independence. That same year Jenny P. d'Héricourt challenged the republican opposition (to the empire) by remarking that the Second Empire (despite its flaws) had done far more for women than republicans ever had. In 1870, months before the abrupt end of the Second Empire, Maria Deraismes also called on the history of the French Revolution and pointed to its universalist principles; the French Revolution, she claimed, *was* the universal revolution; its logic clearly meant to include women – yet both in 1792 and again in 1848, the democrats had cut women out. How so? "The democrats created a universal of their own, a universal without precedent, a pocket-sized universal, leaving half of humankind aside." The political lesson was this: "When you want to attract someone into your camp, the most elementary tactic is to offer that person some advantages. Woman will not appreciate the justice of democracy until that justice extends to her."[2]

---

[2] Maria Deraismes, "La Femme dans la démocratie," *Le Droit des Femmes*, n° 41 (5 February 1870) & n° 43 (19 February 1870); reprod. in Deraismes, *Ce que veulent les femmes*, pp. 82–89. This was a speech that Deraismes gave at a benefit to found a girls' primary school that would prepare them by age 12 to enter vocational (professional) training schools.

The Third Republic was a very much a work in progress in 1870–1871. In October 1871, Deraismes reminded her readers that the term "republic" [*res publica*] signified "the government of all, the will of all, the interests of all. . . . Only the Republic conforms to nature, reason, and truth."[3] To her it seemed logical and obvious that women were included in the notion of "all" – and she would make this point repeatedly. Although most earlier histories of the regime ignore it, the woman question was the "elephant in the room" in the 1870s as the republicans clamored to seize the ring of state power. Most committed republicans, both male and female, did believe that a republican government must address demands for change in the sociopolitical relations between the sexes – demands that were in fact far from "conservative" in character.

Just what the republicans could or would be able to do for women's cause in the short term, as they worked their way toward consolidating power and crafting the new regime, remained to be seen. By 1875 the National Assembly (elected in 1871) would put in place a constitutional parliamentary government with a weak presidency, but only in the 1880s would the republicans take control over the administrative machinery of the French state. Creating an inclusive participatory democracy on the foundations of an inherited top-down authoritarian structure, still staffed by often resistant personnel left over from the imperial regime, was no easy task. Moreover, the extent of the opposition to the Republic and the republicans, from a coalition of monarchist authoritarian men – legitimists, orleanists, and bonapartists – must not to be underestimated. Most of them viewed the republic as lacking authority and the republicans as impertinent scum.[4] They affirmed as foundational the male-headed hierarchical form of "the family" (based on vesting authority in husbands and the subordination of wives) that France had inherited from Greco-Roman antiquity, Roman law, and Roman Catholicism, abetted by centuries of absolutist monarchy and reconfirmed in even stronger terms by the Napoleonic Code. Debates about the form of the state and the form of the family were inseparable. During the late Second Empire and

---

[3] Maria Deraismes, "Liberté et autorité," *L'Avenir des Femmes*, n° 73 (22 October 1871).

[4] On the politics of the monarchist right during the 1870s, see John Rothney, *Bonapartism after Sedan* (Ithaca, NY: Cornell University Press, 1969); Robert R. Locke, *French Legitimists and the Politics of Moral Order in the Early Third Republic* (Princeton, NJ: Princeton University Press, 1974); Karen Offen, *Paul de Cassagnac and the Authoritarian Tradition in France* (New York: Garland, 1991); Steven D. Kale, *Legitimism and the Reconstruction of French Society, 1852–1883* (Baton Rouge: Louisiana State University Press, 1992). None of these earlier works, including my own, took the "woman question" debates into account.

early Third Republic, the followers of Pierre-Joseph Proudhon and Frédéric Le Play were retooling such arguments for a more secular audience.

In face of this multipronged Catholic monarchist resurgence, prominent republican men would maintain that women's support was essential to the success of the secular republic as well as in their own interest. They had long viewed efforts to wrest control of female education from the Roman Catholic Church as central to their strategy. But more was needed; they had to win women's hearts as well as their minds. Already during the revolutionary months of 1848, Ernest Legouvé (who was elected to the *Académie Française* in the 1850s and who wrote for *Le Droit des Femmes* in the late 1860s) had charged that the first French revolution had failed because it was unjust to women; he insisted that the "virile principles of liberty and equality must, in order to be realized, be complemented by the feminine virtue of fraternity," which "grew out of women's love." No republic, Legouvé intimated, would succeed except at this price.[5] This message remained pertinent in the early 1870s, as the remarks of Maria Deraismes indicate. Other committed republicans would similarly under-score the notion that under a newly minted republic women had a special contribution to make to political and societal life. The historian Edgar Quinet, for instance, argued in 1872 (in his book *La République: Conditions de la régénération de la France*):[6]

> What would a republic, a democracy be, that lacked the genius of woman. All those who, in the past, have worked for the revival of a society have called girls, wives, [and] mothers, to their aid. Can we accomplish our work today without them? . . .
>
> Above all else, instead of that false and frivolous idea of the *ancien régime* that men alone make progress, let us reestablish in people's minds the true and new idea, which is this: women cooperate with men in giving birth to societies. They hold not only children but entire peoples in their laps.

---

[5] The quotations are from the first edition of Legouvé's *Histoire morale des femmes* (Paris: Gustave Sandré, 1849), pp. 5, 13. On the impact of this book, see Karen Offen, "Ernest Legouvé and the Doctrine of 'Equality in Difference' for Women: A Case Study of Male Feminism in Nineteenth-Century French Thought," *Journal of Modern History*, 58:2 (June 1986), 452–484, esp. 453. The 6th ed. (1874) of the *Histoire morale* has been digitized by Google. Legouvé's preface to this 1874 edition mirrors his remarks in his lead article, "A M. Léon Richer," in the inaugural issue of *Le Droit de Femmes*, n° 1 (10 April 1869), 1.

[6] Edgar Quinet, *La République: Conditions de la régénération de la France* (Paris: Dentu, 1872), in *Oeuvres complètes de Edgar Quinet*, vol. 26 (Paris: Librairie Germer-Baillière, n.d.), p. 190. On the woman question, chapters 36–40 are relevant. Thirty years later, Françoise Benassis applauded Quinet's contribution, "Le 'Féminisme' d'Edgar Quinet," *La Fronde*, n° 1918 (11 March 1903), even though she remarked that his arguments could be seen as somewhat old-fashioned in comparison with those of early twentieth-century male-feminists.

Quinet, like many other pro-democratic men, adhered without reservation to the deeply entrenched notion of women's influence and promoted the necessity of attaching its force to the new republic as a means of "regeneration." Yet, as the clear-sighted Maria Deraismes argued in late 1871, the route to regeneration lay in improving moral behavior, and for that France was not ready. What the republicans particularly needed to pursue, in her view, was a single standard of morality for both sexes.[7] Building out her earlier assertions, Deraismes called on her fellow republicans to address four major legal changes: *recherche de la paternité* (legalizing paternity suits); separation or divorce to be obtained by a wife in case of her husband's adultery (without the Code's current stipulation that a separation could only be justified if the husband's concubine was lodged under his own roof); recognition of the civil rights of married women; and equal pay for equal work and admission of women to all the liberal professions for which they are qualified. Enactment of these laws, she insisted, would bring about a 100 percent improvement in morality, thereby achieving a big step toward the regeneration of France.[8]

Some republican men did take such observations seriously, and many leading figures (egged on by Richer and Deraismes) openly courted women's support for the new regime. They first insisted that the Third Republic, as an ostensibly anti-authoritarian mode of governance based on the principles, must necessarily apply its principles to individuals *of both sexes.* Some did prioritize major legal changes in the institution of secular marriage that Deraismes had laid out. Some did call for advances in the formal education of girls. A few advocated civil divorce. Their support for women's "right" to work and equal pay for equal work became more energetic as hundreds of thousands of women joined the work force, or failing that, fell into poverty, which in turn produced a rash of illegitimate births, infanticides, abortions, prostitution, and suicide. Acknowledgment of all these so-called social problems reanimated republican men's concern about the falling birth rates and the threat of "depopulation" in an era when calculations of national military and industrial strength would count more than ever before in the international political arena. The press hotly debated these pressing claims, both pro and con. Expeditiously, and for a

---

[7] Deraismes had already made a sharp critique of the double standard in the late 1860s. See the second lecture in her 1868–1869 conference series, "La femme et les mœurs," reprinted in *Ève dans l'humanité* [1868], orig. published in 1891 (Paris: Librairie Générale de L. Sauvaitre), and then as vol. 2 of Deraismes, *Oeuvres complètes de Maria Deraismes*, 4 vols. (Paris: Alcan, 1895–1898). This volume was reprinted in 1990 (Paris: côté-femmes) with an introduction by Laurence Klejman.

[8] Maria Deraismes, "La Régénération de la France," *L'Avenir des Femmes,* n° 75 (5 November 1871).

short time, women's rights leaders would place the quest for political citizenship for all women on the back burner, arguing that resolving all these many other sociopolitical issues must take precedence, via a *politique de la brèche*, that is to say, piece by piece. As historian Arianne Chernock reminds us, "Feminists worked out their arguments in real time, in response to contingencies and conflicts."[9] So, of course, did their opponents. One must understand how these contingencies and conflicts inflected the French debates on the woman question in the short term as well as in the long term. It is equally important to appreciate the earnestness of the reformers and the complexity of the problems they addressed, not only in regard to the law and education but particularly in relation to socioeconomic issues and questions of public morality. It is necessary to recognize that access to political rights for women was but one of many significant reforms being proposed and debated in the 1870s and 1880s. The demand for votes for women would nevertheless reemerge in the late 1870s, when Hubertine Auclert, disgusted with the lack of progress to date, would spearhead a new campaign.

In my earlier book, *The Woman Question in France, 1400–1870*, I laid out five factors or themes in the debates on the woman question that, from the fourteenth century to the mid-nineteenth century seem specifically French. Let me reiterate them briefly here: first, the intensity with which advocates (of both sexes) for women's emancipation attributed immense power and influence to French women (despite the legal incapacities of wives); second, the injustice of men's peremptory exclusion of women from positions of political authority; third, the continuing strategic political importance male opponents of women's emancipation accorded to biomedical thinking; fourth, the political, ideological, and practical emphasis both women and men placed on *civic* motherhood; and, finally, the peculiar character of French republican nationalism – a regime that professed democratic ideals confronted by the distasteful requirements of *realpolitik* in a still-monarchical Europe.

To these one can add another factor that become increasingly visible after 1871: the close relationships that existed between women's rights advocates (of both sexes, who will become known in the 1890s by the neologism "feminists") and a number of important republican political figures. Historian Florence Rochefort has rightly argued that "what was particularly French about French feminism were its ties to the Republic. . . .

---

[9] Arianne Chernock, *Men and the Making of British Feminism* (Stanford, CA: Stanford University Press, 2010), p. 26.

Before feminism allied itself with what proved to be the enduring force of republicanism, the history of French mobilization for women's rights was a discontinuous one, tied to moments of revolution."[10] Rochefort also underscores that, during the early years of the Third Republic, "the movement for women's rights was characterized by the joint participation of women and men."[11] One reason for these connections was, as historian Sylvia Schafer has reminded us, "the new republic's deep investment in civil law as a means of institutionalizing the authority of the state and reconfiguring the moral life of the nation."[12] As the republicans took power, the fact that feminists appealed to the power of the state by turning to legislative remedies (particularly to those that might compel improvements in moral behavior) should hardly come as a surprise, but it also meant that progress would be slow – and that these remedies would be misconstrued by some later historians as "conservative."[13] Realization of

[10] See Florence Rochefort, "The French Feminist Movement and Republicanism, 1868–1914," in *Women's Emancipation Movements in the Nineteenth Century*, ed. Sylvia Paletschek & Bianka Pietrow-Ennker (Stanford, CA: Stanford University Press, 2000), pp. 77–101; quote 78–79. See also Florence Rochefort, "Du droit des femmes au féminisme en Europe 1860–1914," in *Encyclopédie politique et historique des femmes*, ed. Christine Fauré (Paris: Presses universitaires de France [PUF], 1997), pp. 551–570, and her earlier authoritative study with Laurence Klejman, *L'Égalité en marche: Le Féminisme sous la Troisième République* (Paris: Fondation Nationale des Sciences Politiques [FNSP] & des femmes, 1989).

[11] Rochefort, "French Feminist Movement and Republicanism," quote p. 77.

[12] Sylvia Schafer, *Children in Moral Danger and the Problem of Government in Third Republic France* (Princeton, NJ: Princeton University Press, 1997), p. 10.

[13] Much of the 1970s historiography on French feminism and women, read retrospectively, is marked by liberationist values of the era, including marked antipathy for the polemical category "bourgeois feminism," "conventional" ideas about femininity and the family, motherhood, etc. The authors' sympathy for socialist solutions, reproductive freedom, androgynous sex roles, individualism, women's right to work, and their objections to equality-in-difference arguments, plus their repugnance for what they called "purity crusades" made it difficult for them to evaluate the sources and issues within the context of the early Third Republic. The interpretation of Jean Rabaut, *Histoire des féminismes français* (Paris: Stock, 1978), chapters 7–10, is particularly flawed in this respect. In the 1980s the study by Patrick Kay Bidelman, *Pariahs Stand Up! The Founding of the Liberal Feminist Movement in France, 1858-1889* (Westport, CT: Garland Publishers, 1982) captures the anticlerical political context. James F. McMillan responds to Bidelman's dissertation and to Charles Sowerwine's detailed study of *Women and Socialism* in chapter 4 of his book *Housewife or Harlot: The Place of Women in French Society, 1870-1940* (London & New York: St. Martin's, 1981). The most balanced early account is that of Claire Goldberg Moses, *French Feminism in the Nineteenth Century* (Albany, NY: SUNY Press, 1984), chapters 8–9. Also in 1984, Karen Offen introduced two additional elements into the contextual mix with "Depopulation, Nationalism, and Feminism in Fin-de-Siècle France," *American Historical Review*, 89:3 (June 1984), 648–676. The "most comprehensive and balanced study to date" is the joint work of Klejman & Rochefort, *L'Egalité en marche* (cited in n. 9), though their emphasis is on the period after 1889, as is also the case with the contributions of Anne Cova on the importance of motherhood issues in French feminisms, notably *Maternité et droits des femmes en France (XIXe – XXe siècles)* (Paris: Economica, 1997), and *"Au Service de l'église, de la patrie et de la famille": Femmes catholiques et maternité sous la IIIe République* (Paris: L'Harmattan, 2000). See also Anne Cova, *Féminisme et néomalthusianisme*

feminist legal and economic reforms would require the support of a majority of male legislators (not all of whom were convinced republicans in these years). Highly visible republican men did, in fact, support the cause of women's rights, not only promoting demands for radical changes in the Civil Code for married women and initiating major educational institutions for girls but also, as the regime became more stable, supporting campaigns for women's admission to the vote.

One historian of feminism in France, Joan Wallach Scott, has dramatically asserted that republican "universalism" created "paradoxes" for feminists,[14] while another, Charles Sowerwine, has alleged that "the Republic" was unfriendly, even hostile, to women – that it was unrepentantly "gendered" male from the outset.[15] This latter argument focuses specifically

---

sous la IIIe République (Paris: L'Harmattan, 2011). The significant contributions of Steven C. Hause focus particularly on the politics of woman suffrage, with his study (with Anne Kenney), *Women's Suffrage and Social Politics in the French Third Republic* (Princeton, NJ: Princeton University Press, 1984) and his unrivaled biography, *Hubertine Auclert, the French Suffragette* (New Haven, CT: Yale University Press, 1987).

[14] See Joan Wallach Scott, *Only Paradoxes to Offer: French Feminists and the Rights of Man* (Cambridge, MA: Harvard University Press, 1996). What Scott does not acknowledge is the extent to which most French feminists under the republics assertively articulated claims for an expansion and redeployment of women's power and influence "as women," and promoted the sharing of authority with men. Their opponents, on the other hand, continued to think in terms of a topsy-turvy world model, and feared "women on top." Scott's interpretation appears to draw inspiration from the overly emphatic criticism of the masculinism of the French Revolution by Joan B. Landes, *Women and the Public Sphere in the Age of the French Revolution* (Ithaca, NY: Cornell University Press, 1988). Indeed, Landes argues (pp. 203–204) that "the structures of modern republican politics can be construed as part of an elaborate defense against women's power and public presence." But this judgment, with respect to the early Third Republic, lacks traction. Landes views the "private," or domestic, sphere as necessarily a disempowered space, but evidence of French women's historic invocations of women's power and influence along with their demands to value motherhood and to extend it to civil and political space contradict such assumptions. Both Scott and Landes have been influenced by Carole Pateman's broad argument that in the development of political theory, a sexual contract in fact preceded the "social contract." See Carole Pateman, *The Sexual Contract* (Stanford, CA: Stanford University Press, 1988; originally publ. by Polity Press). In fact, Pateman's evidence for this theory comes primarily from British sources.

[15] See Charles Sowerwine's chapter, "Revising the Sexual Contract: Women's Citizenship and Republicanism in France, 1789–1944," in *Confronting Modernity in Fin-de-Siècle France: Bodies, Minds and Gender*, ed. Christopher E. Forth & Elinor Accampo (Houndmills, UK: Palgrave Macmillan, 2010), pp. 19–42, and his earlier articles, "The Sexual Contract(s) of the Third Republic," in *French History and Civilization: Papers from the George Rudé Seminar*, ed. Ian Coller, Helen Davies, & Julie Kalman, vol. 1 (Melbourne: The George Rudé Society, 2005), pp. 245–253 (available online at www.h-france.net/rude/rudepapers.html) and "'La politique, cet élément dans lequel j'aurais voulu vivre': l'exclusion des femmes est-elle inhérente au républicanisme de la Troisième République?" *Clio: Histoire, Femmes et Sociétés*, n° 24 (2006), 171–194. Sowerwine grounds his interpretation of republican hostility to women's "citizenship" (which he equates exclusively with suffrage) in the theoretical analyses of Landes, Pateman, and Michel Foucault, but he ignores the abundant evidence of some republican men's conciliatory, even supportive approach to other aspects of women's rights dating from the late Second Empire and the Third Republic (both before and after 1880). He neither "sees" or acknowledges the extent of French women's activity in "civil society" throughout the

on the absence of male republican support for the single issue of woman suffrage, drawing primarily on evidence from the early 1870s during the immediate backlash against women's activism in the Paris Commune. It does not acknowledge the support that a number of highly visible and influential liberal republicans did bring to other aspects of the debates on the woman question, both during the late Second Empire and in the early years of the Third Republic, recognition of which fundamentally undercuts such assertions. To gain a more valid appreciation of the views of republican men, it seems vital to examine the full range of issues addressed by those women and men who advocated equal rights for women during the early Third Republic, rather than jumping to conclusions on the basis of a single issue, or scrutinizing only the arguments of a few, though admittedly significant individuals (as does Scott with her selection of Hubertine Auclert and Madeleine Pelletier as sites of analysis).

In the chapters of Part I, I will examine the published arguments and political efforts of a number of leading republican men and women who were deeply concerned about one or more aspects of women's status, recuperating the arguments they actually used, in the time in which they used them. This is not to argue either that the Third Republic was a perfect regime that always lived up to its principles, or that all republican men were enthusiastic male-feminists, especially in the years immediately following the Commune. To be sure, there would be some republican men who, even as anticlericals and positivists, were committed to the model of male breadwinner/domestic wives, or who would sympathize either with Jules Michelet's thesis that women were necessarily eternal invalids requiring masculine protection (even as they needed to be liberated from the influence of Catholic priests) or with Auguste Comte's "religion of woman," which required French women to remain on their pedestals – to incarnate virtue – so that men could worship them. Other well-known writers, notably Guy de Maupassant (1850–1893), would issue threats to those who would emancipate women:[16]

---

nineteenth century, especially during the Third Republic – even though women did not have the vote or the right to hold elective office. Does he then mistake Habermas's "Offentlichkeit" (so poorly translated in English as the "public sphere") for the political arena, when in fact the term indicates the opening space for public activism (freedom of the press, assembly, and association, the making of public opinion, etc.) that lies between government and household. For a diametrically different perspective on this issue, see Karen Offen, "Feminists Campaign in 'Public Space': Civil Society, Gender Justice, and the History of European Feminisms," in *Civil Society, Public Space, and Gender Justice*, ed. Karen Hagemann, Sonya Michel, & Gunilla Budde (New York: Berghahn, 2008), pp. 97–116, and Karen Offen, "Is the 'Woman Question' Really the 'Man Problem'?" in *Confronting Modernity in Fin-de-Siecle France*, pp. 43–62.

[16] Guy de Maupassant, "La Lysistrata moderne," *Le Gaulois* (30 December 1880).

> Let us demand of woman that she be the charm and luxury of [our]
> existence. Seeing that woman demands her rights, let us recognize only
> one: the right to please.... Today when she is mistress of the world, she
> calls for her rights! Well then, we, whom she has lulled to sleep, enslaved,
> subdued by love and for love, we are going to judge her coldly with our
> reason and good sense instead of considering her only as a flower that
> perfumes life. Our sovereign is going to become our equal. Too bad for her!

During the formative years of the Republic, the woman question was
clearly on the minds of men of all political stripes, including committed
republicans. Old '48ers or former Saint-Simonians as well as the great
playwright, poet, and novelist Victor Hugo continued to support women's
rights to a remarkable degree, as did the venerable press lord Émile de
Girardin. Younger men on the republican left – and many socialists –
endorsed, attended, and subsequently provided government support for
women's rights congresses and events; they even invited advocates of
women's rights to publish their articles and petitions in organs of the
male-controlled mainstream and working-class press.

The following chapters present a series of significant debates on the
woman question by allies and enemies of women's emancipation in the
singular time frame provided by the early French Third Republic. Readers,
having examined earlier phases of these debates in my companion volume
on 1400–1870 will recognize many familiar themes. Many of the issues raised
about women's citizenship during the monarchies of the Old Regime and
the early years of the French Revolution, but especially in 1848, would be
rehearsed again during the Third Republic, as would the controversies about
"free love" and "immorality" that had swirled around the Saint-Simonians in
the 1830s and 1840s. The ties of women's rights advocates to the republican
idea and to the Third Republic itself, with all the possibilities it provided
to invoke its principles on behalf of women's emancipation, constituted a
huge exception in the European context which, apart from the neighboring
federal republic of Switzerland, remained assertively monarchical and class-
bound. Even in the Swiss republic, democratically enfranchised men in
the German-speaking cantons proved far more resistant to contemplating
women's equality than did most male proponents of the French Third
Republic. Men and women in the French-speaking cantons were far more
supportive; Geneva, Lausanne, and Neuchâtel all provided important allies
in the course of the French campaigns for women's equal rights – Marie
Pouchoulin Goegg, Charles Secrétan, Aimé Humbert, August de Morsier,
and Louis Bridel, to name just a few. Likewise, francophone Belgium,
though still a parliamentary monarchy, would contribute allies such as

Marie Popelin, Louis Frank, and Isabelle Gatti de Gamond, Isala van Diest, and Julia Van Marcke de Lummen, all of whom participated in the debates on the woman question.

Many Francophone feminists would engage with the transnational campaigns to stop the traffic in women and children (known as the White Slave Trade until well after 1900) and to urge the French government to end the government licensing of prostitutes and brothels. After 1900 and the founding of the *Conseil National des Femmes Françaises* (CNFF) and its affiliation with the International Council of Women, the Francophone debates on the woman question, particularly as concerned the Napoleonic Code's strictures on the subordination of wives in marriage that had spread throughout Europe, would influence transnational action on marriage law and the nationality of married women as well as the seemingly interminable debates on women's employment and campaigns for equal pay for equal work. Finally, Francophone feminists would contribute vigorously to campaigns for peace and international arbitration of disputes between countries, only to see their efforts torpedoed by the outbreak of war in 1914.

PART I

Familiarization
Romance with the Republic, 1870s–1889

The more the condition of woman is improved, the more the power of the family is completed and purified.

Ernest Legouvé
Histoire morale des femmes (1849, 1874)

* * *

What we must do is modify the present conditions of women's work; we must moralize the workshop, we must find a way of reconciling . . . the interests of the *ouvrière* with the respect due to every woman and with the obligations of mothers. . . . Woman, even when married, must be able to live from her own salary if she so desires.

Léon Richer
La Femme libre (1877)

* * *

The right of women is the corollary of the right of peoples.

Maria Deraismes
Speech given at the First International Congress for Women's Rights, Paris (1878)

* * *

[A] suffrage that allows you to exclude from the electoral lists nine million women is far too restrictive to bear the name universal. . . . Ladies, we must remind ourselves that the weapon of the vote will be for us, just as it is for man, the only means of obtaining the reforms we desire. As long as we remain excluded from civic life, men will attend to their own interests rather than to ours.

Hubertine Auclert
Le Droit politique des femmes (1878)

* * *

Those who deny our equality in the present, will deny it also in the future. Thus we must count on ourselves to achieve our own freedom.... Without a guarantee, I am truly afraid that human equality, as preached by every socialist school, will still mean the equality of men, and that the women will be duped by the proletarian men just as the latter have been duped by the bourgeoisie.

Hubertine Auclert
Égalité sociale et politique de la femme (1879)

* * *

Let us demand of woman that she be the charm and luxury of [our] existence. Seeing that woman demands her rights, let us recognize only one: the right to please.... Today when she is mistress of the world, she calls for her rights! Well then, we, whom she has lulled to sleep, enslaved, subdued by love and for love, we are going to judge her coldly with our reason and good sense instead of considering her only as a flower that perfumes life. Our sovereign is going to become our equal. Too bad for her!

Guy de Maupassant
"La Lysistrata moderne," *Le Gaulois* (30 December 1880)

* * *

France does not yet know what self-government means. When people express the desire for a reform, they sit down, fold their arms, and wait for the government to act.

Emilie de Morsier
Letter to Theodore Stanton, in *The Woman Question in Europe* (1884)

* * *

At present, war is not only an infamy, a shameful iniquity, but a colossal and sinister stupidity.

Maria Deraismes
Discours (1888)

CHAPTER I

Relaunching the Republican Campaign for Women's Rights

The Banquet of 9 June 1872

On the 9th of June 1872 about 150 French men and women who sympathized with a republican form of government gathered at the Corazza Restaurant in the Palais-Royal to take a symbolic stand on behalf of women's rights. That women were invited was an event in itself; for decades women had been unwelcome at such banquets, even to celebrate the most advanced political causes.[1] Maria Deraismes was prominent among the women present. In attendance were a number of prominent progressive men, including the historian Edouard Laboulaye (1811–1883), who presided at the banquet. Veterans of the Saint-Simonian movement, such as the journalist Adolphe Guéroult (1810–1872) and the peace activist Charles Lemonnier (1808?–1891), and younger republicans, such as Alfred Naquet (1834–1916), were among those present to relaunch the campaign, as was the proud organizer of the event, Léon Richer (1824–1911). Only the previous year Laboulaye had openly complimented Richer for advocating women's rights as human creatures rather than pressing for "equality of functions" on the Spartan model.[2] At the banquet Laboulaye developed a theme that would become a touchstone for republican women's rights advocates in the years following the Paris Commune. "I have in mind," he said, "not merely woman's happiness and the peace of her household; indeed, this question is one of the first

---

[1] Michelle Perrot reports that in 1838 Flora Tristan had been excluded from the banquet commemorating the death of a major champion of women's emancipation, Charles Fourier; see Perrot, *Les Femmes ou les silences de l'histoire* (Paris: Flammarion, 1998), p. 302. On earlier controversies over admitting women to political banquets see Jacqueline Lalouette, "Les femmes dans les banquets politiques en France (vers 1848)," *Clio: Histoire, Femmes, Sociétés*, n° 14 (2001), 71–91. Technically speaking, this 1872 women's rights banquet was not considered a "political" banquet.

[2] Laboulaye's letter to Richer was published in *L'Avenir des Femmes*, n° 76 (12 November 1871).

magnitude for the country. If we want to regenerate France, we must begin with the women."[3]

The political climate in France, however, was still less than auspicious for making drastic reforms in women's status and Deraismes cautioned the audience not to expect that women's demands would be met all at once. Following the Commune and the consequent crackdown, advocates of women's rights had found it necessary to proceed with caution. The government forced Richer's paper, *Le Droit de Femmes,* to rename itself *L'Avenir des Femmes,* tone down its demands, and lower its activist profile in order to continue publication. In the next several years, thanks first to the real possibility of a Bourbon restoration followed by a thwarted Bonapartist effort to restore an imperial system to govern France, republicans felt that their own objectives were seriously threatened. Their ultimate intention was to establish a republican form of government in France, that is, government of the people, by the people, and for the people. But who, then, were "the people"? And what form should such a government take?

Even after the 1875 Constitution was approved, the Republic would not be firmly secured until after the Seize Mai crisis of 1877, when the republican sweep in the ensuing legislative elections, followed by the election (in 1879) of a moderate republican as president of the Republic, would consolidate the change. Only in the 1880s would the republicans, some condemned as "opportunists" and others more radical (or "pure" in the Jacobin sense), have a chance to inaugurate the reforms they considered essential: first of all, freedom of association and the press; then reforms of direct interest to women's rights advocates – secular and obligatory primary education for both girls and boys, a state secondary system of secondary schooling for girls, and civil divorce. Reform of the Civil Code by legislative means would prove far more difficult, even though under the Empire, republicans had repeatedly flayed the Code as a way of attacking Napoléon III's regime. As they edged toward taking power, they became more cautious about undermining it.

---

[3] This banquet was reported *in extenso* in *L'Avenir des Femmes,* n° 89 (7 July 1872). Reprinted by Léon Richer in his *Livre des femmes* (Paris: E. Dentu, 1877), pp. 60–61. Laboulaye became greatly enthusiastic about the United States; his admiration for America apparently became a family tradition (in the 1970s his grandson would served as French ambassador to the United States during the presidency of Giscard d'Estaing). When Laboulaye died in the spring of 1883, Susan B. Anthony attended his funeral in Paris and was deeply moved; see on this point Elizabeth Cady Stanton, *Eighty Years and More* (New York: European Publishing Co.; London: T. Fisher Unwin, 1898), p. 177.

These developments lay far in the future. But the shape of things to come was underscored at the banquet by the veteran '48ers Victor Hugo (1802–1885) and Louis Blanc (1811–1882), who, though absent from the banquet hall, sent lengthy letters applauding the occasion and endorsing the cause. Hugo's letter, read at the banquet and much quoted thereafter, critiqued the Code with a dramatic flourish, drawing on the imagery of slavery and freedom:[4]

> It is sad to admit that slaves exist in our current civilization. The law has its euphemisms, and what I call a slave, it calls a minor. This minor before the law, this slave in reality, is woman. Man has inequitably weighted the two balance pans of the Code, whose equilibrium is important to the human conscience; man has put all the rights on his side and all the obligations on woman's side. Because of this, there is a profound problem. Because of this, woman is in servitude. Under our present legislation, she cannot vote, she does not count, she does not exist. There are *citoyens* but no *citoyennes*. This is a violent situation and it must cease.

Hugo made explicit the current lack of "universal" applicability of republican principles; he believed that women should be full-fledged *citoyennes* – not subordinates, slaves, or serfs. Male privilege must be challenged.

In the following issue of *L'Avenir des Femmes,* Richer celebrated with gusto the success of the banquet demonstration. Other organs of the Parisian press, however, took a less enthusiastic view. "Women's emancipation!" snorted a hostile staff writer at *Paris-Journal*: "That circus is really the last straw!"[5]

Women's emancipation meant something quite different to *Paris-Journal* than to the banquet celebrants and their associates.[6] The latter heartily endorsed the notion of separate but equivalent and parallel "spheres" for women and men; indeed they explicitly insisted on it, but – importantly – with an eye to a parallel, equivalent status, a partnership rather than a domination/subordination hierarchy, in marriage and beyond. These latter applauded the formula of "equality-in-difference." Léon Richer had already underscored in 1870 that the motto of *Le Droit des Femmes* was "*égalité dans*

---

[4] See *L'Avenir des Femmes*, n° 89 (7 July 1872). An excellent account of the occasion and the press responses, drawn from this publication, is Georges Lhermitte's retrospective, "En feuilletant '*Le Droit des Femmes*', 1869–1891," in *Cinquante ans de féminisme* (Paris: LFDF, 1921), pp. 61–74.

[5] Quote from *Paris-Journal* by Lhermitte, "En feuilletant . . . ," p. 67.

[6] In an 1874 book, *La Femme et la civilisation* (Marseille: J. Douat, 1873) by a "Miss Norff," a.k.a. Mme Bouraud of Marseille, the author explained (pp. 72–74) that the emancipation of women did *not* encompass orgies and smoking, but rather equality before the law, in instruction and in work. She went on to state that the law's demand for obedience in marriage was humiliating to women.

la dissemblance."[7] The notion of equality in the law, in fact, assumes the existence of difference, as the sociologist and historian of law Ute Gerhard (among others) has underscored.[8] These French reformers fully understood and adhered to this understanding of "equality-in-difference" and did not view it as either paradoxical or contradictory.

If there was one thing these progressive-minded men and women agreed on, it was that the family, not the individual, remained the basic sociopolitical unit; the sexes must be complementary, and women must remain "womanly." From this "relational" conviction, particular consequences would logically follow, as we will see.[9] These republican men and women were heavily invested in the program of citizen-mothers, mother-educators, and in a program of social regeneration based on enhancing women's role in the household and in society. Their thinking on the matter was in line with the ideas of earlier republican activists including Jeanne Deroin, who had articulated this program during the 1848 revolution, Legouvé, and many others, including Juliette Adam.[10] It fell to other women like André Léo and Maria Deraismes, as adamant liberals, to plead the case for

---

[7]   *Le Droit des Femmes*, n° 64 (17 July 1870). See also Richer's preface to his *Livre des femmes* (Paris: Librairie de la Bibliothèque démocratique, 1872), vii–xi.

[8]   See chapter 1, "The Meaning of Equality with Regard to Difference," in Ute Gerhard, *Debating Women's Equality: Toward a Feminist Theory of Law from a European Perspective* (New Brunswick, NJ: Rutgers University Press, 2001), pp. 7–11. Gerhard is arguing against the misperception that "equality" implies "sameness" or "identity." Equality in law, she argues, is a "relational concept" (p. 1). Only "absolute" equality would lead to "identity."

[9]   The notion of "relational autonomy" has been elaborated by a contingent of late twentieth century feminist philosophers: see in particular *Relational Autonomy: Feminist Perspectives on Autonomy, Agency, and the Social Self*, ed. Catriona Mackenzie & Natalie Stoljar (New York: Oxford University Press, 2000). See also the earlier essays by M. E. Zimmerman, Gary Snyder, & Judith Plant in *Reweaving the World: The Emergence of Ecofeminism*, ed. Irene Diamond & Gloria F. Orenstein (San Francisco: Sierra Club Books, 1990).

[10]   The statements of Jeanne Deroin and Ernest Legouvé can be consulted in the companion volume, *The Woman Question in France, 1400–1870*, chapter 2. Legouvé's *Histoire morale des femmes* (1849) would reappear in a sixth edition in 1874. Juliette Adam, the opponent of Proudhon in the 1850s, stated her version of the complementarity argument in this way: "Je continue à ne pas admettre la formule trop simpliste de l'égalité de l'homme et de la femme. Je n'admets entre eux que des équivalences complémentaires, les facultés de chacun dans un mariage 'assorti', constituant, selon moi, la personne sociale parfait." See Juliette Adam, *Après l'abandon de la revanche* (Paris: A. Lemerre, 1910; orig. publ. 1904), p. 169. Adam admitted to being interested in the 1878 women's rights congress but declined Maria Deraismes's invitation to participate.

The question of whether the notion of "separate spheres" could be construed as positive for women is still being debated. Patrick Kay Bidelman [*Pariahs Stand Up!* (Westport, CT: Garland, 1983), xix] argues that the republicans "tacitly reinforced the social myth of separate spheres." My reading of the sources suggests that this reinforcement was explicit, yet did not of necessity entail a hierarchical notion of male superiority. Obviously "separate spheres" meant different things to different people, but the notion of a sexual division of labor did not inevitably imply either female inferiority or female subordination in the family. James F. Macmillan in *Housewife or Harlot: The Place of Women in French Society, 1870–1940* (New York: St. Martin's Press, 1981) construes separate

women's unrestricted autonomy. But even the latter insisted that women should be able to develop their full potential "as women." This notion (we might now call it "relational autonomy") was grounded in acceptance of bodily specificity, applying equally to both sexes.

Celebrity endorsement for political and social causes had already become fashionable in France. Advocates of women's rights could justly crow about its roster of male supporters, which included some very distinguished names in the political, literary, academic, and artistic world. Besides Laboulaye, Hugo, and Louis Blanc, the cause of women's rights had supporters such as Victor Schoelcher (1804–1893), the champion of slave emancipation in 1848. Some of these men became precious allies. In the 1890s many of these men would acquire the label "male-feminists." Some envisioned more "emancipation" for women than did others.

Undoubtedly the most renowned of these male-feminists was Victor Hugo. He was a champion of women in the old style and a choice ally, for he had the ear of a huge public, not least because of his open opposition to Napoléon III and the Second Empire, which had necessitated his voluntary exile from France, but also for his plays, poetry, and particularly his great social justice novel *Les Misérables* (1862). Hugo firmly believed that talent and genius should serve the social good and that women's cause, in French society, required such champions. His public record was long and honorable. Was it not Victor Hugo who had insisted in the Constitutional Assembly in 1849 that the corollary of the rights of man was the rights of women and children? Was it not Hugo who in 1853, at the funeral of the '48er Louise Jullien on the isle of Jersey, had sounded the clarion: "The eighteenth century proclaimed the rights of man; the nineteenth will proclaim the rights of woman." He chided his fellow men for hedging their bets on this question. Was it not Hugo who, following his triumphant return from exile, publicly denounced the inequalities of women's legal position and called on his fellow men to remedy the situation of "those who make the morals." Because of this record, it was Victor Hugo whom Léon Richer would invite in 1883 to become honorary president of the newly reconstituted *Ligue des Droits de la Femme*.[11]

----

spheres strictly as a domination/subordination paradigm. This is a common, though, I think, misleading view. Then, as now, the reality is more complex.

[11] See Hugo's response to Saint-Marc Girardin at the Académie Française in 1845 as well as his funeral oration for Louise Jullien in Victor Hugo, *Oeuvres complètes*, vol. 48: *Actes et paroles: I – Avant l'exil*, pp. 91–102, and vol. 44: *Actes et paroles: II – Pendant l'exil*, p. 92. His oft-cited letter to Léon Richer in 1872 is sourced above. For a review of Hugo's public statements on behalf of women's rights, see *Le Droit des Femmes*, n° 251 (7 June 1885) & n° 252 (21 June 1885), and shortly thereafter in English,

To claim Hugo as an ally in the cause of women is not to say that he considered women and men to be similar. Virtually every remark he made on the subject belies this view. For Hugo, like so many French men, viewed women as fundamentally different from men, though not at all inferior; he too was wholly committed to the formula "equality-in-difference." His poetry and his oratory both sanctified and eulogized woman as "the hearth, the home, the center of peaceful thoughts." This was the Hugo who in 1858 had enshrined women in his poem "Le Sacre de la femme," but in a rather more positive fashion than either Comte or Michelet, who certainly did not support women's rights as Hugo and Richer did.[12]

Louis Blanc was another political giant, an old '48er who endorsed improving civil (though not political) rights for French women. He nevertheless believed that wives belonged in the *foyer domestique*, as the heart of the family. Since 1848, however, he had been a staunch advocate of civil divorce, arguing that the possibility of dissolving an unhappy marriage was the best guarantee of a sound family. And, to Blanc, the family was everything. "The family! primordial association, elemental unit of every nation, society even predating the individual, truly a sacred and indestructible institution because what comes from nature can never be destroyed." But, Blanc was quick to add, just because woman is in no way like man, it should not be implied that she was not his equal.[13]

In 1872 Blanc restated his views in two articles that appeared in *L'Avenir des Femmes*. Here he developed his case against the "domestic tyranny" of husbands authorized by the Napoleonic Code. This argument had a

"Some of Victor Hugo's Words About Women," *The Englishwoman's Review*, 16 (15 July 1885), 293–306. See also, "Les Présidents d'honneur: Victor Hugo," in *Cinquante ans de féminisme*, pp. 45–49. Hugo also made a number of contributions to the debate on the woman question in his plays during the July Monarchy – on these, see the still valuable works of David Owen Evans, *Le Drame moderne à l'époque romantique (1827–1850): Contribution à l'étude d'un problème dans l'histoire du théâtre en France* (Paris: Éditions de la Vie Universitaire, 1923), and David Owen Evans, *Social Romanticism in France, 1830–1848* (Oxford, UK: Clarendon Press, 1951). Also see Idell E. Siegel, "Feminism in the French Popular Playwrights: 1830-1848" (Ph.D. dissertation, University of Missouri, Columbia, 1975). Two brief commentaries on Hugo's feminism are Jean Rabaut, "Droits de la femme: Victor Hugo, féministe," *L'Histoire*, 40 (December 1981), 79–81, and Nicole Savy, "Victor Hugo, féministe," *La Pensée*, n° 245 (May–June 1985), 7–18.

[12] "The hearth, the home, the center of peaceful thoughts" from his funeral oration for Madame Louis Blanc, 26 April 1876; quoted in *The Englishwoman's Review* article, 1885 (cited in n. 11); "Le Sacre de la femme" appears in Hugo's *La Légende des siècles* (Paris, 1859; in the Garnier ed., 1974, pp. 19–25).

[13] "Aux Femmes; la famille," in Blanc's *Nouveau monde: Journal historique et politique*, n° 4 (15 October 1849), pp. 3, 5. Reprinted as "Le Divorce" in his collections *Questions d'aujourd'hui et de demain*, 3ᵉ série. *Politique* (Paris: E. Dentu, 1880), pp. 103–141.

deliberately anti-Bonapartist thrust to it, and Blanc purposefully lauded the earlier draft of a civil code by the Convention (1792–1793) as his preferred legal model. Restating his thesis of equality-in-difference, he argued that "this lack of resemblance [between men and women] is just one more reason why every project of interest to the destiny of the human being should be completed with the free assistance of woman."[14] This argument had much in common with the case put forth so eloquently in 1849 by Jeanne Deroin in her "Woman's Mission."[15] For Blanc the "human being" [*l'être humain*] was composed of two sexes. This was his resolution of the dilemma posed by "universalism."

The dedication of Victor Schoelcher to the cause of women's rights followed closely from his passion, since childhood, for abolishing black slavery in the French colonies, which he had successfully implemented in 1848 while serving as the Second Republic's minister of the navy and colonies. In Schoelcher's case, as was also the case in England and the United States, the causes of women's emancipation and the emancipation of black slaves were inextricably joined.[16] Not surprisingly, Schoelcher was closely associated with Victor Hugo and especially with Ernest Legouvé. Following the coup d'état by Louis-Napoléon in 1852, he – like Hugo, Quinet, and others – went into exile, not returning to France until late 1870. But only in his later years did Schoelcher become active on behalf of women's rights. After Hugo's death in 1885, Richer would invite Schoelcher to serve as honorary president of the *Ligue*.

The man who was undoubtedly the most important contributor to advancing women's rights in these years was not a celebrity himself, although he knew quite a few. What he lacked in fame, however, he made up for in energy devoted to the cause. Along with Legouvé, Léon Richer epitomized the republican male-feminist. His story has been told many times, but bears summarizing here. Alerted to the legal disenfranchisement of women in French society by the example of his mother and sisters, and by the women whose interests he defended in his practice as a notary's assistant before he came to Paris as a journalist, Richer had thrown himself

---

[14] "La Question des femmes," p. 271.

[15] See Deroin, "Mission de la femme dans le present et dans l'avenir," *L'Opinion des Femmes* (28 January, 10 March, 10 April 1849); English translation in *Women, the Family, and Freedom: The Debate in Documents*, ed. Susan Groag Bell & Karen M. Offen (Stanford, CA: Stanford University Press, 1983); hereafter *WFF*, vol. 1, doc. 77.

[16] The details of Schoelcher's career as a humanitarian political reformer had fallen into obscurity until the publication of *Victor Schoelcher, ou la mystique d'un athée* (Paris: Perrin, 1983) by Janine Alexandre-Debray.

into the fray during the Second Empire, founding the periodical *Le Droit des Femmes* in 1869.[17] Richer was deeply engaged in recruiting the support of other republican men for women's rights. Through his collaboration with Maria Deraismes, whose public lectures in the later 1860s he had promoted, the cause gained new momentum following the June 1872 banquet. This is not to say, however, that these campaigns would not encounter difficult moments.

One of those difficult moments had to do with Alexandre Dumas *fils* (1824–1895), the prolific novelist, essayist, and playwright (best known for *La Dame aux camélias*, 1848) who wrote incessantly about women. Partisans of women's rights hoped to attract the support of this celebrated and influential writer. Earlier in 1872 a Parisian group called the *Association pour l'Émancipation de la Femme* [Association for Women's Emancipation] published a tiny sixty-four-page brochure entitled *La Question de la femme* [The Woman Question].[18] It contained excerpts from Dumas *fils*'s theatre works, from *Un Lettre sur les choses du jour* [A Letter on Current Events], and from his *Nouvelle lettre sur les choses du jour*, with a foreword by Julie-Victoire Daubié, emphasizing what seemed to have become the leitmotif of the era – the necessity of regenerating France by improving the situation of women and children. In the same year, however, Dumas *fils* published a very different, angry work, *L'Homme-femme* [The Man-Woman], of which more later. Because of the tempest this work kicked up, Dumas *fils* was no doubt unwelcome at the 1872 banquet.

Dumas *fils* was a more problematic and perplexing potential ally than the overtly supportive Hugo, or for that matter Louis Blanc, not least because he was less immediately implicated in campaigns for political and social change. Dumas *fils* was above all else a moralist, a skeptical observer, and a severe judge of human behavior. He considered sex love between men and women the great problematic of human existence, and he blamed both sexes for their bad behavior toward one another, and for the way in which each sex let itself be warped. His picture of womanhood was far less idealized than that of Hugo; indeed, amid the crowd of republican male-feminists applauding woman's sphere and the family, amid their calls for reform of the Civil Code, Dumas *fils* was not above claiming (as he did

---

[17] See Bidelman, *Pariahs Stand Up!*, chapter 3, and Claire Goldberg Moses, *French Feminism in the Nineteenth Century* (Albany, NY: SUNY Press, 1984), chapter 9.

[18] Alexandre Dumas *fils*, *La Question de la femme*, préface de J.-V. Daubié (Paris: 5, rue de la Pompe, Passy, 1872).

in *L'Homme-femme* and other works) that women could be just as evil as men, and that women "use" men instrumentally in marriage for strictly reproductive ends. His insights into male and female psychology are at times excruciatingly pessimistic.

Dumas *fils*'s *L'Homme-femme*, followed by the even angrier preface to his 1873 play *La Femme de Claude* (which concerned a husband who murdered his very wicked wife), contained a number of peremptory judgments about the social evil women could engender and, consequently, incensed many women's rights activists including Maria Deraismes (to be discussed later). Offsetting the adverse effect of these two publications was the playwright's preface to *Monsieur Alphonse* (1873), in which he advocated equal rights for women and insisted on the importance of properly educating them so that they could take their rightful place in the world.[19]

In the 1880s Alexandre Dumas *fils* would come out as a proponent of civil divorce and a supporter of the vote for French women and in 1890 as a reluctant supporter of *recherche de la paternité*.[20] But in 1879 he made a point of how little support feminists could expect for the reforms they advocated: neither the "happy," nor the "clever" (who have "made it" in spite of every obstacle), nor the "*abrutis*" (the peasants, who could not even read; literally, the brutes), nor the "pious," who found joy in self-sacrifice, would endorse such reforms. As for those isolated women with talent and intelligence who would like to do more themselves or who represent the best of what intellectual women can be, they fear to adhere publicly to the cause, he insisted; only those who compromise the cause seem to support it openly.[21] Amid his peremptory judgments on the morals of his time, he continued to maintain that women – like men – had a real potential to fulfill. Dumas *fils* did respect what women might

[19] *L'Homme-femme* and the preface to *La Femme de Claude* have been reprinted in *Le Dossier "Tue-la! Constitué, étudié, et plaidé par André Lebois* (Avignon: E. Aubanel, 1969). On this Dumas-Deraismes confrontation, see Angélique Arnaud, "Le vieil Adam – L'Ève moderne," *L'Avenir des Femmes*, n° 92 (6 October 1872). Another critique of Dumas *fils* for libelling women is Louise Audebert, "Le Théâtre de Monsieur Alexandre Dumas *fils*," in supplement to *L'Avenir des Femmes*, issues of 2 January, 6 February, and 5 March 1876. The French laws governing adultery are nicely summarized by Léon Girard in Theodore Stanton's essay, "France," in *The Woman Question in Europe* (New York: G. P. Putnam's Sons, 1884). For an extended scholarly analysis of Dumas *fils* and the *Homme-femme* debate, see Odile Krakovitch, "Misogynes et féministes, il y a cent ans: Autour de l'Homme-Femme d'Alexandre Dumas *fils*," *Questions féministes*, n° 8 (1980), 85–113, and *Nouvelles questions féministes*, n° 2 (October 1981), 75–103.

[20] For a discussion of the later legislative campaigns for legalization of paternity suits, see Part III, Chapter 11 in this volume.

[21] Alexandre Dumas *fils*, *Les Femmes qui tuent et les femmes qui votent* (Paris: Calmann-Lévy, 1880; reprinted, Paris: G. Authier, 1975), p. 111.

become, and even helped a few gifted young women to achieve their intellectual potential.[22]

Of the cluster of women activists who had contributed significantly to the published debate on the woman question during the late Second Empire (see *The Woman Question in France, 1400–1870,* chapter 7), only Maria Deraismes and Julie-Victoire Daubié (the first woman to earn the French *baccalauréat*) remained major figures during the very early Third Republic. By 1874, however, Daubié would be dead. Jenny P. d'Héricourt had long since left Paris for Chicago (she returned to France in 1872 but died suddenly in 1875), and André Léo, after going into hiding during the last days of the Paris Commune, had fled to Switzerland, then to Italy (with another Communard Benoît Malon, whom she subsequently married). Juliette Lambert Lamessine, finally widowed in 1867, had married Edouard Adam in 1868 and had not yet made her political reappearance as the *égerie* [secret counselor] of the charismatic republican leader Léon Gambetta as well as the publisher of *La Nouvelle Revue.* Olympe Audouard was lecturing in and around Paris, but does not seem to have been close to these republican women's rights advocates; in any event she is not listed among those attending the banquet of June 1872.[23] Clarisse Coignet (1824–1918) had plunged into the quest for better girls' education, while another veteran with Fourierist sympathies, Virginie Griess-Traut, advocated coeducation and spearheaded women's antiwar campaigns. The maverick scientist Clémence Royer, a committed republican, juggled her situation as an unmarried mother, living with a journalist and off-and-on republican deputy (Pascal Duprat) who was married to another woman, with her scientific adventures in the Anthropological Society. Although she does not seem to have attended the 1872 banquet, she wrote extensively on the woman question, and she did attend the 1878 International Women's Rights Congress.[24] A younger generation of activists, including Léonie Rouzade,

[22] See the very positive testimony of Jeanne P. Crouzet-Benaben, "Alexandre Dumas *fils* et la femme nouvelle," *La Grande Revue,* 28:7 (July 1924), 166–174, in answer to the question "Alexandre Dumas *fils* a-t-il été féministe?" This important Third Republic educator greatly profited from the guidance of Dumas *fils* during her girlhood; he encouraged her intellectual development and even helped her (at age 18) win admission to Sèvres (the École Normale Supérieure established to train the master teachers for the Third Republic's girls' secondary schools). In sum, she believes that Dumas *fils* was a feminist.

[23] The whereabouts of Olympe Audouard at any given point in the 1870s cannot be determined from the account in Rachel Nuñez, "Between France and the World: The Gender Politics of Cosmopolitanism, 1835–1914" (Ph.D. dissertation, Stanford University, 2006).

[24] See Joy Harvey's biography of Royer, *"Almost a Man of Genius": Clémence Royer, Feminism, and Nineteenth-Century Science* (New Brunswick, NJ: Rutgers University Press, 1997), esp. chapters 6 & 7.

Eugénie Pierre (later Potonié-Pierre), Eliska (Girard) Vincent, and Hubertine Auclert would emerge as champions of women's rights in the later 1870s and would continue their campaigning for several decades.

Maria Deraismes was by far the most prominent of these women activists. Parisian, wealthy, single, some said beautiful, well educated, politically to the radical side of liberal, vehemently anticlerical, she was also an accomplished artist, a published playwright, and a performing musician.[25] Clearly she (like George Sand, Jenny P. d'Héricourt, and Juliette Adam before her) had slipped through the net of social conditioning that attempted to shape a demure, pious, and subservient type of housewifely woman. Articulate and well informed, the 40-year-old Deraismes was no *oie blanche*; she had become a public presence to be reckoned with, a Parisian celebrity in her own right. During the late 1860s she had acquired a substantial reputation as an outspoken public advocate of women's emancipation. What was more, republican politics were her forte and her passion. According to one commentator, her salon (on the Avenue de Clichy) "had become the prolongation not only of the [Masonic] lodge 'Mars and the Arts,' but also of the editorial staff of the newspaper *La Liberté*, which Émile de Girardin had just purchased . . . and taken on as editor-in-chief."[26]

Deraismes always insisted that democracy, the republic, and women's emancipation were all of a piece. The fact that she could not vote did not stop her from becoming an important player in French civil society and in political life. By the late 1870s she would establish herself as a dominant force for republicanism in the department of Seine-et-Oise, where she and her widowed sister Anna Feresse-Deraismes shared an estate at Pontoise. After organizing together the first international congress for women's rights in 1878, Maria Deraismes and Léon Richer would conduct separate campaigns through separate organizations during the 1880s. However, they joined forces again in 1888–1889 to organize the second international congress on women's rights. Both these congresses will be discussed later in this chapter.

---

[25] The fullest contemporary account of the life and career of Maria Deraismes, and the source that continues to inform all others, is Jean-Bernard (pseud. J.-B. Passeriau), "Notice – Maria Deraismes," in the first volume of Deraismes's *Oeuvres complètes* (Paris: Alcan, 1895), vi–lv. The best discussion in English is in Bidelman, *Pariahs Stand Up!*, which includes a comprehensive bibliography, pp. 232–233. See also Odile Krakovitch, ed., *Maria Deraismes: Ce que veulent les femmes. Articles et discours de 1869 à 1894* (Paris: Syros, 1980), which reprints a number of Deraismes's newspaper articles and speeches that were not included in her collected works.

[26] Éliane Brault, *La Franc-maçonnerie et l'émancipation des femmes* (Paris: Dervy, 1953; new ed., revised and augmented, Paris: Dervy-Livres, 1967), p. 76.

To sum up, leading French Republicans were aware of – and generally sympathetic to – the need for change in the disadvantaged legal position of married women. Many of their pet projects, from expanding educational opportunities for girls to regenerating public morality and separating church from state, implicated women directly. In contrast to their more radical socialist contemporaries, they were less apt to engage in critiques of private property, or to prioritize class issues over sex issues. Changes in fundamental structures, whether those based on sex or on class, posed potentially revolutionary implications for the existing socioeconomic structure of French society, as socialist critics would relentlessly point out. For most republicans, even the most liberal, the limits of change were located precisely at that point where private property itself seemed threatened. Some were even hesitant about endorsing changes that might seriously undermine male authority in the family, but others strongly advocated such a change. Those who had absorbed the earlier teachings of Comte and considered themselves positivists, and others who had imbibed the views of Michelet about the pernicious influence of the priests on women and familial relations, still had difficulties with the prospect of considering women as wholly autonomous individuals. Even so, they did not view women as necessarily inferior to men – just different – and most seemed sympathetic to pressing for significant reforms on women's behalf both in the Civil Code and in the Penal Code.

The Du Bourg Affair: Adultery, Divorce, and the Penal Code

"If women wrote the laws, would they permit such revolting measures?" So wrote the Toulouse law professor, Aimé Rodière, in 1874. He was referring particularly to the legal measures in the Penal Codes that outlawed *recherche de la paternité* (Article 340) and to the double standard of sexual morality embodied in the laws on adultery (Article 324).[27] In truth, the many sociopolitical restrictions that gravely handicapped women in the early republic were the products of laws and institutions inherited from the earlier monarchies, both of which were amenable to change by legislative action. But the moral issues cut more deeply and would prove more

---

[27] Aimé Rodière, *Les grands juriconsultes* (Toulouse: E. Privat, 1874), p. 507: "Si les femmes rédigeaient les lois, permettraient-elles des choses aussi révoltantes!" Rodière was professor of law at the law faculty of Toulouse. The American suffrage advocate Elizabeth Cady Stanton praised Rodière in her memoirs as a supporter of woman suffrage – he thought that women were perfectly capable of governing and that, in particular, it was ridiculous to exclude single adult women and widows who paid taxes from municipal suffrage.

difficult to resolve, and many of those were consequences of the highly discriminatory Penal Code. How the republicans would address these issues, as they scrambled for control of the government, remained to be seen.

One of the first intense and lengthy debates about these laws began not long before the June women's rights banquet, spurred by a case of male revenge – a crime of passion. The French law on adultery flagrantly embodied an unequivocal double moral standard. In the spring of 1872 a certain Arthur Leroy Du Bourg had murdered his wife and her lover (who happened to have been her husband's best friend). Had Du Bourg murdered her under his own roof, he would not have been prosecuted, according to Article 324 of the French Penal Code. As this was not the case, Du Bourg was taken to court and tried for murder; he was convicted, but got off with a sentence of five years in prison.[28]

In the French Penal Code, a man convicted for keeping a concubine under the same roof as his wife was subject only to a stiff fine; if he kept the concubine next door – or across the street – the man could not be prosecuted. What was more, a husband who discovered his wife in *flagrante delicto* in their common home and killed her would not be brought to justice; he was within his "right." If he killed her under the roof of another man, he would be tried but more than likely would be acquitted (as several other men had been in recent months). By contrast, a wife who committed an act of vengeance against an unfaithful husband would be dealt with severely by the courts. A woman convicted of adultery could be imprisoned; not so the man.[29]

Thus, the sensational trial of Monsieur Du Bourg, and the French public's amazement that he was actually convicted, brought to the surface many entangled issues about morals and punitive laws. It generated a new outburst of debate on the woman question, focused on the double standard of sexual morality. Women's rights activists uniformly viewed this event as one more example of the unjust prerogatives that men, especially as husbands, enjoyed under French law. Historian Odile Krakovitch calls these debates "the most formidable quarrel over women's rights that has ever taken place in France."[30]

---

[28] The Du Bourg case is exhaustively documented in the works listed in n. 31.

[29] See Patricia Mainardi, *Husbands, Wives and Lovers: Marriage and Its Discontents in Nineteenth-Century France* (New Haven, CT: Yale University Press, 2003), pp. 14–19, for an excellent history of this law.

[30] See the detailed study of this debate in the articles cited earlier (n. 19) by Odile Krakovitch, "Misogynes et féministes, il y a cent ans," quote from the first installment, p. 85. For other

The airing of dirty laundry concerning love and sexual practices, coupled with the vehement protests over the many disadvantages women faced in the law, made it apparent that some men's much-vaunted dream state of "domesticity for women" had an unappetizing, potentially even violent underside. Committed republicans believed that measures must be taken to address this situation – and the sooner, the better. A number of concerns came together: the legal subordination of married women, the tragedies that could ensue when a couple had no possibility of divorce to end an unhappy marriage, the costs (psychological and financial) of extramarital sex and adultery, children born in or out of wedlock, problems of proving paternity for purposes of child support, and, not least, questions about property rights and inheritance. Traditionalists resisted change by arguing that the very future of "the family" was at stake. Reformers argued that this in-fact patriarchal family form, as embodied in the Civil and Penal Codes, which worked to men's great advantage, was extremely disadvantageous for women who married. In their view, both French laws and French morals had to change. But if women "make" the morals, it was indisputably the men who made the laws – and in the 1870s only they could change them.

Some might argue that this debate was really about the French defeat and the bloody Commune, as played out on the bodies and roles of women, but in my view these debates are squarely about the woman question, no doubt energized by the context and psychological consequences of those dramatic events. Many of these debates were even framed allusively in terms of "civilization" versus "barbarism" or even "savagery."

A lengthy and heated debate in print ensued between feminists, male and female, and those who upheld Du Bourg's right to take the life of his

---

briefer accounts of the polemics provoked by the Du Bourg affair, see also Bidelman, *Pariahs Stand Up!* Claire Moses does not discuss this debate, nor does Ruth Harris in *Murders and Madness: Medicine, Law, and Society in the Fin de Siècle* (Oxford, UK: Clarendon Press, 1989), which is based on cases between 1880 and 1892 only (although the author does allude to it in passing on pp. 289–290). Joëlle Guillais extensively documents the Du Bourg case in *Crimes of Passion: Dramas of Private Life in Nineteenth-Century France*, transl. Jane Dunnet (Oxford: Polity Press, 1990; orig. publ. in French, 1986), pp. 134–139. In her study *Breaking the Codes: Female Criminality in Fin-de-Siècle Paris* (Stanford, CA: Stanford University Press, 1996), Ann-Louise Shapiro makes much of Dumas *fils'* 1880 juxtaposition of *La femme qui tue et la femme qui vote*, but only briefly discusses his 1872 harangue *Tue-la!*, drawing on the articles by Krakovitch. In a more recent study of French sexual violence based on the court archives, *Gender and Justice: Violence, Intimacy, and Community in Fin-de-Siècle Paris* (Baltimore: Johns Hopkins University Press, 2010), Eliza Earle Ferguson reports (p. 233, n. 2) that for the Du Bourg case, "The trial dossier no longer exists in the archives of the Cour d'assises de la Seine," though a transcript of the proceedings can be consulted in the *Gazette des Tribunaux*, 15 June 1872.

adulterous wife.[31] Henry d'Ideville, a friend of Dumas *fils*, first engaged the debate, arguing in *Le Soir* (15 May 1872) that the adulterous wife should be exonerated and divorce reestablished. He also critiqued the sexual double standard that allowed men free range before marriage, yet expected brides to be pure and sexually uninformed, and condemned unsuitable arranged marriages. Dumas *fils* then responded to d'Ideville in mid-July with *L'Homme-femme*, a rambling handbook of lacerating misogyny (but also not particularly complimentary to men), which he ended by invoking a wronged husband to defend his honor by killing an unfaithful wife: "TUE-LA!" Not incidentally, this is the publication in which Dumas *fils* appropriated the neologism "*les féministes*," which he used pejoratively, but which Hubertine Auclert would begin to use positively in the early 1880s.[32] This publication, with its outrageous ending, quickly achieved best-seller status (50,000 copies sold in less than three weeks, according to Krakovitch; it was still in print in a forty-fifth edition in 1899) and spawned a public debate that continued for months. Bottom line: in Dumas *fils*'s view, women were inferior, yet cunning beings who must therefore be controlled by masculine power.

Shortly thereafter, also in mid-July, Ideville published *L'homme qui tue et l'homme qui pardonne*, prefaced by a letter to Dumas *fils*, and reprinting Ideville's earlier articles, elaborating his case for forgiving an unhappy adulterous wife and blaming adulterous husbands severely – on the grounds that they should exercise more responsibility. D'Ideville damned the law that permitted husbands to kill unfaithful wives with impunity under certain conditions as "barbarous." As this suggests, some French men were far more sympathetic to the woes of wives than were others.

---

[31] See Henry d'Ideville, *L'Homme qui tue et l'homme qui pardonne* (Paris: E. Dentu, 1872), orig. publ. in *Le Soir*, 15 May 1872, followed by Alexandre Dumas *fils*, *L'Homme-femme: Réponse à M. Henri d'Ideville* (Paris: Michel Lévy, 1872). Dumas *fils*' tract also appeared in English translation: *Man-Woman; or The Temple, the Hearth, the Street*, transl. and ed. by George Vandenhoff (Philadelphia & New York: n.p., 1873). Other significant responses in this debate include: Émile de Girardin, *L'Homme et la femme – L'homme suzerain, la femme vassale – Lettre à M. A. Dumas fils … La liberté dans le mariage par l'égalité des enfants devant la mère* (Paris: M. Lévy, 1872); Maria Deraismes, *Ève contre Dumas fils; réponse à l'homme-femme de Dumas fils* (Paris: E. Dentu, 1872); A. Cool, *La Femme et l'homme, réponse à M. Alexandre Dumas* (Paris: Paul Daffis, 1872); and [Anon.] *La Femme-homme. Mariage - adultère - divorce. Réponse d'une femme à M. Alex. Dumas fils* (Paris: E. Dentu, 1872). Also Hermance Lesguillon, *L'Homme, réponse à M. Alexandre Dumas fils* (Paris: Tresse, 1872); and R. M., *Allez et ne péchez plus! Solutions proposées à M. Alexandre Dumas fils*, pamphlet (Paris: L. Hurtau, 1872). Krakovitch lists a number of other responses, thirty-three in total.

[32] See Karen Offen, "On the French Origin of the Words Feminism and Feminist," *Feminist Issues*, 8:2 (Fall 1988), 47. Dumas *fils* used the word "féministes" on p. 91 of *L'Homme-femme*. In the American translation of Dumas *fils*' *Man-Woman* (1873; cited previously), this term "féministes" was translated as "feminists."

The legendary journalist Émile de Girardin (1806–1881), another friend of women's emancipation, published a lengthy book, replying to both Dumas *fils* and d'Ideville; he challenged Dumas *fils* by insisting that men's superiority over women is man-made, not divinely ordained.[33] Both man and woman, in his eyes, are independent beings with similar needs but different functions. Women required opportunities to exercise responsibility – for their children and for their property. "A woman without direct responsibility is like a ship without ballast parting for a long journey ... destined for shipwreck."[34] Girardin argued that the logical conclusion of Dumas's presentation would have been a call for the legalization of civil divorce; instead the playwright had offered a sermon. Murder, he asserted, is an "ending," not a "solution". In fact, Girardin claimed, the state should not be involved in questions of marriage at all; all children should be equal before their mothers (a radical approach he had already proposed in 1852) – which would, in his view, neatly resolve the "problem" of illegitimacy – and render paternity suits unnecessary.[35]

Over thirty participants contributed to these debates, and their publications have been analyzed in some detail by Krakovitch. For instance, a certain A. de Cool rose to the defense of women, whom he argued were by no means created inferior to men. A breviary for "equality-in-difference" (in de Cool's phraseology, "*égaux quoique dissemblables*"), he insisted that French society had caused the problems by depriving women of any means of action, which led to their increasing oppression and weakness. In addition to critiques of the Civil Code, contributors broached every possible related topic, from women's maternal "role" and the education of girls to women's employment and the vote. Opponents of change dredged up and rehearsed the long litany of arguments against women's rights and emancipation: Biblical authority, Greek philosophy, Catholic theology, biomedical assertions, prescriptions for separate spheres, physical force, Proudhonian calculus of inferiority, and so forth. One contributor who signed only as "une femme" (Krakovitch has identified this author as a male lawyer from Aix-en-Provence, writing under a female pseudonym) charged Dumas *fils* with cultivating immorality and through his plays especially giving French women a bad name; "she" handed Dumas *fils* a

---

[33] Girardin, *L'Homme et la femme*, p, 11.   [34] Girardin, *L'Homme et la femme*; quotation, pp. 67–68.
[35] Girardin, *L'Homme et la femme*; quotation, p. 22. It should be recognized that De Girardin was not afraid of intelligent, gifted women. Following the death of his first wife, the celebrated writer Delphine Gay de Girardin, he courted the widowed Juliette Lambert Lamessine before she linked up with Edmond Adam. He was also a friend of Maria Deraismes.

backhanded compliment of having such talent with words that even what was false could seem true.

Women critics joined in this war of words fostered by the Du Bourg case. One contributor, the well-established writer Hermance Lesguillon (1812–1882), framed her critique as the debate of a group of women assembled in a salon to critique the arguments of Dumas *fils* as well as the laws of marriage in the Civil Code. The gathering (and the book) ends abruptly when a young woman, bursting into the room with her mother, announces that she has called off her wedding – because her husband-to-be had told her he approved of Dumas's ending – Kill her![36] Implied in Lesguillon's not-so-subtle finale was the assertion that the lack of justice for wives in the laws of marriage could (and should) lead some women to refuse to marry.

Deraismes had already critiqued Dumas *fils* in early 1870, taking issue with his preface to *L'Ami des femmes*.[37] Their sparring in print would continue through the decade, but in *Eve contre Dumas fils* (1872), she struck boldly and with precision, dismantling his arguments and attacking him for propagating "immorality." She challenged his ethnological and physiological arguments for women's inferiority, riposting that Nature is not as stupid as men are concerning women's temperament and passions. Again she developed the connection between women and the success of the Republic. "The right(s) of women," she argued, "seem intimately linked to the fortune(s) of the Republic. It is assuredly a logical and necessary result of the principle of democracy, and the democrats who reject it are out of their minds, for they deny their own doctrines. The work of liberating half of humanity is, like the Republic, on its third try; it was tried in 1789, in 1848 and (again) today."[38]

---

[36] Eliza Earle Ferguson has nicely synthesized Lesguillon's critique; see her book, *Gender and Justice*, p. 129. Lesguillon, who has been identified as a member of the Club des femmes of 1848, was a prolific writer whose first work, *Les Femmes dans cent ans: manuscrit de la princesse Hélène* (Paris: A de Vresse, 1859), envisions the building of a community of women; she deliberately presented a woman's perspective. On Lesguillon, see David Berry, "Hermance Lesguillon (1812–1882): The Diversity of French Feminism in the Nineteenth Century," *French History*, 13:4 (1999), 381–416.

[37] Deraismes's article, "Une préface de M. Alexandre Dumas *fils*," originally published in *Le Droit des Femmes*, n° 47 (19 March 1870), was translated into English by Ida Frances Leggett and published as "A. Dumas, Jr., on Woman's Equality," in Stanton & Anthony's *The Revolution*, vol. 5, n° 16 (21 April 1870).

[38] See Maria Deraismes, *Eve contre Dumas fils; Réponse à l'Homme-Femme de Dumas fils* (Paris: E. Dentu 1872); as reproduced in vol. 2 of her *Oeuvres complètes*, pp. 187–222; quote, p. 222. In French: "Le droit des femmes paraît intimement lié à la fortune de la République. Il est certainement une résultante logique et nécessaire au principe de démocratie, et les démocrates qui le rejettent ne sont que des insensés, car ils démentent leurs doctrines."

Léon Richer similarly grounded his arguments in history and in current events. In his publication *La Femme libre* (1877), he would assert that France's recovery from the German defeat necessitated women's emancipation; the republicans must therefore carry out a comprehensive program of reforms in order to attach women to the new regime. The republic, he insisted, would never be truly consolidated if women remained hostile to it. As he catalogued the disabilities of wives in the Civil Code, with respect to their children and to money and property management, Richer continually juxtaposed the terms "servitude" and "liberty: "woman is a serf . . . a vassal."[39] The law always gave the last word to the husband. This situation must change.

Challenging the Civil Code: The International Congress on Women's Rights, Paris, 1878

With the Paris International Exposition of 1878 came a splendid opportunity to promote the republicans' platform for legal changes in the status of women. Following a series of setbacks during the preceding government of "moral order," Léon Richer and Maria Deraismes joined forces to convene the first international congress on women's rights (which they had originally planned for 1873). The gathering attracted a cluster of French republican political dignitaries (male) as well as interested women and men from eleven other nations in Europe and North America. This congress marked a new stage in the development of a truly transnational network among women's rights activists as well as raising the visibility of women's issues on the home front. Sessions took place in the Masonic Hall (rue Cadet) over a two-week period beginning in late July. The congress organizers divided the agenda into five sections: historical, educational, economic, moral, and legislative.

In her welcome speech to the French attendees and foreign visitors, Maria Deraismes proudly (though briefly) reclaimed the revolutionary heritage of 1789, 1830, and 1848 for women. "The right of women," she asserted, "is the corollary of the right of peoples."[40] Despite the organizers' deliberate decision to ban discussion of woman suffrage (of which more below), the congress did address many other controversial topics including government-regulated prostitution and the double moral standard, equal

---

[39] Léon Richer, *La Femme libre* (Paris: E. Dentu, 1877); a translated excerpt is in *WFF*, vol. 1, doc. 124.

[40] Deraismes, in *Congrès international du droit des femmes. Ouvert à Paris, le 25 juillet 1878, clos le 9 août suivant. Actes et Compte-rendu des séances plénières* (Paris: Aug. Ghio, c. 1878), pp. 14–15; quote, p. 14.

pay for equal work, the politics of housework, government subsidies for mothers, unionization, and the relation of war to women's subordination. The published proceedings of this first congress were widely distributed and can still be read with interest today.

Historians Patrick Kay Bidelman, Claire Goldberg Moses, as well as Laurence Klejman and Florence Rochefort have provided some coverage of this congress, of which the latter two, in their joint book, *L'Égalité en marche*, have remarked that it was no longer merely a question of improving the Civil Code but of understanding "oppression" as "an international reality that demanded a globally-organized effort."[41] The congress's resolutions were nothing short of radical – there was nothing "conservative" about its agenda.[42] The resolutions called for the demolition of the French system of government-regulated prostitution (an issue brought to the fore by Josephine Butler's campaigns in England against the Contagious Disease Acts and subsequently, the launching in Switzerland of the British, Continental, and General Federation against the State Regulation of Vice). In the name of women's equality to men in "natural law," the resolutions of the section on legislation included a call for a major overhaul of the entire body of civil legislation, the reestablishment of divorce, equalization in the laws governing adultery, a law on seduction, the right of *recherche de la paternité*, and abolition of the morals police.[43]

Some of these concerns also featured in the resolutions of the section on morals, which, among other things, opposed forced celibacy for (noncommissioned) soldiers. Following an exchange between one woman, who saw no problem with wives being supported by their husbands, and Richer, the latter stated categorically that "there are only two ways for a poor woman to support herself: by remunerative work or by trafficking her body." The congress's economic section insisted that "every woman whose means of living make her dependent on a man is not free," and called for the right to work as well as the recognition of the economic value of household work.[44]

---

[41] Bidelman, *Pariahs Stand Up!*, pp. 99–105; Moses, *French Feminism*, pp. 207–209; Laurence Klejman & Florence Rochefort, *L'Égalité en marche: Le Féminisme sous la Troisième République* (Paris: Presses de la Fondation Nationale des Sciences Politique/des femmes), pp. 54–56: quote p. 54. See the account by E[ugénie] Pierre in *Solidarité*, n° 17 (December 1878), 7–9. An in-depth study of this congress (particularly with regard to its reception in the French and international press) is greatly needed. Of particular importance for the French press would be the accounts in *Le Rappel* and *Le Devoir*.

[42] See the able summary of the resolutions in Moses, *French Feminism*, pp. 207–208.

[43] *Congrès international du droit des femmes.... 1878*, pp. 211–213; see the English translation in Bidelman, reprinted in *WFF*, vol. 1, doc. 125.

[44] See Richer's speech, *Congrès international du droit des femmes.... 1878*, pp. 71–72. He had developed these arguments earlier in *La Femme libre* (1877).

These so-called liberal feminists were, in fact, very radical when it came to proposing legal changes that would improve the moral state of the nation by effectively mandating sexual equality in the family and in society. Feminists are still making these arguments today, particularly with respect to economics. Nevertheless, belief in the male breadwinner philosophy as articulated by Jean-Baptiste Say and others in the early 1800s, and the consequent devaluation of housework, has proved very difficult to dislodge.

The call for the reinstatement of civil divorce, the end to the double standard pertaining to adultery, and *recherche de la paternité* were among the most important legal demands put forward by the 1878 Congress. The legalization of divorce was at the top of the republicans' list of essential reforms. Although Napoléon I had established a limited form of civil divorce in France (after overturning the original, expansive 1792 divorce law) it had been prohibited once again in 1816, under the Restoration. From that date on, the only legal redress available to an unhappy or mistreated spouse was the juridical half-solution known as *séparation des corps*, in which husband and wife lived apart, but in which the husband still retained the bulk of his authority over property and the wife had to seek his permission (or that of a court) to engage in any business and financial transactions. Neither spouse could remarry. Thus the reestablishment of civil divorce became a high priority for radical republicans and feminists, in the name of individual liberty (if not the right to happiness). It was part and parcel of the republicans' anticlerical stance, insofar as they considered civil divorce to be the essential corollary of civil marriage.[45] Needless to say, both civil marriage and civil divorce were anathema to the French Catholic establishment and to many practicing Catholics. As historian Theresa McBride has reminded us, the campaign for divorce was a deliberate effort to change a nationally applicable law; thus it differed from other subsequent social welfare measures insofar as it was not an experimental reform pretested in other private settings.[46]

---

[45] Republican publications advocating divorce included: Léon Richer, *Le Divorce, projet de loi précédé d'un exposé des motifs et suivi des principaux documents officiels se rattachant à la question, ... avec une lettre-préface par Louis Blanc* (Paris: Le Chevalier, 1873); Alfred Naquet, *Le Divorce* (Paris: E. Dentu, 1877; 2nd ed., 1881), and Alexandre Dumas *fils, La Question du divorce* (Paris: C. Lévy, 1880). Following passage of the 1884 law, see Léon Giraud, *La Femme et la nouvelle loi sur la divorce* (Paris: A. Durand, 1885; offprint from *La France judiciaire*), and Alfred Naquet's retrospective, *La Loi du divorce* (Paris: E. Fasquelle, 1903).

[46] See Theresa McBride, "Public Authority and Private Lives: Divorce After the French Revolution," *French Historical Studies*, 17:3 (Spring 1992), 747–768, and Theresa McBride, "Divorce and the Republican Family," in *Gender and the Politics of Social Reform in France, 1870–1914*, ed. Elinor A.

To amend the Civil Code would require a legislative majority in the Chamber of Deputies and in the Senate.

Partisans of civil divorce had tried and failed repeatedly to change the law, both in the legislatures of the early 1830s and again in 1848.[47] By the end of the first decade of the Third Republic, though, unhappy couples still could find no escape from marital difficulties through divorce. But republicans could not agree about whether a new law should reflect the broad approach of the divorce law of 1792 or the more constricted measure embedded in the Civil Code of 1804.

Léon Richer had been arguing for the restoration of civil divorce for years.[48] Others who advocated civil divorce and major changes in the law codes included the young physician Louis Fiaux (1847–1936), who would play an important role in the campaigns against regulated prostitution (which will be discussed later). But it was Richer's colleague Alfred Naquet who led the legislative campaign, arguing that civil divorce was the touchstone of liberty. In fact, in his youth Naquet had come out in opposition to state jurisdiction over marriage per se, favoring "*union libre.*" His book, *Religion, propriété, famille*, which had appeared in early 1869, earned him a conviction by the imperial government for "outraging morals."[49] After participating in the Government of National Defense and getting elected to the National Assembly and then to the Chamber of Deputies, in 1876 he submitted his first private bill to authorize divorce, which did not meet with approval.

Naquet, who still preferred the more expansive 1792 approach to divorce, tried again with a narrower bill in 1882, and finally succeeded in getting the Chamber and Senate to discuss it. After lengthy debates in the

---

Accampo, Rachel G. Fuchs, & Mary Lynn Stewart (Baltimore: Johns Hopkins University Press, 1995), pp. 59–81. An important earlier study is Jacques Desforges, "La Loi Naquet," pp. 103–110, in *Renouveau des idées sur la famille*, ed. Robert Prigent. Institut national d'études démographiques. Travaux et documents, cahier n° 18 (Paris: Presses Universitaires de France, 1994). Desforges takes a skeptical view of the individual freedom arguments put forward by divorce enthusiasts, preferring the constraints of the 1884 law.

[47] See Francis Ronsin, *Les Divorçaires: Affrontements politiques et conceptions du mariage dans la France du XIXe siècle* (Paris: Aubier, 1992), and for 1848 especially, William Fortescue, "Divorce Debated and Deferred: The French Debate on Divorce and the Failure of the Crémieux Divorce Bill in 1848," *French History*, 7:2 (1993), 137–162. For the earlier period to the Restoration, see Francis Ronsin, *Le Contrat sentimental: Débats sur le mariage, l'amour, le divorce, de l'Ancien Régime à la Restauration* (Paris: Aubier, 1990), and Roderick Phillips's sweeping survey, *Putting Asunder: A History of Divorce in Western Society* (Cambridge, UK: Cambridge University Press, 1988).

[48] Richer, *Divorce* (1873); see n. 45.

[49] Alfred Naquet, *Religion, propriété, famille* (Paris: chez tous les librairies, 1869). A third edition appeared in Brussels in 1877, and was reprinted again in 1879 in anticipation of Naquet's next round of legislative divorce campaigns.

two houses, in which a variety of republicans expressed their enthusiasm, reservations, and sometimes outright disagreements, they did come together in favor of the more restrictive approach of the early Civil Code. Naquet believed that this was all that could be obtained in current circumstances.[50] Certainly it was better than nothing – a step in the direction of free choice. Significantly, in 1884, the French chambers "dropped the distinction between male and female adultery which had been a fundamental aspect of the [1804] Code's approach to divorce," but this distinction stayed in place with respect to "grounds for legal separation."[51]

Recherche de la Paternité and the Linked Problems of Child Abandonment and Infanticide

The Civil and Penal Codes contained other elements that severely handicapped women in their relationships to men, particularly with regard to sexual relations and the children born from these relations. The problem known by the pejorative label "illegitimacy" or the kinder term "natural children" is one of long standing in the attempts of men in Western societies to regulate sexual behavior generally and, in particular, to control female sexuality and reproduction. For centuries French governments had been deeply engaged in such regulation.

One of the most egregious offenders was Article 340 of the Civil Code, a post-revolutionary Napoleonic "solution" that stands out for its extreme arbitrariness. This article decreed that within a marriage, the husband was the presumed father of any child born to his wife. Outside marriage, children were simply not supposed to be produced – or if they were, too bad for them! The fathers bore no legal responsibility for such children. The Code prohibited paternity suits (*recherche de la paternité*) or legal actions by single mothers against the men who had made them pregnant outside marriage. This did not stop some single mothers from bringing suit for (and sometimes gaining) child support against putative fathers in French courts, as historian Rachel Fuchs has revealed.[52]

Scholars of comparative law have been quick to point out that the provisions of Article 340 were not only peculiar to nineteenth-century

---

[50] Ronsin provides an excellent account of these debates in *Les Divorçaires*, part II: "Alfred Naquet et le rétablissment du divorce."

[51] McBride, "Divorce and the Republican Family," p. 65.

[52] See the prize-winning study of Rachel Ginnis Fuchs, *Contested Paternity: Constructing Families in Modern France* (Baltimore: Johns Hopkins University Press, 2008).

France but that, also, they ran counter both to canon law and to the customary law of the *ancien régime*. There was, however, a simple explanation for this anomaly: like other restrictive articles of the Civil Code, Article 340 had been instituted at the express wish of Napoléon I, who intended to fortify the "legitimate family," that is, the male-headed, hierarchical family as established through the new national civil laws on marriage. Such a legal prohibition against paternity suits was unknown in any other Western country.[53] It would have serious unintended consequences.

The obvious difficulties inherent in this situation for unmarried mothers and their babies were compounded by the fact that formal adoption of such babies by other families was simply not legal in France.[54] Given the increasingly precarious economic circumstances in which such single women found themselves, particularly in the rapidly growing cities of nineteenth-century France, it is not surprising that some might contemplate abortion or infanticide (if not suicide). For the children of poor mothers, even those who were not surreptitiously "disposed of," infant mortality figures were extremely high. Nor is it surprising that thousands of new mothers would abandon their babies at birth or shortly thereafter.[55]

Infanticide, though probably not frequent, was a solution of last resort for most women, most of them among the single poor, but it had long preoccupied French lawmakers. As was explained in my earlier volume, in the mid-sixteenth century, King Henri II had defined infanticide as a capital crime. This king's edict further required formal written declarations of pregnancy (*déclarations de grossesse*) by unmarried women, a practice that survived well into the nineteenth century in some areas of France. Such declarations were intended both to publicly shame unmarried mothers and to protect the lives of their babies by making their pending arrival public knowledge. Scholars have since recovered and analyzed the sporadic runs of these records, attempting to better

---

[53] X. Torau-Bayle, "Enfants naturels, dépopulation et paternité," *Revue Politique et Parlémentaire* (August 1902), 317.

[54] See Nelly Schargo Hoyt & Rhoda Métraux, "The Family in the French Civil Code: 'Adoption and the tutelle officieuse'," in *Themes in French Culture*, ed. Margaret Mead & Rhoda Métraux (Stanford, CA: Stanford University Press, 1954), pp. 69–88.

[55] See the pioneering work of Rachel Ginnis Fuchs on foundlings and unmarried mothers in *Abandoned Children: Foundlings and Child Welfare in Nineteenth-Century France* (Albany, NY: SUNY Press, 1984), and *Poor and Pregnant in Paris: Strategies for Survival in the Nineteenth Century* (New Brunswick, NJ: Rutgers University Press, 1992). See also her *Contested Paternity* (cited in n. 50).

assess the changing conditions that contributed to rising illegitimacy rates during the later eighteenth century.[56]

Attempts by the revolutionary governments to mitigate the harshness of laws concerning illegitimacy (which fueled the practices of infanticide and abandonment) were astonishingly farsighted. A law of 28 June 1793 had established a government allotment to unmarried mothers to assist them financially so that they could keep their babies. This measure set a controversial precedent, but failed to achieve lasting change.[57] Again under Napoléon I, the Penal Code of 1810 reinstated the death penalty for women convicted of infanticide; the Code punished abandonment less severely but this act nevertheless remained subject to prosecution. Continued state concern with what we now call "human rights" issues fostered the new academic specialty of forensic or legal medicine, in which doctors offered expert testimony in court cases and developed a body of theoretical literature.[58] Meanwhile Napoléon I had authorized (Imperial decree of 19 January 1811) the establishment in the towns and cities of foundling hospitals, which would receive unwanted infants through a revolving turnstile, or *tour*, with the goal of raising them to maturity under public auspices.[59]

The *tour* experiment proved controversial, expensive, and only minimally successful. Some estimates suggested that one out of every thirty babies born each year was abandoned. In 1846 the social critic Alphonse Esquiros had claimed that in Paris alone, between 1816 and 1835, over 100,000 babies had passed through the *Enfants Trouvés*.[60] Esquiros blamed midwives for

---

[56] See, for an institutional overview, Marie-Claude Phan,"Les Déclarations de grossesse en France (XVIe-XVIIIe siècles): Essai institutionnel," *Revue d'Histoire Moderne et Contemporaine*, 22:1 (January–March 1975), 61–88. Cissie Fairchilds studied the records of these pregnancy declarations in Aix-en-Provence, and other scholars based in France have investigated the records in other areas. See Fairchilds, "Female Sexual Attitudes and the Rise of Illegitimacy: A Case Study," *Journal of Interdisciplinary History*, 8:4 (Spring 1978), 627–667, and the subsequent exchange in the same journal between Fairchilds and Jean-Louis Flandrin.

[57] For this legislation, see Crane Brinton, *French Revolutionary Legislation on Illegitimacy* (Cambridge, MA: Harvard University Press, 1936), and Laurence Boudouard & Florence Bellivier, "Des droits pour les bâtards, l'enfant naturel dans les débats révolutionnaires," in *La Famille, la loi, l'État: de la Révolution au Code civil*, ed. Irène Théry & Christian Biet (Paris: Centre Georges Pompidou/ Imprimerie Nationale, 1989), pp. 122–144.

[58] June K. Burton, "Human Rights Issues Affecting Women in Napoleonic Legal Medicine Textbooks," *History of European Ideas*, 8:4-5 (1987), 427–434. See also her book, *Napoléon and the Woman Question: Discourses of the Other Sex in French Education, Medicine, and Medical Law, 1799–1815* (Lubbock: Texas Tech University Press, 2007), chapter 7.

[59] The government closed the *tours* in 1846.

[60] Alphonse Esquiros, "Les Enfans [sic] trouvés," *Revue des Deux Mondes*, 15 January 1846 (211–242) & 15 March 1846 (1007–1044). This lengthy exploration of the problem of the *tours* (which had just been closed) and the putting out of unwanted babies is remarkable for its thoroughness and also for

colluding with unwed mothers in carrying out infant abandonments.[61] That same year (1846), after much debate, many of the *tours* that were funded by the national government were closed. The practical result of this new situation, which provided no alternative solutions for unfortunate mothers and babies, was effectively to condemn to early death many of the children born out of wedlock each year in France. This was not an insignificant number; the illegitimacy rates in major French cities ran to from 30 percent to 50 percent of all registered births, as pregnant women came to seek delivery in the anonymity of urban settings.[62] In 1870 Émile Acollas would quote official figures for the years 1858–1860, showing that children born out of wedlock in France then comprised over 7 percent of the total born; about two-thirds of these babies were never legally recognized (presented to the mayor's office for registration) either by their fathers or their mothers.[63] Republican reformers like Acollas would single out Article 340 as a Bonapartist invention – unjustly penalizing the innocent.

The picture was particularly grim for the babies who had not been formally "recognized" or registered or who had been abandoned to the *tours*. Those who survived were relegated to a sort of legal nonpersonhood as adults. Those whose births had been declared for the *état-civil*, but with "*père inconnu*" as father, carried a comparable social stigma throughout their lives. Since the mothers of such children had no legal possibility for obtaining any financial support from the fathers for the maintenance of a child, however much they might appeal to their charity (although some in fact did go to court, as Fuchs has shown in her study of judicial case law),

---

its humane perspective. Esquiros proposed a cluster of alternative solutions: state subsidies to mothers who keep their babies (as envisioned in 1793), *recherche de la paternité*, and moral support from women in the *Sociétés de Charité maternelles*. On these latter associations and their work, see Christine Adams, *Poverty, Charity, and Motherhood: Maternal Societies in Nineteenth-Century France* (Urbana: University of Illinois Press, 2010). On the general problem, see Angela Taeger, "L'État, les enfants trouvés et les allocations familiales en France, XIXe, XXe siècles," *Francia*, 16:3 (1989), 15–33.

[61] See Esquiros, pp. 215, 225 for these figures, and more generally, Rachel Fuchs, *Abandoned Children*.

[62] In his article, "Illegitimacy, Sexual Revolution, and Social Change in Modern Europe," *Journal of Interdisciplinary History*, 2:2 (Autumn 1971), 237–272, Edward Shorter gives the rates for illegitimacy in France's three major cities (Paris, Lyon, and Bordeaux) as 30 to 50% of all births (see esp. his graphs on pp. 265–267).

[63] Émile Acollas, *Le Droit de l'enfant; l'enfant né hors mariage* (orig. publ. in Paris: Sausset, 1865; 2nd ed., Paris: G. Baillière, 1870), p. 149 in 2nd ed. For earlier analyses, see P.-M. Rozier, *De la Condition sociale des femmes, du taux de leurs salaires, et de la recherche de la paternité à l'occasion des enfants trouvés, suivis de considérations sur les établissements de secours et l'aptitude des femmes à l'exercice de la médecine, avec une notice sur la régence des femmes, et lettres diverses* (2nd ed., Paris: Impr. J. Juteau, 1842) and the two articles by Esquiros (1846), cited in n. 60.

reformers alleged that these mothers were inevitably forced into prostitution in order to earn enough to keep themselves and their babies alive. Thus had the first Napoléon and the framers of the Codes contributed, albeit inadvertently, to the creation of a virtual caste of pariahs, numbering in the tens, even hundreds of thousands, under the guise of protecting the legitimate family.[64]

French children continued to be born out of wedlock, despite the best efforts of the reformers. In fact the situation worsened during the early Third Republic. Victor Schoelcher, who was by the late 1870s a senator for life, pushed for *recherche de la paternité*, publishing articles in *L'Avenir des Femmes* and its rechristened successor *Le Droit des Femmes*, from 1878 through 1885. Along with Senator René Bérenger, he proposed the legalization of paternity suits in the Senate in 1878; in the Chamber of Deputies in 1883, Gustave Rivet, author of the play *Le Châtiment* (1879), became its champion.

Republican reformers could not agree on the best approach. From 1878 through early 1879 Léon Richer published a series of public letters to Schoelcher on the "*paternité*" question, criticizing Schoelcher's bill and stating his opposition to restoring the *tours*.[65] Feminists like Léonie Rouzade invoked the precedent of 1793, and began to campaign for state subsidies for all mothers, to remove them from dependence on fathers or any other man. Even Jeanne Deroin (the first French woman to campaign for office in 1849, now in exile in England) joined the public debate in France. Taking on Richer, she argued for bringing back the *tours* and raising abandoned children communally.[66] Dumas *fils* also supported this position.

[64] On the social problems connected with illegitimate birth, including prostitution, see the publications of Jules Simon, Julie-Victoire Daubié, Émile Acollas, and also Émile de Girardin, *La Liberté dans le mariage par l'égalité des enfants devant la mère* (1852); reprinted in appendix to *L'Homme et la femme*, cited in n. 31. See also the later works by Maria Deraismes, "Les Droits de l'enfant" (1887) in her *Oeuvres complètes*, vol. 2; Léon Giraud, *La Vérité sur la recherche de paternité* (1888); and Gustave Rivet, *La Recherche de paternité* (3rd ed., 1890). A brief summary in English by Giraud is also provided in Stanton, *The Woman Question*, pp. 256–258. For a discussion of the jurisprudence with regard to paternal support, see Torau-Bayle, "Enfants naturels, dépopulation et paternité," (cited in n. 53).

[65] The series begins in the fall of 1878 and continues into 1879: see *Le Droit des Femmes*, n° 170 (January 1879; 6th letter); n° 171 (February 1879; 7th letter); n° 172 (March 1879; 8th letter); n° 173 (April 1879; 9th & last letter). Richer returns to this subject in 1883–1884 (series of letters to M. Achard, deputy). Additional articles on the subject of *recherche de la paternité* would appear in the issues for March & April 1890.

[66] *Le Droit des Femmes* would publish sporadic letters from Jeanne Deroin in the 1880s. See n° 225 (5 August 1883), n° 226 (2 September 1883), n° 227 (7 October 1883), and n° 228 (4 November 1883); also n° 280 (15 August 1886), n° 319 (1 April 1888), n° 385 (4 January 1891), & n° 388 (15 February 1891). In contrast to Deroin, Richer thought that it would be preferable to honor maternity; he viewed the *tours* as tombs.

Republican partisans of abolishing the prohibition against *recherche de la paternité* would make little headway before the early twentieth century. In 1890 Rivet would publish his long book, *La Recherche de la paternité*, which called for passage of a "law of responsibility." Commenting on Rivet's book, Auclert's *La Citoyenne* (n° 162, September 1890) would reproach Rivet for not pursuing the measure energetically from 1883 on, alleging that the "*classe dirigéante*" would prefer to smother this reform. Of the 75,000 children born out of wedlock in France every year, she indicated, only around 5,000 were recognized by their fathers. Still the resistance of legislators to considering the reinstatement of *recherche de la paternité* remained fierce.

Thanks to the efforts of new republican advocates, notably the socialist deputy Marcel Sembat, the legislature would finally, though only partially, reform this law in 1912 (as we will see in Chapter 11). By allowing women to bring suit only against unmarried men, however, the majority of deputies would effectively shield philandering married men, all in the name of "protecting" the family. Fundamental reform, which would fully empower single mothers and equalize the status of children born out of wedlock with those born within, would not come about until 1972.[67] But this is getting ahead of our story. The significant fact is that in the 1870s and 1880s even the most progressive republican legislators still hesitated to undercut male prerogatives by holding men responsible for the consequences of their sexual misdeeds.

Votes for Women: A "Radical" Demand in the 1870s and 1880s

The term "radical" on the spectrum of women's rights came to apply specifically to those who demanded full woman suffrage, namely that the so-called universal manhood suffrage of the Third Republic become *truly* universal by incorporating all adult women. And, indeed, the story of the refusal of the congress organizers to put the suffrage question on the agenda of the International Women's Rights Congress of 1878 is well known; both Maria Deraismes and Léon Richer viewed this claim as "premature." Their refusal provoked strenuous objections from one young associate, Hubertine Auclert (1848–1914), who insisted that political rights for women must necessarily be the first and foremost goal under the new French Third Republic.

---

[67] *L'Express*, 20 August 1972.

In a subsequent pamphlet that published her undelivered speech of 1878, *Le Droit politique des femmes, question qui n'est pas traitée au Congrès international des femmes* [The Political Right(s) of Women, A Question That Is Not Treated at the International Congress of Women, 1878], Auclert denounced her erstwhile colleagues as cowardly. Invoking the history of women's participation in the early years of the French Revolution and quoting such advocates of women's political rights as Condorcet, she dismissed as irrelevant arguments against women's political participation based on their ostensibly weaker physical strength. Intelligence and thoughtfulness were what counted, and women, Auclert claimed, had those qualities in abundance. Like Deraismes in earlier times, Auclert found historical precedents useful for shaming these seemingly recalcitrant republicans.

Addressing the ladies in her audience, she astutely pointed to all the practical reasons why French women – all 9 million of them – should be able to cast their ballots: "We must remind ourselves that the weapon of the vote will be for us, just as it is for man, the only means of obtaining the reforms we desire. As long as we remain excluded from civic life, men will attend to their own interests rather than to ours. . . . The laws will be made against us, and the least possible amount of money will be spent on our behalf."[68] Women should be allowed to vote, just as they are required to pay taxes. Their views, she argued, must be represented in decisions about how government monies are allocated.[69]

In nineteenth-century France, just as in the few other democratizing Western nations (notably the Swiss confederation and the United States, until enfranchisement of women in New Zealand in 1893 and, in Europe, enfranchisement of all women and men together in Finland in 1906), the vote based on the individual and not on property qualifications had become the penultimate symbol of manly status, the primal token of social and political power, the apex of the vision of "equality."[70] For some men

---

[68] Hubertine Auclert, *Le Droit politique des femmes, question qui n'est pas traitée au Congrès international des femmes* (Paris: Impr. L. Hugonis, 1878), as transl. by KO, in *WFF*, vol. I, doc. 142; quotes, p. 515. René Viviani would elegantly restate Auclert's argument in 1900 (see Part II, Chapter 8, in this volume). On Auclert, see Steven C. Hause, *Hubertine Auclert: The French Suffragette* (New Haven, CT: Yale University Press, 1987). A selection of Auclert's articles from this period have been republished in *Hubertine Auclert: La Citoyenne, articles de 1881 à 1891*, ed. Édith Taïeb (Paris: Syros, 1982), and in Steven C. Hause, ed., with preface by Geneviève Fraisse, *Hubertine Auclert: Pionnière du féminisme* (Saint-Pourcain-sur-Sioule: Bleu Autour, 2007).

[69] Auclert, *Droit politique des femmes*, . . . Quote, as transl. in *WFF, vol.* I, doc. 142, p. 515.

[70] See *The Woman Question in France*, chapter 2: "Assessing the Problem of Women and Political Authority in French History."

who, from 1848 on, took this privilege seriously as a prerogative of manhood, women's quest for suffrage amounted to a direct assault on the symbolic marker of masculine authority. Thus, the context for debating women's suffrage in France, already very particular, would be emotionally as well as ideologically charged during the early Third Republic. No one could plead ignorance concerning the issue at hand: the recent British suffrage campaigns (including John Stuart Mill's introduction of a woman suffrage bill in Parliament in 1867) were well known in France, thanks to women journalists such as Clarisse Coignet and republicans such as Jules Favre.[71] Although the British Parliament had denied women the parliamentary vote in 1869, it had enfranchised single adult women property owners to vote and run for office at the municipal level.

Following the death of Julie-Victoire Daubié, who had advocated the vote for single adult women – as well as full economic opportunities for all women – during the later Second Empire and early 1870s, Hubertine Auclert hoisted the woman suffrage banner aloft and waved it energetically. She quickly became the principal and most visible public proponent for woman suffrage, joining Deraismes in calling the newly triumphant republicans to account.[72] Auclert had discovered the women's rights cause

---

[71] See the series of articles by Clarisse Gauthier Coignet in the *Revue Bleue: Revue politique et littéraire:* "*De l'Affranchissement politique des femmes en Angleterre*" (issues of 2 & 9 May 1874); subsequently issued as a 46-page offprint (Paris: G. Baillière, 1874), and "Le Mouvement des femmes en Angleterre: le suffrage politique," 16, n° 11 (11 September 1875), 251–255, and 16, n° 12 (18 September 1875), 274–280. [NB: Mme Coignet, who began publishing on girls' education in the mid-1850s, would continue to be active in advocacy of legal reform in the position of women into the 1890s; see Fonds Kauffmann notes, Bouglé Collection, BHVP.]

The staunch republican Jules Favre, a firm believer in the importance of women's influence, had also endorsed woman suffrage: see his *Discours de M. Jules Favre prononcé a sa réception à l'Académie Française le 23 avril 1868* (Paris: Didier, 1868), p. 30, and in an 1869 speech, he claimed that had he been in the British Parliament in 1867, he would have voted with John Stuart Mill for enfranchising women – and even for extending Mill's proposal to include married women ("De l'avenir de l'enseignement populaire," published in the *Revue des Cours Littéraires*, vol. 6, n° 10 (6 February 1869), 146–154, esp. 152–153. See also his lecture, "De la Condition des femmes dans les sociétés démocratiques, conférence de 4 avril 1874," in his *Quatre Conférences faites en Belgique au mois d'avril 1874* (Paris: Plon, 1874). See the discussion in *The Woman Question in France*, chapter 7, for the French debates about women's suffrage in the later 1860s.

[72] In what follows I have drawn primarily from the "Notice biographique," which introduces Hubertine Auclert's posthumous collection of articles and speeches, *Les Femmes au gouvernail* (Paris: M. Giard, 1923), pp. 1–91. See also A. Leclère, *Le Vote des femmes en France* (Paris: M. Rivière, 1929), pp. 67–69. See especially the excellent (and to date only) scholarly biography, by Hause, *Hubertine Auclert* (cited in n. 68); the essay by Edith Taïeb, introducing *Hubertine Auclert: La Citoyenne 1848–1914, Articles de 1881 à 1891* (Paris: Syros, 1982), and Hause's introduction to *Hubertine Auclert: Pionnière du féminisme* (cited in n. 68). Other scholarly studies that recount various phases of Auclert's campaigns include Bidelman, *Pariahs Stand Up!* (1982); Moses, *French Feminism* (1984); Klejman & Rochefort, *L'Égalité en marche* (1989), all cited earlier. See also chapter 4 in Joan W. Scott, *Only Paradoxes to Offer: French Feminists and the Rights of Man* (Cambridge,

through reading *Le Droit des Femmes,* and had also drawn inspiration from Victor Hugo's 1872 banquet letter on the woman question. When she moved to Paris in 1874, she had joined Richer's editorial staff. In that same year, the National Assembly of the Third Republic took up deliberations on a new electoral law.

In 1874, universal manhood suffrage itself seemed untouchable, though members of the National Assembly's Commission of Thirty made efforts to raise the voting age for men to 25. But adding women to the mix was another matter altogether. All the while the legislators tried their best to ignore (or repress) the issue of votes for women, pausing only to launch some sarcastic humor at the feminists' expense. It is significant that the ensuing Constitutional laws of 1875 did mention *suffrage universel* but left the specifics to be elaborated by an electoral law that was not part of the constitution itself.[73] One could sense the legislators' agreement with the incantation of Prudhomme in 1793: "Let the men make the Revolution!" To women's rights activists, however, such a deliberate exclusion of women from policy-making seemed antithetical to republican principles. Were they not included in *"tous les français?"* Did the term *"tous"* only include women when it came to taxing them?

From the outset, Hubertine Auclert had linked the future of women's rights to the future of the republic and called upon republican men to live up to their principles by enfranchising French women as full-fledged citizens. In 1876 she founded an action group, also called *Le Droit des Femmes.* In the fall of 1876, on the heels of the first French workers' congress, she had issued a fierce manifesto in the press, "Aux Femmes – Femmes de France," in which (echoing a number of her predecessors in the 1830s and 1840s) she linked women and the proletariat as the remaining "outcasts" following the revolution of 1789: the workers had finally

---

MA: Harvard University Press, 1996), which focuses on "the social" and cites only a small number of Auclert's vast editorial corpus through secondary sources and edited collections, notably that of Taïeb. See also Edith Taïeb's more recent publications: "Hubertine Auclert, Fondatrice de La Citoyenne: Une femme, 'seule contre tous'," *Écrivaines françaises et francophones,* special issue (hors série) of *Europe Plurilingue,* (March 1997), 52–74; Edith Taïeb, "Abuses of 'Masculinism' in Hubertine Auclert's *La Citoyenne,*" in *Women Seeking Expression: France 1789–1914,* ed. Rosemary Lloyd & Brian Nelson (Monash Romance Studies. Melbourne: School of European Languages and Cultures, Monash University, 2000), pp. 101–117; and especially Edith Taïeb, "Le politique et le domestique: L'argumentation d'Hubertine Auclert sous la Troisième République," *Mots: Les langages du politique,* n° 78 (2005). Online at www.mots/revues.org/67.

73 See Maurice Duverger, *Constitutions et Documents politiques.* 4th ed. (Paris: Presses Universitaires de France, 1966), pp. 110–114. The electoral laws established voting qualifications and also the mode of voting (*scrutin d'arrondissement, scrutin de liste departemental,* single election, primaries and run-offs, etc.) and were subject to sporadic changes during the Third Republic.

assembled, but women were "shut out from elective and legislative assemblies" in the Republic.[74] Like the workers, women must organize in order to obtain their rights.

In early June 1877 her efforts, along with those of Maria Deraismes, her sister, and others earned ridicule in *Le Gaulois* by Emile Villemot, who labeled them the "seven prophetesses," demeaned them as "*les Politigueuses*," and scorned Auclert, who had dared to write a rebuttal, as "*la Sévigné des deux gares.*"[75] Later that year, just as the legislative elections that would resolve the Seize Mai governmental crisis in favor of the republicans were underway, Auclert returned to the charge with another manifesto, "Les Femmes aux électeurs," in which she argued that "the republican idea excludes the aristocracy of sex just as it excludes the aristocracy of caste." She reminded her readers that there were still "nine million adult women, imbued with reason" that remained "slaves in a nation of free men." She invoked the historical example of "our mothers, *les Gauloises*" to remind the male voters that women were not only watching but did not think that men alone "should be responsible for the destiny of the Republic and the *patrie*.... We want a republican Republic, one which will finally apply our immortal principles of '89. We want equality for all [pour *tous* et pour *toutes*]. We want the reign of justice and law."[76] This manifesto called on the male voters to do the right thing by electing republican candidates, to keep in mind the men of the Revolution: "Choose delegates who put their lives in accord with their principles." She played shamelessly on republican guilt.

In her 1878 post-congress speech/pamphlet, Auclert elaborated at greater length on themes that she had developed in her earlier manifestos and

---

[74] "Aux Femmes" (September 1876), reprinted in *Le Droit des Femmes*, n° 144 (November 1876) and other newspapers; republished in Hubertine Auclert, *Historique de la Société le Droit des Femmes, 1876–1880* (Paris, 1881), pp. 8–10, and in Taïeb, ed., *La Citoyenne*, pp. 19–20. In French: "Si préoccupées que nous soyions du gouvernement de notre pays, nous sommes impitoyablement repoussées de toutes les assemblées, tant électives que législatives. La République n'aurait cependant pas trop du concours de tous et de toutes. Nous comptons moins que rien dans l'État." See also Hause, *Hubertine Auclert*, p. 53.

[75] See *Le Gaulois*, issues of 3, 7, 8, and 12 June 1877. The allusive references are to the famous seventeenth-century letter writer Madame de Sévigné, and to Auclert's street address on the rue des Deux Gares. The word "gueuse" can best be translated as slut; thus political sluts.

[76] "Les femmes aux électeurs" (October 1877), republished in *Historique*, pp. 11–15. "L'idée républicaine exclut l'aristocratie de sexe, comme elle exclut l'aristocratie de caste.... Il y a neuf millions d'êtres doués de raison, neuf millions de femmes majeures qui forment comme une nation d'esclaves dans la nation d'hommes libres.... A l'instar de nos mères, les Gauloises, nous veillons.... Nous voulons une République républicaine, qui applique enfin nos immortels principes de 89. Nous voulons l'égalité pour *tous* et pour *toutes*. Nous voulons le règne de la justice et du droit.... Choisissez des délégues qui mettent leur vie d'accord avec leurs principes."

would continue to pursue throughout her career. She was fed up with nominal republicans who did not act in accordance with their principles. Denouncing the "opportunist" republicans (by whom she referred particularly to Léon Gambetta and his followers) who "closed all its doors," she asserted that "with only a few rare exceptions, the republicans disdain and jeer at woman; meanwhile, the monarchists and bonapartists arm her for combat."[77] She invoked the force of women's influence and challenged French Republicans to deliver full civil and political equality for women, arguing that a republic in which women (including married women) were not considered full citizens was no "true" republic.[78] Addressing republican men, she challenged them, in the name of their own principles, to eliminate the "slavery" of women: "In the name of justice, in the name of liberty, abdicate your masculine kingship. It is time to proclaim equality."[79] Critiques such as these continued to inform Auclert's campaigns throughout the 1880s. No doubt it was from reading texts like this that one scholar-colleague concluded that "the Republic" itself was hostile to women's emancipation.[80] A more careful analysis would suggest that Auclert's critique targeted a particular subgroup of recalcitrant republican men, those whose actions were out of line with the ideals they purportedly embraced – a republic that truly encompassed "every one."

Disappointed with the continuing prudence of her colleagues, in October 1879 Auclert took her campaign for women's political rights to the Marseille congress of the *Parti Ouvrier*. In a lengthy speech that retains its fire over a hundred years later, she insisted that "a Republic that keeps women in an inferior situation cannot make men equal." What was more, workers had no right to seek equality with their bourgeois masters as long as they refused to admit the equality of their women.[81] "We, the women,

---

[77] Auclert, *Droit politique des femmes, question qui n'est pas traitée* ... Quoted in my translation, from *WFF*, vol. 1, doc. 142, p. 514. Gambetta became a particular object of Auclert's scorn – though she did consider him a "grand patriot", she also called him "*masculiniste à outrance*," having founded a regime that excluded women. See her obituary article, "M. Léon Gambetta," at the time of his death in early 1883, *La Citoyenne*, n° 68 (7 January – 4 February 1883), 1.

[78] Auclert, *Droit politique des femmes.*   [79] Auclert, *Droit politique des femmes.*

[80] See the exchange between Charles Sowerwine and myself in *Confronting Modernity in Fin-de-Siècle France: Bodies, Minds and Gender*, ed. Christopher E. Forth & Elinor Accampo (Houndmills, UK: Palgrave Macmillan, 2010), pp. 19–62, and the General Introduction to this volume.

[81] Hubertine Auclert, *Égalité sociale et politique de la femme et de l'homme, discours prononcé au Congrès ouvrier socialiste de Marseille* (Marseille: Impr. de A. Thomas, 1879). The full French text was republished in 1976, with an analysis, in Madeleine Rebérioux, Christiane Dufrancatel, & Béatrice Slama, "Hubertine Auclert et la question des femmes a 'l'immortel congrès' (1879)," in *Romantisme*, n°s 13–14 (1976), 123–142. Excerpts in English in *WFF*, vol. 1, doc. 143. This text is now reprinted in the Hause & Fraisse collection and is also available online at Gallica.

will not busy ourselves with aiding despotism to change hands. What we want is to kill privilege, not merely to reallocate it." Judging from the floor debate that followed her speech, some workers (of Proudhonian persuasion) found Auclert's proposal extremely upsetting. Nevertheless, the assembled delegates voted overwhelmingly in support of equal rights for women and men, demonstrating an enthusiasm that had been absent at the workers' congresses of 1876 and 1878 and would not be allowed to emerge again at subsequent socialist workers' congresses. Auclert's biographer calls this endorsement "the greatest political victory of her life."[82]

Auclert repeatedly underscored the "*masculinisme*" of the French deputies' attitude; in one particularly strongly worded manifesto entitled "*A Tous*" (1880) she addressed voters and those elected: either one must replace the name "republican" by "our regime of masculine law," or else one must install the "real" Republic "by decreeing the abolition of sex privilege, just as our ancestors in the last century decreed the abolition of caste privileges." She called on women to contribute to ending their own "slavery" by supporting the campaign for ideas of "justice and liberty."[83]

From 1881 to 1888 Auclert put her short-lived flirtation with the socialists behind her and devoted herself exclusively to the campaign for women's vote. She repeatedly denounced "masculine autocracy" and "*masculinisme*." In addition to running her association, *Société Le Droit des Femmes*, in February 1881 she launched a weekly publication, *La Citoyenne*, which she published with the financial help of her ally, the attorney Léon Giraud, then with the assistance of the deputy Joseph de Gasté.[84] Repeatedly invoking history, Auclert and her followers organized a women's march to mourn women's plight under the Code at the first Bastille Day celebration (14 July 1881). Citing Lairtullier's history, she applauded the heroism of the revolutionary women: "Women helped the men to take the Bastille, and to make the revolution, but they gained no advantage from either.... The Code makes women slaves, ... a nation of serfs within a nation of free men."[85]

---

[82] Hause, *Hubertine Auclert*, p. 60.   [83] "A Tous," republished in Auclert, *Historique*, pp. 29–32.

[84] Li Dzeh-Djen, *La Presse féministe en France de 1869 à 1914* (Paris: L. Rodstein, 1934), pp. 66–81; Jehan des Étrivières, *Les Amazones du siècle* (Paris: n.p., 3rd ed., 1883), p. 15. Subsidies were no stranger to the nineteenth-century French political press. The women's rights press was unexceptional in this respect. Richer's *Le Droit des Femmes* was aided for many years by the Lyonnais banker and former Saint-Simonian, François Arlès-Dufour (who had promoted the career of Julie-Victoire Daubié in the late 1850s and 1860s) as well as by the wealth of Maria Deraismes. In the early twentieth century, publication of the daily *La Fronde* would devour much of the personal fortune of Marguerite Durand, leading rumor-mongers to suggest that she also received funding from others, including lovers and a member of the Rothschild banking family.

[85] See Hause, *Hubertine Auclert*, p. 80; also Auclert, "La Bastille des femmes," *La Citoyenne*, n° 22 (10 July 1881) and "La Manifestation de la Société le Droit de Femmes," *La Citoyenne*, n° 23 (17 July 1881).

During the 1880s she also organized the first "national" French association to promote woman suffrage, refused to pay her own taxes (arguing "no taxation without representation"), attempted unsuccessfully to register to vote (1880, 1885), put forth electoral programs for republican male candidates (1881, 1885) encouraged women to run for office (which some did in 1885), and with the persistence of a gadfly, goaded her not-so-radical as well as radical republican associates to take action on the issue of woman suffrage.[86]

In 1884, the republican legislature, assembled as a "national assembly" met to consider constitutional revision. The electoral law was revised to substitute *scrutin de liste* for *scrutin d'arrondissement*. Like the earlier electoral law of 1848, the new French electoral law of 1884 [law of 5 April] read: "*Tous les français*." This terminology was equivocal, however, since in French civil and penal law (as was pointed out earlier) the masculine form "*tous les français*" was understood to encompass women as well as men.

The elasticity of "*tous les français*" would be tested in court by Auclert's allies and their male supporters. In 1885 Louise Barbarousse and Marie Richard Picot attempted to register to vote under the revised electoral law of 1884; the Paris Municipal Council denied their request and their appeal was heard by a justice of the peace (*juge du paix*). Two male lawyers who were allies of Auclert, Jules Allix and Léon Giraud, represented the women's case, pleading on the high ground of "imprescriptable rights" of the individual as well as national prestige that women should vote in France.[87]

> It is necessary to the glory of the French laws that they leave a place to woman in this sphere of public power, and it will be to the honour of the declaration of the rights of man to acknowledge also the rights of woman.... Does not *tous les Français* encompass every individual of the French nationality, without exception of sex?

The presiding judge denied the appeal, framing his verdict in terms of legal-historical precedent that dodged the issue of principle. Even issues of grammatical gender could be qualified (when convenient) by invoking

---

[86] For an overview of the woman suffrage question, see Karen Offen, "Women, Citizenship, and Suffrage With a French Twist, 1789–1993," chapter 8 in *Suffrage and Beyond: International Feminist Perspectives*, ed. Caroline Daley & Melanie Nolan (Auckland, London, New York, 1994), pp. 151–170.

[87] The texts below, from the *Gazette des Tribunaux*, are reproduced in English, in "The Recent Decision upon Municipal Suffrage in France," *The Englishwoman's Review*, 16 (14 March 1885), p. 106.

contextual precedent. Judge Carré made the point that precedent from the Revolution on was that voting citizens were males only; indeed the Constitutions of June 1793 and August 1795 had expressly spelled out this point.[88] He noted further that the most recent laws stipulate that "in order to be an elector, one must be a citizen" and that "the citizen is the Frenchman who has full political and civil rights"; therefore since women have neither, and are therefore not citizens, they cannot be electors. In concluding, however, the judge abandoned his air of juridical neutrality, and referred the question of women's suffrage back to the republican legislature:[89] "Whereas, finally, if women repudiating their privileges and inspiring themselves with certain modern theories, believe the hour has come to break the bonds of tutelage with which tradition, law, and custom have surrounded them, they must bring their claim before the Legislative power, and not before the Courts of Law."

Prior to the fall legislative elections, in August 1885 Auclert would put forward a "women's electoral program" in twelve articles that once again demanded women's full inclusion in the French nation. It put forth a series of measures designed to promote the equality of the sexes, including the vote, and to replace what she called the "Minotaur State" (*État minotaur*) by the "Motherly State" (*État mère de famille*), which would assure "security and work to able-bodied French citizens, assistance to children, old people, the sick and the infirm." Here we find seeds of a social welfare program. In conclusion, she insisted that "the human equality it [this program] proposes is the goal of a Republic; for Republic and justice should be synonymous." In Auclert's view – and she was not alone – women (still) had everything to gain under a republic.[90] Among those things was a compassionate state, one that served the needs of all its constituents. In 1888 she advocated organizing an assembly of women in every department to examine and decide on current issues.

Auclert repeatedly invoked lessons from history to chastise the republican legislators. In 1889, she commented on the revolutionary centennial celebrations by refusing to celebrate "the bastard Revolution that has placed us [women], half of humankind, outside humanity." "Women ought not celebrate the masculine '89; they need to make a feminine '89 by taking advantage of the congresses to organize the feminist movement

---

[88] "Recent Decision," p. 108. For the constitutional texts, see Duverger, ed. *Constitutions et Documents politiques*, cited in n. 73.
[89] "Recent Decision," p. 109. My emphasis.
[90] Hubertine Auclert, "Programme électoral des femmes," *La Citoyenne*, n° 99 (August 1885), 1. English translation in Appendix II in Hause, *Hubertine Auclert*.

in the departments."[91] Those who governed France, she insisted, should complete the work of the Revolution on this anniversary of the Revolution by turning France's 9 million slaves (women) into citizens – thereby acknowledging their legal (both civil and political) equality.

Completing the work of the revolution was, however, stymied by anxious speculation about "how" women might vote. At the time Hubertine Auclert first embraced the cause of woman suffrage, both Léon Richer and Maria Deraismes feared that, despite the desirability of the goal (which they endorsed in principle), raising the suffrage question at that moment could only compromise their campaign for women's civil rights – just as had been the case in 1848. The time, Richer argued, was not ripe; women simply weren't ready to exercise the vote.[92] Implicit in this stance, of course, was the vivid republican anticlerical fear (fueled since the 1840s by Michelet's alarm over the pernicious influence of priests and confessors on women) that most French women were still too attached to Catholicism (and, more generally, favorable to a monarchy) to be considered politically reliable.[93] This perception of the suffrage question among republicans would continue to fuel opposition to women voting for many decades. In 1877–1878 republican hostility to "clericalism" (i.e., intervention of the Catholic Church in political life) had been at its peak (Gambetta's "*Le cléricalisme, voilà l'ennemi*"!) and was undoubtedly better grounded than would subsequently be the case when women became better educated and began to think for themselves. But already in 1878 Auclert challenged this deep-rooted fear, criticizing the "cowardice" of her colleagues, and arguing that there was no proof that women "would vote for the priests and the Jesuits"; what was more, under the current electoral laws priests and other Catholic men, including Jesuits, could vote – and certainly they were not electing republicans.

---

[91] Auclert, "Le Quatre-Vingt-Neuf des femmes," *La Citoyenne*, n° 145 (June 1889); partially reprinted in Taïeb, ed., *La Citoyenne*, pp. 126–127.

[92] See Léon Richer, *La Femme libre* (Paris: E. Dentu, 1877), pp. 238–241; in English as doc. 141 in *WFF*, vol. 1. See also pp. 267–272, where the author made the comparison with England, where single propertied women had gained the municipal vote in the late 1860s. He notes that August Nefftzer, the former editor of *Le Temps*, who had retired to England, had changed his mind about woman suffrage, based on his observations that women voters had had a positive effect on municipal affairs and had won over the liberals. For the perspective of Maria Deraismes, who favored woman suffrage in theory but did not think the time was ripe, see *Eve dans l'humanité* (Paris: Librairie Générale de L. Sauvaitre, 1891), pp. 241–242. See also Ferdinand Buisson, *Le Vote des femmes* (Paris: H. Denot & E. Pinat 1911), p. 28.

[93] See the penetrating analysis of Theodore Zeldin, "The Conflict of Moralities," in *Conflicts in French Society: Anti-clericalism, Education and Morals in the Nineteenth Century. Essays*, ed. Theodore Zeldin (London: G. Allen & Unwin; New York: Humanities Press, 1970).

Women were certainly no more clerical than these men.[94] "I say that those who support clericalism – the men – are more clerical than the women who practice [the religion]."[95]

Auclert would subsequently critique republican politicians for continuing to provide state financial support for the church (under the Concordat of 1801, the French state was still responsible for the church budget) and for maintaining an ambassador to the Vatican. Her unrelenting campaigns would ultimately provoke opponents to articulate myriad arguments against women's vote, reflecting their perceived fear for the future of the Third Republic itself, should unschooled, superstitious women dominated by Catholic confessors (and thus presumably monarchists) be enfranchised along with more progressive women.[96] Well after the separation of church and state in 1904–1906, Auclert would continue to critique the hesitancy of some secular republicans to support women's vote, arguing that they were just as bad as the Catholics who deployed "the religious ruse" in their repression and exploitation of women and demanding to know why "women who believe should be treated more harshly than men who believe." "Men are not asked about their philosophical ideas when they pick up their elector's cards. Priests, pastors, rabbis, receive their cards just the same as the freethinkers."[97] Only time would tell whether Auclert was right, or whether these fearful republican men were justified in their concerns.

Another intriguing aspect of the subsequent French campaign for women's suffrage was the effort by partisans to mobilize historic precedent on the side of women's citizenship and suffrage. An important contribution to this effort was Léon Giraud's study on the comparative status of women with respect to public and political rights, which would win a prize from the Paris Law Faculty in 1891. Giraud would share this prize with a widely translated treatise by Moïse Ostrogorski, who argued that, above all else, the question of determining who would vote was a political question.[98]

---

[94] See Auclert's 1878 speech, *Droit politique des femmes,* pp. 13–14.

[95] Auclert, *Égalité sociale et politique de la femme et de l'homme* (1879); p. 129 in 1976 reprint.

[96] Hause (with Kenney) has examined how these anticlerical arguments against women's suffrage played out in the following decades in *Women's Suffrage and Social Politics.*

[97] Hubertine Auclert, "Vous êtes cléricales!" in her book *Le Vote des femmes* (1908), p. 56. This editorial is not listed in the Auclert bibliography prepared by Hause.

[98] Léon Giraud, *De la Condition des femmes au point de vue de l'exercice des droits publics et politiques; étude de législation comparée* (Paris: F. Pichon, 1891). See also Moïse Ostrogorski, *La Femme au point de vue du droit public; étude d'histoire et de législation comparée* (Paris: A. Rousseau, 1892); a revised edition was translated into English as *The Rights of Women: A Comparative Study in History and Legislation* (London: Swan Sonnenschein, & New York: Charles Scribner's Sons, 1893).

With such reputable scholarship at hand, bolstered by the research of legal scholar Paul-Marie Viollet, feminists such as Eliska Vincent would popularize historical evidence of women's participation in political life during the *ancien régime*.[99] These advocates of woman suffrage insisted, on the basis of incontrovertible evidence, that women had repeatedly voted in earlier periods of French history. But then, votes were tied to fiefs or landed property, not to individuals as such, as was currently the case in France.

Auclert was a tenacious crusader. Throughout the 1880s, in her publication *La Citoyenne*, she argued for women's suffrage in every conceivable way. Nevertheless, in private, she became deeply depressed over the lack of results as well as stung by the merciless ridicule of opponents. It was only in the 1890s that her suffrage campaign began to be taken seriously. On one later occasion (1908) she and a few exasperated associates would even invade a polling place and hurl the ballot box to the floor, scattering its contents. Shortly thereafter she would serve (briefly) as chair of the newly established Suffrage Section of the *Conseil National des Femmes Françaises* (CNFF). Finally, in 1909 another group of disgruntled women, who had come to the same conclusions as Auclert, would organize the single-issue *Union Française pour le Suffrage des Femmes* (UFSF) – but without the maverick Auclert's involvement. In 1910 Auclert would run (illegally) for elective office. By the time of her death in April 1914 Hubertine Auclert had transcended the status of a media-created eccentric and had achieved recognition as a pioneer.

We will return to the subject of women's suffrage in Chapter 13.

---

[99] Only in the mid-1890s would Paul-Marie Viollet begin to publish his findings on women's exclusion from political authority; see his article, based on his 1892–1893 lecture series, "Comment les femmes ont été exclues en France de la succession à la couronne," *Mémoires de l'Académie des inscriptions et belles-lettres*, 34 (1895), pt. 2: 125–178; this material would be incorporated in to his chapter "Exclusion des femmes et de leur descendance," in his *Histoire des Institutions politiques et administratives de la France*, vol. 2 (Paris: L. Larose, 1898), pp. 55–86. Advocates of women's suffrage would make good use of such findings. See Eliska Vincent's publications on women and legislation, beginning with "L'Électorat des femmes dans l'histoire," *Revue Féministe*, 1:1 (1 October 1895), 20–26. Hubertine Auclert would draw on this material in "Les Femmes ont voté en France," in her *Vote des femmes* (Paris: V. Giard & E. Brière, 1908), pp. 65ff.

CHAPTER 2

Educators, Medical and Social Scientists, and Population Experts Debate the Woman Question, 1870–1889

If woman suffrage seemed too inexpedient (if not truly threatening) to the majority of male republicans in 1879–1880, what other aspects of the woman question could they successfully address? How could committed republicans best realize the ideals that the "republic" represented when so many things seemed wrong with the relations between the sexes in the society they had inherited? In this chapter we will examine the debates that swirled around three closely interrelated concerns in the period prior to 1890 – 1) the content of education for girls, 2) the debate surrounding women's brains and intelligence, and 3) the growing concerns about the falling French birth rate.[1] In Chapter 3, we will investigate the closely linked debates about women's paid employment and about sexual morality and prostitution.

How Should Women Be Educated under the Republic?

In the 1870s most republican men strongly believed that an expanded and secular state educational system would provide solutions to many of France's challenges. Women's rights advocates agreed; the second most pressing item after legal reform in the 1874 platform of the *Société pour l'Amélioration du Sort des Femmes*, was girls' education – in conjunction with moral and economic reforms.[2] In 1878, the First Section of the International Congress on Women's Rights concerned pedagogy, which

---

[1] This chapter builds on my two earlier articles: "The Second Sex and the *Baccalauréat* in Republican France, 1880–1924," *French Historical Studies*, 13:2 (Fall 1983), 252–286, and "Depopulation, Nationalism, and Feminism in Fin-de-Siècle France," *The American Historical Review*, 89:3 (June 1984), 648–676. I have also drawn on translated documents published in *Women, the Family, and Freedom: The Debate in Documents, 1750–1950*, ed. Susan Groag Bell & Karen Offen (Stanford, CA: Stanford University Press), 2 vols. (hereafter *WFF*).

[2] See *L'Avenir des Femmes* (September 1871 – end of 1878); also the summary of the entire program in *The Englishwoman's Review*, n° 20 (October 1874), 246–249.

in the organizers' inclusive view spanned not only schooling per se but also a mix of moral and practical issues – such as the condemnation of wet-nursing and advocacy of mothers nursing their own babies. The First Section also endorsed the Froebel and "natural" systems for early childhood education. The Congress's resolutions called for a common program of studies for girls and boys, and coeducational classrooms (referred to by some as "integral education").[3] Finally, the Congress resolved (following the presentation of Eugénie Pierre) "that education be accessible to all children of both sexes, and that it be laic, moral, vocational [professional], free at every level, and finally, obligatory."[4] To conclude, as earlier scholars have done, that pressure from women's rights advocates played no part in the passage of the subsequent republican education laws is clearly uninformed.[5] As we have seen in *The Woman Question in France, 1400–1870*, women had been complaining about their inadequate education for centuries; finally the message had gotten through! With a legislative majority in place after 1879, republican men were listening and determined to act.

Given the decades of struggle between secular progressive men and the authorities of the Catholic Church for control of girls' education, the first republican objective was to wrest control of women from the church by taking over, reshaping, and investing in the education of its youth, especially girls. Only a program of mass education would do, they thought, to relax the grip of the clerics and "superstition."[6] Those lay saints of the Republic, Jules Michelet and Edgar Quinet, had both insisted on the centrality of women's improved education – and the importance of laic control over it – to the regeneration of French society

---

[3] For the controversial history of coeducation in France, see the essays in the special issue of *Clio: Histoire, Femmes et Sociétés*, n° 18 (2003): *Coéducation et mixité*, ed. Françoise Thébaud & Michelle Zancarini-Fournel, esp. Rebecca Rogers, "Mixité et coéducation: état des lieux d'une historiographie européenne," 177–202.

[4] *Congrès International du Droit des Femmes, ouvert à Paris, le 25 juillet 1878, clos le 9 Août suivant. Actes. Compte-Rendu des Séances Plenières* (Paris: Aug. Ghio, ed., 1878), "Appendice, Voeux et Resolutions ... ," pp. 207–208.

[5] As, for example, in the still useful English-language treatment of the Ferry laws by Evelyn Acomb, *The French Laic Laws, 1879–1889* (New York: Columbia University Press, 1941; reprinted, New York: Octagon Books, 1967).

[6] One historian has argued that anticlericalism was only a "cover" for other concerns, and that class issues predominated: see Sanford Elwitt, *The Making of the Third Republic: Class and Politics in France, 1868–1884* (Baton Rouge: Louisiana State University Press, 1975) and *The Third Republic Defended: Bourgeois Reform in France, 1880–1914* (Baton Rouge: Louisiana State University Press, 1986). My reading of the evidence as concerns the education of girls confirms that the republicans' anticlericalism was genuine, and that sex was just as important a consideration, if not indeed more important, as class.

(just as Félix Dupanloup and, before him, Joseph de Maistre had defended the church's right to its control for identical reasons).[7]

Already in 1870 the republican lawyer Jules Ferry (1832–1893) had laid out his views on what must be accomplished. In his celebrated speech at the Salle Molière in Paris, this republican lawyer from a textile manufacturing family in eastern France expanded on his program to provide equal education for both sexes, by condemning the "adverse masculine attitude" he had encountered, which he characterized as "the first obstacle to equalizing the conditions of instruction for both sexes."[8] But he blamed women for the second obstacle, which was the overt obsequiousness many displayed in face of men's ostensible intellectual superiority. Ferry invited women to read John Stuart Mill's treatise on the subjection of women, which he praised as "the beginning of wisdom" insofar as it taught that women had the same mental faculties as men. He insisted that "equality of education is a right not only for both classes but for both sexes." In fact Mill's call for the perfect equality of the sexes and the lifting of society's extensive limitations on women, so that they could actually demonstrate what education could do for developing their talents, had set the bar, not only in England and France, but throughout Europe.[9]

Women's rights advocates, who had been promoting equal education for decades, enthusiastically agreed with Mill and Ferry. The veteran educator Clarisse Coignet who had served as a member of the Women's Commission on Educational Reform during the late Second Empire, went further, invoking the French Revolution's original commitment to individual liberty and the right to work, and praising what the republicans had in mind to promote women's development. She believed fervently that the two plans for the secondary education of girls submitted to the Chamber

---

[7] Michelet, *Le Prêtre, la femme, et la famille* (1845) in *Oeuvres complètes de J. Michelet*, vol. 9 (Paris: Flammarion, 1895), and *Woman* (*La Femme*), tr. J. W. Palmer (New York: Carleton, 1873), excerpted in *WFF*, vol. 1, doc. 46, and doc. 97; Edgar Quinet, *La République, Conditions de la régénération de la France* (1872), in *Oeuvres complètes de Edgar Quinet*, vol. 26 (Paris, n.d.), pp. 190, 200; Dupanloup, excerpts from *Studious Women* (1869) in *Victorian Women*, ed. Erna Olafson Hellerstein, Leslie Parker Hume, and Karen M. Offen (Stanford, CA: Stanford University Press, 1981), pp. 65–67 and from his 1867 article in *Le Correspondant* (1867), in *WFF*, vol. 1, doc. 118; Maistre, *Du Pape* (1821), excerpts in *WFF*, vol. 1, doc. 45. See also Auguste Comte, *Catéchisme positiviste: ou sommaire exposition de la religion universelle en onze entretiens systématiques entre une femme et un prêtre de l'humanité* (Paris: Carilian-Goevry & V. Dalmont, 1852).

[8] See Jules Ferry, "Discours sur l'égalité d'éducation (10 avril 1870, Salle Molière)," *Discours et opinions de Jules Ferry*, vol. 1 (Paris, 1893), pp. 301–305; transl. KO in *WFF*, vol. 2, doc. 119, quotes pp. 440, 441.

[9] Mill's treatise, *On the Subjection of Women* (1869), was published in French translation that same year. See Karen Offen, *European Feminisms, 1700–1950: A Political History* (Stanford, CA: Stanford University Press, 2000), chapter 5, on the enormous pan-European impact of this work.

of Deputies in 1879 by Camille Sée (1847–1919) and Paul Bert (1833–1886) had much to offer. She endorsed the rationale of the anticlerical republicans, arguing how important it was to bring women around to support the Republic by overcoming Catholic women's misguided nostalgia for the past. This was a key to modernity: "What modern society teaches [women] is [first] the freedom to think, which makes for independence of mind, and [second] the energy of work which creates independence for life. It is the sovereignty of the conscience, personal responsibility and self-government."[10] In 1881 Coignet would publish *De l'Éducation dans la démocratie*, in which she elaborated many of these earlier arguments.[11]

Once republican men gained control of the government in 1879, they were finally in a position to deliver on this educational program. As French prime minister and minister of public instruction, Jules Ferry would carry out his promise to establish a landmark educational program – no less than a state system of mass, secular public instruction – free and compulsory on the elementary level and open (for a fee) on the basis of social standing and/or merit on the secondary level for girls as well as boys. All these measures sought, in the name of republican progress, to remove formal instruction of the young from the control of the Catholic Church and reshape what they considered to be shallow, unchallenging, and overtly religious instruction. Like their revolutionary predecessors, these republican progressives viewed the arguably "private" role of women as in fact a public service and a quasi-political role; they envisioned the (still male-headed) family with an expanded role for wives and mothers as the principal agents of the state. A century later, historian François Furet would call Ferry's school program "the best symbol of what has been the greatest and only victory of the Left since the French Revolution."[12] It was both bold and, over time, highly effective.

In establishing the new secular schools, however, most members of the new republican legislative majority had no intention of challenging the prevailing conception of the "proper" sexual division of labor in the family and society. Although republican educators initially drew inspiration for the notion of state education of girls from Condorcet during the

[10] Clarisse Coignet, "Enseignement secondaire des jeunes filles," *La Revue Bleue* (19 April 1879), 986–994; quote, 986. See also her subsequent articles in this publication (24 July 1880), 73–82 and (14 October 1880), 155–156. Coignet's first article is reviewed in the Geneva-based *La Solidarité*, n° 20 (August 1879), 15.

[11] *De l'Éducation dans la démocratie* (Paris: C. Delagrave, 1881).

[12] See *Jules Ferry, fondateur de la République: Actes du colloque organisé par l'École des Hautes Études en Sciences Sociales*, ed. François Furet (Paris: EHESS, 1985), quote from Furet's preface, p. 7.

Revolution, and had been mightily impressed more recently by reports on the educational progress of girls in the United States, thanks to mass public instruction and the establishment of institutions of higher education for young women, French legislators shrank from following either the revolutionary *philosophe* or the Americans in endorsing either an identical curriculum for girls and boys – or, for that matter, coeducation.[13] Most genuinely believed that women's capacity to do good – in the home – was indispensable to the success of the Republic. Most saw women's influence in the foyer not only as desirable but also necessary, believing strongly that both the republic and civilization itself could be properly channeled through their post-revolutionary "public" role as mother-educators; thus they would hedge their bets on the sex-role messages to be delivered to girls in the new schools.

This attention to gender role prescriptions based on a strict sexual division of labor informed primary education but would become particularly acute during the parliamentary debates on the new state system of *lycées* and *collèges* for older girls, which was finally and formally established by the law of 21 December 1880. This law became known colloquially as the *loi Camille Sée*, after its principal author and champion.[14] The intimate

[13] Marie-Jean-Nicolas Caritat, marquis de Condorcet, *Sur l'instruction publique, Premier Mémoire*, (1791–1792), in Condorcet, *Oeuvres* (1847–1849 ed.), vol. 9, esp. pp. 215–228. Report by Célestin Hippeau. His summary, "L'Éducation des femmes et des affranchis en Amérique depuis la guerre de sécession," appeared in the *Revue des Deux Mondes*, 15 September 1869.

[14] For the text of the law, see Camille Sée, *Lycées et collèges de jeunes filles; documents, rapports et discours à la Chambre des députés et au Sénat; décrets, arrêtés, circulaires, etc., . . .*, 6th ed. (Paris: L. Cerf, 1896), pp. 434–435; and Gaston Coirault, *Les Cinquante premières années de l'enseignement secondaire féminin, 1880–1920* (Thèse complémentaire, Faculté de Lettres, Université de Poitiers, Tours, 1940), pp. 32–34. The Sée work, an essential compendium of sources, can be consulted in microfiche in the Gerritsen Collection of Women's History (Glen Rock, NJ, 1976) and is now available online. A chart comparing Sée's original proposal with counterproposals and the final text appears in Octave Gréard, *Mémoire sur l'éducation secondaire des filles* (offprint, June 1882), republished in his *Éducation et instruction: Enseignement secondaire* (2nd ed., Paris: Hachette, 1889). See also Antoine Villemot, *Études sur l'organisation, le fonctionnement et les progrès de l'enseignement secondaire des jeunes filles en France, de 1879 à 1887* (Paris: P. Dupont, 1887); Villemot, *Enseignement secondaire: Documents, publications, et ouvrages récents, relatifs à l'éducation des femmes et à l'enseignement secondaire des jeunes filles* (Paris: P. Dupont, 1889), and *Pensées inédites sur l'instruction de la femme et les lycées et collèges de jeunes filles* (Paris: Cerf, 1889). Also essential for appreciating the development of these schools are Sée's periodical, *L'Enseignement Secondaire des Jeunes Filles* (hereafter *ESJF* – 1882–1918), and the *Revue Universitaire* (hereafter *RU* – 1892–1957).

Before Françoise Mayeur's monograph, *L'Enseignement secondaire des jeunes filles sous la Troisième République* (Paris: Presses de la Fondation Nationale des Sciences Politiques, 1977), the only detailed treatment of the history of girls' secondary education after 1880 was the legal study by Coirault, cited in n. 14, which is marred by the author's obsession with proving the illegality of the 1924 decree-reform. Earlier studies of continuing value include Edmée Charrier, *L'Évolution intellectuelle féminine* (Paris: Éditions Albert Mechlinck, 1931), a copiously documented study of women's achievements in the French educational system by a partisan of curriculum assimilation, and

connection between republican anticlericalism and secular control of girls' secondary education was explicit in the Sée law and remained a shared premise for all republican factions during the ensuing controversy over the development of the girls' secondary curriculum.[15] The young republican deputy Camille Sée predicated his law on the now widely shared belief among republicans that "the grandeur as well as the decadence of a people depends ... on its women," and that, therefore, their education was a matter of critical importance to the society in which they would live.[16] But what did that mean in practical terms?

Despite the seemingly enlightened intentions of Sée and his associates in the legislative debates over his bill, most deputies and senators had no interest in empowering women to escape the existing male-headed family structure. Few demonstrated a glimmer of interest in expanding alternative life options open to young republican *bourgeoises* (or, for that matter, to women of the people).[17] The fathers of the Third Republic may have nursed an ineradicable grudge against the church and the monarchy, and the church's educational practices; yet, in fact, their views on the sexual division of labor and the role of women were strikingly similar to those who so antagonized them. Although these republican men were by no means misogynists, they were surely benevolent patriarchs and some could even be considered antifeminists; their support for the improvement of women's status in French society and the deployment of their influence had strict limits. Like their Catholic rivals, they easily acknowledged the equality in moral dignity of man and woman, and like them also, they firmly believed, with Michelet's colleague at the *Académie Française*, the dramatist Ernest Legouvé, that such "equality" could best be exercised in "difference."[18] By

Raymond Thamin, "L'Éducation des filles après la guerre," *Revue des Deux Mondes* (1 October 1919), 512–532, and (1 November 1919), 130–160. Supplementing Mayeur: Offen, "The Second Sex and the *Baccalauréat* in Republican France, 1880-1924" (cited in n. 1 above). An excellent overview is provided by Jo Burr Margadant in chapter 1 of *Madame le Professeur: Women Educators in the Third Republic* (Princeton, NJ: Princeton University Press, 1990). For a new synthesis, see Rebecca Rogers, *From the Salon to the Schoolroom: Educating Bourgeois Girls in Nineteenth-Century France* (University Park: Penn State University Press, 2005), esp. part III.

[15] Acomb, *Laic Laws*; for greater detail see L. Capéran, *Histoire contemporaine de la laïcité française*, 3 vols. (Paris: M. Rivière, 1957–1961); and Mona Ozouf, *L'École, l'Église et la République, 1871–1914* (Paris: A. Colin, 1963).

[16] Camille Sée speech, *Annales, Sénat et Chambre des Députés*, vol. 1:1, 1880, Ch.D., session of 19 January, p. 94; also in Sée, *Lycées et collèges*, pp. 191–192.

[17] Texts of the legislative debates are reproduced in Sée, *Lycées et collèges*; helpful summaries can be consulted in Acomb, *Laic Laws*, pp. 154–157, and Mayeur, *Enseignement secondaire*, pp. 39–61.

[18] Legouvé's influential *Histoire morale des femmes* (Paris: Gustave Sandré, 1849) went through nine editions by 1900; in the 1880s he was instrumental in overseeing the *École Normale Supérieure de Sèvres* to train teachers for the girls' *lycées* and *collèges*. See Karen Offen, "Ernest Legouvé and the Doctrine of

this they meant that women and men were destined to play separate and distinct, albeit complementary, roles in life, in complementary spaces; therefore each sex should be so educated that its members might most advantageously fill their designated function in their respective space. Man's role was a public one, to be exercised in the *forum*; woman's role was a private one, to be exercised in the *foyer* or household, under a husband's protection. Camille Sée spoke directly to this point in presenting his *projet de loi* to his colleagues in the Chamber:[19]

> It is not prejudice but nature herself that confines women to the family circle. It is in their interest, in our interest, in the interest of the entire society that they remain at home. The goal of the schools we want to found is not to tear them away from their natural vocation but to render them more capable of fulfilling their obligations as wives, mothers, and mistresses of households.

Consequently, though these republican men believed that women should be well educated (indeed, educated whenever possible by well-trained members of their own sex), the system they designed was specifically intended to prepare women for cultured domesticity in an open, though nonetheless still hierarchical class society, centered on the core social unit of the family. Its envisioned products were to be skilled, well-read, gracious, and *influential* wives and mothers – suitable companions for the new male republican ruling elite of France.[20]

This was, of course, not new. Indeed, since the revolutions of 1789–1793 and 1848–1851, such beliefs, expressed ever more strongly in terms of the nation's need for *mères-éducatrices* had dominated French approaches to the theory and practice of girls' education. There is no disputing Paul Rousselot's judgment in 1883 that "the figure of the mother, the born teacher, dominates all feminine pedagogy of the nineteenth century."[21]

'Equality in Difference' for Women: A Case Study of Male Feminism in Nineteenth-Century French Thought," *Journal of Modern History*, 58:2 (June 1986), 452–484. An excellent study of the ENS de Sèvres and its graduates is Margadant, *Madame le Professeur* (cited in n. 14).

[19] Sée speech in *Annales, Sénat et Ch.D.*, vol. 1:1, 1880, Ch.D., session of 19 January, p. 90. Sée's intention was further elaborated by Octave Gréard, vice-rector of the Academy of Paris, who was charged with establishing the state secondary schools for girls in that jurisdiction. See Gréard's *Éducation et instruction*, pp. 231–233.

[20] The spirit informing this republican "new woman" as both wife and mother is captured in the historical contributions of Adolphe de Lescure, *Les Mères illustres; études morales et portraits d'histoire intime* (Paris: Firmin-Didot, 1882), and *Les Grandes épouses; études morales et portraits d'histoire intime* (Paris: Firmin-Didot, 1884).

[21] Rousselot, *Histoire de l'éducation des femmes en France*, 2 vols. (Paris, 1883), vol. 2, p. 428. The approaches of earlier nineteenth-century advocates (including Mmes Campan, Rémusat, Necker de Saussure, Guizot, Le Groing La Maisonneuve) of educating women for civic motherhood have been

Indeed, the *mère-éducatrice* argument, which emphasized the practical utility of literacy, learning, and intellectual activity for women and underscored its vital importance for their successful performance as companionate wives and mothers, had become an article of faith among most of the republican founders of the girls' *lycées*, who by the standards of the midnineteenth century (if not by ours) were clearly progressive in their support for women's educational advancement.[22] Their point of view represented a dramatic advance over the not altogether facetious suggestion of certain eighteenth-century French men that women should be denied access to literacy itself, so they would not be diverted from useful domestic labor.[23]

The capstone of the Third Republic's *lycées* and *collèges'* curriculum for girls was the *diplôme de fin d'études secondaires*, a "finishing certificate" attesting to the completion of a five-year course of study. Unlike the *baccalauréat*, which crowned study at the boys' *lycées*, this unique diploma was assigned no practical value whatsoever – it did not allow its holder to enter the university faculties, or to qualify for professional employment of any type, whether in law, medicine, or government service. The intent of

---

analyzed by Barbara Corrado Pope, "Maternal Education in France, 1815–1848," in the *Proceedings of the Western Society for French History*, vol. 3 (1976), 368–377; see also her article, "Revolution and Retreat: Upper-Class French Women after 1789," in *Women, War, and Revolution*, ed. Carol R. Berkin & Clara M. Lovett (New York: Holmes & Meier, 1980), pp. 215–236. An important recent study of these women educators is Jennifer J. Popiel, *Rousseau's Daughters: Domesticity, Education, and Autonomy in Modern France* (Hanover & London: University Press of New England, for the University of New Hampshire Press, 2008).

[22] Thus I find untenable the retrospective verdict of "misogyny" rendered against earlier reformers and opponents alike by such writers as Lillian Jane Waugh, "The Images of Woman in France on the Eve of the Loi Camille Sée, 1877–1880" (Ph.D. dissertation, University of Massachusetts, 1977). The lifelong devotion of Camille Sée (1847–1919) to the advancement of girls' secondary education is unquestionable, and is vividly depicted in Mayeur, *Enseignement secondaire*, pp. 27–28. Sée's vision, in fact, was much more advanced than that of most of his colleagues; he even favored the teaching of classical languages (required for the *bac*) in the girls' schools. The *diplôme* was not Sée's idea but was imposed on his program by more cautious men. On Sée's own views, see C. Suran-Mabire, "Le Latin aux agrégations de l'enseignement secondaire féminin," *Revue Universitaire [RU]* (1920), pt. 1, 23–30, and Léon Brunschvicg, "La Fin d'un bachôtage," *RU* (1920), pt. 2, 16ff. Jules Ferry made explicit his support of equal education for women in his "Discours sur l'égalité d'éducation," 10 April 1870 (excerpted and transl. in *WFF*, vol. 1, doc. 119). Yet with the exception of the article by H. Boiraud, "Sur la création par l'état d'un enseignement secondaire féminin en France," *Paedagogica Historica*, 21:1 (1977), 21–36, Ferry's participation in the women's rights efforts of the later 1860s and 1870s has only been acknowledged as accessory to his anticlericalism. More radical than either Sée or Ferry, Paul Bert, like Condorcet, argued that girls and boys should be given an identical education; see Léon Dubreuil, "Paul Bert et l'enseignement secondaire féminin," *Revue d'Histoire Économique et Sociale*, 18:2 (1930), 205–240.

[23] As in the proposals of Nicolas-Edmé Restif de La Bretonne in *Les Gynographes* (La Haie: Gosse & Pinet, 1777) and the subsequent tongue-in-cheek *Projet d'une loi portant défense d'apprendre à lire aux femmes* (Paris: Massé, 1801) addressed to "Heads of the Household, Fathers, and Husbands" by Pierre-Sylvain Maréchal.

the founders, which they had elaborated at length during the 1880 debates, had been to offer bourgeois girls a substantive yet "general," "disinterested" kind of instruction, explicitly distinguished from the "specialized" kind of learning or "erudition" considered appropriate for young men of their social level. Their pupils were, after all, supposed to marry and found families; as future *mères-éducatrices*, their education was considered instrumental, intrinsic neither to their own self-realization nor to their economic independence. The *baccalauréat* had never been explicitly closed to girls but the necessary preparatory courses in classical languages and philosophy were unavailable to them within any institutional setting. This did not stop a few enterprising girls from acquiring such instruction privately and, like Julie-Victoire Daubié, the first woman to earn the *bac*, registering for and passing the *baccalauréat* examinations.

Women's rights advocates did not find the *diplôme* satisfactory. This credential would serve no purpose, insisted Hubertine Auclert in April 1881; unlike the *bac*, it was useless for entering the liberal professions or the universities. She viewed Sée's law as "sterile," offering young women no training that would provide them with a socioeconomic alternative to marriage and lifelong dependence on men. The Sée law would be "ineffective," she argued, because the deputies had never called on women themselves to debate a measure "which absolutely concerns women" and because "knowledge that women cannot put to use" will not appeal either to the youngsters or to their parents." As a young single educated woman, Auclert doubtless had a better grasp of what the future held: "As long as instruction will not provide a woman with the means of acquiring pecuniary resources, parents will not dream of making the sacrifices necessary to instruct their daughters." Instead, Auclert advocated coeducation of the sexes via the admission of girls to the existing boys' *lycées*, which she believed would temper the personalities of both boys and girls, and offer access to a common – and useful – credential.[24]

In designing the curriculum for the girls' *lycées*, the republican administrators of the university turned away from Condorcet and the American coeducators, instead seeking inspiration in seventeenth-century French precedents, notably Archbishop Fénelon's treatise on the education of daughters (1687).[25] Indeed, the rationale adopted was strikingly Fénelonian, both

---

[24] Hubertine Auclert, "Une loi stérile," *La Citoyenne*, n° 11 (24 April 1881), 1.

[25] François de Salignac de la Mothe-Fénelon, *Traité sur l'éducation des filles* (1687). Fénelon's treatise went through three editions in the late 19th century alone, including one version intended for republican educators edited by Charles Defodon (My thanks to Linda L. Clark for this information). Fénelon's tract thus became required reading in the republican normal schools for

in its primary emphasis on domesticity for women and, more broadly, in its civic humanist aim of providing an appropriate, functional program of instruction for members of a specific social group. In addition to Fénelon and Condorcet, republican pedagogues drew on a number of eighteenth-century educational writers, notably Charles Rollin, J.-H. Bernardin de Saint-Pierre, and not surprisingly, Jean-Jacques Rousseau.[26] Likewise they revisited and republished the treatises written earlier by women educators, from Mme de Maintenon to Mme Campan.[27]

What came next, however, was something of a surprise. The actual course of studies elaborated for the girls' *lycées* in 1882 by the *Conseil Supérieur de l'Instruction Publique* to implement the Sée law far exceeded not only the prescriptions of Fénelon, but also the aims and constraints of Camille Sée himself.[28] The new republican curriculum for girls was surprisingly bookish and intellectual, if not precisely *mondaine* in the sense

women. For an analysis of Fénelon's program, see Carolyn C. Lougee, "*Noblesse*, Domesticity, and Social Reform: The Education of Girls by Fénelon and Saint-Cyr," *History of Education Quarterly*, 14:1 (Spring 1974), 87–113.

[26] In the early 1880s Gréard and Rousselot focused educators' attention specifically on female education, through publication of three reference works: Paul Rousselot, ed. *La Pédagogie féminine: extraits des principaux écrivains qui ont traité de l'éducation des femmes depuis le XVIe siècle* ... (Paris: n.p., 1881); Rousselot, *Histoire de l'éducation des femmes en France*, 2 vols. (Paris: Didier, 1883); and Octave Gréard, *L'Éducation des femmes par les femmes: Études et portraits* (Paris: Hachette, 1886), which went through at least seven editions by 1907. Camille Sée became very cross with the *universitaires'* emphasis on Madame de Maintenon, whom he considered an unfortunate moral example for young republican *bourgeoises* because of her irregular liaison (prior to the morganatic marriage) with Louis XIV. For this quarrel, see Camille Sée, *L'Université et Madame de Maintenon* (Paris: L. Cerf, 1890; reissued 1894); and Mayeur, *Enseignement secondaire*, p. 202. See also John Grand-Carteret, *J. J. Rousseau jugé par les français d'aujourd'hui* (Paris: Perrin, 1890), especially the article by Maria Deraismes, "J. J. Rousseau et l'éducation des filles," pp. 326–334.

Another enormously influential French writer on the education of girls was the bishop of Orléans, Félix Dupanloup, who had disputed with Victor Duruy over girls' public secondary education during the late Second Empire. His broad curricular vision, articulated within a Catholic context, did include the study of the classics. His *La Femme studieuse* (Paris: C. Douniel, 1869) went through seven editions before 1900; and his *Lettres sur l'éducation des filles* (Paris: J. Gervais, 1879) were also widely read. Dupanloup's influence has been reassessed in *Éducation et images de la femme chrétienne en France au début du XXe siècle, à l'occasion du centenaire de la mort de Mgr. Dupanloup*, ed. Françoise Mayeur & Jacques Gadille (Lyon: L'Hermès, 1980).

[27] See the works cited (n. 26) by Rousselot and Gréard.

[28] The subjects to be covered in the curriculum were specified in the law and, apart from the controversy over religious and moral instruction, engendered little debate at the time. The details, notably the number of hours per week to be devoted to each subject, and the number of years over which studies would be spread, were worked out in conjunction with the Ministry of Public Instruction, then headed by Paul Bert, which imposed a more rigorous study program than that envisioned by Camille Sée. Both at the time of its inception and for many years thereafter supporters insisted on the progressive nature of the girls' curriculum, which had been modeled after that of *l'enseignement spécial*. Nevertheless, complaints about *surmnénage* began to surface in the later 1880s: the Academy of Medicine addressed the question on 14 September 1886. See the accounts in the daily press, notably in *La République Française*, 15 September 1886, and *Le Temps*, 16 September 1886.

condemned two centuries earlier by the good archbishop. Not only did it include the humanist classics (though in French translation from the Latin and Greek), but also placed heavy emphasis (as measured in hours of classwork) on the study of French and other modern languages and on the history of civilizations and art. In addition, it required the study of domestic economy and hygiene, as well as the still controversial physical discipline of gymnastics. When the study programs were finally promulgated, they were attacked by the traditionalists for being "too heavy." Too much science, said some critics; too much history, said others. "The end of the sex," warned the constitutional liberal J.-J. Weiss; "the reversal of the laws of nature," cried the editorialist in *Le Français.*[29] "Is your goal to make our daughters into walking encyclopedias?" demanded the distinguished *normalien* and critic Francisque Sarcey.[30]

The reflexive fear of producing "*bas bleus*" [bluestockings] continued to trouble tradition-minded Frenchmen during the later nineteenth century.[31] Historic shadows loomed over the debates about girls' secular secondary education – the shadow of the *précieuses,* the *femmes savantes,* or reconfigured as the highly undesirable "*femme pédante.*" The debates over girls' secondary education contained frequent allusions to the characters fleshed out by Molière some two centuries previously – Chrysale's pronouncements on the limits of female knowledge became a centerpiece.[32] To the fear of learned women was added the newly envisioned threat of Nihilism. Catholic opponents of the Sée law invoked the fearful example of the well-educated and seemingly uncontrolled Russian women, whose reputed immorality had been at least as widely publicized in the West as their campaign of terror against Russian authorities, including the Tsar.[33] They invoked the cautionary tale of Vera Zasulich,

---

[29] Weiss quoted in Ozouf, *L'École, l'Église et la République,* p. 104. For a positive view see Paul Janet, "L'Éducation des filles," *Revue des Deux Mondes* (1 September 1883), 48–85, and for further sampling of opinion, see Ozouf, *École,* pp. 101–107, and Mayeur, *Enseignement secondaire,* pp. 69–84.

[30] Sarcey quoted by Coirault, *Cinquante premières années,* p. 58.

[31] See, for an extreme example, Jules Barbey d'Aurevilley, *Les Bas-bleus* (Paris: V. Palmé, 1878). On the earlier controversies over learned women, see my companion volume, *The Woman Question in France,* chapter 3.

[32] In fact, the first three girls' *lycées* established in Paris were named for seventeenth-century male luminaries – the educator Fénelon, and the renowned playwrights Racine and Molière. For a discussion of the contributions of Fénelon and Molière to the woman question debates, see my companion volume.

[33] Émile Keller speech, *Annales, Sénat et Chambre des Députés,* vol. 1:1, 1880, Ch.D., session of 19 January, pp. 80, 86. In contrast, the Geneva-based women's rights activist Marie Goegg found "Sassoulich" a very high-minded and sympathetic character and applauded her passion for justice; see *La Solidarité,* n° 15 (June 1878), 2–3.

a nihilist who attempted to assassinate the police chief of Saint Petersburg (and was acquitted).[34]

These nineteenth-century republicans had unquestionably conceded literacy and the development of the intellect to women, but few would concede the right of wholly free inquiry or full-time professional (or political) activity – free, that is, from the mediating influence of male authorities. The historian Henri Boiraud reaffirms that the curriculum disputes following on enactment of the Sée law make it clear that producing independent women or preparing them for a profession was never an intended goal: "It is not a question of this education facilitating women's independence but to facilitate her playing an indirect political role through her influence in the family.... The goal is unity of thought within the household but without challenging the sexual hierarchy."[35] Despite this, the fact was that the girls' curriculum was aligned to a substantial degree on that of the boys' *lycées*, though without the "reward" of the *baccalauréat*. Other progressive republican educators such as Octave Gréard (who headed primary education in Paris, then became vice-rector of the University of Paris) would defend the programs from the extravagant accusation that they would change women into men. He argued that "a program for educating girls that, along with moral and literary instruction, did not embrace the elements of the sciences and the general principles of social organization" would be criticized as insufficient; the objective was "to perfect the order of nature."[36]

A second major advocate of such expanded programs was the legislator Paul Bert, a physician-zoologist and physiologist – and the father of three daughters. Bert's own plan for girls' secondary education had initially run parallel to that proposed by Camille Sée, but was far more expansive. Importantly, Bert served briefly as Minister of Education in Gambetta's short-lived cabinet (late 1881–early 1882) and he was responsible for promulgating the ministerial decrees that actually implemented the programs for girls' public secondary education.

---

[34] See G. Valbert, "Le procès de Vera Zassoulitch," *Revue de Deux Mondes* (1 May 1878), 216–227. The fear of the educated Russian women, especially those who studied medicine (which Zasulich did not) was overblown, but no less real for all that; see Barbara Alpern Engel, "Women Medical Students in Russia, 1872–82: Reformers or Rebels?" *Journal of Social History*, 12:3 (Spring 1979), 394–414.

[35] Boiraud, "Sur la création par l'état d'un enseignement secondaire féminin"; quote, 35–36.

[36] See Octave Gréard, "De l'éducation des filles," *Revue Pédagogique*, n.s. vol. 1, n° 6 (15 December 1882), 497–553, quotes, 543 and 551–552. This lengthy article includes an in-depth study of earlier educators' views on girls' schooling, ranging from Fénelon to the women educators of the nineteenth century.

In early 1884 Paul Bert delivered a rousing speech at Salle Wagram in which he called for equal education of the sexes.[37] Reflecting arguments that he, like Jules Ferry, had probably assimilated from John Stuart Mill, he denounced notions that women were inferior or should be in any way subordinate to men. He called women's subordination "an injustice" and argued that there were more than two arguments for institutionalizing girls' secondary education. It was not enough, he claimed, to make mother-educators and intellectual companions of men. We don't educate young men to be good fathers and companions to their wives, he noted. "Do we consider woman as an auxiliary being or as a principal being? Do we choose the thesis of subordination or the thesis of equality?" If the latter, then one needs to provide young women with the same education as men. In fact, he argued that women had already proven their merit in certain professions. Bert went on to critique women's disabilities in the Civil and Penal Codes, and implied that with the good results of a progressive education, they would merit political rights – though not right away. He was still clearly worried about the millions of Catholic women who were under the influence of the clergy – "the worst enemies of the Republic and of freedom of thought." He firmly believed that no one "has the right to limit … the role of women … or even to show her, in theory, the way to happiness." To confine women to the household and to educating her children was, in his eyes, "one of the many forms of masculine egotism." "Women's mission is to find her own happiness, not that of a man." And this meant, in his view, that women might enter professions and support themselves, even become judges and serve on juries and vote.[38]

Audacious views such as those of Paul Bert, Clarisse Coignet, or Hubertine Auclert proved too extreme for some. Nevertheless, many of the republican men who had helped frame the system were clearly pleased with themselves. After almost a hundred years since the Revolution, the secondary public education of girls was in place – and it was secular. Apart from private institutions, the Catholic Church had been evicted from its monopoly on public instruction.

The degree of consensus among republican educators and their support-ers can be grasped from a series of articles concerning women and girls

---

[37] Paul Bert, "L'Éducation de la femme," speech given Salle Wagram, 17 February 1884, reprinted in Léon Dubreuil, "Paul Bert et l'enseignement secondaire féminin," *Revue d'Histoire Économique et Sociale*, 18:2 (1930), 232–239.

[38] Bert's biographer, Dubreuil, is not certain that Bert delivered this particular portion of his address. The quotations above are from pp. 236 and 238 in the reprinted version cited in n. 37.

published in the *Dictionnaire de pédagogie et d'instruction primaire*, edited by Ferdinand Buisson (who later became a major supporter of women's suffrage) and published in 1887–1888.[39] Despite the title of this compendium, these articles also concerned secondary education. In the article "Filles," one Hippolyte Durand crowed about what had been accomplished: "The principle that dominates all the new legislation is the same that inspired Condorcet, without the excessive and utopian views that for so long compromised the fate of his ideas." By this he meant that the two sexes now had equivalent schools, with similar programs (except, of course, for the emphasis on learning needlework, for girls).[40] The venerable republican Ernest Legouvé, academician, playwright, and author of the acclaimed *Histoire morale des femmes* (1849; 1874), had since 1882 become "*inspecteur général, directeur des études*" [inspector general and director of studies] of the new *École Normale Supérieure de Sèvres*, the institution founded to train the master teachers who would then prepare the women *lycée* teachers at the departmental level.[41] Writing on "Femmes" in the first volume of Buisson's *Dictionnaire*, his emphasis remained on mothers as "*éducatrices*," but he acknowledged that this revolution had already happened. He applauded the fact that mothers were now supervising the education both of their daughters and of their sons! "This marvelous maternal intercession has produced very significant results," he claimed. Sisters and grandmothers were also becoming involved, and "maternal education" was spreading into public instruction as well, as women became teachers in primary schools. Legouvé believed firmly that the spread of "*l'esprit de la femme*" in public instruction would be an immense benefit, especially by introducing teaching "through the eyes," which is the way little children learn best. Introducing them to their environment and surroundings was the way to go, rather than immersing them in Latin and Greek grammar. "The University is paternal, but it is not maternal. What the small child needs most is maternal care [*maternité*]" and thus the extension of the family and its loving concern into the school.[42] Legouvé encouraged teaching careers for unmarried women, but (as mentioned

---

[39] *Dictionnaire de pédagogie et d'instruction primaire*, ed. Ferdinand Buisson, 2 vols. (Paris: Hachette, 1887–1888). Twenty years later Buisson would become an ardent supporter of women's suffrage and its lead advocate in the Chamber of Deputies.

[40] Hippolyte Durand, Art: "Filles," in Buisson's *Dictionnaire de pédagogie et d'instruction primaire*, pt. 2:1, pp. 1011–1026.

[41] On Sèvres, its programs to prepare female secondary teachers, and the first generation of Sèvriennes, see Margadant, *Madame le Professeur*.

[42] Ernest Legouvé, Art.: "Femme," in Buisson's *Dictionnaire de pédagogie et d'instruction primaire*, pt.1:1, pp. 997–998.

earlier) he did not approve of equalizing the girls' credentials, preferring the *diplôme* to the *baccalauréat*. For this view he too was roundly chastised by Hubertine Auclert in *La Citoyenne*.[43]

Jules Ferry also believed firmly that women were the best educators, and not only in the home: at the 1881 pedagogical congress he remarked (to an audience that included many women teachers) that even "the schoolmistress who remains unmarried can find in teaching the children of others a satisfaction of that maternal feeling, that great instinct for sacrifice which every woman carries within her, . . . and which establishes the nobility, the dignity and the power of [women's] social action."[44] In Ferry's view, it was women's quality of tenderness that made them such good teachers.

From the standpoint of middle-class educators who, unlike Paul Bert, put the interests of the male-headed family squarely before those of the individual, male or female, a curriculum predicated on separate spheres possessed a certain logical integrity – and it was, in fact, an improvement over most earlier instructional programs for girls, though it also had significant limits. This integrity was, of course, consciously reinforced by the program of moral instruction the educators developed to aid both pupils and members of the teaching corps to increase their appreciation of – and advocacy of – an exclusively familial role for women within French society.[45] Just in case girls and young women got big ideas, republican pedagogues provided strong prescriptions concerning women's duties. Historian Linda L. Clark, who has studied these manuals, points to several that were authored by women. *Francinet*, by G. Bruno (pseud. of Mme Alfred J. E. Fouillée), first appeared in 1869 but became a best-selling reader for 11-to-13-year-old boys and girls during the Third Republic; it

---

[43] Legouvé had restated his preference for the *diplôme* in *Le Temps* in early 1884; see the critique by "Liberta," "Une éducation de jeune fille," in Auclert's *La Citoyenne*, n° 82 (March 1884).

[44] See Ferry's speech in *Congrès pédagogique des institueurs et institutrices de France, en 1881* (Paris: Hachette, 1881), pp. 101–118; quote, p. 112; as translated in Sharif Gemie, *Women and Schooling in France, 1815–1914: Gender, Authority and Identity in the Female Schooling Sector* (Keele, UK: Keele University Press, 1995), p. 70. This speech is also reprinted in Ferry, *Discours et opinions*, vol. 4.

[45] Mayeur, *Enseignement secondaire*, pp. 222–228, discusses the general question of moral instruction but does not specifically address the content of "la morale domestique." My own preliminary sounding of secondary level morale texts for girls indicates that further analysis would probably reveal much the same pattern as Linda L. Clark found in primary instruction; see Clark, "The Molding of the *Citoyenne*: The Image of the Female in French Educational Literature, 1880–1914," *Third Republic/Troisième République*, n°s 3–4 (1977), 74–104; see also her articles, "The Primary Education of French Girls: Pedagogical Prescriptions and Social Realities, 1880–1940," *History of Education Quarterly*, 21:4 (Winter 1981), 411–428; and "The Socialization of Girls in the Primary Schools of the Third Republic," *Journal of Social History*, 15:4 (Summer 1982), 685–697; and Clark's book, *Schooling the Daughters of Marianne: Textbooks and the Socialization of Girls in Modern French Primary Schools* (Albany: SUNY Press, 1984).

included a sympathetic but highly prescriptive chapter, "The Influence of Mothers and the Role of Women in the Family," which underscored women's important but hidden influence in the family."[46] Clark also invokes the example of a widely adopted manual of moral instruction for primary schoolgirls by Mme Henri Gréville, which similarly underscored the sociopolitical significance of women's domestic role. Gréville's manual, with its explicit insistence on women's importance as guardians of the foyer, had been overwhelmingly approved for use in France's departments and already by 1889 had gone through "at least twenty-nine editions." Clark notes that Greville's "Eleven-to-thirteen-year-old readers were also reminded that article 213 of the Civil Code required women to obey their spouses in return for receiving protection and financial support."[47]

An 1888 educational treatise, *Ce que vaut une femme*, by a Mlle Éline Roch, posed the question of women's "natural" mission in terms of France's national future: "What will befall our country when a woman finds herself led astray from her natural destination, when a girl could suppose that she has an alternative to the noble and healthy mission of becoming a wife and mother?"[48] Roch's book won a prize from the Institute. Even so, as historian Margaret Darrow has pointed out, several other manuals for girls' civic instruction did deliver the message that girls could become actors and heroines in defense of *la patrie*.[49]

A leading critic of the *lycée* programs was the venerable Jules Simon (1814–1896), long known for his opposition to women in the workforce.[50] A self-made man, a former minister of public instruction (1871), prime minister (1876–1877) and *académicien*, his words carried considerable weight. Like Talleyrand in 1791, Simon thought education should be

[46] See the various contributions by Linda L. Clark, cited in n. 45. On the works of G. Bruno (Mme Alfred Fouillée) in particular, see also Aimé Dupuy, "Les livres de lecture de G. Bruno," *Revue d'Histoire Économique et Sociale*, vol. 31 (1953), 128–151. Jennifer Michael Hecht provides further insight into the contribution to republican national identity made by "G. Bruno" and her best-selling *Le Tour de France par deux enfants*. Published in 1877, this book reputedly sold 7.4 million copies by 1914; see Hecht, *The End of the Soul: Scientific Modernity, Atheism, and Anthropology in France* (New York: Columbia University Press, 2003), p. 303. An English translation of the chapter on "the influence of mothers" from *Francinet* can be found in *Victorian Women*, ed. Hellerstein, Hume, and Offen, doc. 10-iii.

[47] Clark, "Primary Education of French Girls," both quotes, 414.

[48] Mlle Éline Roch, *Ce que vaut une femme: Traité d'éducation morale et pratique des jeunes filles* (Reims: Dubois-Poplimont, 1888; Paris: Alcide Picard & Kaan, eds., 1893), p. 8.

[49] See Margaret H. Darrow, "In the Land of Joan of Arc: The Civic Education of Girls and the Prospect of War in France, 1870–1914," *French Historical Studies*, 31:2 (Spring 2008), 263–291.

[50] On Simon's important role in the controversies over women's work and education in the 1860s, see *The Woman Question in France*, chapter 6).

aligned with future function. Although Simon was a long-time champion of female literacy, throughout the 1880s and into the 1890s he would express regret and even serious opposition to the substantive girls' *lycée* and *collège* academic programs as a threat to the completion of their womanly apprenticeship. Women's influence strengthened, yes, but also channeled and controlled – that should be the aim. In his 1883 book, *Dieu, Patrie, Liberté*, Simon would acknowledge his support of the new institutions for girls, but objected to providing girls with the same curriculum as boys, which in his view was "unduly long and unduly learned. If our girls learn all that, they will have no time left in their youth to learn how to be women and to be loveable."[51] In his view, Nature could not do the job by itself; dressage was required to avoid bad outcomes. This commitment to gender shaping is so exquisitely French!

By the early 1890s, Simon's views on girls' education would turn increasingly antifeminist. He was all for augmenting women's moral authority in the family, but would express his opposition to civil divorce and to the laicization of schools, instead applauding the legal authority of the father, the force of religion, and tradition. He called on women to reexert their authority in the household.[52] By June 1896, he would be quoted as saying "the intellectual inferiority of women seems established." Women's defenders, he reflected, had long argued that any such inferiority resulted from their bad education, but now this is not the case; they have all the means. "My conclusion is that the elite among men are superior to the elite among women; history establishes this and psychology explains it." He reiterated his views that women should be reserved, timid, sheltered in the home, and modest in their habits. Introducing women into political life would, in his opinion, destroy all that. "Women would have no more master … but they will also lose their protectors. The question is to know whether they can get along without them."[53]

The Catholic critics of the new republican educational system likewise fulminated against the girls' *lycées*. A long two-part article in the Catholic periodical, *Le Correspondent*, by Fénelon Gibon (1850–1926), an ardent Catholic and professed disciple of Le Play's *Réforme Sociale* school, played

---

[51] See Jules Simon, *Dieu, patrie, liberté* (Paris: Calmann Lévy, 1883), quote, pp. 304–305. Simon was also worried about producing nihilists, *déclassées*, and parasites, not to mention bluestockings.

[52] Jules Simon & Gustave Simon, *La Femme du vingtième siècle* (Paris: C. Lévy, 1892), esp. pp. 243–269.

[53] "Pages oubliées: Jules Simon," in *Annales Politiques et Littéraires* (14 June 1896), 377–379; quotes 377ff.

the attack dog.[54] He first insinuated that there were extensive moral irregularities in the new schools (including instances of women teachers not attending church and staying outside the church during funerals!). He then harped on Freemasonic connections of the schools' sponsors, alleged that recruitment of girls students was not going well, and, to boot, called Camille Sée a "*franc-maçon israélite*."[55] He denounced every instance in which republicans had underscored their mission to separate girls, and thereby women, from the church. "*Nihilistes*" *à la russe* and "*déclassées*," not to mention "little walking encyclopedias," would surely result from this new education, Gibon asserted, not to mention suicides. In order to console his cobelievers, he gleefully quoted Jules Simon, *Le Temps*, Francisque Sarcey, and anyone else who had expressed reservations about the programs or their applications. What women needed, in his view, were courses in infant pedagogy and the science of teaching, not science nor mathematics – and certainly not diplomas! In the second part of the article, Gibon (basing his allegations on the inquiries of R. P. Lescoeur) revealed his true object of scorn: Jewish influence. "The Jews have imposed this reform on the [Freemasonic] lodges, the lodges on the Chambers, and the Chambers on the country."[56] There is little doubt that he was an enthusiastic reader of Édouard Drumont's antisemitic newspaper *La Libre Parole*. In Gibon's eyes, Condorcet was nothing more than "a Voltairian materialist" and Lakanel "a defrocked priest."[57] "*La libre pensée*," there is the enemy! He called on Catholic families to "save" religion and society by boycotting these new *lycées*, thus proving "that Christian morals are stronger than bad laws." Other Catholic writers were less vitriolic as well as less doggedly traditionalist. A disciple of Monseigneur Dupanloup and later bishop of Dijon, the *abbé* Pierre Dadolle proposed in 1888 that girls' intellectual education should rather be crowned by the study of philosophy and he emphasized self-development as a young woman's goal.[58]

Thus pressure for changes arose from both secularist republicans and Catholics. But neither efforts to question the instructional goals nor attempts to reform it would originate, as historian Françoise Mayeur has so

---

[54] Fénelon Gibon, "Les Lycées de filles en 1887," *Le Correspondant*, vol. 147 (n.s. 111), n° 6 (25 June 1887), 1106–1126, and vol. 148 (n.s. 112), n° 1(10 July 1887), 142–160. Gibon gleefully quoted Simon's 1883 reservations, 1121.

[55] Gibon, "Lycées de filles en 1887," part 1; quote, 1120.

[56] Gibon, "Lycees de filles en 1887," part 2, 145: "La juiverie a imposé cette reforme aux loges, les loges aux Chambres, et les Chambres au pays."

[57] Gibon, "Lycees de filles en 1887," part 2; this quotation and the following one, 148, 160.

[58] Abbé Pierre Dadolle, *L'Éducation intellectuelle de la femme chrétienne, conférence* ... (Lyon: Vitté et Perussel, 1888).

ably demonstrated, within the educational system itself.[59] Ultimately, both developments would be driven not only by the theoretical and political concerns of French women's rights leaders, who refused to sanction a curriculum for girls that did not prepare them to support themselves and, if need be, their children as well, but also and especially by the practical concerns of lower middle-class families who sought a "union card" for their daughters (whereas the daughters of the *bourgeoisie*, for whom the girls' *lycées* had originally been conceived, were not enrolling).[60] Faced with the unpleasant social and economic realities of the 1870s and 1880s, when many French women had to find paid employment in order to survive and single motherhood was on the rise, the republican "dream" that every woman would be "protected" by a kindly husband in a cozy *foyer* seemed increasingly ethereal.

What these varying views convey is that, in fact, a range of perspectives existed during the early Third Republic, and that the participants in these debates sometimes spoke past one another, offering affirmations of position rather than argument. Viewed from a late twentieth- or early twenty-first-century feminist perspective – with its heightened commitment to individualistic self-fulfillment as a prerogative of both sexes, our insistence on women's right to economic independence, and our suspicion of men's motives in doggedly advocating a sexual division of labor that worked so obviously to their own advantage – it is easy to criticize the republican educators for institutionalizing such a gender-specific curriculum for bourgeois girls. It was perhaps unrealistic on their part to assume that the *lycéennes* – offered a substantive exposure to the humanities and sciences, not only in order to stock their minds, but in order to promote inquiry as well – would, in the name of sexual difference and social order, submit themselves unquestioningly to an "interior life," legally and economically subordinated to husbands. They were supposed to imbibe the knowledge imparted to them, not to critique it. They were certainly not encouraged, *pace* the proposals of Clémence Royer and Jenny P. d'Héricourt in the 1850s, to seek out a more woman-centered form of knowledge.[61] And in the 1880s, they had not yet encountered the visionary, holistic thinker Céline Renooz, inspired by d'Héricourt, whose epistemological vision centered on the power of women's intuition to synthesize all fields of

[59] Mayeur, "Exposé de soutenance," *Le Mouvement Social*, p. 106.
[60] On the reluctance of religious bourgeois families to enroll their daughters, see Émile Levasseur's comments in *La population française*, 3 vols. (Paris: A. Rousseau, 1889–1893), vol. 2, p. 506.
[61] For more about Clémence Royer and Jenny P. d'Héricourt, see the companion volume, *The Woman Question in France*.

knowledge. "Science," she insisted, "must be recast in order to show men who they are and what they ought to be. It is to women that this task is entrusted. With the help of the power that even the most obstinate of men recognize in them – intuition – women can bring to the old world the light that will re-create intellectual life."[62]

In retrospect, we can now clearly see the dilemma that arose for independent-minded women and feminists from this situation. In fact, the "new" model republican women envisioned by republican men did not differ so much from the old model Christian women envisioned by the Catholics – except for one major thing: science and reason were intended to replace blind belief and faith. But whose science? and whose reason? Before turning to the question of women's employment, we must look at the next stage in the continuing debate about women's brains and bodies.

Should Dissimilarities between Women's and Men's Brains and Bodies Have Sociopolitical Consequences?

Why were the French Republicans so cautious in framing their otherwise bold projects for advancing the schooling of girls? For one thing, because opponents of women's rights feared their emancipation and continued to object vociferously to unleashing womanhood, invoking the unity of the family. Frédéric Le Play and his followers at *La Réforme Sociale* would busily strive throughout the early years of the Republic to "save" the "traditional" (read: male-dominated, authoritarian) family. Pierre-Joseph Proudhon's posthumous but still obsessive call for a new patriarchy and the restoration of man as the master in the household (*La Pornocratie*, 1875) would continue to stir up much coverage in French intellectual circles, as would a long article in *Le Gaulois*, "La Lysistrata moderne," by the 30-year-old realist writer Guy de Maupassant, in which he recognized only one right for women – "the right to please."[63] Such warnings about

[62] The largely self-educated Céline Renooz (1840–1928) found the *Revue Scientifique des Femmes* in 1888. On Renooz and her remarkable career, see James Smith Allen, *Poignant Relations: Three Modern French Women* (Baltimore: Johns Hopkins University Press, 2000), chapter 5. The quotation comes from the program statement for Renooz's *Revue Scientifique des Femmes* (1888), as transl. by Smith, p. 135. Later critics of androcentric knowledge include Jeanne Oddo-Deflou (1856?–?) who earned baccalaureate degrees in science and in letters in the 1880s, and in 1898 would found the *Groupe Français d'Études Féministes*. One younger woman who would launch a radical and substantive scientifically based critique of androcentric knowledge was Dr. Madeleine Pelletier (1874–1939), but in the period discussed in this chapter, she was still a schoolgirl.

[63] See Pierre-Joseph Proudhon, *La Pornocratie; ou les femmes dans les temps modernes* (Paris: A. Lacroix, 1875), esp. pp. 374, 382, 463 (his most ferocious antifeminist statements can be found on pp. 369–385. Not everyone was charmed by such fierce antifeminism: the anonymous author of

"denaturing" women or removing them from their quasi-sacred place in the household would echo for decades, as is clear from the later remarks of Jules Simon (cited earlier), not to speak of the stream of early twentieth-century publications by arch-antifeminists such as Théodore Joran.

Thus, to appreciate the measure of the daring as well as the caution of republican legislators and educators in establishing the new secondary schools for girls, we turn to the state of the debates over women's brains, intelligence, and capabilities in the 1870s and 1880s, as reframed both by commentators on women writers and artists and by the founding fathers of the emerging social sciences in France, many of whom were physicians but also budding psychologists, ethnologists, and anthropologists.

A series of publications concerning women writers casts some light on the state of these men's thinking. Remarkably, during the early Third Republic the anxiety about women's intellect, potential genius, and creative ability had begun to subside although it had by no means disappeared; literary figures such as Jules Barbey d'Aurevilly continued to rant (in 1878) that "women who write are no longer women; they are men – bluestockings, which is a masculine term."[64]

A less vitriolic example is provided by Jules Guy's lengthy study of "women of letters," written for adolescent girls (*jeunes filles*) and also published in 1878 (prior to the debates on the school laws).[65] He prefaced his presentation of chapters on individual women writers, ranging from Christine de Pizan (he spelled it Pisan) to Eugénie de Guérin, by remarking that he didn't think much of any woman who displays her knowledge, or has pretentions to science – and neglects her household. He objected to women philosophers, historians, poets, mathematicians, and naturalists. In his view, women should be modest, discrete, and cultivated in domestic virtues. Most of the subjects of his chapters were from the seventeenth and eighteenth centuries, though he did include a few nineteenth-century writers including Mme de Staël and Mme Amable Tastu. But clearly Jules

---

"Le dernier livre de Proudhon," *Revue des Deux Mondes* (15 September 1875), 467–474, criticized his objective of sequestering women. A neglected but very thoughtful linguistic analysis of *La Pornocratie* not surprisingly insists on the androcentric character of Proudhon's prose: see Barbara Kaltz, "Analyse d'un Discours androcentrique: La Pornocratie ou les femmes dans les temps modernes," *Atlantis*, 10:1 (Fall 1984), 15–25. See also Guy de Maupassant, "La Lysistrata moderne," in *Le Gaulois*, 30 December 1880; in Maupassant, *Oeuvres complètes*, vol. 16, pp. 71–74.

[64] See Jules Barbey d'Aurevilly, *Les Bas-bleus* (Paris: V. Palmé, 1878), who insisted in his introduction, "Le Bas-bleuisme contemporain" (xvii), that genius was "immensely virile" ("cette immense virilité"), that sexual difference inevitably implied hierarchy (xxi) and that French men were experiencing a moment of "suprême efféminisation" (xix).

[65] Jules Guy, *Les Femmes de lettres* (Paris: P. Ducrocq, 1878), "Préface," i–vii.

Guy was conflicted. Even as he insisted that women who engaged in such virile work of the mind [*travaux virils de l'esprit*] would lose the qualities of their sex, he had to admit that women had made great contributions to French literature. As he reeled off the list of the contemporary writers he had left *out* of the volume (from Delphine Gay de Girardin to George Sand, via Clémence Royer, André Léo, and Claude Vignon) he remarked that "this brilliant constellation proves that women can give birth to masterpieces [*chefs d'oeuvres*] and that girls can learn from their example. He advised his young readers to cultivate their minds; even as *maîtresses de maison* and future mothers they could then cultivate the minds of their children. And, who knew, there might be one among his readers who could aspire to these literary summits! By 1886, we find an anthology of women writers, probably intended for use in the schools, edited by Paul Jacquinet, along with a history of women writers in France by Henri Carton.[66] Ferdinand Brunetière, editor-in-chief of the *Revue des Deux Mondes*, also published (in 1886) an essay on the "influence of women in French literature."[67] Another anthology of *oeuvres choisis* by François Lhomme, which highlighted women's letters and memoirs, appeared in 1892.[68] To date, I have not come across any collections of women's writings edited by women before 1893, although in 1888 Guizot's daughter Henriette de Witt published an illustrated collection of short biographies of notable women in history from ancient times to "our times" with Hachette.[69] In 1893, however, the widely published Louise d'Alq (pseud. of Louise Alquié de Rieusseyroux) would publish her revisionist prize-winning showcase for women writers, *Anthologie féminine*, which included a preface on the instruction of women and the promise of literary careers for women.[70]

---

[66] Paul Jacquinet, ed., *Les Femmes de France, poètes et prosateurs; Morceaux choisis avec une introduction, des notices biographiques et littéraires et des notes philologiques, littéraires, historiques* (Paris: E. Belin, 1886; 3rd ed. 1895; 4th ed. 1913), 662 pages. Henri Carton, *Histoire des femmes écrivains de la France* (Paris: A. Dupret, 1886).

[67] See Ferdinand Brunetière's "L'Influence des femmes dans la littérature française," *Revue des Deux Mondes* (1 November 1886), 205–224, reprinted in his *Questions de critique* (Paris: Calmann-Lévy, 1889), pp. 23–61. Brunetière's remarks focus on the seventeenth and eighteenth centuries.

[68] François Lhomme, ed. *Les Femmes écrivains; oeuvres choisies* (Paris: Librairie de l'Art, 1892), 546 pages.

[69] Mme de Witt (née Henriette Guizot), *Les Femmes dans l'histoire* (Paris: Hachette, 1888).

[70] See Louise d'Alq, *Anthologie féminine: Anthologie des femmes écrivains, poètes et prosateurs depuis l'origine de la langue française jusqu'à nos jours. Préface sur l'instruction des femmes et la carrière littéraire* (Paris: Bureau des Causeries familières, 1893). This work received a prize from the *Académie Française*. Thanks to Vicki Mistaccio, Wellesley College, for this reference: see her article, "Les Silences de l'Histoire: l'Anthologie féminine de Louise d'Alq," in *La Place des femmes dans la critique et l'histoire littéraire*, ed. Martine Reid (Paris: Champion, 2011), pp. 121–165.

It was seemingly the first such work since that of Louise Kéralio in the late eighteenth century.

A second venue for examining the debates on the woman question with respect to judgments on genius and intellect in the 1870s and 1880s is the world of art. In order to combat the severe discrimination against women in the art world of Paris, in 1881 the energetic and successful sculptor Mme Léon Bertaux (née Hélène Hebert, 1825–1909) founded the *Union des Femmes Peintres et Sculpteurs.* By dissecting the published critiques of women's art and the character of the *Union's* annual all-woman salons, art historian Tamar Garb has unearthed and reconstructed the debate over "genius" (still implicitly gendered male) and "feminine genius" as it manifested itself in the art world. While acknowledging the extent to which "the Sex of Art" remained unrelentingly male in the 1880s and early 1890s, Garb highlights the women artists' deliberate efforts to conduct their own assault on received wisdom by attempting to "undo" the hierarchies of "great art," not only through their choice of subjects and media but also through the arrangement and style of their annual exhibitions. She also documents the group's ultimately successful campaigns, through their publications and public actions, to achieve the admittance of women artists, first to the *Conseil Supérieur des Beaux Arts* in 1890, and then in 1896 to the prestigious *École des Beaux-Arts.*[71] The early activities of this group caught the attention of the veteran feminist campaigner Olympe Audouard, who – back in Paris – featured the Union's artists and activities in her literary journal, *Le Papillon.* Was there such a thing as a womanly genius? Or did "genius" lie beyond sex, as the former Empress Eugénie had claimed when in 1865 she presented the painter Rosa Bonheur with the *Légion d'honneur*? Although it might be an exaggeration to claim, as does Garb, that the 1880s provided "the first major public debate" on women and art, these years certainly did witness a novel and highly visible twist to the venerable subject of women and genius.[72] One critic, writing for *Le Temps* in 1888, thought that the real attractiveness of the *Union's* annual exhibition was "the unique occasion which it offers us [men] to enter into *le génie féminin,* to find out something of the secret feelings of the daughters of Eve."[73] Women might

---

[71] See Tamar Garb, *Sisters of the Brush: Women's Artistic Culture in Late Nineteenth-Century Paris* (New Haven, CT: Yale University Press, 1994), and my review in the *American Historical Review,* 100:5 (December 1995), 1590–1591. Mme Bertaux's effort undoubtedly drew inspiration from its English predecessor, the Society of Female Artists (founded in 1857), which campaigned for the admission of women artists to the Royal Academy exhibitions.

[72] See Garb's claim, *Sisters of the Brush,* p. 105.

[73] *Le Temps,* 25 February 1888; as translated by Garb, *Sisters,* p. 110 (the French is in her note 22, p. 184).

exhibit a sort of genius, but clearly it was not considered the same as that of men; the latter might approach it only as *voyeurs*.

By 1889, Jean Alesson (pseud. of Anatole Alès) could publish his analysis of women's achievements in the arts, letters, sciences, and history, *Le Monde est aux femmes*, in which he also endorsed women's suffrage (because women pay taxes), though not their candidacy for public office.[74] And the woman writer who signed as René Marcil could publish a longer and even more celebratory and pro-feminist "Women Who Think and Women Who Write," in honor of the revolutionary centennial. Appealing to the ideals of the Republic, Marcil denounced the "rights of the male," remarking that "the revolutionary idea has only been half-accomplished: "If, in order to create a human being, the union of man and woman is essential, then why is this not also true for giving birth to a State?" "Who is the Hercules who will say to genius: You will not inhabit the soul of a woman?" "The mind of Woman has reached its majority, and women are absolutely decided to not let it be suppressed again."[75]

A third venue for these discussions was the world of early Third Republic science. Arguments for and against women's intellect and genius, debates over the appropriateness of certain professional activities for women, and more general pronouncements on the woman question emerged in a number of different scientific circles. Some seized on evolutionary arguments, in the aftermath of Darwin's *Descent of Man* (1871), to underscore a growing and possibly unbridgeable gap between women's and men's mental development, which they asserted would cement women's inferiority.[76] Friends of women's education and advancement responded that such gaps, if indeed they existed, were culturally constructed and could be overcome. As we have seen in *The Woman Question in France, 1400–1870*, this was a very old argument, but one that seemed to be gaining traction.

The Third Republic's physician-scientists were unenthusiastic about endorsing the still-revolutionary idea of equality of the sexes. Steeped in medical teachings on physical and biological difference as well as Lamarckian and Darwinian evolutionary theory, most continued to believe that women were irremediably "different" – if not, indeed,

---

[74] Jean Alesson (pseud. of Anatole Alès), *Le Monde est aux femmes* (Paris: G. Melet, 1889).

[75] René Marcil, *Les Femmes qui pensent et les femmes qui écrivent* (Paris: E. Dentu, 1889), quotes from the Preface, pp. 1–12, passim.

[76] See the excerpts from Charles Darwin, *The Descent of Man and Selection in Relation to Sex* (London, 1871). The French translation by J.-J. Moulinié, *La Descendance de l'homme et la sélection sexuelle*, with a preface by Carl Vogt, appeared in two volumes (Paris: C. Reinwald & Cie, 1872). www.darwin-online.org.uk/

inferior – to men.[77] Few of them seemed committed to abstract notions of equality, or, for that matter, even liberty; some even came across as remarkably Burkean in their views on the sociopolitical relation of the sexes. Yet, by virtue of their anticlericalism, most would have considered themselves friends of the new regime, if not outright allies.

The pioneer physician and physical anthropologist Paul Broca (1824–1880) pondered the comparability in size of recently discovered prehistoric skulls of both sexes (found in the caves of *L'Homme mort*) with the significant differences in cranial capacity found between female and male skulls of contemporary Parisians. Echoing Charles Darwin (whose arguments in the *Descent of Man* had in turn been influenced by the arguments of the German/Swiss investigator Carl Vogt), Broca surmised that women's skull size (on the average) had diminished over the centuries. This, he thought, was due to the fact that since prehistoric times women had come under the protection of men – a state of affairs that had spared them (relatively speaking) from the rigorous application of the laws of natural selection and had made possible a differential development.[78] Broca did not think, however, that this situation was immutable.

Other French scientists, partial to furthering women's education in the 1870s, cast a more favorable light on the question of female intelligence. These scientists included the anthropologist Charles Letourneau (1831–1902), whose French translation of the theories on nature and materiality of the German materialist Ludwig Büchner, *L'Homme selon la science* (1870–1872) was repeatedly reissued, and especially Dr. Léonce Manouvrier (1850–1927), a student of Broca's, whose work in comparative skull and brain anatomy in

---

[77] The obsession of physicians and budding sexologists with women's corporeal difference and its social significance was manifested in publications such as: Adam Raciborski, *Traité de la menstruation, ses rapports avec l'ovulation, la fécondation, l'hygiène de la puberté et l'âge critique, son rôle dans les différentes maladies, ses troubles et leur traitements* (Paris: J.-B. Baillière, 1868); Pierre Berthier, *Des Névroses menstruelles; ou la Menstruation dans ses rapports avec les maladies nerveuses et mentales* (Paris: Delahaye, 1874); and Dr. Thésée Pouillet, *Essai médico-philosophique sur les formes, les causes, les signes, les conséquences et le traitement de l'onanisme chez la femme* (1876; 2nd ed. aug. Paris: V. A. Delahaye, 1877; 7th ed. 1897). A relatively progressive summary of the state of knowledge in the mid-1870s is E. Dally, "Femmes," *Dictionnaire encyclopédique des sciences médicales*, ed. A. Dechambre. 4e sér., I(FAA-FET), (1877), pp. 427–439; this article was extensively quoted by Léon Richer in *L'Avenir des Femmes*, n° 159 (February 1878). For a recent scholarly assessment of this literature of the male gaze, see part II of Mary Lynn Stewart, *For Health and Beauty: Physical Culture for Frenchwomen 1880s–1930s* (Baltimore & London: Johns Hopkins University Press, 2001).

[78] Paul Broca, "Sur les Crânes de la caverne de l'Homme-Mort," *Revue d'Anthropologie*, 2:1 (1873) in *WFF*, vol. 1, doc. 110 (Darwin) & doc. 111 (Broca). See also Herbert Spencer's cautious optimism about coming improvements in the status of women, in his *Principles of Sociology*, vol. 1 (London, 1876; New York, 1893), doc. 112 in *WFF*, vol. 1.

the late 1870s and early 1880s (as head of the laboratory of the *Société d'Anthropologie*) would be applauded by champions of women's rights.[79] His contributions will be discussed later.

The progressive scientists and physicians had their work cut out for them, for in 1879 these more positive views of female intelligence would be attacked "scientifically" by Dr. Gustave LeBon (1841–1931). His research findings similarly focused on the diverging skull sizes of men and women over time as "civilization" progressed, but drew from these findings harsh conclusions about the inevitable "inferiority" of women's intelligence in comparison with that of men. Although he did not oppose educating women *per se*, LeBon strongly opposed providing young women and men with the *same* education with the *same* goals (as he believed was happening in America), calling this a "dangerous chimera," that "would result in stripping woman of her domestic role, obliging her to compete with man, and depriving her of everything that constitutes her value, her utility and her charm." "The day that woman leaves the household, disdaining the inferior [sic] occupations that nature has given her, and arrives to take part in our struggles will be the beginning of a social revolution in which the sacred bonds of the family will disappear."[80]

By 1890, the year following the centennial of the French Revolution, LeBon would challenge the notion of "equality" itself, insisting in the eminent *Revue Scientifique* that the pursuit of equality of the sexes or of the races was chimerical and misguided. He insisted that the findings of both anthropology and psychology, plus evolution itself, contested such egalitarian notions; an individual's education must be determined strictly by aptitude and function to be filled. "This education morally, intellectually and physically 'detracks' woman"; "it falsifies her character by making her

---

[79] Letourneau's posthumous work, *La Condition de la femme dans les diverses races et civilisations*, ed. L. Manouvrier & G. Papillault (Paris: Giard & Brière, 1903), would receive effusive praise from the feminist writer Harlor, "Le Féminisme d'un savant," in *La Fronde*, n° 1919 (12 March 1903). Manouvrier's findings, published between 1881 and 1885, would have an international impact; they would be invoked favorably by Jeanne-E. Schmahl, "The Intellectual Inferiority of Women," *The Englishwoman's Review*, 16 August 1893, to combat the theories of Cesare Lombroso (see below, n. 85), and by Dr. Maria Montessori (who took the side of Manouvrier against Broca) in her *Pedagogical Anthropology*, transl. from the Italian (*Antropologia pedagogica*) by Frederic Tabor Cooper (New York: Stokes, 1913), pp. 257–258. In the 1890s and early twentieth century, Manoeuvrier' work would be invoked by Aline Valette and later by Madeleine Pelletier (see the pertinent chapters in parts II and III). See also Marya Chéliga, in *La Revue Encyclopedique Larousse* (1896), pp. 829–830. On the contributions of Letourneau and Manouvrier, see especially the excellent study by Hecht, *The End of the Soul* (cited in n. 46).

[80] See Gustave LeBon, "Recherches anatomiques et mathématiques sur les lois des variations du volume du cerveau et sur leurs relations avec l'intelligence," *Revue d'Anthropologie*, 2e ser., II, 1 (1879), 27–104; quote, 62.

disdain the occupations that nature attributes to her, by inspiring feelings of a dangerous rivalry with regard to man, and by ... developing in her a spirit of revolt and hatred against this society which she believes has victimized her."[81] In Russia, he asserted, "not all women students are nihilists, but all nihilists are women students." Such remarks as these frontally attacked the principles of equality and rights espoused by feminists but also those held dear by the republican elite itself.[82] LeBon would subsequently gain international fame as the popularizer of crowd psychology with his opus *Psychologie des foules*, first published in 1895, in which he characterized crowd behavior as irrational, even hysterical, and thereby feminine.[83] Historian Susanna Barrows has labeled LeBon "a cultural Cassandra," "a precocious and enduring pessimist."[84] He can also be viewed as an arch antifeminist. Could such a man be considered a friend of the Third Republic? Nothing could be less certain.[85]

Another contributor to the scientific literature opposing women's intellectual equality in the early 1880s was Dr. Gaetan Delaunay (dates not known), whose thinking about the sexes ran along the same lines as that of Comte Arthur Gobineau, the theorist of racial differences and dominance. After reviewing a wide range of scientific publications, both French and international, encompassing zoology, anatomy, anthropology, and a variety of other fields, Delaunay concluded that "the preeminence

[81] See LeBon, "La Psychologie des femmes et les effets de leur éducation actuelle," *La Revue Scientifique* (11 October 1890), 449–460; quote, 454.

[82] In this 1890 article, cited in n. 81, LeBon praised the novel *Névrosée* (1890) by Daniel Lesueur (Jeanne Loiseau), who is reputed to have been his mistress; the novel contrasted the fate of two sisters, one domestic and conventional, the other highly educated and unhappy. On Lesueur, see Diana Holmes, "Daniel Lesueur and the Feminist Romance," in *A 'Belle Epoque'? Women in French Society and Culture 1890–1914*, ed. Diana Holmes & Carrie Tarr (New York & Oxford: Berghahn, 2006), pp. 197–210. In the late 1890s Daniel Lesueur would become a regular contributor to the feminist daily, *La Fronde*.

[83] Gustave LeBon, *Psychologie des foules* (Paris: F. Alcan, 1895; many reprints); the first English translation, *The Crowd: A Study of the Popular Mind*, would appear with Macmillan in 1896.

[84] See Susanna Barrows, *Distorting Mirrors: Visions of the Crowd in Late Nineteenth-Century France* (New Haven, CT: Yale University Press, 1981), p. 162 (both quotes).

[85] Le Bon's conclusions would find an echo in the French publications of Cesare Lombroso, the Italian physician and criminologist who argued that although women have abundant talent, they possess little genius. The widely published Lombroso would posit that among all vertebrates females are inferior in size and intelligence to males, and this is because women are organized for maternity, which to him explained everything. In his opinion, great art results from great feeling and erotic urges, which women experience less than men. See Lombroso, "Le Génie et talent chez les femmes," *La Revue des Revues* (1 August 1893), 561–567. Eugénie Potonié-Pierre would take exception to Lombroso's argument in the *Journal des Femmes*, n° 23 (October 1893), as would Dr. Madeleine Pelletier, in "Recherches expérimentales sur les signes physiques de l'intelligence," extr. de *La Revue de Philosophie* (La Chapelle-Montigeon, 1904), and "Les Femmes peuvent-elles avoir du génie?" publication of *La Suffragiste* (undated). Thanks to Marilyn Boxer for the last two Pelletier references.

of male over female represents a higher phase of evolution, because it characterizes the species and the superior races, adulthood and the upper classes. From both the moral and physical points of view, evolution seems to go from the preeminence of the feminine sex to that of the masculine sex." In a second article he argued that "evolution proceeds from equality to inequality, and only retrograde evolution is characterized by a return to equality – which one sees only in species headed for extinction, degenerate varieties or classes, and old persons."[86]

Partisans of women's emancipation vigorously contested such "scientific" claims throughout the 1880s. In *Le Droit des Femmes*, a writer who signed as Louise Lagrave took on Delaunay's assertions, claiming that there was nothing inherent about women's so-called intellectual inferiority. Instead, cultural norms and an impoverished education had distorted women's "natural" equality with men among primitive peoples. Once again the nature/culture debate had emerged, only this round became a contest over the claims of "science" as represented by the up-and-coming field of anthropology, which Lagrave baptized "the master science of our times."[87] Disputing the evidence cited by Delaunay, Lagrave refused his claims of inferiority/superiority for the sexes: "These facts in no way demonstrate some pretended physiological law that would assure unlimited perfection for man, while condemning woman to an inevitable stopping-place." Among the savages, women shared the work with men, she insisted, whereas in so-called civilized societies "woman is condemned to physical and moral atrophy." As for the skull-measuring and brain-weighing efforts, the evidence of sexual differentials may be convincing, but what, she asked, is its significance? Can one conclude absolutely women's intellectual inferiority, based on smaller cranial dimensions? As for the brain studies, the most damning – and unprovable – claim put forth by Delaunay is that women's brains are less perfectible than men's. Lagrave argued that evidence from girls' schooling both in America and in France proved this claim to be ridiculous. She faulted cultural practices: when one tells girls that science makes them ugly, that a learned woman cannot be gracious, that she will not be loved, what can one expect? What

---

[86] See Gaetan Delaunay, "De l'égalité et de l'inégalité des deux sexes," *La Revue Scientifique* (3 September 1881), 304–310, and "L'Inégalité des individus," *La Revue Scientifique* (20 May 1882), 621–626. Delaunay published significant books on evolutionary ethnology in the 1870s and 1880s.

[87] See "Une Question d'anthropologie," a series of four articles signed Louise Lagrave in *Le Droit des Femmes*, n° 219 (5 February 1883), 24–26; n° 220 (4 March 1883), 40–42; n° 221 (1 April 1883), 53–55, & n° 222 (6 May 1883), 71–72. This quotation, and those following, can be found on pp. 24, 25–26, 42, 55, and 72.

really counts is the ability to reason, not to stuff one's head with facts. In the fourth installment of her response, Lagrave laid out the innumerable ways in which French culture hampered women's development. Far from accepting the theory of ongoing divergence in the aptitudes of the sexes, Lagrave concluded, "We believe that one can purify modern societies only by raising up women, through her participation in science, through the development of all her faculties, through her emancipation from the old moral slavery. Only thus can humanity accomplish its higher evolution." In short, Louise Lagrave was not impressed with the detrimental conclusions that Delaunay, LeBon, and others had produced and she bravely disputed both their "scientific" findings and their significance.

Other republican women's rights advocates would latch onto the findings of Dr. Léonce Manouvrier (even though they sometimes systematically overinterpreted his conclusions). In the June 1882 issue of the *Revue Scientifique*, this young physician-anthropologist argued that the volume of the skull and brain weights between women and men were comparable, provided one takes body mass into account. Arguing directly against LeBon, Manouvrier insisted that brain weight differences alone could not be used, as LeBon claimed in his earlier work, to support a case for the intellectual inferiority of women. "The sexual difference in brain weight and skull volume cannot be interpreted scientifically in a way that is unfavorable to the feminine sex. The evidence proves that this difference is due to a difference in body mass and that absolutely nothing in anatomy proves that woman is inferior to man with respect to her intellectual faculties."[88] In a series of later articles published in the *Revue de l'École d'Anthropologie de Paris* and its successor, the *Revue*

---

[88] See Léonce Manouvrier, "La Question du poids de l'encéphale et de ses rapports avec l'intelligence," *La Revue Scientifique*, 3rd series, 29:2 (2 June 1882), 673–683; *Sur l'Interprétation de la quantité dans l'encephale et du poids du cerveau en particulier* (Paris: G. Masson, 1885; offprint, *Mémoires de la Société d'Anthropologie de Paris*, 2ᵉ sér., vol. 3, pp. 137–326); "Indications anatomiques et physiologiques relatives aux attributions naturelles de la femme," *Congrés . . . du Droit des femmes*, pp. 41–51; and "Indications anatomiques et physiologiques rélatifs aux attributions naturelles de la femme," *Bulletin de l'Union Universelle des Femmes*, nᵒ 12 (15 December 1890), 9–12, & nᵒ 13 (15 January 1891), 12–14.

See also the later commentary on Manouvrier's contributions by Marya Chéliga in the *Revue Encyclopédique Larousse*, 1896, pp. 829–830.

Curiously, Manouvrier's findings are not discussed by Paul Topinard in the pertinent sections (on brain differentials for women and men) of his book *Éléments d'anthropologie générale* (Paris: A. Delahaye & E. Lecrosnier, 1885), chapters 13 & 16. This book is based on Topinard's courses at the *École d'Anthropologie*, where he edited the *Revue d'Anthropologie*. Hecht, *End of the Soul*, p. 233, indicates that Manouvrier and Topinard strongly disagreed on whether the findings of anthropology should have a political agenda or apply its findings to contemporary human societies. Topinard was finally eased out of his chair at the École.

Anthropologique, Manouvrier spelled out the political implications of his work. Even as he castigated the influence of "male pride" in the early work of physical anthropologists, he maintained that such prejudices do often carry a grain of truth. In Manouvrier's view, the muscular superiority of males and the gestational requirements of females necessarily resulted in a sexual division of labor that accentuated secondary sexual differences. Although male supremacy was not necessarily eternally destined, he allowed, it had resulted from social necessity. Thus, Manouvrier's support for women's equality, based on his brain weight findings, did have functionalist limits.[89] In May 1883, the obstetrician Eugène Verrier (1824–1910) would give a public lecture, *La Femme devant la science,* in which he summarized Manouvrier's early findings.[90]

The same year, another progressive commentator on the findings of scientists, L. Cosson, would rehash the question of skeletal differences and brain differences, addressing his analysis directly to "*les féministes*" and to "those who are in the camp of the feminists."[91] He also spoke of "*chauvinisme masculin.*" Cosson insisted that the woman question had become the "order of the day" for the civilized world and asserted that indifference was no longer permitted.[92] He supported women's right to employment and to remain single if they so desired, claiming that the individual was the fundamental unit of society (not the family). "Masculine rule," he argued (echoing Maria Deraismes' remarks about masculine aristocracy), "is the last citadel of privilege, of 'might makes right.' It is up to us, in the nineteenth century, to take up once again the work of 1789, which has been diverted from its course."[93] Another male-feminist had entered the lists. And yet, even L. Cosson had his limits; for one thing, he opposed coeducation of the sexes.

The veteran women's rights activist and socialist Léonie Rouzade (1839–1916) would likewise have no patience with functionalist limits on

---

[89] In the early twentieth century, Manouvrier would criticize socialist feminists for advocating the emancipation of women through employment. He argued that this was no road to women's emancipation and that women, for the most part, understood this. He strongly opposed "*concurrence*" (competition) between the sexes in the labor market. In Manouvrier's worldview, men's and women's roles were inevitably (and should remain) distinct and women's role was primarily that of mother and *ménagère*. See, in particular, Manouvrier's "Conclusions générales sur l'anthropologie des sexes et applications sociale," *Revue Mensuelle de l'Ecole d'Anthropologie*, 13:12 (December 1903), 405–423. He would restate such arguments with increasing vigor following the war of 1914–1918.

[90] See the published version: Eugène Verrier, *La Femme devant la science, considérée au point de vue du système cérébrale. Conférence faite à Paris, le 28 mai 1883, à la salle Rivoli* (Paris: Alcan-Lévy, 1883).

[91] See L. Cosson, *Essai sur la condition des femmes* (Paris: P. Dupont, 1883).

[92] Cosson, *Essai*, pp. 59, 121, 125, for these terms.   [93] Cosson, *Essai*, p. 322.

what women could be or do. In her long article, "La Femme devant la démocratie," published in 1887, she would assert (as did most feminists by this time) that any inferiority of women's intelligence had historical and cultural causes and that equal education could overcome any deficits. Positing that women must become "workers for progress," she argued at length against (though without naming her adversaries) the brain size specialists (no doubt LeBon in particular):[94]

> Women respond: our brains are proportional to our size, and insofar as the brain is a precision instrument its quality lies in its organization, not in its dimensions. The same can be said for ears and eyes – small eyes see just as well as large ones, immense ears hear no better than tiny ears; the chronometer measures time just as well as the big clock. The measurement of cerebral dimensions cannot be used to assign us inferiority in reasoning.

Solid education could overcome any such deficits. In the meantime, women's resort to ruse and manipulation remained the great sexual equalizer: it was "her *brevet de capacité.*"[95]

It is easy for us today to criticize the early Third Republic physician-anthropologists on various counts – their sense of racial superiority, or their juxtapositions of civilization and savagery. Even taking these attitudes into account, it is nevertheless essential for us to acknowledge just how important they considered the woman question to be. As one of the more progressive among them, Eugène Dally, put it in his 1877 article "Femmes" in the *Dictionnaire encyclopédique des sciences médicales,* "one must recognize that from the study of the social role of women, their attributes, the conditions of marriage and parenthood, will result, for social hygiene, for future generations, for civilization and for order (which is one of the etiological sources of hygiene) consequences of the highest importance, because they permit us to intervene scientifically in a series of problems on which the future of human societies depends, and which, up to now, have been relegated to haphazard solutions."[96] Finding answers to the woman question seemed central to the future of societal organization, and not only in France. Science to the rescue! But whose science? The biomedical thinking on the woman question by physicians continued, bolstered by a "scientifically" reinforced politics of sexual knowledge (for the earlier

---

[94] Léonie Rouzade, "Les Femmes devant la démocratie," *La Revue Socialiste*, vol. 5, n° 30 (June 1887), 519–534; quote, 529.

[95] Rouzade, "Femmes devant la démocratie," 521.

[96] E[ugène] Dally, "Femmes," *Dictionnaire encyclopédique des sciences médicales*, ed. A. Dechambre. 4e sér., I (FAA-FET, 1877), pp. 427–439.

phases of these debates, see chapters 3 and 4 in *The Woman Question in France, 1400–1870*) that was becoming increasingly transnational in scope.[97] These debates were not purely theoretical; they had practical consequences.

A third venue for examining the state of the question in the early Third Republic is the continuing controversy that would accompany women's entry into the prestigious medical profession through university and hospital training. Opponents of women's higher education and careers – particularly careers in medicine – included the physician Gustave-Antoine Richelot, an officer in the *Société de Médicine de Paris*, who insisted in 1875 that "the study and practice of medicine require virile qualities," and condemned female physicians as a malady of the time.[98] Others disagreed. The English-born physician George Hugh Edwards carefully educated his daughter Blanche Edwards (1858–1941; later Edwards-Pilliet), and after she passed her *baccalauréat*, helped her to enroll (despite the reservations of the dean Dr. Vulpian) in the Paris Faculty of Medicine, where she studied for four years alongside a young American woman Augusta Klumpke, whose family had moved from Lausanne to Paris expressly so she could study medicine.

The French faculties of medicine might enroll and even graduate women, but when Mlles Edwards and Klumpke with their medical degrees ventured to enter the *concours* for the hospital internships in 1884, the first women to do so, the wrath of the opponents in the medical profession exploded. From 1884 until July 1886, when the Prefect of the Seine ordered their registration, the controversy created a media sensation. Medical students gathered at the *Hôtel de Ville*, and at the *Assistance Publique* (where the *concours* took place), they tried to break down the doors; later they burned Blanche Edwards in effigy. Mlle Klumpke placed sixteenth, but Mlle

---

[97] During the early 1870s the English and American medical communities fiercely debated with women's rights advocates over the effects of women's higher education, which certain eminent physicians claimed would dry up girls' reproductive powers. For assessments of these debates in England, see Joan N. Burstyn, *Victorian Education and the Ideal of Womanhood* (London: Croom-Helm, 1980) and Cynthia Eagle Russett, *Sexual Science: The Victorian Construction of Womanhood* (Cambridge, MA: Harvard University Press, 1989). For pertinent documents reconstructing the debate on both sides of the Atlantic (Edward H. Clark, Julia Ward Howe, Caroline Dall, Henry Maudsley, Elizabeth Garrett Anderson), see *WFF*, vol. 1, docs. 115–117. The French-trained American physician Mary Putnam Jacobi would address the subject of menstruation and craft a sharp rebuttal to Clark's theories; her 1876 paper won the Harvard Medical School's Boylston Prize and appeared in print the following year. See Mary Putnam Jacobi, *The Question of Rest for Women during Menstruation* (New York: G. P. Putnam's Sons, 1877).

[98] See Gustave-Antoine Richelot, *La Femme médicin* (Paris: E. Dentu, 1875); originally published as articles in *L'Union médicale* as "Causeries confraternelles." Quote, p. 18.

Edwards was named only as a provisional intern. Harassment of these young women would continue in the hospitals of Paris.[99]

Blanche Edwards had earlier served as an *externe* at the women's hospital of Salpêtrière, under the aegis of the renowned professor of anatomical pathology Dr. Jean-Martin Charcot (1825–1893), who thus found himself in the thick of the subsequent battles over women in medicine. By late 1888, at the thesis defense of the young Polish medical student Caroline Schultze, Dr. Charcot (albeit praising Mlle Schultze's thesis) saw fit to rail against the notion that women should ever become doctors: "If your goal is to prove that medicine is a feminine profession as much as a masculine one, it is impossible for me not to object to such pretension. The woman physician will never be more than an exception. There are exceptional women in every genre – in art, in science, or literature. There are even women who bear arms, and yet the military profession is certainly that which is least suitable for your sex." Charcot went on to criticize women for aspiring to the top positions, not the humble ones – women, he said, always want to become the generals, not the soldiers; they want to practice in the cities, not in the countryside; they want to take the well-paying jobs.[100] Charcot subsequently presided over the 1889 thesis defense of Blanche Edwards, at which point he praised her performance on her exams as "particularly brilliant," but then asked her what she intended to do with her degree. She responded that she would care for all people who were ill, but would consecrate herself especially to the health of women and children.[101] A modest answer, perhaps designed to diffuse the spectre of competition for "men's" positions that so worried Charcot, but it was also sincere in its anticipation of the trajectory her fifty-year-long medical career would follow. Obstetrics would be a big part of her practice, but Blanche Edwards-Pilliet would also become a vocal feminist, devoted to addressing the "politics" of motherhood in the context of population concerns as well as objections to women's employment. By 1900 this pathbreaking woman doctor would become an ardent proponent of required maternity leave and payments to mothers by the state.

---

[99] See the account in Françoise Leguay & Claude Barbizet, *Blanche Edwards-Pilliet, femme et médecin, 1858-1941* (Le Mans: Éditions Cenomane, 1988), pp. 41–49.

[100] Charcot's diatribe is reproduced verbatim in G. Molinari, "Femmes avocats et femmes médicins," *Journal des Économistes*, ser. 4, vol. 45, n° 1 (January 1889), 170–172.

[101] See Leguay & Barbizet, *Blanche Edwards-Pilliet*, pp. 52–53.

Motherhood, the Natality Crisis, and the Resurgence of the "Depopulation" Debates

Everyone recognizes the necessity of motherhood: societies cannot survive without it. For individual women, however, its material consequences can be mixed, at once positive and negative. In the words of women's rights and socialist activist Léonie Rouzade, maternity was both "the secret of women's disarmament" and woman's greatest asset.[102] In early Third Republic France, advocates of women's rights, women and men alike, clearly understood the inescapable importance of producing the next generation of children, without which the French nation could not prosper. If "gender trouble" lay at the center of sociopolitical debate in nineteenth-century France, it was motherhood that held center stage in the debates on the woman question under the new republican regime.

The declining birth rate and high infant mortality figures made it obvious to observers that childbearing was not exactly flourishing in late nineteenth-century France. Finding a solution to the falling birth rate would determine not only the success of the republican project but the very future of the country. From mid-century on, in fact, the debate over lack of population growth in France had both complicated and constrained potential responses to the woman question; the decline in the birth rate was ever present in the elaboration of French debates on the subject of women's status. Jules Michelet had put his finger on the problem already in 1860 when he wrote in *La Femme* that: "The population no longer increases, and its quality is degenerating. The peasant girl dies of labor, the female operative of hunger. What children can we expect from them? Abortions, more and more."[103] This was no mere matter of "the question of women's fertility bec[oming] an ideological prism," as one historian has claimed; the nation's fertility was becoming an issue in its own right and, thus, the key not only to maintaining the ostensible historic grandeur of France but to building a republican future.[104] What could be done?

---

[102] Rouzade, "Femmes devant la démocratie," p. 520.
[103] Jules Michelet, *Woman/La Femme* (New York: Rudd & Carleton, 1860; 1873 ed.), p. 23.
[104] See Joshua Cole, "'There Are Only Good Mothers': The Ideological Work of Women's Fertility in France before World War I," *French Historical Studies*, 19:3 (Spring 1996), 639–672; quote, p. 642. See also Cole's article on the earlier period, "'A Sudden and Terrible Revelation': Motherhood and Infant Mortality in France, 1858–1874," *Journal of Family History*, 21:4 (October 1996), 419–445; and his book, *The Power of Large Numbers: Population, Politics, and Gender in Nineteenth-Century France* (Ithaca, NY: Cornell University Press, 2000).

Abortion, births out of wedlock, infanticide, baby farming/wet-nursing, contraception, malnutrition, venereal disease – all these cultural practices and conditions boded ill for French population growth. For some critics, they could be construed as the symptoms of a dying society, a concatenation of circumstances that encompassed the sexual and moral attitudes and practices of women and men, in an environment highly conditioned by economics, law, and politics. They manifested, in particular, in women's responses to unwanted pregnancies, the consequences of men's unconstrained sexual activity, and laws that effectively condoned men's "sowing wild oats" without taking the slightest responsibility for the results, much less for the fate of their female partners.[105] These were serious, indeed fundamental sociopolitical problems already in evidence during the monarchies, and now it was the turn of French Republicans to address them. Not surprisingly some seized on the idea of a "national make-over" – reshaping a republican woman through education (as we have seen earlier) but also as Judith Surkis has demonstrated, attempting also to shape a new republican man.[106] But this would take time, and time was not on the side of the republicans.

In the aftermath of the Franco-Prussian war and the physical, mental, economic, and moral damage it inflicted, some physicians began to denounce French women as socially, and even patriotically, irresponsible for avoiding pregnancy and for neglecting their infants. Dr. André-Théodore Brochard, for one, had long been appalled by the rise in infant mortality among babies consigned by their working mothers to rural wet nurses and by the increasing numbers of infanticides committed by unwed mothers. As *directeur des nourrices* for the city of Paris, and editor-in-chief of *La Jeune Mère*, he was in a position to know. In 1873 he blamed France's population problems on the indifference of mothers and the incompetence of administrators.[107] By 1876, Dr. Brochard was blowing the whistle on the "immense" numbers of infanticides and the "incalculable" number

---

[105] See Part I, Chapter 1 of this volume, notes 52–55, for citations to the publications by Rachel Fuchs.

[106] See Judith Surkis, *Sexing the Citizen: Morality and Masculinity in France, 1870–1920* (Ithaca, NY: Cornell University Press, 2006).

[107] André-Théodore Brochard, *Des Causes de la dépopulation en France et les moyens d'y remédier* (Lyon, 1873). Also see Brochard, *La Vérité sur les enfants trouvés* (Paris, 1876). Brochard was a staunch advocate of governmental control of the wet-nursing industry, which the Roussel law of 1874 enacted. Also see George D. Sussman, "The Wet-Nursing Business in Nineteenth-Century France," *French Historical Studies*, 9:2 (Fall 1975), 304–328; "The End of the Wet-Nursing Business in France, 1874–1914," *Journal of Family History*, 2:3 (Fall 1977), 237–258; and his pathbreaking book, *Selling Mothers' Milk: The Wet-Nursing Business in France, 1715–1914* (Urbana: University of Illinois Press, 1982).

of abortions – committed by (desperate) women – since the closing of the *tours* that had taken in abandoned infants and the transformation of the hospice service for foundlings. In the preface to his 1876 book, *La Vérité sur les enfants trouvés*, he connected these problems, which compounded the losses caused by the excessive mortality of newborns, to the depopulation question, calling for a mobilization of public opinion to combat these plagues. Something had to be done! He also remarked that the bureaucrats had persecuted him for speaking out.[108]

Already in July 1874, the members of the Anthropological Society of Paris had dedicated several sessions to consideration of the question of fertility [*fécundité*], prompted by the release of the latest figures on population by France's pioneer statistician, the demographer Louis-Adolphe Bertillon. Dr. Gustave Lagneau (who became deeply engaged with the population issue) delivered a paper on the fertility of different classes of society; it was during these sessions that the philosopher and women's rights advocate Clémence Royer (whom we met in *The Woman Question in France*) challenged Lagneau, arguing that (male) anthropologists did not have all the answers and that society should encourage mothers (both married and single) rather than fathers. She laid out a substantive and radical agenda, which historian Jean Elisabeth Pedersen has succinctly summarized: "Instead of socioeconomic incentives for fathers, [Royer] advocated eugenic abortions, legal equality for legitimate and illegitimate children, a married woman's right to work without her husband's consent, legal divorce, and a social system in which new mothers lived with their parents instead of their husbands to receive help with child rearing."[109] Since a number of these measures effectively attacked provisions in the Civil Code, the leadership and editors of the Society's *Bulletin* (Paul Broca and Louis-Adolphe Bertillon in particular) refused to publish her comments in full; Royer's historian-biographer Joy Harvey and Claude Blanckaert rediscovered her text "*Sur la natalité*" in galley proofs more than a century later.[110] This would not be the last time that a feminist scientist would tangle with the physician-anthropologists, asserting her right to

[108] See Brochard, *La Vérité sur les enfants trouvés*, preface; quotes p. 18.
[109] See Jean Elisabeth Pedersen, "Regulating Abortion and Birth Control: Gender, Medicine, and Republican Politics in France, 1870–1920," *French Historical Studies*, 19:3 (Spring 1996), 673–698; quote, 674.
[110] Royer's "Sur la natalité" has been translated and published in appendix (pp. 193–203) to Joy Harvey's book, "*Almost a Man of Genius*": *Clémence Royer, Feminism, and Nineteenth-Century Science* (New Brunswick, NJ: Rutgers University Press, 1997); it is summarized in Harvey's chapter 6. See also Sara Joan Miles, "Evolution and Natural Law in the Synthetic Science of Clémence Royer," Ph. D. dissertation, University of Chicago, 1988, and Pedersen, "Regulating," p. 674.

present alternative knowledge and to promote a more woman-friendly agenda. It may have been the first time that the Anthropological Society of Paris would engage in an effort to censor the perspectives of one of its own members.

By 1876, the same Louis-Adolphe Bertillon would introduce the innovative notion of a "fertility index" to measure annual births in proportion to the number of women of childbearing age in the population.[111] In 1880 his son Dr. Jacques Bertillon (1851–1922) would publish *La Statistique humaine de la France* (*Naissance, mariage, mort*), a statistical overview that would provide fodder for the ongoing depopulation discussion, as well as for debates concerning marriage and divorce.[112] A decade later, in 1887, Jacques Bertillon would proffer a related index for understanding "illegitimate" births by comparing their numbers to the aggregate number of unmarried women of childbearing age. Historian Joshua Cole critiques these indices for pigeonholing women by "describ[ing] a world in which the only measurably interesting fact about birth was the number of potential mothers."[113] What such indices (which have been widely used by demographers ever since) did do, however, was to foreground women, taking them out of the shadow of "the family." From a feminist perspective, it seems significant that women's indispensable role was finally being accounted for.

Women's rights activists were sensitive to these problems, but at the Paris congress in 1878, they addressed them somewhat obliquely, by passing resolutions that advocated *recherche de la paternité* and promoted new laws that would punish seducers of underage girls, through lies or promises of marriage, and provide monetary damages to the young women.[114] During the next few years, the findings of the fertility index, like those of the now discredited ratio of births to deaths, became subjects of increasing public concern, provoking further debates about the irreplaceable contribution of French women and its significance for

---

[111] See Bertillon's article, "Natalité," in the *Dictionnaire encyclopédique des sciences médicales*, ed. A. Dechambre, 11 (sér. 2, 1876), 446–447. According to Joshua Cole ("Only good mothers," p. 653), Bertillon here adopted this innovative concept from the work of a Scottish physician (a gynecological surgeon) named J. Matthews Duncan, but reversed the terminology *fertilité* and *fécondité*. Bertillon also contributed a study to the divorce debates: see Jacques Bertillon, *Étude démographique du divorce et de la séparation du corps dans les différents pays de l'Europe* (Paris: G. Masson, 1883).

[112] Jacques Bertillon, *La Statistique humaine de la France* (*naissance, mariage, mort*) (Paris: G Baillière, 1880).

[113] See Cole, "There Are Only Good Mothers," (cited in n. 104), 654.

[114] Congrès international du Droit des Femmes, "Voeux: Section de législation," in *L'Avenir des Femmes*, n° 166 (1 September 1878), 133–134; as translated in *WFF*, vol. 1, doc. 125.

France's future as a world power in the face of German and English political, economic, and military might.

In 1881 the writer Raoul Frary proclaimed "The National Peril." He pointed out the danger to France posed by population issues, especially with reference to its hereditary enemy Imperial Germany. "The stagnation of the population," Frary insisted, "is the greatest of all the perils, the peril of the future." This condition would disarm France in the face of any future invasion by the Germans as well as the infiltration of "foreign influences." Frary was more concerned by the sorry state of France's morals and by Frenchmen's bad behavior than with women per se. He proposed offering French parents a *"prime"* or bonus to encourage larger families, but it seems clear that by "parents" Frary meant primarily fathers.[115]

This theme of national peril was soon taken up by Dr. Charles Richet (1850–1935), then a young professor at the Paris Faculty of Medicine. His early years had been indelibly marked by the Franco-Prussian war and its aftermath as well as by social Darwinist thinking. In a two-part article on "The Growth of the French Population," published in the *Revue des Deux Mondes* in April and June 1882, Richet sought to bring the findings of demographers to a larger public. Guided by "his concern for the grandeur of France," Richet argued that the principal danger facing France was its falling birth rate. In the second of the two articles, he blamed the decline in the birth rate squarely on "voluntary sterility," his euphemism for birth control.[116] He was particularly concerned with contraceptive practices within marriage, not only among the bourgeoisie but especially among the peasantry. He called on French men and French women to contemplate their duties to the nation – duties that included providing the nation with healthy children. He also underscored the figures for infant mortality, which in 1878 accounted for one-fifth, or 20 percent, of the 839,000 recorded deaths in France. "The fact is," Richer insisted, "that many children die of hunger. Out of every hundred newborns, at least forty die because they don't get enough to eat."[117] Unlike Dr. Brochard, Richet did not directly implicate women; his suggestions for facilitating increase in the birth rate were directed almost entirely to men – restoring primogeniture in inheritance, changing the tax structure to favor large families, etc. Only indirectly, through measures designed to lower infant mortality,

[115] Raoul Frary, *Le Péril national* (Paris: Didier, 1881).

[116] Charles Richet, "L'Accroissement de la population française," *Revue des Deux Mondes,* part 1 (15 April 1882), 900–932, & part 2 (1 June 1882), 587–616.

[117] Richet, "L'Accroissement de la population française;" quotes, part 1, 912, & part 2, 596, 602 respectively.

to increase hygienic practices, to improve housing, etc., did he allude to women – whose responsibilities these things were considered to be. Most importantly, he insisted that for all married couples, giving children to France was becoming a patriotic duty. The nation's power and status could not be maintained without a healthy and numerous population.

Following public debates on the population issue in both the Academy of Medicine and the Academy of Science, Dr. Henri Thulié (1832–1916), director of the new *École Anthropologique* in Paris and a former president of the Paris Municipal Council, advanced quite a different argument. A physician by training, like Brochard and Richet, Thulié specialized in mental illness and had been active in the campaign against state-regulated prostitution. In *La Femme: essai de sociologie physiologique* (1885), he made the birth rate a women's rights issue, arguing – in opposition to Richet – that the principal cause of depopulation was infant mortality, not voluntary sterility, and that this could be attributed to "the legal inferiority of woman, the Code's injustices toward her, and the absence of laws to protect her situation and that of her child." "It is because the woman question encompasses all the others," he continued, "that I have written these pages." Having diagnosed the problem, however, Thulié prescribed a treatment entirely consonant with the still paternalistic attitude then in evidence among certain French republican men. He opposed work outside the home by mothers of small children and, by extension, the wet-nursing industry that made their participation in the labor force possible. In particular, he argued for legislation to obligate putative fathers to support unwed mothers and their common offspring, that is, *recherche de la paternité*. To the extent such measures might have protected French women in the short run, their condition would doubtlessly have improved. But Thulié's solutions, like those of many other republican reformers, were not calculated to deliver French women from male control; rather, they would have effectively ensured women's continuing material dependence on the good will of men.[118]

The perceived enormity of the population question and the vital importance of women's maternal role loomed over the debates about the

---

[118] Henri Thulié, *La Femme: Essai de sociologie physiologique – Ce qu'elle a été, ce qu'elle est, les théories, ce qu'elle doit être* (Paris: A. Delahaye & E. Lecrosnier, 1885), iii. Thulié was echoing the earlier arguments of Émile Acollas and Victor Schoelcher for abrogating Article 340 of the Civil Code, which forbade paternity suits. See Acollas, *Le Droit de l'enfant: l'Enfant né hors mariage* (2nd ed., Paris: G. Baillière, 1870). For an even more focused argument, see Gustave Rivet, *La Recherche de paternité* (3rd ed., Paris: M. Dreyfus, 1890; this is also the original publication date). Rivet would argue that the high rate of abortion, infanticide, and abandonment resulting from "illegitimate" births was responsible for France's population problem; he would lead the legislative campaign for the abolition of Article 340, which would finally be overturned in 1912.

heavily academic curriculum assigned in the new girls' secondary schools. To be sure, the dangers of *surménage* [intellectual overwork] obsessed educators of boys as well as educators of girls during this period. But it was heightened in the case of girls. A growing fear that too much brain-work during adolescence would endanger the reproductive capabilities of the future mothers by disrupting their menstrual cycles had spread from the French medical establishment through European and American educational circles and back again.[119]

In early August 1890, Dr. Gustave Lagneau would again report to the Academy of Medicine on the question of French depopulation.[120] In the right-wing daily *L'Autorité*, Paul de Cassagnac commented on Lagneau's findings, which showed a drop in the number of marriages and a rise in the number of single persons; high rates of infant mortality; and emigration of French citizens to South America (especially Argentina, where approximately 5,000 emigrated in 1885 and 31,000 in 1887). Ever the Catholic anti-republican monarchist, Cassagnac blamed these depressing figures on the "misery" attributable to the Republic.[121] Pro-republican commentators in *Le Droit des Femmes* refused to scapegoat the Republic, but rather remarked that none of the recommendations for stemming depopulation addressed the issue of women's choice. However, news of France's continuing low birth rate would lend a new sense of urgency to advocates of cutbacks in the educational curriculum for girls, to counter charges of intellectual (and physical) exhaustion. Even the most progressive educators of women felt obliged to respond to this concern, but it would take years (until 1897) before the educational authorities would sharply curtail the number of hours assigned to the intellectually demanding curriculum of 1882.[122]

---

[119] Since the 1840s French doctors had been harping on the threat of intense intellectual work to the menstrual regularity and reproductive potential of pubescent girls. American and English doctors trained in Paris had enthusiastically imported these fears, along with their colleagues' gynecologically based regulatory morality, to their respective homelands, and in the 1860s a full-scale transatlantic debate erupted. Among many other French republican educators of the 1880s, Gréard had become greatly concerned about the dangers of *surménage*; see, for example, his 1887 speech at the opening of the Lycée Racine, reprinted in his *Éducation et instruction*, pp. 330–332. On the early nineteenth-century French contributions to this debate, see Yvonne Knibiehler, "Le Discours médical sur la femme: constantes et ruptures," *Mythes et représentations de la femme au dix-neuvième siècle*, special issue of *Romantisme*, n⁰ˢ 13–14 (1976), 41–55; and Yvonne Knibiehler & Catherine Fouquet, *La Femme et les médecins* (Paris: Hachette, 1983).

[120] The full report to the Minister of Commerce from the head of the Division for Accounting and Statistics appeared in the *Journal Officiel* in October 1890.

[121] See Paul de Cassagnac, "La France s'en va," *L'Autorité*, 5 August 1890.

[122] For a resumé of the 1897 reforms, see Mayeur, *Enseignement secondaire*, pp. 210–220. Despite these reforms, the concern over *surménage* would continue to mount as anxiety over depopulation grew; see, for example, the later comments in Charles Turgeon, *Le Féminisme français* (2 vols., Paris: L. Larose, 1902), vol. 2, p. 441, and M.-C. Schuyten, *L'Éducation de la femme* (Paris: O. Doin, 1908).

Infant mortality was one issue that could be addressed. Like Dr. Thulié, Dr. Adolphe Pinard (1844–1934), professor of obstetrics at the Paris Faculty of Medicine and a member of the Academy of Medicine, would focus on bringing down the high rates of infant mortality. Pinard blamed women's ignorance and bad mothering practices for the death of infants and set out to do something about it. In later 1890 and 1891 he would press the case for charitable and governmental assistance to pregnant and postpartum women in order to save infant lives.[123] Such proposals would be welcomed by activists in women-centered philanthropies, such as Marie Béquet de Vienne, founder of the *Société pour l'Allaitement Maternelle* and of maternity homes for indigent women in Paris.[124] But these measures were only a beginning. The next target of the repopulators would be women's employment, on the grounds that it contributed significantly to the declining birth rate.

---

[123] Adolphe Pinard, "De l'assistance des femmes enceintes, des femmes en couches et des femmes accouchées," *Revue d'Hygiène et de Police sanitaire*, 12 (1890), 1098–1112, and *De l'assistance des femmes enceintes*, lecture given at the Sorbonne, 9 May 1891 (Paris, 1891). For a discussion of the birth-weight studies conducted by Pinard and his students throughout the 1890s, see Mary Lynn McDougall, "Protecting Infants: The French Campaign for Maternity Leaves, 1890s–1913," *French Historical Studies*, 13:1 (Spring 1983),79–105. See also Pinard's campaign for the teaching of *puériculture*, his term for the science of caring for infants, especially "De la Puériculture" *La Revue Scientifique*, 31 July 1897. Also see his school text for girls aged 10 to 14 years, *La Puériculture* (Paris, 1904; 3rd ed., 1909). For the postwar history of obligatory *puériculture*, see Linda L. Clark, "Educating Girls to Combat French Depopulation: Puériculture in the Primary Schools of the Third Republic," paper presented to the Duquesne History Conference, held in Pittsburgh, 13 October 1981, and Clark, *Schooling the Daughters of Marianne*, chapter 5.

[124] Marie (Mme Léon) Béquet de Vienne, *Dépopulation de la France: Allocution prononcée par Mme Léon Béquet . . . au Congrès général des institutions féministes tenu à la mairie du VIe arrondissement, le 14 mai 1892* (Paris, 1892). On Béquet de Vienne's career in social services for women, see Dominique Segalen, *Marie Béquet de Vienne: une vie pour l'enfance* (Paris: Conforme Édition, collection Presses Maçonniques, 2003).

CHAPTER 3

The Politics of the Family, Women's Work, and Public Morality, 1870–1890

Women's employment and the monetary resources it could provide threatened to destabilize, even destroy a masculine hierarchy predicated on women's economic dependence. Earned income (and the gendered disparities in earned income) could – and did – encourage working women to question their subordinate status. Maria Deraismes cut to the heart of the matter in 1880: "The human couple is the prototype of every arbitrary hierarchy; there one finds a master, a servant, he who commands, she who obeys; it is there that one must seek the cradle, the primitive origin of every caste and every class."[1]

In the companion volume *The Woman Question in France, 1400–1870* (chapter 6) we have seen that in France fierce disagreements over women's labor force participation (especially in the industrial sector) existed long before the advent of the Third Republic. Debates over paid employment for women (whether single or married) were inextricably intertwined with related issues: the stated objectives for educating girls, women's legal rights as individuals, their childbearing potential and and childrearing capacities, shifts in the sexual division of labor, and, not least, ingrained perceptions of men's assumed requirements for domestic comfort and convenience. Thus, debating the "woman question" was not merely a prism for addressing these "other issues," as some scholars have claimed. On the contrary, the condition of women, the social relations of the sexes, and the production of future generations *were* the core around which every other issue circulated, including – in the later nineteenth century – the entangled issues of public health, population growth (or stagnation), agricultural and industrial productivity, and – in the wake of France's defeat by Prussia and the German coalition – national military strength.

---

[1] "Discours de Mlle Maria Deraismes," in Association Française pour l'Abolition de la Prostitution Réglementée, *La Police des mœurs, réunion de la Salle Lévis du 10 avril 1880* (Paris: AFAPR, 1880), p. 58.

More Facts and Figures

Even today, the facts of women's employment in Third Republic France seem startling. France had the highest proportion of women in the labor force of any country in Europe. As we have already noted, the census of 1866 had revealed that 30.7 percent of the French labor force was female, a figure that then included a significant number of domestic servants. This percentage (including both agricultural and nonagricultural labor) would rise dramatically between 1866 and 1940, rising to 38 percent in 1911 and peaking at 43 percent in 1921. By 1936, a time of high unemployment, the percentage of women in the labor force would only decline to 35 percent, a figure comparable to that for 1906.[2]

As the nineteenth century progressed, women had found employment in new types of jobs, initially in the highly visible industrial production of textiles and in the emerging manufactured garment trades.[3] They subsequently became dominant in other market sectors, such as booksellers in the Hachette Railroad Bookstore network.[4] In fact, between 1866 and 1906 the number of women employed in the nonagricultural sectors would double. The better-educated could be found increasingly in commerce, in white-collar clerical and office jobs, as teachers, and in the health professions. A tiny percentage of women, more highly educated, skilled – and vocal – would challenge the male monopoly in the liberal professions as doctors and lawyers, and in the arts, as writers, painters, and musicians. The government's role in hiring women as teachers, as postal workers and clerks in the ministries, and as school or labor inspectors, became a subject of contention, as did their employment by the state in the manufacture of taxable items including tobacco products and matches.[5] According to

---

[2] For the sources of these figures, see my article "Women: in the Labor Force" for the *Historical Dictionary of the French Third Republic*, ed. Patrick H. Hutton, 2 vol. (Westport, CT: Greenwood Press, 1986), vol. 2, pp. 1072–1074. Of particular value is Madeleine Guilbert, "L'Évolution des effectifs du travail féminin en France depuis 1866," *Revue Française du Travail*, 2, n° 18 (September 1947), 754–777.

[3] See Judith G. Coffin, *The Politics of Women's Work: The Paris Garment Trades, 1750–1915* (Princeton, NJ: Princeton University Press, 1996), and for a comparative view, the pioneering study by Louise A. Tilly & Joan W. Scott, *Women, Work, and Family* (New York: Holt, Rinehart, & Winston, 1978).

[4] See Eileen S. DeMarco, *Reading and Riding: Hachette's Railroad Bookstore Network in Nineteenth-Century France* (Bethlehem, PA: Lehigh University Press, 2006), esp. chapter 4. According to DeMarco (p. 88), the bookstore network "was the first publishing enterprise in France to employ women on a large scale." Usually wives and widows, these women booksellers "represented about 95 percent of the railroad bookstore agents" (p. 89).

[5] See Linda L. Clark, *The Rise of Professional Women in France: Gender and Public Administration since 1830* (Cambridge, UK: Cambridge University Press, 2000). Also Marie-Hélène Zylberberg-Hocquard, "Les ouvrières d'État (tabac-allumettes) dans les dernières années du XIXe siècle," *Le Mouvement Social*, n° 105

historian Marie-Hélène Zylberberg-Hocquard, cigar making alone employed some 10,000 women in the peak year of 1884. Many other young Catholic women joined newly established religious orders that provided essential social services, as school teachers, as nurses in hospitals, even as jailers in women's prisons. Historian Claude Langlois offers these figures: in 1861 religious orders contained over 90,000 women; by 1878 that number had increased to nearly 128,000.[6] But by working for miniscule benefits, these Catholic nuns – and the orphaned girls they took in and put to work – undercut the market for jobs that might otherwise have provided a reasonable living for other women. Consequently, secular women workers objected strongly to convent labor, just as they did to prison labor.

Those who debated the woman question did become increasingly concerned about the entry of women into the skilled trades and professions, but usually they focused more on the overwhelming proportion of unskilled or semiskilled women in the French labor force, especially those newly arrived in the towns and cities, where the debate swirled around the changing patterns and circumstances of their work. Such young women from the provinces, mostly single and unskilled, sometimes found satisfactory employment as domestics, but more often they faced exploitation and sexual harassment, fell back on the worst forms of ill-paying manual drudgery, became increasingly impoverished, and, as a last resort, turned to prostitution, which in both its clandestine and governmentally regulated forms would increasingly be identified as a pressing social problem.

Nineteenth-century social critics, mostly male, continued to view with particular regret and alarm the participation of married women in the labor force, particularly those who were mothers of small children. Physicians, economists, men of science and men of letters, and socialist working men influenced by Proudhon all believed that the best interests of France would be served when a sexual division of labor was strictly enforced, when most women married and, as married women, could dedicate their energies

(October–December 1978), 87–107; employment figures, p. 92. Well before the Third Republic, French government authorities had begun hiring women as postal workers in the provinces, though placing them on a separate career track from men and paying them less; see Susan Bachrach, *Dames Employées: The Feminization of Postal Work in Nineteenth-Century France*, in the monograph series *Women in History*, n° 8 (Winter 1983), especially the Introduction, pp. 1–15. The surge in hiring of women clerks followed the republicans' amalgamation of Postes et Telegraphes in 1878, and Bachrach points out that by 1900 the postal service had become the largest employer of women clerks in France.

[6] Claude Langlois, "Les Effectifs des congrégations féminines aux XIXe siècle. De l'enquête statistique à l'histoire quantitative," *Revue de l'Histoire de l'Église de France*, 60 (January–June 1974), 39–64; charts, p. 56; graphs, pp. 59, 61. Langlois's figures do not include women in contemplative orders.

exclusively to fulfilling their obligations as wives, mothers, and housekeepers within the framework of the male-headed family.

This idealized conception of women's work as lying exclusively in the home did not take into account either the economic realities of family life or the conditions of paid labor in nineteenth-century France. Nor did it address the situation of those women who were, in the nineteenth century, neither married nor leisured. These single women and widows were seen as incipient married women – or old maids. For them, the question was not whether they should compete with men for jobs, but what kind of paid work they might find to ensure their survival. Women's rights advocates acknowledged the importance of women's role and influence in family life, but argued that every woman should have respectable alternatives, that is, choice about her life path. It was clear that to debate the woman question meant debating the "form" of the family and the sexual distribution of labor, and especially after 1877, for the fledgling government of the Third Republic, to address the question of competition, or "*concurrence*," in the labor force. "Competition" and "family" became the keywords in the nineteenth-century debate on women and work, in France as elsewhere in Europe. We will examine each in turn, beginning with "the family."

Male Headship and Sex Roles in "The Family" versus Women's Right to Work

"France was a particularly fertile source of ideas about the family in the early nineteenth century," in historian Michelle Perrot's view.[7] This is putting it mildly! The three sequential generic models (the family economy, the family wage economy, and the family consumer economy) derived by historians Louise Tilly and Joan Scott from careful examinations of family labor practices over time should be supplemented by comparing (as has historian Anne Meyering) the case studies offered by Frédéric Le Play and his followers at *La Réforme Sociale*, as well as the analysis of the many forms of the "European family" by Michael Mitterauer and Reinhold Sieder.[8] Whatever the practices, it is important to remember

---

[7] Michelle Perrot, "The Family Triumphant," in *A History of Private Life*, vol. 4, ed. Michelle Perrot (Cambridge, MA: The Belknap Press of Harvard University Press, 1990), p. 102.

[8] See Tilly & Scott, *Women, Work, and Family* (cited in n. 3) and the critique by Anne C. Meyering, "La Petite Ouvrière surmenée: Family structure, family income and women's work in nineteenth-century France," pp. 132–156 in *Women's Work and the Family Economy in Historical Perspective*, ed. Pat Hudson & W. R. Lee (Manchester: University of Manchester Press; New York: St. Martin's

that "the family" (envisioned then as a specifically male-dominated, hier-archical and authoritarian ideal type) stubbornly inhabited people's heads at all levels of French society. Women, as well as men would uphold the existing model, as for example a certain Caroline d'Ancre, who insisted in her 1877 lecture against the emancipation of women that men needed a place to take refuge from the heartless world, that God knew what He was doing when he created the existing [sexual] order, and concluded that "Woman needs protection, not emancipation."[9]

As thinking about the family shifted from a patriarchal Biblical arche-type to a more fluid, secular conjugal household model, the debates on the woman question began to encompass a spectrum of ideas about family structure that includes at least five (and possibly six) basic variations concerning women's "work" and family "duties", the sexual division of labor, and the responsibilities of husbands and fathers. These notions were highly prescriptive: what "should be" often obscured "what was." Needless to say, all these models presumed heterosexual couples as the norm.

We will present these basic variations in order of appearance:

1) the indissoluble, authoritarian male-headed, often extended family, with the husband/father as supreme monarch and the wife and children completely subordinated to his bidding. This is the Old Testament (Genesis) model most familiar to Christians, with Adam created first and Eve a mere accessory produced from his rib. The Catholic theorist Louis de Bonald articulated the counterrevolutionary version of this model in the early nineteenth century. A still starker version of this model was promoted by the socially minded Catholic Frédéric Le Play; his neo-traditionalist and highly authoritarian "male breadwinner" model likewise invoked Old Testa-ment "Biblical" roots to undergird the sole acceptable and workable model of "the family," an extended, hierarchical family. In 1878 he expressed his indignation at "the social disorders provoked in Paris by several thousands of women who are in open rebellion against the duties of their sex."[10] Who assigned those duties? and for whose benefit?, such women were asking.

Press, 1990), pp. 132–156. See also Michael Mitterauer & Reinhard Sieder, *The European Family: Patriarchy to Partnership from the Middle Ages to the Present* (Oxford: Blackwell, 1982; orig. publ. in German, 1977).

[9] Caroline d'Ancre, *Contre l'émancipation des femmes: Conférence du 9 janvier 1877* (Paris: chez Hurtan, 1877). The published 16-page brochure does not indicate where this lecture took place or what group sponsored it.

[10] Frédéric Le Play, *La Reformé sociale en France deduite de l'observation comparée des peuples européens. 6th ed., corrigée et refondue.* Vol. 2, Livre 3: *La Famille*, chapter 26: "La femme et le mariage," p. 55. Such arguments reappear regularly in the Le Playist publication, *La Reformé Sociale*.

At the other end of the religious spectrum, in a totally secular, even anticlerical and anarchist-socialist context, Pierre-Joseph Proudhon, already infamous for his alternative formulation in the 1840s of "harlot or housewife," in 1875 invoked Molière as he endorsed a comparable approach: "Young man, if you are thinking of marriage, understand first of all that the first condition, for a man, is to dominate his wife and to be master."[11] Proudhon further proposed that a wife perform all the housework herself – no concession here to her hiring servants or working for pay outside the household. A more benevolent paternalistic, moralistic, and "national Catholic" version of the patriarchal family would be articulated in 1875 in the publications of social Catholic industrialists such as Maurice Aubry, a deputy to the National Assembly from the Vosges.[12] But this version was overshadowed in 1878 by Pope Leo XIII's vitriolic encyclical against socialism, *Quod Apostolici Muneris,* which condemned socialist "attacks" on family life, which "rests first of all in the indissoluble union of man and wife according to the necessity of natural law, and is completed in the mutual rights and duties of parents and children, masters and servants," which socialists were ostensibly trying to dissolve. The pope emphatically restated St. Paul's injunction, "as Christ is the head of the Church, so is the man the head of the woman."[13] In 1880, Leo XIII issued another encyclical, *Arcanum,* which articulated the Church's enduring hostility to the secularization of marriage as well as to initiatives for divorce legislation.[14] The pope's subsequent encyclical on the organization of labor, *Rerum Novarum* (1892), would reaffirm this vision and provoke dissent from Christian feminists who, while sidestepping the issue of married women's work, asserted the right of single women to support themselves through paid employment.[15]

---

see, for example, P. de Rousiers, "Le rôle de la femme dans la famille à propos de plusieurs publications nouvelles," in the issue of 15 August 1883, and its sequel in the issue of 1 September. For an energetic account of the mounting support among legislators and pronatalists for Le Playist arguments in opposition to "individualist" universal manhood suffrage during the Third Republic, see Jean-Yves Le Naour, *La Famille doit voter: Le suffrage familial contre le vote individuel* (Paris: Hachette Litteratures, 2005).

[11] Pierre-Joseph Proudhon, *La Pornocratie, ou les femmes dans les temps modernes* (Paris: A. Lacroix, 1875). Proudhon died in 1865. This posthumous publication was reprinted in *Oeuvres complètes de P.-J. Proudhon,* vol. 15 (Paris: M. Rivière, 1939), pp. 325–469, quote, p. 430.

[12] Maurice Aubry, *Le Travail des femmes dans les ateliers, manufactures et magasins* (Nancy: N. Collin, 1875).

[13] "*Quod Apostolici Muneris,*" Encyclical of Pope Leo XIII on Socialism. Accessed at www.vatican.va/ holy_father/leo_xiii/encyclicals/documents/hf_l-xiii_e... on 3 June 2011.

[14] "*Arcanum,*" 10 February 1880, English translation in Joseph Husslein, ed., *Social Wellsprings,* I (Milwaukee, WI, 1940); now also available online at the Vatican website.

[15] The impact of *Rerum Novarum* will be addressed in Part II, Chapter 6

2) the secularized version of the monogamous conjugal family under male authority, as enshrined in the French Civil Code.[16] This vision likewise asserted male headship and a strict sexual division of labor, with separate spheres of activity divided according to location – the classic domestic/public (public/private) division – in which a male breadwinner supports "his" family through paid labor outside the household, and "his" wife presides over the household and raises the children. Internally, this model offered a potential democratic partnership predicated on complementary roles, but it was nevertheless subject to and constrained by male authority. This is, in large part, the model that had been articulated and also reinforced by the post-revolutionary political economists, notably J.-B. Say, and rearticulated by Auguste Comte and his Positivist followers, as well as by Jules Michelet and by Jules Simon. Needless to say, this vision was equally prescriptive. Such views would subsequently congeal into normative laws of social evolution, as is suggested by the remarks of the physician-anthropologist Paul Broca in 1866:[17]

> In the normal condition of things, woman's mission is not merely to bring forth children and suckle them, but to attend to their early education, whilst the father must provide for the subsistence of the family. Everything that affects this normal order necessarily induces a perturbance in the evolution of races, and hence it follows that the condition of women in society must be most carefully studied by the anthropologist.

Should working men ever permit "their" women to work for wages? The envisioned repercussions of the working wife or mother on the fate of the family were debated just as heatedly by articulate working men, who (as the debates at the First International conferences of the later 1860s and the French workers' congresses of the 1870s had highlighted) viewed the "right to work" as a masculine prerogative. They too viewed the woman who worked for pay outside the household [*l'ouvrière*] as a regrettable phenomenon. Indeed, one of the resolutions of the subsequent October 1876 workers' congress in Paris was: "Even as we recognize a woman's right to work, we would prefer that she do nothing outside the household."[18]

---

[16] In my companion volume, *The Woman Question in France, 1400–1870*, see chapter 2 for discussion of the legal status of women in the Civil Code of 1804 and the theorization of the male breadwinner model by male political economists following the French Revolution. Other flashback references (pre-1870) can also be consulted there.

[17] "Broca on Anthropology," *The Anthropological Review*, 6:20 (January 1868), 35–52; quote, 49–50.

[18] Quoted in Christiane Dufrancatel, "Les Amants de la liberté? Stratégies de femme, luttes républicaines, luttes ouvrières," *Les Révoltes Logiques*, n° 5 (Spring–Summer 1977), 61–93; quote, 74.

By the 1880s, the journalist Francisque Sarcey (discussing a recent government move to disallow equal pay to French teachers, depending on their sex) underscored what he took to be wide public acceptance of the male breadwinner model, even as he felt the need to restate it:[19]

> It is understood, at least in our civilized societies, that man must earn his living if he is single, and, if he is married, that of his family as well as his own. It is equally well understood that the wife should be nourished and kept by the man: by her man, to use the energetic expression of the common people, and that, if she works outside her home, where she is assigned the unique care of keeping the house in good order, her salary should be nothing more than a supplement, more or less considerable, to that of the husband who is head of the family. . . . The rule is that the man's responsibility is to earn the money necessary to the upkeep of the family, and the woman to manage the [household] economy.

Such a model could serve as the home of the idealized "mother-educator" but it also had the potential to produce the accomplished homemaker with progressive ideas who would have plenty to say (in due course) about "domesticating the public sphere." From these ranks would come social activists and feminists of the "Belle Epoque" such as Marie Béquet de Vienne (founder of the *Société de l'Allaitement Maternelle* and the *Refuges-Ouvroirs pour les Femmes Enceintes*) and Augusta Moll-Weiss (founder of the *École des Mères*).

3) the secular "mother-centered" family, also entailing a sexual division of labor, with a distinctive sphere of activity for women – to the exclusion of men. In this model, as in the previous two, mothers do not engage in paid labor, but assume full responsibility for raising the children. In its feminist version, the mother heads the family, the father is effectively absent, and the State is called upon to substitute for the husband/father breadwinner in supporting motherhood as a "social function." This model was articulated by Madame E.A.C. (1833) and by Clémence Royer (1874), and championed vigorously in the 1880s and 1890s, particularly by Léonie Rouzade, Aline Valette, and Maria Pognon. Rouzade called repeatedly for direct state financial assistance for mothers, including paid maternity leaves, so that they would not have to depend either on outside employment or on male breadwinners.[20]

---

[19] Francisque Sarcey, "L'Égalité de la femme devant le salaire," *XIXe Siècle*, as reprinted by Léon Richer in his article of the same title in *Le Droit des Femmes*, n° 228 (October 1883), 163–165; quote, 163–164. Richer would reject Sarcey's rationale and would criticize the ministry of public instruction for not according equal pay to women.

[20] This mother-centered model would be most famously elaborated in the mid-1890s by the Swedish educator and reformer Ellen Key, who intended to rehabilitate motherhood (though certainly not

4) the "dual-career" family, another secular model, which entailed a dramatic reorganization of labor, with less onerous requirements of time and energy and a less rigid structure for both sexes. There is no "breadwinner" as such; both adult men and adult women work for pay outside the household. Childcare is delegated to third parties, and/or the community or to the state. Housework is rarely discussed as such, except in Charles Fourier's model, or more frequently, in terms of a woman's "double burden" (viz., in the twentieth century, the Socialist Soviet model and the Israeli Kibbutz model). This egalitarian Fourierist perspective on women and work would barely gain a toehold in French labor circles. This revolutionary perspective would nevertheless be encouraged by a few exceptional working-class movement organizers, notably the socialists Paule Mink and Jules Guesde; its first programmatic victory in France dates from the 1879 Worker's Congress in Marseille.

5) a more recent variant on the "dual-career" family, the "getting to 50/50" or "partnership" model, which also entails a thoroughgoing redistribution of labor, but without relegating childcare to third parties. Partisans of this model reject the assignment of all domestic economy and childrearing tasks to the wife/mother; women and men are both expected to participate in paid labor, and to share equally in household and in-home childcare responsibilities. Hubertine Auclert would articulate this approach in 1881 in response to working men's claims that women were taking jobs away from them. Auclert, in fact, opened up a new line of feminist criticism by challenging the existing sexual division of labor. Women had a perfect right to employment, she maintained, but the precondition for women's paid work was for men to share in the unpaid additional work women were currently doing in male-dominated households. These tasks were not "women's work," she argued. "All those unproductive tasks that are assigned to women in the home are, in society, done by men for money. For money, men sweep, clean, brush shoes and clothes; for money, men sew, for money, men cook, lay and clear tables, and wash dishes. For money, men care for

housework) as women's primary occupation and to oppose the marxist-socialist model, which stipulated that every woman seek independence (from men) through paid labor and delegate childcare to third parties. This statist feminist approach would pick up dramatic support in the early twentieth century, particularly among Scandinavian and German feminists, and foreshadowed certain provisions of twentieth-century welfare states. Opponents of this model, such as Millicent Garrett Fawcett in England, feared what social mischief men might cause if released from their responsibility to support dependents.

young children."[21] Because of the expectations laid on women to do household work in addition to any paid labor they might undertake, employed women had to work far longer and harder than their husbands did. Such household work, Auclert asserted, was not currently valued in French society precisely because women were still treated as men's servants, not as their equals. She clearly laid out the problem of women's "double burden" and proposed the sharing of household labor.

6) a sixth model (or, to some, an "anti-model"), which virtually no one advocated before the twentieth century, but which many French men (and some women) feared: an entirely free-market individualist model, in which women and men are acknowledged as fully independent actors, potentially competing for the same employment – to the presumed disadvantage of men. In fact, the division of the labor market into jobs considered suitable for men and others considered more suitable for women rarely came into play – except in cases where men aspired to capture jobs that women had long held, or resisted women's entry into "male" trades (such as printing). But earlier arguments for women's complete personhood and choice can be found in the publications of Paul Leroy-Beaulieu (see later), and in such statements as that in 1885 of Emilie de Morsier (1843–1896), the Swiss-born cofounder of the French branch of the British and Continental Federation, in an address to the *Oeuvre des Libérées de Saint-Lazare*: "Woman must become independent of man. . . . she can love and respect her husband without sacrificing her intellectual development or her deepest convictions."[22] In the early twentieth century, the radical French feminist physician Madeleine Pelletier would push this individualist argument to its extreme conclusion, treating sexual distinctions as wholly insignificant and discounting the impact of childbearing and childrearing in women's lives.

Countering the free market model was a revolutionary socialist perspective, which called for suppression of the capitalist system as well as the "bourgeois" institutions of marriage and the family. In an 1883 pamphlet, *La Femme et la révolution*, a certain Frédéric Stackelberg would make these arguments; he also called for socialization of the education of children and for basing the *état-civil* of the child on that of the mother alone.[23]

[21] Hubertine Auclert, "Femmes! vous allez prendre notre place," *La Citoyenne*, n° 25 (31 July 1881); transl. in Patricia Hilden, *Working Women and Socialist Politics in France, 1880–1914: A Regional Study* (Oxford, UK: Clarendon Press, 1986), p. 196.

[22] Emilie de Morsier, speech to the *Oeuvre des Libérées de Saint-Lazare*, 25 January 1885; publ. in de Morsier's posthumous collection of speeches and articles, *Mission de la femme: discours et fragments* (Paris: Fischbacher, 1897), p. 75.

[23] See Frédéric Stackelberg, *La Femme et la révolution* (Paris, 1883).

Anarchists such as the geographer Elisée Reclus would object to the institution of marriage itself.[24]

Opponents of women's paid employment staunchly adhered to the prescriptions for the male breadwinner model, in either its Catholic or secular mode. In contrast, proponents of women's paid employment upheld a woman's right to be economically independent, irrespective of her marital status and/or family obligations. In this respect they supported the notion that women were integral individuals, albeit different from male individuals. These were the theoretical bases, underneath which lay two completely opposed approaches to sociopolitical organization – prioritizing the male-headed, hierarchical family unit versus prioritizing the individual's right to independence – for women as well as for men. Today we are still seeking to find the right path between these two approaches. Advocates of both vehemently defended their positions and condemned those of their adversaries. Meanwhile, the mother-centered version, independent of master, husband, or father, remained strictly a minority position, though in the 1890s it would gather increasing traction in feminist circles (as we shall see) among those who opposed *recherche de la paternité* and, indeed, the very idea of women's dependence on male sustenance.

"*Compagnons ou Concurrentes?*" Debating French Women's Employment, 1872–1892

These multiple and seemingly irreconcilable perspectives on "the family" all came into play during the woman question debates that focused on women's employment in France. These debates continued from the early 1870s through the 1880s, culminating in the law of 9 November 1892, which imposed hour limits on employment of all adult women, married or single. Scholars of French women's and gender history have paid extensive attention to the controversies over, implementation of, and objections to protective legislation for women beginning with the law of 1892, but most have glossed over the earlier phase of parliamentary activity, when the legislators of the early Third Republic began to treat women's employment as a problem susceptible to legal intervention – along with that of children.[25]

---

[24] See the speech by the French geographer and professed anarchist Elisée Reclus at the 1882 "free union" celebration for his two daughters, in which he refused to invoke paternal authority or sanction "legal" marriage. "Elisée Reclus – Allocution du père à ses filles et à ses gendres – 1882," *Les Arts de la Vie* (Paris), n° 19 (July 1905), 10–12. Originally published in *L'Art Moderne* (Brussels, no date given).

[25] On the 1892 law and its application, see Mary Lynn Stewart, *Women, Work and the French State: Labour Protection & Social Patriarchy, 1879–1919* (Montreal: McGill/Queens University Press, 1989).

I argue that without understanding the earlier legislative debates on the woman question and the decisions reached during this period one cannot understand the evolution of the debates and how subsequent governmental decisions came to be made.

In the early 1870s, following the Paris Commune and the French defeat, the bitterly divided men who served in the post-imperial National Assembly (from February 1871 to early 1876) found they could only agree on several legislative priorities. One of these was to institute universal *manhood* military conscription. A second was to regulate the labor of women and children. In the latter case, they passed nationally applicable labor legislation that amended and strengthened the earlier child labor law of 1841 and, "for the first time, treated women as specific individuals."[26] This May 1874 law marked the beginning of a long trajectory of French legislation designed to "protect" women in the workplace – to establish (in historian Mary Lynn Stewart's words) a "social patriarchy."[27] And, as historian Joshua Cole points out, it was the debate on this child labor law that effectively authorized a state override on the sweeping paternal authority established by the Civil Code; this override cleared the way for further state incursions on behalf of child welfare, beginning with the regulation of the wet-nursing industry later in 1874 and peaking in the late 1880s with serious encroachments on the sacrosanct paternal authority of the Code (although not on marital authority).[28]

Proposals for new labor legislation had already been under discussion during the late Second Empire, but they came to the floor of the National Assembly in 1871. Some legislators wanted to limit the working hours of all adult women as well as children, but others (including liberal economists who defended employers' rights) resisted the notion of placing any restrictions on the paid labor of adults, whether female or male.[29] In its final form, this new law did not curb the employment of married women (whose employment was in any case legally contingent on a husband's

---

[26] Sylvie Schweitzer, *Les Femmes ont toujours travaillé: Une histoire de leurs métiers, XIXe et XXe siècles* (Paris: Odile Jacob, 2002), p. 35. The book cover subtitle reads *"une histoire du travail des femmes,"* but I am using the title page title here.

[27] The term is taken from the title of Stewart's book (see n. 25).

[28] See Joshua Cole's discussion of the debates on the child (and women's) labor law, "'A Sudden and Terrible Revelation': Motherhood and Infant Mortality in France, 1858–1874," *Journal of Family History*, 21:4 (October 1996), 419–445, esp. 433–436, and Sylvia Schafer, *Children in Moral Danger and the Problem of Government in Third Republic France* (Princeton, NJ: Princeton University Press, 1997).

[29] Lee Shai Weissbach, *Child Labor Reform in Nineteenth-Century France* (Baton Rouge: Louisiana State University Press, 1989), chapter 10.

written permission), but it did create a new juridical category – "*filles mineures*" – young unmarried women between the ages of 16 and 21, and "capped" their work hours in industrial production at twelve hours daily and forbid them to work at night.[30] These were the young working women whose role in the growth of capitalist industry has recently been highlighted by scholars.[31] The male legislators viewed these adolescents, perhaps not surprisingly, as the future wives, homemakers, and mothers of France, who must not be ground down physically and mentally before they could fulfill their maternal mission. This new law also prohibited the employment of all women in underground mining, in line with the English precedent of three decades earlier.[32]

The most significant opposition to women in the workforce came, not surprisingly, from the ultra-Catholic Legitimists, partisans of monarchical restoration to the Bourbon line who supported the God-given order of throne and altar (and therefore were foes of the very notion of a republic, in which authority emanated from "the people"). Their preferred family model was, in Robert Locke's view, not even the conjugal male-headed family favored by many republicans but rather a "hierarchically organized extended family."[33] They would undoubtedly be happy with the vision articulated by Leo XIII in 1878.

The thinking of the Legitimists found articulate allies in the newer Le Play school of social reform, predicated on his quest for "the facts" of social order. Just prior to the debates on women's work, Frédéric Le Play (1806–1882), whom we met (in the companion volume) as a budding social engineer, then senator under the Second Empire and head of the Universal Exposition of 1867, published two books, on the organization of labor (1870) and on the organization of the family (1871) that had important

---

[30] The National Assembly first considered restricting the employment of all women, including adult women, and ultimately decided against doing so in the second reading of the bill, in early February 1873. For an excellent account of the making of the law of 19 May 1874, see Raoul Jay, *Du Travail des enfants et filles mineures dans l'industrie* (Paris: A. Cotillon, 1880); Jay himself supported the prospect of protective legislation for all adult women. See also Cole (n. 28).

[31] Cf. Mary S. Hartman, *The Household and the Making of History: A Subversive View of the Western Past* (Cambridge, UK: Cambridge University Press, 2004), and *Secret Gardens, Satanic Mills: Placing Girls in European History, 1750–1960*, ed. Mary Jo Maynes, Birgitte Søland, & Christina Benninghaus (Bloomington: Indiana University Press, 2005).

[32] See Jay, *Du Travail*, and Weissbach, *Child Labor Reform*, chapters 9 and 10. Other works that address legal issues concerning women's employment include Sylvie Thomas-Buchet, *La Condition juridique des femmes au travail en France au XIXe siècle* (Doctoral thesis, Faculté de Droit et Science Politique, Université de Bourgogne. Lille: Atelier National de Reproduction des Thèses, 2004).

[33] Robert R. Locke, *French Legitimists and the Politics of Moral Order in the Early Third Republic* (Princeton, NJ: Princeton University Press, 1974), p. 144.

implications for the subsequent debates on regulating women's work.[34] In these two works Le Play laid out the issue in stark terms of good and evil. He argued for the restoration of religion (by which he meant strict Roman Catholicism), insisted on a return to the Ten Commandments (the Decalogue), and stipulated that women should have nothing whatsoever to do with the possession or the management of property. In no case should they work outside the home. Invoking "history," scripture, and every other precedent he could muster, Le Play also condemned the "abuse" of the words "liberty," "progress," "equality," and "democracy," and objected to most of the legal changes wrought by the French Revolution. He and his disciples called for complete testamentary freedom for fathers, along with the repression of "seduction."[35] Le Play's followers in the *Société d'Écono-mie Sociale* [Society for Social Economy] continued his investigations in an influential periodical, *La Réforme Sociale* (Social Reform; 52 volumes, 1881–1906), so-called after his important study of the same title, published in 1864.

Other, more forward-looking analysts disputed such assertions. In early 1872 the young liberal political economist Paul Leroy-Beaulieu (1843–1916) published a series of comparative articles on women's employment in the *Revue des Deux Mondes*, which he subsequently issued in book form as *Le Travail des femmes au XIXe siècle* [Women's Work in the Nineteenth Century, 1873].[36] He reminded his readers that the very first public debates following the Second Empire's liberalization of the laws on the press and association in 1868 had been those on women's employment (held at the Vauxhall).[37] More recently, members of the National Assembly's commission on reforms in the child labor laws had engaged the question of women's employment in manufacturing. In his book Leroy-Beaulieu did not mince words, arguing that there was no question more important to the nation than that of women's work:[38]

---

[34] Frédéric Le Play, *L'Organisation du travail, selon la coutume des ateliers et la loi du Décalogue* (Tours: Mame; Paris: Dentu, 1870), and *L'Organisation de la famille, selon le vrai modèle signalé par l'histoire de toutes les races et de tous les temps* (Paris: Tequi, bibliothècaire de l'œuvre Saint-Michel, 1871).

[35] For a recent scholarly analysis of Le Play's later works, see Alan Pitt, "Frederic Le Play and the Family: Paternalism and Freedom in the French Debates of the 1870s," *French History*, 12:1 (March 1998), 677–689.

[36] See Paul Leroy-Beaulieu, *Le Travail des femmes au XIXe siècle* (Paris: Charpentier, 1873); his earlier articles included "Les Ouvrières de fabrique autrefois et aujourd'hui," *Revue des Deux Mondes*, 1 February 1872, and "Le Travail des femmes dans la petite industrie," *Revue des Deux Mondes*, 15 May 1872.

[37] On these important lectures at the Vauxhall, and the earlier contributions of Michelet and Simon, referred to later in this chapter, see *The Woman Question in France*, chapter 6.

[38] Quote, Leroy-Beaulieu, *Travail des femmes*, p. 1.

This question concerns not only the individual interests of the *ouvrière*, but also the general interests of the nation. The constitution of the family, the education of upcoming generations, the conservation, improvement or degeneration of the race, or in other terms, the moral, economic, and even the physical state of a people depends in great part on the organization of women's work in that country.

Leroy-Beaulieu defended women from Proudhonist allegations of inferiority and insisted, against the claims of those who staunchly supported the male breadwinner model, that the individual, not the family was the principal social unit.[39]

Woman is not an incomplete, inferior creature; as an adult she possesses equal rights with men in the law, having also the capacity to acquire [property], and also the capacity to work. Although she may be physically weaker than man, nothing suggests that she is either morally or intellectually inferior.

Leroy-Beaulieu would offer rejoinders to the earlier cries of alarm about the *ouvrière* from Jules Michelet and Jules Simon (see my companion volume, chapter 6) and to the well-meaning projects of philanthropists who wished to prohibit women from working in industry; he addressed some men's concerns about State primacy in decreeing social organization, as well as their fears that women's employment was prejudicial to men.[40] He observed that, in fact, the wages of women employed in factory production had been going up steadily, and that pay by the piece tended to level out the pay to women and men in the same industries. He proposed that one needed to look both to laws and to morals.[41] With regard to morals, he (like Le Play) advocated a law that would punish seducers and strenuously condemned the absence of a law reauthorizing *recherche de la paternité*. In addition, Leroy-Beaulieu argued that "one of the best ways to return mothers to the family is to employ the young [single] women [*jeunes filles*] in the factories from the age of 16 until the ages of 22 or 25. This may seem severe [*rude*] but it is often necessary." That way a girl could earn, put money aside, and provide herself with "independence and to assure the prosperity of her future family." "The young girl who amasses a dowry in the *fabrique* [manufactory] so that she

---

[39] Leroy-Beaulieu, *Travail des femmes*, p. 200.

[40] These aspects of Leroy-Beaulieu's argument are clearly laid out in the review-essay signed "T.S." in the October 1873 issue of the *Journal des Économistes*. See T. S., "L'Émancipation de la femme, considérée dans ses rapports avec le socialisme et l'économie politique," *Journal des Économistes*, 32:1 (October 1873), 5–29, esp. 20–21.

[41] Leroy-Beaulieu, "Ouvrières de fabrique," 645.

can stay home when she marries and raise her family in good conditions, this is true progress."[42] He opposed special legislation directed specifically at women workers, but did call for much shorter workdays. He was enthusiastic about the examples of the Lowell mills in Massachusetts and the silk-working ateliers in southern France (modeled on the Lowell mills) where older girls could earn money for their families and their own dowries while effectively cloistered and thereby protected.

The law of 19 May 1874 was enacted under the government of "moral order," which followed the overthrow of the Thiers ministry. There would be no more legislation of that sort passed until 1892, when the restrictions on the work of all women, including married women, gave rise to acute controversy. But throughout the later 1870s and 1880s, as France's economic situation worsened, debaters on both sides of the woman question (encompassing the leaders of both the nascent workers' movement and the nascent women's rights movement) continued to engage noisily with the question of women's employment and with the even more dire consequences of their unemployment.

In March 1877, federal Switzerland became the first European nation-state to regulate the labor of [all] adult women, by banning their work at night and requiring that any pregnant woman take unpaid maternity leave. Historian Regina Wecker emphasizes that "the 1877 law ... functioned as an opening wedge not only for the terms of international protective legislation but also for a retooled conception of protection: special protection for women only."[43] This legal move set the bar for debates on the woman question in every other European country including France; the Swiss precedent was quickly adopted in the German Empire (1878) and in the Russian Empire (1885). Were women workers consulted about such legislation? Need we even ask?

The leading French male advocate of women's rights, Léon Richer, took up the defense of women's work where Flora Tristan, Pauline Roland, Jenny P. d'Héricourt, Julie Daubié, and Paule Mink had left off. In midsummer 1877 he published *La Femme libre*, a thick book in which he addressed the issue of how women could be free. In addition to advocating major reforms in French family law concerning the adverse situation of wives, Richer forcefully opposed the male-breadwinner solution to

---

[42] All quotes above from Leroy-Beaulieu, "Ouvrières de fabrique," 653.

[43] See Regina Wecker, "Equality for Men? Factory Laws, Protective Legislation for Women in Switzerland, and the Swiss Effort for International Protection," in *Protecting Women: Labor Legislation in Europe, the United States, and Australia, 1880–1920*, ed. Ulla Wikander, Alice Kessler-Harris, & Jane Lewis (Urbana: University of Illinois Press, 1995), p. 72.

women's survival, arguing that "woman, even when married, must be able to live from her own salary if she so desires":[44]

> Far from thinking about removing workers [bras in French] from production, we must give it new ones. What we must do is modify the present conditions of women's work; we must moralize the workshop, we must find a way of reconciling . . . the interests of the ouvrière with the respect due to every woman and with the obligations of mothers.

Richer explicitly confirmed the economic value of a wife's housework, but noted in the same breath that this calculation was rarely made, and that, in appearance, the wife remained dependent on her husband. For dignity's sake, a married mother "had the right to demand" that she be able to contribute to the family's expenses – that she should be able to say, "I too bring something to the household."[45] In conclusion Richer insisted that "every human being, man or woman, should be able to support him/herself."[46] The exploitation of women must end, and wages be equally distributed so that a woman could cover her needs "without being obliged to resort to the vile practice of prostitution."

The question Richer's remarks raised was how women could possibly survive on their own in an economy that, given current conditions, so favored men? Indeed, the specter of prostitution – often referred to, rather disparagingly or facetiously (depending on one's point of view), as the "world's oldest profession," and even more facetiously as the "fifth quarter" of the workday – hovered over these debates. Ever since Dr. Parent-Duchâtelet had first investigated and publicized the surge in the numbers of prostitutes in Paris during the mid-1830s, the flip side of the public obsession about women's employment (or being maintained in marriage) centered around the impossible situation that did not permit poor women to make ends meet when they could not find decently paid work or (as was the case in the highly seasonal garment industry) had been laid off. It also centered on the adverse consequences for maternity.

In 1875 the Francophone English reformer Josephine Butler (1828–1906) had brought her campaign against government-regulated prostitution to continental Europe. She and her supporters targeted the French regulation system, which had inspired so many physicians and hygienists outside France to attempt its importation, as well as the emerging international traffic in women that fed the brothels. Butler, a devout Protestant, framed

---

[44] Léon Richer, *La Femme libre* (Paris: E. Dentu, 1877), p. 90.   [45] Richer, *Femme libre*, p. 91.
[46] Richer, *Femme libre*, "Conclusion," p. 335.

her arguments in terms of Christian morality and justice, as in her tract *Une voix dans le desert* [A Voice in the Desert, 1875; 2nd ed., 1876], but many of her supporters squarely addressed the economic realities of under- or unemployment that drove poor women to prostitute themselves. Thus in Geneva, in September 1877, at the first congress of the British and Continental Federation for the Abolition of Government Regulation of Prostitution, which (in the late 1890s, after several name changes, finally became known as the International Abolitionist Federation), the subject of women's employment, or the consequences of no employment or grossly underpaid or seasonal-only employment occupied center stage. In this Swiss venue, women and men from multiple countries spoke out in a single voice against the appalling difficulties that young women faced in finding safe, sustainable employment.[47] It soon became clear that this problem transcended national boundaries. Caroline de Barrau from France reported that the average wage for women workers in Paris, whose employment was mostly seasonal, was about two francs per day – far from adequate for survival.[48] The Italian women's rights activist Anna Maria Mozzoni even qualified Richer's optimism: "Everyone has the right to live from his work, but women seem to have more of a right to die since it is so difficult for them to find honest and sufficient work."[49]

In late 1877, following resolution of the 16 May ministerial crisis in Paris, leaders of the reborn French workers' movement and the French women's rights movement felt freer to publicize their positions. In October 1876 Jules Guesde (1845–1922), back from Geneva where he had fled to avoid prosecution for defending the Paris Commune in print, had come out strongly in favor of women's right to work in particular, and women's freedom in general, arguing against the die-hard Proudhonians in the

---

[47] See the series of publications from Anne Summers's project on Josephine Butler's international networks, including Summers, "Liberty, Equality, Morality: The Attempt to Sustain an International Campaign against the Double Sexual Standard," *Sextant*, n°s 23–24 (2007), 133–153; republished in *Globalizing Feminisms 1789–1945*, ed. Karen Offen (London & New York: Routledge, 2010), pp. 26–35. See also the special issue, "Gender, Religion, and Politics: Josephine Butler's Campaigns in International Perspective (1875–1959)", ed. Anne Summers, *Women's History Review*, 17:2 (April 2008).

[48] Caroline de Barrau, *Étude sur le salaire du travail féminin à Paris*. Extrait des *Actes du Congrès de Genève, Fédération brittanique, continentale et générale, Sept. 1877* (Neuchâtel: Bureau du *Bulletin continental*, 1877), p. 66. In Geneva, *La Solidarité*, n° 17 (December 1878) praised Barrau's study for pointing out the errors in France's official statistics. An expanded version, Caroline de Barrau, *Le Salaire du Travail féminin* (1879), is cited in *La Solidarité*, n° 19 (June 1879), 15.

[49] Anna Maria Mozzoni, in Rina Macrelli, *Indegna schiavitù: Anna Maria Mozzoni e la lotta contra la prostituzione di Stato* (Rome: Riuniti, 1981); transl. Mary Gibson, in her book *Prostitution and the State in Italy, 1860–1915* (New Brunswick, NJ: Rutgers University Press, 1986), p. 53.

workers' movement. Economic freedom for women was, in his view (as in that of Léon Richer), a necessity. However, for Guesde, the question of women's work was only one part of the picture: he asserted that both men and women were grossly underpaid. They must be assured "of the integral development and free application of their talents," he said. What was more, "Workers must be guaranteed the full value of their labor, irrespective of sex."[50] Guesde's new publication, *L'Égalité* (founded in mid-November 1877), would not address this topic again until late January 1878.[51]

Both the workers' movement and the women's rights movement organized congresses in 1878. The Second Workers' Congress, held in Lyon (28 January – 8 February), was attended by 136 delegates from twenty-four cities.[52] The topic of women's work headed the congress agenda. The day previous to its opening, Guesde again published on "Le travail des femmes" [Women's work], arguing (as historian Patricia Hilden put it) "against widespread male prejudices."[53] He emphasized that women's work was but one part of "the great question of labor in general" and must not be considered separately. In the preceding article, "La loi des salaires" [The law of salaries/wages] Guesde had called (in the short term) for a minimum below which wages must not be permitted to go in order to assure a worker's subsistence and that of his family. As concerned women's work, however, he argued that neither men nor women were being paid what their work was worth, but women were paid less precisely because they could fall back on the exploitation of their own bodies to make up the difference. Under the current abysmal circumstances, he could understand

---

[50] Jules Guesde, articles "Le travail des femmes" & "Le travail et la femme," in *Les Droits de l'Homme* (16 & 18 October 1876); reprinted in Jules Guesde, *Çà et là: de la propriété, la commune, le collectivisme devant le 10ᵉ chambre, la question des loyers, les grands magasins* (Paris: M. Rivière, 1914), pp. 113–122; quote, p. 118. Hearty thanks to Marilyn Boxer and Chips Sowerwine for confirming these references. See Marilyn Jacoby Boxer, "Socialism Faces Feminism in France: 1879–1913" (Ph.D. dissertation, University of California at Riverside, 1975) and Charles Sowerwine, *Les Femmes et le socialisme* (Paris: FNSP, 1978), pp. 24–25.

[51] Contrary to the claims of some scholars, the newly founded workers' periodical, *L'Égalité*, edited by Guesde, did not begin its publication in November 1877 with a series of articles on women's work. I have consulted the entire run in the reprint edition: *Collection complète de L'Égalité, le Socialiste: chronologie et table des matières* (Paris: Éditions Hier et Demain, 1974), vol. 1 (1877–1880), at the Musée Social, 31 May 2011.

[52] See Leslie Derfler, *Paul Lafargue and the Founding of French Marxism, 1842–1882* (Cambridge, MA: Harvard University Press, 1991), pp. 165–166.

[53] Jules Guesde, "Le Travail des femmes," *L'Egalite* (27 January 1878), 2–3; reproduced in *Collection complète* (see n. 50). Patricia Hilden nicely summarizes this article in her book, *Working Women and Socialist Politics in France, 1880–1914: A Regional Study* (Oxford, UK: Clarendon Press, 1986), pp. 177–178.

why male workers wanted women out of the workforce, but he advocated taking a broader view in which women had just as much of a right to work as men, and in which women should not be economically dependent on men or subject to their whims and approval. Taking a shot at the die-hard Proudhonists, Guesde argued that a dependent woman kept in a household by her husband was no less a "courtesan" or harlot than one who worked for pay outside it. Like Paule Mink in 1868, Guesde called for better working conditions, a change in the organization of labor, one that would not only end existing abuses but also allow employment to become "the principal element, the condition *sine qua non* of human happiness."[54] In the issue of 17 February 1878, *L'Égalité* reported on the conclusions of the Lyon congress, which in respect to women's work favored the formation of women's unions, equal pay, the eight-hour day, and many other reforms.[55]

The First International Congress on Women's Rights, held in Paris (25 July–9 August 1878) during the International Exposition had 220 registered participants, hailing from a number of different countries.[56] Its agenda, too, was remarkably radical. Eugénie Pierre (1844–1898; later Potonié-Pierre) acted as secretary of International Women's Rights congress. She also provided a serial account in *Le Devoir*, beginning on 25 August, in which she summarized the congress debates and published its resolutions.[57] During the sessions on economic issues, orators would call for better pay for women workers, equal pay for equal production, equal access to the (liberal) professions, as well as abolition of regulated prostitution, the right to work, and the suppression of privileges accorded to convent and prison labor that seriously undercut the pay of women trying to survive in the free market. Of particular interest is the third resolution, which called for "liberty of work, equal for the woman and the man – and

---

[54] Guesde, "Travail des femmes," p. 3. Emphasis in original.

[55] In this same issue (17 February 1878), Guesde would also report briefly on the resolutions of the January 1878 American women's suffrage congress in Washington, D.C. In March 1880, Guesde returned to the subject in "L'émancipation des femmes et le socialisme," in which he called on women and the proletariat to join hands and march together; liberty, he indicated, can only be founded on economic justice. See *L'Égalité*, issue of 31 March 1880 (2nd series, n° 11) reprinted in *Collection complète*, vol. 1.

[56] See the published proceedings: *Congrès international des droits des femmes, 25 juillet 1878. Actes et compte rendu des séances plenières* (Paris: Auguste Ghio, 1878). The list of registered participants appears on pp. 8–10.

[57] Eugénie Pierre, "Le Congrès du droit des femmes," *Le Devoir; Journal des Réformes Sociales* (25 August, 8 September, & 22 September 1878). Pierre's summary may also have appeared elsewhere in the French press. In Geneva, Pierre's account, "Mes Impressions sur le Congrès du Droit des Femmes," appeared in *La Solidarité*, n° 17 (December 1878). It may also have appeared in Belgium.

affirmation of the value and worth of household and domestic labor [*de la valeur et du mérite des travaux de ménage et d'intérieur*]." This attempt to gain economic recognition for housework is noteworthy, as it offered a direct challenge to the views of the earlier political economists who privileged "production" to the detriment of household work.

Beginning in August 1879, Eugénie Pierre published a series of four articles on "women's work" in *Le Droit des Femmes*.[58] Mlle Pierre based her discussion on two principles that she considered fundamental for the organization of labor for women – the necessity of equal pay for equal work, and the recognition that employment should be decently paid and not exhausting. Like Richer – and Guesde – she contested the notion that women should be economically dependent on a man's family wage. She did allow that a woman's first duty was to nourish and rear her children, and that society should protect mother and child, but she also insisted (as had Juliette Lamber[t)] Adam in the late 1850s) that childbearing and childrearing was not a lifelong project and that, moreover, not all women have children. Muscular strength, she remarked (in this, echoing her predecessor Jeanne Deroin), "is no longer of first importance; it is science and intelligence that makes the world move forward."[59] Thus, she claimed, the playing field for women in the field of employment had been leveled. Elaboration of these new ideas about women's work would continue within women's rights circles, but the principles were firmly in place.

Republican men exhibited a range of views. Some qualified their positions, endorsing specific reforms but objecting to others that might further erode women's domestic roles. For example, in his 1879 synthesis *La Femme au XIXe Siecle* [Women in the Nineteenth Century], the committed secular democrat Adhémard Lecler[e] presented his views on the state of the woman question in a long pamphlet. He affirmed that women were indeed oppressed. Asserting that if woman is man's associate, she is his equal, he argued that both laws and morals would require substantive reform. As concerned her "work," however, he insisted that a woman's duty (*devoir*) was surely to nurse and raise her children; he viewed her employment outside the home as pernicious. Lecler expressed his distress about depopulation, and argued that "the family" needed women's attention; he objected to infanticide and to the practice of farming out babies to wet nurses. Like the abolitionists, he was very critical of legalized

---

[58] Eugénie Pierre, "Le Travail des femmes," series in *Le Droit des Femmes*, n°s 177–180 (3 August, 7 September, 1 October, & 2 November 1879).

[59] E. Pierre, "Travail des femmes," *Le Droit des Femmes*, n° 177 (3 August 1879), 117.

prostitution and called for the suppression of the licensed brothels [*maisons de tolérance*] and the morals police [*police des moeurs*]. Like other secularists, he endorsed legitimization of common law marriages and civil divorce. Work must be reorganized, he said, and shaped to the needs of "nature, justice, and humanity." "We do not have the right to let industry encroach on the rights of maternity, to let exploitation violate morals and engender depopulation." Laissez-faire was not the answer. "Our future depends on woman as mother and citizen, free and virtuous, equal to her husband and her sons, instructed and wise. To let her live the life of the workshop, is to make … an incapable and bad mother." In conclusion, Lecler proclaimed that "the fate of nations lies in women's hands; the morals of the family as well as the entire country depend on her morality." Democratic men must campaign for women's freedom![60] Lecler's tract was not exactly a brief for women's autonomy through earning, but it nevertheless offered a statement that was quite progressive for the time. Clearly, the debates on women's work were far from over.

In June 1884 members of the Paris-based *Société d'Économie Politique* [Society for Political Economy] would take up the question: "Whether woman, from the standpoint of economics, is better placed in the family foyer or in the atelier." Jules Simon and Frédéric Passy had proposed this question for discussion. The renowned peace advocate Passy spoke eloquently against the employment of wives and mothers outside the household, on the grounds that it was contrary to the necessary sexual division of labor. But, having made this declaration of principle, he went on to advocate a series of measures to improve the situation of those women who had no alternative but to work for pay. This, indeed, was progress. The suggested measures included equal pay for equal work, reforms in the Civil Code (Passy insisted, as had Richer, that the articles of the Napoleonic Code which rendered married women legally incompetent were indefensible), and provision of women doctors to attend to the medical needs of women and children.

Several speakers at the session, among them Paul Leroy-Beaulieu and Émile Cheysson, expressed their hopes for the spread of home-based employment for women, utilizing machines powered by electric motors or compressed air. The final speaker, E. Founier de Flaix, countered the naysayers by defending the potential of industrial work for women, arguing that it could be – and indeed had already been in some cases –

---

[60] Adhémard Lecler[e], *La Femme au XIXe siècle* (Paris: Impr. de Claverie, 1879), pp. 20–21, and Conclusion.

organized in a manner that did not erode the domestic commitments of married women workers. He asserted that paid work was a prerequisite for the emancipation of women, and that the group workshop [*atelier*] could in fact contribute to the improvement of women's condition.[61] The audience's reaction to these remarks is not recorded, but it was clear that these economists had begun to confront the harsh realities of women's economic situation, at last taking into account those who were neither married nor mothers.

That same year (1884) the French *Conseil Supérieur du Travail* [Higher Council on Labor] launched an inquiry to businesses and various official bodies, including the chambers of commerce and *chambres syndicales*, concerning the question of prohibiting women's work at night. In November 1886 the government would put forward a proposal to revise the labor laws of 1874 such as to directly address the regulation of women's work.[62] This law would eventually be enacted in late 1892, over the protests of many women's rights advocates who considered it unduly discriminatory to restrict adult women's work without equally restricting the work of adult men. We will say more about this law and its consequences later in the book.

"Morality," Legalized Prostitution, and the Traffic in Women and Children

Challenging the Civil and Penal Codes, implementing public education for girls, and debating women's right to work only began to address some of the major societal problems inherited by Third Republic France. A clear-eyed look at the harsh realities of many poor women's lives, especially in the burgeoning cities and industrial centers of nineteenth-century France rudely challenged republican fantasies of domesticity for all, citizen-mothers and mother-educators. Many of the more objectionable practices can be found throughout history, but the forms they took in later nineteenth-century France were direct responses to legislative discrimination and institutional negligence, which had taken advantage of (or feigned blindness to) poor women's adverse economic status or had dramatized questions of "morality" that did not even address, much less

---

[61] See the report of this debate by Charles Le Tort, *Journal des Économistes*, 26:3 (June 1884), 445–459, as well as the report by Léon Richer in *Le Droit des Femmes*, n° 236 (6 July 1884), 104–106.

[62] See Michelle Zancarini-Fournel, "Archéologie de la loi de 1892 en France," pp. 75–92 in *Différence des sexes et protection sociale* (*XIXe-XXe siècles*), ed. Leora Auslander & Michelle Zancarini-Fournel (St. Denis: Presses Universitaires de Vincennes, 1995), p. 80.

resolve the economic dilemmas of destitute single mothers, who, for one or another reasons, had no male "protector" or "supporter" to rely on. These practices included the legal as well as social stigmatization of children born out of wedlock. As historian Rachel Fuchs has documented, the combination of social and economic difficulties led such unfortunate women, especially young unwed mothers (of which there were a very great number) and poor women workers (often married), to regrettable practices, such as farming out their infants to rural mercenary wet nurses or outright child abandonment, and to criminal practices ranging from stealing to abortion, prostitution, or even, when they were completely desperate, to infanticide and suicide.[63]

Mothers whose babies survived faced continuing problems, not the least of which was infant mortality. Historical demographers who have studied infant mortality in Paris and the immediate region estimate the mortality rate for girl babies at around 20 percent of those born.[64] The "migration" of babies out of Paris due to the wet-nursing industry made keeping track of their fate that much more complicated. The demographers note that in many cases, infant births and deaths were very likely underreported, and that the real infant mortality figures were undoubtedly higher, especially among those born outside marriage. In a situation where depopulation and national strength were becoming increasingly serious concerns (as underscored by the research of Dr. Brochard of Lyon in the 1860s and early 1870s), something absolutely had to be done – but what?[65] Would the best strategy be to do something to assist the mothers in keeping and raising these children, or to intervene in other ways that would directly benefit the children? Or both?

These human problems were immense, and they resulted from abusive consequences for poor mothers and their offspring of the "sexual relation

---

[63] See the invaluable publications of Rachel Ginnis Fuchs on these questions: *Abandoned Children: Foundlings and Child Welfare in Nineteenth-Century France* (Albany, NY: SUNY Press, 1984); *Poor and Pregnant in Paris: Strategies for Survival in the Nineteenth Century* (New Brunswick, NJ: Rutgers University Press, 1992); and *Contested Paternity: Constructing Families in Modern France* (Baltimore: Johns Hopkins University Press, 2008).

[64] See the discussion in Etienne Van der Walle & Samuel H. Preston, "Mortalité de l'infance au XIXe siècle à Paris et dans le département de la Seine," *Population*, 29:1(January–February 1974), 89–107.

[65] See the publications of Dr. André-Théodore Brochard: *De l'Allaitement maternel, étudié au point de vue de la mère, de l'enfant, et de la société* (Paris: E. Maillet, 1868; 2nd revised ed., Lyon: Josserand, 1874); *Des Causes de la dépopulation en France et les moyens d'y remédier; Mémoire lu au Congrès médical de Lyon, septembre 1872* (Lyon: Librairie Médicale de J.-P. Megret, 1873); *L'Ouvrière, mère de famille* (Lyon: Josserand, 1874); *Le Guide pratique de la jeune mère, ou l'éducation du nouveau-né* (Lyon: P.-N. Josserand, 1874; 4th ed. 1899); and *La Vérité sur les enfants trouvés* (Paris: Plon, 1876), in which he expressed his shock at the high number of abortions and infanticides by women since the closing of the *tours* in 1846.

of the sexes." The French often said that "Men make the laws, women make the morals." But when it came to recognizing the dominant pattern of male sexual behavior – irresponsible promiscuity – that prevailed in the mid-to-late nineteenth century, some women and especially feminists, would judge it (and its consequences for women) harshly, and to call for a single standard of behavior, even as many others tried to ignore it or rationalize it.

Identifying the problems was one thing; addressing the causes and implementing solutions was quite another. These problems could hardly be solved by merely changing laws, though that was a starting place. Since the 1830s many reformers had addressed them, raising public awareness but not engendering satisfactory solutions. In the 1860s Julie-Victoire Daubié had spoken of these issues at length in her book, La Femme pauvre. Léon Richer had laid them out repeatedly in his various publications of the 1870s. It was significant, then, that in 1878, at the First International Congress on Women's Rights, the conference organizers bundled all these abuses into a long list of resolutions for action, which they framed in the name of the Republic and liberty.[66]

High on the list was the International Congress's challenge to government-regulated prostitution and the Paris morals police [police des moeurs], which managed it. Certainly French men seeking sexual encounters (not to mention foreigners on holiday) were well aware of its existence, and the French urban culture of the time made it easy for them to find prostitutes. In the nineteenth century, the number of women operating as prostitutes in French cities had begun to grow dramatically, attracting the attention not only of the men who consorted with them, but also that of physicians and various social reformers who worried primarily about the rising rates of venereal diseases and their unintended social consequences.

As explained in my companion book (in chapter 6), France, under Napoléon, had instituted a system for prostitution that was historically unique and, for women, highly invasive of their bodies and erosive of their civil rights. This system existed for the convenience of male clients, ostensibly to "protect" their health by certifying the prostitutes, both those confined to the brothels and the filles en carte [women registered as prostitutes with

---

[66] The 1878 Congress resolutions included repealing the constraints on freedom of speech and association; restoring the tours to receive abandoned children; repealing Article 340 of Penal Code which forbade paternity suits; placing better controls on the wet-nursing industry; providing economic and social alternatives for unwed mothers; providing state subsidies for mothers; raising the age of consent (to marriage and sexual activity) for girls (law on seduction); and, not least, abolishing regulated prostitution and the morals police.

the morals police] who operated outside, as free from venereal diseases. Not only did municipal governments, via the morals police, regulate the brothels but the registered prostitutes had to show up for periodic intrusive (and unsanitary) genital inspections; infected prostitutes would be isolated and treated.[67]

In the 1860s the British parliament decided to copy this French system, by authorizing the Contagious Disease Acts of 1866 and 1869 to apply it in port cities. A small contingent of concerned English women, including Harriet Martineau and Josephine Butler, petitioned the Parliament to cease and desist. This system, ostensibly designed to protect the health of soldiers and sailors by sanctioning the roundup and registration of any woman found out on the street, was, they argued, an outright violation of women's rights.

In the course of a long but ultimately successful campaign against the Contagious Disease Acts in Britain, Josephine Butler learned that France was, in fact, the "mother" of all governmental regulation schemes and that its system of licensing, inspection, and patrolling of prostitution was being imitated to a greater or lesser degree throughout Europe. Among its various effects, the French system had spawned an international network of physicians eager to spread the regulation system, as well as a robust commercial traffic in underage female flesh to feed men's taste for novelty in the brothels. And so, in the mid-1870s, Butler and her associates organized an international coalition of reformers of both sexes (the British and Continental Federation against the State Regulation of Vice, known in French as the *Fédération Britannique et Continentale*). With headquarters in francophone Switzerland, this federation held international conferences in Geneva (1877 and 1889), in Neuchâtel (1882), in Basel (1884), and in Lausanne (1887). Aimé Humbert of Neuchâtel (formerly a Prussian dependency) edited the Federation's monthly bulletin. The ultimate goal

---

[67] See Alexandre-Jean-Baptiste Parent-Duchâtelet, *De la Prostitution dans la ville de Paris*. 2 vols. (Brussels: Hauman, Cattoir, & cie., 1836; 3rd ed. 1857). Also F.-F.-A. Béraud, *Les Filles publiques de Paris, et la police qui les régit* (Paris & Leipzig: Desforges et cie, 1839). Alain Corbin's magisterial study, *Les Filles de noce: Misère sexuelle et prostitution aux 19ᵉ et 20ᵉ siecles* (Paris: Aubier Montaigne, 1978), transl. by Alan Sheridan as *Women for Hire: Prostitution and Sexuality in France after 1850* (Cambridge, MA: Harvard University Press, 1990), provides an in-depth look at the literature and archival traces of regulated (and not-so-regulated) prostitution in Paris and other major French cities; Jill Harsin's complementary work, *Policing Prostitution in Nineteenth-Century Paris* (Princeton, NJ: Princeton University Press, 1985), addresses the early nineteenth-century Parisian prostitution industry and its regulatory literature. See also the important publications on the morals police by Jean-Marc Berlière, "Police et libertés sous la IIIe République: le problème de la police des moeurs," *Revue Historique*, n° 574 (April–June 1990), 235–276; and his book, *La Police des moeurs sous la IIIe République* (Paris: Seuil, 1992).

of this coalition was the demolition of the French regulation system, beginning with the morals police.[68] Accompanying this effort, and closely allied with it was a new religiously inspired organization of women called the *Amies de la Jeune Fille*, which began to track the routes of the traffic in women and send its members to meet underage girls and young women travelling abroad in search of employment at railroad stations and ports; their objective was to keep these girls out of the clutches of the procurers and pimps who frequented these hubs in search of their prey.[69] The work of this association, heavily Protestant in character, would be supplemented a few years later by the founding of a parallel Catholic women's organization based in Fribourg.[70]

Josephine Butler was adamantly opposed to the "double moral standard" and her views on this subject strongly marked the work of the British and Continental Federation. As one historian summarized her position, "Butler's critique of prostitution was economic. She saw it as a totally male-created entity, justified by the equally socially constructed double standard. Men denied women independent employment, then divided them into a double workforce, one part to minister to their domestic comfort, the other to their 'need' for lust without responsibility. Butler sees both sets of women as slaves, their interests set against each other."[71]

In France, the reformer Emilie de Morsier (1843–1896) and the journalist-deputy Yves Guyot (1843–1928), assisted by Maria Deraismes, Auguste Desmoulins, and a number of others, including Mme H[annah] Chapman (the second wife of Dr. John Chapman, proprietor and publisher of the *Westminster Review*, who was then living in Paris and had

[68] On the program, personnel, and politics of the British and Continental Federation, see Anne-Marie Käppeli, *Sublime Croisade: Ethique et politique du féminisme protestant, 1875–1928* (Carouge-Geneva: Éditions Zoé, 1990). Käppeli's biographically focused book must now be supplemented by Anne Summers's investigations of Josephine Butler's international networks for campaigning against government-regulated prostitution and the "white slave trade." See the special issue of *Women's History Review* (London), 17:2 (April 2008), ed. by Summers and cited in n. 47. The papers – and library holdings – of the British & Continental Federation / Fédération Abolitionniste International are housed at the Bibliothèque de Genève (formerly the Bibliothèque Publique et Universitaire).

[69] See Emily Machen's investigation of the French branch of the *Amies de la Jeune Fille*: "Traveling with Faith: The Creation of Women's Immigrant Aid Associations in Nineteenth and Twentieth Century France," *Journal of Women's History* 23:3 (Fall 2011), 89–112.

[70] Catherine Galley, "Les Formes d'un engagement féminin: L'Association catholique internationale des Oeuvres de Protection de la jeune fille (1896–1920)." Mémoire de licence, Faculté des Lettres, Université de Fribourg (Suisse), 1996. My thanks to Catherine Bosshart for procuring a photocopy of this thesis.

[71] See Alison Milbank, "Josephine Butler: Christianity, Feminism and Social Action," in *Disciplines of Faith: Studies in Religion, Politics and Patriarchy*, ed. Jim Obelkevich, Lyndal Roper, & Raphael Samuel (London: Routledge & Kegan Paul, 1987), pp. 154–164; quote, p. 155.

become an authority on the subject of regulated prostitution) raised the banner of a new abolitionism.[72] Outraged over the treatment of women (and not solely poor women) by the Paris morals police, in 1878 these activists founded the French branch of the *Fédération Britannique et Continentale*, which they baptized as the *Association [Française] pour l'Abolition de la Prostitution Réglementée* (hereafter, AFAPR). After encountering some initial obstacles, the group finally received formal authorization from the Paris prefect of police in mid-June 1879. This authorization seems curious, considering that the organization's primary goal was to rid Paris, and France, of the branch called the *police des moeurs*.

This new French organization affirmed individual liberty for women. Its announced goal was to demonstrate not only that the system of government-regulated prostitution was outrageous from every point of view but, in particular, failed the test as a program for public hygiene, its ostensible reason for being. The physician members of the AFAPR would insist, proofs in hand, that this system had not produced any drop in the incidence of male venereal disease. In the short term, the AFAPR announced its very practical and political objective of forcing the abolition of the Paris morals police.[73] The group invited the venerable Victor Schoelcher to serve as honorary president; he was a living symbol of the continuity between the abolition of black slavery in 1848 and the current campaign to end what was now called "white slavery" (and, later, the traffic in women and children). The AFAPR's headquarters were located at the Paris home of the Chapmans, 212 rue de Rivoli.

France's republican government had established freedom of association in 1881, which permitted the establishment of all sorts of groups, charitable, philanthropic, and others; however, ingrained habits of waiting for the government to act seemed hard to overcome. Several years later, Dr. Chapman would severely criticize the French populace as uninterested in supporting philanthropic efforts of any kind, either financially or by their active support, expecting the government to provide what is needed, "to minister to their every need."[74] Emilie de Morsier would echo

---

[72] See Chapman's long review-essay "Prostitution in Paris," *Westminster Review* (April 1883), 494–521, which discussed at length Yves Guyot's 1880 report to the Paris Municipal Council and his 1882 book, *La Prostitution*. Details on Chapman, his second marriage to the widow Hannah Macdonald, and his Paris residency are from F. N. L. Poynter, "John Chapman (1821–1894): Publisher, Physician, and Medical Reformer," *Journal of the History of Medicine and Allied Sciences*, 5 (Winter 1950), 1–22.

[73] *Premier Rapport de l'Association pour l'Abolition de la Prostitution Réglementée 1878–1879* (Rochefort: Impr. Triaud et Guy, 1879).

[74] See Chapman, "Prostitution in Paris," 494, 510.

Chapman's claim: "France does not yet know what self-government means. When people express the desire for a reform, they sit down, fold their arms, and wait for the government to act."[75] However, Chapman made exception for those friends and colleagues who were actually attempting to press for change, especially Yves Guyot, a fearless crusader whom he highly admired (Guyot had launched the initial campaign against the morals police in 1876, with an exposé in *La Lanterne*, for which he went to jail). Chapman was certain that the regulation system and the morals police were "doomed to inevitable extinction"; little did he know that this struggle was far from over.[76]

Early in 1879, the French abolitionists launched a vigorous offensive. In March, members of the AFAPR (including Emilie de Morsier) testified before the *Commission de la Police des Moeurs*, called into being by the Paris Municipal Council, which included several key republican political figures who sympathized with the AFAPR's goals. Emilie de Morsier called for the abolition of the morals police and also condemned the Saint-Lazare prison, where women who might be criminals, prostitutes, or simply detained were all mixed indiscriminately together.[77] Shortly thereafter, the Chamber of Deputies, the Senate, and the Paris Municipal Council each received a petition from members of the morals section of the *Société pour l'Amélioration du Sort des Femmes*, demanding that (as a first step) Article 334 of the French Penal Code be enforced, such that any underage girls (i.e., under the age of 21) be removed from brothels and struck from the registers of the morals police. The petitioners (led by Maria Deraismes) demanded in an accompanying memoir that *free* vocational training schools be established for girls (such free schools already existed for boys) and also that refuges be established for such girls, preferably in the countryside, where they could find shelter, support, and could acquire rudimentary marketable skills. They even suggested that such girls, once trained, might become suitable as colonists.[78]

In early April 1880, the AFAPR, in conjunction with the British and Continental Federation, sponsored a huge public meeting in Paris to call

[75] Emilie de Morsier, letter to Theodore Stanton, in *The Woman Question in Europe* (New York: G. P. Putnam's Sons, 1884), p. 266.

[76] Chapman, "Prostitution in Paris," 519. Although Chapman would die in 1894, Yves Guyot would live another three decades, and for much of that period – as a journalist, a municipal councilor, a deputy, and eventually a cabinet minister – he would continue to spearhead this campaign. Despite the strenuous efforts of these committed abolitionists over the next half-century, the French system of regulated prostitution would endure into the mid-1940s.

[77] *Premier Rapport de l'Association*, pp. 20–21.

[78] This petition and its accompanying memoir is published in *Le Droit des Femmes*, n° 174 (May 1879), 73–75.

for the suppression of the morals police. Chaired by Dr. Henri Thulié, former chairman of the Paris Municipal Council, the gathering drew some 3000 persons to the Salle Lévis. The theme for the entire meeting was an appeal for the realization of individual liberty under the Republic by ending the sexual slavery of unfortunate women "licensed" by the morals police. Speakers included the cream of the international abolitionist crop – including Aimé Humbert from Neuchâtel, Emily Ashurst Venturi, Maria Deraismes, James Stuart, Benjamin Scott (who singled out the population question and France's "infertile" marriages). The various speeches emphasized the necessity of inculcating a single moral standard, of purifying moral life for the success of the republic, of "cleaning out the stables." Everyone appealed to Franco-British friendship and to fostering a joint effort to ensure that the "common law" was properly applied and enforced in France. The personal appearance and eloquent speech by Josephine Butler, the very personification of the international abolitionist campaign, capped the evening. Butler insisted on the necessity of aligning French institutions with the principles of the Declaration of the Rights of Man. The resolutions of the meeting, voted unanimously, called for full application of the principles of 1789 to women, following Guyot's insistence that the Declaration of the Rights of Man "applied equally to the Rights of Woman." The "system called the morals police" is "illegal in its origin, arbitrary in its application, and immoral in its consequences."[79] Such ringing statements issued a challenge to the now all-republican government of the Third Republic.

One question that arose was whether prostitution itself should be criminalized. And, if so, for both sexes? Opponents of this proposal among the abolitionists were very vocal. At a meeting of the AFAPR in Paris in mid-February 1882, Emilie de Morsier spoke out eloquently against such a notion: the State should not *decree* morality, she said, because this would violate hard-won individual rights. What the state could do – and should specifically do – is to punish definable crimes, notably the seduction of minors and their forcible violation [*attentats aux moeurs*]. Moreover, the State should not be in the regulation business; it should simply return to the common law. We are, she reminded her audience, in fact attacking the morals police and the system of licensing in the very name of the law that

---

[79] See the report by Jeanne Mercoeur, "La prostitution réglementée (Réunion de la Salle Lévis)," *Le Droit des Femmes*, n° 186 (May 1880), 73–74, and especially the full published account (95 pp.), Association [Française] pour l'Abolition de la Prostitution Réglementée, *La Police des mœurs, réunion de la Salle Lévis du 10 avril 1880* (Paris: AFAPR, 1880). The resolutions appear on pp. 80–81.

punishes "*excitation à la débauche*" [provocation to debauchery]. A new law "would only provide a national sanction for the injustices committed against women."[80] Léon Richer (writing as Jeanne Mercoeur) agreed, pointing out that with existing laws the State could also take action against soliciting [*raccolage*]. Abolitionists were unanimous in claiming that enforcement of existing laws could accomplish what was needed to put the morals police out of business.

In 1882, the combined forces of the British and Continental Federation, in association with the AFAPR, succeeded in provoking a second investigation of the Paris morals police. In December 1883, in conjunction with Richer's newly founded *Ligue Française pour le Droit des Femmes* [French League for Women's Rights; hereafter LFDF], they sponsored another major public meeting, whose speakers included Morsier, Fiaux, and Jean-Bernard. Among those in attendance were Mme Chapman and Maria Deraismes; Victor Schoelcher sent his regrets.[81] Emilie de Morsier confronted the arguments of the opponents and laid out the necessity of defending individual liberties – for all. She also laid out the raw facts of the international traffic in women (mostly girls), remarking that "in an era where the books by M. Zola go through 150 editions or more, and where the theatres are sold out with plays that are not precisely designed to raise the moral level of society, we are permitted to denounce the abominations that are committed against these poor defenceless [underage] girls under the pretext of morality and public hygiene."[82] Like Josephine Butler, Morsier was both eloquent and fearless. She called on women as well as men to change their attitudes, and especially to eradicate the current stigmatizing language directed at women (privileged women, she indicated, were the worst offenders): no more "fallen women," no more "lost women" – men and women are both involved in sexual encounters. Women must come together to fight this infamy; they must rally the force of love in the service of Justice. Ultimately, in the spring of 1884, the French government proposed transferring jurisdiction over the *police des moeurs* from the Paris municipal authorities to the Ministry of the Interior, a move that would have had national

---

[80] This speech by Emilie de Morsier against criminalization of prostitution was reproduced in extenso in Jeanne Mercoeur, "Une Loi impossible," *Le Droit des Femmes*, n° 208 (March 1882), 38–41; it can also be consulted in Emilie de Morsier, *Mission de la femme: discours et fragments* (cited in n. 22), pp. 35–41. Quotation, p. 40.

[81] An account of the meeting, with the texts of speeches, appeared in *Le Droit des Femmes*, n° 230 (January 1884), 8–14.

[82] De Morsier, in *Le Droit des Femmes*, n° 230 (January 1884), 10.

implications.[83] Apparently this proposal, passed by the Chamber, died in the Senate, and the morals police remained Parisian.

The international abolitionist campaign, which had become, in Butler's own terminology, a "great crusade," produced a burgeoning scholarly and reportorial literature on prostitution. French Federation members, virtually all of whom were deeply engaged republicans (and many were anticlericals) investigated the details of the system, collecting statistics, reading reports, and generally contributing to the "politics of knowledge" as well as militating against government regulation. Yves Guyot's massive (580-page) study, *La Prostitution* (1882) was followed by the thousand-page report of the pro-abolition French physician Louis Fiaux, *La Police des moeurs en France et dans les principaux pays d'Europe* (1888), which revealed the range of the system's abuses as well as the extent of its international reach.[84] Both Guyot and Fiaux would remain prominent figures in the abolitionist campaigns well into the twentieth century. In June 1882 another important abolitionist feminist, the French Protestant pastor Tommy Fallot, founded a related group, the *Ligue Française pour le Relèvement de la Moralité Publique* [French League for the Improvement of Public Morality], which brought women's issues, beginning with "regulation" to the attention of a broader French Protestant community.[85] Through his lecture/pamphlet, "La femme esclave," he made the case for prostitutes as victims of terrible social circumstances that required remediation.[86] Fallot would subsequently campaign, alongside life-senator René Bérenger, against pornographic literature.[87]

---

[83] The first study on this subject, which I found very helpful for initial guidance, is Elisabeth Anne Weston, "Prostitution in Paris in the Later Nineteenth Century: A Study in Political and Social Ideology," Ph.D. dissertation, State University of New York, Buffalo, 1979. Unfortunately, Weston never published an expanded version of her findings.

[84] Guyot's *La Prostitution* (Paris: G. Charpentier, 1882) was translated into several other languages, including English. On Guyot's contributions, see Theodore Stanton, *The Woman Question in Europe* (London & New York: G. P. Putnam's Sons), pp. 265–267. See also [Dr.] John Chapman's earlier publication, "Prostitution at Paris," originally written for the 1878 International Congress on Women's Rights, in Paris; for his 1883 review of Guyot's contributions in the *Westminster Review*, see n. 72. In the same period, see also Armand Desprès, *La Prostitution en France; études morales et démographiques* (Paris: J.-B. Baillière, 1883); and Charles Secrétan's highly philosophical *Le Droit de la femme* (Paris: F. Alcan, and Lausanne: B. Benda, 1886), which was frequently reprinted. See also the many articles on the subject of regulated prostitution in the *Revue de Morale Progressive* (1887–1892).

[85] On Fallot's efforts, see Florence Rochefort, "The Abolitionist Struggle of Pastor Tommy Fallot: Between Social Christianity, Feminism and Secularism (1882–1893)," *Women's History Review*, 17:2 (April 2008), 179–194.

[86] Tommy Fallot, *La femme esclave* (Neuchâtel: Secrétariat général de la Ligue Française pour le Relèvement de la Moralité Publique, 1884); discussed in Rochefort, "Abolitionist Struggle."

[87] On Bérenger, see Annie Stora-Lamarre, *L'Enfer de la IIIe République: Censeurs et pornographes, 1881–1914* (Paris: Imago, 1990).

The abolitionists' investigations of regulation sparked scholarly interest in the culture, condition, and character of the prostitutes, and more broadly raised questions about beliefs in female "deviancy" and "criminality," as opposed to the "innocent victim" characterization favored by the abolitionists, including Fallot, which implied that they could be rescued. This aspect of the debates would peak in 1889 with the challenges laid down by the pro-regulationist Italian physician and criminologist Cesare Lombroso at the International Congress on Criminology in Paris.[88] In the 1890s Lombroso and his son-in-law Guglielmo Ferraro would publish the widely discussed *La donna delinquante*, thereby "secularizing" a far older religious notion (common to Catholics and many Protestants, and often characterized as "Augustinian") that some women were simply "born prostitutes," inveterate sinners who could never be redeemed. Such claims would be assertively contested by feminist abolitionists, particularly those who dedicated themselves to stopping the trafficking of underage girls, raising the age of consent, challenging the double standard of morality, and attempting to rehabilitate adolescent down-and-out girls who found themselves teetering on the brink of prostitution.

In addition to their activism in the AFAPR, a small cluster of French women established a series of practical institutional efforts, based in their commitment to the solidarity of women, to a sisterhood that transcended boundaries of social class and religion. Of particular importance for the future of feminism in France was their Parisian philanthropic association, the *Oeuvre des Libérées de Saint-Lazare* [Philanthropy for the Women Freed from the Saint-Lazare Prison, hereafter OLSL].[89] This organization had originally been founded in 1870 to address the immediate needs of poor and desperate women (excluding those already registered as prostitutes) released from the First Section of the Saint-Lazare women's prison; the Oeuvre's intent was to take them in so that they would not become the prey of either the morals police or the

---

[88] On Lombroso, his verbal duel with Manouvrier at the 1889 Congress, and the aftermath, see Jennifer Michael Hecht, *The End of the Soul: Scientific Modernity, Atheism and Anthropology in France* (New York: Columbia University Press, 2003), pp. 228–235.

[89] The history and mission of the OLSL is recounted by Aline Valette in a 90-page brochure, *Oeuvre des Libérées de Saint-Lazare, fondée en 1870, reconnue d'utilité publique par décret du 26 janvier 1885* (Alençon: Impr. F. Guy, 1889). The Oeuvre's *Bulletin* and annual reports provide detailed chronicles of the group's work. To my knowledge no one has published a scholarly study of the organization, though the broader contributions of some of its second-generation leaders are discussed in other works; Käppeli, in *Sublime Croisade*, focuses on the written contributions of the Swiss-born Parisian Emilie de Morsier.

"white slavers."[90] In 1883, the original founder of the OLSL Pauline Michel de Grandpré retired and the leadership passed to a cluster of progressive Protestant women who were committed to social action. The chevroned reformer and educator Caroline de Barrau (1828–1888) took the helm as the new *"directrice générale,"* seconded by Isabelle Bogelot (1838–1923; the one-time protégée of Maria Deraismes and future promoter of the *Conseil National des Femmes Françaises*), who then succeeded de Barrau as *"directrice"* upon the latter's retirement in 1887. Bogelot's great friend Emilie de Morsier was elected vice-president (the republican deputy Léon Bourgeois was president), and she became one of the OLSL's leading spokeswomen. All three were "respectable" married women of a certain age, open-minded, confident, and dedicated to change under the Republic. Both Barrau and Morsier had attended the 1878 women's rights congress and had also joined the national and international abolitionist campaigns.

These three women all spoke out courageously for the rights of women; they were already far more than "proto-feminists" and there was nothing "conservative" about any one of the three. It was at the January 1885 general meeting of the OLSL that de Morsier asserted, in her speech (quoted earlier) that "woman must become independent of man."[91] In early January 1885, the republican government accredited the OLSL, which observed religious neutrality in its welcome to women, as a work of public utility. During the next few years, the officers of the OLSL succeeded in gaining access to the prison itself and to the *"Dépôt"* (where women were first brought when arrested) at the Paris Prefecture of Police; they had begun to found shelters for the released women and their children (1883, 1884) and they began reporting on their work and networking by attending, speaking, and networking at a variety of international congresses.

The OLSL's reports to the congresses of the British and Continental Federation reveal the organization's current projects and concerns. When Caroline de Barrau reported to the London congress in July 1886, she

---

[90] The Second Section at Saint-Lazare was dedicated to prostitutes or suspected prostitutes 16 and over, and the Third Section to delinquent girls under 16. According to the reports, around half of the women in all three sections were in the Second Section.
[91] "Discours prononcé par Mme de Morsier," *Bulletin de l'Oeuvre des Libérées de Saint-Lazare,* n° 12 (1884), 39–48; quote, 45. In French: " il faut que la femme devienne indépendante de l'homme." In Morsier's *Mission de la femme,* this quotation appears on p. 75 in her speech at the annual gathering of supporters of the OLSL on 25 January 1885, pp. 69–77. I cannot explain the discrepancy in the attributed dates.

observed that two characteristics stuck out among these youngish released *prisonnières*; a bad education (intellectual, moral, and hygienic) and lack of willpower (*la volonté*); they had no self-respect, no sense of dignity, and no hope; instead they were passive, fatally resigned to whatever happens to them, whether a beating or an even worse type of ill treatment from men in their lives. What these girls desperately needed, in de Barrau's view, was an education of the will, a cultivation of self-worth, of self-esteem; questions about employment, salaries, and apprenticeship would also need to be addressed, along with the equal moral standard for both sexes. But without self-respect and the will to make oneself respected, Barrau insisted, none of the other changes would make a difference in these young women's lives.[92]

The following year, in September 1887, Isabelle Bogelot reported on the OLSL's activities to the Federation's meeting in Lausanne. There she insisted that the women's cause could not be won until every woman was, like every man, subject to the common law. Only then, she insisted, would women cease to be scorned; indeed, only when women ceased to believe in the inferiority of their own sex would things change. For the OLSL, a big step forward was taken in 1887 when the Prefecture of Police finally admitted its representatives to the *Dépôt*; with this access, it could more closely align its work with the efforts of the *Fédération Britannique* and the *Amies de la Jeune Fille*; Bogelot celebrated their common cause, their solidarity with these sister organizations. The OLSL could then take custody of any underage girl, legally "standing in" for their absent families until other arrangements could be made. Meanwhile, the OLSL planned to add a third temporary shelter for women and children, also adding *Asiles Temporaires pour Femmes et Enfants* [temporary refuges for women and children] to its organizational name. The organizers' objective was to prevent these young women from ending up in the Second Section of the prison (where the registered, mostly diseased prostitutes were held), by helping them get back on their feet through the provision of shelter, fresh clothing, access to resources, skill training, and in particular friendship and mentoring – with no strings attached, religious or otherwise.[93]

[92] Caroline de Barrau, *Rapport présenté au Congrès de Londres à propos de l'Oeuvre des Libérées de Saint-Lazare à Paris. Séance publique du 1er juillet 1886* (Geneva: Féderation Britannique, Continentale et Générale, 1886). 16 p. pamphlet. BMD DOS 360 OEU.

[93] Isabelle Bogelot, *Rapport présenté à la conference de Lausanne à propos de L'Oeuvre des Libérées de Saint-Lazare à Paris ... Séance publique du 6 septembre 1887* (Paris: Impr. de Ch. Noblet [Féd. Britannique, Continentale et Générale], 1887). 16 p. pamphlet. BMD DOS 360 OEU.

By the time of the *Oeuvres et Institutions Congress* in 1889, the *Oeuvre des Libérées de Saint-Lazare* had much to report in its summary of accomplishments since 1882. In 1887 Isabelle Bogelot had taken over as *directrice-générale* (seconded by a Mme Wagner) when Caroline de Barrau left to found a group devoted exclusively to saving children (*Sauvetage de l'Enfance*); Bogelot then attended the American women's rights congress in Washington, D.C., representing the OLSL, to celebrate the fortieth anniversary of the Seneca Falls convention and the American women's "Declaration of Sentiments." The OLSL increased its range of visitations as well as the number of its members who received authorization to visit the *depôts* and prisons. Its financial position greatly improved and its outreach grew. Above all, Isabelle Bogelot reiterated, the point was to empower these women who came under their sponsorship, to promote their ability to take charge of their destinies with confidence. The Oeuvre's guiding idea and challenge was to turn prisons into hospitals where "moral maladies" could be treated; a place of convalescence that would prepare these released prisoners for the day of liberation, and "hand them the responsibility for their own reconquered liberty." To be sure, it was a conversion they sought, not one that entailed confession and repentance or the embrace of Catholicism or any Protestant sect, but rather a moral and behavioral conversion, which could only be gained "through justice, truth, and affection."[94]

Women reformers had also been advocating major changes in the Saint-Lazare women's prison for decades. Since 1870, Pauline de Grandpré had called out for total organizational reform, a redistribution of the prisoners to other, more suitable detention centers, and had even urged the government to tear down Saint-Lazare. Seven new prisons and other facilities had been built for men but, she complained, nothing had been done for women.[95] The ancient building, once a depository for lepers, then headquarters for the Society of St. Vincent-de-Paul, and subsequently a Lazarist monastery, was sorely (to say the least) inadequate. Upon arrival, women accused, under arrest and awaiting trial, *filles en carte*, women who had been convicted of petty crimes or larger crimes, even women consigned there by their families – were all thrown in together; female procuresses would scout the new arrivals, carefully picking out their prey. Although the

---

[94] Isabelle Bogelot, "Rapport sur l'Oeuvre des Libérées de Saint-Lazare," Congrès des Oeuvres et institutions féminines, Paris, 12–18 July 1889, *Actes* (Paris: Société des Éditions scientifiques, 1890); all quotes, pp. 76–77.

[95] Pauline de Grandpré, "Les Réformes de Saint-Lazare," in *La Prison Saint-Lazare depuis vingt ans* (Paris: E. Dentu, 1889), pp. 5–28; orig. publ. in *Le Moniteur Universel*, 24 February & 4 March 1870.

prison was supervised by the sisters of Marie-Joseph, there was no night supervision; there were no women inspectors, only men. Even though Saint-Lazare prison was divided into three sections, parts of the prison had reportedly become dens of iniquity. Women who passed through its doors, even for the shortest time, were scarred for life. By 1889, some reforms had begun – as Isabelle Bogelot would report at the *Oeuvres et Institutions* congress, administrative changes had already taken place and "an even greater transformation is on the verge of realization."[96] But only in 1896 did some serious changes finally materialize. Juveniles under the age of sixteen, then housed in the Third Section of the prison, were transferred elsewhere and that section was closed; moreover the "absolute and final separation" of the First and Second Sections was achieved.[97]

Another important initiative that involved the women active in the Oeuvre des Libérées de Saint-Lazare was the founding of the *Revue de Morale Progressive* (1887–1892), a "scientific" periodical that appeared six times a year. The names of French collaborators including Isabelle Bogelot, Emilie de Morsier, Yves Guyot, Charles Fauvety, Tommy Fallot, Léon Giraud; Swiss collaborators including Charles Secrétan, Louis Bridel, and Aimé Humbert, and other progressive reformers from Belgium, England (notably Josephine Butler), and more distant cities including Lemburg (later Lviv/Lvov) and Rome, appeared on the list of contributors. This multinational initiative targeted "an absence" in the Francophone literature, notably the legal aspects of the social relation of the sexes – or as the editors referred to it, "*le droit intersexuel*" [intersexual law]. Devoted to individual rights and justice, the publication focused on controversial issues concerning prostitution, the morals police, and abolition. "The facts demonstrate," in the words of the debut editorial (June 1887),[98]

> that there is a close connection [*solidarité*] between the immorality of the institution [*le police des moeurs*] and its bad hygienic results. Moreover, we affirm that exceptional measures are odious and that it is fruitless to seek public security through the crushing [*écrasement*], the setting outside the law, of any category of persons whatsoever. Insofar as we seek to abolish the existing regime, it is to lift up and liberate woman, not to submit her to new arbitrary and repressive laws. . . . To attack an evil, one must first go straight to its causes; all the rest is empirical.

[96] Bogelot, "Rapport sur l'Oeuvre . . .", p. 75.
[97] See the report of Emily M. Hentsch, "Prisoners Aid in Paris," *Public Opinion*, 30:8 (1900), 238.
[98] "Programme," *La Revue de Morale Progressive*, n° 1 (June 1887), 1. This periodical is briefly discussed in Käppeli, *Sublime Croisade*, pp. 146–148, but so far I have not located any more in-depth analysis.

Although the editorial does not explicitly say so, this periodical was effectively the scholarly arm of the British, Continental (and now also General) Federation; its social action program engaged with the legal regimes of Europe. "The woman question is, above all, a question of intersexual law. For the woman, everything depends on the manner in which the law regulates her relationship with the man. It is on this point that our effort will focus." Its supporters aimed to liberate women as individuals and to reformulate relations between the sexes by evolutionary, legal means: "one must not forget that progress is made through slow, gradual evolution and that revolutions are always accompanied by a reversion to the past."[99] Here progressive women and men working together sought to rewrite the law and thereby revise the morals. In the past, as the editorial pointed out, "Almost every injustice that woman objects to is due to the fact that the questions touching on the relations of the sexes have [always] been decided in men's favor."[100] This situation was due for change.

The language of liberalism used by the abolitionists in this new periodical (as elsewhere) is highly significant. The lead writer framed discussion in terms of liberty, autonomy, and personhood, yet never spoke of women as disembodied individuals. In fact, this language was that of the British and Continental Federation – as articulated at its 1886 congress in London: "The Federation upholds, with respect to the special domain of legislation concerning morals, the autonomy of the human person, the corollary of which is individual responsibility."[101] Never, it seems, had the notion of women's autonomy come to the fore so fiercely as in the debates over government-regulated prostitution. Additional articles in the journal, such as "Protection or Justice," published in the spring of 1888, illustrated this ultra-liberal current very clearly. Writing as a woman (and as a believer in evolutionary progress), Louise Gerbert indicated that:[102]

> In the end we are left with two alternatives: war, that is to say the progressive conquest of liberty at the price of suffering and tears, . . . or peace, under the protection of men, which implies an eternal minority and the renouncement of all hope for further development. As for me, my choice is made: I vote for war, because in spite of its perils, struggle is the motor of all progress.

[99] "La Question de la femme au point de vue du droit intersexuel," *La Revue de Morale Progressive*, n° 1 (June 1887), 3–12; quotes pp. 4, 5.
[100] "La Question de la femme," p. 1.   [101] "La Question de la femme," p. 8.
[102] Louise Gerbert [pseud.?], "Protection ou justice," *La Revue de Morale Progressive*, 1:4–5 (April 1888), 208–218; quotes, 218.

This writer designated the freedom to work as the primordial liberty. In France, the positions were clearly marked out: in mid-March, a certain *Association pour la Defense de la Liberté Individuelle* [Association for the Defense of Individual Liberty] convened a headline event, presided by Yves Guyot, and featuring as speakers, among others, Emilie de Morsier, Dr. John Chapman, Caroline de Barrau, and Yves Guyot.[103] They drew the line and they called for action. Their concern, across class lines (to be sure), for poor women, sexually exploited women, embodied and struggling women undergirded their commitment to human autonomy.

[103] Reported in *La Revue de Morale Progressive*, 1:4–5 (April 1888), 238.

CHAPTER 4

The Revolutionary Centennial
Promoting Women and Women's Rights at the 1889 International Exposition in Paris

The centennial celebration of the French Revolution in 1889 provided a long-awaited occasion to bring demands for French women's rights to international attention as well as to publicize the important ways in which French women were exercising their influence in French society. Two international women's congresses would take place in Paris during the summer of 1889.[1] Efforts to organize these congresses overlapped with the Boulanger Affair, in which a combined alliance of monarchists and radical antiparliamentary republicans threatened to overturn the republican parliamentary regime.[2] This political crisis put to rest in early 1889, public attention turned to the International Exposition, the completion

---

[1] The proceedings of the two women's congresses are published. See *Congrès français et international du Droit des Femmes* (Paris: E. Dentu, 1889), and *Congrès des Oeuvres et Institutions féminines, Paris, 12–18 July 1889: Actes* (Paris: Société des Éditions scientifiques, 1890). Both are available on microfilm through the History of Women collection of Research Publications, Inc., and through the Women and Social Movement, International – 1840 to Present documents project edited by Kathryn Kish Sklar and Thomas Dublin (available online through Alexander Street Press).

In her book *French Feminism in the Nineteenth Century* (Albany: SUNY Press, 1984), pp. 221–223, Claire Moses discusses both congresses briefly, noting the difference in their respective programs, but also emphasizing the fact that a number of women's rights advocates also participated in the *Oeuvres et Institutions* congress. Moses alleges (p. 223) that the Rights congress speakers did not speak to the interests of women workers; however, this claim seems unfounded, given that both the economic and moral sections and their ensuing resolutions clearly addressed women's work as well as the prostitution question. In *Pariahs, Stand Up!* (chapter 5) Patrick Kay Bidelman mentions the Oeuvres congress, but focuses primarily on the collaboration between Richer and Deraismes that produced the Women's Rights congress.

[2] The classic account of the Boulanger Affair is Adrien Dansette, *Le Boulangisme* (Paris: Fayard, 1946). More recent accounts, each of which provides a different perspective, include Frederic H. Seager, *The Boulanger Affair: Political Crossroad of France, 1886–1889* (Ithaca, NY: Cornell University Press, 1969); Patrick H. Hutton, *The Cult of the Revolutionary Tradition: The Blanquists in French Politics, 1864–1893* (Berkeley & Los Angeles: University of California Press, 1981); Philippe Levillain, *Boulanger: Fossoyeur de la monarchie* (Paris: Flammarion, 1982). See also William D. Irvine, *The Boulanger Affair Reconsidered: Royalism, Boulangism, and the Origins of the Radical Right in France* (New York: Oxford University Press, 1989), & Karen Offen, *Paul de Cassagnac and the Authoritarian Tradition in Nineteenth-Century France* (New York & London: Garland Publications, 1991; available as an ACLS e-book). Significantly, two of the leading women engaged in the Boulanger Affair, the former actress and then journalist Marguerite Durand and the wealthy Duchesse d'Uzès

and opening of the Eiffel Tower, and the exposition's rich menu of inter-national congresses.[3] French women would take full advantage of the oppor-tunities offered by the revolutionary centennial to publicize their demands.

Why Two Women's Congresses in 1889?

Why were there two women's congresses, one designated as "official" and one "unofficial," one labeled "*féminine*" and the other "*féministe*"? In fact, these two meetings focused on different aspects of the woman question; neither advocated woman suffrage.

With the return of Isabelle Bogelot from the founding conference of the International Council of Women (ICW; *Conseil International des Femmes*, or CIF in French) in the United States (held in Washington, D.C., 25 March–1 April 1888), she and her friend Emilie de Morsier determined to organize a congress during the upcoming international exposition that would bring together, in the spirit of ICW, the women's associations that did exist in France, with the ultimate aim of establishing an affiliate French national council of women.[4] At that time most of these associations, in France as elsewhere, were local philanthropic organizations that were not expressly committed to the pursuit of women's rights. But the two congress organizers had been radicalized through their efforts to ameliorate the plight of France's poor women – both prostitutes conscripted by the morals police and other women prisoners who had been incarcerated in the

(the granddaughter of Veuve Cliquot) who wagered a small fortune on the campaign of the Comte de Paris) would become significant supporters of women's rights in the 1890s.
[3] Florence Rochefort & Laurence Klejman report that seventy-five congresses took place during the Exposition of 1889. See Klejman & Rochefort, *L'Egalité en marche: Le Féminisme sous la Troisième République* (Paris: FNSP & des femmes), p. 82. Other congresses of particular interest to women included the 1st *Congrès Universel de la Paix* (23–27 June 1889; see later in this chapter), which overlapped with the Women's Rights Congress, the *Congrès International de l'Enseignement Primaire* (in August 1889), and the *Congrès International de l'Enseignement Supérieur et de l'Enseignement Secondaire* (opened on 5 August 1889, with many women educators in attendance; a major theme concerned girls' education in science and foreign languages). One particularly important all-male congress was the 1st Intra-Parliamentary Conference, some of whose members also attended the first Congrès Universel de la Paix. Another, with long-term consequences for the women's movement was the workingmen's congress that founded the Second International, also discussed later). Unfortunately, a study of the 1889 Paris Exposition based on an American doctoral dissertation makes no mention of either of the women's congresses held that summer; see Brenda Nelms, *The Third Republic and the Centennial of 1789* (New York: Garland, 1987). On the primary education congress, see the discussion in Linda L. Clark, "A Battle of the Sexes in a Professional Setting: The Introduction of Inspectrices Primaires, 1889–1914," *French Historical Studies*, 16:1 (Spring 1989), 96–125.
[4] As we have seen, both Bogelot and Morsier had long been active in philanthropic and reform circles, particularly in the French branch of the British and Continental Federation and the *Oeuvre des Libérées de Saint-Lazare*.

Saint Lazare women's prison. Emilie de Morsier spearheaded efforts to acquire government endorsement and support for this congress and, after several false starts, ultimately succeeded in February 1889. This was the origin of the *Congrès des Oeuvres et Institutions Féminines* [Congress on Women's Philanthropies and Institutions], strategically scheduled to span the week of 12–18 July (with a brief break for Bastille Day celebrations).

This landmark congress would be the first women's congress to benefit from "official" republican patronage, thanks in particular to the support of Yves Guyot, deputy of the Seine since 1885, who was a committed republican advocate of women's rights and (as we have seen) a staunch opponent of regulated prostitution. For years he had worked closely with Bogelot and Morsier. Conveniently, Guyot had been named minister of public works in the Tirard cabinet (22 February 1889–14 March 1890) and, in this capacity, he became the government sponsor of the Oeuvres congress.

The official conference organizing committee, appointed by the Third Republic's new ministry, designated the distinguished senator, former prime minister, and senior statesman Jules Simon (a member of the *Académie Française* as well as perpetual secretary of the *Académie des Sciences Morales et Politiques*) as honorary president of the *Oeuvres et Institutions* congress. A longtime liberal republican who had been engaged for decades in the debates on the woman question as a strong partisan of educating girls, Simon was additionally becoming, albeit reluctantly, a staunch advocate of protective legislation for women workers.[5] The question of women's employment and what, if anything, should be done to manage it through law, was becoming increasingly divisive, particularly as the Chamber of Deputies had begun to explore the possibility of banning women's night work.

The *Droit des Femmes* [Women's Rights] Congress
(25–29 June 1889)

The government's choice of Simon as president of the official women's congress was not well received by veteran women's rights advocates Léon Richer and Maria Deraismes, who adamantly asserted women's right to economic independence and opposed discriminatory labor legislation of any kind. To protest the government's designation of Simon, Richer and Deraismes and their respective organizations decided to organize a separate congress, the *Congrès français international du Droit des Femmes*

---

[5] Simon's turn toward protective legislation will be discussed in Part II.

[French International Congress on Women's Rights], which they scheduled for late June – that is, prior to the Oeuvres and Institutions congress. Unlike the Oeuvres congress, it was a closed congress, open only to delegates and paid registrants. However, the word quickly spread, the press expressed its interest, and the congress organizers subsequently boasted that their women's rights congress had generated over six hundred articles in the French and international press.[6]

In her opening address at the Women's Rights congress, Maria Deraismes laid out the new terms of the debate, alluding to the differences between liberals, who upheld women's "right" to economic independence, and protectionists, who upheld "privileges" and (in particular) supported the prohibition of women's night work. "This type of protection seems more like a restriction, an oppression, than like an advantageous concession. We know from experience that protection and liberty are two mutually exclusive terms."[7] Moreover, she argued, such "protection" could actually be quite ineffective. Thus it was that her contingent had refused designation as an "official" congress under these terms and had chosen an independent path.[8]

The international women's rights congress heard papers presented in four sections dealing with history, economics, morals, and legislation, and its attendees formulated a set of demands addressed specifically to the French situation. These demands reiterated the program that Richer, Deraismes, and their supporters had laid out since the later 1860s: the complete reform of legislation on married women's civil rights, especially as concerned property rights; equal pay for women and men teachers; access for women to the liberal professions (especially law), apprenticeships for women located in vocational schools rather than in workshops (*ateliers*); suppression of the morals police and demolition of the Saint-Lazare prison;

[6] On the press coverage, see the preface to the published proceedings: *Congrès français et international du Droit des Femmes*, p. I as well as the many newspaper clippings preserved in folders at the Bibliothèque Marguerite Durand, Paris.

[7] Deraismes, opening address, published in the proceedings, *Congrès français et international du Droit des Femmes*, pp. 3–4. The proceedings and accounts in the press offer the most comprehensive view of the congress. But see also the retrospective account in Madame G. Avril de Sainte-Croix, *Le Féminisme* (Paris: Giard & Brière, 1907).

[8] French "liberal" feminists would continue to object to protective legislation for women well into the 1890s, in company with their British counterparts associated with the *Englishwoman's Review*. But on the international level, the tide was turning and during the 1890s feminists in other countries, especially Imperial Germany, would embrace the "privileges" of state-sponsored protective legislation for women as more advantageous in the short term to women workers than any number of hypothetically equal "rights" or "liberties." This would also be the position endorsed by the Second International and the German Socialist Party. Important debates on this subject would take place at the 1899 International Council of Women's Congress in London.

and repeal of the law that prohibited paternity suits.[9] Their earlier demands for divorce and girls' education were no longer on the list; the Third Republic had already addressed those demands (at least partially) in the early 1880s through the massive secular school program described earlier and the 1884 law restoring the possibility (though with limiting conditions) of civil divorce. Even so, the revised list remained very substantive.

The organizers of the 1889 women's rights congress designated History as the first of the four sections around which the June congress would be organized: significantly, the general topic for this section (as elaborated in the conference prospectus) was "On women's influence and their action on the course and development of human societies." The prospectus specifically invoked women's memory of 1789: "The 1889 Centennial being the celebration of the proclamation of Law and Liberty in the world, the time is ripe to organize a great women's demonstration in Paris. At the same time this would render due homage to our mothers who, a century ago, had the initiative and courage to pursue our legitimate grievances."[10]

One might think that the history of women's revolutionary action would have offered an obvious topic of inquiry in this year of revolutionary centennial celebrations. Yet apart from the contribution of Maria Deraismes, it did not materialize as a significant feature of the historical section of the women's rights congress. This was doubtless due to the fact that in 1889 the historical memory of the women's rights campaigns in 1789–1793 was far less well documented than it has since become.[11] Even among professional historians, research on this subject would not develop until the early 1890s, when both Alphonse Aulard, who held the first chair in the history of the French Revolution at the Sorbonne (founded by the Paris Municipal Council), and his student Albert Mathiez would promote and ultimately contribute to scholarly investigation of this topic.[12]

---

[9] *Congrès français et international du Droit des Femmes.* The congress restricted its resolutions to nine, concrete, targeted, and eminently possible legal reforms. These nine resolutions are translated in Bidelman, *Pariahs,* p. 180.

[10] "Circulaire de la Commission d'Organisation," *Congrès français et international du Droit des Femmes de 1889,* dated 26 March 1889; consulted in the papers of Elizabeth Cady Stanton, Library of Congress, Washington, D.C.

[11] For discussion of the plethora of works on women and the French Revolution published at the time of the 1989 bicentennial, see my review essay, "The New Sexual Politics of French Revolutionary Historiography," *French Historical Studies,* 16:4 (Fall 1990), 909–922, and for a fuller discussion of the pre-1889 historiography, Karen Offen,"Women's Memory, Women's History, Women's Political Action: The French Revolution in Retrospect, 1789–1889–1989," *Journal of Women's History,* 1:3 (Winter 1989–1990), 211–230.

[12] More will be said about the contributions of the academic historians in Part II.

The promise of the conference prospectus was developed allusively by Maria Deraismes in her plenary address. "Liberty," she argued, was the fertile principle that determined the Revolution of '89. Yet – and here her language is revealing – in 1789, "it seemed that humanity had attained its manhood [*l'âge viril*]" and "rejected all tutelage and declared its independence."[13] The Declaration of the Rights of Man was not merely a French event, but a universal one. Even so, "half of humanity" [*la moitié de l'humanité*] was "left out of this work of general liberation." Olympe de Gouges and Rose Lacombe led the protest; the names of the others have not, Deraismes claimed, come down to us. Deraismes contrasted the rigorous exclusion of women from political life and the closing of their clubs in 1793 with the visionary claims for sexual equality of the marquis de Condorcet in his "Plea for the Citizenship of Women." But, she had to admit, Rousseau's arguments for women's subordination to men had prevailed, not the egalitarian vision of Condorcet. She also invoked Mirabeau's remarks to the effect that women's participation was needed for the revolution to succeed.[14] To no avail; women's exclusion made them indifferent to the success of the revolution (she argued), and thus the forces of reaction had won the day. Deraismes also offered a partial excuse for the revolution's failure to address the needs of women; that was the immense difficulty of succeeding in one generation to make a change of the magnitude promised by the revolutionary principles.[15] One hundred years later, though, the men were still stalling. For this, Deraismes insisted, there was no excuse.

This was virtually the end of the general comments on the revolutionary centennial at the 1889 meeting. Indeed, within the historical section, what we would now consider proper historical papers were not much in evidence, despite the efforts of Clémence Royer, who alluded more generally to women warriors in French history and summoned women to *study* history as a civic duty, particularly the history of the founding of liberty during the last hundred years. Only one other properly historical paper (by the male-feminist attorney Léon Giraud) rehearsed the historical contributions of two "women worthies" to the Revolution: Charlotte Corday, who assassinated the radical Marat on 13 July 1793, and the ever controversial

---

[13] See Deraismes's speech, *Congrès français et international du Droit des Femmes*, pp. 2–11; quotation, p. 4.

[14] To date I have been unable to identify or verify any such claims by Mirabeau.

[15] Deraismes's speech, cited in n.13. Curiously, the passages concerning the revolution (pp. 4–5) have been omitted in the version reprinted in *Maria Deraismes: Ce que veulent les femmes, articles et discours de 1869 à 1894*, ed. Odile Krakovitch (Paris: Syros, 1980), pp. 103–104.

and colorful Madame de Staël, daughter of the Swiss-born French finance minister Jacques Necker, who had become a key player in the European opposition to Napoléon.[16] But that was all. When one considers the possibilities available from our twenty-first century perspective, this slight array of papers seems very disappointing. A hundred years later, the 1989 bicentennial congress "Les Femmes et la Révolution Française," would demonstrate just how much more there was to be said.[17] New findings on the history of women in the French Revolution are still appearing today.

The list of speakers for the Rights Congress in the other three sections – legislative, morals, and economic – suggests that, to a very considerable degree, every speaker was preaching to the choir. Unfortunately, the published proceedings of this congress do not include transcripts of any debates, making it impossible to tell whether there were any serious disagreements on topics other than the protection of women's work (though controversies of any magnitude would doubtless have been highlighted in the newspaper accounts), given that once again the subject of the vote was, at least in theory, off the table.[18] What debates took place were really between the two congresses and their differing foci and objectives.

Of particular interest in the section on morals at the Women's Rights Congress are the speeches by Maria Deraismes against regulated prostitution and the double moral standard and that of Marie Pouchoulin Goegg, representing the Fédération **B**ritannique, Continentale et Générale [British, Continental and General Federation] on the same topic. The modernity of Deraismes's language stands out, once again, for speaking in terms of "*les deux genres*" [the two genders, rather than the two sexes] and for her insistence on the arbitrariness of the French social construction of sexuality and sexual mores.[19] Goegg's communication assessed the work of the abolitionist Federation from a comparative perspective. In particular she underscored the Federation's guiding principle of complete equality of man and woman in moral law ["*devant la morale*"] and asserted that this approach was the most efficient way to introduce people to and address

---

[16] See the speeches by Clémence Royer (untitled) and Léon Giraud, "La Femme dans la politique contemporaine," *Congrès français et international*, pp. 19–23 and 73–79.

[17] *Les Femmes et la Révolution Française: Actes du Colloque international 12–13–14- avril 1989*, ed. Marie-France Brive, 3 vols. (Toulouse: Presses Universitaires de Mirail, 1990).

[18] The accounts by Bidelman, Moses, and Klejman & Rochefort do not elaborate on the content of the speeches in the three other sections.

[19] Deraismes's address in the proceedings, *Congrès français et international*, pp. 164–168. It was also reprinted in the *Bulletin of the Fédération Brittanique, Continentale, et Générale* (January 1890). For "les deux genres," see p. 165.

the more general issue of women's rights. By bringing people along, especially women, to the point, as had Mrs. Butler, of seeing the "oppression and unhappiness" of their sisters, they begin to grasp the hidden causes "and attack them with a resolution that will [forever] remain the honor of women in our century."[20] This alone, Goegg pointed out, had engendered the public action of thousands of women throughout Europe, forming associations, publishing brochures and tracts, speaking in public, and forcing the public authorities to acknowledge the merit of their complaints. This activity, Goegg insisted, would inevitably, albeit more slowly and by a different path, encourage women to demand their rights. She concluded by pointing out that all eyes are on France, which had invented the morals police and spread it throughout Europe via the armies of Napoléon's empire. "French ideas have a very particular sort of contagiousness about them; it is our deepest wish that the country of the revolution, which has provided such a detestable example on this particular issue, will provide a better one, one that will soon be followed everywhere." She affirmed, with a nod to the presence of the Federation's ally Yves Guyot in the current government, that "this would be a fine way to celebrate the grand Centennial." In conclusion, she invited all interested persons to Geneva for the upcoming September congress of the Federation.

What is notable from perusing the table of contents for the Rights Congress is the number of speakers besides Deraismes and Richer who were veterans of the 1860s and 1870s women's rights movement – Virginie Griess-Traut, Clémence Royer, Léonie Rouzade, and Eugénie Potonié-Pierre (who had served as secretary of the 1878 congress) were all participants. André Léo, who had been living in Italy, did not attend but evidently sent a paper that was not subsequently published.[21] Maria Martin read a communication from Hubertine Auclert, then living in Algeria. Visiting foreigners spoke as well: besides the veteran Swiss campaigner Marie Goegg, both Callirhoé Parren, a Francophone journalist from Greece, and Marie Popelin, the young woman lawyer from Belgium, were becoming prominent as leaders of the feminist movements in their respective countries. Theodore Stanton represented the Americans and "stood in" for his mother Elizabeth Cady Stanton, who had been named as honorary president of this congress. Some younger recruits made their debut at the Women's Rights Congress, including the Polish feminist activist Marya Chéliga (1854?

[20] Speech by Marie Pouchoulin Goegg, *Congrès des Oeuvres et Institutions féminines*, quotes here and later, pp. 171, 175.
[21] See the volume *The Woman Question in France* for their contributions in the 1860s.

or 1859–1927), who applauded the self-possession of American and Russian young women, in contrast to the sheltered innocence of French girls, and René Viviani (1863–1925), a future prime minister of France and a leading supporter of changes in French law that would benefit women. Shortly after this congress, the Chamber of Deputies passed a law that gave business women [*commerçantes*] a vote for the *tribunaux de commerce*. But action by the Senate would be postponed until 1890, while the Tirard government polled the all-male chambers of commerce for their opinion (sixty voted against giving women this voting power, and only thirteen supported the measure).[22]

The *Oeuvres et Institutions Féminines* Congress (12–18 July 1889)

The "official" *Oeuvres et Institutions* congress opened with a flourish on 12 July at the town hall of the 6th arrondissement in Paris. It too encompassed four sections, but with different emphases: philanthropy and morality; pedagogy; the arts, sciences, and letters; and civil legislation. In addition to the usual suspects, the mixed-sex organizing committee included Marie-Anne de Bovet from Juliette Adam's *La Nouvelle Revue*, Mme Léon Bertaux (*présidente-fondatrice* of the *Union des Femmes Peintres et Sculpteurs*; note her deliberate feminization of her title); Mme Marjolin-Scheffer, the founder (*fondatrice*) of the *Société Protectrice de l'Enfance*; Ernest Legouvé and Jean Macé (both old '48ers); Frédéric Passy, the peace activist; Charles Richet, professor of medicine and director of the *Revue Scientifique*; Mme Koechlin-Schwartz, president of the *Union des Femmes de France* (a "patriotic" emergency services organization, attached since 1886 to the French army health services and to the International Red Cross); and, of course, Jules Simon, who took his role as honorary president seriously enough to show up to chair and speak at both the opening and closing sessions. The organizers structured the agenda to include ample time for discussion and debate (though as in the case of the earlier women's rights congress, the debates were not published in the proceedings).

At the opening session, Simon dutifully explained why this congress would not take up all the possible topics, noting that the earlier congress *had* (inadvertently) discussed political rights for women.[23] He encouraged moderation, "calm, peaceful, and honorable" discussions, where "one may

---

[22] Léon Richer roundly condemned the government's "manoeuver"; see his article, "L'Électorat des femmes commerçantes," *Le Droit des Femmes*, n° 366 (16 March 1890), 66.

[23] See Simon's speech in *Congrès des Oeuvres et Institutions féminines, Paris, 12–18 July 1889: Actes*, pp. ix–xv; quotes below, x, xiv, xv.

have adversaries but never enemies." He emphasized women's extraordinarily important role as educators and as teachers of sound morality, and
called on French women to squelch the false charges of dissolute behavior
levied against the French from outside; he praised them for their valor
during the siege of 1870–1871: "if the spirit of France did not bend amidst
all the adversity that we had to endure, we owe it in great part to our
women. They have played a great part in the rehabilitation of our country,
and have provided us all with an example of courage." We must show
everyone how serious we are, what good works women have accomplished
during the last twenty years. This congress, Simon claimed, should demonstrate to all the world "that France is worth something once again, and
we [men] will be the first to rejoice [at the fact] that our women are worth
more than we are." It was with these humble, meditative, and inspiring
words, that Jules Simon ended his introductory address to the congress.

The two principal organizers, Isabelle Bogelot and Emilie de Morsier,
spoke next – followed by May Wright Sewall, president of the National
Council of Women of the United States, who had come to Paris specifically to press for the organization of a French affiliate for the ICW. Isabelle
Bogelot, the one-time protégée of the Deraismes sisters, and co-organizer
of the Oeuvres congress, acknowledged how inspired she had been, at the
1888 Washington congress, despite not speaking English, to discover all
the good works that American women had organized, and how womanly
and intelligent these women were. She concluded that "intelligence and
liberty could not be the privilege of one sex to the prejudice of the other,"
and that the most important right of all was "that every human being be
able to freely choose a career path, to give the widest development possible
to every personal faculty."[24] Bogelot was obviously proud that the government of the French republic had chosen "to honor woman and to consecrate her demands" by sanctioning the congress. "Individual initiative is
the greatest creative force," she declared, but also asserted that the government "has the mission and the duty to encourage people of good will to
come forth and organize." Although she allowed that she had never been at
the forefront of the party of militant demands, the philanthropy she and
the others had engaged with (referring specifically to the *Oeuvre des
Libérées de Saint-Lazare*) offered "the most convincing proof of the need
for certain reforms." Quoting Victor Hugo's celebrated remark about the
nineteenth century proclaiming the rights of woman, she invoked the

---

[24] Bogelot's speech, in *Congrès des Oeuvres et Institutions féminines, 1889: Actes*, xvi–xx; quotes here and
below, xvi, xvii.

theme of justice to emphasize the important ties of 1789 to 1889, especially as concerned women, and to acknowledge the support provided by the current government leaders to ensure the success of the gathering. She concluded by calling on the congress to honor its ancestors, living or dead, and to resolve that future generations might reach their full flowering – physical, intellectual, and moral – under a well-intentioned regime committed to justice and a healthy form of liberty.

Emilie de Morsier's speech was equally moving. She praised the French Republic of 1889 for "comprehending, to its eternal honor, that it owes something more to woman than silent admiration or discrete encouragement."[25] Addressing unnamed critics, who were concerned that such a congress might not be a good idea because it put women in the spotlight, she insisted that publicity for good works is an excellent thing – much better than having one's diamonds or beauty assessed in the press. More explicitly than Bogelot, she demanded that the men who make the laws "modify those that are unjust to woman, because they weigh her down with a brutal tyranny in neglecting to protect her in the struggle for life." "We need to define the nature of the influence we wish to wield in this society . . . which hides so many plagues under its gorgeous gown. . . . Our own country is wherever there is suffering." Invoking the contrast between the brilliant festivities that opened the Exposition on 6 May, and those whom she observed in the shadows, poor women, widows, young working girls dragged down by fatigue, angelic children searching for their mothers, white-haired old women, bent over and dressed in rags, and "all that floating population of misery which passes incessantly, like a black river, under the wheels of our social machine," she argued that only God might distinguish "the criminals from the crazy, the guilty from the victims." What counts, she indicated, is not what one believes but what one has done for the unfortunate. Only good can vanquish evil; "the only lasting religion is that which resides in the heart and translates into acts of kindness." France, she said, "had always been the friend of oppressed peoples, the defender of all liberties, the initiator of social progress." That should be remembered. Her subtext was that France should start cleaning up its own act.

For both these eloquent women, the contributions Jules Simon had made to women's progress seemed enormous and certainly overrode any concern they might have had about his particular stance on the theme of

---

[25] Morsier's speech, in *Congrès des Oeuvres et Institutions féminines, 1889*: Actes, xx–xxv; quote, xxi. Republished in Emilie de Morsier, *Mission de la femme: discours et fragments* (Paris: Fischbacher, 1897), pp. 109–120.

protective legislation. Isabelle Bogelot insisted, rather, on Simon's continuing encouragement of "women's intellectual development and the improvement of their status."[26] This may have been a point of serious personal disagreement between Maria Deraismes's former protégée and Deraismes, who was conspicuously absent at the Oeuvres congress – though both Léon Richer and Mme Griess-Traut were registered and presumably did attend.

In turn, the American visitor May Wright Sewall, representing the National Council of Women of the United States, pitched her message of transatlantic sisterhood, invoking Tocqueville's views on the importance of organizing in America and 1848 as a shared Franco-American date for women's activism. She concluded her remarks by invoking "fraternity" as a founding principle of the ICW: "Why – beloved women of France; it is but one more application of a word dear to your people, of a word whose noble significance was indeed first comprehended by the French people, and by them translated to the world. It is but one more reading of your sublime word – *FRATERNITÉ* – made here to comprehend another evolution in the idea of the unity in destiny of all the peoples of the earth."[27] Alluding to the French government's earlier gift to the United States of the Statue of Liberty to honor its revolutionary centennial, she pointed out emphatically that "[France] has placed the torch that will illuminate the world in the hands of a woman."[28]

One specific "women's history" initiative undertaken by the organizers of the congress on *Oeuvres et Institutions Féminines* was to obtain public recognition of a worthy French woman of the 1789 Revolution. Already in April 1889, writing in *La Citoyenne*, Maria Martin called on republican leaders to provide a concrete tribute to (at least) one woman of the revolution, by extending official recognition to Madame (Manon) Roland (as well as a number of moderate male revolutionaries). Martin conveniently neglected to mention that Madame Roland did not think that women should be actively engaged in political action (even though she herself had been up to her eyeballs in it, behind the scenes). This very fact, however, would insure that she was a "safe" choice; thus, her memory was officially honored by the placement of a memorial plaque at her childhood residence on the Place Dauphine, which – perhaps not coincidentally –

---

[26] Bogelot speech, in *Congrès des Oeuvres et Institutions féminines, 1889: Actes*, xvi–xx.

[27] *Genesis of the International Council of Women and the Story of its Growth 1899-1893*, compiled by May Wright Sewall (Indianapolis, 1914, n.p.), pp. 25–36. The published English-language version of Sewall's text in *Genesis* is considerably longer than the French version published in *Actes*.

[28] See *Congrès des Oeuvres et Institutions féminines, 1889: Actes*, xxvi–xxvii.

had since become the headquarters of the *Oeuvre des Libérées de Saint-Lazare*, close to the Prefecture of Police.[29]

This move could not have pleased Hubertine Auclert, and it was undoubtedly one of the differences that led to her subsequent fall-out with Maria Martin, who had taken over the editorship of *La Citoyenne* in her absence. Although she was still in Algeria, Auclert's editorials continued to appear regularly in *La Citoyenne*. As had been her custom at every Bastille Day celebration since 1881, she invoked the memory of the Revolution as a memory of women's exclusion. "Women should not celebrate the masculine '89; they should organize a feminine '89."[30] How could women celebrate a "bastard revolution" that had excluded them? They would do better to make their own, Auclert argued. Like Deraismes, Auclert was well aware that in 1789 women had demanded admission to the Estates General, that women had contributed to make the Revolution "grand"; she also knew that in 1793 the Convention had shut them out, closing their clubs and forbidding them to take part in public affairs. Reparations were in order, Auclert insisted, and the men who "had neither the courage nor the generosity to complete the work of the Revolution during its anniversary, by making eighteen million French female slaves into *citoyennes*, should at least assure them that they would soon have legal equality." In the meantime, women should take advantage of the exposition and various congresses to organize the "feminist movement" in the provinces.[31]

Efforts to reform the Civil Code in certain particulars were well underway. Already in 1887, male partisans of women's rights, working in association with Léon Richer, introduced a private bill proposing specific reforms in the civil rights of women, beginning with the elimination of the few restrictions still imposed on single adult women. These included the right to witness civil acts, to vouch for another person's identity, to

---

[29] Maria Martin, "Mme Roland au Panthéon," *La Citoyenne*, n° 143 (April 1889). The June issue (n° 145) announced that a commemorative plaque would be placed on Mme Roland's house, 28 Place Dauphine. The plaque remains in place to this day. Mme Roland was also featured prominently (along with Germaine de Staël, Charlotte Corday, Théroigne de Méricourt, and Cécille Renaud) in the large centennial album, *Grands hommes et grands faits de la Révolution français (1789–1804)* (Paris, 1889); I am grateful to Marilyn Yalom for this latter reference. The celebrated seventeenth-century writer Madame de Sévigné was also honored in 1889.

[30] Hubertine Auclert, "Le Quatre-vingt-neuf des femmes," *La Citoyenne*, n° 145 (June 1889); reprinted in *Hubertine Auclert: La Citoyenne 1848–1914*, ed. Edith Taïeb (Paris: Éditions Syros, 1982), pp. 126–127.

[31] Auclert, "Le Quatre-vingt-neuf des femmes." On Auclert's objections to Bastille Day commemorations, see Steven C. Hause, *Hubertine Auclert: The French Suffragette* (New Haven, CT: Yale University Press, 1987), pp. 80–81, and the accompanying note 23.

become a "*tutrice*" (legal guardian), or to serve on a family council.[32] These were small, cautious measures, but they marked the beginning of an effort to reform the Code that would take nearly a century to achieve. The arguments were all in place, but the reformers' efforts to convince the more recalcitrant deputies, or to get a republican ministry to make a governmental priority of eroding the masculine authority that underpinned the Civil Code, would proceed with excruciating hesitation. One feminist attorney, Léon Giraud, challenged his republican colleagues to act: "What the centennial of 1789 requires, above all, is to lay the foundation for a harmonious and just social order that will truly realize, not caricature, the principles of 1789; [it requires that we] halt the bankruptcy of the revolution which will only continue if, out of twenty million adults we consider ten million as [legally] incapable."[33]

Transnational Initiatives: Launching the International Council of Women

Organizing the feminist movement in the French provinces was certainly in order. In fact it would be the necessary complement to organizing a national council. At the *Oeuvres et Institutions Féminines* congress, participants unanimously resolved to establish a permanent international council of women, as proposed by May Wright Sewall. It would take some ten years in order to consolidate and affiliate France's national council of women, but the preliminary efforts to form it date from this congress.

The ICW initiative launched at the Oeuvres congress was but one of several attempts to found international organizations of women. Patrick Kay Bidelman has described Léon Richer's brief but ultimately thwarted countereffort to establish a *Fédération Internationale pour la Revendication des Droits de la Femme* [International Federation for the Demand of Woman's Rights], to rival the ICW initiative.[34] This initiative, launched at the end of the Rights congress, included representatives from nine countries, among them Marie Pouchoulin Goegg and Callirhoë Parren,

---

[32] See *Le Droit des Femmes*, n° 288 (19 December 1886) for coverage of the informal committee's discussions, and n° 294 (20 March 1887), 65–68, for the text of the bill, which would be reintroduced in the subsequent legislature with many more sponsors.

[33] Léon Giraud, "Contradictions du Code Napoléon et nécessité de le reviser" (part 2), *Revue de Morale Progressive*, n° 9 (August 1889), 97–104; quote 104. Also published as a 16-page offprint (Paris: G. Carré, 1889).

[34] Richer first proposed this international initiative in *Le Droit des Femmes*, n° 350 (21 July 1889); it is mentioned in two succeeding issues, n° 352 (18 August 1889) & n° 357 (3 November 1889), and then drops from sight.

Ellen Fries of Sweden, and Isabelle Van Diest of Belgium, as well as English and Scottish representatives.[35] During the next several years, Richer's publication *Le Droit des Femmes* would provide increasing coverage to *le mouvement féminin* in many countries, both in Europe and abroad; in the spring of 1890 Richer changed the subtitle of his publication from "*revue politique, littéraire et d'économie sociale*" [review of politics, literature, and social economy] to "*revue internationale du mouvement féminin, organe officiel de la fédération internationale*" [review of the feminine movement, official organ of the international federation].[36] This ambitious effort, which sought to resurrect the international network built up in the 1870s by Marie Goegg through the organization *Solidarité* (based in Geneva) apparently did not survive the collapse of Richer's paper and his retreat from activism in 1891. The Polish-born women's rights advocate Marya Chéliga-Loévy would sponsor a third transnational initiative, a publication called *l'Union Universelle des Femmes*, which appeared for a brief time in 1890–1891, and her group by that name would help sponsor the 1892 Women's Rights Congress in Paris. However, her group would have no real institutional base until 1909 when she founded another association, which she called the *Congrès Permanent du Féminisme International*, a Paris-based group that organized monthly programs in association with the periodical *La Française*.

The Universal Peace Congress (23–27 June 1889) and the International Workers' Congress (14–20 July 1889)

Among the many international congresses held in Paris during the 1889 International Exposition, two others are of particular interest in conjunction with the debates on the woman question and partisans of women's rights.

The first Universal Peace Congress [*Congrès Universel de la Paix*] convened in Paris from 23–27 June 1889, under the presidency of Frédéric Passy. This congress built on the efforts of the earlier International League for Peace and Freedom [*Ligue international de la paix et de la liberté*, founded in 1867], which had promoted the cause of women's rights since 1868.[37] Some French women had become avid supporters of the peace movement, and a small number of them participated actively in this series of meetings –

---

[35] For an account of the founding meeting at the end of the June congress, see *Le Droit des Femmes*, n° 350 (21 July 1889), 161–162.

[36] The subtitle change occurred in n° 367 (6 April 1890).

[37] On the League and the 1889 peace congress, see especially Sandi E. Cooper, *Patriotic Pacifism: Waging War on War in Europe, 1815–1914* (New York: Oxford University Press, 1990).

not only as part of the organizing committee but also in the debates. Among them were Virginie Griess-Traut and Marie Goegg. A significant number of male-feminists had also embraced the peace movement and played key roles at the universal peace congress. In particular, the now elderly Charles Lemonnier, a former Saint-Simonian and a longtime supporter of women's rights, was chosen to serve as honorary president of the congress.[38] Although the peace conference delegates passed no resolutions concerning women's rights in 1889, they did broach a possible project to consolidate marriage laws across national borders – a project that would gain momentum under the auspices of the ICW in the 1900s.

A second initiative had serious implications for the future of the women's rights movement – the founding congress of the Second International. Scheduled from the 14th to the 20th of July, the International Workingmen's Congress, organized by the Guedists and the *Parti Ouvrier*, took place at exactly the same time as the competing Broussiste-Possibiliste socialist congress. The woman question was on the agenda. Both these socialist congresses actually overlapped with the women's *Oeuvres et Institutions Féminines* congress (12–18 July).

The next stage for debate on the woman question had been prepared by the well-known German socialist August Bebel (1840–1913), in his pathbreaking book, *Women in the Past, Present, and Future*, originally published in German in 1878.[39] In his introduction, Bebel designated the "women's question" [*Frauenfrage*; in the 1884 English translation, it is plural] as "only one side of the whole social question." He had written that "bourgeois" solutions would not resolve the woman question. "The subjection of the sex under men, the pecuniary dependence of the enormous majority and the consequent sexual slavery which finds its expression in modern marriage and in prostitution, will still remain untouched," Bebel asserted. A "complete solution" was required; anything else was merely patchwork. "By a complete solution I understand not only the

---

[38] See the *Bulletin du 1er Congrès Universel de la Paix, 1889* (Berne: Imprimerie Korber, 1901). Consulted on Google, 2 March 2012 (copy from the Harvard Law Library). On this congress and its aftermath, see Sandi E. Cooper, " Pacifism in France, 1889–1914: International Peace as a Human Right," *French Historical Studies*, 17:2 (Fall 1991), 359–386.

[39] August Bebel, *Woman in the Past, Present, and Future*, transl. H(ope) B(ridges) Adams Walther (London: Modern Press, 1885); originally: *Die Frau in der Vergangenheit, Gegenwart, und Zukunft* (1878). Quotations from the "Introduction" to the Walther translation," pp. 1, 3–5. Although this first English translation says "women's question," later translations render the term as "woman question." Bebel's book did not appear in French translation until 1891; Eugénie Potonié-Pierre published a three-part review, with extensive quotations, in *Le Droit des Femmes*, n°s 397–399 (5 July, 19 July, & 2 August 1891). Bidelman's attribution of these articles to *La Citoyenne* is incorrect.

equality of men and women before the law, but their economic freedom and material independence, and, so far as possible, equality in mental development. *This complete solution of the Women's Question is as unattainable as the solution of the Labour Question under the existing social and political institutions.*" [Emphasis in original.]

On the 19th of July 1889, Clara Zetkin – representing the women workers of Berlin at the International Workingmen's Congress – gave a plenary speech in German, "Women Workers—and the Woman Question," which positioned her as an strong advocate for women's issues within the newly revived Marxist socialist labor movement.[40] Building on Bebel's arguments, as well as those of Friedrich Engels, Jules Guesde, and others, Zetkin endorsed the theoretical and practical assertions that would resonate through the socialist movement for more than a hundred years: the struggle of the working class must take precedence over gender issues. Grounded in her own experience as a mother and self-supporting woman, Zetkin addressed the specific issue of women's employment. Anticipating the emerging international efforts to regulate women's labor, particularly night work, she asserted that only the work of pregnant women should be regulated.

Zetkin attempted to convince working men that the central problem was not, as had long been claimed, the threat of women's labor competing with that of men; the real issue, she insisted (as had Marx and Bebel before her), was the capitalist exploitation of women's labor. Like these predecessors, she argued that only the emancipation of labor from capital would resolve this problem: "Only in a socialist society will female and male workers alike gain complete human rights." Women were prepared to be comrades-in-arms to arrive at this new society, Zetkin proclaimed, but they intended to "demand all their rights once victory is achieved."[41] Clearly the socialists were intent on capturing the theoretical and political

---

[40] Orig. publ. as Clara Zetkin, „Für die Befreiung der Frau! Rede auf dem Internationalen Arbeiterkongress zu Paris, 19 juli 1889," *Protokoll des Internationalen Arbeiter-Congresses zu Paris, 14–20 juli 1889* (Nürnberg, 1890). According to Michel Winock, in his introduction to the reprint of the minutes of both socialist congresses held in 1889, the *Protokoll* never appeared in French translation: see *Congrès International Ouvrier Socialiste, Paris 14–21 juillet 1889*, vol. 6–7 (1977), which includes both the Guesdist-Marxist congress and the Broussist-Possibiliste congress. Gilbert Badia notes, in *Clara Zetkin, Féministe sans frontières* (Paris: Les Éditions ouvrières, 1993), p. 37, that Eleanor Marx translated Zetkin's text into English and French (at the congress), but provides no reference to any contemporary published version. The first known published French translation appears in Clara Zetkin, *Batailles pour les femmes*, ed. Gilbert Badia (Paris: Éditions sociales, 1980), pp. 76–81. The first known published English translation of Zetkin's speech is by Susan Groag Bell, in *WFF*, vol. 2, doc. 15 (pp. 87–91).

[41] Zetkin, "Für die Befreiung der Frau!"

high ground in the matter of altering the relations between the sexes by asserting that women's rights could indeed be realized, but only *after* the revolution.

This argument – that class trumps sex – would become the official "party line" of the new Second International and its associated national parties. The notion that Capitalism (with a capital C), not male domination, was the enemy and socialist revolution the answer offered a compelling vision for many. In August 1891 at its second (this time, unified) congress in Brussels, the Second International would endorse complete legal equality for women, even though the woman question had not officially been placed on the congress agenda. Clara Zetkin was not present, and the Belgian socialist leader Emile Vandevelde had reservations about the possibility that equality of functions, of which he disapproved, might also be included. The Congress's resolution on this subject called on the socialist parties and workers from every nation to endorse complete (legal) equality of the sexes. The following October (1891) the German Socialist Party would adopt, as part of its program, the principle of complete equality of the sexes.[42] The French socialists, still fragmented and competing, could not agree on a unified position on the issue. Even so, the relations between French women's rights advocates and the emerging socialist political parties had entered a new period marked both by emulation and by tension. Had the Marxist-socialists effectively hijacked the women's rights agenda in order to keep women workers from turning to support of the feminists? Only time would tell.

Conclusion

The Third Republic had survived the most formidable political challenge to its very existence and celebrated with gusto during the International Exposition of 1889. As the exposition closed, republicans won substantial victories in the fall 1889 elections (runoff on 6th October); they then began to breathe more easily as concerned the future of the secular republic. But more challenges were headed its way – scandals (particularly corruption in the finances of the Panama Canal project), the adhesion [*ralliement*] to the republican regime of some of the leading monarchist and Catholic political

---

[42] See *Congrès international ouvrier socialiste tenu à Bruxelles du 16 au 23 Août 1891, Rapport, publié par le Secrétariat Belge* (Brussels: Impr. Ve Désiré Brismée, 1893), pp. 84–85; pp. 118–119 in the reprint edition, ed. Michel Winock (cited in n. 40). An English translation of the subsequent SPD Program, adopted at the Party Congress, Erfurt, 21 October 1891, appears in Louise Wilhelmine Holborn et al., *German Constitutional Documents since 1871* (New York: Praeger, 1970), pp. 51–53.

figures, controversies over agricultural tariff issues, disputes over colonization in the French empire and, in particular, the convergence of the debates over women's employment with the debates over the population crisis. Women's rights advocacy in France had made enormous headway by the end of the 1880s as French women and their male allies had begun to talk back and to organize, but in the 1890s their "romance" with the Republic would enter a new stage and encounter some harsh realities.

As should be clear from the chapters in Part I, the French debates on the woman question engaged virtually every aspect of sociopolitical organization. It was not only a question of the absence of women's political rights or the subjugation in civil law of wives and, in certain cases, even single adult women, that preoccupied the republican advocates and opponents of women's emancipation; the issues encompassed the expansion of educational and professional opportunities for girls, the focus on women in the investigations of the natural and social sciences, the anxiety about the population problem (linking concern about falling birth rates to questions of national economic and military power), the conflict over the optimum organization of families, the economics and sexual politics of employment (including demands for equal pay), the challenging of "conventional" morality (notably the double standard and the issue of government-regulated prostitution). All these issues had come to a head during the 1889 centennial congresses. The principles of the revolution – liberty, equality, and fraternity – and justice – had by no means fallen by the wayside. Indeed, they never seemed more alive, more essential, than among the supporters of women's civil, economic, social, and political emancipation.

By 1890, secular republican advocates of French women's emancipation had elaborated and definitively articulated a number of principled positions, and had proposed a number of concrete solutions. Catholics, both those of monarchist and republican political persuasion, were cautiously beginning to enter into the debates, as the still divided socialist groups already had. The next decade of the 1890s would see the development of action plans and even more radical proposals for realigning the relations of the sexes. In the meantime, these campaigns and the arguments that undergirded them were acquiring a new and potent label – *féminisme*.

Feminists would disagree among themselves – sometimes vehemently – about how to prioritize their issues and how best to respond to various "solutions" envisaged at the governmental and transgovernmental level, some of which (but not all) they had initiated and even helped to shape. Most feminists would adamantly defend women's right to work as they saw fit; they developed new tactical arguments around "freedom to work" to counter the protectionist pressures based on a male-breadwinner/ dominator model. Perhaps most importantly, they became increasingly bold, not mincing words, in articulating their rights under the Republic. Indeed, the 1890s could be considered French feminism's coming of age as a major political and social force. The chapters in Part II will continue our investigation of the debates on the woman question during the critical period 1890–1900.

Encounter
The Third Republic Faces Feminist Claims, 1890–1900

The woman question, however one envisages it, is a vital question from the perspective of the family, the country, and religion.

Emilie de Morsier
"Conférence de Versailles," *La Femme* (1 July 1892)

* * *

[Woman] is now almost entirely freed from the bonds which once held her captive, a slave to the conjugal hearth. The era of woman's emancipation has commenced.

Juliette Adam
"Woman's Place in Modern Life," *The Fortnightly Review* (1892)

* * *

They [the feminists] want to swallow the entire artichoke at once instead of eating it leaf by leaf.

Francisque Sarcey
"L'Avant-courrière," *Le Petit Journal*, 24 January 1894

* * *

Into this business [of politics] women want to enter? Under the tree of science, Eve, her turn arrived, asks Adam for half the apple ... only to find that the apple Adam holds is spoiled, gnawed to the core by parasites, infected by fungus and infested by vermin. I have no appetite for these little dinners. And if the act of sharing has become necessary, due to man's egoism and ferocity, let us at least pick from the branch a new, healthy, and savoury fruit.

Séverine,
La Revue Féministe (1895)

* * *

My greatest delight is to proclaim that a man who also aspires to be "new," has understood the superiority of the new woman, and bowing before her, accepting her sublime lesson, demands to be one of her soldiers.

Jules Bois
"La Femme nouvelle," *Revue Encyclopédique Larousse* (28 November 1896)

* * *

[T]he feminist movement . . . is a revolutionary movement of the first order; its goal is the emancipation of woman, which is in itself a revolution.

Aline Valette
"Le Féminisme à la Chambre, 1893 à 1898," *La Fronde* (29 April 1898)

* * *

The role of the police is to prevent scandal in public places; by going further [arresting and licensing young women suspected of being prostitutes], it oversteps its rights and violates Articles 1, 5, 6, and 7 of the Declaration of the Rights of Man. . . . We do not want a woman, whoever she is, to be subjected to laws of exception. Like man, she is a human being with a right to her integral autonomy, and we protest against every kind of regulation that, under the pretext of safeguarding the health of men, or even the family, sanctions and consolidates the principle of a double morality for the two sexes.

Ghénia Avril de Sainte-Croix
Speech against state-regulated prostitution at the 1900 *Oeuvres et Institutions* Congress

* * *

Introductory Remarks

The "romance" of the Republic had come to an end. After twenty years of fretting over the stability of the Third Republic, the republican ministries had beaten back the threat of Boulangism and a monarchical restoration. They had sponsored a hugely successful international exposition in Paris to celebrate the centennial of the Revolution, which included an "official" women's congress and one "unofficial" women's rights congress. What was more, republican candidates had won a majority in the parliamentary elections of 1889. Had the day of reckoning for women's rights arrived?

One might have thought that by the 1890s the republican majority could no longer avoid addressing the multiple issues that constituted the woman question, given the challenges posed in 1889 by the two international women's congresses. But even though advocates of women's rights found a number of champions among the republican political establishment to support specific measures, they encountered others who were reticent to support their extensive list of demands. Moreover, those who were wholly opposed became more vociferous in expressing their objections to female emancipation. Reforms in the Civil Code were bottled up in the Chamber of Deputies, and legislative support for women voting still seemed unattainable in the short run. Still there were many other serious issues to be confronted. The time was ripe to address them.

Women's engagement in French civil society and French political life would grow by leaps and bounds in the 1890s. Not only were French women becoming better educated and increasingly self-confident, but their talents would be on display in public places, such as the exhibitions of the decorative Arts of Woman (in 1892 and 1895).[1] During these ten years French women's organizational efforts would gain momentum and the voices of women's rights advocates and other social reformers would multiply, thrusting the woman question debates onto center stage.

In September 1891, Hubertine Auclert would spell out, once again, in *La Citoyenne*, what needed to be done in order for "the Republic in name" to become "the Republic in fact."[2] She proposed:

1) that women, who constitute more than half the nation, be treated according to the rule of common law;

---

[1] See Debora L. Silverman on the exhibitions produced by the Central Union of Decorative Arts, chapter 11 in Silverman, *Art Nouveau in Fin-de-Siecle France: Politics, Psychology, and Style* (Berkeley & Los Angeles: University of California Press, 1989).

[2] Unsigned resolutions, *La Citoyenne*, n° 182 (1 September 1891).

2) that the "limited suffrage" of men alone be accorded to women and thereby become truly universal;

3) that the Constitution, which governs both sexes, be revised by an assembly composed of both women and men;

4) that women have the same opportunities for physical and intellectual development as men do;

5) that women, like men, have access to jobs and to all public offices;

6) that the State pay its women employees the same as men for equal work;

7) that the courts and juries which judge women and men be composed of both women and men.

Auclert's agenda encompassed legal and political equality, economic opportunity, and equal pay.

Other women's advocates sought solutions for several clusters of inter-related issues, both old and new. They focused on legal reforms and social programs that could directly benefit mothers and infants, especially *recherche de la paternité* [paternity suits] and *puériculture* [scientific child development]. They would confront the question of "protective" labor legislation directed solely at women workers and, not least, would strenuously object to claims that their advocacy for women's rights was directly responsible for France's declining birth rate. Critics of the current structure of male–female relations were no longer in short supply; indeed, a critical mass of French women – and men – had begun to talk back to power, condemning male privilege in public lectures and in print (particularly in the periodical and daily press) and they had begun to pressure public officials for action. Their alternative view of women's place – as equals – in French society, which inspired their campaigns for women's rights, acquired a new label.

"Feminism" was born and feminists of both sexes could be found everywhere, energetically pursuing the emancipation of women. Meanwhile the tastes, habits, and activities of these increasingly independent "new women" and "modern women," and feminists more specifically, became subjects of contentious debate, of celebration and regret, provoking alarm among naysayers and defenders of "tradition" (meaning, usually, male defenders of the male-headed authoritarian family) who thought that the subordination of women served men's interests quite nicely. Feminism was fast becoming front-page news in Paris, in the provinces, and, for that matter, throughout Europe.

CHAPTER 5

The Birth and "Take-Off" of Feminism in Republican France[1]

What Is Feminism? Who Is a Feminist? Origins of the Words

Where did this novel terminology, this new "ism" originate? It was actually quite recent, dating from the early 1880s. In the course of her pursuit of women's suffrage in *La Citoyenne*, in 1882 Hubertine Auclert had addressed an open letter to the Prefect of the Seine, opposing the prefect's restrictions on speeches during the civil marriage ceremonies held at the Paris city hall. She asserted the right of *féministes* to criticize the marriage laws during France's obligatory civil weddings. "I have no doubt," stated Auclert, "that the liberty of addressing a few words to newlyweds in the town halls, a liberty I would be most happy to use, is offered to women just as to men, to feminists as well as to freethinkers. It would be incomprehensible that freethinkers could go to the town hall to criticize the Church, whose spirit informs the marriage laws, whereas the feminists could not go to that same town hall to criticize the marriage laws informed by the spirit of the Church." Moreover, she added, "You must make no distinction, Monsieur, between those who attack the effect and those who attack the cause. From the moment a partisan of free thought can speak out, the partisans of women's emancipation [also] have the right to speak out."[2]

---

[1] This chapter draws on several of my previously published articles, including Karen Offen, "Depopulation, Nationalism, and Feminism in Fin-de-Siècle France," *American Historical Review* 89:3 (June 1984), 648–676; "Defining Feminism: A Comparative Historical Approach," *Signs: Journal of Women in Culture and Society* 14:1 (Fall 1988), 119–157; "Sur l'origine des mots 'féminisme' et 'féministe'," *Revue d'Histoire Moderne et Contemporaine* (Paris), 34:3 (July–September 1987), 492–496; and the revised English version, "On the French Origin of the Words 'Feminism' and 'Feminist'," *Feminist Issues*, 8:2 (Fall 1988), 45–51.

[2] Auclert published this letter in her now monthly suffrage newspaper, *La Citoyenne*, n° 64 (4 September – 1 October 1882). *Le Temps* (5 September 1882) discussed it in a lead editorial on the first page; oddly there is no reference to this article under "Auclert" in the published index of *Le Temps* for 1882.

Over the next decade, this new word *"féministe"* and its correlate noun, *"féminisme,"* entered the French vocabulary, characterizing what Auclert also called (further on in the same letter) *partisans de l'affranchissement des femmes* (partisans of women's emancipation).[3] A survey of the headlines in *La Citoyenne* during the latter months of 1885 and thereafter reveals that Auclert also frequently employed the term *"mouvement féministe,"* though this term appears to have found little immediate echo in other periodicals. Auclert's use of *féministes* was, however, picked up in an 1883 publication, *Essai sur la condition des femmes* [Essay on the Condition of Women], whose author speaks both of *féministes* and of *chauvinisme masculin* [male chauvinism].[4] Even so, until 1891 the mainstream French press generally referred to the movement for the extension of women's rights as *"le mouvement féminin* [the women's movement]."[5] As time went on, the distinction between *féminin* and *féministe* would become more pronounced – particularly in the rhetoric of opponents of women's emancipation, who would assert vociferously (albeit inaccurately) that a feminist was, by definition, not feminine – not womanly.

One important precedent for the use of the term "feminist" can be found in the early 1870s, though not as a label claimed by women's rights advocates. In 1872, the well-known French playwright and essayist, Alexandre Dumas *fils* had used the term *féministes* pejoratively in his polemical

---

[3] In a later published version of this letter, published on p. 63 in a collection of Auclert's articles, *Le Vote des femmes* (Paris: V. Giard & E. Brière, 1908), the words *"partisans de l'affranchissement des femmes"* were changed to *"partisans du Féminisme."* This latter version was cited after Auclert's death by her sister Marie Chaumont in her biographical introduction (signed 1922) to another collection of Auclert's articles, *Les Femmes au gouvernail* (Paris: M. Giard, 1923), p. 5. Subsequent commentators, relying solely on the 1908/1922 citation, have mistakenly alleged that the 1882 letter marks the first use of both words, *féministe* and *féminisme*. On this point, Patrick Kay Bidelman is in error; see his otherwise very carefully researched book, *Stand Up Pariahs: The Founding of the Liberal Feminist Movement in France, 1858-1889* (Westport, CT: Greenwood Press, 1982), pp. 153, 194, and 215, note 3.

[4] L. Cosson, *Essai sur la condition des femmes* (Paris: P. Dupont, 1883), pp. 59, 121, 125. Hubertine Auclert also used the word *féministe* repeatedly in an open letter (dated 27 February 1888) to the American suffrage advocate Susan B. Anthony, responding to the latter's invitation to attend the 1888 congress of women in Washington, D.C. See Auclert, "Un mot de marche," *La Citoyenne*, n° 130 (March 1888), reprinted in *Hubertine Auclert: La Citoyenne, 1848-1914*, ed. Edith Taïeb (Paris: Syros, 1982), pp. 128–131. Use of these two terms *féminisme* and *féministe* in *La Citoyenne* is more frequent than might be apparent from the listing of Auclert's signed topical editorials; see the list in appendix 1, in Steven C. Hause, *Hubertine Auclert: The French Suffragette* (New Haven, CT: Yale University Press, 1987).

[5] In spring 1890 (sometime between n°s 365 and 370), the subtitle of *Le Droit des Femmes* changed from "revue politique, littéraire, et d'économie sociale" to "revue internationale du mouvement féminin; organe officiel de la fédération internationale." The *Journal des Femmes* began publication in December 1891 as "the organ of the feminine movement" but quickly substituted the word feminist. Emilie de Morsier also spoke of "le mouvement féminin" in her collected speeches and essays, *La Mission de la femme; discours et fragments* (Paris: Fischbacher, 1897).

tract *L'Homme-femme* (1872; discussed in Part I, Chapter 1). But he did not claim to have invented it himself: "The feminists, if I may use this neologism, say, with the best intentions . . ."[6] Where did he discover – if indeed he did not coin – this "neologism"?[7] My colleague Geneviève Fraisse indicates that the term *féminisme* did appear in an obscure 1871 Paris medical thesis to connote the "weakening" or feminization of the *male* body during illness.[8] It is not impossible that Dumas *fils* could have seen it there (or in some other medical text) and then appropriated it for his own purposes. But of this we have no proof.

A different claim for origins was proposed in 1896, when the Polish-born writer and Parisian journalist Marya Chéliga (ca. 1859–1939; known in the early 1890s as Chéliga-Loévy) insisted that the visionary social thinker Charles Fourier (1772–1837) had invented the expression in the 1808 edition of his major work *La Théorie de Quatre Mouvements*.[9] This claim, though widely reproduced (especially in socialist literature), is unfounded. Certainly, the celebrated paragraph in which Fourier insisted that "progress" in liberty for women was a precondition of general social progress reveals the existence of what we would now consider to be a "feminist" consciousness.[10] However, careful examination of this first edition of the *Théorie*

---

[6] *L'Homme-femme: Réponse à M. Henri d'Ideville* (Paris: Michel Lévy, 1872); republished in *Alexandre Dumas fils, Le Dossier "Tue-La!", constitué, étudié et plaidé par André Lebois* (Avignon: E. Aubanel, 1969), p. 86.

[7] My colleague Geneviève Fraisse, also a scholar of feminism's history in France, has made claims for two earlier appearances in French of the words *féministe* and *féminisme*, but in neither case were the words used by advocates of women's rights. Fraisse's claim is tucked away in her conclusion to *Muse de la Raison: La Démocratie exclusive et la différence des sexes* (Aix-en-Provence: Éditions Alinea, 1989), p. 198. She does not mention this attribution in her earlier article, "Les femmes et le féminisme," in *Encyclopedia Universalis*, 2nd ed., 1984 (Paris), 842–844.

[8] Besides Dumas *fils*, Fraisse points to Ferdinand-Valère Faneau de la Cour, *Du Féminisme et de l'infantilisme chez les tuberculeux* (Paris: n.p., 1871). This short thesis was completed and published amidst France's 1870 defeat and the subsequent civil war in 1871, so it seems unlikely that its title or content would have had much public impact. Significantly, neither word appears in Jean Dubois, *Le Vocabulaire politique et social en France de 1869 à 1872, à travers les oeuvres des écrivains, les revues et les journaux*. Thèse–lettres - Université de Paris (Paris: Librairie Larousse, 1962).

[9] Marya Chéliga, "Les Hommes féministes," *Revue Encyclopédique Larousse*, n° 169 (28 November 1896), 826. Chéliga's misleading claim had a long-term effect – for example, in England, Virginia Crawford picked up this misattribution from Chéliga's article and propagated it in her survey of "Feminism in France," *Fortnightly Review* (April 1897), 525. Somewhat later, the Finnish woman suffrage advocate Alexandra Gripenberg embedded Chéliga's claim in her 77-page survey of French feminism in *Naisasian kehitys era maissa*, vol. 2 (1906); thanks to Prof. Tiina Kinunnen for sharing this information from her current research on Gripenberg.

[10] In the 1980s I spent months chasing this term through the Fourier literature, consulting Fourier scholars, and discovering endless and misleading loops of mystifying citations in etymological dictionaries of the French language. For a more detailed account of this quest, see "Sur l'origine des mots 'féminisme' et 'féministe'," and the revised version in English, "On the French Origin of the Words 'Feminism' and 'Feminist'," both cited in n. 1.

(and subsequent editions, including that of 1841) confirms that the word *féminisme* is nowhere to be found. Nor can it be located in any of Fourier's other published writings, or in the *Dictionnaire de sociologie phalanstérienne*, which does, however, index another related Fourier neologism: "*famillisme*," which does not appear to have entered public usage.[11]

Notwithstanding Dumas *fils*'s use and Chéliga's claim, the evidence shows clearly that Hubertine Auclert deserves the credit for pioneering the use of "*féminisme*" to refer to women's rights and emancipation.[12] Subsequently, in 1888, another longtime women's rights campaigner, historian, and suffragist, Eliska (Girard) Vincent (1844–1913), would found the *Société Féministe Égalité*, as well as the very first feminist library; she also participated actively in the *Amélioration* society of Maria Deraismes.[13] Deraismes's use of this term can also be documented from 1888 on.[14] However, it was Vincent's contemporary, the writer and activist Eugénie Potonié-Pierre (1844–1898) who successfully launched these terms into public debate at both the national and international levels.

In September 1891 Potonié-Pierre, as the organizer and guiding spirit of a new group, *La Solidarité des Femmes*, called for the foundation of a *Fédération Française des Sociétés Féministes*. Her announcement appeared in both *La Citoyenne* and *Le Droit des Femmes*. In its terminal issue of December 1891, Richer's *Le Droit des Femmes* published the federation's charter.[15] In the usage of *Solidarité*, as earlier in the tract authored by Cosson, *féminisme* was juxtaposed with *masculinisme*, which echoed the earlier (1883) term "male chauvinism."

In mid-May of 1892 the *Fédération Française des Sociétés Féministes* in association with Chéliga-Loewy's *Union Universelle des Femmes* would convene a *Congrès Général des Institutions Féministes* in Paris, which included numerous participants from other countries as well as from France.[16] With

---

[11] Edouard Silberling, *Dictionnaire de sociologie phalanstérienne: Guide des oeuvres complètes de Charles Fourier* (1911; republished by Burt Franklin, New York; series "Bibliography and Reference," n° 63).

[12] Auclert would remind her readers of her claim to have pioneered the words *féminisme* and *féministe* in "Les Précurseurs," *Le Radical*, 20 March 1898.

[13] See Bidelman, *Pariahs Stand Up!*, p. 193, on Vincent's society; on the library, see the *Bulletin de la Société pour l'Amélioration du Sort de la Femme et la Revendication de ses Droits*, 4e sér., n° 13 (September–October 1903), pp. 373–375. Eliska Vincent, along with Virginie Griess-Traut, would remain active in this society until their deaths.

[14] Maria Deraismes, presiding at a meeting of the *Société pour l'Amélioration du Sort de la Femme et la Revendication de ses Droits*, *Conférence du 14 mars 1888 sous la présidence de Mlle Maria Deraismes. Discours de M. Yves Guyot [Rapports, Statuts, Commissions]* (Paris: Impr. Mayer & Cie), p. 4.

[15] See *Le Droit des Femmes*, n° 408 (20 December 1891).

[16] See *La Citoyenne*, n° 182 (1 September 1891), n° 183 (15 September 1891), and *Le Droit des Femmes*, n° 402 (20 September 1891) and n° 408 (20 December 1891). The *Congrès Général des Institutions*

this congress the terms *féminisme* and *féministe* entered the mainstream Francophone press – not only in France, where newspapers like *Le Temps* and *Le Figaro* reported daily on "*Le congrès des sociétés féministes.*"[17] Many other papers also reported on the congress and picked up the terminology, according to Auclert's former collaborator at *La Citoyenne*, Maria Martin (1839–1910), writing in the June issue of the newly launched monthly *Journal des Femmes*, which in late 1891 had succeeded both *La Citoyenne* and *Le Droit des Femmes* (and would continue publication until 1911).

The terminology also spread quickly among Francophone writers in Belgium (including Marie Popelin and Louis Frank) and in Switzerland (notably Louis Bridel and Charles Secrétan).[18] Shortly thereafter the well-known Parisian literary critic Émile Faguet, who at that time still objected to women's emancipation, used the word *féministe* several times in the *Revue Bleue.*[19] The venerable Maria Deraismes consecrated the new terminology several months later in an August article on the congress in the *Revue des Revues.*[20] Auclert's neologism *le mouvement féministe* also began to travel; in June 1893 the *Revue Encyclopédique Larousse* appropriated it.[21]

Féministes convened at the sixth district municipal building in Paris on 14 May 1892; its proceedings appeared in the *Journal des Femmes*. See also Maria Deraismes, "A Propos du Congrès de la Fédération des sociétés féministes," *La Revue des Revues* (August 1892), 1–3; and *Dépopulation de la France, allocution prononcée par Mme Léon Béquet, née de Vienne, au Congrès Général des Institutions Féministes, tenu à la mairie du VIe arrondissement, le 14 mai 1892* (Paris: P. Dupont, 1892). The article discussing this congress in the *Englishwoman's Review of Social and Industrial Questions* (15 July 1892), 210, referred to the "General Congress of Women's Societies"; only in 1896 (64, 121) did the *EWR* pick up the terminology of feminism, complete with the French accent marks. The congress of May 1892 is mentioned briefly by Suzanne Grinberg in her *Historique du mouvement suffragiste depuis 1848* (Paris: H. Goulet, 1926), p. 81, and by Frances Ida Clark, *The Position of Women in Contemporary France* (London: P.S. King & Son, Ltd, 1937), p. 18.

[17] See *Le Temps*, series "Le congrès des Sociétés féministes," issues of 14 May through 17 May 1892. *Le Figaro* was more reticent, but did feature Léopold Lacour's front-page article, "L'Assemblée des femmes," 13 May 1892. By 1894, *Le Figaro* had come around to using "féminisme" and "féministe," but in Jules Bois's articles, "Les Apôtres femmes du 'féminisme' à Paris" (9 November 1894) and "Maria Deraismes et le mouvement 'féministe' en France" (17 June 1895), the terms are still set in quotation marks.

[18] See Guy Tomel, "Le Mouvement féministe en Amérique," *Le Figaro* (25 August 1892); by 1896, *Le Figaro* provided daily coverage of the feminist congress – see the issues of 7 April through the 13th. Belgian Francophone feminists established an *Office féministe universel* in 1896 and sponsored publication of the *Cahiers féministes* (March 1896–1905). During August 1897, this group convened an international feminist congress in Brussels; see the proceedings: *Actes du Congrès féministe international de Bruxelles, tenu du 4 au 7 août 1897. Publiés par les soins de Mme Marie Popelin, secrétaire-générale du Congrès* (Brussels: Ch. Eulens, 1898).

[19] Faguet, "Courrier littéraire," *La Revue Bleue* (28 May 1892), 701–703.

[20] See n. 14 for the Deraismes-Yves Guyot 1888 reference; also Deraismes, "Congrès de la Fédération des sociétés féministes," *La Revue des Revues* (August 1892).

[21] For example, Louis Bridel, "Le Mouvement féministe et le droit des femmes," *La Revue Sociale et Politique* (Brussels), vol. 3 (1893), 119–133; Gustave Lejéal, "Le Mouvement féministe," *Revue*

Suddenly the terms *féminisme* and *féministe* had become fashionable, terms the French language could no longer do without – they signified the development of a sociopolitical movement whose emancipationist tenets were gaining a foothold in the press and affecting the consciousness of (at least) the governing elite and the expanding audience of urban newspaper and periodical readers.

By late March 1893 the *Fédération Française des Sociétés Féministes,* now headed by Aline Valette (1850–1899), who had succeeded Eugénie Potonié-Pierre as president, had drafted and published the group's *Cahier de Doléances* (Grievances), commissioned at the 1892 congress with a nod to the pre-revolutionary cahiers of 1789. Based on the central notion that both women and men are human beings, this program called for an "economic right to life" [*le droit à la vie économique*] for women, which included a minimum wage, equal pay for equal work, equal access to the professions, careers, and vocations, public services, and administrative functions. It included as well a claim for the "right to integral development" [*le droit au développement intégral*] which called for legal restrictions on working hours that would allow workers both rest and health to pursue (and thereby enrich) other aspects of their lives. It also encompassed the "right to civil life," which called for the abolition of all the articles of the Code that placed women (particularly married women) in a position inferior to that of men, and the "right to civic life," which called for women's participation in their country's government.

To some, the program of the *Fédération Française des Sociétés Féministes* might seem strikingly "individualist," even libertarian, asking for removal of all barriers, legal and social, that constrained women (à la John Stuart Mill), but it was also interventionist, calling specifically for government action that would improve labor conditions for women workers. Significantly, it alluded to woman as "*génétrice*" [literally, she who gives birth] but did not view women's maternal specificity as a justification for constraining their full participation in society. The Cahier also insisted that, under current circumstances, a woman's "reproductive functions are limited and compromised by her social life as a producer" but that major changes in the laws and the institutionalization of economic equality could mitigate these disadvantages. It also demanded that childhood (to the age of 16) and

Encyclopédique Larousse, n° 61 (15 June 1893), 585–596; Raoul de La Grasserie, "Le Mouvement féministe et les droits de la femme," *La Revue Politique et Parlementaire* 1:3 (September 1894), 432–449; Marie Dronsart, "Le Mouvement féministe," *Le Correspondant,* vol. 184 (10 September & 25 September 1896), 860–893 & 1090–1109, and vol. 185 (10 October 1896), 110–137. See also *L'Éclair,* 11 June 1893 & 12 February 1895.

old age be protected "against physical and intellectual miseries and against familial, pedagogical, administrative, and patronal arbitrariness." This assertive program, reflecting the socialist influence at the 1892 congress, comprised the content and substance of advanced feminist thinking in 1893.[22]

In the accompanying publication *Socialisme et Sexualisme: Programme du Parti Socialiste Féminin,* Aline Valette and Dr. Z. (Pierre Bonnier) went further in emphasizing women's importance as a "producer of humanity" [*productrice de l'humanité*] and expressed the view that individualism on the masculine model would "deform" women: "The masculine form, which encompasses all present human production is a deformation that the woman who wants to emancipate herself must endure."[23] "Sterility is the first consequence of woman's individualist life, as imposed by the masculine economic formula." Their conclusion: "Woman, conscious of her needs, must necessarily be a socialist."[24] Not a party-line socialist, however. That socialist program promoted class struggle, while a sexualist program proposed to resolve the struggle between the sexes.

Valette affirmed that the feminist program was contained in the socialist program. In her weekly publication *L'Harmonie Sociale,* she would also insist – more controversially – that women were neglecting their "natural" role of "*productrice*" in reproduction for the artificial role of "*producteur.*" Ultimately, Valette endorsed the goal of returning women to their "biological role of creator and educator of the species." This was the expressed objective of *L'Harmonie Sociale.* This objective was neither to the liking of certain other feminists who viewed this maternal notion of *productrice* as confining, nor to those socialists who insisted that women's labor force participation was key to their independence.[25] Valette's publication lasted

---

[22] "Cahier de Doléances féminines," published in *L'Harmonie Sociale,* n° 25 (1 April 1893), and reprinted in appendix to *Socialisme et sexualisme: Programme du Parti Socialiste Féminin* (Paris: Beaudelot, 1893), pp. 83–92. This Cahier has been republished, but with one serious omission, in *Femmes et travail au dix-neuvième siècle,* ed. Evelyne Diebolt & M.-H. Zylberberg-Hocquard (Paris: Éditions Syros, 1984), pp. 145–150. These editors inadvertently collapsed the paragraphs on "vie civile" and "vie civique" (see p. 146 and compare with the original).

[23] Valette & Dr. Z, . . . in *Socialisme et sexualisme: Programme du Parti Socialiste Féminin,* p. 63. A key portion of this document is translated and analyzed by Marilyn J. Boxer, as "N° 97. Socialism and Sexualism (1893)," in *Feminist Writings from Ancient Times to the Modern World,* ed. Tiffany K. Wayne (Westport, CT: Greenwood, 2011), vol. 1, pp. 323–326.

[24] *Socialisme et sexualisme,* p. 68.

[25] See Aline Valette's first editorial, "A Nos Lecteurs," *L'Harmonie Sociale,* n° 1 (15 October 1892), 1. For an excellent analysis of Valette's perspective, see Marilyn J. Boxer, "Linking Socialism, Feminism, and Social Darwinism in Belle Epoque France: The Maternalist Politics and Journalism of Aline Valette," *Women's History Review,* 21:1 (February 2012), 1–19.

less than a year (October 1892–July 1893), but she continued her campaign to meld socialism and feminism in *Le Travailleur* and within the *Parti Ouvrier* (Guesdist) itself as party secretary. Her ideas anticipate the far better-known maternalist program of the Swedish writer and reformer, Ellen Key, who in 1896 began her lectures on "the misuse of women's power" and called for government (rather than individual male) support of all mothers, unmarried and married alike. Ellen Kay's writings would eventually become well known in France, as well as in Germany and throughout Scandinavia.[26]

Valette's effort to mesh the feminist program with socialist aspirations became controversial in the years that followed. In fact, the socialists of the Second International (led by the German socialists Auguste Bebel and Clara Zetkin) were developing their own answer: feminism was "bourgeois" (read "class enemies"). For over a hundred years it has been a commonplace of socialist historiography to argue that an irreconcilable gap separated socialists and "bourgeois" feminists, splitting women into warring camps according to class.[27] But this was not the case in the early 1890s. Indeed, the years 1891 to 1896 could be considered the "honeymoon" years of feminism and socialism in France. Assertions by Second International Marxist socialists that feminists were "bourgeois," strictly interested in "reform" and not "revolution," or that prioritizing class struggle between bourgeois and proletariat precluded cooperation with feminists did not become serious assertions, much less compelling

---

[26] On Ellen Key and her ideas, see Karen Offen, *European Feminisms: A Political History 1700–1950* (Stanford, CA: Stanford University Press, 2000), especially for earlier bibliography, and Tiina Kinunnen's doctoral dissertation on Key's enormous influence in the German-speaking world. To my knowledge there is no extant study of Key's reception in France, though several of her works would appear in French translation in the 1900s. See also Part III.

[27] The historian Charles Sowerwine has made this case explicitly in his study of women and socialism in France. See Charles Sowerwine, *Sisters or Citizens: Women and Socialism in France since 1876* (Cambridge, UK: Cambridge University Press, 1982). Claire Moses follows Sowerwine's lead on this point; see her *French Feminism in the Nineteenth Century* (Albany, NY: SUNY Press, 1984), pp. 223–227. Françoise Picq is correct in challenging Sowerwine and others by arguing that the label "bourgeois feminism," used pejoratively by the most radical of the socialist women before 1914, was more polemic than descriptive and based on "a political condemnation, not on a sociological finding." See Françoise Picq,"'Le Féminisme bourgeois': une théorie élaborée par les femmes socialistes avant la guerre de 14," *Stratégies des femmes: Livre collectif* (Paris: Éditions Tierce, 1984), pp. 391–406; quote, p. 392. Since Picq wrote, historian Marilyn J. Boxer has revisited the polemical use of the term "bourgeois feminism" and has demonstrated not only how politically potent it was at the time but also how this pejorative usage inadvertently succeeded in deforming subsequent historical accounts of feminism in France and elsewhere. See Marilyn J. Boxer, "Rethinking the Socialist Construction and International Career of the Concept 'Bourgeois Feminism'," *American Historical Review*, 112:1 (February 2007), 131–158.

arguments in France or Belgium before 1896.[28] There was a good deal of room for maneuver and in fact many of the most active feminists during this period, including Eugénie Potonié-Pierre herself, did consider themselves socialists, though not of the Marxist-Guesdist collectivist persuasion.

Even so, the Second International's unequivocal rejection of "reformist" measures to resolve the woman question, anticipated at its 1889 founding congress in Paris by Clara Zetkin, would be heavily promoted in her periodical *Die Gleichheit* [Equality; founded in Stuttgart in January 1892]. This stance became programmatic in the German Social Democratic Party (SPD) only in 1894, when the intransigent SPD women led by Zetkin (in opposition to the more conciliatory Lily Braun) – publicly refused to collaborate with the leaders of the newly formed German (middle-class) women's federation.[29] It increasingly characterized the politics of left wing socialism in the Second International, whose advocates feared the attraction of feminist claims and projects to the working-class women in its base.

In France, however, such a rift between "bourgeois" and "socialist" feminists was far from a *fait accompli*. Only in late 1896 could Marya Chéliga assert that "Although it is indissolubly linked with the social question, feminism should not be confused with the socialist movement nor subordinated to its various schools," adding that "feminism has its own demands, outside of the socialist factions." She pointed out that as socialism became increasingly identified with Marxist doctrines of class struggle, feminists held themselves increasingly aloof. In Chéliga's view, there was no class in which women weren't oppressed by men. Men were everywhere the *patrons* [the bosses].[30] As late as April 1898 Aline Valette, who had by then become secretary-general of the *Parti Ouvrier*, a committed socialist and an equally staunch advocate of women's emancipation, would insist in *La Fronde* that "the feminist movement . . . is a revolutionary movement of the first order; its goal is the emancipation of woman, which is in itself a revolution."[31]

---

[28] For Belgium, see Julie Carlier, *Moving Beyond Boundaries: The Entangled History of Feminism in Belgium, 1890–1914*. Ph.D. dissertation, Universiteit Gent, 2010.

[29] On socialism and feminism in Germany, see Jean H. Quataert, *Reluctant Feminists in German Social Democracy* (Princeton, NJ: Princeton University Press, 1979), and the important revisionist articles by Richard J. Evans, reprinted in his book, *Comrades and Sisters: Feminism, Socialism and Pacifism in Europe, 1870–1945* (Sussex: Wheatsheaf Books, & New York: St. Martin's Press, 1987). Lily Braun's book would be translated into French in 1908: see Lily Braun, *Le Problème de la femme: son évolution historique* (Paris: E. Cornély, 1908).

[30] Marya Chéliga, "Les Hommes féministes," in the special issue, "Les Femmes et les féministes," of the *Revue Encyclopédique Larousse*, n° 169 (28 November 1896), 825.

[31] Aline Valette, "Le Féminisme à la Chambre, 1893 à 1898," *La Fronde*, n° 142 (29 April 1898), 2.

The immediate historical context in which feminism as well as socialism began to enter the political mainstream in France shows that both movements were embedded in the developing debates about the "social question," which were in turn stimulated and complicated by the Roman Catholic Church. Shortly after the Second International's celebration of May Day 1891, in mid-May the Vatican released Pope Leo XIII's landmark encyclical *Rerum Novarum*, which laid out the Catholic position on the so-called social question; the pope insisted in particular on the centrality of the male-headed family, the eternal necessity of the male breadwinner, the right to private property and inheritance, and he opposed the employment of women, especially wives and mothers, outside the household.[32] A few months later, in August 1891, the socialists of the Second International went on record at their congress in Brussels in favor of full equality between women and men (Hubertine Auclert claimed some credit for this initiative; but so did the Dutch feminist Wilhelmina Drucker).[33] This congress called on all national sections of the International to endorse the measure.[34] In *La Citoyenne*, Maria Martin praised the Second International's 1891 endorsement of the pursuit of full civil and political rights for women, as Maria Deraismes did also.[35]

The timing of these developments strongly suggests that Potonié-Pierre's initiative to federate the feminist societies, *Fédération Française des Sociétés Féministes*, launched the following month, was a direct response to this widely publicized international socialist event, which had strategically positioned the male partisans of socialism, at least in principle, as the flagbearers for women's equality.[36] For the next few years, French socialists

---

[32] Leo XIII, *Rerum Novarum*, 15 May 1891; reprinted in Joseph Husslein, ed., *Social Wellsprings*, vol. 1 (Milwaukee, WI, 1940). See the strategic excerpts in Bell & Offen, *Women, the Family, and Freedom*, vol. 2, doc. 16. These positions had been hinted at in earlier encyclicals, most notably *Quod Apostolici* (1878). All the papal encyclicals are now posted on the Vatican website: www.vatican.va.

[33] See Mieke Aerts & Myriam Evrard, "Forgotten Intersections, Wilhelmina Drucker, Early Feminism, and the Dutch-Belgian Connection," *Revue Belge de Philologie et Histoire*, 77:2 (1999), 440–472.

[34] See *Congrès international ouvrier socialiste tenu à Bruxelles du 16 au 23 Août 1891, Rapport, publié par le Secrétariat Belge* (Brussels: Impr. Ve Désiré Brismée, 1893), pp. 84–85; pp. 118–119 in the reprint edition, ed. Michel Winock (1977). See also Paule Mink, "L'Émancipation de la femme et le socialisme," *La Question Sociale* (1 October & 1 November 1891).

[35] Feminist endorsements of the landmark socialist resolution included Maria Martin, "Remerciements au Congrès de Bruxelles," *La Citoyenne*, n° 182 (1 September 1891) and that of Maria Deraismes, on behalf of the *Société pour l'Amélioration* (reprinted in *La Citoyenne*, same issue).

[36] Surprisingly, Charles Sowerwine does not make this connection in his discussion of the Federation; see his *Sisters or Citizens?*, pp. 60–61 and 67–70. The formation of this feminist federation may also have been a response to the efforts of the American May Wright Sewall to establish a French national affiliate for the newly formed International Council of Women.

and feminists would circle around one another, sometimes aligning, sometimes disagreeing, each faction claiming to have the better answer to the woman question. But the answers varied, of course, depending on the speaker's frame of reference.

Meanwhile, the ongoing fragmentation of the French socialist groups, which continued until the 1905 unification of the party as the *Section Française de l'Internationale Ouvrière* (SFIO) [French Section of the Worker's International], meant that no "national" endorsement for the 1891 resolution would be immediately forthcoming. If anything, socialist developments in France went in the opposite direction as the *Parti Ouvrier* entered parliamentary politics. To quote Paul Lafargue's biographer, "by the mid-1890s, the party dropped its demands for complete gender equality as a result of its efforts to court male allegiance." In fact, well into the early twentieth century, Lafargue continued to pose as the French socialist champion of women's emancipation – *from* paid labor.[37] The influence of Aline Valette can be seen here.

If indeed, legal reform initiatives could be castigated as "reformist" or "bourgeois" it is clear that the pragmatic initiative sponsored by Jeanne-E. (Archer) Schmahl (1846–1916) to enact two specific laws certainly qualified. An English woman by birth (her mother was French and her father English), she had come to France to study medicine in the early 1870s, but had never completed her degree. For a number of years following her marriage to the French Alsacian Henri Schmahl, she worked as an assistant to the male obstetricians with whom she had studied. In the early 1890s she decided to separate the quest for women's legal rights from the anticlerical republican feminists, forming an organization *L'Avant-Courrière* [The Forerunner], which attracted a number of wealthy, well-placed, and reform-minded women across the political – and religious – spectrum; these included, most famously, the immensely wealthy Duchesse d'Uzès (who had bankrolled the Boulangist campaign in the late 1880s) and the writer and editor Juliette Adam, as well as the journalist Jane Misme, who would go on to found *La Française*. The *Avant-Courrière*

---

[37] On Lafargue and his waffling on the woman question, see Leslie Derfler, *Paul Lafargue and the Flowering of French Socialism, 1882–1911* (Cambridge, MA: Harvard University Press, 1998), esp. chapter 16. Quote, p. 246. Not until 1904 would Lafargue rethink his position on the woman question.

In keeping with earlier POF promises, and the founding of a League for the Eight-Hour Day following the 1889 socialist congress in Paris, the socialist deputy Jules Guesde introduced a measure to limit the legal work day for all workers to eight hours, with a forty-eight-hour work week limit. Thanks to Marilyn Boxer for clarification on this point. This measure would take some forty years to enact.

program had two specific objectives: to obtain the right of women to bear witness to public and private legal acts (achieved in 1897) and, most importantly, the right of wives to full control over their own earned income, along the lines of the earlier English Married Women's Property Laws (such a measure would finally be enacted in 1907, after years of obstruction in the French Senate).[38]

In the meantime another distinctively woman-centered variety of feminism had begun to emerge. In October 1895 the French journalist and self-proclaimed "Christian feminist" Clotilde Dissard (dates not known) published the first issue (sixty pages) of a bi-monthly review *La Revue Féministe*.[39] The first issues of this periodical were quite eclectic, containing articles by the already-famous and independent-minded journalist Séverine (pseud. of Caroline Rémy Guébhard, 1855–1929) on "La cause des femmes," articles by Jeanne-E. Schmahl, addressing concerns about economic competition between the sexes, by Marya Chéliga on "childish fears," and many others. Aline Valette wrote on the economic situation of women in the second issue (20 October 1895), and Dissard herself addressed "Feminism and Solidarity" in the third issue (5 November), attempting to explain why the "Latin race" seemed so hostile to the "integral emancipation" of women. Why should feminism be thought to "destroy" women's beauty, why should an egalitarian notion of family bring about "the ruin of the family"? Dissard concluded that there was no serious argument to be made against feminism, and that only people's prejudices and selfishness (*égoisme*) stood in its way.[40] Yet men, she said, will not provide the solution, and only a united front of women ("*une véritable solidarité féminine*") based on their special qualities of love, pity, and awareness of their social mission could bring about the change. She warned that women must not get caught up in the vain quarrels and divisiveness characteristic of men. "The splintering into enemy groups is a masculine proceeding that does not suit women."[41] Moreover, she stated, "Feminism must not become the property of one race, of one religion, of one doctrine, of one party." Feminists must place themselves

---

[38] Jeanne-E. Schmahl and *L'Avant-Courrière* have never attracted the attention they should. Sketches can be found in *Historical Dictionary of the French Third Republic*, vol. 2, 893–894. See also Jane Misme, "Les Grandes figures du féminisme (1): Jeanne Schmahl," *Minerva* (26 October 1930).

[39] Dissard's *La Revue Féministe* published three volumes before it ceased publication in 1897. It began as a bi-monthly publication, a "thick" review. It can be consulted on the Internet via the Gerritsen online collection.

[40] Clotilde Dissard, "Féminisme et Solidarité," *La Revue Féministe*, n° 3 (5 November 1895), 97–101; quote, p. 98.

[41] Dissard, "Féminisme et Solidarité," p. 100.

above doctrines and above political parties. Only thus could feminists, in solidarity, prepare the future. This was a fine idea in principle, but one that would prove difficult to realize.

In April 1896, the *Fédération des Sociétés Féministes* organized a second "Congrès Féministe International" in Paris. It received wide coverage in the press – it was front-page news in *Le Temps* and also heavily reported in *Le Figaro* and other daily newspapers – thereby contributing further to the popularization of the new terminology and the program it represented.[42] This Paris congress stimulated the organization of a number of successor congresses around Europe – in Geneva and Berlin in 1896, in Brussels in 1897, and in The Hague in 1898.[43] The massive London congress of the International Council of Women followed in 1899; and two Parisian congresses would be held in 1900 (to be discussed in Chapter 8). Not all of these congresses would openly designate themselves as "feminist," however.

Several months later, in November 1896, Marya Chéliga edited a special issue of the *Revue Encyclopédique Larousse* devoted to French feminism; it was there she made the claim for inventing *féminisme* on Fourier's behalf. Whether or not she deliberately intended to discredit or disarm Potonié-Pierre's or Auclert's claim is unclear.[44] In any case, other publications soon appeared using one or another of the words *féminisme* or *féministe* in their titles.[45]

---

[42] On the 1896 Congress, see Wynona H. Wilkins, "The Paris International Feminist Congress of 1896 and its French Antecedents," *North Dakota Quarterly*, 43:4 (Autumn 1975), 5–28. Wilkins' article draws on press coverage from *Le Figaro*. However, *Le Temps* provided seven straight days of coverage, including two articles on the front page; see *Le Temps*, 7 (p. 1), 9 (p. 4), 10 (p. 1), 11 (p. 2), 12 (p. 4), 13 (p. 3), and 14 (p. 3) April 1896.

[43] Geneva, 8–12 September 1896; Berlin, 19–26 September 1896; Brussels, 4–7 August 1897; The Hague, 25–26 July 1898.

[44] See the special issue, "Les Femmes et les féministes," *Revue Encyclopédique Larousse*, n° 169 (28 November 1896).

[45] For example, Marie C. Terrisse, *Notes et impressions à travers le "féminisme,"* (Paris: Fischbacher, 1896); Auguste Fabre, *Le Féminisme; ses origines et son avenir* (Nîmes: Imprimerie Veuve Laporte, 1897); and Paul Souday, "Humanisme et féminisme," *La Revue Bleue* (4 December 1897). In August 1896, the *Revue Politique et Parlementaire* launched a series of articles on "féminisme" in England, Italy, the United States, Australia, and Germany. The authors included Millicent Garrett Fawcett, Emiliana Mariani, Harriet Hanson Robinson, Elizabeth Wolstenhume, and Lily Braun-Gizycki. Despite these many examples, the computer search I originally ordered in April 1986 in the database of ARTFL (American and French Research on the Treasury of the French Language) informed me that the first usages discovered were the following, all by male writers: for *féministes*, 1898 (F. Coppée, *La Bonne souffrance*); for *féminisme*, 1900 (O. Mirbeau, *Journal d'une femme de chambre*); and for *féministe*, 1904 (L. Frapié, *La Maternelle*). As of that date, there were very few women authors represented in this database and virtually no periodical literature or political tracts. I trust that the database has since included more women authors.

The related terms *masculinisme* and Aline Valette's alternative term *sexualisme* likewise made frequent appearances.[46]

Importantly, the French words *féminisme* and *féministe* spread quickly into other languages. By 1894–1895 the terms had crossed the Channel to Great Britain.[47] In her report on the status of women in France prepared for the September 1896 Women's Congress in Berlin, Eugénie Potonié-Pierre took credit on behalf of herself and her colleagues for launching the word *féminisme*, and praised the press for carrying it forward.[48] Before the turn of the century the words feminism and feminist were popping up in published sources in Spanish, Italian, German, and also in Greek and Russian. By the late 1890s the words had jumped the Atlantic to Argentina and the United States, though it appears that neither word was commonly used in the United States much before 1910.[49] Detractors in France would nevertheless insist – despite overwhelming evidence to the contrary, including the repeated claims of Hubertine Auclert and so many others – that "feminism" was a concept foreign to France, an undesirable international import.[50]

Defining Feminism? How Did Contemporaries Understand Its Meaning?

From the early 1890s on, despite the calls for unity from Clotilde Dissard and solidarity from Eugenie Potonié-Pierre, feminist factions and fractures

---

[46] Auclert also pioneered the word "*masculinisme*"; see, for example, her editorial concerning the first socialist May Day celebration, "Masculinisme international," *La Citoyenne*, n° 159 (June 1890). "*Sexualisme*" appears to be the contribution of Aline Valette in *Socialisme et sexualisme; programme du Parti Socialiste féminin* (Paris, 1893). This tract also juxtaposes the terms *féminisme* and *masculinisme*; see pp. 60, 64. Subsequently, in 1906, Jeanne Oddo-Deflou would publish a book entitled *Le Sexualisme* (see Chapter 10 in Part III).

[47] According to the 1933 Supplement to the *Oxford English Dictionary* (the 1972 Supplement to the *OED* retains these dates and attributions), the earliest reported use of "feminist" dates from 12 October 1894, in the *Daily News* (London); "feminism" was introduced in April 1895, in a literary book review. The latter reference, a very short unsigned review, was published in the *Athenaeum* (27 April 1895). It introduced a novel entitled *The Grasshoppers*, by a Mrs. Andrew Dean [pseud. Mrs. Alfred Sidgwick]. The author of the review put the word "feminism" in quotation marks. A more significant usage is Virginia M. Crawford, "Feminism in France," *Fortnightly Review* (April 1897), 524–534.

[48] Potonié-Pierre's report appeared in *Der Internationale Kongress für Frauenwerke und Frauenbestrebungen, Berlin, 19–26 September 1896*, ed. Rosalie Schoenflies et al. (Berlin: Walther, 1897), p. 40.

[49] For additional information on the international spread, see my articles, "Sur l'origine des mots 'féminisme' et 'féministe'," and "On the French Origin of the Words 'Feminism' and 'Feminist'," cited in n. 1.

[50] In all her writings, Maria Deraismes insisted on the indigenous (French) origins of women's rights claims, grounded in the principles of the revolution. In his essay on France in *The Woman Question in Europe* (New York: Putnam's Sons, 1884), Theodore Stanton likewise developed a clear case for French origins. Claims to the contrary seem to emerge only after 1896.

did emerge. Like their republican and socialist counterparts in *fin-de-siècle* France, groups and individuals espousing divergent theories of what constituted feminism began to categorize themselves and their rivals through the now familiar practice of exclusionary classification and the formation of separate organizations and publications.[51] By the beginning of the twentieth century, one could find many self-described or attributed feminisms: "familial feminists," "integral feminists," "Christian feminists," "socialist feminists," "bourgeois feminists," "radical feminists," and, of course, "male-feminists." This phenomenon poses interesting questions for the historian of feminism: Who was "really" a feminist? At what point, and over which issues, did some feminists become branded by others (or brand themselves) as antifeminists? Which advocates of which answer to the woman question held women's best interests at heart? Could it be even said, as feminists claimed, that all women shared the same interests? What must the fundamental criteria be? And, most important politically, who would decide? Such questions remain as lively and as troubling in public discourse today as they were in France in the 1890s.

There was certainly no shortage of discussants about the meaning and significance of feminism. The early, very general definitions clearly reveal the tensions between the needs of the woman as an embodied individual of the female sex who sought to escape her subordination (and, beyond that, to contest the androcentric and still patriarchal character of French society and family life) and the demands of a larger society (experiencing a major socioeconomic transition) whose future well-being required some form of ongoing partnership between the sexes to assure the production of children. If indeed this tension could be viewed as "paradoxical" (as Joan Scott and others have claimed), it was a paradox intrinsic to the human condition itself and no mere consequence of the gender-blind revolutionary concept of "universal man."[52]

---

[51] For earlier discussions of the varieties of feminism, see Marilyn J. Boxer, "'First Wave' Feminism in Nineteenth-Century France: Class, Family and Religion," *Women's Studies International Forum* 5:6 (1982), 551–559; and my articles "Depopulation, Nationalism, and Feminism" and "Defining Feminism," both cited in n. 1.

    For several early twentieth century attempts at classification by male authors, see especially Charles Turgeon, *Le Féminisme français* (2 vols., Paris: L. Larose, 1902) and the arch antifeminist Théodore Joran, *Le Mensonge du féminisme* (Paris: Savaète, 1905), pp. 290–294, and his snide comments on the *Almanach féministe* in his book, *Au Coeur du féminisme* (Paris: Savaète, 1908). These authors will be discussed in Part III.

[52] See Joan Wallach Scott, *Only Paradoxes to Offer: French Feminists and the Rights of Man* (Cambridge, MA: Harvard University Press, 1996).

When Hubertine Auclert first claimed the labels *féminisme* and *féministe* in the 1880s, she used them as synonyms for "the emancipation of women" and its partisans, mirroring the allusion to the emancipation of slaves, a well-entrenched metaphoric comparison that continued to resonate in late-nineteenth-century French society. Auclert, of course, insisted on the vote for women and the program she spelled out in 1891 provides further details. Perhaps the best means of understanding what feminism meant to 1890s French feminists can be derived from the unanimous specific resolutions of the 1892 Feminist Congress: 1) preparation of a *Cahier des Doléances* addressed to the public powers in France and also abroad; 2) equal pay for equal work; 3) suppression of night work for women (with several votes against); 4) establishment of a French African Society, with the objective of establishing a laic school for girls in Senegal; 5) equality of women and men before the law; 6) promotion of women in the pharmaceutical profession; 7) opening of refuges for pregnant women; 8) legalizing political candidacy and voting by women, in the interest of ending war; 9) raising children to favor peace not war; 10) abolition of the morals police, and promotion of a single moral standard for the sexes; 11) abolition of the laws governing prostitution and promotion of a living wage for women; 12) call for a law that would allow removal of "child martyrs" from abusive parents; 13) punishments for abortion and for infanticide; 14) promotion of a single standard of justice for both sexes; 15) promotion of unions [*syndicats*] for women in all professions.[53] Nowhere did these resolutions state explicitly that the ultimate objective was to challenge masculine domination. That was, however, the subtext.

The rush to definition, as well as controversy over specific issues, gathered steam following the April 1896 feminist congress in Paris, co-organized by the groups *Solidarité*, headed by Eugénie Potonié-Pierre, and the venerable *Ligue Française pour le Droit des Femmes*, where the former teacher Marie Bonnevial (1841–1918) served as secretary-general under the presidency of Maria Pognon (1844–1925). At this congress controversies broke out over several specific issues: the question of whether or not women's employment should be regulated, coeducation of the sexes, and (by innuendo) the question of family limitation. Moreover, young male socialist hecklers showed up again at the 1896 congress, just as they had in 1892, and attempted to disrupt the proceedings.[54]

---

[53] There being no published proceedings of the 1892 congress, the press provides the best guide to its intentions. See E. P-P [Eugénie Potonié-Pierre], "Congrès Général des Sociétés féministes," *Le Journal des Femmes: organe du mouvement féminin*, n° 7 (June 1892), 1–2.
[54] Socialist or "collectivist" disruptors: see *Le Temps*, reports of 17 May 1892 and 11 April 1896.

As in 1892, the 1896 congress proceedings were published in the press, but its fifty-five resolutions appeared as a separate eight-page pamphlet. Though criticized for being "unable to work out any coherent policy," in fact, the congress advocated, as shown in its resolutions, specific solutions that could be achieved through specific legislation under the Third Republic.[55] The resolutions addressed the problem of married women's nationality and that of their children, proposed amendments to marriage procedures, called for the evaluation of women's work in the family, and demanded a state budget for maternity. The congress resolutions further insisted on the elimination of the legal requirement that a husband sign an authorization allowing his wife to take employment, as well as an equalization of the legal rights of mothers with those of fathers. They advocated abolition of regulated prostitution and the requirement of premarital health certificates for future spouses, equal punishment for adultery, reforms concerning women's prisons, the inviolability of human life, arbitration instead of armed conflict, eligibility of women to serve on expropriation juries and on the councils of *prud'hommes*, an equal voice in questions concerning public instruction, admission to jobs in the public assistance field, inclusion in juries and other public bodies, and, last but not least, political rights.[56] Significantly, this 1896 congress in Paris led to the "conversion" to feminism of several key women journalists – especially Marguerite Durand (1864–1936), who in late 1897 would found the feminist daily *La Fronde*, as well as Eugénie (Ghénia) Glaisette de Sainte-Croix (1855–1939), known in the press as Savioz (and better known after her marriage in 1900 as Madame G. Avril de Sainte-Croix). As the first secretary-general of the *Conseil National des Femmes Françaises* (formed in 1901), she would publish an entire book on the subject – *Le Féminisme* (1907).[57]

It was abundantly clear that what most feminists thought family should and could be, or marriage could be, was not in accord with the French family as defined either by the Civil Code or the Catholic Church. It was

---

[55] See Sowerwine, *Sisters or Citizens?* p. 72.

[56] *Voeux Adoptés par le congrès Féministe International, tenu à Paris en 1896 pendant les journées du 8 au 12 avril.* The copies I have consulted date from 1900, as they list on the final page the several reforms enacted since the congress. Copies can be consulted in the Bibliothèque Marguerite Durand (dossier 37), at the Archives du Féminisme in Angers, Fonds Brunschvicg, 1 AF 571, and in the Gerritsen Collection (microfiche and online).

[57] See coverage in *Le Temps*, cited in n. 42; also the brief summaries by Laurence Klejman & Florence Rochefort, *L'Égalité en marche: Le Féminisme sous la Troisième République* (Paris: FNSP & des femmes, 1989), pp. 101–103, and Anne Cova, *Maternité et droits des femmes en France (XIXe–XXe siècles)* (Paris: Anthropos, 1997), pp. 87–89.

clear, too, that the rights and plights of children and their mothers were importantly on their minds, even as feminists insisted that decently paid employment opportunities be open to women who needed to support themselves. Even so, some had reservations about the implications of such a sweeping program of emancipation. Following the 1896 congress, Clotilde Dissard, the founder of *La Revue Féministe*, began to emphasize the collective interests of society over those of the individual; what others called "integral feminism" made her nervous. She described her publication's mission this way:[58]

> The mission of the *Revue Féministe* is to defend familial feminism. We think that the true social unit is the human couple, that the isolated individual is an imperfect being insofar as his or her principal function, which is to give birth to the society of tomorrow, is rendered extremely difficult if not impossible. The ideal we seek to realize is the more perfect organization of the family, the more harmonious cooperation of man and woman in the common task, the division of functions according to the aptitudes of each sex, whether natural or acquired by education.

Another definition, also dating from 1896, came from the Swiss male feminist, Louis Bridel, a Francophone law professor from Lausanne who published extensively on the woman question. Like Dissard a "relational" feminist, he defined feminism this way:[59]

> Feminism is a doctrine of emancipation and reorganization, intended to raise the status of women: not only to guarantee to woman her individual rights in the name of the principle of the autonomy of the human being, but also in the interest of the collectivity, the sound functioning of which requires the collaboration of the two constitutive halves of the human species. On one hand, a project of justice and liberty; on the other, a project of social utility.

Others whom we would also retrospectively call male-feminists, like the pro-woman writer Léopold Lacour (1854–1939), simply refused to use the neologisms "feminism" and "feminist," preferring the term "Integral Humanism" [*humanisme intégral*]. Lacour published a book with this title in 1897, with the subtitle "*le duel des sexes; la cité future*" [the duel of the sexes; the future community].[60] Not all women liked the terminology either; the English agitator Dora Montefiore, speaking at the Brussels

---

[58] Dissard, in *La Revue Féministe*, vol. 2 (1896), 245–246.
[59] Louis Bridel, *Questions féministes* (Paris: Librairie Fischbacher, 1896), p. 17.
[60] Léopold Lacour, *Humanisme intégral: le duel des sexes, la cité future* (Paris: P. Stock, 1897).

feminist congress in 1897, also asserted her preference for Lacour's term "humanism" over feminism.[61]

Writers for *La Fronde* promptly delineated the meaning of *"féminisme."* In the very first issue (9 December 1897) of this remarkable daily with an all-female staff, Maria Pognon defined feminism as "the common action of individuals of both sexes to demand for woman rights equal to those of men."[62] This definition focused specifically on the campaign for equality before the law. But was this all it was about? Some did not think so; economics and culture were also targets.

Thus, as the words entered popular usage and the elements of the feminist program became more explicit, disputes would break out in print between secularists and Catholics as well as with socialists of differing stripes over the content and degrees of that emancipation, and the best means of achieving it, given the adverse political climate. Educators, politicians, academics, and journalists of both sexes would all make their voices heard in the debates. In 1905, after a decade of debate, one commentator would remark that "many people talk about feminism, but there is much disagreement about the meaning of this word; there are perhaps no more than ten persons, maybe not even five, or even two, who agree on a definition of feminism and who envisage its consequences the same way."[63] Was that really the case?

As often as not, such discussions of definition evolved as "fallout" from defining one's perspective with respect to the claims (and writings) of a particular writer. Feminism's advocates had, in fact, set the bar for the debate; other writers now had to state their positions with respect to what they thought feminism stood for. For example, Anna Lampérière (1854–?), a prominent educator, journalist, a divorced working mother of two daughters, and author of the important Solidarist tract *Le Rôle social de la femme* [Woman's Social Role, 1898], positioned herself as an antifeminist. "Feminism," she claimed, "was based on a false interpretation of the facts."[64] The sticking point for her was the ostensible competition

[61] Montefiore's insistence on prioritizing "humanisme" over "féminisme" was reported by Potonié-Pierre in her report on the Brussels congress in *La Question Sociale*, n°s 40–41 (1897), 635–637.

[62] Maria Pognon, "Féminisme," *La Fronde*, n° 1 (9 December 1897), 2.

[63] "Quelques opinions sur le féminisme," clipping attributed (handwritten) to *L'Information des Lettres*, 15 November 1899, but undoubtedly published in late 1905 or 1906, given that the books under review are from 1905. My attempts to locate the original publication have been unsuccessful.

[64] Anna Lampérière, *Le Rôle social de la femme; devoirs, droits, éducation* (Paris: Félix Alcan, 1898), p. 2. It should be noted that the publisher of her book was also an active member of her *Société de l'Éducation Sociale*. On Lampérière's program and contributions, see Anne Rebecca Epstein, "Gender, Intellectual Sociability and Political Culture in the French Third Republic, 1890–1914"

[*concurrence*] of women and men in the marketplace, which she opposed in absolute terms. Production, in her view, should be the province of men. Lampérière seemed less interested in principle than in function, adhering tightly to the male-breadwinner model; she delineated separate spheres of activity for women and men, and insisted on the importance of woman's role in the home as "the organizer" [*organisatrice*] and as "the artist of human life" [*artiste de la vie humaine*].[65] This situation she defined as "normal." Even single women should not step out of their "sphere," by sticking to womanly professions such as teaching and "social housekeeping" [*ménagère sociale*]. As historian Anne Epstein acknowledges, Lampérière seemed to advocate "difference in equality" rather than "equality in difference," but Lampérière's notion of "equality" was ill-defined.[66] What was more, this campaigner's own public trajectory as a divorced working woman seemed to contradict her prescriptions for limiting women's roles.[67]

Responding to Lampérière's assertions in *La Fronde* in an early 1899 article "Féministes et 'Féminines'," Louise Debor maintained that "Feminism boils down to this absolute principle: the imprescriptible right for every human being, without distinction of sex, to life and to be one's own master."[68] Economic independence, in her view, was the key to women's emancipation. Women must be able to take responsibility for themselves. The following week, Debor addressed the relationship of feminism to the institution of marriage as currently organized. In her view (as in that of virtually all feminists by this time), as a minimum the disempowering legal nonstatus of French wives needed to be ended – and their work in the household valued economically. "We, the wise feminists, want the stability of marriage; and that is why we demand that it [marriage] be legally founded on justice."[69]

Lampérière had been publishing on the education of women in *La Nouvelle Revue* since at least 1891 as well as in *Le Temps, Le Figaro,* and

---

(Unpublished Ph.D. dissertation, Indiana University, 2004). See also Anne Epstein, "Anna Lampérière, solidarité et citoyenneté féminine sous la Troisième République," *Genre et Histoire*, n° 3 (Fall 2008), consulted at www.genrehistoire.revues.org, and Anne R. Epstein, "Pas 'tout a fait des nôtres': Anna Lampérière et les féministes au tournant du XXe siècle," in *Les Féministes de la première vague*, ed. Christine Bard (Rennes: Presses Universitaires de Rennes, 2015), pp. 75–87.

[65] Lampérière's arguments are reminiscent of those used by the American Catharine Beecher, who lauded domesticity for women, even as she, as a single woman, kept busy as a teacher and public speaker.

[66] Epstein, "Anna Lampérière, solidarité et citoyenneté féminine," p. 7.

[67] Epstein, "Anna Lampérière, solidarité et citoyenneté féminine," p. 5.

[68] Louise Debor, "Féministes et 'Féminines'," *La Fronde*, n° 427 (8 February 1899), 1.

[69] Louise Debor, "Féministes et 'Féminines': Situation de la femme dans le mariage," *La Fronde*, n° 434 (15 February 1899).

the *Revue Pédagogique.* She was particularly critical of the heavy curriculum being offered in the girls' *lycées,* which she believed was producing a generation of misfits (she later referred to them as *"féministes frustrées"*).[70] Her own proposals ranged well beyond the earlier notion of "mother-educator"; although this element was part of her vision, her notion of woman as the "artist of human life" clearly transcended it.[71] There was something deeply Comtiste (i.e., the views of Auguste Comte, which entailed placing woman on a pedestal) about Lampérière's views. Curiously, she made no reference to the problem of regulated prostitution or any other pressing social issue of the day, and although a divorced woman herself, she seemed – publicly at least – oblivious to the Civil Code's rigid subordination of wives in the laws governing marriage.

In 1898, Anna Lampérière founded a group called the *Société des Études Féminines* (SEF) [Society for Womanly Studies] – which would be countered by Jeanne Deflou's *Groupe Français d'Etudes Féministes* (GFEF) [French Group for Feminist Studies], also established in 1898, for the study and promotion of legal reforms in the position of women.[72] Deflou's study group became fascinated by the notion of an original matriarchy preceding patriarchy and in 1903 would publish a French translation of the long introduction to Bachofen's *Das Mutterrecht* [Mother Right].[73]

A loud and clear feminist statement defined the "programme" of a new quarterly "thick" journal, the *Revue de Morale Sociale* (*RMS*), first published in the spring of 1899 and endorsed by many Francophone feminists and abolitionists from France, Switzerland, and Belgium in company with women's rights advocates throughout Europe and even North America.[74] Although the word "feminist" does not appear in the first few pages of its statement of purpose, the point of this new publication was unmistakably feminist in spirit, and on its third page its editors stipulated that "the rights of woman" and the "feminist movement" were among its concerns. The mission of the *RMS* was to study the "moral and social relations between the sexes." Its manifesto was decidedly gendered, or one might also say "relational," insofar as it focused on the "reciprocal rights and duties of

---

[70] Anna Lampérière, *La Femme et son pouvoir* (Paris: V. Giard & E. Brière, 1909), pp. 21–25, as cited in Epstein, "Anna Lampérière."

[71] "Artiste de la vie humaine," cited by Epstein from Lampérière's *Rôle social,* p. 32.

[72] The statutes of the Groupe can be consulted in Oddo-Deflou's dossier ODD at the BMD.

[73] *Le Droit de la mère dans l'antiquité: Préface de l'ouvrage "Das Mutterrecht" de J. J. Bachofen. Traduit et publiée ainsi que la table analytique des matières par les soins du Groupe Français d'Études Féministes* (Paris: n.p., 1903).

[74] By "thick" journal, I am appropriating the term used to describe Russian periodical publications, in which each issue comprised several hundreds of pages.

man and woman, the obligations and prerogatives of each in the family and in society, and the regulation of their relations of coexistence: these are vital issues for the community as a whole and for each of its members." Furthermore, the manifesto claimed that "the happiness or unhappiness of individuals, the prosperity or decadence of nations, and even the very future of the human race depend in large part on their resolution."[75] Finally, the program stated loud and clear that women were the "victims of injustice" in virtually every respect.

The authors of this program also addressed the sexual politics of knowledge by remarking that, to date, questions of morals, law, pedagogy, political economy, and sociology had been regarded "from the more or less exclusive perspective of man" – "as if woman were of an inferior essence and only accessory value" and should not be taken into account except insofar as man decides it is important to do so; it was as though "he alone is the goal, the woman is nothing more than the means." This situation, the authors of the program stated, must change. Women's and men's relationship must be addressed "in a spirit of harmony" and "solidarity, not only for women's benefit but for the greater good of the entire society."[76] The editors then spelled out the journal's principles, which included upholding a single moral standard for both sexes; respect for every human being; guarantees of women's rights as well as those of men; intervention of the collectivity on behalf of those whose state of subordination and relative weakness renders them unable to defend themselves; and prohibition of every sort of official organization of debauchery and measures of "exception" on grounds of "morals." "In sum, Pro Justicia!" Justice was the goal.[77] It was the abolitionists' program writ large and it was feminist to the core. This journal was the first thick "scientific" journal to claim programmatically that the relation of the sexes was fundamental to social order and progress, and to undertake investigations of issues that pertained to achieving a more equitable balance in those relations.

Both feminism and internationalism were central to the *RMS* project, which had advisors and French-speaking contributors from outside the French-speaking world as well as within, and made it a point to translate submissions from other languages. *RMS* introduced research on developments

---

[75] "Programme," *La Revue de Morale Sociale*, 1:1 (March 1899), 1; transl. by Anne Epstein, with KO.

[76] "Programme," *RMS*, 1:1 (March 1899), 2.

[77] The *Revue de Morale Sociale* has been studied briefly by Anne-Marie Käppeli, *Sublime Croisade: Éthique et politique du féminisme protestant, 1875–1928* (Carouge/Genève: Éditions Zoé, 1990), pp. 148–150, and more extensively by Anne Epstein, "Gender, Intellectual Sociability and Political Culture," chapter 3.

elsewhere, as a way of quelling French fears, as for example, with regard to experiments in coeducation. Of particular interest is the *RMS*'s first query to readers: "*Quelle mission morale attribuez-vous au mouvement féministe dans l'évolution de la société contemporaine?*" [What moral mission do you attribute to the feminist movement in the evolution of contemporary society?] The German version of the question does not use the word *féministe* but speaks of the *Frauenbewegung*, or women's movement; the English version frames the question in terms of "the participation of women in public life." It is clear from this that the responses, which appeared in the second issue, would vary widely, depending on their point of origin.[78] Most striking is the relative caution expressed by respondents, as though they knew they were juggling a hot potato.

The German-born feminist activist Kaethe Schirmacher (1865–1930), a Ph.D. from Zurich and a longtime resident of Paris who had passed the French *agrégation*, contributed her "Notes on the Present State of Feminism" to the *RMS* in 1899,[79] and she would continue to inform readers of comparative developments in women's rights worldwide, with a particular focus on women's employment. She was one of a handful of Germans who did use the French terminology. What did she think the word "feminism" meant? Beginning with the demand for equivalence of value of the sexes, or what we have referred to earlier as equality-in-difference: "If man and woman are different beings, they are both human beings, two equals, with diverse but equivalent aptitudes. It is the idea that one would translate in Latin as *non similes sed pares*, and in German as *nicht gleichartig aber gleichwertig.*"[80] Her description of feminist demands follows closely on that laid out by the *Cahier des Doléances* of 1892 (published in 1893): equivalent education, economic opportunities, equal pay for equal work; legal rights for married women and rights for single mothers; the vote; a single moral standard. Having attended and spoken at the World's Congress of Representative Women in Chicago in 1893, Schirmacher had acquainted herself with developments in other countries. Like Marya Chéliga (in 1896), she attributed the "birth" of [organized] feminism to the United States, though she was well aware that protests against injustices toward women could be traced much further back in time and she did acknowledge the importance of France's contributions since the Revolution. Schirmacher's interest was clearly comparative; she went on to discuss developments in

---

[78] The responses appear on pp. 197–208.
[79] See Schirmacher, "Notes sur l'état actuel du féminisme," *RMS*, 1:2 (April–June 1899), 220–236.
[80] Schirmacher, "Notes sur l'état actuel," 220–221.

many other countries of the West, separating them by religious group-
ings and distinguishing protestant countries from Roman Catholic countries as well as from Greek (and Russian) Orthodox countries. This
account would provide a summary of her 1898 book, *Le Féminisme aux
États-Unis, en France, dans la Grande-Bretagne, en Suède et en Russie*
[Feminism in the United States, in France, in Great Britain, in Sweden
and in Russia].[81]

Feminists quickly realized that one of their most important projects
would be to combat the hackneyed stereotypes of feminism that were still
deeply embedded in French culture. Marya Chéliga went on the attack in
the first issue of the *Revue Féministe*, with her article "Craintes puériles"
[Childish Fears].[82] The journalists of *La Fronde* would press on with this
campaign. The widely quoted retrospective remark by Marguerite Durand
(in 1903) about the importance of her blonde hair to feminism is well-
known to scholars, if not to general readers; what is perhaps less well
understood is the extent of the active efforts made by the other journalists
[known as *les frondeuses*] to tackle head-on and defuse these malicious
stereotypes, not least the stereotype that feminists were by definition
unwomanly.[83] Already in late March 1898, columnist and novelist Daniel
Lesueur penned a column about women's attire, in which she insisted on
the importance, for progressive women, of charm, seduction, and beauty –
the proverbial tools of women's influence. "Grace is a duty for us, just like
goodness."[84] When Aline Valette died in mid-March 1899, her womanly
qualities (graciousness and charm) would be praised to the skies by Marie
Bonnevial in *La Fronde*, and *La Revue Socialiste* would reproduce Bonnevial's praise in its April issue.[85]

Further feminist statements in *La Fronde* ensued. Louise Debor's
columns of 8 February and 19 July 1899 stand out in particular. In
the course of her debate with Anna Lampérière, she had laid out a

[81] Kaethe Schirmacher, *Le Féminisme aux États-Unis, en France, dans la Grande-Bretagne, en Suède et en
Russie* (Paris: A. Colin, 1898). On Schirmacher's French publications, see Karen Offen, "Kaethe
Schirmacher, Investigative Reporter & Activist Journalist," pp. 200–211, in *Proceedings of the Western
Society for French History, Portland, 2011*, vol. 39 (2013), ed. Joelle Neulander & Robin Walz. Online
at www.quod.lib.umich.edu/w/wsfh/0642292.0039rgn=full+text.
[82] Marya Chéliga, "Craintes puériles," *La Revue Féministe*, 1:1 (1 October 1895), 8–9.
[83] On the importance of blonde hair, see Marguerite Durand, "Confession," *La Fronde*, n° 2003
(1 October 1903). For earlier statements on the importance of beauty, see "Vera," "De l'influence de
la beauté dans le féminisme," *La Fronde*, n° 323 (27 October 1898), & Marcelle Tinayre, "Le Devoir
de beauté," *La Fronde*, n° 424 (5 February 1899).
[84] Daniel Lesueur, "A propos d'une ... robe," *La Fronde*, n° 92 (11 March 1898).
[85] Marie Bonnevial, "Aline Valette," *La Fronde*, n° 470 (23 March 1899), front page; *La Revue
Socialiste*, vol. 29, n° 172 (April 1899), 491–492.

full-fledged version of what feminism meant. She also addressed the
prevailing negative stereotype:[86]

> Feminism is not, as its adversaries pretend to believe, a passionate, violent,
> warlike, illogical, incoherent and problematic opinion, stemming from a
> lack of knowledge of physiological laws that govern feminine nature; [it is
> not] a systematic revolt by woman against her natural destiny; [it is not] a
> demand for rights to the exclusion of duties; [it is not] a refusal to obey the
> laws of social solidarity; [it is not] an infraction of the primordial rule of
> every human group.

Debor then contested the "bourgeois stereotype" of a feminist as "hair cut
short, exaggerated traits, uncontrolled gestures, resolute speech, ugly
matted clothing, cigarette ... asexual, deprived of all physical charm and
of all moral grace, of every delicate feature of woman." This stereotype, she
asserted, was utterly out of date. She added that women have begun to
realize that they are wrong[87]

> to neglect their best weapons, beauty and grace, magic weapons that
> fracture any obstacle they brush up against. . . . the privileges of femininity
> are not beneath the "new women" and that it suffices only to be in the
> right. One can be right with grace and display the most solid intellectual
> gifts with the aid of a becoming hairdo and a flowing dress. What is
> eloquence except the decoration of truth?

Having been extremely impressed by the extraordinary display of feminine
charm and elegance by the women who had convened in London earlier
in July for the congress of the ICW organized by Lady Aberdeen (to be
discussed in a later chapter), Louise Debor offered the hope that the
1900 congress to be held in France could – and would – radiate a
comparable degree of feminine charm. Performing femininity? Yes, indeed!
Quite deliberately so!

New Women? Modern Women? Emancipated Women?

Féminisme was conspicuously performing everywhere, especially following
the French feminist congress of 1896. The debates on the woman question
were by no means restricted to feminist publications; long articles in the
daily and periodical press of the 1890s addressed feminism in particular
and women's issues more generally. Numerous examples can be found in

---

[86] Debor, "Féministes et 'féminines'," *La Fronde*, n° 427 (8 February 1899).
[87] Debor, "Le féminisme en dentelles," *La Fronde*, n° 508 (19 July 1899).

mainstream publications such as the *Revue des Deux Mondes* (*RDM*), the *Revue des Revues* (known after 1901 as *La Revue*), the *Revue Politique et Parlementaire* (*RPP*, which published a series of insightful articles on feminisms in various countries),[88] the *Nouvelle Revue* of Juliette Adam, the *Revue Blanche* and the *Revue Bleue*, *La Quinzaine*, *Le Correspondent*, the *Revue Scientifique*, the *Journal des Économistes*, the *Revue d'Économie Politique*, and the *Revue Philanthropique*. Articles also appeared frequently in the daily press, ranging from *Le Figaro*, the *Echo de Paris*, and *La Libre Parole* on the Right to *Le Temps*, *Le Matin*, and the *Journal des Débats* in the Center, and on the Left *Le Siècle* (ed. Yves Guyot), *Le Radical* (ed. Gustave Rivet, which for many years ran a monthly column by Hubertine Auclert, following her departure from *La Libre Parole*) as well as in the socialist periodicals and press – notably in the *Revue Socialiste* and *La Question Sociale*.

How did the debates on this phenomenon called feminism relate to the other emergent debate of the 1890s – the "*femme nouvelle*" or New Woman? Or to an alternative expression, the "*femme moderne*," or Modern Woman?[89] There are differences between the overarching debates on the woman question per se, the specific debates of the 1890s on the "new woman modern woman" and feminism, that require more systematic scrutiny over time.

In France, the terminology "*femme nouvelle*" was hardly new in the 1890s. It had already made an appearance in the early 1830s as one of the shifting titles (beginning with the fourth issue) of the Saint-Simonian women's publication (first known as *La Femme libre/Apostolat des Femmes*, it also used the title *Tribune des Femmes* and the subtitle *Affranchissement des Femmes*).[90] The notion resurfaced in the Russian literature of the 1860s (particularly in the works of N. G. Chernychevsky, who had been much influenced by French discussions) to describe the "new people" and, in particular, the young Russian women of the 1860s who sought higher

[88] The series in *RPP* included: Millicent Garrett Fawcett, "Le féminisme en Angleterre," vol. 9 (August 1896), 298–315; Marya Chéliga, "Le Féminisme en France," vol. 13 (August 1897), 271–284; Emilia Mariani, "Le Féminisme en Italie," vol. 13 (September 1897), 481–495; Elizabeth Wolstenhume, "Le Féminisme en Australie," vol. 15 (March 1898), 520–545; Harriet Hanson Robinson, "Le Mouvement féministe aux Etats-Unis," vol. 17 (August 1898), 245–272; and Lily Braun Gizycki, "Le Mouvement féministe en Allemagne," vol. 20 (April 1899), 21–65. Cf. n. 45.

[89] In this chapter (as in the other chapters in Part II) I will restrict my analysis of these debates to the publications of the 1890s through 1900. In Part III my analysis will turn to the publications of the early twentieth-century literature (from 1901 to 1914).

[90] For details of the shifting titles, see Claire Goldberg Moses & Leslie Wahl Rabine, *Feminism, Socialism, and French Romanticism* (Bloomington: Indiana University Press, 1993), p. 282.

education and promoted revolution. Not surprisingly many factions in the French public did not welcome the term – or what it stood for – with open arms, though it certainly offered what some would later call "a site for analysis" of the woman question debates.

What did the New Woman signify as the French approached the end of the nineteenth century. In her book *Disruptive Acts: The New Woman in Fin-de-Siècle France,* historian Mary Louise Roberts described the New Women as women who "challenged the regulatory norms of gender by living unconventional lives and by doing work outside the home that was coded masculine."[91] In short, they transgressed what Roberts calls "the liberal ideology of womanhood" that "includes but also transcends republicanism."[92] She ultimately centers her analysis on the women in the circle of *La Fronde,* the all-woman daily newspaper that began publication in December 1897 under the direction of Marguerite Durand, but she focuses especially on the "performativity" of *les frondeuses* as New Women – as well as on the spectacular career of the actress Sarah Bernhardt (b. 1844). As we will see, however, there were many other "new women" active in France during the 1890s. Most of them were also "performing femininity." And, as I have already indicated, there were good reasons for this.[93]

A new phase in European concern about changing gender relations had erupted in 1894, following a media debate in England over the New Woman, a debate fostered by the mass circulation press and by a cluster of new woman novels, including those of Thomas Hardy and Sarah Grand.[94] This debate raised (again) many of the issues that feminists had

[91] Mary Louise Roberts, *Disruptive Acts: The New Woman in Fin-de-Siècle France* (Chicago: University of Chicago Press, 2002), p. 3.

[92] Roberts, *Disruptive Acts,* pp. 3–4. Rather than labeling this latter ideology as "liberal" (or "bourgeois"), it might be more accurate to simply refer to it as "the ideology of domesticity." It is not clear what was "liberal" about it (indeed, leading liberals of the time objected to it as constraining) and as we have seen in the preceding chapters, not all republicans subscribed to it.

[93] Art historian Linda Nochlin summed it up this way in 2011: the New Woman offered "a radical challenge to the status quo. . . . a beacon to the adventurous and a threat to the upholders of traditional values." The New Woman offered "liberation from the ideal of true womanhood, the bondage of marriage and self-sacrifice, the denial of achievement through career and work outside the home, and above all, sexual subordination and submission. It was even liberation from the notion that sexuality and gender were unambiguous givens." Nochlin's last statement is less true of the 1890s than it would become in the later twentieth century when she was writing. See Linda Nochlin, "Foreword: Imagining and Embodying New Womanhood," in *The New Woman International: Representations in Photography and Film from the 1870s through the 1960s,* ed. Elizabeth Otto & Vanessa Rocco (Ann Arbor: The University of Michigan Press, 2011); quote, pp. 2–3.

[94] Sarah Grand published "La Femme nouvelle" in the *Revue des Revues,* vol. 26 (15 September 1898), 616–622. Contrasting the "*femme ancienne*" with the "*femme nouvelle*" she argued that the "*femme nouvelle*" was a great improvement. This piece was translated from an article by Grand in *Lady's Realm,* an English women's magazine.

problematized – marriage, education, economics, morality, and so on.[95] French novelists, playwrights, and journalists quickly joined in the exploration of new woman themes. The Anglo-French writer Claire de Pratz testified to the indistinct boundaries between the "new woman" and the "modern woman" in her 1896 article entitled "L'Esprit de la Femme moderne en Angleterre – 'La Femme nouvelle'," which addressed the "Anglo-Saxon authors." In the words of Pratz, "With what energetic disgust she recoils from two evils that she had for generations supported with dumb patience of despair. The first was marriage without love; the second was maternity without consent."[96] The Parisian poet and journalist Jules Bois (1871–1943), who reported sympathetically on feminist activities and advocates in *Le Figaro*, published his charter for female emancipation, *L'Ève nouvelle* [The New Eve] in 1896, and also published on "La femme nouvelle" in the November 1896 issue of the *Revue Éncyclopédique Larousse* (*REL*), edited by Marya Chéliga and dedicated to "Les Femmes et les féministes."[97] Chéliga was also a contributor to the *Magazine International*, in which the article by Claire de Pratz (cited earlier) had appeared.

In his essay on the new woman, stimulated by what he had heard at the 1896 feminist congress and by Chéliga's invitation, Jules Bois critiqued the long-entrenched authoritarian male-centered perspective, which he called "anthropocentrism" (we would say today "androcentrism"), insisting that woman is not a satellite that revolves around man but is a "free star" [*astre libre*]. To the Proudhonists of the world, who had so repetitiously insisted that woman has only the choice between harlot and housewife (and to the anxious, obedient women who fear change), he answered:[98]

> Harlot, if she wants – housewife if she wants; something in between if she wants (there is lots of space between the two) . . . but a human being, just like man himself, free in mind and body, carrying her own particular mission. . . . Woman, before she is a spouse, lover or mother, is a woman. She is free, she is what she is and not what man wants her to be.

---

[95] For discussion of the European-wide debates on the "new woman," see my *European Feminisms, 1700–1950*, pp. 188–196. See also Elaine Showalter, *Sexual Anarchy: Gender and Culture at the Fin de Siècle* (New York: Viking Penguin, 1990).

[96] Claire de Pratz, "L'Esprit de la Femme moderne en Angleterre – 'La Femme nouvelle'," *Magazine International*, n° 6 (May 1896), 173–182; as quoted by Jules Bois.

[97] See "Les femmes et les féministes," edited by Marya Chéliga, *Revue Encyclopédique Larousse*, n° 169 (28 November 1896). Copies exist in the BMD and in the archives of the League of Nations in Geneva. It can also be consulted on microfilm through Research Publications Inc., History of Women collection, reel 541, no. 4156.

[98] See Jules Bois, "La Femme nouvelle," in *REL* (November 1896), 832–840 ff.; quotes, 832–833.

Invoking the novels of Sarah Grand and Olive Schreiner, as well as the negative notions of the German philosophers Schopenhauer and Nietzsche, Jules Bois invokes the "superior woman" who freely unites with the superior man, along the lines suggested to him by the idealist poets and novelists of the North, who unlike French authors do not "preach vice, cast woman into the mud and then disdainfully spit on her." "My greatest delight," wrote Bois, "is to proclaim that a man who also aspires to be 'new,' has understood the superiority of the new woman, and bowing before her, accepting her sublime lesson, demands to be one of her soldiers."[99] Invoking centuries of efforts by women to raise up other women, Jules Bois expressed his admiration for the Saint-Simonian women and especially Flora Tristan, but also for Pauline Roland, Jeanne Deroin, Julie Daubié, Caroline de Barrau, Marie Béquet de Vienne – whom he called the "*saintes nouvelles.*" "The new society will not be the new society," Bois stated, "unless it becomes feminist; without that, it will only be the old society a bit more off the track, thanks to the sophisms of men."[100]

Following Jules Bois's impassioned essay on the *femme nouvelle* (and the new man) in the 1896 *REL* was a lengthy fifty-five-page feature entitled "La Femme moderne par elle-même," which confirmed that considerable overlap (and perhaps even confusion) existed between "*la femme moderne*" and "*la femme nouvelle.*"[101] Introduced by Marya Chéliga, who insisted that the spirit of the times was to improve society by combatting the "formerly all-powerful principle of authority" and promoting the sacred right of, or at least respect for, the rights of the individual."[102] This stellar catalogue – exquisitely illustrated with Art Nouveau designs – included biographical information (with sketches, portraits, quotations, and even facsimiles of handwritten signatures) on many of the leading women of the day (encompassing writers, artists, feminists, scientists, philanthropists, physicians and lawyers, even a composer) – hailing from France and many other countries including Russia, Finland, and the United States. It offered readers a "Who's Who" of women of achievement, ranging from A (the Countess of Aberdeen, the Scottish aristocrat who then presided over the International Council of Women) to Z (the Russian writer Marie Zebrikova). Chéliga's "modern women" included many French names we

---

[99] Bois, "Femme nouvelle," 834.   [100] Bois, "Femme nouvelle," quote, 840.

[101] The Francophone Russian writer Olga de Bézobrazow, founder of the short-lived *Revue des Femmes Russe* (1896–1897) also published a novel, *La Femme nouvelle,* in 1896. It was first serialized in her periodical.

[102] Chéliga, introduction to "La Femme moderne par elle-même," *REL*, 841.

have already encountered in the course of this book – André Léo and Marie-Louise Gagneur, for example – as well as Virginie Griess-Traut, Léonie Rouzade, and Clémence Royer.

This catalogue also included the Paris-based Irish revolutionary Maud Gonne, the contrarian writer Gyp, the feminist philanthropist Isabelle Bogelot, the journalist Clotilde Dissard (now president of the Syndicat de la Presse Féministe), Maria Martin (editor of the *Journal des Femmes*), Paule Mink, Maria Pognon, Eugénie Potonié-Pierre, the writer Rachilde, Savioz (Mlle de Sainte-Croix), Séverine, and Aline Valette, as well as the explorers Madame R. Bonnetain and Jane Dieulafoy. It included German women such as Minna Cauer, Minna Kautsky, Lina Morgenstern, and Kaethe Schirmacher, Austrian women such as Auguste Fickert and Bertha von Suttner, Swiss women, Italian women, and Portuguese women, as well as a number of Polish or Polish-affiliated women – Pauline Koutschalska Reinschmidt (*"chef du mouvement féministe en Pologne"*), Elisa Orzeozkowa, Dr. Micheleine Stefanowska (who had studied in Geneva, earning a doctorate in the natural sciences), the French novelist Marguerite Poradowska (whose husband was Polish), and the Spanish novelist and feminist militant Emilia Pardo Bazan, as well as French artists, sculptors, and composers including Camille Claudel and Cécile Chaminade. Some were married, some divorced; many were mothers, others single. Many were well traveled or had lived in countries other than those of their birth. Most, with some notable exceptions, championed the emancipation of women. Few of them would have spent their days shopping (or shoplifting) in the great department stores – or riding bicycles and playing golf. These sportive "new women" activities were still marked Anglo-American in the 1890s.[103] As Marya Chéliga remarked in a subsequent 1899 article

---

[103] See Christopher Thompson, "Un troisième sexe? Les bourgeoises et la bicyclette dans la France fin de siècle," *Le Mouvement Social*, n°192 (July–September 2000), 9-39, and Siân Reynolds, "Albertine's Bicycle; or: Women and French Identity during the Belle Epoque," *Literature and History*, 10:1 (Spring 2001), 28–41. It seems significant that none of the most prominent feminists were among the women interviewed for *La Femme à bicyclette: Ce qu'elles en pensent*, ed. C. de Loris (Paris: Librairies-Imprimeries Réunies, 1896); most of the respondents were artists, actresses associated with various Paris theatres, or singers at the opera, and most by far preferred the skirt to the split skirt or pants, which they considered too revealing of the "mystery" underneath. Juliette Adam (pp. 6–8) argued that women should be able to wear whatever they want, but qualified her response by remarking that women who bicycled were revealing far too much leg (*mollet* = calf). The female doctor Madame Gaches-Sarraute (pp. 17–18) was the only respondent who made a point of the new freedom that bicycling allowed women to experience, but even she was opposed to "*travestissement.*" On travestissement, that is, cross-dressing or women wearing pants, see the heavily illustrated volume by John Grand-Carteret, *La Femme en culotte* (Paris: Flammarion, 1899). On concerns about bicycle riding stimulating women's genitals, see Dr. Ludovic O'Followell, *Bicyclettes et organes génitaux* (Paris: J.-B. Baillière et *fils*, 1900); this doctor, who is

entitled *"La femme nouvelle,"* in France the New Woman is known only through literary works by men – but in England she had become a living reality.[104] Given the catalogue of women Chéliga had brought together in 1896, however, this seems something of a misstatement. The "living reality" clearly existed in France.

This roster of achieving women featured in the *Revue Encyclopédique Larousse*, however, included only a few younger university-educated women – notably Marie Popelin (the first Belgian woman lawyer and militant feminist), Dr. Stefanowska (mentioned earlier), Sarmisa D. Bilcesco (a Romanian who was the first woman to earn a French law degree) and Jeanne Chauvin (the second, and first woman lawyer admitted to the Paris bar), Aletta Jacobs (the first Dutch woman physician), Dorothea Klumpke (doctorate in mathematics), Sophie Pereyaslawzewa (doctorate in science, Russian zoologist), and Ernestine Perez-Barahona of Chile (doctorate in medicine, Santiago). Nor did it include many of the new working women – *"les travailleuses"* – who did not fit the category of *"ouvrières."* Most were single women, often from less privileged backgrounds. They were becoming teachers in the new public schools, finding employment as clerks in public administration – working as inspectresses of care facilities, of schools, of the criminal and the poverty-stricken, and of working conditions in factories.[105] To alarmists, it seemed that the New Woman could be any woman, young or old, who left her house without an escort or a chaperone, or who aspired to accomplish anything out of the ordinary – certainly the term was applied to the few women who aspired to practice a profession, or – worse – to talk back to power.

What was certain is that by the 1890s one could see increasing numbers of "untraditional" young women in France. These young women were "stepping out".[106] They were increasingly visible as well as increasingly vocal (especially, but not exclusively, as concerned limits on their opportunities). These were the young women who took to the bicycle and wore split skirts to facilitate their movements, and whose activities were

in favor of the bicycle for women, dismisses the masturbatory concerns but does caution women against riding during menstrual periods or pregnancy. A new and highly amusing study of these controversies is Christine Bard, *Une histoire politique du pantalon* (Paris: Seuil, 2010).

[104] Marya Chéliga, "La Femme nouvelle," *Petit Bleu* (29 June 1899); clipping, BMD, DOS 38.

[105] See Linda L. Clark, *The Rise of Professional Women in France: Gender and Public Administration since 1830* (Cambridge, UK: Cambridge University Press, 2000).

[106] See Michelle Perrot, "Stepping Out," chapter 17 in *A History of Women: Emerging Feminism from Revolution to World War*, ed. Geneviève Fraisse & Michelle Perrot (Cambridge, MA: Harvard University Press, 1993), pp. 449–481.

routinely caricatured in the press.[107] Although there had been equally unconventional women earlier in French history, in the 1890s these exceptions were threatening to become the new "normal." Moreover, this "new Eve" seemed quite threatening to the "old Adam."[108]

In retrospect we can see that France had been blessed with a number of New Women in the course of the nineteenth century, many of whom refused to conform to the prescriptive stereotype of the docile domesticated woman. In addition to the Saint-Simonian women invoked by Jules Bois, we should consider, for example, Maria Deraismes, single and rich, who was still actively campaigning for women's rights until her death in 1894 at the age of 66. Or the accomplished women of previous generations – besides the celebrated writer George Sand (1804–1876) – for example, Veuve Cliquot (Barbe-Nicole Clicquot-Ponsardin; 1777–1866), who as head of the family wine business had transformed it and made an enormous fortune by running naval blockades of French harbors to deliver champagne to the aristocrats of St. Petersburg; or Madeleine Sophie Barat (1779–1865), founder of the elite religious teaching order of the Sacré-Coeur; or Anne-Marie Javouhey (1779–1851), the intrepid nun who founded a teaching order with worldwide reach to teach young blacks in French Guinea and in Africa, and eventually created schools in Asia – and commandeered the French navy to deliver her and her nuns to their posts. Consider the writers Hortense Allart (1801–1879), Flora Tristan (1803–1844), and Delphine Gay de Girardin (1804–1855; the same age as George Sand); or Madame Luce (1804–1882), who founded schools for girls in Algeria; or the writer Louise Colet (1810–1876) and the remarkable painter Rosa Bonheur (1822–1899); or Julie-Victoire Daubié (1824–1874), who pioneered the *baccalauréat* for French women and published the first

---

[107] The most notorious caricature of the decade, "Revendications féminines," appeared in the satirical paper *Le Grelot*, on 19 April 1896. It depicted a woman with cigarette and skirts drawn up for convenience leaving home by bicycle for the feminist congress, while her clearly unhappy husband is left behind doing the dishes, with the crying child in the background, and with orders to prepare dinner punctually. This drawing was surrounded by a number of smaller cartoons, all of which ridicule imaginary feminist claims.

[108] See Michelle Perrot, "The New Eve and the Old Adam: Changes in French Women's Condition at the Turn of the Century," transl. Helen Harden Chenut, in *Behind the Lines: Gender and the Two World Wars*, ed. Margaret Randolph Higonnet, Jane Jenson, Sonya Michel, & Margaret Collins Weitz (New Haven, CT: Yale University Press, 1987), pp. 51–60. This essay goes well beyond the "turn of the century") as does Annelise Maugue, "The New Eve and the Old Adam," in *A History of Women: Emerging Feminism from Revolution to World War*, ed. Genevieve Fraisse & Michelle Perrot (Cambridge, MA: Harvard University Press, 1993), pp. 515–532. The trope of the Old Adam versus the New (or Modern) Eve had been around for decades; see Angélique Arnaud's 1872 article, "Le vieil Adam – L'Ève moderne," *L'Avenir des Femmes*, n° 92 (6 October 1872).

book about the plight of poor women from a female perspective. Other "new women" come to mind: the redoubtable intellectual who translated Darwin's *Origin of Species* into French, Clémence Royer (1830–1902); the journalist and *politicienne* Juliette Adam (1836–1936), fervent republican and founder-editor of the influential *Nouvelle Revue*; and the nonconformist novelist Camille Delaville (1838–1888). Both Bonheur and the renowned explorer and archeologist Jane Dieulafoy (1851–1916) had obtained authorization from the Parisian police to allow them, as women, to wear masculine dress, but other artistic women including Gyp adopted male clothing from time to time. The prolific woman author Th. Bentzon (pseud. of Marie-Thérèse de Solms-Blanc, 1840–1907), an impoverished aristocrat, had become part of the inner circle of writers at the *Revue des Deux Mondes* in 1872 (on George Sand's recommendation), in some sense paving the way for journalists such as the freewheeling Séverine (1855–1929) and uncompromising women's rights campaigners such as Hubertine Auclert (1848–1914), who wrote under her own name and had founded her own periodical.

All these women were conspicuous for their originality, their intellect, their courage, or their pioneering contributions to French (and European) culture; all thought "out of the box." Many (though by no means all) were committed republicans who promoted women's rights in particular and human rights more generally. Some were honored in their lifetime, while others were feared – indeed, even reviled - because of their independent ways and views. Others cautiously endorsed the status quo, even as their lived experience contradicted it. It was simply not true that all nineteenth-century Frenchwomen were repressed and confined to their households.

In the early 1890s, however, the focus of French writers was less on their own "new women" than on the women of England and especially of the United States, who seemed to them to be radically emancipated and increasingly active participants in civil society. Several studies on the subject of American women appeared in French publications in 1893, around the time of the World's Columbian Exposition in Chicago, where French women's exhibits (including 800 books written by French women) impressed visitors to the Woman's Building. The well-traveled Charles de Varigny (1829–1899) published *La Femme aux États-Unis* (1893). He was extremely impressed by the women of America: he applauded their individuality, their adaptability, and their intelligence – as well as their beauty – and, in particular, the fact that they could and did marry for love. "Whether one approves of it or not," de Varigny claimed, "one cannot deny the extent of their feminine influence."[109] Paul Bourget was less enthralled: in a long chapter on American women and girls in his 1895 volume *Outre-Mer (Notes sur l'Amérique)*, he too admitted to being impressed by the extreme liberty enjoyed by American girls, but questioned why men had *allowed* this independence of women to flourish. By way of explanation, he would suggest that in America (in contrast to France) sensuality was not people's number one preoccupation.[110] Bourget represented a stream of thinking that endorsed the venerable androcentric notion that males should keep "their" women under control.

The now-established Parisian novelist and essayist and an expert on American literary works, Th. Bentzon, went to the United States in 1893 on assignment from the *Revue des Deux Mondes*. She was already well connected in American intellectual circles and could access writers and political figures, thanks to her earlier coverage of American literary works in the *RDM*. Bentzon traveled throughout the country for a full year, visiting Chicago (during the World's Columbian Exposition), Boston, the West, and the South and carefully recording her experiences and observations with publication in mind. In 1895 she published the first of several versions of *Les Américaines chez elles*, a work marked particularly by her interest in women's education, settlement houses, and in the still-novel form of women's clubs, which she viewed as an extension of American women's maternal roles. Although exemplary of the "new woman" *à la française*, insofar as she was supporting herself through her writing, Th. Bentzon remained worried about the prospect of antagonism between the sexes and proposed that women should not push their claims for emancipation too far.[111] A new woman? Certainly! Interested in women's issues? Absolutely! But a self-declared feminist? Never.[112]

---

[109]   Charles-Victor-Crosnier de Varigny, *La Femme aux États-Unis* (Paris: A. Colin, 1893). This work also appeared serially, at least in part, in the *Revue des Deux Mondes*.

[110]   Paul Bourget, *Outre-Mer* (Paris: Lemerre, 1895). See vol. 1, chapter 4: "Les Femmes et les jeunes filles," pp. 99–150, esp. p. 105. Some of his observations were originally published in *Le Figaro* in 1894–1895.

[111]   See Th. Bentzon, *Les Américaines chez elles* (Paris: Calmann-Levy, 1895, and subsequent editions). Some chapters had already appeared in the *RDM* in 1894. The book appeared in simultaneous English translation: *The Condition of Woman in the United States*, transl. Abby Langdon Alger (Boston: Roberts Bros., 1895). On Bentzon's publications and journey, see Anne-Caroline Sieffert, "Thérèse Bentzon: itinéraires d'une Française aux États-Unis (1840–1907)," pp. 109–130 in *Le Voyage au féminin*, ed. Nicolas Bourguinat (Strasbourg: Presses Universitaires de Strasbourg, 2008). On this writer's continuing interest in the United States, see Joan M. West, "America and American Literature in the Essays of Th. Bentzon: Creating the Image of an Independent Cultural Identity," *History of European Ideas*, 8:4–5 (1987), 521–535.

[112]   Notwithstanding, Th. Bentzon would later be eulogized by Julie Siegfried (at a meeting of the *Conseil National des Femmes Françaises* in March 1907) as "one of our most valiant feminists" who has brought a considerable number of supporters to the cause. See the *Journal des Femmes*, n° 193 (April 1907).

Another prominent French writer, the multilingual literary critic and historian Arvède Barine [pseud. of Louise-Cécile Boufflé, Mme Charles Vincent, 1840–1908], was clearly fascinated by the woman question and published biographical articles and books about women. Barine "was profoundly preoccupied by the condition of woman without being engaged in the feminist movement."[113] Though she recognized the need for change in the relations between women and men, she was less sanguine than others that male domination could ever be eliminated. In August and September 1894 she published a series of articles in the *Journal des Débats* on the subject.[114] Although she insisted that the relationship between the sexes should be thoroughly reorganized and that *union libre* might indeed provide the ultimate answer, she nevertheless asserted that "the situation of the French woman is one of the best and most beautiful that exists. This should encourage her to leave the experiment of feminism to another nation, for fear of mistaking the shadow for the substance."[115] No mention of reforming the Civil Code or demanding equal pay for equal work appears in Arvède Barine's text; instead she worried that men would crush women in any professional competition. In 1896 she provided an unsympathetic critique of women's rights demands in the *RDM*, through an analysis of new novels by the British writers Olive Schreiner, George Egerton, and Thomas Hardy.[116] Arvède Barine, like subsequent French neo-traditionalist-nationalist writers (including those of *Action Française*), was particularly critical of the "new morality" portrayed by these novelists, considering such [promiscuous sexual] behavior the product of antisocial individualism as propagated by earlier generations of romantic writers; in her view, passion and marriage could not mix. She instead insisted on the necessity of discipline, of repressing the instincts, and wondered why women would attack the institution of

---

[113] On Arvède Barine, see Isabelle Ernot, "Une historienne au tournant du siècle, Arvède Barine," in *Mil Neuf Cent: Revue d'Histoire Intellectuelle*, n° 16 (1998), 93–131; quote, p. 130. An older study by Florence Ravenel, "A Woman Critic of Women: Arvède Barine," appears in Ravenel's *Women and the French Tradition* (New York: Macmillan, 1918), pp. 39–63. Professor Whitney Walton is currently investigating the contributions of Arvède Barine.

[114] See Arvède Barine's four-part feuilleton, "La Question féministe en Angleterre," in the *Journal des Débats*, issues of 7 August, 21 August, 4 September, and 18 September. The last two installments discuss the recent "new woman" novels published by Sarah Grand, George Egerton, and other British writers.

[115] "Suite du roman féministe – Conclusion," *Journal des Débats* (18 September 1894). In this context, *union libre* was generally understood to mean pairing up, and even having children, without the sanction of legal marriage. The foremost exponent of this approach during the 1890s would be the anarchist educator Paul Robin; see his tract *Libre amour, libre maternité* (Paris: Éditions de l'Humanité nouvelle, 1900).

[116] Arvède Barine, "La Gauche féministe et le mariage," *Revue des Deux Mondes* (1 July 1896), 106–131.

Christian marriage, which she asserted had been designed expressly for their protection.[117] Yet by late 1896 she admitted in print that "the feminist movement, shorn of its extravagances ... responds to needs and suffering that are all too real."[118] In the following decade when Arvède Barine would turn to writing history, focusing on women of the seventeenth century, she pondered the meaning of independence for women, the question of marrying or not, of retaining freedom of action, as she studied women in the courts of Louis XIII and Louis XIV, particularly the life of one of the most singular "new women" of the Bourbon monarchy, the wealthy and intrepid Grande Mademoiselle, cousin of Louis XIV and a leader of the uprising known as the Fronde.[119] A new woman? Probably not! A feminist? No, but an increasingly vocal sympathizer with the quandary of women in male-dominated societies.

The theater offered other opportunities to discuss the "new woman" and, for that matter, to discuss feminism. Very often writers confused the two. Did unhappy wives count as "new women"? It depends on how they responded to their situation. Take Ibsen's play, *A Doll's House* [*Une Maison de Poupée*], for example.[120] Some critics deemed the play too Scandinavian and "cold," and yet, despite the actress Réjane's inter-pretation of Nora as a coquette, her proclamation of independence from husband and children to search for self-realization clearly touched a nerve in French society. One contemporary observer, the Catholic feminist Marie Maugeret, remarked in 1899 that Ibsen's play had become such an explosive subject that many Parisian hostesses had forbidden their guests to discuss it at their salons.[121]

---

[117] Arvède Barine, "La Gauche féministe," 130. See the response of Camille Bélilon in *La Fronde*, n° 118 (5 April 1898) to Barine's earlier defense of Christian marriage in *Le Figaro*. The key to saving marriage, in Bélilon's view (here reflecting the feminist consensus of several decades) is to reform the law so that wives are not subordinated to a husband's will; only thus could marriage be a dignified union of two equal and responsible beings.

[118] Arvède Barine, "Progrès du féminisme en Allemagne," feuilleton (front page) in the *Journal des Débats* (2 December 1896).

[119] Ernot, "Une historienne ... " (see n. 113).

[120] According to Mary Louise Roberts, the Parisian premiere in April 1894 did not kick up a particular fuss at the time, while Jean Elisabeth Pedersen argues that, despite only two performances, *Une Maison de Poupée* "created an overnight sensation that left a lasting impression." See Roberts, *Disruptive Acts*, chapter 1; on the reception of Ibsen, p. 22. Jean Elisabeth Pedersen, *Legislating the French Family: Feminism, Theatre and Republican Politics, 1870–1920* (New Brunswick, NJ: Rutgers University Press, 2003), pp. 50–52.

[121] In her open letter to May Wright Sewall, explaining why Catholic feminists found it impossible to join the International Council of Women, Marie Maugeret would chastise Sewall for not "controlling" the ideas expressed by speakers in the series of lectures she sponsored in Paris during the Exposition. Maugeret claimed that French tradition held the mistress of the house responsible for what was said by others at her house; she was to be responsible for determining the

French playwrights would elaborate on Ibsen's unhappy heroine's wish to escape domesticity and "find herself." Both *Les Tenailles* (premiered 28 September 1895) by Paul Hervieu (1857–1913) and *La Vassale* (1897) by Jules Case built on this theme.[122] Significantly, both premiered at the *Comédie Française*, the leading Parisian theatre. These heroines were not "yet" new women, but rather dissatisfied, trapped conventional upper-class wives who had arrived at an impasse in their marriages and had experienced a "consciousness-raising" moment. To this mix one should add Hervieu's next play, *La Loi de l'homme* (premiered on 15 February 1897).

In her study *Legislating the French Family* (2003), historian Jean Elisabeth Pedersen has demonstrated how Hervieu's *Tenailles* "Frenchified" the debate about the untenable position of unhappy spouses (and especially the pathetic position of wives in contemporary French marriage law) by reopening the question of loveless marriages and promoting public discussion of possible liberalization of the extremely restrictive divorce law enacted by republican legislators in 1884. *Les Tenailles* created a sensation. The critic of *Le Gaulois* focused on the buzz during intermission on opening night: "The play instantly brought up the whole series of questions on the matter, from indissoluble marriage in perpetuity to free or liberated unions, including the related subjects of marital authority, women's rights, optional adultery, paternal power, extended or restricted divorce – even the baccalaureate and universal suffrage."[123] Theater critic Francisque Sarcey tried to "naturalize" Ibsen – and demonize Hervieu – by pointing to the "real" origins of Ibsen's rebel women as lying in the novels of George Sand ("thereby preserving the superiority of nineteenth-century French culture"); he considered Ibsen's and Hervieu's female creations as "even worse" than those of Sand. Generally speaking, Sarcey sympathized with the conventional husband.[124]

From that point on, the works of Hervieu and those of Ibsen were inextricably linked in the French literary imaginary, and the expansive

---

subjects to be treated and the way in which they were discussed. She was skeptical that individualist Americans would accept this sort of "collective liberty." See Maugeret, "Lettre ouverte à Mme May Wright Sewall," *Le Féminisme Chrétien*, 5:8 (August 1900), 225–230; quote, 228.

[122] Roberts, *Disruptive Acts*, pp. 28–29. Writing in *La Fronde*, Louise Debor argued that Ibsen should not be counted among the apostles of feminism, because he believed that mothers should and must resolve the human problem; but at the same time she insisted that salonnières in Paris considered the *Maison de poupée* a "hot topic" that would disrupt the congeniality of their salons, requesting their guests not to discuss it. See Louise Debor, "Ibsen et le féminisme," *La Fronde*, n° 190 (16 June 1898).

[123] Pedersen, *Legislating the French Family*, chapter 2. Pedersen's translated quotation from Georges Thiébaud in *Le Gaulois* (the exact date of publication in 1895 not provided) appears on pp. 47–48.

[124] Pedersen, *Legislating the French Family*, pp. 50–52. According to this author (p. 51), Zola had already enunciated the link between Sand and Ibsen.

imagery that developed around the "new woman" quickly evoked feminist questions. Some of the new imagery came in old and familiar packages, such as the trope of the topsy-turvy household. Other imagery tried to imagine what the future held. In the interim, dramatic authors such as Jules Case probed the dilemmas of French marriage: in a response to a review by Jules Lemaître in the *RDM*, Case denied that he was advancing any "thesis," but rather probing "the conflict between man and woman ... dramatic, disquieting, eternal, thus timely. It offers new elements in each era, passion, discussion, sadness. I exploited it; that's all." Jules Case's objective was to immerse his audience in the conflict of the couple – to examine Revolt against Authority, an authority vested in the husband, which he viewed as an unjustified usurpation.[125]

It was amidst this climate of turbulent debate about feminism and the New Woman that Marguerite Durand (1864–1936) founded *La Fronde* in late 1897.[126] Most of her collaborators had been born during the Second

---

[125] See Jules Case, *La Vassale, pièce en 4 actes* (Paris, Comédie-Française, *17 juillet 1897*) (Paris: P. Ollendorff, 1897); and Case, *A propos de La Vassale. Lettre à M. Jules Lemaître* (Paris: P. Ollendorff, 1897).

[126] There has been a flurry of scholarship concerning Marguerite Durand and *La Fronde*, much of which is repetitive and/or focused on coverage of the Dreyfus Case. The most recent book by François Chaignaud, *L'Affaire Berger-Levrault: Le Féminisme à l'épreuve (1897–1905)* (Presses Universitaires de Rennes, 2009) examines Durand's controversial effort to promote women typographers by forming women's unions and exonerates her from accusations of strikebreaking activities in Nancy, when members of the women's union went in to replace the striking printers – at full pay. Jean Rabaut's *Marguerite Durand (1864–1936)* (Paris: L'Harmattan, 1996), is poorly documented and full of errors, while Elizabeth Coquart, *La Frondeuse: Marguerite Durand, patronne de presse et féministe* (Paris: Payot, 2010) offers a well-informed popularization. An early, still valuable study is the dissertation by Sue Helder Goliber, "The Life and Times of Marguerite Durand," Ph.D. dissertation, Kent State University, 1975 (consulted at the Bibliothèque Marguerite Durand in Paris). There is still no in-depth scholarly biography of Durand nor any comprehensive collection of her published writings.

Mary Louise Roberts has contributed several articles on the subject (see below, 1997, 1999), as well as chapters in her book, *Disruptive Acts* (cited n. 91); see also the Bibliothèque Marguerite Durand's publication, *Histoire d'une femme, mémoire des femmes*, by the director Annie Dizier-Metz (Paris: BMD, 1992) as well as the following articles (listed in order of publication): Julie Sabiani, "Féminisme et dreyfusisme," *Les Ecrivains et l'Affaire Dreyfus: Actes du colloque organisé par le Centre Charles Péguy et l'Université d'Orléans (29, 30, 31 octobre 1981)* (Paris, Presses Universitaires de France, 1983), pp. 199–206; Colette Cosnier, "Les 'Reporteresses' de *La Fronde*," in *Les Représentations de l'Affaire Dreyfus dans la presse ... *, ed. E. Cahm & François-Rabelais, 1997), pp. 73–82 (a special issue, hors serie, of *Littérature et Nation*); Máire Cross, "Les Représentations de l'Affaire Dreyfus dans le journal *La Fronde* entre decembre 1897 et septembre 1899," in *Les Représentations de l'Affaire Dreyfus dans la presse ... *, ed. E. Cahm & Pierre Citti (Tours: Université François-Rabelais, 1997), pp. 83–90; Mary Louise Roberts, "Subversive Copy: Feminist Journalism in Fin-de-siècle France," in *Making the News: Modernity and the Mass Press in Nineteenth-Century France*, ed. Dean de la Motte & Jeannene M. Przyblyski (Amherst: University of Massachusetts Press, 1999), pp. 302–350 (an earlier version in French appeared in *Clio*, 1997); Mary Louise Roberts, "Acting Up: The Feminist Theatrics of

Empire; by the 1890s they were in their mid-30s or 40s (or even older; Clémence Royer was born in 1830). Many of them had unconventional backgrounds. Durand was not only an "illegitimate" child and a retired actress; by the early 1890s she was divorced and then became a mother outside wedlock. Several of her best-known collaborators including Séverine and Savioz were a bit older – over 40 (both were born in 1855) and well established as journalists when they began reporting in *La Fronde*. They were the contemporaries of Léopold Lacour (1854–1939), Emile Durkheim (1858–1917), and Paul Margueritte (1860–1918). Yet unlike these men, very few (if any) among these *Frondeuses* had passed the *baccalauréat*, or were part of the newer generation of university-educated women.

The objective of *La Fronde* and *"les Frondeuses"* was to provide a voice to the entire female sex. Although the *Frondeuses* were anything but traditional in their aspirations and behavior and published many articles about feminism and feminist activities, they presented themselves – in dress and behavior – as "womanly" new women.[127] At the headquarters of *La Fronde* (14, rue Saint- Georges in Paris), even as Durand organized women's labor unions while her well-paid reporters were covering the legislature and the *Bourse* (the stock exchange), going on out-of-town assignments to cover the Dreyfus retrial in Rennes, and digging out the facts about government-regulated prostitution, she insisted on providing a "feminine" environment, assiduously holding her banquets and receptions for ladies. While the *Frondeuse* and novelist Daniel Lesueur argued that for feminists grace and goodness were duties, other staff writers not only lauded the founding of cooking schools (where women could be taught the principles of nutrition and hygiene that would contribute to a better *pot-au-feu*) but also propounded the establishment of crèches in all the *quartiers* of Paris as

---

Marguerite Durand,"in *The New Biography*, ed. Jo Burr Margadant (Berkeley & Los Angeles: University of California Press, 2000), pp. 171–217; Michelle Perrot, "La Fronde des femmes au temps de l'Affaire Dreyfus," in *Confrontations: Politics and Aesthetics in Nineteenth-Century France*, ed. Kathryn M. Grossman et al. (Amsterdam: Editions Rodopi, 2001), pp. 287–300; Françoise Blum, "Revues féminines, revues féministes," in *La Belle Époque des revues*, ed. Jacqueline Pluet-Despatin, Marie Leymarie, & Jean-Yves Moller (Paris: IMEC, 2002), pp. 211–222; Sandrine Lévêque, "Femmes, féministes et journalistes: genre et engagement comme ressources professionnelles: le cas des rédactrices de *La Fronde*," in *Le Journalisme au féminin: assignations, inventions, stratégies*, ed. Béatrice Damian-Gaillard et al. (Rennes: Presses Universitaires de Rennes, 2010), pp. 47–68. Earlier publications that discuss *La Fronde* include Li Dzeh-Djen in 1934 and Evelyne Sullerot in the 1960s, both on the more general topic of the French women's press.

[127] Whether this meant that the message of *La Fronde* was "unreadable" to the surrounding culture, as Roberts has alleged, remains to be considered; my sense is that the *Frondeuses* knew exactly what they were doing and that their intended audience understood their mission and message very well. It may have been recalcitrant or antifeminist men (the "old Adams") who had trouble deciphering – or refused to acknowledge – this innovative womanly feminist strategy.

well as cooperative kitchens.[128] Such reforms might ameliorate the condition of women in their prescribed domestic sphere; they did not challenge frontally the sexual division of labor or male supremacy in the family, but – and this is the important point – they sought to subvert it from within. They talked back to (male) power incessantly, albeit in a very womanly way.

To some degree, this behavior was associated with a new movement in the arts in France. Art historian Debora Silverman argues that "French writers, craftsmen, and painters of the 1890s . . . rallied to the celebration of female fecundity and decorative domestic intimacy, rather than obsessing on the *femme fatale*."[129] Centered in the Central Union of the Decorative Arts, this French version of Art Nouveau reflected a concerted effort "to discover a distinctively French modern style." Silverman posits that this "concentration on woman as the queen and artist of the interior emerged in the 1890s as a response to the challenge of the *'femme nouvelle'* . . . who was perceived as threatening to subvert women's roles as decorative objects and decorative artists."[130] This extraordinary effort to perform an elaborate "femininity," whether in personal terms, in journalism, or in the arts was doubtless a response to the negative images of feminists that proliferated in French society to the point of triggering a huge backlash against New Women, feminists, and – more generally – Anglo-American style modernity. Indeed, the responses to women's "stepping out" were multiple and, in some cases extreme. Many of them were merely skeptical, while others revealed themselves as vehemently antifeminist.

Those who opposed the New Woman continued stubbornly to describe her in much the same terms that had been applied in earlier decades to opposing women writers (*les bas-bleus*) or women thinkers – as mannish, "unfeminine," and therefore not "really" women at all. Other opponents waved the red flag of sexual emancipation and voiced their suspicions of flagrant "immorality" by which they meant sexual promiscuity. These two images conveyed widely divergent meanings – but their common

---

[128] Daniel Lesueur [Jeanne Loiseau, pseud.], "A propos d'une . . . robe," *La Fronde*, n° 92 (11 March 1898). Also see Maria Martin, "Le Restaurant à domicile," *La Fronde*, n° 46 (23 January 1898); and Louise Debor, "Une École de cuisine et d'économie domestique," *La Fronde*, n° 602 (2 August 1899).

[129] Debora Silverman, "The 'New Woman,' Feminism, and the Decorative Arts in Fin-de-Siècle France," in *Eroticism and the Body Politic*, ed. Lynn Hunt (Baltimore: Johns Hopkins University Press, 1991), pp. 144–163; quote, p. 145.

[130] Silverman, "New Woman," p. 146. The author identifies this effort as an attempt to align artistic developments with the project of relational feminism (she actually used my earlier, now discarded, term "familial" feminism, which I adopted from Clotilde Dissard).

denominator was acute fear of change in the gender order.[131] Even anarcho-communist artists feared the New Woman, as John Hutton's study of Anarchist antifeminism makes clear.[132] Such men envisioned the "new woman" as free from male control. Some worried that women would be on top and men underneath – the "topsy-turvy" world trope, with its sexual implications, was very old, however, and did not adequately address the complex reality or variety of women's life experiences or their relations with men in the 1890s.[133] The antifeminist novelist Albert Cim (who had dedicated his 1891 novel *Les Bas-bleus* to his predecessors Proudhon and Barbey d'Aurevilly) was obsessed with visions of sex role reversal: "Soon, my friends, we will be the ones who have to make jam and suckle the children."[134] Were such essential tasks so demeaning and, therefore, beneath men's dignity? Obviously, suckling could prove more difficult for men (though nursing bottles did exist), but jam making or, more generically, cooking could be viewed from a feminist perspective as a gender-neutral and necessary task. As Hubertine Auclert had observed several decades earlier, if such jobs were paid, men would have no hesitation at taking them over.[135]

In the 1890s, some older French men – even some who were earlier considered as exemplary male-feminists – had begun to draw the line; this far we will go with emancipating women – but no further. One such critic was the aged Ernest Legouvé, member of the *Académie Française* and advisor to the *École Normale Supérieure de Sèvres*, who since the 1840s had championed women's education, reform of the Civil Code, and many other structural changes in the status of women. In his preface to L. Roger Milès's book *Nos femmes et nos enfants* (1893), Legouvé remarked that where he agreed with the conservative author whose book he was endorsing was that they both condemned some women's desire "to lead the life of a boy." He objected to the secondary curriculum for girls that had become

---

[131] Annelise Maugue, *L'Identité masculine en crise au tournant du siècle, 1871–1914* (Paris: Rivages/Histoire,1987), and Christine Bard, ed., *Un Siècle d'Antiféminisme* (Paris: Fayard, 1999).

[132] See John Hutton, "Camille Pissarro's *Turpitudes Sociales* and Late Nineteenth-Century French Anarchist Anti-Feminism," *History Workshop*, n° 24 (Autumn 1987), 32–61.

[133] See Natalie Zemon Davis's classic analysis of "topsy-turvy world" thinking in her essay, "Women on Top," in *Society and Culture in Early Modern France: Eight Essays by Natalie Zemon Davis* (Stanford, CA: Stanford University Press, 1975), pp. 124–151.

[134] Albert Cim, *Bas-bleus* (Paris: A Savine, 1891), p. 33. Annelise Maugue provides many more choice examples of this topsy-turvy obsession among late nineteenth-century male writers; see *L'Identité masculine en crise*, pp. 45–54.

[135] See Hubertine Auclert, "Femmes! Vous allez prendre notre place," *La Citoyenne*, n° 25 (31 July 1881). I have translated this article in *Feminist Writings from Ancient Times to the Modern World*, ed. Tiffany K. Wayne, vol. 1, doc. 83, pp. 277–283.

"too serious, too scientific, too masculine," preferring to this a "feminized" education – "an education that HAS A SEX."[136] Legouvé thought women should be "womanly" even as they engaged with the world. In 1896, in the *Revue Encyclopédique Larousse*, he reiterated this argument, insisting that because their mission in the world was different than that of boys, the education of girls should be entirely different as well. He reiterated his longstanding argument for equality-in-difference.[137] By the 1890s, though, this argument no longer satisfied those women who wanted to become economically independent and to enjoy professional opportunities heretofore reserved to educated men.

Other opponents appealed to the centuries-old heritage of anti-emancipatory medical literature, adding to it a new twist. French authorities in the emerging social science of psychology, in particular Alfred J. E. Fouillée, and psychological novelists epitomized by Paul Bourget, joined earlier generations of medical men in dissertating on "the psychology of the sexes" as predetermined by their physiological differences, and making authoritative pronouncements on the necessity of limiting women's emancipation.[138] In the most memorable sentence of his long article, Fouillée stated: "What was decided among the prehistoric protozoa cannot be annulled by Act of Parliament."[139]

Victor Cherbuliez, the Swiss-born Protestant writer (another member of the *Académie Française*) who often published under the pseudonym of G. Valbert, was a severe critic of the "New Woman." Valbert had begun publishing on the woman question in the *Revue des Deux Mondes* with his article on the Russian revolutionary Vera Zasulich. In 1880, writing on "the emancipation of woman," he had asserted that the first duty of woman is "grace." He did favor additional education for girls but disdained

---

[136] Ernest Legouvé, preface to L. Roger-Milès book, *Nos femmes et nos enfants: Choses sanglantes et criminalité* (Paris: Flammarion, 1893), as quoted in translation by Ann-Louise Shapiro, *Breaking the Codes: Female Criminality in Fin-de-Siècle Paris* (Stanford, CA: Stanford University Press, 1996), pp. 188–189. Emphasis in original.

[137] Legouvé, in *Revue Encyclopédique Larousse*, n° 169 (29 November 1896), 908.

[138] See Alfred J. E. Fouillée, "La Psychologie des sexes et ses fondements physiologiques," *Revue des Deux Mondes* (15 September 1893), 397–429.

[139] Ibid., 399. Fouillée actually took this quotation (without due credit) from one of the books he reviewed; see Patrick Geddes & J. Arthur Thomson's *The Evolution of Sex* (London, 1889; Paris, 1892), p. 267. Only a few years later Fouillée would invoke the threat of "masculinization" of women, which he feared would accompany women's "invasion" of the male professions in France, as was allegedly happening in the United States; see his *Psychologie du peuple français,* 2nd ed. (Paris: F. Alcan, 1899; 1st ed., 1898), pp. 292–293. Fouillée echoed the analysis of Jules Héricourt (unrelated to, and not to be confused with Jenny P. d'Héricourt). See J. H. [Jules Héricourt], "La Natalité dans les pays à civilisation avancée," *Revue Scientifique* (25 July 1896), 123–124.

women's demand for the vote; women, he suggested, really have all the influence anyhow and will lose it if they aspire to the "appearance" of power that men have.[140] (This argument was becoming a well-known antifeminist trope.) In 1886 he reviewed a study by the German reporter on girls' education in France (which subsequently appeared in French translation).[141] In 1889, as the Centennial Exposition was opening in Paris, Valbert/Cherbuliez reviewed a futuristic book published in Germany, *Das Maschinenzeitalter* [The Age of Machines], by an anonymous author (whom he believed to be Max Nordau, but was actually the Austrian feminist and antiwar activist Bertha von Suttner); the reviewer expressed his distaste both for the depersonalization brought on by the new technologies but also for the prospect of elimination of differences between the sexes. The specter of the "*hommesse*" – portrayed as an austere female man, dessicated and unflirtatious – repelled him and made him fearful for the future.[142] In 1897, he reviewed a study on academic women by another German author, Arthur Kirchhoff, who had interviewed a number of university professors about the prospects of admitting women to the German universities. He found that most were opposed, but resigned to it happening. Notably, Kirchhoff reported that the German university professors of history were the most reluctant to see women enter their discipline.[143]

Not all men (not even all members of the *Académie Française*) were antifeminist in the years of the *fin-de-siècle*; some were fervent advocates of the New Woman and of feminism, more generally. For example, the pro-woman literary critic and journalist Léopold Lacour, along with Jules Bois, launched a series of "feminist" lectures (1895–1897) at the Bodinière theatre in Paris in December 1895, which were very well received.[144]

---

[140] G. Valbert [pseud. of Victor Cherbuliez], "L'Émancipation des femmes," *Revue des Deux Mondes* (1 November 1880), 204–216.

[141] G. Valbert [Victor Cherbuliez], "L'Enseignement des jeunes filles en France à propos d'un livre allemand," *Revue des Deux Mondes* (1 January 1886), 202–213.

[142] G. Valbert [Victor Cherbuliez], "L'Âge des machines," *Revue des Deux Mondes* (1 June 1889), 688–697. I owe this reference to Debora Silverman's article (cited n. 129); Silverman evidently did not know that the author in question was actually Bertha von Suttner, soon to become a celebrated antiwar activist. The book in question was *Das Maschinenzeitalter: Zukunftsvorlesungen über unsere Zeit*, originally published anonymously in Zurich in 1889, then again in Dresden/Leipzig in 1899.

[143] G. Valbert [Victor Cherbuliez], "Ce que pensent les professeurs allemands de l'admission des femmes dans les universités," *Revue des Deux Mondes* (1 April 1897), 674–685.

[144] See the report on the first lecture (of the second series) by Lacour in *Le Journal des Femmes*, n° 49 (January 1896), 2, and the clearly misdated article by Paule Mink, "Les vraies femmes," attributed to *La Cocarde*, 24 December 1893, in *Paule Minck: Communarde et Féministe, 1839–1901*, ed. Alain Dalotel (Paris: Syros, 1981), pp. 149–152. I have not yet been able to consult *La Cocarde* to verify the date (which may have been handwritten) on this archived clipping, but the context strongly

Younger male authors portrayed heroines who were exquisitely "feminine" and, at the same time, exquisitely emancipated. The novelist Marcel Prévost (1862–1941) captured public attention with his best-selling novel *Les Demi-vierges* (1894). The brother-novelists Paul and Victor Margueritte published *Femmes Nouvelles* in the summer of 1899, in which they portrayed their heroine Hélène Dugast as a chaste, highly intelligent New Woman who wanted to marry the man of her choice and to do good to those around her.[145] The reviewer in the *Journal des Débats* (front page) called the brothers "good feminists, generous, clairvoyant, and moderate, as one should be," and referred to the book as "handsome," while Daniel Lesueur, writing in *La Fronde*, praised the brothers not only for their depiction of the New Woman but also for their portrayal of the New Man, who appreciated the heroine as an independent being. Lesueur provided long quotations from the novel to underscore that perspective of the New Man.[146] The lovely, emancipated Hélène exemplified the vast chasm between the old vision of a domesticated, subordinate woman and the New Woman, insofar as a woman could have a mind of her own and make her own decisions about how she would lead her life, irrespective of what men thought she should be doing. But was a woman such as Hélène a feminist? Did she champion legal reforms that might benefit women of all classes? Did she struggle for equal pay for equal work or take a position on protective labor legislation? Did she advocate legalizing paternity suits or ending government-regulated prostitution? Did she critique men's sexuality and penchant for violence? Did she attend feminist meetings and congresses or publish in the feminist press? What was her stance on marriage? On motherhood? What were her professional or career aspirations? What was she reading or thinking or writing about? Was she simply taking advantage of the new educational opportunities for girls and exercising a personal liberty to push herself forward into public view – or into employment that would assure her financial and moral independence? What seems clear is that, to almost everyone, the New Woman signified gender upheaval ahead. Whatever projects she undertook that drew her outside the household were undertaken, not as compensation for maternal loss or conversely in order to support her children, but for their own sake.

---

suggests that it dates from 1895. See also Klejman & Rochefort, *Égalité en marche*, pp. 117–119, and BMD DOS LACOUR. These authors cite another article by Paule Mink, "Conférences de la Bodinière," from *La Petite République*, 17 March 1895.

[145] Paul Margueritte & Victor Margueritte, *Femmes nouvelles* (Paris: Plon-Nourrit, 1899).

[146] "S.", "Femmes Nouvelles," *Journal des Débats* (17 July 1899); Daniel Lesueur, "Femmes nouvelles," *La Fronde*, n° 590 (21 July 1899).

From this a bigger question came to the fore: was the New Woman a feminist? was she even French?

It was Marcel Prévost's two-volume best seller *Les Vierges fortes* (1900) that would link the New Woman to feminism, while at the same time insidiously depicting feminism as an unFrench phenomenon. In Prévost's characterization, the "true" feminist was a man-hating type who wants to live entirely independently of men. This novel presents the story of two sisters, Frédérique and Léa. The heroine, Frédérique, insists she will never marry because of her mother's unfortunate experiences with men (seduced, abandoned, and left to raise an illegitimate child); she commits herself wholly to the feminist cause. Léa, the younger sister, wavers between loyalty to her sister's principles and her love for a young man whom Prévost portrays (as did the Margueritte brothers) as a model of the new Man, the potential companionate husband. Prévost depicted feminism as a new secular religion, international in scope and utterly foreign to France (a judgment that suggests, in light of what we now know, a gravely defective historical perspective). In the course of the book, the author presents sweeping stereotypical contrasts of national character: Nordic versus Latin, English versus French. Frédérique learns of "integral feminism" from a foreigner, portrayed as a Hungarian woman, a boarder in her mother's house.

Frédérique soon becomes the disciple of the foreign woman, a relationship Prévost depicts with unmistakably erotic and suggestively lesbian imagery: "Hers was a total abandonment, delicious, a blind sacrifice at once to a being and to an idea, both confounded and indiscernible from one another. She offered herself passionately to the idea and to its apostle, with the thoughtlessness of one in love." Before departing for England (this choice is significant) to pursue the feminist mission, the Hungarian woman grants Frédérique permission to use her room and books until her return. She then presents Frédérique with her own copy of John Stuart Mill's classic work, *The Subjection of Women*. In a subsequent scene, as sexually explicit as any to be found in a nineteenth-century novel, Prévost portrays Frédérique's conversion to – or, rather, "fertilization" by – Mill's ideas.[147]

The lesson of *Les Vierges fortes* seemed unmistakable: feminist ideas were alien to France, imports from abroad and dangerous. In *La Fronde*, Andrée Téry felt she had to make excuses for Prévost's work; she considered him a

---

[147] Marcel Prévost, *Les Vierges fortes*, volume 1: *Frédérique* (Paris: A. Lemerre, 1900), p. 81. For an extensive extract in English translation, see *WFF*, vol. 2, pp. 51–56.

friend of feminism but suggests that the author was simply trying to "warn against a dangerous interpretation of these theories." She believed that feminists should be thankful to Prévost for forcing them to clarify their ideas – and to insist that "feminism, as we understand it, is not a declaration of war on men; on the contrary it proposes to end hostilities between the sexes by realizing their spiritual, moral, and social equality. [Feminism] tries to reassert the primitive equilibrium, broken by the one-sided development of civilization."[148]

No excuses could be made, though, for the French novelist, Albert Cim. In his 1899 novel *Émancipées*, Cim conjured up an association for the promotion of "*masculisme*" [sic] called the Society of Solomon, whose stated objective was to re-enslave women and thus, allow its members to satisfy their carnal desires efficiently and at the least expense.[149] Such highly negative responses to feminism and to the phenomenon of the New Woman resonated with a number of other critics – critics who, in their effort to foster a nationalist identity for France, had begun to argue that their nation was invaded, indeed infected (these writers were inordinately fond of medical metaphors) by morbid outside influences – Jews, Protestants, and Freemasons – all conspicuously present among the leaders of the French movement for women's rights in the 1890s. Going further than the novelists mentioned earlier, these chauvinistic antifeminists asserted that France was threatened to the core by "Internationalism" and "Cosmopolitanism." In shrill tones they denounced all forms of Anglo-Saxon (by which they meant primarily English and American) cultural imperialism, of which feminism was the most reprehensible element. A work by a Viennese Catholic priest (translated from German into French in 1899) denounced feminism as the major component of a Protestant, Freemasonic, Jewish, and Free-Thinkers' plot; in another lengthy book, the pseudonymous French writer "Anold" asserted that the imported plague of feminism was a primary cause, not only of French demoralization, but of depopulation as well.[150] This current of antifeminist

---

[148] Andrée Téry, "Notre Féminisme, *La Fronde*, n° 892 (19 May 1900).

[149] Albert Cim, *Émancipées* (Paris: Flammarion, 1899). After assessing Cim's plot, the literary historian Annelise Maugue remarked, "One should not underestimate the effects of such a constantly menacing discourse: verbal violence carries its own weight." See Maugue, *Identité masculine en crise*, pp. 151–154; quote, p. 154.

[150] Augustin Rösler, *La Question féministe, examinée au point de vue de la nature, de l'histoire et de la révélation*, transl. J. de Rochay [Juliette Charoy, pseud.] (Paris: Perrin, 1899); Anold, *A quoi tient la supériorité des Français sur les Anglo-Saxons* (Paris: Fayard, 1899), p. 160; and *L'Éternelle enemie* (Paris, 1898).

expression would expand greatly after 1900; at this point, however, the French "masculinity crisis" was still in its early, less insidious stage.

In the interim, the budding contingent of women novelists of the *fin-de-siècle* and *Belle Époque* attempted to distance their "*Ève nouvelle*" heroines, at once consummately professional and feminine as can be, from the caricatures of the old-guard feminists (whom they mercilessly ridiculed). As literary historian Christine Kline-Lataud makes clear, these new heroines, capable and beautiful as they might be, remained caught up in the love plot and faced with heart-wrenching choices between career and family; they still had to contend with the "old Adam" – "who refuses to be New."[151]

---

[151] Christine Kline-Lataud, "Ève Nouvelle, Nouvelle Pandore?" in *Masculin / féminin: le XIXème siècle à l'épreuve du genre*, ed. Chantal Bertrand-Jennings (Toronto: Centre d'études de XIXème siècle Joseph Sablé, 1999), pp. 199–213, quote, p. 203.

CHAPTER 6

Rights or Protection for Working Women?

It is time to take a closer look at the 1890s controversies that swirled around the issue of women's employment– in particular the debates over the Third Republic's legislative efforts to enact "protective" labor laws specific to women workers. This legislation, unapologetically discriminatory on the basis of sex, would restrict adult women's hours of work and, in particular, forbid their night work entirely. As we have seen in Chapter 5, sharp divisions of opinion existed among French socialists and feminists (as was also the case in other European countries) over the necessity of sex-specific labor legislation. Some feminists would uphold women's right to work without restriction and their right to equal pay; they would campaign against discriminatory labor legislation, search for political allies, and combat regulated prostitution. Other feminists and many socialists considered restrictions on women's work as a short-term remedy, a prelude to enactment of restrictions on the work hours and conditions of both sexes. In this chapter, I will examine the debates among feminists as well as those of feminists with the proponents of selective restrictions. I will then address the controversies surrounding France's government-regulated prostitution, an ever-growing concern that cannot be considered apart from the question of women's difficulties in finding sustainable employment and, when they did, in reckoning with the consequences of pathetically inadequate pay.[1]

---

[1] This chapter draws on material from my two earlier published articles, notably, Karen Offen, "Depopulation, Nationalism, and Feminism in Fin-de-siècle France," *The American Historical Review*, 89:3 (June 1984), 648–676, and Karen Offen, "Madame Ghénia Avril de Sainte-Croix, the Josephine Butler of France," *Women's History Review*, 17:2 (April 2008), 239–255.

Did French Feminists Ignore the Question of Women's Work?

In the early 1980s, Geneviève Fraisse posed the question: "Does feminism ignore the question of women's work?"[2] She thereby challenged the assertions of pioneering studies of women's unionization by Marie-Hélène Zylberberg-Hocquard and of the fraught relation between feminism and socialism by Charles Sowerwine, who claimed that feminists had indeed ignored it. Invoking the contributions of Julie Daubié and Elisa Lemonnier (during the Second Empire; she might also have invoked those of Flora Tristan during the July Monarchy), Fraisse's answer was a categorical "no." Fraisse then pointed out that feminism, because it operates through discourse, "can cut through class and socio-professional categories, not because it ignores the female worker, but because the problem of salaried work cannot be isolated from a whole network of difficulties common to women as a whole."[3]

A closer examination of the history of feminist challenges to male domination in France and, in particular, the 1890s debates, confirms Fraisse's judgment. As previous chapters of this book indicate, feminism's concerns have spanned an extremely wide (and shifting) range of overlapping categories and specific issues. Perhaps the most encompassing of these by the 1890s *was* the question of women's "work," or more specifically women's possibilities for – and right to – engage in paid employment, which led directly to discussion of married women's legal inability to control their own earnings. Financial independence was clearly the key to individual independence. Such questions immediately provoked renewed debate over women's "role" in French society and, of course, the "future" of "the [male-headed] family." Thus, the issue of women's participation in paid labor, too often treated as strictly a social and economic question, did crystallize multiple concerns; it was sociopolitical, intellectual, cultural, psychological, and moral, as well as economic. It bridged all these categories (as indeed it still does) precisely because it called into question the deeply rooted, ostensibly "natural" but in fact socially constructed (and heavily enforced) prescriptions concerning the division of labor between the sexes. The ongoing French campaigns to revise the Civil Code, as concerned married women, and to expand educational opportunities and

---

[2] Geneviève Fraisse, "Feminist Singularity: A Critical Historiography of the History of Feminism in France," in *Writing Women's History*, ed. Michelle Perrot (Oxford: Blackwell, 1992; orig. publ. in French 1984), pp. 146–159; quote, p. 152.

[3] Fraisse, "Feminist Singularity," p. 153.

professional certification for girls continued to build momentum, to be sure, but in the 1890s the controversies surrounding women's employment (or lack thereof) and, accompanying that, the challenges to government-regulated prostitution, would become explosive.

Women's rights activists and socialists in France had for decades advocated women's economic independence through employment, but perhaps never with more passion than in the 1890s and early 1900s. Support for this position came from every side of the progressive political spectrum, as for instance from the so-called moderate feminist Jeanne-E Schmahl (1846–1916), who condemned men's opposition to women's admission to the trades, which then forced women to work for less and thereby inadvertently undercut men's pay. She called such opposition an "abuse of force" that "condemned women to servitude." Jeanne Schmahl applauded the "superhuman courage" of women who sacrificed everything to survive and to sustain their children, especially if and when they were not married to the fathers of these children.[4]

When Jeanne Schmahl established the legislative reform group *Avant-Courrière* in 1893 (as a nonpartisan alternative to the fiercely anticlerical republican politics of Maria Deraismes' group), she set two specific goals: to establish the right of women to bear witness to public and private legal acts (achieved in 1897), and the right of wives to fully control their own income (debated in 1894, but stalled until 1907).[5] Like a number of her English counterparts, Schmahl thought that, under the Third Republic, more progress could be made if the legislators could address women's issues singly and serially. Finally recognizing, after a fifteen-year struggle to obtain both goals, that little progress for feminist goals could be made when only men elected the legislators, in 1909 Jeanne Schmahl would become the founder and first president of the *Union Française pour le Suffrage des Femmes*.[6] But this is getting ahead of the story.

---

[4] See Jeanne-E Schmahl, "L'Antagonisme des sexes – La Concurrence économique," *La Revue Féministe*, 1:1 (1895), 7.

[5] It is pertinent to the French debates on married women's property in their earnings that both in the United Kingdom and in many states in the United States, married women's property acts were already in force. As mentioned in Chapter 5, *L'Avant-Courrière* had the support of Juliette Adam as well as the very wealthy duchesse d'Uzes (the great-granddaughter of the champagne magnate Veuve Clicquot) who in the later 1880s had bet (and lost) three million francs on the Boulangist campaign.

[6] See Patrick Kay Bidelman's biographical entry on Schmahl in the *Historical Dictionary of the French Third Republic*, ed. Patrick H. Hutton (New York & Westport, CT: Garland, 1986), vol. 2, pp. 893–894, and, more recently, Karen Offen, "Jeanne Schmahl," in *Dictionnaire des Féministes: France XVIIIe–XIXe siècle*, ed. Christine Bard & Sylvie Chaperon (Paris: Presses Universitaires de France, 2017), pp. 1310–1312.

In the early 1890s, simply gathering meaningful data on women's employment – or lack thereof – was still a priority. The major surveys launched by the *Office du Travail* in 1905 lay in the future.[7] Twentieth-century scholars attribute to Madeleine Guilbert the first systematic academic investigations of French women's participation in industrial production, pointing to the extant data and what it does – or does not – allow us to see.[8] Her careful analysis of daily wages paid to men and women workers doing similar jobs in 1891–1893 is immensely revealing; it was as if the men were being paid proportional to their size and weight, relative to women.

What is less well known is that already in 1892 a group of progressive French women and their associates (originating in the Protestant philanthropic groups whose annual gathering was called the *Conférence de Versailles*) undertook a concerted effort to document women's workforce participation in France.[9] Their project, the *"Statistique Générale de la Femme,"* was prepared by the *Comité des Femmes* [women's committee] with the cooperation of the French Ministry of Commerce and its *Bureau de la Statistique Générale* for display in the Women's Building at the 1893 World's Columbian Exposition in Chicago.[10] This exhibition, which (along with a collection of 800 books by French women authors also sent to Chicago) was a response to American initiatives to consolidate a transatlantic women's movement and, in particular, to promote the formation of a national council of French women that could represent France in the newly formed International Council of Women (ICW).[11]

---

[7] These surveys will be discussed in Part III.

[8] Madeleine Guilbert, *Les Fonctions des femmes dans l'industrie* (The Hague: Mouton, 1966); see especially Part I: "La Perspective historique: l'évolution du travail des femmes dans l'industrie," and Madeleine Guilbert, *Les Femmes et l'organisation syndicale avant 1914: présentation et commentaires de documents pour une étude du syndicalisme féminin* (Paris: Éditions du CNRS, 1966).

[9] Already in 1888 Virginie Griess-Traut had called for the production of such a set of statistics for the 1889 Exposition in Paris. See her remarks in *Société pour l'Amélioration du Sort de la Femme et la Revendication de ses Droits* [SASFRD], *Conférence du 14 mars 1888 sous la présidence de Mlle Maria Deraismes. Discours [de la présidente] et de M. Yves Guyot. [Rapports, Statuts, Commissions]* (Paris: Impr. Mayer & Cie, 1888), p. 52.

[10] Marie Pégard, *Statistique Générale de la Femme en France* (compiled 1895). After years of searching, I finally located and consulted (27 May 2010) this thick volume, classified as manuscript 3467 in the library of the *Institute de France*.

[11] See my unpublished papers, "From Washington to Paris and Back to Chicago: Building a Transatlantic Women's Network, 1888–1893, or 'The French Connection'." Paper given at the American Historical Association, Chicago, January 2012, and "Rendezvous at the Expo," paper given to the conference on "Les Femmes et les Expositions … ," Paris, 23–24 October 2014, forthcoming in *Women in International and Universal Exhibitions 1876–1937*, ed. Rebecca Rogers & Myriam Boussahba-Bravard (London & New York: Routledge, 2017), pp. 215–233.

Marie-Josephine Pégard (1850–1916), the secretary-general of the "official" committee for this venture took charge of the exhibit preparations. She oversaw the development of a visual display of statistics on French women's work and well-being, comprising a comprehensive and colorfully presented series of eighteen large tableaux (the original panels measured 2.65 meters across and 1.65 meters high), which included some 140 graphics. The numbers and graphs included demographic information, a comprehensive survey of women's work in agriculture, industry, and commerce, education, and the arts, as well as comparative data on salaries and wages.[12] Pégard herself wrote in an addendum to the *Statistique* that the *Comité des Femmes* took great satisfaction "in attesting that not one of the other nations taking part in the Exposition de Chicago attempted such a complete survey," a characterization confirmed by the French writer Th. Bentzon who, following her visit to the Chicago Exposition, affirmed that the impressive *Statistique* was "more complete than any other . . . a model in other countries."[13] Jeanne Madeline Weimann, historian of the women's contributions to the Chicago Exposition, would later attest that "the French gathered the first statistics ever attempted of the part played by women in the social economy."[14] Additionally, Weimann remarked, "the colorful French statistical exhibit, mounted on the walls of the south record room [in the Woman's Building], had brightly colored bar graphs which showed Frenchwomen's occupations: they composed 49% of innkeepers and apartment managers or *concierges*, 30.3% of shopowners and retail workers, 20% of the agricultural force, 20.7% of the industrial force, 7.5% of public administrators, and 3.7% of the liberal professions."[15]

---

[12] France. Commissariat Général à l'Exposition internationale de Chicago. Rapports. Ministère du Commerce, de l'Industrie, des Postes et des Télégraphes . . . *Exposition internationale de Chicago en 1893. Rapports publiés sous la direction de M. Camille Krantz. Comité des dames. L'Exposition féminine française à Chicago [en 1893]. Rapport de Mme M. Pégard, Secrétaire générale du Comité des dames.* p.55 (Paris: Impr. nationale, 1895). Bibl. Nat.: 4°V.3695 (14).

[13] See also Th. Bentzon, "La Condition de la Femme aux États-Unis," first installment in the *Revue des Deux Mondes* (1 July 1894), 138–173, quote, 149. Mme Bentzon went to the United States later in the year, so was not present for the World's Congress of Representative Women, but she did visit the Woman's Building in October during the final days of the Exposition. She made an extended tour of the United States, and her articles from the *RDM* series were republished in 1895 as a book, *Les Américaines chez elles: notes de voyage* (1st ed., Paris: Calmann-Lévy, 1895; 2nd ed., 1896, 3rd ed. 1904, Hachette).

[14] See Jeanne Madeline Weimann, *The Fair Women: The Story of the Woman's Building, World's Columbian Exposition, Chicago 1893* (Chicago: Academy, 1981), p. 377.

[15] Weimann, *Fair Women*, p. 389. Also included in the French women's exhibit were (Weimann, p. 377) "a series of monographs and charts illustrating the variation in marriage dates, the longevity of women as compared to men; the number of women immigrants and emigrants; women's participation in schools and universities, and the number that won diplomas, and the kinds of

Indeed, this display did make a huge impression on all who viewed it[16] Although the fate of the original panels remains unknown, we do know that the impressive volume containing hand-painted miniatures of the 140 charts and graphs, commissioned by Marie Pégard, survived and is now lodged at the *Institut de France*. Pégard submitted the *Statistique Générale de la Femme* for the Institut's Prix Montyon (Statistics), winning the award in 1896.[17]

Another early and significant contributor to the effort of documenting French women's workforce participation was Dr. Kaethe Schirmacher (1865–1930), from Danzig, who would become deeply engaged in Parisian feminist activities during the 1890s and the first decade of the twentieth century. She published regularly in the French press and became a sought-after speaker. In Chicago for the 1893 Exposition, she addressed the situation of women in Germany, pointing out that many women, out-numbering men by over a million, had to support themselves out of necessity. While at the Exposition, she must have also seen (and have been impressed by) that pathbreaking exhibition on French women's work and must have decided that there was a great deal more to be done.

Schirmacher's subsequent publications in and about France (rarely, if at all, discussed in the historical literature I have consulted) addressed women's higher education, employment prospects, wages, working conditions, and prostitution. Her 1896 publications make it clear that she was alarmed about the developing split between "bourgeois" and "socialist" feminists in the German context, and wanted to reappropriate the questions of women and work for the nonsocialist side. She also followed the comparative development of feminism, and in 1898 would publish a book on the subject that included the United States, France, Great Britain, Sweden, and Russia.[18] A partisan of "equality in diversity," Kaethe Schirmacher expressed her deep concern about women's degraded economic

merits open to them. On the philanthropic side, there were monographs on orphan homes and other houses of refuge run by the Sisters of Charity."

[16] Carroll Wright, the first head of the U.S. Department of Labor (established in 1888), which had sponsored the quest for reliable statistics to be exhibited at the fair, was very impressed by the French women's exhibit, commending it especially. See Weimann, *Fair Women,* p. 389.

[17] The 140 charts and graphs in the *Statistique Générale de la Femme* (referred to by Marie Pégard as "cartogrammes et diagrammes muraux") are greatly scaled-down versions of the originals. Pégard indicated in her 1895 report that the original panels had returned to France and were on display in Bordeaux. Their current whereabouts is unknown. A team led by Rebecca Rogers at the University of Paris III – Descartes is leading a research project to further investigate and document the French women's contributions.

[18] Kaethe Schirmacher, *Le Féminisme aux États-Unis, en France, dans la Grande-Bretagne, en Suède et en Russie* (Paris: A. Colin, 1898).

status. Her publications confirm that well before 1900, many so-called bourgeois feminists had fully engaged with the broad range of issues that surrounded the paid labor of women.

Reporting on the 1899 London congress of the ICW in the *Revue de Morale Sociale*, Schirmacher underscored the point that, overall, the wages women received were utterly insufficient for survival. In France in particular, according to the early figures gathered by the *Office du Travail* (founded in 1891) and with only a few notable exceptions, "the wages of women in most industries were less than half of those of men."[19] As concerns "average" income, Schirmacher preferred the figures given by the Comte d'Haussonville in his book *Misères et remèdes* (1886; 2nd ed., 1892) which she considered more exact, and she cited a number of other recent studies to confirm her point.[20] To fill the wage gap so that she could survive, a woman without means either had to link up with one man – or many! "The woman who sells herself in the street is not mysterious, not inexplicable, not monstrous. Far from being 'unnatural,' she is only too human, and sorrowfully human."[21]

In 1902, Schirmacher would publish her own study of women's work in France, based on data from the 1896 census (which was published in 1899).[22] *Le Travail des femmes en France* appeared in the *Mémoires et documents* (*supplément aux Annales*) of the *Musée Social* in Paris. Noting a surplus of 434,000 women over men, Schirmacher castigated the French

---

[19] Schirmacher, *Féminisme aux États-Unis*, p. 447.

[20] Schirmacher cites (in text) the following works, for which I have provided full references below: Dr. Oscar Commenge, *Hygiène sociale: La Prostitution clandestine à Paris* (Paris: Schleicher frères, 1897), p.567; Othénin de Cléron, comte d'Haussonville, *Socialisme et charité* (Paris: Calmann-Lévy, 1895), p.500; Dr. Delesalle [*Temps Nouveaux*]. This last author is presumably Paul Delesalle (1870–1940), an anarchist and revolutionary syndicalist. On the weekly *Temps Nouveaux*, see Carole Reynaud Paligot, *Les Temps Nouveaux, 1895–1914: Un hebdomadaire anarchiste au tournant du siècle* (Pantin: Éditions Acratie, 1993). Cf. also Charles Benoist, *Les Ouvrières de l'aiguille à Paris; notes pour l'étude de la question sociale* (Paris: L. Chailley, 1895).

[21] Schirmacher, *Féminisme aux États-Unis*, p. 449.

[22] *Le Travail des femmes en France* (*Mémoires et Documents*, supplément aux *Annales*, Musée social, n° 6, May 1902; Paris: Rousseau, 1902), pp. 321–372. Schirmacher published excerpts from her work in (at least) two French periodicals: "Le Travail des femmes en France," *La Revue* (*ancienne revue des revues*) (15 February 1902), 395–412, and "Le Travail des femmes et la protection ouvrière," *La Revue de Morale Sociale*, 4 (1902–1903), 160–181. On the *Revue de Morale Sociale*, see Anne R. Epstein, "Gender and the Creation of the French Intellectual: The Case of the *Revue de Morale Sociale* 1899–1903," in *Views from the Margins: Creating Identities in Modern France*, ed. & introd. Kevin J. Callahan & Sarah A. Curtis (Lincoln: University of Nebraska Press, 2008), pp. 218–250. The discussion below on Schirmacher's French publications on working women is adapted from Karen Offen, "Kaethe Schirmacher, Investigative Reporter & Activist Journalist," pp. 200–211, in *Proceedings of the Western Society for French History, Portland, 2011*, vol. 39 (2013), ed. Joelle Neulander & Robin Walz. Online at www.quod.lib.umich.edu/w/wsfh/0642292.0039rgn=full +text

census authorities for not counting *ménagères* [homemakers] among the "active" population. "Women's domestic occupations certainly consti-tute professional work, by which homemakers earn their living," she insisted, pointing out that keeping house accounted for some 7.7 million married women. Additionally, she noted, some 2.6 million of these 7.7 married women also worked outside the home. If one counts them all, she insisted, the number of employed women would equal or even outnumber the population of working men. Moreover, Schirmacher demonstrated that French women who worked outside the home found employment in virtually every economic sector, including quarries, mines, and metallurgy.[23]

Significantly, Kaethe Schirmacher (herself a highly educated single woman) listed, as the first category she would discuss, "the work of the wife and mother" [*le travail de l'épouse et de la mère*]. Thereby, she offered a frontal and fundamental critique of the well-entrenched (but increasingly contested) notion about the male breadwinner as provider – a notion that, for most male political economists, Catholic and secular alike, still under-girded their understanding of the how the sexual division of labor should function. She further pointed to the difficulty of marrying faced by girls without a dowry as well as a growing reluctance, due to "modern indi-vidualism," of young women "to embark on a career founded on the legal subjection of the wife." She agreed with her French feminist associates that major changes in the laws governing marriage were essential.[24]

Schirmacher's entire study is replete with figures that bolstered her critique of prevailing views. When it came to the category "industry" (what we would call manufacturing) Schirmacher pointed out that "the number of women occupied in industry is less than the number in agriculture."[25] Looking at pay scales (wages), Schirmacher reminded her readers that most of the women who worked in manufacturing or produc-tion were paid a good deal less than men, and after doing the calculations, she showed that "the majority of the 829,057 *ouvrières industrielles* work 9 to 11 hours per day but cannot without difficulty balance income and expenses." Women's work is worth more than that, she asserted, and it is in fact often of superior quality to men's work; "why," she asks, "is the woman always paid less?" She concluded that the woman is paid less

---

[23] Schirmacher, *Travail des femmes en France*, p. 395. In French: "Les occupations domestiques des femmes constituent, bel et bien, un travail professionnel, par lequel les ménagères gagnent leur vie."

[24] Schirmacher, *Travail des femmes en France*, p. 396.

[25] Schirmacher, *Travail des femmes en France*. This quotation is on p. 398; the ensuing quotations are from p. 400.

simply "because she is a woman ... in an inferior social (i.e., civil and political) condition." And she characterized this situation as a great social danger. Elaborating on a point she had made earlier, on the working woman having to resort to "finding someone," she argued that adding a man to the mix in fact increased that woman's workload by another five to six hours per day spent at home. Such "*surménage*" or overwork, she asserted, could quickly compromise a woman's health and welfare.

Turning to the issue of protective legislation for women workers, in effect in France since late November 1892, Schirmacher remarked the fierce opposition of French feminists to this discriminatory legislation, and, as an alternative, their support for the unionization of women workers. But Schirmacher did not think that, in the short run, unionization would provide the answer; instead "only the legal protection of *ouvrières* will [for the time being] permit the development, among them, of syndical organizations – but this will not provide a noticeable rise in wages until they encompass the mass of women workers."[26] She enumerated the various professions, and the situation of women in them (relative to men), from domestic servants to providers of personal care services, commerce and banking, shipping and transportation, the liberal professions (in which she included law and medicine, the theatre, *musiciennes*, painting and sculpture, and literature), religiously dedicated women, state and local governmental service (including women teachers), and other occupations. She also pointed out that most women workers had no "right" to paid retirement, yet – as things stood – they earned too little to put aside any savings. "What will become of them," she asked, "when they cannot find work or when their strength gives out?"[27] Schirmacher noted that some reformers were working toward a law that would provide retirement benefits for women workers, and that a group of feminists had called for such a law to apply equally to homemakers. In sum, French women were at a serious disadvantage in the workforce, in regard to pay, advancement opportunities, and lack of unionization. If married, a woman worker often faced a "double burden" of work in the workplace and in the household. Concluding, Schirmacher reiterated an earlier published assertion (concerning Austrian working women) that "women who in such conditions, obstinately continue to live, really do merit the label 'the strong sex'."[28] She would subsequently campaign to

[26] Schirmacher, *Travail des femmes en France*, p. 402.
[27] Schirmacher, *Travail des femmes en France*, p. 411.
[28] Schirmacher, *Travail des femmes en France*, p. 412.

include married women's domestic labor in the French labor statistics and to establish the right of single mothers to be paid.

For French feminists, as for Schirmacher, establishing women's right to work and to earn a decent living was central to undercutting the male-breadwinner model and the ideology of domesticity promulgated for so many decades by medical men, economists, and others who dominated the French knowledge establishment, and promoted by so many working-class men. But the feminists' campaigns were complicated by the growing anxiety of men in the public eye over the massive influx of young women into the French labor force, both in Paris and in the provinces, coupled with mounting alarm over depopulation and perceived family erosion (that is to say, "absent" mothers and wives) within the context of reestablishing French national prestige as a democratic republic amid a sea of powerful, populous, and highly militarized monarchies (I will turn to the debates over the demographic issues in Chapter 7). Finding the answers to the woman question, it seemed, would have a direct impact on France's future standing in the society of nations.

The complexity of the problems posed by French women's employment would be underscored once again by the objections of the poetry professor, social critic and moralist Émile Faguet in late 1895, in the course of his remarks in the *Journal des Débats* concerning Jacques Lourbet's new book, *La Femme devant la science*. Lourbet claimed (as had Jeanne Deroin in 1848–1849) that in a world in which physical force was no longer determinant of human capabilities and intelligence counted more than muscles, women would be free to develop and exercise their powers and the world would be the better for it. Lourbet was speaking out in no uncertain terms against the decades of medical and scientific theories about women's "inferiority." Men's pretension to deny women liberty to develop, he insisted, amounted to sheer egoism.[29]

In equally emphatic terms Faguet begged to differ. He pointed to the "bottom line" for France by insisting that "the social interest is antifeminist" (as, indeed, was he, at that time). He concluded his observations with what he believed to be a series of incontrovertible facts. A woman who is employed, he insisted, "will cease to be a woman . . . a woman that society needs in order to perpetuate itself . . . in order not to shrink or perish." This is a serious affair, he asserted ominously. "Any woman who exercises a masculine profession will be lost to the propagation of the species." For Faguet, it seemed, every profession was *de facto* a masculine profession.

---

[29] Jacques Lourbet, *Les Femmes devant la science contemporaine* (Paris: Félix Alcan, 1896).

Women's "invasion" of these professions, he argued, would "reinforce and aggravate" an already existing tendency toward unmarried womanhood. And that would be "perfectly disastrous." "The strong nation, the nation of the future," Faguet dramatically proclaimed, "will be one in which women have no profession other than their traditional role. The access of women to masculine professions is initially the sign, and eventually the cause, of a formidable national degeneration."[30]

Concern about the conditions and consequences of women's employment loomed larger with every passing day. The new discriminatory legislation surrounding women's and children's employment in industrial settings – and its potential consequences – had even begun to attract the attention of doctoral students in law faculties, not only in Paris but also in Caen and Grenoble.[31] Charles Benoist would graphically portray the suffering of young single women working in the garment industry.[32] Serialized articles appeared in learned publications, as for example Victor Mátaja's series on the origins of protective legislation in the *Revue d'Économie Politique*, and Fernand and Maurice Pelloutier's series on women in industry in *L'Ouvrier des Deux Mondes*.[33] Shocking stories about harassment of young women teachers in provincial towns, for example, would arouse public concern.[34] Other equally lurid stories highlighted the social

---

[30] Émile Faguet, "La Femme devant le science," *Le Journal des Débats* (12 December 1895), 1–2. Translation of the last paragraph is adjusted slightly from that in Susanna Barrows, *Distorting Mirrors: Visions of the Crowd in Late Nineteenth-Century France* (New Haven, CT: Yale University Press, 1981), p. 59.

[31] These theses included: Georges Guillaumin, *La Protection des femmes dans l'industrie*. Thèse pour le doctorat, Faculté de Droit (Paris, 1894); César Caire, *La Législation sur le travail industriel des femmes et des enfants*. Thèse, Faculté de Droit, Caen (Paris: A. Rousseau, 1896); Claude Weyl, *La Règlementation du travail des femmes dans l'industrie (Loi du 2 novembre 1892)*. Thèse, Faculté de Droit, Paris (Paris: L. Larose, 1898); J. Mazel, *L'Interdiction du travail de nuit des femmes dans la législation française*. Thèse pour le doctorat, Faculté de Droit, Paris (Paris: L. Larose, 1899); Joseph Vallier, *Le Travail des femmes dans l'industrie française*. Thèse de doctorat, Faculté de Droit, Université de Grenoble (Grenoble: Attier-frères, 1899). See also A. Chazal, *L'Interdiction du travail de nuit des femmes dans l'industrie française*. Thèse, Faculté de Droit, Paris (Paris: A. Pedone, 1902).

[32] See Charles Benoist, *Les Ouvrières de l'aiguille à Paris: Notes pour l'étude de la question sociale* (Paris: L. Chailley, 1895); originally serialized in *Le Temps* in 1893.

[33] Victor Mátaja, "Les origines de la protection ouvrière en France," *La Revue d'Économie Politique*, 9:6 (June 1895), 529–547; 9:8–9 (August–September 1895), 739–768; 10:3 (March 1896), 232–258, and 10:4 (April 1896), 355–369. See also Fernand Pelloutier & Maurice Pelloutier, "La Femme dans l'industrie," *L'Ouvrier des Deux Mondes: revue mensuelle d'économie sociale*, n° 8 (1 September 1897), 113–116; n° 9 (1 October 1897), 129–132; and n° 11 (1 December 1897), 165–166.

[34] A big fuss would develop over Léon Frapié's novel, *L'Institutrice de Provence* (1897), which sparked an inquiry by the critic Francisque Sarcey to test the accuracy of the claims made by the author about the hostile reception confronted by newly minted lay teachers in the small communities of rural France. Some of these letters were subsequently published in *Lettres d'institutrices rurales d'autrefois; rédigées à la suite de l'enquête de Francisque Sarcey en 1897*, ed. Ida Berger (Paris: Association des Amis du Musée pédagogique, 1961). One letter, from a young primary school

consequences of starvation wages, which left women only prostitution as a way out. Benoist, who was sympathetic to the plight of poor women who had to support themselves, dramatized that connection: "Is it really a natural law that a women, after twelve or thirteen hours of unremitting work, earns scarcely enough to house herself in a slum, to dress in rags, and to nourish herself with a sou's worth of milk?" In the new "theory of wages" such a situation represented, he made it clear that the wages paid to women seemed to fall just below what she needed to survive on her own, thus "it's up to her to fill the gap by remembering that she is a woman."[35] In short, the so-called "fifth quarter" of the day . . . exchanging sex for subsistence.

Feminists had, of course, been complaining about this situation for decades. Caroline de Barrau had made the point at an 1878 abolitionist congress and the Italian feminist Anna Maria Mozzoni confirmed the dire situation when she remarked that "everyone has the right to live from their work, but women seem to have more of a right to die since it is so difficult for them to find honest and sufficient work." (See Part I, Chapter 3 in this volume.) For 1890s feminists as well, it seemed incontrovertible that women had a right to work and to earn a living wage, and that they should receive equal pay for equal work and equal training opportunities. Moreover, they opined, women workers should be represented in worker's councils and on the labor exchange [*Bourse du Travail*], and should have a representative on the *Conseil Supérieur du Travail*, as well as the opportunity to join or organize trade unions. But feminists would disagree sharply among themselves as to whether so-called protective legislation should be aimed exclusively at women workers. If workers were to be "protected" by law, whether by limiting their hours or conditions of work, the feminists argued, the laws should apply to both sexes. A commitment to equality of the sexes before the law was essential to their thinking. Yet the pattern for male-headed European governments that intervened in labor relations was (as we have seen in earlier chapters) to legislate separately for women. This pattern developed in the 1840s in Great Britain, but in the 1870s and 1880s Switzerland and the German Empire had also enacted measures to restrict

teacher sent to the department of Loir-et-Cher, can be consulted in English translation in Hellerstein, Hume, & Offen, eds., *Victorian Women* (Stanford, CA: Stanford University Press, 1981), doc. 80. In an early issue, *La Fronde* published another provincial teacher's sad tale of harassment and attempted seduction by the mayor; see "Lettre d'une Institutrice," *La Fronde*, n° 8 (16 December 1897), 2.

[35] Benoist, *Ouvrières de l'aiguille à Paris*, pp. 19–20. Benoist's book is now accessible online through Gallica and through Google Books.

important aspects of women's employment; Austria and the Netherlands would follow suit in 1890.[36] Le Playist ideology and social scientific methodology only bolstered this approach. Increasingly, toward the century's end, a "maternalist" ideology promulgated by many women as well as by men would also endorse it.

The Law of 2 November 1892

The year 1890 marked the convocation in Berlin of a two-week long (15–29 March) intergovernmental congress on worker protection, sponsored by the Swiss and German governments. The all-male delegates to this congress drew up resolutions and stimulated a flurry of subsequent legislative attempts by participating countries to restrict night and Sunday work for women aged sixteen or over, to limit their working hours, to restrict women's employment in dangerous and insalubrious industries, and to forbid their employment during and subsequent to the period around childbirth. It mandated obligatory maternity leave, but declined to propose monetary compensation for work hours lost.

The ubiquitous Jules Simon, a senator and senior statesman as well as permanent secretary of the *Académie des Sciences Morales et Politiques*, headed the French delegation to this 1890 congress. A long-time foe of state intervention in the marketplace, as we have seen earlier, Simon insisted in Berlin that in France respect for individual rights precluded state intervention.[37] Within less than a year, however, due to advancing age, experience, and concern about the French population problem, he had changed his mind and would abandon his earlier laissez-faire economic views, at least as concerned women's employment. In an eloquent speech to the French Senate in July 1891, Jules Simon would unhesitatingly advocate state restriction of women's work in industry, that is, special protective legislation.[38] He favored state intervention to regulate the labor of *all* employed women (including adults), and also to provide government-subsidized maternity leaves. Women workers, he insisted, needed the state's

---

[36] For further comparative insight, see the pathbreaking essays in *Protecting Women: Labor Legislation in Europe, the United States, and Australia, 1880–1920*, ed. Ulla Wikander, Alice Kessler-Harris, & Jane Lewis (Urbana: University of Illinois Press, 1995). See also chapter 6 of Karen Offen, *European Feminisms, 1700–1950: A Political History* (Stanford, CA: Stanford University Press, 2000), esp. pp. 160–164.

[37] For Simon's report on the Congress, 12 May 1890, see Ministère des Affaires Étrangères, *Conférence internationale de Berlin, 15–29 mars 1890: Procès verbaux* ... (Paris, 1890), pp. 17–24.

[38] See *Annales du Sénat, Débats* (session of 7 July 1891), pp. 31, 407–412.

protection.[39] The shift in Simon's views exemplifies the shift toward government intervention in the thinking of European liberals more generally. In comparison to the outright antifeminism of a Proudhon, Jules Simon might still be considered something of a friend to women, of the sort who keeps "women's own good" in his sights. He had, after all, presided at the *Oeuvres et Institutions* congress in 1889, to the consternation of the women's rights feminists, as we have seen in Chapter 4. Promoting educational opportunities for women was one thing, but Simon continued to oppose women, especially married women, entering the labor force.[40]

In the 1890s Social Catholic reformers and Catholic deputies to the French legislature would also advocate protective labor legislation specifically for women, with the full support of the Vatican. Already in February 1886 the Catholic royalist deputy Albert de Mun had proposed to the Chamber of Deputies a measure that would restrict women's employment in industrial plants for four weeks after giving birth, and he intervened again on the question in June 1888, but the time was not then ripe for legislative action.[41] In the French parliament there was no hint of any support for paid leave for mothers prior to the debates on the proposed law in early February 1891, when the moderate socialist deputy Émile Brousse proposed an indemnity for mothers – a suggestion that was ultimately dropped in the law of 2 November 1892.[42] This proposal would not die, however; it would be tossed about for another two decades prior to its resolution in 1913.

---

[39] Simon, new preface to 1891 edition of *L'Ouvrière*, xii–xvi.

[40] Already in 1892, Jules Simon's notion of "reform" had shrunk to augmenting women's moral authority in the family and celebrating paternal authority: see Jules & Gustave Simon, *La Femme du vingtième siècle* (Paris: Calmann Lévy, 1892). By 1896 he would even be quoted as asserting the inferiority of women. On Simon's reported views at age 82 (the year he died), see "Pages oubliées: Jules Simon," *Annales Politiques et Littéraires* (14 June 1896), 377; and on girls getting too much education, Jules Simon, "Il faut rester femme," *La Revue des Revues* (15 July 1896), 135–141. This last article was actually a review of the 1896 revised and final edition of Legouvé's *Histoire morale des femmes*.

[41] The sole mention of this intervention in one historian's political biography of Alfred de Mun does not flesh out the details. See Benjamin F. Martin, *Count Albert de Mun: Paladin of the Third Republic* (Chapel Hill: University of North Carolina Press, 1978), p. 78. De Mun's repeated interventions on the question of women's employment can be followed in the *Journal Officiel* of the Chamber of Deputies through the 1890s, 1900s, and following World War I. Judith Coffin devotes two pages to De Mun's interventionist Social Catholic policies in *The Politics of Women's Work: The Paris Garment Trades, 1750–1915* (Princeton, NJ: Princeton University Press, 1996), pp. 203–204.

[42] See Mary Lynn Stewart, *Women, Work, and the French State: Labour Protection & Social Patriarchy, 1879–1919* (Montreal: McGill-Queens University Press, 1989), esp. chapter 6. Stewart points out (p. 122) that night work in industry had only become possible with the advent of gas lighting, beginning in the 1830s.

The role of the church was not insignificant in attempting to shape legislation on women's work. The Roman Catholic Church has for centuries been a top-down, authoritarian organization, fostering top-down, authoritarian ideas. Catholic views on the woman question are often perceived as monolithic, since they are governed by Biblical doctrine that asserts the "sinful" Eve's subordination to Adam, the dogma of the Immaculate Conception of Mary, the infallibility of the Pope, and the sacramental, hierarchical character of the marriage institution.[43] Thus, the importance of papal pronouncements for restricting the field within which ideological dissidence and factions could develop, either among the laity or the clergy, cannot be overestimated.

Few historians of secular French feminism have taken the trouble to consult the church's texts and their reception or to analyze the specific issues they addressed with regard to the woman question during the Third Republic. Yet two encyclical letters are of the utmost importance. Already in the encyclical letter *Arcanum* (1880), Leo XIII had laid out the reasons (with France utmost in mind) why the faithful must reject all secular claims for jurisdiction over marriage and, in particular, why they must especially oppose the notion of civil divorce. Citing as his authority St. Paul's letters to the Ephesians, Leo XIII underscored the necessity of sexual hierarchy in marriage: "The husband is the chief of the family and the head of the wife. The woman, because she is flesh of his flesh, and bone of his bone, must be subject to her husband and obey him; not, indeed, as a servant, but as a companion, so that her obedience shall be wanting in neither honour nor dignity."[44] According to this view, democracy in the family was unthinkable. Thus, Catholic doctrine coupled with church attitudes on issues of doctrinal obedience set narrow limits on the possibilities for Catholic feminism in France (although one deviation on the question of women's work would appear in the 1890s that certainly appears "feminist" by the standards of the day, if not by those of our own time; it will be discussed later).

On 15 May 1891, *Arcanum* found its supplement in the landmark encyclical on the condition of the workers, *Rerum Novarum*, in which Leo XIII

---

[43] A recent analysis of the complexities and repercussions of the image of Eve for depictions of women in art during the Belle Époque can be found in Elizabeth K. Menon, *Evil by Design: The Creation and Marketing of the Femme Fatale* (Urbana: University of Illinois Press, 2006).

[44] Leo XIII, *Arcanum* (10 February 1880); from Joseph Husslein, ed., *Social Wellsprings*, vol. 1 (Milwaukee, WI, 1940), as excerpted in *Women, the Family, and Freedom*, vol. 2, doc. 44; quote, p. 182. This encyclical elaborated on the position enunciated by Pius IX in the 1864 *Syllabus of Errors*. These documents are now consultable on the Vatican website: www.vatican.va.

rehearsed the now venerable male-breadwinner economic argument: he characterized women's employment as regrettable, and reemphasized men's responsibility to support their families. Here Leo XIII explicitly spelled out the church's position on the required social roles for Catholic men and women in the new industrial age. Reaffirming (echoing J.-B. Say and many other lay political economists, but also the seventeenth-century debates of French and British political theorists who drew an analogy between the family and the state) that man's role was to be head of the family, the pope stated that: "A family, no less than a State . . . is a true society, governed by a power within itself, that is to say, by the father." Moreover, he added, "it is a most sacred law of nature that a father must provide food and all necessaries for those whom he has begotten," and that, collectivist socialist claims to the contrary, fathers must be able to acquire individual property in order to carry out their God-given mission. While critical of "the callousness of employers," "the greed of unrestrained competition," and "rapacious usury," the pope nevertheless condemned the socialist solutions of communalizing private property (as well as the tools of production, then being proposed by the Marxists). The acquisition of property, said the pope, was a vital goal for the workingman.

Characteristically, Leo XIII's remarks on women as wives were enclosed in a single paragraph that dealt primarily with the employment of children, but the message was clear: wives, especially those who were mothers, should not work outside the home, and especially not in industrial occupations. "Women . . . are not suited to certain trades; for a woman is by nature fitted for homework, and it is that which is best adapted at once to preserve her modesty, and to promote the good bringing up of children and the well-being of the family."[45] Few objections could be heard against the proposition that children (including adolescent girls) must be protected, but grown women too? In any event, such arguments provided momentum to the continuing efforts by Catholic laymen and legislators such as Albert de Mun to restrict women's employment.

With the adhesion of some progressive Catholics to the republican regime in 1892 at the demand of the Pope (a political move referred to as the *Ralliement*), the possibilities for cross-class and cross-party social activism increased, especially as regarded issues concerning the working class.

---

[45] Leo XIII, *Rerum Novarum*, (15 May 1891); from Joseph Husslein, ed., *Social Wellsprings*, vol. 1; as excerpted in *Women, the Family, and Freedom*, vol. 2, doc. 16. Quotes WFF, pp. 94–95. Few works on the history of social Catholicism do more than allude in passing to the papal position on the woman question.

These liberal Catholics may have abandoned the monarchy for the republic, but this did not mean that they had abandoned their allegiance to the concept of hierarchical male authority in the family. *Au contraire!* In fact, their adhesion to the Third Republic provided additional ballast for a paternalistic (if indeed not patriarchal) approach to the woman question.

Not all Catholics were thrilled with the pope's determination to discourage women's work outside the household. It is remarkable, then, that within such severe doctrinal constraints, one attempt to formulate a Catholic feminism did emerge in the 1890s. A small contingent of Catholic women who called themselves feminists was able to coexist for some time with the other groups and even to influence them to think a bit more broadly about the implications of women's issues for Catholic believers, particularly single women's right to work, to control property, and – not least – the issue of woman suffrage.[46] The pope had not spoken to the case of single adult women – this loophole was quickly exploited by the founder of Catholic, or Christian feminism, as it was known in 1890s France, the journalist Marie Maugeret (1844–1928), a single professional woman who worked in the printing trades.

In 1896 Marie Maugeret founded the *Société des Féministes Chrétiens* [Society of Christian Feminists]. She also cofounded a journal, *Le Féminisme Chrétien*, in which she would address the woman question during the next eleven years.[47] The introductory program was firm and fierce. Why, Maugeret asked, establish a new feminist society when eighteen others already exist? Those groups, she responded, are all "affiliated with the freethinking school."[48] Christian feminists shared many of the same goals and could cooperate with them whenever "questions of principle" were not on the line. Maugeret took women's rights very seriously: the current of ideas that is feminism, she said, is "the immense complaint of half of humanity, and this constitutes a psychological and historical event which it would be foolish to deny and dangerous not to take into consideration." Dissimilar

[46] Marie Maugeret, "Le Féminisme Chrétien," *La Fronde*, n° 3 (11 December 1897); transl. by KO in *WFF*, vol. 2, doc. 17.

[47] *Le Féminisme Chrétien* appeared from 1896 to 1907. Several historians have dealt at length with Maugeret's proposals; see, in particular Steven C. Hause & Anne R. Kenney, "The Development of the Catholic Women's Suffrage Movement in France, 1896-1922," *Catholic Historical Review*, 67:1 (January 1981), 11–30, James F. McMillan, "Wollstonecraft's Daughters, Marianne's Daughters and the Daughters of Joan of Arc: Marie Maugeret and Christian Feminism in the French Belle Epoque," in *Wollstonecraft's Daughters: Womanhood in England and France, 1780–1920*, ed. Clarissa Campbell Orr (Manchester: Manchester University Press, 1996), 186–198. We will return to Maugeret's post-1900 suffrage and legislative campaigns in Part III.

[48] Marie Maugeret, "Notre programme," *Le Féminisme Chrétien*, n° 1 (1896), 1.

to man, but equal to him, women are "endowed with intelligence as well as heart" and could fill many functions just as well as – or perhaps better than – man. What we want, Maugeret proclaimed, is first of all economic independence, the right to prepare for any career that is compatible with our physical and moral faculties, the right to our salary and to do with it as we please (women might make better use of it!), the right for a married woman to conserve and manage her own property.

The current laws concerning marriage (enshrined in the Civil Code) are bad, Maugeret argued, "because [the Code] consecrates an injustice; it must be changed." These laws, in her opinion condemned wives "to live in chains in perpetuity." Acknowledging God's law that "you will be subjected to man," Marie Maugeret nevertheless insisted that man's privilege in this respect rests wholly on his fulfillment of his obligations: "Is he, for her, the support, the protector, the friend? or is he not more often the exploiter, the tyrant, the enemy?" This state of affairs, she insisted, "is not of divine institution, but a purely masculine institution." Indeed, the contract of marriage must be renegotiated. "Either reform man, or transform woman"; and she remarked, it is probably easier to do the latter. The society's program clearly laid out a forceful feminist position, calling for secular legal, economic, and social reform.

In a subsequent program statement published in late 1897 in an early issue of *La Fronde*, Maugeret elaborated on her program, announcing to the secular world the innovative program of "*féminisme chrétien*." She insisted that "feminism is perhaps the greatest, … the sole, truly great question of social obligation, from which no one has the right to flee." First and foremost on the program for reform was to claim a woman's right to work and to control her own property. On these two points, Maugeret was wholly aligned with the secular and socialist feminists. She opposed any labor legislation that would infringe on a woman's opportunity to earn a living. "We protest with all our energy against any law that, under the fallacious and hypocritical pretext of 'protecting' us, takes away our right, the most sacred of all, to earn our living honestly." Maugeret also advocated that civil laws be changed so that wives could control and dispose of their own earnings and that "salary be based exclusively on the value of her work and not on the sex of the worker." Moreover, she argued for the right of propertied women to retain control of property they bring to marriage. In keeping with the emphasis of *Rerum Novarum* on ameliorating the condition of the working class, Maugeret's arguments stressed the particularly unfortunate situation of the working-class wife who, married under the regime of community property, could be stripped of her meager earnings without recourse, by a dissolute and greedy husband. Husbands often shirked their duty, she asserted. She advocated the establishment of a regime of separate property in all marriage arrangements, and argued for full civil rights for women.

Marie Maugeret did not launch a frontal attack on the principle of female subordination in marriage or on the separation of spheres as delineated by Leo XIII, yet she did not spare the male "head of the family" from criticism. "It is against the husband who so often dissipates the resources of the community property, and not against the fatigues of labor, that women need laws of 'protection'."[49] In all other respects Maugeret's program in the 1890s compares favorably with that of the secular republican women's rights movement. It seems irrefutable that Maugeret did have what we now call a feminist consciousness and that her program placed her on a potential collision course with church doctrine, as well as with the Social Catholic parliamentary advocates of protective legislation for women workers. Not until the 1940s and the advent of Pius XII would Maugeret's emphasis on economic liberty for women become acceptable to the formulators of official Catholic doctrine.[50]

In retrospect, in attempting to promote women's rights in an authoritarian milieu that was resistant if not explicitly hostile to the emancipation of women, Marie Maugeret comes across as a very courageous woman. Her two program statements also reveal that, like Hubertine Auclert and many others, including Kaethe Schirmacher, Maugeret was something of a female chauvinist. Her later antisemitism, her vitriolic objections to Freemasonry, and her hard-core Catholic integral nationalism, painted in vivid and unforgiving color by historian James F. McMillan, were not yet in evidence in the texts discussed earlier.[51] But in the wake of the Dreyfus Case, Maugeret's deeper prejudices would soon reveal themselves, even as her commitment to women's rights remained strong. In 1900 she would refuse to collaborate with the progressive secular women (who included Protestants and Jews along with Freemasons and atheists) who were attempting to found a French national council of women, and she would insist on holding a separate Catholic women's congress.

---

[49] Maugeret, "Le Féminisme Chrétien," *La Fronde*, n° 3 (11 December 1897); transl. by KO in *WFF*, vol. 2, doc. 17.

[50] For the views of Pius XII, see William Barbey Faherty, S. J., *The Destiny of Modern Women in the Light of Papal Teaching* (Westminster MD: Newman Press, 1950). As of 1931, however, the previous pope, Pius XI, still objected to the employment of wives and mothers. See his encylical letter, *Quadragesimo Anno* (1931) at www.vatican.va.

[51] See McMillan, "Wollstonecraft's Daughters," cited in n. 47.

Maugeret's affirmation of women's right to work was exceptional among Catholics. Even as she spoke out, the prevailing social Christian position on women's employment continued to gain momentum following the publications of another distinguished contributor, the aristocratic Catholic social investigator, Paul-Gabriel-Othénin de Claron, comte d'Haussonville (1843–1924), nephew of the former prime minister, the Duc de Broglie, and also an academician and former secretary of the failed Orleanist pretender, the Comte de Paris. In mid-1892 d'Haussonville began to publish his findings from comparative research on women's employment.[52] In the ensuing years he would publish three well-documented and influential studies, a second edition of his 1886 work, *Misère et remèdes, Socialisme et charité* (1895), and *Salaires et misères de femmes* (1900). None of these contained anything that might even remotely be considered a feminist program.

The controversy surrounding women's employment arrived on the threshold of the Chamber of Deputies and Senate in the early 1890s. A cluster of French legislators, some longtime republicans, some socialists, some Catholic *ralliés*, set about placing restrictions on the labor of adult women, which its members who were economic liberals had previously been reluctant to touch. In later 1892, after many years of stalling amid mounting controversy, the all-male legislature broke with its earlier non-interventionist principles concerning the labor of adults to pass a law that specifically regulated the employment of adult women, while still keeping hands off men's labor. Two of the Third Republic's most eminent secular political economists had contributed directly to the law's ultimate passage – Jules Simon, whose reversal of position was discussed earlier, and Paul Leroy-Beaulieu, then professor of political economy at the *Collège de France*, who openly castigated the feminist movement for diminishing women's interest in marriage and maternity by tempting them with "men's jobs."[53] Both had expressed strong convictions on the subject of women's

---

[52] Gabriel-Paul-Othénin de Cléron, comte d' Haussonville, "Le Travail des femmes aux États-Unis et en Angleterre," *RDM* (1 July 1892), 66–88.

[53] See Paul Leroy-Beaulieu, "The Influence of Civilisation upon the Movement of the Population," *Journal of the Royal Statistical Society*, 54 (June 1891), 372–384 (orig. publ. in *L'Économiste Française*, 20 & 27 September 1890). In this article, Leroy-Beaulieu responded to a theory propounded by social anthropologist Arsène Dumont, who attributed the fall in the birth rate to "social capillarity," or the ineluctable movement of men and wealth from the countryside to the city in quest of luxury. See Dumont, *Dépopulation et civilisation: Étude démographique* (Paris: Lecrosnier & Babé, 1890). Also see Leroy-Beaulieu's *Traité théorique et pratique d'économie politique*, 4 vols., 4 (Paris: Guillaumin, 1896; this work had many subsequent editions), esp. pp. 625–626. In later statements, Leroy-Beaulieu expanded on but did not significantly modify the themes he developed in the 1890s. See "La

employment.[54] Their controlling impulses found sustenance in a report issued by the Academy of Medicine in 1891, which endorsed the prohibition on women's night work.[55]

The new French law of 2 November 1892 laid down the first hourly and night work restrictions on *adult* women's labor. It not only restricted the daily hours of women's work in industry but its Article 4 forbade women's employment at night (when their work was often much better paid).[56] The intricacies of debate on this labor law both in the legislature and in the press are lengthy, complex, and fascinating, but what bears underscoring here is the manner in which male legislators thought they could pass laws that vitally affected women without even a nod to the feminists' consolidated campaign for equal rights before the law. It is true, as historian Mary Lynn Stewart points out, that in early 1890 the Labor Committee of the Chamber of Deputies did make an effort to consult a sampling of women workers in potentially affected industries; the biggest employers of women in night work were in braid making (Saint Chamond, in the Loire), cotton mills (in the Vosges), and wool carders (in the Nord), and also, according to Stewart, in "sugar refineries, paperworks, and glass factories." The seamstresses interviewed by Charles Benoist who might be affected by such legislation seemed less concerned about their rights than about convenience of night work for sharing childcare, the possibility of higher pay, and other practical considerations. As Stewart puts it, "The mixture of anxiety about jobs and wages, concern about their dual role, and desire to avoid supervision evident in the working women's statements captures reaction to the proposed ban on their night labour."[57]

However influential French women were deemed to be (or hoped to be) at home, in the arena of legislative politics these hundreds of thousands – even millions – of adult women workers could not vote; thus, they had no political clout. Male legislators could make laws such as these with political

Question de la population et la civilisation démocratique," *RDM*, (15 October 1897), 851–899, and *La Question de la dépopulation* (Paris: F. Alcan, 1913).

[54] See Jules Simon, *L'Ouvrière* (Paris: Hachette, 1861; 9th ed., 1891) and Paul Leroy-Beaulieu, *Le Travail des femmes au XIXe siècle* (Paris: Charpentier, 1873). At the meeting of the *Société d'Économie Politique*, 5 June 1884 (discussed in Part I), Simon and Leroy-Beaulieu had addressed the question, "Où la femme, au point de vue économique, est-elle mieux placée, au foyer de la famille ou dans l'atelier?" See the *Journal des Économistes*, 26:3 (June 1884), 445–459.

[55] See Stewart, *Women, Work, and the French State*, pp. 128–130.

[56] On the law of 2 November 1892, see Hubert-Valleroux, "Loi du 2 novembre 1892, sur le travail des enfants, des filles mineures et des femmes dans les établissements industrials," *Annuaire de la Législation Française*, 1892, 12 (1893), 129–144, and Andrée Lehmann, *De la réglementation légale du travail féminin: Étude de législation comparée* (Paris: H. d'Arthez, 1924), chapter 1.

[57] See Stewart, *Women, Work, and the French State*, pp. 130–133; quotation, p. 133.

impunity, as Benoist and others underscored. Some feminists continued to argue that enfranchising women, including these women, would change things dramatically. Without entry to the decision-making arena, to the realm of political authority, how could they stave off such discriminatory legal incentives?

In the 1890s, not every woman would be that enthusiastic about entering that realm of political authority. The journalist Séverine, while avidly supporting women's economic advancement, was skeptical about the benefits of suffrage for women:[58]

> Into this business [of politics] women want to enter? Under the tree of science, Eve, her turn arrived, asks Adam for half the apple ... only to find that the apple Adam holds is spoiled, gnawed to the core by parasites, infected by fungus and infested by vermin. I have no appetite for these little dinners. And if the act of sharing has become necessary, due to man's egoism and ferocity, let us at least pick from the branch a new, healthy, and savoury fruit.

A decade later Séverine would change her mind about women's need for the vote. For others, such as the founder of *L'Avant-Courrière*, Jeanne Schmahl, it would not take that long.

Since I first explored this topic in the early 1980s, historians Mary Lynn Stewart and Michèle Zancarini-Fournel have published astute analyses of the lead-up to the law of 2 November 1892.[59] Stewart's scholarship addresses and seeks to correct the misconceptions that have entered the historical literature thanks to those who have assumed, or argued from hindsight, that restricting women's work was simply a prelude to "universal" measures that would ultimately apply to the employment of men as well. She has laid out in detail the difference in rationales used when it came to restricting women's work as distinct from men's work. Zancarini-Fournel's analysis further clarifies what was missing in earlier scholarship on labor and social issues in the period: in particular, she emphasizes the convergence in opposition to women's work of the Christian right-wing in the form of Social Catholicism with the Socialist left-wing antifeminists,

---

[58] Séverine in *La Revue Féministe*, 1:1.
[59] On enforcement of the 1892 law, see Stewart, *Women, Work, and the French State*. Also, Mary Lynn Stewart, "Setting the Standards: Labor and Family Reformers," in *Gender and the Politics of Social Reform in France*, ed. Elinor Accampo, Rachel Fuchs, & Mary Lynn Stewart (Baltimore: Johns Hopkins University Press, 1995), pp. 106–127. More recently, see Michelle Zancarini-Fournel, "Archéologie de la loi de 1892 en France," in *Différence des sexes et protection sociale (XIXe-XXe siècles)*, ed. Leora Auslander & Michelle Zancarini-Fournel (St. Denis: Presses Universitaires de Vincennes, 1995), pp. 75–92.

particularly (in the latter case) Henri-Louis Tolain (1828–1897), a life
senator since 1876, who had systematically opposed women's employment
ever since the congresses of the First International Workingmen's Association in the 1860s. The social Catholic spokesman Émile Keller had
advocated Sunday rest and the restriction of night work for women,
especially mothers, since 1881. "If you want the *mère de famille* to be able
to prepare the evening meal, she must be at her stove and table when her
husband and children come home; it is indispensable that her workday
[outside the home] be over by 19 h [7 p.m.]."[60] A focus on women's God-
given responsibility to cook the evening meal for the family had replaced
concern about salting the workingman's soup, but otherwise Keller's
discourse bore a remarkable resemblance to that of the Proudhonist Left
of the 1860s.[61]

It was significant, too, that both Tolain and the much younger Auguste
Keufer (1851–1924), the secretary-general of the *Fédération Française des
Travailleurs du Livre* (FFTL; the printers' union) had been named to the
influential *Conseil Supérieur du Travail*, on which no women served before
1900 when, following years of feminist insistence, the socialist-feminist
leader of a teacher's union, Marie Bonnevial, would be appointed.[62] In
fact, in August 1897, Bonnevial would attend the International Congress
for Protective Labor Legislation in Zurich as a delegate of the *Ligue
Française pour le Droit des Femmes* (LFDF) and of her teachers' union,
with the specific mission of opposing special legislation to protect women
only. According to the report of the French delegates, published by the
Musée Social, Bonnevial "kept the flag of feminist demands waving."[63]
What she encountered at this congress, though, was an intense debate
(provoked by the Swiss convener, Dr. Decurtins) over a Belgian Catholic
delegate's proposal *to eliminate* women, especially married women, from
the labor force – in the interest of preserving "the family," and a "put-
down" to her arguments by the conference organizer. It was clear that for

---

[60] Keller in the Chamber of Deputies, 29 March 1881; cited by Zancarini-Fournel, "Archéologie,"
p. 82.

[61] The gender politics of the First International and the views of Proudhon are discussed in my
companion volume, *The Woman Question in France, 1400–1870.*

[62] Zancarini-Fournel, "Archéologie," pp. 83 ff. Bonnevial would be eased off the *CST* in 1903.

[63] See Ulla Wikander, "Some 'Kept the Flag of Feminist Demands Waving': Debates at International
Congresses on Protecting Women Workers," in *Protecting Women . . .* , pp. 30–62; quotation, in
title, and on p. 42. Wikander references the proceedings, *Amtlicher Bericht des Organisations –
Komittees. Zürich, 28 August 1897*, pp. 261, 207–214. German socialists at the Zurich congress,
including Lily Braun and Clara Zetkin, also defended women's right to work against the Catholic
protectionists. On this congress, see the very useful retrospective report by Albert Duforcq, "Le
Congrès de Zurich," *La Revue d'Économie Politique* 12:7 (July 1898), 598–619.

activist Social Catholics, in particular, anxiety about women's employment remained inextricably intertwined with their effort to defend the patriarchal family and, for that matter, male hegemony in the workplace.

The republican government in France had created a Labor Bureau (*Office du Travail*) in 1891 with a mission that was heavily influenced, as Judith Coffin points out, by Le Playist sociology.[64] This 1892 law marked the real debut of the Third Republic's government's reluctant movement into social intervention and workplace regulation. Zancarini-Fournel has underscored the fact that it was "the first law adopted . . . that marked "the intervention of the French state in 'the social'."[65] It would not be the last. When push came to shove, legislators from both sides of the aisle preferred the approach of restricting women's employment. Although the law concerned only large industrial establishments and would prove difficult to apply, much less enforce, its significance lay (in Zancarini-Fournel's estimation) in its effective discursive exclusion of women from the labor force, by creating a special category of wives and mothers, an exclusion which would remain in place for much of the twentieth century, and which, not incidentally, would also uphold the authority of the father *cum chef de l'atelier* in the smaller family-based manufacturing establishments that were exempt from the law.

What most scholars on the history of French labor legislation have neglected to report are the feminist interventions in the debates that preceded and followed the 1892 law. Despite the long history of feminist claims for women's right to work, which I have detailed in earlier chapters, the legislators as a body seemed reluctant to acknowledge, much less address their claims. Since 1874, with the regulation of child labor and that of underage girls, proposals for more extensive protective legislation had been introduced in the French Chamber of Deputies, but resistance to interfering with adult choices remained stiff, particularly when they concerned the freedom of men and heads of families. Léon Richer had gone head to head on the subject with Dr. Henri Thulié (then president of the Paris Municipal Council) in *Le Droit des Femmes* during the mid-1880s. Even though Thulié blamed all the bad developments such as the already evident drop in the birth rate and high infant mortality on women's legal inferiority rather than on their employment, he did advocate protective legislation, opposed wet-nursing, and argued that fathers must be legally bound to support mothers and children. He insisted, in particular, that mothers of young children must not work outside the home. Dr. Thulié's

---

[64] See Coffin, *Politics of Women's Work*, p. 209.   [65] Zancarini-Fournel, "Archéologie," p. 87.

interventionist solutions were predicated on the notion that good sociology
must have a physiological, not a metaphysical, basis.[66]

The *Parti Ouvrier* under Jules Guesde had, as we have seen, spoken out
strongly for women's emancipation from the mid-1870s on. But during the
1880s, with its turn toward building a political party that would court male
votes, and the 1889 founding of the Second International, women's emancipation began to take a backseat to promoting class conflict (by which
was meant proletarian solidarity and conflict with the bourgeoisie) and the
coming revolution, the goal of which was to overturn capitalist society
and eliminate private property in the name of the proletariat. In later 1891
the former Communarde Paule Mink likewise argued that the "woman
question " was only one part of the "social question," and that socialist
goals must take priority.[67] Disputing Mink's perspective, Eugénie Potonié-
Pierre asserted in the *Journal des Femmes* that women needed their rights in
the current society, so that they could actually influence the construction
of a new society.[68] This difference of opinion did not deter Paule Mink
from participating, later in the century, in the meetings of *Solidarité des
Femmes*, founded and presided by Potonié- Pierre.

In fact, at Aline Valette's recommendation, delegates to the 1892 feminist
congress in Paris would endorse the suppression of night work (though not
restricted hours) for adult women workers. The masthead of her weekly
publication *L'Harmonie sociale* featured the motto: "The Emancipation of
Women lies in Emancipated Labor." Like most socialists and many
feminists, Valette continued to insist on prioritizing women's economic
freedom, arguing that the fundamental solution to the woman question
and women's emancipation lay in "that other revolution – the emancipation of labor."[69] Following passage of the law in November and the
ensuing controversies, some feminist-socialists broke ranks. In 1896, Eugénie Potonié-Pierre came out strongly against protective legislation of any
kind and called for women's "right to work."[70]

---

[66] Dr. Henri Thulié, *La Femme: Essai de sociologie physiologique* ... (Paris: A. Delahaye &
E. Lecrosnier, 1885), passim. Richer's discussion and rebuttals appeared in *Le Droit des Femmes*,
beginning with issue n° 254 (19 July 1885) and continued into 1886.

[67] Paule Mink, "L'Émancipation de la femme et le socialisme," *La Question Sociale*, (1 October &
1 November 1891).

[68] Eugénie Potonié-Pierre, "Congrès Général des Sociétés féministes," *Le Journal des Femmes*, n° 7
(June 1892), 3. Cf. Charles Sowerwine, *Sisters or Citizens, Women and Socialism in France since 1876*
(Cambridge, UK: Cambridge University Press, 1982), pp. 70–71.

[69] Aline Valette, "Le Féminisme à la Chambre de 1893 à 1898," *La Fronde* (in "La Tribune," feuilleton
in 3 parts), n° 142 (29 April 1898), n° 143 (30 April 1898), & n° 144 (1 May 1898).

[70] Eugénie Potonié-Pierre, "Le congrès féministe international," *La Question Sociale*, n°s 21–22 (April–
May 1896), 378–381.

Following the second international congress on "*protection ouvrière*," convened in Zurich in August 1898 (23–28 August), at which Marie Bonnevial, Clara Zetkin, and Lily Braun all spoke, positions would harden. By the time of the 1899 congress of the ICW in London, the debates over protective legislation resembled the "shoot-out" at the OK Corral. Liberals (i.e., noninterventionists) spoke out for the individual's right to work, irrespective of sex, while advocates of labor protection for women continued to insist that restricting women's work was (or in any case, should be) the prelude to equal restrictions on the labor of both sexes.[71]

Although, in retrospect, it might look to some historians as if little progress had been made toward the achievement of women's rights, either legal or economic, in the 1890s, in fact there had been considerable shifts in attitudes, seen notably in the French legislature prior to the revision of the Dreyfus Case. In a series of articles published in *La Fronde's* feature, "La Tribune de la Fronde," in 1898, Aline Valette reclaimed the high ground for the socialist-feminists. She would point to the prominence of the issues raised in the 1893–1898 French parliament by "women's friends," and recounted the multiple initiatives introduced in the Chamber of Deputies by the socialist deputies (especially Jules Guesde, with whom she worked very closely in the *Parti Ouvrier*, but also by Edouard Vaillant, René Viviani, Jean Jaurès, and other left-leaning deputies) to promote the legal changes that would realize the 1893 program put forward by the *Fédération Française des Sociétés Feministes* (FFSF). Valette insisted throughout her presentation, that "the true, the great feminist current is on the side of the masses of working women" who are not misled by the spirit of individualism, but "work each and every day ... toward their economic freedom, which will, in due course, bring them all the other freedoms."[72] She also insisted on the superiority of cooperation to competition, particularly with regard to the two sexes, and to the fact that every time an issue had arisen, the socialists included women with men in their legislative reform projects as a matter of course. After Valette's untimely

---

[71] See Wikander, "Some 'Kept the Flag of Feminist Demands Waving'," pp. 46–49, for further analysis of the debates on protective legislation at the ICW London Congress.

[72] Valette, "Féminisme à la Chambre de 1893 à 1898," second and third installments; quotes, third installment. The 1893 *Cahier de Doléances*, which Valette had compiled, would also be published in appendix to *Socialisme et sexualisme: Programme du Parti Socialiste Féminin* (Paris: A.-M. Beaudelot, 1893). This latter unsigned publication, attributed to Aline Valette and Dr. Z (Pierre Bonnier), circulated widely. See Marilyn J. Boxer, "Linking Socialism, Feminism, and Social Darwinism in Belle Epoque France: The Maternalist Politics and Journalism of Aline Valette," *Women's History Review*, 21:1 (February 2012), 1–19.

death in 1899, Marie Bonnevial would take over Valette's regular column on women's work, "*Le Travail des Femmes*," at *La Fronde* and rebaptize it as the "*Tribune du Travail*."

The feminists faced severe hostility from certain all-male unions, particularly from the FFTL, which for decades had opposed the inclusion of women as typographers.[73] The Federation's leader at this time, Auguste Keufer, was an outspoken critic of women compositors, although he did advocate paying them the same as men; he would speak of a "feminist invasion" [*envahissement féministe*] of the typesetting *ateliers*, and would characterize the shops as "infested by women."[74] Subsequent to passage of the 1892 law, this union's leadership became extremely vigilant in reporting women whom they found working at night as *compositrices* (typographers or typesetters), even in small print shops.[75]

In early September 1898, government work inspectors (no doubt alerted by Keufer and his associates) called on the headquarters of *La Fronde*, which was by no means a large industrial printing firm but did hire (exclusively) women to produce the daily paper, including the typesetting. To no one's surprise, the inspectors "found" fourteen women typographers working at night. They were setting type for the next day's edition, just as they had been doing for nearly a year. What was more, they were earning union wages.

Marguerite Durand, as publisher, was charged with violating the now infamous law of 1892, which restricted women's industrial work hours and which, in Article 4, forbid them to work at night (exceptions being made only for extenuating circumstances). Durand had not filed for an exception. In February 1899, however, the judge hearing the case exonerated Durand and her typesetters, finding the law so full of loopholes and contradictions, and so undermined by a series of administrative "exceptions" based on the industrial necessity of certain employers, that conviction was out of the question. Maria Martin, editor of the *Journal des Femmes*, celebrated this verdict as an "almost unhoped-for success," and urged her readers to ponder "that it is only where men fear the competition of women that they consider 'protecting' them by laws that violate women's right to work."[76] No one, she indicated, had ever contested the

---

[73] On the earlier problems with the printers' union, see my companion volume, chapter 6.

[74] Keufer, quoted in Emmanuel Rivière, *Le Travail de la femme dans l'industrie typographique* (Brochure, publ. in Blois), pp. 27, 28.

[75] See Mary Lynn Stewart's treatment of the Federation's opposition, which she has traced in the archival records of the early and mid-1890s, in *Women, Work, and the French State*, pp. 135–139.

[76] Maria Martin, "La Loi de 1892," *Le Journal des Femmes*, n° 85 (March 1899), 1.

right to work of women who work at night folding newspapers, because such meager earnings are disdained by men. Maria Martin provided a number of other examples where this was the case – in the mines, in the factories which ran nonstop [*les usines à feu continu*], and among the street merchants [*les marchandes de quatre saisons*] who dragged huge loads of goods through the streets at all hours. In early March 1899, Durand founded the *Syndicat des Femmes Typographes*, which quickly affiliated with the *Bourse du Travail*.[77] This was one of a series of all-woman unions that Durand helped to foster in these years.[78]

La Fronde's victory in court turned out to be provisional. When the republican legislature reconvened in the fall of 1899, measures to block women's night work more effectively were introduced. Feminists protested vehemently. In late October Clotilde Dissard published a three-part article for *La Fronde*, in which she sketched the history of women in the printing trades. She even claimed that in its early years, "the typographic art was a womanly art."[79] Dissard alleged that there was indeed a "war against working women." "The printers' unions," she declared, "intended to kick women out of the entire book industry, not only typography but engraving, binding, and the rest." If such ostracism spread to other industries, she claimed, women who needed to support themselves would soon have no recourse except to public assistance or to prostitution.[80] Maria Pognon, president of the LFDF, charged in late December, as the amended law returned from the Senate for reconsideration by the Chamber of Deputies, that the new provisions amounted to "protection in reverse."[81] Echoing the observations of Maria Martin, Pognon argued that:

> The 1892 law was made by antifeminists, who were preoccupied to preserve all the well-paying work for their constituents: this is the real truth! ... wherever night-work is well-paid, someone has found it too tiring for women, or unhygienic, or even dangerous!

---

[77] François Chaignaud, *L'Affaire Berger-Levrault: le féminisme à l'épreuve (1897–1905)* (Rennes: Presses Universitaires de Rennes, 2009) discusses the founding of the *Syndicat des Femmes Typographes*, but not the preceding investigation and court case that triggered it.

[78] In 1898 Durand had founded a dressmakers' co-operative (*coopérative des couturières*).

[79] See the series of articles by Clotilde Dissard on women in the printing industry, "Le Travail des Femmes: Femmes dans l'industrie du livre," in "La Tribune" of *La Fronde*, n⁰ˢ 683, 684, & 685 (22, 23, & 24 October 1899).

[80] Dissard, "Travail des Femmes: Femmes dans l'industrie du livre," *La Fronde*, n° 684 (23 October 1899); in the third installment (24 October), Dissard discussed the founding in Geneva of a typography school for young women.

[81] See Maria Pognon, "La Loi néfaste de 1892," *La Fronde*, n° 743 (20 December 1899). Pognon's article is translated in *WFF*, vol. 2, doc. 55. In the same issue, see Marguerite Durand, "Protection!"

Many thanks for your protection, *Messieurs les députés*. From now on leave women free to work or to rest as they see fit, according to the circumstances. Get used to considering them as responsible beings, capable of directing their own lives and of taking responsibility for their own actions; do not confuse them with their children, whose reasoning powers are not yet fully developed, and, if you want to protect the little ones, let their mothers work in their places.

Help these women to unionize so that they themselves can arrange their terms of work with the employers, but do not deprive them of their jobs on the pretext of safeguarding their health. If the father's health is not good, the children will not be much to brag about either.

Pognon concluded her article by making explicit the underlying concerns about the declining birth rate and the poor quality of children born to working class families: "We can improve the race by requiring of workers only a reasonable expenditure of physical strength. But since both sexes are called upon to procreate, we must be prudent and kind to both; otherwise it is lost labor."

Would the Solidarist Republicans Support Feminist Claims?

By the mid-1890s it had become crystal clear that neither the Social Catholics nor the more extreme Socialists and male-chauvinist unions such as the FFTL would rally in support of feminist proposals to deregulate women's work. However, another group of republican legislators and reformers would play an important role in the debates on the woman question in the 1890s with respect to the role of the state and its responsibilities toward what the French call "the social" (which we would call social welfare).[82] Faced with an increasingly intransigent revolutionary socialism, which at the international level, if not so much in France, aggressively promoted class conflict, progressive republicans promoted the new doctrine of Solidarity to foster harmony between labor and capital, between the working people and the bourgeoisie (or capitalist) class.

The concept of social solidarity, or what the French called *Solidarité* (or occasionally *Solidarisme*), had been around for decades. It appears to have originated with Pierre Leroux in the 1830s; Auguste Comte strongly supported it in his *Cours de Philosophie Positive* (1830–1842). Solidarity was invoked during the 1848 revolutions. In the later 1860s the reformer

---

[82] See Jacques Donzelot, *L'Invention du social: Essai sur le déclin des passions politiques* (Paris: Fayard, 1984).

Charles Fauvety published a monthly periodical entitled *La Solidarité: Journal des principes*; its motto was (as in the novel *The Three Musketeers*) "All for one, and one for all" [*Tous pour chacun et chacun pour tous*]. The future Sorbonne professor Henri Marion (1846–1896) defended his thesis "De la solidarité morale" in 1879.[83] As a political doctrine, *Solidarisme* was further enunciated in 1895 by Léon Bourgeois on philosophical foundations laid by Comte and Alfred J. E. Fouillée, and adhered to by an important contingent of republican deputies, senators, lawyers, educators, and intellectuals who came to power and prominence in the last decade of the nineteenth century. By 1900 it would become, in the words of J. E. S. Hayward, "the official social philosophy of the French Third Republic."[84]

Léon Bourgeois developed *Solidarisme* as a political formula that would go beyond strict laissez-faire market economics to allow the Third Republic to ride the crest of interest in social welfare through state intervention, to pursue humanitarian aims of social reform and mass education within capitalist society, and thereby (it was hoped) to defuse class struggle and all potential revolutionary threats to the existing social order. The quest for national solidarity seemed, to the Solidarist republicans, to offer the perfect antidote to class conflict. One can think of this

---

[83] Marion's revised published version (1883) is discussed at length in Judith Surkis, *Sexing the Citizen: Morality and Masculinity* (Ithaca, NY: Cornell University Press, 2006), chapter 2. Following a professorship in "morale" at the *ENS d'Enseignement Primaire*, Marion moved to the Sorbonne in 1883 as the Third Republic's first professor of educational sciences. He lectured on women's education in 1892–1893 (reported in the *Revue des Cours et des Conférences*, vol. 1 (1892–1893), and his influential posthumously published works included *Psychologie de la femme* (Paris: A. Colin, 1900), and *L'Éducation des jeunes filles* (Paris: A. Colin, 1902). Following Marion's death in 1896, the educator and legislator Ferdinand Buisson was appointed to the educational sciences chair. That same year (1896), Henri Marion's widow succeeded Mme Jules Favre as head of the *École Normale Supérieure de Sèvres*.

[84] Phrase derived from J. E. S. Hayward, "The Official Social Philosophy of the French Third Republic: Léon Bourgeois and Solidarism," *International Review of Social History*, 6, pt. 1 (1961), 19–48; see also his previous article, "Solidarity: The Social History of an Idea in Nineteenth Century France," *International Review of Social History*, 4, pt. 2 (1959), 261–281.
For other scholarly assessments of late nineteenth-century solidarity, see John Anthony Scott, *Republican Ideas and the Liberal Tradition in France, 1870–1914* (New York: Columbia University Press, 1951), 157–186, and William Logue, *From Philosophy to Sociology: The Evolution of French Liberalism* (DeKalb: Northern Illinois University Press, 1983). Also see Theodore Zeldin, *France, 1848–1945*, 1 (Oxford: Oxford University Press, 1973), chapter 21. For a Marxist critique of solidarism, see Sanford Elwitt, *The Making of the Third Republic* (Baton Rouge: Louisiana State University Press, 1975). For an enthusiastic re-endorsement of the solidarist movement by a French socialist militant, see Marcel Ruby, *Le Solidarisme; une doctrine pour la gauche* (Paris: Gedalge, 1971). Linda L. Clark discusses the use of evolutionary theory by French solidarists to support their case for social harmony and cooperation in *Social Darwinism in France* (University, AL: The University of Alabama Press, 1984).

approach as a kind of progressive nationalism, or even as a mild form of socialism on a national scale.[85]

Several successive women's rights groups had already taken up this label as well as pursuing a cross-class approach. Marie Goegg launched *Solidarité* (in Geneva) in the early 1870s, Emilie de Morsier founded an abolitionist feminist group *La Solidarité* in the early 1880s, and in 1891 Eugénie Potonié-Pierre and Maria Martin established the group *Solidarité des Femmes*, which quickly affiliated with the *Fédération féministe* and published accounts of its meetings in the *Journal des Femmes*.[86] In November 1895, in the third issue of the *Revue Féministe*, its editor Clotilde Dissard insisted on the necessity of feminist solidarity in order to achieve women's emancipation.[87] No serious argument against feminism could be found, she insisted; the major obstacle was that men in power could not bear to give up their privileges. Men won't provide the solutions to the woman question, she asserted, and only women acting together could bring about change. Neither religious or party differences should stand in the way. Perhaps, Dissard speculated, women's solidarity could even pave the way toward human solidarity.

Human solidarity seemed a goal worth pursuing. Thus, from the mid-1890s on, French republican feminists sought out allies among the male republican solidarists. Both preferred concrete, scientifically designed solutions to what they perceived as abstract ideals; both sought harmony and association (what we now call consensus) rather than confrontation, conflict, and competition; both called for social justice to rout the inequities of natural justice, for disarmament and international arbitration rather than displays of force, and, in particular, both called for national solidarity across class lines rather than conflict between the rich and the poor. Both solidarists and feminists deemed cooperation of the sexes, as of the classes, preferable to conflict between them. In seeking improvement in the condition of women, they had no intent of toppling capital or the class structure, although they did aspire to minimize class conflict.

---

[85] See, for example, Léon Bourgeois, *Solidarité* (Paris, 3rd ed., 1902; orig. publ. 1896); Léon Bourgeois & Alfred Croisset, *Essai d'une philosophie de la Solidarité: Conférences et discussions (1900–1902)* (Paris: École des Hautes Études Sociales, 1902); & Célestin Bouglé, "L'Évolution du solidarisme," *La Revue Politique et Parlementaire*, 35, n° 105 (10 March 1903), 480–505.

[86] See Klejman & Rochefort, *Égalité en marche*, chapter 3 on the 1891 group; for Goegg's group in 1870s Geneva, see Susanna Woodtli, *Du féminisme à l'égalité politique: Un siècle de luttes en Suisse, 1868–1971* (Lausanne: Payot, 1977), & Beatrix Mesmer, *Ausgeklammert, Eingeklammert: Frauen und Frauenorganisationen in der Schweiz des 19. Jahrhunderts* (Basel & Frankfurt/Main: Helbing & Lichtenhahn, 1988).

[87] Clotilde Dissard, "Féminisme et solidarité," *La Revue Féministe*, 1:3 (5 November 1895), 97–101.

The extent of solidarist support for reforms on behalf of women must, however, be carefully qualified and considered in relation to claims made on behalf of men. Men, the principal theorist of *Solidarisme* Léon Bourgeois argued, are *not* born free, but are enmeshed in a web of obligations by a sort of quasi-contract; so it was for women as well. A higher, even if rigorously secular collectivity – the nation – must necessarily subordinate individual claims. Although radical republicans of solidarist persuasion were bitterly anticlerical, many of them were intellectuals and educators vitally interested in propagating a new morality, a morality that insisted on the functions and obligations of men and women in the name of the nation, and on the family, not the individual, as the basic social and political unit of the nation. They did support a number of reforms that would ameliorate women's position in society by enhancing their assigned roles, through giving married women the right to control their own earnings, allowing all adult women to witness civil acts (the two reforms pursued by Jeanne Schmahl's *L'Avant-Courrière*), liberalizing divorce laws, or even opening professional schools such as the *École des Beaux-Arts* to women – *but always on condition that the time-honored sexual division of labor be respected.* Their touchstone, one that had a long history in republican thought on the woman question, was (yes, you have heard this before) "equality in difference."[88] The Solidarist men were interested, as historian Judith Surkis has demonstrated, in creating "New Man."[89] They were quite willing to consider women as moral equals but did not go so far as to sanction members of either sex acting purely as individuals, in disregard of their functional context in the nation, which in this case was defined in terms of organic biology and the family. Conflict between the sexes, as between the classes, was to be avoided at all cost. Sheer individualism was anathema!

Consequently, the male partisans of solidarity would never consider supporting rights for women independently of – or in conflict with – their assigned responsibilities. They concurred with the relational feminism of a Clotilde Dissard but not with the individualist feminism that would be

---

[88] For discussion of the doctrine of "equality in difference," see Karen Offen, "The Second Sex and the Baccalauréat in Republican France, 1880–1924," *French Historical Studies*, 13:2 (Fall 1983), 252–286, & "Ernest Legouvé and the Doctrine of 'Equality in Difference' for Women: A Case Study of Male Feminism in Nineteenth-Century French Thought," *Journal of Modern History*, 58:2 (June 1986), 452–484.

[89] See Surkis, *Morality and Masculinity in France, 1870–1920*, and my review of this study on H-France Forum, vol. 2, issue 1 (Winter 2007), n° 3, at www.h-france/net/forum/forumvol2/OffenOnSurkis1.html.

articulated in the early twentieth century by Dr. Madeleine Pelletier.[90] In this respect the Solidarists established their distance from the misogyny of Proudhon, but endorsed, in part, the biological imperatives of August Comte. They talked less about the responsibilities of wives than about those of motherhood. Whenever women's demands seemed to augur excessive individualism, that is, to threaten the proprietary familial structure or to transgress the lines laid down for the sexual division of labor (which was considered vital to the national welfare), the solidarist republicans would dig in their heels. Significantly, Alfred J. E. Fouillée, who had invoked the prehistoric protozoa (see Chapter 5), was also a principal theoretician of *Solidarisme*.

The pronouncements of the now mid-career sociologist Émile Durkheim (1858–1917), Fouillée's younger colleague in the university, would coincide in many respects with (and provide scientific reinforcement for) the perspectives of the Solidarist republicans.[91] His study on the division of social labor, published in 1893, was conveniently timed. "The sexual division of labor is the source of conjugal solidarity," Durkheim asserted.[92]

---

[90] On Pelletier, see Marilyn J. Boxer, "When Radical and Socialist Feminism Were Joined: The Extraordinary Failure of Madeleine Pelletier," in *European Women on the Left: Socialism, Feminism, and the Problems Faced by Political Women, 1880 to the Present*, ed. Jane Slaughter & Robert Kern (Westport, CT: Greenwood, 1981), 51–73; & Charles Sowerwine, "Socialism, Feminism, and Violence: The Analysis of Madeleine Pelletier," in *Proceedings of the Western Society for French History, Eugene, 1980*, vol. 8, ed. Edgar Leon Newman (Las Cruces, NM, 1981), 415–422. Pelletier's contributions to the woman question debates will be considered at greater length in Part III.

[91] Although Durkheim never published his early material on family sociology, he did lecture on the topic both at Bordeaux and in Paris prior to 1900. For a surviving fragment from one of his 1892 lectures in Bordeaux, see George Simpson, "A Durkheim Fragment," *The American Journal of Sociology*, 70, n° 5 (March 1965), 527–536.

[92] In his first major publication, *De la Division du travail social* (Paris: Félix Alcan, 1893), p. 58, Durkheim emphasized the "progressive" or evolutionary character of the sexual division of labor as "la source de la solidarité conjugale." Durkheim insisted that the family evolved toward the patriarchal type; significantly, in developing his conclusions he relied on Gustave Le Bon's findings concerning the sexual differentiation of skulls, rather than the counter-findings of Dr. Léonce Manouvrier.

Durkheim's views on what wives offered husbands seem quite conventional and androcentric. These stands and the pattern of his own family life (as revealed by his nephew Marcel Mauss) strongly suggest that his views on the woman question conformed in most respects to (and possibly validated) the thinking of many other republican solidarist intellectuals and politicians, who supported only those reforms in women's legal position that would not erode the sexual division of labor. Also see Herbert Bynder, "Émile Durkheim and the Sociology of the Family," *Journal of Marriage and the Family*, 31:3 (August 1969), 527–533; and Steven Lukes, *Emile Durkheim* (New York: Harper & Row, 1972), chapter 8. On Durkheim's extraordinary intellectual influence in the twentieth century, see Terry Nichols Clark, *Prophets and Patrons* (Cambridge, MA: Harvard University Press, 1973). Recent feminist analyses of Durkheim's views on the woman question include Jennifer M. Lehmann, *Durkheim and Women* (Lincoln: University of Nebraska Press, 1994), and especially the series of articles by Jean-Elisabeth Pedersen, "Something Mysterious: Sex Education, Victorian Morality, and Durkheim's Comparative Sociology," *Journal of the History of*

In Solidarist thinking, women were perceived not necessarily as inferior but invariably as biologically and therefore, irremediably "different." While this recategorization from inferiority to irremediable difference could be viewed as a promotion for women, it certainly did not offer a foundation for any sort of abstract individual equality. In fact, the solidarist republicans would draw the line on reform at the precise point where feminist demands seemed to augur excessive individualism, that is, to threaten the proprietary familial structure or to transgress the lines laid down for that sacrosanct sexual division of labor, which they considered vital to the national welfare.

With partisans of *Solidarisme* in power after 1896, French feminists began to press for the enactment of various legal reforms that had sought political solutions since the 1830s. In an era in which debates over feminist challenges to the sexual status quo were popping up throughout the media and at social gatherings, the New Woman was the talk of the town, and the French press was taking feminist congresses seriously, a group of deputies in the Chamber organized a caucus of sorts on women's rights. The Paris Municipal Council began granting subsidies to congresses on women's rights and bankrolling travel for French women delegates to feminist congresses in other countries.[93] Even so, the republican feminists encountered stiff resistance to some claims. Their efforts to undo the paternalistic and discriminatory regulation of women's work in industry, to end the legal incapacity of married women, and, of course, to achieve suffrage for all women, married and unmarried alike, aroused little enthusiasm among solidarist republicans. These men, after all, were politicians, and as such represented all-male constituencies that were, on balance, less "enlightened" than themselves. As one staunch feminist supporter, the moderate socialist and future *président du conseil* René Viviani, would point out to those assembled at the 1900 women's rights congress, "The legislators make the laws for those who make the legislators."[94] And,

---

the *Behavioral Sciences*, 34:2 (Spring 1998), 135–151; "Sexual Politics in Comte and Durkheim: Feminism, History, and the French Sociological Tradition," *Signs*, 27:1 (Fall 2001), 229–263; and "Confronting the Canon in the Classroom: Approaches to Teaching the Significance of Women, Sex, and Gender in the Work of Emile Durkheim," in *Teaching Durkheim*, ed. Terry F. Godlove, Jr. (Oxford: Oxford University Press, 2005), pp. 187–212.

[93] See the announcement of the Paris Municipal Council's precedent-setting travel subsidy to send delegates from the women's group *Égalité* to the international congress of the FAI in London as well as to the congress associated with the 1898 Dutch exhibition on women's work at The Hague; "Société Féministe L'Égalité," *Le Journal des Femmes*, n° 78 (August 1898), 1–2.

[94] René Viviani, "Rapport de la troisième section (législation)," *Congrès International de la Condition et des Droits des Femmes*, session of 7 September 1900, pp. 195–205; quote, p. 201. Published initially in *La Fronde*, n° 1006 (10 September 1900).

although French men had exercised the so-called universal suffrage since 1848, even by 1900 French women could still not vote. They had no political authority whatsoever. Womanly influence remained important, and was frequently acknowledged, but it was not sufficiently persuasive to get those discriminatory laws changed.

If the intimate prejudices of an all-male electorate harmonized with the biosocial evolutionary functionalism of Fouillée or Durkheim, it could be deduced that voter support for the demands of a thoroughgoing revolution in the status of women and a readjustment of the sexual balance of power would be unenthusiastic indeed. This emerged even more clearly after the Dreyfus Case revealed the implications of challenges to two institutional pillars of traditional social authority, that is, the army and the courts, and the *Ligue de la Patrie Française* of Maurice Barrès and Jules Lemaître would arise to counter the revisionist activities, grounded in claims for individual justice, of the newly founded *Ligue des Droits de l'Homme* of Georges Clemenceau, René Viviani, and Émile Zola. In short, in this climate of opinion, individualistic claims by members of either sex would be viewed with suspicion, if not downright hostility. Feminists would bear the brunt of the nationalist attacks. But they would seize the offensive on the issue of the republic's continuing support for government-regulated prostitution.

Controversies over Prostitution: Debating Licensing and Traffic Issues

The feminists' campaigns against discriminatory labor legislation highlighted the many other problems that plagued most women's employment in France. Undoubtedly one of the worst, as we have remarked earlier, was their abysmal pay. As Maria Martin put it, with her customary sarcasm, "It is incredible that women are reproached for contenting themselves with derisory wages at the same time that one tries to deny them well-paying jobs."[95] A particularly intractable problem in urban areas was that of

---

Viviani, a radical-socialist deputy since 1893, had become a staunch ally of the women's rights movement in France; since 1889 he had been an officer of the *Ligue Française pour le Droit des Femmes*. In 1900 he would push through the law that authorized admittance of women lawyers to the bar. Throughout this period he was closely associated with Durand. For the most thorough discussion to date of the Durand-Viviani relationship, see Sue Helder Goliber, "The Life and Times of Marguerite Durand: A Study in French Feminism" (Ph.D. dissertation, Kent State University, 1975). Sowerwine remarked that, in spite of Viviani's ardent support of women's rights, he did not mention the subject in his 1893 electoral *profession de foi*; in 1898, however, he did speak out for equal civil and political rights for women; *Femmes et socialisme*, p. 258.

[95] Martin, "Loi de 1892," *Le Journal des Femmes*, n° 85 (March 1899).

women's unemployment, sometimes seasonal, sometimes chronic, which often led desperate women to fall back on the world's "oldest" profession – selling sexual access to their bodies.[96]

Campaigns against government regulation (mostly at the municipal level) of prostitution, by licensing and inspecting prostitutes for the ostensible purpose of controlling venereal disease, and establishing sanctioned "houses" of ill-repute, had been going on since the mid-1870s, in conjunction with the *Fédération Britannique et Continentale* (later known as the *Fédération Abolitioniste Internationale* [FAI], or the International Abolitionist Federation), in which a number of leading feminists consistently participated.[97] A new aspect of this problem in the 1890s was the mounting awareness of the developing "white slave trade" [*traite des blanches*] – or more clinically speaking, the international traffic in women and children – that provided "variety" for repeat customers of the brothels. As Yves Guyot and others were making clear in the 1890s, this kidnapping, transporting, and selling of girls for sexual purposes was becoming big business. The abolitionists insisted that the wide range of moral problems then confronting European societies (encompassing alcoholism, pornography, unsanitary and disease-ridden slums in cities, mounting urban crime, and especially the *traite des blanches*) could never be resolved without first closing down these government-licensed brothels, which had, they alleged, become the destinations and transfer points for the trafficked women.[98]

In 1896, following the April feminist congress in Paris, the Paris-based writer and newly converted feminist known in the press as Savioz (Eugénie [Ghénia] Glaisette de Sainte-Croix) led a small group of visiting women from other countries to visit the Saint-Lazare prison.[99] As we know from

[96] This section provides a completely different and far more political understanding of the prostitution problem than one finds in Menon's very interesting analysis in chapter 4 of *Evil by Design*, based on illustrations from the male-dominated French satirical press. Menon's Parisian male caricaturists depicted prostitutes as seductive and dangerous; by contrast, the feminist abolitionists viewed them as underage, naive, poor to the point of desperation, and thus ripe for exploitation in the "white slave" trade.

[97] The group originally established in 1877 as the *Fédération Brittanique et Continentale* still went by that name in 1896 (see n. 98); sometime thereafter the organizers changed the name to the *Fédération Abolitionniste Internationale* (International Abolitionist Federation).

[98] The "traite des blanches," most of whom were underage girls, was already being discussed at the annual conference of the Fédération in 1896; see the report of M. de Memon, quoted in Auguste de Morsier, "La Conférence de la Fédération Brittanique et Continentale à Berne," *La Revue Féministe*, (September 1896), 689–699, esp. 691.

[99] See Savioz, "La prison des femmes – visite des congressistes" in *La Patrie* (ed. Lucien Millevoye), 16 April 1896. In a 1939 obituary tribute to Mme Avril de Sainte-Croix, the Countess Jean de Pange remarked that an article published in *l'Éclair* during the later 1890s had piqued Josephine Butler's initial interest in Savioz: see "In Memoriam, Madame Avril de Sainte-Croix," *Bulletin du Conseil*

Part I, Chapter 3 some positive changes had taken place at the prison during the previous decade thanks to the persistence of Isabelle Bogelot and Emilie de Morsier and their supporters in the *Oeuvre des Libérées de Saint-Lazare*. But much still needed to be done. Rehabilitation of such women was turning out to be very difficult because of the horrific conditions they faced when incarcerated – even temporarily. And they could not look forward to great opportunities upon release.

Shortly following the launch of *La Fronde*, in late 1897, Savioz published a three-part article, "Les Femmes à Saint-Lazare," in "La Tribune" of *La Fronde*.[100] In this series, Savioz denounced the conditions in the prison, which still housed, in the First Section, women charged with misdemeanors and awaiting trial as well as those who had been convicted and were already serving short terms, and, in the Second Section, the prostitutes interned for disease or disorderly behavior. She denounced the conditions – the atrocious overcrowding, the foul odors, the filth, the gloom, the impossibly inadequate nutrition, but she especially condemned the resulting demoralization that thwarted every effort to rehabilitate those so confined. Savioz criticized the extant laws, she castigated the *police des moeurs*, but she became particularly incensed by the seeming indifference of well-off women who ignored (or brushed off) the plight of their much less-privileged sisters. To further shock her readers, she pointed out that the handkerchiefs and dishtowels (serviettes) sewn by the infected prostitutes, to earn a bit of money while in prison, were neither washed nor bleached before being distributed for sale (often, she indicated, the raw materials were stowed in the prisoners' bedding) – thus, the prisoners and their products provided a primary vector of venereal (and other) infections to the unsuspecting buyers – including the indifferent upper-class women she was addressing.

A second series of articles by Savioz in *La Fronde's* feature section, "*La Serve*" [the female serf] followed in mid-January 1898.[101] Here Savioz sought to educate the women readers of *La Fronde* about the long history (from the time of Greece and Rome) of regulated prostitution (no, she asserted: it was not a French invention), about the new arguments for "public hygiene" used to justify regulation on behalf of appeasing men's

---

National des Femmes Françaises, n° 7 (April 1939), 51. Did *L'Éclair* reprint the *La Patrie* article from 1896? or might Butler have been excited by the three-part article series (referenced in n. 100) that Savioz published in *La Fronde* in December 1897 and January 1898?

[100] Savioz, "Les Femmes à Saint-Lazare," *La Fronde*, n°s 7, 8, & 9 (15–16–17 December 1897). Both this set of articles and the following set, "La Serve," appeared as contributions to the three-part investigative reporting series "La Tribune de *La Fronde*."

[101] Savioz, "La Serve," *La Fronde*, n°s 44, 45, & 46 (21, 22, 23 January 1898).

sexual appetites, about the procedures used by the morals police to round up and forcibly register women, and about the humiliating conditions they faced in the prefecture while awaiting administrative action. She particularly blamed the *prostituant*, the man who enjoys sexual release and goes away oblivious of the fate of the prostitute who services him. She then saluted the organization of a French branch of the *FAI* by Auguste de Morsier (1864–1923; the son of Emilie de Morsier) to bring the campaign against government-regulated prostitution to its home turf. Savioz urged more fortunate, happy women to get involved, "if not through kindness or human solidarity, then through self-interest, because by accepting without protest the ignominious stain of inscription, they accredit and fortify – to their own detriment – the concept that woman is inferior and that the two sexes do not have the same rights."[102] In the third installment she discussed how the results of the regulation of prostitution were actually the opposite of what had been intended; for example, there had been a rise in debauchery, a fall in the marriage rate, and a weakening of the birth rate. Not only was concern about individual liberty growing, but what was more, Savioz pointed out, some physicians who had been studying the issue had found that a much higher rate of venereal disease among regulated prostitutes than among those who were not regulated.[103] Some countries, beginning with England, had already abolished the regulation system; France, she pointed out, was the last holdout.

For Savioz, however, the supreme objection to the French system of regulated prostitution was its infringement on women's individual liberty. In his much-cited study of 1836, Dr. Parent-Duchâtelet, the legendary Paris expert on prostitution had insisted that "Individual liberty is a right prostitutes cannot claim."[104] Sainte-Croix would categorically reject such a statement, as would most of the other abolitionists: "No one," she argued forcefully, "has the right to place women outside the law, to make them slaves, subject to degrading measures, in order to assure someone else's

---

[102] Savioz, "La Serve," second installment, n° 45 (22 January 1898).

[103] See Andrew Aisenberg, "Syphilis and Prostitution: A Regulatory Couplet in Nineteenth-Century France," in *Sex, Sin, and Suffering: Venereal Disease and European Society since 1870*, ed. Roger Davidson & Lesley A. Hall (London: Routledge, 2001), pp. 15–28. Aisenberg is wrong about one thing: the abolitionists did indeed draw on scientific counterclaims by physicians to undermine the original arguments used by public hygienist doctors in support of regulation of prostitution. The international conference of physicians at Brussels, meeting 4–8 September 1899, which included many advocates of regulation, would arrive at the conclusion that regulation did nothing whatsoever to stall the spread of venereal diseases. See the proceedings: *Conférence internationale pour la Prophylaxie de la syphilis et des maladies vénériennes, Bruxelles, septembre 1899*, ed. Émile Dubois-Havenith (Brussels: Lamartin, 1899–1900), 5 vol. in 2 vols.

[104] Aisenberg, "Syphilis and Prostitution," p. 20; citing *De la prostitution*, vol. 2, p. 311.

security." "All diseases should be treated as diseases and not as blemishes." French women must speak out, she insisted, just as English women had recently spoken out against the reestablishment of regulation in India. "No one has the right to close herself off in an ivory tower . . . or to ignore the plight of the prostitute." Savioz subsequently reported on the proposal of Dr. Laborde at the Academy of Medicine to suppress the regulation system as well as on developments in the Indian campaign.[105]

Later that year (in July 1898) Savioz traveled to London for the congress of the FAI, where she found inspiration in meeting its founder Josephine Butler.[106] It was there that Auguste de Morsier, leader of the newly established French branch of the FAI, publicly criticized the refusal of Senator René Bérenger, president of the *Ligue Française pour le Relèvement de la Moralité Publique* (a group founded originally in the 1880s by Tommy Fallot to campaign against prostitution, pornography, and obscenity), for refusing to denounce government-sanctioned prostitution.[107] "There is a work of general moralisation to be done, I recognize, but one must attack the evil by its roots," de Morsier said, "and all the moral and social reforms will be sterile as long as regulated prostitution subsists in a country."[108] Savioz herself fully supported Morsier's position and continued to hammer home the FAI's criticism of the Ligue's priorities. In short order, Savioz would become the secretary-general of the French branch of the FAI and a member of the governing council of the international federation, where she developed a reputation as the "Josephine Butler of France."[109] In 1904 she would found a section within the ICW to address the traffic in women and children. In the meantime she became a designated reporter on this subject at the subsequent international congresses convened to address this burning question.

---

[105] Savioz, "À l'Académie de Médicine," *La Fronde*, n° 111 (30 March 1898).

[106] Savioz, "Le Congrés abolitionniste à Londres," *L'Evènement*, (21 July 1898). See also her articles on the congress in *La Fronde*, issues of 12 & 21 July 1898.

[107] As a champion of moral reform, René Bérenger was concerned with a complex mix of issues, ranging from pornography to prostitution. In 1894 he founded the targeted group, the *Société de Protestation contre la Licence des Rues*, and succeeded Edmond de Pressensé as president of the *Ligue Française pour le Relèvement de la Moralité Publique*. On the campaigns of Bérenger and his associates, see Annie Stora-Lamarre, *L'Enfer de la IIIe République: Censeurs et pornographes, 1881–1914* (Paris: Imago, 1990), and *La République des faibles: Les origines intellectuelle du droit républicain, 1870–1914* (Paris: A. Colin, 2005). See also Jean-Yves Le Naour, "Un Mouvement antipornographique: La Ligue pour le relèvement de la moralité publique," *Histoire, économie, et société*, 22:3 (2003), 385–394. Regrettably, this latter article only skims over the 1880s and 1890s.

[108] See Auguste de Morsier, *La Lutte contre la prostitution réglementée en France. Rapport au congrès de Londres, 12–15 juillet 1898* (Alençon: FAI/branche française, Impr. Typogr. Guy, Veuve, *fils* & Cie).

[109] See Offen, "Madame Ghénia Avril de Sainte-Croix . . . ," *Women's History Review*, 17:2 (April 2008), 239–255.

Let us go back to 1899, when Savioz returned to London with Isabelle Bogelot and Anna Feresse-Deraismes to attend the first International Congress on the White Slave Traffic (21–23 June). France sent twenty official delegates to this congress, of whom eight were women and of those eight, several – such as Sarah Monod, Eliska Vincent, and Savioz – were well-known feminists.[110] Many of them would stay on in London for the ensuing ICW congress (26 June–4 July).

This first major congress on the white slave traffic, sponsored by the National Vigilance Association (NVA) in England, had as its objective to collect and compare information on the extent of the traffic in various countries, with the goal of crafting international strategies to address the problem that would involve both nongovernmental agencies and national governments. For political reasons, and by mutual agreement, the question of government-regulated prostitution was deliberately excluded from the agenda. This exclusion upset abolitionists such as Savioz who, like Butler and Morsier, considered it a prime *cause* of the traffic.[111] The NVA first issued an extensive questionnaire, to which each country's delegation was asked to respond in a conference report, which was subsequently published in the proceedings. The organization's main concern was young women under 21, the age of majority.

Alarming reports from eastern Europe, especially from Russia and the Dual Monarchy of Austria-Hungary, furnished lurid stories about the operations of the traffic, especially as it took advantage of naive minor girls; no one could henceforth deny that the "white slave trade" had become a serious problem. Girls from Russia, from Austria, from many other regions of Europe, were being shipped, via Marseille, to South America, especially to Buenos Aires and Brazil. Although Bérenger's report did not so indicate, Savioz made it clear that among those being trafficked were girls from France.[112]

---

[110] See the proceedings: *The White Slave Trade: Transactions of the International Congress on the White Slave Trade, Held in London on the 21st, 22nd, and 23rd of June, 1899, at the Invitation of the National Vigilance Association* (London: Office of the National Vigilance Association, 1899). This publication is available on microfilm: RPI, n.s. 1508, n° 4360. A study of French involvement is Molly McGregor Watson, "The Trade in Women: 'White Slavery' and the French Nation, 1899–1939," Ph.D. dissertation, Stanford University, 1999.

[111] Savioz, "La Traite des blanches," unidentified, undated article, but clearly mid-June 1899, just prior to the opening on 21 July of the London congress on the white slave trade, in Avril de Sainte-Croix scrapbooks of press clippings, BMD, reel 1. I have not been able to locate this editorial in *La Fronde* (checked 14–19 June); it may have appeared in *L'Evènement*, *Le Siècle*, or one of the other mainstream daily papers for which Savioz wrote.

[112] According to Savioz, in "La Traite des blanches."

Several significant arguments stand out in the opening French report, given by Senator Bérenger. First, he did admit that some evidence existed of trafficking in French ports (Marseilles, Bordeaux, Le Havre), but he asserted that this practice was exclusively by and about foreigners. Second, he pointed out that French law did provide remedies to women over 21, as well as the possibility of prosecuting adults who incite girls – or boys – under the age of 21 to debauchery or corruption. But in the current circumstances, where national borders were being crossed, even the current laws were difficult to apply and investigations would require cooperation of several governments. *Souteneurs*, he claimed, were most frequently the ones who seduced young women for the purpose of prostitution.

Bérenger's greater concern, he said, was the large number of French girls recruited to go to Poland and Russia, and the agencies that handled contracts, passports, and other "arrangements" for them. Girls could only get such passports with their parents' consent; women over 21 were made aware of the hazards that may await them. He singled out for special praise the important work of the (nonsectarian, but mostly protestant) *Amies de la Jeune Fille* and its Catholic counterpart, the *Oeuvre Catholique International de la Protection de la Jeune Fille*, in addressing the threats to the girls who emigrate.[113] He called especially for preventive measures, then made a point of mentioning that those who argued for the abolition of regulated prostitution had agreed not to bring it up, for the sake of achieving unanimity of the Congress on "the more general and more urgent question it is summoned to discuss, and would incite the grave suspicion and opposition of several Governments, and thus risk compromising the unanimity which is so much to be desired."[114] Bérenger, a lawyer by training, then proposed a series of concrete measures, both legal and

---

[113] Founded in 1877 and based in Neuchâtel, Switzerland, the association *Amies de la Jeune Fille* developed branches and correspondents in many countries, including France, where its supporters included many leading Protestant philanthropic women. The organization can be followed in the abolitionist publication, *Journal de Bien Public*, and a later publication, *Amies de la Jeune Fille*. Monique Pavillon (emerita, University of Lausanne) has prepared an excellent summary of its activities (private communication, 2008). For a comparative perspective on the French immigrant aid societies, see Emily Machen, "Traveling with Faith: The Creation of Women's Immigrant Aid Associations in Nineteenth and Twentieth Century France," *Journal of Women's History* 23:3 (Fall 2011), 89–112. For an international comparison, see Christine Machiels, "Les féminismes face à la prostitution aux XIXe et XXe siècle (Belgique, France, Suisse)," doctoral thesis, jointly awarded by the Catholic University of Louvain (BE) and University of Angers (F), 2011.

On the Catholic counterpart of the *Amies*, founded in Fribourg in 1896, see Catherine Galley, "Les Formes d'un engagement féminin: L'Association catholique internationale des Oeuvres de Protection de la jeune fille (1896–1920)," Mémoire de licence, Faculté des Lettres, Université de Fribourg (Suisse), 1996.

[114] *White Slave Trade: Transactions*, p. 54.

procedural, for consideration by the Congress. None of these proposed measures, however, addressed the root causes of young women's emigration – the lack of job opportunities in their own countries and the problem, for those young women who could find jobs, of inadequate pay.

Bérenger's report was followed by that of his French colleague Henri Joly, who reported on the numbers of French philanthropic projects (over 1300 by his count) devoted to helping orphaned and abandoned girls. More importantly, in the view of Savioz, Joly did address the problem of women's inadequate earnings and made it very clear that even those French women who did find employment could not earn enough to sustain themselves – a point feminists had incessantly reiterated. Dr. Bonmariage from Belgium, who nevertheless insisted on examining the causes of prostitution and the traffic, concurred. Thus, as Savioz underscored in her first report in *La Fronde*, with considerable satisfaction, "the economic situation of woman is one of the major reasons for her enrollment in prostitution."[115]

The Swiss reporter A. de Meuron, from the Grand Council of Geneva (and an active member of FAI), acknowledged the complexity of his country's cantonal laws, but his report focused primarily on the necessity of prosecuting procuration and procurers [*pronéxétisme*]. He then introduced the purportedly "banned" subject of the government-regulated brothels, making the significant point that although he understood that some governments [e.g., France] considered the morals police an "indispensable social necessity," "we are profoundly convinced that there can be no effective suppression of the white slave traffic as long as this, which is its principal support, exists."[116] The "official" houses, he said in no uncertain terms, "constitute the principal market for the white slave traffic." He pointed the finger directly at France which, he said, provided over 53 percent of the girls in the licensed brothels of Geneva, and remarked that in France alone, there would have been about "18,000 commercial transactions, of which a large number would drag into prostitution girls who had not yet fallen into it." Several women were among the speakers on the third day, notably Mme de Tscharner, from the Swiss committee of the *Amies de la Jeune Fille*, and the Baronne de Montenach, from its Catholic counterpart. The issue of regulation refused to be silenced. "One member of the French delegation" (presumably Savioz) proposed that the

---

[115] Savioz, "La Traite des Blanches (Ire Journée)," *La Fronde*, n° 564 (25 June 1899), 1. This is a later article, but with the same title as that cited in n. 111.

[116] *White Slave Trade: Transactions*, p. 95.

terminology be changed from "*traite des blanches*" to "*traite des femmes*," since especially in the countries with colonies not only white women were concerned; the organizing committee demurred, sticking with the earlier label. (Savioz would pursue this change in nomenclature throughout the next decade; ultimately it would be adopted officially by the League of Nations.)

The post-conference report authored by M. Moncharville provides an excellent summary of the various positions represented at the congress, reiterating Bérenger's point that the abolitionists had publicly ceded to the necessity of bracketing discussion of regulated prostitution (at the national, local level) in order to allow the Congress to succeed in coming to conclusions on the question of how to address the problem of the traffic. Also off the table were the potentially complicating questions of women's inadequate salaries (considered to be fundamentally part of the "worker/ labor question") and, more generally, of women's lack of equal rights.[117] But as we see from the proceedings, these issues had indeed been brought up. Significantly, this author made no mention in his report of the proposal for a change in terminology.

The NVA congress on white slavery was followed almost immediately by the "women's parliament," the quinquennial meeting of the fledgling ICW. This congress, organized by the ICW president, the Scottish aristo- crat Ishbel Aberdeen (her husband, Lord Aberdeen, had played a major role at the white slavery congress), opened in London in late June 1899; it clearly impressed all observers, including much of the world press, with its superb organization, its articulate, splendidly well-dressed women "per- forming their femininity," its massive attendance (over 3,000 persons), its inclusion of men, and, not least, its evening receptions hosted by duch- esses, "ladies," and other British aristocrats in the most elegant homes in and around London. It also impressed some French commentators as overwhelmingly Anglo-Saxon.[118] A number of French feminists attended and spoke, including Savioz.

On the fifth day of the ICW congress, the focus turned to questions of women's pay as well as the promotion of a single standard of morality for women and men. Savioz again brought up the question of regulated prostitution and again criticized those women who either ignored the issue

[117] M. Moncharville (of the Paris Faculty of Law), *La Traite des blanches et le congrès de Londres. Rapport présenté au comité français de participation au Congrès* (Paris: P. Mouillot, 1900), 26 p.
[118] See, for example, the coverage by Marya Chéliga in *Le Petit Bleu*, 11 July 1899. Clipping in BMD, DOS 38 (Congrès).

or still thought prostitution necessary in order to "save" the family, for their smug, self-satisfaction; the question of the white slave trade apparently did not emerge – as such.[119]

However, these questions were discussed at greater length at a separate women-only meeting, held on 30 June.[120] At that gathering Savioz joined with women from several other countries to denounce the government regulation of prostitution; she also called for laws to permit paternity suits, and to engage fathers' legal responsibility in cases of infanticide. Again, she castigated women who turned their backs on the manifold problems created by male promiscuity.[121] The French writer Th. Bentzon reported that the publication (1900) containing these speeches on prostitution, considered too "hot" for public consumption, was issued separately and available only on demand.[122]

The issue of women's abysmal pay would be kept very much alive by partisans of the FAI. Its 1899 annual congress in Geneva (home to the last bastion of regulated prostitution in Switzerland) took place following the July London congress on the white slave trade, the ICW congress, and, in early September, the international physicians' conference in Brussels.[123] The aging Josephine Butler attended in person. The final session was

---

[119] See the four-page account/compte-rendu by Jeanne Deflou in the monthly *Journal des Femmes*, n° 89 (July 1899). The series of reports in *La Fronde* (all on the front page) on the ICW congress by Savioz provides selective insight: see *La Fronde*, n° 560 (21 June 1899); n° 568 (29 June 1899); n° 569 (30 June 1899). Unfortunately, the ACRPP microfilm copy of *La Fronde* does not include the issues of 1–14 July, but I retrieved the articles for 1–8 July 1899 from Marguerite Durand's files at the BMD, DOS 38.

[120] The seven-volume set of ICW proceedings is readily available, but it took some sleuthing to track down the separately published report on the special session on the equal moral standard. I finally located a copy in the ICW papers at the Women's Library @ LSE in London: *An Equal Moral Standard for Men and Women. Report of Papers Read at a Special Meeting for Women Held in Connection with the Social Section at the International Congress of Women, Convocation Hall, Church House, Friday, June 30, 1899* (London: T. Fisher Unwin, 1900). (Located and consulted, 27 Aug. 2013; in 5 ICW/B/04 – Box 12). With the exact title in hand, I discovered that it is also available in the RPI microfilm collection on women's history. In the RPI microfilm set at Stanford University, however, the reel that should contain this item is missing.

[121] Mlle de Sainte-Croix was one of five women who spoke at this woman-only meeting. Her speech appears in *Equal Moral Standard for Men and Women*, pp. 20–26. She made similar observations in the article "Responsabilité paternelle," in *Le Relèvement Social* (1 July 1899). Thanks to Rachel Fuchs for transmitting a photocopy of this latter article, in which Savioz discusses the differences of opinion between the leaders of the *Ligue Française pour les Droits des Femmes* (LFDF; Maria Pognon was president and chief spokeswoman), who preferred setting up *caisses de maternité* to support poor single mothers and their children (funded by taxes on men), and those feminists who, like herself, thought that overturning the law that prohibited paternity suits through legislative action would be more achievable in the short run.

[122] See Th. Bentzon [pseud. of Marie-Thérèse Blanc], "Le Conseil international des femmes," *RDM*, vol. 163 (15 February 1901), 825–854, & vol. 164 (1 March 1901), 87–119; this observation is on p. 835.

[123] On the physicians' conference, see the proceedings, cited in n. 103.

dedicated to "Les salaires féminins et la prostitution," and featured detailed reports by three women speakers – Anna Pappritz from Berlin, Kaethe Schirmacher from Paris, and Olympe Gevin-Cassal, also from Paris. At the public session, attended by some 2,500 people, 2 feminist abolitionists spoke (Emma Pieczynska and Mlle de Sainte-Croix [Savioz]) along with Yves Guyot, Marcel Huart, and other well-known anti-regulationists.[124] Writing in *Le Siècle*, Auguste de Morsier proclaimed the congress a complete success.[125]

A sympathetic male writer remarked in *La Suisse* that feminism, which he called "one of the most important phenomena of our time," was far and away the dominant stream of thought at this FAI gathering. He praised its representatives at the congress as being of the first order, contradicting the notion that women were intellectual inferiors: "The best-run sessions were presided by women; the most solid and powerful speeches were presented by women, and the majority of the audience was women." These feminist speakers reiterated the point, with plenty of facts at hand, that inequality of the sexes, and especially women's inferior pay, lay at the root of disadvantaged women's recourse to prostitution. The question was, then, how to remedy this now thoroughly documented situation, given that so many male-dominated governments remained reluctant to take action.[126]

In France, one further facet of the woman question debates, perhaps the most fundamental of all in the context of the French nation-state, dampened the possibilities for realizing feminist economic demands under the Third Republic. Here we must turn to the 1890s phase of the "depopulation" scare, amplified by the continually falling birth rate and the growing concern about the nation's demographic strength, which would loom more ominously than ever over France's national future and international position.

---

[124] Mlle de Sainte-Croix's speech in the FAI congress's public session in Geneva was not mentioned in an article by Henry Nice (DOS 351 FED), but see her reports on this congress in *La Fronde*, n°s 655–658 (24–28 September 1899). See also A. de Morsier's account of this conference, "La Conférence de la Fédération abolitionniste internationale à Genève," *Le Siècle*, hand-dated 27 September 1899, and misfiled in BMD DOS 40 – Congrès 1908 – Paris. Date subsequently verified on Gallica; this article appears on p. 2. The traffic per se was not an agenda item at this conference, which focused on three specific issues: the question of hygiene, of legislation and criminalization, and the question of the links between prostitution and women's low pay.

[125] De Morsier, "Conférence de la Fédération abolitionniste internationale," *Le Siècle* (27 September 1899).

[126] Paul Pictet, "Après le Congrès abolitionniste," attrib. to *La Suisse*, (24 September 1899). AdeSC clipping books, reel 3, BMD.

CHAPTER 7

Must Maternity Be Women's Form of Patriotism?

In his domestic drama *Francillon* (1887), the indefatigable and invariably provocative playwright Alexandre Dumas *fils* sketched a disagreement between a bourgeois husband and wife over her protracted nursing of their first child, who had just been weaned and moved out of the marital bedchamber. The author implied that the wife, Francine, now wanted her husband to stay home and go to bed with her. The husband, who following the child's birth had cultivated the habit of going out at night to his club with his male friends instead of keeping company with his wife, insisted on leaving for the evening. The wife suspected something else; she responded to her husband's implied criticism of her motherly duty (the implication being that she had not been sexually available to him during this nursing period and, in consequence, he had taken a mistress) by comparing her nursing the child with a man's military duties that took him away from a wife for extended periods. Drawing a parallel, Francine claimed that she would not seek distractions with another man but would stand by the cradle of her child. "Maternity," she argued, "is women's form of patriotism, and the blood that you are so proud to spill for your country is the milk that we give you." She then accused him of having taken up with another woman.[1] Although the husband denied this, her suspicions did not abate.

What is significant about Dumas *fils'* framing of this spousal exchange is the clear assumption by the author and his public that an intimate connection existed between motherhood and the future of the French nation. Maternity had never been a strictly a private matter in France, but in the context of the national anxiety about "depopulation" – signified by the falling birth rate – it was becoming a worrisome public concern. Was, indeed, maternity a woman's form of patriotism? Must it be women's primary – or sole – form of patriotism? What about women's aspirations

---

[1] Alexandre Dumas *fils, Francillon* (1887), *Théatre complèt, avec notes inédites* (Paris: Calmann Lévy, 1893), pp. 301–302.

to full personhood and citizenship in the Republic? During the decade of the 1890s these questions became inextricably entangled with feminist campaigns for full legal, economic, social, and cultural emancipation.[2]

Debating the Causes and Consequences of Depopulation in the 1890s: Abortions and Birth Strikes

Both supporters and adversaries of women's emancipation invoked the links between their objectives and the incessantly declining birth rate. The controversy had begun to heat up again in the latter part of 1889, when a new series of articles by eminent secular medical and academic spokesmen (including Dr. Charles Richet, Dr. Jacques Bertillon, and the political economist Émile Levasseur) appeared in the *Revue Scientifique*. They fretted over the continuing slow French population growth in comparison with the galloping birth rates of England and Germany. Already in 1882 Dr. Richet had blamed "voluntary sterility" for the decline, and thumped the nationalist drum by insisting that married couples owed children to France as their patriotic duty. His counterpart Dr. Henri Thulié had meanwhile framed the issue squarely as a women's rights issue. Despite these radically different positions, and questions about how to stimulate the birth rate, both Thulié and Richet agreed that something must be done in the short term about the unduly high – and potentially avoidable – rates of infant mortality. This concern became even more acute following Dr. Lagneau's discouraging report to the Academy of Medicine in August 1890, which received considerable attention in the press.[3]

---

[2] When I published these lines in 1984, early in my career as a historian of France, I felt an urgent need to demonstrate the heretofore ignored intersections of what were, in earlier historical writing, very separate debates over depopulation, nationalism, and feminism in Third Republic France. I argued that each of these strands could not be understood without addressing its entanglement with the other two. Previous studies on depopulation and nationalism had virtually ignored the "woman question," and scholars had only recently begun to publish on the history of French feminism. Nowadays the population question, and its links to the woman question as well as the national question, are present in virtually every book that has been published on this period. For the detailed historiographical references, see Karen Offen, "Depopulation, Nationalism, and Feminism in Fin-de-Siècle France," *American Historical Review*, 89:3 (June 1984), 648–676. In this chapter, I will revisit those connections during the period 1890–1900, adding evidence to and refining my earlier analysis by drawing on additional contributions to the debates by French men of science and by feminist writers, and taking into account subsequent scholarly contributions by Rachel Fuchs, Anne Cova, and others (all referenced later in this chapter).

[3] In addition to the figures on infant mortality, Dr. Lagneau also remarked the diminution in the number of marriages and the rise in numbers of single adults; he noted as well the stunning increase in French emigration to Argentina. None of Lagneau's recommendations, however, directly addressed the woman question. See "La Dépopulation," *Le Droit des Femmes*, n° 376 (17 August 1890).

In early October 1889 the attorney Léon Giraud, a close friend and associate of Hubertine Auclert, had endorsed Thulié's 1882 perspective in a paper presented to the International Congress of Ethnographic Sciences on "depopulation in France, causes and means of remedying it," in which he squarely blamed the decline in the French birth rate on women's inferior status in the law, and, in addition, on the "unjust and inhumane" legal position of the "natural child" (Article 340). Changing these laws, he argued, would be "the most efficient means" of remedying the situation.[4] Not surprisingly, Giraud's presentation was discussed at length by "Camille" in four successive issues of *La Citoyenne*.[5]

In 1890 the sociologist Arsène Dumont took the depopulation debate to an entirely new level when he published *Dépopulation et civilisation*.[6] In a book that was clearly engaged in the politics of knowledge, "full of disagreeable facts and some new perceptions," Dumont argued that the economists since Adam Smith had gotten it all wrong: the most important wealth for a nation is not monetary, but the quantity of its citizens. The new sciences of anthropology, ethnography, and demography must replace political economy, Dumont insisted; riches and resources are not the whole story. Dumont blamed France's falling natality squarely on a concatenation of circumstances peculiar to French culture that influenced couples, in order to get ahead socially and economically (he baptized this phenomenon as "the law of social capillarity"), to decide not to bear children. Although he did not single out as preponderant either women's or men's role in such decision-making, he did insist that decisions not to have children were conscious, not inadvertent. The causes were moral and they were specific to the French.

Dumont was very concerned (often citing Michelet) about the adverse influence of the church on women and children, and about the disagreements this produced within marriages. He also critiqued the Catholic Church's enthusiasm for virginity and its treatment of sexuality as sinful. The legal remedies Dumont proposed included placing a tax on bachelorhood, making it legally easier for young people to marry earlier, legalizing *recherche de la paternité*, and enacting legislation to address

---

[4] See *Congrès international des Sciences ethnographiques, tenu à Paris du 30 septembre au 7 octobre 1889* (Paris: Imprimerie nationale, 1890), p. 22, for a resumé, which does not provide a stenographic account of what appears to have been a "very lively" discussion.
[5] See *La Citoyenne*, "La Question des questions," n° 153 (December 1889), then in follow-up articles, "La Fin prochaine de la France," n° 154 (January 1890), 2; n° 155 (February 1890), & n° 156 (March 1891).
[6] Arsène Dumont, *Dépopulation et Civilisation: Étude démographique* (Paris: Lecrosnier et Babé, 1890).

the employment of women and children in factories as well as abolishing convents (which housed tens of thousands of single, childless women). He argued that the wealthier classes, in particular, needed to produce more children. Dumont strongly advocated legalizing paternity suits as a means of providing recourse to unwed mothers but he did not advocate (as had Léon Girard) improving the legal status of wives.[7] Arsène Dumont's sociocultural interpretation became the foundation and springboard for all subsequent French debates on population and on the emancipation of women.

Among the first social practices to be addressed in the context of depopulation was the practice of abortion, which was, of course, illegal in France as elsewhere. In late 1891, a sensational trial in the Paris *Cour d'Assises* rekindled public anxieties about the connections between the practice of abortion (which French women were clearly then using as a form of birth control) and depopulation. The trial of the self-educated and quite disreputable abortionist Constance Thomas and her consort Abélard Floury, plus some fifty other individuals, began in early November 1891, after a long preparatory investigation set off by the discovery of a possible homicide, presumably caused by an attempted abortion. According to one scholar who has studied the case, the judicial dossier can no longer be located in the archives. The best account he found, and carefully verified, is by the Parisian writer and judicial reporter Maurice Talmeyr, who carried out his own investigation of the case, dramatizing it in a series of well-researched articles in the daily paper *Gil Blas*.[8] Both the accused abortionists and their accomplices, who lived at Place de Clichy, were disreputable types, and the details of their exploits are sordid; casual sex, drunkenness, extortion, collusion, and many other questionable practices came together with filth and contagion in running – over a period of twenty years – an abortion "mill" frequented by hundreds, even thousands, of women from every social class. The trial of this abortionist known as "*la Morte aux Gosses*" [lit., death to the kids] and the forty-five other women inculpated (those who had undergone abortions) in addition to the four men who served as accomplices lasted for several weeks. The two principal suspects, Thomas and Floury, were convicted on 28 November. Their appeal failing, they would serve (respectively) sentences of ten

---

[7] Dumont, *Dépopulation et Civilisation*, pp. 508–509.

[8] Maurice Talmeyr's series "Les Avorteuses de Paris," has been republished by René Le Mée in his article, "Une affaire de 'faiseuses d'anges' à la fin du XIXe siècle," *Communications*, n° 44 (1986), beginning on 143.

years hard labor and eight years in confinement; their accomplices were let off more lightly, and the charges against most of the women (the majority were working-class women including many domestic servants) were dismissed, given the difficulty of "proving," well after the fact, either that the women had actually been pregnant or that abortions had been performed on them. In his analysis of the case, the physician for the *Palais de Justice*, Dr. Charles Floquet, had no hesitation about linking the specific issue of abortion to the more general concern about French depopulation.[9]

Where did the feminists stand on abortion? It is revealing that in the 1890s both Eugénie Potonié-Pierre and Paule Mink publicly condemned the practice.[10] In *Le Droit des Femmes* (1 November 1891), Potonié-Pierre, who had no children, published an article entitled "The Inviolability of Human Life," while in an article dated 2 August 1892, the socialist-feminist Paule Mink, the mother of several children out of wedlock, commented on a wave of prosecutions for abortion, mentioning not only the Thomas-Fleury affair (which she referred to as the *affaire de Clichy*) but also to a series of abortion trials in Germany, England, and Russia.[11] "Humanity seems to be plunging into a panicky extinction of the race," she observed, "and abortion is becoming the supreme remedy for people's pathetic and miserable situations." In 1890s France, Mink claimed, abortion was a habitual practice and was prosecuted only when some unhappy woman died or the scandal became too great; it was endemic, in the countryside as well as in the cities.

Mink criticized the hypocrisy of the bourgeoisie who rattled on about children for the nation, but had very few of their own. "Abortion, this crime against nature, this injury to the race, enters more and more into our customs. It has become a frequent practice, almost a general one, and it is the consequence of our economic state of affairs, our social state of affairs, of the harsh struggle for life that is devouring us; it is the result, a fatal result, of our morals, of our laws."[12] If only society could guarantee life and work to every being that came into the world, there would be no more "*suppression d'enfant*." If *recherche de la paternité* were legal in France, to

---

[9] See Dr. Ch[arles] Floquet, *Avortement et dépopulation* (*Affaire Constance Thomas-Floury*) (Paris: Policlinique de Paris, 1892).

[10] The references to Potonié-Pierre and Mink are discussed by Anne Cova, *Maternité et Droits des Femmes en France* (*XIXe–XXe siècles*) (Paris: Anthropos, 1997), pp. 242–243.

[11] Paule Mink, "Le Droit à l'avortement," *Almanach de la Question Sociale, 1893*, ed. P. Argyriades, pp. 63–69. Thanks to Marilyn Boxer for sharing her photocopy. The quotations translated below are scattered throughout this seven-page document.

[12] Mink, "Droit," p. 66.

hold men accountable for their sexual conduct, they might think twice before engaging in seduction. If France really valued mothers and maternity – "woman's pedestal, woman's redemption" in Mink's words – it would not inadvertently force pregnant women to abort. In the meantime, they have every right to do so. "As long as our capitalist society – unjust, pleasure-seeking, depraved and ferocious – continues to exist, there will be disasters and more and more abortions. Society will have no right to punish these crimes against the race, because it is you, Society, who encourages this terrible massacre of the innocents, by your iniquitous laws and your easy and venal morals."[13]

On 27 October 1892, just a few days prior to the enactment of the Law of 2 November 1892 for the protection of working women, the deputies of the *Parti Ouvrier*, led by Paul Lafargue, proposed an additional series of measures that would especially benefit working-class mothers and mothers-to-be, including the creation of *caisses de maternité*, which would provide mutually funded insurance for working women who became mothers.[14] Thus, they promoted the program of those feminists who, for years, had been advocating maternity as a social function. The French Chamber of Deputies was far from ready to move in such a direction, however.

That said, the plight of mothers, especially desperate single mothers, was stirring up considerable public attention. It was indisputable that "in nineteenth-century Paris, poor working women, whether single or married, lived in a world where motherhood could present great hardship."[15] Feminists closely followed the debates on birth rates, abortions, poverty, etc., among the male physicians, legislators, and reformers, and continued to advocate a variety of woman-friendly solutions, which ranged from legalizing *recherche de la paternité* to providing government subsidies to single mothers and their children. Above all else, they continued to press for legal reforms in marriage law and economic measures that could empower poor women.[16]

---

[13] Mink, "Droit," p. 66.

[14] In 1891–1892, the socialist deputies Émile Brousse and Paul Lafargue submitted bills to the Chamber of Deputies proposing subsidized maternity leave for women workers. Lafargue argued that childbearing was a social function and should be subsidized by taxing employers. See *Annales de la Chambre des Députés: Documents (1891)*, n° 1187 (Brousse) and *(1892)*, n° 2369 (Lafargue).

[15] Rachel G. Fuchs, *Poor and Pregnant in Paris: Strategies for Survival in the Nineteenth Century* (New Brunswick, NJ: Rutgers University Press, 1992), p. 178.

[16] An important work on the subject of maternity allowances by male-feminists is Louis Frank, J. H. Keiffer, & Louis-J. Maingie, *L'Assurance maternelle* (Brussels: H. Lamertin, 1897). Many more such works would be published in the following decade.

The *Journal des Femmes*, the monthly publication edited by Maria Martin (which had succeeded the now defunct *La Citoyenne* in late 1891), continuously monitored the propositions of male physicians, scientists, and legislators on the population question. In an August 1892 editorial, "Dépopulation," Maria Martin advocated (as had Léon Richer, Maria Deraismes, and Hubertine Auclert before her) legal reforms designed to protect children born out of wedlock and to facilitate marriages. Martin (yet again) advocated amending the Civil Code to improve the legal status of married women, with respect to both husbands and children. Young women, she claimed, did not want many children, having seen their mothers suffer greatly from childbearing. *Women*, not men, she implied, were making these decisions.[17]

That was not all. In early October 1892, a certain Marie Huot lectured before an audience of two thousand persons at the Salle de Géographie in Paris. Huot had "a taste for and a talent for brilliant and spectacular actions" – hers was a strong personality, but not one much interested in moderation or in organized propagandizing.[18] An activist in the Anti-Vivisection League and an opponent of bullfighting, Marie Huot also came out as a proponent of birth control or abstention [*l'abstention génésique*] if that's what it would take to precipitate a new kind of society! No evidence supports the claim that she specifically used the term "*grève des ventres*" [birth strike] though she is often credited with launching this term. Nevertheless, the evocative notion of a birth strike took wing and would be exploited dramatically in the early twentieth century by Nelly Roussel and other neo-Malthusian birth control advocates, developing in parallel with the socialists' call for a workers' general strike.

A birth strike was the last thing republican reformers wanted to be identified with. Nor were most 1890s republican feminists eager to take Huot's bait; they preferred sticking to demands for legal and economic reforms, coupled with practical intervention. This strand of philanthropically oriented reformism "is not preoccupied," remarked the historians of French feminism Laurence Klejman and Florence Rochefort, "with

---

[17] Martin, "Dépopulation," *Le Journal des Femmes*, n° 9 (August 1892).

[18] Huot's speech is mentioned briefly in several works: Francis Ronsin, *La Grève des ventres: Propagande néo-malthusienne et baisse de la natalité en France, 19e-20e siècles* (Paris: Aubier, 1980); quote, p. 44; also Angus McLaren, *Sexuality and Social Order: The Debate over the Fertility of Women and Workers in France, 1770–1920* (New York & London: Holmes & Meier, 1983), p. 161. In Cova's book, *Maternité et Droits des Femmes en France* (pp. 114–115), she debunks the attribution to Huot of the phrase "grève de ventres;" Cova repeats this assertion in *Féminismes et néo-malthusianismes sous la IIIe République: "La liberté de la maternité"* (Paris: L'Harmattan, 2011), pp. 32–33.

making feminism into an actor for social change but to remedy, efficiently and punctually, the deficiencies in the legislation."[19] From the perspective of other contemporaries, however, even these "moderate" proposals still seemed far too radical, though not as radical as proposals such as Huot's. The following winter (early 1893) Maria Deraismes underscored Martin's earlier argument – that women were making the decisions about child-bearing – in her lecture at a benefit for Marie Béquet de Vienne's *Société d'Allaitement Maternelle*. It was, Deraismes insisted, neither the love of luxury (as Arsène Dumont had suggested) nor partible inheritance (as Bertillon and the followers of Le Play had insisted) that retarded the birth rate, but rather the miserable legal and moral situation of women and children in French society.[20]

By the end of 1893, in fact, support by republican men for certain types of legal reforms in women's status seemed to be growing. Members of the *Alliance des Savants et des Philanthropes* resolved in September to work for the "disappearance of all legislative measures or prejudices that tend narrowly to delimit and restrain the number of women for whom mater-nity is socially permitted."[21] Although limited in scope, this resolution did recognize the *political* significance of women as mothers. The savants' awareness of the need for such reforms had no doubt been stimulated not only by the Affaire de Clichy (Constance Thomas – Floury) and the socialists' initiatives in late 1892, but also by reading the recent mono-graphs on women's inferior standing in French law written by legal scholars with reformist sympathies.[22] Most of these scholars, like the

---

[19] Klejman & Rochefort, *L'Egalité en marche*, p. 87.

[20] Deraismes, "De la dépopulation," *Bulletin de la Société de l'Allaitement maternel et des Refuges-ouvroirs pour les Femmes enceintes*, n° 8 (1893). For the report of this lecture, see *Le Journal des Femmes*, n° 14 (January 1893).

[21] For a report on the meeting of the *Alliance des Savants et des Philanthropes*, see *Le Journal des Femmes*, n° 22 (September 1893).

[22] Léon Richer's pioneering publications on laws adversely affecting women in the 1870s and 1880s inspired a flurry of academic successors. Works on women's position in French law (both public law and private law), all published in Paris during the 1890s, include the following: Sarmisa D. Bilcesco, *De la Condition légale de la mère en droit romain et en droit français* (Paris: A. Rousseau,1890); Moïse Ostrogorskii, *La Femme au point de vue du droit public; Étude d'histoire et de législation comparée* (Paris: A. Rousseau,1892); Louis Frank, *Essai sur la condition politique de la femme; Étude de sociologie et de législation* (Paris: A. Rousseau, 1892); and Léon Giraud, *De la Condition des femmes au point de vue de l'exercice des droits publics et politiques; Étude de législation comparée* (Paris: F. Pichon, 1891). For an astute survey of this legal scholarship, see Raoul de La Grasserie, "Le Mouvement féministe et les droits de la femme," *Revue Politique et Parlementaire* (*RPP*), 1:3 (September 1894), 432–449. For works published in the 1870s and 1880s, including those by Richer, see the chapters in Part I. By the end of the 1890s, additional legal studies had appeared (originally law theses): Lucien Leduc, *La Femme et les projets de lois rélatifs à l'extension de sa capacité* (Paris: Giard & Briere, 1898); Charles Krug, *Le Féminisme et le droit civil français* (Paris: Imprimerie nancéienne, 1899); and Poirier [no

savants themselves, were socially conservative men. Their perspective, a cautious variant of relational feminism, was summed up in 1893 by Louis Bridel, the Francophone Swiss professor of law, who would assert optimistically that[23]

> the true feminists do not intend in any way to tear woman away from her natural vocation. What they desire and demand is that woman be better armed and better protected, so that the task she has been given [that is, motherhood] can manifest itself in all its grandeur, and not as a fatal servitude to whose yoke she must resign herself. To grant woman her rights and to guarantee them will facilitate her accomplishment of her duties, not turn her away from them.

Marie Huot was not the only radical voice in the 1890s. In late 1895 the venerable, still active Clémence Royer (who in the 1850s had sought to develop a woman's form of knowledge and in the 1860s had asserted, well before Dumas *fils*, that motherhood was women's form of patriotism) responded to the arguments of Arsène Dumont in his 1893 memoir on the movement of the population – and implicitly to Louis Bridel. Her letter, published as "Diminution de la population de la France" [The Diminishing Population of France] asserted that all of Europe was enroute to depopulation because each citizen upon birth already carried a tax debt, because tiny farms could not even provide subsistence for small families, because men went off to serve in the military and acquired bad [read: moral and sexual] habits, etc. Royer argued that only a thorough revision of France's civil laws that would include abandonment of the venerable principles of Roman law and also of Canon law, could save it. Then Royer proposed a dramatic solution: total reorganization of the family, with inheritance only through the female line and a form of dower that would assure the lives of children along with the life of their mother. "A return to primitive matriarchy is required," she insisted. Children should be raised by the mothers and daughters living together, which would free the daughters to earn a living. It was unclear from her letter what she thought men should be doing, but the implicit message was that they weren't doing enough. Implying that the equality of (social and economic) condition sought by socialists was a mirage, the skeptical Royer argued that the

---

surname provided], *L'Infériorité sociale de la femme et le féminisme* (Paris: Marchal et Billard, 1900). Most of these authors favored pro-woman reforms in the Civil Code.

[23] Louis Bridel, "Le Mouvement féministe et le droit des femmes," *La Revue Sociale et Politique* (Brussels), 3 (1893), 123.

progress of civilization "consists of multiplying the layers of the social pyramid; the bottom always stays the same."[24]

Some critics had, of course, begun to blame women's employment for the fall in the birth rate. Not so, Marya Chéliga retorted, women went to work not for amusement, but in order to survive. She pointed out that the majority of women attending meetings of the *Fédération Française des Sociétés Féministes* were mothers themselves; they understood all too well the legal liabilities women faced in French society. Clotilde Dissard (who reported Chéliga's rebuttal) remarked that for working-class women the attraction of better-paying jobs had nothing to do with feminism, but derived rather from poverty, the bitter consequence of industrialism. "Feminism," asserted Dissard, "is in no way directed against marriage; it asks quite simply that woman in the *foyer* be conscious and free, sharing with man all the rights, all the responsibilities, all the obligations."[25] To sum up, these feminists did not object in principle to the concepts of marriage and family, but they certainly did oppose preservation of the authoritarian, hierarchical form of male-headed family then institutionalized by the French Civil Code as well as advocated by the Roman Catholic Church.

1896 – Pronatalists versus Birth Controllers

The debates on depopulation entered a new stage in 1896. Early that year the French government released the latest census figures. These showed a continuing decline in the absolute number of births, but more alarming still, France's 834,000 births for 1895 were exceeded by 852,000 deaths. The deficit suggested to pessimists like the physician-savants Jacques Bertillon and Charles Richet that the French population, far from continuing its pattern of ever-so-slow growth, was about to enter upon an era of absolute decline. France had gained only one-quarter million inhabitants in the past decade, whereas its rival across the Rhine had gained eight million. "*Finis Galliae!*" would be Bertillon's mournful verdict.[26]

---

[24] Clémence Royer, "Diminution de la population de la France," *Bulletin de la Société d'Anthropologie de Paris*, 4th. sér., 6 (7 November 1895), 653–656; quote, 655.

[25] Clotilde Dissard, "Féminisme et natalité," *La Revue Féministe*, 1:4 (20 November 1895), 174–181, quote, 180; and Chéliga-Loewy as reported in Dissard's article, 176.

[26] Jacques Bertillon, "Le Problème de la dépopulation. Le Programme de l'Alliance Nationale pour l'Accroissement de la Population Française," *RPP*, vol. 12, n° 36 (June 1897), 531–574; quote, p. 538. Bertillon had used this phrase in an earlier letter to *Le Temps*, 26 February 1897.

In the face of this depressing demographic news, delegates to the April 1896 international women's rights congress in Paris scandalized republican moderates and the general public by provoking a confrontation between proponents of two radically different approaches to the subject of motherhood itself.[27] The first line of thought, reiterated by the French socialist-feminist Léonie Rouzade, was that "motherhood is women's principal social function and deserves to be subsidized by the State."[28] The second, alternative line of thought, espoused by the neo-Malthusian anarchists Paul Robin and Marie Huot, was that since, in any case, women were primarily producing cannon fodder for the armies of the State, they should be given the wherewithal to refuse; in short, women, especially women workers, should have unrestricted access to contraceptive information and devices.

The following month Jacques Bertillon, best known as chief demographer for the department of the Seine, founded the *Alliance Nationale contre la Dépopulation* (later amended to *Alliance Nationale pour l'Accroissement de la Population Française*), with the stated purpose of encouraging republican *men* to father large families.[29] Just three months later Paul Robin founded the *Ligue de Régéneration Humaine*, expressly to propagandize for

---

[27] For contrasting contemporary perspectives on the 1896 congress, see Clotilde Dissard, "Le Congrès féministe de Paris en 1896," *La Revue Internationale de Sociologie*, 4:6 (June 1896), 537–552, & Baron J. Angot des Rotours, "L'Agitation féministe," *La Quinzaine*, 2, n° 41 (1 July 1896), 111–120. For a scholarly survey of this congress reconstructed through press coverage in *Le Figaro*, see Wynona H. Wilkins, "The Paris International Feminist Congress of 1896 and its French Antecedents," *North Dakota Quarterly*, 4:4 (Autumn 1975), 5–28.

[28] Rouzade, as quoted in Wilkins, "International Feminist Congress," 23. Rouzade's advocacy of state-supported childrearing dated from the early 1880s, according to historians Charles Sowerwine and Marilyn J. Boxer. See Sowerwine, "Women and the Origins of the French Socialist Party," *Third Republic/Troisieme République* (*TR/TR*), n°ˢ 3–4 (1977), 119–121, and Boxer, "Socialism Faces Feminism: The Failure of Synthesis in France, 1879–1914," in *Socialist Women: European Socialist Feminism in the Nineteenth and Early Twentieth Centuries*, ed. Marilyn J. Boxer & Jean H. Quataert (New York: Elsevier, 1978), 79–80. Sowerwine's *Femmes et socialisme* is highly critical of the socialist women's insistence on motherhood. He is silent on Rouzade's later views and on the entire discussion of legislation affecting women's employment and marriage law reform, including the Brousse-Lafargue proposals mentioned earlier. For the contrasting view, see Marilyn J. Boxer, "Linking Socialism, Feminism, and Social Darwinism in Belle Epoque France: The Maternalist Politics and Journalism of Aline Valette," *Women's History Review*, 21:1 (February 2012), 1–19.

[29] Alliance Nationale pour l'Accroissement de la Population Française, *Programme, statuts et compte rendu des travaux de l'exercice 1896–1897* (Paris: Alliance Nationale, 1897). Despite his primary focus on the *familialistes* who eventually split off from the *natalistes* to form their own organization, Robert Talmy reported on the subsequent activities of the pronatalists in his *Histoire du mouvement familial en France (1896–1939)*(Paris: Union Nationale des Caisses d'Allocations Familiales, 1962), vol. 1. Bertillon's subsequent personal history took an ironic twist with regard to the birthrate: neither of his two daughters ever married or bore children, but instead became career women. Meanwhile, Mme Bertillon, née Caroline Schultze, a trained physician, returned to work in 1900.

birth control as a weapon against the state.[30] In the interim the French Senate had approved a bill, passed by the Chamber the preceding year, that simplified the formalities for marriage, thereby hoping to encourage the founding of more legitimate families, along the current model, in the national interest.[31] Although it is difficult to establish cause and effect, it seems clear that these developments were intimately connected.

Alluding to the confrontation over birth control at this 1896 feminist congress, Jacques Bertillon would insist that France's declining birth rate, or "depopulation," was strictly a *man's* issue. He dismissed as "fantasies" claims that the distress of French women over their inferior legal status was affecting reproduction and that feminism itself was to blame for the decline, which had potentially grave implications for France's claims to be a world power. Bertillon argued that the trend could be reversed simply by amending tax laws that affected men's property and patrimony and thereby bolstering patriarchal pride.[32] Nor did Bertillon or his associates welcome women's participation in discussions of the population problem – an attitude that vexed Maria Martin. "It appears," she remarked in an 1897 editorial in the *Journal des Femmes*, "that some think it possible to have *too many* women to discuss the matter of population growth. But no one has yet discovered a means of achieving it without them."[33]

Bertillon persisted in his male-focused approach. In June 1897 he would present the program of his Alliance Nationale in the *Revue Politique et Parlementaire* (*RPP*). Men, he declared, were to blame for the falling birth

---

[30] There is considerable information about Paul Robin and the Ligue (though the interpretation is hostile) in Bertillon's *Dépopulation de la France*. For a more sympathetic discussion of Robin's Ligue, see Roger H. Guerrand, *La Libre maternité, 1896–1969* (Tournai & Paris: Casterman, 1971); and Ronsin, *La Grève des ventres*. On Robin's unorthodox career as an educator, see Angus McLaren, "Revolution and Education in Late Nineteenth-Century France: The Early Career of Paul Robin," *History of Education Quarterly*, 21:3 (Fall 1981), 317–335. In *Sexuality and Social Order: The Debate over the Fertility of Women and Workers in France, 1770–1920* (New York: Holmes & Meier, 1983), McLaren exaggerated the importance of French neo-Malthusian feminism. On Robin's overall career, see Christiane Demeulenaere-Douyère, *Paul Robin (1837–1912): Un militant de la liberté et du bonheur* (Paris: Publisud, 1994).

[31] On the marriage reform law of 20 June 1896, see Darlan, minister of justice, to the procureurs-généraux, circular of 23 June 1896, reprinted in *La Revue Féministe*, 2 (1896), 636–640. See also Esther Kanipe, "The Family, Private Property and the State in France, 1870–1914" (Ph.D. dissertation, University of Wisconsin, Madison, 1976).

[32] Jacques Bertillon, as quoted in Désiré Descamps, "Le problème de la population," *La Revue Socialiste*, 24:1 (September 1896), 274. Bertillon repeated this statement the following year in his major article, "Problème de la dépopulation," cited in n. 26. See also Bertillon's later book, *La Dépopulation de la France, ses conséquences, ses causes, mésures à prendre pour la combattre* (Paris: F. Alcan, 1911).

[33] Martin's remarks appeared in her front-page editorial, "Savants et philanthropes," *Le Journal des Femmes*, n° 60 (January 1897).

rate. Drawing on the theories of Frédéric Le Play, he traced the decline to men's unwillingness to split up family patrimonies.[34] Moreover, he categorically rejected the earlier arguments of those men, notably Henri Thulié and Paul Leroy-Beaulieu, who did take seriously women's claims for legal reform. Bertillon thus discounted the role not only of feminism but also of women themselves in the decline of the birth rate. Such claims were in any event unquantifiable! He denied that legal reforms would have any effect (though he did look with favor on the new law easing legal formalities for marriage). His proposed solution was to tax the childless and grant tax relief for *fathers* with three or more children, a solution that Émile Levasseur, Bertillon's colleague and an economist and demographer, opposed as "illiberal" and, thus, heretical from the standpoint of republican doctrine.[35]

From the socialist camp came a different objection. In 1893 Aline Valette had made motherhood the foundation of the socialist-feminist program.[36] Writing in 1896 in the *Revue Socialiste*, Désiré Descamps, while implicitly accepting the masculine bias of Bertillon's economic argument, turned it topsy-turvy by blaming depopulation on *men's* lust for property. The problem would never be remedied by fiscal reform, but only by the abolition of private property; only then could prolific families flourish. "Capital," he argued, echoing Marx and Engels, "is what tears woman away from her role of wife and mother; it imposes sterility upon her."[37]

---

[34] Bertillon, "Problème de la dépopulation," 537–538. For the views of Frédéric Le Play, see his *La Réforme sociale en France*, 2 vols. (Paris: Plon, 1864; 8th edn. 1901), and *L'Organisation de la famille* (Paris: Tequi, 1871). In 1881, shortly before Le Play's death, his followers founded a monthly review, also entitled *La Réforme Sociale*, which continued to have a substantial impact on French social thought. For one reinterpretation, see Catherine Bodard Silver, transl. & ed., *Frederic Le Play: On Family, Work, and Social Change* (Chicago: University of Chicago Press, 1982). [Cf. my earlier discussion of Le Play and his analyses in Part I, Chapter 3.]

[35] Bertillon, "Problème de la dépopulation," 550. For Levasseur's rebuttal, see "La Dépopulation de la France: Lettre à M. Marcel Fournier, directeur," *RPP*, 14, n° 40 (October 1897), 5–30. In March 1897 Bertillon would argue that sterilized milk was preferable to mother's milk for infants in childcare facilities, which prompted an angry reply from Dr. Pinard, "De la Puériculture," *La Revue Scientifique*, 4ᵉ série, 8:5 (31 July 1897), 135–140; quote 137.

[36] For the ringing defense of motherhood by socialist-feminist women in the mid-1890s, especially Aline Valette, see Marilyn J. Boxer, "French Socialism, Feminism, and the Family," *TR/TR*, n° 3–4 (1977), 128–167; and "Linking Socialism, Feminism, and Social Darwinism." See also Sowerwine, *Femmes et socialisme*, 53–64.

[37] Descamps, "Le Problème de la population," *La Revue Socialiste* 24:1 (September 1896), 282. For the antecedents of late nineteenth-century French socialists' attitudes toward sex and birth control, see Angus McLaren, "Sex and Socialism: The Opposition of the French Left to Birth Control in the Nineteenth Century," *Journal of the History of Ideas*, 37:3 (July–September 1976), 475–492. Although McLaren does not address the fin-de-siècle period, his emphasis on the continuing moral conservatism of socialist writers during the earlier period is also borne out by evidence from 1890–1914. "The Left did not break," he wrote (492), "with traditional Judeo-Christian

Women and their "natural" instincts were, in this view, simply the victims of capitalist greed.

A heated debate soon arose over the relationship between feminism and socialism. Some feminists responded by insisting that their brand of feminism was quite distinct from socialism. According to Marya Chéliga (echoing Hubertine Auclert), women were oppressed by men in every social class; extensive legal, educational, and economic reforms, such as the proposal by Jeanne Schmahl's *L'Avant-Courrière* to give married women legal control over their own earnings, would be required to guarantee women's well-being within a familial context.[38] Meanwhile, Martin and her associates at the *Journal des Femmes* continued to press for other legal reforms for women, married or unmarried. Why, she demanded in June 1896, should women bear children at all when they were treated so badly by the nation? "It is unjust," she argued later, "to impose duties on those who have no rights."[39]

Amidst this perfect storm of conflicting perspectives on how to stimulate the birth rate, writers for the *Journal des Femmes*, sensitive to the arguments of Dr. Adolphe Pinard and others, began to press for legislative action to ensure better care for the children who *were* born. At the December 1896 meeting of the *Alliance des Savantes et des Philanthropes*, a number of women activists in attendance spoke out boldly for economic assistance to mothers, for the "rehabilitation" of maternity (especially for unwed mothers), and for improvements in women's means of self-support.[40] The last of these demands, supplemented by advocacy of women's "right to work" would become the special concern of Marguerite Durand, *directrice* of *La Fronde*. Yet even in that pathbreaking daily newspaper,

morality." For an exploration of subsequent anarchist, socialist, and syndicalist responses to neo-Malthusian arguments in the early twentieth century, see André Armengaud, "Mouvement ouvrier et néo-malthusianisme au début du XXe siècle," *Annales de Démographie Historique* (1966), 7–19; Léon Gani, "Jules Guesde, Paul Lafargue et les problèmes de population," *Population*, 34:6 (November–December 1979), 1023–1043; and Alfred Sauvy, "Les Marxistes et le malthusianisme," *Cahiers Internationaux de Sociologie*, n° 41 (1966), 1–14.

[38] See "Les Femmes et les féministes," *Revue Encyclopédique Larousse*, n° 169 (28 November 1896). Also see Chéliga, "Le Mouvement féministe en France," *RPP*, 13, n° 38 (1 August 1897), 271–284.

[39] Maria Martin, "Dépopulation," *Le Journal des Femmes*, n° 54 (June 1896), and "Savants et philanthropes," *Le Journal des Femmes*, n° 60 (January 1897). Both Martin's editorials are lead articles on the front page.

[40] Reported by Maria Martin in "Savants et philanthropes." For further information on the campaign for maternity insurance in the French legislature to 1913, see Mary Lynn McDougall [Stewart], "Protecting Infants: The French Campaign for Maternity Leaves, 1890s-1913," *French Historical Studies*, 13:1 (Spring 1983), 79–105. On the development of private maternity insurance plans, see Fuchs, *Poor and Pregnant*, pp. 148–151.

columnists would take up the campaign of Pinard for obligatory *puéricul-ture* (infant care training) for schoolgirls.[41] *La Fronde* would also advocate *recherche de la paternité*, as indicated by the three-part article on the subject by Savioz in April 1898 and the forty-seven part feuilleton, "L'Article 340: Grand roman parisienne," signed by Anna D'Auray and published between 25 July and 19 October 1899.[42] By 1900, the pioneer woman doctor and staunch republican advocate of women's rights, Blanche Edwards-Pilliet, was urging (not unlike Rouzade, Brousse, and Lafargue a few years earlier) that motherhood be made a fully subsidized social function of the French nation-state.[43] Thus did French feminists highlight the patriarchal character of some republican men's efforts to resolve the population problem; they called on the republican government to provide woman-centered and woman-friendly solutions.

These debates about who was responsible for the falling birth rate and what could be done about it would continue throughout the 1890s, culminating (as we shall see in the next chapter) at the international women's congresses held in Paris in 1900. In late May 1896, the world-famous French novelist Émile Zola (1840–1902) offered his analysis of the depopulation issue in *Le Figaro*. In an editorial that took up nearly half of the front page, he condemned the literature of decadence, of adultery and infertility, and urged French women to once again become mothers: "O French mothers, bear children, so that France can maintain its rank, its power, and its prosperity, for it is necessary for the salvation of the world that France lives, France which has launched human emancipation, and from which will flow all truth and all justice!"[44] Zola's panegyric to France

---

[41]   Marie-Anne de Bovet, "Oh! Ces économistes . . . ," *La Fronde*, n° 7 (15 December 1897); and Andrée Téry, "Faisons des mères," *La Fronde*, n° 741 (19 December 1899). For a positive endorsement of *puériculture*, see Ida R. Sée, "L'Apprentissage de la maternité," *La Fronde*, n° 1859 (11 January 1903).

[42]   Savioz, "La Recherche de la Paternité," (Tribune de *la Fronde*), *La Fronde*, n°117 (4 April 1898); n° 118 (5 April 1898); & n° 119 (6 April 1898). The writer calls for legalizing paternity suits, for an equal standard of moral responsibility of both parents for the children born out of wedlock; she rehearses the laws of other countries that permit such suits and award economic sustenance to the mother and child, and closes with a very sad case study of a young woman who killed her baby and ended up in Saint-Lazare, where she could at least get something to eat. On the long serialized novel by Anna d'Auray, see Anne Cova's doctoral thesis, "Droits des femmes et protection de la maternité en France, 1892–1939" (Florence: European University Institute, 1994), vol. 1, p. 145, note 193.

[43]   See "Rapport de Mme la docteur Edwards-Pilliet," *Congrès Internationale de la Condition et des Droits des Femmes, Paris, 1900*, 66–68, transl. Karen Offen in *WFF*, vol. 2, doc. 32. In 1901, Edwards-Pilliet, in association with Augusta Moll-Weiss, would found the *Ligue des Mères de Famille*, a philanthropic organization of middle-class women reformers dedicated to bringing assistance and advice to working-class mothers in their homes.

[44]   See Zola, "Dépopulation," *Le Figaro* (23 May 1896), rept. in *Nouvelle campagne* (Paris, 1897), 217–228.

and fertility was only the prelude to his quartet of evangelical novels, beginning with *Fécondité* (1899; translated as *Fertility*), written during his exile in England following the pandemonium that ensued in the wake of his public letter in defense of Captain Dreyfus, "*J'Accuse!*"[45]

In this first novel of the quartet, this author would elaborate his vision of France's new moral man and woman. As goddesses of fertility, women play a central role in Zola's new republican vision. The novel traces the saga of a vast family founded by a virtuous and hard-working artisan named Mathieu Froment and his agreeable and bounteously fertile wife-companion, who is symbolically named Marianne, the incarnation of Liberty and the Republic. The young couple returns to the land to make it flower through hard work. Mathieu's fields, warmed by the sun and worked conscientiously, yield abundant harvests; so also do the Froment women, first Marianne, then her daughters and her daughters-in-law, all impregnated every two years by their wholesome, hard-working, and virile husbands.[46] Several writers for *La Fronde* exuded praise for the vision of womanhood elaborated by Zola's new novel.[47] However, another reviewer, Gustave Kahn, described the novel as "a hymn to the new patriarchy."[48]

Others such as the much younger budding novelist and journalist Marcelle Tinayre (1870–1948) took a more skeptical, if not downright dismal view. Tinayre published several articles about motherhood in *La Fronde*.[49] In two of her early novels, *La Rançon* (1898) and *Hélle* (1899), she

---

[45] The previous year, Savioz had applauded Zola for his strong defense of Captain Dreyfus; see "Liberté de conscience," *La Fronde*, n° 42 (19 January 1898), and "Valets et parasites," *La Fronde*, n° 88 (6 March 1898).

[46] Émile Zola, *Fécondité* (Paris: E. Fasquelle, 1899); in English, *Fruitfulness*, transl. & ed. Ernest Vizetelly (New York: Doubleday, 1900). For a selection from this novel, see *WFF*, vol. 2, doc. 27. On Zola and the woman question, excellent scholarship was published in the 1970s: see David Baguley, *Fécondité d'Émile Zola: roman à thèse, evangile, mythe* (Toronto: University of Toronto Press, 1973); Anna Krakowski, *La Condition de la femme dans l'oeuvre d'Émile Zola* (Paris: Nizet, 1974); Chantal Bertrand-Jennings, *L'Eros et la femme chez Zola: de la chute au paradis retrouvé* (Paris: Éditions Klincksieck,1977); Mieczyslaw Kaczynski, *"Les Quatre Évangiles" d'Émile Zola: entre la vision catastrophique et la vision utopique* (Lublin: University Marie Curie-Sklodowska, 1979).

[47] Zola's *Fécondité* received a flurry of coverage in *La Fronde*. See May-Armand Blanc, "La Femme dans l'oeuvre d'Émile Zola" *La Fronde*, n° 692 (31 October 1899) & n° 693 (1 November 1899); Manoel de Grandfort, "Fécondité," *La Fronde*, n° 703 (11 November 1899), 1, & Henriette Lefébure, "Opinion d'Émile Zola sur l'allaitement maternel," *La Fronde*, n° 711 (19 November 1899), 1. According to Lefébure, Zola opposed using wet nurses or nursing bottles (as do the English, as he had observed); he was an enthusiastic advocate of motherly nursing and thought that "women's beauty is to be a mother, with an infant on her knees." If this practice were to become fashionable, he maintained, France "would be the queen of nations, mistress of the world."

[48] The review of *Fécondité* referred to here was by Gustave Kahn in *La Revue Blanche*, 20:2 (October 1899), 284–293. The *Frondeuses* did not appear to be perturbed about the patriarchal aspects of Zola's novel.

[49] See, for example, Marcelle Tinayre, "L'Assistée," *La Fronde*, n° 40 (17 January 1898), front page.

would probe the deeper complexities of maternity from a female perspective. In *La Rançon*, Tinayre questioned the sacrosanct belief in an innate maternal instinct, while in *Héllé*, she explored the unpleasant material physicality of motherhood among the poor during a visit she made to the Baudeloque maternity hospital in Paris: "Lamentable maternal flock, the flotsam and jetsam of misery and love, by which life and suffering are perpetuated."[50] The literary historian France Grenaudier-Klijn interprets Tinayre's effort as "dismantling an archetype" (maternal love), then dwelling on "communal pain and suffering," drawing on naturalist techniques.[51] In her fourth novel, *La Rebelle* (1905), Tinayre would continue her interrogation of the "maternal," demonstrating just how difficult it would be to deconstruct the androcentric idealization of motherhood, even when a woman confronted its harsh physical reality. For obvious reasons, Tinayre's brutally frank observations about the realities of motherhood in these novels did not endear her to the natalist crowd.

In another novel of the period entitled *Stérile* (1899), a writer who signed as Daniel Riche, also probed the darker corners of maternity by placing this analysis of poor women's difficulties into the mouth of an abortionist:[52]

> You should see ... the difficulties, the anxiety, and the complications that arise in a crowded room upon the arrival of a new existence; you should see the women, their youth destroyed, their strength exhausted, and their lives spoilt by over-fatigue, to understand that in the slums many children are a misfortune. You wish to suppress this misery? But you should then teach women not to have children when they are unwilling to have them. If you leave women in ignorance, they will continue to have need of my assistance. ... when women learn how to avoid maternity, without any operation, which is always dangerous, they will no longer come to seek our assistance.

These were but several of the French novels that plumbed the brutal realities and challenges of the "maternal" in the later 1890s and early twentieth century.[53]

[50] Marcelle Tinayre, *Héllé* (Paris: Calmann-Lévy, 1899), pp. 159–160.
[51] France Grenaudier-Klijn, "Mater Dolorosa: Motherhood Reclaimed in Three Novels by Marcelle Tinayre," *Women in French Studies*, 9 (2001), 40–53; quotations, pp. 43, 45.
[52] Daniel Riche, *Stérile* (1898). This translation (slightly amended) is from p. 483 of Angus McLaren, "Abortion in France: Women and the Regulation of Family Size, 1800–1914," *French Historical Studies*, 10:3 (Spring 1978), 461–485.
[53] See the analysis of Leonard R. Koos, "Making Angels: Abortion Literature in Turn-of-the-Century France," in *Confrontations: Politics and Aesthetics in Nineteenth-Century France*, ed. Kathryn M. Grossman, Michael E. Lane, Bénédicte Monicat, & Willa Z. Silverman (Amsterdam: Rodopi, 2001), 259–285.

The birth rate decline was not the only demographic figure that *fin-de-siècle* Frenchmen found worrisome. In one its first issues, *La Fronde* reminded readers that women now outnumbered men:[54]

> In France, women constitute the majority of the population. Millions of women, single or widowed, live without the legal support of men. Women pay taxes that they do not vote for, contribute to the national wealth through their manual or intellectual work, and they claim the right to officially give their advice on all the questions that interest society and humanity, of which they are members just like men.

In early 1901, the members of the Statistical Society in Paris would address the population question. According to the journalist Louise de Marnes, writing in *La Fronde*, one of the society's distinguished male members insisted that the birth rate drop was clearly due to the "progressive improvement in the condition of women" [*relèvement de la condition de la femme*] and now that women were free to participate in men's liberties and pleasures, they weren't having children. Doubtless he was thinking of those much-discussed New Women who were ostensibly breaking the mold. Certainly he had not been reading Tinayre or the investigative articles in *La Fronde*, much less the other literature that delineated the plight of poor women in the workforce.

Louise de Marnes countered vigorously. On the contrary, she asserted, "The improvement of women's condition has not yet been obtained.... Woman remains the serf of man who doesn't want to hear, at any price, about an equality that is more apparent than real."[55] The birth rate might be falling among the middle classes, but not because women's condition was improving; instead such women were copying the vices of the former aristocracy and, in order to pursue those pleasures, couldn't be bothered with children. Such behavior, Marnes asserted, had nothing to do with improvements in the condition of women as a whole. A strange understanding of feminism, indeed! Our feminism, she said, aims higher than a mere effort to aspire to men's "pleasures and liberties." We want concrete reforms, she declared: to obtain equal pay for equal work and freedom to work; to end the rule of exception in the question of morals (here she was referring to licensed prostitution and the morals police); to improve women's moral and intellectual level and to obtain the right for a woman

---

[54] Back-page advertisement, *La Fronde*, n° 3 (11 December 1897). See also "On dit . . . ," *La Fronde*, n° 586 (17 July 1899).

[55] Louise de Marnes, "La Condition de la femme et la dépopulation de la France," *La Fronde*, n° 1139 (21 January 1901).

(following marriage) to retain her nationality of birth; to dispose of her earnings and to manage her own property as she sees fit; to end the exclusivity of paternal authority over children. "This is what we mean by improving the condition of woman. Should that have any effect on the drop of French natality? Quite the contrary!" These men who present "such sophisms," she charged, simply ignore the justice and moral impact of feminist demands. Her subtext was clear: that women, once in possession of their rights, would probably be *more* willing to bear children. The question was how to make that happen in a nation whose men (and many women) still seemed so attached to the notion of masculine domination, even though women now constituted the majority of the population. Would the dawn of a new century bring any answers?

CHAPTER 8

The New Century Greets the Woman Question, 1900

The French daily *Le Gaulois* devoted its New Year's editorial of 1 January 1900 exclusively to the woman question.[1] "Of all the changes that have disassembled and reconstructed aspects of everything in our land, the greatest change is that which has modified the personality of woman and redirected her orientation." According to this editorialist, the first thing women were doing with their newly developed faculties was "to judge man" and to find him wanting. "Why should he be master?" they ask. Women have, the editorialist alleged, become the rivals and antagonists of men; antifeminist men seemed to think that New Women were rising from the ashes of French masculinity! "What will you become, emancipated woman of the twentieth century?" What will become of you, the new Eve?

This editorialist was undoubtedly exaggerating for effect. He had, of course, noticed that, as the new year rang in, the feminist critique of women's subordination in French society had reached new heights of visibility and was dramatically expanding its range of concerns even as it reiterated long-standing calls for change. Just a year earlier, the editors and collaborators of the newly founded francophone review, the *Revue de Morale Sociale* (*RMS*) had declared in their introductory program that "amongst the numerous 'burning questions' of our day ... none is of greater importance than the problem of the moral and social relations between the sexes."[2] Indeed, for them gender injustice had become "the central problem of human rights."[3] They weren't speaking solely of France,

[1] "Soir de fin de siècle," *Le Gaulois* (1 January 1900), front page.
[2] "Programme," *La Revue de Morale Sociale*, 1:1 (January–March 1899), 1. Transl. Anne R. Epstein, with KO.
[3] See Anne R. Epstein, "Gender and the Creation of the French Intellectual: The Case of the *Revue de Morale Sociale* (1899–1903), in *Views from the Margins: Creating Identities in Modern France*, ed. & intro. Kevin J. Callahan & Sarah A. Curtis (Lincoln: University of Nebraska Press, 2008), pp. 218–250; quote, p. 230.

but it was clear that the continuing imbalance of power between the sexes in France was central to their transnational perspective.

There was, admittedly, an eerily familiar ring to most of the claims made by French feminists on women's behalf in 1900 (especially as concerned demands for legal and economic changes), but thanks to the press, it looked as though their oft-repeated message was finally reaching a broad spectrum of the population. Feminists continued to challenge man-made laws that had proved unfavorable to women, the most recent of which was the Law of 2 November 1892, which placed restrictions on women's work, but also the older Article 340 of the Penal Code, which forbade *recherche de la paternité*.[4] They repeatedly condemned the Civil Code (as they had for decades) and demanded equal pay for equal work (as they had for decades), but some had also begun to critique masculine cultural habits and practices that had visibly detrimental effects on women (alcoholism, venereal disease, prostitution and the traffic in women, pornography, and physical violence, both domestic and public). Feminists were, in fact, analyzing and critiquing the male-centeredness of the culture in which they found themselves. Some had begun to demand the right for women to control their own bodies as well as their own finances, and to have a say about questions of war and peace. No wonder some French men were purportedly experiencing a "masculinity crisis."[5]

The Woman Question in French Art and Letters

Although the journalist Séverine had been skeptical about the health of the Republic, doubting that French women would really want anything to do with that "rotten apple, gnawed to the core by parasites, infected by fungus and infested by vermin" as she had described it in 1896, others saw things in a far more optimistic (or at least wishful) light.[6] Certain republicans had begun to celebrate women. The composer Gustave Charpentier envisioned the young French woman of the people as a Muse, an embodiment of the nation; his musical pageant, "The Coronation of the Muse," launched in 1897, would become "a central feature of Bastille Day celebrations, local

---

[4] See Maria Pognon, "La Loi néfaste de 1892: Protection des femmes et des enfants dans l'industrie," *La Fronde*, n° 743 (20 December 1899), and in the same issue, Marguerite Durand's angry editorial, "Protection!"

[5] Christopher E. Forth calls it a "crisis of French manhood"; see his book, *The Dreyfus Affair and the Crisis of French Manhood* (Baltimore: Johns Hopkins University Press, 2004).

[6] *La Revue Féministe*, 1896 (see Chapter 6 in this volume).

festivals, and commemorations" throughout France.[7] A Muse was not a citizen, however, and generally speaking, Muses did not talk back to authority.

An even bigger celebratory moment was the inauguration of Jules Dalou's monumental bronze sculpture, "The Triumph of the Republic," on 21 September 1899 at the Place de la Nation in Paris. Commissioned by the City of Paris to commemorate the establishment of the first French republic in September 1791, this acclaimed *chef d'oeuvre* represented political allegory at its best.[8] For centuries, "Liberty" had been represented by an allegorical female figure, as had, more recently, the Republican "Marianne," but Dalou's dynamic and massive sculpture seemed to take the symbolism in a different and more equitable direction. Flanking the female figure of *"la Republique"* – an energized Marianne *"dominatrice et maternelle"* (according to the reporter from *La Fronde*) – are four massive figures representing Work [*Travail*], Justice [*Justice*], Liberty [*Liberté*] and Peace [*Paix*].[9] Two figures, Liberty and Work, are represented as brawny working-class males. The other two, Justice and Peace, were depicted as bounteously, if not voluptuously, female. Two children also adorned the sides of the wagon, pulled by two immense lions, on which all the figures stood.

In the climate of high political anxiety that marked the autumn months of 1899, consequent on nationalist and antisemitic agitation in response to the high court's reopening of the Dreyfus Case (but also fuelled by the omnipresence of the woman question, as the three previous chapters have indicated), Dalou's monument would be read in a number of ways. The Paris Municipal Council, making a deliberately pro-republican statement, sponsored a massive parade, inaugural ceremonies, a concert and a banquet (attended by mayors from all over France), with speeches by the president of the Republic (Émile Lourbet) and Prime Minister (René Waldeck-Rousseau) in support of the triumph of the Republic. These events were reported at length in *La Fronde* (by Maria Vérone and Marie Bonnevial)

---

[7] See David M. Pomfret, "'A Muse for the Nation': Gender, Age, and Nation in France, Fin de Siecle," *American Historical Review*, 109:5 (December 2004), 1439–1474. According to Pomfret, Charpentier subsequently included the "crowning of the muse" scene in his opera *Louise* (1900).

[8] The sculptures of Jules Dalou were the subject of two major exhibitions in Paris during the spring and summer of 2013. See the catalogue raisonnée, *Jules Dalou, le sculpteur de la République: catalogue des sculptures de Jules Dalou conservées au Petit Palais* (Paris: Paris-Musees, 2013). See also Maurice Dreyfous, *Dalou – Sa Vie, Son Oeuvre* (Paris: Librairie Renouard/H. Laurens, Éditeur, 1903). One can find considerable information on the internet about Dalou's "Triomphe de la République," commissioned by the City of Paris.

[9] Jeanne Brémond, "La Fête du 'Triomphe'," *La Fronde*, n° 711 (19 November 1899).

and most other Parisian newspapers.[10] Several hundred thousand marchers representing trade unions, including the women's and mixed unions, freemasonic lodges, and other organized groups convened for an imposing demonstration at the Place de la Nation.

Hubertine Auclert, reporting on the installation of the monument in the Parisian press, chose to interpret the sculpture literally and politically. She wrote that the sculptor Dalou "had so visibly indicated that this triumph would take place with the aid of women that, the other day, a citizen was applauded by the excited crowd in front of the monument when he declared loudly that the triumph of the Republic was the triumph of the oppressed woman." The Republic, she pointed out, "whether cast in bronze or sculpted in stone, is represented by the feminine sex." And only through the Republic, she posited, would French women gain their rights. She called on French women to declare themselves republicans in their own self-interest. "The Republic whose base is liberty and equality cannot refuse your rights without abdicating its principles," Auclert asserted, "whereas the empire or royalty, which base their claims in authority, would violate their own principles in granting those rights."[11]

Auclert, like Marguerite Durand in *La Fronde*, invoked the preponderant numbers of women in France: "By tolerating that the majority of the nation is subordinated to the good pleasure of the minority, by putting up with the fact that twenty million women bound by laws of exception sustained by a couple of million male electors and a couple of hundred of male deputies, they [French men] retard the coming of the true republic." Neither the "*plébiscitaires*" nor the "*nationalistes*" nor the "*antisémites*" would deliver the true Republic, she claimed; so far only the radical-socialists were supportive of women's rights and political participation. "The eloquent work of Dalou, forever showing the Republic triumphing with women's help," Auclert insisted, would do more for "the reconciliation of the human couple" than newspapers or books. "It would anchor in everyone's head [the idea that] the happiness of the French people [*les Français*] can only be achieved through the power of woman to be

[10] Maria Vérone reported at great length on the speeches and the parade, as well as the concert and dinner that followed. See *La Fronde*, n° 712 (20 November 1899), 2–3. Marie Bonnevial reported in the same issue on the events at the *Bourse de Travail*, making much of the representation of the women workers' unions as they marched to the Place de la Nation.

[11] Hubertine Auclert, "Le Féminisme: Le Triomphe de la Femme," unidentified press clipping found in BMD, DOS AUC. This undated clipping, presumably published in *Le Radical*, is not listed in Steve Hause's published list of Auclert's editorials. It likely dates from late September 1899, following installation of the bronze version of the monument. An earlier version sculpted in stone had already been exhibited in 1889.

involved in public affairs, so that they can foster abundance and joy of life everywhere." The best way to honor the Republic, she ventriloquized through the representation of the Republic that crowned the monument, was to "apply my principles of equality. . . . You crowds who acclaim me – know that the best way to honor me . . . is to turn twenty million French female serfs into twenty million sovereigns." In fact, Auclert reported, a group of women was agitating to have Dalou's energy-charged statue moved to the Place de la Concorde, precisely and deliberately to displace the more placid figure of Marianne.[12]

Dalou's "Triumph of the Republic" was not the sole work of art to celebrate French womanhood as the nineteenth century came to a close. Half a year later, the male republicans who organized the Paris Universal Exposition of 1900 crowned *"La Parisienne"* as the queen of the new century, installing her massive statue over the entrance to the Expo.[13] In sharp contrast to the sturdy working-class figures celebrated by Jules Dalou, Paul Moreau-Vauthier's elegant *La Parisienne* symbolized to the world the importance of well-bred, fashionably "feminine" French women and their cultural influence under the Republic. *La Parisienne* effectively asserted her elegance, seemingly in deliberate defiance of the cigar-smoking caricature of the *femme nouvelle* promoted by satirical journals and anti-feminist writers during the later 1890s.[14]

Feminism may not have become a "mass movement" in France by 1900, but the woman question was unquestionably on many people's minds. Its most outspoken advocates and the remedies they sought were making serious inroads in public opinion and, what was more, they were gaining public distinction for their achievements, if not unanimous public support for the passage of the laws they demanded. In addition to the symbolic tribute to womanhood epitomized by the two sculptures mentioned above, the governments of the Third Republic had begun to honor women who had made outstanding contributions to the nation with the cross of the Legion of Honor; to a list dominated in earlier decades by obscure but brave Catholic nuns who had served in wartime situations and a sprinkling of secular women educators, the choice of honorees was beginning to include women who could be considered feminists. The list from 1894

---

[12] Auclert, "Triomphe de la Femme."

[13] The 15-foot high sculpture of "La Parisienne" stood atop the Porte Binet entrance to the 1900 Paris Exposition. Its image was widely reproduced in the contemporary press.

[14] See Debora L. Silverman, "The 'New Woman,' Feminism, and the Decorative Arts in Fin-de-Siècle France," in *Eroticism and the Body Politic*, ed. Lynn Hunt (Baltimore: Johns Hopkins University Press, 1991), pp. 144–163.

through 1901 included the philanthropist and feminist Isabelle Bogelot (decree of 2 April 1894); the educator Pauline Kergomard (decree of 31 December 1895); Marie Pégard, for her contributions to organizing the French exposition in Russia (decree of 31 May 1900); the outspoken and controversial scientist Clémence Royer and the novelist Daniel Lesueur (both, decree of 16 August 1900); and the popular novelist Marie-Louise Gagneur (decree of 21 February 1901).[15]

What was more, women were forcing public recognition as *"intellectuelles."*[16] In addition to publishing analytical articles in progressive, transnational publications such as the *Revue de Morale Sociale*, they were also furnishing articles and editorials for the principal organs of the mainstream French press – *Le Journal des Débats, Le Figaro, Le Temps, Le Radical, Le Siècle* – as well as for the feminist press. The theatre would become another venue for women's creative activity. In 1897, the energetic Marya Chéliga launched a "Théatre Féministe International" to perform works by women playwrights.[17] In October 1901, the *Revue d'Art Dramatique* would dedicate an entire issue of analysis and criticism to the subject of "feminism in the theatre."[18] The actress Sarah Bernhardt reigned supreme on the Paris stage.[19] In the world of art, the women artists of the *Union des Femmes Peintres et Sculpteurs* continued to mount highly successful annual exhibitions of their works.[20]

---

[15] The excitement and pride over the selection of Clémence Royer and Daniel Lesueur is palpable in the three articles devoted to the event and to these accomplished women in *La Fronde*, n° 983 (18 August 1900). See also Haryett Fontanges, *La Légion d'honneur et les femmes décorées; étude d'histoire et de sociologie féminine* (Paris: Alliance coopérative du livre, 1905).

[16] See the articles in the theme issues "Figures d'intellectuelles," *Mil Neuf Cent: Revue d'Histoire Intellectuelle*, n° 16 (1998) and "Intellectuelles," *Clio: Histoire, Femmes et Sociétés*, n° 13 (2001). Also Epstein, "Gender and the Creation . . ." (cited in n. 3). In fact, the term "intellectuelle" appears in the *Journal des Femmes*, n° 19 (March 1902), 3, in reference to a Belgian feminist, Julia Van Marcke. In the feminist publication *L'Entente* (begun in 1905), the term "intellectuelle" appears repeatedly in early 1908, and in the February 1908 issue (n° 49) the publication calls for "Droits de l'intellectuelle" along with "Droits de la mère." Cf. also the 50-page publication by the Swiss writer Wieland Mayr, *L'Intellectuelle: un chapitre du féminisme* (La Chaux de Fonds: Baillod, 1908).

[17] See Odile Krakovitch,"Théâtre féminin ou féministe? Les créations du Théâtre Féministe International," *Bulletin de la Société de l'Histoire de Paris et de l'Ile-de-France*, 131 (2004), 65–97, and especially Jean Elisabeth Pedersen, "Le Théâtre féministe de Marya Chéliga (juin 1897-février 1898)," *Bulletin de la Société de l'Histoire de Paris et de l'Ile-de-France*, 131 (2004), 33–64.

[18] This special issue included articles by Marya Chéliga, Léopold Lacour, Jane Misme, and Harlor.

[19] On the outsize presence of Sarah Bernhardt, see Mary Louise Roberts, *Disruptive Acts: The New Woman in Fin-de-Siècle France* (Chicago: University of Chicago Press, 2002), esp. chapter 6.

[20] On the first fifteen years of the Union (1881–1896), see Tamar Garb, *Sisters of the Brush: Women's Artistic Culture in Late Nineteenth-Century Paris* (New Haven, CT: Yale University Press, 1994). See also the *Dictionnaire de l'Union des femmes peintres et sculpteurs (1882–1965)* in 3 vols. (Dijon: Échelle de Jacob, 2010).

Some French feminists fiercely critiqued the sexual politics of formal knowledge. Like Clémence Royer before her, the self-taught intellectual Céline Renooz sought to elaborate an intuitive feminist science that would free women "from all the infamous historical lies and to rehabilitate her glory."[21] She was a vigorous proponent of the notion that all knowledge is connected – what we now call a holistic approach.[22] Jeanne Oddo-Deflou and her associates in the study circle *Groupe Français d'Études Féministes* had begun to read, discuss, then translate and publish the long introduction to Bachofen's "Mother-Right"; on the basis of his historical philology, they reclaimed a matriarchal past and matriarchal power for women.[23] In the next decade this group would launch a monthly periodical entitled *L'Entente* and appropriate the term "*intellectuelles*" – in the feminine. Eliska Vincent (1844–1913) was studying the history of the old regime to validate her claims that women in France had once exercised the vote.[24] The artist and savante Marguerite Souley-Darqué was writing about Nietzsche in *La Fronde*.[25] She subsequently developed a lecture course on

[21] Quoted by Ann Taylor Allen (in translation) from Renooz, *La Religion naturelle restituée* (1907). On the eccentric Renooz, see James Smith Allen, *Poignant Relations: Three Modern French Women* (Baltimore: Johns Hopkins University Press, 2000), chapter 5, and Ann Taylor Allen, *Feminism and Motherhood in Western Europe, 1890–1970: The Maternal Dilemma* (Houndmills, UK: Palgrave Macmillan, 2005), pp. 26–27.

[22] Although Renooz's approach to a holistic knowledge echoes the approach in the 1850s by Clémence Royer to developing a women's form of knowledge, according to James Smith Allen (personal communication) these two women found themselves at odds.

[23] *Le Droit de la mère dans l'antiquité: Préface de l'ouvrage "Das Mutterrecht" de J. J. Bachofen. Traduit et publiée ainsi que la table analytique des matières par les soins du Groupe Français d'Études Féministes* (Paris: n. p., 1903). *La Fronde* published a series of articles (signed J. Hellé) "Matriarcat et Gynécocratie," in its monthly issues for November & December 1903 (n°s 2004 & 2005), and January 1904 (n° 2006). See also Jacques Lourbet, who dismissed the claim for matriarchy, citing evidence from biology and the law of the strongest, in "La Signification du Matriarchat," *La Revue de Morale Sociale*, 1:2 (April–June 1899), 158–173, and the defense of Bachofen's theory by Jeanne Deflou, "De Droit de la mère dans l'antiquité," *RMS*, 4:16 (1903), 497–502.

On the feminist fin-de-siècle fascination with matriarchy, see the analyses of Françoise Picq, "Par delà la loi du père: le débat sur la recherche de la paternité au congrès féministe de 1900," *Les Temps Modernes*, n° 391 (February 1979), 1199–1212, & Ann Taylor Allen, *Feminism and Motherhood in Western Europe*, pp. 19–28.

[24] In the *ancien régime*, votes were generally local and represented fiefs (real property), not individuals; thus when women inherited such property they could cast their vote, or delegate a male relative to cast it for them. Eliska Vincent (and her sister Flor Mauriceau) put together a very impressive library and archive of women's history and Vincent attended and spoke at a number of national and international congresses (Berlin, 1896; Brussels, 1897; The Hague, 1898; and London, 1899) on the subject of women's voting rights. See "Madame Vincent," in the *Bulletin de la Société pour l'Amélioration*, 4th sér., n° 13 (September–October 1903), 373–375. Her earlier publications include: "L'Électorat des femmes dans l'histoire," *La Revue Féministe*, 1:1 (1 October 1895), 20–26; and "Le Vote des femmes dans les élections consulaires," *La Revue féministe*, 1:3 (5 November 1895), 106–111.

[25] Marguerite Souley-Darqué, "La Philosophie de Nietzsche," *La Fronde*, n° 997 (1 September 1900); n° 1000 (4 September 1900); n° 1001 (5 September 1900); & n° 1008 (12 September 1900).

"féminologie," which she would teach at the innovative *Collège Libre des Sciences Sociales.*[26] Her course was the first interdisciplinary women's studies course in Europe, and possibly the first in the entire world.

A new generation of feminist novelists had begun to judge French men and their behavior, as well as to critique the bourgeois "ideal" of hierarchical and authoritarian separate spheres, as the pioneering studies of literary historian Jennifer Waelti-Walters have demonstrated.[27] These female writers, perhaps inspired by the audacity of famous male writers like Henrik Ibsen, were tipping the tables on the earlier prevailing novels of adultery by exploring the parameters of women's constraint and unhappiness in marriage from an explicitly female standpoint. These new novels were "subversive novels by politically astute and socially conscious women."[28] Although many of this "small army" of novelists would become far better known after 1900, Marcelle Tinayre, Pierre de Coulevain, Daniel Lesueur, Jeanne Marni, Camille Pert, Georges Peyrebrune, Liane de Pougy, Rachilde, and even young Colette published their first novels before 1901. Tinayre had in fact published four before the turn of the century.

Feminists had already begun to address the sexual politics of the French language. They continued to point to examples of sexual discrimination in vocabulary and grammar: in a culture where the *Académie Française* (which "controlled" the French language) insisted that the gender of words was strictly a matter of grammar derived from Latin (and not based on sex), French feminists exposed the blatant sexism that lay behind this claim, with particular reference to the naming of professions, where the masculine form invariably prevailed. Already in July 1891 Marie-Louise Gagneur had challenged the *Académie Française* to acknowledge the feminization of names such as *le sculpteur* (*la sculptrice*).[29] Her request was summarily dismissed. Others continued the campaign for the feminization of

---

[26] See Edmond Char, "Un cours de Féminologie: Mme Souley-Darqué," *Femina*, n° 30 (April 1902), 125. See documents in translation and analysis by Marilyn J. Boxer, in "Women's Studies in France circa 1902: A Course on Feminology," *International Supplement to the Women's Studies Quarterly*, n° 1 (January 1982), 25–27. The lectures were later published in book form: Mme Souley-Darqué, *L'Évolution de la femme* (Ghent: Société coopérative Volksdrukkerij, 1908). Her pamphlet, *Le Servage de l'épouse*, would be published by the Lyon-based group *L'Éducation Féministe* in 1907.

[27] Jennifer Waelti-Walters, *Feminist Novelists of the Belle Epoque* (Bloomington: Indiana University Press, 1990). See her invaluable list of these novels, pp. 193–198.

[28] Waelti-Walters, *Feminist Novelists*, p. 1.

[29] On Gagneur's initiative, see Claudie Baudino, "Une initiative inaboutie mais prémonitoire," *LHT*, n° 7, Documents, publié le 01 janvier 2011 [En ligne], URL: www.fabula.org/lht/7/index.php?id= 177. On the general question, see Baudino's longer study, *Politique de la langue et différence sexuelle: La politisation du genre des noms de métier* (Paris: L'Harmattan, 2001).

professional titles (*le docteur/la doctoresse, le pharmacien/la pharmacienne, le professeur/la professeure*, etc.) as women entered professional fields from which they had earlier been barred.[30] Marguerite Durand would pointedly refer to herself as *la directrice* of *La Fronde*. In 1900, however, *La Fronde* queried three women physicians as to their thoughts about adopting the term "*la doctoresse*". All three preferred "*Madame le docteur*," on the grounds that *docteur* was the official term used on their diplomas.[31]

Other irritating linguistic conventions also came under feminist scrutiny. For decades they had been insisting on the feminine form of "citizen" – *citoyenne*. Additionally, they attacked the inconsistency of claims made by courts that in some cases (taxpayers, for instance) the category *les français* included the female half of the population, but in others (such as voters) it did not.[32] Additionally, they sought to find a title that could be employed to address a woman without distinguishing her marital status. The suffrage advocate Hubertine Auclert advocated using "Madame" for all adult women, a practice that ultimately did take root in France.[33] Controversies broke out over allowing women who married to keep their

[30] The issue of feminizing professional titles had come up as early as the 1830s; see the petition to the king and the Chamber of Deputies in *La Gazette des Femmes*, 2:1(1 January 1837), 1–6, demanding that women be able to be *jurées*, just as men were *jurés* (i.e., to serve on juries), and the following year (issue 3:1[1 January 1838], 1–5) arguing that women be allowed to qualify as "docteures" in medicine, law, letters, and sciences. Subsequently Maria Deraismes concerned herself with this matter; she adopted the usage "*consoeur*" to address women. See the "Notice" to Deraismes's *Oeuvres complètes*, vol. 1 (Paris: F. Alcan, 1895), xl–lii. See also Hubertine Auclert's deliberate feminizations: "Pharmacienne" (and "doctoresse"), *La Citoyenne*, n° 107 (April 1886), "Des Prud'femmes," n° 113 (October 1886), and n° 114 (November 1886); also "Les Doctoresses et le service médical de l'exposition," *Le Radical* (22 March 1897); "Doctoresses de l'état civil," *Le Radical* (27 November 1898); "Doctoresse oculiste," *Le Radical* (23 February 1899); "Les Législatrices," *Le Radical* (3 September 1901), etc. By contrast, the feisty Dr. Blanche Edwards-Pilliet objected strenuously to the term "doctoresse," according to Leguay & Barbizet, *Blanche Edwards-Pilliet, femme et medicin*, p. 63. See *La Fronde*, n° 1033 (7 October 1900).

[31] *La Fronde*, n° 1033 (7 October 1900).

[32] For examples, see Auclert, "Féminisez la langue," *Le Radical* (12 August 1900). Calls for feminization of the language had been stimulated (once again) by concerns about the inclusivity of "*tous les français.*" In 1885, Louise Barbarousse and Marie Richard Picot, who had attempted to register to vote locally under the rubric of "tous les français," challenged the electoral law of 1884 in court; see "The Recent Decision upon Municipal Suffrage in France," *The Englishwoman's Review*, 14 (14 March 1885), 106. In 1900, Andrée Téry discussed "feminization of the language" in *La Fronde*, n° 999 (3 September 1900). See Klejman & Rochefort, *Égalité en marche*, pp. 313–317, for more examples of linguistic subversion by feminists.

[33] See Auclert, "Madame ou mademoiselle," *Le Radical* (22 December 1896); "Le Nom de la femme mariée," *Le Radical* (3 October 1897); and in a speech at the mairie of the 11th arrondissement [s.d.], reprinted in *Les Femmes au gouvernail* (Paris: M. Giard, 1923), pp. 83–84. Although Auclert's suggestion finally entered common usage in the later twentieth century, it was only in 2012 that the French government would finally eliminate from official documents the distinction of "Mademoiselle" for unmarried women.

original patronymic, or for those who divorced, to take back their surname of birth.[34] All these proposals would generate debate in the early twentieth century.

In *La Fronde* Clémence Royer promoted the use of *consoeur* as the feminine form of *confrère* (the neologism *consoeur* had been coined decades back by Maria Deraismes).[35] Other proposals included attempts to find new ways of labeling unwed mothers that did not emphasize the "illegitimate" status of their children. In 1897 Paule Mink proposed substituting *femme-mère* and in 1898 Daniel Lesueur promoted *fille-mère* (in 1922 Jane Misme would propose *mère célibataire*).[36] Others objected to calling a single woman over the age of 25 *vieille fille* [old maid]. Maria Pognon advocated abolishing the word *bâtard* [bastard] to qualify babies born outside marriage.[37] At the 1900 Congress (*Condition et Droits*), Eliska Vincent would propose dignifying "*domestiques*" [domestic servants] with the title "*ouvrières ménagères*" [household workers].[38] This congress also voted a resolution to rename streets in Paris after their recently deceased feminist predecessors Jeanne Deroin, André Léo, and Eugénie Potonié-Pierre.[39] By the early twentieth century, feminists such as Nelly Roussel would openly object to the terminology "*La Femme*" used so frequently (by men) to refer to "women" in the plural – "We do not recognize 'The Woman,' a vague abstraction," she insisted. "We see around us women, concrete creatures with very diverse aptitudes, tastes, tendencies, and temperaments."[40]

---

[34] See Andrea Mansker, *Sex, Honor, and Citizenship in Early Third Republic France* (Houndmills, UK: Palgrave Macmillan, 2011), pp. 176–177. I will have more to say about these terminology quarrels in Part III.

[35] See Clémence Royer, "Confrère ou consoeur," *La Fronde*, n° 33 (10 January 1898). Royer also write a three-part piece on "Nos Titres de politesse," for the "Tribune" section of *La Fronde*; see especially the final installment, *La Fronde*, n° 303 (7 October 1898), where she too proposed using "Madame" for all adult women.

[36] Paule Mink, "Le Congrès féministe de Bruxelles," *La Revue Socialiste*, n° 153 (September 1897), 339–349; quote, 348; Daniel Lesueur, "Les Mères," *La Fronde*, n° 191 (17 June 1898). But nothing changed: see Jane Misme "Carnets d'une féministe – Il n'y a pas des filles mères," *L'Oeuvre*, 16 March 1922.

[37] *Deuxième Congrès International des Oeuvres et Institutions Féminines. 18–23 juin 1900, compte rendu des travaux par* Mme M. Pégard, 4 vols. (Paris: C. Blot, 1902), vol. 1, p. 277.

[38] *Congrès International de la Condition et des Droits des Femmes, 5–8 septembre 1900, questions économiques, morales, et sociales: Éducation, législation, droit privé, droit public* (Paris: Imprimerie des Arts et Manufactures, 1901), pp. 74–75.

[39] *Condition et des Droits des Femmes*, p. 288.

[40] Nelly Roussel, "Qu'est-ce que le 'féminisme'?" *Le Petit Almanach féministe illustré* (1906; orig. publ. 1904 in *La Femme affranchie* [September 1904]), pp. 4–5; quote, p. 4. Note, though, that Marie Pape-Carpantier had made exactly the same point in 1862, in *L'Économiste Français*, n° 22 (10 November 1862), p. 299.

The feminist campaign against the sexism of the French language would be ongoing.[41]

In the wake of the revival of the Olympic Games (an all-male affair) in 1896, some feminists, such as Caroline Kauffmann, from the group *La Solidarité des Femmes*, promoted physical exercise and sports for women.[42] And although the most visible feminists in France were conspicuously performing femininity by their dress and demeanor (if not by their speech) in the later 1890s, critics such as Charles Turgeon, author of the landmark book, *Le Féminisme français* (1902), would continue to criticize them for affirming the liberating character of the bicycle, for challenging the deforming, constraining character of the corset, and for daring to wear *culottes* [split skirts] or *pantalons* [trousers or undergarments with two legs] to enhance their mobility.[43] Harlor, one of the staff writers at *La Fronde*, would give a lecture tour at the *Palais de Costume* on the subject of women's dress at the opening of the 1900 Rights congress; under the shadow of *La Parisienne*, she called for practical, hygienic but still elegant wearing apparel. "Does woman decide the fashion – or does she submit to it? Or both at once?"[44]

Turgeon would further claim that feminists resisted men's gentlemanly acts of courtesy on the grounds that they were condescending and, thereby, insulting to women; he charged the late Eugénie Potonié-Pierre with this offense.[45] Other critics, such as the *faits divers* columnist in the *Journal du Peuple*, reported that the feminists of Avesnes-les-Aubert

---

[41] This campaign is still underway in our own time. Besides Baudino (cited in n. 29), see Julia Penelope, *Speaking Freely: Unlearning the Lies of the Fathers' Tongues* (New York: Pergamon Press, 1990); Thérèse Moreau, *Le Nouveau Dictionnaire féminin-masculin des professions, des titres et des fonctions* (Geneva: Métropolis, 1991); Fabienne H. Baider, *Hommes galants, femmes faciles: étude socio-sémantique et diachronique* (Paris: L'Harmattan, 2004); and the publications of Edwige Khaznadar. See especially "Genre, le désaccord," in *Le Monde* (14 January 2012), at www.lemonde.fr/societe/article/2012/01/14/genre-le-desaccord_1629145_3224.html.

[42] Caroline Kauffmann founded a *Ligue Féminine de Culture Physique* in the 1890s. See Mary Lynn Stewart, *For Health and Beauty: Physical Culture for Frenchwomen 1880s–1930s* (Baltimore: Johns Hopkins University Press, 2001), esp. chapter 8: "Gymnastics, Sports, and Gender." See Paule Mink & Caroline Kauffmann [delegates of *Solidarité des Femmes* to the London Congress], *Importance de l'éducation physique scientifique combinée avec l'éducation intellectuelle morale," (Idées générales sur les travaux du Congrès International Féministe de Londres). Rapport au Conseil Municipal de Paris, 1899*; partially reprod. in *Paule Minck* [sic], ed. A. Dalotel (Paris: Syros, 1981), pp. 176–181. The original report can be consulted at the BHVP, côte 619195 and online through the Gerritsen Collection (Chadwyck & Taylor).

[43] Charles Turgeon, *Le Féminisme français*, 2 vols. (Paris: L. Larose, 1902), vol. 1, 39ff.

[44] "Causerie de Mlle Harlor au Palais de Costume," *Congrès International de la Condition et des Droits des Femmes* (1901), pp. 3–7; quote, p. 4.

[45] According to Turgeon, *Féminisme français*, vol. 2, p. 453.

refused to be buried by men following their deaths.[46] No doubt this was a bad joke, but jokes of this sort – often accompanied by allegations (usually from antifeminists) that feminists were "anti-male" or, on the other hand, wanted to become men – would refuse either to die or be buried, despite every feminist effort to dismiss or neutralize them. In sum, the woman question continued to highlight the changing relations of the sexes, changes that struck at the very organizational core of French society and culture. It would continue to provide a theme of choice for male artists, novelists, and especially playwrights around the turn of the century, offering endless topics for debate in various learned societies and in the press.[47] It would also provide a host of research topics for professional as well as amateur historians.

By 1889, the year of the centennial, revolutionary historiography and women's history had intersected. In the 1890s, with the establishment of the chair in French revolutionary history at the Sorbonne and the founding in the early 1880s of the scholarly journal, *La Révolution française*, the historiography on the Revolution became increasingly professionalized. Michelet's *Women of the French Revolution* (1854) was still in circulation, but the meticulous archival research by Alphonse Aulard (1849–1928) and his students in Paris was getting underway. In the 1890s both the giants of the next generation of revolutionary historiography, Aulard and the younger Albert Mathiez (1874–1932), published short, well-documented articles on revolutionary women's history.[48] In 1896 Marya Chéliga had published a densely packed article, "L'Évolution du féminisme," in the *Revue Encyclopédique Larousse*.[49] There she considered the history of women in the French Revolution, praising the abbé de Sièyes and the marquis de Condorcet for their recognition of women's role and rights. Chéliga then recounted the saga of the colorful Théroigne de Méricourt and discussed the first women's societies, mentioning various women's names that are hardly known to us today such as Mlle d'Orbe. She incorporated a long excerpt from Olympe de Gouges's "Declaration of

---

[46] "Féminisme macabre," *Le Journal du Peuple* (22 April 1899); cited by Madeleine Guilbert, *Les Femmes et l'organisation syndicale avant 1914* (Paris: Éditions du CNRS, 1966), p. 308.

[47] See Jean Elisabeth Pedersen, *Legislating the French Family: Feminism, Theater, and Republican Politics, 1870–1920* (New Brunswick, NJ: Rutgers University Press, 2003).

[48] See Aulard's articles, "Le Féminisme pendant la Révolution," *La Revue Bleue*, (19 March 1898), and "La Formation du parti républicain (1790–1791)," *La Révolution Française*, 35:4 (October 1898), 296–347. Mathiez published "Catherine Théot et le mysticisme révolutionnaire," in *La Révolution Française*, 40:6 (June 1901), 481–515.

[49] Chéliga, "L'Évolution du féminisme," *Revue Encyclopédique Larousse*, [special issue, "Les Femmes et les féministes"] n° 169 (28 November 1896), 910–913.

the Rights of Woman," remarked the presence in Paris of the English women's rights advocate Mary Wollstonecraft, and rehashed the drama of the closing of the women's clubs in 1793. This literature served to naturalize the history of feminism for the French, against the claims by nationalist antifeminists that feminism was a dangerous imported movement, originating in England and America. It is in this context that one must consider the important contribution by the journalist Léopold Lacour's *Les Origines du féminisme contemporain. Trois Femmes de la Révolution: Olympe de Gouges, Théroigne de Méricourt, Rose Lacombe* (1900), a reexamination of three of the best-known female figures of the revolutionary period.[50] Many more historical studies on women and the French Revolution would appear in the following decade.

The 1900 International Women's Congresses at the Paris Universal Exposition

The ongoing debates on the woman question would provide multiple topics for discussion at two major women's international congresses held during the 1900 Universal Exposition in Paris – at which French feminists again laid their demands on the table, including a call for the vote. These congresses would sanction the founding of the *Conseil National des Femmes Françaises* (CNFF) in 1901, which would quickly join the International Council of Women.

French feminists had already been out and about, building international networks, for several decades. Previous to the 1900 Universal Exposition in Paris, they had sent delegates to two important international congresses held in London during the summer of 1899 – the First International Congress on the White Slave Trade and the ensuing congress of the International Council of Women.[51] Another small contingent of French women activists

---

[50] Léopold Lacour, *Trois Femmes de la Révolution: Olympe de Gouges, Théroigne de Méricourt, Rose Lacombe* (Paris: Plon, 1900). On this work, see Laurence Klejman, "Léopold Lacour, les origines du féminisme contemporain ... ," in *Les Femmes et la Révolution française: L'effet'89*, vol. 3, ed. Marie-France Brive (Toulouse: Presses Universitaires du Mirail, 1991), 215–220. Another major historical study of women's history published in the 1890s, but which dealt with an earlier period, was *Les Femmes de la Renaissance* by René-Marie-Alphonse Maulde de Clavière (Paris: Perrin, 1898). This erudite work would appear in English translation as *The Women of the Renaissance,* but with the subtitle, *A Study of Feminism,* transl. George Ely (London: Sonnenschein, 1900; rev. ed., 1905).

[51] French delegates to the international congress on what was then called the "White Slave Trade" included Mlle Sarah Monod, Mme Oster, Mme Vincent as well as Senator René Bérenger & Henri Joly; other French feminists in attendance were Isabelle Bogelot, Mme Veuve Feresse-Deraismes, Mme Ferd. Dreyfus, Miss Gillian[?], and Mlle de Sainte-Croix (Savioz).

participated in the 15 May 1899 "international manifestation," a statement by women from eighteen countries that was presented at the opening of the Peace Conference convened in The Hague by the Tsar of Russia.[52] Feminists from France also traveled to Geneva for the annual conference of the *Fédération Abolitionniste Internationale* (FAI) [International Abolitionist Federation] in September 1899. In conjunction with the 1900 Universal Exposition, two clusters of French feminists decided to host their own international congresses, one in June and one in September, with differing objectives.[53] One group, headed by Marie Pégard, even attempted to secure a *Palais de la Femme*, modeled on the Woman's Building at the 1893 Chicago Columbian Exposition; lacking a government subsidy, the organizers nevertheless made it happen as a private initiative, offering a library and a reading room.[54] Another coalition of well-established feminist groups, including the *Société d'Amélioration* (SAFRED), *Égalité, Solidarité des Femmes*, the *Groupe Français d'Études Féministes* (GFEF), and the *Ligue Française pour les Droits des Femmes* (LFDF), organized an exhibition in the *Palais de l'Économie Sociale*, which displayed the history, founders, and contributions of their respective groups.[55]

The organizers of the first major congress to take place during the exposition, the *Deuxième Congrès International des Oeuvres et Institutions Féminines*, held in Paris from the 18th to the 23rd of June 1900, had obtained official backing (and financing) from the government of the French Third Republic. They invited the promoter of *Solidarité*, Léon Bourgeois, to lend his patronage to this gathering of women's charities and institutions. In the historiography of feminism, this congress has taken a back seat to the September 1900 women's rights congress, where calls to

---

[52] See *La Manifestation internationale des femmes pour la Conférence de la Paix, du 15 mai 1899, publiée par Mme L. Selenka* (Munich: A Schupp, 1900), in French, German, and English. This group assembled around Princess Wiszniewska (née Hucot) and Marya Chéliga's *Ligue des Femmes pour le Désarmament International*, subsequently known as the *Alliance Universelle des Femmes pour la Paix par l'Éducation* (founded in 1896; authorized in 1897). Their manifesto was framed in the name of "mothers, sisters, daughters, and wives, pleading in the name of the household and the child." See the materials in BMD dossiers Paix DOS 327 ALL, Paix DOS 70, and Paix DOS 327 GRO.

[53] The proceedings of the two 1900 congresses are published: see notes 37 and 38. Both are available on microfilm and online through the Gerritsen Collection of Women's History and through the website Women and Social Movements International.

[54] BMD, DOS: Congrès de 1900. Organized by Marie Pégard, the *Palais de la Femme* was situated between the Eiffel Tower and the Pont d'Iena, along the side of the Champs de Mars. See "Sylvie," "La Femme à l'Exposition," *Le Figaro*, (5 February 1900), for additional details.

[55] *Bulletin bimestriel* of the *Société pour l'Amélioration du Sort de la Femme et la Revendication de ses Droits* [*SASFRD*], 3rd sér., vol. 7, n°ˢ 2–3 (January–April 1900), 2–3. For a summary of the exhibition contents, see Klejman & Rochefort, *Égalité en marche*, pp. 140–141.

solidarity would also feature prominently. Its proceedings deserve to be examined in greater detail.[56]

The roots of this congress date back to 1888–1889, when Isabelle Bogelot attended the American suffragist congress (in Washington, D.C.) that founded the International Council of Women (ICW); she was named an officer of the ICW. In 1889, the American representative (and stalwart organizer) of the ICW, May Wright Sewall, had attended and spoken at the earlier (1889) First International Congress on Charities and Institutions, with the hope of jumpstarting the founding of a French national council of women to affiliate with the ICW. The Franco-American courtship continued through the 1890s, thanks to Sewall's series of visits to France and meetings with leading French feminists. Isabelle Bogelot and Sarah Monod sought to foster the development of common bonds among French women through the annual Conférence de Versailles (first convened in 1891), bringing together women philanthropists and leaders of charitable organizations throughout France, as well as a sprinkling of feminists, to discuss their common interests, and ultimately to encourage the charitable women to explore the causes of social problems, rather than to offer mere remedies. Bogelot continued her involvement, traveling to the Chicago Exposition in 1893, where she presented a copy of Jenny P. d'Hericourt's *La Femme Affranchie* to the World's Congress of Representative Women (organized by Sewall). In 1899 selected French feminists received personal invitations from the London organizing committee to attend the June London ICW congress, which would discuss both philanthropic and women's rights issues.

In June 1900, the Second International Congress on *Oeuvres et Institutions* convened, specifically to further the dual goals of national association and international collaboration by inviting representatives of the various French women's associations to report on their concerns and findings. The promotion of the national council project was uppermost in the organizers' minds.[57] It was a project-oriented congress, not an issue-oriented congress,

---

[56] On the educational efforts of the Solidarists, see *Congrès International de la Condition et des Droits des Femmes*, and especially *Congrès International de l'Éducation Sociale, 1900, tenu à Paris du 26 au 30 septembre 1900. Procès-verbal sommaire, par Mme Anna-M. Yon-Lampérière* (Paris, 1902).

Several authors spelled out the implications of Solidarist thought for women's education. See Anna Yon-Lampérière, *Le Rôle social de la femme* (2nd ed., Paris: F. Alcan, 1898); the posthumous works of Henri Marion, *Psychologie de la femme* (Paris: A. Colin, 1900) and *L'Éducation des jeunes filles* (Paris: A. Colin, 1902); and, subsequently, in Dr. Baptiste Roussy, *Éducation domestique de la femme et rénovation sociale* (Paris: Delagrave, 1914). Also see *La Grande Encyclopédie*, 17 (Paris, 1903), 143–170, s.v. "Femme" [articles by Henry de Varigny, Henri Marion, and other Solidarist writers].

[57] On Sewall's efforts to recruit the French women, see Karen Offen, "Overcoming Hierarchies through Internationalism: May Wright Sewall's Engagement with the International Council of

and it did ultimately contribute to the founding (1901) of the *Conseil National des Femmes Françaises* (CNFF), which will be discussed in the next chapter.

There was one major obstacle to the quest for a truly all-encompassing French umbrella association: the Catholic feminist women, led by Marie Maugeret, refused to take part, charging that there were too many Protestants (Maugeret also objected to fraternizing with Freemasons, socialists, and other free-thinking types). She especially objected to rubbing elbows with Jewish participants. Provoked by Émile Zola's *J'accuse* in early 1898, which had precipitated the revision trial of Captain Dreyfus's case later in the year, Maugeret's publication, *Le Féminisme Chrétien*, had begun to exhibit a virulent antisemitism (along with anti-immigrant sentiments), even as the secular feminists – particularly those associated with *La Fronde* – stood up for Dreyfus's innocence in the light of newly discovered evidence. The president of the LFDF Maria Pognon (who had succeeded Léon Richer upon his retirement), writing in *La Fronde* in January 1899 on behalf of "republicans and free thinkers," expressed her shock at this turn of events:[58]

> Is it true, Mesdames, that under the pretext of nationalism, you are preaching holy war? ... You speak of union, but you try to sow hatred and discord.... Is this the role that women should be playing? ... If we women do not demand justice for a condemned man who we have reason to believe is innocent, we have no right to demand justice for ourselves.

Marie Maugeret and her followers subsequently organized their own Catholic women's organization, the *Union Nationaliste des Femmes Françaises contre le 'Peril Juif'* [Nationalist Union of French Women Against the 'Jewish Peril'], and in June 1900 their own, exclusive congress, *Oeuvres catholiques des femmes*, a subcongress held from 3rd to 10th June (prior to the Oeuvres congress and the Rights congress) under the umbrella of the *Congrès International des Oeuvres Catholiques*.[59] Despite being a poorly

---

Women (1888–1904)," in *Unequal Sisters in Global Historical Perspective*, ed. Margaret Allen, June Purvis, Francisca de Haan, and Krassimira Daskalova (London: Routledge, 2013), pp. 15–27, and Offen, "From Washington to Paris and Back to Chicago: Building a Transatlantic Women's Network, 1888–1893, or 'The French Connection'," paper delivered at the American Historical Association, Chicago, January 2012.

[58] Maria Pognon, "Au Féminisme Chrétien," *La Fronde*, n° 441 (24 January 1899). Marguerite Durand was equally upset with the antisemitism exhibited by the writer Gyp, as several of her articles in *La Fronde* attest.

[59] See the issues of *Le Féminisme Chrétien* for April, May, July, and August 1900. There is no June issue in the Gerritsen online sequence. Maugeret's congress report appears in the May issue. Judging from internal context, the May issue appeared only after the congress ended, i.e., after 10 June. That

publicized and poorly attended gathering, closed to the press, Maugeret was nevertheless jubilant at the outcome, having introduced her pet feminist issues to other Catholic women and to the church: "Feminism in the hands of free-thinkers, with its mixed baggage of good and bad, with its personnel who are no less mixed than its theories, is the supreme artifice for snatching woman, and through woman the entire society, from the Church. It is important to expose this trap. This is the special mission of Christian Feminism."[60] Catholics must lead the way to "true" liberty, Maugeret insisted, so that French women are not misled by "false" liberty. Even so, Maugeret did consider the legal reform of property rights for wives to be an important goal, along with *recherche de la paternité* and the "right" to work (i.e., opposition to protective labor legislation for women).[61] Needless to say, the Oeuvres congress in June took place without the Catholic feminists, as would the Droits congress in September.

In August 1900 Maugeret would patiently but firmly lecture the ever hopeful May Wright Sewall, the American president of the ICW, about how impossible it would be for Catholic women to work with the secular feminists in establishing a national council: the ideas behind this made-in-America feminism were simply too Protestant, too free-thinking, and too contrary to the "true" French national tradition. "To hope that French Catholic women will rally to an organization initiated by foreigners, by Protestants and which, up to this time, has only been adopted in Europe by Protestant nations and in France by Protestant and free-thinking circles," wrote Marie Maugeret, "would be absurd. However ardent our feminism, it would never lead us to such a monstrosity."[62] Moreover, now that our group has been recognized by the Catholic congress, she said, we

---

report indicates that she was very unhappy that the Catholic women's congress sessions ran in parallel with the main Catholic congress, so that no one interested in the main congress could attend the women's meetings, and vice versa.

[60] Marie Maugeret, "Congrès Catholique des Oeuvres de Femmes: Compte-Rendu," *Le Féminisme Chrétien*, 5:5 (May 1900), 129–137; quote, 137.

[61] On Maugeret's activities, see Steven C. Hause, with Anne R. Kenney, *Women's Suffrage and Social Politics in the French Third Republic* (Princeton, NJ: Princeton University Press, 1984), pp. 61–67, and James F. McMillan, "Wollstonecraft's Daughters, Marianne's Daughters and the Daughters of Joan of Arc: Marie Maugeret and Christian Feminism in the French Belle Epoque," in *Wollstonecraft's Daughters: Womanhood in England and France, 1780–1920*, ed. Clarissa Campbell Orr (Manchester: Manchester University Press, 1996), pp. 186–198; and on Maugeret's publication, Anne Cova, *"Au service de l'église, de la Patrie et de la famille": Femmes catholiques et maternité sous la IIIe République* (Paris: L'Harmattan, 2000). Notwithstanding these excellent studies, it seems extremely difficult to find precise documentation on the Catholic women's "works" congress of 1900.

[62] Marie Maugeret," Lettre ouverte à Mme May Wright Sewall," *Le Féminisme Chrétien*, 5:8 (August 1900), 225–230.

are under a moral obligation to speak only with its agreement. "I have difficulty," she said, "seeing the members of a congress gathered together under the auspices of the archbishop of Paris, specially blessed by the sovereign Pontiff, adhering to a Protestant organization." If individual Catholic women want to do so, that is their business, but they may not speak on behalf of – or represent – the Catholic party. Maugeret's position couldn't be clearer – or less conciliatory.

Oeuvres et Institutions, June 1900

We must backtrack a bit to June 1900, before Marie Maugeret issued her ultimatum, to consider the Second Oeuvres et Institutions Congress and its impact. The executive committee of the *Conférence de Versailles* had taken the initiative and won governmental authorization as an "official" congress; they also obtained financial support from the Paris Municipal Council. Savioz announced the upcoming congress in *La Fronde* (24 July 1899). Significantly, Isabelle Bogelot, president of the *Oeuvre des Libérées de Saint-Lazare*, who had been engaged both officially (as treasurer) and unofficially with the ICW since 1888, was named honorary president of the organizing committee, along with Mme Jules Simon.[63] Sarah Monod, the highly respected Protestant deaconess and the longtime head of the *Conférence de Versailles*, served as president of the congress. According to the journalist Jane Misme, Monod was the "singlemost powerful person of the movement" [*unique grande puissance du mouvement*], the only leader capable of bringing together and governing the entire spectrum of femi-nists (though, in fact, Monod disclaimed the feminist label for herself) and of welcoming foreign delegates with dignity.[64] The champion of *Solidarité*, Léon Bourgeois was (as we have mentioned earlier) named as honorary president, and Marie Pégard, secretary-general of the *Société Française d'Émigration des Femmes* [French Society for Women's Emigration], would serve as secretary-general of the congress and as editor of the four volumes of proceedings. Maria Martin, editor of the *Journal des Femmes* (and also, earlier, succeeding Bogelot, as treasurer for the ICW), served as conference treasurer. In addition to the leaders of French Protestant philanthropy, the general staff of republican secular feminism was present at the Oeuvres

---

[63] Mme Jules Simon had been active in women's rights circles since the later 1860s, but we know virtually nothing about her, except that in 1900 she was the widow of Jules Simon, who had figured so prominently in the earlier woman question debates.

[64] Jane Misme, "Émancipatrices," *Le Figaro* (7 July 1899), p. 2.

congress, including Maria Pognon and Marie Bonnevial from the LFDF, Caroline Kauffmann from *Solidarité des Femmes*, the newly minted attorney Jeanne Chauvin, Eliska Vincent from *Égalité*, Marya Chéliga, and Savioz (since her marriage in May, now officially known as Mme Avril de Sainte-Croix). Although Marie Maugeret was not present, the Christian (Catholic) feminist Paule Vigneron did attend. The university-educated German feminists Kaethe Schirmacher and Anita Augspurg joined in the debates, as did Hanna Bieber-Böhm. Dr. Elizabeth Garrett-Anderson (one of the first three women admitted to the Paris Faculty of Medicine) attended, as did Alice Salomon (Germany), Camille Vidart and Pauline Chaix-Chaponnière (Switzerland), Callirhoë Parren (Greece), and a number of women from the Netherlands, Russia, Sweden, Finland, and other European countries. Also present was May Wright Sewall, the newly elected president of the ICW.

The agenda for this congress had to be negotiated with the government, so there were certain topics that could not be directly addressed. However, the problem of the legal situation of wives in marriage was on the agenda, as were other ongoing topics of concern such as establishing alimentary and educational support to children born out of wedlock, along with monetary support for their mothers. Maria Pognon argued for the establishment of publicly funded *caisses de maternité* in France, as the preferred alternative to either legalizing lawsuits for economic support (without admission of paternity), or legalizing paternity suits by abolishing Article 340 of the Civil Code. The resolutions put forward by Jeanne Chauvin and Marc Réville, on behalf of the congress's second section (Legislation and Morality), advocated maintaining the interdiction against *recherche de la paternité*, but amending the current law to allow – as the jurisprudence had already established – the possibility of mothers going to court for a maintenance allowance for the child (with no formal consequences about acknowledging paternity for the father) and a monetary subsidy for the mother. They argued that the law already provided such tools for addressing seduction and abandonment. The education section, on the initiative of Dr. Blanche Edwards-Pilliet, pushed through a resolution to establish preparatory courses for the *baccalauréat* in the girls' *lycées*.

The debates in the fourth section on women's work, chaired by Ghénia Avril de Saint-Croix (Savioz), proved particularly contentious. Under the title "The Freedom to Work," Maria Martin (the editor of the *Journal des Femmes*) gave a blistering report on the injustices caused by the so-called protective legislation of 1892, which had effectively put many women out of work. She claimed unfettered work as the "right to life" [*droit à la vie*] for women as well as for men. "If the law had been applicable to both sexes, we would have had nothing to complain about." She cited example after example to demonstrate how the current labor laws worked against women: "The laws are not made by women for women, but by men against women." This was strong language – and it would get even stronger![65]

> In the name of justice, in the name of equality, sacred principle of our Republic, in the name of humanity, we protest against every law that restricts the work of the *ouvrière* by placing unfavorable conditions around it and which leaves her no choice but a life of misery and privations – or prostitution. . . . Women, not being voters, cannot impose their will, but in the meantime we call upon just and humanitarian men to obtain for women and to conserve for them this most precious right: 'Free labor in a free country'.

Savioz focused her remarks on "the ill-starred influence of penal institutions, convents, and [even] philanthropic projects on forcing down women's wages." Charity, she claimed, makes its clients dependent. This was, to be sure, a classic liberal argument. The work done by girls and women in "caring" institutions, she emphasized, is done on the cheap and undermines the pay of women who are working outside such institutions; one particular religious order, she claimed, exploits over 47,000 girls in this way. Not only do these girls get no education, but they are also badly nourished. When these girls finally leave such establishments, they are good for nothing [*inaptes à faire quoi que ce soit*]. These girls are fodder for Saint-Lazare, even for the bordellos [*maisons de tolérance*]. A great proportion of them come from such industrial convents and from orphanages. Work is not a punishment; these workers should be paid the going wage – one called for by the *ouvrières* themselves and negotiated by the unions. Solidarity should and must replace charity, according to Savioz.[66]

Not everyone favored women's employment. Anna Lampérière spoke up in favor of women's mission in the home, regretting their propensity to want to leave it.[67] Raising children is women's "normal work" [*travail normal de la femme dans la société*], she insisted.[68] The men are meant to be

---

[65] Maria Martin's blistering report appears in *Deuxième Congrès International des Oeuvres et Institutions Féminines,* vol. 3; quotes, pp. 334, 337, 338.

[66] Avril de Sainte-Croix, in *Deuxième Congrès International des Oeuvres et Institutions Féminines,* vol. 3; quotes, pp. 428, 429, 431.

[67] See Anne Epstein, "Anna Lampérière, solidarité et citoyenneté féminine sous la Troisième République," *Genre & Histoire,* n° 3 (Fall 2008), consultable at www.genrehistoire.revues.org.

[68] Lampérière, at the *Oeuvres et Institutions* congress; the following quotes come from vol. 1, pp. 434, 435.

the breadwinners; thus, she declared, "we seek to give women the means to stay at home." When it came to a vote, the congress rejected as unrealistic Lampérière's proposal that women should not work outside the home. Certainly, given the hideous economic conditions that so many poorer women faced in 1900, her arguments were dismissed as so much wishful thinking.

Such radical proposals notwithstanding, a certain Léon Parsons, writing in the *Revue Bleue* in mid-July, characterized the Oeuvres congress as "more conservative than revolutionary, both in morals and in economics and politics."[69] He proclaimed the upcoming Droits congress as "*purement féministe*," and stated that the only way women would get what they want was to constitute themselves as a "class." "The feminist movement is a historical necessity," he insisted. The economic and juridical causes of their problem must be addressed, and men needed to understand its causes, to study them "and to give immediate satisfaction to the "*revendications féminines*." In a second article, following on the Droits Congress, Parsons insisted that "Feminism is a [political] party, having for its objective to demand certain economic, civil, and political rights for all women."[70] From the chaos of 1896, he posited, order has come forth, "a homogeneous party, seeking immediate and practical reforms, has replaced the party of vain agitation that early on characterized feminism." Parsons was clearly impressed. He had reason to be.

The editor and organizers of the *Oeuvres et Institutions* congress viewed the publication of the immense 2,500-page proceedings, with all the reports and precise transcriptions of the discussions, as a monument that "will pinpoint the state of the question at the end of the nineteenth century."[71] Writing in the *RMS*, a subsequent commentator, Madeleine Saint-Morand, provided the public with a summary of these four volumes, which she aptly characterized as a foundational work.[72] In contemporary terms we would consider this publication to be a "*lieu de mémoire*." It has yet to be thoroughly analyzed by historians.

---

[69] Léon Parsons, "Les Congrès de l'exposition: Oeuvres et Institutions féminines," *La Revue Bleue* (14 July 1900), 56–59, and "Les Congrès de l'exposition: Entre féministes," *La Revue Bleue* (20 October 1900), 501–504. The quotes are on pp. 56, 58, and 59.

[70] Parsons, "Les Congrès," pt. 2, p. 501.

[71] To date historians of French feminism have skipped lightly over this congress and its contributions. However, its four volumes of published proceedings deserve closer examination as concerns the French debates on the woman question. See *Oeuvres et Institutions* Proceedings, Introduction, p. 8.

[72] Madeleine Saint-Morand, "Livre d'Or du Féminisme," *RMS*, n° 16 (vol. 4, 1903), 483–497.

Condition et Droits Congress – 5–8 September 1900

The September congress, organized by Maria Pognon (LFDF), Marie Bonnevial and Eliska Vincent (*Égalité*), with Marguerite Durand of *La Fronde* serving as secretary-general,[73] threw the spotlight on the issues of economic rights, women's education, and civil rights – but it also highlighted a call for women's suffrage. One might view its program as fully complementary to that of the *Oeuvres et Institutions* congress that preceded it. Unlike the Rights congress of 1889, it was not a "breakaway" congress. Like the Oeuvres congress it too sought and acquired official status. The Prospectus bragged that "the acceptance by the Government of the French Republic of a program to study feminist demands proves how far things have come and should encourage those whose goal is the improvement of women's condition in their efforts."[74] This congress and the issues it planned to address had the government's seal of approval. Who could dare maintain, in the face of such evidence as this, that "the Republic" was bad for women?

At the Rights congress, unlike its predecessor (designated as an all-female affair, except for the presidency of Léon Bourgeois), a number of men were involved in the planning committee and as speakers.[75] The committee included Hubertine Auclert, a number of women from the LFDF including the veteran feminist Amélie Hammer, Jeanne Oddo (Oddo-Deflou) and Camille Bélilon from the *Groupe Français d'Études Féministes*, two women from the national federation (mixed) of tobacco workers, Mme Allpeter and Mme Jacoby, Caroline Kauffmann from *Solidarité des Femmes*, and a number of women who held administrative positions in the public assistance sector such as Olympe Gevin-Cassal and Flor Mauriceau, along with several men who also held official governmental positions. Mrs. Chapman, now "*directrice*" of the *Westminster Review*, also served on this committee, as well as Mary Léopold Lacour and Savioz.

---

[73] In fact, Marguerite Durand replaced Savioz as secretary-general of the Rights congress; the latter had withdrawn in later 1899 for reasons of health; see Savioz, "Le Féminisme à l'Exposition universelle," *RMS*, n° 8 (vol. 2, n° 4, December 1900), 505–512.

[74] Official Congress Prospectus issued by the *Ministère du Commerce, Industrie, des Postes et des Telegraphes, Exposition Universelle de 1900. Direction Générale de l'Exploitation. Congrès Internationaux. Congrès international de la Condition et des Droits des Femmes* (Paris, 1900). Consulted in the Gerritsen Collection of Women's History, microfilm n° 573.1.

[75] In *Women's Suffrage and Social Politics*, Hause & Kenney provide only one paragraph on the Droits congress, focusing on the suffrage debates (admittedly, the focus of their book is on suffrage in the period after 1900); Klejman & Rochefort offer a somewhat more extensive treatment in *Égalité en marche*, pp. 141–147.

Speakers who had also attended the previous congress included Vincent, Elisabeth Renaud from the *Groupe Féministe Socialiste* (GFS), Blanche Edwards-Pilliet, and the LFDF's Maria Pognon (again pushing her notion of establishing *caisses de maternité* as an alternative to legalizing *recherche de la paternité*). Contemporaries such as Léon Parsons, whose articles are cited earlier in this chapter, were impressed by the presence of a sizeable number of working-class women and the overall tenor of the congress.

The Rights congress program had three parts: 1) economic, moral, and social questions; 2) education; and 3) legislation (civil law and political rights). In each section, the organizers called for some form or another of state action to ensure equality of treatment: on behalf of single mothers, integral education for both sexes, access for girls to programs leading to the *baccalauréat* and to the careers it opened for them, etc.

In fact, the debates of the first section focused heavily on problems concerning women's employment, further proof – if further proof were needed – that feminists were greatly concerned about women's work. As Marie Bonnevial remarked in her report to the congress, "The organizing committee of the congress thought it necessary to give questions concerning work first place in its program, because it deemed that the economic enfranchisement of woman is the point of departure and the basis for her complete liberation."[76] Given the huge discrepancies between men's pay and women's pay, women's work "is shamefully exploited."[77] "By what right is it decreed that the woman should be paid less than the man because she does not have the same needs as he does?" Bonnevial did not mince words when it came to critiquing the shortsightedness and selfishness of employers under the capitalist regime. She spoke harshly as well of women's timidity and resignation, and of the convent labor that undercut the wages other women could earn in the marketplace. "Who gave men the right to say to us: 'The domain of your activity extends only to here; mine encompasses everything'?" As for the question of *la femme au foyer*, Bonnevial reminded her listeners that (as Juliette Lamber[t] Lamessine Adam had so eloquently done nearly fifty years earlier), "the period of maternity does not absorb a woman's entire life." Bonnevial reminded her audience that many women in France were, in fact, single or widowed, or if married, had sick, disabled, or unemployed husbands. She praised the efforts of Marguerite Durand to stimulate the formation of unions for women workers in some female-only fields. It would be ridiculous to deny

[76] "Rapport de Mlle Marie Bonnevial, rapporteur," Droits congress, p. 28–29.
[77] Droits congress, p. 29. The subsequent quotes are on pp. 31 and 37.

that these feminists of 1900 were addressing head on the myriad problems and issues concerning women's work. They had laid the major issues on the table for debate; the next step would be to identify and implement solutions. The biggest disagreements came to a head over the question of protective legislation for women only; in the end the congress voted against all laws of exception, and for equal treatment of both sexes.[78]

There was, to be sure, a brief confrontation over the question of employers providing a full day off for household servants, provoked by Elisabeth Renaud, a former governess in Russia and spokeswoman for the GFS. She confronted a speaker named Mme Wiggishoff (from the *Société pour l'Amélioration du Sort de la Femme et la Revendication de ses Droits,* or SASFRD), who had asked where such workers would eat on their day off. *"Chez vous,"* Renaud retorted.[79] This exchange comes up again and again in one historian's analysis as indicative of the bad faith of bourgeois women with respect to the women of the working class; indeed, it has taken on the status of an urban legend.[80] When viewed from within the broader context of the Second International's dissatisfaction with the advances being made by the feminist movement among working women, it seems perfectly clear that Renaud was deliberately baiting Wiggishoff.[81]

To blow this incident up into a major conflict in class relations seems not only inaccurate but also irresponsible; what is more, it deforms our understanding of the sizeable achievement of this congress. It is time to set the record straight. What is not reported is Mme Wiggishoff's full response, after she jokingly said that she would probably not make lunch for her domestic help on the day off. To the prospect of a full day off for a young domestic worker, which might throw her out on the streets where only trouble awaited her, Wiggishoff proposed an alternative solution, that

---

[78] Some historians, heavily influenced in the 1970s by the tone and vocabulary of the socialist left, nevertheless criticized the Rights congress as overwhelmingly "bourgeois" in character, highlighting a particular moment in the debates on women's work as exemplary of an unbridgeable divide between "bourgeois" and "proletarian" women. See notably Charles Sowerwine, *Sisters or Citizens? Women and Socialism in France since 1876* (Cambridge, UK: Cambridge University Press, 1982), chapters 3 & 4. For his analysis of the 1900 Droits congress, see pp. 74–80.

[79] *Congrès International de la Condition et des Droits des Femmes,* p. 75.

[80] See Sowerwine, *Sisters or Citizens,* p. 88.

[81] Despite efforts by subsequent historians of French feminism to place this incident in perspective, Sowerwine's interpretation persists. See Marilyn J. Boxer, "Socialism Faces Feminism in France: 1879–1913," Ph.D. dissertation, University of California, Riverside, 1975, as well as Klejman & Rochefort, *Égalité en marche* (pp. 142–144) who underscore Renaud's ulterior motive –which was to dissuade women workers from aligning with the "bourgeois" feminists. In fact, Elisabeth Renaud subsequently became very involved with the LFDF, attending its meetings, and writing in its publications.

of limiting daily hours of work for servants, especially for those who were underage, so they would have some time to themselves each day. This response effectively silenced Renaud. In fact, no irreconcilable rift developed between working women and the philanthropic women and feminists, either at the Rights congress or later, despite the efforts of Renaud and her associate Louise Saumoneau to provoke one (much as Clara Zetkin and Alexandra Kollontai would continue to do in their respective German and Russian settings). In fact, in her closing speech the president of the congress, Maria Pognon, addressed this seemingly deliberate effort to create a rift, emphasizing that "we must tear down this wall of hatred that you are trying to establish between us. We hold out our hand to you, loyally and genuinely. Why don't you grasp it? Have you perhaps come here to provide systematic opposition because you are *ouvrières* and you call us bourgeois?"[82]

It was also in this first section of the Droits congress that Savioz presented her impassioned report on the history and consequences of state-sanctioned prostitution internationally.[83] Drawing on evidence from around the world (the practices of the British Army in India; the Heinze Law in imperial Germany; a litany of abuses in the Netherlands and their colonies; in Belgium, Italy, Switzerland, Russia, and the United States), Savioz issued a battle cry for a single moral standard for both sexes. This bar-no-holds speech would quickly propel her to the forefront of the international campaign against the traffic in women as well as against regulated prostitution, a campaign she would spearhead during the next thirty-odd years.[84] She also forcefully articulated her public disagreement with Senator Bérenger's insistence that the government regulation of prostitution had little to do with the flagrantly growing international "white slave traffic." To Savioz, it was essential to demonstrate the links between these two phenomena and to use this connection as a lever to combat and end regulation. "Iniquitous in principle, the regime of the morals police is deplorable in its consequences, because, having suppressed

[82] Pognon, in *Condition et des Droits 1900*, p. 291.
[83] "Rapport de Mme Savioz de Sainte-Croix," *Condition et des Droits*, pp. 97–111; subsequently republished as *Une Morale pour les deux sexes* (Paris: Imprimerie Paul Dupont, 1900). An autographed copy dedicated to Louise Michel resides in the collection of the International Archive for Social History (Amsterdam); thanks to Marilyn J. Boxer for this information. This text was also published in Dutch translation as *Een moraal voor de twee geslachten. Rede uitgesproken door Savioz (Madame Avril de Sainte-Croix) op het internationaal congres over den toestand en de rechten der vrouw, gehouden te Parijs van 5–8 september 1900. (Vertaald door P.B.)* (Amsterdam: Versluys, 1900); my thanks to Petra de Vries for this reference.
[84] Savioz quotes below from *Condition et des Droits 1900*, pp. 108, 100, 101, 102.

women's liberty, it also suppresses – in the same breath – men's responsibility," she asserted. In her view, the State thereby infringes women's liberty, obviates equality, and also affronts morality. She tied the growing problem of prostitution squarely to the perceived problems of falling off rates of marriage and births and highlighted again the 1899 medical findings that showed the rate of infected women as actually higher in the regulated brothels than among the prostitutes who lived and practiced their trade outside the control of the morals police.

In the course of her report, Savioz publicly thanked Marguerite Durand for having had the courage to publish her earlier articles on this subject "that no other paper would publish."[85] Invoking history from ancient to modern times, Savioz insisted that the sole role of the police should be to "prevent scandal on the streets." In going beyond this mission, she charged, the state violated Articles One, Five, Six, and Seven of the Declaration of the Rights of Man regarding liberty, equality, and morality as they concerned women. Since women did not yet have the vote, she asserted that politicians only accorded these injustices "a relative importance." No woman could ignore this outrage; women must begin to fight back: [86]

> We do not want a woman, whoever she is, to be subjected to laws of exception. Like man, she is a human being with a right to her integral autonomy, and we protest against every kind of regulation that, under the pretext of safeguarding the health of men, or even the family, sanctions and consolidates the principle of a double morality for the two sexes.

This strongly phrased argument, invoking women's human rights as individuals, along with a higher, single standard of morality, was utterly in line with the approach of the great British abolitionist, Josephine Butler.[87] Following this speech by Savioz, the Congress passed a resolution: "Considering that the principle of different morals and responsibilities for the two sexes is inadmissible, the Congress demands that all exceptional measures as concerns morals be abrogated."[88] This resolution too was entirely in line with the earlier resolutions concerning women's

---

[85] *Condition et des Droits 1900,* p. 107.   [86] *Condition et des Droits 1900,* p. 110.

[87] Note that in 1889, the centenary of the French Revolution, Josephine Butler wrote to her Swiss colleagues (Aimé Humbert and Charles Secrétan) as follows: "Il nous paraît propice d'annoncer à très haute voix le fait que la moitié de la race humaine, c'est-à-dire les femmes, n'est pas satisfaite de cette célébration, car, en pratique, les 'droits de l'homme' n'ont jamais été étendus egalement à la femme." Quoted in Anne-Marie Käppeli, *Sublime Croisade: Ethique et politique du féminisme protestant, 1875–1928* (Carouge-Genève: Éditions Zoé, 1990), p. 33.

[88] *Condition et des Droits 1900,* p. 111.

employment. Liberty and equality – for women as well as for men – these were the guiding principles of the Rights Congress.

Calling for Equal Rights for Women, 1900

The third section of the Rights congress actually encompassed two parts: private (i.e., civil) law and public law. The session began with the most significant issue in public law, namely, women's demand for the vote. Presiding at the session, Marguerite Durand expressed again the argument that generations of her predecessors had put forward: the vote is "the weapon without which no struggle can succeed today.... We must not solicit it as a favor but we must demand it as a right ... in order to obtain the power to make the laws, and to enact the reforms that cannot be achieved in the present state of affairs."[89] Durand did not mention "universalism," but she made it clear that no distinction between the sexes should be possible in France's "general laws." "The French Revolution, which proclaimed the rights of man, suppressed the rights that women formerly enjoyed. Later, Napoléon was similarly unjust to them." Durand pointed out that public opinion was turning in favor of reforming the Code; even the judges, she noted, were ruling in women's favor. Nevertheless, the laws forbidding paternity searches and punishing adulterous wives remained stubbornly in place.

With that, Durand ceded the floor to René Viviani (the socialist-feminist deputy and longtime supporter of the LFDF who had agreed to present the feminists' resolutions to the Chamber of Deputies) for his report. Viviani, who would play a stellar role in the debates on woman suffrage, introduced his remarks by stating that he was a proponent of a new kind of family, an alternative to the (authoritarian) family constructed by the current code in which all privileges were vested in the husband. In his vision, this new family would be an association "where, with respect to the children, the mother is the equal of the father."[90] "We want marriage to be a free association where the spouses have equal rights." This has nothing to do, he assured his listeners, with what some call "free love." That, he claimed, is an "ambush" and a "trap" for women; he also rejected the notion of "term marriage," at the end of which the husband could

---

[89] Marguerite Durand, introducing the debates in the third section, *Condition et des Droits 1900*, p. 193.
[90] René Viviani, in *Condition et des Droits 1900,* p. 196. Viviani's remarks were reported in extenso in *La Fronde*, n° 1006 (10 September 1900), and his speech was republished early the following year as "La Femme," in *La Grande Revue* (1 February 1901), 331–356.

throw out the wife.[91] He rejected the male-breadwinner argument as justification for giving husbands all the legal authority, calling it inapplicable to current conditions in which so many men could not earn enough to support families, and women must find paid employment to make ends meet for their families.

In Viviani's view, there was no getting around the hard fact that French women must become voters in order to realize the feminist program. "In the name of my relatively long political and parliamentary experience," he declared to the assembled delegates at the women's rights congress, "let me tell you that the legislators make the laws for those who make the legislators."[92] That is to say, only voters count and those without a vote have no power or influence as concerns legislation. He stated his objections to the various arguments raised against giving women political rights. First, the argument that political rights for men hinged on their military service; "Right(s) do not depend on force," he stated; "they are attached to the individual." Viviani supported a woman's right to invoke her special mission of maternity as the equivalent of men's military service, and he also pointed out that there were a number of men who were exempt from military service: priests, teachers, professors, and those with certain types of diplomas. He then addressed the economic arguments, and finally he spoke to the objections by those who actually favored women's emancipation and political rights in principle but were fearful for the future of French democracy, given that most French women were allegedly still under the thumb of the Catholic Church. If that were really the case, he proposed, then the secular and laic regime had not done its job. Men, he concluded, had not done such a great job in France to date either; given the ravages of alcoholism, gambling, and other vices, it seemed that these were signs of the emergence of a new kind of barbarism. In sum, Viviani maintained that it was becoming urgent to defend the patrimony of civilization. Without adding women as voters, he insisted, "society will lurch from torment to torment and from abyss to abyss."[93] Without women's input into French political life, he implied, human progress would encounter a rough road going forward.

In the debates on the various congress resolutions proposed by the organizing committee concerning civil laws, two men spoke up against the provisions of marriage law that decreed women's obedience; a German

[91] Viviani, in *Condition et des Droits des Femmes*, p. 198.
[92] Viviani, in *Condition et des Droits des Femmes*, p. 201.
[93] Viviani, in *Condition et des Droits des Femmes*, p. 204.

spokesman (von Gerlach) insisted that the congress's resolution should go beyond French law to address the laws of all countries, at least those that were "civilized." The congress accepted his proposition, unanimously voting that "all laws that impose on the wife obedience to her husband must be abolished."[94] The congress also accepted a resolution on behalf of adding divorce by mutual consent (with a built-in timetable) to the possible grounds on which (civil) divorce could be demanded. This proposal engendered significant debate and a number of amendments, all of which were voted down. Many other resolutions concerning changes in the law were presented, amended, debated, and accepted (or rejected). A resolution calling for legalization of *recherche de la paternité* was disputed, as usual, by Maria Pognon, who (as she had at the earlier Oeuvres congress) promoted the alternative solution of a *caisse de maternité*. Not wanting to favor one option over the other (or offend Pognon), the congress voted in favor of both.[95]

With regard to proposals for amending public law, many addressed discriminatory restrictions on applying for jobs in public administration (such as requiring military service as a prerequisite, which effectively excluded women candidates). The culmination of all these reports and debates was the comprehensive resolution proposed by the committee: "The Congress resolves that civil, civic and political rights should be equal for both sexes."[96] Léon Richer could be proud! The time was ripe. The question was called and the proposition voted unanimously. This measure, of course, encompassed political rights (without stipulating exactly how those might be parsed out). The final piece of business was the approval of the congress for naming three delegates to participate in the founding of a National Council of French Women (*Conseil National des Femmes Françaises*; CNFF).[97]

In *La Fronde* Marguerite Durand offered a summing-up statement in mid-September. She highlighted her effort to publish a stenographic transcript of the proceedings, day by day, to ensure that the public had access to what was actually being said. She denied allegations that the congress was either beholden to the socialists or opposed to the socialists, making explicit her view that feminism was beholden to no political party

---

[94] *Condition et des Droits des Femmes*, pp. 209–211, 215.

[95] The stenographic report of the debates on these two topics extends from pp. 261 to 274.

[96] "Le congrès émet le voeu que les droits civils, civiques et politiques soient égaux pour les deux sexes." *Condition et des Droits des Femmes*, resolution 25, p. 305.

[97] The story of the founding of the CNFF and the development of its program for answering the woman question will continue in the next chapter.

and would not be identified with one. "[Feminism] should call on all parties and not believe blindly in the promises of any party." Which [party] will help us protect the labor of the *ouvrière* against the competition of child labor? Which [party] will help us protect the child against its exploiter and against its own family? Since neither the clericals or the socialists will do so, she said, we call on the men of other political parties and we will be happy to acknowledge whatever help they can provide. She also made clear her belief that the future of feminism lay with proletarian women: "they will make the revolution for their bourgeois sisters," she said. But she also reminded readers that the "arms" require the leadership of the "head," and thus her "constant preoccupation has been and will be to interest those women in the feminist cause who are knowledgeable and who reason, those who are not guided solely by instinct." Such women were once reticent, but they are now coming aboard, she indicated; even some who publish in *La Fronde*, who were initially skeptical about our ideas, "are now our most heated partisans, our most devoted defenders."[98]

Marie Bonnevial, who had taken such an active role in the Droits congress, published her own summary in *Le Mouvement Socialiste* (15 October & 1 November 1900). Opposing the perspective of separatist socialists like Elisabeth Renaud, she argued that it was the *duty* of socialist women (like herself) to get involved in the feminist movement, even if it were "bourgeois," because in her view, the so-called bourgeoisie was well worth conquering, and once won over, it would follow through. "Many of them [bourgeois women], very sincere, march hand in hand with the *ouvrières* toward the conquest of our rights, toward emancipation not only of woman, but of humanity."[99]

Camille Vidart, from Switzerland, lectured in Geneva on both congresses in early November 1900. She appropriately noted the significant differences between the "*deux grandes fractions*" as well as the Catholics' separate congress.[100] She was particularly impressed with the collaboration of both sexes at the two congresses: at the Droits congress she remarked that "the women put forth claims not only for themselves, but also for men, on the questions of wages, hours of work, etc. There was a feeling of solidarity between the sexes," she maintained. Everyone agreed on a number of points: that wives should be able to control their own property;

[98] Marguerite Durand, "Après le Congrès," *La Fronde*, n° 1010 (14 September 1900), 1.

[99] Marie Bonnevial, "Le Congrès de la Condition et des Droits des Femmes," *Le Mouvement Socialiste*, n° 44 (15 October 1900), 503–512, & n° 45 (1 November 1900), 539–548.

[100] "Les Congrès féminins," clipping attributed to *Le Signal de Genève*, (17 November 1900), in the Avril de Sainte-Croix scrapbooks, reel 3 (1898–1900). BMD: DOS AVR mf.

that children born outside marriage should also have rights; that there should be a single moral standard for both sexes, as well as integral education and equal pay. Disagreement still existed, however, on the question of regulating women's work. She did not make much of the confrontation of Renaud with Wiggishof, merely indicating that relations between employers and employees, including domestics, had been a subject of discussion.

Summing up both congresses later that year, Savioz applauded the way in which both had converged in their goals, especially as concerned revising the Civil Code articles concerning wives.[101] The major point of disagreement, she pointed out (as had Camille Vidart), came over the subject of whether or not women's work should be regulated by the state. Interestingly, the *Oeuvres et Institutions* congress came out for women's unrestricted right to work, while the Rights congress voted in favor of protective legislation – but protection that would encompass both sexes. Both congresses had endorsed coeducation, thanks to the leadership of Pauline Kergomard. The biggest criticism made by Savioz was that both congresses had been more French-centered than internationalist.[102] She welcomed the advent of "the grand national party of women" [*le grand parti national des femmes*] in France. As well she might. "It is by love, I speak here in the elevated sense of that word, that the New Eve will triumph."[103]

The leaders of the Third Republic had cooperated in making these congresses possible. Now the men who governed had been put on notice as to what was expected from them to advance women's interests in the years ahead. The case for change was well argued and it would be heard, though the road to implementation would be strewn with legislative obstacles and, therefore, progress would be excruciatingly slow.

---

[101] Savioz, "Le féminisme à l'Exposition universelle," *RMS*, n° 8 (vol. 2, n° 4, December 1900), 505–512. A copy can also be consulted at the BMD: DOS Congrès 84.
[102] Savioz, "Féminisme à l'Exposition universelle," p. 512.
[103] Savioz, "Féminisme à l'Exposition universelle," p. 507.

PART III

Climax
Mainstreaming the Woman Question, 1901–1914

France, is, in the opinion of the entire world, the paradise of woman.
Inaugural issue of Femina (1 February 1901)

* * *

We have risen up in solidarity, all of us, women of all classes whom injustice and sorrow have made sisters and – all of us, the enchained, the sacrificed – we are rising up menacing, against the abominable, accursed Law, and the clamor of our revolts will rise higher than the smoke of your incense, wicked or stupid adorers of this monument of infamy [the Civil Code]. All women, in whatever situation chance has allowed them to be born into, have an interest in a profound upheaval. There are not, among us, "governing classes" or "privileged classes." We can all go to war against the present Society, for we are all, according to the law, more or less plundered, battered, and violated in our bodies, our hearts, and our consciences.

Nelly Roussel, speech protesting the centennial of the Civil Code
La Fronde, 1 November 1904

* * *

Feminism is, like Socialism, an anti-French sickness! . . . I object to feminism because it allows women to envisage happiness as independent of love and external to love.

Théodore Joran
Le Mensonge du féminisme (1905)

* * *

The forward march of feminism is a fact that no one can deny, a movement that no force can henceforth bring to a halt. Woman has become a social and political factor to be reckoned with.

Ghénia Avril de Sainte-Croix
La Revue, Revue des revues, 1906

* * *

Not content to exercise his omnipotence over persons and to bend
everything according to his interest or his fantasy, HE has even
disequilibreated the sciences, which by their abstract nature, would
seem to be able to escape the influence of caprice and partiality. Man,
in effect, has not even wanted the two sexes to be equal in
grammar.... . Since childhood we have been inculcated with the
notion that ..."The *masculin* always takes precedence over the
féminin."

Jeanne Deflou
Le Sexualisme, 1906

* * *

The generative function – with all its physiological and moral consequences – is certainly the most serious thing, the primordial and dominant thing about feminine existence. Adversaries and partisans of feminist
theories agree on this fact. And it is somewhat curious to attest that this
generative function furnishes both sides with their supreme argument,
their climactic point, in support of their reasoning. But, insofar as the first
insist on seeing in this [function] only a cause of woman's essential and
irremediable inferiority and a rationale for her subordination (a primitive
notion, worthy of barbarous times when the "right of the strongest" was
the only rule), the second, inspired by the modern ideal of justice, would
like it to become, for she who accomplishes it, a source of material and
moral advantages, independence, influence, and well-being; and in its
name they formulate their principal demands.

Nelly Roussel
"Pour les Mères," *L'Almanach Féministe, 1907*

* * *

Under no pretext should a feminist prefer the [political] party she has
entered to feminism itself, for while she serves the party, she belongs
only to feminism and to no other cause. A woman, like any individual, may be a socialist, a republican, or a monarchist according to her
convictions, but before all else she should be a feminist. For under a
monarchy, a republic, or socialism, she will not be counted unless the
political equality of the sexes becomes a reality.

Dr. Madeleine Pelletier
La Revue Socialiste (April 1908)

* * *

To obtain a venue [for a candidate meeting], one must be a candidate; to be a candidate, one must be eligible; to be eligible, one must
be a voter; to be a voter, one must be of the masculine sex ... and to
be of the masculine sex?"

Maria Vérone, 1908
Quoted in *Le Matin*, (28 avril 1908)

* * *

People have called us [women] the eternally wounded, but we don't want to be the wounded, the infirm who need to be nourished [by someone else]. You want to condemn us, along with yourselves, to marriage; and if we don't want to marry, we will be eternally prostituted, because the men [will] still need to nourish us; we do not want to be kept women, neither legally nor illegally. . . . It is a question of dignity – when a woman can work, she ought to work.

Maria Vérone,
Bulletin de la Ligue des Droits de l'Homme, 1909

* * *

The woman should work, like the man, with the same pay as he gets, not only because she needs to eat or to feed others, as he does, but because she has the right to the full independence of a free being. *Earning one's living is a guarantee of dignity.*

Louise Compain
La Femme dans les organisations ouvrières, 1910

* * *

And I return from Budapest more persuaded than ever that women's suffrage is the key to every humanitarian, philanthropic or social movement. We must have it first. Without it we can do nothing. It's putting the cart before the horse to occupy ourselves with antialcoholism, equal moral standard, worker legislation, protection of children without having the ballot. Let us conquer that first. Let us unite for that. We will even abandon immediately our daily tasks, our most pressing duties, which we will again take up once we have won it – with success as women citizens and as women legislators.

Emilie Gourd (Geneva)
Le Mouvement féministe, 10 August 1913

* * *

There can be no class struggles between women, no more than there can be racial struggles, because from top to bottom of the human condition and from one end of the earth to the other, for century after century, [women] have formed an immense class, a universal race, oppressed by a single domination under which, in diverse forms, they all suffer.

Jane Misme
La Française, n° 322 (13 June 1914)

* * *

Introductory Remarks

The first decade of the new century witnessed the full flowering of the woman question debates as well as the beginnings of feminist institutionalization in France. Following the Third Republic's enactment in 1901 of laws that granted freedom of association, new women's organizations began to spring up everywhere, and debates on the woman question proliferated at public and private meetings and in a host of new periodicals and books, as well as in the daily press.[1]

Significant debates continued on a wide range of subjects, many ongoing and some new: among these were amending the Civil Code, legalizing paternity suits, ameliorating conditions surrounding women's employment, addressing regulated prostitution and the traffic in women, combatting unhygienic urban slum conditions which had become host sites for rampant alcoholism and tuberculosis, and asserting women's role in fostering peace. The intersection of women's demands for legal and economic emancipation, the population crisis, worries about the future of French democracy, and concerns over French national security continued to provide the contextual framework in which these debates were articulated.

What was new would be the far more overt critiques of the prevailing double standard in sexual customs, proposals for sex education of girls prior to marriage, conflicts over sexual freedom, including women's right to control their own bodies by championing contraception or, alternatively, by proclaiming the virtues of virginity. Heated controversies broke out over women's employment, especially the explosion of exploitative *travail à domicile*, or home work, the unionization of women workers, claims for equal pay for equal work, and for married women's right to

---

[1] See Laurence Klejman & Florence Rochefort, *L'Egalité en marche: Le Féminisme sous la Troisième République* (Paris: FNSP & des femmes, 1989), chapter 5, for the details of the various feminist organizations and study groups founded from 1900 on. On the proliferation of women's philanthropic organizations after passage of the new law on associations in 1901, see Evelyne Diebolt, *Les femmes dans l'action sanitaire, sociale et culturelle, 1901–2001: Les associations face aux institutions* (Paris: Femmes et Associations, 2001), and *Un siècle de vie associative: quelles opportunités pour les femmes? Colloque international tenu à l'Assemblée nationale et au Centre historique des Archives nationales les 14–15–16- mai 2001 pour la commémoration du centenaire de la loi 1901*, ed. Evelyne Diebolt & Christiane Demeulenaere-Douyère (Paris: Femmes et Associations, 2002), and Evelyne Diebolt, ed., *Militer au XXe siècle. Femmes, féminismes, Églises et société: Dictionnaire biographique* (Paris: Michel Houdiard Éditeur, 2009). These organizational histories will not be discussed here, except insofar as members of these organizations contributed in print to the debates on the woman question or became leaders in the major national feminist groups such as the CNFF, the UFSF, or the LFDF.

work. By the end of the decade, there was a significant resurgence of activity among feminists in obtaining votes for women, so that they could effect the wide range of legal, economic, and social changes they demanded and could have a say on questions of war and peace. Indeed, the tide was slowly turning in favor of emancipating French women, especially as wives and mothers: feminist perspectives continued to acquire traction in French public opinion and to attract support from a widening circle of women and men. Not surprisingly, the opponents of feminist goals would become far more vociferous, if not more convincing. The arguments for and against women's emancipation would become more elaborate, even as positions for and against would solidify.

CHAPTER 9

Building a Force to Reckon with the Republic
The Conseil National des Femmes Françaises *and Its Allies, 1900–1914*

The *Oeuvres et Institutions* congress of 1900 voted unanimously in favor of founding a national council of French women. But the necessary unity of the various factions of feminists was far from assured. Writing on "the three segments of feminism" in the *Le Journal des Femmes* issue of July–August 1900 (prior to the Rights congress in September) Jeanne Deflou characterized the segment on the right as the "cautious" reformers (those interested primarily in revising married women's legal position and in opening the professions to women); the segment on the left would comprise the socialists – especially the collectivist socialists – who insisted that change in women's situation would come only through class struggle and the defeat of capitalism. A third segment, she argued, had now emerged (with the Oeuvres congress), which, though branded by some as "conservative," had dared to debate two of the most important issues of the day: married women's lack of property rights and *recherche de la paternité.*[1] She likened these segments to three parts of a dismembered serpent, the head, the tail, and the body, arguing that if and when they could be reunited the serpent would indeed be a creature to reckon with. Building out on the unsuccessful attempt by Eugénie Potonié-Pierre in the 1890s to establish an enduring *Fédération féministe*, the mostly Protestant women behind the *Conférence de Versailles* had taken up the challenge, spearheading current efforts to establish a national council to affiliate with the International Council of Women (ICW). Would they succeed? Nothing seemed less clear to Jeanne Deflou in the summer of 1900, given the acuity of the religious differences – Catholic on the Right, Protestants in the middle, and Free-thinkers on the Left. This writer was also concerned about the preponderance (to date) of England and its colonies in the ICW and insisted that if France joined, it must enter through the main door, with

---

[1] Jeanne Deflou, "Les Trois Tronçons du Féminisme," *Le Journal des Femmes: organe du mouvement féministe*, n° 101 (July–August 1900), p. 2.

the rank it deserved – that France must be treated as an equal and not as a subject. Extending the serpent analogy, Deflou hoped that in the interim, "the head doesn't eat the tail, or the tail eat the head."

The *Conseil National des Femmes Français* (CNFF; the Council) was far from a done deal in 1900. Even after the second endorsement of the national council project by the Droits congress in September, it would take months (until the following April) for the organization to crystallize. The defection of the Catholic feminists led by Marie Maugeret from this effort to achieve feminist solidarity dealt a blow (though not a terribly surprising one) to the unification efforts but the organizing committee, consisting now of three representatives each from the Oeuvres and Droits congresses, soldiered on throughout the fall.[2] Achieving unity would not be simple or swift, even without the Catholics.

The organizing committee successfully completed its task and announced the formal establishment of the CNFF, convening the first meeting of the thirty-five newly affiliated organizations on 18 April 1901.[3] Ninety women, representing some 21,000 women in the thirty-five affiliated organizations, including the *Société d'Amélioration* (SAFRED) and the *Ligue Française pour les Droits des Femmes* (LFDF), came to the April meeting, approved the statutes with just a few modifications, and elected the slate of officers for a three-year term. As befitting the occasion and in recognition of her strenuous efforts since 1888 to foster a French national council, Isabelle Bogelot was named honorary president, with the eminently diplomatic Sarah Monod from the *Conférence de Versailles* elected as president. Maria Pognon and Julie Siegfried were elected as vice-presidents and Ghénia Avril de Sainte-Croix (the journalist known as Savioz, and, following her marriage in 1900 to François Avril, as Mme Avril de Sainte-Croix or G. Avril de Sainte-Croix – hereafter Mme Avril, Sainte-Croix, or Savioz) as secretary-general (the latter would serve in this capacity until 1922, when she would succeed Julie Siegfried as president). Mme Alphen-Salvador and Marie Bonnevial were named as adjunct secretaries; and as treasurer Mme Isaac (Eugénie) Weill. The CNFF specifically welcomed Jewish philanthropic women as participants and officers. Some of the more radical feminist organizations remained outside the CNFF, at least for the time being. For her part, Marguerite Durand preferred to focus her

---

[2] The delegates were, from the Oeuvres congress, Sarah Monod, Julie Siegfried, and Ghénia Avril de Sainte-Croix, and from the Rights congress, Maria Pognon, Marie Bonnevial, and Mme Wiggishoff.
[3] See Maria Martin, "Le 18 avril 1901," *Le Journal des Femmes*, n° 110 (May 1901), 1, and Savioz, "Le Conseil National des Femmes Françaises," *La Contemporaine: Revue illustrée*, 5:1 (10 November 1901), 342–349.

attention on publishing *La Fronde* and organizing women's labor unions. Jeanne Deflou's *Groupe Français d'Études Féministes* (GFEF) did affiliate subsequently, but Hubertine Auclert and her suffrage group would remain aloof for several more years.[4] Maria Martin celebrated the founding of the CNFF in the *Le Journal des Femmes*, declaring this event to rank among the most important of the new century.[5] It was, as Laurence Klejman and Florence Rochefort have correctly pointed out, "a secular organization where the protestant ethic of a great number of its adherents conjugated perfectly with the [Dreyfusard] republican ethic."[6]

The initial program of the CNFF – "the amelioration of woman's situation from an educational, economic, social, philanthropic or political perspective" – seemed both inclusive enough and (at least at the outset) vague enough to please most parties. The specifics of its broad program would emerge in due course. These mainstream feminists did not lay out the kind of grand plan enunciated by the earlier congresses of 1893 and 1896, but would pursue a series of strategic initiatives through its various sections, as we shall see.

Writing in *La Contemporaine* later that year, Mme Avril de Sainte-Croix (signing as Savioz) retraced the French origins of feminism, but acknowledged how long it had taken the feminists to get organized. She pointedly acknowledged the missteps of some earlier advocates of women's cause who thought that by becoming more masculine, they were serving the cause. Mme Avril clearly articulated the notion that feminists must be feminine; they ought not to neglect "the weapons and gifts that nature has given them in order to make their cause triumph."[7] "Today one cannot even count the number of feminists in France; they are legion," she asserted. They have come together to pursue a common ideal: "the safeguard of feminine dignity and the defense of women's rights."[8] Announcing the first general assembly of the CNFF (scheduled for 14 November 1901), Savioz emphasized the growth of the movement since

---

[4] One feminist missing from this organizational phase of the CNFF is Clotilde Dissard, who seems to drop from sight by 1900.

[5] Maria Martin, "Le 18 avril 1901," *Le Journal des Femmes*, n° 110 (May 1901).

[6] Laurence Klejman & Florence Rochefort, *L'Égalité en marche: le féminisme sous la Troisième République* (Paris: FNSP & des femmes, 1989); quote, p. 152.

[7] Savioz, "Le Conseil National des Femmes Françaises," quote, p. 345. Mme Avril would repeat her counsel concerning the importance of women's elegance in her book, *Le Féminisme* (Paris: Giard & Brière, 1907), pp. 155–156. Another summary of what the CNFF represented can be found in an article by Marie-Georges Martin (not to be confused with Maria Martin, editor of the *Le Journal des Femmes*), "Le Conseil National des Femmes Françaises: La Lutte contre la tuberculose," *La Revue Philanthropique*, 13:3 (July 1903), 308–312.

[8] Savioz, "Conseil National ... ," p. 346.

April, and declared that at the upcoming meeting "the women will, for the first time, hold their own Estates-General."[9] The French women's parliament was about to become a reality. At this November meeting, Sarah Monod reported that the ICW executive board, meeting at The Hague in mid-July 1901, had duly ratified the CNFF's application for affiliation. The delegates then voted to establish four working sections: Legislation, Education, Work, and Assistance.[10] By the time of the first General Assembly of the CNFF in early February 1902, the organization of these sections was well underway. The *Le Journal des Femmes* diligently published the minutes of each of these early meetings, until such time as the CNFF began to publish its own General Assembly proceedings (1903 on) and, from 1909 on, its bulletin, *L'Action féminine*.[11] *La Française*, a weekly founded in October 1906 by Jane Misme and her associates (including the novelist Marcelle Tinayre), supplemented the monthly reporting of the *Le Journal des Femmes* (which would not survive the death in late 1910 of its editor Maria Martin).

Historians who have written about the founding of the CNFF have tended to underplay the actual achievement of the unification effort, treating the organization as if it had sprung into action fully formed rather than as what we would now call a "start-up" and still fluid coalition of highly capable but independently minded volunteers; most gloss over the importance of the affiliation with the ICW, which was itself still a work in progress.[12] Too often qualified as "conservative" or "moderate," or

---

[9] Savioz, "Conseil National . . . ," p. 349.

[10] Maria Martin, "Conseil National des Femmes Françaises," *Le Journal des Femmes*, n° 116 (December 1901), 1–2.

[11] I first consulted these CNFF publications in 1981 at the Widener Library, Harvard University. *L'Action féminine* can also be consulted (on microfilm) at the Bibliothèque Marguerite Durand. Progress on the specific issues addressed by the four initial CNFF sections can be tracked in this monthly periodical.

[12] Scholars who have written about the early years of the CNFF have provided somewhat different assessments of its political stance.

In *Sisters or Citizens* (1982; pp. 79–80), Charles Sowerwine interprets the founding of the CNFF as a defeat for Marguerite Durand and "social feminism," viewing half of the founders as "staunchly conservative." Hause, with Anne R. Kenney, in *Women's Suffrage and Social Politics* (1984; pp. 36–40, 58–60, 87–90), speak of the CNFF in terms of "moderate" or "restrained" feminism, with a commitment to the "feminine." In *L'Égalité en marche*, Klejman & Rochefort, question the qualifiers "un parti féministe," "image modérée," and being more about duties than about rights. None of these historians cite the early documents, especially those penned by Ghénia Avril de Sainte-Croix and Maria Vérone, which paint a different picture. For full references to these studies, see the earlier chapters.

The Canadian historian Yolande Cohen has explored the contributions of the Jewish women among the CNFF founders (Gabrielle Alphen-Salvador, Eugénie Weill, Louise Crémieux Cruppi). See her "Le Conseil National des Femmes Françaises (1901–1939): ses fondatrices et animatrices

dismissed (typically by the more extreme socialists) as "bourgeois," in fact, the CNFF was from the start a remarkably progressive (though admittedly not "revolutionary") association. The Council, as Mme Avril pointed out in her brief retrospective account of 1907, "was constituted not only with bourgeois and intellectual elements, but also with the socialist element represented by the female delegates of the women workers' unions."[13] Marie Bonnevial, one of the six founders, considered herself a socialist, although temperamentally she was a solidarist, not a proponent of class struggle. She would end her affiliation with one socialist faction following a congress that refused to add the terms "of both sexes" to "emancipation of the proletariat." Other younger feminists such as Maria Vérone also identified as socialists. After 1904, Bonnevial and Vérone would assume organizational responsibilities (president and secretary-general respectively) in the LFDF, and both would continue their participation in the CNFF Section on Suffrage.

President Sarah Monod reported on the first year of CNFF operations at the June 1902 meeting of the *Conférence de Versailles*.[14] By that time the council had issued a statement of endorsement in principle for women's suffrage: "The National Council of French Women, envisaging that the question of woman suffrage should be fundamental to every womanly demand, that only by the vote will they obtain the autonomy to which they have a right, as well as the moral and material improvement of their

---

juives," *Archives juives*, 44:1 (2011), 83–105. It is not clear that Cohen envisions the CNFF as the "start-up" project and umbrella coalition that I have found it to be during the first decade; instead she treats it as a well-established and rather conventional organization. In an earlier article, she explored contributions to the development of secular family policy by Protestant and Jewish women in the CNFF: "Protestant and Jewish Philanthropies in France: The Conseil National des Femmes Françaises (1901–1939)," *French Politics & Society*, 24:1 (Spring 2006), 74–92.

    The CNFF does not lie at the center of Anne Cova's story in *Maternité et Droits des Femmes en France* (Paris: Economica, 1997), except in respect to its positions on issues related to maternity (see pp. 133–136). None of Cova's recent articles comparing the CNFF with its counterparts in Italy (fd. 1903) and Portugal (fd. 1914) address developments during the first decade of the CNFF's existence, nor does she reference its early publications and reports. See, inter alia, Anne Cova, "Femmes et associations: Le Conseil national des femmes françaises sous la IIIe République," in *Femmes, familles, filiations – Société et histoire: En hommage à Yvonne Knibiehler*, ed. Marcel Bernos & Michèle Bitton (Aix-en-Provence: Publications de l'Université de Provence, 2004), pp. 75–88; "International Feminisms in Historical Comparative Perspective: France, Italy and Portugal, 1880s–1930s," *Women's History Review*, 19:4 (September 2010), 595–612; "Feminisms and Associativism: the National Councils of Women in France and Portugal, a Comparative Historical Approach, 1888–1939," *Women's History Review*, 22:1 (February 2013), 19–30; and "The National Councils of Women in France, Italy and Portugal: Comparisons and Entanglements, 1888–1939," in *Gender History in a Transnational Perspective: Biographies, Networks, Gender Orders*, ed. Oliver Janz & Daniel Schönpflug (Oxford & New York: Berghahn Books, 2014), pp. 46–76.

[13] Mme Avril de Sainte-Croix, *Le Féminisme* (Paris: Giard & Brière, 1907), pp. 146–148; quote, p. 148.

[14] See "Allocution de Mlle S. Monod," *La Femme: Organe des Institutions Féminines, Chrétiennes, Sociales*, vol. 24, n° 12 (combined issue for 15 June - 1 July - 15 July 1902), 91–93.

situation, demands for women in principle the vote and eligibility for office at every level." The organization then added the caveat that women should first undertake an apprenticeship in civic affairs, limiting their initial demand to participation in municipal affairs.[15] This caveat would disappear in mid-June 1906 when the CNFF hosted the executive committee of the ICW in Paris in conjunction with its yearly assembly, and would authorize a new working section on women's suffrage, launched in November and headed by Hubertine Auclert. Even though the CNFF would not endorse the 1908 congress on women's civil and political rights organized by Jeanne Oddo-Deflou and Marguerite Durand, it did subsequently organize an impressive consolidated congress, incorporating both the Oeuvres and Droits tendencies, in early June 1913. This latter congress would be baptized as the Tenth International Congress of Women, thereby situating it in the long line of international women's congresses that had begun in Paris in 1878. We will have more to say about the debates at this 1913 congress later in this chapter and in Chapter 13.

The CNFF Becomes the Official "Voice" of French Women to the Governments of the Republic

The activities and commitment of the CNFF's most energetic supporters testify to its importance and its moderate but firm and forward-looking positioning. The officers of the CNFF, with Mme Avril de Sainte-Croix serving as its highly efficient and committed secretary-general, were quickly becoming masters of what we now call "leverage" to push for the reform legislation they had agreed to promote. The CNFF repeatedly invoked their growing numbers (73,000 women claimed circa 1907), the prestige of hosting the ICW Executive Board in Paris in 1906, and, not least, it touted the prestige of its "honorary" members, in particular the Polish-born, French-educated physicist Marie Curie (1867–1934). In 1903 she and her husband Pierre Curie were awarded the Nobel Prize in physics for the discovery of radioactivity. After his untimely death, Marie succeeded Pierre as professor of physics at the Sorbonne.[16] The CNFF leadership took great pride in "annexing" Mme Curie as it had already annexed the venerable polymath Clémence Royer. Subsequently the

---

[15] See *La Femme*, vol. 24, n° 12 (combined issue for 15 June -1 July -15 July 1902), p. 92, for the CNFF suffrage endorsement.

[16] Concerning Madame Curie's honorary membership, see the secretary-general's report, CNFF, *Quatrième Assemblée Générale Publique, le 7 juillet 1907* (Paris: Siège de la société, 1 Avenue Malakoff, s.d.), pp. 16–17.

CNFF would confer additional honorary memberships on the longtime feminist Clarisse Coignet (1824–1918) and to the enterprising intellectual and well-connected educational administrator Mlle Dick May (Jeanne Weill, 1859–1925), who did not consider herself a feminist.[17]

In the early years, the CNFF executive officers devised various strategies for publicizing its existence and for influencing officialdom and public opinion. For example, the council repeatedly sent official delegations to cabinet ministers, communicating directly with the successive presidents of the council of ministers and with members of the legislature. The Council launched petitions, dispatched representatives to the International Woman Suffrage Alliance (IWSA) congresses, joined the ICW's international effort to commemorate the opening of the first peace congress at The Hague by hosting a peace rally in Paris (18 May 1907), and claimed credit for a number of modest but nevertheless significant legislative reforms as those were enacted from 1907 on. In consequence of such activity, government officials began to respect the CNFF and to consult its leaders for advice and assistance on issues affecting women.

In what follows, my emphasis will focus less on the mechanics of the CNFF's organization than on its choice and presentation of specific issues. Its officers and section leaders drafted legislative measures with the express intention of recruiting male deputies to carry them forward and to exert the necessary peer pressure to pass the desired legislation. The Council also lobbied for the appointment of women to positions on commissions and as government inspectors. This would, of course, be a long-term project. Still, during the next decade and a half, the CNFF could boast of multiple successes. It helped women's cause enormously to speak to French officialdom with one voice and to have the ear of strategically placed republican deputies and senators as well as editors of newspapers and magazines with national circulation.

By June 1906, the CNFF's four active sections, rank ordered as Assistance, Education, Legislation, and Travail [Work] had expanded to encompass a fifth Section on Suffrage, and by 1907 a sixth Section on Sciences, Arts, Belles-Lettres. At this point in the council's development, there was neither a Peace

---

[17] The latter two honorary members are reported in: "Report of the National Council of Women in France," in *International Council of Women. Report of Transactions of The Fourth Quinquennial Meeting held at Toronto, Canada, June 1909* (London: Constable & Co., 1910), p. 66. Coignet was an important women's rights activist from the 1860s on; Dick May had administered, first, the innovative Collège Libre des Sciences Sociales, and subsequently (from 1900 on), the École des Hautes Études Sociales. Her contributions to these innovative private educational institutions have attracted the attention of a number of historians.

Section nor (despite Mme Avril's active interest) a Section on "Morality" aimed at ending the government regulation of prostitution and the so-called white slave traffic; the latter section would only be organized in 1916.

The Assistance Section, headed by Eugénie Weill, focused in its early years on getting women appointed to the *Conseil Supérieur de l'Assistance Publique* and to inspectorship positions for *Assistance Publique*, and on the campaign against alcoholism (particularly the ultimately successful campaign to outlaw the production and sale of absinthe). By 1907, this CNFF section had met its first goal, with the appointment of Isabelle Bogelot (the CNFF's honorary president) and a Mme Perouse, president of the *Union des Femmes de France*, to the *Conseil Supérieur*. Its next campaign would be to "feminize" the women's prisons and boards.[18] This effort met with success in July 1907, according to the report by Mme Weill.[19] By 1913 a new section devoted to Hygiene would spearhead the CNFF's stepped-up campaigns to combat alcoholism and tuberculosis.[20]

The Education Section, established under the aegis of the widowed philanthropist Gabrielle Alphen-Salvador (1856–1920) and by 1906 taken over by the feminist educator Pauline Kergomard (1838–1925), promoted the principle of coeducation, which the CNFF preferred to label "*enseignement mixte*" because the latter term seemed more neutral. Under Kergomard, this section pushed initially for the appointment of women as inspectors in the educational system at all levels (not solely at the level of the *écoles maternelles*) and to restore autonomy to the *inspectrices* of *écoles maternelles*, who were then subordinate to and under pressure from the all-male primary level inspectors.[21] In 1908–1909 it would take up the question of teaching Greek and Latin in the girls' *lycées*, so that those who intended to become teachers in secondary education would be on the same footing as the boys.[22] In 1910 the Education Section would endorse the

---

[18] *Quatrième Assemblée Générale . . . 1907*, pp. 15–16.

[19] *Quatrième Assemblée Générale . . . 1907*, p. 24.

[20] The French feminists' campaigns against alcoholism and efforts to close off or regulate the number of drinking establishments, or to halt production and sale of noxious distilled products such as absinthe, accelerated in the early twentieth century, as their international exposure widened. The CNFF did pass a resolution in early 1907 against absinthe, which was sent to Émile Cheysson, President of the *Ligue Anti-alcoolique* and to the presidents of the anti-alcohol groups in the Chamber of Deputies and the Senate; see CNFF, *4th General Assembly publique*, 7 July 1907, p. 17. The CNFF involvement would become much more vigorous in 1913–1914; the topic took up considerable space at the 1913 international congress. *La Française* reported regularly on the progress of the campaigns and the women's petitions to restrict the number of sales outlets: see, among others, the issues n° 254 (9 November 1912); n° 256 (23 November 1912), and n° 257 (30 November 1912).

[21] Avril de Sainte-Croix, report in the *Le Journal des Femmes*, n° 166 (June 1906), 2.

[22] See *La Française*, n° 114 (21 March 1909), 2.

demand of the primary teachers in the *Fédération Féministe Universitaire* (FFU) for equal pay with the male teachers who did the same work.[23] In 1912 the Education Section, still under Kergomard, would propose the teaching of sex education in the state schools along with maternal education courses in the normal schools.

The third section on Legislation, chaired by Mme d'Abbadie d'Arrast, initially prioritized the question of *recherche de la paternité* (authorization of paternity suits by unwed mothers); her section demanded a law that would provide strictly an alimentary allowance for the unwed mother and child from the purported father, without allowing the latter to assert any legal claims over the child – thereby to stabilize and institutionalize a judicial practice that already had been developing for decades in the courts.[24] Its initial proposal, drafted by Jeanne Oddo-Deflou of the GFEF, who became the section's secretary, argued for complete suppression of Article 340, which since 1804 had forbidden paternity suits. This proposal asserted that acknowledgement of paternity only for purposes of child support should be possible without creating "civil ties" between the father and the child. Either marry the mother – or "pay up." Oddo-Deflou had investigated practices in other countries and on this basis drew up a seven-point proposal, which the CNFF general assembly endorsed.[25] The socialist deputy Marcel Sembat introduced the CNFF's proposal in the Chamber of Deputies on 2 July 1903 but it never made it to the floor for discussion.[26]

In late January 1905, a competing proposal was introduced in the Senate by senators Gustave Rivet (who had been elected to the Senate in 1903) and René Bérenger.[27] Rivet, a committed republican, had been unsuccessfully

---

[23] See *L'Action féminine*, n° 11 (August 1910), report of the secretary-general, 7 July 1910, and Mme Pichon-Landry's article on the FFU. The FFU campaign for equal pay will be taken up at greater length in Chapter 12.

[24] Report by Mme d'Abbadie d'Arrast, in CNFF, *Première Assemblée Générale Publique, le 17 mai* (Dole: Impr. Giardi & Audebert, 1903).

[25] Reported by Maria-Georges Martin, in *La Revue Philanthropique*, vol. 13, n° 6 (October 1903); see 696–701. See also Maria Martin, "La Recherche de la Paternité," *Le Journal des Femmes*, n° 134 (July 1903). Oddo-Deflou likely drew on the prize-winning work of Abel Pouzol, *La Recherche de la paternité, étude critique de sociologie et de législation comparée* (Paris: V. Giard & E. Brière, 1902).

[26] "Rapport pour la France au Conseil International des Femmes: Année 1903," by Jeanne Deflou [aka Jeanne Oddo-Deflou], *Le Journal des Femmes*, n° 142 (April 1904), for the upcoming ICW congress in Berlin. It is Rachel G. Fuchs, *Contested Paternity: Constructing Families in Modern France* (Baltimore: Johns Hopkins University Press, 2008), p. 151, erroneously gives the date for Sembat's *proposition de loi* as 1905.

[27] Journal Official, *Documents du Sénat*, 28 January 1905, annex 16; see Jean-Elisabeth Pedersen, *Legislating the French Family: Feminism, Theater, and Republican Politics, 1870–1920* (New Brunswick, NJ: Rutgers University Press, 2003), chapter 5.

promoting the abolition of Article 340 in the Chamber of Deputies since the 1870s (he was opposed to putting "natural" children in the custody of the state) but finally, with the mounting concern over depopulation and national strength, he was determined to push men into taking legal as well as economic responsibility for the children they fathered outside of marriage.[28] This proposed legislation, coauthored with the morality crusader Bérenger, was Rivet's fifth attempt. The principal difference between the CNFF bill and that of Rivet-Bérenger was that the latter measure gave the putative fathers legal rights over the "natural" child in addition to requiring financial support, whereas the CNFF/Sembat proposal stipulated paternal financial support for mother and child but without any legal strings attached.[29] The CNFF did not then support the more radical alternatives favored by some speakers at the congresses of 1900, that would simply eliminate the question of fathers' responsibility for child support from the picture by establishing either a *caisse de la maternité* funded by taxes on men, as Maria Pognon had advocated, or by recognizing maternity as a "social function" fully supported by the state (in that respect, analogous to soldiers) as Dr. Blanche Edwards-Pilliet had proposed. I have seen no evidence that, during these early years, the CNFF advocated a paid maternity leave for pregnant employed women, but the *Ligue des Droits de l'Homme* (LDH) [League for the Rights of Man], would endorse such a paid leave at its 1909 Congress.[30] Two laws would be passed that year, providing this broader group of women with both paid maternity leave and job guarantees.[31]

The Legislation Section also pressed for reform of the Civil Code as concerned wives (the CNFF supported in principle the wholesale abolition of married women's civil incapacity), and – unsuccessfully – the appointment of women as members of the official government commission on reform of the Code. Nevertheless, several council leaders (including Ghénia Avril de Sainte-Croix and Jeanne Oddo-Deflou) were appointed to the "unofficial" commission on the reform of marriage organized by Henri Coulon and René Chavagnes under the sponsorship of the newspaper *Gil Blas*, where they intensified pressure on the government for thorough

---

[28] See Gustave Rivet, *La Recherche de la paternité. Préface par Alexandre Dumas fils* (3rd ed., Paris: M. Dreyfus, 1890). Cf. the commentary by "X" in *La Citoyenne*, n° 162 (September 1890).

[29] See the report of the section on legislation at the 10 March 1910 meeting of the CNFF, in *Le Journal des Femmes*, n° 205 (April 1910), 2.

[30] The *Ligue des Droits de l'Homme* did endorse a resolution at its May 1909 conference in support of a paid maternity leave of six weeks previous to delivery and four weeks following for employed women. See *Bulletin* of the *Ligue des Droits de l'Homme*, n° 15 (15 August 1909), 995.

[31] We will return to the development of CNFF positions with regard to evolving legislative action on *recherche de la paternité* in Chapter 11.

reform of the sections of the Code that still so severely constrained married women.[32] Oddo-Deflou had developed considerable expertise on the civil laws concerning marriage in comparative perspective and she strongly advocated separate property regimes in marriage as well as married women's control over their own earnings. Her reports at the 1899 ICW Congress in London had provided exemplary surveys of the topics of French civil law and divorce.[33] At the 1900 *Oeuvres et Institutions* Congress she had presented a more extensive study on the extant property laws concerning married women in France, which led to invited lectures in Belgium as well as in France.[34] Oddo-Deflou served under Mme Charles (Marie, born Coulomb) d'Abbadie d'Arrast until 1908, when she broke away to organize her own conference on the law and to initiate a more aggressive campaign for women's suffrage.[35]

Later in the decade (following the ICW's 1909 quinquennial conference in Toronto), the ICW Board would authorize its own standing committee on the laws, chaired by France's Mme d'Abbadie d'Arrast of the CNFF's Section on Legislation, to proceed with a generalized survey of its members on the status of women in the law – "in the home, the family, the municipality, and the state." Entitled *Women's Position in the Laws of Nations*, this landmark comparative legislative study of married women's legal situation (published in 1912 by the ICW, in English, French, and German) was the first such report ever assembled by a collective international group of women. The stated objectives of the report were, first, to encourage a broad audience of women to familiarize themselves with the law, and secondly, "to provide a clear statement, suitable for circulation in many lands, which should serve to show that existing laws often bear adversely and with entire injustice upon women, and can no longer be regarded as in

---

[32] Avril de Sainte-Croix, report in the *Le Journal des Femmes*, n° 166 (June 1906), 2. See also Henri Coulon & René de Chavagnes, *Le Mariage et le divorce de demain* (Paris: E. Flammarion, 1908) for the ex-officio commission's verbatim proceedings.

[33] Mme [Jeanne] Oddo-Deflou, "Civil Disabilities of Women in France," in International Council of Women (ICW), *Report of Transactions of the Second Quinquennial Meeting, held in London, July 1899*, vol. 6, pp. 139–144, and "Divorce Laws in France," vol. 6, pp. 126–128. See also her review of Charles Krug's book, *Le Féminisme et le droit civil français* (Paris: Impr. Nancéienne) in the *Le Journal des Femmes*, n° 90 (August 1899).

[34] Jeanne Deflou "Du Régime des Biens de la femme mariée: Rapport présenté le 21 juin 1900, à Paris, au Congrès des Oeuvres et Institutions féminines, qui en a adopté les conclusions à l'unanimité moins une voix," offprint [1900]. She spoke on this subject to the *Ligue Belge du Droit des Femmes*, 10 December 1900, and her report was republished in *La Ligue* (*Organe belge du Droit des femmes*), 8:3 (1900), 57–68, and in the first two issues for 1901. Born in 1856, Jeanne Deflou had earned two *baccalauréats* in the 1870s, the first in sciences, the second in letters (according to the sketch in Coulon & Chavagnes, *Mariage et divorce* [1908], pp. 202–205).

[35] The suffrage campaigns will be discussed at greater length in Chapter 13.

harmony with that higher standard of enlightenment, that broader culture, and stronger grasp of public duties and responsibilities which are characteristic features of present-day womanhood in every great nation of the world."[36]

The Section on Work (Travail), initially organized by CNFF cofounder and suffrage advocate Eliska Vincent, and unique among national councils of the ICW, was – by mid-1906 when the French Ministry of Labor was being established – reorganized and taken over by the capable Marie Pégard. The compilers of an official *enquête* on *travail à domicile* (industrial home work) for the ministry of Commerce (which had housed the Office du Travail, organized in 1891, until the latter was transferred to the new ministry of labor in 1906) had called on the CNFF for assistance.[37] By 1907 this section could boast of several concrete achievements: it had organized a series of public lectures aimed at working women to explain the benefits of unionization, and it had lobbied hard for passage of the law that finally authorized women's election to the *Conseils de Prud'hommes* as well as for the law that granted married women control over their own earnings (the second of the two legal reform projects promoted since the early 1890s by Jeanne Schmahl and *L'Avant-Courrière*). Importantly, the CNFF successfully opposed the inclusion of an insidious clause that would have permitted women, by marriage contract, to permanently renounce their earnings in favor of their husbands. Ultimately, from early 1913 to December 1915, the social reformer Gabrielle Duchêne, seconded by Louise Compain and Cécile Brunschvicg, would head the council's Section on Work which would endorse legislation to protect home workers and would campaign vigorously for a minimum wage and for women's right to work.[38]

---

[36] *Women's Position in the Laws of Nations, a compilation of the laws of different countries, prepared by the I.C.W. Standing committee on laws concerning the legal position of women, with an introduction by Mme d'Abbadie d'Arrast* (Karlsruhe-in-Breisgau: G. Braunsch Hofbuchdruckerei & Verlag, 1912). Quotation from the Foreword by Ishbel Aberdeen, on behalf of the Board of Officers, v. For the significance of this study, see Karen Offen, "National or International? How and Why the Napoleonic Code Drove Married Women's Legal Rights onto the Agenda of the International Council of Women and the League of Nations: An Overview," in *Family Law in Early Women's Rights Debates*, ed. Stephan Meder & Christoph-Eric Mecke (Cologne: Böhlau Verlag, 2013), pp. 42–59.

[37] On the Office du Travail, see the comprehensive study by Isabelle Lespinet-Moret, *L'Office du Travail 1891–1914: La République et la réforme sociale* (Rennes: Presses Universitaires de Rennes, 2007). Cf. also Marilyn J. Boxer, "Protective Legislation and Home Industry: The Marginalization of Women Workers in Late Nineteenth/ Early Twentieth Century France," *Journal of Social History*, 20:1 (Fall, 1986), 45–65.

[38] See Emmanuelle Carle, "Gabrielle Duchêne et la recherche d'une autre route: entre le pacifisme féministe et l'antifascisme" (Ph.D. dissertation, McGill University, Montreal, 2005), pp. 51–71. These issues around women's labor will be considered further in Chapter 12.

By November 1906, the CNFF activated its fifth section on Suffrage. The council's leaders tapped the redoubtable champion of women's suffrage Hubertine Auclert to lead it. By mid-March 1907 the suffrage section had drawn up an important petition to the French legislators for unrestricted women's suffrage, which was duly conveyed (for endorsement) to the LDH by Mme Avril de Sainte-Croix.[39] Auclert resigned as section head in March 1907, at which point she was named its honorary president.[40] Maria Georges-Martin then succeeded Auclert as head of the suffrage section; she was in turn succeeded by Marie Bonnevial and Maria Vérone of the LFDF, who would breathe new energy into the campaign for women's suffrage.[41]

In mid-June (12th through the 17th) 1906, the CNFF proudly hosted the ICW Executive Board meeting in Paris. This meeting included joint sessions with the *Conférence de Versailles* and with the General Assembly of the CNFF. For this occasion the National Council had sought and obtained monetary sponsorship from the City of Paris and the Paris Municipal Council, thereby aligning itself with and receiving sanction from local officialdom.[42] These meetings obtained broad press coverage, as attested by an abundance of press clippings in the archives.[43] In a long article published simultaneously with the ICW/CNFF meetings, in *La Revue: Revue des revues* (18 June 1906) Mme Avril summed up how far the CNFF and ICW had come prior to the joint board meetings.[44]

> The forward march of feminism is a fact that no one can deny, a movement that no force can henceforth bring to a halt. Woman has become a social and political factor to be reckoned with . . . a factor whose power will be underscored by the upcoming Conference of the International Council of Women. . . . Paris can flatter itself that for a few days the leaders of global feminism will be here.

---

[39] See the account and a copy of the suffrage petition, presented by Mme Avril, in the LDH *Bulletin* (cited in n. 30), vol. 7, n° 9 (15 May 1907), 440–442. See also "Conseil National des Femmes Françaises – Séance du 5 mai 1907," *Le Journal des Femmes*, n° 174 (May 1907), 1.

[40] Steven C. Hause, *Hubertine Auclert: The French Suffragette* (New Haven, CT: Yale University Press, 1987), pp. 188–189

[41] Maria Georges-Martin and her husband Dr. Georges Martin were prominent in the mixed-lodge freemasonry and in local government circles. The suffrage section's further efforts and arguments, along with those of other feminist groups, will be elaborated in Chapter 13.

[42] See the minutes of these meetings in the *Le Journal des Femmes*, n° 166 (June 1906) and n° 167–168 (July–August 1906), with transcripts of speeches and section reports, as well as Avril de Sainte-Croix, *Le Féminisme*, pp. 169–175.

[43] See my notes, photocopies from Avril de Sainte-Croix scrapbooks, reel 4, at the BMD; also Nelly Roussel's coverage of the events in *L'Action*, 20 June 1906 (quoted by Avril de Sainte-Croix in *Le Féminisme*, p. 172).

[44] Copies of this article consulted in BMD (AdeSC Scrapbooks, reel 4) and in DOS 396 CON FEM 1914–1931; also on file at the Musée Social. Mme Avril repeated the quotation in the paragraph below in her 1907 book, *Le Féminisme*, p. 6.

"In coming to us," she asserted, "these women do not abdicate a thing – they have brought their flags, just as we conserve our own, but it is no longer in order to make them symbols of massacre and hate that they have been up till now; the women want to use them to form a harmonious cluster, the image of peace and fraternity. The task that feminism has traced for itself, and consequently, for the International Council of Women," she claimed, "is not only to free women from secular oppression, but also to deliver humanity from its ancient barbarism."[45] This was admittedly an ambitious goal, one worthy of an international "Parliament of Women."

The secretary-general's subsequent report on the year's activities of the CNFF, presented to the General Assembly in June 1907, applauded the founding of the parliamentary group of male legislators, whose leaders kept in close touch with CNFF leadership, and acknowledged that, thanks to the impact of the CNFF petition for the vote – on precisely the same conditions as applied to men – great strides had been made in gaining public support for women's suffrage.[46]

By 1913, the CNFF would be considered part of the republican "establishment" and, indeed, a power to be reckoned with. Its seasoned leaders and spokeswomen had proved themselves to be patriotic supporters of the Third Republic and had gained the trust and respect of progressive ministers and deputies. Some, like Marie d'Abbadie d'Arrast, Ghénia Avril de Sainte-Croix, and the young lawyer Maria Vérone (1874–1938) had also become players of consequence in the ICW and advocates of international collaboration on issues such as marriage law reform and the traffic in women.[47] Although to date these feminists had not always gotten legislation passed in the form they deemed most desirable – the 1912 law on *recherche de la paternité* would provide a case in point – they would enjoy

---

[45] Mme Avril de Sainte-Croix's remarks here are aligned with the general transnationalist philosophy of the ICW, as developed by May Wright Sewall and Lady Aberdeen. See Karen Offen, "Understanding Feminisms as 'Transnational' – An Anachronism?" commissioned for *Gender History in a Transnational Perspective: Biographies, Networks, Gender Orders*, ed. Janz & Schönpflug, pp. 25–45.

[46] See *Conseil National des Femmes Françaises, fondé à Paris, le 18 avril 1901. Quatrième Assemblée Générale Publique, le 7 juillet 1907* (Paris: Siège de la Société: 1, Avenue Malakoff, Paris). On the CNFF suffrage petition of March 1907, see the LDH *Bulletin*, vol. 7, n° 9 (15 May 1907), 440–442.

[47] On Abbadie d'Arrast and her participation in the effort to mount a joint international effort to address the laws of marriage, see Offen, "National or International?" in *Family Law in Early Women's Rights Debates*, pp. 42–59. On Avril de Sainte-Croix's activities as head of the ICW's section on prostitution and the international traffic in women, see Karen Offen, "Madame Ghénia Avril de Sainte-Croix, the Josephine Butler of France," *Women's History Review* (London), 17:2 (April 2008), 239–255.

success in their push for legislation that would make motherhood a more economically secure situation for poor women and their children.[48]

Spectacularly, the CNFF leaders would gain substantive governmental support for their sponsorship of the Tenth International Congress of Women in Paris (2–8 June 1913), which was attended by nearly a thousand persons. The Congress opened in the grand amphitheater of the Sorbonne, inaugurated by the minister of the interior, L.-L. Klotz, who presided over the session, and by Lady Aberdeen, vice-reine of Ireland and president of the ICW.[49] Two other officers of the ICW attended: Alice Salomon (Germany), secretary of the ICW, and May Wright Sewall (United States), now its honorary president.[50] The congress delegates were feted at the Elysée palace by the recently elected President of France Raymond Poincaré and his wife, and at the Quai d'Orsay by the minister of foreign affairs Stéphen Pichon. A tacit, albeit deliberate goal of the congress organizers was to demonstrate that, suffragette violence across the English Channel notwithstanding, reasoned discussion and cooperation between feminists and the government could actually effect positive change on behalf of women (as well as men and children), and not only in a national context. The journalist and novelist Victor Margueritte made much of this contrast between violent and reasonable tactics in his report on the congress published in *Le Journal*.[51] Jane Misme of *La Française* underscored how orderly the proceedings were, how eloquent the various speakers, and how those in the audience were well-behaved and paid rapt attention – in

---

[48] See Offen, "Exploring the Sexual Politics of French Republican Nationalism," in *Nationhood and Nationalism in France*, ed. Robert Tombs (London: HarperCollins Academic, 1991; subseq. acquired by Routledge), pp. 195–209.

[49] *Dixième congrès international des femmes: Oeuvres et institutions féminines, Droits des femmes, 2-8 juin 1913, compte rendu des travaux par* Mme Avril de Sainte-Croix (Paris: V. Giard & E. Brière). The working sessions took place at the Hôtel des Ingénieurs Civils. The title vice-reine was given to the wife of the then viceroy of Ireland, Lord Aberdeen.

[50] The ICW had held its "interquinquennial" meeting in The Hague, 20–27 May 1913, in preparation for its Fifth Quinquennial congress planned for Rome in May (16–23), 1914. The FAI Eleventh Congress (9–12 June) began just after the 10th International Women's Congress in Paris ended. The Seventh Congress of the IWSA would convene a few days later in Budapest (15–21 June), the culmination of a feminist progressive trip that began in The Hague, proceeded to Paris, then to Vienna, before arriving in Budapest.

[51] See Victor Margueritte, "Le Congrès des Femmes," *Le Journal*, (hand-dated 7 June 1913); clipping in LLF 65 at the Mundaneum (Mons). The same point is made by Senator Paul Strauss, in "Le Congrès de Paris," *Le Progrès du Nord*, (10 June 1913) [reprod. in *L'Action féminine*, n° 28 (June 1913), 501], and by Jeanne Crouzet-Benaben, "Une Assemblée des femmes en 1913: Le Congrès international de Paris (2-7 juin)," *La Grande Revue* (10 July 1913), 56–77; quote, 59). The daily press coverage in the mainstream press (including *Le Temps, Le Matin, Le Journal,* and the *Journal des Débats*) was substantial, and some of it was contributed by the principal feminist journalists of the day, including Jane Misme and Louise Compain.

pointed contrast to the behavior seen in France's all-male legislative bodies.[52] "Never," wrote Jeanne Crouzet-Benaben in *La Grande Revue*, "had one seen in the newspapers such an interest in feminist concerns as during this past month. The papers were full of allusions to feminist demands, to the feminist congress, and unanimously they rendered homage to the wisdom of the first and to the orderliness of the second ... in sum, it had a resounding glow that accompanied and followed it like a halo."[53] The 1913 Congress was hailed at the time as a triumph and it posed a benchmark for national and international collaboration. "It gave the congress *Droit du cité* in the Republic and gave the foreign delegates the impression that France regarded the feminists as elements of progress for today's society and as precious elements for the future society."[54]

Not only did the congress bring together the spectrum of women's rights advocates in France (Hubertine Auclert, Séverine, and Marguerite Durand were all in attendance) with those who worked in *Oeuvres et Institutions* but it also assembled a substantial international crowd, including one Parsee (Parsi) woman from India, a Madame Cama, then living in Europe. It was not specifically a congress of the ICW, even though twenty national councils were represented in addition to its president Lady Aberdeen. In the congress's eight sections (assistance, hygiene, education, legislation, work, suffrage, science-arts-letters, and peace) the organizers insisted on rapporteurs treating each of the topics in a comparative, transnational manner based on a series of international inquiries; Mme Avril de Sainte-Croix, as secretary-general and congress organizer, would constantly emphasize this point.[55] This was a concerted move away from the practice at previous international congresses held in France, where the focus had been far more exclusively national and navel-gazing. Delegates from many countries debated sex education, suffrage, and voted some far-reaching resolutions, amid serious differences of opinion on matters such as protective legislation for women only versus equal protection of workers of both sexes (the congress would overrule the recommendation of the rapporteur, Louise Compain, to support

---

[52] Jane Misme, "Un Congrès féministe à Paris," *La Revue (ancienne Revue des Revues)*, (1 July 1913), 54–61.

[53] Crouzet-Benaben, "Assemblée des femmes en 1913," quotes, 56, 57.

[54] Ibid., p. 57. Klejman & Rochefort take a less celebratory view, criticizing the CNFF for timidity in not challenging their republican allies to push through enactment of the measures they recommended. See *L'Égalité en marche*, pp. 156–158. My reading of the record does not support the charge of "timidity."

[55] *Dixième congrès international*, pp. 427, 429.

protective legislation, following the interventions and objections of Marguerite Durand and Maria Vérone).

What is striking as one reads the bulletins published by the CNFF between 1901 and 1914 is the extent to which the various articles exude increasing self-confidence and optimism. The leadership was putting out important and well-documented studies and reports and succeeding in obtaining a hearing for its arguments at the highest levels. The manifest contrast between the French women's intention of working with government officials and the English suffragettes' sustained opposition tactics is glaring. The CNFF leadership considered WSPU tactics counterproductive, as they made clear at the final general assembly of the 1913 congress, when the leadership rebuffed Séverine's impromptu effort to obtain a resolution congratulating the English suffragettes for their courage and suffering. To fend off this initiative, Mme Avril countered by tactfully remarking that "we can admire them for their courage, without affirming that their method is right."[56]

That the women of the CNFF were making an impact both within France and in the ICW is incontestable. At the ICW's congress in Rome in May 1914, four highly competent CNFF leaders would be elected to positions of leadership in that international organization. The CNFF had claimed its place not only in the French republican establishment but also in the international women's movement.

The CNFF Builds Alliances with Other Progressive Groups

In addition to lobbying the government ministries and parliamentarians, the women of the CNFF attempted to form coalitions with other progressive nongovernmental organizations, such as the French section of the *Fédération Abolitioniste Internationale* (FAI) [International Abolitionist Federation] and the *Ligue des Droits de l'Homme* as well as with the emerging political parties, in particular the newly unified (1901) *Parti Radical et Radical-Socialiste* (PRRS) and the *Section Française de l'Internationale Ouvrière* (SFIO), which finally united the competing socialist factions in 1905.

One of the first alliances was with the newly founded French branch of the FAI. The two groups were closely aligned on the issues – and, not coincidentally, Ghénia Avril de Sainte-Croix, the secretary-general of the CNFF, also served as secretary-general of the French section of the FAI and as editor of its publication, the *Bulletin Abolitionniste*, which began monthly publication in January 1902. In late May 1901, as Savioz, she had

---

[56] *Dixième congrès international*, pp. 541–546, esp. 545–546.

given a sensational speech at the FAI congress in Lyon.[57] In this speech, subsequently published as "La Serve" [The Female Serf], Savioz colorfully portrayed government-regulated prostitution as "the last, most solid link that rivets the new Eve to the old slavery." Abolish regulation and promote a single standard of morality for both sexes, she argued.[58] She assured her listeners that all the French women's groups supported this position. The recently founded CNFF, she remarked, was too new (at that time) to have taken a position, but she reminded her audience that its officers also endorsed the arguments she was presenting. She denounced the "hygienic" arguments (long put forth by the male medical establishment) for regulating prostitution (by regular, arbitrary medical inspection of the genital health of the licenced prostitutes) as specious and an affront to the individual liberty of women. By such speeches in support of the FAI's official positions, Savioz began to build her well-deserved reputation as the Josephine Butler of France.[59] The links between the CNFF and the FAI grew tighter when a number of women who were also active in the CNFF were elected to the council of the FAI's French section.[60]

By August 1902, following the French government-sponsored international conference on the traffic in women, held in July, Savioz was publishing detailed and timely information in *La Grande Revue* on recently reported revelations concerning the expansion of the traffic.[61] Her fundamental argument, which she had also made in Amsterdam the previous

[57] Mme Avril de Sainte-Croix's speech is noted and summarized but not published in the account (reprinted from the *Signal de Genève*) of the proceedings of the *Congrès international de la Fédération abolitionniste*, Lyon, 1901); see A. de Morsier, *La Police des Moeurs en France et la campagne abolitionniste. FAI. Congrès de Lyon 1901* (Paris: P. V. Stock, 1901).

[58] The offprint of this speech, which can be consulted at the Musée Social, is Savioz [Mme Avril de Sainte-Croix], *La Serve: une iniquité sociale* (Paris: Imprimerie Paul Dupont, 1901). A partial, annotated English translation, "The Female Serf," is published in *Feminisms of the Belle Epoque*, ed. Jennifer Waelti-Walters & Steven C. Hause (Lincoln: University of Nebraska Press, 1994), pp. 169–174.

[59] See my article "Madame Ghénia Avril de Sainte-Croix, the Josephine Butler of France," cited in n. 47.

[60] See the *Bulletin Abolitioniste*, n° 5 (May 1902), 62: the French women elected to the committee included Mmes Chapman, Sarah Monod, Gevin-Cassal, Legrain, Bogelot, Schmahl, Hudry-Menos, Moriceau, Schirmacher, Vincent, Alphen-Salvador, Pégard, Bonnevial, Pognon, and Avril de Sainte-Croix. Several of these – Alphen-Salvador, Chapman, Vincent, and Avril – served on the executive committee.

[61] Savioz, "La Traite des blanches," *La Grande Revue*, vol. 23:2 (1 August 1902), 281–294. Consulted in the AdeSC scrapbooks/clippings, BMD, reel 5; thanks to Marilyn J. Boxer for transmitting a photocopy of the full article from the holdings of the University of California, Berkeley. The governmental conference, held in Paris from 15–25 July 1902, resulted in a minimal Convention that was signed by sixteen countries; see France, Ministère des Affaires Étrangères, Documents diplomatiques, *Conférence internationale pour la repression de la traite des blanches (15–25 juillet 1902)* (Paris: Imprimerie nationale, 1902).

year and would frequently reiterate, was that the white slave traffic could never be eradicated without first putting a stop to government-regulated prostitution and the licensing of brothels whose clients clamored for novelty and rapid turnover in the "merchandise."

At its General Assembly (6 June 1903) in Lyon, the French section of the FAI launched another public attack on the morals police. Yves Guyot had returned to lead the charge, replacing Auguste de Morsier as president. Mme Avril reported on the branch's efforts to get the government to convene an Extraparliamentary Commission on the Morals Police.[62] Several scandalous round-ups of innocent women by the police in Paris and Rennes in early May had finally precipitated ministerial action. "Apart from those men interested in retaining the system," she asserted, "there is not one republican worthy of the name who dares openly to defend the morals police and the present regime."[63] In particular, she pointed out, the doctors who were worried about public hygiene had themselves begun denouncing this French system as ineffective. The CNFF, she declared, had unanimously demanded the suppression of the government regulation of prostitution, seeing it as "an offense to the entire feminine sex."[64] This institution, she concluded, is "the shame of France and the most absolute negation of the Declaration of the Rights of Man."[65]

Less than two weeks later (18 June 1903) the Combes ministry authorized the Extraparliamentary Commission and selected, among many others, the CNFF's and FAI's general secretary, Mme Avril de Sainte-Croix – the first and only woman ever appointed to a government commission under the Third Republic. She played a very active role in the Commission's discussions, and, as its published proceedings indicate, was never afraid to challenge officialdom.[66] Leveraging that experience from her double

---

[62] See *Fédération Abolitionniste Internationale*, 1903, *Contre la police des mœurs: Critiques et rapports. Assemblée générale du 6 juin 1903*, with preface by Dr. Victor Augagneur, mayor of Lyon (Paris: Edouard Cornély et cie., 1904). Guyot's speech is pp. 1–20; Mme Avril's, pp. 21–30. A third speaker was Dr. L. Queyrat.

[63] *Contre la police des mœurs*, p. 24.   [64] *Contre la police des mœurs*, p. 29.

[65] *Contre la police des mœurs*, p. 30. In a late May speech to the Union des Étudiants Républicains, Marguerite Durand similarly invoked the Rights of Man and called the republicans to task for not observing its principles when they allowed the regime to place prostitutes, and especially minors, "outside the law." See the account of the public meeting by "Parrhissa," "Les Arrestations arbitraires et la police des moeurs," *La Fronde*, n° 1901 (23 May 1903); Durand quoted Mme Avril's 1900 congress report at length.

[66] See the published proceedings, edited by Louis Fiaux, *La Police des moeurs devant la Commission extraparlementaire du régime des mœurs*, 2 vols. (Paris: F. Alcan, 1907). Cf. also the official transcripts of the sessions (also available in the Fiaux volumes previously cited): France. *Commission extraparlementaire du régime des mœurs. Procès verbaux des séances* (Melun: Imprimerie administrative, 1909). For an assessment of the extraparliamentary Commission and Mme Avril's

secretary-generalships, in 1904 (at the Berlin congress of the ICW) Mme Avril agreed to serve as the first head of the ICW's new committee on the "'White Slave Traffic' and Equal Moral Standard," and was duly praised by the ICW president Lady Aberdeen in 1906 for her effectiveness in organizing this international section.[67] Yet despite the prominence of the secretary-general in both these organizations, and the back-to-back alignment of the international congresses organized by the CNFF (2–10 June 1913), the FAI (9–12 June 1913), and the London Congress on Suppression of the White Slave Traffic (30 June–4 July 1913), no section would be formed within the CNFF to address these issues before 1916, when Mme Avril proposed adding a section on "the unity of morality and repression of the trade in women."[68] This new section would be headed by Marguerite de Witt-Schlumberger, with assistance from Marcelle Legrand-Falco, both of whom would become important figures in the abolitionist and anti-trafficking movements for years to come.

The CNFF built a second significant alliance with the LDH, which was itself only a few years older than the women's council and included women as members. The LDH's actions took the form of "publications, petitions to the Chambers, intervention with government and administrative officials, meetings, and lectures."[69] The CNFF utilized the same practices, including active publicity in the Parisian (and provincial) daily press. This was how "marketing" a cause was done in an era in which radio and television had not yet been invented. This alliance provided the CNFF

---

contributions to it, see Andrea Mansker, *Sex, Honor and Citizenship in Early Third Republic France* (Houndmills, UK: Palgrave Macmillan, 2011), chapter 6.

[67] For Lady Aberdeen's high praise of Mme Avril de Sainte-Croix, see her speech as reported in the *Le Journal des Femmes*, June 1906. One of Mme Avril's first moves was to compile and circulate a questionnaire to all the national councils and their affiliates; it is published (in English) as "Report of the Committee on 'White Slave Traffic' and Equal Moral Standard" by Mme Avril de Sainte-Croix in *International Council of Women, Report for 1905–1906*, ed. Mrs. Ogilvie Gordon (Aberdeen: Rosemount Press, 1906), pp. 45–49.

[68] See Julie Christine Miller, "The 'Romance of Regulation': The Movement Against State-Regulated Prostitution in France, 1871–1948" (Ph.D. dissertation, New York University, 2000), p. 251. Remarkably, this dissertation does not draw either on the published proceedings of the FAI or of its French section.

[69] Anne-Martine Fabre, "La Ligue des Droits de l'Homme et la femme des origines à 1914," mémoire de D.E.A. d'Histoire Contemporaine, Sciences Po, 1987–1988, p. 27. Consulted at Sciences Po, 25 January 2013. Thanks to Pascal Cauchy for facilitating access to this thesis. Fabre's thesis is sporadic and not always reliable in dates and citations. I have provided correct dates in this chapter, based on my own subsequent consultation of the LDH *Bulletin* at Cujas library, place du Panthéon. Anne R. Epstein has also written about the LDH in the context of her doctoral dissertation, "Gender, Intellectual Sociability, and Political Culture in the French Third Republic, 1890–1914," (Bloomington: Indiana University, 2004), pp. 117–127. Epstein views women's participation in the LDH as a "political apprenticeship" (p. 127).

with many opportunities to underscore the intrinsic links between the woman question and the Declaration of the Rights of Man. The founders of the LDH were clearly aware of the centrality of women's issues to their concerns. According to the political scientist Anne-Martine Fabre, who surveyed the *Bulletin* of the LDH during the 1980s, already in 1898 the organization had selected three women for its initial thirty-six-member central committee: Jeanne Schmahl (*L'Avant-Courrière*), Matilde Salomon (head of the Collège Sévigné, a private girls' secondary school) and a Mme Fontaine.[70] But the three only attended a few meetings before they disappeared from the bimonthly reports.[71]

As of December 1901, the LDH had gone on record in favor of suppressing the morals police, which would effectively end the government regulation of prostitution.[72] And this declaration was, of course, of great significance for its future links with the CNFF (and, of course, also with the FAI). It would become even more important following the election in late 1903 of the deputy, journalist, and abolitionist Francis de Pressensé as president of the LDH. From that time forth, the *Ligue* moved beyond defending existing rights, including the rights of women wrongly arrested by the morals police as suspected prostitutes (whose cases the LDH took up), to call for new rights. The LDH began to organize its annual congresses around such themes as the treatment of indigenous peoples in the colonies, peace and arbitration, and women's rights, including the vote. Under Pressensé's leadership, the *Ligue's* 1907 Congress again addressed the issue of the morals police and endorsed the abolitionist position, in the name of individual rights.[73] Fabre remarks that "of all the themes concerning women's condition taken up by the LDH, the greatest consensus developed around the issue of prostitution," though she queried with some skepticism whether this was because the topic was more about "society" than about women.[74]

In her capacity as secretary-general of the CNFF, Mme Avril de Sainte-Croix gave at least one presentation on regulated prostitution to a Parisian

---

[70] Fabre, "Ligue des Droits de l'Homme et la femme," mémoire, pp. 25, 35–36. Epstein, "Gender, Intellectual Sociability, and Political Culture" (pp. 119, also 126) identifies Mme Fontaine as "Mme Lucien Fontaine, wife of the industrialist, also a founding member" of the LDH.

[71] See also Anne-Martine Fabre's short article, "La Ligue des Droits de l'homme et les femmes au début du 20ème siècle," *Materiaux pour l'histoire de notre temps*, 72 (2003), 31–35.

[72] Fabre, "Ligue des Droits de l'Homme et la femme," mémoire, pp. 16–17.

[73] Fabre, "Ligue des Droits de l'Homme et la femme," mémoire, p. 85; cf. also pp. 88–89.

[74] Fabre, "Ligue des Droits de l'Homme et la femme," p. 94.

LDH branch at a meeting on 13 February 1903 and chaired another.[75] In June 1904 she was elected to the LDH Central Committee, on which she served until December 1909.[76] During her tenure, she would press the *Ligue* to promote women's rights as part of its mission; at one point she suggested – unsuccessfully – that the Central Committee establish separate groups for women in those local sections throughout France that had more than twenty-five women members.[77] As we have seen, in mid-March 1907, on behalf of the CNFF, Mme Avril addressed a letter to the central committee of the LDH, asking for its support of the CNFF petition to the legislature (drafted by Hubertine Auclert during her brief tenure as chair of the suffrage section) demanding women's suffrage on the same terms as men. "Universal suffrage," Mme Avril wrote, "cannot achieve its full significance as long as half the nation, that is, the women, are deprived of their political rights."[78] The *Ligue*, she asserted, could not avoid endorsing this request if it wished to remain faithful to its mission of supporting the principles of the *Declaration des Droits de l'Homme*. The Central Committee did, in fact, endorse the CNFF's request and circulated the petition for discussion in its sections.[79] The *Ligue* would do more to support women's right to vote in the years to follow.

On 31 May 1909, the annual LDH congress (in Rennes) devoted a half-day session of its long and varied program to women's rights. Although the CNFF's Mme Avril was incapacitated by health issues in early 1909, the

---

[75] I have verified that Mme Avril's February 1903 talk on regulated prostitution to a Paris section is indeed summarized and commented in the LDH *Bulletin*, vol. 3, n° 8 (1 May 1903), 495–496. She also chaired an earlier session at which Dr. Sicard de Plauzoles spoke. In May 1909 Mme Avril went on a speaking tour in the Midi, on behalf of the *Ligue*. According to Wendy Ellen Perry, "Remembering Dreyfus: The Ligue des Droits de l'Homme and the Making of the Modern French Human Rights Movement" (Ph.D. thesis, University of North Carolina, Chapel Hill, 1998), Mme Avril gave several presentations on feminism to the LDH. Anne Epstein also refers to this first talk, in 1903, misleadingly, as about feminism. Curiously, Fabre does not mention this talk or any other talk presented at *Ligue* meetings by Mme Avril. It bears pointing out that both Fabre and Perry (and many others) have misidentified the husband of Mme Avril as a magistrate (rather than an engineer) and characterize her as a "*grande bourgeoise*," which she was manifestly not, at least not by birth. Rather, one might view her as a "self-made" modern woman who "performed" the persona of a *grande bourgeoise* whenever it suited her.

[76] See clipping in reel 4, AdeSC scrapbooks, from October 1906. Fabre, p. 36, says (mistakenly) that Mme Avril resigned in 1910. In fact, the LDH *Bulletin*, vol. 10, n° 1 (15 January 1910), 4, reports that the Central Committee accepted Mme Avril's resignation at its 6 December 1909 meeting.

[77] Fabre, "Ligue des Droits de l'Homme et la femme," p. 32.

[78] See LDH *Bulletin*, vol. 7, n° 9 (15 May 1907), 440–442; quote, 441.

[79] Concerning the suffrage petition, see the LDH *Bulletin*, vol. 7, n° 9 (15 May 1907), 440–442, for the report on this agenda item and the text of the CNFF's letter (Fabre has mis-cited this reference). See also "Conseil National des Femmes Françaises – Séance du 5 mai 1907," *Le Journal des Femmes*, n° 174 (May 1907), front page.

young attorney Maria Vérone, who was secretary-general of the LFDF (a CNFF affiliate) had stepped in to draft the succinct (eleven pages) yet comprehensive report on women's rights (drawn up by a nine-member LDH commission, with the imprimatur of the Central Committee, and circulated to delegates in advance) that would be discussed at this congress.[80]

The Vérone report and the ensuing debates set the benchmark for the *Ligue*'s embrace of women's rights.[81] The report opened by quoting Article 1 of the Declaration of the Rights of Man, followed by Article 6, which posited equal opportunity for all citizens. Yet, the report remarked, from revolutionary times on these articles had been interpreted as not encompassing women, and Vérone called on the LDH to ensure that "liberty, equality, and justice, as inscribed in the Rights of Man" would be equally applied to "all human beings." The report was structured so as to consider economic rights first, followed by civil rights, political rights, maternity, and prostitution.

With respect to economic rights, Vérone's report forcefully argued that "women's activity [in the labor force] has developed to the point where one had to take into account this enormous quantity of women workers of every sort, and to accord them some rights."[82] To date, she noted, women in commerce could vote for consular elections, *ouvrières* could vote and stand for election to the *conseils du travail*, the *Conseil Supérieur du Travail*, and even the councils of *prud'hommes*. Working women should also be eligible for the tribunals of commerce, the report asserted. But the most pressing issue concerned the principle of equal pay for equal work. Expressing the general consensus among feminists, Vérone's report underscored the unpleasant fact that women who worked for pay did not earn enough to live on, and all too many were forced to turn to prostitution to survive. It was false to claim that women had fewer needs than men; there were many women who also had to support families. Of particular interest to the committee were those women who were employed by the State such as teachers and as employees in the post office, telegraph, and telephone system. Equal pay for equal work, plus opportunities for advancement, were the objectives, and the place to begin was with the State itself. The *Ligue* must intervene, the report concluded.

---

[80] Other members of the commission included Fernand Corcos, Girard, E. Kahn, and Rousselet, all of whom spoke out during the debates.

[81] The full text of Vérone's report is published in the LDH *Bulletin*, vol. 9, n° 17 (15 September 1909), 1094–1104. See also the LFDF *Bulletin*, vol. 3, n° 8 (July–October 1909), 7.

[82] See Vérone's report, LDH *Bulletin*, 1096.

The absence of civil rights for married women had been on the feminist agenda for many decades. The Vérone report insisted on the fact that it was the "condition" of marriage that denied women their rights; "this was neither just nor logical" since single adult women enjoyed comprehensive rights. It called on the LDH to urge the legislature to pass the *proposition de loi* introduced by the parliamentary feminists to abolish the civil incapacity of married women. As for mothers, they must have equal opportunity to exercise parental power; this should not be the prerogative of fathers alone. Moreover, the report asserted, women must be granted political rights, although for the time being the demand was for political rights at the level of local governance. The report concluded with a series of resolutions, which would be voted on at the LDH congress. One of these indicated that the *Ligue* would put pressure on the government to enact equal pay for equal work, beginning with the State's employees.

The debate over this report at the 1909 congress offers an index of how far progressive republican men were willing to go, despite some misgivings, in support of women's rights with respect to the principle of equality. Presenting the report and its accompanying resolutions to the assembled delegates, Maria Vérone pointedly reminded delegates that she had framed the question of women's rights "as being the prolongation of the Declaration of the Rights of Man," which clearly placed the question on the agenda of the LDH.[83] She discounted the arguments used for so long against women's rights – their ostensible physical and intellectual inferiority – by remarking not only the importance of mechanization for diminishing the necessity of physical strength but also the diminution of the handicaps women previously faced due to inadequate schooling.[84] All that women required now, Vérone insisted, was equality before the law. She remarked that in the nine-member commission that had worked on the report, the economic question had provoked the most controversy but, nevertheless, the commission had voted 5-4 in favor of economic liberty for women, including access to all careers.[85]

---

[83] The stenographic account of Vérone's oral presentation of the report to the LDH and the ensuing debate (all on 31 May) is published in an earlier LDH *Bulletin*, vol. 9, nos 14–15 (31 July–15 August 1909), 969–999.

[84] The argument about changes in the requirement of physical strength due to mechanization echo earlier arguments by Jeanne Deroin and other nineteenth-century feminists. The arguments about women's intellectual inferiority, and objections to them, date back to the eighteenth century – and before – in conjunction with the nature/culture debates.

[85] Vérone's oral presentation, 970–971 (see note 83).

It was precisely this issue, dear to the heart of the CNFF executive officers and to Maria Vérone, that engendered some contestation and much discussion during the LDH congress's debates. Despite Vérone's eloquent oral presentation, several members of the commission's minority spoke up in opposition to the notion that women's employment was either desirable or necessary. The long-standing feminist claim that women should and could support themselves through paid labor met with strong resistance from these partisans of the male-breadwinner model.[86] Even so, it seemed clear that the male-breadwinner model was unsustainable in the face of France's current economic realities.

Addressing such opposition, Vérone marshalled the statistics: men are now a minority in the population, she reported, and thus not all women could marry even if they so desired. Even if one forced all men to marry, she joked, there would still be single women who would have to find a means to survive economically. Women's employment was a fact, one that would not go away simply through wishful thinking. Moreover, she asserted, to work [for pay] was a right: [87]

> People have called us [women] the eternally wounded, but we don't want to be the wounded, the infirm who need to be nourished [by someone else]. You want to condemn us, along with yourselves, to marriage; and if we don't want to marry, we will be eternally prostituted, because the men [will] still need to nourish us; we do not want to be kept women, neither legally nor illegally.

These remarks met with applause. For us, she continued, "it is a question of dignity – when a woman can work, she ought to work." Vérone boldly criticized the republicans for having provided such a good education to women if there was no intent to let them put it to use. Why not, then, forbid women from entering educational institutions? Keeping women in ignorance – as an "animal de luxe" or "as a baby-making machine" – was not an option; social progress would be impossible under such conditions.[88] What was needed was a resolution in favor of "equal pay for equal work" – and that could and should be applied first to the female employees of the State, in its industries, in administration, in teaching, and others, where the

---

[86] See especially the objections of Fernand Corcos, LDH *Bulletin*, vol. 9, nᵒˢ 14–15 (31 July–15 August 1909), 974–978, and Rousselot, ibid., 979–980.

[87] Vérone, oral presentation; see the compte-rendu of the debates in the LDH *Bulletin*, vol. 9, nᵒˢ 14–15 (31 July–15 August 1909), 972. Vérone's reference to "eternally wounded" is, of course, to Michelet.

[88] Debate, LDH *Bulletin*, vol. 9, nᵒˢ 14–15 (31 July–15 August 1909), 973. Cf. Fabre, "Ligue des Droits de l'Homme et la femme," 56.

qualifications and work requirements were exactly the same for men and women.

At the conclusion of the debate, the LDH congress delegates voted down a counterresolution that favored the male-breadwinner model to support wives, with subventions based in men's collective labor to support those who were unmarried or widows with children. Instead, they affirmed the *Ligue*'s support for women's right to work and for equal pay for equal work. The delegates further supported a resolution that this principle be applied to all government employees. Then, during the debates on maternity policy, they also supported an amended resolution favoring an obligatory extended (six weeks before birth and four weeks following birth) maternity leave for women workers, to be indemnified by public funds.[89] The LDH congress delegates likewise endorsed a resolution to legalize *recherche de la paternité*, and with respect to prostitution, they supported a resolution to abolish the morals police and to bring the bill [*projet de loi*] recommended by the Extraparliamentary Commission to the floor of the legislature, and even called for punishment of those who exploited prostitutes.[90]

The debates concerning the second major issue addressed by the Vérone report and its ensuing resolution – to end the disempowerment of wives in French civil law – put the LDH delegates to the true test of what they believed about the "gender" of the rights of "Man." Vérone argued pointedly in the debate that it was time to "admit in the family the principles you have admitted in society," that is to say, democracy. Equal rights, she insisted, would "assure good understanding and harmony" and she called for the suppression of the infamous articles of the Civil Code (Article 212 and those immediately following) that bound the hands of wives. The LDH congress did support the resolution to suppress the civil incapacity of the wife as established in the Civil Code. The delegates also agreed on a further resolution, to the effect that *"puissance paternelle"* [paternal authority] should be shared by both parents (following the intervention of the *Ligue*'s legal counsel, who pointedly reminded delegates of Napoléon's pronouncements concerning wifely "obedience" in the debates on the code a century earlier, and prodded the delegates to get rid of "this outdated obedience which is nothing more than a superannuated form of religion and authority").[91] Both measures were ratified by the

---

[89] Debate, LDH *Bulletin*, vol. 9, n[os] 14–15 (31 July–15 August 1909), 995. Cf. Fabre, "Ligue des Droits de l'Homme et la femme," 59–60.

[90] Debate, 997–999.   [91] Debate, 982–987.

delegates, but the question of revising marital property regimes was postponed for consideration at a later date.

Although Fabre expressed her skepticism about the authenticity of the LDH's support for women's rights, my reading of the Vérone report and the 1909 convention debates suggests that, in the context of the times, the men of the LDH were, on the whole, extremely supportive.[92] The resolutions proposed and passed at the 1909 congress represented some very progressive, pro-feminist positions for the time. They encompassed everything that the CNFF and its affiliated organizations had asked for.

The debate on granting women political rights at the 1909 LDH congress climaxed in a surprise ending. Vérone's eloquent arguments, in her report, for granting women the vote in gradual steps, beginning at the municipal, arrondissement, and departmental level, were both assertive in principal and cautious in practice.[93] "The woman works, woman pays taxes, thus she has the right to vote." To objections such as lack of military service, women can respond with maternity, she said; military service may one day disappear, but maternity will remain with us. She pointedly reminded the audience that although there were indeed a few feminists who argued that women should neither be wives nor mothers, "a great majority of feminists are wives and mothers and by that alone have fulfilled their social obligations."[94] She reminded the delegates that the first measure to be proposed in the legislature (by M. Gautret, in 1901) would give the vote to single women, widows, or *divorcées* – with the effect that "in order to exercise their political rights, married women would either be obliged to divorce or to kill their husbands."[95] The second, by Dussaussoy in 1906, removed eligibility for office but extended the vote to all women. Action, Vérone affirmed, needed to be taken before the end of the present legislature.

In the ensuing debate, the *Ligue*'s president Francis de Pressensé proposed, in the spirit of full equality, that women be granted not only eligibility to run for national office but to vote as well; since the British House of Commons had recently endorsed full woman suffrage, why shouldn't the LDH, he asked.[96] With little further debate (was it perhaps

---

[92] Fabre, "Ligue des Droits de l'Homme et la femme," p. 65.

[93] Fabre, "Ligue des Droits de l'Homme et la femme," pp. 78–80. See Debate, LDH *Bulletin*, vol. 9, n°s 14–15 (31 July-15 August 1909), 991–992.

[94] Maria Vérone, during the debate, 991.

[95] No laughter is recorded following Vérone's impertinent remark, 991.

[96] Pressensé was probably referring to the House of Commons vote (271 to 92) on the second reading of the Stanger Women's Enfranchisement Bill on 28 February 1908 (which was subsequently

because the afternoon was long) the Congress voted on an amended resolution, rallying to the principle of woman suffrage without restriction.[97] The question then was whether this resolution would have a practical effect on the French legislators. It is worth remarking that the deputy who would carry the suffrage bill forward in the Chamber of Deputies was none other than Ferdinand Buisson, who in 1911 would succeed Pressensé as president of the LDH. Buisson's endorsement of women's suffrage carried considerable weight, though not enough to force the Chamber of Deputies to actually discuss the matter (prior to resolving the issue of proportional representation). Even so, up to 1914, some members of the LDH were still of the opinion that women should first be better educated, lest a clerical vote on their part lead to the downfall of the republic. After the war, when suffrage for women seemed a real possibility, the *Ligue*'s support for woman suffrage would remain firm in principle but more tepid in practice.[98]

Following this triumph for women's rights with the *Ligue des Droits de l'Homme*, in early 1910 Maria Vérone was elected to the organization's Central Committee, where she served throughout the war years. In 1920, however, Vérone would be removed without cause, by which time she had succeeded Marie Bonnevial, also active in the LDH at the local level, as president of the LFDF, and would play a leading role in the continuing suffrage agitation.[99]

The CNFF also reached out to the emerging political parties. In the same year (1901) that the national council was founded, the political factions known subsequently as the *Parti Radical et Radical-Socialiste* (PRRS) came

---

blocked from advancing by the Speaker). See June Purvis, *Emmeline Pankhurst: A Biography* (London: Routledge, 2002), p. 104. This vote was briefly reported in the *Le Journal des Femmes*, n° 183 (March 1908), 1. The WSPU began to raise the stakes with public demonstrations, initially with its great rally of 21 June 1908 in Hyde Park. In 1909, the liberal prime minister Asquith would refuse to receive a delegation of WSPU suffragettes or their petitions, arrests would be made, and that summer the infamous forced-feeding of WSPU prisoners would begin.

[97] See Debate, LDH *Bulletin*, vol. 9, n°ˢ 14–15 (31 July – 15 August 1909), 991–999. Cf. Fabre, "Ligue des Droits de l'Homme et la femme," 78–80.

[98] See William D. Irvine, "Women's Right and the 'Rights of Man'," in *Crisis and Renewal in Twentieth-Century France*, ed. Martin S. Alexander & Kenneth Mouré (New York & Oxford: Berghahn Books, 2002), pp. 46–65, and, more generally, Irvine's book *Between Justice and Politics: The Ligue des Droits de l'Homme 1898–1945* (Stanford, CA: Stanford University Press, 2007). Although the dates in the book title suggest otherwise, Irvine's research focuses primarily on the interwar period.

[99] Fabre notes that other feminists such as Marie Bonnevial, Maria Pognon, and Séverine, were active in local LDH branches in Paris prior to 1914, though not at the national level. She does not mention ("Ligue des Droits de l'Homme et la femme," mémoire, p. 38) the names of the six other women candidates who were not elected to the Central Committee.

together in June for their first congress. Many of the CNFF's male-feminist supporters such as Ferdinand Buisson were also engaged in this effort at political consolidation. Nevertheless, as Maria Martin underscored in the *Le Journal des Femmes* (in an editorial that was even more caustic than usual) the congress was nearly devoid of female delegates; there were just four women, adrift in a sea of a thousand men who were all talking at once. No woman was appointed to the congress's study commission. But when several supporters introduced a measure in favor of integral rights for women, supplemented by the statement that the Rights of *Man* must be applied to women, the commission demurred – and the conclusions of its rapporteur, Louis Andrieux (a male-feminist who was obviously unhappy with the subcommission's decision not to consider, much less affirm, this resolution) was challenged from the floor by Dr. Georges Martin.[100] The congress subsequently endorsed a far weaker statement, calling for "the progressive and reasoned admission of woman to public affairs," and also approved an amendment that demanded the same pay for women civil servants as for men." At its 1902 congress in Lyon, the president reminded delegates – importantly – that "woman's accession to civil rights is part of the republican program."[101] Political rights for women, on the other hand, remained controversial. The male-feminists were certainly a minority in the PRRS; at their 1907 congress in Nancy party officials were still talking about "woman" in the abstract singular and would adopt only a tepid program statement on women's rights, proclaiming its support for "the gradual extension of rights to woman," but adding the caveat that a woman "must be protected by law in every circumstance of her life."[102] Hubertine Auclert, who since 1896 had been publishing weekly articles in *Le Radical,* kept pestering the PRRS leaders and had high hopes, but at its 1907 congress the party did not even consider her [the CNFF's] suffrage petition.[103] Auclert's editorials for *Le Radical* terminated in late 1909. It was by then quite clear

---

[100] As reported by Maria Martin in her front-page editorial, "Le Féminisme au Congrès Radical Socialiste," *Le Journal des Femmes,* n° 112 (July 1901). The men who submitted the resolution for full equal rights for women and application of the principles of the Rights of Man were Jean-Bernard, Lucien Le Foyer, and Ch. Robet.

[101] For the final resolutions, see Armand Charpentier, *Le Parti Radical et Radical-Socialiste à travers ses congrès (1901–1911)* (Paris: Giard & Briere, 1913), p. 406. This book breaks down the party positions by topic; half a page concerns "Le Féminisme," but under the rubric "Oeuvres de solidarité". Concerning the woman question, Charpentier makes the Radical congress look far more supportive of women's issues than it actually was.

[102] The Radical Party programme is partially reproduced in translation in *France: Empire and Republic, 1850–1940,* ed. David Thomson (New York: Harper & Row, 1968), p. 281.

[103] Hause, *Hubertine Auclert,* pp. 192–194.

that, despite its small cohort of male-feminists, the PRRS as a whole was resistant to endorsing women's emancipation.

The CNFF leaders also cultivated the parliamentary socialists. We know that Mme Avril de Sainte-Croix and Jean Jaurès exchanged letters in 1902.[104] Following the unification of the socialists into the *Section Française de l'Internationale Ouvrière* (SFIO) in 1905, the feminists reminded its leaders of their earlier promises to act on behalf of women's emancipation. Other non-CNFF affiliated feminists were also actively pressing on the SFIO to introduce a bill on women's suffrage; the young Dr. Madeleine Pelletier (1874–1939) would speak to this very point at the Third SFIO congress in November 1906, addressing the musty old arguments that had been circulating for so long, and challenging the party to follow up earlier declarations of principle with an action plan.[105]

In mid-January 1907, the CNFF's secretary-general Mme Avril, again signing as Savioz, published a front-page editorial in the SFIO's daily paper, *L'Humanité*, claiming the feminist movement as a child of the French Revolution and pressing on the French socialist party to follow through on its earlier promises to women, as other socialist parties in England, Belgium, and Germany were doing. Seventy percent of French women today, she pointed out, pursued economic independence and this fact alone brought them closer to the socialists. By this time, Savioz claimed 11 million adherents for the CNFF and underscored the Council's insistence on the economic emancipation of women, a goal clearly dear to the hearts of the Socialists. Ever leveraging, she laid out the seven programmatic goals of the CNFF's Section on Work, which included unionization of women workers and equal pay for equal work. The inferiority of women's pay represented an economic danger, a social danger, and a moral danger, she insisted. "By claiming women's revendications as its own, the Socialist party has not only accomplished an act of justice, but at the same time it has made an excellent political move since, by its attitude, it has drawn over to its ideas thousands of women."[106] As the Socialist party prepared a bill to give women political rights, she indicated, it should heed the words of Jean Jaurès who, upon receiving a delegation of feminists at the Palais-Bourbon, stated that it was inappropriate to reject women's claims on the grounds that the majority were "clerical." If this were really

[104] On their correspondence, see Miller, "'Romance of Regulation'," p. 226 (cited in n. 68).

[105] Madeleine Pelletier, "Extension du droit de suffrage à la femme," Parti Socialiste (Section Française de l'Internationale Ouvrière), *3e Congrès National, tenu à Limoges, les 1er, 2, 3, et 4 novembre 1906. Compte Rendu analytique* (Paris: Au Siège du Conseil National, s.d.), pp. 146–149.

[106] Savioz, "L'Indépendance économique de la femme," *L'Humanité* (17 January 1907), front page.

so, she noted, the events around the separation of Church and State (in 1905) would have been far more turbulent.

In the year 1907, the first International Socialist Women's Conference, meeting in August in Stuttgart, concurrently with the International Socialist Congress, endorsed the still-radical principle of unrestricted suffrage for both sexes, whether married or single.[107] This women's conference, organized by Clara Zetkin, also reaffirmed the argument that working-class women should make no common cause with "bourgeois feminism" as concerned the suffrage (or any other matter). The Second International's congress overwhelmingly endorsed these pro-suffrage resolutions.

How would the newly unified SFIO respond? In *L'Humanité* (6 September 1907), the socialist deputy known as "Bracke" (Alexandre Desrousseaux; 1861–1955) spoke out in support of the Stuttgart resolution and emphasized that the socialists' campaign for women's suffrage had nothing in common with that of the "bourgeois feminists," who – he claimed – were only interested in material gain for their class, whereas proletarian women were interested in the victory of the proletariat. Writing in *L'Action* (17 September 1907), another young feminist named Nelly Roussel (1878–1922) spoke against Bracke's party-line assertions, insisting that he was attributing to the so-called bourgeois feminists arguments that she had never encountered among them. What was more, she asserted, bourgeois and proletarian women had far more in common – that is, their subjection to masculine domination – than women of either class did with the men of their own class. "One cannot repeat enough times that with us [women] there are no '*classes dirigéantes*' – because all women are – or at least according to the law, should be – the '*dirigées*'. . . . the social question is for us women far less simple than for the men. The struggle against capitalism, which interests a great number of women, is complicated by the struggle against *masculinisme*, e.g., *the principle of male superiority*, which interests *all* women" (emphasis in original). Even though socialists would claim that feminism was no longer relevant, once the socialists had embraced women's demands in its program, Nelly Roussel queried the absence of results to date: what had the socialists actually accomplished for women without being pushed by the feminists who made the party understand that "woman counts and that she is a force."[108]

---

[107] For the English-language text of the socialist women's statement endorsing integral suffrage for women at the Stuttgart congress, see Bell & Offen, *Women, the Family, and Freedom*, vol. 2, doc. 59, pp. 231–232.

[108] See Bracke, "Le Vote des femmes," *L'Humanité* (6 September 1907), front page, and Nelly Roussel, "Feminisme et socialisme," *L'Action* (17 September 1907), reprinted in Nelly Roussel, *Quelques Lances rompues par nos libertés* (Paris: V. Giard & E. Briere, 1910), pp. 45–50; quote, pp. 48–49.

In late October 1909, another socialist deputy for Paris, Marcel Sembat, would speak out for women's suffrage in the Chamber of Deputies, a move much appreciated by the feminists of the LFDF.[109] In March 1910, the leadership of the LFDF (Bonnevial and Vérone, both of whom were very active in the CNFF as well as committed socialists) challenged the deputies, socialist and otherwise, to act on behalf of women's vote in the coming elections. However, despite Sembat's intervention, little action was forthcoming from the socialist deputies; the preoccupation of the legislature with a proportional representation bill meant that suffrage for individual women was relegated to the back burner. To be sure, in the 1910 legislative elections, the socialists and feminists would put forward a cluster of symbolic female candidates for the deputation, including Elisabeth Renaud (also active in the LFDF), Madeleine Pelletier, Caroline Kauffmann, and Marguerite Durand. Even though leading socialists such as Eugène Fournière, editor of the *Revue Socialiste*, would speak positively at the LFDF's 1910 banquet concerning the interests that ought to unite socialism to feminism, the prospects for alliance remained questionable.[110] In February 1912 a delegation of fifty feminists, including Bonnevial and Vérone, would call on Marcel Sembat, following which the socialist parliamentary group would discuss ways in which its deputies might intervene on the question of women's suffrage.[111]

At one of the LFDF's monthly lectures in later 1910, a young Russian woman, Lydie Pissarjewski, lectured on the parallels between socialism and feminism, but remarked that feminism had no firm doctrine or "method" such as that established for socialists by Karl Marx with the method of class struggle; even so, she accorded immense credit to the "bourgeois" feminists for the work they were doing. The ensuing discussion indicated that audience participants were divided on the question of whether sex solidarity was, or was not, more important than class solidarity. A Mr. Moufilet thought that an alliance between socialism and feminism was out of the question; although many socialist leaders were sympathetic to feminist aims, he stated, the vast bulk of its supporters were not. Maria Vérone's husband, the attorney Georges Lhermitte, insisted that bourgeois and working class women had many interests in common. The lecturer, Mlle Pissarjewski, concluded that, since men and women did not constitute two distinct classes, feminism

---

[109] See the LFDF *Bulletin*, n° 10 (April–July 1910), 11–13, reprinting the transcript of Sembat's intervention in the Chamber of Deputies, 29 October 1909.

[110] LFDF *Bulletin*, n° 12 (January 1911), 4.   [111] LFDF *Bulletin*, n° 3 (March 1912), 12–13.

had nothing to do with class struggle.[112] Meanwhile, socialist feminists who, like Madeleine Pelletier, attempted to maneuver politically within the SFIO, found it a frustrating experience, as did the feminists who supported women's right to work and equal pay. In fact, in 1913–1914, it would be the feminists, not the socialists, who would stand up for women's economic independence.[113]

In late 1912, a new socialist women's group called the *Groupe des Femmes Socialistes* (GDFS), distinct from the earlier *Groupe des Féministes Socialistes*, would form. Initially it included a number of leading socialist feminists such as the LFDF's Maria Vérone, Marie Bonnevial, and the educator Elisabeth Renaud (who became the group's first secretary-general). Louise Saumoneau, however, would ultimately succeed in eliminating these more conciliatory women from the group's leadership, insisting that membership in the SFIO itself must be a prior requirement for membership in the GDFS. By the end of 1913 the GDFS would fully embrace the Zetkin anti-bourgeois-feminist noncooperation line. Already in July Suzanne Lacore (1875–1975; known as Suzon) restated this position in *L'Équité*, asserting that class struggle must take precedence over any revolution in women's position.[114] In the wake of the triumphal congress of the International Woman Suffrage Alliance (IWSA) in Budapest in July 1913, Saumoneau's condemnation of feminists would become ever more virulent; she praised her Hungarian socialist counterparts for not letting themselves be "duped by this amalgam of intriguers, naïve, misguided and hysterical [women] who constitute bourgeois feminism in every country."[115] But Saumoneau's hard-core approach would not succeed either in engaging more committed women in the GDFS or in inflecting the SFIO's quest for electoral success with a still heavily masculinist male electorate.[116]

---

[112] On the Pissarjewski lecture (undated), see LFDF *Bulletin*, n° 12 (January 1911), 10–12. Her brochure, *Socialisme et féminisme* (Paris: Impr. L'Union typographique), on which her lecture was presumably based, was published in 1910; and reprinted in 1978, under the spelling Pissarjevsky.

[113] This is the conclusion of Marilyn J. Boxer, "Socialism Faces Feminism: The Failure of Synthesis in France, 1879–1914," in *Socialist Women: European Socialist Feminism in the Nineteenth and Early Twentieth Centuries*, ed. Marilyn J. Boxer & Jean H. Quataert ((New York: Elsevier, 1978), pp. 75–111. This article provides a condensed version of Boxer's arguments in her earlier dissertation, "Socialism Faces Feminism in France: 1879–1913" (University of California, Riverside, 1975).

[114] The ensuing polemic in *L'Équité* will be discussed in Chapter 12, in connection with the Couriau Affair.

[115] Louise Saumoneau, comment on article from *L'Humanité*, in *La Femme socialiste*, 2, n° 11 (1 September 1913), 5.

[116] See Sowerwine, *Sisters or Citizens*, chapters 5 and 6.

Much of the scholarship on French feminism in this period has focused on the quest for woman suffrage, to the neglect of other issues. It seems clear from a reexamination of the sources that French feminists, especially those associated with the CNFF, did advocate and campaign for a comprehensive range of specific alterations in the institutions, laws, and practices of the Third Republic, which they hoped to accomplish by invoking republican principles and by working through official channels. However, the women's proposed alterations in the political, economic, and social structure continued to encounter resistance from the majority of France's elected legislators. Thus it was that years of legislative frustration would lead the women's advocates to conclude (as had Hubertine Auclert and her supporters decades earlier) that only the vote would provide them with the political clout they needed to succeed. Electoral authority in the form of the vote (and candidacy for office) promised to be the tools that could unleash women's political and social power. But, as the feminists constantly claimed, attaining the vote was never the ultimate objective, nor an end in itself; it was the essential means to achieve a series of concrete reforms. Let us then see how, and in what manner, the debates about feminism itself as well as its major objectives, its strategies and its tactics, were developing in the interim, as the frustration grew and the suffrage option gathered momentum. We will address, first, the varied representations of feminism and feminists in the early twentieth century, then move to the debates surrounding the population issue, the issues raised by women's employment, and finally, the campaigns for the vote.

CHAPTER 10

Defining, Historicizing, Contesting, and Defending Feminism
Early Twentieth-Century Developments

By 1901 the terms *féminisme* and *féministe* had become well established in the Francophone world and were spreading fast into other languages. In Chapter 5, I discussed the first phase of the debates over defining, contesting, and defending the new terms feminism and feminist during the decade of the 1890s. In this chapter, this investigation continues by pinpointing certain significant trends and developments in the period from 1901 to 1914. Of these perhaps the most important is the continuing assertion of embodied womanhood (which cannot be reduced to merely a "performance" of femininity or womanliness) by most of the leading feminists, from Marguerite Durand and Marcelle Tinayre to Ghénia Avril de Sainte-Croix and Maria Vérone, in the face of repeated accusations by critics that feminism stood for women wanting to become "like" men, or indeed to become men. These "feminine" feminists vigorously demanded legal and economic equality for their sex, even as many sought to convince skeptics and opponents that such equality would not put an end to womanliness *à la française*, but would in fact enhance it. There were, of course, some notable exceptions to this trend, such as Madeleine Pelletier and Arria Ly, whose objections to this "femininity"-centered approach will be addressed in conclusion to this chapter. But it is worth remarking that this concern with "remaining a woman" preoccupied socialist women as well.[1] A second major development was the beginning of a scholarly historiography of feminisms, including feminism during the French Revolution. A third was the proliferation of antifeminist critiques, as the masculinist backlash mounted against women's emancipatory claims. In fact, as my colleague Florence Rochefort has remarked, and as we will see, antifeminist criticism "only became more vigorous" and "found an unprecedented amplitude" in

---

[1] See the militant socialist-feminist monthly, *L'Équité*, 15 December 1913 and 15 January 1914, 3, for the exchange between Suzanne Gibault and Marie Laignier over the question of "rester femme." This was not a new concern in socialist circles; in 1898 the various obituary announcements for socialist-feminist Aline Valette (see Chapter 2) had all stressed that she had "remained a woman."

these years.[2] But the responses by feminists to the antifeminists became more vigorous still as public opinion began to recognize the merit of the feminists' demands for institutional and attitudinal change.

During the first decade of the twentieth century, feminist arguments reached an unprecedented audience through lecture series and publications and through the Francophone daily and weekly press. In 1902, the writer Marguerite Souley-Darqué launched her public lectures on "feminology," offering the first interdisciplinary courses in what we would now call "women's studies" at the innovative *Collège Libre de Sciences Sociales* in Paris. In 1908 she would publish a broad-ranging book based on her lectures, *L'Évolution de la femme* [Woman's Evolution], in which she argued that industrial capitalism had made obsolete the conditions that had hindered women's full development.[3] Ghénia Avril de Sainte-Croix would also deliver a series of lectures at the *Collège* on "*féminisme.*"

Women's magazines offered an interesting array of analyses. For example, the new twentieth-century Parisian women's magazines such as *Femina* [fd. 1901] and *La Vie Heureuse* [fd. 1902], which targeted a "genteel" (leisured and well-heeled) bourgeois audience, deliberately skirted the label "feminist" even as they discussed aspects of the woman question and discretely promoted the modern woman.[4] The late twentieth-century expression "I'm not a feminist – but . . ." exemplifies their approach. The same could be said of another magazine for women, *La Femme française* (1902–1904), which had a great deal to say about what was (or was not) acceptable with regard to women's sports.[5] The editors of the newly minted Catholic periodical *La Femme contemporaine,* launched in Besançon in late 1903 by Abbé Jean

---

[2] Florence Rochefort, "L'Antiféminisme à la Belle Époque, une rhétorique réactionnaire?" in *Un Siècle d'antiféminisme,* ed. Christine Bard (Paris: Fayard, 1999), pp. 133–147; quotes, p. 133. A fourth important development was the blossoming of public forums on feminist issues, such as the gatherings of the *Société de Sociologie de Paris* or the "Libre Entretiens" sponsored by the Union de la Vérité, where women as well as men were invited to debate aspects of the woman question. The latter gatherings are currently under study by Jean Elisabeth Pedersen and will not be discussed here.

[3] See Marguerite Souley-Darqué, *L'Évolution de la femme* (Ghent: Soc. coopérative Volksdrukkerij, 1908). Marilyn J. Boxer first brought Souley-Darqué's courses and her ensuing book to public attention in "Women's Studies in France circa 1902," *International Supplement to the Women's Studies Quarterly,* n° 1 (January 1982), 26–27. See also Boxer's article, "Feminology," in the *Women's Studies Encyclopedia,* ed. Helen Tierney (Westport, CT: Greenwood Press, 1999), vol. 1, pp. 490–491.

[4] Rachel Mesch, *Having It All in the Belle Epoque: How French Women's Magazines Invented the Modern Woman* (Stanford, CA: Stanford University Press, 2013). On *Femina,* see also Lenard Berlanstein, "Selling Modern Femininity: *Femina,* a Forgotten Feminist Publishing Success in Belle Epoque France," *French Historical Studies,* 30:4 (Fall 2007), 623–649; and Colette Cosnier, *Les Dames de* Femina: *Un féminisme mystifié* (Rennes: Presses Universitaires de Rennes, 2009).

[5] Françoise Labridy-Poncelet, "Imaginaires féminins et pratiques sportives. L'imaginaire de la femme bourgeoise et son usage des pratiques sportives: l'exemple de la revue *La Femme française* (1902–1904)," in *Les Athlètes de la République,* ed. Pierre Arnaud (Toulouse: Privat, 1987), pp. 317–329.

Lagardère, however, had no compunctions about using these f-words; under his pseudonym "C. Mano" the progressive abbot published on "true feminism" in the third and fourth issues, admitting that women did have some justifiable grievances, while in early 1904 the academician and Catholic convert (and, not incidentally, the influential director of the *Revue des Deux Mondes*) Ferdinand Brunetière published his own two-part article about the "two feminisms" – in which he distinguished Christian feminism (good) and revolutionary feminism (bad), condemned class struggle, and called for unity of the sexes in the family.[6] In 1905, the secular Paris-based *Groupe Français d'Études Féministes* (GFEF) launched the monthly (later weekly) *L'Entente: journal féministe*, with Héra Mirtel (pseud. of Louise Jacques, 1868–1931), as editor-in-chief and Jeanne Oddo-Deflou as one of its most prominent contributors. Its proud motto was "Feminism is the re-establishment of the human being in one of its most downtrodden factors until now: Woman."[7] By 1908, Maria Martin, writing in the *Journal des Femmes* (whose subtitle was *Organe du Mouvement Féministe*), had had enough of the notion of "two feminisms," the good and the bad. She argued that there was but one feminist goal: "Equality of man and woman before the law" through the pursuit of civil and political rights.[8] There was no point, she stated, in using euphemisms like "*progrès féminin*" when "*féminisme*" said it all.[9] In fact, she opined (perhaps too optimistically), that public opinion had evolved and that vociferous antifeminism was slowly losing public support.

Historiography of Feminism: A New Growth "Industry"?

Feminism as a historical subject began to attract the attention of French writers and scholars, most of them sympathetic men. Importantly, the

---

[6] C. Mano, "Le vrai féminisme," *La Femme contemporaine*, 1:3 (December 1903), 173–180, and 2:4 (January 1904), 31–38; Ferdinand Brunetière, "Les deux féminismes," *La Femme contemporaine*, 2:4 (January 1904), 8–16, and 2:5 (February 1904), 109–122. Cf. also Jean Lagardère, "La Femme contemporaine: son but, sa méthode, ses moyens d'action," *La Femme contemporaine*, 2:4 (January 1904), 1–7, and 2:7 (April 1904), 305–310. On Lagardère and his publication, see Florence Rochefort, "La revue *La Femme contemporaine*, quel féminisme catholique?," in *Femmes, Genre, et Catholicisme: Nouvelles recherches, nouveaux objets (France, XIXe–XXe siècles)*, ed. Anne Cova & Bruno Dumons (Lyon: RESEA/LARHRA, 2012), pp. 121–134.

[7] Founded in April 1905, *L'Entente* continued publication until 1908/1909, often in tandem with *Le Semeur*. "Le féminisme est le relèvement de l'être humain dans un de ses facteurs trop anéanti jusqu'ici: la Femme." I have translated "anéanti" as downtrodden rather than annihilated. The slogan was adopted by Mirtel's *Le Petit Almanach féministe*.

[8] Maria Martin, "Les Deux Féminismes," *Le Journal des Femmes*, n° 183 (March 1908), front page. Martin's editorial provides one of the most succinct summaries of feminist goals in the legal area.

[9] Maria Martin, "La Signification des mots," *Le Journal des Femmes*, n° 191 (January 1909), 1.

topic of feminism engaged the first professor to hold the newly created chair of history of the French Revolution at the Sorbonne, Alphonse Aulard.[10] If, indeed, to speak of feminism in the French Revolution was anachronistic, it was a conscious anachronism, one embraced early on by the Sorbonne.[11] A major contribution to this literature was Léopold Lacour's *Trois Femmes de la Révolution: Olympe de Gouges, Théroigne de Méricourt, Rose Lacombe* (1900); the author dedicated his first chapter on the author of the Declaration of the Rights of Woman, Olympe de Gouges, to Professor Aulard.[12] Aulard's scholarly journal, *La Révolution française; revue d'histoire contemporaine*, published articles on the women of Orléans during the Revolution and on women serving as soldiers, based on new research in departmental archives.[13] Other, more ambitious works soon followed, such as the lavishly illustrated *Les Femmes de la Révolution française (1789–1795)* by Maurice Dreyfous, published in 1903; Alfred Dessens's 1905 doctoral thesis, *Les Revendications des droits de la femme au point de vue politique, civil, économique, pendant la Révolution*, and Adrien Lasserre's *La Participation collective des femmes à la Révolution française; les antécédents du féminisme* (1906).[14] Léopold Lacour supplemented his earlier *opus* with articles on the feminism of Condorcet and

---

[10] A[lphonse] Aulard, "Le Féminisme pendant la Révolution," *La Revue Bleue* (19 March 1898), 361–366; and "La Formation du parti républicain (1790–1791)," *La Révolution française*, vol. 35, n° 4 (October 1898), 296–347; and especially A. Aulard, *Histoire politique de la Révolution française: Origines et développement de la Démocratie et de la République, 1789–1804* (Paris: A. Colin, 1901), vol. 1, p. 93ff.; also in the English edition, *The French Revolution: A Political History 1789–1804*, transl. Bernard Miall, from the third French edition (New York: Charles Scribner's Sons, 1910), vol. 1, pp. 231–237. Aulard's younger colleague Albert Mathiez also began publishing on women in the revolution, though not necessarily on the feminist elements; see his "Catherine Théot et le mysticisme révolutionnaire," *La Révolution française*, vol. 40, n° 6 (June 1901), 481–518. In Brussels, another study appeared: Rienzi [pseud. of Henri Hubert van Kol], *Les Femmes de la Révolution française* (Brussels: La Presse socialiste, 1898), 85 p. This work (which has no scholarly reference apparatus) focuses on the sad fates of four women, Théroigne de Méricourt, Charlotte Corday, Madame Roland, and Olympe de Gouges. Consulted at Smith College, The Sophia Smith Collection, France, Box 11. Cf. the brief discussions in Chapters 4 and 8 of the beginnings of this historical writing on women and feminism during the French Revolution.

[11] See Christine Fauré, "La naissance d'un anachronisme: 'le féminisme pendant la Révolution française'," *Annales Historiques de la Révolution française*, n° 344 (April–June 2006), 193–195.

[12] Léopold Lacour, *Trois Femmes de la Révolution: Olympe de Gouges, Théroigne de Méricourt, Rose Lacombe* (Paris: Plon, 1900).

[13] E.g., Camille Bloch, "Les Femmes d'Orléans pendant la Révolution," *La Révolution française*, 43:1 (July 1902), 49–67. On the women soldiers, see F. Gerbaux, "Les femmes soldats pendant la Révolution," 47:1 (14 July 1904), 47–61; Léon Deschamps, "Les Femmes-soldats dans la Sarthe," 47:4 (October 1904), 326–335; and Camille Bloch, "Reine Chatton, Volontaire (1793)," 49:5 (November 1905), 440–441.

[14] Maurice Dreyfous, *Les Femmes de la Révolution française (1789–1795)* (Paris: Société française d'éditions d'art, 1903); Alfred Dessens, *Les Revendications des droits de la femme au point de vue politique, civil, économique, pendant la Révolution*, doctoral thesis, Faculté de Droit (Toulouse: C.

Marat. Joseph Turquan published a two-volume study of *Les Femmes de l'émigration*.[15] New documents supporting claims for feminist activity during the revolution would be discovered, as, for example, a 1789 petition from Marseille, "Réclamations des femmes de Provence pour leur admission aux États-Généraux," which would create a buzz in 1913 after it had been published in an Italian newspaper (*Il Secolo*) by a certain Giuseppe Guisti; Marcelle Tinayre would republish it in *Le Journal*, and in May 1914 an English translation made its way into the British suffrage journal *Common Cause*.[16]

This anachronistic use of the term feminism quickly became the flavor of the month among historians. Doubtless in order to attract public attention, French scholars began to apply the term "feminism" to describe early modern writers including Erasmus, Thomas More, and especially François Poul[l]ain de la Barre as well as to explore the relationship between women's rights and early socialism.[17] Even the English got into the act: the translator (1900) of *Les Femmes de la Renaissance* (1896) by René-Marie-Alphonse Maulde de Clavière – one of the first full-length historical studies of women's history – added the word "feminism" in its subtitle.[18] In 1906 Georges Ascoli published a bibliography on the "history of feminist ideas" from the mid-sixteenth to the end of the seventeenth centuries in the *Revue de Synthèse Historique*.[19] In March 1908, Jules Tixerant defended his doctoral thesis, *Le Féminisme à l'époque de 1848 dans l'ordre politique et dans l'ordre économique*, at the Faculty of Law of the University of Paris.[20] Another doctoral thesis, defended in 1911 at the

---

Marquès, 1905); Adrien Lasserre, *La Participation collective des femmes à la Révolution française; les antécédents du féminisme*. (Paris: F. Alcan, 1906).

[15] See Léopold Lacour, "Le Féminisme de Condorcet," *La Revue Hebdomadaire*, n° 28 (14 June 1902), 162–171 and n° 29 (21 June 1902), 273–283, and "Marat féministe," *La Grande Revue*, 6, n° 9 (1 September 1902), 575–602; and Joseph Turquan, *Les Femmes de l'émigration* (Paris: Emile-Paul, 1911; a third edition in two volumes appeared in 1912).

[16] See *L'Équité*, n° 11 (15 December 1913), and *The Common Cause* (29 May 1914), p. 171.

[17] In addition to the articles by Léopold Lacour (cited in n. 15), see Louis Chabaud, *Les Précurseurs du féminisme: Mesdames de Maintenon, de Genlis et Campan, leur rôle dans l'éducation chrétienne de la femme* (Paris: Plon, 1901); Emile Dessignolle, *Le Féminisme d'après la doctrine socialiste de Charles Fourier* (Lyon: A. Storck et Cie, 1903; orig. thèse de droit, Lyon); and Charles Thiébaux, *Le Féminisme et les socialistes depuis Saint-Simon jusqu'à nos jours* (Thèse de doctorat, Faculté de Droit, Université de Paris, 1904; Paris: A. Rousseau, 1906).

[18] *Les Femmes de la Renaissance* (Paris: Perrin, 1898). In English as *The Women of the Renaissance: A Study of Feminism*, transl. George Ely (London: Sonnenschein, 1900; rev. ed., 1905).

[19] Georges Ascoli, "Essai sur l'histoire des idées féministes en France du XVIe siècle à la Révolution," *La Revue de Synthèse Historique*, 13 (1906), 25–57, 99–106 (bibliography), 161–184.

[20] Jules Tixerant, *Le Féminisme à l'époque de 1848 dans l'ordre politique et dans l'ordre économique* (Thèse de doctorat, Faculté de Droit, Université de Paris; Paris: Giard & Brière, 1908). Tixerant had shared some of his findings on the history of feminism in the lecture series sponsored by the *Ligue Française pour le Droit des Femmes* (LFDF); see the LFDF bulletins for 1910 and 1911. Léon Abensour also published on 1848: see "Le Féminisme en 1848" in vol. 73 of *La Grande Revue*, issues of 10 May 1912, 105–120, and 10 June 1912, 544–564.

French-speaking University of Neuchâtel in Switzerland, was Rose Rigaud's *Les Idées féministes de Christine de Pisan* [sic; the authoritative spelling is Pizan, not Pisan].[21] In his extensive studies of the history of feminism in France, the young scholar and journalist Léon Abensour would use the term "feminism" freely, notably in his articles "Le Féminisme pendant le règne de Louis-Philippe" (1908) and "Un mouvement féministe au XIIIe siècle" (1911).[22] Abensour's important book, *Le Féminisme sous le règne de Louis-Philippe et en 1848*, would be published in 1913, but his still unsurpassed magnum opus, *La Femme et le féminisme avant la Révolution française* (1923), would not appear until 1923.[23]

Anachronism was becoming as fashionable as feminism itself. Scholars and feminist writers began to identify signs of historical feminism in every conceivable time and place. Scholars applied the term feminism rather wildly to studies of classical antiquity, as (e.g.,) Cleyre Yvelin, *Étude sur le féminisme dans l'antiquité* (1908), and J.-M.-F. Bascoul, *La chaste Sappho de Lesbos et le mouvement féministe à Athènes au IVe siècle avant J.-C.* (1911).[24] The terms would even be applied to some of the earlier nineteenth-century male writers. Françoise Benassis, for example, evaluated the feminism of Edgar Quinet.[25] Charles Jacquard assessed "the feminism of Auguste Comte," but in fact the article celebrated the Comtean cult of womanhood; the author seemed somewhat confused about what might constitute the feminist element in Comte's writings.[26] The literary critic Émile Faguet would contemplate the feminism of Sainte-Beuve, a judgment that will greatly surprise today's feminist literary scholars.[27]

By 1906, the history of feminism would make its debut as front-page news in the mainstream daily press. Scholars were sending letters to the editor on such questions, as for example, Abel Le Franc, professor of French literature at the Collège de France, who published on Rabelais and the so-called

[21] Rose Rigaud, *Les Idées féministes de Christine de Pisan* (doctoral diss., Neuchâtel: Attinger frères, 1911; reprinted, Geneva: Slatkine Reprints, 1973).

[22] Léon Abensour, "Le Féminisme pendant le règne de Louis-Philippe," *La Révolution française*, vol. 55 (1908), 331–365; "Un mouvement féministe au XIIIe siècle," *La Nouvelle Revue* (1 March 1911), 107–116.

[23] Léon Abensour, *Le Féminisme sous le règne de Louis-Philippe et en 1848* (Paris: Plon-Nourrit, 1913); *La Femme et le féminisme avant la Révolution française* (Paris: E. Leroux, 1923; reprinted, Geneva: Slatkine Reprints, 1977).

[24] See Cleyre Yvelin, *Étude sur le féminisme dans l'antiquité* (Paris: V. Giard et E. Brière, 1908), and J.-M.-F. Bascoul, *La chaste Sappho de Lesbos et le mouvement féministe à Athènes au IVe siècle avant J.-C.* (Paris: H. Welter, 1911).

[25] Françoise Benassis, "Le 'Féminisme' d'Edgar Quinet," *La Fronde*, n° 1918 (11 March 1903), 1.

[26] Charles Jacquard, "Le Féminisme d'Auguste Comte," *La Revue Pédagogique* (15 September 1909), 217–237.

[27] Émile Faguet, "Sainte Beuve et le féminisme," *La Femme contemporaine*, n° 18 (March 1905), 193–203.

querelle des femmes (1904). In May 1906 Lefranc wrote to the editor of *Le Temps* to correct the record on the woman question debates in the seventeenth century. On "*la une*" [the front page] Lefranc objected to an earlier published claim that political rights and women were not a mix that reflected French tradition. On the contrary, said Lefranc, pointing to the comedies of Molière; it was precisely in response to such wickedness [*méchancité*] by Molière and others that Poulain de la Barre had risen to the defense women's rights in his 1673 *Treatise on the Equality of the Sexes*.[28] The following day Henri Pieron, who had previously published on the subject, weighed in to discuss Poulain's Cartesianism and the dramatic effect for the future of France of his promulgation of equality for women.[29]

Others investigated related topics in women's history, such as Mario Schiff's study of Poulain de la Barre's predecessor, the outspoken seventeenth-century rights advocate Marie le Jars de Gournay.[30] The links between socialism and feminism also attracted professors outside Paris and their doctoral candidates: Émile Dessignole wrote a thesis on feminism in the writings of Charles Fourier, and his findings were soon supplemented by Charles Patureau-Murand, who published a doctoral thesis on the Saint-Simonian writings on women.[31] In 1903, law professor Paul Viollet published volume 3 of his magnum opus, *Histoire des Institutions politiques et administratives de la France,* followed in 1905 by his *Histoire du droit civil français;* based on his reading of sources in French legal history, he had

[28] See Abel Lefranc, "Le Féminisme au temps de Molière: Au directeur du Temps," *Le Temps*, clipping dated 25 May 1906 (date verified online), in Avril de Sainte-Croix scrapbooks, reel 4, BMD. This letter appears on the front page, cols. 4–5. Lefranc was an expert on Rabelais and edited the latter's collected works (1912). See especially his article, "Le Tiers livre du Pantagruel et la Querelle des femmes," *La Revue des Études Rabelaisiennes*, vol. 2, n°s 1 & 3 (1904); also published separately by H. Champion in 1904.

[29] Henri Pieron, "Un précurseur du féminisme et de la Révolution sous Louis XIV: Au directeur du Temps," *Le Temps* (26 May 1906; date verified online), in Avril de Sainte-Croix scrapbooks, reel 4, BMD. His earlier scholarly article is "De l'Influence sociale des principes cartésiens: un précurseur inconnu du féminisme et de la révolution: Poulain de la Barre," *La Revue de Synthèse historique*, vol. 5 (1902), 153–185 & 270–282. Another Henri, this time Henri Grappin, also examined Poulain as a feminist in the *Revue d'Histoire Littéraire de la France*: see his two articles, "Note sur un féministe oublié: le cartésien Poullain de la Barre," vol. 20 (1913), 852–867 and "A propos du féministe Poullain de la Barre," vol. 21 (1914), 387–389. Cf. also, G. Lefèvre, "Poullain de la Barre et le féminisme au XVIIIe siècle," *La Revue Pédagogique*, n.s. vol. 64, n° 2 (15 February 1914), 101–113. The authoritative work on Poullain is now Siep Stuurman, *François Poulain de la Barre and the Invention of Modern Equality* (Cambridge, MA: Harvard University Press, 2004).

[30] Mario Schiff, *La Fille d'alliance de Montaigne, Marie de Gournay* (Paris: H. Champion, 1910).

[31] Émile Dessignolle, *Le Féminisme d'après la doctrine socialiste de Charles Fourier*. Thèse de droit, Lyon (Lyon: A. Storck et Cie, 1903); Charles Patureau-Murand, *De la Femme et de son rôle dans la société, d'après les écrits saint-simoniens: Exposé analytique*. Thèse de doctorat, Faculté de droit et des sciences économiques, Université de Poitiers (Limoges, 1910).

exposed not only the fraud of the Salic Law, but had also demonstrated authoritatively that women had voted in the French past.[32] The historian Victor du Bled (1848–1927) published the final volumes of his *Histoire de la Société française*, spanning the period from 1500 through the nineteenth century; this author highlighted elite women's activities and contributions in every one of his nine volumes.[33] The socialist writer Charles Vérecque would publish his *Histoire de la famille des temps sauvages à nos jours* (1914), with an appendix containing the supportive motions concerning women's emancipation endorsed by various socialist congresses.[34]

Additional copious tomes by male scholars and intellectuals addressed the comparative status and cultural situation of women around the world, painting with a broad brush and raising uncomfortable questions about the status quo. In *L'Affranchissement de la femme* (1903) the libertarian sociologist Jacques Novicow, of the *Institut International de Sociologie*, would offer a lengthy and incisive comparative cultural critique of women's unhappiness in institutionalized marriage and in custom as it was currently constituted and its adverse effects on wives and mothers. Citing examples of unfortunate situations in which women found themselves, ranging from France to China, via Poland, Russia, Italy, and elsewhere in the world, he advocated full liberty for women to love freely, find sexual pleasure, bask in their motherhood, and to become economically independent of men. He insisted that families could exist without marriage.[35] His objective was to demonstrate "how society should be organized in order to procure for woman the sum of happiness to which she was entitled – a sum of happiness absolutely equal to that enjoyed by man."[36]

Anthropologist Charles Letourneau's massive (over 500 pages) posthumous treatise on the comparative condition of women also appeared in 1903.[37] Harlor, reviewing Letourneau's work in *La Fronde*, observed that sooner or later, most investigators of a scientific mind would come around to favoring equity and emancipation for women, whatever their initial

---

[32] See Chapter 13 on suffrage for more about Paul Viollet's learned contributions to the feminist cause.

[33] Victor du Bled, *Histoire de la Société française*, 9 vols. (Paris: Perrin, 1900–1913). His emphasis was on court life and cultural developments.

[34] Charles Vérecque, *Histoire de la famille des temps sauvages à nos jours* (Paris: Giard & Brière, 1914). It could be interesting to compare this author's treatment with the earlier classic works of Friedrich Engels and Auguste Bebel.

[35] Jacques Novicow, *L'Affranchissement de la femme* (Paris: F. Alcan, 1903). Of Slavic background, this man's works are also filed under Novicow, Iakov Aleksandrovich.

[36] Novicow, *Affranchissement*, p. 38.

[37] See Charles Letourneau, *La Condition de la femme dans les diverses races et civilisations*, ed. L. Manouvrier & G. Papillault (Paris: Giard & Brière, 1903).

reservations may have been. Even the once skeptical Letourneau now acknowledged that woman had become man's first domesticated animal, and had remarked wonderingly that some women had managed, in spite of their long history of oppression, to attain a level of high cultural distinction. It was precisely because of this "in spite of," Harlor attested in her review of Letourneau's study, that one could hope for an end to women's subjection.[38] But all these studies paled before the impressive thousand-page study of French feminism by Charles Turgeon, to which we will now turn.

Historicizing and Evaluating Feminism: Charles Turgeon's Landmark *Le Féminisme français* (1902)

Complementing this proliferation of interest in the history of feminism (and the anthropological past and present of women), a dense two-volume study, *Le Féminisme français*, appeared in French bookshops early in 1902.[39] When it appeared, the *Conseil National des Femmes Françaises* (CNFF) was still in the first year of its existence. The author of this weighty tome (comprised of two fat volumes, each one nearly 500 pages long), was Charles Turgeon (1855–1934), a middle-aged professor of political economy and dean of the faculty of law in Rennes, who was also a correspondent of the *Académie des Sciences Morales et Politiques* in Paris. In this well-documented, learned study (subsequently "crowned" by the *Académie Française*) which had obviously been in preparation for some time, Turgeon argued that feminism in France must not and cannot be ignored, particularly because it "implicates the very constitution of the family" and that "both the demanders and the defenders are both judge and party in the case."[40] The author posited that feminist demands "threaten to seriously trouble the [existing] social and familial order."[41] Approaching the subject from a Christian perspective, he was clearly perturbed by aspects of feminism that he considered to be violations of Biblical law, but he was haunted as well by what he perceived to be challenges to French cultural specificity and the much-vaunted Gallic spirit.

Le Féminisme français is a dense and argumentative book and it is impossible to do full justice to it here. It is deeply researched, well-documented, and

---

[38] Harlor, "Le Féminisme d'un savant," *La Fronde,* n° 1919 (12 March 1903), 1.
[39] Charles Turgeon, *Le Féminisme français,* 2 vols. (Paris: L. Larose, 1902).
[40] Turgeon, *Féminisme français,* I, ii.   [41] Turgeon, *Féminisme français,* I, p. 6.

remarkably comprehensive, touching on virtually all the issues under discussion at the turn of the century, and it is as well informed concerning the general context as it is by a close reading of feminist publications through 1900. The work is presented as "reasonable" and "equitably impartial."[42] At the outset, though clearly speaking from a man's perspective, Turgeon sounds cautiously pro-feminist, but then he quickly states that in his opinion some advocates of women's emancipation have gone too far – especially those who seek to exercise "masculine" professions. Cutting to the chase, he insists that *"these ladies and demoiselles take on science in order to lift woman up in society and attack marriage, more or less openly, in order to lower man in the family."* "That's what feminism is about," he declared.[43] He feared the threat of war between the sexes as much as (or even more than) the threat of socialism.[44]

Turgeon admitted to being impressed by the extraordinary scope of feminism at the turn of the century as well as its international reach:[45]

> Today we have a feminist propaganda, a feminist literature, feminist clubs, a feminist theater, a feminist press, headed by a major newspaper, *La Fronde*, whose projectiles whiz past our ears every day and fall with great fracas in the gardens of Peter and Paul, without heed to the quality or status of the owners. We know, moreover, that feminism has its (labor) unions and its councils, and that every year it holds its plenary sessions in a major city of the old or new world. It has become international.

He categorized the feminists' grievances in terms of reaction to women's inferiority on seven counts: intellect, pedagogy, economic, electoral, civil, conjugal, maternal – the last three having to do with the legal subordination of married women. He boiled these seven categories down to two: 1) individual emancipation and social emancipation and 2) political and familial emancipation. Individual emancipation was sought through education, whereas social emancipation was sought through paid employment. The latter (i.e., women's right to work for pay, especially in the professions dominated to date by men) had clearly become a sticking point.

Charles Turgeon opined that even though the word *"féminisme"* might well be French (though he wrongly attributed it to Fourier, as had Marya Chéliga in 1896), the observed phenomenon seemed to him actually to be American in origin. Its scope, in his view, was very widespread, and he distinguished four varieties: 1) a *worker* feminism, 2) a *bourgeois* feminism, 3)

---

[42] Turgeon, *Féminisme français*, I, p. 113.
[43] Turgeon, *Féminisme français*, I, p. 5. "Tout le féminisme est là." The italicized quotation conveys the author's emphasis.
[44] Turgeon, *Féminisme français*, I, p. 112.   [45] Turgeon, *Féminisme français*, I, p. 5.

a *mondain* feminism, and 4) a *professional* feminism.[46] Each, he insisted, had as its goal the shrinking of male privilege and authority (about which the author exhibited considerable ambivalence). Here he was totally on the mark: challenging masculine domination is the core feature of feminism, whether or not it is overtly acknowledged.

Turgeon was harshest on "mondain feminism," where he saw examples of the *"femme libre,"* whose "greatest pleasure is playing with [moral] fire."[47] He attributed such risky behavior to "the contagion of bad examples," most of which appeared to be Anglo-American (in other words, "un-French"). He had nothing good to say about "new women," or about the so-called professional feminists, who (in his opinion) stood for free love, the suppression of marriage, and the overthrow of the family. His chapters 5 and 6 abound with observations critical of such women, especially the overeducated "intellectual proletariat of women"; indeed, this author speaks of the "revenge of the old maids."[48] Turgeon's invective became particularly virulent on the subject of young women pursuing physical culture, sport, riding bicycles, and especially engaging in *"traves-tissement,"* or cross-dressing, or even the adoption of certain elements of male costume. He warned his readers ominously that the more women try to imitate men, the more they would lose their influence over men. Such statements as this one concerning a loss of "femininity" leading to a loss of influence would become a commonplace among antifeminist men – and some women.[49]

Charles Turgeon further identified three strands of feminism: revolutionary, Christian, and independent (which he would later refer to in his fifth chapter in a different order, as "left, right, and center"). In the first category, he insisted that the socialist efforts since around 1896 to capture the feminists, and to castigate proletarian women for cooperating with bourgeois women, were simply about annexing women in order to assault the rich. As for Christian feminism (with which he was clearly more sympathetic), he expressed his doubts, though he did insist on the historic role of Christianity in decreeing the equality of women and men before God; moreover, he emphasized the importance of the Catholic dogma of Immaculate Conception (promulgated in 1852) for glorifying the female sex. The Church's identification of Eve with sin notwithstanding, he

---

[46] Turgeon, *Féminisme français,* I, p. 12.   [47] Turgeon, *Féminisme français,* I, p. 29.
[48] Turgeon, *Féminisme français,* I, quotes, pp. 35–36.
[49] Turgeon, *Féminisme français,* I, p. 47. The well-known (and well-off) woman novelist Lucie Delarue-Mardrus would express similar sentiments in her interview with Joseph Bois. See "La Femme de demain: chez Mme Lucie Delarue-Mardrus," *Le Temps* (11 September 1911).

believed that the entire spirit of Church doctrine had led to the rehabilitation of the wife and the glorification of the mother; nevertheless, he
admitted, the Christian tradition had never endorsed equality between
husband and wife. He praised Catholic feminists for resisting the "virus"
[of secular feminism].[50] He subsequently agreed with the Vatican's objections to women's work in industry, and judged the protective law of
1892 to be in conformity with the spirit of Leo XIII's 1892 encyclical on
work.[51]

Turgeon further acknowledged that there could be feminists of both
sexes, but he was particularly critical of what he considered to be the
"exalted" views of male-feminists such as Jules Bois and Louis Frank. He
also strongly excoriated the contemporary interest of some feminists in
"matriarchy," and their ostensible attribution of all good qualities to
women.[52] He assessed the contributions of various groups, individuals,
and congresses as of 1900.[53] He blamed these feminists for fomenting "an
unfortunate hostility between the two sexes that constitute the human
family.... Feminism tends to disunite that which nature has manifestly
wanted to associate." In fact, he reminded readers, every strain of feminism
"is attacking more or less directly the current prerogatives of man."[54] Or,
more precisely, the prerogatives and privileges that contemporary French
men preferred to think of as "normal" components of their masculine
identity!

But after some steamy analysis of qualities that repelled him, Turgeon
calmed down again and insisted that men must, in fact, judge the feminist
phenomenon using their reason (i.e., with cool heads), admitting the
reasonable and just demands while condemning those that are "excessive."
Above all, he cautioned, readers must not opt wholly for – or against –
feminism.

Turgeon insisted on (and frequently reiterated) his belief in the importance of sexual complementarity, of cooperation within the couple; in his
view, the rights of the individual *must* cede to the rights of the species, of
the family, of society: "This subordination of the parts to the harmony of
the whole should neither wound nor humiliate anyone. The sexes are not
made to struggle separately, and even less to be jealous of one another and

---

[50] Turgeon, *Féminisme français,* I, p. 74.   [51] Turgeon, *Féminisme français,* I, p. 437.

[52] See Turgeon, *Féminisme français,* II, chapters 3 and 4.

[53] Turgeon did not have access to the printed proceedings of the two 1900 congresses when he was
writing his book, but relied on published reports and accounts in the press, including those in *La
Fronde.*

[54] Both quotes, Turgeon, *Féminisme français,* I, p. 111.

to combat one another in the pursuit of egotistical satisfactions that would imperil the future of the race." He allowed that "woman should be legally everything that she can be naturally. Nothing more, nothing less." Equality in every aspect, but also reciprocal coordination, equal consideration, and solidarity ... for the greater good. Competition between the sexes found no favor in his eyes.[55] This may be relational thinking, but it is not relational feminism. The author does ultimately acknowledge male superiority in intelligence, genius, etc., but insists on "grace" as God's sovereign gift to women.

Turgeon's account of women's education (in his chapter 6) resonates with all the old antifeminist commonplaces about "*femmes savantes,*" "*bas bleues,*" "*l'éternelle blessée,*" "*cet être artificiellement virilisé,*" and in his chapter 7 he invokes the time-honored saying, "*les femmes font les moeurs,*" accompanied by an undisguised nostalgia for the innocence of the old model "*jeune fille*" and "*la femme vraiment femme.*"[56] Although he recognized that some women must earn their own keep, he contradicts his earlier endorsement of "equality in every aspect" by dismissing outright the idea of equality of the sexes; he waxes lyric about the "natural differences" between the sexes and how these inevitably necessitate a sexual division of labor. "Wives and mothers, those are the two functions of woman, the alpha and omega of her destiny." [57] He does not stand outside the society in which he lives sufficiently to allow him to appreciate the feminists' critique of fundamental problems in the relation of the sexes, but simply calls for women of leisure to engage less in frivolity and more in patching up social problems through charitable activities. Moreover, even as he admits the right of needy women to seek remunerative employments, especially in sedentary jobs, he depicts the aspirations of younger, educated women to white-collar jobs as an "invasion" of the offices, the courtrooms, and all the virile employments."[58] You get the picture – his views are conflicted! To be sure, Turgeon's views of women can, in many respects, be considered antifeminist, although, for the most part, his language seems relatively moderate in comparison with some of his predecessors, and even more so with respect to the most vociferous of his successors. He seems to be trying hard to be objective, but it is clear where his sympathies lie.

As concerns political rights, Turgeon admits in his second volume that adult women should have the vote as a matter of equity and he argues adamantly that the so-called universal suffrage should become truly

---

[55] Turgeon, *Féminisme français,* I, p. 128.   [56] Turgeon, *Féminisme français,* I, chapters 6 and 7.
[57] Turgeon, *Féminisme français,* I, p. 343.   [58] Turgeon, *Féminisme français,* I, p. 345.

"universal." "Our so-called universal suffrage is today only a limited suffrage, a virile privilege, a masculine monopoly." Citing reports of the positive effects of women's vote in America and Australia, Turgeon concedes that there are no convincing objections to feminist claims for women's *right* to vote, including married women. He admits that, in fact, on this issue, the feminists have the best of the argument. But while conceding women the suffrage, he qualifies his generosity by insisting that women should not run for, or be elected to, public office.[59]

Even so, invoking the hallowed old Roman notion of the "*office virile*" that closed off access to public offices to women, Turgeon suggests getting rid of it. He approves of the loi Schmahl (1897), which gave women the possibility of witnessing civil acts. He argues that women should be eligible to serve as guardians or as members of family councils. Employed women should have equal rights in matters of commerce, including the right of elections to councils of *prud'hommes*. Turgeon even posited that women should be able to vote on the same terms as men – although he didn't think it would happen "in our free and gallant country of France." He fully endorsed suffrage for *les françaises*, not finding convincing any of the arguments against it, including that concerning military service. "Sovereignty," Turgeon argued, "has no masculine essence. Its nature is twofold – it is, in some sense, male and female . . . it is bisexual."[60] Turgeon was hereby making enormous and authoritative breaches in received opinion.

As for the Civil Code's construction of husbandly power, Turgeon – wearing his law professor's hat – squarely addressed Article 213, the notorious article that posited wives' obedience, which feminists had been contesting since its inception in the early nineteenth century.[61] Turgeon's view on this subject supported the status quo; he wrote that "order is not possible without a certain hierarchy." In a household, he asserted, somebody has to have the last word; otherwise there is no end to the struggles: "Equal power for husband and wife? I deny the possibility."[62] For Turgeon, the notion of equal rights stops at the threshold of marriage. Or, as he put it later in the chapter: "The civil equality of the two sexes ceases in conjugal relations: by engaging in the ties of marriage, the wife alienates a part of her rights and submits to a sort of temporary incapacity."[63] (Husbands, however, retain their rights and capacity). Concerning dowries

[59] Turgeon, *Féminisme français*, II, chapter 3; quotes, pp. 26, 48.
[60] Quotes and observations above, II, pp. 18, 22, 35.
[61] Turgeon, *Féminisme français*, II, Book 2, chapter 3.
[62] Turgeon, *Féminisme français*, II, pp. 101, 102.   [63] Turgeon, *Féminisme français*, II, p. 162.

and the option of community property in marriage, Turgeon favored giving wives more control over community property, rather than total separation of property regime; as for the dowry regime, he thinks it should be suppressed. But the earnings of wives who must work must be protected, he admitted, implicitly endorsing the ongoing campaign of *L'Avant-Courrière* for the right of married women to control their earnings.

Turgeon's lengthy treatise addressed many more aspects of the woman question, but this account covers the essentials of his major arguments. Now we turn to the reception of this important work.

Reception, Aftermath, Supporters and Antagonists

The Catholic feminist and editor of *Le Féminisme Chrétien,* Marie Maugeret, had nothing but praise for Turgeon's book, calling it "a monument, almost perfect and definitive."[64] Reviewers of differing persuasions also had many good things to say about it, and in every case their analyses seemed to have helped them to sharpen and solidify their own positions.

The writer and literary critic Émile Faguet (1847–1916), recently elected (1900) to the *Académie Française,* launched his *Revue Latine* in early 1902 with a long essay on "Féminisme," inspired by his reading of Turgeon's book. Faguet immediately proclaimed himself a feminist (in the [liberal] tradition of the British philosopher/economist John Stuart Mill), and "perhaps even more so" than Turgeon. He hailed Turgeon's book as a "classic" – "the must-read book that dispenses one from reading all the others."[65]

Turgeon's conclusions, Faguet insisted, are formally feminist, although at times he seems to be taking the part of the most hostile antifeminists, which could (and undoubtedly did) cause confusion for readers. Faguet pointed to Turgeon's tendency to address the extremist aspects of feminism in ways that made him seem to be "taking off on the most bellicose antifeminist crusade"[66] – as, for example, when he critiqued the lyrical extravagances of a Jules Bois or a Léopold Lacour, or for that matter those of Jean Izoulet, or the unfeminine behavior of certain female advocates.

---

[64] Marie Maugeret, "Lettre ouverte à M. Turgeon," *Le Féminisme Chrétien,* 6:12 (December 1901), 353–364. Translated by Steven C. Hause, in Steven C. Hause, with Anne R. Kenney, *Women's Suffrage and Social Politics in the French Third Republic* (Princeton, NJ: Princeton University Press, 1983), p. 82. This issue is included in the ACRPP microfilm, but not in the Gerritsen online holdings.

[65] Émile Faguet, "Le Féminisme," *La Revue Latine,* vol. 1, n° 1 (25 January 1902), 5–37; quote, 2.

[66] Faguet, "Le Féminisme," 6.

But Faguet quickly qualified this criticism by remarking that on certain points the antifeminists had some important points to make.

The essential elements of feminism, Faguet detailed, lie in the answers to the question: "Should woman be the equal of man in the school, in the family, in civil life, in social life?" Faguet's answer was "yes." But in what remained of his very long review essay, Faguet posed a distinction between "*droit*" ("right," or theory) and "*pratique*" ("practice"), and addressed the distinctions between them. What he seemed to mean was "yes – but . . ." Or, perhaps, he meant "yes – but not now."

Faguet's witty thirty-page essay can be characterized as a personal feminist manifesto. He questioned certain ingrained practices and beliefs, as for example, why the famous division of labor had to be by sex. He posited that one of the reasons so many young women had to support themselves was because young men were not marrying, in order to spare themselves the expense of a wife – it's the men's fault! Because men are not marrying, the women they might have married become their competition and drag down their pay. He insisted that women must have the "right" to do whatever they pleased, but that they not make use of that "right," observing that the law permits many things that are not recommended behaviors, especially for men.

With any revolution in human affairs, Faguet stated, comes both good and bad. The realization of feminist goals would undoubtedly provoke quarrels in some families; among other things, it would create "*déclassées.*" Feminism, he posited, is above all else a revolt by woman against herself: "Woman revolts against the defects that her subordination to man has developed within her . . . frivolity, ignorance, thoughtlessness, childishness, coquettishness." He remarked that he applauded, even adored feminist women "when they critique men's gallantry and affectations as insults, when they want to be treated seriously, looked squarely in the eye instead of being ogled from bottom to top, when they assert that they are as educated as we are, as solid as we are, as brave as we are, that they have as good a head as we do, and a better heart." All this was to the good – it would create the "*femme forte,*" the competent woman sketched in the Bible (presumably in Proverbs 31) – this is the woman that a man could love with all his heart and would seek in marriage. "Thus, what was invented to divide women and men would finish by reuniting [them]."[67]

Faguet, after Turgeon, complained about the continuing situation where men took jobs that women could do. This practice had been the

---

[67] Faguet, "Le Féminisme"; all quotations in this paragraph, 31–32.

subject of complaint since before the 1789 revolution, but in the course of the nineteenth century had been repeatedly castigated by Julie-Victoire Daubié, author of *La Femme pauvre*, and many others. Similarly, he objected to women taking jobs that men thought were "theirs." He favored the redistribution of labor according to aptitude, not sex. "In a word, professions have no sex," a remark Yvette Roudy (France's first minister of women's rights) would have approved! Faguet insisted that one doesn't need a law, one needs "liberty and feminism accepted, practiced, and integrated into our morals." He thought that civil and social life would benefit greatly by the entry of women, who he viewed, overall, as more moral than men: "She is less brutish; alcoholism is not womanly; crime is not feminine."[68] Are you convinced, men? If not, then you are judging all women by the example of your own wife. Take a step back, he insisted, and consider what others think of her, which may be quite different, and take the average. Both women and men, he asserted, have a mixture of good and bad qualities. On the whole, it is better to adopt feminism without illusions – and with occasional recourse to antifeminism whenever you have a household quarrel, though one ought not draw conclusions from the latter.

Mme d'Abbadie d'Arrast (who headed the Section on Legislation of the CNFF), reported positively on Turgeon's book at the annual *Conférence de Versailles* (12 June 1902).[69] Calling the book "a veritable encyclopedia of feminism, surprising by its alert and independent style [*allure alerte et indépendante*]," she remarked that Turgeon "was not afraid to become the advocate of a women's political and familial liberation that would please the most convinced feminist." She interpreted the fact that the book and its author had been recognized by the *Académie Française* as a "sign of the times." She characterized the author as a moderate and the advocate of a "wise" [*sage*] feminism, one who is comfortable quoting both Victor Hugo and Ibsen on the coming revolution. Her report focused on the author's treatment of Christian feminism and on the question of women's employment, pointing out that Turgeon wanted to conserve the monopoly of justice, of judges and courts, for men and that he frowned on women entering the liberal professions, notably law. Skipping over a number of chapters, d'Abbadie remarked on Turgeon's conclusions, and recommended that her associates get hold of a

---

[68] Faguet, "Le Féminisme"; quotes in this paragraph, 33–34.
[69] Mme d'Abbadie [d'Arrast], "Travail de Mme d'Abbadie sur le *Féminisme français*," *La Femme: Organe des Institutions Féminines, Chrétiennes, Sociales*, vol. 24, n° 12 (combined issue for 15 June–1 July–15 July 1902), 100–103; quotes, pp. 100ff. Consulted BNF-Gallica, 15 November 2012.

copy: it is "a good book, an excellent book," she underscored. "You will gain more maturity in your feminist opinions, more true knowledge, more wise ponderation," she said, by reading Turgeon's book. There was, in her view, simply no equivalent.

In the wake of Turgeon's book, other French men and women would step up to offer their own assessments of feminism. In a 1905 brochure, *Qu'est-ce que le féminisme*, Odette Laguerre, an associate of Marguerite Durand, claimed that feminism was "an impulse for justice that tends to equalize the rights and responsibilities of man and woman." And, she added, "feminism is not only an impulse for justice; it is also an impulse for liberty that marks the end of the reign of Man, or what Jules Bois calls '*anthropocentrisme*'."[70] This pamphlet, the first of a series published by the Lyon-based *Société d'éducation et d'action féministes* (of which Laguerre served as secretary-general), provided a clear statement of what I have called elsewhere "relational feminism," centered on the possibility of self-definition for women and the end of male domination over and male definition of woman. Laguerre was reshaping the language of equality-in-difference, but with a twist that spun it in the direction of a liberating individual potential.

Some definitions of feminism were more abstractly philosophic, even romantic in character. Note, for example, that of Mme S. Poirson, in her book, *Mon Féminisme*, published in 1905:[71]

> It is a moral revolution, women's effort toward betterment; it is a revolutionary ferment that has thrown their consciences into confusion, and that makes men of narrow and limited judgment smile. Feminism is also the terrain of legitimate grievances which are temporarily smothered or torn by the brambles and thorns of ridiculously false and grotesque theories. Feminism can yet be defined as a powerful evolutionary march forward of present-day thought. A sure, vigorous march that we submit to just as we submit to that of cosmic laws; a march forward that will be necessarily retarded or accelerated by events. . . . Feminism is an ubiquitous fluid.

Poirson distinguished between a "sectarian" or extremist feminism and a "rational" feminism; the difference was, in her mind, that adherents of

---

[70] Odette Laguerre, *Qu'est-ce que le féminisme?* (Lyon: Société d'éducation et d'action féministes, 1905), pp. 1, 3. Odette Laguerre's definition seems to have traveled widely; in late 1921, it was appropriated, translated, and published (without attribution) by the editor of the short-lived Turkish Armenian feminist journal *Hay Gin*. See Lerna Ekmekçioğlu, *Recovering Armenia: The Limits of Belonging in Post-Genocide Turkey* (Stanford, CA: Stanford University Press, 2016), p. 182, n. 45.

[71] See Mme S. Poirson, *Mon Féminisme* (Paris: E. Bernard, 1905), pp. 35–36.

"rational" feminism did not desire to appropriate men's place in society while rejecting their own. Poirson's feminism was undeniably "relational"; her aim was "equivalence" of the sexes, not equality, and she also insisted on the importance of the family.[72] Even so, her brand of feminism was not deemed attractive by the editors of the Catholic *La Femme contemporaine*. She was doubtless too much of a secularist for their taste.[73]

Further definitions of feminism would pop up in scholarly publications, as for example, Georges Ascoli's definition, premised on liberty and justice, which prefaced his bibliographical article, "Essai sur l'histoire des idées féministes en France du XVIe siècle à la révolution," published in the *Revue de Synthèse historique* in 1906:[74]

> In its broadest and most comprehensive sense, feminism is the mental attitude of those who, repelled by insuperable boundaries and arbitrary exclusions, refuse to admit a natural and necessary inequality between the abilities of men and women, and consequently, between their rights; it is the attitude of those who believe that women can, insofar as their physical nature permits them, pursue the same occupations as men, and that they can succeed at them as well, when, prepared by an appropriate education, they are no longer faced by the ill will and jealous hostility of the other sex; the attitude of those who, desiring a more complete liberty, a more generally extended liberty and more liberal justice, hope that this day will come as soon as possible, for the greater well-being of women and for the greater well-being of humanity.

As these contributions make clear, in the early twentieth century there were a number of approaches to defining feminism by both men and women. Even so, all of them pointed, some more discretely, some more blatantly, toward one goal – the dismantling of male privilege in Francophone society.

Le Sexualisme (1906): The Analysis by Jeanne Oddo-Deflou

In early 1906 Jeanne Deflou (a.k.a. Oddo-Deflou), activist in the GFEF and in the CNFF Section on Legislation, and a specialist in married women's property law, published a volume of acerbic meditations on the cultural aspects of the woman question under the title *Le Sexualisme*.[75] By

---

[72] Poirson, *Mon Féminisme*, p. 56.   [73] See *La Femme contemporaine* (November 1905), 471.

[74] See Georges Ascoli, "Essai sur l'histoire des idées féministes en France du XVIe siècle à la Révolution," *La Revue de Synthèse historique*, vol. 13 (1906), 25–57, 99–106 (bibliographie), 161–184; quote, part 1, 25–26.

[75] Jeanne Deflou, *Le Sexualisme: Critique de la prépondérance et de la mentalité du sexe fort* (Paris: J. Tallandier, 1906).

this term *sexualisme* she meant "the domination of one sex over the other and the effects that flow from that." Deflou's critique was aimed beyond the law, to critique certain discriminatory practices that had become deeply embedded in French thinking and sociopolitical practice. She indicated that she was fed up with male supremacy (she uses the term "*la suprématie du mâle*") and saw through the systems of ideas and practices by which women had been enslaved and demeaned by men through the centuries.[76]

Beginning with "*sexualisme*" in grammar, Deflou picked apart the notion that, in French, "the masculine always takes priority over the feminine."[77] Critiquing accepted customs and practices affecting women in marriage, she pointed out the absurdity of giving a child the father's family name, of a wife taking the husband's name even effacing her own given name: "Branded by the name of their husbands like a flock of sheep by the name of their owner, the code of 'civility' does not even permit wives to conserve their given name." They are in "total eclipse behind the masculine sun"; widows are even more "eclipsed" in their widow's weeds, the "widow" of someone or another. Not so for the husband whose wife dies. Why must widows not put their address on their visiting cards, she asked? Because they have no home of their own – only that of their spouse. In southern France, still in the twentieth century, wives serve their husbands at the table, and only eat the leftovers – should there happen to be any leftovers. They are forbidden to sit in the husband's chair, next to the fire. Why, she queried, do women put up with this state of affairs?

Deflou, herself a double *bachelière*, did not mince words. In one chapter she denounced the French propensity to teach Latin to boys yet to forbid it in the girls' *lycées*; Latin, she said, is an "old fossil of organisms that have been destroyed forever."[78] It is effectively useless. Every work in Latin worth knowing has been translated more than once. Moreover, many so-called classical works in Latin are obscene – our sons don't need this! Nor do our daughters. The old Latin *baccalauréat*, she claimed, was nothing more than a status symbol for certain bourgeois men, closed to women and to "*plebes*." It provided nothing that allows one to succeed in the modern world.

As for the writing of history, Deflou was quite aware that men had monopolized it: "an epitome of horrors, a catalogue of massacres, an

---

[76] Deflou, *Sexualisme*, v–vi.

[77] Deflou hereby anticipated by over a century the current debates on the same question. See, most recently, Eliane Viennot's astute historical and political analysis of how the masculine gender came to predominate in French grammar: *Non, le Masculin ne l'emporte pas sur le Féminin! Petite Histoire des résistances de la langue française* (Paris: Éditions iXe, 2014).

[78] Deflou, *Sexualisme*, p. 121.

anthology composed of features capable of lowering a human being below the most vile and ferocious animals, who at least do not eat each other. It is the tableau and glorification of the great facts of masculine politics, of cunning united with cruelty. And these are the examples one is proposing to our youth."[79] Besides that, women's contributions, she insists, even when they have been powerful, has been consigned to the shadows, even blotted out. Knowledge as we have known it, she claimed (in the wake of Jenny P. d'Héricourt, Clémence Royer, Céline Renooz, and others), must be entirely reconstructed. Deflou was well aware of the sexual politics that underlay knowledge formation and propagation. Her chapter on "Le Sexualisme en Philosophie" drew readers' attention to the misogyny and masculinist attitudes of pagan, Christian religious, and secular philosophers, beginning with the Greeks and ending with Comte, Schopenhauer, and Nietzsche.

Small wonder, then, that Maria Martin praised Deflou's book in the *Journal des Femmes* as highly valuable, pleasing for the "hardiness of its views, the simplicity and clarity of its style, and the author's ability "to say aloud what many others among us have been quietly thinking." Martin particularly praised Deflou's deconstruction of French "gallantry" as a façade for male egotism.[80] She recommended Deflou's arguments as ammunition for all feminists to deploy against their adversaries.

Le Féminisme (1907): The Affirmation by Ghénia Avril de Sainte-Croix

In July 1907, Mme Avril de Sainte-Croix published her book entitled *Le Féminisme*. This work included a lengthy historical summary of the campaigns for women's rights in Europe and especially France, a glance at other lands, and an account of the founding and activities of the CNFF and ICW. It was intended to provide a sort of handbook for the French women's movement. With a preface by Victor Margueritte, the book appeared as the sixth volume in a series "Collection des doctrines politiques," by the very reputable publishing house of Giard & Brière.[81] The

---

[79] Deflou, *Sexualisme*, p. 170.
[80] M. M. [Maria Martin], "Le Sexualisme," *Le Journal des Femmes*, n° 164 (April 1906), 3.
[81] Mme Avril de Sainte-Croix, *Le Féminisme* (Paris: V. Giard & E. Briere, 1907). Here and there, *Le Féminisme* contains some "facts" that are simply wrong (as, for example [p. 83], that Napoléon III rather than Eugénie overrode the council of ministers to assure the entry of women to the Paris Faculty of Medicine) and a plethora of typos in English (and some French) names that attest to a certain haste in production. Overall, however, the book is extremely informative.

historical chapters point to Condorcet as the first apostle of feminism (there is no trace of such illustrious predecessors as Christine de Pizan, Marie Le Jars de Gournay, or Poulain de la Barre, despite the recent debates in *Le Temps*) and to the French Revolution as its crucible. It is clearly a militant book, one that "naturalized" (and, for that matter, "nationalized") feminism. Overall, the book was recognized as a landmark, hailed a standard reference.[82] Copies can still be found today in a number of national libraries outside France, including the National Library of Mexico; it was even translated into Bulgarian.[83]

How did Mme Avril characterize feminism? The feminist movement, she said, was "the modern manifestation of a woman's coming to consciousness of her feminine individuality." "Today, after a century of struggle, women's quest for more justice, more independence, seems about ready to be realized. No one laughs at feminisms any longer." More and more women are staking their claim to "an integral life" and, "attentive to the transformations going on around them, are rising up, are protesting against the state of inferiority in which they have been kept until now."[84] Women have always exerted influence, she acknowledged, but that has "nothing to do with feminist claims," which are about *rights*. Optimistically, she argued that economic evolution would eventually resolve the question of sexual inequality and that feminism (along with masculinism) would then disappear with the arrival of "integral humanism" (Léopold Lacour's term), which would witness men and women working harmoniously together, side by side.[85] Mme Avril denied earlier claims that America was the cradle of feminism, tracing its emergence to eighteenth-century France.[86] As for the nineteenth century, she was particularly impressed by Flora Tristan and her concern for the working class and insisted that feminism is intrinsically linked to the cause of the oppressed, the weak, and the disinherited.[87] She remarked, too, that "feminists have finally understood that, in abdicating their charm, they diminish their power."[88]

After recapping various developments in favor of women's rights in France and its neighboring European countries, Mme Avril concluded

---

[82] The article "Féminisme" in A. Compère-Morel's *Grand Dictionnaire socialiste du mouvement politique et économique, national et international* (Paris: Publications sociales, 1924), for example, is entirely "lifted" from Mme Avril's book.

[83] Thanks to Prof. Krassimira Daskalova for locating a copy of the published Bulgarian translation and photocopying it for me.

[84] Avril de Sainte-Croix, *Le Féminisme*, pp. 5–6.

[85] Avril de Sainte-Croix, *Le Féminisme*, p. 37, pp. 203–204.

[86] Avril de Sainte-Croix, *Le Féminisme*, pp. 49–50.   [87] Avril de Sainte-Croix, *Le Féminisme*, p. 65.

[88] Avril de Sainte-Croix, *Le Féminisme*, p. 158, repeated on p. 171.

that "human harmony would be realized on the day that man gives woman the place that is due to her, and that man and woman would march side by side, each one supporting the other, each one completing the other." She envisioned that day as on the horizon. "Feminism has got wind in its sails," she proclaimed.[89] She might also have added: "at last."

Mme Avril's historical treatment of feminism capped a five-year long debate about "*féminisme*," which had by then consumed a great deal of paper and ink. For the most part, *Le Féminisme* was well received in the press. Not only did French newspapers and learned journals (such as the *Revue Internationale de Sociologie*) praise it, but so did the *Tribune de Genève*, and the *Neues Frauenleben* in Vienna.[90]

"C. Mano" [Jean Lagardère], reviewing *Le Féminisme* in *La Femme* (March 1908), approved of the book's conclusion, but faulted its historical account especially as concerned the author's treatment of the role of the Catholic church. Mano depicted it as more of an "advertisement" (*réclame*) for the ICW – and remarked on the resignation from the CNFF of Jeanne Oddo-Deflou (author of the earlier *Le Sexualisme*) in 1908, who had apparently complained that it was "dominated by the Protestant and Jewish element."[91] Which was, of course, true. Had there been a falling out between Deflou and Mme Avril over the general issue of inclusiveness or, more specifically, over Catholic antisemitism?

Another shorter but useful publication that also appeared in 1907 was a twenty-four-page brochure, "State of the Feminist Question in France" by a Countess Pierre Lecoîntre.[92] It was not, according to the reviewer in *La Française*, a polemical work but rather a compendium of "facts" that also included a chronology and statements and resolutions from the congresses of the Christian feminists, of the CNFF, of the GFEF, and the inter-national women's rights congress of 1900. The brochure ended with references to Hubertine Auclert's suffrage group and to the feminist library run by Eliska Vincent and her sister Flor Mauriceau, which the author highly recommended.[93]

---

[89] Avril de Sainte-Croix, *Le Féminisme*, pp. 197–203 passim; quote, p. 197.

[90] *Neues Fraunleben*, 21:7 (September 1909), 189.

[91] Oddo-Deflou's remarks from an interview in *La Patrie*, cited by C. Mano [pseud. of Jean Lagardère], in *La Femme*, n° 53 (March 1908), 258–269.

[92] Comtesse Pierre Lecoîntre, *État de la Question féministe en France* (Paris: École professionel de l'imprimerie, 1907). This author was an "amateur" naturalist, who also published on fossils in the Touraine.

[93] For the unsigned review, see *La Française*, n° 65 (26 January 1908), 2.

The "*Chevalier du Masculinisme*": Théodore Joran

Not all commentators on feminism were as anxious as CharlesTurgeon, or as enthusiastic as Faguet, d'Abbadie d'Arrast, Odette Laguerre, Georges Ascoli, or Ghénia Avril de Sainte-Croix. In 1905, a new champion of insurgent antifeminism rode into the arena of French print culture, lance drawn, horse panting, prepared for mortal combat – Théodore Joran (1858–?). A grammarian and teacher by profession by day, a mortal enemy of liberated womanhood in his off hours, Joran's profile was that of the (ostensibly) chivalrous hatchet man; drawing heavily on medical metaphors, his self-appointed mission was to scourge the feminist plague. "Feminism is, like Socialism," he proclaimed in his first book, *Le Mensonge du féminisme* (1905, 459 pages), "an anti-French sickness!" But that was not all. "I object to feminism," Joran thundered, "because it allows women to envisage happiness as independent of love and external to love." "In reality, if not in law," Joran asserted, "good households are those where the man considers the woman as an object made for his own personal pleasure and well-being, and where the woman believes she ought to please her husband, to serve him, and applies herself exclusively to that end."[94] Jean-Jacques Rousseau himself never put it so baldly. To the great annoyance of the feminists, this book won the Prix Montyon of the *Académie Française*. It also attracted the scorn of the feminist writer Camille Bélilon, writing in the *Journal des Femmes*, who called Joran's arguments "a monument of illogicality," especially as concerned his defense of male authority over women and the now infamous Article 213 of the Civil Code, which commanded the obedience of the wife.[95] She once characterized Joran in the *Journal des Femmes* as "this valiant cavalier of *masculinisme*."[96]

From the outset, Joran's rantings epitomized a form of male-supremacist thinking and expression that is not only unremittingly anti-feminist, but borders on sheer misogyny, as Nelly Roussel quickly pointed out in a commentary, "Misogynie," in *L'Action*, in which she refused either to name the author or provide the title of the book.[97] The titles of Joran's

---

[94] Théodore Joran, *Le Mensonge du féminisme* (Paris: Jouve, 1905), pp. 120–121, 128–129, 295.

[95] Camille Bélilon, "Réponse à M. Théodore Joran,"*Le Journal des Femmes*, n° 159 (November 1905), 3. This long riposte took up two and a half columns.

[96] Camille Bélilon, in *Le Journal des Femmes*, n° 191 (January 1909), 4.

[97] Nelly Roussel, "Misogynie," *L'Action* (16 November 1905); reprinted in Roussel, *Quelques lances rompues pour nos libertés* (Paris: V. Giard & E. Brière, 1910), pp. 23–29. Roussel was particularly annoyed by Joran's constant references to "la femme," as though there were not many different varieties of women.

subsequent diatribes, which rolled off the presses on an almost annual basis, suggest the extent of his obsession with slaying the feminist dragon: *Autour du féminisme* (1906), *Au cœur du féminisme* (1908), *La Trouée féministe* (1909), *Les Féministes avant le féminisme* (1910), and ultimately *Le Suffrage des femmes* (1913). Camille Bélilon, commenting at length on *Au cœur du féminisme* in April 1907, took her cue from Joran's extravagant language to call him "a brain stricken by misogynist prose" ["*un cerveau en mal de prose misogynique*"] and to castigate him for castigating feminists for "*crime de lèse-masculinisme.*" She found extremely offensive his attacks on Mme X (Jeanne Deflou) for translating Bachofen's introduction to *Das Mutterrecht*. Nor did it end there: Joran would also pillory in print some of feminism's other leading figures, including Ghénia Avril de Sainte-Croix and Céline Renooz. His rantings were effectively a declaration of war on feminism – or at least on Joran's comprehension of it. Not surprisingly, Joran's publisher from 1908 on was Arthur Savaète, who during the first decade of the twentieth century specialized in publishing antisemitic and ultra-conservative extremist Catholic literature, also not known for its friendliness to women's aspirations.[98] His polemical publications would quickly furnish ammunition for right-wing nationalist and antisocialist antifeminism.

Why did Joran find feminism and its advocates so objectionable? According to his own account in *Le Mensonge du féminisme*, Joran's crusade against the feminists began in response to the death (a suspected suicide) of his best friend, Léon H. The friend was unhappily married; he couldn't seem to make his wife love him by bringing her the most beautiful dresses and costly gifts – the "necessary luxuries." The wife in turn shut herself in with her books, recognizing herself and her plight in Jules Case's play *La Vassale* (1897). Both spouses were deeply unhappy. But neither Joran nor his friend appeared to comprehend why, to recognize that their characters may simply have been incompatible, or to consider that she did not wish to have her husband "devote himself to her" – that is to say, whenever it was convenient for him to furnish expensive presents. In his 1906 book, *Autour du féminisme*, Joran stated his objections even more strongly: "Feminism is above all revolt, discord, disorganisation, and jealousy of our masculine nature."[99] He dedicated this latter volume to Frédéric Masson, the Bonapartist *académicien*, who in turn wrote a preface

[98] It is unclear whether Joran was acquainted with the slightly earlier antifeminist, antisemitic publication *Geschlecht und Charakter* by his Viennese counterpart Otto Weininger.
[99] *Autour du féminisme* (Paris: Plon, 1906), pp. 20–21.

for Joran's subsequent volume, *Au Coeur du féminisme* (1908), in which he denounced feminism as a sickness imported from the Nordic and Anglo-Saxon countries.[100] "Women, at least Christian women," Joran wrote in his "Introduction" to the volume, "must understand that by enrolling in feminism, they are sticking their finger into a machine that will catch them up and conduct them straight to socialism, communism, neo-malthusianism, and even to anarchy.... We must open their eyes."[101] Joran positioned himself as a well-meaning yet self-aggrandizing Prince Charming, who would awaken Sleeping Beauty (*La belle en bois dormant*) and return her to the right path.

Some feminists had thought it possible to open Joran's eyes – and diffuse his polemics – by meeting with him. Jeanne Oddo-Deflou and the GFEF invited him to speak on 10th June 1908 at one of their "confrontational" gatherings.[102] It appears that the circle around *La Française* had also invited him (at least once) to meet with them. But following the publication of his third book, *Au Coeur du Féminisme* (in the fall of 1908), the editor of the weekly *La Française*, Jane Misme, announced that she was fed up with Joran's attacks. In an article entitled "Le Mensonge de M. Joran," Misme remarked that Joran's books would give a reader "a singularly false idea" of feminism; his mind, she charged, "possessed a marvelous power of deformation, which is to say – he lies."[103] In fact, she insisted, Joran's books were full of lies, along with "a fastidious string of all the commonplaces that the 'prejudice of sex' (to quote Jeanne Schmahl) had put in place over the centuries." "In truth," Misme claimed, Joran's current book is "unworthy of being read or refuted."

When Jane Misme first met Joran, she had criticized him in person for writing two books on feminism "without being acquainted with either its history or its philosophy, its serious manifestations, or its important personalities." To which he replied (before witnesses, Misme claimed), "Well, if one had to wait to know a cause before combatting it one would never ever begin." She was particularly annoyed by Joran's trashing of Mme Avril (whom he professed not to know at all) and her 1907 book *Le Féminisme*. In his response to Misme, published the following week, Joran

---

[100] Frédéric Masson, "A M. Th. Joran," in Joran, *Au Coeur du féminisme* (Paris: Arthur Savaète, 1908), ix. Masson (1847–1923), a staunch proponent of authoritarian Bonapartism and historian of Napoléon and his family, was hostile to anything that threatened his hierarchical ideal of "authority."

[101] Joran, "Introduction" to *Au Coeur du Féminisme*, vii.

[102] The GFEF session with Joran was announced in the *Journal des Femmes*, n° 186 (June 1908).

[103] Jane Misme, "Le Mensonge de M. Joran," *La Française*, n° 99 (29 November 1908), front page.

coupled indignation with a passive-aggressive gallantry, demanding her to prove that he had set forth anything in his works that was not factual. Giving tit for tat, she declared that his letter only confirmed her critique. She went on to highlight one particularly significant misstatement of fact when he claimed that feminism's orators neither knew how to speak in public or to improvise. Untrue, Misme retorted, pointing to very able speakers who professed feminist opinions – orators such as Nelly Roussel, Marie Bonnevial, Maria Vérone, and a long list of others, including Mme Avril.[104] Jane Misme then cut off the debate, affirming that the circle around *La Française* had tried "to open his eyes to the 'true' feminism. But he didn't want to see it." We want it to be known, she said, that . . . "we are not his accomplices."

This ultimatum did not silence Joran. In a private letter to Jane Misme, in February 1909, he complained about no longer being welcome "in the small circle of spiritual and distinguished women" at the luncheons of *La Française*, after having once been invited. He blamed his exclusion directly on Mme Avril de Sainte-Croix (whom he claimed had felt his blows and was taking revenge), and promised to return to the charge as concerned her . . . "*qui n'est ni de, ni Sainte* (*oh! non!*) *ni Croix.*" He vowed to redouble his blows: "too bad for her!"[105] Decidedly, the influential Mme Avril had become one of his preferred targets. Antifeminist men like Joran had made up their minds in advance; they did not wish to be confused by facts – or by closer acquaintance with the foe. In an earlier article, he had claimed flatly that "Feminism is the bankruptcy of French gallantry," the consequences of which would be to treat women like men.[106] The notion of sex role confusion seemed frightening to such men. On the front page of *Le Matin*, the writer Rémy de Gourmont labeled women who would not stay in their place as "*hoministes*."[107] Equality, he stated flatly, made love impossible.

Catholic commentators, though not antifeminist in the style of Théodore Joran, also drew the line at maintaining sharply separate roles and spheres for women and men, even though during the next decade the

---

[104] "La Réponse de M. Joran," *La Française*, n° 100 (6 December 1908), front page.

[105] Letter from Théodore Joran to Jane Misme, dated 7 February 1909 – in Jane Misme dossier, BMD. Thanks to Helen Chenut for alerting me to this curious letter, a mixture of fawning compliments with outraged self-pity and threats of revenge. In fact, Joran's "ni, ni, ni" remarks paraphrased Voltaire's criticism of the Holy Roman Empire as being "ni sainte, ni romain, ni empire". In fact, Mme Avril's claim to the name "de Sainte-Croix," disputed by Joran, was wholly legitimate.

[106] See Joran, *Le Féminisme à l'heure actuelle*, offprint from the *Revue Internationale de Sociologie*, 1907.

[107] Rémy de Gourmont, "Un mot nouveau: les hoministes," *Le Matin*, (20 September 1909), front page.

church would move toward enhancing women's education and even supporting women's suffrage. One Catholic writer, Étienne Lamy, in *La Femme de demain* (1901), invoked history to insist that the institutional Church had treated women equitably; it was rather the revival of the pagan tradition with the Renaissance, he argued, which had contributed to the deterioration of woman's position. In contrast, during the seventeenth century, the Catholic revival in France had been instrumental in restoring respect for women; was it not, after all, a Catholic bishop (Fénelon) who had renewed interest in the education of women?[108] Abbé Jean Lagardère acknowledged in his opening editorial in *La Femme contemporaine* that feminism was indeed a major component of the social question. But this progressive priest, whose mission was to promote the political and social education of his female readers, insisted that the family must nevertheless take precedence over the individual's aspirations and that he would never challenge male authority in marriage.[109] The Thomist philosopher A.-D. Sertillanges also took a great interest in the woman question, publishing *Féminisme et christianisme* in 1908.[110]

The lines were firmly drawn in 1909 by none other than the pope, Pius X. In an audience granted that spring to three Catholic women's organizations from Italy and France (the two French groups were the *Ligue des Femmes Françaises* and the *Ligue Patriotique des Françaises*), the Pope restated Church doctrine as enunciated by his predecessor Leo XIII:[111]

---

[108] Étienne Lamy, *La Femme de demain* (Paris: Perrin, 1901). Christian feminists such as Lamy perceived the woman problem as one of maximizing the development and exercise of women's capacities within a framework in which, nevertheless, the complementarity of the sexes centered on the male-headed family. See also his articles that preceded publication of the book: "La Femme et les penseurs," *Le Correspondant* (25 February 1901), 680–705, & (10 March 1901), 912–947; and "La Femme et l'enseignement de l'État," *Revue des Deux Mondes* (1 April 1901), 601–629.

[109] Abbé Jean Lagardère, "Notre programme," *La Femme contemporaine*, n° 1 (October 1903), 7–15; cf. also n° 4 (January 1904), 1–7, and n° 7 (April 1904), 305–310.

[110] A.-D Sertillanges, *Féminisme et christianisme* (Paris: V. Lecoffre, 1908). Other significant contributors to Christian feminism catholic-style include Abbé Henri Bolo, *La Femme et le clergé* (Paris: René Hoton Librairie, 1902), Abbé Paul-Antoine Naudet, *Pour la femme: études féministes* (Paris: A. Fontemoing, 1903; considered by Mme Avril de Sainte-Croix to indicate a tactical change on the part of the Catholic feminists) and the bulky tome (566 pages) by Abbé P. Jardet, *La Femme catholique: Son apostolat, son action religieuse et sociale* (Paris: H. Oudin, 1913). Cf. Hause with Kenney, *Women's Suffrage and Social Politics*, pp. 82–83.

[111] "Audience pontificale accordée à l'Union des femmes catholiques d'Italie, à la Ligue des femmes françaises, et à la Ligue patriotique des françaises," *Echo de la Ligue Patriotique des Françaises* (May 1909), 2–4. As quoted and translated by Odile Sarti, *Ligue Patriotique des Françaises (1902–1933): A Feminine Response to the Secularization of French Society* (New York: Garland, 1991), p. 196. For additional remarks on the views of women's role prevalent or professed in the L.P.D.F. and, more generally, in the Catholic Church, see Sarti, chapter 5, and the more recent publications of Magali Della Sudda. Thanks to Magali Della Sudda for forwarding photocopies of the article cited above in the *Echo* and of the Italian version of the papal address.

> Women are under men's authority.... However, a woman is neither a slave nor a servant of men. She is a companion, helper, associate.... Their functions are different but equally noble and have a unique goal: to raise children and form a family. A man has the duty to provide by his work that which is necessary to the family. A woman must care for the domestic economy and primarily for the education of the children.

Then, the pope added, alluding directly to the more extreme secular advocates of women's rights: "Those who seek for women the same rights and social role as men are in error." Thus had the most authoritative voice in the Roman Catholic Church made it clear that to contest male authority in the family would not be acceptable, to advocate an extrafamilial role for wives would not be acceptable, and to demand "the same rights and social role as men" would not be acceptable. This did not appear to leave much room for feminism among the Catholic faithful, except in the area of female education.

Following the papal pronouncement, a certain Pierre Suau, writing in the Jesuit periodical *Études*, reasserted the notion of two feminisms. Skeptical about women's emancipation, he persisted in claiming (as had Rémy de Gourmont and others) that the objective of [advanced] feminism was to make women be like men.[112] When men begin from the premise that "certain [women] have abdicated their true role, that which they held in Christian society, in a quest for a new use of their lives, they will not find it, because they misunderstand ... their reason for being and their grandeur," you know that they cannot see beyond stereotypes. But Suau counseled a second sort of feminism, where women better understood their "mission" and "desiring to fulfill it more perfectly, wanted to raise themselves to the level of intelligence and influence it required." This latter feminism is "wise and generous," sympathetic. Suau agreed that there were "pagan" elements in the [secular] laws that do oppress women, and that those must be eliminated. He also argued, for example, for legal measures to raise the wages of homeworkers, measures that would "guarantee for women the accomplishment of their maternal mission," but he strongly objected to measures that would give women the civil and political rights of men or allow them to pursue "men's careers." Catholic men had a clear, if conventional, understanding of where to draw the line.

On the secular side, a new surge of book-length publications, supporting and contesting feminism and feminists, appeared in 1907 and 1908, particularly in the wake of the 1908 congress on women's rights and

---

[112] Pierre Suau, "Féminisme et féminisme," *Les Études*, vol. 119 (5 June 1909), 655–676.

suffrage.[113] These included works by Camille Bos, major antifeminist treatises by the eminent Parisian zoologist Edmond Perrier and the Genevan William Vogt, books (1909 and 1914) by the positivist critic Georges Deherme, and a French translation of "the ideas of a woman on feminism," by an Italian antifeminist writer known as Neera (featuring a preface by Théodore Joran).[114] This surge also included the first major publication by Dr. Madeleine Pelletier. Space does not allow an extended analysis of all these works; in what follows I will highlight the exemplary and contrasting contributions of Perrier and Pelletier, while referring to several other works that contributed to the debates on the woman question. Perrier would restate old arguments against feminist goals, while Pelletier would propose novel ways of thinking about women, the family, and the state.

As in the periods following the Revolution, the upheavals of 1848, and the Paris Commune, the big guns of French academic science would oppose further progress for women's emancipation. According to the director of the Museum of Natural History in Paris, a distinguished zoologist and member of the Academy of Sciences, Edmond Perrier (1844–1921), writing on the front page of *Le Matin* (22 November 1908), "*féminisme*" was impossible.[115] But Perrier was not merely editorializing: a far longer version of his editorial, an extended essay (nearly 400 pages) on "Woman in Nature," would grace the first volume (1908) of a luxuriously produced and lavishly illustrated four-volume publication, *La Femme dans la nature, dans les moeurs, dans la légende, dans la société*, accompanied by another essay by a Dr. Verneau on the physical characteristics of women of

---

[113] The 1908 Congress on women's rights and suffrage will be discussed in Chapter 13.

[114] On the antifeminist side: Neera [Anna Radius Zuccari, connue sous le nom de], *Les Idées d'une femme sur le féminisme*, traduit de l'Italien (Paris: V. Giard & E. Brière, 1908); Georges Deherme, *Démocratie vivante* (Paris: B. Grasset, 1909), and *Le Pouvoir social des femmes* (Paris: Perrin, 1914) was strongly anti-individualist, envisioning women primarily as mothers; see the review by F. D. of Deherme's 1909 book in *La Française*, n° 135 (31 October 1909). Earlier, the literary critic and future leader of the *Action Française*, Charles Maurras, criticized "romantisme" in literature as feminine, calling instead for hard, cold reason, and women to be "kept" by men; see his *L'Avenir de l'intelligence* (Paris: Flammarion, 1905). The novels of Colette Yver figure in this category, but will be discussed at greater length in Chapter 12. See, on the profeminist side, the articles of Jacques Bonzon, and especially Jean Finot's *Préjugé et problème des sexes* (Paris: Alcan, 1912; this work was subsequently translated into English), Marguerite Martin, *Les Droits de la femme* (Paris: M. Rivière, 1912), and the published articles of Arria Ly. See later in this chapter for discussion of Pelletier's first book-length feminist publication.

[115] Edmond Perrier, "Le Féminisme impossible," *Le Matin* (22 November 1908), front page. Christine Bard cites this article in her essay, "Les antiféministes de la première vague," in *Un Siècle d'antiféminisme*, ed. Christine Bard (Paris: Fayard, 1999), p. 47.

different races.[116] Three more volumes would appear by the end of 1910, each featuring lengthy essays by a number of well-known (and some less well-known) writers including Frédéric Loliée, Jules Claretie, and Marcel Prévost. Only one essay in the four volumes, that on "woman's work," was written by a woman – in fact, by a well-published female novelist, Camille Pert (pseud. of Louise-Hortense Cyrille Grille de Rougeul, b. 1865).

In contrast to the rants of Théodore Joran, Perrier's contributions were characterized by a calmer, more "objective" approach. His major question was this: "Is this movement [for women's emancipation] in accordance with the findings of biology?" His answer was, in effect, "No." Sexual difference is fundamental, he asserted; it pervades the entire organism of each man and each woman. "The feminine sex is the sex of intensive nutrition" and stores up potential food – in contrast to the masculine sex. Experience, Perrier asserted, confirms these findings – in plants and animals it is the same: "The differences that separate them [the sexes] are fundamental and profound." Psychologically, it was the same thing: "the entire psychology of the feminine sex turns around a single pivot: to assure the security and alimentation of her progeny." A woman cannot escape this, he claimed, but this neither made her superior or inferior – just different. The two sexes, he said, complement each other, physiologically and psychologically. Each has its distinct role. He did not recognize that roles ought not to preclude rights!

Edmond Perrier could not think his way out of a deep-seated belief in sexual hierarchy. Very much aligned with the earlier antifeminist tradition of Rousseau, Roussel, Virey, Comte, and Michelet, whose medically informed views I have discussed in my companion volume, and with Henry de Varigny, who authored the article "Femme. I. Anthropologie et Physiologie" in the *Grande Encyclopédie* (vol. 17, 1903), Perrier situated his views in a perspective that later feminists would condemn as "essentialism."[117] Woman's physiology and psychology, he claimed, is totally

---

[116] *La Femme dans la nature, dans les moeurs, dans la légende, dans la société; tableau de son évolution physique et psychique,* 4 vols. (Paris: Bong & cie., 1908–1910). Until 2013 I had found no analysis of the longer piece that precipitated Perrier's article in *Le Matin,* nor of the other essays in these landmark volumes. A first step is Helen Harden Chenut, "L'esprit antiféministe et la campagne pour le suffrage en France, 1880–1914," *Cahiers du Genre,* vol. 52 (2012), 51–73 – and copublished in *Recherches féministes* (Canada), vol. 25:1 (2012), 37–53. Chenut discusses Perrier's views strictly within the context of the suffrage question.

[117] See *La Grande Encyclopédie,* vol. 17 (1903). Articles by Henry de Varigny, "Femme: I-Anthropologie et Physiologie"; H. Marion, "Femme: II-Psychologie;" also III-Sociologie; and IV-Politique. Varigny's article stated unequivocally that "Woman is defined by her sexuality, and most of her moral and even physiological features must be attributed to her sexual organization" (vol. 17, p. 146). Perrier's approach is slightly different.

constructed around reproduction. "Even the non-existent child invades the woman's entire existence"; her monthly cycles were a preparation for conception. Alluding to the declining French birth rate, he argued that "No matter what she does, woman cannot conquer her independence vis à vis her [male] companion without sacrificing her very reason for being: maternity." "To encourage women's pretension to independence, when the French birth rate is falling in such alarming fashion, could be fatal to the race and to themselves." Women need men's protection, in Perrier's estimation, in order to fulfill their mission. Men must be the breadwinners, he insisted. Woman "is before all else, the property of the child [*l'enfant*]." In sum, the equality of the sexes was impossible (Perrier was speaking here of an equality that went well beyond the notion of mere "equality before the law").[118]

In the concluding chapter of his essay on "Woman in Nature," Perrier reiterated, in a moderate albeit firm language, that "woman could never escape the laws that regulate the evolution of her sex." The good society, he believed, would be founded on the sexual division of labor, with young women instructed as well as educated to fulfill their motherly roles and young men educated to understand their role as sustainers and companions. This would be in accordance with the laws of nature and the best interests of social organization. A feminism built on such an understanding, he believed, should be encouraged.[119]

Neither Perrier nor the other authors in these volumes actually responded to the specific sociopolitical issues and problems that women's advocates in France were then addressing. It is clear, though, from such works that the very existence of a campaign for women's emancipation was really irritating some men. The francophone Swiss writer William Vogt (1859–1918; the son of professor Carl Vogt, who had participated in the Darwin debates) was more specific in his disparagement of feminism (just as he was of freemasonry). In a 350-page work on the "weak sex," he responded to what he called on the title page "the exaggerations, the absurdities, and the utopias" of feminism, and asserted that feminism could only be put down by men's arbitrary use of force and repression.[120] It seemed to such writers that men must take drastic measures in order to reestablish their sovereign authority and assure the future of France. A far

---

[118] Perrier, "Le Féminisme impossible," *Le Matin* (22 November 1908).

[119] See Edmond Perrier, conclusion to his "La Femme dans la nature," pp. 379–390 in vol. 1 of *La Femme dans la nature, dans les moeurs,* etc.

[120] See William Vogt, *Sexe faible; une riposte aux exagérations, aux absurdités, et aux utopies du féminisme* (Paris: M. Rivière, 1908), v.

less learned work than that of Perrier, the first half of Vogt's book consisted of denigrating reflections such as women's "absence of ponderation," "their meanness," and "their ferocity." The latter half of the book consisted of short essays on various French queens and women writers since the seventeenth century, ending with George Sand, whom Vogt actually admired to some degree (he devoted five sketches to her). Adding fuel to the antifeminist fire, a certain Paul Flat condemned "literary feminism" as a "monster," as anti-natural; he insisted that women need, indeed "demand to be dominated by men" and that principles of authority and hierarchy must be upheld.[121] Even as he praised the novels of the best-selling author Marcelle Tinayre for their vigor and virility (by which he meant objective and intellectual), he could not resist repeating the old saw that women had never produced any masterpieces.[122]

Still Defining Feminism

As these debates continued, some advocates of women's rights began to see a need to define feminism for general audiences in less provocative terms. They backed off from Odette Laguerre's explicit insistence (in 1905) that feminism was "an impulse for liberty that marks the end of the reign of Man." And they spun it more positively, as so many champions of women's emancipation have done since, leaving the overt challenge to masculine domination unspoken.

In 1907, Héra Mirtel, the editor of *Le Petit Almanach Féministe* (1906), published by the Paris-based *Union Fraternelle des Femmes*, featured Nelly Roussel's article "What is Feminism?" in which she argued that "Feminism is the doctrine of natural equivalence and social equality of the two factors of humankind."[123] The following year, the *Almanach* surveyed leading figures in the feminist movement to present their own definitions. From the CNFF, Isabelle Bogelot asserted that, for her, feminism meant "working for the intellectual and moral development of woman and for the improvement of her condition in the name of justice," while Ghénia Avril de Sainte-Croix optimistically intoned (in the wake of Léopold

---

[121] Paul Flat, *Nos femmes de lettres* (Paris: Perrin, 1909), pp. 218–231, and passim.

[122] Flat, *Nos femmes de lettres*, pp. 149–151. For an analysis of the misgivings, if not outright hostility, of most male literary critics to women writers in the early twentieth century, see the excellent study by Melanie Collado, *Colette, Lucie Delarue-Mardrus, Marcelle Tinayre: Émancipation et Resignation* (Paris: L'Harmattan, 2003), esp. pp. 43–45.

[123] Nelly Roussel, "Qu'est-ce que le féminisme?" in *Le Petit Almanach Féministe illustré* (1906), pp. 4–5. Roussel's article originally appeared in *La Femme affranchie*, n° 2 (September 1904).

Lacour) that "Feminism, the effort of an elite to achieve more harmony and justice, should disappear, for the good of society, the day its efforts have succeeded. Then feminism, like masculinism, must make way for integral Humanism."[124] Neither would disappear in her lifetime and, even today, integral humanism remains a utopian vision.

The leaders of the other grouplets in the French feminist movement provided additional definitions. Jeanne Oddo-Deflou posited that "Feminism is a social movement that encompasses all the efforts made to improve the condition of woman – economically, intellectually, and legally." Anna Feresse-Deraismes (the younger sister of the famed feminist Maria Deraismes) added that "The name of our Society – Amelioration of the Condition of Woman and the Revendication of her Rights – seemed to her to summarize all the objectives of Feminism." Eliska Vincent remarked that Feminism was the "doctrine or theory that places woman on a footing of equality with man" (without specifying law or rights), while Hubertine Auclert insisted that "the word Feminism synthesizes the efforts made to provide women with the rights men possessed." Mlle J. Van Marcke (Julia van Marcke de Lummen, from Brussels) asserted that "The word Feminism is a banner. It is the philosophic term for militantism – the opposite of selfish resignation." Mme Marbel put it this way: "Feminism is a reaction against all the forces that attempt to inferiorize woman, in other words, a struggle against everything that prevents her from attaining her maximum value as an individual and as a social being."[125] "Everything" was clearly a code word for masculine domination.

It seemed clear by this time that feminism's critics either refused to read or could not digest what various feminist writers were actually saying. The writer Gaston Richard felt it necessary in 1909 to lay out an evolutionary history of women, in which he disparaged the definitions of feminism offered to date as "unscientific." The term, he insisted archly, should not enter the terminology of the social sciences: "It sins, in effect, by an extreme impropriety. It is easy to see what influence the inventors of the word were under when they created it. They had been nourished by literary, moral, and juridical prejudices that established the inequality of the sexes as the very foundation of the social order."[126] Prejudices? Scientific proof? Fact? Fiction? It was left to the Olympic fencer and male-

---

[124] *Le Petit Almanach Féministe illustré* (1907), pp. 4–5.
[125] *Le Petit Almanach Féministe illustré* (1907), pp. 4–5.
[126] Gaston Richard, *La Femme dans l'histoire; étude sur l'évolution de la condition sociale de la femme* (Paris: Doin, 1909), pp. 294–295.

feminist writer Jean-Joseph Renaud (known as Joseph-Renaud, 1873–1953) to provide a tool for feminists that could set straight critics such as Richard, Joran, and the others. In *Le Catéchisme féministe* [The Feminist Catechism, 1910], a small book of a little over a hundred pages, which he dedicated to Marguerite Durand, Joseph-Renaud laid out the ten most frequent objections made against feminism and in plain, reasoned language, provided thoughtful rebuttals to each.[127] This catechismic form was completely understandable to any French woman or man who had been raised Catholic. As one sympathetic commentator put it, "Thanks to [Joseph-Renaud] the old arguments [against feminism] have lost their value – he has killed them off."[128] Opponents of feminism would have to find new ones. Could they do so?

The debates over definition heated up once again in 1912. In January, Jane Misme, editor of *La Française*, laid her emphasis on women's right to work. She exposed the absurdity of the view (which she labelled antifeminist) that a woman had to choose between following her heart and using her brain, especially professionally; she singled out for criticism the recent novels of Colette Yver and, more recently, Yvette Prost, and stated that the heart vs. head/brain dualism/opposition was, without a doubt, "one of the most absurd inventions of antifeminism."[129] Shortly thereafter, in mid-January 1912, Misme launched a series on "feminist doctrine" in *La Française*. She defined feminism as "a doctrine and movement for social reform, tending to establish via laws and morals the equality of rights and duties between man and woman."[130] No more, no less.

---

[127] See Jean Joseph-Renaud, *Le Catéchisme féministe: Résumé de la doctrine sous forme de réponses aux objections* (Paris: Rey, 1910). The specific objections to which the feminist catechism responded were: 1) Woman's place is at home with her husband and children; 2) thanks to women's employment, male salaries go down; 3) feminism masculinizes woman; 4) feminists are partisans of free union and want to disorganize the family; 5) woman is not man's equal but is inferior to him, thus she cannot have the same rights; 6) despite all the progress that woman has made, or will make, woman will always be inferior because of her periodic indisposition [i.e., menstruation]; 7) her extravagant coquetry makes her morally inferior; 8) *recherche de la paternité*, which a number of feminist groups inscribe in their programs, cannot produce serious results and will lead to limitless blackmail; 9) there have been innumerable great men but very few great women; and 10) why should women become either voters or candidates?

[128] See "Aurel," "Le Féminisme et l'homme nouveau," *La Grande Revue* (25 August 1910), 833–839; quote, 835. This article provides an enthusiastic endorsement of Joseph-Renaud's catechism. See also the positive review by Alice Berthet in *La Française*, n° 176 (13 November 1910); this reviewer also remarks the publication of Nelly Roussel's new collection of articles, *Quelques lances rompues pour nos libertés* (1910; cited in n. 97), which also contains refutations of antifeminist claims.

[129] Jane Misme, "Coeur ou Cerveau," *La Française*, n° 224 (21 January 1912).

[130] J. M. "La Doctrine féministe," in *La Française*, n° 224 (21 January 1912).

In the second installment (28 January) Jane Misme addressed the issue of "natural equality of the sexes," praising the forthcoming book, *Préjugé et problème des sexes*, by Jean Finot (1858–1922), a well-known Parisian male-feminist who addressed and refuted the "scientific" arguments for female inferiority of men like Edmond Perrier. Finot, a solidarist republican and editor of *La Revue*, was a keen advocate of equality-in-difference (he made a firm distinction between equality and identity); he also published on race prejudice. *Pacé* Finot and others, he entitled one of his chapters "Creative genius and intelligence have no sex." Finot's book attracted considerable attention in the French press and was welcomed with open arms in *La Française* by Misme. In March she responded to the allegation by Gaston Rageot, in *Le Temps*, that Finot was not a feminist, asserting that Rageot had a misguided idea what feminism was – that he seemed to think it was about turning women into men, "and men becoming nothing at all." *Au contraire.* Finot's book, Misme indicated, had been adopted by feminists as a foundational book, "universally celebrated in the press for its feminist *profession de foi.*"[131] Finot endorsed woman suffrage, unity of morality, equality of rights and duties for both sexes. Although he did not think that women should abandon their role as "queen" of the household, he also advocated that women bring the fruits of science into their homes and that their access to professions and professional growth not be constrained by domestic responsibilities. At the same time Misme, developing another strand of feminist thinking, argued that men must be brought into the foyer to help with household responsibilities, with the cooking, with the children.[132]

> It is just as unjust to forbid men to get involved in household matters, under threat of ridicule, as it is to ridicule the *femmes savantes*. It would be, for both, inhumane to not permit women to exercise a profession except in case of immediate necessity, that is to say, when they have no man to subsidize them. Alas! All too often the male provider, prevented [from working] or suddenly ill, will perish before his companion has been able to force open the doors that she has let entrap her, in order to support herself.

More help was on the way. Not long after the publication of Finot's book, in the late winter of 2012, Jules Bois published *Le Couple futur*. And in early 1913, two pro-woman dramatists premiered their latest plays: Eugène Brieux's *La Femme seule*, and Maurice Donnay's *Les Éclaireuses*.

---

[131] Jane Misme, "M. Jean Finot 'n'est pas féministe'," *La Française*, n° 232 (17 March 1912).
[132] Jane Misme, "La reine du foyer," *La Française*, n° 241 (26 May 1912).

Jane Misme applauded Brieux's efforts to bring women's problems to the attention of larger audiences, and especially the "problem" of single women who needed to support themselves. Brieux, she claimed, did not understand the problem from the "inside"; Brieux's heroine Thérèse "had not figured out the reason for women to have professional work – no light is shed on this." Brieux seemed to indicate that paid work was still a temporary solution for women. As Thérèse blames the workers for forcing women into the labor force because they would rather support their vices than their families, and threatens that women will chase them out of the skills where they are currently being persecuted – because "not having vices, they have fewer needs and work for less than you," Jane Misme classified this "heroine" as an angry woman, but certainly not a well-informed feminist. It is up to the feminists, Misme declared, to say what Brieux was not able to convey.[133] Around this same time, *La Française* was running a series of articles on women's job opportunities, among which was one on sales girls in the department stores. As for Donnay's play, certainly it ends with marriage, but of a young woman whose young man shares her ideas, recognizes and even welcomes the necessity of partnership.[134]

A Dissenting Voice: Dr. Madeleine Pelletier Publishes *Woman in Combat for Her Rights*

In 1908 a new voice entered the debates on the meaning and significance of feminism, Dr. Madeleine Pelletier (1874–1939). Physician, socialist, and by this time an ardent feminist, Pelletier would publish a short book, her first, *La Femme en lutte pour ses droits*.[135] At the outset, she affirmed provocatively that "in either sex, the individual is an end in itself." This claim would, of course, not sit well with the Edmond Perriers, much less the other more extremist objectors to feminism mentioned earlier, who insisted that either "the family," "society," or "love" should forever trump individual liberty, especially in the case of women. Pelletier made her position clear from her very first publication.[136]

[133] Jane Misme, "Après-dernière de 'La Femme seule'," *La Française*, n° 267 (15 February 1913).

[134] Jane Misme, "Les Éclaireuses," *La Française*, n° 268 (22 February 1913).

[135] Madeleine Pelletier, *La Femme en lutte pour ses droits* (Paris: Giard et Brière, 1908).

[136] On Pelletier, see (in chronological order of publication) Marilyn J. Boxer, "When Radical and Socialist Feminism Were Joined: The Extraordinary Failure of Madeleine Pelletier," in *European Women on the Left*, ed. Jane Slaughter & Robert Kern (Westport, CT: Greenwood Press, 1981), pp. 51–71; Felicia Gordon, *The Integral Feminist: Madeleine Pelletier, 1874–1939* (Minneapolis:

Historian Joan Scott characterizes Pelletier's feminism (correctly, in my view) as "radically individualistic," even positing that Pelletier did not think that feminism was "a means to enhance the social status of women, but a way of dissolving the category [woman] entirely."[137] While dissolving the category may have been Pelletier's utopian ideal, practically speaking, she did advocate a particular set of rights for women – as women – rights that challenged the understanding of more conservative French men and women. In fact, in 1906, at the request of Caroline Kauffmann, Pelletier took over the leadership of the action group *Solidarité des Femmes*.[138] From that time on she would be a vocal presence in the French women's rights movement as well as in the SFIO; she would attract criticism for her repugnance toward the outward manifestations of "femininity" as it was then manifested, declaring her preference for masculine dress (at least a man's jacket and tie, and close-cropped hair) and activity in defiance of criticism. Physical sex, she had concluded, was far less important than psychological sex – which seems a surprising perspective for anyone who had undergone medical training, with its focus on the materiality of the

University of Minnesota Press, 1990); Charles Sowerwine & Claude Maignien, *Madeleine Pelletier, une féministe dans l'arène politique* (Paris: Éditions ouvrières, 1992); and *Madeleine Pelletier (1874–1939): Logique et infortunes d'un combat pour l'én comb*, ed. Christine Bard (Paris: côté-femmes, 1992), and Anne Cova, *Maternité et droits des femmes en France (XIXe–XXe siècles)* (Paris: Anthropos, 1997). See also Marilyn J. Boxer's important review-essay, "Placing Madeleine Pelletier: Beyond the Dichotomies Socialism/Feminism and Equality/Difference," *History of European Ideas*, 21:3 (1995), 421–438, and Joan Wallach Scott, "The Radical Individualism of Madeleine Pelletier,"chapter 5 in *Only Paradoxes to Offer: French Feminists and the Rights of Man* (Cambridge, MA: Harvard University Press, 1996).

Some of Pelletier's most significant texts have been republished as *Madeleine Pelletier. L'Éducation féministe des filles et autres textes, préface et notes par Claude Maignien* (Paris: Éditions Syros, 1978), and her later autobiographical novel *La Femme vierge* (Paris: V. Bresle, 1933; Indigo & côté-femmes éditions, 1996), and in Albistur & Armogathe's collection. Pre-1914 texts available in English include translations by Marilyn J. Boxer of two pamphlets, *Féminisme et la famille* (undated) and *Pour l'abrogation de l'article 317: Le Droit de l'avortement* (1913), in the *French-American Review*, 6 (1982), 3–26; by Jennifer Waelti-Walters & Steven C. Hause of "A Feminist Education for Girls," "One Morality for Both Sexes," and "The Right to Abortion" (from *L'Émancipation sexuelle de la femme* [1911]), in *Feminisms of the Belle Epoque* (Lincoln: University of Nebraska Press, 1994); and by Felicia Gordon & Máire Cross in *Early French Feminisms, 1830–1940* (Cheltenham: Edward Elgar, 1996), chapters 5 & 6. Specific texts in translation will be referred to later in this volume. In this chapter I refer only to the position statements that Pelletier published prior to 1910.

[137] Scott, chapter 5: "The Radical Individualism of Madeleine Pelletier," in *Only Paradoxes to Offer*, p. 126. Scott here refers to Pelletier's article, "Les Femmes et le féminisme," *La Revue Socialiste* (January 1906), 44: "Elle sera un individu avant d'être un sexe." See also Boxer, "When Radical and Socialist Feminism Were Joined."

[138] Pelletier later recounted this story in her obituary tribute to Caroline Kauffmann, in *La Fronde*, n.s., n° 74 (16–17 August 1926), 2. It seems paradoxical that Pelletier, the arch-individualist, would agree to preside over the action group *Solidarité des Femmes*.

body. Blessed with a brilliant mind and a penetrating talent for psychological analysis, trained in anthropology, psychology, and medicine, Madeleine Pelletier consciously cultivated the persona of a rugged individualist on the manly model, fueling the criticism of those who thought feminists were really *hominists*. She was a radical feminist who leaned strongly toward socialism (at least insofar as shared housekeeping and child-rearing were concerned). But she always prioritized feminism over socialism, and even over *la patrie*.[139]

Some found Pelletier's propositions extremely disturbing. They represented the antithesis of solidarist collaboration and efforts to put the good of the national community above all else that, for example, characterized the approach of the CNFF. Her four chapters in *La Femme en lutte pour ses droits* addressed the "sociological factors of feminine psychology," "feminist demands," "feminist tactics," and "the social consequences of emancipating women."[140] She thought in terms of social evolution, and affirmed that no social institution or social role was cast in concrete. Even mentalities could change, she affirmed. Certainly, equality-in-difference feminism was not her cup of tea.

Pelletier's first chapter lucidly critiqued the social role conditioning of girls. In her second chapter, she castigated feminist colleagues who flaunted their femininity through dress or behavior even as they posed their demands for change; it was not possible to be emancipated, she indicated, without renouncing these accoutrements and mental habits of femininity. Payment for housework? for maternity? "How wrong the defenders of masculine privilege are to reproach feminists for abandoning their sex; 'femininity,' that is to say weakness, bursts out of every one of their ideas!" Only women who earn their keep will be given consideration – never housewives, Pelletier asserted. "One cannot transform by decree the ideas husbands have about their wives; in order to change ideas, one must modify the conditions of existence." As for "maternity as a social function," this idea seemed no better than the earlier one. "Motherhood," Pelletier indicated, "will never constitute an entitlement to social

---

[139] See Madeleine Pelletier, "Féminisme bourgeois et féminisme socialiste," *Le Socialiste* (5–12 May 1907), 2. See also articles in her monthly publication, *La Suffragiste* (1907–1914).

[140] To my knowledge, only one of these essay/chapters has been published in English translation: the earlier version of "La Tactique féministe," which was originally published in *La Revue Socialiste*, 47, n° 280 (April 1908), 318–333, appears in partial translation (pp. 318–321, 325) by Karen Offen in *Women, the Family, and Freedom*, ed. Susan Groag Bell & Karen Offen (Stanford, CA: Stanford University Press, 1983), vol. 2, doc. 21, pp. 105–106. This essay proposes tactics for getting the vote for women by working through the existing political parties.

importance. Future societies may build temples to maternity, but only to confine the feminine sex inside."[141] Fundamentally, she attested, "women lack courage." They want masculine prerogatives without being willing to fight for them. And so Madeleine Pelletier went on (in this chapter) for thirty more pages, telling it as she saw it – and offending virtually every one of her nominal allies. She even advocated military service for women as a way to toughen them up. "If, for the general good of humanity, men should become more feminine . . . , it is even more necessary for the greater good of their sex, that women become more virile, and a couple of years in a regiment would be very good for them." They would become stronger, used to discipline, and they would even learn how to bear arms. In current circumstances, the army was a "school of energy."[142] Women could be introduced at first in the medical services, as clerks, and as administrators [*intendants*], freeing up men for active service. These proposals attracted some coverage in the daily press.[143]

Pelletier's final chapter on social consequences was doubtless considered the most outrageous at the time, even as it may seem commonsensical to many readers today. Here Pelletier directly addressed the sacred cow of the patriarchal family and posited its disappearance, though not that of motherhood or children. Severe social and economic reorganization was ultimately Pelletier's goal. She asks:[144]

> What will happen to the husband, what will happen to the children, what will happen to the family when, as we desire, woman is emancipated intellectually, morally, and socially – this is the question that those all too numerous persons who are frightened to death of any social transformation will not neglect to ask. As concerns the husband, I avow that my apprehensions are not excessive; he is the strong one, thus there is no need to be preoccupied with protecting him.

"Nor is the perspective of the family's disappearance so terrifying," Pelletier proposed.

> In order to render their privileges intangible, the oligarchies of antiquity designated their origins in the hereafter, but for us who believe that

---

[141] Pelletier, *Femme en lutte pour ses droits*; quotations above from pp. 35–36.

[142] Pelletier, *Femme en lutte pour ses droits*; quote, p. 42.

[143] See, for example, "Les Femmes doivent le service militaire: C'est ce que nous expose ici Madame Madeleine Pelletier, docteur, féministe et . . . antimilitariste," *Le Matin* (28 October 1908) and "Chronique Bruxelloise," *Le Petit Bleu* (5 December 1908). I found both these clippings in the papers of Léonie La Fontaine, LLF 62, Institut International de Bibliographie, at the Mundaneum, Mons, Belgium.

[144] Pelletier, "Social Consequences of Women's Emancipation," unpubl. translation by KO.

everything is of this earth, there is by definition nothing either sacred or intangible. We can undo those things our ancestors did when we think we can do better; if the institution of the family oppresses woman – and this is the case – then there can be no hesitation about suppressing it. What society needs to aim for is the protection of childhood. In an equitable and well-organized society, everything should be so organized that the least possible number of individuals suffer, and children who are weaker even less than the adults.

But, Pelletier asserted, "from the moment the child develops normally, it doesn't matter much whether he receives care from his own mother, from another woman, or from a public service. However interesting the child may be, it is excessive to have to sacrifice to it the entire life of half of humanity, as our present society does. Everyone has the right to happiness, but it is both unreasonable and unjust that this happiness depends on constraining another individual." Heresy? Or common sense?

Madeleine Pelletier then laid out four alternative scenarios, some of which she would further develop in post-war publications. "In the society toward which we are moving, I hope, woman would be able, if she so desired:

1.   To renounce love altogether;
2.   To devote herself to the pleasures of love and have no children;
3.   To have children and turn them over to society to be brought up;
4.   To have children and to raise them herself.

None of these options, in Pelletier's view, would have any moral coefficient attached.

After laying out some thoughts about the suppression of marriage, how women would eventually be able to support themselves, and how children would be supported, Pelletier added that "one must not forget that if we move toward feminism, we move also toward socialism. Do you think that the revolution, whether peaceful or violent, which will have socialized the laboratory, the office, and the workshop, will not socialize the household? All the transformations that we have sketched [here] will be realized by socialism, and they will be for the greatest happiness of both sexes."[145]

---

[145] As of 1908, Madeleine Pelletier had not yet made public her ideas on abortion and contraception. This would only happen in 1911–1912 with the publication of "The Sexual Emancipation of Woman." I will take up these later contributions by Pelletier in Chapter 11, in conjunction with the debates on the population question.

Arria Ly Champions Female Celibacy in the Name of Feminism

The spectacular and controversial journalist Arria Ly (1881–1934; pseud of Joséphine Gondon), from Toulouse, was even more extreme than Madeleine Pelletier in her understanding of what feminism must require: unconditional celibacy, ergo no carnal relations with men, an argument she had begun to put forward in the early years of the century, even as other feminists were engaged in thinking about matriarchy, the reform of the Civil Code, combatting the traffic in women, realizing a fair wage for employed women, advocating *recherche de la paternité*, and improving the conditions surrounding motherhood. Not so Arria Ly. Historian Andrea Mansker has treated Arria Ly's brief career as a feisty, single, self-proclaimed virgin as a case study in the gendering of the concept of "honor" and in her dissertation has probed the development of her views on female purity within the context of an ultra-Catholic upbringing.[146] Mansker interprets Ly's campaign as a defense of the single professional woman.

Arria Ly had actively displayed the banner of feminism since 1902 when she began publishing articles on that subject in the provincial press.[147] In 1905 she published an article, "Restons Mademoiselle" [Remain 'Miss'] in *La Femme affranchie*.[148] But it was her belligerence in arguing for complete female autonomy, in an article entitled "Vive Mademoiselle," published in late June 1911 in Toulouse, that brought her nationwide, and even international, notoriety. There she asserted that "Mademoiselle is the privileged woman who has remained pure, virginal, free, independent! It is she who is not '*en puissance du mari*,' who has not sworn obedience to man and for whom the masculine law recognizes the most civic rights."[149] Ly went on

---

[146] See Andrea Mansker, *Sex, Honor and Citizenship in Early Third Republic France* (Houndmills, UK: Palgrave Macmillan, 2011), which sets the debate squarely with respect to crumbling concepts of male honor, the feminine "surfeit," and the prospective citizenship of the single woman. See also Mansker's dissertation, "'The Pistol Virgin': Feminism, Sexuality, and Honor in Belle Époque France," Ph.D. dissertation, University of California, Los Angeles (2003), and her earlier articles, "Sexuality and the Self in the French Feminist Movement: The Case of Arria Ly," *Proceedings of the Western Society for French History* (2001), vol. 29, ed. Barry Rothaus (University Press of Colorado, 2003), 154–163; "'Mademoiselle Arria Ly Wants Blood!' The Debate over Female Honor in Belle Epoque France," *French Historical Studies*, 29:4 (Fall 2006), 621–647; and "Shaming Men: Feminist Honor and the Sexual Double Standard in Belle Époque France," in *Confronting Modernity in Fin-de-Siecle France: Bodies, Minds, and Gender*, ed. Christopher E. Forth & Elinor Accampo (Houndmills, UK: Palgrave Macmillan, 2010), pp. 169–191.

[147] A list of Arria Ly's articles can be consulted in Mansker's dissertation (cited in n. 146), pp. 351–354.

[148] Arria Ly, "Restons Mademoiselle," *La Femme affranchie*, n° 13 (August 1905).

[149] Arria Ly, "Vive Mademoiselle," first published (according to Mansker) in *Le Rappel de Toulouse* (28 June 1911), and quickly reprinted in *La Renovation morale* (30 June 1911). The bulk of this translated quotation appears in Mansker's dissertation, "The 'Pistol Virgin,'" p. 105; a slightly different translation (and I think less acccurate) is given in the FHS article. I have amended it slightly here, based on consultation of the reprint from *Gil Blas*, 6 September 1911; I thank Andrea Mansker

to argue that "physical relations between men and women are abominable and immoral both within and outside of marriage."[150] Furthermore, she added: "Whether they admit it or not, married women are sullied women and those who refuse to recognize this only prove that they do not have a sense of purity. On the contrary, the more lively the horror and disgust inspired in a married woman by the physical relations she is obliged to have with her husband, the more developed the elevation of her sentiments."[151] She issued a clarion call for virginity, and insisted that it would be the supreme honor for feminism "as I understand it" to turn resolutely in this direction. Feminists, she indicated, must take up the cry "Vive Mademoiselle." And "Masculina" be hanged! She had nothing good to say about men.

This single article, which was subsequently reprinted in the Parisian press (*Gil Blas*, 6 September 1911), provoked a swarm of responses, but one annoyed journalist, writing in a regional paper, *Le Rappel de Toulouse*, indirectly insinuated that Arria Ly must be a lesbian. This deliberate insult provoked her to step over a previously unbreachable cultural boundary set by men's double standard. In defense of her personal "honor" and to make the point that women, just as men, could defend their honor, Arria Ly directly challenged the editor of the paper (who was by law responsible for its content) to a pistol duel "in the name of feminism." This incident made front-page news throughout France and abroad.

Why was Arria Ly so adamant about defending "Mademoiselle" in the name of feminism? Previously, in early September and October 1910, *La Française* had opened its columns to a debate over whether all women should be referred to as "Madame" (Mme), so as not to distinguish between single women and married women. Most respondents leaned toward applying the term Madame to married and unmarried women alike, in order to obliterate the stigmatized treatment of adult women who remained single (stigmatized culturally even though they, unlike their married counterparts, did possess full civil rights).[152] This is the debate into which Arria Ly strode with her decidedly original perspective. Had she simply made the case for "Mademoiselle," she would undoubtedly not

---

for sharing her digital photo of the *Gil Blas* reprint, which I have confirmed on Gallica. Although Arria Ly said "droits civiques," it is likely she actualy meant "droits civils," since no women, single or married, yet enjoyed civic/political rights.

[150] "Vive Mademoiselle" (1911), as quoted in translation in Mansker's dissertation, p. 216; this quotation and the next one have been checked against the photoprint.

[151] "Vive Mademoiselle" (1911), as quoted in translation in Mansker's dissertation, p. 132.

[152] See in *La Française*, Claire Galichon in n° 169 (7 August 1910), n° 170 (4 September 1910), & n° 171 (2 October 1910); see also the responses in n° 170 (4 September 1910) by Th. Reinach, Amélie Hammer, Elisabeth Hamburger-Courdès; "Djénane" in n° 172 (16 October 1910) and "Aylol" in n° 173 (23 October 1910).

have triggered such an adverse response in the press and in the feminist community. But by basing her case on the "unsullied" chastity of the single woman and demeaning all married women as unclean, putting them in the same category as prostitutes, she provoked a very strong and mostly negative response.[153]

In an era of great concern about the French lack of population growth, such views as Arria Ly's concerning sex (and its consequences) seemed tantamount to treason – and a number of Arria Ly's less radical feminist counterparts found her arguments disturbing. Even the outspoken Madeleine Pelletier was concerned and in an earlier personal letter she had observed to Arria Ly that it was impolitic to say out loud – or print – everything that one thought: "I believe, and I tell you as your friend, that you are mistaken in your ideas. . . . Feminism should not be a feeling but an idea born of reason."[154] Undeterred, in 1913 Arria Ly founded a short-lived periodical called *Le Combat féministe, organe du mouvement féministe arrialyste*, in which she effectively declared war between the sexes, and against sexual intercourse itself. Population growth, be damned!

---

[153] On the reaction, see Mansker's prizewinning article, "Vive 'Mademoiselle'!" The Politics of Singleness in Early Twentieth-Century French Feminism," *Feminist Studies*, 33:3 (Fall 2007), 632–658.

[154] Pelletier's letter to Arria Ly, 27 June 1908, as translated by Felicia Gordon in *Integral Feminist: Madeleine Pelletier*, p. 91. The original letter can be consulted in the Marie-Louise Bouglé collection, Fonds Arria Ly (Série 83 – féminisme) at the BHVP.

CHAPTER 11

Refocusing the State
Depopulation, Maternity, and the Quest for
a Woman-Friendly State

Arria Ly and Madeleine Pelletier were certainly the outliers among those who identified as feminists in France during the early twentieth century. More common was the attitude expressed by the feminist novelist Marcelle Tinayre in 1910, who remarked in *La Française* that:[1]

> I believe that woman is made, above all, for love, marriage, maternity, the education of children, the government of the household, and not for heavy labor or vast responsibilities. I believe that the secular tasks of woman are in no way inferior to those of man, that they require a special intelligence, considerable reason, judgment, patience, goodness, courage, and perseverance. These tasks that are particular to women also are clearly useful, something that some jobs of man are not always, for France could probably get along without politicians, but not without mothers of families.

But in early twentieth-century France the situation of wives and mothers was compromised in virtually every respect.

Concerned as they were with the "the grand problems of today," as Odette Laguerre characterized them, that is, those defined as such by French men, they believed that questions of peace and war, of religion, and of socialism could not be resolved without first confronting and resolving the major and still unresolved problem of the legal, economic, and social disparities in the relationship between the sexes.[2] In particular, and because feminists were deeply concerned about the future of France, they paid keen attention to fundamental issues surrounding sex and reproduction, which could in turn not be disentangled from questions of family formation and the diminishing birth rate and, of course, the distressing conditions surrounding the possibility of maternity for poor women.

---

[1] Marcelle Tinayre, in *La Française*, n° 176 (13 November 1910).
[2] See Odette Laguerre, "Le Féminisme et les grand problèmes actuels," *La Fronde*, n° 1902 (24 May 1903), front page.

The ongoing population question lay at the very heart of French politicians' national concerns under the Third Republic.[3] Indeed, depopulation, nationalism, and feminism had clearly become inextricably linked concerns that cried out for resolution, most likely through some form of government action. We will address the concerns swirling about women's economic predicament and questions about their employment in Chapter 12; here we will explore the debates about women's control of their own bodies and their fertility, debates that encompassed heterosexual love, sex, babies (especially those born outside marriage who were highly vulnerable), sex education, and, more broadly, women's "role" and responsibilities to themselves and to the nation in the context of concerns about the future of France. Talking back to men who would restrict women's access to contraception and sex education in 1905, the fiercely anticlerical feminist journalist Nelly Roussel phrased her challenge boldly: "The liberation of the flesh is the first of all liberations, the foundation of all the others."[4] Even more foundational, she believed, than economic independence. But these several forms of liberation were, in fact, most difficult to separate.

Like Marcelle Tinayre and even Nelly Roussel, most turn-of-the-century feminists would freely acknowledge the importance of women's maternal role and responsibilities, but they were deeply concerned about how these were put to use. In early 1901, stimulated by Eugène Brieux's most recent play, *Les Remplaçantes*, which questioned the practice of employing rural wet nurses who would sacrifice their own babies in order to make money by nursing those of wealthier women,"Harlor," writing in *La Fronde*, came down firmly in favor of maternal nursing. Only reasons of health, she said, are an excuse for mothers not to nurse their own infants. In fact, Harlor insisted, women's beauty can be enhanced by nursing, as can a man's love. Even so, there should be more day nurseries [*crèches*], where poorer women could safely leave their babies while they went to work. "The importance of the question of maternal nursing must be recognized by the State especially and by the communes; they must make

---

[3] Some material in this section is adapted from my articles, "Depopulation, Nationalism, and Feminism in Fin-de-Siècle France," *The American Historical Review*, 89:3 (June 1984), 648–676, and "Exploring the Sexual Politics of French Republican Nationalism," in *Nationhood and Nationalism in France*, ed. Robert Tombs (London: HarperCollins Academic, acquired by Routledge, 1991), pp. 195–209.

[4] Nelly Roussel, "Lettre ouverte à MM Paul et Victor Margueritte," *L'Action*, (16 December 1905); reprinted in Nelly Roussel, *Quelques Lances rompues pour nos libertés* (Paris: V. Giard & E. Brière, 1910), p. 125.

it easy," Harlor insisted; "Feminism is by no means against the 'responsibilities of motherhood' – nothing could be more false." The organization of labor must be changed, so that poorer mothers can fulfill their responsibilities.[5] A few months later, examining the question of household responsibilities, Andrée Téry argued in *La Fronde* that a woman could be a good wife and mother without having to master every household task; get rid of the kitchen, she said, by turning food preparation over to specialists.[6] Later that same year,"Mytha" expressed her concern that the enemies of feminism were blaming depopulation on women – but, she said, such persons had strange misconceptions about what they thought feminism was. She asserted that it was the frivolous rich women who didn't want motherhood, but that what the feminists wanted for all women, and especially for poor women, was better education and serious preparation for their maternal role. "It is less important to augment the population numbers than to enhance their value."[7] "Quality over quantity" increasingly characterized the attitude of vocal mainstream feminists. "One must recognize that the women's solution is the good one; that maternal love and the very legitimate desire of the woman to not suffer too much, are not, as has been claimed, in disagreement with the requirements for the defense of the country."[8] In short, as Nelly Roussel would repeatedly insist, women should not be forced to become mothers without their wholehearted consent.

The First Depopulation Commission (1902–1903)

In the shadow of concerns about depopulation, some republican politicians began to take seriously the feminist women's arguments and to reconsider their priorities. As feminists increasingly framed their arguments in terms of national concerns, these men's responses became increasingly explicit and detailed. These responses ranged from a defensive, traditionalist (and clearly antifeminist) commitment to the authoritarian male-

---

[5] Harlor, "Maternité totale," *La Fronde*, n° 1169 (20 February 1901).
[6] Andrée Téry, "Le Home sans pot-au-feu," *La Fronde*, n° 1229 (24 April 1901).
[7] "Mytha," "Maternité et féminisme," *La Fronde*, n° 1353 (23 August 1901).
[8] See the report on this work by Camille Bélilon and Hyacinthe Bélilon, *Rapport sur Qualité Prime Quantité*, supplement au *Journal des Femmes*, n° 138 (December 1903), 5–6. The author of the tract under consideration, Julia van Marcke de Lummen, was a well-off Belgian feminist who was close to Léon Richer and had a residence in Paris. She had founded a Belgian group, *Union pour la Solidarité des Femmes*, and published a monthly, *La Revendication des droits féminins*. See Julie Carlier, "Moving Beyond Boundaries: An Entangled History of Feminism in Belgium, 1890–1914," Ph.D. Dissertation, University of Ghent, 2010.

headed family as the core unit of the state, resting on a hierarchical division of labor between the sexes, to a relatively more liberal, secular, and egalitarian view that nevertheless upheld a division of labor along sexual lines as both a fundamental principle and an axiom of evolutionary progress. The controversy showed again that support from many republican men for the autonomous existence of women – or, for that matter, of men – would remain qualified, although there would be some significant exceptions.

By 1902, three schools of thought on the relationship between the woman question and the population issue could be identified among anticlerical republican men active in public life. In an earlier article on depopulation, nationalism, and feminism I baptized these as the "patriarchal patriots," the solidarists (who advocated state intervention on behalf of the national community, but were not socialists), and the "integral individualists," some of whom during this period adopted an anti-statist perspective.[9] Nelly Roussel would refer to the first group (and their Catholic counterparts) as "patriotards," and "apostles of fecundity."[10] The first two lines of thought were well represented among the seventy members of the all-male and all-republican Extraparliamentary Commission on Depopulation, established by the French Senate late in 1901 and appointed by prime minister René Waldeck-Rousseau early in 1902.[11]

Somewhat after the fact, in the spring of 1902 French feminists in the *Solidarité des Femmes* group published a letter to Senators Piot and Maignin, complaining that no woman had been appointed to serve on the Depopulation Commission.[12] Complaints continued to be filed, but

---

[9] See Offen, "Depopulation, Nationalism, and Feminism . . ."

[10] Nelly Roussel, "L'Église et la maternité," in *L'Action*, 6 December 1904; reprinted in *Quelques Lances rompues*, pp. 105–108; quote, p. 108.

[11] This commission consisted of deputies, senators, professors of law, political economy, and medicine, magistrates, hospital administrators, educators, high civil servants, and a smattering of men of letters. At the commission's first meeting, two subcommittees, one on natality and one on mortality, were established. The published records of the Commission include: France. Commission de la dépopulation: (1) *Séance du 29 janvier 1902* (Paris, 1902); (2) *État des travaux de la commission extra-parlementaire contre la dépopulation, dressé par M. Ogier, secrétaire générale de la commission* (Melun, 1902); (3) *Tableaux statistiques recueillis ou établis par les soins du comité d'études* (Melun, 1902); (4) [G. Delamotte] *Note sur les mesures fiscales susceptibles dans les principaux pays d'influencer le mouvement de la population* (Melun, 1902); (5) [Arsène Dumont] *Rapport sur l'âge au mariage et son influence sur la natalité* (Melun, 1903); (6) [Charles Gide] *Rapport sur la moralité publique* (Melun, 1903); (7) [Adolphe Pinard & Charles Richet] *Rapport sur les causes physiologiques de la diminution de la natalité* (Melun, 1903); (8) Sous-commission de la mortalité, *Séance du 2 juillet 1902* [compte rendu].

[12] The French group *Solidarité des Femmes* protested the exclusion of women from the Commission, exchanging correspondence with Senator Piot, and planned to go straight to the Président du

the government did not act. The novelist Marcel Prévost, writing in *Le Figaro* in March 1903, insisted that women's opinions on the Commission's projects, inasmuch as they were central to its concerns, must be taken into account. He argued, in particular, that the pronatalists consider the needs of working women, who required guarantees – "before, during, and after" – for their childbearing.[13]

The published discussions and reports of the Depopulation Commission and its two subcommittees on natality and mortality, as well as the publications of various committee members, enable us to identify their explanations for the falling birth rate, their general views on the position of women – which often touched on assessing women's responsibility (or, conversely, lack of responsibility) for depopulation – and their attitudes toward state intervention.

Partisans of the first tendency, the patriarchal patriots (or "patriotards"), exhibited little enthusiasm for the feminists' assertion that women, even as wives and mothers, must be perceived as responsible individuals capable of independent action. Their full attention was focused gloomily on threats to the "traditional" family, in which patriarchal control was assumed to be necessary, especially over children; they feared that such control would be jeopardized by intrusion of the state. These men manifested outright hostility to the notion of economic independence for women, though they sometimes seemed less hostile to giving women the vote, perhaps on the assumption that women would vote as their husbands wished. They perceived "the family" to be under obligation to fulfill the manpower needs of the French state. To this end, they viewed state intervention as necessary *only* insofar as it might promote natality by restoring as much formal authority as possible to the *chef de famille*. They advocated amendments to the inheritance and tax laws that would restore paternal disposition of the patrimony of landed capital as fathers saw fit and urged the adoption of financial incentives through tax exemptions to foster the fathering of large numbers of children.

This school of thought (as we have seen in previous chapters) had deep roots in Le Playist sociology. In the wholly republican Depopulation Commission, it was espoused by some secular republicans, who in this respect at least found themselves in accord with social Catholics. These

---

Conseil; see the minutes of its 5 March meeting in the *Journal des Femmes*, n° 120 (April 1902), 2. Cf. also n° 122 (June 1902), 3, and n° 123 (July 1902), 2.

[13] See Marcel Prévost, "La conquête des mères," *Le Figaro* (15 March 1903); date verified on Gallica, 7-1-2012; the hand-dated clipping can also be consulted in BMD DOS 312 NAT.

secularists viewed natality and family building as exclusively male concerns; indeed, they even presented the phenomenon of depopulation itself as evidence of male degeneracy – a crisis in French virility! This orientation was epitomized by the arguments of the doctor-demographer Jacques Bertillon, who (as we have seen in earlier chapters) discounted not only the role of women but even the possible importance of abortion (the classic female solution to the problem of unwanted children, as historian Angus McLaren has reminded us) in contributing to the decline.[14] The essence of this argument is conveyed, not in jest, by the title of an article by Bertillon's lieutenant Fernand Boverat, which appeared some years later in the magazine of the Alliance Nationale – "Prepare our children for the idea of becoming fathers" [*Préparons nos enfants à l'idée d'être pères*].[15] As if all children were male – and the sons of fathers alone.

A second prominent "patriotard" in the Depopulation Commission was the elderly Edme-Georges Piot (1828–1909), senator for Côte d'Or.[16] Piot's arguments on the population question are also remarkable for their infrequent references to women's role in reproduction. Although he called for reforms in public health practices that would facilitate maternity, his principal objective was to encourage paternity – within the bounds of marriage, that is. Piot did acknowledge women's importance in one respect; he thought they could be bribed. It was Piot who in 1903 reintroduced in France the old Roman notion of state-awarded medals for motherhood.[17] Advocates of women's rights had a field day with this suggestion. In the *Journal des Femmes,* Maria Martin observed, with some sarcasm, that although the idea of honoring mothers might be quite

---

[14] Angus McLaren, "Abortion in France: Women and the Regulation of Family Size, 1800–1914," *French Historical Studies,* 10:3 (Spring 1978), 461–485.

[15] Fernand Boverat, "Préparons nos infants à l'idée d'être pères," *La Revue de l'Alliance nationale,* n° 147 (October 1924), 306. See also Boverat, *Patriotisme et paternité* (Paris: B. Grasset, 1913). Not surprisingly, many of the patriarchal patriots also supported the sports movement of Pierre de Coubertin, with its emphasis on restoring virility, and later helped found the French eugenics movement. On these men and movements, see Robert A. Nye, "Degeneration, Hygiene, and Sports in Fin-de-Siècle France," in *Proceedings of the Western Society for French History, Eugene, 1980,* ed. Edgar Leon Newman, pp. 404–412; John M. Hoberman, "Pierre de Coubertin: Hygienist of the Third Republic," ibid., p. 413; and William Schneider, "The Origin of Eugenics in France," ibid., p. 414. Also see William Schneider, "Toward the Improvement of the Human Race: The History of Eugenics in France," *Journal of Modern History,* 54:2 (June 1982), 268–291.

[16] See Edme Piot, *La Question de la dépopulation en France: Le Mal, ses causes, ses remèdes* (Paris: Société anonyme des Publications périodiques, 1900), and *La Dépopulation; enquête personnelle sur la dépopulation en France: Documents, discours et rapports* (Paris: Société anonyme des Publications périodiques, 1902).

[17] Piot, "Une Décoration pour les mères de familles," *La Revue Philanthropique,* 13, n° 74 (June 1903), 273–274.

acceptable, it should certainly take a more concrete form; in *Le Radical,* Hubertine Auclert argued for a monetary indemnity *to be paid directly to mothers,* or, that failing, the award of the medal of the *Légion d'honneur.*[18]

Solidarism, the second and more complex line of thought that had developed among anticlerical republican men, espoused a more limited form of state intervention. This vision was personified in the Depopulation Commission by Paul Strauss (1852–1942), former Paris municipal councilor, member of the *Conseil Général* of the Seine, and from 1897 on senator for the department of the Seine, and director (since its founding in 1897) of the *Revue Philanthropique.*[19] Strauss, a radical republican, acknowledged women as competent beings (though always in the context of the family), and, in his private philanthropic activities, he worked closely and congenially with advocates of women's rights. Stressing the reciprocity of men's and women's obligations in the social division of labor, however, he invariably stereotyped women as mothers, including even young, unmarried girls who were perceived, first and foremost, as potential mothers. Men of solidarist persuasion preferred to view the population crisis as a moral issue, one that could be successfully addressed by the state through education and intervention, if only the government could be induced to adopt and finance the costly programs necessary to correct certain structural and environmental defects. They, too, were interested in enhancing French natality in the national interest; as Senator Strauss put it in 1900, "First the Fatherland, then Humanity" [*La patrie d'abord, humanité ensuite*].[20]

---

[18] Documents from the 1903 controversy were reprinted in successive issues of Paul Robin's neo-Malthusian periodical, *Régénération.* For women's views, see Maria Martin, "La Grève des mères," *Le Journal des Femmes,* n° 133 (June 1903); and Hubertine Auclert, "Recompensez la maternité," *Le Radical* (18 March 1902), and "La Dotation des mères françaises," *Le Radical* (30 November 1903). In addition, a series of Auclert's articles on this subject were reproduced (without dates) in *Les Femmes au gouvernail* (Paris, 1923), pp. 317–358. Also see "Lettre ouverte à M. Piot, sénateur de la Côte d'Or," from the president of "Le Dû aux mères," *La Fronde,* n° 2011 (12 June 1903); and Marcel Prévost, "La Conquête des mères," *Le Figaro* (15 May 1903), who insisted that women's opinions in reproductive matters must be considered; clipping in Dossier 312 NAT, Bibliothèque Marguerite Durand. NB: when in 1920 the French government did inaugurate a program to reward *mères de famille nombreuses,* it would be strictly honorific – medals with ribbons and merit citations but no bonuses.

[19] For further insight into the ideas of Paul Strauss, see especially Mary Lynn Stewart, *Women, Work, and the French State: Labour Protection and Social Patriarchy, 1879–1919* (Toronto: McGill-Queen's University Press, 1989), chapter 8, and Rachel G. Fuchs, "The Right to Life: Paul Strauss and the Politics of Motherhood," in *Gender and the Politics of Social Reform in France, 1870–1914,* ed. Elinor A. Accampo, Rachel G. Fuchs, & Mary Lynn Stewart (Baltimore: Johns Hopkins University Press, 1995), pp. 82–105. See also Rachel Fuchs, *Poor and Pregnant in Paris: Strategies for Survival in the Nineteenth Century* (New Brunswick, NJ: Rutgers University Press, 1992), chapter 2.

[20] Paul Strauss, "La Puériculture avant la naissance," *La Revue des Revues* (15 January 1900), 140. Also see Strauss's contributions to the *Revue Philanthropique,* which he edited, his article in the *Revue des Revues* (1 August 1900), 229–237, and his subsequent book, *Dépopulation et puériculture* (Paris:

In contrast to the patriarchal patriots, Solidarists like Strauss did take seriously the importance of women's role in population formation and in *puériculture* [the French term for scientific child-rearing]. They generally gave credence to women's views and listened attentively to the claims of the mainstream feminists when the latter made an effort to present their demands in a respectful, conciliatory, and ladylike (though nevertheless forceful) manner. The solidarists' solutions for women's concerns, however, had a way of coming down on the side of an intrusive, if benevolent paternalism, the *"police des familles"* of Donzelot's classic analysis.[21] This is evident in Strauss's arguments for obligatory school programs for girls in *puériculture*, and in the later response of another Solidarist, the political economist Charles Gide, to the findings of a Depopulation Commission subcommittee report. In that report, Dr. Adolphe Pinard had blamed women's contraceptive practices for 80 percent of the benign tumors observed in women's reproductive organs after their surgical removal. Gide concluded from Pinard's finding that doctors should counsel bourgeois women against these unhealthy "neo-Malthusian practices"; he further proposed that the state educate married couples to believe that they owed four children to *la patrie*.[22]

Men like Strauss and Gide were never so obsessed with the need to reaffirm male virility and authority as were the patriarchal patriots. But, as the birth rate decline continued with no sign of abatement through the first decade of the twentieth century, the tolerance of the Solidarists for claims to rights based on individual liberty, whether made by men or by women, diminished markedly, and their public utterances were marked by increasingly fervent patriotic rhetoric. That this decreasing tolerance would affect the possibilities for reform open to campaigners for women's rights, whose leaders were so closely affiliated with these men, there can be little doubt. Rachel Fuchs put it squarely when she concluded that "Strauss's concept of liberty ... like that of his republican cohort, applied to men. His discourse and programs ignored, or denied women's right to liberty." For Strauss, social hygiene and producing and maintaining infants for the future of France were the goals, and women as "mothers were the

---

Bibliothèque Charpentier, 1901). These publications offer insight into the thinking of male-feminist solidarist republicans. Strauss's writings ring with appeals to solidarity and science within a republican patriotic framework.

[21] Jacques Donzelot, *La Police des familles* (Paris: Éditions de Minuit, 1977); in English, *The Policing of Families* (New York: Pantheon, 1979).

[22] Charles Gide, "Le Dépeuplement de la France; Y a-t-il quelque remède à la dépopulation de la France?" *La Revue Hebdomadaire*, 5:2 (8 May 1909), 141–148.

vehicles."[23] He once claimed that the protection of infants was "the keystone of the entire social edifice."[24] Strauss was nevertheless generous in advocating for feminist social welfare concerns during his years on the Paris Municipal Council and in opening the pages of the *Revue Philanthropique* to feminist contributors who spoke to the social welfare concerns of the nation. He became a key figure in obtaining funding for projects that would save infants by sustaining their mothers. Unlike earlier charitable groups (such as the venerable and very Catholic *Société de Charité Maternelle*, which would provide aid only to married mothers with more than two children), he was entirely willing to support the provision of aid to single mothers, without worrying about their "morality" – or their religious affiliation (or lack thereof). Above all else, Strauss wanted to deter desperate poor mothers from falling back on child abandonment or, far worse, infanticide. In his view, France simply could not afford such losses. He strongly supported *recherche de la paternité* in the Senate (and fought against various amendments that sought to water down the proposed bills). But perhaps Strauss's greatest contribution in the decade we are considering here would be to patiently but persistently advocate in the *Conseil Supérieur de l'Assistance Publique* and in the Senate for a law that, finally, in mid-1913, would provide an obligatory, partially paid maternity leave for expectant women workers. Throughout this decade – and for several more thereafter – Paul Strauss served as a champion of state intervention to address grave, and possibly crippling, social problems that endangered not only the lives of infants and the health of their mothers, but the life and health of the French nation itself.

The third tendency among the secularists, unlike the first two, was not well represented on the Depopulation Commission. The advocates of integral individualism brooked no barriers to the rights of the individual, man or woman, no limitations on self-determination, irrespective of the perceived needs of state or society. In their ranks were both anarchists and neo-Malthusians, campaigning for the right of women not only to control their own bodies but also to employ active contraception – which they viewed as a woman's ultimate act of civil disobedience.[25] One member of the commission, the social dramatist Eugène Brieux, though silent during committee discussions, subsequently espoused these libertarian views. In his earlier play, *Three Daughters of M. Dupont* (1897), he had warned

---

[23] Fuchs, "Right to Life," p. 86.   [24] As quoted by Fuchs, "Right to Life," p. 90.
[25] See Roger-Henri Guerrand, *La Libre maternité, 1896–1969* (Tournai: Casterman, 1971) and Francis Ronsin, *La Grève des ventres* (Paris: Aubier Montaigne, 1980).

against the evils of Malthusianism; given a political climate already sensitive to the population question, this play – along with *Les Avariés* (*Damaged Goods*, a 1901 play about the dangers of syphilis), and *Les Remplaçantes* (*The Replacements*, 1902, which addressed the hazards that awaited infants farmed out to commercial wet nurses) – presumably established Brieux's credentials as a defender of the nation and led to his appointment to the Depopulation Commission.

It was precisely during Brieux's tenure on the commission, ironically, that he wrote *Maternité* (*Maternity*), the play that scandalized his colleagues when it opened in Paris in December 1903. The play depicted the fate of a young woman, seduced, pregnant, and abandoned (for lack of a dowry), who sought a clandestine abortion and died from complications. Through the play's female characters, notably the older, married sister of the unfortunate young mother-to-be and the clients of the midwife who performed the fatal abortion, Brieux vocalized the rank injustices confronting women in French society. In defending the right of women to control the disposition of their own bodies for procreation – against both husbands they did not love and predatory, egotistical seducers, Brieux's *Maternity* confronted Parisian theatergoers with another stark reminder not only of women's inferior legal status in marriage, but also of the appallingly inferior economic status of women outside marriage, and it presented a powerful case for change.[26] More than one of his associates on the Depopulation Commission were not pleased. Dr. G. Drouineau, writing in Strauss's *Revue Philanthropique* in March 1904, after the play closed, criticized Brieux for not offering any new solutions. He was particularly disturbed by Brieux's unkind depiction of male officialdom, but said nothing further about the dilemmas of the women. During the next decade, Brieux would go on to compose several more pathbreaking plays that addressed further contemporary dilemmas in women's lives, such as *La Déserteuse* (1904) and *La Femme seule* (1912). Although Brieux seems a forgotten literary figure today, the great British playwright George

---

[26] Eugène Brieux, "Maternity," transl. Mrs. Bernard Shaw, in *Three Plays by Brieux*, ed. and introduced by Bernard Shaw (New York: Brentano's, 1911). Brieux's pithy social plays of this period are important documents for studying the debates on the woman question. For a commentary following the opening of *Maternity*, see M. de Morsier, "M. Brieux," *La Revue Bleue* (12 December 1903), 753–755. The public exchange between Brieux and Senator Piot continued in *Le Matin* (11 December & 16 December 1903), and *L'Éclair* (14 December 1903). Also see G. Drouineau, "Maternité," *La Revue Philanthropique*, 14, n° 83 (10 March 1904), 553–560. On the sociopolitical impact of Brieux's plays, see Jean Elisabeth Pedersen, *Legislating the French Family: Feminism, Theater, and Republican Politics, 1870–1920* (New Brunswick, NJ: Rutgers University Press, 2003).

Bernard Shaw considered him to be the "most important dramatist west of Russia" after the death of Ibsen.[27] Certainly, Brieux's topical plays captured the anguished consequences for women of male dominance in French society.

Feminists Talk Back to the Pronatalists: Nelly Roussel, Ellen Key, and Léon Blum

As indicated previously, women had absolutely no voice in the meetings of the Depopulation Commission – much to the dismay of French feminists. At that time only a few women had begun to publish objections to the notions being debated in the commission. Of particular importance would be the intrepid Nelly Roussel (1878–1922), who burst into public prominence as a feminist writer and orator during these years.[28] Like Camille Bélilon, Hubertine Auclert, and Marguerite Durand and other feminist journalists, she was not shy about talking back to power. In March 1903 she spoke on "freedom of maternity" and invoked the notion of a mothers' strike.[29] Not long after, she introduced her short allegorical play, *Par la Révolte*, which she would perform in many venues throughout France, including the Theatre Sarah-Bernhardt in Paris.[30]

---

[27] Bernard Shaw in *Three Plays by Brieux*, vii.

[28] The landmark publications of Elinor Accampo on Nelly Roussel include: "The Rhetoric of Reproduction and the Reconfiguration of Womanhood in the French Birth Control Movement, 1890–1920," *Journal of Family History*, 22:3 (July 1996), 351–371; "Private Life, Public Image: Motherhood and Militancy in the Self-Construction of Nelly Roussel, 1900–1921," in *The New Biography: Performing Femininity in Nineteenth-Century France*, ed. Jo B. Margadant (Berkeley & Los Angeles: University of California Press, 2000), pp. 218–261; "The Gendered Nature of Contraception in France: Neo-Malthusianism 1900–1920," *Journal of Interdisciplinary History*, 34:2 (Autumn 2003), 235–262; and her biographical chef d'oeuvre, *Blessed Motherhood, Bitter Fruit: Nelly Roussel and the Politics of Female Pain in Third Republic France* (Baltimore: Johns Hopkins University Press, 2006). See also Anne Cova, "Féminisme et natalité: Nelly Roussel (1878–1922)," *History of European Ideas*, 15:4–6 (August 1992), 663–672, and Anne Cova, *Féminisme et néomalthusianisme sous la IIIe République* (Paris: L'Harmattan, 2011).

Nelly Roussel's published works (before 1914) include *L'Éternelle sacrifiée*, préface, notes et commentaire par Maïté Albistur & Daniel Armogathe (Paris: Syros, 1979) and *Quelques Lances rompues* (cited in n. 4). Several of Roussel's major texts are translated in *Feminisms of the Belle Epoque*, ed. Jennifer Waelti-Walters & Steven C. Hause (Lincoln: University of Nebraska Press, 1994).

[29] This speech is discussed in Accampo, *Blessed Motherhood*, p. 35. Accampo consulted the manuscript version; I have not located a published version.

[30] The text of "Par la Révolte" appeared in *La Fronde*, n° 1974 (6 May 1903). It was also published in brochure form. One of the characters maintains that the republic's principles of liberty and quality do not apply to women. It would be republished on the eve of the war in *L'Équité*, n° 22 (1 July 1914), 3–4.

Writing in *Le Rappel* in October 1903, Roussel squared off against Senator Piot for blaming wives for the falling birth rate, and for suggesting that child subsidies should be granted to fathers. These sorts of "solutions" stoked her anger at the way in which these influential men seemed to ignore women's role and responsibilities. Taking up the theme that Léonie Rouzade had promoted for decades, Nelly Roussel countered by championing salaried compensation for mothers. She also argued that motherhood should be "de-naturalized," that young women should receive sound education about their own physiology, and should be alerted to the hardship and suffering of childbirth.[31]

Married and a young mother herself (her second child died, and a third – unplanned – arrived in 1904) when she began writing columns for *La Fronde* and its successor, *L'Action*, Nelly Roussel quickly became one of the most eloquent public speakers on the roster of the *Ligue pour la Régéneration Humaine* (LRH), which, under the leadership of the anarchist educator Paul Robin, had launched a deliberately provocative campaign to spread birth control propaganda and contraceptive information among working-class women. Sustained in her public activities by her husband (her husband's sister had married Robin's son), she became well known in neo-Malthusian circles, both in France and abroad, and would publish many articles in the league's publication, *Régéneration*.[32] In mid-November 1903, as chair of a public meeting sponsored by the LRH, she implicitly critiqued the pronatalist members of the Depopulation Commission – "our good repopulators" – making a point of the fact that the session organizers had understood the need to have a woman's voice speak directly to the subject of "avoiding large families."[33] The repopulators, she asserted, thought of woman only as "a machine for turning out cannon-fodder," or a "breeding animal, whose suffering is of slight moment." "Such a conception of their sublime role can only revolt all intelligent mothers; and 'feminism' ought to proclaim, above all, the 'freedom of Maternity'," she insisted. "The worst of all slavery, fellow citizens, is for us sexual slavery; and the enfranchisement of the body is no less desirable than that of the mind." The hardships of giving birth would not disappear in any new social order imaginable, but the important point for Roussel was that, in

---

[31] Accampo, *Blessed Motherhood* (pp. 48–49) nicely summarizes Roussel's response to Piot's pamphlet, *La Question de la Dépopulation en France*. See Roussel's article, "Féminisme et fécondité," in *Le Rappel* (19 October 1900).

[32] A number of Roussel's articles appeared in English translation in *The Malthusian*.

[33] At their meetings, including this one, the *Ligue* sold copies of a pamphlet, *Les Moyens d'éviter les grandes familles*. Reported in *The Malthusian* (January 1904), 2–3.

the future, women "will understand that her body is her own, and that she alone has the right to wisely make use of it, according to her powers of endurance, whilst choosing the right time." And, she added, "The type of worn out woman – worn out before she is old by over-numerous births, doomed to continual suffering, and not even retaining the strength to make a gesture of revolt, or to refuse the use of her poor body to a brutal and thoughtless husband – will disappear."[34]

In December 1903 Nelly Roussel chaired and spoke at the National Freethinker's congress in Paris, making the case for the integral, independent development of woman. No longer should women be "confined" to the mother-educator role, or – once freed from the influence of the church – be subject to "*lois et moeurs hominists*" [laws and morals dictated by men].[35] Feminists and Free-thinkers, she proclaimed, had need of one another. Raised as a Catholic, Nelly Roussel was acutely aware of the church's authoritarian, patriarchal views on the woman question, but she was equally critical of the subordination wives and mothers in the Civil Code inherited by the Third Republic. In February 1904 she took issue with an article by Dr. Edouard Toulouse who, although insisting that pronatalists needed to speak directly to women, fretted about the fact that educated women were not reproducing. Objecting strenuously to this last point, Nelly Roussel countered by insisting that "the 'strike' is declared, in the circle, restricted as yet, of those who reflect, who understand, but the circle will extend unceasingly." Only when woman "shall occupy in humanity the place that belongs to her" and "shall no longer be refused the rights corresponding to her duties, and the compensations due to her sacrifices; on that day when maternity shall become a social function, the most honoured and the best remunerated of all," only then could one say to a woman "Sacrifice thyself to society."[36] In March 1904, writing in *La Fronde* in response to a recently opened play, *Le Droit des Vierges*, by another profeminist dramatist, Paul Hyacinthe-Loyson (1873–1921), Nelly Roussel demanded premarital sex education for young women.[37] Older girls should understand the physiology of reproduction and should be alerted to what marriage implied physically,

---

[34] These quotations are from the translation in *The Malthusian* (January 1904).

[35] "Conférence de Mme Nelly Roussel," *La Fronde*, n° 2006 (1 January 1904); republished in Roussel's *Paroles de Combat* (1919), pp. 9–16.

[36] Nelly Roussel, "Open letter to M. le Docteur Toulouse," in response to his article, "Peut-on arrêter la dépopulation," *Le Journal* (16 February 1904). Reprinted in *La Femme affranchie* – clipping in BMD, DOS ROU, hand-dated October 1904. This article was subsequently translated and published in *The Malthusian* (April 1904), 30. I have quoted parts of this translation here.

[37] "Le Droit des Vierges," in *La Fronde*, n° 2098 (1 March 1904). Transl. KO and published as doc. 24 in Bell & Offen, *Women, the Family, and Freedom*, vol. 2, pp. 177–179.

instead of being delivered over in complete ignorance of sex to husbands. Young men should also be better educated as to their responsibilities, instead of learning about sex in covert and unhealthy ways that only fed their disdain for women.

Nelly Roussel's speeches and writings became increasingly bold and increasingly critical of the existing society and its double standard of morality, but she was also suspicious of utopias. In an open letter to women, published in late 1904 in *La Femme affranchie*, Roussel threatened that the "hour of revolt" must come; "unlimited fecundity" was not a good thing and, turning the tables on the repopulators, she alleged that – in fact – the real evil was not depopulation, "but, on the contrary, over-population." It was not only a right, but a sacred duty, for women "to regulate wisely, and freely, our fertility as mothers; and only to conceive knowingly and willingly, according to the measure of our strength and our resources, ourselves choosing the opportune moment." "Civilized human-ity already possesses sufficient knowledge to direct in a certain measure the blind forces of nature," she claimed. "We can arrange ... that the indul-gence of the affections has not necessarily for consequence the creation of a new life." By making this claim, she disagreed sharply with Auguste de Morsier, of the *Fédération Abolitioniste Internationale* (FAI), who also advocated autonomy for women but, when it came to sexuality, allowed them only two choices: maternity or chastity.[38] In any case, she asserted, quality (of children) was preferable to quantity, and "the perfectionment of the race is only possible by means of selection." "The day is coming when we mothers shall decide to create fewer degenerates and paupers, fewer competitors for labour, less fodder for [gun]powder and enslavement; when that day comes we shall see, spreading itself abroad over the surface of the globe, a new renaissance of intelligence, of strength, and of beauty."[39] This was the type of argument that would inform the develop-ing eugenics movement, which would not take organized form in France before the end of 1912, following the attendance of a large French all-male delegation at the 1912 International Eugenics Congress in England.[40]

---

[38] See Auguste de Morsier, *Le Droit des femmes et la morale intersexuelle – une question d'éducation sociale* (Geneva: H. Kundig, 1903).

[39] Nelly Roussel, "Aux Femmes. To Women (Translated from La Femme Affranchie)," *The Malthusian* (December 1904), 94–95.

[40] On the French eugenics movement, see William H. Schneider, *Quality and Quantity: The Quest for Biological Regeneration in Twentieth-Century France* (Cambridge, UK: Cambridge University Press, 1990), chapter 4. The founders, reports Schneider (p. 94), were virtually all men (he does not name any women). He also notes that the French eugenics advocates, of whom many were physicians, came to the cause through *puériculture*, rather than (as in the Anglophone world) through the social

Significantly, the French delegation shied away from endorsing programs for sterilization, pleading France's commitment to individual liberty. Social controls to better the French population would take other, less invasive forms.

A frequent lecturer in the popular universities of Paris, Nelly Roussel subsequently toured France – and Europe – for many years as a public speaker and actress, dramatizing the plight of "the eternal victim" to mass audiences, and making the case, always allusively, for woman-controlled contraception.[41] In late 1904, she was a featured speaker at the women's protest meeting in Paris on the 100th anniversary of the Civil Code. "[All] women, in whatever situation they were born," she argued, "have an interest in a profound [social] upheaval. Among us there are no 'ruling classes,' no 'privileged classes.' *All of us* can declare war on today's society, for all of us are more or less ruined, our bodies, our hearts, our consciences brutalized by its laws." Especially mothers![42]

> Oh, yes indeed, mothers, the noble working women of life, whom Society does not acknowledge and denigrates, even while it dares ask them to multiply their troubles and to work for it unceasingly and without reprieve! And this, my sisters, this is the supreme inequity, among so many others! The most odious aspect of the situation we find ourselves in is that they invoke against us precisely that thing that ought to plead on our behalf. They see as an obstacle to our re-establishment – a pretext for drenching us with sorrow and humiliation in this maternal function – this terrible and sublime function that ought, on the contrary, to assure us every honor and every solicitude!

Young, beautiful, and articulate – Nelly Roussel embodied the "New Woman," one with very advanced sociopolitical ideas – the integral feminist who performed her femininity as no other had before her; she

---

sciences. Even so, this did not produce much female involvement. Paul Strauss, Jacques Bertillon, and Léonce Manouvrier were among the founders, and the Solidarist Léon Bourgeois was named honorary president.

[41] See the reprint ed., *Nelly Roussel, l'éternelle sacrifiée*, cited in n. 28. English translation: "She Who Is Always Sacrificed," in *Feminisms of the Belle Epoque*, ed. Waelti-Walters & Hause, pp. 18–41. Roussel's accounts of several of her lecture tours in southern France and Francophone Switzerland (1904–1905) and in Europe (1908, as far east as Budapest) are published in *Quelques Lances rompues*, part IV. Three of her most important lectures (1907, 1908, 1914) are reprinted in *Trois Conférences de Nelly Roussel*, préface d'Odette Laguerre (Paris: Marcel Giard, 1930); of particular importance is "La Liberté de la Maternité" (1907), pp. 17–52.

[42] Nelly Roussel, speech given at the women's meeting called to protest the centennial of the Civil Code, 29 October 1904. Published in *La Fronde*, n° 2106 (1 November 1904). Transl. KO and published as doc. 29 in *Women, the Family, and Freedom*, vol. 2, pp. 134–136. Emphasis in italics is in Roussel's original text.

had a magnetism, theatrical "star power," eloquence, and, as her biographer Elinor Accampo points out, she delivered her ultra-radical message in the persona of an elegant and yes, even seductive, bourgeois wife and mother. But opponents saw through her persona and drew back in horror at her message, which was that in a civilized society women must exercise the right to control their own bodies, and especially their own fertility. And that maternity must become a social function.[43] One French court referred to her teaching as an immoral and antisocial doctrine.[44] In certain respects, Nelly Roussel's arguments found their counterparts in works such as writer Camille Pert's marriage manual for women, based on women's testimonies, *Le Bonheur conjugal* (1905), which denounced the hypocrisy surrounding birth control. The real crime, according to Pert, was that husbands were "inflicting too many pregnancies on their wives."[45]

Roussel's arguments ran parallel in some respects to those of the Swedish writer Ellen Key (1849–1926), whose publications were being translated into French.[46] These translations came out after Nelly Roussel had begun her campaign for women's control of their own fertility. Key's introduction to the Francophone world was prefigured by a 1905 notice in the *Journal des Débats* and in a well-informed work, *A Travers le féminisme suèdois*, by a writer who knew Ellen Key and had even visited her in Sweden.[47] How the pronatalists in France must have relished Key's

---

[43] See Nelly Roussel, "Pour les mères," in *Quelques Lances rompues,* pp. 40–44; orig. publ. in *Le Petit Almanach féministe*, 1907, pp. 12–14.

[44] Cova, "Féminisme et natalité, p. 664.

[45] On Pert and others novelists and writers concerned with women's sexual fulfillment and pleasure, see Rachel Mesch, "Husbands, Wives and Doctors: Marriage and Medicine in Rachilde, Jane de La Vaudère and Camille Pert," in Masha Belenky & Rachel Mesch, eds., theme issue: "State of the Union: Marriage in Nineteenth-Century France," *Dix-Neuf: Journal of the Society of Dix-Neuvièmistes*, n° 8 (October 2008), 90–104; published online at www.sdn.ac.uk/dixneuf and available through Ingenta. On Pert's novels, see Rachel Mesch, "Housewife or Harlot? Sex and the Married Woman in Nineteenth-Century France," *Journal of the History of Sexuality*, 18:1 (January 2009), 65–83.

[46] See the references for Ellen Key in my article "Ellen Key" in *The Oxford Encyclopedia of Women in World History*, ed. Bonnie G. Smith (New York & Oxford: Oxford University Press, 2008), vol. 3, pp.16–17. In French, see Dominique Ottavi, "Ellen Key et le 'puérocentrisme'," *Les Femmes dans les sciences de l'homme (XIXe-XXe siècles)* (Paris: Seli Arslan, 2005), pp. 31–48. The most comprehensive study of Key and her influence is by the Finnish historian Tiina Kinunnen, but so far it has not been translated into English.

[47] For the reception of Ellen Key's ideas in France, see Jane Michaux, "Ellen Key," *Le Journal des Débats* (26 August 1905), and Marc Helys (pseud. of Maria Léra), *A travers le féminisme suèdois* (Paris: Plon-Nourrit, 1906). See also Louise (Crémieux) Cruppi, "Les Idées d'Ellen Key," offprint from *La Revue scandinave*, vol. 3, n° 4 (April 1912), 205–216 & n° 5 (May 1912), 297–306, along with Cruppi's book, *Femmes écrivains d'aujourd'hui*, vol. 1: *Suède* (Paris: A. Fayard, 1912). Whitney Walton has learned that Key was in Paris for the 1900 Universal Exposition and met the French writer Arvède Barine at that time.

celebration of the child and the mother-educator – as well as her insistence (not unlike that of Aline Valette in the 1890s) that women who worked for pay were "misusing" their womanpower!

In 1906 the publishing house Flammarion would publish a French translation of Ellen Key's *De l'amour et du mariage*, with a preface by the noted historian Gabriel Monod.[48] What the pronatalists couldn't accept, however, was Key's disregard for conventional morality – that a woman bear a love child or several outside of institutionalized marriage – and that she be subsidized by the community for doing so. This was what radical feminists had been calling for as a "*fonction sociale*," but without the accompanying assertion of "*union libre*." Ellen Key's celebration of Love with a capital "L" offered another bone of contention. Her eugenics ideas were also controversial, insofar as she (like the Bélilon sisters and Nelly Roussel) emphasized that in the bearing of children, quality must trump quantity; lovers must be physically and mentally healthy, even flourishing, in order to produce children who would flourish. An unsigned review in the women's publication *La Vie Heureuse* (April 1907) skirted around some of these issues in comparing the main points of Key's book with the parallel and, for the French, even more scandalous work of Léon Blum, *Du Mariage* (1907).[49] Both authors, said the reviewer, were totally individualist and focused strictly on the idea of happiness [*bonheur*], with little regard for society [*l'organisme social*]. "Neither of them recognizes traditional morality … or seems to take account of the practical value of these duties, which by posing a ring of obstacles, even put the damper on aspirations." Ellen Key, the optimist-idealist, posited Love as the sole basis for contracting a marriage (or bearing a child). Léon Blum had no such grandiose idea; he simply wanted to render conventional marriage more habitable – by proposing for young women the same liberty for sexual exploration before marriage that young men in France had, so that, once a marriage choice was made, the couple could stick it out for the duration. To many French men and women this was a shocking idea, one that would haunt Blum's later political career.

---

[48] Ellen Key, *De l'amour et du mariage* (Paris: Flammarion, 1906), with a preface by Gabriel Monod. Monod's preface was republished as a separate article (in two parts): "Ellen Key et ses idées sur l'amour et le mariage," *La Revue Bleue*, 5e sér., vol. 7, n° 18 (4 May 1907), 550–554, & n° 19 (11 May 1907), 592–596.

[49] Anon., "Autour du mariage," *La Vie Heureuse* (April 1907), [no page number]. I thank Rachel Mesch for sending me a photocopy of this article.

In October 1907 Émile Faguet published a long and eloquent essay concerning the books by Ellen Key and Léon Blum.[50] He admitted to be deeply impressed with *De l'amour et du mariage*, "*un beau livre*" full of penetrating psychological insights about the fundamental differences in attitude of men and women toward love and sex. He admitted to agreeing with many aspects of Key's thought, but viewed her objections to women working outside the home as "too antifeminist" for him. Overall Faguet thought Key's book was full of contradictions – "very lucid" on each subject, but "no comprehension of the whole."[51] As for Blum's provocative book, which argued that young women should have the same sexual freedom as young men before marrying, Faguet considered it "a wager of impertinence and cynicism" and replete with paradoxes; he compared it to Denis Diderot's notorious work, *Supplément au Voyage de Bougainville* (1772, 1796), which posited the separation of moral concerns from physical sex acts. Faguet argued that Léon Blum ignored fundamental psychological principles, especially that what is true for the male is not true for the female. Both sexes, Faguet proposed, should marry early and as virgins, and that their parents should support young couples until the age of 30.[52]

Depopulation *Bis*: The Search for Institutional Solutions

From 1905 on, following the release of new population statistics that showed the birth rate still in decline, French men's efforts to identify and seek institutional solutions accelerated. In late November 1906, the *Académie des Sciences Morales et Politiques* would launch a prize competition for the best submission on the "causes and moral and social consequences of the decline of French natality," which would garner twenty-two entries – all submitted by male authors.[53] The following year (1907) the French statistical office would release a new set of census figures; deaths in France again exceeded the number of births. The perceived population crisis only seemed to get worse. Why did the birth rate keep going down?

---

[50] Émile Faguet, "L'Anarchie morale: Deux livres contre le mariage," *La Revue Latine*, 10 (25 October 1907), 577–605. This essay was later republished in Faguet's book, *Le Féminisme* (Paris: Boivin, 1910), along with a number of his other long reviews on books concerning the woman question, all from *La Revue Latine*.

[51] Faguet, "Anarchie morale," 570.   [52] Faguet, "Anarchie morale," 597–604.

[53] The Stassart Prize, awarded every five years, conveyed the impressive sum of 3000 francs. For the announcement by Mr. Waddington, see *Séances et Travaux de l'Académie des Sciences morales et politiques*, vol. 166 (1906), p. 187. For the report of the prize committee by Henry Joly in June 1909, see ibid., vol. 171 (1909), pp. 106–130. Jacques Bertillon won the prize. Accessed on Gallica, 21 June 2013.

The explanations followed much the same lines as before. Nationalists on the right continued to insist that it was a male problem: that Frenchmen were experiencing a crisis of virility, or at least a disinclination to marry and father legitimate children, due (they claimed) to erosion of the legal and economic authority vested in husbands and fathers (feminists had certainly not noticed such an "erosion"). Others blamed the feminist movement and women's increasing access to life options other than childbearing. But the explanation that reform-minded men found increasingly convincing, and that indeed bore on the situation of the vast majority of women, was poverty and women's employment, which was thought (not completely without reason) to restrict their ability to bear and raise significant numbers of legitimate children.[54]

In a political climate marked by increasing anti-French belligerence and sabre-rattling by the German emperor Wilhelm II, populationist propagandists (still mindful of the German defeat of France in 1871) had little trouble linking the issues of national population deficit, the French state's readiness (or not) for war, and motherhood. "Maternity is the nursery of the nation," Henri Vedette had exhorted in a 1906 book, *L'Art de vaincre les Allemands*.[55] In 1907 a certain Jean de Valdor, author of *Le Vrai féminisme* (also published by Savaete, Théodore Joran's publisher) asserted that women who demanded independence would only be "crushed by men's force." "Demand, insist on maternity; it is your right and your duty. God will aid you!"[56] God's aid not being immediately forthcoming, French Republicans were forced squarely to confront – at last – the enormous significance of the woman question for the future of the French nation. In this sense, and due to the pressure of right-wing nationalists, the discourse of republican nationalism itself was becoming woman-focused, if not indeed "feminized." Would the leadership of the Third Republic henceforth be willing to address the population issue in a way that might serve both the interests of women and the requirements of a male-dominated and increasingly military-minded political establishment?

In 1909 a series of carefully orchestrated pronatalist articles by members of the first Depopulation Commission began to appear in the *Revue Hebdomadaire*. Writers ranging from the bishop of Versailles to one of Professor Pinard's physician-disciples espoused the most conservative

---

[54] The issues that swirled around women's employment will be addressed in Chapter 12.
[55] Henri Vedette, *L'Art de vaincre les Allemands: Protection de l'enfance et de la maternité, l'enfant et les éducateurs laïques; le soldat et les éducateurs militaires* (Auxerre: Laulanié, 1906), p. 35.
[56] Jean de Valdor, *Le Vrai Féminisme* (Paris: Savaète, 1907), pp. 7, 219.

slogans, voicing strong opposition to the increasingly vociferous birth control advocates and urging the government to take steps to address the seriousness of the population issue.[57] Such male writers were absolutist in their insistence on maternity; clearly, men could not repopulate the nation by themselves. "Woman is essentially designed to give birth; she cannot arrive at her complete realization unless she realizes her destiny by becoming a mother," asserted Dr. Burlureaux in the issue of 22 May. Indeed, he believed that women must bear three children in order to attain flourishing health. Henri Joly condemned the advocates of quality over quantity, branding them as sophists – and as even more dangerous than the Malthusians.[58]

There was, however, a broader range of male opinions as to what ought to be done to improve the situation of women, especially of mothers and infants, than those expressed in the *Revue Hebdomadaire*. Although many men still considered women as instrumental, the means to an end – walking wombs to provide population growth and more regiments – others articulated more sophisticated and more woman-friendly positions. Progressive republican members of the medical establishment, citing the turn-of-the-century studies by Dr. Pinard and his students, insisted less on breeding than on improving the conditions for maternity in France, especially for the great number of employed women. Their primary goal was to reduce infant mortality, and only then to assist women as individuals with particular sets of sex-specific needs.[59] In late 1904, a Dr. Klotz-Forest launched a public opinion survey in the *Chronique medicale* on the question: "Are anticonceptional measures [*prophylaxie anticonceptionnelle*] legitimate?" The responses, published in the February 1905 issue, spanned the gamut from "no, absolutely not" to "yes, absolutely"; they came from physicians, writers, and feminists such as Odette Laguerre, Nelly Roussel, Séverine, and concluded with a poem entitled "Refus" by Lucie Delarue-Mardrus. Responses ranged from "maternity is woman's battlefield; she

---

[57] *La Revue Hebdomadaire*, 1909, issues of 1 May through 5 June. Contributors included Alfred de Foville, Charles Gide, the bishop of Versailles, Dr. Burlureaux, Ch. Lyon-Caen, and Henri Joly. In the first installment, Foville accused the former prime minister Émile Combes of torpedoing the work of the First Commission (by claiming there were no funds available to print its reports) and urgently called on the government to face up to the magnitude of the depopulation peril.

[58] Joly's contribution, "Le dépeuplement de la France: Rapport au public sur un concours de l'Institut," appeared in the issue of 5 June 1909, 5–27. Joly reported that the competition had received twenty-two entries.

[59] See Pinard's publications, among others (with Charles Richet) "Rapport sur les causes physiologiques de la dimunition de la natalité en France," *Annales de gynécologie et d'obstétrique*, vol. 59 (January 1903), 15–24.

cannot desert it," from Dr. Félix de Backer, to a reminder from Jeanne Dubois that, after all, "it is woman who plays the primary role in procreation and that she must be the one to decide ... how she will deploy her forces. The partisans and adversaries of contraceptive measures should address themselves to [women]."[60] Between 1907 and 1913 longer studies by male authors contemplated what needed to be done.[61] In this flurry of publication, and angst about producing more babies, most feminists fought hard to insist on the needs of the women themselves.

Reluctantly, some republicans began to consider legal and institutional solutions. They also had to contend with a set of influential and extremely far-reaching proposals from the medical establishment. Among the most radical proposals put forth by any male writer prior to 1914 was that of the physician Just[in] Sicard de Plauzoles (1872–1968), a doctor with ties to the *Collège Libre des Sciences Sociales* in Paris and with socialist political leanings (he denounced "individualist and capitalist barbarism"), who had also replied to Klotz-Forest's survey. Sicard de Plauzoles published two important books on the population question, *La Fonction sexuelle au point de vue de l'éthique et de l'hygiène sociales* (1908) and *La Maternité et la défense nationale contre la dépopulation* (1909), in which he called for a national maternity service.[62]

In his second book (which I will focus on here), Sicard de Plauzoles proposed that the national state be substituted for the family by underwriting motherhood as a paid service to the nation. Placing the French

---

[60] Klotz-Forest launched the survey in the November 1904 issue of the *Chronique medicale* (vol. 11, nᵒ 21), with an article that wholeheartedly favored contraception, illustrated with stories about the fervent opposition of the Catholic hierarchy. The responses appeared in the issue of 15 February 1905 (vol. 12, nᵒ 4, 97–138). Nelly Roussel comments extensively on this survey in *L'Action*, articles of 6 December 1904 and 6 March 1905, both republished in *Quelques Lances rompues,* pp. 105–108 and 113–119. Consulted at www2.biusante.parisdescartes.fr.

[61] As, for example, Jean Trouette, *Les Mutualités maternelles; leur action sur la mortalité infantile,* thèse de médecine, Université de Paris, 1906; J. Fauconnet, *L'Assistance aux filles-mères et aux enfants illégitimes du premier âge en France,* Thèse, Faculté de Droit, Université de Paris (Paris: V. Giard et E. Brière, 1907); Sébastien-Charles Leconte, *L'Assistance nationale aux mères, projet de loi Sébastien-Charles Leconte, texte et motifs [suivi de "Pour les mères,"* par *M. Henri Coulon*] (Paris: Marchal & Godde, 1910); Dr. Felix Saporte, *Assistance et maternité,* Thèse de doctorat, Bordeaux (Bordeaux: Imprimerie de l'Université, 1910); Jacques Mornet, *La Protection de la maternité en France; étude d'hygiène sociale* (Paris: M. Rivière, 1910); Dr. Jacques-Gilbert-Joseph Mornet, *Les Mutualités maternelles* (Paris: Bloud, 1911); La Mutualité maternelle de Paris, *La Maternité chez l'ouvrière en 1911; la situation des femmes et des enfants de nos soldats en 1911* (Paris: La Mutualité maternelle de Paris, 1911). See also the proceedings of the *Congrès national de la mutualité maternelle,* beginning in 1908.

[62] See Just Sicard de Plauzoles, *La Fonction sexuelle au point de vue de l'éthique et de l'hygiène sociales* (Paris: Giard & Brière, 1908), and *La Maternité et la défense nationale contre la dépopulation* (Paris: Giard & Brière, 1909).

situation in comparative perspective, he pointed out that countries such as Germany, Austria, and Switzerland had set a precedent by insisting on a period of rest from work by wage-earning women before and after confinement and by compensating them through national health insurance.

> France should do still better; it should outlaw work for women who are pregnant or just delivered; mercenary nursing and artificial feeding should be prohibited; maternal nursing should be made compulsory; mothers should be indemnified, put on salary, subsidized; a [state] budget for maternity must be created.

Sicard's thoughts on the protections of maternity ranged from the teaching of *puériculture* through improved diet, assistance and legal protection of expectant and parturient women, maternal nursing, and assistance and protection to nursing mothers, including unwed mothers and their "natural" children. In the final section of the book, he laid out a plan, including a draft law, for the organization of maternity as a national service. Sicard de Plauzoles was by no means the first to insist that the state must recognize maternity as a social function; as we have seen in earlier chapters, many feminist and socialist women before him had advanced this claim, including Léonie Rouzade in the 1880s and 1890s, Dr. Blanche Edwards-Pilliet in the 1890s, Nelly Roussel in the early twentieth century, and, of course, Ellen Key, whom Sicard de Plauzoles quoted at some length.[63] Not surprisingly, his proposal included a number of arbitrary restrictions and supervisory intrusions to which mothers would be subjected in order to experience maternity "freely and fully." Sicard's argument favored a collectivist solution, with the mother returned to the home:[64]

> The State must necessarily substitute itself for the disorganized family in order to watch over the upbringing and education of its future citizens. In the interest of the individual and the species, as in the collective interest of the nation, the State must assure the normal and complete development of the child. For that, the child must get its mother back, and the woman permitted to remain in her household, where she can fulfill her natural function and her social duty; if need be, she must be obliged to do it; but maternity must be recognized and organized as a social function. This is still maternity at the expense of the collectivity, but it is baby confided to its

---

[63] Rachel Fuchs, *Contested Paternity: Constructing Families in Modern France* (Baltimore: Johns Hopkins University Press, 2008), p. 147, argues that Olympe de Gouges was the first to claim maternity as a social function, citing her Declaration of Rights of Woman, article XI and Conclusion.

[64] Sicard de Plauzoles, *Maternité et la défense nationale*, pp. 248–249.

mother, raised in the best conditions, and it is the salvation of the future of the nation.

Following the happy expression of Madame Doctor Edwards-Pilliet, "The woman, in her rule as *créatrice*, is a social functionary who has the right to have her existence assured by society on the same grounds as the soldier who defends its territory."

In Article 12 of his draft law, Sicard called for the establishment of a national budget to support these services, to which the state would contribute an amount equal to one-third of the defense budget, complemented by contributions from the departments and the communes.[65] Other works, both scholarly and popular, followed, all advocating some form of state assistance to mothers.[66] Hundreds of books, articles, and pamphlets addressed the population question, though unlike Sicard's studies, few considered the woman question as integral to its resolution. But the press would keep the focus on the woman question by publishing articles such as that of the British writer H. G. Wells, who thought the state "should pay for all children born in proportion to their number and quality."[67]

Republican feminists, however, rejected the pronatalist nationalist men's conviction that the falling birth rate was the primary issue. Some, such as Maria Martin, endorsed the arguments for "quality not quantity," which had already become fashionable in eugenics and family-planning circles.[68] More frequently they insisted on the necessity to halt the dramatic losses due to infant mortality, and some, such as Ida R. Sée (another columnist for *La Fronde*), even judged others of their own sex harshly for providing inadequate maternal care for their infants.[69] Dr. Blanche Edwards-Pilliet, whose principal work was in the area of gynaecology and obstetrics (and who presided over the *Ligue Française des Mères de Famille* as well as working in the *Conseil National des Femmes Françaises* (CNFF), had already called in 1900 for the establishment of shelters for pregnant women, for a two-week rest-leave from employment for women

---

[65] Sicard de Plauzoles, *Maternité et la défense nationale*, p. 282.

[66] Other works included Jacques Mornet, *La Protection de la maternité en France: Étude d'hygiène sociale* (Paris: M. Rivière, 1910); and A. Vallin, *La Femme salariée et la maternité*. Thèse de doctorat, Faculté de Droit, Paris (Paris: A. Rousseau, 1911).

[67] H. G. Wells, "Ou les mères seront dotées suivant le nombre et le vigueur de leurs enfants, ou la civilisation reculera," *Le Matin* (25 November 1909), front page.

[68] Martin, "Quantité ou qualité," *Le Journal des Femmes*, n° 201 (December 1909).

[69] Ida R. Sée, "Féminisme et dépopulation," *La Revue Philanthropique*, vol. 31, n° 181 (15 May 1912), 23–26; quotations from 23, 26.

workers and for a four-week *paid* maternity leave following birth.[70] Such constructive ideas did not go unheeded either by other women or by the radical republican ministries. The first step, the law of 21 November 1909, would prohibit employers from firing women who took a six-week maternity leave, but it would take several years longer to make an extended maternity leave obligatory and to allocate funds to subsidize it.[71] By 1913 Edwards-Pilliet (like Sicard de Plauzoles) would be calling for full governmental support for mothers, on the grounds that both soldiers and mothers were social servants and should be financially acknowledged as such.[72]

Historian Anne Cova has provided a comprehensive account of the circuitous legislative complexities that finally produced the 1913 *Loi Strauss*.[73] Following the passage by the Senate of yet another measure that might satisfy, and its return (again) to the Chamber of Deputies, the Tenth International Congress of Women, meeting in Paris in early June, would apply pressure, calling for an obligatory four-week rest leave for parturient women in every country, to be indemnified either by an insurance law or through the public assistance bureaus.[74] Shortly after the conclusion of this congress, the Chamber would finally authorize the mandatory four-week maternity leave for new mothers following birth; it became known as the Strauss Law, after the Solidarist senator Paul Strauss, who had actually fought for a more substantial financial allocation for mothers than was finally provided. This law took effect on 17 July 1913. It was followed by another law, the law of 30 July 1913, which enacted allocations for large families. The Strauss law did not address the necessity of leave for working mothers prior to delivery, to allow the expectant mothers some rest that would enhance the survival chances of their babies, a measure that had been promoted by the physicians who worried about the high infant mortality rates. Nor did it apply to women who did industrial home work, who (as we will see in the next chapter), constituted

---

[70] Rapport de Mme le docteur Edwards-Pilliet, *Congrès international de la condition et des droits des femmes, Paris . . . 1900* (Paris: Impr. des Arts et Manufactures, 1901), pp. 66–68; KO transl. in Bell & Offen, *Women, the Family, and Freedom*, vol. 2, doc. 32, p. 145.

[71] See Gabrielle Rosenthal, "La Protection de la maternité," *La Française*, n° 143 (26 December 1909), 1.

[72] Blanche Edwards-Pilliet, "Le Dépopulation; à propos de la loi d'assistance aux mères," *L'Action féminine: Bulletin officiel du Conseil National des Femmes Françaises*, n° 27 (April 1913), 480.

[73] See Anne Cova, *Maternité et droits des femmes en France (XIXe-XXe siècles)* (Paris: Economica, 1997), pp. 147–169.

[74] *Dixième Congrès international des femmes: Oeuvres et institutions féminines, Droits des femmes, 2-8 juin 1913, compte rendu des travaux par* Mme Avril de Sainte-Croix (Paris: V. Giard & E. Brière, 1914), "Voeux," p. 575.

a large and particularly exploited subgroup of laborers. Despite these lacunae and other imperfections that would emerge during the early stages of their application, these laws marked an important first step. In the shadow of the perceived population crisis and in face of the threat of war – and at the behest of the establishment feminists – the government of the Third Republic would provide the beginnings of material assistance to needy French mothers and their babies at the time when they could best benefit from it.

Legal Reform? Feminists Focus on *Recherche de la Paternité*

Given the distress over depopulation, the critical question raised in the early twentieth century was how to provide economic support for expectant and new mothers, and for the raising of children. French feminists were divided on this question. Some wanted to force men who fathered children, especially outside marriage, to accept their paternal responsibilities, in support of the male-breadwinner model; others wanted to remove irresponsible men entirely from the picture. This latter option, however, would require state intervention, and the treating of maternity as a socially desirable function that should be subsidized by the collectivity.

Women in philanthropic organizations affiliated to the CNFF pressed forward with a broad-based program of woman-centered social action to enhance women's status in (and contributions to) French society, and especially to address the problems faced by poor women. Their projects included the establishment of homes for unwed mothers, refuges for released female convicts and prisoners, shelters and job training for rescued prostitutes, *crèches* and other childcare facilities, and concerted efforts to combat the ravages of alcoholism, tuberculosis, and, more generally, unhygienic and inadequate urban housing that facilitated such plagues. These social welfare efforts, important as they were, could alleviate some of the misery, but they did not address the root causes of the pressing social problems that besieged urban France. Legal reform provided another avenue for redress.

Following extensive debates at both the 1900 women's congresses, the newly founded CNFF, through its Section on Legislation, designated *recherche de la paternité* as its first legislative priority and in 1903 set about drafting legislation to be submitted to the Chamber of Deputies.[75] The

---

[75] Repeal of Article 340 (*recherche de la paternité*) had, of course, figured prominently in the programs of Léon Richer and other women's rights activists during the early decades of the Third Republic. Gustave Rivet (editor of *Le Radical*) had become an early and ardent supporter of its abolition. The campaign for legislative action was reinvigorated at the 1900 congress on women's condition and rights and became a priority for the CNFF. Subsequent to the congresses, both René Viviani (in the

dilemma for these mainstream feminists was how best to address the question of children and the birth rate while centering on the plight of the unmarried mothers, young and poor. The CNFF's bill [*proposition de loi*] called only for monetary support from the purported father, without giving him any legal rights over the child. Maria Martin qualified this proposal as one that, while drafted in a juridical form, "maintained the feminist character that the CNFF had given it." Having been accepted in many other countries, such a reform is "desired by humanity, justice, and social progress."[76] But the legislature took no action. In early 1905 another, very different *proposition de loi* was introduced by Senators Gustave Rivet and René Bérenger, which focused on qualified punishment for fathers of children out of wedlock. The women in the Section on Legislation of the CNFF analyzed this new measure, concluding that it would be impossible to meld the Rivet-Bérenger proposal with their own (deposed earlier in the Chamber of Deputies by Marcel Sembat), but nevertheless indicated that their proposal be submitted as an amendment.[77]

It was true that, in an era before DNA analysis, "proving" paternity was fraught with problems. Sometimes the debates over *recherche de la paternité* took on a comic aspect, as many male legislators fretted about the prospect of unscrupulous, manipulative women attempting to blackmail innocent men by filing unsubstantiated paternity suits. Feminist advocates, on the other hand, were looking out for their less fortunate sisters, whose poverty and naiveté was being sexually exploited by unscrupulous, manipulative men, who then left the women to deal with the consequences of their deception. It seemed clear that the present situation could only lead to tragedy – and, of course, it did. One desperate mother, Marie Davaillant, took revenge on the seducer who had fathered her child and refused to help her when she was pregnant; she stabbed him to death! Even the radical republican and current prime minister Georges Clemenceau was outraged when a judge found Davaillant guilty. Critical of men's hypocrisy and the double standard of morality that victimized women, he queried when France would pass a law reauthorizing paternity suits? "What

Chamber of Deputies) and Gustave Rivet (in the Senate) introduced new bills. For analysis of the debates at both 1900 congresses, see Cova, *Maternité et droits des femmes,* pp. 169–177; Pedersen, *Legislating the French Family,* chapter 5; Fuchs, *Contested Paternity,* pp. 148–149, and Chapter 9 in this book. See also Françoise Picq, "Par delà la loi du père: le débat sur la recherche de la paternité au congrès féministe de 1900," *Les Temps Modernes,* n° 391 (February 1979), 1199–1212.

[76] Maria Martin, "La Recherche de la Paternité," *Le Journal des Femmes,* n° 134 (July 1903).

[77] See the report on the 17 February meeting of the CNFF, *Le Journal des Femmes,* n° 152 (March 1905), esp. 2.

advantage is there to being in a Republic, if we can't even rise to respect maternity which the laws of certain monarchies honor?"[78] The allusion was, of course, to Imperial Germany, which had initiated protection and paid maternity leave for mothers decades earlier.

Maneuvering in the shadow of France's population concerns, both sides were committed to ensuring the survival and welfare of the "innocent" bastards, but from very different perspectives. In late 1907, the feminist writer Louise Compain published a comprehensive series of articles in *La Française* concerning *recherche de la paternité*.[79] In early 1908, she reported to the *Ligue Française pour les Droits des Femmes* (LFDF) about the sticking points concerning the legislative proposals. According to her report, the CNFF was still insisting that mothers of "natural" children have complete legal control over them, and also that putative fathers cover the expenses of delivery and support mother and child for three months. Questions concerning criteria for proof of paternity remained contentious matters, as was the question of a whether a "proven" father should have any legal relationship whatsoever to the "natural" child. Would paying entail giving the father legal rights of some sort over the child or its mother? The earlier propositions by Viviani and Rivet were still floating about in the legislature. Jeanne Deflou made certain that *recherche de la paternité* would be on the agenda at the suffrage conference she and the GFEF organized in midsummer 1908; Compain would be one of three reporters on the issue.[80]

---

[78] Georges Clemenceau, *Le Justice du sexe fort* (Paris: Librairie de la Raison, 1907). In the same brochure Clemenceau also advocated civil rights for married women.

[79] Compain's series "La Recherche de la paternité," in *La Française*, comprised a series of weekly articles, beginning on 3 November 1907 (issue n° 54) through 15 December (n° 60). She laid out the three propositions de loi (Viviani, Rivet, Sembat on behalf of the CNFF), examined their similarities and differences, argued the case for the CNFF proposition (which asked for monetary support only from presumptive fathers), discussed the exceptions enumerated in the other two bills, and opposed the notion of state support (viz. Maria Pognon's earlier proposal for complete state support of motherhood, supported at the time by the LFDF), which would let men off the hook entirely. The issue of 8 December 1907 (n° 59) is missing in the ACRPP microfilm of *La Française*.

[80] Compain presented the results of her investigation to the LFDF in early January 1908, pointing out the differences between the three bills and making some other suggestions as well; her main point was that the fathers of these children born out of wedlock should be held responsible by the law for supporting them. See the *Journal des Femmes*, n° 182 (February 1908), 2 and *LFDF: Bulletin Trimestriel*, 3:4 (April 1908), 4. The LFDF decided to form its own study commission; its report and recommendations, based in study of comparative laws, appeared in the *LFDF: Bulletin Trimestriel*, 3:4 (April 1908), 1–2. It recommended that the law offer two options: a regular paternity suit, with all its legal consequences, and an option for financial support only. Pognon's advocacy of state support for mothers and their babies ended when she resigned as president in 1904 to move to Australia. See also the reports by Bokanowski, Moufflet, and Compain, plus discussion in *Congrès national des droits civils et du suffrage des femmes . . ., 26–28 juin 1908, compte rendu des travaux par* Mme Oddo-Deflou (Paris, 1910), pp. 55–76.

In the interim, the CNFF Section on Legislation, still headed by Mme d'Abbadie d'Arrast, with Jeanne Oddo-Deflou at her side, had been working on the repeal of Article 340, which since 1804 had prohibited paternity suits. At its 6th May 1909 general assembly, Marguerite Pichon-Landry placed two resolutions before the delegates, the first on protection of the child before birth, and the second concerning the situation of children of divorced parents.[81] The Council stood by its demand for the abolition of the much-criticized Article 340. Pichon-Landry then reported what appeared to be a compromise with the legislators, focusing on "the protection of the unborn infant," on the grounds that the prohibition of *recherche de la paternité* had become a *primary cause* of abortion. The CNFF would then affirm its support for a government proposal for the "decriminalization" of abortion (which would effectively remove abortion trials from lenient juries who acquitted the women defendants, by placing their fates in the hands of judges, but would also lower the penalties for women who were convicted); it also urged that an educational effort be launched to inform women about the dangers abortion posed for their health. Pichon-Landry assured the assembled delegates that the CNFF's endorsement of the decriminalization measure was contingent on the prior repeal of Article 340. The report further called on the state and welfare agencies to provide adequate financial assistance to mothers.

Shortly thereafter, Maria Martin, alarmed by the number of reported cases of infanticide, complained in the *Journal des Femmes* that the legislature had still not acted on the CNFF proposal deposed by Sembat in 1903. Most of these infanticides could have been avoided, she insisted, had the fathers done their duty: "How many tiny lives will be sacrificed before this [proposal] is taken up for discussion by the legislature?"[82] She said nothing about the question of abortion.

In early 1910, however, the CNFF Section on Legislation would revisit the question, given that the stricter, more complex Rivet-Bérenger bill on *recherche de la paternité* was actually coming up for discussion in the Senate. Shifting its position, in light of the possibility of getting some kind of legislative action, just to get something on the books that could be amended later, the CNFF leaders decided to endorse this far more restrictive proposal, even though they greatly preferred the Sembat proposal.[83]

---

[81] See Marguerite Pichon-Landry, "La Protection de l'enfant," *L'Action féminine*, n° 4 (1 August 1909), 57–59. Evidently Ghénia Avril de Sainte-Croix [subsequently] convinced the CNFF to prioritize the legislative abolition of Article 340, and only then to support the decriminalization of abortion.

[82] Maria Martin, "Mères coupables," *Le Journal des Femmes*, n° 195 (May 1909), front page.

[83] See CNFF, *L'Action féminine*, n° 8 (March 1910), 134–135.

But the CNFF put forward three specific demands: 1) it objected to restricting the paternity claim to within one year of the birth, and asked that it be two years; 2) it stipulated that the language in one clause saying that the father owed a pension to the child that "bears his name" be amended to read "*en qualité de père*"; and 3) it objected to the Rivet measure's requirement of written proof, suggesting that there were other kinds of proof that should be considered, such as "*cohabitation notoire*," that is to say that people in the neighborhood recognize the man and woman as living together.[84]

As for one-night stands, what would constitute proof? Mme Pichon-Landry reported that the CNFF had been successful in its demands on the first two counts.[85] But agreement on a comprehensive, substantive text would not materialize until 1912, and when it did, the legislators specifically exempted from prosecution men who were already married. In mid-March 1912, Mme d'Abbadie d'Arrast invited the Paris law professor A. Tissier to speak to the CNFF's Section on Legislation to lay out the differences between the proposal that had gone to the Chamber from the Senate and the national council's earlier proposal for a subsistence allowance for the mother and child, which would have none of the legal ramifications of the current bill. The bill made it clear, as well, that a mother could only go to court on behalf of her minor child, not in her own right. The section members voted, reluctantly, to support the project under consideration.[86] This bill was far narrower and more stringent than equivalent laws that had recently passed in Belgium and in Switzerland. The Senate debates began in June and lasted into July. On 7 July 1910 Mme d'Abbadie d'Arrast reported on the history and progress of the bill at a special general assembly of the CNFF. Amid much praise for the senators and for the sponsors of the bill, Mme d'Abbadie also complained that a double standard had entered the bill, with strict penalties to protect men from false suits by women, but nothing to protect women from false allegations and slander by the men being sued.[87]

In early 1912 another controversy would again arouse the objections of the feminists: the question of whether the law authorizing *recherche de la paternité* would apply in the French colonies, and if so, to whom. The

---

[84] It must be remembered that proof of paternity was highly problematic before the advent of DNA testing.

[85] *L'Action féminine*, n° 8 (March 1910), 134–137. See also n° 11 (August 1910), 172–174, which discussed the Senate debate on the paternity bill, and the report of the CNFF's statutory assembly of 13 November 1910, *Le Journal des Femmes*, n° 212 (December 1910), front page.

[86] *L'Action féminine*, n° 8 (March 1910), 134–137.

[87] *L'Action féminine*, n° 11 (August 1910), 172–174.

1910 Senate version (Article 4) stated simply that "The law will apply in Algeria and in the colonies." But by 1912, when the Senate bill returned to the Chamber of Deputies, red flags had gone up – following a survey of colonial administrators by the ministry of colonies and strenuous objections from the colonial press. The *rapporteur* on the bill then proposed amending Article 4 to grant local control to administrators in applying the law (or not), in particular with regard to possible paternity suits by indigenous women and their children against French male citizens.[88] On 22 January the Chamber quietly passed this version of the bill. So amended, it would then have to return again to the Senate.

The establishment feminists strenuously protested the new addition to Article 4 as discriminatory and, moreover, anti-republican and unworthy of France. The LFDF took the lead in objecting to two articles of the most recent Chamber of Deputies amendments, the first placing the mechanism for enforcing penalties for intended fraud or blackmail in the correctional courts (as a means of discouraging blackmail of well-heeled men by unscrupulous women), and the second, the especially contentious addition to Article 4. In late January 1912, L[ouise] Frappier, who acknowledged growing up in the French colonies of the West Indies, gave a report to the LFDF that called for comprehensive application of the pending law in *all* French colonies and protectorates: "Wherever the French flag flies, wherever our modern schools are established, the same laws must protect the indigenous woman, raise her up and especially make her children citizens who are proud of France and its justice."[89] This French feminist claimed sisterhood with indigenous women and demanded that they too be enabled to file paternity suits.[90]

---

[88] On the social issues surrounding *métis* (mixed-race) children in the French colonies, see Owen White, *Children of the French Empire: Miscegenation and Colonial Society in French West Africa, 1895–1960* (Oxford, UK: Clarendon Press, 1999), esp. p. 132, and Jean Elisabeth Pedersen, "'Special Customs': Paternity Suits and Citizenship in France and the Colonies, 1870–1912," in *Domesticating the Empire: Race, Gender, and Family Life in French and Dutch Colonialism*, ed. Julia Clancy-Smith & Frances Gouda (Charlottesville: University of Virginia Press, 1998), pp. 43–64, and also, more briefly, in *Legislating the Family*, by which time Pedersen had discovered the Frappier letter. It appears from the inquiry undertaken by the ministry of colonies that the colonial governors in West Africa were the most reluctant to contemplate the authorization of racially unrestricted paternity suits in their territories.

[89] L[ouise] Frappier, report presented to the LFDF, meeting of 24 January 1912, *Le Droit des Femmes: Revue mensuelle*, vol. 7, n° 5 (March 1912), 3–5. This author's first name is attached to a later article, "Le Féminisme à la Réunion," in *La Française*, n° 315 (25 April 1914), 2. She had already written columns for *La Française*, including one in which she told her personal story as the heiress to a sugar plantation and refinery (see issue n° 135, 31 October 1909).

[90] According to *Le Droit des Femmes: Revue mensuelle*, n° 7 (July 1913), 11–12, Mme Frappier had first engaged with the status of women in the colonies in April 1911 at a meeting of the Paris-based *Congrès Permanent du Féminisme International* (Marya Chéliga & Mme Orka's group) at the Musée Social. She was also a member of the executive committee of the LFDF.

Frappier subsequently addressed a letter to the French Senate (published in *La Française* on 18 February 1912), asking that the original inclusive text be restored to Article 4 and not compromised by the Chamber of Deputies' addition of the clause on optional local control. She characterized the addition as "an attack on the principle of Republics" and out of place in "a new 'century of equality'." She further claimed that the original text would serve to bring French men in the colonies into line and check their blatant sexual conduct with black women. Moreover, it would reduce the production of mixed-race children, who would be discriminated against and thereby learn to hate France and cause trouble. It would also benefit white French wives:[91]

> What! One would no longer be free to "have fun" out there. One would have to recognize and assist the small beings born of relations with the *savages*. For the white man has *two hearts* for his children, as the blacks [*noirs*] in the old colonies say, and he detests his mulatto bastards. Thus, if the law does not cover all cases of illegitimate paternity, nearly always it would apply to the colonial, who normally has his bastards with a companion who lives with him.

Louise Frappier reckoned (as had many of the colonial governors consulted by the Ministry of Colonies) that *recherche de la paternité* legislation (if extended to all women) would indeed change men's behavior for the better. In the future they should come to the colonies already married to a French wife, rather than single and therefore prone to seek sexual comfort in the arms of indigenous women.

The Senate paid attention but did not relent. M. Guillier, the *rapporteur* for the bill in the Senate, acknowledged in a letter to Mme Frappier (which was published in *La Française* in mid-March) that he himself had preferred the earlier Senate version of the text, but in the interest of finally getting the legislation on the books, decided that it would be better to leave the local control option in the bill and thereby avoid further delays. But delay there was, despite Guillier's efforts to "fast-track" the legislation. The Senate would not approve the bill until early November 1912, and then only after voting against the changes desired by the feminists, civil liberties advocates, and argued for by Senator Paul Strauss. The final text of the law of 16 November 1912, published in *l'Action féminine* (December 1912)

---

[91] L. Frappier, "A Messieurs les Sénateurs: Contre l'Article 4 de la loi sur la Recherche de la Paternité – Les Raisons d'une coloniale," published in *La Française*, n° 228 (18 February 1912), front page. Emphasis in original.

reveals that the feminists had lost this particular battle.[92] The local option had been retained, and, in fact, could only be exercised by women of French nationality. The LFDF would pointedly publish the record of the legislative debates on Articles 3 and 4 in *Le Droit des Femmes*, so that all could see.[93]

With the repeal of the notorious Article 340, *recherche de la paternité* would be restored to French law. Yet the severe restrictions that the legislators introduced to hedge the use of the law that was finally enacted satisfied no one. Not only did the new legislation effectively exempt married men from possible paternity suits by women who were not their wives, but in addition, it contained draconian penalties to be enforced (without a hearing) against any woman who brought false suit. The latter provision upset the legal establishment and triggered the public opposition of both the *Ligue des Droits de l'Homme* (LDH) and the *Ligue Française pour le Droit des Femmes* (LFDF). Moreover, the law retained the local enforcement option clause in Article 4, and it did not provide a subsistence allowance for mothers and children, as the CNFF had demanded earlier. Despite the attempts of the minister of justice, Aristide Briand, to put a positive spin on the law, it was damaged goods. The novelist and social critic Victor Margueritte characterized this newborn law as "a monster."[94] In an unpublished letter, Cécile Brunschvicg (secretary-general of the *Union Française pour le Suffrage des Femmes* [UFSF, founded in 1909] as well as head of the CNFF Section on Work) remarked sourly that it was a "law made for women – without women."[95]

The establishment feminists had won a hollow victory. As historian Rachel Fuchs rightly concluded, "The law of 1912 ignored the mother except as agent for the child."[96] Its apparent counterweight, the decriminalization of abortion, would be brought up in 1914 but not enacted until after the war, and then by ministerial decree.[97] What seems clear, though,

[92] *L'Action féminine*, n° 25 (December 1912), 425–426.

[93] See *Le Droit des Femmes: Revue mensuelle*, issues of December 1912 and January 1913.

[94] *Le Droit des Femmes: Revue mensuelle*, issues of January and February 1913, published the full text of Briand's circular and various editorial assessments in the mainstream press. Victor Margueritte's statement appeared in *Le Journal* (10 January 1913).

[95] C. Brunschvicg to H. Auclert, s.d., in Bouglé collection, BHVP. Quoted by Anne Cova, "Cécile Brunschvicg (1877–1946) et la protection de la maternité," in *Colloque sur l'histoire de la sécurité sociale, Strasbourg, 1988 [Actes du 113ᵉ Congrès national des Sociétés savantes]* (Paris, 1989), p. 89. For a summary analysis of the new law, see Marcel Sauvagnac,"Loi du 16 novembre 1912 modifiant l'article 340 du Code civil (reconnaissance judiciaire de la paternité naturelle)," *Annuaire de Législation Française 1912*, vol. 32 (1913), 185–190.

[96] Fuchs, *Contested Paternity*, chapter 3, quote p. 109.

[97] On the so-called decriminalization of abortion, see Ronsin, *La Grève des ventres*, chapter 17. See also Angus McLaren, *Sexuality and Social Order: The Debate Over the Fertility of Women and Workers in*

in retrospect, is that the feminists – these women citizens who had no vote – had nevertheless made significant input into the legislative process; although they did not get every change that they thought necessary, their voices had been heard loud and clear in the places that counted – the press and the legislature. The LFDF promptly began a fund-raising effort to support a campaign for revision of Articles 3 and 4, especially the provisions that authorized "prison and the non-authorization of residency for single mothers" and "mixed-race persons."[98]

Rachel Fuchs has noted that this law's ultimate passage was, in part, a matter of national pride: legislators did agree that it was "'humiliating for France to be the only nation without a law allowing judicial recourse to paternal child support,' and that children needed protection from poverty, degeneration, and death."[99] French legislators and public opinion had become highly sensitive to the exceptional nature of France's century-long prohibition of paternity suits. But even though concerns about depopulation weighed heavily on the legislators, they did not offset the legislators' caution about "protecting" the ostensibly innocent men from ostensibly scheming women who would bring false lawsuits. In their logic, the plight of the single, poor mothers simply faded from view – at least for the time being.

Educational and Cultural Reform? Sex Education and a Single Moral Standard

Legalizing paternity suits was by no means the sole answer to the population problem, the woman question more broadly, or the specific plight of unwed mothers. What else could be done? Some moderate feminists proposed cultural and educational solutions. Here social class became a huge issue because of the efforts by social conservatives to keep upper-class girls in ignorance of sexual activity up to the time of their marriages. For decades many assumed that lower-class girls and women were well-versed in knowledge of sex, though the sheer numbers of young, unwed mothers

---

France, 1770–1920 (New York: Holmes & Meier, 1983). The law of 27 March 1923 would technically "decriminalize" abortion.

[98] The fundraising effort is reported in *Le Droit des Femmes: Revue mensuelle 1913*, beginning with n° 1 (January).

[99] Fuchs, *Contested Paternity*, p. 140. Fuchs includes a useful summary discussion (pp. 140–141) of the legal situation in other countries that had long allowed (Germany, England), or had recently legalized (Belgium, Switzerland) paternity suits within certain limits. For a contemporary analysis, see Abel Pouzol, *La Recherche de la paternité, étude critique de sociologie et de législation comparée* (Paris: V. Giard & E. Brière, 1902).

would seem to belie this claim. Historian Anne Fugier-Martin discusses the efforts made by bourgeois mothers to protect their ostensibly innocent *jeune filles* (the *oie blanche*, or white goose – discussed in my companion volume) from contamination by the household's maids, not to mention contact with newspapers or with lascivious literature of the sort penned by Rachilde, Jane de la Vaudière, or Camille Pert, which, as literary historian Rachel Mesch indicates, did not spare the details about sex.[100] Did these novels (or other salacious *romans des moeurs* by male writers) ever circulate in clandestine fashion among adolescent girls?[101] Jo Margadant cites a case from the National Archives in which the director of the girls' *lycée* in Montauban expelled a lower-middle-class girl student for "sharing" with another girl (of upper-bourgeois background) not only details about intercourse but also the fact that women might have babies outside marriage.[102] Republican educational authorities worried that fears of such possible "contamination" might provoke bourgeois parents either to withdraw their "innocent" pubescent daughters from the girls' secular *lycées* or, worse, to avoid enrolling them in the first place.

Already in 1895, according to Fugier-Martin, Jules Bois had suggested during his lectures at *La Bodinière* that sex education be provided, in particular, to these young upper-class women, whose very innocence portended a huge shock upon marriage. Others began to press forward with programs for sex education, especially for girls, as a persistent prudery slowly gave way to discrete discussion. The subject was on the agenda at the 1900 congress of *Oeuvres et Institutions*, where debates were marked by serious differences, with Dr. Blanche Pilliet-Edwards and Marie Pégard on the side of frank sex education, and Clarisse Coignet and others

---

[100] Anne Fugier-Martin, *La Bourgeoise: Femme au temps de Paul Bourget* (Paris: Bernard Grasset, 1983), pp. 56–60; Rachel Mesch, "Husbands, Wives and Doctors," cited in n. 45. Of particular salience here were Rachilde, *La Marquise de Sade* (1880s), which contained a speech by the main character Mary on not having children; Camille Pert, *Les Florifères* (1899); and La Vaudière, *Les Demi-sexes* (1897). The last-mentioned novel concerned bourgeois women who deliberately underwent surgery for removal of their ovaries (ovariotomies) in order to avoid having children. To my knowledge, none of these novels were mentioned, much less discussed, in the feminist press. Other novels, by Colette, Marcelle Tinayre, and Lucie Delarue-Mardrus would affirm women's desire and their expectations of sexual pleasure; on these writers, see Melanie Collado, *Colette, Lucie Delarue-Mardrus, Marcelle Tinayre: Émancipation et Resignation* (Paris: L'Harmattan, 2003) and Rachel Mesch, *The Hysteric's Revenge: French Women Writers at the Fin de Siècle* (Nashville: Vanderbilt University Press, 2006).

[101] See Peter Cryle, "The Open Secret: Hiding and Revealing Sexuality in the *Roman des moeurs* (1880–1905)," *Romanic Review*, 97:2 (March 2006), 185–200. The novels discussed in this article were all authored by men, and most could be considered pornographic.

[102] See Jo Burr Margadant, *Madame le Professeur: Women Educators in the Third Republic* (Princeton, NJ: Princeton University Press, 1990), p. 215.

opposing it.[103] In the meantime, Dr. Alfred Fournier had launched a *Société Française de Prophylaxie Sanitaire et Morale* (SFPSM) to focus on the problem of rampantly spreading venereal disease among young men. In 1899 Fournier had convened the first international conference for the prevention of syphilis and venereal disease, and in 1901 he published the first sex education manual directed at young men: *Pour nos fils, quand ils auront dix-huit ans*. According to historian Jennifer Burek Pierce, the French (in this case Dr. Fournier) were the first in the world to originate sex education for adolescents.[104] But initially, sex education for young men preached continence (i.e., stay away from prostitutes) in order to avoid venereal disease.[105] Questioning their conduct with respect to their future wives was a related but different matter, best left to physicians, who, critical of men's sexual ham-handedness, did publish marriage manuals during this period that counseled young men on how best to approach their new, sexually innocent wives so as not to scare them out of their wits.[106]

The question of adolescent sex education reemerged in 1905 in the Extraparliamentary Commission on the Morals Police, especially as concerned instruction to warn young men in the army and in secondary schools about the problem and peril of contracting venereal diseases. Mme Avril de Sainte-Croix informed the commission that the CNFF Section on Education had presented a project to the Ministry of Public Instruction recommending that such a course be offered in girls' secondary schools.[107] But, according to

---

[103] Fugier-Martin, *La Bourgeoise*, p. 59. See the congress proceedings, *Deuxième congrés international des oeuvres et institutions féminines, 18-23 juin 1900. Compte rendu des travaux par* Mme M. Pégard. 4 vols. (Paris: Impr. typographique Charles Blot, 1902).

[104] See Jennifer Burek Pierce, *What Adolescents Ought to Know: Sexual Health Texts in Early Twentieth-Century America* (Amherst & Boston: University of Massachusetts Press, 2011), chapter 1: "French Origin of International Sexual Health Communication with Adolescents," and chapter 2: "Initial Transnational Intersections: French Texts and American Culture."

[105] Historian Judith Surkis provides an extended analysis of Fournier's brochure in *Sexing the Citizen: Morality and Masculinity in France, 1870–1920* (Cambridge, MA: Harvard University Press, 2006), chapter 7. She does not address sex education for girls.

[106] See Peter Cryle, "'A Terrible Ordeal from Every Point of View': (Not) Managing Female Sexuality on the Wedding Night," *Journal of the History of Sexuality*, 18:1 (January 2008), 44–64. The early twentieth-century marriage manuals discussed by Cryle, published between 1903 and 1909, were all written by male doctors to counsel young husbands. Their advice can be summed up as "act as lovers, extend the foreplay and be gentle."

[107] See Louis Fiaux, *La Police des moeurs devant la Commission extraparlementaire du régime des moeurs.* 2 vols. (Paris: F. Alcan, 1907). Also: *Rapport Général sur les Travaux de la Commission Extraparlementaire du Régime des Mœurs*, présentés par M. F. Hennequin, ... secrétaire-général de la commission (Melun: Imprimerie Administrative, 1907). Those appointed to this commission included many names that we have encountered so far in this book, notably Alfred Fournier, René Bérenger, Paul Strauss, Francis de Pressensé, Louis Fiaux, Charles Gide, Yves Guyot, Eugène

the commission minutes, the Ministry was reluctant to introduce any such instruction in the public schools, even for boys, given the hostility of some fathers and the fear that students (of either sex) might be pulled out and sent to the Catholic schools (where they would presumably not be exposed to such scandalous information). One physician-member of the Extraparliamentary Commission reported that his effort to develop a text for use in the schools had encountered heavy opposition. The Extraparliamentary Committee on the Morals Police would present its findings and recommendations in 1907.[108] As for the French army, officials were worried primarily about stopping the spread of venereal disease via setting up regulated brothels or by providing "cleansing stations" and private medical exams.[109] Beyond that there seems to have been little official interest before 1914 in counseling either prudence – or continence – to young soldiers who were performing their compulsory military service.[110]

The earliest French tract devoted to sex education for girls, *Pour Nos Jeunes Filles quand elles auront 16 ans*, by Dr. Charles Burlureaux, buried in vol. 2 (1902) of the *Bulletin* of the SFPSM, was the subject of contentious debate at one of the society's meetings.[111] Note that the tract for girls was targeted at 16-year-olds, while Fournier's tract for boys was designated for 18-year-olds. A third edition, with an amended subtitle "when their mothers deem this advice necessary" [*quand leurs mères jugeront ces conseils nécessaires*], and a preface by Dr. Fournier, made a more public debut and, along with Fournier's 1902 tract for boys, had an important international ripple effect.[112]

French feminists would soon develop their own approaches to sex education for girls. As we have seen earlier, Nelly Roussel would denounce virginal ignorance at marriage. Shortly thereafter, in 1907, the CNFF activist Jeanne Leroy-Allais would publish a sex education tract for girls, built around a tasteful dialogue between mother and daughter.[113] This author was a staunch opponent of both neo-Malthusian family limitation

Brieux, and the sole woman, Ghénia Avril de Sainte-Croix. The latter's remarks are reported in Fiaux, *Police des moeurs*, vol. 2, pp. 340–341.

[108] See Fiaux & Hennequin, references in n. 107.

[109] For a more extended discussion of army measures before 1914, see Surkis, *Sexing the Citizen*, chapter 8.

[110] Communication with Prof. Michelle Rhoades, 15 February 2014.

[111] Reported by Burek Pierce, *What Adolescents Ought to Know*, p. 196, n. 15. See the *Bulletin de la Société Française de Prophylaxie Sanitaire et Morale*, vol. 2 (1902), circa p. 523.

[112] Dr. Charles Burlureaux, *Pour nos jeunes filles quand leurs mères jugeront ces conseils nécessaires* (Paris: C. Delagrave, 1905).

[113] Jeanne Leroy-Allais, *Comment j'ai instruit mes filles des choses de la maternité* (Paris: A. Maloine, 1907); also Leroy-Allais, *Une Campagne criminelle; avortement et néomalthusianisme* (Paris: Maloine, 1909).

(birth control) and of abortion, which she condemned as criminal. Yet she was no blind pronatalist; she advocated responsible sex. She specifically insisted that mothers inform their daughters about what to expect in bed once they married; there should be no more instances of sexually ignorant virgins being effectively raped by husbands who learned their techniques from prostitutes. The writer Djénane published a long article in support of Leroy-Allais's tract in the *Journal des Femmes* in the fall of 1907, which contained quotations from literary works by male and female authors that denounced the practice of keeping "well-bred" girls in sexual ignorance.[114] In May 1910, sex education for girls was broached in a session on "instruction by women" [*l'enseignement par la femme*] at the *Société de Sociologie de Paris*, and was roundly ridiculed by the ubiquitous antifeminist Théodore Joran, who upheld the view that young women must come to marriage as innocents.[115] In the fall of 1911, another feminist, a more radical women who signed "Remember" and helped finance Madeleine Pelletier's periodical *La Suffragiste*, would raise the stakes on the subject of young women's sexual ignorance by pointing not only to the act but to its frequent results: the prevalence of venereal disease and the "crime" husbands committed (not always inadvertently) against unsuspecting wives and unborn children by transmitting those diseases to them. "Three quarters of the male race," she indicated, "come to marriage with this filthy and incurable malady that has been given the scientific name 'syphilis'."[116] Thus did the respective interests of the woman-focused feminists, the man-focused venereal specialists, and the demographers obsessed by depopulation converge. For the consequences of syphilis included sterility, blindness, even death, and contributed to miscarriages and stillbirths. There was no cure before 1910, when the drug Salvarsan (arsphetamine) was introduced.

---

[114] See Djénane, "Lettre d'une féministe sur l'ignorance des jeunes filles," *Le Journal des Femmes*, n° 177 (September 1907), 3, & n° 178 (October 1907), 3–4. The author cited lines supporting her views from Brieux, Prévost, Tinayre, Dumas *fils*, and others. By way of introduction, the *Journal des Femmes* reported that the local paper in Brittany had refused to publish this letter, stating that it was "too indelicate and too contrary to received ideas."

[115] See the minutes of this session, 11 May 1910, in the *Revue Internationale de Sociologie*, 18:6 (June 1910), 434–443. Théodore Joran ridiculed the feminist speakers (Dr. Edwards-Pilliet and Lydie Martial) who defended early sex education against the critique of the first speaker, an actress from the Comédie Française, in "Le Féminisme et la morale," *La Revue Parlementaire, Économique et Financière* (clipping hand-dated 28 May 1910), 284–285 (clipping in DOS 396 FEM - Coupures de presse 1910–1914, BMD). The session ended with a rousing defense of feminist aims by Paul Vibert.

[116] Remember, "Faut-il instruire les jeunes filles des réalités du mariage?" *La Suffragiste* (October 1911); as quoted and translated by Andrea Mansker in *Sex, Honor, and Citizenship in Early Third Republic France* (Houndmills, UK: Palgrave Macmillan, 2011), p. 206. On this topic, see also chapter 5: "Sexual Initiation and Sex Education" in Mary Lynn Stewart, *For Health and Beauty: Physical Culture for Frenchwomen, 1880s–1930s* (Baltimore: Johns Hopkins University Press, 2001).

Marguerite de Witt-Schlumberger, speaking in May 1909 at a public debate about women and the morals police (at the *Union de la Vérité's Libres Entretiens*), upheld the conclusions of the Extraparliamentary Commission on the Morals Police: close the licensed brothels and abolish the morals police, which were targeted exclusively at women. She insisted that was the solution "that every woman worthy of the name of mother, wife or sister, must not hesitate to support."[117] These matters of morality are *women's business*, she argued, and she advocated that mothers instruct their sons about sexual matters and inculcate a single standard of morality from a very young age. "Who will warn our sons, who will fortify them against their 'undesirable urges' [*mauvais penchants*], who will inform them of the dangers of life, if we mothers don't do it?"[118] How can we teach them if we turn our heads the other way and pretend to know nothing about these matters? She believed that sex education was best done within the family. As for the necessary evil argument in favor of regulation, Mme Schlumberger objected vehemently, invoking a sisterhood of all women: "No sensible woman would accept this pretended protection, which consists of putting a number of her sisters outside the law. ... there is no such thing as a 'necessary evil'."[119] A critique of contemporary girls' education published in *La Nouvelle Revue* around the same date argued that neither ignorance nor bookishness were satisfactory. In particular, Maria Garcia-Mansilla argued that girls needed to be acquainted with life, to learn – from their mothers – that physical love [*l'amour physique*] was a good thing in its proper place, but also that girls should be trained in household management and even practical law so that, once married, they could run their households with competence.[120]

In 1912, Jane Misme of *La Française* would wade into the debate on sex education, following the publication of yet another allusive guide by a Catholic writer along with educator Pauline Kergomard's proposal that the

---

[117] Mme Paul de Schlumberger (Marguerite deWitt-Schlumberger), published in Union de la Vérité, *Libres Entretiens*, 6e Entretien, 21 March 1909, pp. 307–313; quote, p. 309. The question of sex education came up again later in the session; see the remarks of Mlle Jeanne Chambon, p. 346. Consulted at the BN, m'film M-487. My thanks to Jean Elisabeth Pedersen for subsequently transmitting a printout of the entire session, pp. 307–353.

[118] Schlumberger, Union de la Vérité, *Libres Entretiens*, 6e Entretien, p. 312. Other feminists who spoke out against regulation at this meeting included Simone Bodève, the CNFF's Mme d'Abbadie d'Arrast and Louise Compain. A number of men, including Dr. Just Sicard de Plauzoles and Frédéric Passy, condemned the system of regulated prostitution as wholly incompatible with the republic's principles of equality before the law.

[119] Union de la Vérité, *Libres Entretiens*, 6e Entretien, pp. 347–348.

[120] Maria Garcia-Mansilla, "L'Éducation des jeunes filles au XXe siècle," *La Nouvelle Revue* (15 May 1909), 165–176.

"facts of life" be taught in the republic's schools.[121] Misme strongly preferred that mothers provide such education, especially for their daughters, and urged that they themselves, rather than their daughters, read the new manuals so they could provide correct information. Certainly, she said, the "system of total silence has caused much unhappiness; total silence is hypocritical and, therefore, a mistake." But even so, such knowledge should not be delivered prematurely. And, most importantly, when it is delivered, it should be accurate.[122] Fugier-Martin reports that the publication *Le Flambeau* (edited by Jacques Lourbet) launched a survey on the subject of sex education for girls in 1912: "Should girls be instructed about the realities of marriage?" was the topic proposed, and responses were forthcoming from a number of highly visible feminists, including Jeanne Oddo-Deflou, Nelly Roussel, and Arria Ly.[123] As the remarks of Marguerite de Witt-Schlumberger and others make clear, the mainstream feminists considered sex education as part of the answer to eradicating the double standard of morality (and in this they made common cause with the abolitionists). By 1913, such progressive republican women were openly advocating sex education at the Tenth International Congress of Women, in conjunction with their campaign for a single moral standard for both sexes. One of the major resolutions (under the rubric of sexual education) was "that parents consider as one of their most important duties to give their sons and daughters an appropriate sexual education, and that such education be based on the principal of the single standard of morality [*unité de la morale*], which is respectful of order and justice." Additionally, "wherever the mother cannot provide this education, it should be assured to young people by others."[124]

[121] The Catholic book in question is Françoise Harmel, *Une grave question de l'éducation des jeunes filles: La chasteté* (Paris: Perrin, 1912; also 1926 and 1932 editions).

[122] Jane Misme, "Ce qu'on ne dit pas," *La Française*, n° 233 (24 March 1912), lead editorial. Apropos an upcoming congress in Geneva addressing the traffic in women, Misme had severely criticized her compatriots who "closed their ears" when the subjects of prostitution or the traffic in women came up. See also her editorial, "Les Oreilles closes," *La Française*, n° 89 (6 September 1908), in which Misme argues that prostitution is a logical consequence of the male breadwinner argument, since society is then organized so that it becomes impossible for a woman to support herself.

[123] Fugier-Martin, *La Bourgeoise*, pp. 59–60.

[124] For these resolutions, see *Dixième congrès international des femmes, 1913*, p. 572. It was Marguerite de Witt-Schlumberger who provided a report on the sex education question, but remarked that the subject would be discussed further at the upcoming abolitionists' congress. During the discussion, most participants were of the opinion that it was far better for parents to provide this education rather than public school teachers, because of the possible hostility of public opinion (and, presumably, its adverse consequences for enrollment in the state schools).

The sex education of young men and women was not, however, the sole focus of debate during this decade. Married men and their standard of "honor" were also called into question by the mainstream feminists, who called for *"unité de la morale."* This meant in practice to demand a single standard of morality for both sexes, both within and outside marriage, one that would effectively rein in the sexual promiscuousness of men and hold them to a more stringent, less forgiving standard of sexual behavior – a standard set by women. These feminists understood that "the personal is political." Historian Andrea Mansker does not exaggerate when she argues that "by breaking the silence and declaring themselves the overseers of male sexuality, feminists subverted the patriarchal implications of the honor code and insisted on the connection between the personal aspects of their lives and their political exclusion. Though they couched their demands partly in customary language, these women nonetheless advocated *a complete reform* of French sexual culture, and saw the single moral standard as the foundation of political change." Their challenge to the venerable male "code of honor" and their advocacy of a female code of honor "ultimately mark the attempted adaptation of a code based primarily on blood and patrimony to the egalitarian and national demands of republican citizenship for both men and women."[125] The French debates on *recherche de la paternité*, sex education, the morals police and government regulation of prostitution, the traffic in women, single mothers and abandoned children would all revolve around this fundamental challenge.

In its summer issue (August–September 1909), the *Journal des Femmes* announced the founding (9 July) of a new action group, the *Ligue Française de Preservation Morale et Sociale de la Jeunesse*, in which both Maria Martin and Hyacinthe Bélilon were engaged. Then, in later 1909, *La Française* launched a survey on the single moral standard [*"Enquête sur l'unité de la morale"*] which lasted into the following year.[126] The publication's editor, Jane Misme, explained in the issue of 24 October that "the feminists do not advocate 'free love'." Rather, they "want the unification of

---

[125] See Mansker, *Sex, Honor, and Citizenship*, p. 233. Emphasis in original.

[126] Andrea Mansker gives a good summary of this survey in her book, *Sex, Honor, and Citizenship*, chapter 6, notes 109–119 & pp. 227ff., and also in her article, "Shaming Men: Feminist Honor and the Sexual Double Standard in Belle Époque France," in *Confronting Modernity in Fin-de-Siecle France: Bodies, Minds, and Gender*, ed. Christopher E. Forth & Elinor Accampo (Houndmills, Basingstoke, UK: Palgrave Macmillan, 2010), pp. 181–182. Lucie Stanislas-Meunier (1852–1940), married to the naturalist of that name, was a well-known French writer. Other published respondents included Dr. Blanche Edwards-Pilliet, Aurel, Jeanne Oddo-Deflou, the Duchess of Rohan, Augusta Moll-Weiss, Ida R. Sée, Paul Bureau, Maria Vérone, Ghénia Avril de Sainte-Croix, Lucy Bérillon, Jane Misme, and a number of others who wrote in.

morality . . . in love. But they want a single good morality, not a single bad morality. They demand that free love be prohibited to men as it is for women. It's that simple."[127] By "free love," the feminists meant irresponsible, predatory sex (*libertinage*), especially that of men who spawned unwanted children without the sanction of marriage, children who would be severely disadvantaged in life in every way, and whose mothers would struggle, not always successfully, to survive.[128]

The first responders to the inquiry, the novelists Colette Yver and Mme (Lucie) Stanislas Meunier, however, both upheld the well-entrenched "necessary evil" argument and, by extension, the double standard of sexual behavior for husbands and wives, in order to "protect" the family line and property. They suggested that women should "rise above this," or as the writer Myriam Harry remarked, be "indulgent" toward men and their sexual pecadillos.[129] Jeanne Oddo-Deflou, on the other hand, presented a compelling argument for chastity for both sexes, blaming women for not shaming men for their dissolute behavior rather than tacitly approving it – and calling on them to use their influence to censure such behavior and attach consequences to it.[130] But shaming men, as Andrea Mansker has emphasized, was only part of the story; the other significant aspect was that these feminists called directly on women, especially those of the educated classes, to exert their influence in the family as well as their educational authority to put stop to such male behavior and to demand better of them. Women who looked the other way were a big part of the problem, but once made aware of the issues, these same women could also become part of the solution.

Both the Duchesse de Rohan and Augusta Moll-Weiss pointed to the importance of women's influence and teachings within the family to be deployed in shaping everyone's moral behavior.[131] Ida R. Sée (in a letter to the editor) condemned the double standard and the practice of delivering sexually innocent young women over to men whose "experience" had come from consorting with prostitutes. "We say that this is immoral. A family established on this basis is fatally corrupted. . . . Desire [*l'amour*]

---

[127] Misme, in *La Française,* n° 134 (24 October 1909).
[128] The plight of these mothers is the subject of Rachel Fuchs's pathbreaking study *Poor and Pregnant in Paris* (cited in n. 19).
[129] Yver, issue n° 134 (29 October 1909); Stanislas-Meunier, issue n° 137 (14 November 1909); Myriam Harry, issue n° 140 (5 December 1909).
[130] Jeanne Oddo-Deflou, "Une Seule morale pour les deux sexes," *La Française,* n° 148 (21 November 1909).
[131] *La Française,* issues n° 139 (28 November 1909) and n° 140 (5 December 1909).

never justifies debauchery." Sée asserted that the tacit approval of male promiscuity so characteristic of French society might even be "the key to our degeneracy, to the bastardization of the race, to that 'slow death' that seems to be slaughtering our nation."[132] In other words, such behavior was not simply a private matter. The Catholic social reformer Paul Bureau, though suggesting that feminists had not taken up the issue of morals (a mistaken view, in light of this survey and earlier concerns expressed in tandem with the FAI since the late 1890s), was primarily concerned about the cluster of provocations in the current society that served to stimulate the sexual excitability of already volatile men, especially adolescents. "The novel, the theatre, the newspaper and the press, the street and the work-shop, the school and the peer group, all converge to raise the excitation of the male to its highest peak." And, he added, "Our pagan notion of honor is so outrageous and so egotistical that, very often the first obligation of a man of honor is to close his ear[s] to the perfidious advice that is offered to him." But, Bureau noted, that would entail confronting issues of morality and religion, which were currently off the table.[133]

To this mix, the attorney Maria Vérone added consideration of a neglected element in the discussion: the exclusion from the "rights of man" of the prostitutes ("human cattle," "*véritable chair à plaisir*") who were subjected to the humiliating regime of government-regulated prosti-tution in order to provide outlets for male sexual expression. This anom-aly, she indicated, was a direct consequence of the double standard of sexual morality and ostensibly justified by "social hygiene," yet the doctors had shown that this sordid institution did not cut down on the risk of transmitting "certain contagious diseases" (by which she meant specifically the dreaded venereal diseases). In fact, Vérone pointed out, the last congress of the LDH had voted in favor (unanimously, minus one vote) to suppress this regime and thereby to restore "unity of legislation for both sexes."[134] Following a number of others, Ghénia Avril de Sainte-Croix joined the critique of "the strange mentality" of women who are quite aware of what was going on, and yet condone and excuse the promiscuous sexual behavior of men. "The principle of equal responsibility for man and woman in intersexual matters" is the "foundation of equality," she asserted: "Respect for woman should be inculcated in everyone, by every possible means – the education of children and young people, at school and at the

---

[132] Ida R. Sée, letter to the editor, *La Française*, n° 141 (12 December 1909), front page.
[133] Paul Bureau (a Catholic moralist), in n° 142 (19 December 1909).
[134] Maria Vérone, in n° 143 (26 December 1909).

university." Even as Mme Avril condemned the collusion of members of her own sex, she praised the many male-feminists who have understood feminist claims for promoting a higher standard of morality and personal responsibility.[135] Lucie Bérillon, a professor at the Lycée Molière (for girls) in Paris, insisted that, over generations, morals could improve as "better educated and more respected" women used their influence to build the character of their sons; as women advanced and lifted themselves up, men would submit to a more stringent morality in order to be worthy of them.[136]

Their stance was not, however, what some have branded as puritanical or prudish. Many historians, including Edward Berenson (in his study of the case of the July 1914 trial of Mme Joseph Caillaux for assassinating Gaston Calmette, the editor of *Le Figaro*, in mid-March) have inadvertently misrepresented what feminists in France actually had to say about the single standard of morality.[137] In contrast to the opinions of an Arria Ly, who endorsed lifelong virginity, the establishment feminists were not opposed to sexual intercourse; rather their concerns centered on establishing mutual fidelity and responsibility in marriage. In particular, these feminists disputed the well-entrenched point of view that men, and in particular married men, should be allowed to exploit an entire class of poorer women as prostitutes to vent their sexual impulses, ostensibly in order to "protect" their wives and their families. They objected to the notion that men could not – or would not – control their sexual desires just as women had to. One respondent memorably cited these lines from Beaumarchais's *Figaro*: "How many men would be able to practice the restraint demanded of women?" Another cited Alexandre Dumas *fils*'s advice to a son, to confine his sexuality to marriage.[138] They thought it ridiculous that French society gave young men tacit permission to sow their "wild oats" while young women of their class were expected to be virginal until marriage. Others, following the lead of Maria Pognon and later Mme Remember, would object publicly to married men bringing home the "gift" of venereal disease to their wives and unborn children. None would have endorsed the extramarital promiscuity of women like the notorious socialite Meg Steinheil, who traded sex for commissions of paintings by her artist husband (and much more), or the sexual hanky-panky of the

---

[135] Mme Avril de Sainte-Croix, in n° 146 (23 January 1910).
[136] Lucie Bérillon, in n° 147 (30 January 1910).
[137] See Edward Berenson, *The Trial of Madame Caillaux* (Berkeley & Los Angeles: University of California Press, 1992), p. 129.
[138] See *La Française*, n° 147 (30 January 1910).

politician Joseph Caillaux that led his wife (and former mistress) to assassinate the editor of *Le Figaro*.[139] Nor would they have welcomed the demeaning defenses developed by these women's defense attorneys. "Madame Caillaux is by no measure a feminist," asserted Jane Misme in *La Française*, but merely the product of a poor education and "oblivious to intellectual and social preoccupations."[140] There is no denying that a puritan streak existed, especially among certain French protestants (Steven C. Hause calls it "social control puritanism") and pious Catholics, such as Paul Bureau. But the views expressed by the feminist women surveyed by *La Française* did not mirror it.[141]

The Question of Reproductive Choice for Women: Abortion and Paid Maternity Leave

Given the intensity of concern with the population issue and the demographic future of France, both abortion and birth control remained controversial and relatively hush-hush topics in France during the first decade of the twentieth century. Nonetheless, the limited public debates about abortion that had taken place in France from 1893 to 1907 (see Chapter 7) had even inspired a wave of fiction based on what literary historian Leonard Koos calls "the abortion plot." The elements of this plot included abortionists who were not medically certified (neither midwives nor physicians), the consequent failure of the abortive procedure, and the male doctors who were trying to establish their hegemony over the practice. It seems significant that most of these novels were written by male authors, but Koos does not analyze the significance of this fact, nor does he allude to the portrayal of the psychology of the women who are aborting.[142] The feminists' outspokenness on sex education notwithstanding, many women remained reluctant to address the topic, much less to insist on women's

---

[139] On Meg Steinheil, see Benjamin F. Martin, *The Hypocrisy of Justice in the Belle Epoque* (Baton Rouge: Louisiana State University Press, 1984), chapters 1 & 3.

[140] Jane Misme, "Le Crime d'une femme," *La Française*, n° 311 (21 March 1914), front page. She reiterated this point in passing in "Ce qui n'est pas du féminisme," *La Française*, n° 319 (23 May 1914).

[141] See Steven C. Hause, "Social Control in Late Nineteenth-Century France: Protestant Campaigns for Strict Public Morality," in *Confronting Modernity in Fin-de-Siecle France: Bodies, Minds, and Gender*, ed. Christopher E. Forth & Elinor Accampo (Houndmills, Basingstoke, UK: Palgrave Macmillan, 2010), pp. 135–149.

[142] See Leonard R. Koos, "Making Angels: Abortion Literature in Turn-of-the-Century France," in *Confrontations: Politics and Aesthetics in Nineteenth-Century France*, ed. Kathryn M. Grossman, Michael E. Lane, Bénédicte Monicat, & Willa Z. Silverman (Amsterdam: Rodopi, 2001), pp. 259–285.

right to control their own bodies. We will discuss the notable exceptions later in the chapter.

Republican feminists did criticize the selection of the Third Republic's Second Commission on Depopulation, appointed in late 1912. As before, in 1902, every one of the 250 members selected by the ministry was male; no women were appointed, despite the precedent set earlier by the extraparliamentary commission on the morals police. In *La Française*, Pauline Rebour complained mightily about the exclusion of women from this new body.[143] Shortly thereafter, in a short note published in the CNFF's *L'Action féminine* (December 1912), an anonymous writer huffed: "How ridiculous is this chaotic and interminable list of members of the 'depopulation commission'. It would have been far more useful to ask women from different social strata. Then one would learn a lot more about why people don't want children and whose fault it is."[144] There would be no solution to this or other major national problems, these mainstream feminists maintained, without consulting French women. The LFDF, receiving no response to its published complaint about the omission of women, decided to constitute its own commission; its plan was to investigate the apparent lack of enforcement of the Roussel Law (on the wet-nursing business and the protection of nurslings) in the provinces.[145] Subsequently, in *La Française*, editor Jane Misme noted the absence of any concern with such moral issues among the repopulators; their societies, she remarked, "content themselves with preaching to men the obligation to procreate, to promise them in response the plural vote, if they are poor, puny hand-outs to be reinforced by laws off in the future."[146]

Only a few French women would publicly defend women's right to make reproductive choices, campaigning both against male authority in the matter and against the intrusion of the state. These women included the ever-eloquent Nelly Roussel and the even more vociferous Gabrielle Petit (1860–1952), whose publication, *La Femme affranchie* (established 1904), had particular ideological and propagandistic significance. Historian

---

[143] Pauline Rebour, "Les Lois d'intérêt féminin au Parlement," *La Française*, n° 257 (30 November 1912).

[144] "La Dépopulation et les femmes," *L'Action féminine*, n° 25 (December 1912), 436.

[145] See Marie Bonnevial & Maria Vérone, "Contre la Dépopulation. A Monsieur le Ministre des Finances," in *Le Droit des Femmes: Revue mensuelle*, n° 12 (December 1912), 1–2, and Maria Vérone, "Sauvons les Poupons," *Le Droit des Femmes: Revue mensuelle*, n° 1 (January 1913), 1–2. Attorney Suzanne Grinberg (a.k.a. Grunberg) would lead this investigation.

[146] See Jane Misme, "Le Bonheur d'être mère," *La Française*, n° 320 (30 May 1914), front page.

Francis Ronsin has described Petit's paper as "revolutionary feminist, violently antimilitaristic, and neo-Malthusian."[147]

Joining Roussel and Petit as advocates of women's right to control their own bodies was Dr. Madeleine Pelletier, whose frank and uncompromising views have been much discussed by scholars.[148] Claiming a state of celibacy for herself, Pelletier nevertheless became one of the most forceful champions of women's right to express their sexual desire, to take contraceptive measures, and if impregnated despite those precautions, to seek abortions. As we have seen, in her 1908 publication, *La Femme en lutte pour ses droits*, she scornfully dismissed the current French obsession with maternity. Taking her distance from most other feminist activists who could not say a bad word about motherhood as such (even as a claim to full citizenship, and a female equivalent of men's military service), Pelletier asserted flatly that "childbirth will never provide women with a title to social importance."[149]

Pelletier's most daring statement on this subject dates from 1911, with the publication of her book, *L'Émancipation sexuelle de la femme*, which included a notoriously controversial chapter on the right to abortion, which was later republished in pamphlet form.[150] In this chapter she laid out a logical, articulate argument for the legalization of abortion – simply by abolishing Article 317 of the Penal Code.[151] Maternity, Pelletier insisted, should not be imposed on a woman who has satisfied her sexual desire: "It is up to the woman alone to decide if and when she will become a mother."[152] She discussed the extent to which abortion (which French courts continued to treat as a criminal offense) had become a "common practice" in large cities, and how women could always find an

---

[147] Ronsin, *Grève des ventres*, p. 159. This Gabrielle Petit should not be confused with the Belgian woman of the same name who spied for the British during World War I.

[148] For the scholarship concerning Pelletier's earlier ideas and actions, see Chapter 10.

[149] Madeleine Pelletier, *La Femme en lutte pour ses droits* (Paris: Giard & Brière,1908), p. 37; my translation.

[150] Madeleine Pelletier, *L'Émancipation sexuelle de la femme* (Paris: M. Giard & E. Briere, 1911). Two of the chapters from this book, "Feminism and the Family" and "The Right to Abortion" are published in full English translation by Marilyn J. Boxer in *The French American Review*, 6:1 (Spring 1982), 3–26. A second translation of major parts of "The Right to Abortion" is available in *Feminisms of the Belle Epoque*, ed. Jennifer Waelti-Walters & Steven C. Hause (Lincoln: University of Nebraska Press, 1994), pp. 253–262.

[151] Madeleine Pelletier, chapter 3, "Le Droit à l'avortement," in *L'Émancipation sexuelle*; republished (2nd ed.) as a 24-page pamphlet, *Le Droit à l'avortement* (Paris: Éd. du "Malthusien," 1913). The quotations that follow are from the 1913 pamphlet edition, as transl. by M. Boxer.

[152] *Le Droit à l'avortement*, p. 7 of the 1913 offprint.

agency or an individual to help her self-induce, generally through her neighborhood networks.

Contrary to what prominent male doctors were claiming, Dr. Pelletier asserted that if abortion were legal, it would not be dangerous. Up to three months into a pregnancy, she affirmed, the procedure was simple and routine; there would never be an accident. However, Pelletier considered abortion as always a last resort [*pis-aller*]. She argued forcefully (against Church authorities and the pronatalists) that, unlike infanticide, abortion was not a criminal act; French law was simply wrong on this point. Drawing on her medical knowledge, she argued that until a child was born, it was not a person; until birth a fetus is a part of its mother's body. "It is not possible to compare a germ to a person who has the right to life, without falling into absurdity. Men as well as women harbor germ cells. Would it be possible to require them not to waste a single one, to use them all for impregnation?"[153] Only the child, once born, had a right to life. A woman who bears a child, she argued, "is not obligated to raise it," but she has no right to destroy it. "It is no more permissible to destroy an infant than to kill an adult."[154] Acknowledging the correctness of French law in this particular instance, however, Pelletier did consider infanticide a criminal offense.

Not many agreed with Dr. Madeleine Pelletier that maternity should be optional, or that it amounted to a cage for women. By 1908 or so, most republican feminists and their male allies asserted that in order to preserve that life and make it blossom, something must be done to assist the mothers, especially those women who were holding down, laid off from, or seeking poorly paid jobs, under the constant threat of resorting to prostitution to make ends meet. One solution repeatedly proposed was maternity leaves for employed women and compensation for their time away. Others (as we have seen) were arguing even more strongly for maternity as a paid social function. The lawyer A. Vallin (who had made a comparative study of medical literature and pertinent foreign legislation) did not think it possible to eliminate arbitrarily the employment of working-class women. But he did advocate compensating women for obligatory maternity leaves (on the German model) in order to reduce infant mortality, which still ran to roughly 14 percent of births.[155] The solutions envisaged by the men of Bertillon's *Alliance Nationale pour*

---

[153] *Droit à l'avortement*, p. 23.   [154] *Droit à l'avortement*, p. 22.

[155] A.Vallin, *La Femme salariée et la maternité*, doctoral thesis, Faculty of Law, University of Paris (Paris: A. Rousseau, 1911), pp. 3, 19, 23 24.

l'Accroissement de la Population Française continued to run along a line that culminated in Fernand Boverat's *Patriotisme et paternité* (1913). Boverat emphasized men's primary responsibility, even headlining one chapter "The duty of paternity should be joined to the duty to serve in the military." He did, however, accord limited agency to women: in fact, he lectured women that the only way to establish a lasting peace was through French population growth. All healthy women, he insisted, should give their country *at least* four children. Women who did not fulfill this foremost duty were "no better than deserters!"[156]

It was one thing to condemn women who did not produce four children as "deserters" and another thing to improve the sociopolitical conditions that surrounded motherhood. French republican feminists staked their claims on making maternity feasible. Even as they sought major changes in family law, including *recherche de la paternité*, they also called for government intervention on behalf of the welfare of mothers. Most early twentieth-century French feminist activists, particularly those affiliated with the CNFF, tried to work closely with progressive republican legislators such as Paul Strauss and René Viviani to compel state action on behalf of mothers. Their preferred solutions were articulated at the governmental level by Strauss, the solidarist republican senator who worked closely with the republican women's movement on a comprehensive body of legislation to benefit women as mothers and workers, and by the deputy Fernand Engerand in the Chamber of Deputies. I will not rehearse the slow development of this legislation, which has been perceptively analyzed by Mary Lynn Stewart and Rachel Fuchs.[157] Suffice it to say that before the outbreak of war in 1914 only two modest laws and one program resulted from their efforts. The law of 27 November 1909 provided job guarantees to women who took (voluntary) maternity leave from their jobs. A private program of mutual maternity insurance, partially subsidized by the government, was successfully established. Private groups organized *mutualités maternelles* to assist the needy wives and children of French on-duty soldiers.[158] The law authorizing paternity suits in restricted circumstances became law on 16 November 1912.[159]

---

[156] Fernand Boverat, *Patriotisme et paternité* (Paris: Grasset, 1913); quotations, chapter 9 subtitle and p. 361.

[157] See Stewart, *Women, Work, and the French State,* cited in n. 19.

[158] See A. Pinard, "La protection des enfants de nos soldats," *La Grande Revue,* vol. 85 (25 May 1914), 185–198.

[159] See Marcel Sauvagnac, "Loi du 16 novembre 1912 modifiant l'article 340 du Code civil (reconnaissance judiciaire de la paternité naturelle)," *Annuaire de Legislation Francaise 1912,* vol. 32 (1913), 185–190, and the summary by Maria Vérone, "La Recherche de la paternité," *Jus Suffragii,* 7:5 (15 January 1913), 50–51.

By early 1913 Dr. Edwards-Pilliet would be using the term *fonctionnaire social* in the pages of the CNFF's *L'Action féminine* to advocate for full state support of mothers from pregnancy through breastfeeding.[160] Finally, in the wake of the Tenth International Congress of Women, which encompassed both the areas of women's works and women's rights, feminists celebrated what had been accomplished to date and pressed for further changes. Shortly thereafter, the pathbreaking law of 17 June 1913 established obligatory paid maternity leaves, both pre- and post-partum, for all waged women workers.[161] Nevertheless, the quest for fully paid, extended maternity leave would continue.

Rachel Fuchs has argued (against others who have focused solely on legislation affecting male workers) that, in fact, the legislation passed before 1914 to foster maternity and save the lives of children signals the true origins of the French welfare state. She attributes this legislation directly to the population crisis, and to the perceived plight of poor women and children. "Only in France did the threat of depopulation loom so central in reform debates," she indicates. Moreover, Fuchs argues (again, against other male-focused interpreters who have not taken gender into consideration) that "social reforms leading to the welfare state embodied a blurring of the lines between the public and private spheres." She notes that "the politicians of the social welfare state have made *la vie intime* of the family and reproduction public," a finding that confounds a variety of assumptions made by social theorists. "In fact, France was a European leader in designing family policies and family allowances." That French legislatures did enact such measures at a relatively early point was because of the population decline concerns: "If the cry of depopulation was a means to get women back into the home, it may have been louder in France because there was a much higher rate of married women's participation in the workforce there than elsewhere."[162] Thus, it is to the debate over women in the workforce between 1901 and 1914 that we now turn.

---

[160] Dr. Edwards-Pilliet, "La Dépopulation: A propos de la loi d'assistance aux mères," *L'Action féminine*, n° 27 (April 1913), 179–181; quote, 181. Commenting on the law under consideration, already passed by the Senate, she argued that it must be pushed further: "obligatory insurance" was necessary in order to provide assistance to all needy mothers.

[161] See Hubert-Valleroux, "Loi du 17 juin 1913 sur le répos des femmes en couches," *Annuaire de Législation Française, 1913*, vol. 33 (1914), pp. 83–91.

[162] See Rachel G. Fuchs, "France in a Comparative Perspective," in *Gender and the Politics of Social Reform*, pp. 157–187; quotes scattered throughout this essay.

CHAPTER 12

Emerging Labor Issues
Equal Pay for Equal Work, Travail à Domicile and Women's Right to Work

The 1906 census had verified the presence of some 7 million women in the French labor force, twice as many as in 1866, representing some 37 percent of the total workforce. In fact these figures would disclose the highest point of women's industrial workforce participation in the twentieth century.[1] After that, women's employment in this sector would decline somewhat, but their work in other sectors continued to rise as some reasonably well-paying opportunities had begun to open up for more educated, lower-middle-class women. Nevertheless, employed working-class women would continue to suffer from poor working conditions, exhausting labor, and, most devastating, abysmally low wages.

Many of these women who worked for pay were married. According to the male-breadwinner model that so many French people carried around in their heads, married women were not supposed to be working for pay outside the home. Yet in France, during the *Belle Époque*, it would become increasingly difficult for many working men to earn a wage that would sustain a wife and family, notwithstanding the prescriptions of liberal economists and popes.[2] Even working-class families in which both spouses were employed often faced severe financial challenges, because both men and women were so poorly paid for their long hours of physically exhausting and thankless labor. That countless French wives had to go out to work was a well-known fact, as the working-class novelist Simone Bodève (1876–1921) would explain in 1909 to the audience at the *Union de la Vérité*: "Poor women who work don't do it for their pleasure.... She goes out because the man's income is not sufficient, or because the man doesn't

---

[1] The first authoritative scholarly analysis of women's employment statistics is Madeleine Guilbert, "L'Évolution des effectifs du travail féminin en France depuis 1866," *La Revue Française du Travail*, vol. 2, n° 18 (September 1947), 754–777. I will refer here to Guilbert's figures.

[2] This situation is amply documented in Susan Pedersen, *Family, Dependence, and the Origins of the Welfare State: Britain and France 1914-1945* (Cambridge, UK: Cambridge University Press, 1993).

bring enough of it home. Everybody knows that, especially the workers."[3] Social critics were deeply concerned that some significant part of men's wages went for alcohol – no doubt to drown their misery – and the little money that was left, even when supplemented by the wife's meager earnings, was insufficient to provide a nutritious diet, a healthy habitation, or a comfortable existence, not to mention time for leisure activities for the rest of the family.

The typesetter Emma Couriau would underscore the point in 1913, even as she (like many other committed advanced socialist women and men) blamed this predicament on Capitalism.[4] There can be no doubt that capitalist exploitation of the proletariat certainly existed in the nineteenth and early twentieth centuries, but as we now know, even centuries before industrial capitalism came into existence, the pay for nonhousehold work by women had been scandalously undervalued, and not only in France, as the German socialist-feminist Lily Braun would point out to her French readers.[5]

Maria Vérone would bemoan the persistence of this regrettable fact in her 1909 report to the *Ligue des Droits de l'Homme*. "If men's pay is often derisory and insufficient, that of women is even less."[6] And then there were the single women – the unmarried, the widowed, the divorced – who significantly outnumbered single French men: these "surplus" women had to find a way to support themselves. This increasingly imbalanced sex ratio had huge sociopolitical and economic significance. Even if every single man in France were forced to marry, Vérone pointed out, there were simply not enough "breadwinners" to go around.[7]

---

[3] Simone Bodève in *Union de la Vérité*, "Troisième Entretien, 10 janvier 1909. Le Travail féminin en concurrence avec le travail masculin," *Libres Entretiens*, 3ᵉ entretien (10 January 1909), quote, 139–140. In 1913 Simone Bodève would publish a book of stories about proletarian Parisian women, *Celles qui travaillent* (Paris: P. Ollendorff, 1913). She also published several novels, including *La Petite Lotte* (1907), *CLO* (1908), and *Son Mari* (1911).

[4] Emma Couriau, in *L'Équité*, 15 December 1913; as republished in Maïté Albistur & Daniel Armogathe, *Le Grief des femmes*, 2 vols. (Paris: Éditions Hier & Demain, 1978), vol. 2, p. 127.

[5] Lily Braun's study, *Die Frauenfrage, ihre geschichtliche Entwicklung und ihre wirtschaftliche Seite* (Leipzig: Hirzel, 1901), appeared in French translation as *Le Problème de la femme: son évolution historique* (Paris: E. Cornély, 1908). I have encountered only two references to its reception in France, the first in an article by a Belgian sociologist, in the *Revue d'économie politique* (July 1909), and the second in the brochure by Marianne Rauze, *Féminisme économique* (Paris: Éditions de l'Équité, 1914; reprinted 1915), which extensively quotes Braun's historical findings. Braun's biographer, Alfred G. Meyer, describes the bulk of Braun's book as "a guided tour through hell, the hell of women working in the capitalist economy." See Alfred G. Meyer, *The Feminism and Socialism of Lily Braun* (Bloomington: Indiana University Press, 1985), p. 74.

[6] The full text of Vérone's report is published in the *Bulletin de la LDH*, vol. 9, n° 17 (15 September 1909), 1094–1104; these remarks, 1096.

[7] Vérone, in her remarks during the discussion at the LDH congress, as reported in the compte-rendu of the debates in the *Bulletin de la LDH*, vol. 9, nᵒˢ 14–15 (31 July–15 August 1909), 972.

Out to Work: Old Circumstances, New Forms of Exploitation

From 1901 to 1914 the circumstances surrounding most wives who had to work outside the home in France remained much the same: horribly low pay, which everyone agreed fostered malnutrition, disease, miscarriages, prostitution, and neglected children. It also fostered public disputes over whether or not the protective legislation for women in industrial settings, initiated by the law of 2 November 1892, was either necessary or effective, and, given the surplus of single women, to what extent it actually disadvantaged those who needed to support themselves. The anarchist Charles-Albert, a Proudhonian, attacked his version of the *"modern woman,"* dramatizing what an outrage it was to behold "these women, creatures of gentleness, of grace, and of fertile repose, enfeebled and withered by hard labors on the land, in the mine, in the factory or the workshop, these precious and fragile wombs, depositories of future humanity, crippled by virile tasks."[8] Shades of Michelet and Jules Simon! In contrast, some men such as the Francophone Hungarian doctor André [Andor] de Máday, active in the *Association Internationale pour la Protection Légale des Travailleurs* (AIPLT) [International Association for the Legal Protection of Working Men] and its Hungarian affiliate, argued in his comparative "scientific" study *Le Droit des Femmes au Travail: Étude sociologique*, that, given the nature of society's evolution (the movement of women's conventional tasks outside the home) every woman has an "inviolable right to work."[9] Others, such as the positivist Alfred Lambert and all the leading male-antifeminists continued to insist that everything possible must be done to keep wives and mothers out of the labor force and in the household (keeping house, cooking, and tending children).

Was Lambert's vision only a masculinist pipe dream, in light of the new twentieth-century economic realities underscored by Máday's evolutionary perspective and Maria Vérone's unassailable, troubling figures about a surfeit of women? If so, it was a dream that was widely shared, even by many women. As Charles Sowerwine acknowledges, "to both men and

---

[8] Charles-Albert, *L'Amour libre*, 4th ed. (Paris: P.-V. Stock, 1902), p. 285, as translated in John Hutton, "Camille Pissarro's *Turpitudes Sociales* and Late Nineteenth-Century French Anarchist Anti-Feminism," *History Workshop*, n° 24 (Autumn 1987), 32–61; quote, variously, 43, 48.

[9] André de Máday, *Le Droit de la femme au travail: Étude sociologique* (Paris: V. Giard & E. Brière, 1905; Geneva: Atar, 1905); quote, p. 252. For France, Máday draws heavily on the statistics provided by Kaethe Schirmacher (1902), cited in n. 55, and in Chapter 6. See also Alfred Lambert's review of this book in the *Revue Internationale de Sociologie*, 14, n° 9 (September 1906), 659–671, in which he asserts, against Máday, that wives and mothers should be in the home, not in the workforce.

women workers, 'woman by the hearth' signified not only a defense against proletarianization but also a utopian vision."[10] It was on this point, he indicates, that the men in the labor movement parted company with the socialists. And, as had been the case for several decades, the printers' federation would lead the efforts to keep women out of their shops. By 1913, Auguste Keufer, the general secretary of the *Fédération du Livre*, would still be arguing that women, especially wives, should not be in the workforce – but he also agreed that their labor in the home should be considered valuable, an argument that been made earlier by many feminist social critics including Kaethe Schirmacher and the socialist-feminist Elisabeth Renaud.[11]

In the meantime, socially responsible legislators, recognizing that many women did indeed need to earn money in order to survive, often under extraordinarily adverse conditions, slowly pressed forward with some remedial solutions, including mandatory seating laws, hours laws, obligatory paid maternity leave, and a minimum wage. Even Catholic spokesmen such as Eugène Duthoit admitted the necessity of equal pay for equal work, of unionization, and laws that would protect women workers during and after childbirth.[12] But the path to legislative action was strewn with obstacles, and as was the case for *recherche de la paternité*, the laws ultimately passed would be partial, unsatisfactory, and often difficult to enforce.

Supplementing the evolutionary changes in women's workforce participation between 1866 and 1906, recognized at the time by Máday and others, a second significant change had taken place within this workforce of women: the emergence of the "*travailleuse*" as distinct from the "*ouvrière*." According to the authoritative figures put forward by the historical sociologist Madeleine Guilbert and elaborated by historian Marie-Hélène Zylberberg-Hocquard in the late 1970s, the number of women working in

[10] See Charles Sowerwine, "Workers and Women in France before 1914: The Debate over the Couriau Affair," *Journal of Modern History*, 55:3 (September 1983), 411-441; quote, 419. The focus of this article is on shifts of male attitudes in the C.G.T. away from corporatism and mutualism toward revolutionary syndicalism and solidarity of the sexes in class struggle.

[11] See Sowerwine, "Workers and Women," p. 422, quoting Keufer's remarks on this subject from *La Bataille Syndicaliste*, 25 August 1913. This was the daily paper published by the revolutionary syndicalists, who supported class struggle against the corporatist/mutualist factions and were also more supportive of women's right to work.

[12] Eugène Duthoit, *Le Travail féminin dans l'industrie; deux leçons données à la Semaine Sociale de Dijon (30 et 31 Juillet 1906)* (Paris: E. Vitté, 1906). This 35-page pamphlet reviews the reforms advocated by feminists with regard to women's employment in light of the Catholic ideal.

the tertiary sector had quadrupled during this period.[13] The *travailleuse* was "not merely the *ouvrière* condemned to the same fate as the men of her social class, but she could have some instruction, some professional training, that prepared her for a life of paid work ... and attain or had already attained, thanks to her labor, a relative ease of existence." And, this historian remarked, "some of these women did not feel themselves to be proletarians."[14] In English, we would call them white-collar workers.

By 1908, a new monthly publication, *Les Travailleuses,* directed by Marie-Louise Bérot-Berger (of the *Union Fraternelle des Femmes*), would address the needs of this expanding category of working women.[15] These young women with some educational credentials could make choices: to marry or not to marry, to have children or not; to give up employment upon marriage, or to continue their work after marrying. The novelist and social investigator Louise Compain (1869–1940?) laid out these young women's options in *La Grande Revue* in 1913, emphasizing their increasing freedom of choice and the opportunities for personal growth and empowerment that their training and well-paid work could provide.[16] Finally, the arguments made by the well-known South African Anglophone novelist and social critic Olive Schreiner, especially those that mapped the evolution of women's labor out of the home and castigated the leisured wife (who was neither employed outside the home nor active in her community) as a "parasite," made their way into Francophone feminist circles, thanks to a translation of Schreiner's *Woman and Labour* published in Lausanne by Payot in 1913, with a preface by the leading Swiss suffrage activist Emilie Gourd.[17]

Schreiner's observations attracted the attention of both the French labor activist Marie Guillot (1880–1934), secretary of the teachers' union in the

---

[13] See Madeleine Guilbert, *Les Femmes et l'organisation syndicale avant 1914: présentation et commentaires de documents pour une étude du syndicalisme féminin* (Paris: Éditions du CNRS, 1966), and Marie-Hélène Zylberberg-Hocquard, *Féminisme et syndicalisme en France* (Paris: Éditions Anthropos, 1978).

[14] Zylberberg-Hocquard, *Féminisme et syndicalisme*, pp. 19–21; quote p. 21.

[15] *Les Travailleuses* appeared from 1908 to 1919. In 1908, Marie-Louise Bérot-Berger also published an *Annuaire des Oeuvres et des Travailleuses*. She published many works from 1905 on and would become very active in social reform efforts in the 1920s and 1930s.

[16] See Louise Compain, "Les Conséquences du travail de la femme," *La Grande Revue*, vol. 79 (25 May 1913), 364–376 ("Pages Libres," n° 544, 308–320). This text is published in English translation in *Feminisms of the Belle Epoque*, ed. Jennifer Waelti-Walters & Steven C. Hause (Lincoln: University of Nebraska Press, 1994), pp. 133–145.

[17] See Olive Schreiner, *La Femme et le Travail*, trad. par Madame T. Combe (Lausanne: Payot, 1913; and Paris: Fischbacher, 1913) with a preface by Emilie Gourd. The book was originally published in English in 1911 as *Woman and Labour*.

department of Saône-et-Loire, and the veteran suffrage activist Marguerite de Witt-Schlumberger (1853–1924).[18] Guillot pointed out that Schreiner's analysis focused on the situation of privileged bourgeois women, omitting recognition that poor women had no choice but to go out to work; they could not afford the luxury of becoming parasites. Guillot considered the book good and well translated. But, as she rightly observed in conclusion, Schreiner had ignored "the questions raised by the exploitation of women's labor ... which count among the most 'interesting' problems raised by the issue of women's work."[19] Witt-Schlumberger compared Schreiner's evolutionary vision to that of Condorcet in his *Tableau historique des progrès de l'esprit humain* (1795). As concerned women's fertility, Witt-Schlumberger remarked that Schreiner was by no means endorsing "the evil caused in our country by egotistical and criminal neo-malthusianism," but that she did insist that in the future only families who had the "physical, intellectual, and moral means" of raising children properly should have children and that fertility for its own sake was no longer relevant to humanity's progress.[20] Finally, she underscored Schreiner's critique of the fact that women's domestic labor of childcare and housekeeping remained unpaid, and therefore considered of little value, but that in the future those women who chose this role should be accorded value equivalent to that of the man who worked outside the household. Moreover, women should receive equal pay for equal work. That women were discriminated against exclusively on the basis of sex, and that men did nothing to remedy this, Schreiner said, made her incredibly angry. Witt-Schlumberger, clearly inspired by Schreiner's ideas, concluded her commentary by insisting that it would be "through the efforts of women that woman would acquire her place in the world."[21]

A third major change in this period was the dramatic internationalization of labor issues. In France, as elsewhere in the western world, governments would initiate ministries of labor; women's bureaus would spring up to address the special needs of employed women; international congresses, including women's international congresses (both the International Council of Women [ICW] and the International Woman

---

[18] See Marie Guillot's review in *La Vie ouvrière*, n° 82 (20 February 1913), 248–249, and Witt-Schlumberger's 22-page brochure (with extensive quotations from the translated work), *Les Idées de Mrs Olive Schreiner sur la femme et le travail* (Paris: Union Française pour le Suffrage des Femmes, 1913).

[19] Guillot review, quote, 249.

[20] Witt-Schlumberger, *Idées de Mrs Olive Schreiner*; Condorcet comparison, p. 2; on fertility, p. 6.

[21] Witt-Schlumberger, *Idées de Mrs Olive Schreiner*, p. 22.

Suffrage Alliance [IWSA] held regularly scheduled congresses), would bring concerned individuals from many countries together to discuss the pressing issues.[22] Francophone readers could henceforth access significant analyses (in French translation) of the problems surrounding women's work – especially those by Ellen Key and Olive Schreiner, but also those by the German socialist-feminist Lily Braun. Building on the initiatives of the AIPLT in May 1905, European government officials (all male) convened again in September 1906, in Bern, Switzerland, to sign an international convention banning night work for women. Arthur Fontaine, head of the *Office du Travail*, and René Viviani, the Minister of Labor, represented and signed on behalf of France. The Chamber of Deputies voted to ratify the Convention rather quickly, also amending several of the 1892 laws to meet its requirements, but the Senate held out for several more years; France finally ratified the Bern Convention in December 1911.[23] Should we be surprised that, in the wake of national precedents to date, the first international convention on labor laws should (again) endorse restrictions that applied specifically to women workers? Should we be surprised that feminists in France would begin to cite examples from other countries when they proposed reforms affecting women's work? Should we be surprised that many feminists would approve of protective legislation for women workers, even though a highly vocal minority who favored equal rights in law for both sexes would continue to advocate applying these labor laws to men as well as women?

   In the wake of these international initiatives, and thanks to pressure from the socialist left, French legislators finally began to confront the most serious issues and to propose some cautious remedies, recognizing increasingly that France was "behind" its neighbors in addressing the economic and social problems of the modern industrial age. While hard-liner collectivists

---

[22] A book by Bérot-Berger reports on three such congresses: the *Congrès international des habitations ouvrières à bon marché*; the *Congrès international de la tuberculose*; and the *Congrès international de la goutte de lait*. See Bérot-Berger, *Enquêtes sociales: A tous ceux qui pensent, agissent, et se dévouent* (Paris: Sansot, 1906).

[23] On the developments leading up to the Bern Convention, see Marcel Caté, *La Convention de Berne de 1906 sur l'interdiction du travail de nuit des femmes employées dans l'industrie*. Thèse, Faculté de droit (Paris: Larose, 1911). See also *Actes de la Conférence diplomatique pour la protection ouvrière réunie à Berne du 17 au 26 septembre 1906* (Bern: Staempfli, 1906). For an international perspective, see the essays in *Protecting Women: Labor Legislation in Europe, the United States, and Australia, 1880–1920*, ed. Ulla Wikander, Alice Kessler-Harris, & Jane Lewis (Urbana & Chicago: University of Illinois Press, 1995); there is no study of the French case in this otherwise very important book. For the ratification, see Mary Lynn Stewart, *Women, Work, and the French State: Labour Protection and Social Patriarchy, 1879–1919* (Montreal: McGill-Queens University Press, 1989), pp. 144–147. Stewart informs us (p. 146) that "Political consensus on the 1911 law, transferred to the Labour Code, held until the 1970s."

continuously condemned Capitalism (with a capital "C") for France's growing problems, most feminists continued to insist that legislative remedies
could be found for many of these problems within the existing system. For
them, it was primarily a question of bringing France's antiquated civil laws
into alignment with contemporary morals and practices, as a pro-reform law
professor from Dijon indicated at the inaugural meeting of the *Société
d'Études Législatives* in 1902.[24] Feminists in France may have still been
divided over the question of "protective legislation" that applied only to
workers of one sex, but they unanimously agreed that women – married
women as well as single women – must have the right to work and to receive
equal pay for equal work. By 1909 even Armand Fallières, the president of
the French Third Republic from 1906 to 1913, would endorse ending the pay
differential between women and men.[25] That meant raising women's pay to
the level of men's pay (for the same work) within any given industry or
occupation; the time had come to defuse the claim that hiring cheaper
women would drag down men's wages or put them out of work.

Equal Pay for Equal Work? The Public Sector

As the twentieth century began, the government of the Third Republic did
take some steps toward pay equity for the growing numbers of *travailleuses*
who were becoming public servants, though without acknowledging the
justice of the principle. This initiative began by equalizing pay for certain
comparable professional civil service appointments – first, of women
primary school inspectresses with male inspectors; then of inspectors of
social services, and of labor inspectresses.[26] But these precedent-setting
developments anticipated further demands: there seemed to be no stopping the influx of young women into teaching and into inspectorships, a
development that the primary school inspector Émile Bugnon, writing in
1914, considered worrisome.[27]

---

[24] *Bulletin de la Société d'Études Législatives*, vol. I (1901–1902), 26–28. Report of M. Tissier at the first
meeting (20 February 1902) on modifications of rights and powers of married women with respect
to property and earnings, followed by discussions throughout the year.

[25] Armand Fallières, "Discours de l'inauguration de l'Hôtel de la Ligue de l'Enseignement,"
30 October 1909; reproduced in *L'Action féministe*, 2:2 (November 1909), 24–25.

[26] See Linda L. Clark, *The Rise of Professional Women in France: Gender and Public Administration since
1830* (Cambridge, UK: Cambridge University Press, 2000), pp. 60, 110. In each case, controversy
arose over the appropriateness of equal pay for equal work. Of course, this demand for equal pay was
much older, as shown in my companion volume.

[27] For a resumé, see Émile Bugnon, "Les Institutrices," *La Grande Revue*, vol. 84 (25 April 1914), "Pages
Libres," n° 562, 713–733, esp. 724–731. Bugnon is critical of these teachers' increasing militancy and,
especially, their support for women's suffrage.

The next step would be to equalize the pay (at the same rank) of the massive body of women and men teachers. Public school teachers in France were, of course, state employees, as were also women and men in state-run industries including the railways and the *Postes, Télégraphes, et Téléphones* (PTT), not to mention the increasing numbers of female and male employees in the various state ministries.[28] Although unionization was forbidden to state employees, they nevertheless would organize as associations and friendly societies (known as *amicales*) in pursuit of their professional goals. In 1903, a cluster of women teachers, led by Marie Guérin (1864–1945) from Nancy, organized a group that would become the *Fédération Féministe Universitaire de France et des Colonies* (FFU), following the 1903 congress of the *Ligue de l'Enseignement*; at that congress they protested a measure that would raise salaries for teachers while retaining the existing inequality between men's and women's pay at the same rank.[29] As one teacher pointed out to Nelly Roussel in the spring of 1904, "The famous principle of equal pay for equal work should be applied to us first of all."[30] By 1909, the FFU's demand for equal pay was accepted by the *Fédération des Amicales*, but it would only be partially realized by 1913, notwithstanding the supporting letter of the *Conseil National des Femmes Françaises* (CNFF) to the President of the Budget Commission in December 1912.[31]

The FFU's publication, *L'Action féministe*, would carefully track the debates on the equal pay question in the Chamber of Deputies and would reproduce the salient speeches for the benefit of its readers.[32] Significantly, René Viviani was the reporter for the Chamber's budget commission and came out strongly for equal pay for equal work [which is abbreviated in the minutes as "l'E. de T." or "*égalité de traitement*"]. The government, Viviani insisted, must confront the issue head on, and set an example for those major employers who would otherwise hire women in order to undercut

---

[28] See Leslie Page Moch, "Government Policy and Women's Experience; The Case of Teachers in France," *Feminist Studies*, 14:2 (Summer 1988), 301–324, which focuses on governmental efforts to encourage marriage of male and female teachers (rather than on the campaign for equal pay). However, the big issue for women teachers in the 1901–1914 period was equal pay, and this initiative, which succeeded partially in 1913, was spearheaded by the FFU and its publication *L'Action féministe universitaire*. See also Bugnon, "Institutrices," cited in n. 27.

[29] See the account by Marie Guérin, "Historique de la Fédération Féministe Universitaire" (1913), as reproduced in Marguerite Bodin, *L'Institutrice* (Paris: G. Doin, 1922), chapter 5.

[30] Reported by Nelly Roussel, "Impressions de Militante," *L'Action* (8 June 1904); reproduced in Nelly Roussel, *Quelques Lances rompues pour nos libertés* (Paris: V. Giard & E. Briere, 1910), p. 204.

[31] CNFF, letter to the Budget Commission, *L'Action féminine*, n° 25 (December 1912), 426–427.

[32] See *L'Action féministe*, n° 21 (March 1913) and n° 22 (April 1913). The summary provided below comes from this account.

men's pay. Deputies Kerguezec (reporter for the Education commission) and Louis Marin seconded Viviani's claims. Deputy Breton asked for a family supplement, according to the number of children, in case the "E. de T." was enacted. A compromise reached overnight in conciliation committee, however, sacrificed endorsement of the E. de T. principle in exchange for a 300 franc raise for both men and women teachers, which narrowed the pay gap between them but left the principle of equal pay unresolved. The next day the socialist leader and deputy Jean Jaurès publicly upheld the principle and emphasized the moral importance of E. de T., whereas Viviani had to admit that in the previous evening's conciliation committee negotiations meeting he had found it necessary – for the time being – to sacrifice the principle in favor of the raise.

Marthe Pichorel of the FFU was unhappy with this result: it was not about the money, she indicated in *L'Action féministe*, but about the principle of equal pay itself. It was, for her, "a question of dignity, corresponding to a principle of high moral value that interests not only the teachers but all women who live from their work, all women for whom we want a bit more justice."[33] Posing the question "Why Equality?" in the May issue, another FFU activist, J. Méo, went further. "What we care about most is to see the State recognize the legitimacy of our demand [for equal pay]. It is to see the State-boss cease to exploit the work of a woman because she is a woman. What we care about is to work for the emancipation of the entire feminine proletariat, for we have miserable sisters, exploited by private industry, whose sad condition is to die slowly of hunger while working, or to prostitute themselves in order to be able to live." This teacher and union activist considered her group, the FFU, to be the vanguard, the group of women that would establish the principle which would help to improve the fate of other, far less fortunate women.[34] For the time being, these energetic women teachers would have to wait. No French finance law would endorse the principle and practice of complete equal pay for teachers of both sexes – or anyone else – before 1920–1921. In the interim, and for obvious reasons, the women of the FFU would become a force in the pursuit of women's suffrage.[35]

---

[33] Marthe Pichorel, "Réflexions sur le vote de la Chambre," *L'Action féministe*, n° 22 (April 1913), front page.

[34] J. Méo, "Pourquoi l'Égalité?" *L'Action féministe*, n° 23 (May 1913), 1.

[35] This effort among women primary school teachers to attain equal pay apparently did not extend to the teachers and *directrices* in girls' secondary education. Jo Margadant claims that the women in these Amicales, "asked for exactly the same treatment as the state provided men regarding sick leave, promotions, and professional discipline," but that "no one for the moment mentioned salaries." See Margadant, *Madame le Professeur: Women Educators in the Third Republic* (Princeton. NJ: Princeton University Press, 1990), pp. 260–261.

The legislature's reluctance to endorse the principle of equal pay for equal work for teachers hung, to a considerable degree, on its practical financial implications for other state employees – or at least that was the excuse given. The public employees' sector in France was immense and many of its members were women; their sheer numbers had budgetary significance. An FFU pamphlet circulated in 1913 provided numerical evidence of the thousands of women teachers employed by the state – 70,693, to be precise. Moreover, 37,120 women were employed in the administration of departments and communes; 19,466 women worked for the PTT, 15,072 in the *Services et Finances*, and 6,356 for the state railways. In fact, according to the FFU figures, a total of 155,028 women were employees in public services.[36] These impressive figures did not include the twenty-one state-owned and operated factories (state monopolies) that produced matches and tobacco products, and which in 1901 employed 17,140 individuals, of which a staggering 91 percent were women.[37] Other feminists continued to criticize the low wages paid to women by other government agencies in specific locales, such as the government-run mineral water spas.[38] In 1903, the government initiated a thirty-five-day maternity leave for the "*dames employées*" of the PTT, a policy that historian Susan Bachrach indicates was "one of the first of its kind in France, its passage owing much to the intense lobbying efforts of women employees in organized groups."[39]

The French state did not require PTT women or women teachers to resign from their jobs when they married, in contrast to the practices developing in other countries such as Imperial Germany, Switzerland, and

[36] See *Fédération Féministe du Sud-Est (FFSE), Extraits de 3 siècles de féminisme: Condorcet et le "Journal de la Société de 1789": Stuart Mill et "L'assujettissement des femmes". Suivies d'opinions féministes modernes et des Statuts de la Fédération Féministe du Sud-Est* (Lyon: FFSE, 1913), p. 31. This little brochure is sometimes catalogued under the name of Venise Pellat-Finet.

[37] See Marie-Hélène Zylberberg-Hocquard, "Les ouvrières d'État (tabac-allumettes) dans les dernières années du XIXe siècle," *Le Mouvement social*, n° 105 (October–December 1978), 87–107. This article underscores the point that the factories of the state monopolies aimed to manufacture perfect products and to be model employers; they provided full employment, better than average pay, retirement benefits, and even granted a maternity bonus to women workers. The tasks in these factories seem to have been highly sex-segregated, which reinforced disparities of pay between male and female workers.

[38] See *l'Équité*, n° 12 (15 January 1914), 1, for Jeanne Robin's complaint about the poor pay of the *masseuses* at the *Établissements d'Eaux de l'État*, who worked for only four months of the year at very low pay and were expected to supplement this with tips from clients.

[39] See Susan Bachrach, *Dames Employées: The Feminization of Postal Work in Nineteenth-Century France*, published as issue 8 (Winter 1983) of *Women & History*, published by the Institute for Research in History (New York) and The Haworth Press; quote, 81. See also Dominique Bertinotti, "Carrières féminines et carrières masculines dans l'administration des postes et télégraphes à la fin du XIXe siècle," *Annales: E. S. C.*, 40:3 (May–June 1985), 625–640.

The Netherlands. When news reached France of a 1904 Dutch decree evicting married women from government jobs, specifically from teaching and from positions in its postal service, the outcry against it was not limited to the Netherlands. French feminists learned about these dismissals through the network of the ICW. In the *Journal des Femmes*, editor Maria Martin vented her indignation, remarking that "few among the French antifeminists would [even] dare to propose such a radical measure." She insisted that the question of whether a married woman should work was ultimately up to the individual, and that if one tried such an eviction by decree in France, all it would accomplish would be to discourage women from marrying or to force them into clandestine relationships. Martin concluded: "We hope that the example given by the Dutch antifeminists will not inspire the French misogynists."[40] In 1912 Dutch feminists would beat back a fiercer government-initiated measure to exclude married women, but elsewhere such rules remained in place.[41] Female teachers in France were actually encouraged by the government to marry.[42]

Even as the French state slowly began to address the question of equal pay in public sector employment and to provide various perquisites including paid maternity leaves, nursing rooms, etc., inducing private businesses to follow its example would remain a challenge. If (and when) the tasks assigned to each sex were not deemed equal or of equivalent value, how could one justify the case for equal pay? Attitudes would have to change.

Unintended Consequences in the Private Sector: *Travail à Domicile*

French workplace conditions were still very far from rendering possible that "independent, responsible, well-instructed woman worker." The *travailleuses* found themselves in a far better (though far from perfect) position than their poorer compatriots, the *ouvrières*, who could count neither on the parsimonious generosity of the state nor on regular employment that would provide anything close to a living wage. A particularly excruciating, even scandalous new problem that attracted much public attention in the early twentieth century had emerged in France's biggest industry, the garment industry; it was referred to as *travail à domicile*

---

[40] See Maria Martin, "Célibat forcé," in *Le Journal des Femmes*, n° 152 (March 1905), front page.
[41] See Mineke Bosch, "History and Historiography of First-Wave Feminism in the Netherlands, 1860–1922," *Women's Emancipation Movements in the 19th Century: A European Perspective*, ed. Sylvia Paletschek & Bianka Pietrow-Ennker (Stanford, CA: Stanford University Press, 2004), p. 62.
[42] See Moch, "Government Policy and Women's Experience," cited in n. 28.

(sometimes also called *travail au foyer*) or industrial homework (also referred to in English, and sometimes in French, as sweated labor – or the sweating system). Historian Judith Coffin calls it, following a contemporary source, "the factory in the home."[43] In France, as elsewhere, such home-based industry was not covered by the extant labor laws, due to concerns about preserving the sanctity of "the family," by which its defenders almost always meant the male-headed family. That concern notwithstanding, many industrial employers had responded to the legislation limiting women's hours and night work in industry, the ostensibly "protective" legislation of 1892, by decentralizing their labor force; they outsourced piecework to be done by women at home, where their hours could not be monitored. The garment industry, or at least its employers, flourished as never before – on the backs of poor, even desperate, French mothers and their children.

The studies published in the early twentieth century on home-based industry reveal the most appalling work conditions, the most devastating levels of starvation wages, exploited children, high mortality from tuberculosis among the workers, and diseases spread from the workers to consumers via their products.[44] Social investigators at the time overwhelmingly agreed that this resurgence of home-based industry was the unintended consequence of the 1892 law, which had forced many women workers out of the *ateliers* into even more marginal, exploited situations, not only in the cities but also in the French countryside.

---

[43] Judith G. Coffin, *The Politics of Women's Work: The Paris Garment Trades, 1750–1915* (Princeton, NJ: Princeton University Press, 1996), title of Part II, p. 119. The term was used by contemporaries; Coffin (p. 163) references Henri de Boissieu, "L'usine au logis à Lyon et à Sainte-Etienne," *La Quinzaine*, 230 (May 1904).

[44] In chronological order of publication, the important studies on the French sweating system (mostly written by men) are: Charles Benoist, *Les Ouvrières de l'aiguille à Paris: notes pour l'étude de la question sociale* (Paris: L. Chailley, 1895); Albert Aftalion, *Le Développement de la fabrique et le travail à domicile dans les industries de l'habillement* (Paris: L. Larose & L. Tenin, 1906); Paul Pic & A. Amieux, *Le Travail à domicile en France, et spécialement dans la région lyonnaise, rapport présenté à l'Association internationale pour la protection légale des travailleurs, Assemblée de Genève, 1906* (Paris: F. Alcan, 1906); Gabriel-Paul-Othénin, comte d'Haussonville, *Le Travail des femmes à domicile* (Paris: Blond, 1909); Paul Gemaehling, *Travailleurs au rabais; la lutte syndicale contre les sous-concurrences ouvrières* (Paris: Bloud, 1910), esp. pt. II, chapter 2 – "La Concurrence féminine"; Étienne Martin Saint-Léon, *Travail de la femme et de la jeune fille* (Lyon, 1911); and the 700+ page comparative study by Paul Boyaval, *La Lutte contre le sweating system* (Paris: F. Alcan, 1912; orig. a doctoral thesis). Most of these authors were either law students or social investigators engaged in various social action groups, from the Catholic *Action Sociale* and the *Ligue Sociale d'Acheteurs* to the *Association Nationale Française pour la Protection Légale des Travailleurs*. The reports by Edouard Payen in the *Économiste français* throughout these years are also very useful, as are, of course, the official inquiries by the *Office du Travail* and the *Conseil Supérieur du Travail*. On the latter, see Coffin, *Politics of Women's Work*.

Historian Marilyn Boxer confirms that "protective labor laws should be considered among the factors deemed responsible for the marginalization (and impoverishment) of women workers . . . and for the related failures to attend seriously to the unionization of women workers and to provide for the problems of working mothers."[45] In the garment trades, only a select few could earn well. The "queens of the needle trades," as the high-end *couturières* in Paris fashion houses were called, did earn good money, as did the highly skilled artificial flowermakers studied by Boxer.[46] But the majority of seamstresses who made mass-market garments by the piece were abysmally remunerated. Ironically, as Boxer points out, some of these home workers actually defended these developments, preferring to have a little income that would help make ends meet for their families than to having none at all.[47] Not surprisingly, French translations of Thomas Hood's plaintive poem, "The Song of the Shirt" (orig. 1843) found their way into a number of publications that considered the plight of the home workers.[48]

Jules Simon's earlier nostalgic notion that women could best produce for the market in their homes had, by 1901, spawned a colossal nightmare. In her important 1914 report to the ICW Congress in Rome, the feminist social critic and philanthropist Gabrielle Duchêne would estimate (based on the best evidence then available) that there were "more than 850,000 women working at home" in the garment industry alone, and out of a total of home workers of both sexes in all industries, at least 1.2 million women.[49] With this massive shift to piecework done at home, these women's earnings kept on going down compared to what they had been

---

[45] Marilyn J. Boxer, "Protective Legislation and Home Industry: The Marginalization of Women Workers in Late Nineteenth-Early Twentieth-Century France," *Journal of Social History*, 20:1 (Fall 1986), 45–65.

[46] See Marilyn J. Boxer, "Women in Industrial Homework: The Flowermakers of Paris in the Belle Epoque, *French Historical Studies*, 12:3 (Spring 1982), 401–423.

[47] Boxer, "Protective Legislation and Home Industry," p. 53.

[48] Among these: Charles Benoist, *Les Ouvrières de l'aiguille à Paris; notes pour l'étude de la question sociale* (Paris: L. Chailley, 1895); A. de Máday, *Le Droit de la femme au travail* (Paris: Giard & Brière, 1905), p. 133; Mlle A. Couvreur, *La Femme aux différentes époques de l'histoire; conférences faites aux dames égyptiennes* (Le Caire: Université égyptienne, 1910), pp. 587–589; and *L'Équité*, n° 21 (15 June 1914). This list is far from definitive.

[49] See Gabrielle Duchêne, *Le Travail à domicile. Ses misères, ses dangers. Les Causes. Les Moyens d'y remédier* (Paris: Secrétariat de l'Office Français du Travail à Domicile, 1914). 16-page pamphlet. As chair (succeeding Cécile Brunschvicg) of the CNFF's Section on Work, she also presented this as a report, "Le Travail à domicile," to the International Council of Women's meeting in Rome, May 1914; see *Atti del Congresso internazionale femminile, Roma, 16–23 maggio 1914* (Torre Pelice: typografia Alpina di Augusto Coisson, 1915), pp. 144–158. See also *L'Action féminine* [CNFF], n° 34 (June 1914), 644–646.

paid by the hour in the shops, which had never been that much to begin with. This was largely due to the fact that so many women had learned how to sew, that they were competing with one another and driving down their own pay, which was now accorded by the piece. Zylberberg-Hocquard put it bluntly: *"Les Travailleuses à domicile* all share a common trait: they are overexploited; officials as well as unionists and feminists insisted particularly on this fact."[50]

In 1900, at the Droits congress in Paris, feminist-socialists such as Marie Bonnevial had advocated for the right to work, equal pay for equal work, and an eight-hour day. Bonnevial observed in her report that this congress had given first place on its program to questions concerning women's work "because it considers the economic emancipation of woman as the jumping off point and foundation for her total liberation. All misery – intellectual misery, moral misery, as well as physical misery – stems from inadequate pay, which is inequitably fixed for each sex, but especially for woman whose work is shamefully exploited." In fact, she argued, "waged labor [*le salariat*] was the last form of serfdom." The guiding principle for the section, she asserted, must be the "right to life and to personal development [*personnalité*], assured by the right to work, for woman as well as for man."[51] The congress section also endorsed the formation of professional associations, including labor unions, cooperatives, etc. But the issue of *travail à domicile* itself only came up indirectly at this congress, in the form of an appeal to make protective laws apply equally to both sexes.[52] A resolution concerning a minimum wage was voted down. In the next decade, however, the campaign for a minimum wage would be reactivated by new recruits to the cause, including Gabrielle Duchêne (1870–1954), who (after founding the pioneering working women's cooperative, *l'Entre'aide*, mentioned earlier) would appoint herself secretary of the *Office du Travail à domicile*, and in late 1913 would also take over the Section on Work (*Travail*) of the CNFF, succeeding Cécile Brunschvicg (1877–1946) and the *ouvrière* Jeanne Bouvier (1865–1923).

---

[50] Zylberberg-Hocquard, *Féminisme et Syndicalisme*, p. 36.

[51] *Congrès international de la condition et des droits des femmes, 5-8 sept. 1900, questions économiques, morales, et sociales: éducation, législation, droit privé, droit public* (Paris: Impr. des arts et manufactures, 1901), "Rapport de Mlle Marie Bonnevial," pp. 28–39, and the ensuing discussion.

[52] See Judith Coffin's summary of the discussions on women's work at the 1900 Droits Congress, in her *Politics of Women's Work*, pp. 237–239. At that time, there was not sufficient legislative support for a minimum wage bill, but that would change in the next decade, following the outbreak of war.

The immediate problems surrounding home-based piecework would first be addressed by volunteer philanthropic groups. One such group, the *Association Nationale Française pour la Protection Légale des Travailleurs* (ANFPLT) [French National Association for the Legal Protection of Workers, affiliated with the previously mentioned AIPLT], lobbied for a minimum wage for homeworkers (a campaign begun by Count Albert de Mun decades earlier), which would ultimately succeed in 1915. Another innovative effort to raise the miserable pay of home-based seamstresses had begun with the founding of the *Ligue Sociale des Acheteurs* [Consumers' League] in December 1902, thanks to the initiative of Henriette-Jean Brunhes, her husband Jean Brunhes, and their social Catholic associates.[53] Inspired by the Consumers League in New York, the Christian women and men engaged in this action group aspired to assist the workers themselves through bettering their pay. The Ligue did not oppose home work in principle, but insisted that, in the words of Henriette-Jean Brunhes, "In present circumstances [it] is false family work [*pseudo-travail familial*], even more contrary to the moral and physical hygiene of the family than work in the factory, and still more contrary to the interests of women."[54] Because the law of 1892 exempted "family" workshops from regulation, some had become a front for employers with no conscience to avoid the legal restrictions on women's industrial work. The group focused its efforts to help working women in addressing and convincing well-off women consumers to act morally and responsibly by purchasing their goods only from vendors who could show they were paying their seamstresses a living wage and by spreading out their orders through the year – so as to mitigate the pernicious effects for seamstresses of lack of income during the "dead season."

As we have seen in Chapter 6, in 1902, the German feminist and longtime French resident Kaethe Schirmacher weighed in with an extensive study on women's work in France, published by the Musée Social. This study was, however, based on employment statistics from the 1896 census, so did not address the ever-worsening situation of home workers in any detail. Schirmacher, like many of her counterparts, was scandalized by the disproportionately low pay given to women. In her accompanying

[53] See Marie-Emmanuelle Chessel, *Consommateurs engagés à la Belle Époque: La Ligue sociale des acheteurs* (Paris: Presses de Sciences Po, 2012), which is based on the Brunhes papers at the Archives Nationales.

[54] H.-J. [Henriette-Jean] Brunhes, "Les conditions du travail de la femme dans l'industrie," *La Quinzaine*, vol. 57 (1 March 1904), 1–16, on "*travail à l'usine*," and (16 March 1904), 187–210, on "*travail à domicile*"; quote, 208.

article in the *Revue de Morale Sociale*, she did provide comparative findings, and did discuss briefly the question of unregulated *travail à domicile* and its negative effects. Overall, Schirmacher favored sex-specific regulation as the best solution for women workers in the short run.[55] But she also called for the economic evaluation of housework done by women in the home, a concern that would gather momentum in the 1900s. Moreover, she insisted that French women were handicapped not only by marriage laws but also by their political incapacity. This was becoming an all-too-familiar refrain.

Another initiative, which followed up on these earlier works, was the call by the social investigator Caroline Milhaud for an official investigation of *"Travail au foyer."*[56] In the *Revue Politique et Parlementaire* (December 1903), she asked for specifics: How many of these workers are there? What is the average pay? the length of their workday? In 1907 she published the results of her investigation, *L'Ouvrière en France: sa condition présente, les réformes nécessaires,* in which she argued for (additional) state intervention to protect domestic workers. As long as there are socioeconomic classes and antagonism between capital and labor, Milhaud argued, the exploitation of the *ouvrière* would continue. Only with the triumph of socialism, she indicated, would it end.[57] This refrain would be sung over and over again by the advocates of class struggle during the so-called *Belle Époque*.

The republican government was, of course, not interested in fomenting revolution – or class struggle. As we have seen, many of its leading personalities fostered class solidarity and sought solutions of a practical nature to the manifold problems that had arisen in the world of labor. In 1905 its *Office du Travail* (which in later 1906 would become a full-fledged ministry) embarked on its own investigation of industrial homework (the first of several it would sponsor in the next decade) in lingerie production, a category that included a wide range of articles from ladies' nightgowns and undergarments to men's shirts and household linens.[58] Between

---

[55] See Kaethe Schirmacher, *Le Travail des femmes en France* [*Mémoires & Documents*, Suppl. aux *Annales*, Musée Social, n° 6 (May 1902), pp. 321–372] (Paris: Rousseau, 1902), her article "Le Travail des femmes en France," *La Revue (ancienne revue des revues)* (15 February 1902), 395–412, and her overview in "Le Travail des femmes et la protection ouvrière," *La Revue de Morale Sociale*, 4:14 (September 1902), 160–181.

[56] Caroline Milhaud, "De la Nécessité d'une enquête officielle sur le travail à domicile des femmes," *La Revue Politique et Parlementaire* (December 1903), 579–589.

[57] Caroline Milhaud, *L'Ouvrière en France; sa condition présente, les réformes nécessaires* (Paris: F. Alcan, 1907).

[58] See Coffin, *Politics of Women's Work*, p. 143, for the breakdown of products associated with the category "lingerie."

1907 and 1911, the Office published five volumes of findings on conditions in Paris and in the provinces.[59] These included case studies built on interviews of women working in the industry, which have been carefully analyzed by historian Judith Coffin.[60] Investigators found that most of the women homeworkers were either married or widowed; it was the young single women who worked in the better-paying *ateliers*. Coffin has affirmed (reflecting the views of many at the time) that in this field, "the 'marriage bar' structured the female labor market as much as did the gender division of labor."[61] But weren't marriage and real or potential motherhood intrinsic to constituting the gender division of labor in the first place?

Efforts to ameliorate the situation of these poorly paid female domestic laborers would result in some piecemeal reforms. In late October 1906, the new Clemenceau ministry would establish France's first ministry of labor (and social welfare), to be headed by the feminists' great friend René Viviani. Shortly thereafter, the *Ligue Française pour Le Droit des Femmes* (LFDF), now led by Marie Bonnevial (who was also a vice-president of the CNFF) and lawyer-activist Maria Vérone, petitioned the new minister of labor, congratulating him on his new position and asking him to press for two concrete reforms: first, passage of the law that would enable married women to control their own earnings (*L'Avant-Courrière's* long-sought legal initiative, launched in the 1890s), and second, the appointment of women to the councils of *prudhommes*.[62] In July 1907, the first of these finally achieved legislative approval. This was – at least in theory – a big breakthrough, another step toward dismantling the Civil Code's concept of *puissance marital*. It would take some time to work in practice, however, due to doubting officials at banks and savings associations. Once in force, however, the new law removed a significant handicap on a wife's economic empowerment, whether as an *ouvrière* or as a *travailleuse*, as demonstrated in a story told by Louis Delzons about a young married woman, an author who before 1907 had written a novel, but as a wife, had no legal standing and could not sign a contract for publication with an interested Parisian publisher. The young author claimed that her husband would have refused

---

[59] See France, Ministère du Travail, *Enquête sur le travail à domicile dans l'industrie de la lingerie*, 5 vols. (1907–1911).

[60] See Coffin, *Politics of Women's Work*, chapter 5. See also the excellent new study by Colette Avrane, *Ouvrieres à domicile: Le combat pour un salaire minimum sous la Troisième République* (Rennes: Presses Universitaires de Rennes, 2013).

[61] Coffin, *Politics of Women's Work*, p. 148.

[62] "Lettre au Ministre du Travail: A Monsieur René Viviani, ministre du Travail," dated 15 November 1906, signed by Bonnevial as president of the LFDF and Vérone as secretary-general; published in the *LFDF Bulletin Trimestrial*, 2:2 (October 1907), 8.

to sign the contract for her – and, of course, he could have confiscated and spent her royalties as he wished.[63] After the 1907 law passed, this scenario was no longer possible. Indeed, the law had serious practical consequences for married women of all classes, but especially for those who needed to work for pay or who wanted to market their wares and retain ownership in – and control over – the proceeds. It empowered married homeworkers, underpaid as they were; any pittance they earned would remain theirs to keep or spend as they themselves saw fit.[64] Despite this success, the prospects for minimum wage legislation would remain poor.

In conjunction with the new ministry of labor, Marguerite Durand, a close personal friend of Viviani, embarked in the fall of 1906 on a campaign to establish a women's labor bureau (*Office du Travail féminin*). In December the French legislature approved this initiative in principle – but, significantly, did not appropriate funds for its immediate realization.[65] Thus, Durand decided to fund its activities herself, a unprecedented move by a private individual.

As we know from Chapter 6, Marguerite Durand had long concerned herself with problems of women's employment. During the early years of *La Fronde* (1897–1900) she had already begun to foster women's unions, notably in typography, to serve the interests of her women typesetters in face of the opposition of the strongly antifeminist typographers' union, the *Fédération du Livre*. Durand had been brought to court for employing women typesetters at night but the judge had dismissed the case.[66] Unjustly accused of fostering strike-breaking when some members of this women's union journeyed to Nancy in the spring of 1902 to work for union wages in the face of a male typographers' strike at the printing firm Berger-Levrault, the evidence now suggests that the allegation of "scabbing" was false but it nevertheless served at the time to stir up trouble and

---

[63] Louis Delzons, "Contre la puissance maritale," in *Idées modernes*, 1:2 (February 1909), 246–256.

[64] For interpretations of the 1907 law on married women's earnings, see Henri Lalou, *Droits de la femme mariée sur les produits de son travail et les produits du travail de son mari depuis la loi du 13 juillet 1907* (Paris: A. Rousseau, 1909); Bertrand de Lesseps, *Les Droits de la femme mariée sur ses gains et salaires en France et à l'étranger*. Thèse pour le Doctorat (Paris: A. Rousseau, 1910); and Pierre Guyon, *La Femme mariée commerçante sous le régime de la loi du 13 juillet 1907*. Thèse de doctorat, Faculté de Droit, Paris (Paris: A. Rousseau, 1910).

[65] See Elizabeth Coquart, *La Frondeuse: Marguerite Durand, patronne de presse et féministe* (Paris: Payot-Rivages, 2010), chapter 22. The legislature did extend a credit – but for 1908, not 1907. Coquart's account closely follows the account in Jean Rabaut, *Marguerite Durand (1864–1936)* (Paris: L'Harmattan, 1996).

[66] See Maria Martin's account of the trial and the verdict, "La Loi de 1892," *Le Journal des Femmes*, n° 85 (March 1899), front page.

foment distrust.[67] In early 1901, *La Fronde* had provided close coverage of the month-long strike of the Parisian dressmakers and tailors.[68] The all-women's daily would cover women's labor issues until its demise in 1903, but Marguerite Durand, who would continue her journalistic career at *L'Action* and later at *Les Nouvelles*, never lost her focus on issues surrounding women's paid labor. She counted among the many feminists who opposed protective legislation for women workers and who protested against the restrictions placed on wives by the Civil Code.

In March 1907, on behalf of the fledging *Office du Travail féminin* – and again at her own personal expense – Durand organized a congress on women's work, to which she invited union leaders and women workers. It attracted some sixty women's unions and a bevy of women workers who spoke up about their concerns, notably the lack of apprenticeship opportunities for women, the dreadful working conditions they faced, and the prospects for unionization. Attendees at Durand's congress also included the prime minister Georges Clemenceau, the minister of labor Viviani, and the foreign minister Stéphen Pichon, whose presence provided enormous luster and visibility to the proceedings. Durand's congress reintroduced issues that had been on the agenda since 1900 such as equal work for equal pay, the eight-hour day, the *semaine anglaise* (granting women the possibility to leave work Saturday noon instead of working a full day), and the regulation of *travail à domicile*. Not surprisingly, given Durand's staunch opposition to the 1892 labor laws, the congress voted against "protective" legislation for women workers, stipulating that only mothers should benefit from special protection.[69] Despite the hostility of male union leaders and a part of the press, Durand's biographers consider the congress to have succeeded.[70] Durand would continue to lead the charge against protective

---

[67] For details and analysis see François Chaignaud, *L'Affaire Berger-Levrault: le féminisme à l'épreuve (1897–1905)* (Rennes: Presses Universitaires de Rennes, 2009). See also the earlier analysis by Joan Wallach Scott, "Féministes contre syndicalistes dans l'industrie typographique: Guerre des sexes ou lutte des classes?" in *Militantisme et histoire (Mélanges offerts à Rolande Trempé)*, ed. Marie-Danielle Demélas & Alain Boscus (Toulouse: Presses Universitaires de Mirail, 2000), pp. 181–198.

[68] See *La Fronde*, issues of 18, 20, 23, 27 February 1901 (n°s 1167, 1169, 1172, & 1176).

[69] On this congress, see Rabaut, *Marguerite Durand*, p. 100; also Klejman & Rochefort, *L'Égalité en marche*, pp. 242–245. Madeleine Guilbert, *Les Femmes et l'organisation syndicale avant 1914: présentation et commentaires de documents pour une étude du syndicalisme féminin* (Paris: Éditions du CNRS, 1966), pp. 401–403, discusses the hostility of some worker's press publications to Durand's initiative.

[70] Rabaut, *Marguerite Durand*, pp. 99–102; Coquart, *La Frondeuse*, pp. 205–208, emphasizing Durand's personal involvement. Of interest is the fact that the *Journal des Femmes* appears to have published no coverage of Durand's 1907 congress during the spring months.

legislation at the CNFF-organized Tenth International Congress of Women in 1913.

Gabrielle Duchêne pioneered one hopeful approach to the problem of *travail à domicile* in the Parisian garment-making sector, founding in 1908 a small production cooperative called *L'Entre'Aide* [Helping One Another]. Its objective was to eliminate the intermediaries (notably sub-contractors), and to sell the women's products made in a local workshop/boutique directly to consumers at prices that would provide a good living for the women who did the sewing. According to historian Colette Avrane, however, it never attained the success its founder had hoped for, since prospective buyers continued to seek bargains in the big stores.[71]

Duchêne then turned to working with a quasi-official *Office Français du Travail à Domicile*, headed by the law professor Roger Picard; as secretary-general of this organisation, she promoted legislation for a minimum wage for home workers.[72] It was in conjunction with this effort that she drew closer to the women of the CNFF and in 1913 became head of its *Section du Travail*. As Duchêne (on behalf of the CNFF) put it, in her oft-quoted report to the 1914 ICW Quinquennial Congress in Rome, "The mass of homeworkers constitutes a labor reserve that is 'almost indefinitely com-pressible' and permits the bosses to remain the masters in decisions about salary."[73] In her thinking, only a legislated minimum wage could amelior-ate this situation.

Unionization of Women Workers and the Quest for Equal Pay

Unionization was another strategy being promoted heavily by feminist activists during this first decade of the twentieth century. Marguerite Durand was by no means alone in fostering labor unions for women workers. In fact, the slow acceleration of their unionization would mark a big step forward in the world of women's employment. In her wonder-fully documented study of women's unionization before 1914, Madeleine Guilbert attests to considerable progress in organizing women after 1900, but remarks (in her conclusions) the tensions that continued to exist between male and female workers, the strikes by men's unions against the employment of women and opposition to their entering unions, and

---

[71] See Avrane, *Ouvrières à domicile*, pp. 126–130.
[72] The *Office Français du Travail à Domicile* should not be confused with Marguerite Durand's pet project, the *Office du Travail Féminin*, discussed earlier.
[73] Gabrielle Duchêne, "Le Travail à domicile," in *Atti del Congresso internazionale femminile, Roma, 16–23 maggio 1914* pp. 144–158; quote, p. 151.

the fact that women's actual participation in strikes and/or in union leadership remained minimal.[74] Subsequent studies, such as those by Marie-Hélène Zylberberg-Hocquard (1979), Joceline Chabot (2003), and Sandra Salin (2014) testify to the complexities of organizing women workers in various French trades.[75] In certain industrial centers in the provinces, however, women workers did participate in strike actions, including the 1900 general strike in the knitting center of Troyes, without as yet being union members, though many seem to have joined during that dispute. Historian Helen Chenut reports that subsequent to this strike there were great fluctuations in women's membership in the mixed-sex, industry-wide union in Troyes, the *Association syndicale des ouvriers et ouvrières de toutes les professions se rattachant à la bonneterie*, and a serious falling off after 1905.[76]

In 1900, the Parisian Mme A. Blanche-Schweig organized a white-collar union of women cashiers, accountants, and employees (*Syndicat des Femmes Caissières, Comptables employées aux Écritures et Employées du Commerce*, according to her visiting card). She soon became active in the CNFF and the LFDF, and had intervened with the government on the question of equal pay for men and women teachers. Blanche-Schweig would also publish in *La Française*, where, in an article on women's unions, she posed the question, "Who has the right to pay women less than men?" Disputing the oft-repeated argument that women had fewer needs than men, she staked a claim for comparable needs. She focused on the question of teachers' pay, insisted on the equivalence of the credentials required as well as on their personal needs, and, often, their need to support others (parents, siblings, etc.). The same criteria apply to (female) *employées* and *ouvrières*, she said. "If the work is well-executed," Blanche-Schweig indicated, it is that which should be remunerated, not the sex of the executor." To develop a sense of the value of their work and to combat

---

[74] See Guilbert, *Femmes et l'organisation syndicale avant 1914*.

[75] See Marie-Hélène Zylberberg-Hocquard, *Féminisme et syndicalisme en France* (Paris: Éditions Anthropos, 1978), and Zylberberg-Hocquard, *Femmes et féminisme dans le mouvement ouvrier français* (Paris: Éditions ouvrières, 1981). On the Catholic initiatives to unionize women, beginning in Lyon, then in Paris, see Joceline Chabot, *Les Débuts du syndicalisme féminin chrétien en France, 1899–1944* (Lyon: Presses Universitaires de Lyon, 2003). See also Sandra Salin, *Women and Trade Unions in France: The Tobacco and Hat Industries* (Bern: Peter Lang, 2014). I was surprised to find that there were no studies addressing issues of women workers and secular unionization before 1914 in *Syndicats et associations: concurrence ou complémentarité?*, ed. Danielle Tartakowsky, with Françoise Tétard (Rennes: Presses Universitaires de Rennes, 2006).

[76] See, for example, Helen Chenut's masterful study of Troyes, *The Fabric of Gender: Working-Class Culture in Third Republic France* (University Park: Pennsylvania State University Press, 2005), esp. chapter 1, and pp. 144–147.

exploitation by the employer [*le patron*], and wages of famine, women workers must not remain in isolation. In groups, women could improve their social education and discuss the economic and professional issues that concern them. To some degree, she explained, the present situation was women's own fault; they needed to develop the "spirit of association." With respect to homeworkers, she indicated, the potential for association was thwarted because of their isolation. Joining unions would give women the strength to fight for just pay, to have confidence in themselves, and to develop the courage to fight back.[77] In short, Blanche-Schweig envisioned unionization as a means of empowerment for women who worked for pay.

Another early effort on which we have only bits and pieces of information is the attempt by the writer and exposition organizer Pauline Savari to unionize women of letters (those who did mostly anonymous hack work and thus did not qualify for membership in the *Société des Gens de Lettres*) and lyric artists (singers), in a *Fédération féministe: Union des syndicats professionnels de femmes*.[78] Following her "Appeal to Women," published in *Voltaire* in early December 1900, she also founded a short-lived periodical *L'Abeille*, which began publication in January 1901.[79] The first issue featured Savari's rejoinder to Marguerite Durand's snide criticism in *La Fronde* of her unionization efforts, especially as concerned singers, whom Durand referred to disparagingly as "sluts [*les grues*] of the café-concert." The two exchanged insults in their respective publications. A more revealing article published in the first issue of *L'Abeille* was a letter of support from Mme Blanche-Schweig, in which she intimated that the women she and Savari were attempting to organize were subject to constant sexual harassment from bosses; they should be able to support themselves and keep their jobs without having to submit to employers' sexual demands. This, too, was a major objective of such unions for working women in 1901. In 1902 Savari and her associates organized an international exposition of women's arts and crafts, but little further information on her efforts seems to be available.

In late November 1900, the *Groupe Féministe Socialiste* (formed following the death of Aline Valette by Louise Saumoneau [1879–1950]) organized a union of seamstresses. Called the *Chambre Syndicale des*

---

[77] A. Blanche-Schweig, "Syndicats Féminins," *La Française*, n° 57 (24 November 1907), lead editorial.
[78] See Klejman & Rochefort, *L'Égalité en marche*, pp. 240–243.
[79] Savari's "appeal" was republished in *L'Abeille*, n° 1 (20 January 1901), 3. This publication published at least four issues. The microfiche from the Bidelman Collection at Stanford contains only the first two issues, but Marilyn Boxer located a copy of a fourth issue, dated 1 March 1901 at the Institute for Social History in Amsterdam.

Travailleuses de l'Aiguille [Women's Needleworkers' Union], it was initially intended for needleworkers engaged in sweated labor, but following the divisive strike of shop-based tailors and seamstresses in May 1901, its members disbanded in favor of joining the men's union. *L'Abeille* indicates that Saumoneau served as its secretary-general.[80]

Concerning the failure of the socialist women's group efforts, Charles Sowerwine has remarked that "the problem of the twentieth century was not doctrine but organisation."[81] This was also true of efforts to organize women workers into the other newly forming political parties and into unions, either all-women's unions or mixed unions. Indeed, many men's unions continued to express hostility to the notion of women-only unions, even as they seemed unwilling to invite women working in the trades to join theirs. The debates of the decade (especially the Couriau Affair in 1913, which we will discuss at greater length) amply reveal the frustration of those who were attempting to unionize women workers. Not the least of the issues would be that the centennial celebration of Proudhon in 1909 would rekindle the antifeminist objections of many male union members and leaders who objected to women's presence in the workforce, especially if they were wives.

Less well known is the fact that in 1906–1907, the CNFF's Section on Work joined the effort to encourage the unionization of women workers. Under the leadership of Marie Pégard, members of the section organized a series of educational lectures to promote unionization, which they coproduced in Paris with the *Société Républicaine des Conférences Populaires* during the fall of 1906 and spring of 1907. The Section also produced a small two-page handout laying out a definition of labor unions, indicating their goals, the facts concerning unionization in France (at the time unionized women represented only 8.56 percent of organized workers) and called on working women to get involved and campaign for women's economic independence.[82]

---

[80] See *L'Abeille*, n° 2 (February 1901), 3.   [81] Sowerwine, *Sisters or Citizens*, pp. 89–91; quote p. 98.

[82] See the report of Marie Pégard for the Section du Travail in *Conseil National des Femmes Françaises … Quatrième Assemblée Générale Publique, le 7 juillet 1907* (Paris: CNFF, n.d.), pp. 41–51, esp. pp. 48–51. See also the *Journal des Femmes*, n° 174 (May 1907), 1–2, reporting on the CNFF meeting of 5 May, and the insert, "Conférences féministes," on 3. The flier announcing these lectures on "Les Femmes et l'Esprit d'Association (Syndicats)" is posted on the website for the Paris Municipal Libraries/Bibliothèque Marguerite Durand. The CNFF Section du Travail's small handout (printed on cardstock), "Les Syndicats Ouvriers," is reproduced in Zylberberg-Hocquard, *Féminisme et syndicalisme*, as document n° 5, pp. 301–303, but this author dates it as 1908 or 1910. The evidence from the CNFF records indicates that it was first drafted and distributed in early 1907. An example can be consulted in BMD 396 CON.

Jean Rabaut recounts that following Durand's 1907 congress, the race was on to unionize women; the *Confédération Générale du Travail* (CGT) even launched an "ephemeral" committee to promote feminist syndicalist action.[83] But it would take many years for unionization to make much of an impact among women workers. Madeleine Pelletier sourly observed in July 1912 that the problem was, in part, due to the fact that married women workers carried the double burden of housework in addition to their long days of paid labor; they had no time to participate in union organization and militancy.[84] In July 1913, the teacher and union organizer Marie Guillot could still point to the "almost insurmountable difficulties" that stood in the way of women's unionization.[85] By December 1913, another well-informed commentator, the novelist and journalist Louise Compain, would mourn the failure of women's union organizing in Paris.[86]

In early 1909, however, the prospects for women's unionization seemed more promising. Louise Compain would publish (in the new periodical *Idées modernes*) the initial results of an important survey of women's unionization, based on her personal investigation of extant French trade unions [*syndicats*] and their attitudes towards women's work.[87] Under the rubric "*Le Féminisme au XXe siècle*," her serialized account provided a detailed analysis of recent developments, union by union, mixed and single-sex alike. In the first part she paid particular attention to the objections of the *Fédération du Livre*, the jeweler's union, and the shoe-makers' union, in which male adherents continued to insist that women belonged in the home and not in their shops (even with equal pay). Those men seemed deaf to the arguments that all women were not married and could not marry since they outnumbered the men. Compain reported that the response of the working men to her claims that women must have a profession in order to have some independence was simply that "not all men are brutes, and women should simply change their man" if her

[83] Jean Rabaut, *Marguerite Durand*, p. 102.

[84] Madeleine Pelletier, "La Class ouvrière et le féminisme," *La Suffragiste*, n° 30 (July 1912), 1–3; also consultable on the website of Marie-Victoire Louis, www.marievictoirelouis.net. Pelletier proposed that working-class men treat their wives as equals and pitch in by sharing housework and cooking. "Remember" had advocated the same solution in an earlier issue, n° 25 (February 1912).

[85] Marie Guillot, "La Femme hors du Foyer," *La Vie ouvrière*, n° 91 (5 July 1913), 1–15; quote, 11. Partially reproduced in Albistur & Armogathe, *Grief des femmes*, vol. 2, pp. 130–132. An earlier Guillot article, "Les Femmes et l'action dans la vie publique," dated July 1912, is reproduced in *Fédération Féministe du Sud-Est* (FFSE), *Extraits de 3 siècles de féminisme*, pp. 24–28.

[86] L.-M. Compain, "L'Initiation sociale de la femme: Histoire d'un échec," *La Grande Revue* (25 December 1913), 816–824 ["Pages Libres," n° 554, 760–768].

[87] See L.-M. Compain, "Le Féminisme au XXe siècle," *Idées modernes*, I, n° 1 (January 1909), 149–159, & n° 2 (February 1909), 339–352.

current man was being violent. As Compain remarked in exasperation, "The entire antifeminist doctrine of the workingman is contained in these words."[88] She noted that a young woman worker who was listening to this exchange protested; this action personified, for Compain, "the budding revolt of woman against the theory that has so long held her in slavery."[89] She went on to discuss the unions where women and men cooperated, as well as the exclusively female unions. The hatmakers' union [*Syndicat des Chapeliers*], in contrast to those discussed previously, had unionized a significant number of women, included them in their governing council, and held assiduously to the formula of equal pay for equal work. The gardeners' union [*Syndicat des Jardiniers*], included both the *fleuristes* [florists] and the unfortunate *maraîchères* [garden workers], who performed hard physical labor for up to fifteen hours per day and were very poorly paid. In January 1909 Compain participated in the "*Libres Entretiens*" session, sponsored by the *Union de la Vérité*, that addressed the question of competition of women's work with men's work.[90]

In 1910 Louise Compain would publish these articles from *Idées modernes* in book form. Entitled *La Femme dans les organisations ouvrières*, Compain dedicated the volume to Marguerite Durand.[91] In this book the author affirmed the support of so-called bourgeois feminism for women's right to work and to enter every profession for which their qualifications entitled them. She then called for the vote, as the "most effective weapon in [women's] combat for life, without which every other claim would not be granted for a very long time."[92]

In conclusion, Compain optimistically characterized women's entry into the industrial labor force as a "practical feminism" that would "irresistibly" lead to their economic emancipation. Labeling it as such, she said, was justified by the violence of the attacks against it by men such as the author and anarchist activist Georges Deherme (a founder of the short-lived popular university movement) – who surely had claimed the title of

---

[88] Compain, "Féminisme au XXe siècle," part 1, p. 158.

[89] Compain, "Féminisme au XXe siècle," part 1, p. 159.

[90] Historian Jean Elisabeth Pedersen is currently engaged in a study of the "Libres Entretiens." For the first fruits of this work, see her article, "'Speaking Together Openly, Honestly, and Profoundly': Men and Women as Public Intellectuals in Early-Twentieth-Century France," *Gender & History*, 26:1 (April 2014), 36–51.

[91] L.-M. Compain, *La Femme dans les organisations ouvrières* (Paris: V. Giard & E. Brière, 1910), 148 pages.

[92] Compain, *Femme dans les organisations ouvrières*, quote from the author's Introduction, p. 8. Compain would become an activist in the *Union Française pour le Suffrage des Femmes*, and would represent that organization to the CNFF.

antifeminist. She summarized the three principal (and by now highly repetitive) arguments of the "anti's" against women's employment: 1) women's industrial work effectively lowers the wages of men, which is harmful to women themselves; 2) women's work in unhealthy workshops is dangerous not only to the woman but to the race; and 3) women's work outside the home leads to the "disorganization" of the family – the men taking refuge in the cabaret, the children thrown out into the street to become juvenile delinquents. In sum, opponents insisted that women should not become competitors with men for jobs, but should stick with their role as guardians of the household and mother-educators.

Compain's solution was twofold: women should receive equal pay for equal work, but in addition work tasks should be divided "according to the capacities of each sex." For instance, women were well suited for cutting shoe leather and for setting type, both of which paid well and allowed them to sit down. Why, she queried, couldn't print shops provide washing facilities for both sexes to mitigate their exposure to lead? Why couldn't Parisian print shops hire women as proofreaders, which didn't entail any lead exposure? Why couldn't women who work in fatiguing or dangerous jobs be provided with a paid maternity leave (as had been granted to the state workers in tobacco and match production)? Even sewing had its hazards for women's health, Compain asserted. Should mothers, then, be sustained by the collectivity, as the socialists advocated? Like her predecessor Paule Mink, Compain restated the feminists' arguments: "The woman should work, like the man, with the same pay as he gets, not only because she needs to eat or to feed others, as he does, but because she has the right to the full independence of a free being. *Earning one's living is a guarantee of dignity.*"[93]

However, almost to a man, the workers Compain spoke with opposed the employment of married women, who, they believed, had important, and equivalently valuable work to do in the household and with the children. Compain conceded the point about the value of women's work in the working-class household (so eloquently stated decades earlier by Flora Tristan and more recently by Kaethe Schirmacher). Other male respondents objected that living conditions being so unhealthy, it would be better not to spend much time in lodgings; still others advocated communal solutions, including communal childrearing. Compain reported that the married women workers she had interviewed all said that they did not go out to industrial workplaces by choice and would

---

[93] Compain, *Femme dans les organisations ouvrières*, p. 134. Emphasis in original.

rather stay home. But, she argued, if they did stay home, they ought not take on additional homework (sweated labor), tasks that would drive down the pay of single women and thus inadvertently force them into prostitution.

Louise Compain proposed three short-term actions that could provide solutions: to increase union propaganda for women workers in the mixed unions, to advocate for equal pay, and to create within each mixed union a women's section that could work with the men's section on finding a better distribution of labor within the *métier*. Women should have the work that "requires the most skill and agility with less expense of muscular force." But men had taken over many of these less taxing jobs. How unsuitable it was, Compain remarked (here echoing the long-standing complaints of Julie-Victoire Daubié and other earlier French critics) to see men selling hats, ribbons, scarves, and gloves to women. Women themselves should discuss the problems in their union sections and arrive at suitable solutions. They should study the issue of half-time work at the same rates as full-time work. They could propose these solutions to the unions, and to the *Union des syndicats*. The unions should address the problem of women's poor pay in the garment trades and incorporate the home workers. Finally, Compain said, the unions should insist that their members not allow women in their households to do poorly paid piecework. But most importantly, she called on the working men [*les ouvriers*] to recognize that their wives are their "associates," not their competitors or their servants, and that their interests are "*solidaires.*" Women who are economically independent, she argued, can be better companions, better counselors, and more capable mothers. She called on the state to provide vocational instruction for girls, especially girls in the provinces, as a capstone to the primary education that would assure their independence. Echoing the concerns of Gabrielle Duchêne, with whom she had worked closely at the cooperative *L'Entr'Aide*, Compain stated that the Ministry of Labor should investigate the possibilities for instituting a minimum wage; without this, Compain insisted, it would be "impossible" to improve the pay for homework. In addition, the state should provide financial encouragement and support to the aspiring women's production cooperatives.

The point, ultimately, Louise Compain assured her readers, was to "shape an independent, responsible, well-instructed woman worker," a woman who with these attributes would be even more womanly than before. It is less important to make predictions about the future form of society, she insisted, than to assure that it should be "just, moral, happy, insofar as a woman will be free through her work and honored in her family functions."[94]

Compain would publish much more on the question of poor women who had to work to survive. Perhaps the most widely circulated of these would be her columns on feminism and economics in the daily *La Petite République*, beginning in mid-January 1912, and, in particular, her moving novel (also 1912) *La Vie tragique de Geneviève*, about a young widow, a starving homeworker whose eighteen-hour days as a seamstress did not pay enough to support herself and her two little daughters; out of sheer desperation, this woman killed her children (and attempted her own suicide), and was tried for murder.[95] Compain also published a series of articles in *La Grande Revue* ("Pages Libres") in 1912–1913 addressed at the issues facing the slightly less desperate middle-class women who wanted to – or needed to – find jobs or to contribute to the betterment of society. In one of these articles, Compain would attribute the failures of the various initiatives addressed to women workers (by educated women) to the overall absence of a sense of social solidarity and mutual responsibility among French women of all classes (as compared to their counterparts in England, the United States, and Germany), and among young women, an appalling ignorance of and disinterest in economic issues.[96] Compain would subsequently produce the report on protective legislation for the 1913 international women's congress in Paris, which advocated the continuation of protective legislation for women. At the behest of Marguerite Durand, who strongly opposed differential legislation, the congress would vote to override the Compain report's resolution.

Many others published on these questions as well.[97] What is important to underscore here, however, is the effort made by a number of French feminists not only to address the problems and issues of women workers, but thereby to invite working women into the feminist camp. Madeleine Pelletier, however, was skeptical about the feminists' prospects for success:

---

[94] Compain, *Femme dans les organisations ouvrières*, p. 146.

[95] Compain's novel, *La Vie tragique de Geneviève*, was published by Calmann-Lévy in 1912. See Jane Misme's glowing tribute, "Geneviève ou l'Ouvrière à domicile," *La Française*, n° 243 (9 June 1912), front page. Misme characterizes the author as the first woman novelist to address feminist issues head-on and to participate actively in the women's movement. Excerpts would subsequently appear in *L'Équité*, n° 4 (15 May 1913) and n° 5 (15 June 1913).

[96] Louise Compain, "L'Initiation sociale de la femme," *La Grande Revue* (25 December 1913), 816–824, esp. 816–817.

[97] In 1912 alone, besides Boyaval's magistral *Lutte contre le sweating system* (cited in n. 44), see Marguerite Gemaehling, *Le Salaire féminin* (Paris: Bloud, 1912), and Maurice Guerrier, *Le Salaire de la femme: Ses conséquences sociales et économiques*. Thèse pour le doctorat, Faculté de Droit, Paris (Paris: Impr. H. Jardin, 1912).

"The working class will be the last to come over to feminism. This is in the natural order of things; ignorant folks only respect brute force and one wastes one's time in wanting to interest them by presenting the spectacle of feminine intelligence crushed by the law of man."[98] It did not help that the feminists' efforts to attract working class women, in particular, were staunchly opposed by the socialist women such as Suzanne Lacore (known as Suzon) and Louise Saumoneau, who had embraced the Clara Zetkin line.[99]

When one looks at the so-called *Belle Époque* through the prism of the plight of working women, it is justifiable to ask what, indeed, could be considered "belle" about this "époque"? Jules Simon's 1860s vision of the happy French housewife producing wares at home in her spare time to earn a little extra money had turned into a nightmare with a cast of millions. The "woman question" in its new economic guise, was threatening to become the number one obsession of France. But, of course, the woman question is not and never was only a question about women. The sweating system of industrial homework threatened not only the future of poor women and children, but also the health and well-being of men, women, and children (born or unborn), and with that, the very future of the nation. Even the reticent felt that there was no option but government intervention, particularly on the questions of a minimum wage, addressing the unhygienic conditions in urban slums, confronting alcoholism (which would garner increasing concern from social reformers and feminists in the decade we are examining here), and providing working-class girls with a more applied education and especially with expanded apprenticeship opportunities. But in France, the struggle for social welfare solutions to these problems by legislators would be slow and immensely painful.

Do Women (Especially Wives) Have a Right to Work?
The Question of Work-Life Balance for Middle-Class Women in the Liberal Professions and the Arts

What of the small elite of "exceptional" women, including (but not limited to) university educated professional women – the physicians, the newly empowered lawyers, or the professors? Or the journalists, the novelists,

---

[98] Pelletier, "La Class ouvrière et le féminisme" (see n. 84).

[99] See Sowerwine on Saumoneau and the *Groupe des Femmes Socialistes*, in chapter 6 in *Sisters or Citizens? Women and Socialism in France since 1876* (Cambridge, UK: Cambridge University Press, 1982).

artists, and actresses? Such women were still relatively few and far between, but the fact that they worked to support themselves, rather than being supported by husbands, still engendered controversy. When they worked for pay in public venues in particular, they were singled out for comment. Some combined their professional interests with marriage and children, though many others did not. Some, though certainly not all, became feminist activists. There were some prominent examples of very successful working women: the distinguished actress Sarah Bernhardt (1844–1923) ranks high on the list, along with the somewhat younger investigative journalist Séverine (1855–1929). The physician-activist Blanche Edwards-Pilliet (1858–1941) had broken through the barriers to medical internship, practiced medicine, and became an important feminist activist; a widow since 1898, she was raising three children in the interstices of her medical practice. The Polish-born Marie Curie (1867–1934), educated at the Sorbonne, co-Nobel laureate in 1903 (with her husband Pierre Curie) in physics, successor to her late husband's chair in physics at the Sorbonne, Nobel laureate again in chemistry in 1911, and mother of two gifted daughters, achieved celebrity status. The sculptresses Mme Léon Bertaux (1825–1909), founder of the *Union des Femmes Peintres et Sculpteurs*, and Camille Claudel (1864–1943) were well known. The writer Daniel Lesueur (pseud. of Jeanne Loiseau, later Lapauze [1860–1921]), whose novels examined women's plight (and who thought that women still needed men's protection), was awarded the *Légion d'Honneur* in 1900, as was also the prolific progressive novelist Marie-Louise Gagneur in 1901.[100] The venerable Juliette Adam (1836–1936), who had combatted Proudhon's misogynism as a young woman, had founded and for many years directed *La Nouvelle Revue*, and who was publishing her memoirs in the first years of the twentieth century, symbolized the continuity of a tradition of highly visible, outspoken, and successful working women.[101]

Women of the next generation were beginning to make their mark. Maria Vérone (1874–1938) wrote for *La Fronde*, passed her *bac*, studied for a law degree and became the fifth woman to join the French bar. In 1908, this divorced mother of two acquired a second husband (Georges

---

[100] In 1891 Marie-Louise Gagneur challenged the *Académie Française* to feminize the names of the skilled crafts [*métiers*]. See Claudie Baudino, "Une Initiative inaboutie mais prémonitoire" *LHT*, N° 7, Documents, publié le 01 janvier 2011 [online]: URL: www.fabula.org.lht/7/index/php?id= 177. Consulted 5 November 2012.

[101] For a comparative perspective on such distinguished French women, see Linda L. Clark, *Women and Achievement in Nineteenth-Century Europe* (Cambridge, UK: Cambridge University Press, 2008).

Lhermitte) and soon became a highly successful defense attorney as well as a strenuous campaigner for juvenile courts and for the vote.[102] The energetic young writer and free spirit who came to be known simply as Colette (1873–1954) earned her keep, ghostwriting naughty novels for her first husband, then branching out to work as a music hall performer and cohabiting with a wealthy lesbian before marrying the powerful editor of *Le Matin*, Henri de Jouvenal, in 1912, with whom she bore a daughter. Although her first signed novel, *La Vagabonde*, was published in 1910, the bulk of her literary work would appear only after 1914.

An important feature of the first decade of the twentieth century was the publication of best-selling novels by women of this new generation that would explore the perils and problems of the professional woman in relation to the work-family conflict.[103] In 1900, Gabrielle Reval published *Les Sèvriennes*, to analyze the training, lives, and emotions of the gifted young women who would become the professors in charge of training other women professors to teach in the secular girls' *lycées*. Unlike their celibate Catholic predecessors, some are torn between the demands of their vocation and their desire to live a "normal" life.[104] As one critic (Jules Case) put it, in considering Reval's novel, "Solitude is awful for a man; it is impossible for a woman."[105]

Of particular significance for the debates on the woman question are the novels of Marcelle Tinayre (1870–1948), who took her *bac* at the age of 17, married young to an engraver (whose mother had been a Communard), and would bear four children; she also published regularly in *La Fronde*. Her novels began with *La Rançon* (1894, 1898), *Avant l'Amour* (1896), *Hellé* (1899), and *La Maison du Péché* (1902; considered by some to be her masterpiece), and would peak with her best-selling 1905 "new woman"

---

[102] On Vérone's contributions, see Sara L. Kimble, "No Right to Judge: Feminism and the Judiciary in Third Republic France," *French Historical Studies* 31:4 (Fall 2008), 609–641, and Kimble, "Feminist Lawyers and Legal Reform in Modern France, 1900–1946," in *Women in Law and Lawmaking in Nineteenth and Twentieth-Century Europe*, ed. Eva Schandevyl (Farnham, Surrey, UK: Ashgate, 2014), pp. 45–73.

[103] Waelti-Walters has published a pioneering analysis of these novels in *Feminist Novelists of the Belle Epoque* (Bloomington: Indiana University Press, 1990); see especially chapter 6: "Profession: Struggles and Solitude." Juliette M. Rogers has followed up with a very interesting study of eleven of these novels (by Colette, Gabrielle Reval, Colette Yver, Marcelle Tinayre, Louise Compain, & Esther de Suze), focusing on the work-family conflicts; see her *Career Stories: Belle Epoque Novels of Professional Development* (University Park: Penn State University Press, 2007), on which I have relied here.

[104] Gabrielle Reval, *Les Sèvriennes* (Paris: P. Ollendorff, 1900).

[105] Jules Case, "Les Idées et les faits," *La Nouvelle Revue* (15 May 1901), 294–298; quote, 298.

novel, *La Rebelle*.[106] Even the skeptical literary critic for the *Revue des Deux Mondes*, René Doumic, had to admit in 1906 that Tinayre was no run-of-the-mill romance writer but had achieved the status of an *écrivain*.[107] This was high praise indeed, although Doumic deliberately left off the *e* (which would have "feminized" the word as *écrivaine*). If any woman writer of the *Belle Époque* seemed headed for inclusion in the canon of French literature, it was certainly Tinayre.[108] An English critic would report in 1908 that "among modern novelists [in France] none is more widely read than Marcelle Tinayre."[109] She just missed, by her own insouciance, being named a chevalier of the Legion of Honor.[110]

Tinayre's *La Rebelle* provided readers with a psychologically penetrating analysis of one middle-class woman's tortuous effort to "be free" to pursue her own ideal of happiness. (If Ibsen had written a sequel to *A Doll's House*, it might have read something like *La Rebelle*.) The heroine, Josanne Valentin (who works at a feminist women's magazine, supporting herself and her invalid husband, and who has a child with her lover before she becomes a widow and meets her true love), would not fit my definition of a feminist (or indeed the definition of the time), but she was certainly engaged in an argument with herself and other women and men about how to "free herself from social shackles, from the prejudices that prevented her from earning her keep," as she put it. But, as Josanne also observed, it was another matter for a woman to cut free of herself; "a woman who has 'a man in her blood' belongs in a servile fashion to that man," a trap that she hoped to avoid. In fact, the principal feminist in the

---

[106] On Tinayre's novels, see Waelti-Walters, *Feminist Novelists*, and, most recently, Mélanie Collado, *Colette, Lucie Delarue-Mardrus, Marcelle Tinayre: Emancipation et Résignation* (Paris: L'Harmattan, 2003); France Grenaudier-Klijn, *Une Littérature de circonstance: Texte, hors-texte et ambiguïté générique à travers quatre romans de Marcelle Tinayre* (London & New York: Peter Lang, 2004); and Rogers, *Career Stories*. Contemporary evaluations include: Winifred (Whale) Stephens, "Marcelle Tinayre, 1877, " *French Novelists of Today*, 2nd series (London & New York: John Lane, 1915), pp. 45–94; and Benjamin M. Woodridge, *The Novels and Ideas of Madame Marcelle Tinayre, Bulletin of the University of Texas*, n° 6 (25 January 1915). 24 pp.

[107] René Doumic, "Romans de femmes," *Revue des Deux Mondes*, 33:2 (15 May 1906), 447–458, esp. 450. The bulk of this review-essay concerns Tinayre's novels, though it also references works by Anna de Noailles and Gérard d'Houville.

[108] See France Grenaudier-Klijn, "Omission ou exclusion? Marcelle Tinayre et le canon littéraire," *Voix plurielles*, 8:2 (2011), 65–78.

[109] Violet Stuart Wortley, "Feminism in England and France," *The National Review*, 51 (March–August 1908), 789–799; quote, 798.

[110] Tinayre's nomination was withdrawn after she publicly ridiculed the honor. A dossier on this affair appeared in *Le Censeur politique et littéraire*, n° 3 (1908), 65–94. See the analyses by Gabrielle Houbre, "L'Honneur perdu de Marcelle Tinayre," in *Les Ratés de la littérature* (Tusson, Charente: Du Lérot, 1999), pp. 89–101, and Rachel Mesch, "A Belle Epoque Media Storm: Gender, Celebrity, and the Marcelle Tinayre Affair," *French Historical Studies*, 35:1 (Winter 2012), 93–121.

story is the new lover, Noël, who had published a book *La Travailleuse* in which he addressed the challenges facing women who must work for a living. Another is a single woman, Mlle Bon, an older employee at the magazine. Tinayre's point in the novel was to demonstrate that her rebel heroine was in revolt against society and its constraints but not against "nature," and that a woman and a man together could build a true, richer type of partnership.

La Rebelle was controversial for several reasons, among them that Josanne had an affair while still married to her disabled husband and bore a child by the lover. It provided a "happy ending" when the heroine found love with an enlightened man and finally married him. Some feminist critics then and since have considered this ending, in which Josanne threw herself at the feet of her lover, a "cop-out"; indeed, the antifeminist Théodore Joran considered this book to represent "the bankruptcy of feminism."[111] Yet Tinayre's concern was not whether or not women should work per se, but what the effects of their efforts to support themselves might be: as she put it in an interview published in *Femina*, a woman who worked (for her keep) could "conquer something else besides her daily bread, her clothing and her housing: moral independence, the right to think, to speak, and to act as she sees fit, this right that man has always had and that he always refused to her."[112] The point that most critics seem to have missed is that Tinayre portrayed Josanne's ultimate act of submission to love – and also, implicitly, to the husbandly authority incarnate in the still unamended Civil Code – as an act of free will – of choice – informed by the harsh experience of a mature woman.[113]

Tinayre's important novel appeared in between three significant novels about the conflicts faced by intellectual women, written by the slightly younger, more pessimistic, and more traditionalist Catholic novelist Colette Yver (1874–1953; pseud. of Antoinette de Bergevin Huzard). Beginning with *Les Cervelines* (1903, reissued 1908), which examined the trajectory of a woman historian and teacher who refuses marriage in order to continue with her research, and *Princesses de Science* (1907), which explored work-family conflict in the world of Parisian medicine and hospitals and won the

---

[111] Théodore Joran, *Autour du Féminisme* (Paris: Plon, 1906), p. 9.
[112] Henri Duvernois, "Une Interview de Marcelle Tinayre," *Femina*, n° 126 (15 April 1906), 169.
[113] A somewhat similar point would be made by Daniel Lesueur in her 1908 novel, *La Nietschéenne* (1908), which she refers to as "a novel of feminine energy." There she argues (as reported in *Le Matin* [4 June 1908], p. 1) that obedience (to social conventions) was itself a form of discipline, and reiterated the point that women should be womanly. She placed all her hopes in women, as distinct from feminism, and argued what was essentially a stoic position, ornamented by grace.

1907 *Prix Vie Heureuse* (later *Prix Femina*), Yver continued her inquiry with a novel about women entering the legal profession, *Les Dames du Palais* (1909), which was initially serialized in the *Revue de Paris*.[114] All three of Yver's novels engage with the "problem" of marriage and maternity for young professional women, who are generally educated middle-class women who lack dowries. Of course, as in Tinayre's novels, a love story always drives the action and creates dilemmas for young women, but Yver also demonstrates a considered appreciation of men's biases as well as their desires and their efforts to accommodate the needs of their spouses. In fact, the literary historian Jennifer Waelti-Walters considers Yver's psychological analysis of the women and men in *Les Cervelines* as "a model of analytic perspicacity which has few peers to this day."[115]

Colette Yver was deeply skeptical that intellectual women (whom she considers to be primarily daughters of *petit bourgeois* families) could "have it all" and strongly, if regretfully, believed that women who married must sacrifice their careers. Thus, most commentators then and since have considered her works to be antifeminist tracts. But it may be more complicated than that, as Waelti-Walters has demonstrated; Yver's novels, she remarks, "are novels of pragmatic and subversive feminism."[116] Yver's knowledge of the obstacles that stood in women's way in these professions is astute and her analyses insightful. She explained her position as of May 1909 in *L'Écho de Paris*, in an article on "the marriage of the *intellectuelle*."[117] Yver claimed not to understand men who objected to young women's entering well-paying professions, especially the intellectual professions, over which men claimed proprietary rights. In fact, she defended women's right to pursue a career. But what happens, she queried, if they do marry? Sometimes Prince Charming does find (and fall for) these young women without dowry, but with professional capital that can serve them in the event something might happen to their male breadwinner. Even so, Yver reminded readers that "this fragile and delicate structure that some

---

[114] Colette Yver was the pseudonym of Antoinette de Bergeron, Madame August Huzard. Calmann-Lévy published *Princesses de Science* (1907) and *Les Dames du Palais* (1909). *Les Cervelines* was published by F. Juven. Her novels seems to have been widely read and frequently republished and translated into English, and still in 1943 she published *Madame sous-chef*, which considered the same marriage/family conflicts for a bright woman working in administration. After 1918 she published many articles in *Le Correspondant* and in the *Revue des Deux Mondes,* in addition to career advice for girls. Her fundamental message to women was that loving a man requires her submission to him and the casting off of pride [*orgueil*] and ambition. For a sensitive discussion of Yver's novels and others of the genre, see Rogers, *Career Stories* (cited, n. 101). Apart from *Career Stories*, there seems to be scant critical literature on Yver's works.

[115] See Waelti-Walters, *Feminist Novelists*, p. 101.   [116] Waelti-Walters, *Feminist Novelists*, p. 101.

[117] Colette Yver, "Le Mariage de l'Intellectuelle," *L'Écho de Paris* (14 May 1909), front page.

call the happiness of the household [*le bonheur du ménage*] rests almost entirely on one principle: the presence of the wife in the household. Nothing perturbs a married man more," she indicated, "than finding that his wife is not there when he returns home" and is not available to share his successes, his worries and concerns. Yver believes that, in general, a woman should abandon her career when she marries, for the sake of conjugal happiness. "The dream would be that from the top of society to the bottom the married woman would stay at home: no more factory, no more courses, no more functions outside, nothing but the most august feminine function." They will not be bored there, but can put their intellect to use in different ways, she asserted. We will recognize their rights but will also speak to them about their future duties, Yver concluded. Was Yver too sympathetic to the needs of husbands (and children)? Or was she simply acknowledging the realities of conjugal togetherness in the still male-dominated *Belle Époque*, when many bourgeois husbands still expected wives to act as their mirrors, reflecting them at twice their normal size?

Yver's novels in various ways illustrate a long-standing generalization about French society that was underscored once again in 1908 by an American observer: "the family is the prime social fact" and "the social unit . . . is not the individual but the family group."[118] Such "social facts" were accompanied by attitudes, emotions, prejudices, practices, and (of course) laws of long standing, all of which proved difficult to change.

Princesses de Science opens with a proposal of marriage, during which the young doctor Fernand Guémené, who has fallen for the heroine Thérèse Herlingue, asks her to give up medicine and her medical research so she can belong entirely to him. She is shocked. A man of very conventional ideas, he tells Thérèse that he wants a wife who can keep his house, provide him with a refuge from his hard day's work of medical rounds in his neighborhood; he indicates also that he does not want to be known as "the husband of the *doctoresse*."[119] Thus, does Yver set the scene for trouble ahead. The two debate the question of whether women are inferior or just

[118] See Barrett Wendell, *The France of Today* (New York: C. Scribner's sons, 2nd ed., 1908; orig. publ. 1907); quotes, pp. 125–126. Wendell, a professor of English at Harvard, also repeated (p. 112) the deeply held belief that within the French family the man is the minister of foreign affairs and woman the minister of the interior, "virtually absolute in her domestic authority." This book also appeared in French in 1910.

[119] Colette Yver, *Princesses de Science* (Paris: Calmann-Lévy, 1907), p. 13. The bulk of this important scene is translated in Jennifer Waelti-Walters & Steven C. Hause, ed. *Feminisms of the Belle Epoque* (Lincoln: University of Nebraska Press, 1994), pp. 211–214.

"different," as well as what to do about the big surplus of women who can't marry and must support themselves. Thérèse upholds the feminist arguments for equality and companionship in marriage and Fernand denies that his male-centric views are retrograde and bourgeois. He admits that there are many women who will have to support themselves, but he upholds the view that for those who do marry, "everything falls back into place," the husband supports the family, and a married woman takes on her "sovereign mission," which is to "live for her husband and her children." These arguments are all out on the table by page 19. On page 20, Thérèse counters, insisting that he must either take her with her profession or forget about her. Impasse. But, of course, Yver's story – because it was a love story – does not end there. On page 82, Fernand gives in and Thérèse revels in the idea that she can pursue her profession and marry Fernand. But the business of combining a career with a family for a woman was not so simple, as the rest of the novel would demonstrate. Yver knew the arguments on both sides of the question, she was sympathetic to the plight of the young educated women, and she had a profound understanding of the prejudices of the day, as she would also demonstrate in her subsequent novel about women lawyers, *Les Dames du palais* (1909). She also made it clear that these professional women could afford to hire help and live in nice places. The question of work–life balance would play out very differently among poorer, less educated women of the working class. There a wife's income, as insignificant as it might be, could make the difference between economic hardship and a modicum of well-being.

Do Working Class Wives Have a Right to Work?
Revisiting *L'Affaire Couriau*

The Couriau Affair thrust all these questions about women, employment, and unionization into high relief. The story of the expulsion in 1913 of Louis Couriau from the Lyon section of the *Fédération du Livre* for "allowing" his wife Emma Couriau (also a veteran typographer) to work and encouraging her union membership has been told many times from various perspectives.[120] Madeleine Guilbert's comprehensive survey of the workers' press during the summer and fall of 1913 confirms that some key

---

[120] In order of publication: Guilbert, *Femmes et l'organisation syndicale*, pp. 409–412, 414–429; Marilyn Jacoby Boxer, "Socialism Faces Feminism in France: 1879-1913" (Ph.D. dissertation, University of California at Riverside, 1975), chapter 9, pp. 279–308; Marilyn J. Boxer, "Socialism Faces Feminism: The Failure of Synthesis in France, 1879-1914," in *Socialist Women*, ed. Marilyn J. Boxer & Jean H. Quataert (New York: Elsevier, 1978), pp. 75–111; Sowerwine, *Sisters or Citizens*,

figures in the workers' movement (notably the revolutionary syndicalists) had come to oppose the dominantly Proudhonesque positions of earlier times and had endorsed women's right to work – for equal pay.[121] In fact, at its 1910 congress in Bordeaux, the *Fédération du Livre* had actually voted to admit women. This did not, however, mean that female typographers would be welcome in all-male workshops at the local level, nor that there would be no backlash against the 1910 decision. What is important for our purposes is the breadth of the published debates Couriau's expulsion engendered, which went well beyond the syndicalist and socialist press that is usually quoted, to attract the attention and intervention of French feminists on behalf of Emma Couriau and, more generally, in defense of women's right to work.

Perhaps the most entertaining of the documents in this case was Louis Couriau's published appeal of his expulsion from the Lyon local to the Central Committee of the *Fédération du Livre*, in which he stated that even if (as the Lyon local would have liked) he ordered his wife not to work, "my companion would obstinately refuse to obey me," and would insist that her right to work could not be denied, "that it was a condition of life and independence for her." What was he supposed to do, he queried; "what means could he employ to force her to 'do nothing'?" Should he beat her? throw her out? he asked the union authorities, tongue-in-cheek. He prided himself on his career as a longtime militant in the printers' union, as well as being a husband who did not tell his wife what to do.[122] Not coincidentally, he was also part of the faction of revolutionary syndicalists that was challenging the leadership of the *Federation*'s secretary-general Auguste Keufer, who they viewed as too chummy with the employers and the government, and not doing enough either to raise the pay of the typographers or to enforce the 1910 resolution to admit women.

When the Lyon section's general assembly met in late July 1913, it overwhelmingly supported the expulsion of Louis Couriau and the refusal to consider the membership application of Emma Couriau. The majority

pp. 135–136, but see esp. his long article "Workers and Women in France before 1914: The Debate over the Couriau Affair," *Journal of Modern History*, 55:3 (September 1983), 411–441; and Zylberberg-Hocquard, *Féminisme et Syndicalisme*, esp. pp. 263ff. See also Jeremy Jennings, "The CGT and the Couriau Affair: Syndicalist Responses to Female Labour in France before 1914," *European History Quarterly*, 21:3 (July 1991), 321–337.

[121] Guilbert, *Femmes et l'organisation syndicale*, pp. 409–413.

[122] Louis Couriau, letter to the Central Committee of the C.G.T., published in *Le Reveil Typographique* (June 1913); republished in *La Vie ouvrière*, n° 91 (5 July 1913), 52–54, and in *L'Équité*, n° 6 (15 July 1913), 1; reproduced in Zylberberg-Hocquard, *Féminisme et Syndicalisme*, pp. 305–307 as Document 5.

of its board had threatened to resign if the local's earlier decisions (to exclude women and punish men who allowed their wives to work) were not upheld. A number of other local sections, however, protested; their members supported the Bordeaux resolution – let the women join the union and receive equal pay – as a way of warding off the undercutting of men's wages. The writer for *La Vie ouvrière,* the periodical of the revolutionary syndicalists, seemed hopeful that Couriau could be affiliated directly with the *Fédération du Livre* (which ultimately did happen), and that the 1910 decision to admit women would be decisively upheld at the next congress of the Federation in 1915.[123]

In the interim, *La Vie ouvrière* published a hard-hitting general article on women's work by the feisty Marie Guillot. Making her debut in *La Vie ouvrière* (after complaining earlier that year that the publication never printed anything by women), Guillot came out swinging in the early July issue, explaining to the largely male readership that "ineluctible economic facts" were driving women into the workforce.[124] Appropriating Olive Schreiner's enumeration of all the household tasks formerly done by women that, in the course of economic evolution, had been displaced from the home or replaced by industrial products (from socks to bed linens and mattresses, and mass-produced food items), leaving wives with more time (as well as more need for cash to purchase what they needed), Guillot criticized capitalism for focusing on profit rather than on furnishing solid products. She nevertheless admitted that many of these innovations, those that were solid products, were beneficial for women. Freed from the heavy charge of domestic labor, but needing money to pay for the improvements, with industrialization women had been called into the workforce, but paid a pittance, which then brought down the pay of men as well. And, in a much-quoted phrase (mirroring Schreiner), Marie Guillot insisted that "the force that pushes woman out of the home is irresistible: it has economic causes and nothing can stop it."[125] What working men needed to do, rather than dig in their heels in opposition to women's paid labor, was to offer women a social education, which Guillot claimed would help

---

[123] F. Million, "L'Affaire Couriau," *La Vie ouvrière,* n° 93 (5 August 1913), 189–191.

[124] Guillot, "La Femme hors du Foyer," *La Vie ouvrière,* n° 91 (5 July 1913), 1–15 (cited in n. 85). Guillot's arguments closely follow those laid out by Olive Schreiner in *La Femme et le Travail* (see my introductory remarks & n. 17). As noted earlier, Guillot had reviewed the French edition of Schreiner's work. On Marie Guillot's activism on behalf of women teachers, see Persis Hunt, "Teachers and Workers: Problems of Feminist Organizing Before World War I," in *Third Republic/ Troisième République,* n⁰ˢ 3–4 (1977), 168–204, in a special issue on "Aspects of the Woman Question During the French Third Republic," ed. Karen Offen.

[125] Guillot, "Femme hors du Foyer," 15.

to protect the level of men's pay. She did not mention (as had Madeleine Pelletier) sharing the housework.

The Paris-based feminists, preoccupied by their upcoming Tenth International Congress (2–8 June 1913), had in the meantime been covering the ultimately successful strike of women workers at the Lebaudy sugar refinery, who were protesting proposed cuts in their already meager pay. Writing in *La Française* on 7 June 1913, Hélène Brion (1882–1962) had denounced as an affront to civilization the acts of men wielding whips to force striking wives to go back to work; she further denounced the lack of intervention by other male workers, or by the police agents and the absence of denunciation of this "uncivilized" behavior by the workers' press (the exception being *La Bataille Syndicaliste*).[126] From this episode Brion concluded that the feminist campaign must come first, must precede women's struggle for economic rights, and that even as women join the unions and the socialist party, they must also stick together to fight for women's rights. The international feminist congress, which had drawn some thousand participants from various countries, debated the report of the section on work presented by Louise Compain, and voted on a series of resolutions concerning women's work.[127] Among these was (as has been previously mentioned) a counterresolution by Marguerite Durand, opposing the Compain report's recommendation of supporting protective legislation for women only; Durand's counterresolution, supported on the floor by the LFDF's Maria Vérone, was adopted by the general assembly of the congress. This resolution read as follows: "That laws which exceptionally regulate the work of women should be abolished and replaced by the application to the entire working population of a law of equal protection that does not distinguish between the sexes."[128]

---

[126] H. B. [Hélène Brion], "Les Enseignements d'une Grève," *La Française*, n° 282 (7 June 1913), front page.

[127] See *Dixième congrès international des femmes: Oeuvres et Institutions féminines, Droits des femmes, 2-8 juin 1913, compte rendu des travaux par* Mme Avril de Sainte-Croix (Paris: V. Giard & E. Brière), and the coverage in *La Française* in June 1913. The subsequent congress of the International Abolitionist Federation, which followed immediately (9–12 June), discussed (as its fourth question), "Les conditions du travail féminin et la prostitution." See *Prostitution réglementée et hygiène. Rapports présentés au congrès de la Fédération Abolitionniste Internationale, Paris, juin 1913. Extraits du Compte rendu des travaux du congrès avec annexe* (Geneva: Bureau international de la Fédération, 1914), pp. 221–312. The debates at these two congresses are neither mentioned nor tied in to the discussions on women's right to work and the Couriau Affair in the studies by Boxer, Sowerwine, and Zylberberg-Hocquard. This omission doubtless reflects the long-standing and arbitrary separation between "bourgeois" and "socialist" feminists – which was long accepted uncritically by their historians; I owe this observation to Marilyn Boxer.

[128] *Dixième congrès international des femmes*, p. 519. The general assembly delegates also voted to support a 48-hour week for workers of both sexes and the 10-hour day restriction for employees of both sexes. Both these congresses took place before the Couriau Affair had attracted significant public attention. See Klejman & Rochefort, *Égalité en marche*, pp. 245–247.

In the ensuing issue of *La Française* (14 June 1913), Hélène Brion followed up with a call for female solidarity: "For this struggle, there are neither *bourgeoises* nor *ouvrières*, there can only be women in struggle against a common oppression."[129] She argued that bourgeois women should intervene *directly* to help the working women. Cécile Brunschvicg, then secretary-general of the *Union Française pour le Suffrage des Femmes* (UFSF) and also head of the CNFF's Section on Work, disagreed with this proposed tactic. In a subsequent editorial, Brunschvicg spoke out against direct intervention, noting that the *bourgeoises* were standing by and would help when and if the *ouvrières* called for their assistance, but in the meantime would keep a discreet distance, as they had in the Lebaudy strike, even as they offered both moral and material support (collections of funds, in particular) to the striking *ouvrières*. She asked Hélène Brion to carry this message to the workers.[130] Neither Brion nor Brunschvicg alluded to the Couriau affair during this exchange.

The Couriau Affair would pop into the headlines again in late July and August, following the 27 July General Assembly of the Lyon local which upheld the expulsion of Louis Couriau and the refusal to admit Emma Couriau. It provided context and fodder for another, closely related, and rather leisurely debate in the new monthly publication *L'Équité: Organe Éducatif du Prolétariat Féminine*, founded and directed by Marianne Rauze (pseud. of Marie-Anne Comignan, née Gaillarde, 1875–1964).[131] Stimulated by a note from a typographer insisting that wives should be forbidden by law from working for pay, the ensuing debate in *L'Équité* was about, first, defending women's right to work, and subsequently challenging and defending the compatibility of feminism and socialism, with a concerted effort by some contributors to prioritize Marxist socialism, and others to prioritize feminism. Most of the participants (if indeed not all) were members of the newly formed *Groupe des Femmes Socialistes* (GDFS; discussed in Chapter 9). These debates introduced a new generation of left-leaning and feminist female journalists that included Suzanne Lacore (writing as "Suzon"), Hélène Brion, Madeleine Vernet, Marguerite

---

[129] Hélène Brion, "Ouvrières et Bourgeoises: Les Enseignements d'une Grève," *La Française*, n° 283 (14 June 1913), front page.

[130] C.-L. Brunschvicg, "Bourgeoises et Ouvrières: Réponse à Hélène Brion," *La Française*, n° 284 (21 June 1913), front page.

[131] On Rauze / Comignan Gaillarde, see Boxer, "Socialism Faces Feminism in France," pp. 287–288. Her husband was a military officer. She had been publishing articles in *La Française* before founding her own journal. Rauze specifically presented *L'Équité* as the French counterpart to Clara Zetkin's *Die Gleichheit*, and its sister publications in Switzerland, Belgium, and Austria.

Martin, and Fanny Clar, as well as veterans such as Gabrielle Petit, who strongly disagreed with one another about strategic priorities. Should class solidarity or sex solidarity be prioritized?

The more general discussion of women's right to work, launched already in the first issue of *L'Équité* (15 February 1913), had begun with a response to the typographers by Nelly Roussel, who called for liberty for women in their choices of occupation, by Hélène Brion who defended equal pay, and subsequently (15 June) by Mélanie Rolland, who urged women to join unions. As of the 15 June issue, the focus shifted to a consideration of feminism and socialism (with reference to the right to work issue), and the lead article, "*Féminisme et Socialisme*," by "Suzon" raised (once again) the interminable question: "What is feminism?" Suzon defined it as the quest for equal rights, based on "natural" law, as exemplified in 1789 by Condorcet and Olympe de Gouges. Acknowledging the struggles of women in the nineteenth century, she spoke of the triumph of the principle of the right to work and women's quest "to cease being considered man's subordinate"; but she expressed concern that women's success in gaining rights equal to those of men would only reinforce the bourgeois capitalist regime. Proletarian women, on the other hand, were the victims of capitalism, and "must understand that their own enfranchisement is linked to that of the working class." Both, she insisted, would be liberated together. Suzon went on to assert that the women of the bourgeoisie fear class struggle, that they are (necessarily) the supporters of the capitalist regime. Thus, in Suzon's view, socialism and feminism were wholly incompatible. "Socialism's national and international congresses support political equality for women, so socialist women do not have to climb aboard the ship of bourgeois feminism." Moreover, she claimed, the vote was not an end in itself, but a means (which was exactly what the feminists had been saying for decades) to arrive at economic equality which only socialism could provide.[132] Suzon was, of course, mouthing the quintessential Clara Zetkin line.[133]

---

[132] Suzon, "Féminisme et socialisme," *L'Équité*, n° 5 (15 June 1913), front page. Excerpts from this debate are reprinted in Albistur & Armogathe, *Grief des Femmes*, vol. 2, pp. 115–121.

[133] That Zetkin's ideas, especially her strictures of noncooperation of socialist women with "bourgeois feminism," were known to and acted upon by some French socialist women, notably Louise Saumoneau, is incontestable, though it is unclear just how wide Zetkin's influence (or, for that matter, that of the Second International) actually was. See Marilyn J. Boxer, "Clara Zetkin and France: Eight Year Exile, Eighty Year Influence," in *Clara Zetkin: National and International Contexts*, ed. Marilyn J. Boxer & John S. Partington. Occasional Publications Series No. 31 (London: Socialist History Society, 2013), pp. 9–21. The French socialist-feminist periodicals in 1913–1914 do reference Zetkin's perspective on prioritizing class struggle and her acknowledgment of the first International Women's Day in Paris, as we will see later.

In the issue of 15 July, the editor Marianne Rauze announced that, following a number of protests against Suzon's article, *L'Équité* would sponsor a referendum on the question of feminism and socialism, even as she insisted that the publication would remain faithful to its mission as "an organ for the interests of the female proletariat, with the fundamental principle of class struggle."[134]

A vehement refutation of Suzon's arguments by Hélène Brion followed in the August issue of *L'Équité*. Asserting that as women, from childhood on "we suffer from sexual inequality before we suffer from economic or political inequality," Brion underscored the constraints that surround girls in all classes of society, as well as the historic protests against those constraints. "Who demanded more games, more liberty, more reason, more serious and focused study for girls," she asked, answering her own question by remarking that "all those who protested in earlier times, long before socialism was even born, had 'bourgeois' names." It is feminism, not socialism, that is attempting to change women's condition: "There is a perfect solidarity in inequality among women. And it is in the name of this sexual solidarity, more durable and deeper than all the social categories, that I preach, the absolute and necessary entente between the *ouvrières* and the *bourgeoises*." Brion fervently denied the claim that women's interests divided according to class: [135]

> It is not in order to consolidate the society that men have made that women want to become involved, it is to reform it, to profoundly modify it, and in the direction of their sex interests not in the direction of their class interest.... What right have you to deform their intentions? ... Learn your feminist history, women comrades who only swear by socialism! Read the writings, listen to the claims and the conquests of Flora Tristan, Jeanne Deroin, Pauline de Grandpré, Maria Deraismes, Paula Mink, Mauriceau, Vincent and others and you will no longer dare to think that the *bourgeoise* is the born enemy of the *ouvrière*. No, there cannot be a question of class struggle between the *bourgeoises* who are *féministes* and the women who work. I say the *bourgeoises* [who are] feminists, that is to say those who think and act socially.

Brion would add that the Couriau Affair offered a perfect case in point. Women are women's best allies, even as men are deciding where women's ostensible happiness lies. It was not just Proudhon's "housewife or harlot,"

---

[134] *L'Équité*, n° 6 (15 July 1913). Louis Couriau's initial letter appeared in this same issue.

[135] Hélène Brion, "Solidarité féminine," *L'Équité*, n° 7 (15 August 1913), 3. This article takes up all of page 3, in four full columns; all the quotations following are from this page. This powerful article is only partially reproduced in Albistur & Armogathe, *Grief des femmes*, vol. 2, pp. 127, 130.

but one could eliminate the word housewife and just say harlot, because, in her view, the bed (and men's sometimes unwelcome intentions) is included in the work of the housewife.

Who protested in the Couriau case? Not the socialists, Brion pointed out to Suzon. "The socialists held back from interfering with union matters ... not even the socialist women's group said anything ... It was the feminists," she asserted, "who brought this case to the attention of *L'Humanité*, i.e., to the general public. And among these feminists there are *bourgeoises*, women not affiliated with the socialist party, women who are not *ouvrières*." Brion concluded by making two points: "1) the feminist struggle is primordial for woman and should be undertaken by her in parallel with any other and 2) in this feminist struggle, woman should have as allies all women who think, whether they are *bourgeoises*, housewives, or intellectual or manual *ouvrières*."

Subsequent issues of *L'Équité* published further contributions to what was becoming a no-holds-barred debate. The veteran socialist Marguerite Martin laid out the reasons why she was taking her stand on the feminist side, arguing that some socialists seemed to have a false idea of feminism. "True feminism," Martin indicated, "is uniquely based on the egalitarian principle, and what is more, it signifies a reaction against ancestral prejudices and established traditions, it is thus revolutionary by definition and thus entirely reconcilable with the socialist and even syndicalist ideal." While it may be true that feminism offers only a partial solution, the fact is that we currently live under a system in which women are very unjustly treated, and feminism offers solutions to immediate problems. Marguerite Martin argued that socialist women should work together with bourgeois women wherever their interests coincide but nevertheless in the meantime women should organize around class struggle so that they can come down on the side of the proletariat when the time is right.[136] Martin seemed to want to have her cake and eat it too.

In the same issue, Fanny Clar, acting as "angel of peace" between Brion and Suzon, would indicate that terminology was part of the problem. Being from the bourgeois class was not the problem; the real question, she claimed, concerned the "bourgeois mindset" [*esprit bourgeois*]. "All those, from whatever class they come, who have good will and sincerity, devoting themselves to the triumph of the exploited, should be welcomed with open arms. Those happy women who have not had to struggle for themselves and who nevertheless claim solidarity with those who suffer from the bad

---

[136] Marguerite Martin, letter for "Notre referendum," *L'Équité*, n° 8 (15 September 1913), 3.

state of work, have broken with the bourgeois mind-set and belong to us."
Moreover, there are working-class women who are tainted by a bourgeois
mind-set, jealous little sisters of the bourgeois, who discourage their
menfolk from participating in the social struggle. For Clar, "feminism
should not become detached from socialism, [which is] the great human
question. Socialism cannot ignore intelligent feminism, under penalty of
denying itself." She called instead for struggle against a bourgeois mind-set
and for socialists and feminists to make common cause.[137]

Suzon responded to Fanny Clar and Hélène Brion in the October issue,
correcting what she viewed as Clar's misimpressions concerning "*la bourgeoise*," a term she said she had never used, but most importantly, underscoring that she and Brion had diametrically different perspectives on the
woman question as well as answers to it. Suzon made it clear that she did
not think masculine domination was the main problem, as did Brion, but
that the economic system was. Only "a change in the mode of production
and the appropriation of riches" would resolve the problem; "women's
legal inferiority was only the distant consequence of her economic subjection." Invoking history since ancient times, Suzon briefly recounted the
development of private property, etc., along the lines laid out by Engels
and Bebel. The emancipation of the proletariat was, for her, the key to
ending every type of servitude. If the women of the *bourgeoisie* come over
to us, she indicated, they will have to accept "the integrality of our ideal."
Decidedly, Suzon had embraced a vision of radical social change that only
the revolution could bring about.[138] Nobody at the time was pointing out
that the economic system was gendered male.

Hélène Brion concluded the debate in the November 1913 issue, with a
final reply to Suzon:[139] "Nowhere," Brion asserted, "does man offer woman
her economic freedom."

> Show me a single line in the socialist credo that proclaims women's absolute
> right to work outside the home if she so desires, the absolute right to take
> up any profession [*métier*] and to be paid exactly the same as a man. This is
> what the feminists demand, whereas the socialists and their avant-garde –
> for example, the *typos* [typographers] – want to keep woman at home and
> nothing else. They want her to be economically dependent on man, kept by
> him – housewife or harlot, in the words of Proudhon.

---

[137] Fanny Clar, letter for "Notre referendum," *L'Équité*, n° 8 (15 September 1913), 3.
[138] Suzon, untitled response to Fanny Clar and Hélène Brion, *L'Équité*, no 9 (15 October 1913), 3–4.
[139] Brion, "'Dernière' à Suzon," *L'Équité*, n° 10 (15 November 1913).

Moreover, Brion admitted that once a child arrives, equality is impossible. "More suffering and more duties should lead to more rights, and the equilibrium is broken in favor of woman. It is she and not the man who is the true and natural foundation of the family; it is she who should be its head [*le chef*]. Her children should bear her name and belong to her and not to the man." She warded off Lacore's possible accusation that this was a step backward, toward matriarchy, by asserting that "this is my conception of feminism." Inviting further exchanges, Brion concluded by remarking that there was nothing about any of this in the socialist program. In appendix to Brion's article, Marianne Rauze invited women comrades, as members of the socialist party, to get engaged in moving its program, as concerned women, beyond economic and political rights. As editor and publisher of *L'Équité*, she also responded to a number of letters received from suffrage advocates among others, ending her column with an invitation to the rich *bourgeoises* and suffragists to come over to the socialists "to work for the integral liberation of the feminine proletariat via economic independence."[140]

The debates over women's right to work and the Couriau Affair in *L'Équité* would not end there. Another group of feminist activists would intervene during the summer of 1913. In mid-July, the *Fédération Féministe du Sud-Est* (FFSE) endorsed women's unrestricted right to paid work and to join unions, "and especially those who work in the book trades." Writing in the 15 August issue of *L'Équité*, Venise Pellat-Finet, self-proclaimed "*socialiste et syndiquée*" and secretary of the FFSE, summarized the case, calling it a "brutal exclusion" and announcing that the FFSE was taking up the Couriau couple's defense. She queried whether it was men alone who were deciding the fate of women typographers, and called for a female typographer to speak out about what was going on in Lyon.[141]

Emma Couriau herself responded to the FFSE's call in the September 1913 issue of *L'Équité*, with her article, "*Les Typotes*," proposing the formation of a separate union for women typographers. Such a proposal was, of course, anathema to skilled workingmen such as the typographers, who staunchly opposed separate unions for women workers, following their experience earlier in the decade with the women's union organized in their craft by Marguerite Durand (even though its members worked for union wages). Emma Couriau did indeed found such a group on 14 September, and its

---

[140]   Marianne Rauze, [no title], *L'Équité*, n° 10 (15 November 1913), 2–3.
[141]   Venise Pellat-Finet, "Les Femmes dans la Fédération du Livre: les Syndicats lyonnais votent une brutale exclusion," *L'Équité*, n° 7 (15 August 1913). See also Boxer, "Socialism Faces Feminism," p. 294.

existence was duly reported in the issue of 15 October (but its application for affiliation with the *Fédération du Livre* would be rejected in early 1914).

Following its long Parisian summer holiday, *La Française* would renew its coverage of the Couriau Affair, beginning with a summary, "*Les Femmes dans la Fédération du Livre*," by the FFSE's Pellat-Finet in the issue of 6 September. Two weeks later, it reported on the congress of the *Fédération Féministe Universitaire* (FFU), which (in light of Pellat-Finet's report on the Couriau Affair) passed a resolution in favor of women's right to work and to join unions, and in support of Emma Couriau.[142] Only in November, though, did the Couriau Affair garner additional attention, with updated coverage by Cécile Brunschvicg on the intervention of the *Ligue des Droits de l'Homme* (a public letter from the LDH president, Francis de Pressensé, to Keufer, of the *Fédération du Livre*) and an announcement of a public meeting on the subject of women's right to work, to be held on 15 December.[143] On the 17th November, the UFSF organized a public discussion of the Couriau case at the Musée Social, affirming women's right to work; speakers included Marcelle Tinayre, Mlle [Stéphanie] Bouvard (head of the artificial flowermakers' union), Marie Bonnevial (LFDF), Elisabeth Renaud (GDFS), Pauline Rebour (UFSF). Marguerite de Witt-Schlumberger, the president of the UFSF, wrapped up the evening with a declaration of female solidarity across classes.[144] This event provided a kind of dress rehearsal for the upcoming December event.

The LFDF, led by Marie Bonnevial and Maria Vérone (who also held positions in the CNFF and, throughout 1913, in the GDFS) also reported on the Couriau Affair in the LFDF monthly bulletin, beginning in its September–October issue. Their reporting was primarily informational, without commentary, though it seemed clear from the context which side the LFDF leadership was on. Subsequent issues included publication of the correspondence between Pressensé and Keufer, who announced that in light of the Lyon section's continuing refusal to reintegrate Louis Couriau, the central committee had decided to affiliate him directly to the *Fédération* and to take up his case again at its 1915 congress.[145]

---

[142] See Pauline Rebour's report, "Troisième Congrès National de la Fédération Féministe Universitaire," *La Française*, n° 289 (11 October 1913). This congress took place in Bordeaux, 16–18 August.

[143] See *La Française*, n° 295 (15 November 1913), 1–2.

[144] *La Française*, n° 295 (22 November 1913), front page.

[145] Pressensé / Keufer correspondence, published in LFDF, *Le Droit des Femmes*, n° 11 (November 1913), 1–3, and n° 12 (December 1913), 4–5. The renaming of this periodical began with the first issue in 1912, when the old *Bulletin Trimestrielle* became a monthly.

On 15 December 1913 a coalition of ten feminist groups in Paris, (including the UFSF, the CNFF, LFDF, FFU, *Amélioration*, plus *L'Équité*, though with the conspicuous absence of the GDFS) responded to the uproar caused by the Couriau Affair by organizing a massive "Grand Meeting" at the *Salle des Sociétés Savantes* in Paris on the question "Do Women Have the Right to Work?"[146] In conjunction with this public event, *L'Équité* would publish a forum on the subject of the right to work of the human being in its mid-December 1913 issue.[147] Virtually every respondent supported women's right to work, though some – including Emma Couriau – considered it a regrettable necessity in the current economic system. Generally speaking, the feminists surveyed, ranging from Hubertine Auclert and Madeleine Pelletier to Jeanne Oddo-Deflou, Nelly Roussel, Cécile Brunschvicg, Hélène Brion, all strongly supported women's right to work as absolute – and they also called for equal pay. Virtually every issue surrounding women's work surfaced in this forum: the current tragedy of minimal pay, exorbitantly long hours, *travail à domicile*, the threat of poor women falling into prostitution or committing suicide when ends didn't meet, the efforts to unionize women in the interests of equal pay, the question of protective legislation, the condemnation of greedy employers who preferred to hire cheap female labor so as to undercut male wages, the human costs of capitalism, the visions of harmony following socialist revolution. The speakers also addressed questions such as the choice of occupation, the availability of apprenticeships and other job training, the exclusion of married women, and unhygienic or even dangerous or toxic working conditions. Everyone agreed that women should have the absolute right to work, but that in practice, they faced a veritable potpourri of problems, the most significant of which was exploitation – long hours and miserable pay. Although, as we have mentioned, minimum wage legislation was in the pipeline, as well as legislation to impose a ten-hour law for all workers, none of it had yet achieved legislative ratification.

---

[146] The poster/flier advertising this meeting was published, among other places, in *La Française*, n° 297 (6 December 1913) and n° 298 (13 December 1913) and in the monthly *Bulletin* of the LFDF, *Le Droit des Femmes*, n° 12 (December 1913), 4–5. A tiny notice appeared in *La Bataille Syndicaliste*, n° 963 (14 December 1913). It can also be consulted at the BMD in DOS 396 CON (CNFF 1901–1914) and is reproduced in Zylberberg-Hocquard, *Féminisme et syndicalisme*, p. 266. According to Sowerwine, (*Sisters or Citizens?*, pp. 136–137), the *Groupe des Femmes Socialistes* conspicuously refused an invitation to participate: "Rauze, Renaud, and Vérone nevertheless spoke at the protest meeting, but only as individuals disavowed by their group" (p. 137).

[147] See *L'Équité* (15 December 1913). Boxer, "Socialism Faces Feminism," pp. 299–303, analyzes the nineteen published opinions, providing extensive quotations in translation.

The organizers of the Grand Meeting itself deemed it a great success. Presided over by Marguerite de Witt-Schlumberger of the UFSF and Professor Célestin Bouglé of the Sorbonne, the program included speeches by the major women orators of the feminist movement: Mme Avril de Sainte-Croix, Maria Vérone, Marianne Rauze, Elisabeth Renaud, as well as by sympathetic men including Francis de Pressensé (president of the LDH), Villeval (*Syndicat des Correcteurs*), and Chenevier (*Ligue d'Électeurs pour le Suffrage des Femmes*). Auguste Keufer from the *Fédération du Livre*, though listed on the program, bowed out two days before (on the grounds that he needed to stay in Marseille where a strike was underway), and no substitute filled his place.[148] Bouglé made it clear that the intent of the meeting was not to attack the *Fédération du Livre* but rather to critique "the tyranny that certain people wanted to exercise in expelling women from typography." Many of the speakers insisted on the necessity of unionizing women workers.[149]

The Grand Meeting's single public resolution demanded that the Central Committee of the *Fédération du Livre* take measures to apply the (still-controversial) decision of its 1910 Bordeaux congress, which was favorable to women's joining the union and earning equal pay for equal work.[150] The text of this resolution indicated that it was the voice of the eight hundred persons who attended.[151] The gathering and the resolution itself provoked the wrath of a Monsieur Mamelle, a member of the central committee of the Fédération. Writing in *La Typographie française*, Mamelle publicly blasted the organizers of the December gathering for making a public issue of what was, in his view, a private matter strictly pertaining to the typographers' union. He engaged in name-calling, insults, and much other impolite expression. *La Française* published a rejoinder, with choice citations from Mamelle's letter, disparaging his objections to the meeting and its resolution as "incompetent" [*sans qualité*] to judge a "private" matter, and pointing out that in a democracy disputed issues such as women's right to work are certainly worthy of being discussed publicly.[152]

---

[148] See the *compte-rendu* by Pauline Rebour in *La Française*, n° 300 (27 December 1913), 1–2. Keufer's long letter of apology for his absence, due to a strike in Marseille, is published in this same issue, with commentary by Jane Misme. Keufer outlines there what he would have said at the gathering. Another account of the Grand Meeting is in the *Bulletin* of the LFDF, n° 1 (January 1913), 7–8.

[149] See the summary and resolution, "Le Meeting féministe," *L'Équité*, n° 12 (15 January 1914).

[150] This resolution was published, without comment and in small print, in *La Bataille Syndicaliste*, n° 966 (17 December 1913), 4.

[151] Marilyn Boxer gives the figure of 600, while Charles Sowerwine indicates that the police report estimated 1,000 in attendance.

[152] J. Bosquet, "L'Affaire Couriau: Un nouveau Dogme," *La Française*, n° 303 (24 January 1914), 2. Mamelle's angry letter originally appeared in *La Typographie française* (1 January 1914).

In the aftermath, nothing much would change, though the boundaries between socialists and feminists would calcify. Louise Saumoneau, declining to debate either the Couriau Affair or women's right to work, had nevertheless published an angry response in *La Femme Socialiste* to Hélène Brion's August article "Solidarité féminine" in *L'Équité,* and over the course of several issues would underline her support in the fiercest terms for the position of socialist noncooperation with feminists outlined earlier by Suzon.[153] What was more, by early 1914, Saumoneau had engineered the expulsion of those members including LFDF leaders Maria Vérone, Marie Bonnevial, and Elisabeth Renaud, who, effectively defying Saumoneau, had taken part in the Grand Meeting on their own initiative. Henceforth, the GDFS, under Saumoneau's leadership, would insist on a hard-core line – class struggle and socialist revolution. Thus did this group's leadership cut itself off definitively from the feminist campaigns for women's rights, and by mid-1914, had ended any further possibility of cooperation with the feminist women, who, as Marilyn Boxer reminds us, had become the primary champions of the cause of working women and equal pay. "The old assumption that feminism had a special place in the socialist movement, and that socialism could contribute toward success of a women's movement had proven false in France," Boxer concluded. "In essence, the socialists told the feminists to return to their foyers and wait for the revolution."[154] Charles Sowerwine, speaking specifically of the GDFS under the leadership of Saumoneau, concurs: "The sentiment of class overwhelmed that of sisterhood once again."[155]

Nor did the all-male unions rise to the challenge of recruiting women coworkers. In April 1914, Emma Couriau complained: "What have they done up to now, the syndicats, the unions, the federations and the CGT, to organize women?"[156] The one group to champion the Couriaus and the inclusion of women in the union movement were the revolutionary syndicalists, whose publication, *La Bataille Syndicaliste,* closely documented the Couriau Affair and also published an important series of articles by the investigative journalist Marcelle Capy (pseud. of Marcelle

---

[153] See Saumoneau's riposte in *La Femme Socialiste*, issues n° 12 (1 October 1913), and n° 13 (1 November 1913), under the title "Solidarité humaine et Prolétarienne." These issues are unpaginated. Saumoneau would continue her fierce opposition to any cooperation with bourgeois feminists through the spring of 1914 and well beyond. I consulted Saumoneau's periodical at the Hoover Institution Library, Stanford University.

[154] Boxer, "Socialism Faces Feminism," p. 308.   [155] Sowerwine, *Sisters or Citizens?*, p. 141.

[156] Boxer, "Socialism Faces Feminism," p. 306; Couriau quote attributed to *La Voix du Peuple*, 6 April 1914; transl. MJB.

Marquès, 1891–1962) concerning the dubious conditions surrounding women's employment.[157] The LFDF Bulletin for June 1914 editorialized on the positive effects of women entering unions.[158] But, although momentum was picking up, the effort to unionize women workers in France would remain a work in progress.

Meanwhile, the leaders of the CNFF Section on Work would continue to pursue the Couriau Affair in 1914, pulling off their gloves in the face of objections put forth by the *Fédération du Livre*. Following the refusal of the federation's Central Committee to accept the application of the union of women typographers founded by Emma Couriau (on the grounds that no city could affiliate more than one union, in this case, the all-male *Section Lyonnaise*), the CNFF section established a Couriau committee. The Couriau Affair, Cécile Brunschvicg insisted in mid-January, was about much more than the particular case of Emma Couriau; the threat concerned all employed women:[159]

> It is the woman who works they want to target, track, and chase from the workshop. The 'defenders of the foyer' in the *Fédération du Livre* scarcely disguise their objective; they are fearful of the women's competition, even when they are paid the same. And, what's more, they are worried that woman, liberated by the possibility of supporting herself, will no longer be the docile, respectful, admiring servant.

They don't even bother to consult the women on these matters, she huffed. "Aren't they [the women] habituated to obey?" Brunschvicg then delivered her parting shot, branding as retrograde the arguments of the *Fédération du Livre*. The unions in Germany, England, and America, she said, "open their doors wide to women." Invoking these comparative examples, Brunschvicg issued a fundamental challenge to the *Fédération* – hop on the bandwagon, or be left in the dust.[160]

Louise Saumoneau and the GDFS struck back at the feminists in March by organizing the first International Women's Day ever held in France, with a *"Grande Manifestation Internationale"* scheduled for the evening of

---

[157] A number of Marcelle Capy's articles, which ran from 25 August 1913 through 3 June 1914, have been republished in whole or in part in Marcelle Capy / Aline Valette, *Femmes et travail au XIXe siècle: Enquêtes de La Fronde et La Bataille syndicaliste, présentation et commentaires par M. H. Zylberberg-Hocquard & E. Diebolt* (Paris: Syros, 1984). Five Capy articles are republished in Armogathe & Albistur, *Grief des Femmes*, vol. 2. I consulted these and other Capy articles from *La Bataille Syndicaliste* at the Hoover Institution, Stanford University.

[158] See LFDF, *Le Droit des Femmes*, n° 6 (June 1914), 124.

[159] C.-L. Brunschvicg, "L'Affaire Couriau," *La Française*, n° 302 (17 January 1914), 2.

[160] Brunschvicg, "L'Affaire Couriau."

the 9th at the same location that the feminists had been using for their public events, the large hall of the *Société des Savantes*. The major socialist daily *L'Humanité* announced the event and its list of speakers on the back page of its issue for 8 March. The socialist deputy "Bracke" (Alexandre Desrousseaux) contributed a front-page editorial in the issue of the 9th, "*La Journée des Femmes*," in which he made the point that German proletarian women were resisting the siren song of the "*bourgeois*" feminists and joining the Socialist Party by the thousands; he also touted Suzon's recent brochure, *Féminisme et Socialisme*, an outgrowth of the articles she had published in 1913 in *L'Équité*.[161] The following day a short article provided a sketch of the event and its speakers, who included Marianne Rauze, along with Alice Joanne, Marguerite Martin, and of course Louise Saumoneau. Also on the roster were speakers from the Russian Social Democratic Party, England's Independent Labour Party, and the Spanish socialists. *Citoyen* Grumbach from the *Club Allemand* read the letter that Clara Zetkin, international secretary of socialist women, had sent to Paris to commemorate the occasion, urging French working women to demand the right to vote. "Never," Zetkin affirmed, "will [women's] hunger for justice and liberty be appeased, as long as the capitalist order exists."[162] The message of the evening event was clear: only Socialism could fully liberate women. The resolution passed indicated that two thousand people (not a mere eight hundred) were in attendance and that each had engaged to "energetically support the integral emancipation of women by attaching it to the grand cause of international socialism, which is working to suppress every injustice and every exploitation."[163]

In the short term, though, Clara Zetkin urged French socialist women to work for the vote. But in that department, the so-called bourgeois feminists had clearly taken the lead (as we will see in Chapter 13). What has been less noticed by scholars is that at the ICW quinquennial congress in Rome in May 1914, the French delegates of the CNFF's Section on Work, Gabrielle Duchêne and Maria Vérone, succeeded in goading the assembled national councils into approving an international section on work (*Travail*). By so doing, the ICW confronted the pretensions of

---

[161] Bracke, "La Journée des Femmes," *L'Humanité* (9 March 1914). Consulted on Gallica, 17 March 2014.

[162] See Klara Zetkin, "Les Femmes socialistes allemandes à leur soeurs françaises," *L'Équité*, n° 14 (15 March 1914).

[163] "Une Belle Demonstration des Femmes Socialistes," *L'Humanité* (10 March 1914), 3. Consulted on Gallica, 17 March 2014.

Zetkin's international socialist women's boycott of "*bourgeois feminism.*"[164]
What has been less noticed as well is the momentum that feminism was
building in France. In mid-June 1914, Jane Misme published a long (three-
column) article in *La Française* entitled "What the Bourgeois Feminists do
for Women Workers."[165] Categorically rejecting the tactic of class struggle
proclaimed by the socialist women, Misme argued that the status of
women improves more quickly when there is no rift between classes of
women. Feminists must defend French women against this "disadvantageous" tendency, which has been so successful in Germany (in blocking
feminist reform) though not in the Scandinavian countries or in England.
The feminist movement, she argued, may have initially been created by
bourgeois women, who enjoyed the opportunity for more enlightenment
and more freedom, but it is directed toward the working women [*les
travailleuses*], in which category she also included *les ouvrières*. Invoking
history, Misme argued that from 1830 on, feminists had demanded equal
education and the right to work. Feminists soon realized, she insisted, that
justice (not charity) was essential, and that "one could not definitively help
the poor without giving them the means to help themselves." Concluding
her strongly stated rebuttal to the Zetkins, the Suzons, and the Saumo-
neaus, Jane Misme insisted that:

> there can be no class struggles between women, no more than there can be
> racial struggles, because from top to bottom of the human condition and
> from one end of the earth to the other, for century after century, [women]
> have formed an immense class, a universal race, oppressed by a single
> domination under which, in diverse forms, they all suffer.

On the very day this article appeared, the 13th of June 1914, the UFSF
would sponsor a "*Grande Réunion*" in Paris to promote women's suffrage.

---

[164] See the ICW Quinquennial Proceedings (Rome) (referenced in n. 49).
[165] See Jane Misme, "Que font les Féministes bourgeoises pour les Ouvrières?" *La Française*, n° 322
(13 June 1914), front page.

CHAPTER 13

"The Alpha and Omega of Our Demands" – The Women's Suffrage Campaigns Heat Up, 1906–1914

Summing up the results of the Tenth International Congress of 1913 in Paris (sponsored by the *Conseil National des Femmes Françaises* [CNFF]), the educator and feminist Jeanne Crouzet Ben-Aben could claim that "*la patrie* needs its women." One of the three French feminists named "Jeanne" engaged in the suffrage campaign (the other two were Jeanne Oddo-Deflou and Jeanne-E. Schmahl), she further claimed that "this word suffrage, so scary only twenty years ago, doesn't frighten anyone anymore," and that "when the political [national] vote is accorded to women, it won't be a revolution but the continuation of an evolution begun long ago." The dozens of congress resolutions, she indicated, were expressed "with a profound and tranquil sentiment of dignity and equity, and the ardent wish to obtain the vote as a means, not as an end."[1] This perspective on the vote – as a means, not an end – had been a constant refrain since the early campaigns of Hubertine Auclert. Already in 1878, Auclert had reminded the French public that "a suffrage that allows the exclusion from the electoral lists of nine million women is far too restrictive to bear the name universal. . . . the weapon of the vote will be for us, just as it is for man, the only means of obtaining the reforms we desire. As long as we remain excluded from civic life, men will attend to their own interests rather than to ours."[2] In 1885, she would call the vote "the Alpha and Omega of our demands."[3] Events would prove that Auclert's analysis – and her claim – was absolutely on target.

---

[1] Jeanne Crouzet Ben-Aben, "Une Assemblée de femmes en 1913," *La Grande Revue*, vol. 80 (10 July 1913), 56–77; quotes, 76, 74–75.

[2] Hubertine Auclert, *Le Droit politique des femmes, question qui n'est pas traitée au Congrès international des femmes* (Paris: Impr. de L. Hugonis), p. 13.

[3] "Une Liseuse," "Un Stuart-Mill français," *La Citoyenne*, n° 99 (August 1885), in analyzing a recent text by the Franco-Swiss philosopher Charles Secrétan, "La Femme et le Droit," *Revue Philosophique de la France et de l'Étranger*, vol. 20 (1885), 37–67. Secrétan's work was frequently republished as an offprint under the title *Le Droit de la Femme*; the 4th edition (Paris: Alcan; Lausanne: Benda, 1888) includes replies from supporters and critics, along with the author's responses. To be touted as France's John Stuart Mill by Hubertine Auclert was no small compliment.

During the early twentieth century, variations on this argument would appear repeatedly in feminist publications. "Suffrage," argued Jeanne Oddo-Deflou in 1905, "is the key without which the other doors, even [those now] open, can close definitively. It is the alpha and omega of our demands."[4] To Ghénia Avril de Sainte-Croix, the vote for women was "the keystone for the edifice."[5] To Maria Martin, as for Auclert, the vote was a weapon, a necessary weapon in the struggle for life.[6] The CNFF publication, *L'Action féminine*, asserted in 1909 that "we must not forget that it is by obtaining our political rights that we can realize our just demands."[7] Schmahl characterized the vote as "the only means of obtaining adequate reforms ... [that will] relieve the disorder and unhappiness that desolate our country today."[8] Oddo-Deflou called civil and political rights "the two mistress columns of the structure," and argued that political suffrage "dominated all the rest."[9] Although when, in 1926, the suffragist attorney Suzanne Grinberg would publish her short history of the women's movement since 1848, claiming that "the right of suffrage is no longer considered as an end in itself, but as a means," she was fudging the adverbs when she wrote "no longer." [10] The evidence from the earlier decades demonstrates decisively that feminists in France had *never* considered the vote for women as an end in itself. In France as elsewhere in the Western world, the vote represented an enabling tool: the endgame was the full empowerment of women as citizens in civil, economic, and political life. By making possible the radical restructuring of the legal, economic, and social status of women in French society, feminists thought they could finally achieve serious woman-friendly sociopolitical reform in France (as was already happening in other countries where women were voting). What French women sought was the political authority that accompanied the vote, the authority to put their less tangible though much-acknowledged power and influence to work for

---

[4] Mme [Jeanne] Oddo-Deflou, "Ce que nous reste à conquerir, *L'Entente*, 1st issue (1905), 2.

[5] *Le Féminisme* (1907), p. 181. Also see note 17.

[6] Maria Martin, "L'Exemple des autres," *Le Journal des Femmes*, n° 181 (January 1908), front page.

[7] "Le Suffrage des femmes," *L'Action féminine*, n° 3 (1 June 1909), p. 35.

[8] Jeanne-E. Schmahl, "Propos d'une suffragiste: l'antisuffragette," *La Française*, n° 111 (28 February 1909).

[9] Jeanne Oddo-Deflou, "Préface" to *Congrès national des droits civils et du suffrage des femmes, Tenu les 26, 27, & 28 juin 1908. Compte rendu in extenso, recueilli, mis en order et publié par les soins de Mme Oddo Deflou* (Paris: n.p., 1910) (Asnières: chez Mme Vincent, 1910), vi. These proceedings are available on microfilm through the Research Publications microfilm collection, n.s. 1508, reel 718, n° 5739.

[10] Suzanne Grinberg, *Historique du mouvement suffragiste depuis 1848* (Paris: H. Goulet, 1926), p. 9.

the greater good. In the section on Suffrage at the 1913 Congress, Marguerite de Witt-Schlumberger put it this way:[11]

> Women need the vote for the exact same reasons as men do – to defend their particular interests, the interests of their children, the interests of their country and of humanity, which they often envision differently than men do.... Women's sphere is everywhere, because she represents half of humanity, whose life is intimately linked with that of the other half. The interests of men and women cannot be separated. Woman's sphere is therefore everywhere that man's sphere is, that is to say in the entire world.

As we have seen, members of the new generation of women's movement leaders had come around to the position long asserted by Auclert; by 1900–1901 they agreed that the main reason why substantive and sensible reforms in the laws governing women's situation were not forthcoming was because women had no political clout. Due to frustration with the lack of positive legislative response to their demands for radical reforms in the Civil Code and economic freedoms during the early years of the twentieth century, many feminists did finally designate women's suffrage as their most pressing political goal. When, in September 1900, the reformer and newspaperwoman Marguerite Durand and her associates convened an *international* congress on women's condition and rights in Paris, the suffrage question occupied a very prominent place on its agenda (see Chapter 8). It was then that René Viviani, deputy and future prime minister of France, had cautioned the assembled delegates: "In the name of my relatively long political and parliamentary experience, let me tell you that the legislators make the laws for those who make the legislators."[12] There was no getting around the fact that the so-called universal suffrage, which left out over half the adult population, was in no way "universal." And, due to the disputes about national belonging that arose during the Dreyfus Affair, the inclusiveness, or noninclusiveness of "universal" rights was spotlighted – not only as concerned Jewish military officers but also as concerned women. From that time on *"La femme doit voter"* [Woman

---

[11] *Dixième congrès international des femmes: Oeuvres et institutions féminines, Droits des femmes, 2-8 juin 1913, compte rendu des travaux par Mme Avril de Sainte-Croix* (Paris: V. Giard & E. Brière, 1914), sixième section: Suffrage. Report of Mme de Witt-Schlumberger, pp. 320–321. Her report and that of Maria Vérone occupy pp. 319–354 and rehearse all the laws and practices that need to be changed.

[12] René Viviani, reported in *La Fronde* (10 September 1900). For Viviani's full speech, see *Congrès International de la Condition et des Droits des Femmes, 5-8 septembre 1900, questions économiques, morales, et sociales: Éducation, législation, droit privé, droit public* (Paris: Imprimerie des Arts et Manufactures, 1901), pp. 195–205.

Must Vote] became a constant refrain in the feminist literature and gained increasing public support.

In the tense political climate of early twentieth-century France – where the major challenges confronting the fabric of French society included not only depopulation and women's employment, but also the Dreyfus Affair, separation of church and state, a proposed income tax, anarchism and assassinations, and industrial worker unrest – it may not surprise readers to learn that the first bills for women's suffrage made their political debut in an extremely timid, noncomprehensive form. Two woman suffrage bills by pro-feminist legislators were introduced into the all-male Chamber of Deputies during the first decade of the twentieth century.[13] The first, in 1901, introduced as a private bill by a friendly deputy from the Vendée, Fernand Gautret, sought municipal and legislative suffrage for unmarried women, including divorced women and widows (thus skirting the issue of married women's subordinate legal status in the family); it was referred to committee and quietly buried there.[14] The second, introduced in l906 by Paul Dussaussoy, a liberal Catholic deputy from the Pas-de-Calais, sought to confer the vote on all adult women in both municipal and cantonal (but not national parliamentary) elections. Both bills signified small steps forward, but neither reached the floor of the Chamber for debate. By this time, the question of woman suffrage had become inextricably intertwined with the broader – and highly emotional – discussion on overall electoral reform via proportional representation, brought on by an ever-growing concern for the future of parliamentary democracy in France. Many apprehensive legislators thought this proposal should be addressed first.

A change in pace lay around the corner, as French campaigns for woman suffrage would begin to gather momentum once again. The year 1906 was, first of all, a year for legislative elections in France, and suffrage activity would pick up, with various propaganda measures – postcards and postage stamps, posters, manifestos, even small parades through the streets of Paris, sponsored by one or more feminist groups.[15] Jeanne Oddo-Deflou's

---

[13] I use the terms "woman suffrage" and "women's suffrage" interchangeably in this section.

[14] The historical arguments made in support of women's suffrage by Gautret in 1901 merit our consideration. Gautret's charges anticipate the later investigations of Joan Kelly and others into the sexism of the early humanist scholars. In effect, Gautret blamed Renaissance biblical and talmudic scholars for undercutting and distorting the earlier, more favorable position of women in France by dredging up "orientalist" arguments to reestablish women's inferiority. On Gautret's position, see André Leclère, *Le Vote des femmes en France; les causes de l'attitude particulière à notre pays* (Paris: M. Rivière, 1929), p. 101.

[15] See the accounting of activities in 1906 by Maria Martin, "La Propagande suffragiste," in the 1907 *Petit Almanach féministe*, pp. 14–15.

Groupe Français d'Études Féministes (GFEF) spearheaded at least one consolidated effort to publicize the question, as did *Solidarité des Femmes* (under Caroline Kauffmann and Madeleine Pelletier) and Hubertine Auclert's group, *Suffrage des Femmes*. Women began to show up at male candidates' meetings. International developments also provided an impetus, following the pathbreaking and inspiring enfranchisement – and election to parliament – of Finnish women in the summer of 1906 – the first women in Europe to vote. Cheered on by this breakthrough in Finland, supplemented by the news that impatient English women (suffragettes, as distinct from suffragists) were mounting an ever more intensive and bellicose campaign for the vote through the Women's Social and Political Union (WSPU), and the forthcoming congress of the newly organized International Woman Suffrage Alliance (IWSA) in Copenhagen, journalist and editor Maria Martin applauded how women were coming together internationally to pursue their goals. Might not French women also mobilize to pursue theirs? "In general," wrote Maria Martin in the *Journal des Femmes*, "public opinion indicates that it is only just to grant women the right to vote. Only – there are always those who say 'only' and 'but' – some would prefer that women not ask for it. According to them, it would be preferable if they wait silently until the socialists, or the catholics, or the radicals offer women the ballot on a silver platter."[16] The silver platter not being forthcoming, the CNFF founded its suffrage section in late 1906, with none other than Hubertine Auclert as its initial president; in the spring of 1907 the Council, with the help of the *Ligue des Droits de l'Homme*, would launch a nationwide petition for unrestricted women's suffrage.[17]

Historiography of the French Suffrage Movement

Historians of France have long treated the French suffrage movement during the Third Republic as the wallflower among the suffrage movements of Europe and America. Until very recently, their guiding question

---

[16] Maria Martin, "L'Union fait la force," *Le Journal des Femmes*, nᵒˢ 167–168 (July–August 1906).

[17] The correspondence between Auclert and Avril de Sainte-Croix concerning Auclert's CNFF appointment and resignation is archived in Auclert's papers at the BHVP; see Steven C. Hause, *Hubertine Auclert: The French Suffragette* (New Haven, CT: Yale University Press, 1987), pp. 188–189. On the 1907 petition, see also Chapter 9. The text of the CNFF petition is reproduced in Mme [Ghénia] Avril de Sainte-Croix, *Le Féminisme* (Paris: V. Giard & E. Briere, 1907), pp. 197–198.

was: "Why did it take so long for women in France to obtain the vote?"[18] Since the early twentieth century the standard for comparison was swiftly becoming the militant, media-savvy movement of the WSPU in England, which pioneered the use of dramatic and publicity-seeking nonviolent militant tactics that quickly made headlines in the press worldwide. Measured against this "gold standard," which fixated on the unprecedented exploits of the Pankhursts and their associates, or that of the multipronged (state-by-state) mass suffrage campaigns in the United States, the French campaign did look relatively sedate. Thus it took some time before investigators decided to look into the actual development of the French campaigns for suffrage.

The much-appreciated pioneering studies published in the 1980s by Steven C. Hause (with Anne R. Kenney), followed by the contributions of Florence Rochefort and Laurence Klejman, have done much to reestablish the chronology and significance of the French women's suffrage campaigns.[19] Indeed, their interpretations had to overcome the dismissal of

---

[18] Anne-Sarah Bouglé-Moalic points out that this view that France was "retarded" as concerned the vote began with contemporaries; see *La Vote des Françaises: Cent ans de débats, 1848–1944* (Rennes: Presses Universitaires de Rennes, 2012), pp. 166–170. Many contemporary sources do remark on the granting of the franchise to women in Wyoming in 1869, followed by the successful campaign for the vote in New Zealand and the Australian territories. In 1911 these sources would make much of the successful statewide referendum for women's suffrage in California. It seems clear that, for suffragists, to claim that France was "*en retard*" was to shame the Republic and its legislative bodies.

[19] See Steven C. Hause, with Anne R. Kenney, *Women's Suffrage and Social Politics in the French Third Republic* (Princeton, NJ: Princeton University Press, 1984); see also Hause & Kenney, "The Limits of Suffragist Behavior: Legalism, Militancy, and Violence in France, 1876–1914," *American Historical Review*, 86:4 (October 1981), 781–806. See also, and especially, the following articles by Florence Rochefort, which supplement the chapters in Klejman & Rochefort, *L'Égalité en marche* (Paris: FNSP & des Femmes, 1989): Florence Rochefort, "La citoyenneté interdite, ou les enjeux du suffragisme," *Vingtième Siècle*, n° 42 (April–June 1994), 41–51; Florence Rochefort, "Démocratie féministe contre démocratie exclusive ou les enjeux de la mixité, " in *Démocratie et représentation*, ed. Michèle Riot-Sarcey (Paris: Kimé, 1995), pp. 181–202; and Rochefort & Laurence Klejman, "Au nom du droit et de la spécificité féminine: Diversité des tactiques et ambiguïté du mouvement suffragiste avant la première guerre mondiale," in *La Démocratie 'à la française', ou les femmes indésirables*, ed. Éliane Viennot (Paris: Publications de l'Université Paris 7 – Denis Diderot, 1996), pp. 223–231. For post-1918 developments, see Christine Bard, *Les Filles de Marianne: Histoire des féminismes 1914–1944* (Paris: Fayard, 1995) and the important account in English by Paul Smith, *Feminism and the Third Republic: Women's Political and Civil Rights in France, 1918–1945* (Oxford, UK: Clarendon Press, 1996). A popularized anniversary account is *Citoyennes! Il y a cinquante ans, le vote des femmes* by Albert & Nicole du Roy (Paris: Flammarion, 1994). A short overview in English is provided by Karen Offen, "Women, Citizenship, and Suffrage with a French Twist, 1789–1993," in *Suffrage and Beyond: International Feminist Perspectives*, ed. Caroline Daley & Melanie Nolan (Auckland: Auckland University Press; copublished with New York University Press and Pluto Press, London, 1994), pp. 151–170; in French translation as "Les Femmes, la citoyenneté et le droit de vote en France, 1789-1993, " in *Le Processus d'intégration des femmes au politique: Féminismes et cultures nationales*, ed. Yolande Cohen & Françoise Thébaud (Lyon: Centre Jacques Cartier, 1998), pp. 44–70.

women's suffrage by the 1970s women's liberation movement. In the heyday of women's liberation, it had become fashionable, in the United States and elsewhere, for post-1968 feminists to criticize their predecessors for their fixation on the vote to the exclusion of other more radical sexual reforms, including the legalization of abortion. In her book *Sexual Politics* (1st edition, 1970), for example, Kate Millett (whose work also appeared in French translation in 1971 as *Le Politique du mâle*) condemned the pursuit of the ballot as "the red herring of the revolution," "so minimal an end."[20] It took the determination of historians like Ellen Carol DuBois to almost singlehandedly rehabilitate the historical suffrage campaigns, demonstrating how radical – and significant – these actually were in the American context, while other historians began to reassess suffrage movements in other countries, beginning in 1893 with New Zealand, the first nation-state to enfranchise all its women.[21] The new studies of the French suffrage movement followed on this newly aroused enthusiasm, but perhaps did not appreciate the extent to which French suffrage advocates rested their case on "equality-in-difference." These earlier publications have been supplemented by the recent study (2012) by Anne-Sarah Bouglé-Moalic, which reexamines the suffrage campaigns primarily through the eyes of the male-dominated mainstream press and parliamentary debates, and the valuable new political biography of Cécile Brunschvicg by Cécile Formaglio.[22] Yet, there is more to be said concerning the historical debates on suffrage in Third Republic France as part of the greater "woman question."

What earlier historians downplayed or even overlooked is the evidence that indicates that most French suffrage movement leaders deliberately and repeatedly foreswore, resisted, failed to endorse, and occasionally

The foundational account is Ferdinand Buisson, *Le Vote des femmes* (Paris: H. Denot & E. Pinat, eds., 1911) in the publisher's series Encyclopédie Parlementaire des Sciences Politique et Sociales, which republished Buisson's favorable report to the Chamber of Deputies (see n. 92). See also Grinberg, *Historique du mouvement suffragiste* (cited in n. 10), and Leclère, *Vote des femmes* (cited in n. 14), for further analysis and commentary.

20 Kate Millett, *Sexual Politics* (1st ed., Garden City, NY: Doubleday, 1970). The quotes come from pp. 83 and 85 in the Equinox/Avon paperback edition of 1971.

21 See Ellen Carol DuBois, *Feminism and Suffrage: The Emergence of an Independent Women's Movement in America, 1848–1869* (Ithaca, NY: Cornell University Press, 1978). See also Patricia Grimshaw, *Women's Suffrage in New Zealand* (Auckland, NZ: Auckland University Press, 1972; reprinted, 1987). An excellent retrospective on the world's woman suffrage campaigns is provided by the articles in *Suffrage and Beyond: International Feminist Perspectives* (cited in n. 19), and the classic articles by Barbara Molony, Patricia Grimshaw, Rochelle Ruthchild, and Louise Edwards in *Globalizing Feminisms, 1789–1945*, ed. Karen Offen (London & New York: Routledge, 2010).

22 See Bouglé-Moalic, *Vote des Françaises*, cited in n. 18, and Cécile Formaglio, *"Féministe d'abord": Cécile Brunschvicg (1877–1946)* in the series Archives du Féminisme (Rennes: Presses Universitaires de Rennes, 2014), which appeared only after I had written this chapter.

condemned the tactics of Britain's militant suffragettes. Mass mobilization and direct actions that included dramatic public demonstrations and deliberate acts of violence against property never became part of the French suffrage strategy. Virtually all French woman suffrage advocates (with the notable, and very temporary, exception of Madeleine Pelletier and Hubertine Auclert) insisted that French women could – and must – obtain the vote and eligibility to run for office by dignified, well-reasoned and "ladylike" means. Why was this? Because, strategically speaking, they thought they could gain the vote by working through their very numerous contacts and "influence" in high places. Marguerite Durand had become a master of using her contacts in the ministries, thanks (in par at least) to her personal relationship with René Viviani, even though she continued to insist that French feminists should express their admiration and support for the imprisoned and force-fed suffragettes.[23] The women of the CNFF and LFDF opposed violent tactics, got behind the Dussaussoy project for women's suffrage at the municipal level, and demonstrated their talents at "working" their government contacts. As time went on, it looked as though this strategy was highly effective. In 1913, Jane Misme quoted Ghénia Avril de Sainte-Croix, who with amusement pointed out to ministers and legislators that "you have been forced to get to know us, because we are always on your doorstep."[24] In fact, by 1913, the leaders of the CNFF had induced Third Republic officialdom to roll out the red carpet for the Tenth International Congress of Women, including substantial subsidies, receptions at the Elysée Palace, hosted by President and Mme Poincaré; at the Quai d'Orsay (ministry of foreign affairs), hosted by Foreign Minister Stephen Pichon; use of the Sorbonne amphitheatre for its opening session granted by Louis Liard, then rector of the Academy of Paris; and the escort services of another minister for the grand entry of Lady Aberdeen, president of the International Council of Women (ICW), at the opening session of the congress. The municipal suffrage bill would be revived in 1914 and sent on to the newly elected legislature for consideration.

Indeed, these energetic French feminists were playing a conspicuous part in the expanding French civil society from 1900 on, even though they were not voting citizens. Freedom of the press (1881), coupled with the vast new opportunities for women's education (if not economic opportunity)

[23] See Durand's unsuccessful effort to force a resolution to this effect at the Tenth International Women's Congress in Paris, 1913.

[24] Quoted by Jane Misme, "Un Congrès féministe à Paris," *La Revue* (1 July 1913), 54–61; quote p. 55.

and passage of the new laws on association (1901) stimulated a flurry of activity, and in the first decades of the twentieth-century Third Republic, a broader cohort of women would (again) swing into action in order to claim full citizenship as their entitlement.[25] The leaders of the newly formed *Union Française pour le Suffrage des Femmes* (UFSF) put it this way in 1909: "Surely in France more than anywhere else women deserve to be enfranchised. By contributing their taxes to the State and municipal funds, by their participation in industrial, commercial and intellectual work, by their devotion to their family [sic] and their country, Frenchwomen have the same right to vote as Frenchmen have."[26]

By proceeding cautiously, opting to pursue the municipal ballot as a first step, while maintaining the principle that women deserved both the municipal vote and, ultimately, the parliamentary vote, the feminists thought they could attract the necessary parliamentary support. British women had exercised the municipal vote since 1870, even as they had failed to obtain the parliamentary vote; their current campaigns for the latter were inspiring, but their French counterparts (with only a few exceptions) thought they should not ask for everything at once, and that aggressive behavior would not work in their favor.

French Women Claim Rights and Reform as Capable Embodied Female Citizens

During the early years of the Third Republic most women – and their male supporters – had presented their claims for equality in the law, including suffrage, by arguing that women's differences from men, in particular their incipient motherhood, gave them an irrefutable claim on citizenship in the French nation, including full civil and political rights. Jeanne Deroin had already developed this argument eloquently in 1849, as we have seen, and many more had deployed it since. Feminists increasingly

---

[25] Material in this section has been revisited and revised from earlier work, beginning with my article on "Women: Political Rights," in *Historical Dictionary of the IIIe Republic*, ed. Patrick H. Hutton (New York: Greenwood Press, 1986), pp. 1077–1079; and subsequently in the following articles: "Exploring the Sexual Politics of French Nationalism," in *Nationhood and Nationalism in France: From Boulangism to the Great War, 1889–1918*, ed. Robert Tombs (London: HarperCollins Academic, 1991), pp. 195–209; "Women, Citizenship, and Suffrage with a French Twist, 1789-1993," *Suffrage and Beyond: International Feminist Perspectives* (cited in n. 19). See also Karen Offen, "Des modèles nationaux (1900–1945)?" in *Le Siècle des féminismes*, ed. Éliane Gubin et al. (Paris: Les Éditions de l'Atelier, 2004), pp. 65–79.

[26] The UFSF statement is reprinted in English translation in *Jus Suffragii*, vol. 4, n° 2 (15 October 1909), 10–11; quote, 10.

made their claims on the rights of women *as individuals of the female sex*, by virtue of their differences from men – and their acknowledged importance to the French state as citizen-mothers.[27] Since the French Revolution, this had been the dominant (though not the only) French feminist approach to renegotiating what political theorist Carole Pateman has called (for the British case) "the sexual contract."[28] Another strand of this "relational" argumentation focused on the interdependency of the male/female couple. In the population-conscious political atmosphere of the early Third Republic, such "relational" arguments appealed to many women and had the potential to appeal far more to contemporary male sensibilities (at least those of progressively minded men, including many republican Solidarists, albeit not to the Proudhonistes and others who continued to parrot their assertions about women's inferiority) than did arguments based on generic individual rights and abstract justice.[29] In one of my first published articles, I argued that "the emphasis on motherhood by French republican feminists ... was a realistic, even astute, response to difficult political circumstances."[30] The evidence I have reviewed since then confirms this judgment, and, what is more, I understand these French feminists to be speaking sincerely and strategically when they affirmed women's right to a sexually embodied and culturally distinct individuality. In the game of Bridge that was French sexual politics, this was, in fact, their trump card.

Most French feminists thought they could best achieve their goals by using their powers of feminine persuasion on republican leaders and legislators. They understood that the venerable notion of "women's influence" was a tool they could utilize, especially when they lacked "authority."[31] After all, since 1880 they had lived in a secular parliamentary republic, ostensibly devoted (and here the contrast with England, with its property-based franchise, was explicit) to democratic development; the French franchise had included all men since 1848, and the pursuit of women's rights could be documented not only from 1848 but from 1789;

[27] Karen Offen, "Depopulation, Nationalism, and Feminism in Fin-de-siècle France," *The American Historical Review*, 89:3 (June 1984), 648–676, esp. 674–675. See also Offen, "Defining Feminism: A Comparative Historical Approach," *Signs: Journal of Women in Culture and Society*, 14:1 (Autumn 1988), 119–157.

[28] Carole Pateman, *The Sexual Contract* (Stanford, CA: Stanford University Press, 1988).

[29] For an excellent statement of the individual rights and justice arguments, see Raoul de la Grasserie, "Le mouvement féministe et les droits de la femme," *La Revue Politique et Parlementaire*, 1:3 (September 1894), 432–449. The author, clearly a male-feminist, was a lawyer and a judge for the tribunal of Rennes.

[30] Offen, "Depopulation," p. 674.

[31] See my chapters on the questions of French women's influence and their historical exclusion from political authority in my companion volume, *The Woman Question in France, 1400–1870*.

indeed, history was on their side, given that historical research (Vincent, Viollet) supported feminist assertions that that French women had enjoyed political and civil rights for centuries prior to 1789. But also, in retrospect, most French republican suffrage advocates seemed confident of their ultimate success. Why was that? To Jeanne Oddo-Deflou it was all about acknowledging and sanctioning women's influence. In her view,[32]

> Success is assured because, in the final analysis, it is only a question of putting legislation in agreement with the real position of woman in our society. The translation of fact by law is logical, thus certain. The evolution consists of transforming an occult influence into an open influence; subterranean machinations do not suit either elite minds or honest souls. And we hope that women's power, exercised in broad daylight, will be the power of feminine virtues substituted for the power of feminine wiles.

Moreover – and this was a significant consideration – women had become the majority of the French adult population: Marguerite Durand (in 1908), Jeanne-E. Schmahl and Maria Vérone (in 1909, based on recent census data) would all pointedly attest that women outnumbered men by around one million, out of a total population of 39.2 million.[33] How, they queried, in a real democracy, could the minority (men) make laws for the majority (women)? Surely, in their view, the current situation was absurd. They felt that both logic and republican principles were on their side.

In the 1900s, a decade marked by a surge in patriotic consciousness but also fiercely nationalistic political challenges on the Right, the leaders of the French republican women's movement made a concerted effort to identify feminism with the national community; *les Françaises* repeatedly asserted their claims to equal standing with *les Français*. Witness, for example, the emphasis on the term **Française** at the founding in 1901 of the *Conseil National des Femmes Françaises* (which by 1909 boasted of 75,000 members, through affiliated groups), the naming of the feminist newspaper *La Française* in 1906, and of the *Union Française pour le Suffrage des Femmes* in 1909. In 1908, two feminist groups, *Solidarité des Femmes* and the *Groupe Français d'Etudes Féministes*, would convoke a *national* congress on women's rights and suffrage; the organizers appealed to French women's solidarity above and beyond differences of religion, politics, and

---

[32] Jeanne Oddo-Deflou, in her long congress summary in *La Liberté d'Opinion*, vol. 2, n° 3 (May–June 1908), 72–128; quote, 127.

[33] See Durand's speech at the 1908 *Congrès national des droits civils et du suffrage des femmes . . . compte rendu*, p. 137; and Jeanne-E. Schmahl, "Propos d'une suffragiste," *La Française*, (6th article) n° 113 (14 March 1909). The exact number for the French population (census of 4 March 1906) was 39,252,267.

socioeconomic class.[34] Such efforts by French feminists to assert their intrinsic connection with the national community may seem exaggerated in retrospect. But they should not surprise us. Such emphases are extremely meaningful; they deserve our attention, not least because they suggest the sheer force of national sentiment on both sexes in early twentieth-century France. Few republican men, including those of the dominant radical parties, dared to stand apart. And some women from all points of the political and religious spectrum – Catholics, Protestants, Jews, even atheists – had begun to insist that they be fully included. Those who had attended the new secular primary and secondary schools had, after all, been educated to become *citoyennes* of the democratic French republic.[35] For growing numbers of them, the unanswered questions became not "would they be admitted" but how soon, and subject to what conditions? Under the Third Republic, feminist suffrage advocates in France thought they could simply hold the feet of republican men to the fire, invoking republican and national principles to play on their liberal guilt. Some played the politics of righteous indignation, arguing that among French men even idiots could vote, while intelligent, educated French women could not.

Others would question whether the majority of French women were really committed to obtaining the vote. Opinions differed. In 1902, the journalist Louise Faure-Favier (1870–1961) insisted in the *Revue Bleue* that overall, even though "politics" had seemingly "invaded everything," women were not especially interested. "They" (*elles*) were this and they were that, and they were emotional rather than rational, and basically they could not care less.[36] Politics, to "*elles*" were sentimental, not about "interests." But even Faure-Favier invoked the "influence" argument – women will become "councilors," "to give counsel is often the best means of action." "The men," she indicated, "would continue to frequent the parliamentary assemblies, but it is the women who will direct them. . . . They will not vote. The men will vote for them. Why then aspire to

[34] See the proceedings, *Congrès national des droits civils et du suffrage des femmes . . . compte rendu*. The best general account of feminist politics and organizing during the Third Republic, especially after 1889, is Laurence Klejman & Florence Rochefort, *L'Egalité en marche: le féminisme sous la Troisième République* (Paris: FNSP/des femmes, 1989). On suffrage in particular, see Hause, with Kenney, *Women's Suffrage and Social Politics*.

[35] See Linda L. Clark, *Schooling the Daughters of Marianne: Textbooks and the Socialization of Girls in Modern French Primary Schools* (Albany, NY: State University of New York Press, 1984).

[36] See Louise Faure-Favier, "Les Femmes et la politique," *La Revue Bleue* (3 May 1902), 574–576.

become the equals of men in politics? This would diminish us, since it is so easy to become or to remain their superiors."[37]

The English journalist Charles Dawbarn explained to his readers in 1910 that in France, for the most part, "one of the most significant facts about the movement is that men are more bent upon it than women."[38] "Silent and insidious is the march of Feminism, and the more dangerous in consequence." Impressed with the forward march of feminine achievement in France, which he equated with feminism, in the final analysis Dawbarn fell back on a concern not only about a loss of "feminine charm" but also about "the growing effeminacy of the male." "It would seem," he proposed, that "Nature had only a certain amount of virility to bestow, and that the masculinity of woman is at the expense of the manliness of man." (Dawbarn's thought exemplifies the venerable topsy-turvy, zero-sum notion of how societies work). In conclusion, this author from across the Channel dwelt upon the theme of womanly influence that Faure-Favier had spoken to earlier: "In France the woman has succeeded in the astonishing feat of capturing man by her natural charms and yet in imposing herself upon the world by her intellectuality and capacity. It is quite likely that part of her indifference to the actual symbol of power resides in the fact that she prefers to exercise that subtler force, which is occult."[39]

In the 1780s the champion of women's rights and equality, the marquis de Condorcet had fretted about this very problem: had nothing then changed in over a hundred years in the entrenched belief of men in (and concern about the potency of) women's influence – a belief that was certainly shared by many French women, including many feminists, as we have seen earlier? But such views about the potency of women's influence were also shared by men of the working classes, exemplified by the revolutionary syndicalist Maxime Vasseur, who in 1913 wrote against the granting of the political vote to women. His concern was that unenlightened wives, mothers, and even daughters, were influencing their working-class husbands, sons, and brothers adversely, that is, against

---

[37] Faure-Favier, "Les Femmes et la politique," 576. Several recent books have underscored the importance of women's continuing influence as *égéries*, the secret but highly effective counselors of male political actors. See Marie-Thérèse Guichard, *Les Égéries de la République* (Paris: Payot, 1991), and Susan K. Foley & Charles Sowerwine, *A Political Romance: Léon Gambetta, Léonie Léon, and the Making of the French Republic, 1872–82* (Houndmills, UK: Palgrave, 2012).

[38] See Charles Dawbarn, "The French Woman and the Vote," *Fortnightly Review* (August 1911), 328–335; quotes here and following, 329, 334, 335.

[39] Dawbarn, "French Woman and the Vote," 335.

joining unions or striking for higher wages and better working conditions. Interestingly, his rant ignored the proposition that was actually up for discussion: the modest Dussaussoy-Buisson bill, which would grant women municipal suffrage but not the parliamentary vote.[40]

The French Suffrage Campaigns Begin to Gather Steam, 1906–1909

As we have mentioned earlier, 1906 proved to be a turning point. This had, in part, to do with developments in the separate, but mutually entwined spheres of Catholics and Socialists, interacting with the feminists, in the anxiety-producing context of the definitive separation of church and state. On the first of May, *Le Temps* reported that the pope Pius IX had denounced woman suffrage and female politicians during a private audience accorded to the Viennese feminist journalist and novelist, Camille Theimer.[41] Reports of this event attracted further coverage, including an interview with Theimer, in the June issue of the women's magazine, *Femina*.[42] Not all French Catholics were happy with the pope's opposition to women in politics; in a speech at the Catholic women's conference (*Congrès Jeanne d'Arc*) in late May, the pro-woman abbé Jean Lagardère argued that women should engage in political life. Votes for women was a coming idea and "we" [i.e., Catholics] don't want the Freemasons telling women how to vote.[43] Of course, the secular republicans (whose ranks indeed included many Freemasons) had long been obsessed by precisely the opposite idea – that priests would tell women how to vote. The feminists, not surprisingly, would argue that to claim women could be told by anyone how to vote was to underestimate them: women could perfectly well make up their own minds about how to vote, given the opportunity to do so.

In June, anticipating the meeting in Paris of the Executive Council of the ICW, the distinguished Isabelle Bogelot, former director of the *Oeuvre des Libérées de Saint-Lazare*, currently the honorary president of the CNFF and a former officer of the ICW (as well as a much applauded recipient of the medal of the *Légion d'Honneur*), insisted not only on the immense size of the organization, its character as "a federation of working women" (she

---

[40] Maxime Vasseur, "Notre Féminisme," *La Bataille Syndicaliste*, n° 794 (28 June 1913).

[41] "Une interview du pape Pie X," *Le Temps* (1 May 1906), from the *Neue Wiener Tageblatt*.

[42] See Max Rivière, "Le Pape et le féminisme," *Femina* (1 June 1906), 241.

[43] Jean Lagardère, "La Femme et la politique," discours prononcé au Congrès Jeanne d'Arc à L'Institut Catholique de Paris le 30 mai 1906, published in *La Femme Contemporaine*, n° 36 (October 1906), 785–796.

used the word *travailleuses*), but also on its commitment to obtaining women's suffrage in every country that had a representative form of government. She noted, however, the resistance in the Latin countries, where skepticism existed about the efficacity of the vote, "even though it might seem unjust that a Madame Guizot de Witt, a Madame Curie, or a Madame Kergomard – to mention only our honorary members – cannot vote, whereas the most illiterate peasant can give his advice on public affairs." She reiterated the commitment of ICW/CNFF women to address the plight of poor working women, "demanding the vote for women, in order to obtain more respect for their rights and those of their children," and to fostering "a more perfect union of ideas and feelings among the *travailleuses* of all classes, all parties, and all religions in view of the most extensive application of the grand principle 'Do unto others, as you would have others do unto you'."[44]

French socialist spokesmen seemed worried that in the wake of the defeat of the political Right in France's spring 1906 legislative elections, its forces would offer their own woman suffrage bill – "in the hopes that the enfranchisement of this 'half' of humanity might bring them back into power." The *Revue Socialiste* therefore launched a survey of European socialist leaders, the question being whether women should be enfranchised immediately or whether a transition was necessary; what, in short, should be the response of French socialist deputies to such an initiative from the Right? The periodical drew responses from as far away as Russia, but also included socialist party leaders such as Emile Vandervelde (Belgium), Karl Kautsky (Germany via Austria), Keir Hardie (Britain), etc., all of whom affirmed their commitment to women's equality and to the pursuit of women's suffrage. Most of these men doubted that the much-vaunted clerical menace was really the threat to the Republic that some perceived it to be, and were skeptical that the right-wing deputies would actually propose a women's suffrage measure.[45] Would the socialists then propose one first?

In anticipation of action, Dr. Madeleine Pelletier joined the newly unified Socialist party, known as the *Section Française de l'Internationale*

---

[44] Isabelle Bogelot, "Les Femmes qui agissent," *L'Écho de Paris* ([mid-June] 1906). Clipping at the BMD: DOS 396 CON/Conseil International des Femmes, 1897–1914. The Golden Rule ("Do unto others . . . ") was the ICW's motto or mission statement.

[45] See *La Revue Socialiste*, n° 260 (15 August 1906), 145–166. At the end of the article, Louise Chaboseau-Napias spoke of the possibility of an international conference of women socialists, to be organized by the German socialist women's organization. Such a conference did take place in 1907 in Stuttgart.

Ouvrière (SFIO). She had been publishing in the socialist press for some time.[46] She had also taken part in public debates, such as those at the Paris Sociology Society, on women's social role. There she defended women's right to object to men's assigning them a constrained social role; all individuals should have the right to choose their place in society, she argued.[47] In a subsequent meeting of the society she attempted to set the record straight that "feminism is not the struggle of women against men, as a sex." Such a view was a complete misunderstanding, she argued: what feminists demanded was the elimination of the obstacles that society had thrown in women's way. Pelletier objected to the Positivist notion that "the differentiation of the sexes was the necessary corollary of the progress of civilization," and against the views of Auguste Comte she invoked those of his opponent on the woman question, John Stuart Mill (which at the Sociology Society, dominated by Comtists, could be construed as heresy).[48] No one, she asserted, should be telling women what to do or what to be; in her view, individuals had the right to make their own choices.[49] Although Pelletier did not specifically address the suffrage question in these two sessions, another woman speaker, Mme J. de Maguerie, did – pointing out how the fact that women could not currently vote was being used to disqualify them from having any input into resolving France's severe social problems.[50]

Votes for women quickly attracted Madeleine Pelletier's attention. In her capacity as the new secretary of the feminist group *Solidarité des Femmes*, Pelletier spoke on behalf of women's suffrage at the SFIO congress in Limoges in November 1906, cleverly refuting the various "practical" objections she had heard voiced by members of a political party that had, since 1891, accepted the

---

[46] See Pelletier's article "Les Femmes et le féminisme," n° 253, *La Revue Socialiste* (January 1906), 37–45. She defended the feminists from the allegation by opponents that they wanted to turn women into men, but at the same time criticized the use made by some (presumably she was alluding to Marguerite Durand and her associates) of their feminine charms to achieve their ends.

[47] See Madeleine Pelletier, remarks in opposition to the positivist claims of Émile Cheysson, "Séance de Sociologie de Paris; séance du mercredi 8 november 1905)," *Revue Internationale de Sociologie*, 13:12 (December 1905), 886–887.

[48] See *Lettres inédites de John Stuart Mill à Auguste Comte, publiées avec les réponses de Comte et une Introduction par L. Lévy-Bruhl* (Paris: Felix Alcan, 1899). This publication seems to have reinvigorated French interest in the British philosopher's active support of women's rights, especially women's suffrage, a cause that Mill had vigorously supported in the British parliament in the later 1860s. Prior to this time, only Comte's letters to Mill had been published (Paris: Ernest Leroux, 1877).

[49] Pelletier, remarks in the session of January 1906, *Revue Internationale de Sociologie*, 14:1 (February 1906), 139.

[50] Mme J. de Marguerie, session of January 1906, *Revue Internationale de Sociologie*, 14:1 (February 1906), 140.

principle of equal suffrage. In fact, the SFIO congress adopted the resolution she proposed to stimulate the party to take action on the woman suffrage question.[51] To ensure that the suffrage question did not fall off the SFIO's radar, in January 1907 Pelletier organized a deputation of socialist-feminist women to call on the socialist deputies at the Palais Bourbon, to remind them of their obligation to take action. In May she addressed the question of "bourgeois feminism" in the pages of the Guesdist publication, *Le Socialiste*, arguing that feminism signified political and social equality for both sexes, and that "its triumph would benefit all women," whether working class or middle class.[52] It seems clear that Pelletier was acting simultaneously as a feminist and a socialist.[53] But this balancing act would prove to be a difficult one: even as Pelletier was militating in various SFIO factions, first *guesdiste*, then the even more extreme *hervéiste* (even representing the latter on the central committee of the SFIO), she was publishing the monthly *La Suffragiste* (1908–1920), the mottos of which were "*Droit de Travail, Droit de Vote*" [Right to Work, Right to Vote].

In mid-June 1907, Pelletier and the former secretary of *Solidarité des Femmes*, Caroline Kauffmann, organized a combined delegation of French suffrage supporters, visiting English "suffragettes" (members of the WSPU) and feminists from a number of European countries, to parade through Paris, then to call on Georges Clemenceau (then prime minister as well as minister of the interior) and on the French socialist leader Jean Jaurès at the Chamber of Deputies. They subsequently paid a visit to the offices of the leading socialist daily, *L'Humanité*. Their group photo appeared on "la une" of *L'Humanité*, along with their message: "We want the right to vote. Feminists from every European nation understand that they will obtain nothing as long as they cannot vote."[54] They invoked the

---

[51] Pelletier's speech to the SFIO's Limoges' congress can be accessed through Gallica – *3e Congrès national, tenu à Limoges, les 1, 2, 3, et 4 novembre 1906: compte rendu analytique*, pp. 146–151. See Charles Sowerwine, *Sisters or Citizens?*, pp. 117–123, and Felicia Gordon, *The Integral Feminist: Madeleine Pelletier* (Minneapolis: University of Minnesota Press, 1990), chapter 5, esp. pp. 111–113. Cf. also Marilyn J. Boxer, "Socialism Faces Feminism in France: 1879-1913" (Ph.D. dissertation, University of California at Riverside, 1975), pp. 232–238.

[52] Madeleine Pelletier, "Féminisme bourgeois et féminisme socialiste," *Le Socialiste* (5–12 May 1907), 5–12.

[53] See Charles Sowerwine, "Madeleine Pelletier, fut-elle socialiste?" in *Madeleine Pelletier (1874–1939): Logique et infortunes d'un combat pour l'égalité*, ed. Christine Bard (Paris: côté-femmes, 1992), pp. 145–155.

[54] See the front page of *L'Humanité*, 18 June 1907. According to the account, the women included English suffragettes, members of *Solidarité des Femmes*, and a contingent of "Russian, Dutch, Italian, Swiss, and Polish feminists." A photograph of the group at the offices of *L'Humanité* accompanied this article.

"no taxation without representation" trope, but also emphasized the social good that enfranchised women could accomplish.

In August 1907 the German socialist leader Clara Zetkin (who, already in the mid-1890s, had declared her opposition to cooperating with "bourgeois" feminists, asserting that class struggle must take precedence over sex struggle), convened the first international congress of socialist women in Stuttgart. This conference endorsed unrestricted women's suffrage, resolving as follows: "Women's suffrage is the correlate of the economic emancipation of women from the household and of their economic independence from family owing to their professional work. With the sharpening of the class struggle, the question of women's suffrage rises in importance."[55] The ensuing, larger congress of the Second Socialist International also endorsed the pursuit of unrestricted women's suffrage within the existing order (even as they claimed that private property was the real problem). As one of the delegates from the SFIO to the Second International's congress and in her capacity as secretary of *Solidarité des Femmes*, Pelletier found herself in opposition to the prevailing Zetkin line. In September Hubertine Auclert would likewise respond to Zetkin's formulation, arguing that "there cannot be a bourgeois feminism and a socialist feminism because there are not two female sexes."[56]

In the interim, the French SFIO responded equivocally to the Second International's suffrage imperative: as Charles Sowerwine summarizes the situation, "the party voted to present a bill for women's suffrage which was never written and ... in 1907 the SFIO deputies named a sub-committee on women's rights which never met."[57] Steven Hause concurs: "The SFIO offered many words and little action."[58] Madeleine Pelletier kept pressing on the party to take positive action, to honor their commitment, but with no success.

In June 1908, both Pelletier and Kauffmann journeyed to England to attend the massive militant suffrage demonstration on the 21st at London's Hyde Park. This event would draw a crowd of over 500,000 women. Discouraged by her inability to foster such a public display of militance among Parisian feminists, Pelletier subsequently expressed her disillusionment both with her socialist comrades, whom she suggested were just as egoistically male as the rest, as well as with the timidity of her erstwhile

---

[55] Resolution of the International Socialist Women's Conference (Stuttgart, Germany, August 1907).
[56] Auclert, "Socialistes et bourgeoises," *Le Radical* (3 September 1907).
[57] See Charles Sowerwine, *Sisters or Citizens?*, p. 109.
[58] See Hause, with Kenney, *Women's Suffrage and Social Politics*, p. 162.

feminist associates.[59] Neither she nor Hubertine Auclert would ever succeed in mobilizing the kind of mass support for women's vote that had
suddenly become possible in England.

Historians Florence Rochefort and Laurence Klejman are skeptical of
Pelletier's ultimate contribution to the suffrage cause: "on a theoretical
level, she did not push the argumentation forward, and on the practical
level, she followed the lead of the radical feminists."[60] Her subsequent
contributions to feminist arguments concerning women's bodies and their
sexual emancipation were far more pathbreaking.[61] But it must be acknowledged that Pelletier was exquisitely clear-sighted when it came to underscoring the necessity for feminists to get organized and to join political
parties. Her book, *La Femme en lutte pour ses droits* (published in early
1908), which contained her article "La tactique féministe," emphasized the
necessity of organized efforts by women to achieve feminist goals, especially the vote, irrespective of political commitment. "For under a monarchy, a republic, or socialism," she assured her readers, "[a woman] will
not be counted unless the political equality of the sexes becomes a
reality."[62]

As mentioned earlier, the women of the CNFF had organized their
suffrage section in 1906, with Hubertine Auclert as its first president, and
in early 1907 it drafted and circulated a firmly worded mass petition,
calling for women's suffrage on the same conditions as those applied to
men. This petition, meant to impress (though not radical enough to satisfy
Auclert, who wanted action in the street) was certainly straightforward:[63]

> The National Council of French Women, which currently has 73,000
> members and whose goal is the amelioration of women's situation

[59] Madeleine Pelletier, "Le féminisme et ses militantes," *Documents du Progrès* (July 1909), 9–26;
accessed at www.marievictoirelouis.net on 11 May 2013.

[60] Laurence Klejman & Florence Rochefort, "L'action suffragiste de Madeleine Pelletier," in *Logique et
infortunes*, pp. 63–71; quote, p. 70.

[61] Pelletier's arguments about sexual emancipation for women are discussed in Chapter 10.

[62] Madeleine Pelletier, "La Tactique féministe," *La Revue Socialiste*, 47, n° 280 (April 1908), 318–321,
325. Partial translation by KO, as published in *Women, the Family, and Freedom*, vol. 2, doc. 21, pp.
97–98; quote, p. 98. This article is reprinted in *Madeleine Pelletier, L'éducation féministe des filles et
autres textes*, ed. Claude Maignien (Paris: Syros, 1978) and is also available in text form on the
website www.marievictoirelouis.net. This article also appeared as part of Pelletier's book, *La Femme
en lutte pour ses droits* (Paris: V. Giard & E. Briere, 1908), now online through the Gerritsen
Collection. The *Revue Socialiste* reviewed the book in its March 1908 issue (n° 279, 269–270),
emphasizing Pelletier's call for militant women to "renounce their feminine prerogatives" (what we
would now call their performance of femininity) and assume the allures of virility. The reviewer
thought that Pelletier went too far, but applauded her energy.

[63] CNFF 1907 Petition, published in *Bulletin de la Ligue des Droits de l'Homme*, vol. 7, n° 9 (15 May
1907), 441–442, and elsewhere.

economically, socially, and politically, has frequently protested against the exclusion of women from the voters' lists.

Woman, like man, responsible for her actions in relation to society, should have, like him, the right to fight for her opinions in public life as well as in private life.

Like man, subject to the laws of her country, she should also have the right to discuss them.

Like man, a taxpayer, she should no longer be unjustly deprived of any power to examine the finances of the State.

As a spouse and mother, she should be legitimately empowered to prepare the best possible future for her descendants.

In 1908 the CNFF followed up its petition by organizing public events. In early April 1908, the Suffrage Section sponsored a rousing lecture at the Geographical Society in Paris by a teacher named Thérèse Mercier on women's role in society; a mixed audience of some 500 people, including many public officials and the entire general staff of the CNFF, heard her make the case for women's full participation in French civic life.[64] Sketching the subordinate status of married women and single women alike, Mercier addressed directly the question of "what women want": respect, opportunities, the right to choose their own life path. The rights women want, she argued, are those that all people want, and "that we can read in the Declaration of the Rights of Man" as well as in Olympe de Gouges's Declaration of the Rights of Woman.[65] Today's "modern woman," Mercier asserted, wants "equal rights for women and men, admission to all employment for which she is suited, and the right to participate in the sovereignty of the nation." Whoever enjoys the right to suffering and labor, she indicated, should also enjoy the right to liberty and happiness. "She demands equal work and equal pay, and even in advance of her civil and political rights, her moral elevation in the family and in society, and the means to expand her intelligence and to enlighten her reason." Why, in particular, she queried, alluding to the Civil Code, should a single woman have to sacrifice her civil rights when she marries? Addressing the now shopworn arguments used against women's equality, beginning with the argument of physiological inferiority, then the allegation that women

[64] See Thérèse Mercier, "Le Rôle de la Femme dans la Société," 20-page offprint of her lecture of 9 April 1908, published by the Suffrage section of the CNFF. Consulted in dossier 1AF232 (Papiers de Cécile Brunschvicg) at the Archives du Féminisme, Angers, 2003. A concert followed the lecture, according to the published account, "Conférence féministe," Le Journal des Femmes, n° 185 (May 1908). The quotations below are on pp. 12 and 13 of the Mercier offprint.

[65] Not every feminist was enthusiastic about Olympe de Gouges; see the remarks by Cécile Brunschvicg concerning the 1911 IWSA congress, in La Française, n° 206 (25 June 1911).

would lose their femininity, and the fear that women's emancipation would threaten the family, Mercier countered and dismissed each objection. To the argument that women's rights would lead to moral licentiousness, she argued that men were judging women (unjustly) in their own promiscuous image. To the final argument, that women were intellectually and morally inferior to men, she blamed any traces of this on the past conditions in which women had been confined, miseducated (i.e., culture, not nature, was to blame), and singled out the Catholic Church for special opprobrium, thanks to its doctrines on Eve's "original" sin. Mercier applauded the efforts of the ICW and, earlier, Mixed Freemasonry for their work in lifting up women by combatting centuries of "ignorance and error," and for accelerating the mission of the women's movement. Acquiring the right to vote, she affirmed, "seems like nothing in appearance, but it represents an enormous victory over all the prejudices that hold us back, and it opens the door to all the reforms that will bring about the amelioration of our situation." Women, she said, should not rely on their male champions but must take the initiative: "women's cause can best be defended by women themselves." Woman must participate in making the laws, because – like Man – she is subject to them; to become really equal, she must share the rights as well as the duties. "Social harmony is at this price, and the future *cité* [civil society] that we all dream of will only be born when woman will be emancipated and lifted up, and when the united forces of all humanity will flourish and bloom in a climate of liberty and justice." This, from an organization, the CNFF, that some have labeled "conservative." Mercier's pro-suffrage speech provided a comprehensive summary of what mainstream republican feminists in France demanded in 1908.[66]

Not only did some women want to vote, but they also wanted to run for office. Women candidates began to challenge the rules that barred them from doing so. In April 1908 a young Parisian journalist named Jeanne Laloë decided to run for the Paris Municipal Council, putting forward her candidacy in the ninth arrondissement. Thus, she would contest the unwritten rules and customs that ostensibly barred her from seeking elective office. Neither the election law of 1848 nor its revision in 1884 specifically excluded women's candidacies. Laloë's campaign had been instigated by the important daily *Le Matin* (which provided extensive press coverage) and was assisted by the feminist attorney Maria Vérone, secretary-general of the LFDF in obtaining a venue for an electoral

---

[66] Quotes in this paragraph in Mercier, "Rôle de la Femme," pp. 19, 20.

meeting. Hubertine Auclert and Madeleine Pelletier both made speeches on the candidate's behalf. On 3 May 1908, Laloë received some 900 votes.[67] Subsequently Jeanne Laloë would recount the story of her candidacy in *La Nouvelle Revue*, affirming her distress over women's impotence in French law and embracing a feminism which, in her view, had nothing to do with old clichés such as aspiring to virility, cutting one's hair short, or wearing pants.[68]

In the course of this election day feminist demonstrators had marched from one polling place to another (under police escort), provoking two incidents – including the invasion by some 200 women of a polling place in the seventh arrondissement and the overturning of a ballot box by Hubertine Auclert. Much to their dismay, the demonstrators were not arrested and the incidents apparently got very little press, except for a quickly rendered (and inaccurate) color drawing on the cover of *Le Petit Journal* (3 May 1908), although their actions were duly publicized and praised by the English suffragette paper, *Votes for Women*.[69] During the subsequent run-off election (10 May) Madeleine Pelletier, inspired by Auclert's militant action, threw a rock through the window of a polling precinct. Writing in the *Journal des Femmes*, the veteran feminist Camille Bélilon praised these "delinquents": "Honor to these courageous women who mounted the assault, braving the prejudices and exposing themselves to danger with no other profit than the satisfaction of having served the cause." "The first and third of May," Bélilon claimed, "will be landmarks in the annals of feminism."[70] Other articles in the mainstream press would be less complimentary. Auclert, charged with a misdemeanor, went to court a month later. She expressed her exasperation over the lack of progress on women's political rights: "I do not regret having committed this act, but being obliged to commit it."[71] As Steven C. Hause characterizes her message, it was "*nolo contendere* rather than *mea culpa*. . . . she

---

[67] An overview of this campaign is provided by Steven C. Hause & Anne R. Kenney, "Women's Suffrage and the Paris Elections of 1908," *Laurels*, 51:1 (Spring 1980), 21–32.

[68] Jeanne Laloë published an account of her experience as a candidate in *La Nouvelle Revue* (1 June 1908), 405–410. Laloë was particularly offended by all the bureaucratic hoops that she and Maria Vérone were forced to jump through at the Prefecture of the Seine in order to get authorization for a venue to hold an electoral meeting. Cf. her remarks in the minutes of the LFDF meeting of 4 May, *Le Journal des Femmes*, n° 186 (June 1908), 2.

[69] See especially *Votes for Women* (14 May 1908), p. 155, and a few pages later (p. 161) "The French Suffragette," a first-person account of Laloë's campaign by "An English Visitor."

[70] Bélilon, "Conseillères municipales," *Le Journal des Femmes*, n° 185 (May 1908), 1.

[71] Auclert's statement to the court, as reconstructed from the press and translated by Steven C. Hause in his biography, *Hubertine Auclert*, p. 199. She would repeat substantially the same message at the June 1908 congress (see below), where she would be received in triumph.

managed to concede without capitulating."[72] Meanwhile Auclert's compendium of earlier newspaper articles, *Le Vote des femmes*, appears to have
come out in late June or early July, probably timed to coincide with the
upcoming mid-June IWSA conference in Amsterdam and Oddo-Deflou's
suffrage conference in Paris.[73]

Public lectures and solo candidacies were not enough to satisfy Jeanne
Oddo-Deflou of the GFEF, who had been active for years in the Legisla-
tive section of the CNFF. In January 1908, she resigned from the CNFF.[74]
She then quickly took the initiative by convening a congress (the first in
Paris since 1900, she said – not counting the ICW meeting in Paris in
1906 hosted by the CNFF), to present the case, yet again, for women's
civil, economic, and political rights. Teaming up with Eliska Vincent (of
Égalité; one of the six original founders of the CNFF) and Marguerite
Durand (*Office Féminin du Travail*), Oddo-Deflou scheduled a *Congrès
National des Droits Civils et du Suffrage des Femmes* for 26–28 June 1908,
immediately following the massive London suffrage demonstration and the
Amsterdam IWSA congress.[75] Well attuned to international women's
suffrage developments, Oddo-Deflou, secretary-general of the congress,
translated into French and published the 1906 Copenhagen IWSA Declaration of Principles and Statutes for French readers, complaining bitterly
(once again) about the unfortunate "*masculinisme*" of French grammar,
which required putting so many articles, adjectives, and neutral substan-
tives into the masculine form.[76]

This 1908 congress was a spirited affair. Among the eight hundred
persons in attendance, virtually every pro-suffrage group would be represented – only the CNFF, the Catholic groups, and the socialists were
absent. One highlight was Auclert's speech, which earned her a standing

[72] Hause, *Auclert*, p. 203.
[73] See Klejman & Rochefort, *L'Égalité en marche*, p. 274, citing Schmahl's letter to Auclert. Auclert
subsequently tried to submit her book for the Botta Prize of the *Académie Française*, only to be told
that works to be considered could not be submitted directly by their authors; see her editorials, "Le
Prix Botta," *Le Radical* (13 December 1908), and "Une Donation enlevé aux femmes," *Le Radical* (20
June 1909). Consulted at the BHVP.
[74] Oddo-Deflou's resignation from the CNFF board was announced at the 19 January assembly; see
the *Journal des Femmes*, n° 182 (February 1908), 1. It appears that she was annoyed by directives from
the ICW to the CNFF, encouraging its participation in 1907 pacifist initiatives. See her explanatory
article, "Féminisme national et international," *La Suffragiste*, n° 28 (May 1912), 8–10.
[75] This congress and its objectives were announced in the *Journal des Femmes*, n° 184 (April 1908), 1–2.
The CNFF sent Cécile Cahen as its "fraternal" representative to the Amsterdam IWSA congress
(15–20 June 1908); the Catholic feminist Marie Maugeret sent a written greeting, which was read at
the congress.
[76] See Jeanne Deflou, "L'Alliance Internationale pour le Suffrage des Femmes," *Le Journal des Femmes*,
n° 185 (May 1908), 3.

ovation! Pursuing reform by legal means was the primary message of the congress. One of its organizers' objectives was to highlight once again the many civil laws, and by extension economic laws, that required changing, and – in contrast to the ICW's international congresses in London (1899) and Berlin (1904) – to encourage an actual discussion rather than passive listening to a series of reports. For instance, four years after the centennial of the Civil Code and the formation of an all-male commission to consider revision, Jeanne Oddo-Deflou pointed out that no results had been forthcoming and that the commission had virtually disappeared from public view.[77] Meanwhile the private Coulon-Chavagnes commission, which had appointed six women (including Oddo-Deflou herself), had completed and published its report, with many suggestions for legal changes that would specifically benefit married women. Old issues were revisited, such as *recherche de la paternité* and the increasingly troublesome question of married women's nationality.

During the third and final part of the congress, the congress "gave great attention to women's suffrage."[78] Seventeen speeches were given on the suffrage question, including Hubertine's brief but triumphal presentation. The pro-suffrage deputy Louis Marin expressed his concern that a commitment in principle to equality and justice seemed insufficient to sway the opposition; he advocated the development of practical reasons based on social scientific studies plus stimulating pressure from public opinion to bring resistant legislators on board. A delegate from the WSPU in England (a Mrs. Rigby) reported how no one would have believed, just two years ago, that such a suffrage movement as theirs in England could have sprung forth, engaging hundreds and thousands of women in picketing, going to meet with ministers, going to jail, and the like. Perhaps it was not impossible in France. Another Englishwoman, Mrs. Manson, recently active in the Women's Franchise League, also spoke at this congress.

After yet another rehearsal by Eliska Vincent of the historical voting rights women in France had enjoyed for centuries prior to the Revolution, and Marya Chéliga's report on women's voting rights in other countries, came Maria Vérone's detailed analysis of the current complexities of the qualifications for voting at the municipal level. Vérone concluded with a resolution that favored backing the simpler Dussaussoy proposal of local

---

[77] See *Congrès national des droits civils et du suffrage des femmes ... compte rendu*, p. 12.

[78] Hause, *Hubertine Auclert*; quote, p. 202. In contrast, Klejman & Rochefort remarked that insofar as these feminists all agreed that women must have political rights, the congress actually didn't spend much time discussing the matter; see *L'Égalité en marche*, p. 259.

suffrage for all women, and of leaning hard on the members of the universal suffrage parliamentary committee to send the measure on to the Chamber, but Marguerite Durand countered with a resolution in favor of pursuing full civil and political rights, including political suffrage, which the congress voted by acclamation.[79] Nobody spoke directly about the vote being the keystone to further change, but as much was implied by the very organization of the congress, which first considered a series of changes to be made in the Civil Code, then focused on the issue of suffrage and what should be done to obtain it. The congress attracted a lot of press, but as Nelly Roussel (who could not attend) observed in *L'Action*, it also precipitated many old, worn-out antifeminist clichés.[80] In fact, there was little to discuss further, except for how to proceed. And on that point, there was serious disagreement.

Founding the *Union Française pour le Suffrage des Femmes* – 1909

In early 1909, as a follow-up to the 1908 congress, the third Jeanne – Jeanne-E. Schmahl – riding high on the 1907 legislative success (women's controlling their own earnings) of her *L'Avant-Courrière* group, would organize the UFSF to spearhead the French drive for woman suffrage.[81] Among her lieutenants were the former general staff members of *L'Avant-Courrière*, the Duchesse d'Uzès, Jane Misme (the editor of *La Française*, who became the group's first secretary-general), and two important recruits (whom we have met in Chapter 12), Marguerite de Witt-Schlumberger and the young and energetic Cécile Brunschvicg, who would succeed Misme as secretary-general and, with Witt-Schlumberger as president, lead the organization vigorously for several more decades.[82]

Schmahl's pragmatic one-issue-at-a-time approach to earlier legislative reforms on behalf of women had proved very successful, first in obtaining

---

[79] *Congrès national des droits civils et du suffrage ... compte rendu*, pp. 227–232.

[80] See Nelly Roussel, "Le Féminisme ... tout court," *L'Action* (15 July 1908); reprinted in Roussel's *Quelques Lances rompues pour nos Libertés* (Paris: V. Giard & E. Brière, 1910), pp. 51–55. Her article responded to another, by a deputy from Tours, René Besnard, "Le bon féminisme" (source not indicated).

[81] For a retrospective account of the UFSF founding and activities, see Grinberg, *Historique du mouvement suffragiste*, chapter 5, and subsequently, Leclère, *Vote des femmes en France,* pp. 85–90. The founding of the UFSF in 1909 is analyzed in Hause, with Kenney, *Woman Suffrage and Social Politics*, pp. 109–114, and in Klejman & Rochefort, *L'Égalité en marche*, pp. 274–281. Bouglé-Moalic, *Vote des françaises*, devotes only two pages (pp. 182–183) to the UFSF, which then drops from sight.

[82] Brunschvicg became very active as secretary-general of the UFSF before 1914, in addition to chairing the Section on Work of the CNFF, but her major contributions to the suffrage cause came after 1919. See especially Formaglio, "Féministe d'abord," chapters 8 & 9.

legislative action to permit women to serve as witnesses of official acts (1897) and, second, legislation that empowered wives to keep and control their own earnings (1907), which was a potentially a big step forward in mitigating the civil disempowerment of married women and asserting their rights as individuals. Schmahl and her associates, who spanned political party and religious affiliations, were not opposed to suffrage being granted by gradual steps, beginning with the municipal vote, even as the political education of women proceeded apace. Obtaining the vote for women had become less of a question of elaborating reasons why it should be enacted – everyone knew by 1909 what those arguments were – but of actually getting some form of woman suffrage approved by the legislators. The UFSF circular, quoted earlier, foregrounded women's "right" and economic contributions: women produce, contributing to the French economy; women are taxed but not represented; women devote themselves to family and country – in sum, French women deserve the vote in their own right.[83]

Schmahl's series of articles in *La Francaise*, "*Propos d'une suffragiste*," during the first three months of 1909, spelled out her approach.[84] In those articles she remarked on the obstacles (uncertainty as to where women's suffrage would lead, which she categorized as implicitly an antifeminist argument, and questions of tactics, militancy vs. gradualist). She acknowledged but did not dwell on the existence of a purported social class difference between *suffragistes* (bourgeois) and *suffragettes* (working class), and characterized anti-suffrage women as lazy, spoiled, and uninformed. The overarching argument for women's suffrage, she insisted in her final column, was practical: since women were taxed, they should be represented and have a say in how decisions were made as to the distribution of tax revenue. It is "tyranny," Schmahl asserted forcefully, "to render financially responsible those who are denied the privilege of citizenship. This is legalized theft!"[85]

Jeanne Schmahl's speech at the UFSF's second meeting in March 1909 welcomed new recruits of a younger generation. She implored these women to speak up in defense of their rights, affirming that neither suffragism nor feminism were directed *against* men as enemies. Suffrage, she argued, was not simply a matter of party politics, or even restricted to

---

[83] See the UFSF circular, cited in n. 25.

[84] Jeanne-E. Schmahl, "Propos d'une Suffragiste," series of six articles in *La Française*. See issues n° 106 (24 January 1909); n° 107 (31 January 1909); n° 108 (7 February 1909); n° 110 (21 February 1909); n° 111 (28 February 1909), and n° 113 (14 March 1909).

[85] Quote, last article in series, "Propos d'une Suffragiste," *La Française*, n° 113 (14 March 1909).

one people, but rather "a vast phenomenon of human evolution."[86] She envisioned launching a concerted propaganda campaign, and – impressively – solicited the necessary funds to underwrite it. The reporter (probably Jane Misme) observed that many reached deep into their pocketbooks, "subscribing fifty, a hundred, even two hundred francs," which was a great deal of money at the time. Hinting at a certain trans-Channel rivalry, the reporter asserted that "*les Françaises* owed it to themselves not to lag behind *les Anglaises*, whose zeal was working miracles."[87] Jane Misme also explained that efforts to work with and include Hubertine Auclert in the UFSF had come to naught.[88] Within a few months, the UFSF had successfully achieved affiliation with the IWSA, which in late April 1909 welcomed the French delegates at its London congress.[89]

Meanwhile the suffragists in the CNFF Section on Suffrage were mobilizing. One of the new faces – a particularly important one for the future of women's suffrage – would be the newly minted attorney Maria Vérone (1874–1938), who then served both as secretary-general of the LFDF (under Bonnevial) and would also serve as head of the suffrage section at the CNFF, where Bonnevial was also involved. It was Vérone in fact who had presented suffrage resolutions at the 1908 Women's Rights and Suffrage conference, discussed earlier. She also prepared an important report on the suffrage question in France, destined for the ICW's Toronto meeting, and would also draft the suffrage section's comprehensive report "Appeal to Justice" (1909), which the CNFF addressed to the Chamber of Deputies and the Senate, accompanied by a resolution favoring the electorate and eligibility of women for the municipal councils, arrondissement councils, and departmental councils.[90] Vérone's expertise would also contribute to the preparation of the Buisson report, on behalf of the Chamber of

---

[86] "Union Française pour le Suffrage des Femmes," *La Française*, n° 115 (28 March 1909), 1.

[87] Ibid., 1.   [88] "L'UFSF et Madame Hubertine Auclert," *La Française*, n° 115 (28 March 1909), 1.

[89] Schmahl arrived at the 1909 IWSA congress while still in recovery from a recent illness, while the second delegate Jane Misme, recovering from a traffic accident, missed a number of sessions and networking opportunities. See Schmahl's account, "Impressions de congressistes," in *La Française*, n° 121 (16 May 1909), and her report in the IWSA, *Report of the Fifth Conference and First Quinquennial, London, England, April 26, 27, 28, 29, 30, May 1, 1909* (London: Samuel Sidders & Co., 1909), pp. 96–98. A third delegate, Julie Auberlet, "Impressions de Congressistes," *La Française*, n°ˢ 122–123 (23 May 1909), reported how impressed she was by the WSPU suffragettes, who appeared at two of the public meetings. Audebert represented both the UFSF and the CNFF at the IWSA congress.

[90] See Maria Vérone, *Appel à la justice adressé par le Conseil National des Femmes Françaises à la Chambre des députés et au Sénat [Rapport de la section du suffrage du Conseil national présenté par Mme Maria Vérone (CNFF, 1909)]*.

Deputies's Commission on "Universal" Suffrage.[91] Her intervention at the annual convention of the *Ligue des Droits de l'Homme* in May 1909 (discussed in Chapter 9), confirmed the CNFF's gradualist approach to suffrage, but her proposal would be outflanked by the LDH president Pressensé's enthusiastic move to declare for unrestricted women's suffrage – and eligibility for office, which the LDH congress then strongly endorsed. The LFDF under Maria Vérone's leadership would become an indispensable advocate of women's suffrage in France.

On 16 July 1909, Ferdinand Buisson, a longtime woman suffrage sympathizer and Radical party deputy (and future president [1911–1926] of the *Ligue des Droits de l'Homme*), and rapporteur for the Chamber of Deputies' Commission on Universal Suffrage, finally deposed the commission's report on the 1906 Dussaussoy bill, the cautious suffrage proposal that would enfranchise all women, whether single or married, but only at the local levels.[92] This measure, similar to one enacted in England in the late 1860s, would simply amend the wording of the 1884 municipal elections law, "*tous les français*" by adding the words "*des deux sexes.*"[93] The Buisson report, as it became known after it was officially printed and distributed in 1910, was a landmark of research and composition; it quoted every suffrage advocate from Condorcet and Olympe de Gouges to Hubertine Auclert and incorporated much of the CNFF report, plus many appendices pertaining to the state of women's suffrage around the world.[94]

[91] See the suffrage section report from May 1909 in *Conseil National des Femmes Françaises. Assemblée générale publique*, n° 4 (1907), and subsequently Vérone, *Appel à la justice adressé par le Conseil National des Femmes Françaises à la Chambre des députés et au Sénat*. This report (or a version of it) also appeared in the CNFF's *L'Action féminine*, n° 3 (1 June 1909), 35–47. Also reported in *La Française*, n° 121 (16 May 1909).

[92] Chambre des Députés. Dixième Législature. Impressions: Projets de Lois, Propositions, Rapports, Etc. Vol. II, n°s 31 to 101. N° 31: *Rapport fait (au cours de la précédente législature) au nom de la Commission du Suffrage Universel, chargée d'examiner la proposition de loi tendant à accorder Le Droit de Vote aux Femmes dans les Élections aux Conseils municipaux, aux Conseils d'arrondissement et aux Conseils généraux*, par M. Ferdinand Buisson. Repris le 10 juin 1910, par application de l'article 18 du Règlement. (Paris: Imprimerie de la Chambre des Députés, Martinet, 1910). This report is 278 pages long, including 38 appendices. Available on Gallica. The core of the Buisson report (pp. 151–166) with the major arguments of the commission and text of the proposed law, was translated and published in English by the National American Woman Suffrage Association (NAWSA); see France. Chamber of Deputies. Session of 1910. *Official Report of the Commission on Universal Suffrage, on the Proposition to Give Women the Right to Vote* (New York: NAWSA, 1910). 16 pages. The expanded version of the Buisson report was published as a 300-plus page book in 1911. See Ferdinand Buisson, *Le Vote des femmes* (Paris: H. Dunot & E. Pinat, éditeurs, 1911).

[93] See Buisson, *Rapport*, p. 164; in *Vote des femmes*, p. 335. Two alternative formulations of the wording (suggested later, in 1923) would be "*sans distinction de sexe*" or "*hommes et femmes.*"

[94] The extensive documentation on which Buisson based his report can be consulted in the Marie-Louise Bouglé collection at the BHVP, Fonds Ferdinand Buisson.

One knowledgeable commentator, André Leclère, would remark some years later that "this report represents a great amount of work and we must congratulate its author who, in making himself a realistic champion of the feminist cause, understood that he must gather together all the historical and experimental elements of the problem.... This [report] constitutes the first serious study in France of this delicate question.... It made the legislature understand the high importance and gravity of the problem."[95]

The legislative remedy was easy – but legislative resistance would remain stiff; the votes weren't yet there. The deputies remained preoccupied with the question of proportional representation.[96] Thus, getting the Chamber of Deputies to schedule a discussion of Buisson's report on women's suffrage prior to the next general elections in early 1910 would be no simple matter. Then the Clemenceau ministry, which refused to put its weight behind the woman suffrage question, fell on 20 July. On 6 October Jeanne Schmahl paid a visit to the new prime minister, Aristide Briand, to press the case for government endorsement of the suffrage bill. A well-known figure because of her campaigns with *L'Avant-Courrière*, she too had entrée to high government officials.[97] But Briand was noncommittal (though not opposed) and in the end, lacking endorsement from the ministry, the bill did not go forward.

Other initiatives in support of women's suffrage took cultural forms. The *Bibliothèque de la Ville de Paris* (now the BHVP) organized an exhibition of prints and pamphlets concerning the women of 1848, "Les Vesuviennes," which gained the attention of *Le Monde Illustrée* and other papers, including *L'Étoile Belge*.[98] In mid-1909, the *Oeuvre des Libérées de Saint-Lazare*, so instrumental in bringing public attention to the plight of poor women prisoners and to launching the CNFF, also sponsored an

---

[95] Leclère, *Vote des Femmes en France*, pp. 114–116. This author did criticize Buisson, though, for not including any of the history of women representing fiefs and debating public matters in towns prior to 1789.

[96] The competing issue of proportional representation and proposals for the "family vote" greatly complicated consideration of women's suffrage for individuals. On this issue, see Jean-Yves Le Naour, avec Catherine Valenti, *La famille doit voter: Le suffrage familial contre le vote individuel* (Paris: Hachette Littératures, 2005). This book provides an exemplary compendium of patriarchal, authoritarian male thinking dedicated to muffling women's political expression. See also Hause, with Kenney, *Women's Suffrage and Social Politics*, pp. 128–131.

[97] Meeting reported in *Jus Suffragii*, vol. 4, n° 2 (15 October 1909), 10, noting that this meeting was reported in *Le Figaro* and the *Journal des Débats*.

[98] Clippings on this exhibition found in at the Mundaneum (Mons, Belgium), Léonie La Fontaine papers, LLF 044 (four illustrations published in *Le Monde illustrée*) and LFF 62, clipping of an article by Paul Ginisty, "Notes Parisiennes: Les 'Vesuviennes'," from *L'Étoile Belge* (3 July 1909).

exhibition in Paris, accompanied by a limited-edition book/catalog publication, depicting through works of art and literature the plight of poor women, which one commentator described as "an iconography of feminine misery."[99] Later in the fall of 1909, the suffrage cause gained the support of another important ally, Jacques Flach, professor of comparative legislation at the *Collège de France*, who would open his course in early December 1909 by saluting the women's quest for political rights as the dawn of a new era, characterizing it as a positive force in reestablishing balance in French society.[100]

The spring of 1910 would bring an election for the Chamber of Deputies. Suffrage supporters hoped to bring in new deputies who might actually be able to break the logjam and pass a women's suffrage bill. They were keenly aware that the moment had come for them to clinch their case with the general public and to provoke candidates to declare themselves for women's suffrage. In November 1909 Jane Misme indicated in *La Française* that collaboration between the UFSF and the LFDF, and both of these groups with the CNFF, was underway, intimating that Hubertine Auclert's *Suffrage des Femmes* group would do well to associate itself with their gradualist program and consolidate efforts at petitioning on a mass scale.[101] Misme was also pursuing subscribers for a French edition of the IWSA's monthly publication, *Jus Suffragii*.

Beginning in mid-February 1910, Jane Misme (like Jeanne Schmahl in 1909) would launch a series of articles, "*Pour le Suffrage des femmes*" in *La Française*.[102] She blamed women's own inertia for the slow progress of women's suffrage, but insisted that, even though suffragists' arguments for justice did not seem to sway opponents, progress was being made thanks to increased awareness of the "desolating [economic] realities that propel women into misery." Marriage law, Misme argued, was "the citadel in

---

[99] The catalog, *La Misère sociale de la femme, d'après les écrivains et les artistes du XVIIe au XXe siècles* (Paris: Devambreez, 1910), contained a preface by that icon of Solidarism, Léon Bourgeois. I have found one press clipping concerning the exhibition, "Le Misère sociale de la Femme," *Le Soir*, 8 July 9, signed "Colomb," in LLF 62 at the Mundaneum.

[100] Jacques Flach, *La Souveraineté du peuple et le suffrage politique de la femme, leçon d'ouverture faite au Collège de France, le 11 décembre 1909. Extrait de la Revue Politique et Littéraire (Revue Bleue)*, 29 January & 5 February 1910. 33-page brochure.

[101] Jane Misme, "Le Vote des femmes," *La Française*, n° 137 (14 November 1909), 1.

[102] Jane Misme, "Pour le suffrage des femmes," *La Française*, n°s 149 (13 February 1910); 151 (27 February 1910); 154 (10 March 1910); & 156 (10 April 1910). These articles subsequently appeared in brochure form, *Pour le suffrage des femmes; esquisse du mouvement pour le suffrage des femmes. Le Féminisme et la politique; études extraites de la revue Idées Modernes*, which Misme dedicated to its publisher, A. Le Chatelier. Consulted in the Bidelman collection, Stanford University Special Collections.

which the final efforts of masculine self-love are entrenched, and especially the last laziness – or may I say feminine servility." The key to obtaining the vote for women, she believed, lay in stimulating *women's* interest in public affairs. Henri Coulon and René de Chavagnes (who had convened the marriage reform committee), publishing in *La Nouvelle Revue*, urged caution, arguing that women must be educated on civic matters first; only then should they be granted political rights. English women, they insisted, had had a fifty-year apprenticeship; the same could not yet be said of French women. The mistake made with male suffrage in 1848, which enfranchised uneducated men *en masse* (and led to the election of Louis-Napoléon Bonaparte as president of the Republic, followed by his *coup d'état*) must not be repeated.[103] The Dussaussoy-Buisson *proposition de loi* for municipal suffrage was designed precisely to allay such fears by providing a mechanism for women to gain essential education and experience in public affairs at the local level.

The first round of legislative elections was scheduled for the 24th of April 1910. On 11 March (spearheaded by the LFDF in the person of Maria Vérone, who by this time also chaired the CNFF suffrage section), five of the pro-suffrage organizations (LFDF, Auclert's *Suffrage des Femmes*, the GFEF, *Amélioration*, and UFF) organized a huge public meeting in Paris on the suffrage question, presided by the socialist deputy Marcel Sembat, who had become a highly vocal champion of votes for women in the Chamber of Deputies. It was attended by some 2,000 persons.[104] Speakers included Hubertine Auclert, Jeanne Oddo-Deflou, Nelly Roussel, and Maria Vérone, in addition to a number of leading male deputies including the author of the suffrage bill report, Ferdinand Buisson, and other public officials, but – conspicuously – without the participation of the UFSF's Schmahl and Misme – and without either Marguerite Durand or Madeleine Pelletier. In *Le Matin* (23 March 1910), Auclert praised the effort that had resulted in this immense public meeting even as she criticized the rivalries that continued to hinder unified feminist collaboration. She blamed "those who only seek aggrandisement for themselves and their coteries." She was evidently referring to the leadership of the UFSF, notably Jeanne Schmahl, and to Marguerite Durand, who in the meantime

---

[103] Henri Coulon, & René de Chavagnes, "La Femme et ses droits politiques," *La Nouvelle Revue* (1 April 1910), 289–301.

[104] On the 10th of March public meeting, see Maria Vérone's long article, "L'Oeuvre de la Ligue," *Cinquante Ans de Féminisme* (Paris: LFDF, 1921), esp. pp. 22–23; see also Hause, with Kenney, *Women's Suffrage and Social Politics*, pp. 145–151; Klejman & Rochefort, *L'Égalité en marche*, p. 281; these authors give the attendance figures at 1,200 persons.

had decided to declare her candidacy for the deputation along with six other women, including Pelletier (running in Paris), Elisabeth Renaud (running in the department of l'Isère), and Arria Ly (in Toulouse).[105] These women had tried to place female candidates in every district, but this effort at propaganda by the deed would not work out as they had hoped. Surprisingly, in the case of Durand, whose published electoral program addressed women's issues, especially economic issues, ranging from pay for housework, equal pay for equal work, and the ending of protective legislation for women workers, the demand for women's suffrage itself was conspicuously absent![106]

In the meantime, Jeanne Schmahl, on behalf of the UFSF, had organized a survey of male opinion on the question of women's vote. The question posed was: "What do you think of women's suffrage, and are you in favor of it?"[107] Many male allies in the press came forth to promote the cause, including the editor of *La Revue*, Jean Finot, who in the issue of 15 May 1910, promulgated "La Charte de la Femme" or Women's Charter. In the June and July issues Finot published the results of the survey.[108] Such a survey, he mentioned in a footnote, had been requested of the UFSF by the IWSA, of which the UFSF had become the French national affiliate. The respondents, which included deputies of various political persuasions, members of the *Académie Française* and the *Institut de France*, professors, journalists, etc., were, for the most part, familiar with the pro-suffrage arguments and favorable to women voting. The socialist deputies were wholly in favor. But others issued caveats – start with single women first; educate women before giving them the vote; begin at the local level, etc. Only a few, including the venerable Alfred Fouillée, mentioned the anticlericals' feared specter of women voting as their priests told them to. A number of respondents, however, did resonate to the oft-repeated assertion that suffrage without women could certainly not be called "universal." Kauffmann and Pelletier called it "unisexual."

[105] Hubertine Auclert, "Les Femmes ont de la peine à se mettre d'accord, même contre les hommes," *Le Matin* (23 March 1910), front page. Accessed on Gallica, 14 May 2013. On the 1910 campaigns, see the documented account by Auclert's sister Marie Chaumont, *Les Femmes au Gouvernail* (Paris: M. Giard, 1923), pp. 72–77, and Hause, *Hubertine Auclert*, pp. 209–212.

[106] See the flier announcing Durand's election meeting, 13 April 1910. "Réunion publique et contradictoire. Madame Marguerite Durand et le citoyen Charles Marest, candidats aux élections législatives dans le IXe arrondissement exposeront leurs programmes." Thanks to Steve Hause for forwarding a photocopy of this flier, on file at the BMD.

[107] The questions are restated by Paul Viollet, in *La Revue*, part 2 (15 July 1910), p. 37. See n. 110.

[108] See Jean Finot article, "La Charte de la Femme et la Société de Demain," *La Revue* (15 May 1910), and then the survey, "Les Femmes française doivent-elles voter?" in the issues of 15 June 1910 (446–463) and 15 July 1910 (23–39).

It is curious that in 1910 not one of these men framed his response in terms of the "republic": respondents spoke instead in terms of democracy and the parliamentary regime. Suffrage partisan and deputy Louis Marin made it clear that women's suffrage was one part of a tripartite reform he desired, which would include proportional representation. Others invoked the "no taxation without representation" pro-suffrage argument. Only one expressed his complete disillusionment with manhood suffrage, though many others were critical of it and supported women's suffrage as a means of improving its results. One criticized the absurdity of the antifeminists, while another objected to the violent, unwomanly behavior of the English suffragettes. Most expressed support for the moral equality or equivalence of the two sexes, but several spoke out against eligibility for office accompanying the woman's vote. Charles Turgeon reiterated his support for women as voters on the same terms as men, which he had earlier stated in his book *Le Féminisme français*. Some respondents thought that the social interventions resulting from women voting in other countries had provided a splendid example, while others doubted that the experience in "new" countries could be applied to "our old societies."[109]

Finally, the distinguished historian Paul Viollet provided a brief summary of women's earlier political participation in France, and mentioned in particular the sanction given it by Pope Innocent IV in the thirteenth century.[110] Viollet was not, to be sure, the sole individual to document that French women had exercised certain forms of political rights in olden times, but he was undoubtedly the most authoritative, having published three volumes of his magnum opus, *Histoire des Institutions politiques et administratives de la France* (1890, 1898, and 1903; a fourth volume on the modern period would appear in 1912). Importantly, he came down on the side of the suffrage advocates. The veteran feminist Eliska Vincent had raised this point many times in the previous decade, in speeches, in conference presentations, and in print, but Viollet's scholarly knowledge

---

[109] Survey (15 July 1910), p. 36.
[110] Paul Viollet, in the survey in *La Revue*, part 2 (15 July 1910), p. 39; he referred interested readers to his *Histoire des Institutions*. See Paul Viollet, "Exclusion des femmes et de leur descendance," in his *Histoire des Institutions politiques et administratives de la France*, vol. 2 (Paris: L. Larose, 1898), pp. 55–86, and vol. 3 (Paris: L. Larose, 1903), esp. pp. 188–190, where he provides several documented examples of women voting in local assemblies in the 14th and 15th centuries. The endorsement by Pope Innocent IV (1243–1254) is invoked in vol. 2, p. 3. Viollet had earlier published his findings on the forgery of the Salic Law: see "Comment les femmes ont été exclus en France de la succession à la couronne," in *Mémoires de L'Institut National de France. Académie des Inscriptions et Belles Lettres*, 34, pt. 2 (1895), pp. 125–178. Cf. also Marie Denizard, *Les Droits de la femme française avant 1789* (Amiens, 1911). See also my chapter on "Women and the Problem of Political Authority" in my companion volume *The Woman Question in France, 1400–1780*.

was undoubtedly better suited to convince male legislators.[III] No one could henceforth invoke a historical precedent to oppose women's voting. Although the Buisson report did not go back prior to 1789 in its search for precedents, it was clear from the research of Viollet and Vincent that there were favorable arguments to be made for women's participation in public life well before the Revolution.

The UFSF leadership changed in December 1910. Eliska Vincent (one of the six original founders of the CNFF and a longtime advocate of political rights for women) replaced Jeanne Schmahl as president; Cécile Brunschvicg became secretary-general.[112] The new UFSF leadership believed that widespread propaganda was the key to bringing the French population on board the women's suffrage bandwagon. Only politically empowered women could successfully address the social ills that plagued French society. "Social housekeeping" was the name of the game.[113] On 2 April 1911 the reconstituted UFSF would sponsor its own *Grande Réunion* in Paris, with Ferdinand Buisson discussing the beneficial results of women's suffrage in other countries, attorney Suzanne Grinberg rehearsing the arguments for suffrage, Brunschvicg reporting on the upcoming IWSA meeting in Stockholm and the UFSF's propaganda efforts, and Louis Marin, wrapping up.[114] Indeed, Cécile Brunschvicg's approach to the suffrage question was, in fact, not dissimilar to that elaborated over the decades by Hubertine Auclert. Like Auclert, she argued that the vote was the means to an end, the end in this case being the enactment of a significant program of reforms that would benefit women and children.[115] But she was in some respects more conciliatory than Auclert. In a December 1913 article, Brunschvicg would make it clear that

---

[III] See Eliska (Girard) Vincent, "L'Électorat des femmes dans l'histoire," *La Revue Féministe*, vol. 1, no. 1 (1 October 1895), 20–26; and "Le Vote des femmes dans les élections consulaires," *La Revue Féministe*, vol. 1, no. 3 (5 November 1895), 106–111. In 1889 she had submitted a proposal to the international socialist congress for the election of women to the councils of *prud'hommes*, an issue that particularly interested her. See her presentations on this subject from the proceedings of the feminist congresses held in Brussels in 1897 and 1912, and especially "De la condition et du vote politique des femmes en France," in *Der Internationale Kongress für Frauenwerke und Frauenbestrebungen in Berlin, 19. bis 26. September 1896* (Berlin: H. Walther, 1897), pp. 267–272. The sources she listed were from older books; to my knowledge Vincent never acknowledged the Viollet memoir (1895), cited in n. 110.

[112] Klejman & Rochefort, *L'Égalité en marche*, p. 279.

[113] The mother/social housekeeping argument had developed much earlier in France, most notably in the 1848–1849 publications of the French feminist-socialist Jeanne Deroin.

[114] A flier for this big meeting is in the Kauffmann papers, box 1, folder 4, in the Marie-Louise Bouglé collection at the BHVP. See the short report in *La Française*, n° 196 (9 April 1911). Another major public meeting took place in Clermont-Ferrand, according to the previous issue (2 April 1911).

[115] Compare Brunschvicg's statements with Hubertine Auclert's 1885 electoral program.

the UFSF took a "relational" feminist position: "It is precisely because men and women have different qualities and distinct aptitudes that society must invite the collaboration of all men and all women in the interest of the collectivity."[116]

The spring of 1911 marked the appearance of Ferdinand Buisson's fat book, *Le Vote des femmes*, based on his earlier report to the Chamber of Deputies.[117] This bulky and authoritative reference work provided interested readers with a detailed survey of the suffrage question in other countries around the world, emphasizing those countries where women's suffrage had already been adopted and had produced far-reaching and much-needed social reforms. Buisson's tome provided fuel for another practical pro-suffrage argument, adding to those that were gradually being recognized as meriting consideration. No one who cared about the pursuit of women's vote, including vociferous anti-suffragists, could ignore these findings.[118] It was grounded in extensive correspondence and publications collected specifically for this purpose by participants ranging from the CNFF's secretary-general Ghénia Avril de Sainte-Croix to Dr. Madeleine Pelletier.[119] Documentation from the United States, for example, was collected with the cooperation of the French embassy in Washington, D.C., and of the president of the IWSA, Carrie Chapman Catt. Indeed, this extensive survey could be considered a response to Louis Marin's earlier call for social science data. What happened between 1910 and 1914 would prefigure the impasse that would continue for the next thirty years. Women's suffrage advocates scurried to find the best formulations for presenting their case: would it be philosophical (the appeal to the principles of rights, equality, and justice), expedient (the vote as a means to further reforms benefitting women and children, notably combatting social evils that included alcoholism, prostitution, etc.), economic (the vote as means to address the miserable situation of working women),

---

[116] Cited in Klejman & Rochefort, *L'Égalité en marche*, p. 277, from C. Brunschvicg, "Le suffrage des femmes en France," *Les Documents du Progrès* (December 1913), 297–301; quote, 298.

[117] Ferdinand Buisson, *Le Vote des femmes* (Paris: H. Denot & E. Pinat, eds., 1911) in the publisher's series Encyclopédie Parlementaire des Sciences Politiques et Sociales.

[118] Although some did try; see Théodore Joran's book, *Le Suffrage des femmes* (Paris: A. Savaète, 1913), pp. 69–84.

[119] The abundant survey materials on which Buisson's book was based can be consulted at the BHVP in the Bouglé Collection, Fonds Buisson. Correspondence in these files indicates that these responses and publications were solicited by and collected primarily by the CNFF, through the network of national councils of the ICW, as well as through the contacts of Madeleine Pelletier. Internal evidence suggests that the book came out in the late spring [cf. Mme Avril de Sainte-Croix, letter 2 June 1911, thanking Buisson for sending her a copy of the book, as she was just leaving for Berlin; see Folder 4 (1)-Correspondance France, Bouglé collection, BHVP].

commercial (no taxation without representation), moral (women's moral superiority to men), or pragmatic/comparative (women with votes are making positive differences in other countries. Why not here? Why wait?).[120] Suffrage partisans even went to court, following the example of their predecessors Louise Barbarousse in 1885 and Eliska Vincent in 1893. Marguerite Durand filed suit against the prefect of the Seine over his refusal to register her candidacy in 1910, but his action was upheld by the *Conseil d'État* in early 1912. In 1913, Jeanne Halbwachs, Maria Vérone, Blanche Edwards-Pilliet, and two other members of the LFDF attempted to register to vote. In each of these cases, the result was the same; only the legislature was deemed competent by the courts to empower women to register to vote and pose their candidacies for office.[121] And if they did run, the votes they received would not be counted. High hopes, and energetic promotion of votes for women were invariably followed by a mixture of delays, temporizing, compromises, complications, resistances, repeated expressions of overt hostility, and outright fear on the part of many of France's elected legislators as well as local bureaucrats.

Suffragists' enthusiastic efforts notwithstanding, there were still French women's rights advocates who either ignored or opposed prioritizing woman suffrage. A notable example was Lydie Martial, who had become president of the *Société pour l'Amélioration du Sort de la Femme*, the group initially founded by Maria Deraismes. In 1914, suffrage would appear as the thirty-second and last demand on this group's list of desired reforms.[122] There were others such as Mme Remember who took a dim view of masculine behavior and did not hesitate to criticize it. She was frankly skeptical that most men knew how to behave themselves. In *La Suffragiste* she wrote that "Men find running to cabarets and spending the household's money there more worthy of their masculine *majesty*. The lowliest member of the male tribe feels dishonored by having to cook the soup; he vests his male pride on crossing his arms and smoking."[123] Although she

[120] Bouglé-Moalic provides a thoughtful analysis of the various arguments for and against women's suffrage; see *Vote des Françaises*, chapter 6, esp. pp. 162–179. With the advent of war in 1914, another argument would emerge: the women's vote as a reward for services rendered to the nation in wartime.

[121] On these lawsuits, see Bouglé-Moalic, *Vote des Françaises*, pp. 190–191.

[122] See Lydie Martial, "Le Vrai féminisme," *La Republique de l'Ariege* (dated 5 April 1914); clipping in BMD, DOS 396 FEM. Martial's notion of feminism was philosophically liberal, i.e., unfettered masculine and feminine development toward forming the complete human being of either sex; she was more committed to educational advancement than to political rights.

[123] Mme Remember, "Le Travail ménagère," *La Suffragiste*, n° 25 (February 1912), 5. Emphasis in original.

admitted that exceptions did exist, she observed that overall men (especially working-class men) enjoyed lording it over their womenfolk.

When the IWSA met in Stockholm in June 1911, the UFSF made a substantial showing. Ten members made the journey from France to Sweden. "France cut quite a figure at an international feminist congress," secretary-general Cécile Brunschvicg reported in *La Française*, "the enthusiasm that surrounded us from suffragists of the entire world was enormous and we listened with emotion not only to nearly all the Swedish women, but the Russians, the Germans, and even a Bulgarian woman who congratulated us in French and sang the praises of our country. . . . and they asked why, France being so avant-garde, intelligent, and courageous, we didn't yet have the vote."[124] Marguerite de Witt-Schlumberger headed the delegation, as proxy for Eliska Vincent (who could not attend), and Cécile Brunschvicg seconded her.[125] Others who went to Stockholm from France included Mme C. Legrelle de Ferrer, who had recently published an important tract ("Why They Would Vote"),[126] and a Mme Compain (presumably the novelist and social investigator Louise Compain). One of the French delegates, a man, represented the newly formed *Ligue d'Électeurs pour le Suffrage des Femmes*. The French report to the conference emphasized that suffragists were "only in the educational stage" but that their 3,000 members were "nevertheless a power sufficient to conquer public opinion."[127] The IWSA appointed Brunschvicg to produce a French translation of Colorado's Judge Ben Lindsey's opinion on the benefits of woman suffrage in his state, and designated Maria Vérone, in absentia, to work with Marie Stritt (Germany) and Chrystal Macmillan (Scotland) to "compile a booklet of suffrage facts for propaganda purposes."[128]

[124] Cécile Brunschvicg, "Les Suffragistes Françaises au Congrès de Stock[h]olm," *La Française*, n° 206 (25 June 1911), 1.

[125] IWSA, *Report of the Sixth Conference of the International Woman Suffrage Alliance, Stockholm, Sweden, June 12–17, 1911* (London: Women's Printing Society, 1911). The list of French delegates appears on p. 16.

[126] Madame C. L. de Ferrer, *Pourquoi voteraient-elles? Cahiers exposant quelques unes des revendications féministes les plus urgentes à solutionner pour le relèvement de la natalité en France* (Paris: Les Publications encyclopédiques et littéraires, 1910). 69 pages. This author gave her affiliation as the GFEF.

[127] IWSA, *Report of the Sixth Conference*, pp. 96–99; quote, p. 98.

[128] The Colorado testimony appeared in French as *Le Suffrage des femmes au Colorado*, by George Creel and Judge Ben B. Lindsey (U.F.S.F., [1911]). The translator is not named. A second IWSA pamphlet that was translated into French prior to the Stockholm meeting was Alice Zimmern's *Le Suffrage des femmes dans tous les pays* (U.F.S.F., 1911). Both are advertised in *La Française*, n° 222 (4 January 1912), 4.

This extensive handbook (p. 157) compiled by Vérone, Stritt, and Macmillan appeared in 1913 as *Woman Suffrage in Practice* (NUWSS and NAWSA). A second, corrected and updated edition

Subsequently, other notable French suffrage leaders, including Jeanne Schmahl, Jeanne Oddo-Deflou, and Maria Vérone, journeyed to London to take part in the massive suffrage parade organized by the WSPU, with the National Union of Women's Suffrage Societies (NUWSS) and the Women's Franchise League (WFL) on 17 June.[129]

Public opinion surveys on the topic of women's rights more generally and women's suffrage in particular continued to proliferate in early twentieth-century France. In 1911, the results of another survey appeared in four succeeding issues of *Les Documents du Progrès*, from December 1910 through March 1911.[130] In July 1912, *La Grande Revue* published "Les Résultats du vote des femmes," by Marie-Louise Le Verrier on behalf of the UFSF. This article drew heavily on the Buisson publication to argue the case for the beneficial consequences of women's suffrage in many parts of the world. Here again the social housekeeping argument was prominent. The message of this article, however, was that neither philanthropic works nor municipal suffrage was sufficient – that full political equality was absolutely necessary to enable women in France, as elsewhere, to "clean house." "We need to clean up the cities, materially and morally, we need to build workers housing, improve salaries and working conditions, and first of all, we need to close the cabarets. We cannot achieve these reforms without the vote."[131]

New Issues Emerge and Old Issues Revive in the Suffrage Campaign: Alcoholism and Peace

New problems required vigorous solutions. In addition to – or indeed, as intrinsic to the concern over depopulation, the growing problem of alcoholism and its nefarious consequences for individuals and families would come to the attention of French reformers and especially the women in the French suffrage movement. Two aspects were of particular interest to suffragists: the vast expansion (since 1880, when limits were removed) in the number of authorized public houses (*débits*) where

appeared later the same year. It provided an important complement to the ICW's publication on the comparative status of women in the law (1912), ed. by Mme d'Abbadie d'Arrast.

[129]   Reported in *La Française*, n° 207 (2 July 1911).

[130]   Elements of this survey in *Documents du Progrès* are cited sporadically by Bouglé-Moalic in *Vote des Françaises*, e.g., pp. 163, 177; the responses are dissected more systematically by Théodore Joran, *Suffrage des femmes*, pp. 77–84.

[131]   Marie-Louise Le Verrier, "Les Résultats du Vote des Femmes," *La Grande Revue* (10 July 1912), 129–147; quote, 147.

alcoholic drinks could be purchased, and secondly, the vast increase in the commercial production and sale of distilled spirits – especially absinthe – and the illicit production of the misnamed and potentially poisonous *eau-de-vie*.

The campaigns against alcoholism had come together with the suffrage question in the English-speaking world through the work of the temperance societies, especially those affiliated with the World Woman's Christian Temperance Union (WCTU), and had provoked fierce opposition from the liquor interests to the prospect of women obtaining the vote.[132] News of these campaigns – and their successes – had quickly filtered into the IWSA congresses and from there into the consciousness of suffragists in a number of countries.

But debate on the problem was not new. In Francophone Europe, a significant literature on alcohol abuse had already built up during the 1890s, both in France and Belgium. The book *La Femme contre l'alcool* (1897) by the Francophone Belgian feminist Louis Frank was important in bringing the two issues together and in raising public awareness.[133] In commenting on Frank's book in *La Française*, the lawyer Jeanne Chauvin pointed out that only a quarter century earlier alcoholism was almost unknown in France, but had since gained considerable ground in the working classes, due to the distilling of grains, beets, and potatoes, "to the point that the French are becoming almost as alcoholised as their neighbors to the North." Wine and wine-derived products were not implicated in alcoholism, she maintained, a view that seemed to be well accepted in France and other Latin countries. But even in these countries, wherever the traffic in hard liquor was growing, profits were significant and the health and social consequences dreadful. Meanwhile, she alleged, the State was raking in some 500 million francs per year through taxes, and the liquor interests were beginning to influence elections. Louis Frank suggested that one answer to alcoholism lay in the emancipation of women and their engagement in public affairs, especially (though not exclusively) at the municipal level; Jeanne Chauvin heartily concurred.[134]

---

[132] See Ian Tyrrell, *Woman's World, Woman's Empire: The Woman's Christian Temperance Union in International Perspective, 1880–1930* (Chapel Hill: University of North Carolina Press, 1991). Of France, Tyrrell remarks (p. 63) that [in the 1890s] "among the unpromising fields that the sowers of the WCTU gospel surveyed, none presented such an inhospitable prospect as France."

[133] See Louis Frank, *La Femme contre l'alcool: Étude de sociologie et de législation* (Brussels: H. Lamartin, 1897).

[134] Jeanne Chauvin, "L'Alcoolisme et la question féministe," *Le Journal des Femmes*, n° 59 (December 1896), 1–2.

Commentators at the time suggested that most of the drunkards were men, who spent their earnings on drink and came home soused to beat up their wives and children. This was another motive for the feminists' pursuit of the law of 1907 that would give married women control of their own earnings, so that their husbands couldn't appropriate that money too and drink it up. The question of alcoholism among women emerged as well. In his 1899 article on women's alcoholism, Raymond de Ryckère remarked that it had first appeared among women of the working class, but was percolating up into the leisured middle classes, and even manifesting among women of the social elites.[135] In 1900 a student in medicine published a dissertation, *Alcoolisme chez la femme*.[136]

The first international congress concerned with alcoholism in European settings dated from 1878, in Paris. The 7th International Congress Against the Abuse of Alcoholic Beverages [*VIIe Congrès International contre l'abus des boissons alcooliques*] met in Paris in early April 1899. In a public lecture, Mme Elisabeth Selmer, head of the Danish women's temperance society, called on French women to confront the problem of alcoholism. Shortly thereafter, a group known as the *Union Française des Femmes pour la Temperance* came into being; to be an officer one had to pledge total abstinence. Its particular concern was the rehabilitation (*relèvement*) of drunkards. But total abstinence would never attract mass support in France. A number of French feminists attended the congress, but evidently few joined the temperance union.[137] There was virtually no French representation at the subsequent international congress in Vienna (1901), except for Dr. Legrain who spearheaded the French national temperance effort and his wife, the president of the French women's group, who gave an

---

[135] Raymond de Ryckère, "L'Alcoolisme féminin," *Archives d'Anthropologie Criminelle*, 14 (1899), 70–92 and 205–222; observation on social mobility of alcoholism among women, p. 92. See also his book with the same title (Paris: Masson, 1899).

[136] Alphonse-Joseph-Louis-Calixte Cat, *Alcoolisme chez la femme*. Thèse, Faculté de Médicine, Paris (Paris: Rousset, 1900).

[137] *VIIe Congrès International contre l'Abus des Boissons Alcooliques. Session de Paris 1899* (Paris: L'Union Française Antialcoolique, 1900). Feminists in attendance included Mme Béquet de Vienne, Mme d'Abbadie d'Arrast, Mme Isabelle Bogelot, Mlle Brès, Marie Guérin, also Jules Siegfried, Dr. Charles Richet, Dr. Edward Toulouse, Dr. Théophile Roussel, etc. Proceedings consulted at the Musée Social, May 2012. Savioz covered this anti-alcohol conference for *La Fronde*: see her five articles in n°s 483–486 (5–8 April 1899); these clippings can also be consulted in her scrapbooks, reel 1, pp. 49–50, at the BMD. In her fifth article, "Les Femmes et l'alcoolisme," n° 489 (11 April 1899), Savioz documented the reservations expressed at the women's meeting by Maria Pognon and Eliska Vincent, concerning the requirement for total abstinence to serve on the executive board of the proposed women's temperance society; these militant feminists defended the French enjoyment of wine. Mme Vincent thought that activism should be directed primarily toward closing the many cabarets where hard liquor was served.

update on French women's efforts since 1899.[138] Mme Legrain would then remark that the requirement for total abstinence to be a leader in the women's group was off-putting to some French women, who did like their glass of wine or sherry; thus, the organization's membership remained small.

At the 1900 *Oeuvres et Institutions* Congress in Paris, nearly a dozen speakers addressed the role of women in combatting alcoholism with Mme Legrain leading off a roster that included women from Belgium, England, Germany, Sweden, Switzerland, and one speaking about alcoholism in the colonies.[139] At some point the CNFF had passed a resolution against absinthe. In early 1907, the now-consolidated *Ligue Nationale contre l'Alcoolisme* (formed in 1903 by merging the *Union Française Anti-Alcoolique* and the French temperance society) petitioned to join (via its Ladies' Auxiliary) the CNFF.[140] At the March meeting, CNFF members debated the links between alcoholism and crime, and whether criminals who are alcoholics should be subject to the full force of the law or institutionalized for possible rehabilitation.[141] In May, the CNFF agreed to give the *Ligue Anti-Alcoolique* the floor at its General Assembly to make an appeal to women to fight against alcoholism.[142] The CNFF took the antialcoholism campaigners very seriously (it bears mentioning that the husband of Julie Siegfried, the second president of the CNFF, was the prominent deputy Jules Siegfried, who was deeply engaged in the French anti-alcohol league).[143] In fact, it seemed at times that in the press the suffragists were placing more weight on addressing the "hot" topic of alcoholism than on the longtime goal of revising the laws that subordinated married women in the Civil Code, though certainly that issue had not subsided (as was evidenced by the ICW's publication on the comparative status of wives in the law, compiled by France's Mme d'Abbadie d'Arrast, which singled

---

[138] *Bericht über den VIII. Internationalen Congress gegen den Alkoholismis abgehalten in Wien, 9–14. April 1901*, ed. by Dr. Rudolf Wlassak (Leipzig und Wien: F. Deuticke, 1902). Mme Legrain's presentation is on pp. 228–230.

[139] See *2e Congrès International des Oeuvres et Institutions . . . Compte Rendu des Travaux*, ed. Mme Pégard, vol. 1, pp. 166–169. Cf. Klejman & Rochefort, *Égalité en marche*, p. 138.

[140] See the report on the CNFF meeting of 13 February, reported in the *Journal des Femmes*, n° 171 (February 1907), 1–2. The letter of intent, on behalf of the Ladies' Auxiliary of the anti-alcohol league, appeared in the *Journal des Femmes*, n° 172 (March 1907), 3.

[141] See the report in the *Journal des Femmes*, n° 173 (April 1907), 2.

[142] *Le Journal des Femmes*, n° 174 (May 1907), 1.

[143] See Jules Siegfried's report "La Lutte contre l'alcoolisme en France," in the *Compte-Rendu du XIV Congrès International contre l'Alcoolisme. Milan, 22–25 September 1913* (Milan: n.p., 1921), pp. 417–421. At this time, the Senate version of the proposed law was still awaiting action in the Chamber of Deputies. Siegfried says nothing about the question of women's suffrage in his report.

out the French Civil Code as a pan-European obstacle).[144] The sale and production of absinthe was successfully outlawed in 1907. The next step was to limit (at the local level) the number of outlets for alcohol; to this end, the prospect of municipal suffrage for women offered formidable potential, as it had in other countries.

In consequence, the anti-alcohol campaigners and pro-suffrage forces came together further following the formation of the UFSF in 1909. By 1911, the two groups would be working closely together. Hause, with Kenney, remark that Cécile Brunschvicg, the new secretary-general of the UFSF, set out to capture the anti-alcohol supporters in the provinces as allies for the women's suffrage quest. Indeed, such an alliance could benefit both causes. Brunschvicg argued in *La Française* for the benefits this alliance would bring; the results in other countries had shown that "everywhere the advent of women's vote has been accompanied by legislation that represses alcohol, and the same countries that, in the statistics of alcohol furnished the biggest numbers for the consumption of alcohol, have since merited citation as the most memorable examples of victory for the cause of temperance and health."[145] Women's voting, she indicated, would have serious practical effects.

The two groups collaborated on organizing a huge public meeting in Paris on 31 May 1911, chaired by none other than Ferdinand Buisson, the *rapporteur* of the suffrage bill.[146] The UFSF published a December 1911 lecture by a certain Mlle Levray, *L'Alcoolisme et le vote des femmes*.[147] Other publications by women included Marie-Louise Le Verrier's article on suffrage in *La Grande Revue* (previously quoted) and Cécile Brunschvicg's lecture reprinted in the *Revue Medico-Sociale* (March 1912).[148] In 1912, *La*

---

[144] See Karen Offen, "National or International? How and Why the Napoleonic Code Drove Married Women's Legal Rights onto the Agenda of the International Council of Women and the League of Nations: An Overview," in *Family Law in Early Women's Rights Debates*, ed. Stephan Meder & Christoph-Eric Mecke (Cologne: Böhlau Verlag, 2013), pp. 42–59.

[145] Cécile Brunschvicg, "Le Suffrage des femmes et l'Anti-Alcoolisme," *La Française*, n° 202 (28 May 1911), 1.

[146] See Hause, with Kenney, *Women's Suffrage and Social Politics*, pp. 154–155, and Klejman & Rochefort, *Égalité en marche*, pp. 277–278. In *Drink and the Politics of Social Reform: Antialcoholism in France since 1870s* (Palo Alto: Society for the Promotion of Science and Scholarship, 1988), Patricia E. Prestwich devotes a mere four pages (pp. 187–190) to the relationship between the French women's movement and the anti-alcohol campaigns. W. Scott Haine, *The World of the Paris Cafe: Sociability among the French Working Class, 1789–1914* (Baltimore: Johns Hopkins University Press, 1996), does not address the fin-de-siècle anti-alcoholism crusade at all.

[147] Mlle Levray, *L'Alcoolisme et le vote des femmes: Conférence* (Paris, 1911), 13 pages.

[148] These publications were recommended by Mme Meynadier at the 1913 International Congress (see n. 153), p. 111. The article by Le Verrier is cited in n. 131.

Française would publish the petitions, including a women's petition, calling for a cutback in the number of retail outlets for liquor and demanding immediate action on the subject in the Chamber of Deputies.[149] This publication would also launch an occasional feature, "Tribune d'Antialcoolisme" in October 1913.[150] Madeleine Vernet would publish a pamphlet on the "problem" of alcoholism in 1913.[151] In *L'Équité*, Hélène Brion would call for "war on alcohol," one of several articles on the subject that would be published there.[152]

At the June 1913 international women's congress in Paris, the campaign to combat alcoholism held a prominent spot on the agenda of the section on hygiene, along with the campaign against tuberculosis. A long, comprehensive and internationally focused report by a Mme Meynadier presented the startling fact that in France, the number of bars in France alone rose in recent years from 354,000 to 480,000, while the quantity of absinthe consumed rose from 700,000 to 1,363,000 liters. She concluded, however, that women, the housewives, were key to resolving the problem; they were the "front-line soldiers in this worthy combat" – notably by maintaining clean, inviting households that would keep their menfolk out of the bars but also by campaigning for the reduction in the number of bars.[153]

The overall agenda of the very successful congress was very broad. The resolutions fell into three principal categories:[154] 1) those having for objective to raise the moral dignity of the woman, including *l'unité de la morale* (the single moral standard for both sexes), sex education, protection of women's work, amendment of the Civil Code, and education/instruction, along with coeducation; 2) those having for object the improvement of the condition of the family, including housing, *puériculture*, campaigns against tuberculosis and alcoholism, joint parental authority, prohibition

[149] See "Aux Françaises," in *La Française*, n° 254 (November 1912), and "Pétition Nationale des Femmes pour la Limitation des Débits," n° 256 (23 November 1912), and n° 257 (30 November 1912).
[150] See, for example, *La Française*, issue n° 290 (18 October 1913), n° 292 (1 November 1913), n° 294 (15 November 1913), n° 298 (13 December 1913), and n° 300 (27 December 1913).
[151] Madeleine Vernet, *Le Problème de l'alcoolisme*. 2nd ed. (Paris: La Renovatrice, 1913); a 3rd ed. appeared in 1917 (Epône: L'Avenir social). I have found no traces of a "first" edition.
[152] See Hélène Brion, "Guerre à l'alcool, " *L'Équité*, n° 4 (15 May 1913), and "Les Femmes contre l'alcool, " in n° 14 (1 March 1914).
[153] *Dixième congrès international des femmes: Oeuvres et institutions féminines, Droits des femmes, 2–8 juin 1913* (cited in n. 11). See pp. 100–118 for the report of Mme Meynadier and its resolutions and annexes.
[154] According to Jeanne Crouzet Ben-Aben's article, "Une Assemblée de femmes en 1913," *La Grande Revue* (10 July 1913; cited in n. 1).

of night work by adolescents (under 18), kindergartens and *écoles ménagères* [housekeeping schools] for both sexes; 3) those having for object the perfecting of the *cité*. These campaigns thus encompassed the fight against alcoholism and tuberculosis, as well as addressing the major issue of war and peace, of which more later; and, of course, 4) the right to vote. Clearly, there was a great deal of work that French women could do in collaboration with men.

It was at this 1913 congress also that debates about the possibility of war and prospects for peace reemerged vigorously. The threat of war had grown substantially since the middle of the 1900s, as the German emperor Wilhelm II began to rattle his saber (both figuratively and literally) and dramatically expand his navy, making several tentative moves on Morocco, which ultimately (1912) became a French protectorate. The wars in the Balkans in 1912 and 1913 did nothing to dissipate fears. War fever mounted, and with it questions about the "gender" of war.

Mainstream feminists periodically expressed their concerns about how women should view warfare, even as they sought to participate in national – and international – decision-making. In 1904 – at the ICW quinquennial meeting in Berlin, a gigantic meeting on behalf of peace took place in the Philharmonic concert hall. The speakers included the great peace advocate Bertha von Suttner, followed by Isabelle Bogelot who, in name of the women of the CNFF, called for an international arbitration tribunal to resolve conflicts between nations.[155] In 1907 feminists from the CNFF had again taken a strong stand for peace, helping to organize a public meeting in May, in association with several more established peace societies.[156] In mid-June of that year the CNFF secretary-general, Ghénia Avril de Sainte-Croix, journeyed to The Hague to join the ICW delegation in commemorating the tenth anniversary of the landmark 1899 Hague Conference (during the opening of the second Hague Conference). This international delegation of women would succeed in organizing an unprecedented audience with the elected conference president, M. Nelidow, the Russian ambassador to France, to express "the ardent desire of all women to see the second conference result in solutions that would push back a bit further the risks of war."[157] Slowly, very slowly,

---

[155] Quotes from Bogelot in Mme Avril de Sainte-Croix, *Le Féminisme*, pp. 156–157.

[156] See the account of this big meeting by Parrhisia, "Pour la Paix," *La Française*, n° 32 (26 May 1907), 2–3.

[157] See the two articles in *La Française* by the appellate court attorney Maurice Bokanowski, "La Deuxième Conférence de La Haye," in n° 35 (16 June 1907) and "Les Femmes à La Haye," in n° 37 (30 June 1907); the quotation, in Bokanowski's words, is from the second article.

some sectors of French public opinion would come around to rethinking their views on war and peace, even in the face of mounting nationalist efforts to stir up chauvinistic and pro-war feeling.

Historian Margaret Darrow has sketched a scathing account of Right wing nationalist thinking in the early twentieth century, portraying war as a purely masculine experience, one in which women had no part.[158] Indeed, the young men who responded to the landmark survey by "Agathon," *Les Jeunes Gens d'aujourd'hui* (1913), exhibited such attitudes, emphasizing nationalism, religious revival, the need for virility, action, and associated features.[159] Darrow has observed that the respondents in *Jeunes Gens* "were remarkably silent about their attitudes towards the opposite sex, especially considering all the brouhaha at the time about the emancipated woman."[160] It seemed that, among others, the publications of the nationalist deputy and writer Maurice Barrès in his trilogy, *Le Roman de l'énergie nationale*, had widely influenced young people's thinking. In her chapter, "Women's War Imagined," Darrow discusses the Agathon survey as well as the parallel survey in 1914 of young women by Amélie Gayraud, which reflected some of the same sentiments, and on which I will comment later.[161]

Another influence promoting warlike thinking came from avant-garde writers such as the Italian poet Filippo Thommaso Marinetti, author of the shocking "Futurist Manifesto" (1909), published in *Le Figaro* in February of 1909 (the newspaper declined responsibility for Marinetti's ideas). Marinetti considered peace as "effeminate" and demasculinizing.[162] Among its choice morsels:

---

[158] Margaret H. Darrow, *French Women and the First World War: War Stories of the Home Front* (Oxford: Berg, 2000), esp. chapters 1 and 2.

[159] See Agathon (pseud. of Henri Massis & Alfred de Tarde), *Les jeunes gens d'aujourd'hui* (Paris: Plon-Nourrit, orig. publ. 1913). This work, which went through many editions, has been republished with an introduction by J. J. Becker. For an extended analysis, see Robert Wohl, *The Generation of 1914* (Cambridge, MA: Harvard University Press, 1979).

[160] See the discussion in Darrow, *French Women and the First World War: War Stories of the Home Front*; p. 14.

[161] Amélie Gayraud, *Les Jeunes filles d'aujourd'hui* (Paris: G. Oudin, 1914). See Darrow, *French Women and the First World War*, pp. 23, 39, & 44–45. Darrow's conclusion is that for most of these young women, their idea of patriotic action in face of war would be to join the Red Cross.

[162] Filippo Tommaso Marinetti, "Le Futurisme," *Le Figaro* (20 February 1909), front page. Reprinted in F. T. Marinetti, *Le Futurisme*, préface de Giovanni Lista (Lausanne: Éditions l'Age d'homme, 1980); quote, p. 153. Note that in the latter reprint, the word "féminisme," which figured in the original text in *Le Figaro*, is absent. My retranslation here is based directly on the article in *Le Figaro*. See also, for a full translation of the Manifesto and other works, *Marinetti: Selected Writings*, edited by R. W. Flint; translated by R. W. Flint & Arthur A. Coppotelli (New York: Farrar, Straus, and Giroux, 1972).

We want to sing of love for danger, the habit of energy and courage. . . .

The only beauty lies in struggle. . . .

We want to glorify war – the world's only hygiene – militarism, patriotism, the destructive act of the anarchists, beautiful ideas that kill, and contempt for woman. We want to destroy museums, libraries, to combat moralism, feminism, and all such opportunistic and utilitarian acts of cowardice.

At that time and since, this was enough to make some people's hair stand on end, not least that of the feminists.

Marinetti's perspective would be followed up in 1912 by another Futurist writer – this time a woman named Valentine de Saint-Point – who would propose that both men and women of the early twentieth century lacked virility. What women needed, asserted Saint-Point, was not "rights" but an infusion of spilled blood, of instinct; she called for a resurgence of heroic warriors, warrior women, and ferocious mothers. Then, she indicated, masculinity and femininity would resume their proper places. "Let Woman rediscover her cruelty and violence, which assure that she will tear apart the vanquished." Sentimentalism, softness, compassion, humane values were the enemy: feminist claims, to Saint-Point, incarnated these. "Feminism," she assured her readers and audiences, "is a political error . . . a cerebral error, which woman's instinct recognizes as such."[163]

Some feminists such as the UFSF secretary-general and editor of *La Française*, Jane Misme, would reiterate her view that feminism is pacifist but also patriotic, that the two notions were not mutually exclusive.[164] Yet not every feminist was happy about the continued emphasis of the mainstream feminists of the CNFF on peace and peacekeeping. In contrast to many of her counterparts, Jeanne Oddo-Deflou would insist that pacifism had nothing to do with feminism, and expressed her concern that the ICW was ordering its national affiliates to demonstrate for peace. Perhaps this conviction influenced her decision to resign from the CNFF in early 1908 and embark on a different path.[165] In another venue, in *La Suffragiste*, several of the more radical feminists dissented on questions of war and peace. Arria Ly queried whether war was in fact a bad thing, while Caroline

---

[163] Valentine de Saint-Point, "Manifeste de la Femme Futuriste: Réponse à F. T. Marinetti" (dated 25 March 1912); reprinted in *Futurisme: Manifestes, proclamations, documents*, ed. Giovanni Lista (Lausanne: Éditions d'Age d'homme, 1973), pp. 329–332; quote, p. 330. This text was read by the author at avant-garde gallery presentations in Brussels and Paris during the late spring and summer of 1912, and published in Italian, French, and German.

[164] See Jane Misme, "Les Femmes et la guerre," *La Française*, n° 278 (10 May 1913), lead article.

[165] See Jeanne Oddo-Deflou's article, "Le Féminisme national ou international," *La Suffragiste*, n° 28 (May 1912), 8–10.

Kauffmann (a champion of physical culture, it should be remembered) declared that although she used to be a pacifist, she was "not an enemy of war."[166] Indeed, Kauffmann began to echo the themes developed by Marinetti in the "Futurist Manifesto" – war excites energies and combats softness – "it is physical and moral weakness that one must exterminate."[167] A third contributor to the same issue of *La Suffragiste*, a Mlle S. Renkin, opined, however, that armies should exist only for defense of the country, and that once women get their rights there would be no more war.[168]

A proposal for girls' national service, mainly aimed at preparation for motherhood, provoked further controversy. Another alternative, that of military service for French women, had been proposed earlier by Dr. Toulouse, but Nelly Roussel would strongly oppose it. Roussel agreed with the critique of Augusta Moll-Weiss, who thought that soldiers should not be relieved of their responsibilities (by bringing in women to take care of things) to rustle up their food, take care of their own clothing, and clean up their living space. Men should learn, in their regiments, to get used to taking care of themselves! In response to a subsequent proposal for women's military service by Madeleine Pelletier, Roussel insisted that women's current maternal "service" to the nation was quite enough to ask of them.[169] Indeed, such proposals kept coming up. Marguerite Durand promoted the idea of women's national service during her 1910 legislative campaign, which created a buzz but also provided fodder for some off-color jokes in the press.[170]

In 1913, however, the introduction of a legislative proposal to extend the current two years of men's compulsory military service (initiated in 1905) to three years provoked further debate, not least about its potentially adverse implications for the population question. Surprisingly, some of the ensuing literature scarcely took women's role in population increase into account; one deputy's proposal, loaded with comparative statistics on German and French military manpower, ignored women completely – or perhaps simply assumed that if young conscripts were more available, or encouraged to found families, young wives would happily cooperate in producing

---

[166] See Arria Ly, "La Guerre est-elle un mal?" *La Suffragiste*, n° 28 (May 1912), 10–12, and Caroline Kauffmann, "Paix ou Guerre," *La Suffragiste*, n° 29 (June 1912), 9–11.

[167] Kauffmann, "Paix ou Guerre," 9.

[168] Renkin, "Sur la Guerre," *La Suffragiste*, n° 29 (June 1912), 11.

[169] See Nelly Roussel, articles in *Quelques Lances*, pp. 185–186 (from an article in *L'Action*, 6 September 1907) and pp. 191–192 (from an article in *L'Action*, 21 November 1908).

[170] See Darrow's remarks in *French Women and the First World War*, pp. 34–36.

offspring.[171] In July 1914, *L'Équité* would point out that virtually none of the chief legislative proponents of the three-year law had sons; in fact, some were bachelors and none, except for Raymond Poincaré, who was then president of the Republic, had ever served in the French military.[172]

Women writing on the topic were far less engaged with the technical details of conscription law, but very wary of the frightening prospects implied by increasing the number of men under arms. Writing in *L'Équité* in opposition to the three-year military service law, Fanny Clar warned her readers about the prospects ahead: "We are before a precipice, over the edge of which the European nations dizzily lean and are about to slide, if . . . they don't straighten up and pull back from the chasm . . .. War is hideous!"[173] Leading feminists agreed. The LFDF's Maria Vérone would give a fiery speech at the IWSA's 1913 congress in Budapest, in which she reputedly declared "war against war."[174] This was a longtime slogan of the European peace movement, dating back to the 1860s at least and deployed by many progressive women, including Bertha von Suttner and Clara Zetkin.

Not all well-known women proposed waging "war against war." In March 1913 the celebrated cross-dressing *exploratrice* Jane Dieulafoy suggested to the minister of war that French women be called into military service (as had the Austrian women), and she offered to be the first to sign up. Her objective was not to call women into combat but rather to replace men (officers and sous-officers) currently assigned to administrative offices, so they could go to the front if and when they were needed.[175] Some eight

---

[171] See, for example, André Honnorat, "Le service de trois ans et le problème de la natalité," *La Grande Revue*, vol. 78 (25 March 1913), 318–330.

[172] "Leur Famille," *L'Équité: Journal du Prolétariat féminin*, n° 23 (15 July 1914), 2.

[173] Fanny Clar, "Le mensonge des trois ans," *L'Équité*, n° 2 (15 March 1913); reprinted in *Le Grief des femmes: Anthologie des textes féministes du Second Empire à nos jours*, ed. Maïté Albistur & Daniel Armogathe (Paris: Éditions hier et demain, 1978), p. 202. See also *L'Équité*, n° 6 (15 July 1913), 3.

[174] I have had no luck in tracking down the text of Maria Vérone's "war against war" speech. In Vérone's report on the Budapest IWSA congress in *Le Droit des Femmes*, n° 7 (July 1913), 1–3, she does not mention her speech. In the Report of the 7th Congress, a Tuesday evening session in the Academy of Music (Budapest) with six featured speakers is indicated, but not reported on: the six designated speakers were Marie Stritt, Maria Vérone, Rosika Schwimmer, Jane Addams, Gilli Tetrini, & Anna H[oward]. Shaw. The only report concerning the Rome speech is in *Le Droit des Femmes*, via *Le Journal*, in July issue 1914. Vérone evidently repeated this cry during her lecture tours. See *La Française* (23 May 1914), and Mary Sheepshanks, "The Suffrage Meeting in Rome, 15 May 1914," *Jus Suffragii*, 8:11 (1 July 1914), 137–138.

[175] See "Si les femmes voulaient: Elles donneraient à l'armée française 2,672 officiers et 5.000 sous-officiers de plus, de quoi encadrer deux corps d'armée," *Le Matin* (2 June 1913), and Paul Ginesty, "Notes parisiennes: 'Les officières'," *L'Étoile Belge* (28 June 1913). Clippings from LLF62, Mundaneum, Mons. Evidently the minister of war was pleased with this initiative and with the idea of sponsoring classes at which women (presumably not those of child-bearing age) could volunteer to learn the skills they needed; see the positive report by Marie Louise Le Verrier, "French

hundred women thought this was a good idea and signed up. Mme d'Abbadie d'Arrast of the CNFF, though skeptical about Jane Dieula-foy's notion of service, would speak enthusiastically to the *Société Général des Prisons* about the many different types of social service that French women were providing, with the hope that working with imprisoned young people could be added to that list. The French woman, she asserted grandly, "has proved that for *la patrie*, she is ready for all sacrifices and ready to provide every service that might be demanded of her."[176] The notion that all demands for rights must be cognizant of the necessity of fulfilling duties was deeply embedded in the culture of French feminism. Women were deeply engaged in "duties" in France, but where were the rights?

The Regrettable Fate of Woman Suffrage Legislation in 1914 France

Feminists in France wanted desperately to become functioning *citoyennes* of the Third Republic. They complained that France had fallen behind other countries; indeed, everyone who cared about suffrage for women was keenly aware of this fact.[177] That Finnish women had not only obtained the vote in 1906 but that nineteen women had been elected to the Finnish parliament provided an impetus for other suffrage campaigns in the Scandinavian countries. British women were campaigning madly for the vote. This state of affairs was embarrassing to the French feminists in the court of world opinion and to their own self-image. Maria Vérone, among others, complained repeatedly about "*le rétard*." Mme Remember's *La Suffragiste* complained that even Chinese women were being enfranchised before the French, who seemed to be losing their position of world leadership in forward-looking ideas. Madeleine Pelletier reported writing to Sun Yat-Sen, recently elected president of the new Chinese republic, on the subject – and claims to have received an answer, in which he said that women's education would have to come first. However, she did receive a reply from the president's secretary, announcing the election of four Chinese women to the provincial assembly in Canton. "Thus even China,

---

Women and Conscription," *Jus Suffragii*, 8:4 (1 December 1913), 26. Cf. also Darrow, *French Women and the First World War*, pp. 40–42.

[176] Madame d'Abbadie d'Arrast, "Le Service social de la femme," *La Revue Pénitentiaire*, vol. 37, n°s 7–10 (July–October 1913), 934–939. Session of 28 June 1913.

[177] See Bouglé-Moalic, *Vote des Françaises*, on the creation of "*le retard*," pp. 166–170; and *La Suffragiste*, n° 27 (April 1912).

a country that we thought forever mired in thousand year old traditions," she moaned, "is now more advanced than we are."[178]

Throughout 1913 the Chamber of Deputies continued to drag its feet on debating the revised Buisson report, which (again) called for municipal suffrage for all French women. Concerned about the resurgence of monarchist and neo-traditionalist nationalist political factions in the early years of the twentieth century, even many pro-suffrage radical republicans were reluctant to broaden the electorate still further without "properly educating" the massive potential female electorate. The mainstream women's rights activists themselves would take such concerns very seriously. Early in 1910, the house organ of the UFSF, *La Française*, had published a "course in political education for women." Beyond that, nothing much would happen.

Republican politicians would endorse the principle of woman suffrage but then separate principle from application; such a bifurcated view occupied a prominent place in republican public opinion, as is clear from numerous statements published in the press.[179] One significant exception was the deputy Louis Andrieux, who in November 1913 did invoke the republic's principles when he demanded the vote for all women.[180] To date French legislators had proved themselves more interested in enacting laws to protect maternity and early infancy, and had even passed the ultimately unsatisfactory measure legalizing *recherche de la paternité*. But coming to agreement on any number of other proposals, from taxes to the method of voting itself, had hamstrung the legislature. As Bouglé-Moalic emphasizes, "the principal obstacle to political rights for women from 1910 on was no longer the 'nature' of women, but was manifestly political."[181] What, then, would it take to get the legislators to act positively on the suffrage question?

Ever the optimists, the campaigners for suffrage continued to press on. They had some reason to be hopeful. They continued to play the citizen-mother card, and to emphasize sexual difference and relationality, along with women's capacity for local and national "social housekeeping" and

---

[178] Madeleine Pelletier, "La Chine nous devance," *La Suffragiste*, n° 27 (April 1912), 10–11.

[179] See, among others, Henri Coulon & René de Chavagnes, "La Femme et ses droits politiques," *La Nouvelle Revue* (1 April 1910), 289–301 [Juliette Adam, still famous for her refutation of Proudhon in the 1850s, was the editor of this well-respected publication]. See also "La Charte de la femme et la société de demain," *La Revue* (15 May 1910); and the public opinion poll organized by Jeanne-E. Schmahl, "Les femmes françaises doivent-elles voter?," *La Revue* (15 June 1910), 446–463, and (5 July 1910), 23–39.

[180] See Bouglé-Moalic, *Vote des Françaises*, p. 195.   [181] Bouglé-Moalic, *Vote des Françaises*, p. 200.

service to the nation. Equality-in-difference continued to be their dominant argument. As they sought entry into local and national decision-
making, French feminists would become thoroughly nationalized, even
as French maternity found some "protection." How could it have been
otherwise? In 1913, the activists of the UFSF put together a pro-suffrage
petition that was signed by 200 deputies.[182]

Steven Hause and Anne Kenney rightly call 1914 "the apogee of suffragist activity" and devote an entire chapter to it.[183] The challenge suffrage
advocates faced was how to demonstrate, for the benefit of the more
skeptical deputies and senators, that many women really did want to vote
and had the capacity to do so effectively. Several initiatives got underway
during the spring, including one spearheaded by the LFDF, where Marie
Bonnevial and Maria Vérone also had charge of the suffrage section of the
CNFF (a fact that has not been sufficiently recognized by earlier scholars).
It began with a kiosk selling suffrage gifts for holiday present-giving.

A survey of young women (alluded to earlier) in parallel to the "Agathon" survey of young men, and like it initially published serially in
L'Opinion, was organized by a woman, Amélie Gayraud, who would
inquire into attitudes of young women ages 18 to 25 with some education,
young women who could be considered "cultivated." Like Agathon, she
gathered information through conversations, rather than "interviews" as
such. Invoking the longstanding French saying, "if men create politics and
laws, women make the morals," Gayraud sought to understand her subjects' thinking "as women" on moral issues.[184]

Gayraud introduced the resulting book with the affirmation that bolts
of feminist lightning have accompanied every revolution, then supplied her
readers with a list of outstanding nineteenth-century women who had
promoted women's emancipation. But, Gayraud remarked, these were
exceptional women, isolated women, whereas the current generation of
young women is the first to be systematically educated, thanks to the
efforts of the Third Republic and the forerunners and promoters, Ernest
Legouvé and Camille Sée.[185] She underscored the patriotic character of
such a laic education, provided by *la patrie*, which valued and enhanced

---

[182] Brunschvicg, "Le suffrage des femmes en France" *Les Documents du Progrès* (December 1913), cited
in n. 116.

[183] Hause, with Kenney, *Women's Suffrage and Social Politics*, quote, p. 169.

[184] Gayraud, *Jeunes filles*; quote, p. 16. On this survey, as well as that by "Agathon," (mentioned in
n. 159) see Darrow, *French Women and the First World War*, pp. 13–15, 44–46. Darrow does not
mention the 1914 survey by Abensour, which I will discuss next.

[185] Gayraud, *Jeunes filles*, pp. 20–24.

motherhood, marriage and the household ... and emphasized women's moral duty. Even though the recent explosion of women's writing, especially by its poetesses, was celebrating freedom, voluptuousness, and so forth, Gayraud claimed that young modern French women were not enthusiastic about that: they "are against licenctiousness" and take a dim view of these "Amazons of love." Instead, she remarked, they align themselves with the critics of these works. This generation relishes notions of discipline, Gayraud insisted; their guide is Auguste Comte [!] ... They are not enthusiastic about the idea of *union libre*. These young women, Gayraud found, all want to marry, but they are more particular than before about their choice of spouse, who should be mentally and physically healthy, and they want to become companions to their future husbands. In concluding her introduction, Gayraud would fall back on literary examples (all by male novelists) of how today's young women should (or should not) be, praising in particular the character of Antoinette in Romain Rolland's *Jean Christophe* (10 vols., 1903–1912) as exemplifying *la jeune fille française*.

Another survey, also published in *L'Opinion* (weekly, 28 March through 25 April 1914) was organized by the young male feminist Léon Abensour; its subject was "*Le Féminisme et la Jeunesse Française*" [Feminism and French Youth]. Begun on the eve of the spring legislative elections, it promised a follow-up to the highly masculinist picture provided by the Agathon book, and to the enlightened but conservative view of femininity revealed by the Gayraud survey. Abensour addressed his questions to the young people of both sexes by asking a more focused question: "Are you in favor of women's emancipation, and especially of votes for women?" His subsequent five questions inquired about the possible consequences, from the point of view of the family, of morality, of politics, of economics, of the social. The respondents included a variety of educated women and men along with workingmen from the mixed unions and the typographers.

The published opinions in Abensour's survey were not encouraging for suffragists; they exhibited much support for male authority in the family and separate spheres of labor for the sexes. One self-professed Catholic respondent, Robert Vallery-Radot by name, invoked St. Paul as the final word on the matter, along with God's curse on women from the Book of Genesis; this respondent could not resist (à la Théodore Joran), calling feminists names such as "*les évaporées et les énergumènes de l'intellectualisme*," "*ces mégères*," as authors of "*cette littérature de bacchantes ivres et d'hystériques dévergondées*," terms that translate as feather-brained/flighty, ranters, shrew/scold, drunken bacchantes, and licentious hysterics. Such viputerative language seems, in and of itself, hysterical. Abensour also commented on the antifeminism he encountered among women teachers, but noted that some young men did favor economic and social emancipation for women, though not political rights. He also provided a dialogue between two workers who stood on opposite sides of the woman question, one of whom reflected the intransigence of the *Fédération du Livre* in the wake of the Couriau Affair, and the other, more optimistic, partially supported women's rights.[186] For Abensour, a dedicated young feminist himself, these results must have been extremely disappointing.[187] It seems that even the most conservative advocates of women's suffrage and political participation were operating well in advance of French public opinion.

In anticipation of the legislative elections of 1914, a new type of suffrage campaign sprang forth, organized by the pro-suffrage mass circulation newspaper *Le Journal*, now edited by Gustave Téry, a longtime supporter of women's suffrage and former vice-president of the LFDF. The idea was simple but ingenious: ask the women of France, via this important newspaper, to vote in a poll on women's suffrage itself by depositing or mailing in a ballot (between the 26 April and 3 May) marked *Je désire voter*. Over 500,000 French women responded, both in Paris and, by mail, from the provinces.[188] Maria Vérone crowed over the results: "we had not dared count on such a success . . . the results exceeded our wildest hopes."[189]

One unfortunate result of the April 1914 legislative elections was the defeat of Ferdinand Buisson. For over a decade he had been the chief advocate of women's suffrage, and especially of the Dussaussoy-Buisson bill to enfranchise all women at the local level. As the Chamber of Deputies regrouped, however, the new reporter for the suffrage bill, Pierre-Étienne Flandin, did manage to get the issue onto the agenda of

---

[186] See Léon Abensour, "Enquête: Le Féminisme et la jeunesse française," *L'Opinion* (28 March 1914), 402–404; (4 April 1914), 436–438; (11 April 1914), 467–468; (18 April 1914), 497–498; and (25 April 1914), 533–535.

[187] Léon Abensour would go on to publish well-documented scholarly histories of feminism: see his *Histoire générale du féminisme – des origines à nos jours* (Paris: Delagrave, 1921), and his magisterial *La Femme et le féminisme avant la Révolution*. Thèse de doctorat, Faculté des lettres, Université de Paris (Paris: E. Leroux, 1923). He would also publish books of contemporary analysis on the woman question, notably *Les Vaillantes; héroines, martyres et remplaçantes* (Paris: Chapelot, 1917) and *Le Problème féministe; un cas d'aspiration collective vers l'égalité* (Paris: Radot, 1927).

[188] See Hause, with Kenney, *Women's Suffrage and Social Politics*, pp. 179–184; Klejman & Rochefort, *Égalité en marche*, pp. 285–286; and Elizabeth Coquart, *La Frondeuse: Marguerite Durand, Patronne de presse et féministe* (Paris: Payot, 2010), chapter 27, pp. 243–253.

[189] Maria Vérone "505,972 Femmes réclament le suffrage," *Le Droit des Femmes*, 9:5 (15 May 1914), 1–2, quotes, 2.

the newly elected chamber. In mid-June 1914, the proposed law based on the Buisson report was finally presented to the Chamber of Deputies.

This was the moment everyone had been waiting for. In early July (5th) an unprecedented alliance of French pro-suffrage groups, under the leadership of the celebrated journalist Séverine, staged a massive Sunday afternoon rally to stimulate action on the bill. Much touted by Jane Misme as a "*Jour Suffragiste*," this would be their first – and, as it turned out, their last – major public demonstration. Speeches at the Orangerie prepared the groundwork for a silent mass procession through the streets of Paris to lay garlands at the statue of the Marquis de Condorcet, "the father of feminism" in the words of Ghénia Avril de Sainte-Croix.[190] An estimated 5,000 to 6,000 individuals turned out for the event. That evening, at a banquet sponsored by the LFDF, French feminists celebrated the prospect of realizing their supreme goal wholly within the framework of the French Third Republic.[191]

La Française published a special issue for the 5th of July event, featuring articles about the suffrage question and profiling its supporters; this would be its last issue before the summer break, and as it turned out, the last issue for several months. It featured endorsements of women's suffrage by distinguished advocates, including a quotation from René Viviani's 1901 article on the subject, and messages from Julie Siegfried, president of the CNFF, and Marguerite Witt-Schlumberger, president of the UFSF. It included a long, unsigned article in support of suffrage that detailed all the practical reasons why women, single and married, needed the vote and dismissed all objections raised against their voting as "childish."[192] Cécile Brunschvicg, secretary-general of the UFSF, provided an up-to-date report on the progress of the suffrage question in the Chamber of Deputies, urging supporters to contact those members of the commission on universal suffrage who were not already declared partisans of women voting. Jane Misme's lead article celebrated the upcoming event as an end to the war between the sexes: for the first time, the feminists of France were going to add to their daily tasks of propaganda, the grand public gesture of the symbolic festival; she praised the symbol of the vote as "the guarantee of every other right." "A celebration of justice, it will also be a

---

[190] See Mme Avril de Sainte-Croix, "Le père du Féminisme: Condorcet," *La Française*, n° 325 (5 July 1914).

[191] The most comprehensive account of the 5 July event is in Hause, with Kenney, *Women's Suffrage and Social Politics*, pp. 184–190; see also Klejman & Rochefort, *Égalité en marche*, pp. 286–288. Bouglé-Moalic, *Vote des Francaises*, p. 183, barely mentions it in passing.

[192] "Pourquoi les femmes doivent voter," *La Française*, n° 325 (5 July 1914), 2.

celebration of devotion."[193] Those who had worked so hard for this result, she indicated, would not live to see its fruition. Little did she know.

In the 15 July issue of *Fémina*, which, after disparaging feminism, had come around to publishing on its advances, Hélène Miropolsky, in guise of an obituary for Eliska Vincent and Hubertine Auclert, the two prominent suffragists who had recently died, indicated that following the recent campaigns "one thing is certain; never before has the movement in favor of the political equality of the sexes taken as bold and resounding a turn."[194]

And turn it did. But not in the expected direction. Within weeks France was at war. The woman suffrage bill in particular, and the feminist campaigns for far-reaching legal, economic, and social reforms were among the first major casualties. The key to all other reforms had been wrested from their hands, just as it seemed within reach. War had slammed shut the window of opportunity.

---

[193] Jane Misme, "Jour Suffragiste," *La Française*, n° 325 (5 July 1914).
[194] Hélène Miropolsky, "Les Précurseurs du féminisme," *Femina* (15 July 1914), 414.

PART IV

Anti-climax
The Great War and Its Aftermath

To the Women of France.

The war was unleashed by Germany, despite the efforts of France, Russia, and England to maintain the peace. At the call of *La Patrie*, your fathers, your sons, your husbands rose up and tomorrow they will have met the challenge. The departure of all those who could bear arms for the army leaves the work of the fields interrupted: the harvest is unfinished, and the grapes must soon be picked. In the name of the government of the Republic, in the name of the entire nation assembled behind it, I call on your courage and on that of your children, which only their age and not their courage keep out of the fight. I ask you to maintain the activity of the countryside, to finish the year's harvest, to prepare that of the coming year. You can render no higher service to your country. It is not for you, it is for her that I speak to your heart. We must save your subsistence, the provisioning of the urban populations and especially the provisioning of those who defend the frontier, along with the independence of the country, civilization, and the law. Arise, then French women, young children, daughters and sons of *La Patrie*! Replace on the field of work those who are on the field of battle. Prepare to show them, tomorrow, the cultivated land, the harvests brought in, the fields once again sowed. In these grave times, there is no labor too small. Every [labor] is grand that serves the country. Arise! to action! to work! Tomorrow there will be glory for everyone. Long live the Republic, long live France.

René Viviani, president of the Council of Ministers
Le Figaro, 7 August 1914

* * *

Never has there been so much talk about civilization.

Marcelle Capy
La Bataille Syndicaliste, 14 February 1915

* * *

Feminism leads to the abolition of familial duties, to the destruction of the family, to the suppression of marriage. It was, and is the most active agent in [causing] depopulation.

Frédéric Masson,
L'Écho de Paris, 27 June 1915

* * *

Cease to be man's shadow; cease to be the shadow of man's passions, of his pride and of his impulse towards destruction. . . . How many of you in Europe to-day are carried away by the gusts of passion that have overpowered the minds of men; how many of you, instead of enlightening men, add your own fever to the universal delirium!

Romain Rolland
To the Undying Antigone, 1915

* * *

How can we reconcile the need for a vigorous birthrate, the protection of newborns, the caring – not only material but also moral – that childhood requires with this feverish industrialization of women's lives? How can we safeguard women's morality in the workshop and the stability of the family? This is the problem. We were poorly prepared for it. And, it has to be said, we have not yet resolved it. What the future requires is the establishment of a great charter of female work which will be the law that preserves the race.

Hélène Miropolsky
Le Journal, 17 February 1918

* * *

France had 200,000 fewer births in 1915. Even fewer than that in 1916. For five million young men ran to the invaded frontiers. Many of them will never return. The health of many others has been ruined. The war is bleeding the future itself. Already several [prospective, for 1933] French armies have been destroyed in embryo. Moreover, among the babies that are born, the already terrible mortality rate has increased during the war. How could it be otherwise? . . . In the least industrialized, most fertile departments, convoys of women have left their children and their homes to go work in the munitions factories. They owe this assistance to the fighters. . . . But what happens to maternity as concerns these workers?

Dr. Clotilde Mulon
La Française, 30 November 1918

* * *

It is humiliating to think that we are Frenchwomen, daughters of the land of the Revolution, and that in the year of grace 1919 we are still reduced to demanding the "rights of woman."

Cécile Brunschvicg
L'Humanité, 19 May 1919

* * *

"The right to vote . . . is not compensatory, but rather a means to better fulfill our duties toward our children, our families, our country, humanity."

Maria Vérone
La Française, 25 October 1919

* * *

Introductory Remarks

By all accounts, and despite the constant concern about impending war during the previous several years, the sudden declarations of war in early August 1914 took the French population by surprise. Historian Florence Rochefort attests that "on the first of August 1914, the feminists were, like the rest of the population, stupefied by the order for general mobilization. In no way prepared for this terrible drama that lay ahead, they saw their dreams of equality, peace and internationalism brutally shattered and they felt that they themselves were victims of the German aggression."[1]

Only a few men at the top – and no women – knew the secret terms of the diplomatic and military alliances, including the Franco-Russian alliance, that would cascade irrevocably into place following the 28 June assassination in Sarajevo of the heir apparent to the throne of the dual monarchy.[2] What the French authorities certainly did not know were the aggressive invasion plans that had been concocted by the German general staff and which stood ready for immediate execution. As German troops swiftly marched through Belgium, pillaging, raping, and torching, strewing chaos, enroute to invading France in early August, the men and women of France would face the future with uncertainty and considerable anxiety. The novelist Marcelle Tinayre captured the emotions of the days from 31 July to 2 August in her moving novel *La Veillée des armes: Le Depart, août 1914* (1915).[3]

General mobilization began in France on the first of August, and like the hundreds of thousands of hastily mobilized reservists, women rallied overwhelmingly to the defense of their country (or, at least, to the support of their mobilized menfolk). The German army crossed the French border on 23

---

[1] Florence Rochefort, "Les Féministes en Guerre," in *1914–1918: Combats de femmes. Les femmes, pilier de l'effort de guerre*, ed. Évelyne Morin-Rotureau (Paris: Les Éditions Autrement, 2004), pp. 17–31; quote, p. 17.

[2] On the diplomatic complexities and missteps, see Christopher Clark's extraordinary study, *The Sleepwalkers: How Europe Went to War in 1914* (London: Allan Lane/Penguin, 2012; New York: HarperCollins, 2013); and the oldie but goodie by George F. Kennan, *The Fateful Alliance: France, Russia, and the Coming of the First World War* (New York: Pantheon, 1984). On the response of the international peace movement leaders to the outbreak of war in 1914, see Sandi E. Cooper, *Patriotic Pacifism: Waging War on War in Europe, 1815–1914* (New York: Oxford University Press, 1991), chapter 8.

[3] Marcelle Tinayre, *To Arms! (La Veillée des Armes): An Impression of the Spirit of France.* Authorized translation from the French of Marcelle Tinayre by Lucy H. Humphrey, with a preface by John H. Finley (New York: E. P. Dutton, 1918; originally published in France in 1915 by Calmann-Lévy).

August. Only with the battle of the Marne (4–8 September) and after many casualties did the French army turn back the German advance on Paris.[4] Only then would begin the seemingly interminable months, then years of trench warfare on the Western front. In the press there was much talk of civilization sliding back into barbarism. "Never," the investigative journalist Marcelle Capy would remark in *La Bataille Syndicaliste*, "had there been so much talk about civilization."[5] In 1917 *La Voix des Femmes* would justifiably castigate the war as "horrible," "this hideous, savage, and useless massacre."[6] There were many more condemnations along these lines, including a retrospective one by a key player in the government: "this horrible tragedy unworthy of a grand civilization."[7] As if at a gigantic pagan potlatch, men were deliberately sacrificing and destroying material goods and one another.

In this chapter, I want to examine briefly the shock of the war and its short-term effects in reconfiguring the debates on the woman question, even silencing them temporarily before new participants began to refocus on the question of women's relationship to war, work, motherhood, and the state, and in particular the significance for official recognition of their citizenship (the vote) of women's wartime contributions to their countries. In contrast to some other historians, I do not propose to examine these events from the retrospective vantage point of the end of the war, or to

---

[4] For an excellent recap of the war experience itself, see Leonard V. Smith, Stéphane Audoin-Rouzeau, & Annette Becker, *France and the Great War 1914–1918* (Cambridge, UK: Cambridge University Press, 2003, 2008). One of the earliest scholarly investigations of French women's wartime experience is Part II of James F. McMillan, *Housewife or Harlot: The Place of Women in French Society, 1870–1940* (New York: St. Martin's Press, 1981), which was based on the author's doctoral thesis. The classic work is Françoise Thébaud, *La Femme au temps de la Guerre de 14* (Paris: Stock, 1986; revised ed. 2014); see also her long comparative essay, "The Great War and the Triumph of Sexual Division," in *A History of Women: Toward a Cultural Identity in the Twentieth Century*, ed. Françoise Thébaud (Cambridge, MA: Harvard University Press, 1994), pp. 21–75; & Thébaud, "Work, Gender, and Identity in Peace and War: France, 1890–1930," in *Borderlines: Genders and Identities in War and Peace, 1870–1930*, ed. Billie Melman (London & New York: Routledge, 1998), pp. 397–420. For more recent analyses of women and the "great war" in France with respect to feminism in particular, see n. 8.

[5] Marcelle Capy, "L'Enfant du viol," *La Bataille Syndicaliste* (14 February 1915); translated as "The Child of Rape," in *Lines of Fire: Women Writers of World War I*, ed. Margaret R. Higonnet (New York: Penguin, 1999), pp. 116–118; quote p. 116. Anne Cova analyzes this debate in *Maternité et droits des femmes en France (XIXe–XXe siècles)* (Paris: Economica/Anthropos, 1997), pp. 196–202.

[6] *La Voix des Femmes*, n° 2 (7 November 1917) and n° 5 (28 November 1917).

[7] Marcel Frois, *La Santé et le travail des femmes pendant la guerre. Publications de la Dotation Carnegie pour la Paix Internationale* (Paris: Presses Universitaires de France, & New Haven, CT: Yale University Press, 1926), p. 149. This publication, in the series sponsored by the Carnegie Endowment, provides a comprehensive overview of the issues concerning women's war work; it is the sole publication in the Carnegie series on the economic and social history of the world war that singles out women's issues.

focus on the question of whether or not the war was "good" for women. Instead, I wish to highlight the immediacy of events, the uncertainties that characterized the debates during the war's beginning and middle phases and their impact on the campaigns for women's legal, economic, and political rights.[8] What would war mean for the debates on the woman question in France, or for its resolution?

[8] In his essay, "More Minerva than Mars," (in *Behind the Lines: Gender and the Two World Wars*, ed. Margaret Randolph Higonnet, Jane Jenson, Sonya Michel, & Margaret Collins Weitz [New Haven, CT: Yale University Press, 1987], pp. 99–113), Steven C. Hause reads the French women's rights campaign retrospectively, looking back through the lens constituted by the war's end to assess whether the war was good or bad for women, a perspective also shared by McMillan and others who focus on the eviction of women from the wartime labor force c. 1919 and the failure of women's suffrage in the Senate in 1922. Hause does, however, insist on the upheaval in female employment in the 1914–1915 period (p. 105).

The best general account to date of feminist politics and organizing during the Third Republic, especially from 1889 to 1914, is Laurence Klejman & Florence Rochefort, *L'Égalité en marche: le féminisme sous la Troisième République* (Paris: FNSP/des femmes, 1989), though these authors pass lightly over the war years. On suffrage in particular, see Steven C. Hause, with Anne R. Kenney, *Women's Suffrage and Social Politics in the French Third Republic* (Princeton, NJ: Princeton University Press, 1984). Françoise Thébaud and Florence Rochefort have both published thoughtful articles about the impact of the coming of war on French feminism: See Thébaud, "Le Féminisme à l'épreuve de la guerre," in *La Tentation nationaliste*, ed. Rita Thalmann (Paris: Éds. DeuxTemps Tierce, 1990), pp. 17–46, and Rochefort, "Féministes en guerre" (cited in n. 1). See also the perceptive analysis of the wartime activities of the feminists in Christine Bard, *Les Filles de Marianne: Histoire des féminismes, 1914–1940* (Paris: Fayard, 1995), chapters 1–3; Susan R. Grayzel, *Women's Identities at War: Gender, Motherhood, and Politics in Britain and France during the First World War* (Chapel Hill: University of North Carolina Press, 1999), chapter 5; & Margaret H. Darrow, *French Women and the First World War: War Stories of the Home Front* (Oxford: Berg, 2000). See also Cova, *Maternité et droits des femmes*, chapter 4: "Concilier maternité et travail, 1914–1918," pp. 179–232. An important collection of articles by leading scholars concerning differing views of the impact of the war on gender relations is *Evidence, History and the Great War: Historians and the Impact of 1914–18*, ed. Gail Braybon (New York & Oxford: Berghahn Books, 2003); see especially the essay by James McMillan, "The Great War and Gender Relations: The Case of French Women and the First World War Revisited," pp. 135–153, in which he disputes the assertions of Mary Louise Roberts, instead taking sides with Susan Grayzel's interpretation (shared by Françoise Thébaud and myself), that the war actually reinforced gender differences, even as it provided opportunities for women to step, at least temporarily, into new and unfamiliar roles.

CHAPTER 14

The Great War and the Woman Question

Just a few weeks earlier, in early July, the momentum for women's suffrage had reached a high point, only to be "truncated … at its apogee," in the words of historian Steven C. Hause.[1] Historian Margaret Darrow observes that "the move to war virilized society by valorizing the masculine; the feminine was left behind, subordinated, saddened, silenced."[2] She also ably characterizes the varying discourses that swirled around women shortly thereafter, telling them what they should do, counseling them on how they should present themselves to others, and how they should respond to the war effort: ought they to model themselves on the Spartan mother, the Corneillean heroine, or the *Mater Dolorosa*?[3] Would the national crisis caused by the outbreak of war and the German invasion effectively put stop to six centuries of debate on the woman question?[4] In fact, no, though

---

[1] See Steven C. Hause, "More Minerva than Mars," in *Behind the Lines: Gender and the Two World Wars*, ed. Margaret Randolph Higonnet, Jane Jenson, Sonya Michel, & Margaret Collins Weitz (New Haven, CT: Yale University Press, 1987), p. 109. Surprisingly, this is the sole essay in this important collection that studies the French situation during the 1914–1918 war. See also Hause, "Women Who Rallied to the Tricolor: The Effects of World War I on the French Women's Suffrage Movement," in *Proceedings of the Western Society for French History* (San Diego, 9–11 November 1978), ed. Joyce Duncan Falk, vol. 6 (1979), 371–378, and Hause, with Kenney, *Women's Suffrage and Social Politics in the French Third Republic* (Princeton, NJ: Princeton University Press, 1984), chapter 7: "The World War and the Suffragist Truce." See also chapters 2 & 3 in Christine Bard, *Les Filles de Marianne: Histoire des féminismes 1914–1940* (Paris: Fayard, 1995).

[2] Margaret H. Darrow, *French Women and the First World War: War Stories of the Homefront* (Oxford: Berg, 2000), p. 54.

[3] Darrow, *French Women and the First World War*, pp. 58–71.

[4] Although French suffragism has received attention in the publications of Steven C. Hause, the woman question debates as such do not figure significantly in historic treatments of the Great War, even in the studies that provide and promote a "women's history of the war": see, e.g., James F. McMillan, *Housewife or Harlot: The Place of Women in French Society, 1870–1940* (New York: St. Martin's Press, 1981), chapter 5; Françoise Thébaud, *La Femme au temps de la guerre de 14* (Paris: Stock, 1986; reissued by Payot, 2013); Darrow, *French Women and the First World War*; & Susan R. Grayzel, *Women's Identities at War: Gender, Motherhood and Politics in Britain and France during the First World War* (Chapel Hill: University of North Carolina Press, 1999). Not surprisingly, many of the novels and short stories studied by Nancy Sloan Goldberg, *"Woman, Your Hour is Sounding": Continuity and Change in French Women's Great War Fiction, 1914–1919* (New York: St. Martin's

some of the many issues currently on the table would be temporarily relegated to the shadows. In the meantime, the mainstream feminists would develop their positions on war, peace, women's participation in the destiny of the French nation, and France's destiny as the flagship of civilization.[5]

The Outbreak of War

It was ironic that France's prime minister when the war began was René Viviani, who was without question one of France's most ardent proponents of women's suffrage, in particular, and of women's emancipation, more generally. Viviani, who had supported the Condorcet suffrage demonstration of early July, now had to call for mobilization of the French military to defend the nation, but also on French women to "man" the home front by bringing in the harvest and preparing for next year's crops. "You can render no higher service to your country. It is not for you, it is for her that I speak to your heart. We must save your subsistence, the provisioning of the urban populations and especially the provisioning of those who defend the frontier, along with the independence of the country, civilization, and the law."[6] One thing seems clear; as historian Françoise Thébaud points out, the outbreak of war put an end, for the time being, to the earlier stream of antifeminist rhetoric. Suddenly, Frenchmen acknowledged that their female counterparts could be patriots, could become valuable contributors to the war effort, and – most importantly – that this war could not be won without women's help. This initial period was indeed "the time of praise."[7]

One feminist (presumably Madeleine Pelletier) had written in 1910 that "women have no country," arguing that "where only men may be citizens, women can know nothing of patriotism." Woman, she asserted, "should

Press, 1999), emphasize women's conventional roles of self-sacrifice in solidarity with the war effort along with their mourning. Exceptions include Françoise Thébaud, "Le Féminisme à l'épreuve de la guerre," in *La Tentation nationaliste*, ed. Rita Thalmann (Paris: Éds. DeuxTemps Tierce, 1990), and Anne Cova, *Maternité et droits des femmes en France (XIXe–XXe siecles)* (Paris: Economica, 1997), chapter 4.

[5] An excerpt from this chapter will be published in *From the Balkans to the World: The Globalisation of the Great War, 1914–1918*, ed. Catherine Horel & Robert Frank (Bern: Peter Lang, forthcoming 2018), based on papers given at UNESCO in November 2014.

[6] René Viviani, "Aux Femmes Francaises," 6 August 1914; published in *Le Figaro*, 7 August 1914. The original document can be viewed online at www.lefigaro.fr/histoire/centenaire-14-18/2014/08/07/26002-20140807ARTFIG00061-appel-aux-femmes-francaises-de-rene-viviani-1914.php.

[7] Thébaud, *Femme au temps de la guerre de 14*, p. 36.

put the emancipation of her sex ahead of her country."[8] Such a choice was moot after Imperial Germany declared war on France. As men became soldiers, the women of France – including the feminists – became instant patriots, putting their campaigns for rights on hold and stoically sending their husbands, lovers, and sons off to defend their country. The establishment feminists quickly rallied to the support of the French nation. Indeed, how could it be otherwise? Were they not *Françaises*? Viviani's old friend Marguerite Durand would argue (in *La Fronde*) that "so long as the trial facing our country lasts, no one will be permitted to talk about their rights. We only have responsibilities toward her."[9]

Indeed, from 1900 on, the leaders of the French republican women's organizations had made a concerted effort to identify feminism with the national community and to integrate themselves within it as full partners; *les Françaises* had repeatedly asserted their claims to citizenship and equal standing with *les Français*, even as they invoked the specificity of their womanhood. Those French women who campaigned for women's rights and especially women's suffrage anticipated a complete integration of women into the public polity, even as they made their voices heard at the international level. For a time it had seemed that the national and international playing fields for women's activism were not mutually exclusive. Yet these new and precarious international alliances would be sorely tested by the outbreak of the war and especially by the German army's invasion and occupation of Belgium and northern France.

In the short term, the war forcibly invigorated national cohesion, halted the feminists' momentum, and reinforced the traditional gender order. Marcelle Tinayre's novel, *La Veillée des armes,* deftly depicts the conventional attitudes about the sexual division of labor and the cult of virility associated with military men as she writes about a couple and their neighborhood during two days at the outset of the war. She also wove in, through the voice of an old concierge, her thoughts about how there might be no war if women ran the government. How hard war was on the mothers of sons: "If there were women in the government, war would

---

[8] [Unsigned article, probably by Madeleine Pelletier], "Les femmes n'ont pas de patrie," *La Suffragiste*, vol. 2, n° 18 (September 1910), 13.

[9] Marguerite Durand, in *La Fronde,* August 1914, as cited by Thébaud, "Féminisme à l'épreuve," p. 21. In *Filles de Marianne*, pp. 58–59, Christine Bard cites four issues of Durand's new weekly series (17 & 24 August, and 1 & 3 September 1914). These four issues of *La Fronde* are not included on the ACRPP microfilm, which does include four issues for July (3rd, 9th, 16th, & 23rd) but none thereafter.

be ended! It is the soldiers who make the battles, but it is the women who make the soldiers."[10]

> Between you and me, we always think about saving our children. I cannot think that a German mother has a different heart from mine! There are not two ways of bringing a child into the world, and not two ways for him to leave it, and not two ways of suffering when we lose him. Nature is everywhere the same.

Marguerite de Witt-Schlumberger, president of the *Union Française pour le Suffrage des Femmes* (UFSF), drafted a circular letter in early August to her "dear sisters of the Union," urging them to repress their tears and support the war effort as outlined by Viviani. Renouncing action against the war, Witt-Schlumberger called on members to "show by our calm and courageous attitude, by our devoted hearts and hands, and by our intelligent action, that we are worthy to help to direct our country since we are capable of serving it."[11]

The president of the *Conseil National des Femmes Françaises* (CNFF), Julie Siegfried, revealed her distress in a private letter to Lady Aberdeen (the president of the International Council of Women [ICW]), dated 9 August 1914.[12] Several weeks later, she and the CNFF secretary-general, Ghénia Avril de Sainte-Croix (who had been stranded in Switzerland at the time of mobilization) sent out a circular letter to member associations, invoking women's strength in face of "this terrible assault, this war against war," and calling on "their love of *la Patrie*, . . . their faith in the ideal and in the triumph of justice and truth."[13] They too believed that civilization itself seemed at risk in the face of the German attack.

> We do not say to ourselves: "what use is our work because we seem to be returning to barbarism?" No, wiping away our tears and anguish, we go on with our work just as our soldiers go into the line of fire, without reproach and without fear. And, in the midst of torment, we feel proud to be women of our times, those who have finally become the true companions of men, those who, in Félix Pecaut's wonderful words, "Dare to be". . . . We will

---

[10] Marcelle Tinayre, *La Veillée des armes: Le Départ: août 1914* (Paris: Calmann-Lévy, 1915); in (authorized) English translation as *To Arms!* Transl. Lucy Humphrey (New York: Dutton, 1918); quote, pp. 145–146. Feminist literary critics have judged this novel harshly, not least because of its conventional characterization of relations between the sexes.

[11] "Chères Soeurs de l'Union," 12 August 1914, printed circular in Bibliothèque Marguerite Durand, Paris. DOS UFSF 396 UNI. English translation from *Jus Suffragii*, 8:13 (1 September 1914), 161.

[12] Letter from Julie Siegfried to Ishbel Aberdeen, 9 August 1914, in Lady Aberdeen's correspondence, box 3. 5ICW/A/08, The Women's Library @ LSE, London. Consulted 27 August 2013.

[13] Circular letter to members of the *Conseil National des Femmes Françaises*, 25 August 1914. BMD DOS. 396/Con (CNFF, 1901–1914).

consent with courage and absolute faith in the final victory to the sacrifices that are demanded of us.

Witt-Schlumberger, whose moral authority was greatly enhanced by the fact of having five sons and a son-in-law all serving in the French army, would report to the International Woman Suffrage Alliance (IWSA) in late September:[14]

> Whilst the women of all countries are waiting to obtain the vote and make impossible the wars in which their sons are massacred, they continue in all countries to play their part as the menders of humanity. They try as far as is possible to remedy the evils, poverty and sufferings that war brings in its train, sufferings that ought to fall in curses like molten lead not on the nations, but on those who in their mad and criminal arrogance dare to declare war and hurl the nations one against the other.

Her anger was palpable, her resolve steely, her tone somber – and authoritative.

For several months, the French women's press remained in disarray. *La Fronde* had made only an ephemeral reappearance. *La Française* would not appear in print again until mid-November 1914, and would then highlight the varied forms of women's wartime service under the rubric "French women during the war. What they do. What one does for it" [*Les Françaises pendant la guerre. Ce qu'elles font. Ce qu'on fait pour elle*]. But by the spring of 1915, the litany of earlier feminist demands began to creep back into view. Advocates of women's rights began to remind the French public of their commitments to combat alcoholism, regulated prostitution, and violence against women; they likewise began to hammer home their claims on women's behalf, not least as concerned the fight against depopulation, which due both to war losses and a dramatic decrease in the number of babies born, looked even more menacing than before. Thébaud's analysis of *La Française* also reminds us that these mainstream republican feminists continued to defend women's right to work and pushed for measures, as before the war, that would allow women to combine paid employment with family responsibilities. They continued to demand equal pay for equal work and to fight against the threatened cuts in women's pay in wartime jobs. Overall, the feminists' claims and goals during wartime would demonstrate a remarkable consistency with those of the years before the war when they fiercely defended women's economic interests, including their entry into new careers, at all levels.

---

[14] [Marguerite] De Witt-Schlumberger, "France," *Jus Suffragii*, 9:1 (1 October 1914), 180.

Given the harsh reality of war, however, the question of peace rose to the forefront of feminist concerns. The invasion of the German army had solidified French women's opposition to a number of well-meaning but unacceptable attempts to halt the war. Arbitration was acceptable, but an armistice that would allow the Germans to consolidate their territorial gains in France and regroup was deemed unacceptable. How to end the war quickly and to rid French soil of the German army would be the *sine qua non* for any further international cooperation.

La Française, the CNFF, and the UFSF soon became the sustainers of "women's brand of patriotism." And in the instance, this meant envisioning a French military victory in the face of severe wrongs – the German invasion of their country, the violation of Belgian neutrality, and the atrocities committed by the invading army, especially during the first months of the war. Jane Misme made this position very clear in December 1914 when she addressed the efforts of women in the neutral countries and the published disclaimers by the German women, denying the atrocities. "Today, the soul of the most pacifist French woman combats the enemy at the side of our soldiers," Misme insisted. "As long as the war lasts, the women of the enemy will also be our enemy.... Diplomacy can do nothing; only arms and the flow of blood can decide the outcome."[15]

In fact, the major representatives of French feminism, including the feminist-socialists, had become thoroughly nationalized – even, one might say, super-patriotic.[16] In retrospect, such efforts to affirm French women's intrinsic connection to the national community may seem exaggerated. But they should not surprise us. In the feminist and feminine associations, women from all points of the political and religious spectrum – Catholics, Protestants, Jews – and many socialists and anticlerical republicans would come together to support the "*Union Sacrée*." Although French girls had not, even since 1880, been educated to become either patriots (or voting *citoyennes*) of the democratic French republic, they would nevertheless rally

---

[15] Jane Misme, "Une campagne féminine des pays ennemis et des pays neutres en faveur de la paix," *La Française*, n° 339 (19 December 1914).

[16] I have written elsewhere about two interlocking developments that set the stage for developments in women's quest for the vote (and every other major reform, legal, social, and economic, advocated by women in France) from 1900 to 1914. I referred to these as "nationalizing feminism" and "feminizing nationalism." To counter claims by opponents that feminism and its emancipatory objectives were somehow "unFrench," women's rights advocates emphasized its roots in French history, especially in the principles that underlay the French Revolution, and they repeatedly invoked the promise of the Third Republic's living up to its principles. See Karen Offen, "Exploring the Sexual Politics of French Republican Nationalism," in *Nationhood and Nationalism in France*, ed. Robert Tombs, (London: HarperCollins Academic, acquired by Routledge, 1991), pp. 195–209.

in support of the war effort.[17] The women would anchor their claims not only in justice and law, but also in the very preservation of civilization against the barbarians of the north. They believed fervently that France was the country of the Rights of Man and Citizen. They took the moral high ground and occupied it with fervor, as the response of socialist feminist Marie Bonnevial, head of the CNFF's suffrage section as well as president of the *Ligue Française pour le Droit des Femmes* (LFDF), to the American president of the IWSA (Carrie Chapman Catt) made clear.[18] Bonnevial was seconded by Maria Vérone, who also endorsed socialist solidarity behind the defense effort.[19] Already the previous month the socialist women of *L'Équité* had stood resolutely behind the defense of the nation, refusing the prospect of a peace that would "consecrate the advantages acquired by the offensive of the feudal and brutal Prussian militarism on a neutral and inoffensive nation and on the country of the Rights of Man and the Citizen."[20] The women of the CNFF and UFSF helped unemployed women find work, produced or purchased warm clothing for soldiers, opened workshops for unemployed women and popular restaurants to feed them; they reached out to refugees and orphans. They threw themselves into philanthropic and Red Cross work. They would establish a highly successful register for refugees and families torn apart, to help them find one another again. They would invent ingenious ways to be useful to the nation at war, some of which entailed constructive criticism.[21]

---

[17] See Linda L. Clark, *Schooling the Daughters of Marianne: Textbooks and the Socialization of Girls in Modern French Primary Schools* (Albany, NY: State University of New York Press, 1984). Jo Burr Margadant remarked that in girls' schools, "patriotism had been a muted theme," but that in 1915, "given the exigencies of war, the ministry [of education] determined to end this hesitant practice;" see *Madame le Professeur: Women Educators in the Third Republic* (Princeton, NJ: Princeton University Press, 1990); quote, p. 231. Margadant also reports (p. 232) that the schools, especially the girls' *lycées*, plunged into organizing charitable activities on behalf of soldiers.

[18] See Marie Bonnevial's letter, published in *La Française*, n° 332 (9 January 1915), under the rubric "Les Socialistes françaises et la guerre."

[19] Maria Vérone, in *La Française*, n° 333 (16 January 1915).

[20] "Notre Réponse," dated 14 December 1914; published in *L'Équité*, n° 25 (15 February 1915), front page. In an editorial "Inconséquences? . . . " published in this same issue, "Mater" (presumably Marianne Rauze) warned her associates not to be tempted by campaigns for an immediate peace, including those promulgated by Clara Zetkin; to go that route, she indicated, would be treasonous. "We are against war in principle," but the war at hand must be pursued to a conclusion that is good for democracy. "To agitate for the triumph of democracies, is to agitate for future peace, and for the coming of socialism."

[21] See Cécile Formaglio, *"Féministe d'abord": Cécile Brunschvicg (1877–1946)* (Rennes: Presses Universitaires de Rennes, 2014), esp. part II, for a comprehensive survey of these philanthropic projects.

During the winter months came the official reports on the sexual attacks by German officers and soldiers against French and Belgian women and girls.[22] Were these women, then, simply the victims of German lust? In *La Française* Jane Misme responded by insisting that it was the social permission given to men to seek their pleasure in abandoning themselves to their instincts that lay beneath such behavior, and returning to the earlier feminist pursuit of a single moral standard, criticized women (in general) for condoning such behavior.[23] In response to protests that Misme was inadvertently blaming the victims and that men's bad behavior was simply the result of the law of the strongest, she retorted by invoking France's commitment to equality as an ideal and denounced the lingering prejudices of those who insisted on women's "natural" inferiority. Back to the debates on the woman question, with Misme as a thought leader!

As concerns the results of such sexual violence, Misme also addressed the "unhappy subject" of the "little undesirables," the babies who inadvertently resulted from the rapes.[24] Discussion on this topic, including controversy over whether or not abortions should be permitted, or whether these unfortunate mothers should raise these unwanted children, continued in the women's press into early March 1915.[25] Marcelle Capy, writing in *La Bataille Syndicaliste*, pondered the question of what should be done, given the circumstances, and published a series of letters from readers on the issue, a number of whom supported legalizing abortion.[26] Irrespective of the circumstances, Jane Misme would argue in *La Française* that motherhood was sacred and that the child was likewise sacred; mothers must do their duty and not worry about the bloodlines; the children could become exemplary French citizens, given the proper education. In the meantime, families and the state must come to the assistance of the mothers and the children, perhaps by granting them a war service pension. In *L'Équité*, Marguerite Martin dissented; she would argue that

---

[22] On these reports and their consequences, see Stéphane Auzouin-Rouzeau, *L'Enfant de l'ennemi 1914–1918: Viol, avortement, infanticide pendant la Grande Guerre* (Paris: Aubier, 1995); also Ruth Harris, "The 'Child of the Barbarian': Rape, Race and Nationalism in France during the First World War," *Past & Present*, n° 141 (November 1993), 170–206; and Judith Wishnia, "Natalisme et nationalisme pendant la première guerre mondiale," *Vingtième Siècle*, n° 45 (January–March 1995), 30–39. According to Christine Bard, who cites an opinion survey in *Le Journal*, 17 December 1914 (*Filles de Marianne*, pp. 61–64), this debate was already underway in December. See also Cova, *Maternité et droits des femmes* on "l'enfant du barbare," pp. 196–201.

[23] Jane Misme, "Les femmes outragées,"*La Française*, n° 333 (16 January 1915).

[24] Jane Misme, "Que ferait-on des petits indésirés?" *La Française*, n° 336 (6 February 1915).

[25] *La Française*, n°s 337 through 340 (13, 20, & 27 February & 6 March 1915).

[26] See Marcelle Capy, "L'Enfant du viol," *La Bataille Syndicaliste* (14 February 1915), lead article, and subsequent issues (17th, 20th, and thereafter) for the letters from readers.

these "little undesirables" should be turned over to public assistance; no mother should be forced to keep such a child with such bad memories associated with it. "Repopulating France is a good thing," but "it is not with the children of chance, the children born via brutality and rape, raised in tears … that one can build a great and strong France. It is with the children of love, the children of happiness who will be conceived when peace is finally reconquered." The others will bring only "disgust, revolt, and hate."[27]

Patriotism or Pacifism? The Hague Congress and the Brion Affair

French feminists also spoke out when they received invitations to attend a special conference that was being organized in The Hague in late April 1915, in lieu of the cancelled IWSA international conference which was supposed to have taken place in Berlin. The "Call to the Women of All Nations" appeared in the IWSA's *Jus Suffragii* in early March. "War, the *ultima ratio* of the statesmanship of men, we women declare to be a madness, possible only to a people intoxicated with a false idea; for it destroys everything the constructive powers of humanity have taken centuries to build up." This manifesto called for the enfranchisement of all women, who could then become a force for world peace. Its objective was to foster an "immediate truce," so that the warring parties could "define the terms on which they are willing to make peace." The organizers' intentions seemed good. But from the perspective of the French feminists, the call posed several serious concerns, including the statement that "people in each of the countries now at war believe themselves to be fighting not as aggressors, but in self-defense and for their national existence."[28] Certainly this was how the French felt, as well as the Belgians, but they would deny this status to the Germans whose army had clearly taken the offensive. Moreover, the draft agenda being circulated contained two restrictions on debate that were unacceptable to the French feminists, not least of which was the condition that there would be no discussion at the congress of the *causes* of the war – or of the methods used to pursue it.

The CNFF's Marie Bonnevial and Julie Toussaint (who headed the CNFF's Section on Peace) would respond firmly to earlier letters from German and Dutch women affiliated with the ICW and from the

---

[27] Marguerite Martin, "Les 'Indésirés'," *L'Équité*, n° 26 (15 April 1915), 2.
[28] "Call to the Women of All Nations," published in "International Congress of Women," *Jus Suffragii*, 9:6 (1 March 1915), 245–246.

Women's Peace Committee. "We are attacked, we will defend ourselves." The time, they indicated, was not ripe for a premature peace effort, not even for an arbitrated effort.[29] On behalf of the LFDF, Maria Vérone likewise refused the organizers' invitation to meet at The Hague. Her speech at the meeting of 21 March (the group's first meeting since the outbreak of war, in the presence of the CNFF president Julie Siegfried) ridiculed the idea of banning consideration of the causes of the war. "What do you take us for?" she asked. "Isn't the game all too clear?" Before the war, we were betrayed, she said (speaking as a socialist and a pacifist herself), by the German socialists and pacifists. "Once is enough." It would not happen again. "You won't get us to call for peace as long as the enemy is on French and Belgian soil." To do so would be "cowardly" and "treasonous." Her refusal, supported almost unanimously by the LFDF, was reported in *Le Temps*.[30] Vérone's objections were seconded the following day by the venerable Juliette Adam, known for her fierce commitment to the return of Alsace-Lorraine to France. "To ask French women to discuss arbitration and mediation at this moment, to discuss an armistice, is to demand of them a national abdication." And she added, "What they should be doing at the moment ... is to awaken the conviction, in their children, their husbands, their brothers, even their fathers, that a defensive war is a holy war."[31]

In *La Française*, 27 February 1915, Hélène Brion and three associates (Marthe Bigot, Lazarette Frier, and Marianne Rauze) posted a "Declaration of French Socialist Women," in which they argued that the time was not ripe for disarmament – not until German militarism was vanquished.[32] Furthermore, they called for the inclusion of women in any commissions that might be established to discuss disarmament, the rights of oppressed minorities, the ordering of war crimes by officers, and conditions in the metallurgy industry, and they asked for women to be appointed to any bodies charged with administering and enforcing the decisions made by such commissions. Theirs was a plea for inclusion, not revolution.

[29] In *L'Action féminine: Bulletin Officiel du Conseil National des Femmes Françaises*, n° 37 (March 1915), 2–9ff.

[30] "Les féministes et la paix," *Le Temps* (23 March 1915), 3.

[31] Juliette Adam's remarks appeared in *Le Temps*, 24 April 1915, following the joint CNFF-UFSF manifesto, to be discussed on p. 557.

[32] "Une Déclaration des Femmes socialistes françaises," in *La Française*, n° 339 (27 February 1915), front page. This declaration was presumably issued in anticipation of the March socialist anti-war women's conference being organized by Clara Zetkin in Switzerland. A version truncated by the censors appeared in *L'Équité*, n° 26 (15 April 1915).

Generally speaking, French feminists viewed the organizers of the 1915 congress at The Hague to be sincere but misguided (this would be a recurring trope); clearly, the latter did not appreciate the extent of the French revulsion against the German invasion and the horror it brought in its wake to France and especially to Belgium, whose neutrality had been egregiously violated.[33] In a joint statement prepared by the CNFF and UFSF officers in April, they would object firmly (albeit graciously) to the initial draft program for the upcoming congress, implicating the women of the enemy in their government's decision:

> How could we meet with the women of enemy countries? . . . Have they disavowed the political crimes and the violations of common law by their government? Have they protested against the violation of Belgian neutrality? against the attacks on human rights [*droits de gens*]? against the crimes of their army and navy? If their voices have been raised, it was too weakly to be heard in our violated and devastated land. We cannot renew our collaboration until, for them as for us, respect of the law will be the foundation of all social action.

French women's societies, they said, would continue to pursue their goals: "1) obligatory arbitration of any international conflict before a conciliation council; 2) the education of children for peace; 3) the absolute respect of nationalities in the attribution of territories." . . . How can one speak of an armistice in light of the current conditions?[34] Unfortunately this joint

---

[33] The story of The Hague congress of 1915 has generally been told from a perspective sympathetic to its organizers, who in 1919 would found the Women's International League for Peace and Freedom. The focus is on the Dutch-British-American-German-Austro-Hungarian peace initiatives personified by Dr. Aletta Jacobs, Jane Addams, Emily Greene Balch, Rosika Schwimmer, Anita Augspurg, and Lida Gustava Heymann. See, in particular, Lela B. Costin, "Feminism, Pacifism, Internationalism and the 1915 International Congress of Women," *Women's Studies International Forum*, 5:3–4 (1982); the excellent book by Anne Wiltsher, *Most Dangerous Women: Feminist Peace Campaigners of the Great War* (London: Pandora, 1985); and Jo Vellacott, "Feminist Consciousness and the First World War," *History Workshop*, n° 23 (Spring 1987), 81–101. With only a few exceptions (the names of Gabrielle Duchêne and Jeanne Mélin are occasionally invoked), the responses of the French women and their perspectives, which are discussed here, are absent from these studies, and there seems to be no comparable account in French, which may be due to the fact that the French feminist leaders boycotted the congress. For the proceedings, see *Women at The Hague: The International Congress of Women and Its Results*, assembled by Jane Addams, Emily Greene Balch, & Alice Hamilton (New York: Macmillan, 1915; now available online through Women and Social Movements International). On Jeanne Mélin, who did consider going, see Isabelle Vahé, "Jeanne Mélin (1877–1964), les évolutions d'une féministe libre-penseuse,"*Archives du Féminisme*, n° 9 (December 2005), 42–45.

[34] "Aux Femmes des Pays neutres et des Pays alliés," a joint declaration of the CNFF and the UFSF in *La Française*, n° 346 (24 April 1915). Reprinted in Jane Misme "Le Rôle international des femmes pendant la guerre," *La Revue*, vol. 112 (issue of 15 August–1 September 1915), 442–462, and in full (329–331) in Louise Compain, "Les Femmes et l'action internationale," *La Grande Revue*, vol. 19, n° 10 (December 1915), 327–336 ["Pages Libres," pp. 55–64]. See also the article by Mme Avril de

statement was not read to attendees at the congress (the organizers insisted, perhaps disingenuously, that it had not reached the congress before it adjourned, although it seemed to have reached the press in The Hague). *Le Temps* blew the whistle on this excuse, however, by reporting that the bureau of the congress had *refused* to read the French protest, and that the representatives of the French press were planning to file a joint protest.[35] In any event, the boycott by the French mainstream feminists of the Hague congress received a ringing endorsement, also published in *Le Temps,* from none other than the British WSPU leader, Christabel Pankhurst![36]

Subsequently, Marguerite Pichon-Landry, writing on behalf of the UFSF, objected vociferously to the Hague Congress's omission from its agenda of any discussion of "the causes of the war and the manner in which it has been conducted." "What is the good of the slow elaboration of international right," she queried, "if its decisions are to be a dead letter, and if no condemnation of its violations may be expressed? *Intellectual and moral neutrality is nothing but recognition of the right of force.*" She criticized the "bleeding heart" character of the proceedings:[37]

> . . . a war is not a cataclysm of nature; there is no analogy between it and an earthquake or volcanic eruption. This universal pity, when it absorbs the mind, effaces the clear idea of right [law], which looks for the responsible and guilty on the one side and the victim on the other; it is the most serious menace to our common pacifist faith. If we wish to see our hopes revive, we must all seek to know the causes of the war; we must have the courage to know and to judge. To weep and be silent is for the conscience of mankind to abdicate.

Sainte-Croix, correcting some of Misme's assertions and, in particular, objecting to Misme's proposal that the two great women's associations be attached to the French government ministries. [G.] Avril de Sainte Croix, "Les Françaises dans les grandes sociétés féminines internationales," *La Revue*, vol. 113 (1–15 November 1915), 456–460, and Misme's conciliatory rejoinder, "L'Action internationale des femmes et le gouvernement," *La Revue*, vol. 113 (1–15 November 1915), 488. All of these articles concern the "fall-out" from the late April women's international congress at The Hague.

[35] See the news for "Hollande" on the closing of the congress; *Le Temps*, 3 May 1915, 2.

[36] Christabel Pankhurst's statement of solidarity with the French feminists' boycott of the congress is embedded in an article, "Le gouvernement et le congrès pacifiste féminin," *Le Temps* (29 April 1915). Pankhurst also published English translations of the French statements (by C. Brunschvicg, on behalf of the UFSF, and M. Vérone of the LFDF) in *The Suffragette*, n° 98 (23 April 1915), 21 & 24. The NUWSS leadership split over support of the war and also over attendance at the congress, with president Millicent Garrett Fawcett strongly supporting the war effort and opposing British participation against a group of younger, more radical NUWSS women who opposed the war and favored going to The Hague; ultimately the British government did not allow any women to leave England to attend the congress.

[37] Mme Pichon-Landry (on behalf of the UFSF), "French Women and the Hague Congress," *Jus Suffragii*, 9:9 (1 June 1915), 308.

This unanimous declaration of solidarity with the military defense of France by the three major national women's associations would, however, be challenged by a small group of dissenters led by Gabrielle Duchêne (head of the CNFF Section on Work), who with several dozen other French supporters engaged in the quest for peace, addressed a missive to the international women's congress at The Hague which laid out a call for pacifism and an end to the violence. This document quickly became known by its headquarters' address, 32 rue de Fondary.[38] Both Gabrielle Duchêne and Jeanne Halbwachs would subsequently be recruited by the Dutch suffragist Dr. Aletta Jacobs to form the French section of the International Women's Committee for a Permanent Peace.[39] Not surprisingly the CNFF leadership was distressed by this initiative; in September a polite exchange of correspondence between the secretary-general Ghénia Avril de Sainte-Croix and Gabrielle Duchêne made it clear that a "malaise" had developed over this issue.[40] The final break came several months later, when a newly formed *Section Française du Comité international des Femmes pour la Paix Permanente* circulated a brochure with a pacifist theme, *Un Devoir urgente pour les femmes* [An Urgent Duty for Women] which quickly drew unwelcome attention from the French military authorities.[41] This brochure incited disavowals of Duchêne's project by feminist leaders including Jane Misme, Marguerite de Witt-Schlumberger, and Maria Vérone.[42] Louise Compain, who up to that time had been working closely with Duchêne at *L'Entre'Aide*, would characterize this initiative as "the attempt of several isolated persons," against which the major national

---

[38] Duchêne's manifesto is published in English translation in *Towards Permanent Peace: A Record of the Women's International Congress Held at the Hague, 28 April–1 May, 1915* (June 1915), pp. 3–4. A partial version of the French text is reproduced in Maïté Albistur & Daniel Armogathe, *Le Grief des femmes: Anthologie de textes féministes*, vol. 2: *Du Second Empire à nos jours* (Paris: Éditions Hier et Demain, 1978), pp. 207–208.

[39] See Charles Sowerwine, "Women Against the War: A Feminine Basis for Internationalism and Pacifism?" *Proceedings of the Western Society for French History* (San Diego, 9–11 November 1978), ed. Joyce Duncan Falk, vol. 6 (1979), pp. 361–370. This study examines the tensions (even hostility) between the socialist pacifist women associated with Louise Saumoneau and the so-called bourgeois peace advocates associated with Duchêne.

[40] The exchange is presented, with quotations from the letters in the BDIC, by Emmanuelle Carle, "Gabrielle Duchêne et la recherche d'une autre route: Entre le pacifisme féministe et l'antifascisme" (Ph.D. Dissertation, McGill University, Montreal, 2005), pp. 111–112.

[41] Section Française du Comité international des Femmes pour un Paix permanent, 32, rue Fondary, *Un Devoir urgent pour les femmes* (1915). See Bard, *Filles de Marianne*, pp. 99–102, and especially Carle, "Gabrielle Duchêne," for more on this publication and the ensuing controversy.

[42] See *La Française*, n° 365 (11 December 1915), including Jane Misme's "Réponses à une manifestation pacifiste" and disavowals of this initiative by the LFDF and UFSF. The main objection seems to be that this brochure placed all the warring states on an equal moral footing, irrespective of the German aggression.

associations protested.[43] In consequence of this overt breach of solidarity on the question of the war, the CNFF would ultimately evict Duchêne from her presidency of the Section on Work, which she had ably chaired while successfully promoting the minimum wage law of 10 July 1915.[44] The women of *L'Équité* seemed surprised by the harsh response from the mainstream feminists.[45] According to Duchêne's biographer Emmanuelle Carle, not only was she subsequently shunned by her former associates but the members of the new *Section française* were subjected to heavy police surveillance.

In short, overt opposition to the war would not be tolerated by French establishment feminists, who aligned themselves completely with the French and Allied war aims and, even, according to Léon Abensour, developed a propaganda campaign in 1915 that prepared and distributed printed materials presenting the French position (and grievances) vis à vis Germany. They sent feminist speakers on the road to promote the French and Allied cause in other countries, from Switzerland, Italy, and Spain to Romania and the United States, and to The Netherlands, where the 1915 women's congress had taken place.[46]

Other feminists would express disagreement with the war, but from differing perspectives. Nelly Roussel published a series of thoughtful articles in *La Libre Pensée Internationale* (published in Lausanne, Switzerland), in which she reflected sorrowfully on the meaning of war and conflict and objected to the climate of hatred being stirred in the press against entire peoples.[47] In *L'Équité*, however (just prior to the Hague congress) she raised again the associated ideals of pacifism, socialism, rationalism, malthusianism, and feminism, reminding her readers of the heroic story of what French women had done to date in support of the war effort, and posing the question of how anyone could now dare refuse to

---

[43] Compain, "Femmes et l'action internationale," 336. Compain subsequently left her position at *L'Entr'aide*; along with C. Brunschvicg, Compain was second in command at the CNFF's Section on Work.

[44] Duchêne's last report as president of the Section on Work appeared in *L'Action féminine*, n° 40 (September–October 1915), 70–75. For the correspondence between the CNFF and Duchêne, see Carle, "Gabrielle Duchêne . . .," pp. 112–116.

[45] See Marguerite Martin, "Autour de la rue Fondary, " *L'Équité*, n° 31 (31 December 1915), front page. Martin did not read this tract as a particularly subversive document.

[46] See Léon Abensour, *Les Vaillantes: héroïnes, martyres et remplaçantes* (Paris: Chapelot, 1917), pp. 130–134.

[47] See Nelly Roussel's articles in *La Libre Pensée Internationale*: "Quelques réflexions sur la guerre," (12 December 1914) and "Atrocités" (6 February 1915), reprinted in Roussel, *Derniers Combats: Recueil d'articles et de discours* (Paris: L'Émancipatrice, 1932), pp. 59–64. I am deeply grateful to Elinor Accampo for sharing her copies of Roussel's articles from *La Libre Pensée Internationale*.

women "the title and rights of *'citoyennes,'* conquered through their privations and tears." But not only that, there was the problem [for women] of obtaining daily bread, and acting to "prevent the return of the horrors that have torn [humanity] apart."[48]

> For it is from us, the *créatrices*, who know the price of life, that must come the abolition of the work of death. It is our overt influence, exercised in the daylight, directly, officially, from which must come – not the end of struggle, for struggle is a vital necessity, a constituent of progress, and the satisfaction of a profound, eternal and magnificent instinct – but the end of international wars, which are only an erroneous and hideous application of this grand principle [of struggle].

The sensitive Roussel was appalled not only by the violence of war, but also the verbal violence and passionate hatred that it generated, as is made clear in her response to the condemnation (by the editor of *Le Journal*, Gustave Téry) of the feminists she had met from Germany and Hungary who were engaged in the 1915 congress as "Austro-German shrews."[49] She deeply regretted the fact that no French representative had attended the Hague congress to present the consolidated French perspective in person – "to declare loudly and clearly that, as true partisans of peace, we did not think it realizable until after the crushing of the ferocious beast who unremittingly troubled it, the Prussian imperial eagle." She made a sharp distinction, however, between condemning the imperial regime and condemning the German people as a whole, much less the sympathetic colleagues she had met while on a lecture tour in Austria-Hungary and Germany – naming Rosika Schwimmer, Vilma Glüchlich, and Adele Schreiber (for whose book *Mutterschaft* [1912] Roussel had written an article on the status and condition of motherhood in France).[50]

A different and forceful expression of dissent came from Louise Saumoneau, who objected wholeheartedly to the French socialists' (and presumably also the feminists') embrace of the *Union Sacrée*. She would distribute a number of socialist anti-war tracts and manifestos on behalf of the dissident socialists of the Second International and was finally arrested

---

[48] Nelly Roussel, "Notre Idéal," *L'Équité*, n° 26 (15 April 1915); reprinted in *Derniers Combats*, pp. 65–69.

[49] Nelly Roussel, "Mégères austro-boches," *La Libre Pensée Internationale* (15 May 1915); reprinted in *Derniers Combats*, pp. 70–73.

[50] Nelly Roussel, "Frankreich," in *Mutterschaft: Ein Sammelwerk für das Probleme des Weibes als Mutter*, ed. Adele Schreiber, introduction by Lily Braun (Munich: Albert Langen, 1912), pp. 487–494.

and jailed (for a short time) by the French police.[51] Such disagreements were about strategy and tactics with respect to supporting – or not supporting – the French and Allied effort to drive out the invaders.

The debates on the woman question itself would pick up again following the 1915 appeal of Romain Rolland, from his self-imposed exile in Switzerland, exhorting women to "be a living peace in the midst of war – the immortal Antigone who refuses to hate, and who cannot, when they suffer, distinguish between her brothers and her enemies.[52] "To wage war against the war," Rolland wrote, "your action comes too late. You could have fought, you ought to have fought against this war before it broke out; to have fought it in the hearts of men." He invoked women's power and influence: "You do not realise your power over us. Mothers, sisters, helpmates, friends, sweethearts, you are able, and you will, to mold man's soul. The soul of the child is in your hands; and in relation to a woman whom he respects and loves, a man is ever a child. Why do you not guide his footsteps?" And, Rolland added, "If a woman can save one man's soul, why do not you women save all men's souls?"

> The reason, doubtless, is that too few among you have as yet saved your own souls. Begin at the beginning. Here is a matter more urgent than the conquest of political rights (whose practical importance I am far from under-rating). The most urgent matter is the conquest of yourselves. Cease to be man's shadow; cease to be the shadow of man's passions, of his pride and of his impulse towards destruction.... How many of you in Europe to-day are carried away by the gusts of passion which have overpowered the minds of men; how many of you, instead of enlightening men, add their own fever to the universal delirium!

Romain Rolland's clearly heartfelt appeal boiled down to an evocation of the time-honored moral power and influence of the mother-educator/muse and a critique of what women had *not* done in generations past. He was clearly less interested in women's attaining political authority or

---

[51] Several of these tracts are reproduced in the volume *Le Mouvement ouvrier français contre la guerre, 1914–1918*, vol. 2: *L'Opposition des Femmes*, ed. Aude Sowerwine & Charles Sowerwine (Paris: EDHIS, 1985).

[52] Roman Rolland, "L'Antigone éternelle," published in French in *Towards Permanent Peace* (cited n. 38), p. 3, and partially in Bard, *Filles de Marianne*, pp. 97–98. Subsequently reprinted in various places, including *Les Précurseurs* (Paris: Éditions de L'Humanité, 1920). *Jus Suffragii* published an English translation, "The Immortal Antigone," in its issue 9:11 (1 August 1915), 330, but another 1915 translation by the British writers Eden & Cedar Paul, *To the Undying Antigone* is more poetic, and I have cited it here. Earlier in 1915 Ellen Key invoked the Antigone image ("I was born for love and not for hate") in her article, "La Guerre, la paix et l'avenir," *La Française*, n° 335 (30 January 1915).

embracing the war effort than in telling women, especially the French feminists of the great associations, how they should think and what they should be doing differently than the warriors.

To Rolland's evocation of Antigone who could not hate, Nelly Roussel would respond with an article entitled "Hate." Roussel defended hate as the other side of love, but specified that she could not hate those whom other people told her to hate. Roussel admitted her hatred for those who, on both sides of the divide, were responsible for "the great slaughter" ["*la grande tuerie*"]: the Pan-Germanists, France's "*revanchards*," those who hated the French, or those who hated the Germans, the handful of those responsible who "by their declamations or their intrigues have pitted against one another millions of poor souls who were too credulous and too docile." These were "the yeast that spoiled the loaf," . . . "the infectious germ against which insufficient prophylactic measures were taken." Once people wake up, she insisted, they will join together against such "bad shepherds" and find there "the ground for understanding and reconciliation." "We women have the responsibility to guard jealously the sacred flame of this kind of hate, justice-giving and generous, a source of love and happiness, a safeguard of Peace."[53]

Already in the fall of 1915, the officers of the UFSF pushed still further, complaining to the American president of the IWSA, Carrie Chapman Catt, in an open letter published by *Jus Suffragii*, that the international suffrage alliance (some of whose members had organized the peace congress at The Hague) should stick strictly to promoting women's vote and, in particular, retain its neutrality by refraining from taking a position on the war, from morphing into "a pacifist organ," a move that would violate its statutory neutrality.[54]

Meanwhile, other disaffected feminists would speak out against the war in more general terms. In 1916 the journalist Marcelle Capy published her mournful sketches of the human costs of the war, with individual sketches, small stories of love, affection, and mostly of loss, with an introduction by the now notorious Romain Rolland.[55] Far from idealizing the "heroes" or

---

[53] Nelly Roussel, "Haïr," *La Libre Pensée Internationale* (22 January 1916); reprinted in *Derniers Combats*, pp. 74–75, and in *Grief des Femmes*, ed. Albistur & Armogathe, vol. 2, pp. 218–219.

[54] "France. French Union for Woman Suffrage. Open Letter to Mrs. Chapman Catt, President of the International Woman Suffrage Alliance," *Jus Suffragii*, 10, n° 1 (1 October 1915), 7.

[55] Marcelle Capy, *Une voix de femme dans la mêlée* (Paris: Paul Ollendorff, 1916). On Capy's publications, see Mary Lynn Stewart, "Marcelle Capy's Journalism and Fiction on War, Peace, and Women's Work, 1916–1936," *Proceedings of the Western Society for French History*, vol. 39 (2011), ed. Robin Walz & Joelle Neulander, pp. 212–223. Online: www.quod.lib.umich.edu/w/wsfh/0642292/0039.

"heroines," Capy tried to deflate the pseudo-enthusiastic official and media-generated heroic war rhetoric; the French censors made many cuts in the published version of her work. "A natural solidarity unites women around the earth, and what injures some also injures the others.... They are governed by a common instinct, against which laws, governments, and interests are powerless." Their main concern, in Capy's estimation, was to preserve those near and dear to them to the best of their ability. Capy's sympathetic depictions of the miseries of working-class and peasant women confronted by war, like those of the soldiers whose stories she also tells, invariably render them as victims of forces wholly beyond their control.

A subsequent milestone in the debates over the relationship between pacifism and feminism was marked by the arrest on 17 November 1917 and military trial for treason (March 1918) of the outspoken feminist teacher and union activist Hélène Brion, whom we met already in Chapter 12. She was arrested the day following the nomination of the new no-nonsense wartime cabinet organized by Georges Clemenceau.[56] Already in July 1917, Brion, who headed a national federation of teacher's unions, while also actively participating in several feminist organizations including the UFSF and LFDF, had been dismissed from her teaching post as a state-employed nursery school teacher in suburban Paris because of her pacifist activities. She would be prosecuted for treason under a wartime law that curtailed freedom of speech, which the French government had enacted immediately after the outbreak of war in 1914. The specific charge was that she had been engaged in distributing printed anti-war propaganda to soldiers in the trenches. It was clear that the Clemenceau government, in an attempt to squelch all anti-war and/or pacifist outbursts (which came to be known in 1917 as "defeatism," the code word for proposals for immediate peace without victory, or "*paix blanche*") intended to make an example of her. Indeed, her friend Madeleine Vernet considered this case to take on the stature of a new Dreyfus Affair and published a lengthy pamphlet on the subject just two weeks after the arrest.[57] Historian Susan Grayzel has remarked that "the importance of Hélène Brion's case comes from the precise nature of her status as a feminist activist and of the place of women

---

[56] See "Une Institutrice arrêtée à Pantin," *Le Matin* (18 November 1917; 4th edition), front page, and "La Propagande défaitiste. Du pacifisme à l'anarchie. La correspondance et les tracts saisi montrent sous leur véritable jour les agissements d'Hélène Brion et de ses affiliés," *Le Matin* (19 November 1917; 4th ed.), also front page. Consulted, Gallica-BNF, 13 June 2014.

[57] Madeleine Vernet, *Hélène Brion: Une belle conscience et une sombre affaire* (Epône: L'Avenir Social, 1917).

in supporting or resisting the war effort."[58] It was also due to her visibility as a dissident in a teaching profession that was supposed to inculcate patriotic values in young people.

Already in July 1917, during the height of the strikes, *La Française* had spoken out against defeatism. Since the German invasion in August 1914, the leading women's organizations had declared a moratorium on talking about the subject of Peace. In July 1917 they deemed that the time had come to discuss it, particularly in light of the new efforts underway by others, including a number of vocal women, to (again) propose an immediate peace.

According to *La Française*, "good" pacifists were those who thought war should be abolished for all time, and the feminist weekly proudly aligned itself with them. Bad pacifists, on the other hand, were those who wanted an immediate peace without victory, one which the editorial insert insisted would benefit only the Germans and the profiteers. This type of pacifism was to be feared. Accompanying this succinct statement, and an editorial by Jane Misme, "Faut-il parler de la Paix?" [Must We Speak of Peace?] were four additional front-page articles, by the playwright Marie Leneru, the sculptress Yvonne Mille-Serruys, Julie Siegfried (CNFF), and Marguerite de Witt-Schlumberger (UFSF), each evaluating the state of affairs from her perspective. They all agreed that war was horrible, but that peace without victory was not a viable solution for ending this particular conflict. The thrust of all their arguments was to confirm their support for the goals of the Allied leaders; in order to arrive at long-lasting, hopefully even permanent peace, victory was essential. As Jane Misme put it, "Renouncement of the principle of war must be imposed by the most civilized nations on the states that wanted and ferociously prepared and conducted this war. And in order to impose [this renunciation of war] . . . we must first win."[59] Julie Siegfried quoted Abraham Lincoln, who refused a peace without victory in the American civil war. Marguerite de Witt-Schlumberger argued that[60]

> it is because women who reflect and who love are as passionately pacifist as they are patriots, it is because they have an ardent faith in the necessity and possibility of a peaceful future organization of the world, it is because they want to work and force it to come about, that they now repudiate any peace

---

[58] See the extensive account of the Brion case in Grayzel, *Women's Identities at War*, pp. 164–186; quote, p. 167.
[59] Jane Misme, "Fait-il parler de la Paix?," *La Française*, n° 431 (28 July 1917).
[60] Julie Siegfried, "Pas de Paix hâtive," and Marguerite de Witt-Schlumberger, "Courage et Pacifisme," in *La Française*, n° 431 (28 July 1917).

that does not assure the future peace and that does not finish off [literally, give the *coup de grace* to] the idea that Might makes Right. They must stubbornly demand the participation of women in the governance of their countries, for the women of the entire world will work, each in her own way, efficiently, to strangle the hideous monster of war that nourishes itself on their children.

Juliette François-Raspail discussed the possibility of a League of Nations, proposed most recently by the American president Woodrow Wilson, as a vehicle for ending war forever.

In early December 1917 Jane Misme published an editorial concerning the arrest of Hélène Brion, in which she dissented from those who were protesting Brion's arrest and imprisonment. The article was kind enough as concerned Brion herself, who in the past had indeed contributed articles to *La Française*, but Misme remained firm in the conviction that those who called for an immediate peace and, in particular, distributed printed propaganda to that effect *should* be arrested and judged, since she believed they were playing (whether consciously or inadvertently) into the hands of the enemy. She regretted that such arrests had not happened sooner, as in the case of the group around Duchêne and the rue Fondary.[61] Only after the holiday break did a fierce rejoinder from Louise Bodin (1877–1929) appear in *La Voix des Femmes*. Bodin was clearly upset and criticized Misme for what Bodin characterized as a high and mighty, absolutist attitude, suggesting that anyone who did not agree with the stand taken by the mainstream feminists and *La Française* should be put in prison. But that was not what Misme actually said; in her anger, Louise Bodin had twisted the argument of Misme's article.[62]

Additional articles on the subject of defeatism would appear in early 1918. Again, *La Française* would judge those who advocated this position as possibly sincere, but also dupes of the enemy. Jane Misme enjoined all French women to fight against defeatism, to join the league that supported restrictions, to do everything in their power to convince others that a "short order" peace was not to France's advantage or to that of its allies.[63] On 9 February 1918 a huge public meeting at the Sorbonne, attended by 5,000 people (with a typically all-male cast of speakers) reaffirmed the

---

[61] Jane Misme, "Hélène Brion et la propagande défaitiste," *La Française*, n° 441 (8 December 1917). Misme made it clear that she was speaking only for herself and not for the national feminist organizations.

[62] Louise Bodin, "Réponse tardive, mais nécessaire," *La Voix des Femmes*, n° 13 (23 January 1918).

[63] See Jane Misme, "Toutes les Vraies Françaises debout contre la Propagande Défaitiste," *La Française*, n° 449 (9 February 1918).

Union Sacrée.[64] Not long thereafter *La Française* participated in the commemoration of the annexation, in 1871, of Alsace-Lorraine, reminding its readers of the stakes that lay in victory: the return of the lost provinces.[65] The CNFF issued yet another manifesto, "Appeal to French Women," calling on women to support the additional restrictions (rationing) and to simplify their lives as much as possible: "It is in order to render war impossible [in the future], that we must hold tight to the end."[66] The battle of the Somme had just begun, the American troop reinforcements were in place, and the German army had rolled out "Big Bertha" and had begun to bombard Paris. Meanwhile, a group of women from other countries which, following the 1915 congress at The Hague, called itself the International Committee of Women for Permanent Peace (ICWPP, not to be confused with the International Council of Women) would convene for a second time in April, meeting in Bern, Switzerland, to discuss the prospects for peace.[67] And – women over 30 in England had just obtained the parliamentary vote.

Thus, in late March 1918, when Hélène Brion's trial, held in a military court, began, tensions (and expectations) ran high. The trial received heavy coverage in the daily press. Speaking in her own defense, Brion argued eloquently and bravely that she was "first and foremost a feminist" and that, "it is because of my feminism that I am an enemy of war." "I have never," she indicated, "reflected on the horrors of the present without noting that things might have been different if women had had a say in matters concerning social issues. . . . I am an enemy of war because I am a feminist. War represents the triumph of brute strength, while feminism can only triumph through moral strength and intellectual values."[68] Many of Brion's neighbors, close friends, and colleagues including Marguerite

---

[64] "Manifestation Nationale d'Union Sacrée," *La Française,* n° 450 (16 February 1918).

[65] *La Française,* n° 452 (2 March 1918).

[66] "Appel aux Femmes Françaises" from the CNFF, published in *La Française,* n° 455 (23 March 1918).

[67] This group of women would form the core of the Women's International League for Peace and Freedom. On the ICWPP, see Leila Rupp, *Worlds of Women: The Making of an International Women's Movement* (Princeton, NJ: Princeton University Press, 1997), pp. 28–29. Rupp does not mention the two interim meetings in Berne.

[68] "L'Affaire Hélène Brion au 1e Conseil de Guerre," *Revue des Causes Célèbres,* n° 5 (2 May 1918), 152–154. Transl. Karen Offen, orig. publ. in *Women, the Family, and Freedom, 1750–1950: The Debate in Documents,* ed. Susan Groag Bell & Karen Offen (Stanford, CA: Stanford University Press, 1983; hereafter WFF), vol. 2: 1880–1950, doc. 71, pp. 273–275. The French text of Brion's "Déclaration" is reprinted in *Hélène Brion: La Voie féministe,* ed. Huguette Bouchardeau (Paris: Syros, 1978), pp. 109–117; in *Grief des Femmes,* ed. Albistur & Armogathe, vol. 2, pp. 223–226, 228 (cited in n. 38); and in the collection *L'Opposition des Femmes,* ed. Sowerwine & Sowerwine, cited in n. 51 (which also includes other texts related to the Brion affair). For additional insights into the French war government's obsession with "defeatist" activities, including the Brion case, see Thébaud,

Durand and Séverine testified at the trial as character witnesses on her behalf. This show of support notwithstanding, the judges convicted Hélène Brion and sentenced her to three years in prison – but then quickly suspended her sentence. Having observed a spring break, *La Française* published only a short article on the trial, taken from another Paris paper that praised the humane verdict.[69]

Peace at any price was not an option that any committed French patriot, man or woman, could entertain in 1915 or 1916. The mass deportation by the Germans of women and girls from the occupied zones of France and Belgium to perform forced labor in Germany, following the earlier episodes of sexual violence, reinforced the French in their determination to win the war. But victory would not come easily. In the meantime, during 1916 and 1917, several other significant aspects of the woman question would attract public attention, not the least of which was the effect of young women's employment in the French defense industries on the ever-troublesome birth rate.

Babies? Or Bombs and Bullets? Or Both?

Babies? Or bombs and bullets? Which did France need most in order to win the war? The answer, of course, was both – and simultaneously! The concern over the now-plummeting birth rate and how to stimulate it meant that the public debates on the woman question would refocus – more than ever before – on motherhood. The immediate concern of pro-natalist men was how to stimulate the birth rate; the associated question was whether women's burgeoning employment (especially in war industries from 1915 on), was bad for natality. The question in 1914–1918, as before, was (in historian Anne Cova's words): how to "reconcile maternity and employment."[70]

Already in May 1915, Dr. Charles Richet reminded readers of the *Revue des Deux Mondes* of the increasingly acute population problem.[71]

Femme au temps de la guerre de 14, pp. 254–256, and Mona Siegel, *The Moral Disarmament of France: Education, Pacifism, and Patriotism, 1914–1940* (Cambridge, UK & New York: Cambridge University Press, 2004, 2011), pp. 42–49. An earlier study is Judith Wishnia, "Feminism and Pacifism: The French Connection," *Women and Peace: Theoretical, Historical, and Practical Perspectives*, ed. Ruth Roach Pierson (London: Croom Helm, 1987), pp. 103–113.

[69] "Le Procès d'Hélène Brion," *La Française,* n° 457 (13 April 1918). Brion did not get her teaching job back until 1925, when the consolidated Left (*Cartel des Gauches*) came into power.

[70] See especially chapter 4 in Cova, *Maternité et droits des femmes,* and Thébaud, *Femme au temps de la guerre de 14,* chapter 5.

[71] Charles Richet, "La Dépopulation de la France," *La Revue des Deux Mondes* (15 May 1915), 425–432; quotes below, scattered over 426, 427, & 428.

Concerned that everyone was wringing their hands but no one was prescribing remedies, he spoke of depopulation as "the devouring cancer that menaces our national existence, . . . an inexorable and slow cataclysm that envelops us." . . . "Why all this courage [demonstrated] on the battlefield, if France commits itself to suicide? . . . France has played too grand a role in history to content itself with becoming nothing but a shining historical memory." Certainly it was necessary to combat the German armies, Richet asserted, but this other danger seemed even more fatal, more menacing; over the course of a 25-year marriage, fertile couples could produce "at least ten children; . . . if they don't, it's because they do not want to." Yet Richet (like Fernand Boverat of the *Alliance Nationale pour l'Acroissement de la Population*) remained preoccupied with the choices of *men* not to produce children. He does not mention women, potential mothers of all these potential children. Richet posits that only a radical remedy will work, by which he meant a substantial "prime " or bonus that will mitigate (for prospective fathers) the expenses of raising a child. He recommended at least 1,000 francs as a minimum – but not for the first child, only for those that follow. Richet's alarmist article dramatically refocused public attention on the population problem in wartime.

And the existing and prospective mothers? Left to fend for themselves following mobilization of the army reserves, they would try to find means to support themselves. After facing a severe unemployment crisis during the first year of the war, muted only by women's taking over the agricultural work done prior to the war by men and accepting jobs that would keep the urban economy running, many women – young and old – would ultimately enter the industrial labor force. The importation of thousands of foreign male workers from Asia had not provided enough manpower to staff the war economy, so in 1916 the French government decided to actively recruit women. In contrast to England and Germany, Russia, and, eventually, the United States, France would not officially "mobilize" nor "militarize" its women, but that did not stop the government from exhorting them to become workers, most visibly in the munitions industry. Almost immediately, a hue and cry went up about how such work, with heavy metals, chemicals, gunpowder, and other toxic substances would threaten young women's prospects of becoming mothers or being successful mothers.

Soldiers' home leaves were not authorized until the summer of 1915, the year that the birth rate fell to *half* of the average for previous years. At the beginning of the war, soldiers' contact with the home front had been limited to letters and the omnipresent patriotic picture postcards, many of which advocated, however unsubtly, procreation and defense of the French family and home as signal objectives of winning the war. Some of these, according to the fascinating findings of Marie-Monique Huss, equated the thrust of the bayonet or the repeating rifle with the thrusting penis, producing bundles of little children for *la patrie*.[72] These postcards suggested, without a trace of subtlety, that soldiers should be making babies, especially boy babies, when they went on leave.

At the same time that most feminists threw themselves into the national defense effort, the French government was becoming increasingly aware of how essential women's work might be to victory; one might say that the government's concerns were becoming increasingly woman-centered, or one might also say "feminized." By this time, government officials were listening intently to what the mainstream feminists had to say on behalf of French women's interests. For example, the *Conseil Supérieur du Travail* had sponsored a report on infant mortality due to gastroenteritis, based on investigations from early 1914; the report concluded by advocating the establishment of childcare and nursing facilities that would enable employed mothers to combine their work with motherhood. This report would be published by the Labor Ministry in early 1916.[73]

In April 1916, the Ministry of Armaments and War Production (headed by the socialist Albert Thomas) convened a committee on women's work (*Comité du Travail Féminin* [CTF]), headed by the solidarist Senator Paul Strauss, to make inquiries and propose solutions that would facilitate women's employment in munitions factories – as well as facilitate their becoming mothers. This time leading feminists were appointed to the committee.[74] One of the women who served as social investigators for this committee was Marcelle Capy, who would go "underground" for a week as

---

[72] See the classic study of pronatalist postcards by Marie-Monique Huss, "Pronatalism and the Popular Ideology of the Child in Wartime France: The Evidence of the Picture Postcard," *The Upheaval of War: Family, Work, and Welfare in Europe, 1914–1918*, ed. Richard Wall & Jay Winter (Cambridge, UK: Cambridge University Press, 1989), pp. 329–367.

[73] See France. Ministère du Travail et de la Prévoyance Sociale. Conseil Supérieur du Travail. *Allaitement maternel au magasin et à l'atelier. Rapport de M. Abel Craissac, au nom de la Commission permanente. Procès-verbaux, enquête et documents* (Paris: Imprimerie Nationale, 1916). BN: 4° R. Piece 1871. Much of the data used in this report dates from early 1914, i.e., before the war.

[74] See "Les Femmes dans les usines: Un comité du travail," *L'Action féminine*, n° 43 (May 1916), 40. This article provides the list of names of twenty-five committee members, which include, from the CNFF and LFDF, Julie Siegfried and Marie Bonnevial. It promised the addition of other women who would serve as social investigators. Anne Cova indicates (*Maternité et droits des femmes*, p. 211) that the ten women initially appointed to the CTF were all members of the newly established *Section d'Études Féminines* (SEF) of the *Musée Social*.

an employee in a munitions factory and publish a series of articles in *La Voix des Femmes* about her experiences.[75]

In response to the CFT's inquiry, the UFSF promptly put the population question under study. At a public meeting on 19 March 1916, president Marguerite de Witt-Schlumberger had delivered a rousing call to action. She framed the question of having children and raising children (even without acknowledged fathers) as a choice between devotion and egotism. She forcefully characterized as deserters healthy (heterosexual) households that would refuse to provide a child for *la patrie* in the year following the end of the war.[76] The deputy Jules-Louis Breton went so far as to claim that "the current war is the consequence of depopulation. If we had been more numerous than the enemy, it would never have dared to attack us." Moreover, France has had to import Chinese and Vietnamese workers. Breton worried that France would be taken over by foreigners. Thus, he declared, "the question of the birth rate is a social question." He called on the suffragists not only to campaign for the women's vote but also for a plural vote for heads of families, whether these were men or women. Dr. Doizy, deputy from the Ardennes, also elaborated on the theme of being overtaken by foreigners: "Our country is enroute to being denationalized" and he called for additional measures of social hygiene, a theme developed further by the attorney Suzanne Grumberg (a.k.a. Grinberg).[77] Another contributor was Paul Bureau of the publication *Pour la Vie*, and founder of a new secular and nondenominational association by that name, intended to draw support from various sectors of French society. This meeting anticipated the subsequent formation in May 1916 of a close alliance between feminists and this pro-life group: its first executive committee included Julie Siegfried, Marguerite de Witt-Schlumberger, and Cécile Brunschvicg, who were also leaders in the CNFF.[78] The UFSF would cement its alliance with *Pour la Vie* in May 1917 and *La Française* would publish a special issue (12 May 1917) devoted to the natality question and the prospect of a joint feminist/pronatalist campaign. In the interim Witt-Schlumberger took charge of the CNFF's

[75] See Marcelle Capy, "La Femme à l'usine," serialized in *La Voix des Femmes*, issues n° 5 (28 November 1917); n° 6 (5 December 1917); n° 7 (12 December 1917); n° 8 (19 December 1917); & n° 10 (2 January 1918).

[76] Marguerite de Witt-Schlumberger at UFSF meeting, 19 March 1916; as quoted in *La Française*, n° 378 (25 March 1916), front page. A report on this meeting, filed by a police spy, can be consulted in AN F⁷13266, dos. 4.

[77] Sometime after this March 1916 gathering, Suzanne Grumberg (with her husband, who was from Romania) evidently changed their surname to the less Germanic Grinberg.

[78] For the names, see "La Lutte pour la Vie," *La Française*, n° 385 (13 May 1916).

new Section on Unity of Morals and Repression of the White Slave Trade, on which she reported at the CNFF's 1916 general assembly.[79] The directorates of these two major associations were becoming ever more interlinked and interlocking than before.

Others would suggest measures that could ostensibly benefit some women, but in their capacity as widows or as mothers (rather than as individuals). Additional legislative proposals included one actually voted on by the Chamber of Deputies (and sent to the Senate) that would provide state maternity benefits to *all* mothers, not only those who worked in certain industries (as provided for by the 1913 law), and, of course, the new law of 10 July 1915 that established a minimum wage for home-based workers in the garment industry, a prelude to raising women's wages in other industries so that they could no longer undercut the wages of men. Baby bonuses were also on the agenda; one employer in Meudon offered his women workers a bonus of 200 francs for a boy baby, but only 100 for a girl.[80] Obviously, equality of the sexes was far from this employer's mind. Julie Siegfried, president of the CNFF and also of the *Ligue d'Éducation morale*, called for celebrating Mother's Day on 12 May.[81] Two events, in Paris and in Lyon in mid-1918, both launched by Catholic groups, would celebrate mothers, but Mother's Day as a state-sponsored celebration would only become official in 1926.[82] In the midst of all these ideas, feminists began to push for reform of girls' secondary education, especially for the inclusion of the curriculum for the *baccalauréat* in the girls' *lycées*, so that girls could access, on an equal footing with the boys, higher education and the university degrees that would provide entry to professional opportunities other than school teaching.[83]

---

[79] Mme de Witt-Schlumberger, "Unité de la morale et répression de la traite des blanches," *L'Action féminine*, n° 45 (August 1916), 91–96. Surprisingly, in this issue, Ghénia Avril de Sainte-Croix, who edited *L'Action féminine*, did not enforce the new terminology "*traite des femmes*" which, before the war, she had insistently advocated on the grounds that not all trafficked women were white.

[80] Quoted in Thébaud, *Femme au temps de la guerre*, pp. 265–266.

[81] "Le Jour des mères," *La Française*, n° 461 (11 May 1918).

[82] See Thébaud, *Femme au temps de la guerre*, pp. 279–280.

[83] See Mme Suran-Mabire, "La Réforme de l'enseignement secondaire féminin," *La Revue Universitaire*, 1916, vol. 2, pp. 204ff; Augusta Moll-Weiss, "A Propos de la réforme de l'enseignement secondaire des jeunes filles," *La Française*, n° 406 (21 January 1917), 1; Louise Cruppi, "La Réforme de l'enseignement secondaire féminin," *La Revue* (1 July 1917), 40–54; and Raymond Thamin, "L'Éducation des filles après la guerre," *Revue des Deux Mondes* (1 October 1919), 512–532, and (1 November 1919), 130–160. NB, in passing, that the Extraparliamentary Commission appointed to investigate the reform of girls' secondary education was called into existence by none other than the feminist/socialist René Viviani (minister of justice, education, and beaux-arts in the sixth Briand cabinet, formed in December 1916) and that several women were appointed to serve.

In early 1916 other nonlegislative proposals of a more radical nature were floated, for example, to introduce polygamy as a means of addressing the population problem. In *La Française*, Jane Misme opposed this "solution" as a "return to barbarism," and condemned its advocates for having "a singular deformation of moral sensibility." Lifelong marriage with a single moral standard was her ideal, even though it could be and had been compromised by divorce and by prostitution. So what if many young women could not marry because of the growing deficit of young men due to the war; they too could be considered war casualties.[84] Marguerite de Witt-Schlumberger likewise rejected such notions, which she claimed had been introduced for discussion in Germany.[85] Another proposal from a certain Martin de Torina, addressed to young women and widows in 1917, proposed that such women *must* become mothers outside of marriage. Only women, he argued, could save *la patrie*, not only by fulfilling their natural role as mothers under new conditions, but also by demanding that the public powers furnish the now 3.5 million single French women with the means to accomplish the task to which they would consecrate their lives.[86] Jane Misme also addressed this proposal: she emphatically denied that any woman had the "right" to have a baby outside wedlock whenever she pleased. Single motherhood, she indicated, must be respected when it happens, but certainly not encouraged or thought of as a right. In fact, such a notion "is contrary to the entire moral stance of feminism, the goal of which is to encourage social progress by ennobling relations between man and woman. It [single motherhood] is degrading for the woman, humiliating for the man, and is prejudicial for the child; it is dangerous for public order and intimate happiness."[87]

Already in May 1916 Marguerite Clément had presented a report to the UFSF's General Assembly based on consultation with its affiliate groups throughout France. Her findings neatly refocused the population debate on the needs of mothers, which included many additional reforms that could benefit women generally (and that had been demanded for decades).[88] High on the list was the facilitation of mothers' employment,

---

[84] Jane Misme, "Les Français seront-ils polygames?" *La Française*, n° 370 (23 January 1916).

[85] Witt-Schlumberger, "Unité de la morale," esp. 96.

[86] Martin de Torina, *Mère sans être épouse pour la France et pour soi-même; étude psychologique et physiologique*. 2nd ed. (Paris: l'auteur, 1917); quotes, pp. 11, 20–23.

[87] Jane Misme, "Mères libres," *La Française*, n° 435 (27 October 1917).

[88] "Ce que les Suffragettes pensent de la Répopulation. Rapport présenté par Mlle Marguerite Clément à l'Assemblée générale de l'Union Française pour le Suffrage des Femmes," *La Française*, n° 385 (13 May 1916). Also published in the *UFSF Bulletin 1914–1916*, 22–26.

with well-supervised crèches to provide day care and facilities in the workplaces where mothers could nurse their babies. Childcare emerged as a critical topic: "Similar institutions, if they were sufficiently numerous, that is to say innumerable, would do more for repopulation than any sort of tax" [on single men]. Other proposals of long standing included building new urban housing that could accommodate larger families and combatting alcoholism. More subversive suggestions for cultural reform also surfaced, such as not stigmatizing single mothers and teaching boys how to do household chores. This was apparently the first extensive survey of French women's own proposed solutions for stimulating the birth rate. Not surprisingly, progress on such reforms would be slow.

By the autumn of 1916, some feminists were optimistic about the prospects for the full integration of women in the war effort – and, thereby, in the nation. In a November 1916 article in *La Revue* on women and the war, Jane Misme provided a historically grounded assessment of where things stood. She emphasized that French women were the ones keeping the country afloat, and she demanded that they be recognized for their contributions: "Just as history will recognize the zeal of the Finnish and Norwegian women as their countries were seeking independence, it will remember the role of today's French women in the defense of France." She insisted that all these activities by women prove "again, and in a striking fashion, the value of feminine collaboration in the life of nations." To what extent, she asked, can feminism claim credit for this? "Whether they call themselves feminists or not," she indicated, women in France have benefitted "from the last 125 years of feminist propaganda." "The feminist doctrine is the demonstration of these principles – that men and women are born equal before Nature, that society should treat them as equals, according them the same rights, and imposing the same duties – that these are the price of for the happiness of individuals, the public good and the grandeur of nations." The great international congress of 1913 (Jane Misme mistakenly wrote 1912) demonstrated to all what feminists want and what they can do. "Women demand their rights so that they can do their duty," Misme exclaimed. Indeed, the case for women's emancipation had come a long way since the Revolution of 1789.[89]

> A society cannot flourish under a regime that arbitrarily limits the activity of its members and thus annihilates a part of its forces; this crisis of civilisation, of which the war is an aggravating symptom, will not be resolved except by

[89] Jane Misme, "La Guerre et le rôle des femmes," *La Revue de Paris* (1 November 1916), 204–225; quotes, 208, 209, 211.

a larger and more enlightened collaboration of women in production and in general governance. The reconstruction of France depends on the manner in which it will deploy feminine values.

There will doubtless be opposition, she continued, but "feminists believe that henceforth the attempts to confine woman to the household will fail against the force of the situation which will result for her from the war." "The major change will be that in women's feelings toward employment [*travail*]." The celebration of "a lady who does nothing" will recede. "Everything leads us to believe that the women workers [*travailleuses*], exalted by the public glorification of their merits, have finally understood their dignity." "Penetrated by the nobility of work, women have been able to look at it more lucidly than when they viewed it as a sign of social slippage." Women, Misme believed, were beginning to understand how dangerous it was to rely on a man for support – and how dangerous to accept inadequate pay. Meanwhile an inter-union action committee against the exploitation of women (*Comité Intersyndicale d'Action contre l'Exploitation de la Femme*) had formed to support equal pay and good working conditions. "This kind of progress," Misme predicted, "will be difficult to un-do."[90]

As for motherhood and the population question, Jane Misme argued that the war had shown the bankruptcy of the notion that women should do nothing else but be mothers. "It is clear that it would be much better for the birth rate if the mother could be assured that she could, if necessary, furnish subsistence for her little ones, and would not be condemned, in the name of maternity, to every abdication." "She needs to be provided with all the possibilities to be a joyful mother." With the reduction in the number of men, so many widows and so many girls that would have to support themselves after the war, "France would have to call on its women to aid its production, its administration, and to combat all the internal plagues that menace it."

Jane Misme's long article was fundamentally a manifesto. It provided a road map for a feminist future, grounded in the circumstances of the war and the sense that the accelerated progress toward the emancipation of French women had reached the point of no return. She laid out the constituent elements of the feminist program: educational improvements; hygienic affordable housing; a single standard of morality; reform of marriage via the Civil Code – all the reforms that had been targeted during

---

[90] Misme, "Guerre et le rôle des femmes," quotes, 213–215.

the nineteenth and early twentieth centuries. There was so much to be done! But thanks to the help of the women of France, "Civilization will always have France for its center – a France rebuilding its population, conserving its idealism and its graces, but resolutely progressing by every path of reformative action toward the realization of its ideal."[91]

Was Jane Misme's celebration of women's paid labor and a change of attitude on the part of the unions premature? Was her call for a combination of earning power and maternity too optimistic? Was her satisfaction justified by the number of small but significant legal reforms achieved to date (which included the ban on the sale of absinthe; the minimum wage for domestic workers; the legitimation of children of adultery; the legitimation of bastard war orphans; obligatory vocational instruction; the granting to women of the power of guardianship over orphans and the right to participate in family councils; or the acceleration in naming women to official committees)? Certainly, the war had significantly changed the climate in which the woman question could be addressed. But in late 1916 was it, perhaps, too soon to claim victory for feminist reforms? There would be pushback; the only question was what forms it would take.

The pushback arrived in December 1916, when the spotlight shifted to mothers, including potential mothers, who were being recruited for work in the munitions factories. This time it was driven by leading spokesmen for the medical profession. In early December 1916, in *Le Matin*, the obstetrician Dr. Adolphe Pinard, whose longstanding worries about premature births and high mortality rates were well known not only to the Academy of Medicine but also to the French public through the daily press, made his move with an article entitled "Cry of Alarm: the Factory is Killing Babies."[92] By all accounts, Pinard's article created a firestorm.[93] In

[91] Misme, "Guerre et le rôle des femmes," 225.

[92] A. Pinard, "Cri d'alarme, l'usine tueuse des enfants," *Le Matin* (6 December 1916).

[93] See the discussion of this controversy in Matilde Dubesset, Françoise Thébaud, & Catherine Vincent, "Les Munitionnettes de la Seine," in *1914-1918, l'autre front*, ed. Patrick Fridenson, with J.-J. Becker (Paris: Éditions Ouvrières, 1977), pp. 202–205; Cova, *Maternité et Droits des Femmes*, chapter 4, esp. pp. 213ff.; Darrow, *French Women and the First World War*, chapter 6; Laura Lee Downs, "Women's Strikes and the Politics of Popular Egalitarianism in France 1916–1918," in *Rethinking Labor History: Essays on Discourse and Class Analysis*, ed. Lenard R. Berlanstein (Urbana: University of Illinois Press, 1993), pp. 114–148, and Downs, *Manufacturing Inequality: Gender Division in the French and British Metalworking Industries, 1914–1939* (Ithaca, NY: Cornell University Press, 1995). Mary Lynn Stewart, *Women, Work, and the French State: Labour Protection and Social Patriarchy, 1879–1919* (Montreal: McGill-Queens University Press, 1989), touches only briefly on wartime developments in her conclusion, pp. 191–194. The major elements that led to this controversy are documented in Frois, *La Santé et le travail des femmes pendant la guerre* (cited in n. 7).

fact, this concerned doctor had been pushing this line of argument, in an effort to get pregnant women excluded from factory labor, for over a year.[94] Meanwhile, the Academy of Medicine had appointed a commission to study the matter and issued a report, compiled by Dr. J.-A. Doléris and released in early January for discussion, which deemed nonviable Pinard's proposal for the total exclusion of pregnant and nursing women.[95] By late December, Dr. Bonnaire, a member of the CTF and chief obstetrician at the Paris Maternity Hospital, had contradicted the project of Dr. Pinard, by publishing a report which he had previously presented to the CTF.[96] Margaret Darrow remarks that the ensuing argument over Pinard's allegations "involved little that was new," and that "scientific evidence in this debate was sparse."[97] This is undoubtedly true, but the repetition did nothing to mitigate the vehemence with which Pinard and his respondents stated – and restated – their respective positions, in direct contrast to the optimistic forecast of Jane Misme. The labor leader and feminist Jeanne Bouvier issued a rebuttal to Pinard and called for major reforms in the workplace that would enable women's employment in the factories.[98] Closing the factories to women workers would do absolutely nothing, she stated, to solve the problems that faced French working-class women and mothers.

Finally in March 1917, and after several additional sessions, the medical academy agreed to accept the practical proposals put forward by Doléris and Paul Strauss, rejecting an amendment by Drs. Pinard and Richet that would extend the commission's proposals (for monetary compensation for wages lost due to obligatory maternity leaves, and for the establishment of on-site nursing facilities and childcare centers) to *all* women workers in *all* factories, not just the new munitions factories in and around Paris. It was the opinion of Dr. Doléris and his backers that it was better to begin with

---

[94] See Cova, *Maternité et droits des femmes*, p. 214.

[95] See Jacques-Amadée Doléris, *La Protection des femmes et des enfants dans les usines* (Paris: Maretheux, 1917), which includes his report for the commission and summaries of the ensuing debates in February and March 1917 along with his responses to objections, mainly to those who wanted to broaden the scope of the report beyond the immediate subject of the munitions factories. With Jean Bouscatel, Dr. Doléris would publish a longer work, *Hygiène et morale sociales: Néomalthusianisme, maternité et féminisme, éducation sexuelle* (Paris: Masson, 1918).

[96] Dr. E. Bonnaire, "Le Travail féminin de munitions dans ses rapports avec la puerpéralité," *Bulletin des Usines de guerre*, n° 35 (25 December 1916), 276–279. Consulted at the Hoover Institution, Stanford.

[97] See Darrow, *French Women and the First World War*, quotes pp. 207, 209.

[98] See Jeanne Bouvier, "L'Usine de guerre, tueuse d'enfants," in the CNFF's *L'Action féminine*, n° 47 (March 1917), 144–145.

more modest measures that could actually be realized in the short term, rather to attempt solving France's entire depopulation problem.[99]

The question of women's industrial work and its potential contributions to the population problem was, of course, not new (as we have learned in earlier chapters); since the war began it had been carefully studied again by the *Association Nationale Française pour la Protection Légale des Travailleurs* (ANFPLT). Already in May 1915 Mme Paul (Marguerite) Gemähling had presented a report on the legal protection of maternity, following on the Strauss law of 1913.[100] This report insisted that the interests (or "rights") of infants must take precedence over those of women; it called on the government to do more in support of new births and healthy babies: to extend the obligatory repose for pregnant women to four weeks before delivery; to provide obligatory maternity insurance rather than merely assistance to needy mothers; and to embark on a government-sponsored system of substantial bonuses for births. During the discussion of this report, Dr. Pinard invoked the Convention and demanded even more. Mme Gemähling's plan, he said, is not revolutionary enough – a minimum of three months' rest before delivery must be provided; more governmental money must be found; and the "rights of the child" must be proclaimed. But little happened, though the new group, *Pour le Relèvement de la Natalité Française*, known as *Pour la Vie* (viewed as a rival by Bertillon's and Boverat's *Alliance Nationale pour l'Acroissement de la Population*), focused on moral education, which embraced anti-alcoholism and other social campaigns; these commitments provided the common ground for cooperation with the feminist groups.[101]

Following Dr. Pinard's cry of alarm, *La Française* (23 December 1916) would publish a rejoinder by Mme Le Grelle de Ferrer, representing yet another group, the *Alliance Féministe pour l'Union Sacrée des Mères*. She argued forcefully that during this war France simply had no option: women (whether pregnant, postpartum, or nursing) *must* work and the government *must* therefore provide support services to make it possible. In the meantime, the number of women working in the munitions factories continued to climb: from 100,000 at the end of January 1916 to 204,000 at

---

[99] See Doléris, *Protection des femmes et des enfants,* especially the debates for 6th March.

[100] See Association Nationale Française pour la Protection Légale des Travailleurs. *La Maternité ouvrière et sa protection légale en France, rapport de Mme Paul Gemähling, agrégée de l'Université. Allocutions du Dr. Bonnaire et du Pr Pinard. Réunion du 3 mai 1915 de l'Association* (Paris: F. Alcan/ M. Rivière, 1915).

[101] See *L'Action féminine,* n° 43 (May 1916), 42. See Cova, *Maternité et droits des femmes,* pp. 204–213, on the formation of *Pour la Vie* and its alliance with the UFSF, esp. pp. 204–206.

the end of June, and 300,000 by the end of December, the numbers kept on rising and kept the French armies supplied with their deadly products.[102] Small wonder that the medical community was concerned.

On the first of January 1917, Dr. A.-A. Lesage published his report (endorsed by the CTF), which called for proactive measures such as on-the-job nursing locales, nurseries and crèches for the women employees, and time off to nurse without penalties; it also demanded that extra attention be paid to hygiene and prevention of illnesses![103] The debates between Pinard and Paul Strauss made the front page of *Le Petit Journal* in mid-February, and doubtless other papers as well.[104] Shortly thereafter, the CTF would issue a circular stipulating the measures industrialists must take in order to ensure safe employment for expectant working women. These included medical surveillance, assurance of appropriate pay, and in particular the establishment of on-site facilities for nursing mothers.[105] A law to this effect would finally be promulgated on 5 August 1917. All these measures would sound very good on paper, but getting the private sector munitions establishments to set up such facilities in a timely manner would not be easy, nor would they materialize in time to be truly useful, except in exceptional establishments such as the brand new Citroën plant, reported on in *La Française* by Dr. Clotilde Mulon in March 1918.[106]

Men's concern about women working in the war industries would continue to grow, even as men's numbers declined; by mid-1916 war casualties had already produced over 600,000 war widows who had to

---

[102] Gaston Rageot, *La Française dans la guerre* (Paris: Attinger freres, 1919), p. 19, gives these figures.

[103] Dr. A.-A. Lesage, "L'enfant de l'ouvrière d'usine," *Bulletin des Usines de Guerre,* n° 36 (1 January 1917), 285–287.

[104] See "La mère et l'enfant dans les usines de guerre," *Le Petit Parisien* (14 February 1917), 1. Accessed on Gallica 19 August 2014.

[105] "Décisions, Circulaires et Avis: La Protection de la Maternité," *Bulletin des Usines de Guerre,* n° 38 (15 January 1917), 299. Circular from the Minister of Armaments and War Production [Albert Thomas] addressed to the Controllers of the Workers, n° 13235/0. For discussion of the CTF, "whose work inspired the decisions taken," see Yvonne Delatour, "Le Travail des femmes pendant la Première Guerre mondial et leur rôle sur l'évolution de la société," *Francia: Forschungen zur Westeuropäischen Geschichte,* vol. 1 (1974), 482–502; quote, 493. For more on the CTF, see Rageot, *Française dans la guerre;* McMillan, *Housewife or Harlot,* chapter 5; and the more extended discussion in Downs, *Manufacturing Inequality,* pp. 168–174.

[106] All the major automobile manufacturers in and around Paris evidently turned to munitions production. Thébaud, *Femme au temps de la guerre de 14,* p. 172, reported that at Citroën, women constituted some 60% of the wartime labor force; she refers readers to Sylvie Schweitzer's study, *Des engrenages à la chaine, les usines Citroën 1915–1935* (Lyon: Presses Universitaires de Lyon, 1982). Downs, *Manufacturing Inequality* (pp. 15–16) provides a long quote in translation from Dr. Clotilde Mulon's report on her visit to the Citroën's Javel plant; see Mulon, "Une visite à l'usine de guerre Citroën," *La Française,* n° 452 (2 March 1918), 4 (feuilleton).

find ways to survive! Although the work performed by women workers in munitions factories was relatively well paid in the beginning, mounting inflation and price increases continually eroded their purchasing power. Meanwhile their numbers continued to grow. By mid-May 1917, 684,000 French women would be employed in war industries, plus 150,000 employed in the administration of the army.[107] Yet the projects to protect their maternity had barely gotten underway and the birth rate continued to drop precipitously. In the interim, France experienced a wave of mutinies in the military, strikes in Paris, and general unrest among the civilian population, plus what appeared to be sinking morale among the thousands of soldiers in the trenches.[108] The influenza epidemic also took a heavy toll. The war was dragging on and victory seemed far from certain.

In May 1917, the Academy of Medicine made public its report on the depopulation question, with emphasis on how to stimulate natality. This report reiterated the need to raise the birth rate; the authors blamed depopulation squarely on the conscious use of birth control, deliberate and agreed on by both spouses. Additionally, it called for monetary allocations for mothers, from conception on.[109] The Academy's report was followed later that year by a special issue of the monthly obstetrical and gynecological medical journal (which actually appeared only in 1918).[110]

As ever looking out for women's interests, the UFSF and CNFF filed complementary reports on the question of women's employment and maternity during the war. Marguerite Martin of the UFSF framed her April 1917 report squarely in terms of the population crisis. "Because it is a RIGHT for the *ouvrière* to experience the joys of maternity, it is also a DUTY for the industrialist who profits from her work and for the country that has need of her collaboration to watch over her and her child, in consequence of which one cannot leave this care to philanthropy, [which is] inevitably humiliating and arbitrary. The measures taken must be

---

[107] Figures from the *Journal Officiel*, 15 May 1917, as cited by Edouard Herriot, *Créer* (Paris: Payot, 1919), vol. 2, p. 199. Rageot, *Française dans la guerre*, p. 19, also cites this figure for mid-May 1917.

[108] See Downs, "Women's Strikes and the Politics of Popular Egalitarianism in France 1916–1918," pp. 114–148.

[109] *Sur la Dépopulation de la France. Rapport au nom d'une Commission, composée de MM. Gariel, Président; Delorme, Doléris, E. Gley, A. Pinard, Paul Strauss et Charles Richet, rapporteur. Académie de Médecine, 15 mai 1917*; this report is reproduced in Martin de Torina, *Mère sans être épouse*, pp. 87–145.

[110] See the special issue "Quelques problèmes d'ordre social intéressant la mère et l'enfant," *Archives Mensuelles d'Obstétrique et de Gynécologie* (October–December 1917), published 31 March 1918. In addition to articles on protection of mothers and infants, this issue contained articles on the fight against criminal abortion and on the necessity of (further) regulating the midwives' profession.

measures of justice, uniform and obligatory." Both the child and the woman worker must be protected, this report indicated. There must be facilities for maternal nursing and childcare at all levels, close to the workplace or even as part of it; the personnel (in charge of those facilities) must be upgraded. The report called for a thoroughgoing overhaul of existing institutions, and provisions for taking care of sick children. For the women, improvements were envisioned in hygiene in the workplace, changes in the nature of their work, and especially its length. The eight-hour day, with three shifts, was essential as was the possibility of half-time work; the *semaine anglaise* must be introduced and, especially, equal pay for equal work. The demands for communal services to serve working mothers and their children and for upgrades in the requirements for the personnel who would staff them were such that any partisan of collective solutions would be pleased.[111]

Supplementing Marguerite Martin's report for the UFSF was the longer and more comprehensive report of Dr. Clotilde Mulon (dated 19 May 1917) on behalf of the CNFF Section on Hygiene, which was addressed directly to the Undersecretary of Labor.[112] It took up nearly a full page (four-and-a-half of five columns) in *La Française* and laid out twelve specific measures that required enactment. The thrust of this report was to strongly encourage the passage of a law that would require employers to institutionalize a series of specific practices that would make maternity less onerous for their women workers, including the establishment of nursing rooms and crèches at the factories.[113] A law to this effect was promulgated in August 1917 but the administrative regulations required to activate it would not be in place for another *nine* years.[114] Still, France had made a significant step in the right direction.

[111] See Marguerite Martin, Rapport au Congrès de l'UFSF, 5 avril 1917: "Le Travail féminin et la maternité," in *La Française*, n° 420 (5 May 1917). This report and its demands anticipate both the arguments and demands that would be put forward by Alva Myrdal in Sweden during the 1930s.

[112] Dr. Clotilde Mulon, "La Maternité et le travail," *La Française*, n° 430 (14 July 1917), 2.

[113] Dr. Mulon would continue to remind readers of the serious collapse of the birth rate in 1915 and 1916, accompanied by the exceedingly high rates of infant mortality. Among other proposals, she touted the benefits of organized classes on *puériculture* (scientific child-rearing). See her subsequent articles in *La Française*: "La Campagne américaine contre le dépeuplement de la France," n° 459 (27 April 1918); "Le Puériculture pour toutes," n° 475 (12 October 1918); and "Travail des mères et dépopulation," n° 482 (30 November 1989). In the latter article, Dr. Mulon would lament the ineffectiveness of the law of 1917 and the continued high infant mortality rates, due, she believes, to the insouciance of most employers of women workers.

[114] Cova, *Maternité et droits des femmes*, pp. 220–221. Cova considers this law to have been more beneficial to infants than to their mothers but remarks that it was ineffective despite its good intentions.

In the meantime (in May) feminists in the UFSF (led by Marguerite de Witt-Schlumberger and Cécile Brunschvicg) had joined forces with the pronatalist league to campaign forcefully for more babies for France. Given the overt hostility between pronatalists and feminists since the 1890s, this alliance was unprecedented. In a dedicated issue of *La Française*, the president of *Pour la Vie*, Paul Bureau, raised the stakes, indicating ominously that "France would no longer be able to pursue its international destiny" if the French continued to restrain the "bursting forth of life." "Systematic sterility" was not, he indicated, an option that the French nation could afford. Reproduction had become a patriotic duty. Gabriel Garcia-Ramon, secretary-general of the league, provided facts and figures. "From 1856 to today, our country, in terms of population, has fallen from second place among global powers to seventh place, and it is on the verge of falling to eighth place." This decline was due squarely to a "voluntary restriction of births." The result was that "France's military strength was compromised, its colonial empire menaced, its agriculture, industry, and commerce paralyzed, and its political, linguistic, moral and cultural influence in the entire world would diminish." "Depopulation," in sum, was synonymous with "the death of France." These were strong words indeed. And this time, this natalist called for engagement by the women of France: "Do you have faith in France's mission and in France itself? Do you want it to live?" We are calling on you and we place our faith in you, he concluded.

Marguerite de Witt-Schlumberger followed these two presentations with her discussion of the "particular duty" of women.[115] "Although it is not the duty of women to kill and destroy, it is their special duty to give children to *la patrie* and to reconstruct the country after the war. They represent the power of the future," she indicated. Framing her text in terms of the duties that would accompany future rights, and evoking the concern about French decline and the necessity of more population to fill the gaps left by the war in order for France to retain its preeminent position in the hierarchy of nations, she addressed her remarks to the "mothers of the race." This summons to reproduce, she argues, is not about providing future cannon fodder, but about assuring a lasting peace

---

[115] See *La Française*, n° 421 (12 May 1917). In May 1920, Witt-Schlumberger would go still further, insisting in a tract published jointly by the CNFF and *Pour la Vie* that women would either be "mothers of the fatherland or traitors to the fatherland" [*mères de la patrie, ou traîtres à la patrie*]. See *La Française*, n° 525 (15 May 1920), for discussion of this tract by A. B. who indicates that it is one of the first works to address directly women and their responsibilities as mothers of the next generation of French citizens.

and the possibility for France of "playing its role in the enlightened civilization of humanity." She considered any young married couple in good health that would not provide a child in the year following the war, to be considered deserters or traitors: "Either France will be reborn or it will disappear." These suffragist feminists and repopulators laid the action item squarely on women. What a change from the discourse of the 1890s!

Stimulating maternity was the overarching cause of the moment, but another social problem again raised its ugly head, a practice that not only did not facilitate legitimate maternity but could also enhance the threat of venereal diseases to men, women, and children: prostitution, this time abetted by the army. Already in 1916 the CNFF had learned of the establishment of brothels near the front lines and had issued a new condemnation of regulated prostitution and the morals police.[116] In the spring of 1918 the CNFF and UFSF leaders would get wind of an Army circular (dated 13 March 1918) promoting the establishment of "tolerated" brothels near the front.[117] In its 29 June issue, the lead article in *La Française* read "Should the State Encourage Debauchery?"[118] Both these French feminist organizations responded forcefully and, on 17 July, they would lead an imposing delegation representing twelve feminist and pronatalist groups to call on the minister of war. In early August, the ministry responded only that it would "review the matter."

Marguerite de Witt-Schlumberger (speaking in her capacity as head of the Section on Morals of the CNFF) was incensed. In a long article in *La Française* (21 September 1918), she framed the issue as, above all, a moral question. She would remind her readers why it was that government-regulated prostitution was so demeaning for all women: "It is an injust and immoral institution, an offense to our entire sex because it permits an arbitrary police to act against women whereas it does not regulate the men."[119] Invoking the solidarity of feminist women with the prostitutes, she called on women to remind the menfolk of their complicity. There is

[116] See the report of Marguerite de Witt-Schlumberger for the Section on Morals and repression of the white slave trade, *L'Action féminine*, n° 45 (August 1916), 93–94.

[117] On the French army's efforts to address the problem of venereal diseases, see Jean-Yves Le Naour, *Misères et tourmentes de la chair durant la Grande Guerre: Les moeurs sexuelles des Français, 1914–1918* (Paris: Aubier, 2002), pp. 136–139, & chapter 3, esp. pp. 189–218. Le Naour does mention the feminists' protests.

[118] See *La Française*, n° 468 (29 June 1918).

[119] Marguerite de Witt-Schlumberger, "Ce que les Femmes peuvent pour le relèvement des moeurs," *La Française*, n° 473 (21 September 1918), 1. The texts of the CNFF and UFSF protests are also published in English in *Jus Suffragii*, 12:11 (1 August 1918), 170, followed by several other protests in the issue of 1 September 1918, 185–186. I have retranslated Witt-Schlumberger's remarks from the original French.

no such thing as a "necessary evil," she insisted; it is rather a question of "willpower, education, and habit." For centuries, she remarked, men have insisted that women be virtuous; now the time had come for women to insist that men apply the same principles to themselves. No more double standard of virtuous women and profligate men! Regulated prostitution has proven ineffective against the increasingly terrible flood of venereal disease, she indicated, and it was a big lie that hygienic examinations [of the women] can put a stop to it. "The fight against the venereal diseases that are poisoning our people [she used the word *race*] should now be one of the major preoccupations for conscious women." The first step, she indicated, is to prevent contamination; the second, to care for those who are diseased. Punishment and regulation are fruitless; care is necessary, along with education about the contagiousness of these diseases and their connection with debauchery. Free – and discrete – medical care should be made available to those who contract the diseases. The Ministry of the Interior had begun to move in this direction, but Witt-Schlumberger would call on women at the local level to ensure that such dispensaries got established and would run effectively. "No woman," she stated, "has the right to ignore this problem." Linking this issue to suffrage, which had reappeared on the feminist agenda in 1917, Witt-Schlumberger argued that no women merit their rights as citizens "as long as they support and condone the regulation of prostitution that allow placing a woman outside the law simply because she is a woman." Quoting the petition handed to the ministry of war earlier that year by the coalition of women's and men's associations mentioned earlier, she emphasized that "'one cannot create morality by immoral means, nor sanitize a situation by unclean means'" and, furthermore, "'a State cannot diminish debauchery by taking on the inauspicious role of organizing debauchery'." In closing, Witt-Schlumberger called for the vote for women, which she deemed "a necessity for acting on all these moral questions that lie at the base of all social questions."

The flip side of the emphasis on raising the birth rate would be the prospect of legislation addressed at curbing contraception and abortion. Already in 1917 (as we have previously indicated), the Academy of Medicine was taking a long, hard look at the role of contraception and abortion in fomenting the natality crisis. In May 1918 the CNFF's Mme Chevalier, who now chaired the Section on Legislation, filed a report on a private bill proposed by the Senate's Commission on Depopulation (reported out by Senator Cazeneuve) to crack down on abortion – by, among other things, "decriminalizing" the act so that it could be tried by strict judges rather than by lenient juries in the assize courts. The CNFF report objected adamantly to the notion of criminalizing the victim – in this case, the poor single mothers, who were in any case acting out of fear of misery and/or dishonor. Importantly, it opposed the "correctionalization" of abortion, remarking that judges of the correctional courts had no option but to enforce the existing law. "At present, the jury effectively has full power to take into account the facts that are provided in the Assize court. It can acquit a woman who pleads guilty, or a woman whose crime is proven if it finds that the circumstances are an excuse for the crime. The correctional judge does not have this right. His hands are tied by the law. If the violation is admitted to or proved, the punishment must be endured. The National Council cannot vote for this uniform and inevitable punishment as long as the social conditions surrounding pregnant women have not been improved."[120]

Before cracking down on women who have aborted, the CNFF section report stated that the government should first provide a full program of adequate financial and institutional aid to pregnant women so as to allow them to complete their pregnancies and deliver their babies safely and, if need be, in secret. Specifically, it advocated that each department should provide a refuge or home for pregnant women, and that maternity clinics should be attached to hospitals, open to all women. The report also proposed that the Strauss Law of 1913 (on maternity leaves) be extended to *all* women. Finally, and significantly, it proposed that equal penalties be reserved for fathers of illegitimate children; masculine responsibility and complicity must be addressed. Only when these conditions had been met, the report said, could the CNFF consider supporting the various punitive elements of the Cazeneuve report, which its section had gone through article by article to stipulate which elements were unacceptable, which were supportable, and why.[121]

In this report, however, the women of the CNFF did not contest the articles (16, 17, 18) of the proposed law that would sharply limit access to contraceptive information. There is no question that the CNFF approved of the articles that intended to act against "neo-Malthusian" propaganda in

---

[120] See "L'Action des Femmes sur les Lois. Rapport de la Section de Législation du Conseil National des Femmes sur la Proposition de Loi de la Commission sénatoriale de la Dépopulation, tendant à la répression des avortements criminels," signed by Mme Chevalier, in *La Française*, n° 461 (11 May 1918), 1–2; quote, 2. This report was reprinted in the *UFSF Bulletin, 1918–1919*, 88–93, as "Rapport de Mme Chevaley [sic], de la Section de Législation du CNFF, sur la proposition de loi de la Commission sénatoriale de la Dépopulation, tendant à la répression des avortements criminels."

[121] Chevalier report in *La Française*, 1–2.

any shape or form. Seen from a twenty-first century feminist perspective, this seems shocking, to say the least. We must remember, however, the context: the extreme concern about the huge drop in the French birth rate during the war. Deep concern for the post-war population/birth deficit doubtless provided extenuating circumstances, overriding concern for what we now call women's freedom of reproductive "choice." Mme Chevalier's report did, however, propose that such measures be part of a broader, omnibus bill that would allow action against the circulation of any information (contraception or promoting abortion being only one aspect) that was "against good morals."[122] And we must take into account the CNFF's statement of reservations (discussed earlier), which insisted that *before* any such punitive laws were put into place, society first needed to make a number of major changes in the circumstances surrounding pregnant women, especially those who were poor and needed assistance during this critical time of their lives. Then and only then would such laws make sense, the feminists indicated. The question was whether the legislators would "hear" this message as they proceeded toward a crackdown.

It seems incontestable that without the efforts of French women to "man" the home front, France could not have won the war. But as the end of the war came into sight, it was unclear whether French women would retain the right to continue serving *la patrie*. It depended, of course, on the mode of service being envisioned. In 1917, Léon Abénsour attested to the outsized contributions of these women to the war effort: "The facts speak for themselves; . . . for our allies, and even for our enemies, the patience and courage of [French] women are the brightest rays of the national glory. The action of the women can no longer be debated. It imposes itself with the clearest evidence, with the force of a *fait accompli*."[123] In a 1919 report on the mobilization of women for the war effort, Mme Émile Borel (a.k.a. the writer Camille Marbo), who served as secretary-general of the society *L'Effort féminin français* (a joint venture of Catholic women and secular republican women), would applaud the contributions of women workers, especially those in the defense industries.[124]

---

[122] Chevalier report in *La Française*, 1; surprisingly, neither this report nor the rest of the discussion on this bill prior to 1919 is discussed in Cova, *Maternité et droits des femmes*.

[123] Abensour, *Les Vaillantes*, p. 305 (cited in n. 46).

[124] Mme Émile Borel [Camille Marbo], ed. *La Mobilisation féminine en France, 1914–1919. Documentation rassemblée par la Société "l'Effort féminin français"* (Paris: Impr. Union, 1919), quote, p. 52. This author, née Marguerite Appell, was better known to the public as the prolific novelist Camille Marbo, winner of the *Prix Femina* [*La Vie Heureuse*] in 1913. She would later become the president of the *Société des Gens de Lettres*.

The employment of women in the factories was not always happy, either from the perspective of their health or especially from the very serious perspective of maternity. It made many nervous, but it was not a question, for France, to discuss in theory whether or not one should employ women in manufacturing – the products they made were just as necessary as soldiers in the trenches were necessary. The intensive labor of women was one of the consequences of the war; one could try to alleviate the inconveniences and to organize it, but one could not hope to avoid it.

Writers such as Gaston Rageot expressed their amazement and admiration at the contributions to the war effort of the women of France: "The victory of the allies has been the victory of the French woman."[125] There was no question that the women of France had made heroic sacrifices on behalf of French victory; the question was what would happen after the war was over.

These relatively well-paid economic opportunities for women in the factories would be among the first casualties of the armistice; returning soldiers would, of course, need jobs. Two days after the Armistice was signed, on the 13th of November 1918, the Ministry of War would call for the demobilization of women who worked in munitions factories and set a deadline of 5 December, by which date women who voluntarily gave up their jobs would receive thirty days' severance pay. The ministerial memo made it clear that these women were not being fired, but rather that their jobs, making munitions, were no longer necessary.[126] In an article published in January 1919 on the demobilization, Léon Abensour underscored that the expectation was that women would indeed continue to work.[127] As he put it,

> it was clear that in order to fill the holes made by the cannons in the masculine elite, it would be necessary to call on women. Individual interest coupled with social interest, the necessity for single women to support themselves, for married women to add to the family income, and the necessity for the country not to give a preponderant place to foreigners during its industrial renaissance, all combine to require imperiously a mobilization of women for peacetime. Women can furnish the workers' army with numerous and solid forces.

---

[125] Rageot, *Française dans la guerre*, p. 5.

[126] "Avis du Ministre de l'Armament aux ouvrières des usines et établissements de l'État travaillant aux fabrications de guerre, 19 novembre 1918."

[127] Léon Abensour, "Le Problème de la démobilisation féminine," *La Grande Revue*, vol. 98, n° 3 (January 1919), 488–502 ("Pages Libres," n° 414 [January 1919], 80–94); quotes (here and below), 501–502.

Abensour seemed to be suggesting that the old ideal of the sexual division of labor in families, the male-breadwinner model, might never snap back into place. Women's paid labor was all too necessary.

Women's labor in heavy industry, however, should be exceptional; to Abensour it seemed obvious that French women would be steered to other, less strenuous kinds of employment. What was snapping into place was a sexual division of jobs in the workplace (something feminists had long advocated). The implication was that, leaving behind the heavy industrial jobs deemed men's work, French women would return to more "suitable" work in the luxury trades, in textiles and the arts, in which they had long dominated (but in which, with only a few exceptions, they had suffered from minimal pay, dead seasons, and lack of respect for their skills). The long-standing problem in this older economic sector was, of course, not about the tasks, but about raising the pay to levels that could sustain the women who did the work. Abensour seemed optimistic about the possibilities: "An immense domain is open to women: the luxury industries, which were formerly the uncontested prerogative of France, then downgraded and claimed by Germany, should be reborn tomorrow from the ashes of war and bring back millions to our cities." He waxed lyric about the options:

> From the textile industries to the Articles of Paris, from fashion to bookbinding, from the lamination of threads of gold and silver to clock and watchmaking, from ceramic art to furniture, from toys to decorative arts, from furniture to jewelry, women can [exhibit] those qualities that are truly those of the French woman: good taste, ingenuity, inventiveness. [These are] the most lucrative jobs for women and the most fruitful for the country. For the renovation of these luxury industries which, going forward, should become one of the essential preoccupations of our ministers of commerce and of labor, we must call on women. Previously, even in these industries, women played only a subordinate role.

Abensour argued that the war had shown that French women, once well trained, could handle any task. Their skills should be fully developed through improved vocational education. Moreover, women should become managers and administrators [cadres], who could even manage foreign workers [who would be imported to fill the gaps left by the million-plus deceased men]. They would be able to choose their occupation and support themselves independently, working in establishments that would benefit from the best scientific and hygienic advances. "Women, armed for the economic struggle through professional education and the vote, could ride the wave of the future," Abensour predicted, and not be stuck in the industrial backwater of the past. Little did he foresee what direction the French economy would actually take – historian Laura Levine Frader points to the growth in the 1920s and 1930s of new industrial sectors – consumer goods, pharmaceutical manufacturing, and food processing, in addition to the expansion in the numbers of teachers and state employees.[128] What Abensour did not address was the problem of how women could be employed in long-term, responsible jobs, either in the arts and crafts or in management, when they could not control their own fertility, when even the very circulation of information about contraception was under attack.

The old arguments for the necessity of a male breadwinner and the *femme au foyer* would not, however, disappear after the war; in fact they would be reintroduced by a growing "familial" movement bolstered by "the rhetoric and practices of employers, the state, and organized labor."[129] What had disappeared, however, were the prospective breadwinners: some 1.4 million men of marriageable age, some already married, others potential bride-grooms, had died in the war. Many thousands more were maimed for life. Even though new cohorts of young men and women would reach maturity after the war, their numbers were reduced due to the falling birth rate of the pre-war period. Frader's research demonstrates how employers and organized labor would exert their combined efforts in attempts to restore traditional gender norms and to bolster the male-breadwinner model.[130] It was not the case that in the post-war period "civilization ... no longer had sexes," as Pierre Drieu La Rochelle would claim mournfully in 1927, but it was certainly true that neo-traditionalist efforts to reconstitute the pre-war sexual order would be unremitting, even as women's labor force participation continued and women's relative independence would grow.[131]

Suffrage and Citizenship? Or?

These closely related uncertainties – about women's employment in the future, about the continued legal subordination of women in marriage, restrictions on contraceptions, etc. – bring us back to the question of the

---

[128] Laura Levine Frader, *Breadwinners and Citizens: Gender in the Making of the French Social Model* (Durham, NC: Duke University Press, 2008), p. 10.

[129] Frader, *Breadwinners and Citizens*, p. 243, n. 21.

[130] Frader, *Breadwinners and Citizens*, pp. 12–13, and chapters 2 and 3. Cf. also Susan Pedersen, *Family, Dependence, and the Origins of the Welfare State: Britain and France, 1914–1945* (Cambridge, UK: Cambridge University Press, 1993), part 1.

[131] See Pierre Drieu La Rochelle, *La Suite des idées* (Paris: Au Sans Pareil, 1927), p. 125. Drieu La Rochelle's complaint provides the reference for Mary Louise Roberts' book title, *Civilization without Sexes: Reconstructing Gender in Postwar France, 1917-1927* (Chicago: University of Chicago Press, 1994).

vote – the "alpha and omega" of women's demands. Now that the war was over, now that French women had proved how indispensible they were to the nation, to the Republic itself, what would become of women's quest for citizenship?

To recapitulate: in mid-June 1914, the municipal women's suffrage bill based on the Buisson report was finally presented to the Chamber of Deputies. In early July French suffragists had staged a massive, celebratory rally on behalf of the proposal at the Condorcet monument in Paris. Just seven days later France was at war. The woman suffrage bill was eclipsed by the German invasion.

When, in early 1916, the nationalist deputy Maurice Barrès suddenly proposed enfranchising war widows or mothers of fallen soldiers, the women's suffrage issue bounced back into public consciousness – as "*le suffrage des morts*" [the vote of the dead]. While this initiative may have appealed to some women, others objected to this offer of a second-hand vote. The eloquent Nelly Roussel (who had not been heard from for some time) burst into print in *L'Équité* with a resounding "No." She rejected the Barrès proposal out of hand, calling it "injurious generosity."[132]

> Nothing is less feminist than the intentions of M. Barrès.... We do not want to *think via another*, to *speak for another*, however infinitely dear to us that other was.... We do not want to vote by procuration, as delegates, as substitutes. We want to vote as free *citoyennes*, enjoying all the rights and prerogatives attached to that dignity.... If the vote must be compensatory, let it then not compensate their heroism, but our own labor, our own courage. No, not the vote of the dead! What is due to us, without unjust distinctions or humiliating restrictions, is the *suffrage of the living*.

Like others, Nelly Roussel made it clear that French women's prodigious effort to keep the country afloat during the war offered an overriding argument for women's full enfranchisement.

The national feminist associations would also remind legislators that women's suffrage was an individual matter. Any adult woman, married or not, must be able to cast her own vote. A report by Marguerite Clément to the General Assembly of the revived UFSF reported on "What the Suffragettes think about Depopulation" and asserted that motherhood and the welfare of children were at the top of the list of concerns that their

---

[132] Nelly Roussel, "Le 'Suffrage des Morts'," *L'Équité*, n° 33 (March 1916), 3; reprinted in Nelly Roussel, *Derniers combats: Recueil d'articles et de discours* (Paris: L'Émancipatrice, 1932), pp. 76–78; quote, p. 77. The censors did not cut this article although they did heavily amputate others in the same issue.

anticipated political rights might make it possible to address.[133] At its 21 December meeting, the Paris section of the UFSF began to consider launching a series of public lectures on behalf of women's suffrage. Marguerite de Witt-Schlumberger "reminded" members of the UFSF and readers of *La Française* of the importance of the vote, and reported on the present state of the suffrage struggles beyond the French hexagon, where women were winning the vote right and left. For France, however, it would be particularly important. "It is for the reconstruction of the country that the right of suffrage is necessary for us, for the country will have need of the strength and intelligence of all its children together, men and women." The views of women must be represented as the problems are addressed, she indicated.[134]

On 7 January 1917, in response to the "Appeal of the Women of Occupied Belgium," the CNFF, the UFSF, and several other groups moved once again into public space when they organized a mass protest meeting against the deportation by the German military of French, Belgian, and Serbian girls and women from the occupied zones. Cécile Brunschvicg read a passionate statement from the feminist groups, in which they called on women of the world to make their voices heard; to be silent was to be complicit in the crimes, which constituted clear violations of the rules of war and international law.[135] In the ensuing weeks, *La Française* renewed its coverage of the doings of the Chamber's Commission on Universal Suffrage, which had acquired a new socialist chairman. On 5 April 1917 the UFSF convened its annual congress, which was duly reported in the CNFF's *L'Action féminine.*[136]

In addition to their many social welfare projects, targeted to help those in need during wartime, the feminist activists of the big associations continued to intervene in matters of public policy.[137] In late 1917, for example, a petition addressed to the Minister for Provisions [*ravitaillement*] by the *Union des Grandes Associations Françaises contre la Propagande*

---

[133] "Ce que les Suffragettes pensent de la repopulation," *La Française*, n° 385 (13 May 1916). Clement's text, "The duty of women in the struggle against depopulation," was republished in the UFSF's *Bulletin 1914–1916*, 22–26.

[134] See "État actuel de la Question du Suffrage féminin en France et à l'étranger," and the report on the meeting in *La Française*, n° 405 (13 January 1917), 2.

[135] See "Protestation solonnelle contres les Déportations," *La Française*, n° 405 (13 January 1917), 1–2; the text of the Belgian protest of 16 December 1916 evidently took some time to reach France and was not published in *La Française* until the issue n° 425 (9 June 1917).

[136] See the report on the UFSF congress by Mme Witt-Schlumberger in *L'Action féminine*, n° 48 (May 1917), 164–166.

[137] See their association reports in *La Française*, n° 430 (14 July 1917), 1.

Ennemie (signed and submitted by Julie Siegfried and Ghénia Avril de Sainte-Croix of the CNFF) asked that women be included in the decision-making process as to the provisioning of the country. No response had come by May 1918, much to the disgust of Jane Misme. "Permit me to remind you, *Monsieur le Ministre*, that it is in your department that it is especially important to have the women with you." Sarcastically invoking the German emperor's notorious 4-K's (Kinder, Kirche, Küche, Kleider), Misme remarked that indeed women are the ones who run the households, who know how to economize, how to observe restrictions. "The first good housekeeper you encounter," she wrote, "can tell you more than the most learned economist about whether or not the measures you are projecting have any chance of being effective; and they will tell you why. They know what the conditions are for your obtaining the indispensible collaboration of consumers. For in fact they *are* the consumers."[138] This editorial was followed by a comparative survey of what foodstuffs were being restricted in the allied and enemy countries and a list of items that one could possibly do without.

The feminist associations made another intervention concerning the pricing of gas in May/June 1918, in a "*Cahier de Doléances des Ménagères*" [Grievances of the Housewives]. This time the feminists were telling the ministry for provisioning that it was making mistakes precisely because it had not consulted the women, "the sole class of French people that are still refused inclusion in national sovereignty by the Republic. In face of men, the absolute sovereigns, women are always in the situation of the old Third Estate, [whose members] could only present its cahiers of grievances on their knees, but at least they could present them." What must they do to get the ministry to request and then follow women's advice on things such as food supplies and gas prices? Alluding to history, and to French women's historic roles in fomenting food riots when prices rose too high or shortages appeared, they presented to the members of the Paris Municipal Council a *Doléance des Mères de Familles nombreuses à propos du prix du Gaz* [Grievance of Mothers of Large Families Concerning the Price of Gas]. The thrust of the complaint was that gas rationing should not be allotted equally per residence, but rather according to the number of persons living in that residence. These mothers pointed out that, for example, more gas is required to cook for more persons, or to [heat water] to bathe them or to do the laundry for them. "Revise your system!"

---

[138] Jane Misme, "Les Françaises offrent leur aide au Ministère du Ravitaillement. L'offriront-elles en vain?" *La Française*, n° 463 (25 May 1918), 1. Emphasis in original.

"Hasten, Messieurs, to revise this question of gas [pricing]. We ask it of you in the name of Repopulation."[139]

In September 1918, the national women's organizations weighed in again on the question of morals, prostitution, and sex education – and the relation of all these issues to women's suffrage. Marguerite de Witt-Schlumberger, in her capacity as head of the CNFF Section on Morals, and president of the USFS, detailed "what women could do for the improvement of morals."[140] The anti-alcoholism campaign was never far from the front page of *La Française*.

After the Armistice: In Search of Peace and Women's Rights

With the conclusion of the Armistice on 11 November 1918 and the ensuing celebrations, the time had come for the showdown on women's suffrage. As we have seen, there was one new argument for women's citizenship, and it was a potent, practical one: the extraordinary service of French women of all social classes to the nation during the war – without which (no one denied) France could never have achieved victory. Many reports applauded the contributions of women to the war effort. Celebrating the armistice, Jane Misme published a reminder that women, having contributed so much, stood ready for further assignments. "Will they be permitted to employ their full value and would it be that all the French, men and women, of the Glorious Republic, would not be citizens? Could one so offend the unity of the reconstituted *patrie*? If women of good will refuse to remain an 'inferior class,' don't forget that it is because they need their rights in order to fulfill their duties."[141]

The campaigns for women's suffrage would find new life and new supporters in 1919. In the meantime, French feminists would affirm their right to citizenship through various public actions. To a plea from the German feminists to the CNFF, asking them to intervene with their government to lighten the severe conditions of the armistice, the French feminists would proudly refuse, pointing out that throughout the war, the German women had never apologized for the crimes committed by their government and military against the French and Belgians and had stood by the decisions made by their men. The UFSF offered a similar response to a request from the

---

[139] "Cahier de Doléances des Ménagères," and "A Messieurs les Conseillers Municipaux de la Ville de Paris. Doléances des Mères de Famille nombreuses à propos du prix du Gaz," *La Française*, n° 464 (1 June 1918), 1.

[140] *La Française*, n° 473 (21 September 1918), 1.

[141] Jane Misme, "Le Reveil," *La Française*, n° 480 (16 November 1918), 1.

president of the German women's suffrage organization who asked for merciful intervention with the Allied governments to lift the blockade that was keeping food from German women and children.[142] The French suffragists would stand by their government and invoke the cause of justice. A subsequent plea from Swedish feminists, signed by Ellen Key and the Nobel prizewinning novelist Selma Lagerlof, for pity toward the now starving women and children of the former enemy states failed to bend the French women's determination to hold the line.[143] The UFSF response to the Swedish women underscored that their sympathies would continue to lie with the innocent, while retaining the memory of the atrocities and bad deeds committed by the German invaders and remarking that the German women had apparently made no effort to protest their misdeeds. (The French feminists would finally get their apology in Geneva in 1920, when a small delegation of German and Austrian women expressed their "regrets" at a special meeting during the first post-war IWSA congress.)[144]

Having the previous day buried Marie Bonnevial (the president of the LFDF was killed in a traffic accident), the CNFF would convene a public meeting in Paris on the 8th of December 1918 to bring pressure on both the Chamber of Deputies and the Senate. If eloquence alone could have won French women the vote, surely this meeting would have put the cause over the top. The speakers, who rolled out every old and new argument for suffrage and disputed every old tired argument against, included H. Berthélemy from the Paris law faculty; Cécile Brunschvicg, secretary-general of the UFSF; Ferdinand Buisson of the LDH, champion of women's suffrage and *rapporteur* of the earlier suffrage bill; the lawyer Suzanne Grinberg (standing in for Marguerite de Witt-Schlumberger); Juliette François-Raspail of the UFF; and Maria Vérone, who would succeed Bonnevial as president of the LFDF. The assembly's resolution "demanded" that the Chamber of Deputies schedule discussion on the recently released Flandin report, "so that France, which gave to the world the Charter of the Rights of Man would not be the last of the great nations to accord the right to vote to women."[145]

---

[142] See *La Française*, n° 482 (30 November 1918) and n° 484 (14 December 1918) for these exchanges with the German women.

[143] Ellen Key, "Appel aux Femmes des Pays Victorieux" and Selma Lagerlof, "Aux Mères des Pays de l'Entente," both in *La Française*, n° 488 (19 January 1919), front page, and "A Ellen Key, à Selma Lagerlof, aux signataires de l'appel des Femmes suédoises," same issue.

[144] See Suzanne Grinberg's letter to *Le Matin*, published 19 June 1920, correcting the record on this meeting of reconciliation.

[145] See S. G. [Suzanne Grinberg], "Il faut que les femmes votent en 1919," *La Française*, n° 484 (14 December 1918), 1.

The Flandin report on the women's suffrage bill, which had been put on hold until the war was over, was finally distributed to the deputies in December 1918; it was published in full (although without the annexes) in *La Française* over the next several weeks.[146] The new bill included several compromises from the earlier Dusaussoy bill, namely the raising of the age for women's vote to 30 (as the British had recently done) and restricting their eligibility to serve on any of the councils except at the municipal level, or to elect senators. Flandin explained these restrictions as necessary "to disarm the opposition," even as he provided a summary of how the world had changed in the last one hundred years and why it was necessary to include women in French political life. But once again reform of the electoral system, the long-standing controversy over installing (or not) a system of proportional representation (of political parties), delayed action on the women's suffrage bill. It seemed that there was always some other issue, deemed more important by those who governed, that stood in the way of considering women's vote.

In the months following the armistice, the leaders of the major women's associations made it clear that these socially conscious women were prepared to fight hard for the vote. They had a significant number of allies. One of them was Jules Siegfried himself, husband of the CNFF's Julie Siegfried and the senior member [*doyen d'âge*] of the Chamber of Deputies, who in his speech opening the 1919 session, put forward an eloquent argument for women's suffrage. These deputies, elected in 1914, had been in office throughout the Great War; new elections had not yet been scheduled, but would ultimately be held in November 1919. The feminists had high hopes that the vote for women was in sight. Also in sight, and of more immediate interest, was the Allied Peace Conference, which would convene in Paris in February to embark on drafting the major treaty of peace with the vanquished powers that would subsequently be known to history as the Treaty of Versailles. Among its many other components, this treaty would also establish the League of Nations and the International Labour Office. These new bodies would be of great interest to the feminists of the Allied powers, as they offered new opportunities for women to engage in the building of the post-war world.

In the interim, the international feminist leaders had developed a greatly expanded worldview, enhanced by their experience of the war. In anticipation of the opening of the peace conference, and led by the French and

---

[146] The Flandin report was serialized in *La Française*, n° 484 (14 December 1918); n° 485 (21 December 1918); n° 487 (11 January 1919); and n° 488 (18 January 1919).

British feminists, along with their American counterparts, the major women's groups would accelerate their participation in international public space by calling for a conference of Allied women's suffragists in Paris (10–17 February) to study the women's suffrage situation in various countries, and to lead the charge to right wrongs that could no longer viewed as strictly national. Their particular goal was to foster the representation of women and their specific concerns in the design and drafting of the peace settlement, which was to be handled topically by a series of internal commissions, all of whose members were men.[147]

Representatives of the IWSA-affiliated UFSF had already written to the American President Woodrow Wilson in January 1919, requesting a meeting with him. Their request was granted on the opening evening of the Inter-allied Women's Suffrage Conference. The women quickly drafted a petition to Wilson, asking for the formation of a committee that would represent women's interests to the peace conference, its members to be nominated by the international women's associations and appointed by their respective governments. They requested that Wilson transmit their demand to the plenipotentiaries. Although Wilson told the women that he couldn't do it personally as he was about to leave Paris, he did promise to discuss the matter with his associates; in fact, according to documents in the U.S. Archives, on 13 February he did transmit the Allied women's demands to the secret meeting of the Council of Ten – meeting with resistance from several members who, concerned that the demand for a committee of women was really a demand for the peace conference to act on women's suffrage, spoke strongly against it. Wilson then withdrew his proposal.[148]

---

[147] See the precious account of these meetings by Suzanne Grinberg in *La Française*, n° 493 (22 February 1919), front page. The copy on the ACRRP microfilm is poor; a legible copy can be consulted at the BMD in PAIX/DOS 76. *Conférence des femmes suffragistes alliés 1919 à Paris.*
 The details of the Allied feminists' campaign at the peace conference are reported (in English) by Suzanne Grinberg, in "Women at the Peace Conference," *Jus Suffragii*, 13:6 (March 1919), 71–73, and "The Inter-Allied Suffrage Conference," *Jus Suffragii*, 13:7 (April 1919), 88–89. I have also drawn on Grinberg's account in *La Française*, n° 493 (22 February 1919) and M.-L. Puech's, "Le Conseil international des Femmes et la Conférence des femmes suffragistes reçues par la Commission de la Société des Nations," in n° 501 (26 April 1919), 1–2. Other progress reports signed S.G. can be consulted in *La Française*, n° 497 (22 March 1919; on the campaign to rescue the "martyred sisters") and n° 498 (29 March 1919). Grinberg's more detailed and personalized reports can be consulted in *La Renaissance politique, littéraire, économique* (29 March 1919), 20–23, and (26 April 1919), 9–12. Maria Vérone's reports are published in *Le Droit des Femmes*, issues of February, March, April 1919. Additional information can be found in dossiers at the Bibliothèque Marguerite Durand, Paris.

[148] See the discussion of this point by historian Glenda Sluga, based on her consultation of the records of this "secret" meeting of 13 February, located in the American and French archives, in "Female and National Self-Determination: A Gender Re-Reading of 'the Apogee of Nationalism'," *Nations and Nationalisms*, 6:4 (October 2000), 495–521, esp. 498–500.

In the meantime, the Allied women organized a study committee to develop the form and content of their resolutions. The IWSA leaders agreed (under some pressure from the ICW, it appears) to collaborate closely with the ICW leadership (who had, over the years, developed a series of highly effective international theme sections to study the various issues) in orchestrating and presenting the women's demands to the plenipotentiaries from all the Allied countries who would make the decisions at the Peace Conference.[149]

Both Woodrow Wilson and, subsequently, Georges Clemenceau (who proposed a very different approach, namely a Women's Commission as part of the treaty elaboration process) did express interest in assisting the women. In the ensuing weeks (late February through April) the leaders of both major French associations (the CNFF and UFSF), who were ready and available in Paris, would play an outsize role in representing the Allied women from the international organizations (the ICW and IWSA) in engaging the plenipotentiaries to argue their case for women's inclusion in the conference.[150] On behalf of the LFDF, Maria Vérone would address an open letter to Clemenceau, who had just appointed Léon Jouhaux, secretary of the *Confédération Général du Travail* (CGT; the major association of labor unions), as the French delegate to the Commission on International Legislation. The LFDF asked specifically for representation of women workers, given that many unions were closed to women, or forbade women from exercising certain professions. In addition to full representation, the related issues of concern included the protection of children, rest for women workers who had given birth, and equal pay for equal work for both sexes. "You have made it known to the delegation of Allied women that you are favorable to the principle of admitting women to the commissions of the peace conference, so we have the hope that you will favorably welcome our demand." Appealing to French pride, the LFDF announced, "We would be happy and proud if the French government could be the first to apply this principle of feminine representation."[151]

---

[149] See Alice La Mazière, "Les Femmes à la Conférence de la Paix. Préparation des Voeux," *La Française*, n° 494 (1 March 1919), 1. They would begin with the resolutions concerning women's employment. It should not be forgotten that Cécile Brunschvicg, who was leading the charge here, was both the secretary-general of the UFSF and head of the Section on Work of the CNFF.

[150] It should be mentioned that both Julie Siegfried and Ghénia Avril de Sainte-Croix were officers of the ICW as well as of the CNFF, and that Marguerite de Witt-Schlumberger of the UFSF was also an elected vice-president of the IWSA.

[151] Maria Vérone, "Ligue Française pour le Droit des Femmes," *La Française*, n° 494 (1 March 1919), 2.

Having scurried about to meet with the many peace conference pleni-potentiaries from around the world to rally their support for women's representation through the aforesaid committee, the Allied women could report good news. In *La Française* (8 March) they published the list of all those they had met with and who were supportive of their demands. "The peace that is being prepared would not merit the lovely name of "the Peace of Peoples" [*la Paix des Peuples*], if half of humanity, that is to say the women, are not admitted so that their voices can be heard." They then spelled out the issues that needed to be addressed:[152]

> The nationality of married women; the White Slave Trade, the return home of the Serbian, Greek, and Armenian women who were captured and sometimes even auctioned off by the Turks and the Bulgarians; questions relating to hygiene, to alcohol, to women's employment, and so many others that are of special interest to women, will certainly come up for discussion in the various Commissions. It is indispensable that women are called on to be seated in these Commissions.

Following up in March, the Allied women addressed a resolution to the secretary-general of the Peace Conference, demanding that the women and girls from the Allied countries who had been deported, abducted, and even sold during the war, be located, repatriated, and indemnified.[153] On 11 March, the Allied Supreme Council authorized the women's organizations to testify before the various Commissions that would deal with the issues that concerned them.[154] This was doubtless an important step, though not as gratifying as agreement to have women appointed to and serving on those Commissions would have been.

The Allied women's coalition succeeded in scheduling its first hearing with the Commission on Labor, chaired by the American labor leader Samuel Gompers. On 18 March an all-star delegation would present the women's demands concerning women's employment to the commission-ers. This delegation included Julie Siegfried, Ghénia Avril de Sainte-Croix, and Cécile Brunschvicg as delegates of the international women's organiza-tions, supplemented by other prominent French women leaders in labor and women's rights issues including Jeanne Bouvier, Maria Vérone, Gab-rielle Duchêne, and Mlle Bouilliot from the CGT's women's unions. It

---

[152] "Conférence des Femmes Alliées," *La Française*, n° 495 (8 March 1919), 1.

[153] "Requête des Suffragistes interalliées," *La Française*, n° 497 (22 March 1919), front page. This campaign is discussed briefly by Thébaud, *Femmes au temps de la guerre de 14*, p. 57.

[154] See "Les Commissions entendront officiellement des déleguées interalliées," *La Française*, n° 497 (22 March 1919), 1.

also included women leaders from Great Britain, the United States, Belgium, and Italy.[155] No discussion with the commissioners was allowed. Their visit made front-page news in Paris and was heralded by Madame Jules Siegfried as "a red letter day in the history of the feminist movement."[156] Apparently their visit was successful; the following week, *La Française* announced that "many of the resolutions they had presented" were taken into consideration and adopted in part in the Charter of Labor prepared by the Commission.

In the meantime, the president of the ICW, Lady Aberdeen had arrived in Paris and joined Siegfried and Avril de Sainte-Croix in the Allied women's delegations that called on the most powerful men at the Peace Conference, Vittorio Emanuele Orlando (the Italian prime minister), General Jan Smuts from South Africa, and Lord Robert Cecil of Great Britain. They also paid a call on the president of the peace conference, the French prime minister Georges Clemenceau, who agreed that women "should have their place, the same as men, in the permanent commissions that would be named." He did, however, think that women's voices were most important in those areas of "touching the family, work, hygiene, etc."[157]

On the 10th of April 1919 another equally impressive joint delegation of women's rights advocates testified before the Commission on the League of Nations, chaired by President Wilson. The resolutions and speeches in support covered various areas: morals, education, hygiene, and finally disarmament. The eloquence of the feminists on that day (the transcript of the resolutions and speeches was published in *La Française* by Marie-Louise Puech) spoke to the right of self-determination, for individuals as well as peoples; to hopes for civilization as opposed to barbarism, for recognition of the principle of women's right to suffrage, and an end to the "waste" of arms races (not surprisingly, many of these themes are still under discussion today). The speeches by the French delegates, Mme Avril

---

[155] The full list of names in the Allied women's delegation is provided in Suzanne Grinberg's coverage, both "Les Démarches de la Conférence suffragiste interalliée," in *La Française*, n° 498 (29 March 1919), 1, and in her article in *La Renaissance*, pt. 2 (26 April 1919), 10. The texts of the resolutions conveyed to the commission by Duchêne, Avril de Sainte-Croix (ICW), and Brunschvicg (Conference of Allied Women's Suffragists) at this hearing are published in International Labour Office, *The International Protection of Women Workers. Studies and Reports, Series I*, n° 1 (15 October 1921), pp. 4–7.

[156] As cited in the commission proceedings, republished in *The Origins of the International Labor Organization*, ed. James T. Shotwell. 2 vols. (New York: Columbia University Press, 1934), vol. 2, p. 275.

[157] "Visites aux Plénipotentiaires de la Paix," *La Française*, n° 499 (5 April 1919), 1.

de Sainte-Croix, Suzanne Grinberg, and Dr. Girard-Mangin, were inspiring as well as to the point. Other French feminists present at this hearing, but not speaking, included Cécile Brunschvicg, Marie-Louise Puech, and Maria Vérone.[158] The resolutions on suffrage did not neglect to invoke, in conclusion, the oft-repeated observation that "the position of women has always been recognized as being the criterion of the degree of civilization," adding to that "and the liberalism of States." According to the subsequent account published by Vérone, the delegation asked that no nation be admitted to the League of Nations unless its leaders agreed to the following points: 1) "to prohibit the sale of women and children; 2) to respect women's right to self-determination, and thus to forbid any sale of women or children in view of marriage; and 3) to repress severely and prosecute the traffic in adult or minor women and children for purposes of prostitution."[159] These feminists had become all too aware of the fact that even if the so-called civilized nations did not officially sanction these practices, that in other lands religion and custom still upheld them unconditionally. They spoke in the name of the self-determination of individuals, which they considered as important as the self-determination of nations.[160] The pitch was perfect, not only for the Wilsonians but also for the French audience, as these women, a few recently enfranchised and most others still seeking the vote, clearly recognized.[161] In his response, after praising the delegation for the excellence and pertinence of their presentations, Wilson delivered some good news, which was that in the project for the League, women and men would be put on the same footing and that in referenda on national self-determination women as well as men were being authorized to vote. More than that he couldn't promise at the moment.

Following the 10th of April interview with the Commission, Maria Vérone of the LFDF sent President Wilson a letter to in which she argued for a worldwide Women's Charter.[162]

---

[158] See the extended report of this meeting by M.-L. Puech, "Le Conseil international des Femmes et la Conférence des femmes suffragistes reçues par la Commission de la Société des Nations," *La Française*, n° 501 (26 April 1919), 1–2.

[159] Cited by Maria Vérone, in her account of the 10 April meeting in *Le Droit des Femmes* (April 1919), 58.

[160] See Maria Vérone's articles "A la Conférence de la Paix," "Memorandum," and "Au Comité de la Ligue des Nations," all in the April 1919 issue of *Le Droit des Femmes*, and "Les Femmes et la Ligue des Nations," in the May issue.

[161] The entire story is admirably recounted by Suzanne Grinberg in her articles in *La Renaissance politique, littéraire, économique* (29 March 1919), 20–23, and (26 April 1919), 9–12.

[162] "A Monsieur le Président," letter signed by Maria Vérone, as president of the LFDF. Reproduced in *Le Droit des Femmes* (April 1919), 58–59; quote, 58.

The entire civilized world has been unanimous in protesting against the atrocities committed by the central empires during the war, but is it tolerable that in peacetime, millions of women and children should still be considered as livestock, and sold, whether into labor, or into prostitution, or in view of marriage? Slavery, abolished in principle, has been maintained when it comes to these women, these children, in whose name we raise our voices today, because it is impossible for them to make themselves heard.

The Allied leaders did deliver on some of the feminists' demands. In the final version of the Treaty of Versailles (Preamble and Articles 389 and 427) we find certain provisions for equal rights, notably equal pay for equal work. It made specific provision for the inclusion of women in the work of the International Labour Organisation (ILO) and the League of Nations itself.[163] Once the League of Nations began to function, it did begin to address the issues of particular interest to the feminists, notably the international traffic in women and children for purposes of prostitution, the adverse international implications of national marriage laws that forced women who married foreigners to give up their citizenship for that of their husbands, and the treatment of women in the League's mandate states and in international concessions. Assuring women's presence and participation in the League, either as governmental delegates or experts, on committees, and as ranking staff members would be a continuing challenge throughout the 1920s.[164]

The French women had done an outsize job as citizens of the world; it was now time for them to turn back to their own country. Even as they struggled for women's suffrage at home, women in other countries – including (much to the great chagrin of the French feminists) the defeated countries of Germany and Austria – had obtained the vote. In the interim, the French Senate had voted affirmatively on measures designed to outlaw abortion and to punish neo-Malthusian propaganda, in the interests of combatting depopulation.[165]

While the suffragists had been busy lobbying the peace conference, their male allies in the Chamber of Deputies had continued their work for women's suffrage. In March, the stalwart feminist deputy Louis Andrieux,

---

[163] For the text of the Treaty of Versailles, see *Major Peace Treaties of Modern History, 1648–1967*, ed. Fred L. Israel, vol. 2 (New York: Chelsea House, 1967). It can also be easily accessed online.

[164] See the annual volumes compiled by D. M. Northcroft, *Women at Work in the League of Nations* (London: Page & Pratt, 1923) and subsequently; I have seen a 4th ed., 1926. These provide lists and potted biographies of women who had any kind of official appointments at the League.

[165] See the article by Pauline Rebour, in *La Française*, n° 499 (5 April 1919).

deposed a report in which he ridiculed the restrictions embedded in the Flandin report's recommended text, especially the clause that set the voting age at 30, and mocked the men's fear of being outnumbered. He then called for the removal of such restrictions and the granting of full suffrage.[166] In mid-May the CNFF, with five other associations (LFDF, *Amélioration*; *Droit Humain*, UFF, and the UFSF), distributed a straight-shooting, no nonsense propaganda poster/flier "*La Femme Doit Voter.*"[167] It headlined seven points: "It is her right; it is her duty; it is in her interest; it is in the interest of the family; it is in the interest of society; it is in the interest of the race; it is in the interest of *la Patrie.*" The poster makes the point that women are now voting in nine European countries, plus the United States, Canada, Australia, and New Zealand. It concludes by proclaiming that French women want to vote in 1919 – that is, in the upcoming elections. Every week in *La Française*, Juliette François-Raspail would keep readers informed of developments in the Chamber of Deputies.[168] Readers should be reminded that even in the United States, the campaign for the federal constitutional amendment that would enfranchise all women, was still underway; this is doubtless why the president of the IWSA, Carrie Chapman Catt, who was also orchestrating the American campaign, could not come to Paris for the peace negotiations. However, Margery Corbett Ashby, who would succeed Catt as international president, was there in her stead.[169]

Historians Steven Hause and Anne Kenney have detailed the progression and complexity of the various women's suffrage proposals in the Chamber of Deputies during 1919; only after the Chamber had authorized proportional representation over the individual vote did the deputies finally agree to discuss the Flandin report and the various proposed amendments concerning women's vote. Nothing new was added to the arguments for and against, but each speaker vehemently and eloquently stated his position.[170] Finally, after the Treaty of Versailles had been

[166] See "Vers le suffrage des femmes," *La Française*, n° 497 (22 March 1919), 2.

[167] This poster/flier is reproduced in *La Française*, n° 504 (17 May 1919), 1. I also consulted a copy in the *Archives du Féminisme* (Angers), in 1 AF 232.

[168] See *La Française*, n° 504 (17 May 1919) & n° 505 (24 May 1919).

[169] See Jacqueline Van Voris, *Carrie Chapman Catt: A Public Life* (New York: The Feminist Press, 1987), chapters 15 & 16.

[170] See Suzanne Grinberg, *Historique du mouvement suffragiste depuis 1848* (Paris: H. Goulet, 1926), esp. part II, for an extended account of the parliamentary debates, and André Leclère, *Le Vote des femmes en France; les causes de l'attitude particulière à notre pays* (Paris: M. Rivière, 1929), part II, pp. 129–213 for developments to 1929. A short, good English-language account of the situation regarding suffrage by the mid-1930s is provided by Frances I. Clark, *The Position of Women in*

finalized in mid-May 1919 (though not yet signed; that would only happen on 28 June, the fifth anniversary of the assassination of the Austrian archduke in Sarajevo, the tragic event that had triggered the war) and after the French Chamber of Deputies had finally affirmed proportional representation, the deputies would hold their initial debate (8 May) on the women's suffrage bill as outlined in the Flandin report. A majority of the deputies would vote to take up discussion of the articles; this was already a breakthrough. The socialist deputy Bracke quickly proposed an amendment that would give women integral (unrestricted) suffrage. The next debate, on 15 May, was marked by the strenuous opposition of the deputy from Pas-de-Calais, Edmond Lefebve du Prey, father of thirteen children who (he said) had all been breastfed by his wife, who made an eloquent, if truly rear-guard plea for the *femme au foyer*. On the 19th of May, writing in *L'Humanité*, suffragist advocate Cécile Brunschvicg depicted the woman suffrage question in terms of national honor: "It is humiliating to think that we are Frenchwomen, daughters of the land of the Revolution, and that in the year of grace 1919 we are still reduced to demanding the 'rights of woman'."[171]

On the 20th of May, thanks to a last minute counterproposal to the more cautious municipal suffrage bill put forward by the chamber's committee on suffrage (and to powerful speeches by the long-time suffrage advocate and now former prime minister René Viviani as well as Aristide Briand), the Chamber of Deputies voted by a margin of 344 to 97 to

---

Contemporary France (London: P.S. King, 1937; reprinted Westport: Hyperion Press, 1981), pp. 241–251.

   The first detailed scholarly analysis of the Senate's opposition is Hause, with Kenney, *Women's Suffrage and Social Politics*, pp. 221–229. Paul Smith, in *Feminism and the Third Republic: Women's Political and Civil Rights in France 1918–1940* (Oxford, UK: Clarendon Press, 1999), pp. 106–116, does discuss developments between 1919 and 1922, underscoring the fact that the membership of the Senate Commission on Women's Suffrage became heavily stacked against granting women's suffrage in any form. Bouglé-Moalic, *Vote des Françaises*, pp. 220–222, stresses the importance of the Chamber's vote of 20 May and, through her study of its reception in the press, suggests that indeed the tide of public opinion, both nationally and internationally, was turning in favor of women's voting, and that the causes of its later failure in France should be sought in the subsequent period. This author, however, does not closely examine the dynamics of the years between May 1919 and the Senate vote in 1922, nor does Bard in *Filles de Marianne*. A recent article by Anne Verjus dissects and compares the votes in the Chamber and in the Senate, noting how both deputies and senators shared what she calls a "*sexualiste*" discourse (which is certainly true), but she disputes Hause & Kenney's suggestion that the 1919 vote in the Chamber may have been cynical. See Anne Verjus, "Entre principes et pragmatisme; députés et sénateurs dans les premiers débats sur le suffrage des femmes en France (1919–1922)," *Politix*, vol. 13, n° 51 (2000), 55–80. Online, through Persee.fr.

[171]   Cécile Brunschvicg, "Les Femmes et le suffrage," *L'Humanité* (19 May 1919).

approve unrestricted woman suffrage and eligibility.[172] Without mentioning women at all, the new wording indicated that "the laws and regulations
on voting and eligibility to all elected assemblies are applicable to all
French citizens without distinction of sex."[173] It was a huge victory! In
L'Humanité, Marcel Cachin hailed the vote as a victory for socialism:
"Thus is crowned with success the campaign to which our socialist party
has consecrated itself, without pause and almost alone, and for many
years."[174] Cachin reminded readers of the fact that women were now a
majority, and that most of them were working women who must be
recruited to the socialist cause. In *La Française*, Jane Misme described
the 20th of May as "the 4th of August for the privilege of sex," referring to
the revolutionary night in 1789 when the First and Second Estates gave up
their privileges.[175] For Marguerite de Witt-Schlumberger, "The date of
20 May 1919 will remain engraved in our annals and in our hearts by a
sentiment of profound joy." But, she cautioned, there was much work to
do to get the Senate to approve as well, and she urged women to write to
the senators from their departments to urge them to support integral
suffrage.[176] Juliette François-Raspail, covering the triumphal session, cautioned: "We have won the first round, *Mesdames*, but there is another
Bastille to conquer."[177] The following day, in Washington, D.C., the U.S.
House of Representatives approved the constitutional amendment on
women's suffrage by a vote of 304 to 89.[178] The French had gotten there
before the Americans, and by a bigger margin! Both still faced a hurdle in
their respective senates, but the French Senate would present the bigger
challenge.

---

[172] "La Chambre accorde aux femmes le droit de voter et d'être élues," *Le Matin* (21 May 1919). This
unsigned and noncommittal article provides extensive coverage of the speeches by Viviani and
Briand. "La Chambre vote le Suffrage intégral des Femmes," *La Française*, n° 505 (25 May 1919), 1.
This issue and subsequent issues detailed the debates in the Chamber of Deputies. For the official
version, see *Annales, Chambre des Députés, Législature II, session ordinaire 1919*, pt. 2, Sessions of 8
May, 15 May, 20 May 1919.

[173] Grinberg, *Historique*, pp. 144–145, provides the new text with the wording that the Chamber
approved: "Les lois et dispositions réglementaires sur l'électorat et l'éligibilité à toutes assemblées
élues sont applicables à tous les citoyens français sans distinction de sexe."

[174] Marcel Cachin, "Le Vote des Femmes," *L'Humanité* (22 May 1919).

[175] Jane Misme, "Le Sénat sera-t-il à la hauteur de la Chambre?" *La Française*, n° 506 (31 May 1919).

[176] Marguerite de Witt-Schlumberger, "Trois-cent-quatre-vingt contre quatre-vingt-dix-sept," *La
Française*, n° 506 (31 May 1919), front page.

[177] Juliette François-Raspail, "La Séance du Vingt Mai," *La Française*, n° 506 (31 May 1919).

[178] Van Voris, *Carrie Chapman Catt*, p. 154. The Nineteenth Amendment for women's suffrage had to be
ratified by the states; it finally triumphed (but only by one vote in Tennessee) in August 1920.

Six of the major women's rights associations (the CNFF, UFSF, LFDF, UFF, *Amélioration,* and *Droit Humain*) quickly issued a joint communiqué to all the senators:[179]

> The Chamber has understood that the daughters of the French Republic should not and cannot be put in the same class as minors, criminals, and the incompetent. She [the Chamber] has understood our humiliation in face of the women of the entire world who, almost all, now have the vote, while our country seems still to lack confidence in us.... We are certain that all true Democrats are on our side.

They pulled out all the stops, rhetorically and politically, working throughout the summer and into the fall to bolster support in the Senate.

As before, debates and public opinion surveys would continue in the press over whether or not women should vote, or whether or not they really wanted to vote, or whether or not it was a good idea in the first place. Some leading Frenchmen remained skeptical, as for example the editor of *Le Matin*, Stéphane Lauzanne, who had been quoted the previous year in the *New York Times Magazine*: "Woman suffrage will not come in France in the immediate future because the women do not want it. There is no demand for the vote by Frenchwomen. The women will be a power in French political life, but they will prefer to exercise it through their husbands and in their social life, rather than through the coarse medium of the ballot box."[180] Here we find a restatement of the old argument about women's covert influence. Other men took a different position. In the interim, according to the press, the Senate tried to figure out how to handle the question.

In October 1919, pope Benedict XV issued a veiled endorsement of women's suffrage, which would propel the Catholic suffrage supporters into high gear, leading to the founding in 1920 of the *Union National pour le Vote des Femmes* (UNVF) and a reinvigorated Catholic suffrage campaign.[181] This development, which was perhaps not entirely coincidental, given that the French parliamentary elections had finally been scheduled for November (on the 16th and 30th), immediately reinvigorated the fears of the anticlerical Radical republicans in the Senate about the ostensible

---

[179] "Les Sociétés féministes aux Sénateurs," *La Française*, n° 506 (31 May 1919).

[180] Quoted in William S. Crawford, "A Changed World for the Women of France (an interview with Stéphane Lauzanne, ed. of Le Matin)," *New York Times Magazine*, 23 June 1918, 4–5.

[181] The papal endorsement of women's suffrage is generally attributed to the message of Benedict XV to the head of the Catholic Women's Union of Italy, "Sono avventurati," published in French as "Allocution sur la mission de la femme dans la société (21 October 1919)," in *Actes de Benoit XV*, 3 vols. (Paris: Bonne Presse, 1924–1934), vol. 2, pp. 68–72.

clerical menace. Even so, in early 1920 the venerable republican demographer and pronatalist advocate Jacques Bertillon (who years earlier had denied that women had anything to do with the declining birth rate) would actually take the side of the suffragists, insisting that the women's vote would be necessary to refocus candidates' platforms on family protection issues and on the campaign against alcoholism and debauchery; he was particularly impressed with the importance of women's vote in other countries for resolving the problem of (male) alcoholism.[182]

On 3 October 1919, the Senate *rapporteur*, Alexandre Bérard, deposed his report on the Chamber's *proposition de loi* plus two other proposals by senators, and he rolled out the clerical menace to the Republic at full volume, dismissing sarcastically the suffragists and their intense efforts as "the isolated opinions of small groups nearly all of whom are enclosed in the boundaries in Paris," and – as Suzanne Grinberg pointed out – ignoring the resolutions of the many departmental and municipal councils throughout France who had come out in favor of women's voting. "We do not want to seal the tombstone of the Republic," Bérard threatened, also making a big issue of the "surplus" of several million women in France, who, following the war, outnumbered the men even more than before. This, of course, was calculated to evoke an age-old male fear of what would happen to men in a numerically topsy-turvy world, in this case a political democracy in which they were no longer in control. Such fearmongering arguments as these would deliver the kiss of death to women's voting in the near future.

Several days later (7 October) the Chamber passed a resolution, formulated by the socialist deputy Bracke, urging the Senate to get on with consideration of the bill. It was clear to these deputies what the suffragists stood for, and they were fed up with the Senate's stalling on the vote; in the meantime they passed a resolution complementing women on their "conduct" during the war.[183] On 8 November, the UFSF organized a massive rally where they restated their arguments and endorsed candidates for the deputation who had come out for women's suffrage.[184]

It was clear that the senators were stalling – and would continue to stall well after the November elections for the Chamber of Deputies, at which time voters returned (using the new system of lists and proportional

---

[182] Jacques Bertillon, "Un essai de vote féminin," *La Femme et l'Enfant*, n° 31 (15 January 1920), 745. See also "Vote féminin - vote familial," in n° 25 (15 October 1919), 555–556.

[183] See *La Française*, n° 515 (25 October 1919), and "Protestation contre le Sénat," in *Le Droit des Femmes* (May 1919), 198.

[184] See *La Française*, n°s 519 (November 1919) and 520 (December 1919).

representation) an extremely conservative, fiercely nationalist legislature. It was then clear that the earlier Chamber's enthusiastic support for "universal" women's suffrage was not going to transfer itself to the Senate, either in its old incarnation or in its new one. *La Française* would counter by ridiculing Berard's "Fourteen Points," but it was clear that the new Senate, like its predecessor, was not going to act.[185]

Political analyst Odile Rudelle blames the French prime minister Georges Clemenceau's refusal to demand priority ["*urgence*"] in the Senate for the delay and ultimate failure of women's suffrage in 1919. Rudelle admits, however, that this point was never really brought up at the time. Nor does she mention the fact that during the women's campaign to be heard by the Peace Conference in the spring, Clemenceau had publicly affirmed his support of municipal suffrage. But the Chamber's decision to support full suffrage and eligibility for women undoubtedly went well beyond what the sitting prime minister, who had privately objected earlier to the notion of women voting, could easily tolerate.[186]

Clemenceau clearly had other issues on his mind. Already in October 1919, in a speech to the Senate in which he urged ratification of the Treaty of Versailles, Clemenceau sketched his concerns about France's future in the postwar world:[187]

---

[185] See *La Française*, n° 520 (20 December 1919), front page.

[186] See Odile Rudelle, "Le vote des femmes et la fin de 'l'exception française'," in *Vingtième Siècle: Revue d'Histoire*, n° 42 (April–June 1994), 52–65, and Léon Abensour, *Clemenceau intime* (Paris: Radot, 1928), pp. 145–146. A student of feminism himself and from 1909 to 1912 a part-time research assistant to Clemenceau, Abensour reported trying – in vain – to encourage the "Tiger" to support woman suffrage. He reported that Clemenceau was not feminist; he was even violently hostile to any efforts on behalf of women's emancipation. The former prime minister did have a soft spot for chorus girls and actresses, but as for women in politics, that was out of the question. When the young man continued to bring up the topic, he reports Clemenceau as responding, not very nicely: "Don't bother me with your women's suffrage." But Abensour admits that nowhere in Clemenceau's writings or speeches can one find him expressing such an opinion, and according to Rudelle, his biographers have ignored the issue entirely. This is not exactly the case. The delegation from the Inter-Allied Women's Conference in February 1919 (including Mmes Witt-Schlumberger, Compain, and Brunschvicg) called on Clemenceau to get his support for including women in the commissions that were drafting various portions of the peace treaty; he agreed to carry their request forward himself, but when asked his view about women's suffrage in France, he said that he was completely in favor of municipal suffrage for women but not an advocate of the political vote. See S. G., "Une première victoire: Réception chez M. Clemenceau," *La Française*, n° 493 (22 February 1919), 1. Shortly thereafter (19 February) an attempt was made on Clemenceau's life – not, however, by suffragists. The next issue of *La Française*, n° 494 (1 March 1919), published its expression of regret, condemnation of the attack, and best wishes for a quick recovery.

[187] Georges Clemenceau, in the French Senate, 12 October 1919. As quoted in Edouard Bonnefous, *Histoire Politique de la IIIe République*, vol. 3 (Paris: Presses Universitaires de France, 1968), p. 58. Also quoted in Cova, *Maternité et droits des femmes*, p. 233.

The Treaty doesn't say that France engages itself to have many children, but that is the first thing that should have been included. For if France turns its back on large families, you could jolly well put the most beautiful clauses you want in the treaties, you could jolly well take all the cannons in Germany, you could jolly well do whatever you please, but France would be lost because there would be no more Frenchmen.

Clemenceau's message was not lost on members of the pronatalist and profamily associations. Or, as it turned out, on the French legislature. In late October, just prior to the upcoming legislative elections, a new law came into existence, endorsed by the Chamber on 28 August and seconded by the Senate in October, which provided a financial benefit from the State to mothers who nursed their own babies.[188]

In early 1920 the new French legislature, since the elections of November 1919 under the control of the Right, decided to act with regard to the birth rate problem. What could the legislators actually do? Their first line of defense was to legislate – in this case, against abortion and against the projects of the birth-controllers. What, indeed, could the council of ministers actually do? They found several possibilities for action.

On 20 January 1920 the new Millerand government (replacing the Clemenceau war ministry) took office, under a newly elected president of the Republic, Paul Deschanel. One of its first acts was to establish a Ministry of Hygiene, Assistance and Social Insurance [*Ministère de l'Hygiène, de l'Assistance et de la Prévoyance Sociales*], and to appoint the pronatalist deputy Jules-Louis Breton to run it. Promptly thereafter, by a decree issued on 27 January 1920, the government would establish a *Conseil Supérieur de la Natalité* (CSN). This was not exactly what Dr. Clotilde Mulon had in mind when she proposed the previous October that such a body could lead to a proper Ministry of Maternity.[189] More attention, she indicated, should be given to keeping babies alive via the science of child-raising [*puériculture*]. The new government did appoint two women to the CSN – Marguerite de Witt-Schlumberger of the UFSF and CNFF and Marie-Louise Bérot-Berger from the UFF.[190] What steps would this new body take, both to satisfy the earlier demands of the feminists and those of the pronatalists?

---

[188] This was known as the Law of 24 October 1919; see Cova, *Maternité et droits des femmes*, pp. 246–247.

[189] See Dr. Clotilde Mulon, "Pour repeupler la France il faut restaurer le culte de l'enfant," *La Française*, n° 513 (11 October 1919), 1. Mulon was reporting on the Congress on Natality, which had recently taken place in Nancy, under the auspices of the Nancy Chamber of Commerce.

[190] See Cova, *Maternité et droits des femmes*, p. 250. Cova expresses surprise that no woman doctor, such as Clotilde Mulon, was appointed to this higher council.

Under Alexandre Millerand's two cabinets (prior to his election as president of the republic in September 1920), several symbolic steps were taken. According to one authoritative source, the Ministry of the Interior decreed the celebration of Mother's Day on 9 May, and shortly thereafter a decree of the Ministry of Hygiene, etc., issued on 28 May 1920, established medals for motherhood.[191] This Mother's Day [*La Fête des Mères*] would turn into a Festival for Large Families; an actual Mother's Day would not become an official government-endorsed celebration until 1926.[192] In "honor" of this event, Nelly Roussel, writing in *La Voix des Femmes*, called for a birth strike![193]

> No more babies! until our maternal labor, facilitated, reimbursed, honored, has ceased to be a cause of inferiority, of dependence, of physical and social collapse for us. No more babies, until we can be certain that we are not laboring and suffering in order to fertilize battlefields; and until, by our direct participation in public affairs, we can assure ourselves of lasting Peace.

As for the medals, Nelly Roussel commended Breton for at least thinking of the women who are the mothers, although she objected to the provision that these medals could only be awarded to mothers of "legitimate" children.[194]

An even more dramatic action took place in the legislature in July 1920. As we have seen, the Senate's Cazeneuve report to repress abortion had been under discussion since 1918. It was taken up again in 1919 and passed on 28 January 1919, providing heavy penalties (both monetary and prison terms) for abortion, but (despite a favorable report) it did not meet with the approval of the Chamber in October 1919. In 1920, however, a new proposal would pass the Chamber on 23 July by an astounding majority of 521 to 55; the Senate approved this version on 29 July, and it became law on 31 July. This law, passed just before the legislature adjourned for summer break, can only be described as draconian in its crackdown on advocating, propagandizing for, or supplying materials that would make abortion – or contraception – possible. It authorized stiff penalties for advocating

---

[191] See Robert Talmy, *Histoire du mouvement familial en France (1896–1939)* (Paris: Aubenas, 1962), vol. 2, pp. 10–14; the decree establishing medals for motherhood is translated in Bell & Offen, *Women, the Family, and Freedom*, vol. 2, doc. 84 pp. 308–309.

[192] On the story of Mothers' Day, see Cova, *Maternité et droits des femmes*, p. 253.

[193] Nelly Roussel, "La Journée des Mères de Familles Nombreuses," *La Voix des Femmes* (6 May 1920); reprinted in *Derniers Combats* (Paris: 1932), pp. 106–109.

[194] Nelly Roussel, "La Médaille des Mères," *La Voix des Femmes* (3 June 1920); reprinted in *Derniers Combats*, pp. 110–113.

abortion or abetting it in any way (Articles 1 & 2); or for conveying or teaching information that would prevent pregnancy (Article 3).[195] Only Dr. Pinard stood firmly against it, insisting (with the CNFF) that "mothers must be given everything they need to have when they accomplish the function that, only, can assure the future of the nation."[196]

Critics quickly baptized this law of 31 July 1920 as the "Loi Scélérate" (the wicked, villanous law). "Wicked law or law of public safety, according to its adversaries or its partisans, it is one of the most repressive European legislative acts," concluded historian Anne Cova.[197] (In 1923 another law promulgated on 27 March, amending the notorious Article 317, would change the jurisdiction for abortion trials from the criminal courts [Assizes] to the correctional courts, in order to shut down lenient juries.) Little had been done, in the meantime, to improve the conditions for maternity, as the mainstream feminists had demanded prior to the war. And given the fact that women could not yet vote, they could not do much about it except to complain bitterly. What women did do, however, was to not comply with the pronatalist offensive. The birth rate would continue to drop, as the work of Françoise Thébaud on maternity in France during the interwar period has made clear.[198] Had potential mothers been moved by Nelly Roussel's words? Or were they simply making their own choices within the socioeconomic circumstances in which they found themselves?

Both socialists and the more radical feminists were outraged by the 1920 law. L'Humanité published two scathing editorials following promulgation of the law, one by Anatole Sixte-Quenin (a former socialist deputy), which argued that in the eyes of this new law, almost every Frenchman was a criminal, and Louise Bodin attacked "the justice of men."[199] The columnists of La Française kept silent. Some months earlier, however, it had announced the birth of a son, her fourth child, to the UFSF secretary-general, Cécile Brunschvicg, and her husband, the philosophy professor

---

[195] For an English translation of the law of 31 July 1920, see WFF, vol. 2, doc. 85, pp. 309–310; from Roger-Henri Guerrand, La Libre Maternité (Tournai: Casterman, 1971), pp. 149–150. The debates are summarized in several works: Roger-Henri Guerrand & Francis Ronsin, Le Sexe apprivoisé: Jeanne Humbert et la lutte pour le contrôle des naissances (Paris: Éditions La Decouverte, 1990), chapter 5; Bard, Filles de Marianne, pp. 209–215; & Anne Cova, Féminismes et Néo-malthusianismes sous la IIIe République: "La liberté de la maternité" (Paris: L'Harmattan, 2011), chapter 3.
[196] Pinard quoted by Cova in Féminismes et néo-malthusianismes, p. 138; from the Annales de la Chambre des Députés, 2ᵉ séance du 12 janvier 1923, p. 45.
[197] Cova, Maternité et droits des femmes, p. 255.
[198] See Françoise Thébaud, Quand nos grand-mères donnaient la vie: La maternité en France dans l'entre-deux-guerres (Lyon: Presses Universitaires de Lyon, 1986), esp. p. 26.
[199] See Sixte-Quenin, "Les Français sont-ils presque tous des criminels?" and Louise Bodin, "La Justice des Hommes," both in L'Humanité (9 August 1920), front page.

Léon Brunschvicg. It seems that the Brunschvicgs had taken seriously the mission of repopulation – a salient fact that is not mentioned in Brunschvicg's recent biography.

It seemed as though the roof was caving in on efforts to emancipate French women. The backlash was fierce and it would continue to accelerate. The aftermath of the war was indeed terrible in many ways, but this was one of its overlooked features. In December 1920 a group of Catholic notables (men) drafted a *"Déclaration des Droits de la Famille,"* which was adopted at their first Congress on the Family. It began as follows: "The family, founded upon marriage and hierarchically constituted under paternal authority, has as its goal to transmit, to uphold, to develop, and to perpetuate human life. To this end it has at its disposal rights that are irrevocable, anterior to and superior to all positive law." Its intent was to reassert patriarchal authority over the other members of the family – namely the wife and children – even advocating the weighting of a father's vote according to the number of his minor children.[200]

Throughout these debates and the aggressive antifeminist legislation, the women of the CNFF and the UFSF continued to stand up for the right of all women to combine paid work with motherhood, a right that would increasingly be threatened. The feminists would defend a woman's right to work, including the right of women who were – or about to be – mothers.[201]

Despite the venerable socialist Jules Guesde's proposal (in the Chamber in January 1920) for complete equal rights for women, progress in answering the woman question in France had been derailed for the time being. Two-thirds of the French Senate was renewed on 11 January 1920, but even these elections did not give the proponents of women's vote a majority. After delaying for three years, on 21 November 1922, the new Senate would vote *against* proceeding to discussion on the women's suffrage bill, thus inaugurating a pattern of repeated Chamber passage and Senate refusal that would plague suffragists throughout the duration of the Third Republic. Even the presence of a new senator, the once eloquent champion of women's vote, René Viviani, longtime member and honorary president of the LFDF, wartime prime minister, could not deflect this resurgent backlash, which would continue, through the disenchanted 1930s, and beyond the cataclysmic French defeat in 1940.

---

[200] "Déclaration des Droits de la Famille" (December 1920); in English as doc. 88, *WFF*, vol. 2, p. 317.
[201] Anne Cova makes a point of this in her study of motherhood and rights in France, and my reading of the sources concurs with hers.

"Long live the Republic, in spite of everything" ["*Vive la République, quand même!*"] proclaimed Maria Vérone when in 1922 the Senate refused to discuss the women's suffrage report. She and her colleagues would doggedly continue to press for Senate action. But victory would not be forthcoming in her lifetime. It was not "the Republic" but a particular coterie of resistant republican senators who blocked the way. Generally, the blame has been placed on the senators' fear of a clerical vote, but there were many other contributing factors. Undoubtedly the fact that in postwar France adult women far outnumbered adult men and that the population issue was far from resolved must have weighed heavily in the thinking of those senators who consciously denied women access to political and economic decision-making authority in what were indisputably troubled times. But it was also the case that it was precisely those European republics that had early on enfranchised all men in the name of democracy – namely France and Switzerland – that women found it the most difficult to attain full citizenship. Even in the United States, the campaign for women's rights that also began in 1848 did not succeed until 1920, when the federal constitutional amendment passed by both houses of Congress was finally ratified by a two-thirds majority of the states.

Women's suffrage in France became a reality in 1944; it was ultimately a gift of the Liberation and General Charles de Gaulle, not of the French parliament. Few would have dreamed in 1900, much less in 1919, that it would take so long. Or that the Civil Code's provisions on marriage would not be rewritten or women's reproductive freedom sanctioned before the 1960s and 1970s. Why, indeed, did it take so long?

CHAPTER 15

"Half the Human Race"
Epilogue and Conclusions

In November 1920, the Third Republic celebrated its fiftieth anniversary. On that occasion, the secretary-general of the *Conseil National des Femmes Françaises* (CNFF), Ghénia Avril de Sainte-Croix (who, along with Cécile Brunschvicg, had just been awarded the medal of the *Légion d'Honneur* by the French government) published an editorial entitled "Women and the Republic," in which she expressed her annoyance that women had not been included on the official program for the ceremonies (which included interment of the "unknown soldier" at the Arc de Triomphe). Taking a historical perspective on women's support for the Republic, and the support for women's rights by a sizeable contingent of eminent French male republicans, she asserted that:[1]

> Women, and more particularly those who desire the emancipation of woman in the highest meaning of this word, do not forget that it was ardent republicans who, since before the Revolution, would present their demands and defend their rights. From Condorcet, reclaiming the equality of the sexes in unforgettable terms: "Among the advances in the progress of the human mind that will contribute most to the general happiness, we must count the thorough destruction of the prejudices that have established an inequality of rights between the two sexes, an inequality deadly even to the party it seeks to favor," to Viviani, Briand, Jules Siegfried, Doizy, Merlin, Flandin, Bracke, demanding women's right to vote in the Chamber of Deputies, with only a few exceptions, all those who championed our cause were the enthusiastic defenders of the republican regime.

[1] G. Avril de Sainte-Croix, "Les Femmes et la République," *La Française*, n° 529 (11 November 1920). The quote she provides from Condorcet is from his *Esquisse d'un Tableau historique des progrès de l'esprit humain* (1795), ed. Monique & Francois Hincker (Paris, 1966), p. 274; the Victor Hugo quote, much invoked by feminists for the next century, comes from his 1853 funeral oration for Louise Jullien, one of the women activists exiled from France when the counterrevolutionaries crushed the 1848 revolution and abolished universal manhood suffrage. See Victor Hugo, "Sur la Tombe de Louise Jullien" (1853), *Oeuvres complètes de Victor Hugo* (Paris: Éditions Hetzel-Quantin, 1880–1889), vol. 44, p. 92. The translations are mine. The same 11 November issue of *La Française* announced the award of the cross of the *Légion d'Honneur* to Sainte-Croix and Brunschvicg.

And if one of them, one of the greatest, made a mistake when he prophesied that "The eighteenth century proclaimed the rights of man, the nineteenth will proclaim the right[s] of woman," [women] are nevertheless convinced that Victor Hugo was only off by one number and that the twentieth century will see the triumph of women's cause in France.

Mme Avril added, optimistically, that "women have sufficiently proved their attachment to France during these five years of war such that the Republic, in acquitting its debts of recognition, will take this into account." As it turned out, the acquitting of "debts" would take several decades longer.

However pragmatic and realistic the feminists' arguments for change, and however many times they repeated those arguments, the political possibilities in the quasi-counterrevolutionary postwar climate that marked the 1920s and 1930s would not allow their specific demands to advance very far. Yet persistent repetition has its advantages, as more and more French women and men would begin to consider the merit of the arguments and public support for women's rights would slowly but steadily increase. It is noteworthy that many of the same individuals who had been major participants in the woman question debates during the Belle Époque, such as Mme Avril, Mme Brunschvicg, and Maria Vérone, still held leadership positions well into the 1930s.[2]

In the 1920s, the mainstream French women's rights leaders would become extremely active in the international arena through the International Council of Women and the International Woman Suffrage Alliance, and particularly at the League of Nations, where they pursued issues that ranged from the campaign to stifle the traffic in women and children to the campaign for the right of married women to maintain their nationality of birth; ultimately they convinced the League to sponsor an investigation of the status of women worldwide.[3] The CNFF itself would look beyond the hexagon, organizing three sequential conferences which they called, following revolutionary precedent, the Estates General of Feminism [États-Généraux du Féminisme; 1929, 1930, and 1931], the last of which would focus squarely on colonial affairs and the situation of French and indigenous women in the colonies.[4] Maria Vérone and

---

[2] Among others, Paul Strauss, Dr. Sicard de Plauzeoles, Ghénia Avril de Sainte-Croix, Cécile Brunschvicg, Dr. Toulouse, Bracke, Jane Misme, and Maria Vérone.

[3] See my *European Feminisms, 1700–1950: A Political History* (Stanford, CA: Stanford University Press, 2000), chapter 11.

[4] See Régine Goutalier, "Les États Généraux du féminisme à l'Exposition coloniale, 30–31 mai 1931," *La Revue d'histoire moderne et contemporaine*, 36:2 (April–June 1989), 266–286.

France's other younger women lawyers (Yvonne Netter, Marcelle Kraemer-Bach) would activate an international women lawyers association.[5] Marcelle Legrand-Falco, who had worked closely with Mme Avril in the CNFF and on the issue of regulated prostitution and the traffic, would lead a *Union Temporaire contre la prostitution réglementée et le traffic des femmes*. Others, notably Gabrielle Duchêne, would engage in the 1930s in antifascist political activities at the international level, and another pacifist feminist, the war widow Camille Drevet, would serve as secretary-general of the Women's International League for Peace and Freedom, headquartered in Geneva.[6] Younger feminists would take advantage of the opportunities presented by the League of Nations and the international peace and antifascist organizations to channel their activism. New women's groups were being founded to press for specific issues, and even right-wing organizations such as the war veterans' organization, the *Croix de Feu*, would begin to encourage women's participation.[7]

Yet the political and economic climate of the 1920s and 1930s was unhospitable, to say the least.

The challenge was how to make major changes in the relations between the sexes happen in a society that was still suffering from the aftereffects of the trauma of war, aftereffects that included a pronounced political backlash, troubled economic times, the rise of antiparliamentary and authoritarian antirepublican movements, and deep divisions over religious and moral issues. Externally, in the 1920s the French would grapple with the tempting mirage of Communism (the example of the newly communist USSR, where radical reshaping of the institution of marriage and campaigns for the full employment of women loomed large), and in the 1930s would experience political stalemate in face of the threats to democracy in its neighboring nation-states – Fascism in Italy, Francoism in Spain (the Spanish Civil War), and Nazism in Germany, each of which was

---

[5] Sara Kimble is currently investigating "Transnational Networks for Legal Feminism," including the existence of an international association of women lawyers.

[6] See especially Siân Reynolds, *Alternative Policies: Women and Public Life in France between the Wars*, Stirling French Publications, n° 2 (Stirling, Scotland, 1993) and, more generally, Reynolds, *France Between the Wars: Gender and Politics* (London & New York: Routledge, 1996).

[7] See, for example, Kevin Passmore, "'Planting the Tricolor in the Citadels of Communism': Women's Social Action in the Croix de Feu and Parti Social Français," *Journal of Modern History*, 71:4 (December 1999), 814–851; Cheryl Koos & Daniella Sarnoff, "France," in *Women, Gender, and Fascism in Europe, 1919–1948*, ed. Kevin Passmore (Manchester: Manchester University Press, 2003), pp. 168–188; and Caroline Campbell, "Building a Movement, Dismantling the Republic: Women, Gender, and Political Extremism in the Croix de Feu / Parti Social Français, 1927–1940," *French Historical Studies*, 35:4 (Fall 2012), 691–726.

conspicuously antifeminist.[8] Even the left-wing Popular Front government under Léon Blum (1936–1937), with its commitment to appointing three female undersecretaries, could not muster the political support necessary among legislators to realize the political, economic, and social reforms that feminist leaders had been calling for since the nineteenth century.[9] The collapse of the Third Republic, the outbreak of a second world war, and the occupation of France by the Nazis would thwart efforts to emancipate French women, as the measures implemented by the Vichy regime would demonstrate.[10]

The obstructions became particularly visible not only with respect to the campaign for the vote, but also in the endless debates around the reform of the Civil Code, and the dogged resistance to change that continued through the 1930s and, indeed, well into the 1960s. Although the legislative committee charged (in 1926, with René Renoult as chair) with amending the Civil Code would report out in 1932, vocal opponents with entrenched convictions continued to block any effort to dismantle the Civil Code's authoritarian, hierarchical family model and the subordination of wives and mothers within it. A nonhierarchical partnership of the sexes still seemed a strange and unwelcome idea to these opponents, especially those who invoked Catholic doctrine on the subordination of women and the male breadwinner economic model, yet it was key to feminist demands in the French context. Here is what Cécile Brunschvicg, president of the UFSF, had to say on this subject in May 1933 (in conjunction with the French celebration of Mother's Day):[11]

> Some people in France are not afraid to assert that the development of women's role can only harm the family and they oppose what they call "the development of individualism" against the idea of the family.
>
> In reality we [feminists] do not share the same understanding of the family.
>
> For them, the family is a small group entirely dominated by the authority of the father. In exchange for the bread he wins, he has the right to command as a master to the servant-wife and to the children, in whom

---

[8] For the international context, see Offen, *European Feminisms,* part III: The Twentieth Century, chapters 10–12.

[9] The latest assessment of the Blum cabinet is Cécile Formaglio, *"Féministe d'abord": Cécile Brunschvicg (1877–1946)* (Rennes: Presses Universitaires de Rennes, 2014), chapter 10.

[10] See especially Sarah Fishman, *We Will Wait: Wives of French Prisoners of War, 1940-1945* (New Haven, CT: Yale University Press, 1991); Miranda Pollard, *Reign of Virtue: Mobilizing Gender in Vichy France* (Chicago: University of Chicago Press, 1998); and Hanna Diamond, *Women and the Second World War in France 1939–1948: Choices and Constraints* (London: Longman, 1999).

[11] Cécile Brunschvicg, "Mères, osez être!," *La Française,* n° 1067 (27 May 1933).

he seeks more to develop blind submission than to develop their personalities.

For us, on the contrary, the family is the union of two beings who share the same spiritual and intellectual ideal, who decide to give life to healthy and happy children. The common household is the source of energy, with the possibility to increase the radiance of each by the free development of his or her own faculties.

How is it possible not to understand that it is the perfectioning of the individual that will give birth to the most perfect family, and by what aberration can one oppose a healthy individualism to a healthy family.

How is it possible to dispute the logic of this quintessential statement of French feminist aspirations? The systematic identification of women as individuals of the female sex and as visibly "half the human race," asserted by Condorcet and many others since, seemed a statement of fact, a conclusive argument for liberty, equality, and justice in the relations between men and women.

Despite the negative arguments and efforts in the 1920s by Catholic neo-traditionalists to push through a "family vote" (in which wives and children would be only secondarily represented by husbands and fathers) or in the 1930s to propose that family allowances be paid to fathers rather than to mothers, and even the interventions in the 1930s of the Vatican on behalf of Catholic perceptions of the necessity for hierarchical male-female relations, it would become increasingly apparent that in France, women, and in particular married women, had to acquire legal and economic status as rights-bearing individuals, must be able to retain their nationality of birth (this was accorded in 1927), and that maternity – whether "legitimate" or out of wedlock, must be facilitated and protected.

After years of study and negotiation, in which women lawyers participated, some significant changes in the position of married women in French law did finally come about, with promulgation of the law of 18 February 1938. As one Parisian legal commentator, favorable to the changes, remarked, "the rules of the [1804] Code rested on assumptions [that were] no longer defensible." At last, married women gained full civil rights.[12] Nevertheless, the feminist attorneys who had pressed for broader

---

[12] There are many published commentaries on the Code, both before and after the 1938 changes concerning the effective civil emancipation of married women. See, notably, the feminist legal analyses of Maria Vérone, *La Femme et la loi* (Paris: Larousse, 1920) and Suzanne Grinberg & Odette Simon, *Les Droits nouveaux de la femme mariée, commentaire théorique et pratique de la loi du 18 février 1938* (Paris: Sirey, 1938). A good summary in English is A.-F.-P. Herchenroder, "The Capacity of Married Women in French Law," *Journal of Comparative Legislation and International*

changes were less than thrilled by the details of this outcome.[13] Their dissatisfaction focused on the infamous Article 213 that required wifely obedience in exchange for husbandly protection; the original wording was in fact removed, but the legislators, under pressure from Catholic interests, substituted another phrase that maintained the husband as "head of the family" – as opposed to an alternative phrase that would have stipulated equal responsibility of the spouses.

As for women's suffrage, the sparring would continue. Vitriolic arguments were used against giving women the vote in 1919, and even though they would continue to be heard, they would seem feebler, more repetitive, less convincing, and – to many – more ridiculous with every passing year.[14] As the politologue Odile Rudelle put it, the debates against women's voting in the French legislature from 1922 on offered "an anthology of stereotypes" [une florilège de stereotypes].[15] No new arguments would emerge – a claim confirmed by Cécile Formaglio in her excellent political biography of Cécile Brunschvicg.[16] The advocates of women's enfranchisement would continue to appeal, variously, to republican principles, to expediency and to the potential of women's special contributions as women, and through comparisons they would emphasize the sheer injustice – even humiliation – of French women being "behind" those of the rest of the civilized world. What would it take to break the logjam?

Despite the French defeat in 1940 at the hands of the Nazis and the retrograde family policies implemented by the Vichy regime of 1940–1944 (which have been studied in detail by feminist historians), women in France would ultimately obtain the vote as individuals in 1944–1945. One of the provisions of the ordinance of 21 April 1944 framed by the Consultative Assembly in Algiers, was to inscribe the enfranchisement of women on the same terms as men, that is, without conditions; the old "suffrage universal masculin" would be replaced by a "universal" suffrage

Law, 20:4 (1938), 196–203. For the later, most dramatic legal changes, see Dorothy McBride Stetson, Women's Rights in France (Westport, CT: Greenwood Press, 1987).

[13] See Françoise Blum & Janet Horne, "Féminisme et Musée Social (1916–1939)," Vie Sociale, 8–9 (August–September 1988), esp. pp. 351–360. These authors remind us that, over the objections of the Musée Social, Mme Pichon-Landry would reinvigorate its Section d'Études Féminines in 1936 precisely to promote the reform of the Civil Code. See also Sara L. Kimble, "Feminist Lawyers and Legal Reform in Modern France, 1900–1946," Women in Law and Lawmaking in Nineteenth and Twentieth-Century Europe, ed. Eva Schandevyl (Farnham, Surrey, UK: Ashgate, 2014), pp. 45–73.

[14] E.g., in the parliament alone, the notorious antifeminists included Edmond-Charles Lefebvre du Prey (député, Pas-de-Calais, 1909–1927), François Labrousse (sénateur, Corrèze, 1932–1945), Raymond Duplantier (sénateur, Vienne, 1920–1936).

[15] Rudelle, "Vote des femmes," p. 60.   [16] Formaglio, Cécile Brunschvicg, pp. 213–215.

that specifically included women. Historian Siân Reynolds has called for a rethinking of the historical significance of this decision, namely, how to get past the prevailing notion that General De Gaulle (or the Resistance) was personally and primarily responsible for "granting" women the vote.[17]

From the ruins of the occupation and the Resistance a new set of French institutions would emerge. The constitution of the Fourth Republic (1946) would enshrine equal rights for women, and these provisions would be incorporated also into the constitution of the Fifth Republic (1958). By the mid-1960s the reforms long advocated by the Third Republic's mainstream feminists would begin to be realized. Finally, in 1965, would come the final round of changes in the Civil Code concerning married women's property rights.

In the wake of these changes, French women would gain full access to educational and professional opportunities, as well as to physical and sporting activities that had earlier been denied them. They had already gained access to significant social services and economic benefits for mothers, but in the 1970s, most importantly, women gained legal access to modern contraceptive technology that would permit them to control their own fertility. Viewed in retrospect, one might argue that today French women and men are probably closer to achieving partnership and mutual respect than at any earlier time in history. "The Family" has not gone away, and most French women, including many feminists, continue to celebrate their femininity, to bear children – and to exercise their right to speak out. The French educated public has even begun to grapple with the notion that "gender" is not an American invention, and that, in fact, *"genre"* (masculine and feminine, referring explicitly to the social construction of sex) has been the subject of public debate for centuries in France; moreover, women's history is making inroads into the universities, schools, and public consciousness – challenging the sexual politics of historical writing and teaching in the Francophone world. Even the sexism of French grammar (priority given to the masculine) has again come under attack. In 2014 France witnessed a renewed campaign to admit a symbolic heroine Olympe de Gouges, author of the Declaration of the Rights of Women, to the Pantheon, where France's heroes (including the Geneva-born antifeminist Jean-Jacques Rousseau) are entombed. In early May 2016, Audrey

---

[17] See Reynolds, *France between the Wars*, esp. pp. 212–221, where she argues that, retrospectively, France's "lag" in granting women voting rights was not such a lag at all, and that the prevailing historiography on the question of women's suffrage needs to be entirely rethought. See also, for the particulars, Albert & Nicole du Roy, *Citoyennes! Il y a cinquante ans le vote des femmes* (Paris: Flammarion, 1994).

Azoulay, the current French minister of Culture and Communication, announced a major initiative to foster the systematic collection of source materials pertaining to French women and women's groups by national and departmental archives.[18] Christine de Pizan would be extremely pleased.

* * *

Deeply rooted prejudices and fixed ideas are hard to change in any culture, but especially excruciating to change when they concern relations between the sexes and the family – arguably, the fundamental sociopolitical unit of any society. What is remarkable in the French case is the extent to which change did ultimately come about. The repeated upheavals of France's political and economic history, compounded by the highly intellectualized and artistic culture it fostered, ensured that ultimately ideas and principles did matter and that sustained debates would take place on the woman question, with women and their male allies challenging conventional beliefs about masculine hegemony. They insistently and repeatedly talked back to the men (and some women) who affirmed that the sole model for relations between the sexes must be a hierarchical one in which men must subordinate and dominate (albeit not enclose and shroud) women – when they did not justify such arrangements by claiming that women were "naturally" inferior to men. For centuries this had been the prevailing view, and even by the 1920s there were individuals of both sexes who would fiercely uphold male supremacy, unwilling to contemplate, much less concede its erosion. Nevertheless, a growing number of men in Third Republic France came to understand that, due to drastically changing social and economic circumstances, the discontents and protests of the feminists did have a solid basis, and that women, however influential they might be perceived to be (or perceived themselves to be) in the home as wives and mothers, were in fact severely handicapped and disenfranchised whenever they stepped beyond its threshold. These men would support women's quest for legal, educational, economic, and social equality, personal independence, and participation in public life.[19]

---

[18] "Conseil superieur des archives – Mardi 3 mai 2016. Discours d'Audrey Azoulay, ministre de la Culture et de la Communication," text forwarded by the listserve of *Mnémosyne*, the French women's history organization.

[19] See Alban Jacquemart, *Les Hommes dans les mouvements féministes: Socio-histoire d'un engagement improbable* (Rennes: Presses Universitaires de Rennes, 2015).

The French debates on the woman question during the Third French Republic were indeed exceptional in the history of the world. There (as I have explained at far greater length in my companion volume) public debates on the woman question began earlier – and continued longer – than in any other country. Those countries besides France that also have a lengthy history are limited, in effect, to England, Spain, and some Italian city-states (notably Venice) – all were both precociously urban and wealthy, and had produced an intellectual elite that included literate women.[20] Few other countries (nation-states) in the world can claim a debate on the woman question as extensive or enduring as that of France; even in England these controversies arose only in the sixteenth century, and in the United States of America, they began only in the 1830s and 1840s. In other parts of the world there are still no systematic and lasting critiques of male hegemony, much less critiques with a long, well-documented history.

The debates in France, however, began in the early 1400s, thanks to the concerted effort of Christine de Pizan to challenge men's slanders of women; by the sixteenth century her manuscripts would become print volumes and her ideas would inform tapestries that hung in the castles of great queens and princesses. From the courts these debates would inform city dwellers and townspeople. By the early seventeenth century, French advocates of women's emancipation were postulating the equality of the sexes – and by mid-century French women writers were condemning marriage as slavery. Debates during the European Enlightenment pushed claims on women's behalf incessantly and the French Revolution expanded (and exported) them; they provided French women and their champions with both an intellectual and a political springboard for challenging masculine domination. Rare it was before that event that a nation-state would develop a dedication to secular ideals, to principles of liberty, equality, and justice, in ways that would empower women. Just how rare it was would become evident in the course of negotiations for the Treaty of Versailles and the founding of the League of Nations, when plenipotentiaries from an assortment of less "enlightened" nations objected strenuously, usually on religious or cultural grounds, to some

---

[20] For the early centuries, see the references in my companion volume, *The Woman Question in France, 1400–1870*, including especially Constance Jordan's comparative study of sixteenth-century texts, *Renaissance Feminism: Literary Texts and Political Models* (Ithaca, NY: Cornell University Press, 1990), and the many documents subsequently republished in English translation in the University of Chicago series, "The Other Voice in Early Modern Europe."

of the proposals for international intervention made by the French and British Inter-Allied Women.[21]

Great opportunities for change opened up with the advent of the Third Republic, whose leaders purposefully grounded the infant regime in the revolutionary principles of liberty, equality, and fraternity. In consequence, the debates on the woman question mushroomed in scope and intensity during the first fifty years of the regime; these debates are, of course, the subject of this lengthy volume. By 1914, however, the mainstream republican French feminists (of both sexes) had explored virtually every aspect of the question and had laid all the significant issues on the table, and by 1920, they had exhaustively elaborated the arguments for women's emancipation on the premises of "equality-in-difference" for individuals with sexed bodies. Here, some might prefer to use the word "equity," for the equality demanded by establishment feminists was specifically legal equality, taking into account women's distinctiveness as embodied individuals. To them, empowering women had nothing to do with turning women into men, or achieving sexual "neutrality," but rather with attaining some further progress toward partnership of the sexes, with providing women with opportunities to demonstrate their intellectual and economic potential while also providing protection for motherhood and for children. In the interwar period, women in the labor market, especially those who campaigned for greater access to administrative positions, would make greater use of nondiscriminatory "equality" arguments, as Linda L. Clark's study of women in public administration affirms.[22] But they would never abandon their conviction that women were "different" from

---

[21] When, in the 1920s and 1930s, France attempted to displace religious laws on personal status with the Civil Code in the postwar protectorates of Syria and Lebanon, the backlash was tremendous; see Elizabeth Thompson, *Colonial Citizens: Republican Rights, Paternal Privilege, and Gender in French Syria and Lebanon* (New York: Columbia University Press, 1999). In French Algeria in the 1930s, there were three separate legal systems: the Civil Code for French citizens, Berber law and Muslim personal status law for the locals; see Sara Kimble, "Emancipation through Secularization: French Feminist Views of Muslim Women's Condition in Interwar Algeria," *French Colonial History*, vol. 7 (2006), 109–128. Even in today's Morocco, an "enlightened" monarchy tempered by parliamentary input and a relatively benign form of Islam, Shari'ia law still governs the relations between the sexes – and leaves little space for contestation of injustices. In the Jewish state of Israel, religious law governs personal relations including marriage, there is likewise little secular space for contestation and no such thing as civil marriage. As concerns promoting the education of girls, we are all too familiar with the violent responses today in certain areas of Muslim countries like Afghanistan and Pakistan, in Iraq and Syria, and even in some sub-Saharan countries.

[22] Linda Clark remarks (in a 2014 e-mail exchange) that "I agree that the arguments are already on the table by the interwar period but, with the women administrators' book, I was struck by the much greater emphasis on the equal abilities argument and less use of the special feminine qualities arguments. Of course, the special qualities arguments do continue – in the administrative case with the continued gendering of certain positions." See Linda L. Clark, *The Rise of Professional Women in*

men; the question was whether, as the public sector expanded, they could perform certain administrative tasks equally well (or even better) than men. The major challenge in the 1930s, however, would be to defend women's right to employment in the face of the Great Depression.[23]

Thus, from the fifteenth century on, and increasingly from the eighteenth century into the twentieth century, French women found their voices; one by one, they moved relentlessly into public space, publishing and petitioning, founding periodicals and newspapers, writing novels in which they talked back to masculine authority, insinuation, and slander, and asserted their rights and prerogatives as women. The advent of the Third Republic and its relative longevity gave them the space needed to fully articulate their claims and to mount campaigns to achieve them. The Great War had made it abundantly clear that, while "conventional" gender roles might be reinforced temporarily, middle-class and upper-middle-class men could no longer "protect" their wives and daughters from the realities of contemporary life by cordoning them off in the ostensibly safe space of the household or by shielding them from the "facts of life"; the need for women in the workforce and in the social services that supported the war effort was simply too great. What was more, women were playing a new and significant role in combatting social evils such as alcoholism, slums, licensed prostitution and the traffic in women, and addressing other difficult issues that male politicians were reluctant to tackle. Feminists of both sexes continued to demand the requisite political authority to implement their agenda.

Amidst all these developments, what I have called (in my companion volume) the "peculiar traits of French republican national identity" continue to resonate. Overt recognition of women's power and influence, in contrast to concern about their relative absence in positions of political authority, remain central to and characteristic of the French debates today, even though they are not often distinguished in the way I have done in my two books. Even in authoritative contemporary works, feminist scholars have often talked in terms of power when they mean "authority" – as, for example, the authors in a landmark collection of essays, *La Démocratie "à la française," ou les femmes indésirables*, published in 1996, which included analyses by feminist scholars and leaders such as Françoise Collin,

---

France: Gender and Public Administration since 1830 (Cambridge, UK, & New York: Cambridge University Press, 2000).
[23] See Karen Offen, "Body Politics: Women, Work, and the Politics of Motherhood in France, 1920-1950," in *Maternity & Gender Policies: Women and the Rise of the European Welfare States, 1880s-1950s*, ed. Gisela Bock & Pat Thane (London: Routledge, 1991), pp. 138–159.

Geneviève Fraisse, and Françoise Gaspard.[24] Certainly we understand what they mean when they speak of power and object to women's exclusion from it, but I think that the preferable term here must be "authority," which highlights the officeholder's decision-making authority and responsibility, and provides more clarity. For, as I have argued throughout my work, women in France have always had influence and power, but for centuries they were deliberately excluded from wielding public authority.[25]

In the French case, especially with the advent of universal male suffrage from 1848 on, what we see is that, with the exception of the minority of committed male supporters of the suffrage for women, so many of the men who did possess some political and economic authority were extremely reluctant to give it up or even to acknowledge a willingness to share. This tendency was manifest during the time of the Third Republic, but it was constantly questioned and critiqued. Even today, when women do have a vote equal to that of men, French feminists insist that women are far from exercising their proportional share of political authority, despite the inclusion of a parity [in representation] amendment to the constitution of the Fifth Republic. The philosopher/*historienne* Geneviève Fraisse remarked sardonically on a time-honored distinction: "still today, women make the morals and the men hold onto the privilege of making the laws."[26] The sponsors of that parity measure in the 1990s argued, ingeniously and within what has come to be called the "universalist" tradition, that the much-vaunted "abstract individual" came in two sexes and that both were necessary to represent the French nation. However, they carefully sidestepped any discussion of women's "difference" from men.[27] Despite this attempt at theoretical slight-of-hand, for most people – including most French people – "women" still constitute a category that has its specific concerns. The moral of this story may be that having "power" and "influence" is a very fine thing, but that exercising authority, especially in political life, is even more desirable. In fact, women have exercised significant authority in France as heads of religious orders, as missionaries, as executives in family-owned businesses – indeed, everywhere except in formal political decision-making. Even though Edith Cresson served briefly under President François Mitterrand as president of the council of

---

[24] See *La Démocratie "à la française," ou les femmes indésirables*, ed. Éliane Viennot (Paris: Publications de l'Université Paris 7 – Denis Diderot, 1996).

[25] See the General Introduction to my companion volume.

[26] Geneviève Fraisse, "Quand gouverner n'est pas représenter," in *Démocratie "à la française,"* p. 41.

[27] On the parity campaign, see Joan Wallach Scott, *Parité: Sexual Equality and the Crisis of French Universalism* (Chicago: University of Chicago Press, 2005), and my review in *History: The Journal of the Historical Association* [UK], 92:2 (n° 306), April 2007, 281–282.

ministers and Ségolène Royale has run for president of France, the face of political authority remains heavily masculine.

A second distinctive factor, the population question, remains alive in France, but arouses far less anxiety today than in earlier centuries. In the twentieth century, France's demographic profile changed considerably. Thanks to extensive immigration and an end to the wars that drastically and repeatedly decimated the male population, demographic "suicide" is no longer the concern it once was, although the French birth rate remains low and some worry about the impact of in-migration from the former French colonial possessions, especially as it concerns Muslims. According to 2014 figures from *Index Mundi*, there are now slightly more men than women in the 15–54 age group, although women outnumber men in the 55–64 and 65-and-over age groups.[28] Indeed, the demographic balance has tilted slightly in favor of French men. Yet support for families, and especially for motherhood, remains essential for a society's survival, and feminist historians such as Yvonne Knibiehler remind us that mothers have a history, in France as elsewhere, and that ongoing issues such as "who will take care of the children?" must not be allowed to become sticks with which to beat women who insist on the right to combine maternity with their professional interests.[29] France as a nation, it has to be said, has done a better job than most others at mitigating this ostensible conflict of interests.

Perhaps the biggest change has been in French attitudes toward a woman's right to control her own fertility. The demographic hysteria of the last few centuries having subsided, this is now taken for granted by secular French women and even by many practicing Catholics. In fact, today, a cluster of French "activists, politicians and health practitioners ... are pushing to have those benefits expand beyond their country's borders" and are pressing for a common European Union policy.[30] One of these groups, the International League for Women's Rights, led by Annie Sugier, is pressing for the decriminalization of abortion "on the European level and eventually worldwide," beginning with a revision of the European Union's Charter of Fundamental Rights. It will be an uphill struggle, but in France itself the battle has been won.

---

[28] "France Demographics Profile 2014" (source: CIA World Factbook). Accessed at www.indexmundi .com/france/demographics_profile.html on 4 December 2014.

[29] See Yvonne Knibiehler & Catherine Fouquet, *L'Histoire des mères du moyen âge à nos jours* (Paris: Éditions Montalba, 1980) and Yvonne Knibiehler, *Qui Gardera les enfants? Mémoires d'une féministe iconoclaste* (Paris: Calmann-Lévy, 2007).

[30] See "France Pushes Abortion Rights Beyond Its Borders," on Women's eNews at www.womensenews .org/story/reproductive-health/141212/tweet-tweet-our-reporters-track-eureprorights.

A third factor, the heavy emphasis on biomedical considerations in debating the "roles" and "values" of women and men continues to resonate, except that nowadays women trained as gynecologists and obstetricians, and as psychologists and neurologists, have joined these debates – on both sides of the issue.[31] The nineteenth-century debates over the implications of brain size and body mass have given way to brain configuration (and now genetic) questions. Explanations that the uterus of a woman controlled her entire being gave way to the ovarian explanation, which featured a glandular approach to explaining the distinctiveness of the feminine body.[32] But modern medicine has also recognized that men, as well as women, have glands, and that indeed the two sexes are mutually complementary. Arguments over men's superiority are no longer fashionable; indeed, the entire discussion of sexual superiority or inferiority now seems quite silly. Most recognize that men's physical strength arguably gives them an edge in certain activities, but that women have indeed become physically stronger than they once were. Mentally, they have more than proven their capabilities, as the surge of women into French higher education and the professions clearly attests.

A fourth factor, the intense competition between Catholic and secular educators for controlling the education of girls has been reduced to a simmer; a Catholic education is still available for those families who want it for their children. And the once dominant political and ideological emphasis on educated motherhood, which provided such a powerful tool for women who pursued advanced schooling in the nineteenth century, has given way to an emphasis on education for professional and economic equality, accompanied by the provision of social services that support parenthood. Indeed, the notion of the mother-educator is far from dead; it would be given a new twist when, in 1917, as the world war dragged on, the French teacher and feminist activist Madeleine Vernet founded a new periodical, *La Mère Éducatrice*, to promote this specific mission among

---

[31] E.g., see Luc Ferry, "Y a-t-il des 'valeurs féminines'?" *Le Figaro* (18 September 2014). Ferry is commenting on the arguments of gynecologist Anne de Kervasdoué, who insists that feminine values, i.e., nurturing, compassionate values, do have a genetic basis, and that testosterone informs aggressivity in male values. Opponents of such assertions include the philosopher and public intellectual Elisabeth Badinter, who denies that women have a built-in mothering instinct and asserts that women and men are fundamentally the same.

[32] See especially Félix Jayle's *La Gynécologie*. Vol. 1: *L'anatomie morphologique de la femme* (Paris: Masson, 1918). For a discussion of Jayle's importance (he was also a founder and editor in 1897 of the *Revue de Gynécologie*, and proponent of the ovarian focus and environmental explanations of women's health), see Mary Lynn Stewart, *For Health and Beauty: Physical Culture for Frenchwomen, 1880s–1930s* (Baltimore: Johns Hopkins University Press, 2001).

mothers – and by extension, among female primary school teachers – of inculcating peace and peaceful values in children.[33]

It is now accepted in France that women have the right to work and to obtain equal pay for equal work – and that married women can take employment, open bank accounts, and transact business of various kinds without the written permission of their husbands. As these chapters on the woman question debates reveal, however, it took enormous effort to arrive at this point.

The republican vision – a government based on principles of moral, legal and educational equality, government of and by the people, and a growing concern for human rights – while never perfect, promised much and has actually achieved a great deal as concerns women. Already in the early 1790s the Francophile Englishwoman Mary Wollstonecraft had asserted, in her *Vindication of the Rights of Woman*, that "the divine right of husbands, like the divine right of kings, may, it is to be hoped, in this enlightened age, be contested without danger."[34] And, indeed, the demise of a male-exclusive monarchy has diminished the credibility of the authoritarian father/husband figure. But it could not and did not eliminate acknowledgement of sexual difference. Indeed, the historical French republican configuration of "equal-ity-in-difference" (and not the post-1945 dedication to the "abstract individ-ual") belies the calculus of opposites that some have tried to draw between equality, on the one hand, and identity on the other. Never did those earlier generations of vocal French women accept the notion that the "individual" *l'Homme* was abstract. Instead, they persisted in underscoring its sexual concreteness, even as they began to investigate and expose the underpin-nings of *masculinisme*. Repeatedly French feminists of both sexes have insisted – and continue to insist – that equality (before the law) is not the same thing as "identity" of persons.[35] There is no "paradox."

* * *

---

[33] See Anne Cova, "Féminismes et maternité entre les deux guerres en France: Les ambiguités et les divergences des féministes du passé," *Les Temps Modernes*, n° 593 (April–May 1997), 49–77; Anne Cova, *Maternité et droits des femmes en France (XIXe–XXe siècles)* (Paris: Economica, 1997); and especially, on the teachers, Mona Siegel, "'To the Unknown Mother of the Unknown Soldier': Pacificism, Feminism, and the Politics of Sexual Difference among French Institutrices between the Wars," *French Historical Studies*, 22:3 (Summer 1999), 421–451.

[34] Mary Wollstonecraft, *A Vindication of the Rights of Woman* (1792), chapter 3. (In the new Yale edition of *A Vindication of the Rights of Woman*, ed. Eileen Hunt Botting [New Haven, CT: Yale University Press, 2014], the quotation appears on p. 67.

[35] See, for example, Wilfred Monod, *Masculin et féminin. Discours prononcé au Musée Social, à l'assemblée annuelle de la Ligue d'Électeurs pour le Suffrage des Femmes, le 11 février [1913], sous la présidence de M. Ferdinand Buisson* (Épinal: Impr. Nouvelle, n.d.), p. 7. By contrast, the American philosopher Wendy Brown asserts that in what she calls "the liberal tradition," "equality presumes sameness"; see her essay, "The 'Jewish Question' and the 'Woman Question'," *differences: A Journal*

Analysis of the woman question would take off in a different direction after World War II. In *Le Deuxième sexe* [*The Second Sex*, 2 volumes, 1949], the existentialist philosopher and social critic Simone de Beauvoir would posit that "She [woman] determines and differentiates herself in relation to man, and he does not in relation to her; she is the inessential in front of the essential. He is the Subject, he is the Absolute. She is the Other."[36] Beauvoir certainly put her finger on how, for centuries, many articulate French men had characterized the relation between the sexes. By extension, and not surprisingly, philosophers who had been steeped in the male way of thinking about the relations between the sexes would exude such sentiments. Yet Beauvoir was not a man, and at the time she wrote, was certainly not a feminist. How do we explain that she was so caught up in this mind-set? How could she have ignored or failed to discover the depth of evidence of French women – and their male allies – talking back over the centuries? Was it because of the backlash against women's emancipation that characterized the 1920s and 1930s during which she was growing up and studying? Or was it, more generally, because she had not yet recognized, much less acknowledged or grappled with, the sexual dimension of the "politics of knowledge" in France? This would seem surprising, given that she wrote her doctoral thesis under Léon Brunschvicg, vice-president of the *Ligue d'Électeurs pour le Suffrage des Femmes* and, even more importantly, the husband of the well-known women's rights advocate Cécile Brunschvicg, who long presided over the *Union Française pour le Suffrage des Femmes*. Beauvoir, however, studied, worked, and thought within a long "masculinist" tradition of men in philosophy, psychiatry, and literature – not the works of the less well-known feminist authors who had for six long centuries contested those masculine "truths." For the most part, and until the 1940s, hers was a "male gaze"; she seemed ignorant of the bounteous historical literature of contestation or even of the arguments in the contemporary feminist press. Unlike her nineteenth-century predecessors Clémence Royer (seeking a woman's form of knowledge) or Jenny P. d'Hericourt (who also criticized male-dominated knowledge) or her

---

of Feminist Cultural Studies, 15:2 (2004), 1–31. In the French and European tradition, however equality presumes difference and is a "relational concept"; see Ute Gerhard, *Debating Women's Equality: Toward a Feminist Theory of Law from a European Perspective* (New Brunswick, NJ: Rutgers University Press, 2001), chapter 1: "The Meaning of Equality with Regard to Difference," esp. p. 7.

36 Simone de Beauvoir, *Le Deuxième Sexe*, vol. 1 (Paris: Gallimard, 1949, 1976), p. 14. The translation cited here is from the new Constance Borde/Sheila Malovaney-Chevalier translation, *The Second Sex* (London: Johnathan Cape, 2009), p. 6.

early twentieth-century predecessors Marguerite Souley-Darqué and Jeanne Oddo-Deflou, she had not engaged with "women's studies." She was apparently unaware that at least since the later nineteenth century feminists had even contested the very structure and rules of French grammar that favored the "masculine." She began to ask her questions in *The Second Sex* as if writing on a bare slate. What is more, ignorance of women's history allowed many in her audience, including many mid-twentieth century feminists, to anoint her as "the" pioneer in discussing women's condition. Impressed by Beauvoir's unprecedented intellectual achievement, many readers including budding feminist scholars long overlooked the extent to which her analysis of women's condition was skewed by the influence of socialist ideology, with its commitment to prioritizing class.

The conclusions I have reached from exploring six centuries of debates on the woman question in France suggest that, in fact, contrary to Beauvoir's aforementioned observation, the reality may be the other way around – and that Man "determines and differentiates *him*self in relation to woman." The debates reveal, in my reading, that in France many educated, but still "traditionalist" men devoted enormous effort to differentiating themselves from women. In attempting to situate and control the feminine *in order that* they could assert the primacy and power – and authority – of the masculine, they attempted to strengthen their hold onto masculine privilege, even to the point of controlling the politics of "remembering" and "forgetting" as they channeled and institutionalized in schools and universities an ostensibly "un-gendered" approach to "knowledge." It would seem that Sigmund Freud – and by extension Jacques Lacan – came closer to the truth when they spoke about masculine differentiation from and separation from the Mother. Is it then the case that what was long called the "woman question" is really the "man problem"? Is that why for so many centuries, male artists would obsessively paint and sculpt the female nude, or why so many male poets would wax lyric over the "eternal feminine," or obsessively castigate and malign women when they thought women weren't paying attention – and not the other way around? Perhaps the astute Natalie Clifford Barney, American denizen of the Parisian Left Bank, was closer to the truth than Beauvoir, when she insisted in 1920 that: "One must liberate man from man" and "There is no enemy sex; the enemy of man is man himself."[37]

---

[37] Natalie Clifford Barney, in *Pensées d'une Amazone* (Paris: Émile-Paul frères, 1920), pp. 8–9.

The feminist philosopher Françoise Collin remarked in the early 1990s on the exclusion of women from the "democracy" of the Greek polis on the basis of their proximity, not to sexual life per se (which for men encompassed homosexual as well as heterosexual relations), but to the formidable processes of generation. What, then, in light of such earlier views, could be more radical, even revolutionary, than the claims made by French feminists in the late nineteenth and early twentieth centuries for women's inclusion in democracy precisely on the grounds of their capacity for motherhood and their identities as mothers.[38] Yet this woman-centeredness, this matrifocality, the historic source of enormous cultural power and influence, has been disparaged and dismissed by some later twentieth-century feminists as "maternalism" or "essentialism." It is time to acknowledge that these earlier French feminists may have been wiser than some of their successors, and that, by embracing their sexual difference as enviable and estimable, and staking their demands for sociopolitical responsibility on it, they may have played their winning card.

---

[38] Françoise Collin, "Mythe et réalité de la démocratie," in Démocratie "à la Française," p. 30.

Afterword

This book (and its companion volume) has taken me over forty years to write. Yet as I go through my files, my earlier notes, and publications, I find that I have forgotten many things that I already knew in 1972, when the first version of this project, all eighty pages of it (with its 190 endnotes), began to circulate among friends and colleagues as a sort of underground quasi-publication (*samidzat,* as one colleague called it). Another good friend and colleague said to me at the time: "what you've written is either too long to be an article or too short to be a book. But it looks like a book (in embryo) to me." Others said, yes, but . . . how does the debate on the woman question in France compare with that in America or England? Or Germany? Or Russia? Or China? It was this quest that launched me in the direction of comparative history, and explains to some degree why this project on France and the Francophone world took so long to complete.[1] In addition, studying the historical progression of a multifaceted debate requires finding out exactly who was speaking to whom, when exactly, and in what order. This could take years to figure out – which it did. I now think I am able to explain the singular features of the French debates on the woman question within the historical context that made them so unique.

Generally speaking, the study of the woman question (except as it impinged on women's labor) was not of much interest to professional historians of my generation until the bicentennial of the Revolution (in 1989) loomed on the horizon and engaged the curiosity of feminists. Before that, most of the work published on French women and politics,

---

[1] The fruits of this comparative study include *Women, the Family, and Freedom: The Debate in Documents, 1750–1950.* 2 vols. (Stanford, CA: Stanford University Press, 1983), with Susan Groag Bell; *European Feminisms, 1700–1950: A Political History* (Stanford, CA: Stanford University Press, 2000), and *Globalizing Feminisms* (London: Routledge, 2010), along with many articles, especially concerning the international women's organizations. For a list of articles published since 1998, see my website www.karenoffen.com.

or women in political thought, or women thinking politically, or on the history of French feminism and socialism was produced by historians outside France, including Patrick Kay Bidelman, Linda L. Clark, Charles Sowerwine, Marilyn J. Boxer, Persis Hunt, Steven C. Hause, and myself – all of whom published pioneering articles on "Aspects of the Woman Question during the Third Republic" in the 1977 special issue of *Third Republic/Troisième République*.[2] Subsequent books on French feminism by Bidelman, Clark, Sowerwine, Hause, and Claire Goldberg Moses, in addition to numerous articles by Marilyn J. Boxer and, on the earlier period, by S. Joan Moon and many others, all added to our knowledge base.[3] In France, the exceptions to this generalization were Yvonne Knibiehler, whose landmark articles on the post-revolutionary medical discourse on women appeared in 1976; the younger politologue Christine Fauré, whose book *La Démocratie sans les Femmes* appeared in 1985; and Florence Rochefort and Laurence Klejman whose joint thesis (under Michelle Perrot) was published in 1989, along with Geneviève Fraisse's *Muse de la Raison*.[4] These were the early works.

Between those days and now, many things have changed and new possibilities for research have opened up. For one thing, the accessibility of sources has vastly improved. Publications are now available on the internet that were formerly only available on microfilm, and even that was an improvement over seeking out the originals (often in bad shape and "unconsultable") in the monumental *Bibliothèque Nationale* (BN; rue de Richlieu), or consulting them at the Réserve where photocopying was both expensive and vigorously controlled. This was well before the BN's successor, the *Bibliothèque National de France* (BNF), sprouted its air-conditioned book towers, dauntingly steep escalators, and deeply

---

[2] "Special Issue: Aspects of the Woman Question," ed. Karen Offen, in *Third Republic/Troisième République*, n°ˢ 3–4 (1977). These pioneering essays can now be consulted online at www.box.com/s/790700647aeda5371ffi.

[3] These books have all been cited in the course of my chapters.

[4] See Yvonne Knibiehler, "Le Discours médical sur la femme," *Romantisme: Revue du Dix-Neuvième Siècle*, n°ˢ 13–14 (1976), 41–55, and "Les Médecins et la 'nature féminine' au temps du Code Civil," *Annales: Économies, Sociétés, Civilisations*, 31:4 (July–August 1976), 824–845; also Christine Fauré, *La Démocratie sans les Femmes: Essai sur le Libéralisme* (Paris: Presses Universitaires de France, 1985). 1989 saw the publication of both Laurence Klejman & Florence Rochefort, *L'Égalité en marche: Le Féminisme sous la Troisième République* (Paris: FNSP & des femmes, 1989), and Geneviève Fraisse, *Muse de la Raison: La Démocratie exclusive et la différence des sexes* (Paris: Alinea, 1989). Fauré's *Encyclopédie Politique et Historique des Femmes* (Paris: Presses Universitaires de France, 1997) contains many important articles.

submerged reading "caves" on the Left Bank of the Seine. My American colleagues from the 1970s ordered quantities of very pricey microfilm. We also discovered the precious smaller libraries, particularly the *Bibliothèque Marguerite Durand* (BMD), the *Bibliothèque Historique de la Ville de Paris* (BHVP), the *Musée Social*, and from the 1990s on, the newly developed *Archives du Féminisme* at the University of Angers. In the meantime, I investigated libraries and archives in Switzerland, Belgium, and The Netherlands, seeking other traces of the francophone debates on the woman question.

In France, works that once had to be painstakingly searched out in the printed catalogues of the *Bibliothèque Nationale* or by combing the series of card catalogs on the library's lower level can now be located – and found – online! Who would ever have thought in 1972 that, from a personal computer, one could log onto the Stanford library catalog, or onto OCLC World Catalogue? much less to the *Bibliothèque Nationale de France* itself? Unbelievable! Google has now scanned many older, out-of-copyright books and pamphlets, and has made them freely available online, which enhances one's ability to locate heretofore obscure quotations. The BNF has introduced Gallica, where we can now consult legible scans of old French newspapers with the flick of a finger. Such technical progress seems astounding! Our younger colleagues can do four or five times the work in the same amount of time it took us – and, even as we veterans remain astounded, they take this immense progress entirely for granted. They will wonder why we, who had to work so slowly, were – by comparison – so relatively unproductive. We set up elaborate photographic equipment on easels and with proper lighting to take photos of documents, which then had to be developed and printed; our younger colleagues (and now we ourselves) take endless photos with iPhones and store them digitally for later consultation.

Word processing did not exist – at least for scholars – when I began this research. For ten years I typed out my own manuscripts, retyped the revised drafts of chapters, and then retyped again – and again, and again. Stacks of unpublished manuscripts lay in a desk drawer, for want of being retyped yet another time. Word processing has been a godsend! Watching the little characters fall into line on my vintage "Superbrain," or cut sentences align themselves in new parts of one's text, without the endless, mind-numbing retyping of each character, is an unprecedented power trip for the author-typist (or should we say, keyboarder)! Embedded endnotes are another wondrous development, allowing one to cut and paste a sentence or paragraph with the endnotes moving right along with it. We can finally throw away the Scotch tape, the glue sticks, and the carbon paper, and abandon the scissoring of sentences and paragraphs that had to be reassembled on the floor.

I began my graduate research in French history by studying the political career of a male politician – a right-wing one at that. Yet even then, I kept stumbling across fragments of information concerning French women and feminism. The more I looked the more I found.[5] I started filing notes about it. But, of course, I had no framework readily available in which to interpret what I had found; nothing concerning the woman question had made it into our earlier textbooks. And, of course, Simone de Beauvoir had told us in her book, *The Second Sex*, that "they [women] have no past, no history, no religion of their own."[6] Thus, when I embarked on this project, I knew next to nothing about the woman question debate or the feminist campaigns in France, but I had my suspicions that there was a story to be told.

In the early 1970s we expressed our amazement at new scholarly studies that revived the views of endless men on the woman question, with their mostly antifeminist images and fantasies; then we began digging out other sources, uncovering the published voices of women (and men) who challenged these antifeminist men in print, who framed their own demands, elaborated their own visions of what women could and should be. Today we continue to unearth quantities of published texts as well as manuscript texts. We can now hear a multitude of voices where once only "silences" were thought to exist. Admittedly, historians piece their stories together from scraps, but in the case of France this scrap pile has acquired prodigious proportions. Already by the nineteenth century, it was no longer a question of deciphering "women's silences" but of acknowledging multiple voices, articulate, well-informed – indeed, even eloquent. We are finding that women, historically, and not least in France, had some very important things to say – and they have expressed them well, just as have the better-known men. We have discovered that there is a "politics" of knowledge and that it is deeply gendered, and we have arrived at an understanding of those earlier decisions as to what gets

---

[5] I have discussed the steps in this intellectual trajectory in "Going Against the Grain: The Making of an Independent Scholar," in *Voices of Women Historians*, ed. Eileen Boris & Nupur Chaudhuri (Bloomington: Indiana University Press, 1999), pp. 86–101.

[6] Simone de Beauvoir, *Le Deuxième Sexe*, vol. 1 (Paris: Gallimard, 1949, 1976), p. 17. The quotation is from the new Constance Borde/Sheila Malovaney-Chevalier translation, *The Second Sex* (London: Johnathan Cape, 2009), p. 8.

included and what gets left out in any given historical (or, for that matter, contemporary) account. Which is perhaps an explanation as to why we never learned about either the woman question – or, for that matter, the man problem – in our schoolbooks, at our universities, or in graduate school. At that time, we did not know to ask those questions.[7]

We have learned to appreciate the deeper features of the "modern" human condition: that essential to it is the notion that the order of things is changeable, and can (and does) change; that even relations between the sexes can evolve, can be reconfigured, and that neither God, Nature, nor parenthood totally foreclose women's (and men's) options. In a secular world, law and institutions, state social and economic policies, and changing needs have played and continue to play a major role in organizing those relations and authorizing the particular forms they take from one society to another.

Studying the debates on the woman question in France raises other questions about the reception of our findings. Why do some people immediately understand the importance of feminist demands and others do not? Why, even today, do some women not "get it" – for example, why do they not appreciate what Hubertine Auclert, Jeanne Schmahl, Cécile Brunschvicg, and their counterparts were so agitated about when they demanded the vote as the keystone to obtaining legislative changes? Do young women today, like some French women throughout history, think that the power of their influence combined with their material dependence offers a more attractive way of living than "equality" or "justice" or "independence"? Why do some young women, especially those from privileged families, insist that they "are not feminist, but ... "? Why do they think that few obstacles bar their way to fame or fortune? Or that those obstacles that their mothers and/or grandmothers confronted no longer exist? All too frequently, their tune changes around the time they hit forty – just about the time that Simone de Beauvoir (among many others who had acquired some experience of the world) began to ask the woman question – and to do such an inadequate job of assessing its very long history.[8] It is because Beauvoir's highly influential book provided such an unsatisfactory historical component that I began to ask: "was there ever a women's movement in France?" and to launch an inquiry that led to

---

[7] The allusion here is to the title of Marilyn J. Boxer's fine book, *When Women Ask the Questions: Creating Women's Studies in America* (Baltimore: Johns Hopkins University Press, 1998).

[8] See my as yet unpublished article, "History, Memory, and Simone de Beauvoir, in which I elaborate on the poor treatment of history in *The Second Sex*."

the recovery of the very *long* history of the woman question debates themselves, the many challenges to masculine domination (and efforts to quell those challenges) that now seem central to understanding the history of France and the Francophone world. The results of that quest have become this book and its companion volume. Consider them Prolegomena to *The Second Sex*.

Important Dates for the Woman Question Debates in France, 1870–1920 and Beyond

1870   March: First meeting of *Association Internationale des Femmes* (fd. Marie Goegg), in Geneva

16 April: *Association pour le Droit des Femmes* founded by Léon Richer, in Paris

1870–1871   Franco-Prussian war: France defeated by Germany; end of Second Empire; proclamation of the Republic; unification of Germany proclaimed at Versailles

Paris Commune (March–May 1871): *Union des Femmes* founded; many women's rights leaders in exile; period of political uncertainty and cautious activity until 1875

1871   *Association pour l'Émancipation Progressive de la Femme* founded (Léon Richer)

24 September: *L'Avenir des Femmes: Journal Politique* launched by Richer (after thirteen-month shutdown of *Le Droit des Femmes*)

1872   May–December: The Du Bourg affair, followed by months of polemic over "right" of husbands to assassinate adulterous wives with impunity

9 June: First Women's Rights banquet, Paris (amidst the DuBourg affair debates)

27 July: *Loi organique militaire* prescribed obligatory military service by all French men [*tout Français*] – men could be called up between ages 20 and 40. No soldier on active duty allowed to vote

1874   19 May: Law enacted regulating employment of children and (for the first time) underage women (16–21); forbids women's underground work in mines; forbids night work for young women ages 16–21; establishes twelve-hour day maximum

July: Clémence Royer takes on the Anthropological Society of Paris on the subject of measures to raise the French birthrate

11 December: Josephine Butler arrives in Paris to launch her continental crusade against government-regulated prostitution

23 December: Roussel law enacted, regulating the wet-nursing industry to protect infants

1875 25 February: Adoption and promulgation of constitutional laws for the Third Republic

19 March: Founding in Liverpool of the British, Continental and General Federation for the Abolition of Government Regulation of Prostitution [*Fédération Britannique, Continentale et Générale pour l'Abolition de la Prostitution Réglementée*]

Founding in Paris of the *Société pour l'Amélioration du Sort des Femmes* [Society for the Amelioration of Women's Condition] by Léon Richer and Maria Deraismes

1876 8 June: Death of George Sand

3–10 October: First Workers' Congress debates women's rights and employment

1877 16 May: Government crisis; monarchist-bonapartist threat; severe repression

17–23 September: First International Congress (in Geneva) of the British and Continental Federation Against the State Regulation of Vice (founded 1875) and the *Amies de la Jeune Fille*

October: French legislative elections held – the republicans gain a majority in the Chamber of Deputies

22 November: Paris Municipal Council votes to establish a (secular) nursing school for women

1878 28 January–8 February: Second Congress of Workers, Lyon

20 May–10 November: Paris Universal Exposition

June: Women workers strike at Saint-Chamond

25 July–9 August: First International Congress on Women's Rights, Paris–elaboration of demands for women's rights; Hubertine Auclert not allowed to discuss women's suffrage

Émile Zola publishes *L'Assommoir*

1879	Early 1879: The republicans establish dominance in the Senate and take the presidency with election of Jules Grévy on 30 January
	Mid-June: The Paris prefect of police authorizes the establishment of the French section (founded in 1878) of the British and Continental Regulation for the Abolition of State-Regulated Prostitution
	20–31 October: Third Workers' Congress, Marseille. Hubertine Auclert delivers feisty speech and provokes a congress resolution in support of women's rights
1880	Émile Zola publishes his scandalous novel *Nana*
	Early April: Huge public meeting in Paris to call for suppression of the morals police
	Law of 21 December: Sée law establishes secular secondary education for girls; teacher training institutes for women follow. Ferry law establishes universal secular primary education
1881	13 February: Hubertine Auclert publishes first issue of *La Citoyenne*
	Law of 29 July: Establishes freedom of the press in France
	Law of 26 July: Founds the *École Normale d'Enseignement Secondaire des Jeunes Filles*
1882	14 January: Decree and *arrête ministeriel* elaborate the organization and programs for the girls' *lycées* and *collèges*
	Suffrage advocate Hubertine Auclert calls herself a *"féministe"* in letter to Prefect of the Seine
	Léon Richer founds the *Ligue Française pour le Droit des Femmes* (LFDF) [French League for Women's Rights]
1883–1884	Much legislative discussion (including Senate) of *recherche de la paternité*
1883	Protestant women (led by Caroline de Barrau, Isabelle Bogelot, and Emilie de Morsier) take over leadership of the *Oeuvre des Libérées de Saint-Lazare*, following retirement of its founder Pauline de Grandpré
	7 December: Grand Meeting on subject of the Paris morals police, jointly sponsored by the *Ligue Française pour le Droit des Femmes* and the French section of the British and Continental Federation
1884	Law of 27 July 1884: Divorce (illegal since 1816) again legalized, though with restricted conditions

Law of 14 August: National Assembly (Chamber of Deputies and Senate) amends the constitution of 1875 to perpetuate the republican form of government and deny the presidency to members of former royal families

Voting system changed to *scrutin de liste*

1885   Suffrage activists put together an electoral list with women candidates in conjunction with the Socialist Republican Federation after failing in earlier attempt to register to vote

1886   July: Prefect of the Seine (Poubelle) grants women physicians the right to compete for hospital internships; mid-October: doctors Blanche Edwards and Augusta Klumpke enroll in the competition for internships

1887–1889 The Boulanger Affair; threat to the Third Republic from alliance of the antiparliamentary Left and monarchist Right

1888   25 March–1 April: Isabelle Bogelot attends the congress of women in Washington, D.C., and is elected treasurer of the newly formed International Council of Women

1889   June–July: Two international women's congresses held in Paris during the International Exposition celebrating the centennial of the French Revolution: *Droit des femmes* (25–29 June) and *Oeuvres et Institutions* (12–18 July)

14–20 July: Founding congress of Second International Workingmen's Association in Paris (Clara Zetkin's address on the 19th)

Law of 19 July: Authorizes appointment of women primary school inspectors on same terms as male inspectors

Law of 24 July: Enables divestiture of *puissance paternel* (paternal authority) when children are mistreated or morally abandoned

December: Marya Chéliga-Loewy founds the *Union Universelle des Femmes* in Paris

1889–1892 Chamber of Deputies (again) considers regulation of adult women's work

1890   January: Marya Chéliga's *Union Universelle des Femmes* (founded December 1889) publishes its program statement

1891   25 April: first general assembly of the *Union Universelle des Femmes*

11 June: first assembly of the *Conférence de Versailles*, at "Les Ombrages"

June: *Solidarité des Femmes* founded by Eugénie Potonié-Pierre and Maria Martin

22 August: The Brussels Congress of the Workers' International (Second International) endorses social and political equality of the two sexes

November: Federation of "feminist" and "feminine" societies established; last issue of *La Citoyenne*; trial of Affaire Thomas-Floury for abortion, *cour d'assises*; verdict on 28 November

December: first issue of the monthly *Le Journal des Femmes*, edited by Maria Martin

1892   13–15 May: First "feminist" congress held in Paris in May [*Congrès Général des Sociétés Féministes*, organized by the *Fédération Française des Sociétés Féministes* and Chéliga's *UUF*]; called for, drew up and published (in May 1893) a widely circulated *Cahier des Doléances*

August–November: First Exhibition of the Arts of Woman (*Exposition des Arts de la Femme*) at the Palais de l'Industrie in Paris, sponsored by the *Union Centrale des Arts Décoratifs*

27 October: Deputies of *Parti Ouvrier Français* propose measures concerning maternity and *caisses de maternité*

Law of 2 November: Establishes maximum eleven-hour day for all women workers; forbids night work for women

Preparation of *Statistique Générale de la Femme*, effort led by Marie Pégard, for the 1893 World's Columbian Exposition in Chicago

1893   Mid-February: Incident at the Sorbonne, protest of male students against women in literature class of Prof. Gustave Larroumet

4 April: Maria Deraismes founds *Le Droit Humaine*, a mixed Masonic order

1 May: *Fédération Française des Sociétés Féministes* circulates its *Cahier des Doléances* to the city halls (*mairies*).

Jeanne-E. Schmahl founds group *L'Avant-Courrière* [The Forerunner] to work specifically on achieving a married women's property law and a law allowing women to witness civil acts

Committee headed by Marie Pégard sends exhibition on French women's work (with statistics and graphics) to Chicago, for display in the Women's Building at the World Exposition; World's Congress of Representative Women in May opens the Exposition

1894   6 February: Death of Maria Deraismes

1895   January–March: Lecture series at [theater] La Bodinière, Paris: "L'évolution de l'amour et de la femme" – Léopold Lacour and Jules Bois

27 April–10 June: Second Exhibition of the Arts of Woman, in Paris

October: Founding of monthly *La Revue Féministe* by Clotilde Dissard (first issue, October 1895)

1896   February: Marie Maugeret founds *Le Féminisme Chrétien*

18 March: Founding of the *Ligue des Femmes pour le Désarmement International* (authorized 28 August 1897).

8–12 April: Second "feminist" congress (*Congrès Féministe International*) in Paris; lots of press; proliferation of groups

8–12 September: Swiss feminists organize the *Congrès des Intérêts Féminins* in Geneva during the Swiss national exhibition

28 November: Publication of special issue #169 of the *Revue Encyclopédique Larousse*, "La Femme et le féminisme," ed. Marya Chéliga

Marie Pégard's *Statistique Générale de la Femme en France* (1896) crowned by the Institut de France

1897   Publication of Léopold Lacour's *Humanisme intégral: le duel des sexes, la cité future*

June 1897–February 1898: *Théâtre féministe* presented by Marya Chéliga

4–7 August: Feminists in Brussels host an international congress

Law of 7 December 1897: empowers women to serve as witnesses of private or public legal acts

9 December: Marguerite Durand launches first issue of the daily, all-woman paper, *La Fronde* (1897–1903)

10 December: LFDF petitions the Paris Municipal Council to establish minimum wage for needleworkers

1898   13 January: Émile Zola publishes "J'accuse" in Clemenceau's *L'Aurore*

24 February: Formation of *Ligue pour la Défense des Droits de l'Homme* (LDH)

May: Joint Manifesto of four feminist groups, and the editors of the *Journal des Femmes* and *La Fronde*, stating their program for change and calling for electors to support pro-feminist candidates in the general elections

12 June: Death of Eugénie Potonié-Pierre

1899 Founding of the *Revue de Morale Sociale* (Program statement dated March 1899)

21 March 1899: Death of Aline Valette

15 May: "Appeal from Women of All Countries," petition of women from eighteen countries addressed to the International Peace Conference meeting at The Hague, advocating disarmament

June–July: International Congress on the White Slave Trade (21–23 June) in London; followed by the Quinquennial Congress of the International Council of Women (26 June – 4 July) also in London

July: Founding of *Groupe Féministe Socialiste* (GFS) in Paris by Louise Saumoneau and Elisabeth Renaud

7 August–8 September: Retrial of Captain Dreyfus in Rennes; new evidence

1900 Law of 30 March (Loi Millerand): Limits workday to eleven hours, and ten hours for women and children

14 April: Opening of the Paris Universal Exposition: "La Parisienne" reigns

June–September: Two international women's congresses, Paris: *Oeuvres et Institutions* (18–23 June) and *Condition et des Droits des femmes* (5–8 September). A Catholic women's congress, organized by Marie Maugeret, is embedded in a general Catholic congress, *Congrès International des Oeuvres Catholiques*, 3–10 June.

17 September: Decree empowering women to vote and serve on tribunals for labor dispute arbitration

Law of 1 December 1900: Admits women with law degrees to the bar

1901 18 April: Founding of the *Conseil National des Femmes Françaises* (CNFF)

April–May: Feminist postage stamp campaign, initiated by Hubertine Auclert

Law of 1 July: Grants freedom to organize (nonprofit or cultural) associations

1 July: First (limited to unmarried women) suffrage measure introduced in legislature by deputy Fernand Gautret

31 December: "Marbel" (Marguerite Belmant) founds *Union Fraternelle des Femmes*

Dr. Blanche Edwards-Pilliet founds the *Ligue des Mères de Famille*

1902   June–October: *Exposition Internationale des Arts et Métiers Féminins* organized by Pauline Savary

15–25 July: *Conférence Internationale pour la Repression de la Traite des Blanches*, in Paris

4–9 August: *Congrès du Travail Féminin* organized by Pauline Savary

Le Féminisme Français published in two volumes by Charles Turgeon

1903   Marie Curie and Pierre Curie awarded Nobel Prize for physics; discovery of radioactivity

14 March: Decree empowers women to vote on and run for the *Conseil Supérieur du Travail*

April: Premiere of Nelly Roussel's *Par la Revolte!* at Sarah-Bernhardt theater in Paris

7 May: l'Affaire Forissier (arrest of journalist, his sister, and his fiancée by the Paris morals police)

27–29 May: First [Catholic] *Congrès Jeanne d'Arc*

6 June: FAI decides to move forward on campaign for abolition of regulated prostitution and abolition of the *police des moeurs*

18 June: Government authorizes the Extraparliamentary Commission to look into the morals police and regulation of prostitution; appoints women to the commission

9 December: Premiere of Eugène Brieux's play, *La Maternité*

1904   24–26 May: Second *Congrès Jeanne d'Arc*

Early June: French feminist delegates journey to Berlin to attend IWSA conference (3–4 June) and ICW Third Quinquennial Meeting (8–10 June)

29 October: Hubertine Auclert organizes march to Place Vendôme to burn copy of Civil Code – her effort is foreclosed by massive police action; demonstration against

centennial of Civil Code in front of Chamber of Deputies also closed down by police

30 October: Caroline Kauffmann (*Solidarité des Femmes*) arrested for disturbing the peace during the banquet celebrating the Code by releasing balloons with the slogan "The Code Crushes Women"

December: *Prix Femina* in various fields inaugurated by the magazine *Femina*

1905   January: formation by group of women writers with Hachette's *Vie Heureuse*, and first award (28 January) of *Prix Vie Heureuse* to Myriam Harry

April: *Section Française de l'Internationale Ouvrière* (SFIO) founded, uniting the competing socialist factions

28–30 September: *Congrès Féministe Socialiste,* Paris

Theodore Joran publishes *Le Mensonge du féminisme,* the first of his attacks on feminism

Marcelle Tinayre publishes best-selling novel, *La Rebelle*

Law of 9 December: formalizes the definitive separation of Church and State in France

1906   Early 1906: Madeleine Pelletier becomes leader of *Solidarité des Femmes*, at request of Caroline Kauffmann

Early 1906: Jeanne Deflou publishes *Le Sexualisme*

18 March: Suffrage rally at *Musée Social*, followed by small parade

April: Pope Pius X opposes suffrage for women; interview with Austrian feminist

Late May: *Congrès Jeanne d'Arc* includes session on women and politics

29 May: Finnish Diet enfranchises all Finnish women and men – a "first" for Europe

3 June: *Solidarité des Femmes* leaders Pelletier and Kauffmann visit the Chamber of Deputies on opening day and throw leaflets from gallery down on the deputies

12–17 June: ICW/CIF executive board meets in Paris, in conjunction with CNFF General Assembly, which approves formation of a suffrage section

Early July: Municipal/cantonal woman suffrage measure introduced in Chamber of Deputies by M. Dussaussoy; educator and deputy F. Buisson designated as *rapporteur*

21 October: Launch of weekly *La Française* (1906–1939; Jane Misme and colleagues)

22–25 October: Third International Congress for the Repression of the White Slave Trade, in Paris

November: CNFF announces activation of its Suffrage section, with Hubertine Auclert as chair (she served only four months, until early March 1907)

24 December: Pelletier and Kauffmann of *Solidarité des Femmes* lead delegation to the Chamber of Deputies, to meet with Jean Jaurès and other socialist deputies and pressure them to act on women's suffrage

1907   March: CNFF Suffrage Section (under Auclert) launches nationwide pro-suffrage petition in tandem with *Ligue des Droits de l'Homme*

Early 1907: Marguerite Durand founds the *Office du Travail Féminin*, while awaiting affiliation with Ministry of Labor and credit voted for 1908 (which never materialize)

25–27 March: *Congrès du Travail Féminin*, Paris, organized by Marguerite Durand at the Grand Orient

Law of 27 March: Gives women the vote for the *conseils des prud'hommes* (to resolve differences between employees and employers)

18 May: CNFF organizes peace rally as part of ICW commemoration of 1899 peace congress

17 June: Pelletier organizes joint delegation of French and English suffragettes – to Chamber of Deputies to call on Jean Jaurès, and on *L'Humanité*

7 July: Fourth General Assembly of CNFF

Law of 13 July 1907: Married women gain control of their own earnings

Summer: Ghénia Avril de Sainte-Croix publishes *Le Féminisme*

July: Madeleine Pelletier joins the Hervéist faction of the SFIO and for next three years advocates militant (extremist) anti-republican and anti-parliamentary tactics. Elected to the main board of the SFIO in 1909, replacing Hervé

17 August: International Socialist Women's Conference, preceding the Seventh International Socialist Conference (18–24 August) in Stuttgart. Resolution supporting unrestricted suffrage. Pelletier attends; disputes Zetkin

Léon Blum's *Du Mariage* published; his advocacy of premarital sex for unmarried women was considered scandalous

1908 April–May: journalist Jeanne Laloë runs for Paris Municipal Council in the ninth district, with aid of Maria Vérone; she protests noncounting of votes she received

3–4 May: Two militant actions during municipal elections. Hubertine Auclert and friends demonstrate at polling place, breaking urns in WSPU style; later repudiates her action in late June; on 4 May Dr. Madeleine Pelletier and friends in *Solidarité des Femmes* break window panes; they are arrested, tried, and fined

15–20 June: Fourth IWSA Conference, Amsterdam

21 June: Massive suffrage demonstration in London attended by M. Pelletier and C. Kauffmann

26–28 June: *Congrès National des Droits Civils et du Suffrage des Femmes* (organized by UFF, GFEF in Paris, Jeanne Deflou); Hubertine Auclert recants on propaganda of the deed

Hubertine Auclert publishes *Le Vote des femmes;* Madeleine Pelletier publishes *La Femme en lutte pour ses droits*

1 September: ICW executive board and delegates convene business meeting in Geneva, in preparation for the upcoming quinquennial congress in Toronto in 1909

24–26 September: First International Conference of Consumers' Leagues, Geneva

22 November: E. Perrier publishes blast against feminism in *Le Matin*

1909 13 February: *Union Française pour le Suffrage des Femmes* (UFSF), founded by Jeanne Schmahl and others; affiliates with International Woman Suffrage Alliance at their London meeting (26 April – 1 May); demands municipal and regional vote for women, based on women's "difference"

20 February: Marinetti's *Manifeste du futurisme* published in *Le Figaro*

Spring 1909: Two exhibitions of women's portraits in Paris

31 May: LDH debates women's rights at their annual convention, following Maria Vérone's report prepared for/by the CNFF

16 July: F. Buisson submits his report on the suffrage bill to the Chamber of Deputies

Fall: Suffrage petition organized (4,000 signatures) and sent to the parliament by Auclert's group *Suffrage des Femmes*; it was referred to Commission on Universal Suffrage

Law of 27 November 1909: Loi Engerand guarantees that employed women taking eight-week (unpaid) maternity leave do not lose their jobs

1910   Late January: major flooding of the Seine River in Paris.

11 March: 1st major Parisian suffrage meeting organized by five feminist groups (*Suffrage des Femmes*, LFDF, GFEF, UFF, *Amélioration*)

April: Parliamentary commission OK's measure on woman suffrage

24 April: Feminist candidacies in the legislative elections in Paris (Durand, Auclert, Pelletier, Kauffmann, Renaud, Arria Ly)

Paid maternity leave of two months initiated for female teachers (civil servants); in 1911 extended to women employees of *Postes, Téléphones, et Télégraphes* (PTT)

Colette (Sidonie-Gabrielle Colette) publishes novel, *La Vagabonde*

1911   24 January: French Academy of Sciences refuses candidacy of Marie Curie (because of her affair with Langevin); later in the year she wins the Nobel Prize for Chemistry)

18 February: Introduction of the *jupe-culotte*

Spring: Publication of Buisson's *Le Vote des Femmes*

2 April: Grand Meeting to promote women's vote sponsored by UFSF

31 May: Grand suffrage meeting in Paris (organized by UFSF, chaired by F. Buisson); seals alliance of UFSF with *Ligue Nationale contre l'Alcoolisme*

12–17 June: IWSA Sixth Congress, Stockholm – attended by large contingent of French suffrage advocates

17 June: Immense suffrage parade in London, attended by Maria Vérone and others

27 June: LFDF with other groups sponsored a Grand Meeting to push for authorization of juvenile courts, presided by Senator Ferd. Dreyfus

late June: First International Congress on the Juvenile Courts, Paris

28 June: Arria Ly publishes "Vive Mademoiselle!" touting permanent virginity/celibacy for women

F. Buisson and Jean du Breuil de Saint-Germain found *Ligue d'Électeurs pour le Suffrage des Femmes* (LESF)

M. Pelletier publishes *L'Émancipation sexuelle de la femme* (including essay on women's right to abortion)

Paid maternity leave initiated for female postal clerks (public sector)

1912 Big flap over the discriminatory amendments to the bill authorizing *recherche de la paternité*; drags on from February, March, through the fall (awaiting reconsideration by Senate). Continuing campaign for juvenile courts (LFDF) and women's suffrage (LFDF)

28–30 April: *Congrès International Féministe* in Brussels

17 May: Grand Meeting on Suffrage, Paris (*Sociétés savantes*), sponsored by CNFF Suffrage section (led by LFDF women, Bonnevial and Vérone)

Law of 22 July: Establishes new procedure for grappling with juvenile crime, establishes juvenile courts and opens position of *rapporteur* (investigator) on cases to women, but not juvenile judgeships

16 November: Law promulgated authorizing *recherche de la paternité* (though not against *married* men, with local option concerning application in the colonies)

1913 23 January: *Groupe Des Femmes Socialistes* (GDFS) founded

20 February: Death of Eliska Vincent

Opening of Maurice Donnay's play, *Les Éclaireuses*

14 March: Big feminist meeting "Les Éclaireuses" at the Comédie Marigny (Durand, Vérone, and others)

15 April: Grand Meeting to oppose governmental regulation of prostitution at Hôtel des Sociétés Savantes, Paris; Ghénia Avril de Sainte-Croix gives major speech, *L'Esclave blanche*

29 May: Stravinsky/Diagelev's ballet *Rites of Spring* premiers (Paris, Théâtre des Champs-Elysées) and provokes scandal, riot

2–8 June: Tenth International Congress of Women combined *Oeuvres et Institutions/Droit des Femmes,* in Paris, organized and hosted by CNFF

9–12 June: Eleventh Congress of the *Fédération Abolitioniste Internationale* (Paris, Musée Social)

Law of 17 June: Strauss Law authorizes mandatory four-week maternity leave following birth; prenatal four-week break optional. Daily allowance to be provided. Applies to all women who work for wages outside home; includes private sector firms and domestic service; peasant women and homemakers excluded

Law of 14 July: First family allocations authorized for large families (three children or more)

15–21 June: IWSA/AISF Seventh Congress, Budapest

June–July: Couriau Affair begins to attract national notice in the press

M. Pelletier publishes 2nd ed. of *Le Droit à l'avortement,* retitled *Pour l'abrogation de l'article 317*

Fall: Controversy over Couriau Affair, socialism and feminism, continues between Suzon, Brion, Rauze, and others

15 December: Feminists (all groups, incl. CNFF, but without the GDFS) organize mass public meeting (Grand Meeting) on l'Affaire Couriau and women's right to work

Théodore Joran publishes *Le Suffrage des femmes*

1914   18 January: Founding of *Ligue Nationale pour le Vote des Femmes* (LFVF) by Mme Ducret-Metsu

6 February: Grand Meeting on questions concerning women's work (G. Duchêne et al.)

9 March: First French celebration of International (Socialist) Women's Day

13 March: Grand Meeting on suffrage, organized by CNFF, UFSF, and LFDF

16 March: Henriette Caillaux shoots Gaston Calmette, editor of *Le Figaro,* for insulting her husband

10 April: Death of Hubertine Auclert

26 April (day of national legislative elections): LFDF (and CNFF suffrage section) and *Le Journal* sponsor national referendum on women's vote: "Je désire voter" in Paris and by mail attracts 505,972 supporters

16–23 May: ICW Fifth Quinquennial Congress, Rome –
French feminists in attendance

22 May: Grand Meeting in Paris, to prepare a federated
attempt to win the vote

13 June: Formation of Viviani ministry

28 June: Assassination of Austrian Archduke Franz
Ferdinand in Sarajevo (the incident that provoked the
Austrian declaration of war on Serbia and would
ultimately unleash the world war in August)

5 July: Mass suffrage demonstration in Paris to honor
Condorcet; 6,000 persons join the parade organized by
federation of women's suffrage societies

20–28 July: Trial of Madame Caillaux, for assassinating
Calmette

31 July: Assassination in Paris of Jean Jaurès, socialist leader
and anti-war stalwart

1 August: War declared; general mobilization begins in
France: martial law in effect (curtailment of freedom of
the press and unauthorized public meetings)

26 August: Second Viviani ministry formed (in place until
October 1915)

December: First news received of rapes of Belgian and
French women in occupied zones by German soldiers

1915 27 February: "Declaration of [French] Socialist Women,"
defending their patriotic stance

26 March: International Conference of Socialist Women for
Peace, Bern, organized by Clara Zetkin

Late winter/early spring: public controversy about the fate of
the children of rapes (*"les petits indésirés"*) by German
soldiers in Belgium and France

28 April–1 May: International Congress of Women for
Permanent Peace, The Hague (leaders of CNFF, UFSF,
LFDF decline to attend)

10 July: Minimum wage law ratified for women home
workers (sweated labor in garment industry)

29 October: Briand ministry replaces Viviani ministry
(remains in place until March 1917)

End of 1915: Founding of *Ligue National Contre
l'Exploitation du Travail Féminin*

Romain Rolland publishes *Au Dessus de la Melée*

1916 Marcelle Capy publishes *Une Voix de Femme dans la Melée*

Early February: Deputy (and president of the League of
Patriots) Maurice Barrès floats the notion of a "*suffrage des
morts*," which would transfer the vote of men who died in
the war to their widows, mothers, or other relatives

Early 1916: Founding of *Comité du Travail Féminin (CTF)*,
to advise government on policies concerning women war
workers

Quarrel about Barres's "*suffrage des morts*" versus
N. Roussel's "*suffrage des vivantes*"– convocation of a
"grand meeting" at *Le Journal.*

8 April: CNFF founds its Section on Unity of Morals and
Repression of the White Slave Trade

16 April: Anti-alcohol rally LDH – founding of *Union des
Femmes contre l'Alcool*

20 April: UFSF Grand Meeting

4 October: Opening of *École des Hautes Études Commerciales
pour les Jeunes Filles* (HEC-JF; Louli Sanua)

1917 7 January: Feminists' protest meeting against forced
deportations by Germans of Belgian, French, and Serbian
women to labor in Germany

February: P.-E. Flandin deposes bill to enfranchise women
24 and above for municipal suffrage

8 March [23 February, Julien calendar]: women march and
demonstrate in St. Petersburg on International Women's
Day; Russian revolution begins

5 April: UFSF Congress calls on the French state to recognize
maternity as a national service

First lady-superintendents in wartime factories; first
government-authorized infant care facilities (*crèches*) in
armaments factories

17–25 May: Strike by women garment workers (*les
midinettes*) in Paris; followed by multiple strikes by other
workers, threatening to shut down the country's
industries in wartime

29 June: Small contingent of American soldiers arrives in
France; thousands more to follow

5 August: Law providing working mothers an hour off per
day to nurse babies, and creates *chambres d'allaitement* in
plants of 100+ employees

17 September: Call for minimum wage in the couture industry; strike called (resolved 18 March 1918)

31 October: *La Voix des Femmes* launched by Colette Raybaud and Louise Bodin

17 November: Clemenceau ministry takes office

18 November: Hélène Brion arrested for pacifist activities

December: Jeanne Mélin and friends found *Comité d'Action Suffragiste*, calling for integral suffrage and cite examples of other countries that have recently enfranchised the women

1918 25–29 March: Hélène Brion tried for treason by military tribunal for distributing pacifist literature

17 July: Protests of CNFF and UFSF against the Army's brothel plan; delegation visits the Minister of War

18 October: Flandin report on universal suffrage bill; 9 November: Senate establishes a Committee to consider it

11 November: Armistice – end of war and call for immediate demobilization of women workers in armaments industry

4 December: death of Marie Bonnevial in traffic accident

8 December: CNFF-sponsored Grand Meeting in Paris to call for women's suffrage

1919 19 January: Opening of the Allied Peace conference in Paris

February–March–April: Inter-Allied women's rights delegations meet in Paris to influence the negotiations for the Peace Treaty

Law of 23 April: Establishes eight-hour day and forty-eight-hour work week

8 May: Deputy P.-E. Flandin reports out the decision to offer municipal vote to women, but with restrictions of age, etc.

20 May: Chamber of Deputies approves *unrestricted* woman suffrage bill and eligibility, 344 to 97

28 June: Signing of Treaty of Versailles

15 July: Pope Benedict XV endorses women's suffrage

8–9 October: CNFF meets at the university in Strasbourg, to celebrate the end of the war and the return of Alsace-Lorraine to France

24 October: Law providing nursing French mothers with a small monthly allocation from the State (follow-up to Strauss law of 17 June 1913)

16 November: Legislative elections by (new) *scrutin de liste*, proportional representation system, resulting in election of a very conservative, nationalist (*"Bleu Horizon"*) majority

1920   20 January: Formation of cabinet of ministers under Alexandre Millerand, succeeding Clemenceau

27 January: Formation of the *Conseil Supérieur de la Natalité* (CSN)

18 February: Election of Paul Deschanel as president of the Republic; second Millerand ministry

9 May: First [quasi-official] French celebration of Mother's Day [*Fête des Mères*]

16 May: Jeanne d'Arc canonized in Rome by the Catholic Church (Benedict XV)

28 May: Decree establishing medals for motherhood

6-12 June: Eighth IWSA/AISF Conference, Geneva

30 July–3 August: First International Conference of Communist Women, Moscow

31 July: Law outlawing antinatalist propaganda, i.e., circulating information about abortion, contraceptive practices

8-18 September: ICW Quinquennial meets in Oslo, Norway

24 September: Millerand elected president of the Republic; new cabinet formed under Georges Leygues

Autumn: Founding of *Union Nationale pour le Vote des Femmes* (UNVF; Catholic woman suffrage organization)

25–30 December: Tours Congress of the SFIO and schism; establishment of the *Parti Communiste Français*

* * * * *

1921   16 January: Aristide Briand heads a new cabinet of ministers *Exposition Nationale de la Maternité et de l'Enfance*

May–June: Repression of the neo-Malthusian leaders – Eugène and Jeanne Humbert convicted under law of 31 July 1920 and sent to prison

1–7 July: *Congrès des Institutions d'Assistance et d'Hygiène morale*

1922   15 January: Raymond Poincaré heads new cabinet of ministers (continues into June 1924)

18 March: CNFF sponsors Grand Meeting (3,000 persons) in favor of women's suffrage

April: Ghénia Avril de Sainte-Croix nominated by
  CNFF and appointed to the League of Nations
  Consultative Committee on the Traffic in Women
  and Children, the first of a number of appointments
  for her at the League

June: CNFF elects Ghénia Avril de Sainte-Croix as president
  to succeed Julie Siegfried (who died in late May)

12 July: Victor Margueritte publishes the best-selling novel,
  La Garçonne

12 October–15 November: *Exposition des Femmes Célèbres du
  XIXe Siècle*, organized by Marguerite Durand, to benefit
  the *Club des Femmes Journalistes*

21 November: French Senate refuses to proceed to discussion
  of the woman suffrage bill, after stalling for several years

1923 January: French and Belgian military forces occupy the
  Ruhr, in response to Germany's failure to pay reparations

26 January: CNFF organizes a Grand Meeting, Salle Wagram,
  to protest Senate refusal to act on woman suffrage bill

27 March: Law "correctionalizing" [decriminalizing]
  abortion; abortion changed to a misdemeanor, places
  trials in the hands of strict judges not lenient juries

18 October–4 November: First "Salon des Appareils
  Ménagers" (Exhibit of Household Appliances) in
  1926 renamed as the Salon des Arts Ménagers

1924 Mid-March: Program of preparation for *baccalauréat* authorized
  within the girls' *lycées* (secondary schools); creation of a
  unified "*bac*" examination for girls and boys alike

May: *Cartel des Gauches* (alliance of left-wing parties) wins
  the legislative elections

Clément Vautel publishes antifeminist novel, *Madame ne
  veut pas d'enfant*

1925 Maternity leave of two months granted for all women in
  public service

17 May: Canonization of Thérèse de Lisieux in Rome

9 June: Foundation of *Union Féminine Civique et Sociale*, by
  Andrée Butillard (Catholic social action group; favors
  familial vote and married women in the home)

July: School curricula for boys and girls aligned

1926 6 January: First meeting of (new) Extraparliamentary
  Commission on Women's Rights

30 May–6 June: International Woman Suffrage Alliance Tenth Congress, Paris; changes name to IAWSEC

July: UFSF takes over *La Française* from CNFF; Cécile Brunschvicg becomes editor

Creation of the *Union Temporaire Contre la Prostitution Réglementée* (Marcelle Legrand-Falco)

1927   27 January: First meeting of Natalie Clifford Barney's *Académie des Femmes* (on rue Jacob) honors Colette

February: Henriette Alquier publishes "La Maternité, fonction sociale," in *L'Ecole Émancipée* and in December is prosecuted, along with Marie Guillot, (in Saumur) under the law of 31 July 1920; Alquier is acquitted

29–30 July: International Conference of Women Workers, Grand Palais, Paris

14 August: Law on Nationality promulgated; Article 8 stipulates that women who marry automatically retain their birth nationality unless they make different arrangements

Measure floated to authorize conscripting women (Paul-Boncour) and feminist protest

1928   Mandated, eight-week, fully paid maternity leaves for women employed in public sector

27 August: Signing of Kellogg-Briand Pact, outlawing war

28 August: Women's protest at Rambouillet; call for Equal Rights Treaty (Doris Stevens and US Women's Party members involved)

30 October: Public meeting, Paris (Salle des Sociétés Savantes), "Femmes et relations internationales" orchestrated by the U.S. Woman's Party committee for international action (and LFDF), presided by H. Vacaresco

Founding of *Fédération Internationale des Femmes des Carrières Juridiques* (FIFCJ)

1929   14–16 February: *États-Généraux du Féminisme*, Paris (CNFF)

27 May: Grand Meeting in support of woman suffrage, organized by Maria Vérone (LFDF)

24–29 October: Wall Street – crash of the US stock market

Creation (in Berlin) of Open Door International for the Emancipation of the Woman Worker, opposing any and all legal restrictions on women's employment

1930   13 March–mid-April: World Conference on Codification of
        International Law, The Hague – Maria Vérone
        participates on behalf of ICW
        22–23 March: Second CNFF *États-Généraux du Féminisme*,
        Paris
        9–11 June: the reconstituted SFIO debates the woman
        question (Bordeaux)
        31 December: Papal encyclical "Casti Connubii" condemns
        contraception as immoral

1931   15 May–15 November: *Exposition Coloniale Internationale*
        15 May: Papal encyclical "Quadragesimo Anno" reminds
        Catholics that women's place is in the home
        30–31 May: Third CNFF *États-Généraux du Féminisme*
        addresses the woman question in France's colonial empire
        Formation of Consultative Committee on Nationality at
        League of Nations, chaired by Maria Vérone
        Depression hits France; economic situation deteriorates
        5 November: Blast of Dr. Charles Richet against women's
        employment in *Le Matin* provokes national debate over
        women's employment; all women's groups rise to defend
        women's right to work

1932   January: CNFF presidency changes: Marguerite Pichon-
        Landry replaces Mme Avril de Sainte-Croix; serves as
        president until 1952
        21 January: Law on Family Allocations/Allowances
        6 February: International petition of women for peace
        (8 million signatures) delivered to the Disarmament
        Conference in Geneva
        February: Chamber of Deputies again votes favorably on
        unrestricted women's suffrage (then Senate again refuses
        to discuss it)
        29–30 March: *Congrès des Femmes Méditerranéennes* (First
        Mediterranean Women's Conference), Constantine, Algeria
        23 June: René Renoult introduces the bill (in the Senate) to
        revise the Civil Code to authorize married women's legal
        capacity

1933   30 January: Adolf Hitler (NSDAP) named chancellor in
        Germany, following NAZI majority in elections
        15 May: CNFF's German counterpart, the *Bund Deutscher
        Frauenvereine*, dissolves itself to avoid Nazi takeover

4–5 June: First national conference of French socialist women, in conjunction with the congress of the SFIO

6-11 June: International congress in Paris to consider question of mothers' employment and well-being of the household, sponsored by the *Union Féminine Civique et Sociale* (a social Catholic organization for women)

Ligue de la Mère au Foyer (LMF) founded

1934   6 February: Fascist riots in Paris; 12 February: protest march by Socialists and Communists

July: Women's international organizations meet in Paris; CNFF hosts ICW Executive Board meetings plus massive International Congress of Women (delegates from many international women's organizations; 600 attendees from around the world), featuring big public meetings on questions concerning women and intellectual cooperation, peace, women's employment, and vestiges of slavery; LFDF and UFSF hold national congresses; Soroptimists hold their international conference, etc.

4–6 August: World Congress [*Rassemblement*] of Women against War and Fascism, Paris

6 October: Louise Weiss's organization *La Femme Nouvelle* (pro-suffrage organization) opens its doors on the Avenue des Champs-Elysées; public meeting called

1935   *Comité de Liaison pour la Défense du Travail Féminin* formed

1 March: Chamber of Deputies votes favorably on Bracke's proposal to give women the same voting rights as men

19 March: Rally sponsored by the *Comité Mondial*, resulting in *Comité de Défense des Droits de la Femme* (CDDF), mainly to protect women's right to work but also to demand civil and political rights for women

23 May: Death of Jane Misme

14 July: Radical Party joins forces with PCF and SFIO to establish a "popular front" alliance against the fascists

Payments established for mothers who nurse their own children

1936   16 March: Death of Marguerite Durand

April–May: Legislative elections – victory for the Popular Front

4 June: Léon Blum's Popular Front ministry: three women appointed undersecretaries of state

30 July: Chamber of Deputies again approves unrestricted woman suffrage (in October, the Senate once again refuses to discuss it)

28 September–9 October: ICW meets at Dubrovnik

1937   25 May–25 November: *Exposition Internationale des Arts et Techniques dans la Vie Moderne*, Paris

21 June: Popular Front ministry falls

21–27 June: International congress to promote mothers remaining in the home as workers for human progress (UCFS)

26–30 June: *Congrès International des Activitiés Féminines*, Paris, accompanied by an *Exposition des Oeuvres Féminines* (CNFF, ICW)

League of Nations agrees to launch a worldwide inquiry into the legal situation of women

1938   Law of 18 February 1938: eliminates legal incapacity of married women

13–15 May: *Congrès International des Femmes pour la Défense de la Paix, de la Liberté, de la Démocratie*, Marseille (Germaine Malaterre-Sellier)

24 May: death of Maria Vérone

11 July: Law Paul-Boncour authorizes conscription of women in the military

September: Founding of *Ligue des Femmes pour la Paix* (Jeanne Alexandre, Magdeleine Paz)

30 September: Signing of Munich Agreement with Hitler, acquiescing in his annexation of parts of Czechoslovakia

1939   First birth premiums; payments established to indemnify mothers who stay at home to raise children instead of going to work for pay

21 March: Death of Ghénia Avril de Sainte-Croix

31 July: Promulgation (by decree-law) of the *Code de la Famille*; Article 213 of Code rewritten (obey clause removed); payments established to indemnify mothers who stay at home to raise children instead of going to work for pay

29 December: Death of Madeleine Pelletier in an insane asylum

1940–1944   War, defeat, and German occupation; Vichy family laws; growth of the Resistance

1940
10 May: German invasion of The Netherlands, Belgium, Luxemburg

12 May: German Wehrmacht enters France at Sedan; by 4 June the British expeditionary forces and French troops evacuate at Dunkerque

June issue of *La Française*, deprived of paper, is the last issue

10–14 June: French government flees Paris for Bordeaux; Paris declared an "open city" and on the 14th the Nazi *Wehrmacht* arrives, occupies the northern half of France; panic and mass evacuations to the south ensue

17 June: Marshal Philippe Pétain calls for armistice with the Nazis; on 18th General Charles De Gaulle, in London, issues his call for resistance

9 July: Full powers granted to Pétain by France's National Assembly; end of the Third Republic

8–11 October: *L'État français* defines its ideology: "Travail, famille, patrie." Its mission includes putting women "back" in their place

11–13 October: French State issues new rules governing women's work in the public sector, including purging them from the civil service

1941
12 April: French State initiates restrictions on the laws governing divorce

25 May: Mothers' Day made official

14 September: Abortion declared an "*acte contre le people français et l'unité nationale*"

1942
15 February: The "300" Law – abortion declared a crime against Society, the State, and the Race, an act of treason, punishable by death

18 March: Instruction in domestic science made obligatory for girls

1943
June: *Conseil Supérieur de la Famille* established

1944
11 January: Creation of women's auxiliaries for the army, navy, and air force

21 April: Ordinance of Algiers – women will have the right to vote

18 August: End of the Vichy regime

21 August: Liberation of Paris: women not allowed to participate

5 October: Provisional government extends "universal suffrage" to encompass women

1945 April: French women vote for the first time in municipal elections

June: Paris Congress of the *Union des Femmes Françaises* (UFF), founded in 1944

26 November–1 December: International Congress of Women, Paris. Founding of the Women's International Democratic Federation (WIDF; headquarters in the DDR; closely associated with the Third Communist International)

1946 Law of 11 April: Opened posts in the judiciary to women, either through competition or by nomination

13 April: *Loi Marthe Richard* ends municipal government regulation of prostitution in Paris, closes the brothels

July: Government introduces state family allowances

Law of 27 October: Constitution of the Fourth Republic: Preamble states that "*La loi garantit à la femme, dans tous les domaines, des droits égaux à ceux de l'homme*"; Article 4 confirms voting rights of adult women

1948 Constitution of the Fourth Republic promulgated: grants equality to French women; establishes right to work; social security system takes over family allowances, grants to mothers, etc.

1949 *Le Deuxième Sexe* published by Simone de Beauvoir

Index